MEANS
MAN-HOUR
STANDARDS
FOR
CONSTRUCTION

REVISED SECOND EDITION

Publisher

E. Norman Peterson, Jr.

Editor-In-Chief

William D. Mahoney

Senior Editor

Allan B. Cleveland

Contributing Editors

Donald D. Denzer
Roger J. Grant
F. William Horsley
Carl W. Linde
Bernard M. McInerney
Paul L. Miskel
Melville J. Mossman
John J. Moylan
Jeannene D. Murphy
Kornelis Smit
Arthur Thornley
Edward B. Wetherill
Rory Woolsey

Technical Coordinator

Marion Schofield

MEANS MAN-HOUR STANDARDS
FOR
CONSTRUCTION

REVISED SECOND EDITION

R.S. MEANS COMPANY, INC.
A Southam Company

CONSTRUCTION CONSULTANTS & PUBLISHERS
100 Construction Plaza
P.O. Box 800
Kingston, MA 02364-0800
(617) 585-7880

10 9 8 7 6 5

Library of Congress Catalog Card Number 88-140499
ISBN 0-87629-089-6

TABLE OF CONTENTS

FOREWORD

GENERAL INTRODUCTION

Almost anyone in the construction industry would agree that accurate productivity information is an important starting point for any cost estimate. It may be the most common problem an estimator faces: finding out how long it takes a particular crew of workers to get a job done. On the surface, that may seem an easy task. Productivity is easy to calculate for the straightforward jobs that a contractor repeats time and time again under the same job conditions. However, no two construction projects are totally alike, and there are literally thousands of separate construction activities, each with its own productivity figures and specialized equipment.

Getting the right figures should be easy with the right reference. A reference of productivity data should be comprehensive if it is going to be useful, and it must be presented in a "per unit" format to be versatile for projects of various sizes. *Means Man-Hour Standards* takes all these variables into consideration.

This book is an extensive listing of crew information, daily output, and man-hour figures presented in an easy-to-use format. It's a man-hour reference for thousands of separate construction-related activities. Users will find it easy to locate almost any area of construction with a minimum of confusion, because this book has been developed with the construction industry in mind. Since no cost information requiring annual updating is included with the man-hour listings, all of this information should remain a reliable reference for years to come. For up-to-date information on labor costs and data on other areas of the construction industry, refer to any of the R.S. Means cost manuals which are published for many specialties in this field.

If used carefully, *Means Man-Hour Standards* can help increase profits by providing comprehensive information about labor productivity. Included as part of each item in the listing is a full description of that particular construction activity, plus the crew needed to do the work, the daily output of that crew, the units that the daily output is defined in terms of, and a unit man-hour figure. In all, there are more than 25,000 separate items covered in this book.

The listings conform to the Construction Specifications Institute's MASTERFORMAT, which places all elements in one of 16 basic "divisions" or areas of construction. Within each of these divisions are the many items that go into a building. Over the years, the MASTERFORMAT has become the accepted standard of the industry because it is comprehensive and easily adapted to different types of construction. In addition to the actual listings, each division has its own introduction describing important job considerations and special aspects of labor and trade productivity information.

All of the information in this book reflects the accuracy of extended research that has gone into the preparation of the thousands of unit prices which make up the R.S. Means Company, Inc., data file of construction cost information. The company has assembled information covering a wide variety of building construction items.

THE COMPANY AND THE EDITORS
Since 1942, R.S. Means Company, Inc., has been actively engaged in construction cost publishing and consulting throughout North America. The primary objective of the company is to provide the construction industry profession — the contractor, the owner, the architect, the engineer, the facilities manager — with current and comprehensive construction cost data.

A thoroughly experienced and highly qualified staff at R.S. Means works daily at collecting, analyzing, and disseminating reliable cost information for your needs. These staff members have had years of practical construction experience and engineering training prior to joining the firm. Each contributes to the maintenance of a complete, continually-updated construction cost data system.

With the constant flow of new construction methods and materials, the construction professional often cannot find enough time to examine and evaluate all the diverse construction cost possibilities. R.S. Means performs the function by analyzing costs in all facets of the industry. Data is collected and organized into a format that is instantly accessible. The data is useful for all phases of construction cost determination — from the preliminary budget to the detailed unit price estimate.

The Means organization is always prepared to assist you and help in the solution of construction problems through the services of its four major divisions; Construction and Cost Data Publishing, Computer Software Services, Consulting Services, and Educational Seminars.

FACTORS AFFECTING THIS DATA

Quality: The information given in this book is in accordance with the Model Building Codes and represents good, sound construction.

Overtime: No allowance has been made for overtime.

Productivity: All man-hour figures for installation are based on an eight-hour day in daylight hours.

Location: All information pertains to projects in metropolitan areas. Beyond a 20-mile radius of large cities, extra travel can affect productivity.

Important Factors That Affect Productivity: There are several important factors that must always be considered when analyzing productivity information. These factors, as they relate to each area of construction, are dealt with in greater detail in the introduction to each separate division in this book.

Job Conditions: In general, it is important to be aware of the job conditions at the construction site. This involves knowing the scope of the project and actual site conditions. The difficulty of moving material to the site and the amount of mechanized operation, as well as the number of labor-saving methods involved in the specific project, can have a direct effect on worker productivity. Factors such as the height at which tradesmen work and the relative amount of space in which they operate are important.

Supervision: No amount of economy in operation can make up for a lack of proper supervision at the job site. The potential effectiveness of supervisors should be evaluated by experience, the rate of pay, and the status of the labor pool that they are drawn from. The level of construction activity in the area of a proposed project can have a direct effect on the availability of quality supervision. In other words, if there is a high activity level of new construction in any given area, it may be difficult to acquire top-notch supervision.

Other Factors: Other factors which affect productivity include weather, season of the year, contractor management, local labor restrictions, building code requirements, natural disasters, as well as availability of skilled labor and materials. The influence of general building conditions is another factor. Substitute materials and construction methods may affect the rate at which work can be done at the job site. It is also important when calculating actual man-hour figures to know if the particular job is subcontracted. A considerable portion of all large construction jobs is usually subcontracted. In fact, the percentage of work performed by subcontractors is constantly increasing and may often run over 90% of one project. Since the workmen employed by these companies do nothing else but install their particular product, they soon become proficient at installing that line. The result is that installation is accomplished so efficiently that man-hour figures have been known to vary.

When specific information is available about the installation of a complex or new building system, whether it is historical information from a previous job or a well-educated guess, use the productivity information in this book as a starting point and alter the figures to suit specific job conditions and materials.

TABLES FOR MAN-HOUR STANDARDS

The coding system used in this book is identical to the unit price cost file coding system used in all R.S. Means Company, Inc., cost publications.

The listings in this book have six columns of information. Although not every item in the listing utilizes all of the columns, each line item is assigned a "Line Number" and occupies a complete horizontal line in the listing. Line Numbers are shown in the first column. The "Subdivision" code is always shown at the upper left corner of the table in reverse type for easy identification. There are 16 separate C.S.I. divisions covered by the listings. Once working within a subdivision, locate the appropriate "Classification" for each item needed. Classification codes and descriptions are listed at the head of each grouping in bold type and always consist of three numbers.

Actual line items are then listed with their productivity information to the right. Sub-items are indented beneath appropriate line items. Each line item is described briefly under the heading "Description". Then, a variety of productivity information is listed in the right-hand columns under the headings: Crew, Daily Output, and Man-Hours.

How to Use Man-Hour Standards

Daily Output

The Daily Output figures given in this book represent the number of units that the crew completes in an 8-hour day. To develop the Total Crew Days required to complete a specific task, use this basic formula:

$$\frac{\text{Quantity}}{\text{Daily Output}} = \text{Crew Days}$$

Assume that a total of 1500 C.Y. of soil need to be compacted with an Air Tamper. Producitivity figures are listed on line **022 204 1000**

$$\frac{1500 \text{ C.Y.}}{285 \text{ C.Y./Day}} = \textbf{5.26 Total Crew Days}$$

Total Crew Days can be multiplied by 8 to develop **Total Crew Hours.**

5.26 Crew Days x 8 = 42 Total Crew Hours

Note: Always adjust the **Quantity** used to agree with the **Unit Of Measure** listed in the tables for the line item being used.

Man-Hours

Man-Hour figures are expressed as units. Because of this, they can be easily used with Daily Output figures to develop the Total Daily Crew Hours required for a particular task. Conversely, if there is a change in Total Daily Crew Hours, the new total can be divided by the indicated Daily Output to develop a new unit man-hour figure.

Total Daily Crew Hours/Daily Output = Unit Man-Hours

The Man-Hour figures given in this book represent a unit figure for how many hours it takes a crew to perform a specific task in terms of the unit of measure listed. To calculate the **Total Man-Hours** required to complete a job, multiply the **Unit Man-Hour** figure times the **Quantity.**

Unit Man-Hours x Quantity = Total Man-Hours

Assume, once again, that 1500 C.Y. of soil need to be compacted. The **Unit Man-Hour** figure is listed on line **022 204 1000**.

.140 Man-Hours/C.Y. x 1500 C.Y. = 210 Total Man-Hours

CREW	MAKEUP
B-9	1 Foreman (outside)
	4 Building Laborers
	1 Air Compr. 250 C.F.M.
	Air Tools Accessories
	2 50' Air Hoses, 1.5" Diam.

Equipment Hours

The figures in the crew listing shown next to equipment can be used to develop a **Unit Equipment Hour** figure. Simply multiply the total of the numbers next to all equipment in the crew listing times 8 (the number of hours in a work day) and then divide that figure by the **Daily Output**. This figure can then be used to develop **Total Equipment Hours**. To calculate **Total Equipment Hours** required to complete a job, multiply the **Unit Equipment Hour** figure times the **Quantity:**

$$\frac{\text{Crew Equip. Qty. x 8}}{\text{Daily Output}} = \textbf{Unit Equipment Hour}$$

Unit Equipment Hour x Quantity = Total Equipment Hours

Assume, once again, that 1500 C.Y. of soil needs to be compacted. The **Unit Equipment Hour** figure is based on the number **1** listed next to **air compressor, 250 C.F.M.** in a crew listing for line **022 204 1000**. The **Daily Output** figure is taken directly from the tables:

$$\frac{\text{1 (Crew Equip. Qty.) x 8}}{285} = \textbf{.028 Unit Equip. Hrs.}$$

.028 Unit Equipment Hours x 1500 C.Y. = 42 Total Equipment Hours

Total Equipment Hours can be divided by 8 to develop **Total Equipment Days**

$$\frac{\text{42 Equipment Hours}}{\text{8 Hours}} = \textbf{5.26 Equipment Days}$$

Daily Output
To the right of every crew in this book, a Daily Output figure is given. This figure represents the number of units that the crew will complete in an 8-hour day.

Man-Hours
Man-hours are a unit figure that represents how long it takes one worker to do the task in terms of a specific unit of measure

Unit Designation
To the right of the Man-Hour column is the Unit column. The abbreviated unit designations listed under this heading describe the unit upon which the production and crew are based.

Line Number Determination
Each line item is identified by a unique ten-digit number.

MASTERFORMAT

Division

022 204 1000

Subdivision

MASTERFORMAT

Mediumscope

022 204 1000

022 **204** 1000

Major

Classification

022 204 **1000**

Individual
Line Number

Description
Each line item has a Description of a particular aspect of construction. In many cases this brief listing is all that is required to identify the appropriate item. Indented items offer a range of dimensions, sizes or varieties.

Crew
The Crew column shows a code reference for the typical crew needed to install the item described on that line. The number of workers or pieces of equipment are indicated, along with an exact description of the trade involved and the equipment used by that trade.

022 | Earthwork

022 200 | Excavation, Backfill, Compact

			CREW	MAKEUP	DAILY OUTPUT	MAN-HOURS	UNIT
204	204	BACKFILL By hand, no compaction, light soil	1 Clab	1 Building Laborer	14	.571	C.Y.
	0100	Heavy soil			11	.727	C.Y.
	0300	Compaction in 6" layers, hand tamp, add to above			20.60	.388	C.Y.
	0400	Roller compaction operator walking, add	B-10A	1 Equip. Oper. (med.)	100	.120	C.Y.
				.5 Building Laborer			
				1 Roll. Compact., 2K Lbs.			
	0500	Air tamp, add	B-9	1 Labor Foreman (outside)	190	.211	C.Y.
				4 Building Laborers			
				1 Air Compr., 250 C.F.M.			
				Air Tools & Accessories			
				2 50 Ft. Air Hoses, 1.5" Dia.			
	0600	Vibrating plate, add	A-1	1 Building Laborer	60	.133	C.Y.
				1 Gas Eng. Power Tool			
	0800	Compaction in 12" layers, hand tamp, add to above	1 Clab	1 Building Laborer	34	.235	C.Y.
	0900	Roller compaction operator walking, add	B-10A	1 Equip. Oper. (med.)	150	.080	C.Y.
				.5 Building Laborer			
				1 Roll. Compact., 2K Lbs.			
	1000	Air tamp, add	B-9	1 Labor Foreman (outside)	285	.140	C.Y.
				4 Building Laborers			
				1 Air Compr., 250 C.F.M.			
				Air Tools & Accessories			
				2 50 Ft. Air Hoses, 1.5" Dia.			
	1100	Vibrating plate, add	A-1	1 Building Laborer	90	.089	C.Y.
				1 Gas Eng. Power Tool			
	208	BACKFILL, STRUCTURAL Dozer or F.E. loader					
	0020	From existing stockpile, no compaction					
	2000	75 H.P., 50' haul, sand & gravel	B-10L	1 Equip. Oper. (med.)	1,100	.011	C.Y.
				.5 Building Laborer			
				1 Dozer, 75 H.P.			
	2020	Common earth			975	.012	C.Y.
	2040	Clay			850	.014	C.Y.
	2200	150' haul, sand & gravel			550	.022	C.Y.
	2220	Common earth			490	.024	C.Y.
	2240	Clay			425	.028	C.Y.
	2400	300' haul, sand & gravel			370	.032	C.Y.
	2420	Common earth			330	.036	C.Y.
	2440	Clay			290	.041	C.Y.
	3000	105 H.P., 50' haul, sand & gravel	B-10W	1 Equip. Oper. (med.)	1,350	.009	C.Y.
				.5 Building Laborer			
				1 Dozer, 105 H.P.			
	3020	Common earth			1,225	.010	C.Y.
	3040	Clay			1,100	.011	C.Y.
	3200	150' haul, sand & gravel			670	.018	C.Y.
	3220	Common earth			610	.020	C.Y.
	3240	Clay			550	.022	C.Y.
	3300	300' haul, sand & gravel			465	.026	C.Y.
	3320	Common earth			415	.029	C.Y.
	3340	Clay			370	.032	C.Y.
	4000	200 H.P., 50' haul, sand & gravel	B-10B	1 Equip. Oper. (med.)	2,500	.005	C.Y.
				.5 Building Laborer			
				1 Dozer, 200 H.P.			
	4020	Common earth			2,200	.005	C.Y.
	4040	Clay			1,950	.006	C.Y.
	4200	150' haul, sand & gravel			1,225	.010	C.Y.
	4220	Common earth			1,100	.011	C.Y.
	4240	Clay			975	.012	C.Y.
	4400	300' haul, sand & gravel			805	.015	C.Y.
	4420	Common earth			735	.016	C.Y.

DIVISION 1

GENERAL REQUIREMENTS

DIVISION 1

GENERAL REQUIREMENTS

Some of the items in the General Requirements Division include: Safety Nets, Scaffolding, Surveying, Swing Staging, Tarpaulins, and Temporary Construction.

An important first step in any construction project is to ascertain all safety requirements and create a full inventory of all items that are included in this division. Although the number of items in this division is not very large in comparison to others, it is one of the most commonly overlooked parts of an estimate. Always evaluate these items to avoid lengthy construction delays.

When assigning crews to install such items as staging, make sure that the work force is well matched to the task. Many times either an over-qualified or under-qualified crew is assigned to this work, and there is a corresponding loss in overall productivity. Check to see that the workers assigned to this work are familiar with it. For example, don't expect a plumber to be proficient at erecting staging. It may be more efficient to assign a special crew to the task, no matter how small the job.

In some cases there are trades that prefer to install their own staging and scaffolding. Bricklayers are among the tradesmen who work most efficiently when they assemble the platforms where they work.

Weather conditions often dictate heat or special protection for workers on the job site. This is an added cost that falls under General Requirements.

Always fully evaluate the need for temporary construction to protect workers and passers-by, especially on multi-story jobs in urban areas. Urban work sites also call for extensive temporary construction when there are any access problems and the potential for material theft. In many cases, these circumtances call for sidewalks with overhead protection, special roadways, fencing, and special lighting.

010 | Overhead

010 000 | Overhead

			CREW	MAKEUP	DAILY OUTPUT	MAN-HOURS	UNIT
094	094	**WINTER PROTECTION** Reinforced plastic on wood					
	0100	framing to close openings	2 Clab	2 Building Laborers	750	.021	S.F.
	0200	Tarpaulins hung over scaffolding, 8 uses, not incl. scaffolding	↓	↓	1,500	.011	S.F.
	0300	Prefab, fiberglass panels, steel frame, 8 uses			1,200	.013	S.F.

013 | Submittals

013 300 | Survey Data

		CREW	MAKEUP	DAILY OUTPUT	MAN-HOURS	UNIT
306	**SURVEYING** Conventional, topographical, minimum	A-7	1 Chief Of Party 1 Instrument Man 1 Rodman/Chainman	3.30	7.270	Acre
0100	Maximum	A-8	1 Chief Of Party 1 Instrument Man 2 Rodmen/Chainmen	.60	53.330	Acre
0300	Lot location and lines, minimum, for large quantities	A-7	1 Chief Of Party 1 Instrument Man 1 Rodman/Chainman	2	12.000	Acre
0320	Average	"	"	1.25	19.200	Acre
0400	Maximum, for small quantities	A-8	1 Chief Of Party 1 Instrument Man 2 Rodmen/Chainmen	1	32.000	Acre
0600	Monuments, 3' long	A-7	1 Chief Of Party 1 Instrument Man 1 Rodman/Chainman	10	2.400	Ea.
0800	Property lines, perimeter, cleared land	"	"	1,000	.024	L.F.
1100	Crew for building layout, 2 man crew	A-6	1 Chief Of Party 1 Instrument Man	1	16.000	Day
1200	3 man crew	A-7	1 Chief Of Party 1 Instrument Man 1 Rodman/Chainman	1	24.000	Day
1300	4 man crew	A-8	1 Chief Of Party 1 Instrument Man 2 Rodmen/Chainmen	1	32.000	Day

015 | Construction Facilities and Temporary Controls

015 100 | Temporary Utilities

		CREW	MAKEUP	DAILY OUTPUT	MAN-HOURS	UNIT
104	**TEMPORARY UTILITIES**					
0100	Heat, incl. fuel and operation, per week, 12 hrs. per day	1 Skwk	1 Skilled Worker	8.75	.914	CSF Flr
0200	24 hrs. per day	"	"	4.50	1.780	CSF Flr
0350	Lighting, incl. service lamps, wiring & outlets, minimum	1 Elec	1 Electrician	34	.235	CSF Flr
0360	Maximum	"	"	17	.471	CSF Flr

015 200	Temporary Construction	CREW	MAKEUP	DAILY OUTPUT	MAN-HOURS	UNIT
204	**PROTECTION** Stair tread, 2" x 12" planks, 1 use	1 Carp	1 Carpenter	75	.107	Tread
0100	Exterior plywood, 1/2" thick, 1 use			65	.123	Tread
0200	3/4" thick, 1 use	↓	↓	60	.133	Tread

015 250	Construction Aids	CREW	MAKEUP	DAILY OUTPUT	MAN-HOURS	UNIT
254	**SCAFFOLD**					
4000	Scaffolding steel tubular rented, no plank, 1 use per month					
4100	Building exterior 2 stories	3 Carp	3 Carpenters	17.72	1.350	C.S.F.
4150	4 stories	"	"	17.72	1.350	C.S.F.
4200	6 stories	4 Carp	4 Carpenters	22.60	1.420	C.S.F.
4250	8 stories			20.25	1.580	C.S.F.
4300	10 stories			19.10	1.680	C.S.F.
4350	12 stories	↓	↓	17.70	1.810	C.S.F.
4500	One tier 3' high x 7' long x 5' wide 1 use per month	1 Carp	1 Carpenter	14.90	.537	C.S.F.
4550	2 uses per month			14.90	.537	C.S.F.
4600	4 uses per month			14.90	.537	C.S.F.
4650	8 uses per month			14.90	.537	C.S.F.
5000	5' high x 7' long x 5' wide 1 use per month			20.65	.387	C.S.F.
5050	2 uses per month			20.65	.387	C.S.F.
5100	4 uses per month			20.65	.387	C.S.F.
5150	8 uses per month			20.65	.387	C.S.F.
5500	6'-6" high x 7' long x 5' wide 1 use per month			26.85	.298	C.S.F.
5550	2 uses per month			26.85	.298	C.S.F.
5600	4 uses per month			26.85	.298	C.S.F.
5650	8 uses per month	↓	↓	26.85	.298	C.S.F.
6000	Scaffold steel tubular, suspended slab form supports to 8'-2" high					
6100	1 use per month	4 Carp	4 Carpenters	31	1.030	C.S.F.
6150	2 uses per month			43	.744	C.S.F.
6200	3 uses per month	↓	↓	43	.744	C.S.F.
6500	Steel tubular, suspended slab form supports to 14'-8" high					
6600	1 use per month	4 Carp	4 Carpenters	16	2.000	C.S.F.
6650	2 uses per month			22	1.450	C.S.F.
6700	3 uses per month	↓	↓	22	1.450	C.S.F.
255	**SCAFFOLDING SPECIALTIES**					
0050						
1200	Sidewalk bridge, heavy duty steel posts & beams, including					
1210	parapet protection & waterproofing					
1220	8' to 10' wide, 2 posts	3 Carp	3 Carpenters	15	1.600	L.F.
1230	3 posts	"	"	10	2.400	L.F.
1500	Sidewalk bridge using tubular steel					
1510	scaffold frames, including planking	3 Carp	3 Carpenters	45	.533	L.F.
6500	Stair unit, interior, for scaffolding, buy					Ea.
6550	Rent per month					Ea.
256	**SWING STAGING**					
2000	Swing staging for masonry, 5' wide x 7', hand operated					
2050	Cable type with 150' cables, rent & install, per week	E-4	1 Struc. Steel Foreman	18	1.780	L.F.
			3 Struc. Steel Workers			
			1 Gas Welding Machine			
2100	Catwalks, no handrails, 3 joists, 2" x 4"	2 Carp	2 Carpenters	55	.291	L.F.
2150	3 joists, 3" x 6"	"	"	40	.400	L.F.
2200	Move swing staging	E-4	1 Struc. Steel Foreman	37	.865	L.F.
			3 Struc. Steel Workers			
			1 Gas Welding Machine			

015 | Construction Facilities and Temporary Controls

015 300 | Barriers And Enclosures

		Description	CREW	MAKEUP	DAILY OUTPUT	MAN-HOURS	UNIT
302	302	BARRICADES 5' high, 3 rail @ 2" x 8", fixed	2 Carp	2 Carpenters	30	.533	L.F.
	0150	Movable			20	.800	L.F.
	1000	Guardrail, wooden, 3' high, 1" x 6", on 2" x 4" posts			200	.080	L.F.
	1100	2" x 6", on 4" x 4" posts	↓	↓	165	.097	L.F.
	1201	Portable metal with base pads					
	1250	Typical installation, assume 10 reuses	2 Carp	2 Carpenters	600	.027	L.F.
304	304	FENCING Chain link, 5' high	2 Clab	2 Building Laborers	100	.160	L.F.
	0100	6' high			75	.213	L.F.
	0200	Rented chain link, 6' high, to 500'			100	.160	L.F.
	0250	Over 1000' (up to 12 mo.)	↓	↓	110	.145	L.F.
	0350	Plywood, painted, 2" x 4" frame, 4' high	A-4	2 Carpenters 1 Painter, Ordinary	135	.178	L.F.
	0400	4" x 4" frame, 8' high	"	"	110	.218	L.F.
	0500	Wire mesh on 4" x 4" posts, 4' high	2 Carp	2 Carpenters	100	.160	L.F.
	0550	8' high	"	"	80	.200	L.F.

015 500 | Access Roads

		Description	CREW	MAKEUP	DAILY OUTPUT	MAN-HOURS	UNIT
552		ROADS AND SIDEWALKS Temporary					
	0050	Roads, gravel fill, no surfacing, 4" gravel thickness	B-14	1 Labor Foreman (outside) 4 Building Laborers 1 Equip. Oper. (light) 1 Backhoe Loader, 48 H.P.	715	.067	S.Y.
	0100	8" gravel thickness	"	"	615	.078	S.Y.
	1000	Ramp, 3/4" plywood on 2" x 6" joists, 16" O.C.	2 Carp	2 Carpenters	300	.053	S.F.
	1100	On 2" x 10" joists, 16" O.C.	"	"	275	.058	S.F.
	2200	Sidewalks, 2" x 12" planks, 2 uses	1 Carp	1 Carpenter	350	.023	S.F.
	2300	Exterior plywood, 2 uses, 1/2" thick	↓	↓	750	.011	S.F.
	2500	3/4" thick			600	.013	S.F.

015 900 | Field Offices And Sheds

		Description	CREW	MAKEUP	DAILY OUTPUT	MAN-HOURS	UNIT
904		OFFICE Trailer, furnished, no hookups, 20' x 8', buy	2 Skwk	2 Skilled Workers	1	16.000	Ea.
	0300	32' x 8', buy			.70	22.860	Ea.
	0400	50' x 10', buy			.60	26.670	Ea.
	0500	50' x 12', buy	↓	↓	.50	32.000	Ea.
	1000	Portable buildings, prefab, on skids, economy, 8' x 8'	2 Carp	2 Carpenters	265	.060	S.F.
	1100	Deluxe, 8' x 12'	"	"	150	.107	S.F.
	1200	Storage vans, trailer mounted, 16' x 8', buy	2 Skwk	2 Skilled Workers	1.80	8.890	Ea.
	1300	28' x 10', buy	"	"	1.40	11.430	Ea.

017 | Contract Closeout

017 100 | Final Cleaning

		Description	CREW	MAKEUP	DAILY OUTPUT	MAN-HOURS	UNIT
104		CLEANING UP					
	0050	Cleanup of floor area, continuous, per day	A-5	2 Building Laborers .25 Truck Driver (light) .25 Light Truck, 1.5 Ton	12	1.500	M.S.F.
	0100	Final	"	"	11.50	1.570	M.S.F.

018 000	Facilities Maintenance	CREW	MAKEUP	DAILY OUTPUT	MAN-HOURS	UNIT
020	**SITE WORK FACILITIES MAINTENANCE**					
0800	Flower bed maintenance					
0810	Cultivate bed-no mulch	1 Clab	1 Building Laborer	14	.571	M.S.F.
0830	Fall clean-up of flower bed, including pick-up mulch for re-use			1	8.000	M.S.F.
0840	Fertilize flower bed, 3 lb./c.s.f. of nitrogen, potash, phos.			85	.094	M.S.F.
1110	Plant (flats)			800	.010	S.F.
1130	Police, hand pickup	↓	↓	30	.267	M.S.F.
1140	Vacuum (outside)	A-1	1 Building Laborer	48	.167	M.S.F.
			1 Gas Eng. Power Tool			
1200	Spring prepare	1 Clab	1 Building Laborer	2	4.000	M.S.F.
1300	Weed mulched bed			20	.400	M.S.F.
1310	Unmulched bed	↓	↓	8	1.000	M.S.F.
1550	General site work maintenance					
1560	Clearing brush with brush saw & rake	1 Clab	1 Building Laborer	565	.014	S.Y.
1570	By hand	"	"	280	.029	S.Y.
1580	With dozer, ball and chain, light clearing	B-11A	1 Equipment Oper. (med.)	3,675	.004	S.Y.
			1 Building Laborer			
			1 Dozer, 200 H.P.			
1590	Medium clearing	"	"	3,110	.005	S.Y.
1595	Garbage can, 32 gal., clean with soap & water	1 Clab	1 Building Laborer	16	.500	Ea.
1610	Grounds, policing, incl. picking up trash & other debris	"	"	300	.027	M.S.F.
1650	Mowing brush, tractor with rotary mower					
1660	Light density	B-84	1 Equip. Oper. (med.)	22	.364	M.S.F.
			1 Rotary Mower/Tractor			
1670	Medium density			13	.615	M.S.F.
1680	Heavy density	↓	↓	9	.889	M.S.F.
3000	Lawn maintenance					
3010	Aerate lawn, 18" cultivating width, walk behind	A-1	1 Building Laborer	95	.084	M.S.F.
			1 Gas Eng. Power Tool			
3040	48" cultivating width	B-66	1 Equip. Oper. (light)	750	.011	M.S.F.
			1 Backhoe Ldr. w/Attchmt.			
3060	72" cultivating width	"	"	1,100	.007	M.S.F.
3100	Edge lawn, by hand at walks	1 Clab	1 Building Laborer	16	.500	C.L.F.
3150	At planting beds	"	"	7	1.140	C.L.F.
3200	Using gas powered edger at walks	A-1	1 Building Laborer	88	.091	C.L.F.
			1 Gas Eng. Power Tool			
3250	At planting beds			24	.333	C.L.F.
3260	Vacuum, 30" gas, outdoors with hose	↓	↓	96	.083	M.L.F.
3400	Fertilize, push gravity spreader, nitrogen, potash, phos. mix	1 Clab	1 Building Laborer	24	.333	M.S.F.
3450	Push rotary	"	"	140	.057	M.S.F.
3460	Tractor towed spreader, 8'	B-66	1 Equip. Oper. (light)	500	.016	M.S.F.
			1 Backhoe Ldr. w/Attchmt.			
3470	12' spread			800	.010	M.S.F.
3480	Truck whirlwind spreader	↓	↓	1,200	.007	M.S.F.
4000	Lawn mowing, improved areas, 16" hand push	1 Clab	1 Building Laborer	48	.167	M.S.F.
4050	Power mower, 18"-22"	A-1	1 Building Laborer	80	.100	M.S.F.
			1 Gas Eng. Power Tool			
4100	22"-30"			120	.067	M.S.F.
4150	30"-32"	↓	↓	140	.057	M.S.F.
4160	Riding mower, 36"-44"	B-66	1 Equip. Oper. (light)	300	.027	M.S.F.
			1 Backhoe Ldr. w/Attchmt.			
4170	48"-58"	"	"	480	.017	M.S.F.
4175	Mowing with tractor & attachments					
4180	3 gang reel, 7'	B-66	1 Equip. Oper. (light)	930	.009	M.S.F.
			1 Backhoe Ldr. w/Attchmt.			
4190	5 gang reel, 12'			1,200	.007	M.S.F.
4200	Cutter or sickle-bar, 5', rough terrain			210	.038	M.S.F.
4210	Cutter or sickle-bar, 5', smooth terrain	↓	↓	340	.024	M.S.F.

018 000 | Facilities Maintenance

		CREW	MAKEUP	DAILY OUTPUT	MAN-HOURS	UNIT
020	4221	Lawn mowing w/tractor, drainage channel, 5' sickle bar	B-66	1 Equip. Oper. (light)	5	1.600	Mile
				1 Backhoe Ldr. w/Attchmt.			
	4250	Lawnmower, rotary type, sharpen (all sizes)	1 Clab	1 Building Laborer	10	.800	Ea.
	4260	Repair or replace part	↓	↓	7	1.140	Ea.
	4500	Rake leaves or lawn, by hand, (cavex)			7	1.070	M.S.F.
	4510	Power rake	A-1	1 Building Laborer	45	.178	M.S.F.
				1 Gas Eng. Power Tool			
	4900	Water lawn, per 1" of water	1 Clab	1 Building Laborer	21	.381	M.S.F.
	4910	50' soaker hoses, set up			82	.098	M.S.F.
	4920	60' soaker hoses, set up	↓	↓	89	.090	M.S.F.
	5900	Road & walk maintenance					
	5910	Bituminous concrete paving, cold patch, 2" thick	B-37	1 Labor Foreman (outside)	390	.123	S.Y.
				4 Building Laborers			
				1 Equip. Oper. (light)			
				1 Tandem Roller, 5 Ton			
	5913	3" thick	"	"	260	.185	S.Y.
	5915	De-icing roads and walks					
	5920	Calcium Chloride in truckload lots see Division 025-112					
	6000	Ice melting comp., 90% Calc. Chlor., effec. to -30°F					
	6010	50-80 lb. poly bags, med. applic. 19 lbs./M.S.F., by hand	1 Clab	1 Building Laborer	60	.133	M.S.F.
	6050	With hand operated rotary spreader			110	.073	M.S.F.
	6100	Rock salt, med. applic. on road & walkway, by hand			60	.133	M.S.F.
	6110	With hand operated rotary spreader			110	.073	M.S.F.
	6130	Hosing, sidewalks & other paved areas	↓	↓	30	.267	M.S.F.
	6260	Sidewalk, brick pavers, steam cleaning	A-1	1 Building Laborer	950	.008	S.F.
				1 Gas Eng. Power Tool			
	6300	Snow removal from sidewalk by hand	1 Clab	1 Building Laborer	780	.010	C.F.
	6310	Power (24")	A-1	1 Building Laborer	1,200	.007	C.F.
				1 Gas Eng. Power Tool			
	6400	Sweep walk by hand	1 Clab	1 Building Laborer	15	.533	M.S.F.
	6410	Power vacuum	A-1	1 Building Laborer	100	.080	M.S.F.
				1 Gas Eng. Power Tool			
	6420	Drives & parking areas with power vacuum	"	"	150	.053	M.S.F.
	6600	Shrub maintenance					
	6640	Shrub bed fertilize 3 lb. of nitrogen, potash, phosp./C.S.F.	1 Clab	1 Building Laborer	85	.094	M.S.F.
	6700	Prune, shrub bed			7	1.140	M.S.F.
	6710	Shrub under 3' height			190	.042	Ea.
	6720	4' height			90	.089	Ea.
	6730	Over 6'			50	.160	Ea.
	6750	Spray, pest control (labor only)			8	1.000	M.S.F.
	6770	Water, shrub			32	.250	Ea.
	6780	Shrub bed			7	1.140	M.S.F.
	6800	Weed, by handhoe			8	1.000	M.S.F.
	6810	Spray out			32	.250	M.S.F.
	6820	Spray after mulch	↓	↓	48	.167	M.S.F.
	7100	Tree maintenance					
	7200	Fertilize; nitrogen, potash, phosphate mixture	1 Clab	1 Building Laborer	16	.500	Ea.
	7350	Prune from ground			20	.400	Ea.
	7360	High work			8	1.000	Ea.
	7420	Pest control, spray			24	.333	Ea.
	7430	Systemic			48	.167	Ea.
	7500	Water, under 1" caliper			34	.235	Ea.
	7550	1"-3" caliper			17	.471	Ea.
	7600	3"-4" caliper			12	.667	Ea.
	7650	Over 4" caliper	↓	↓	10	.800	Ea.

018 000	Facilities Maintenance	CREW	MAKEUP	DAILY OUTPUT	MAN-HOURS	UNIT
030 **030**	**CONCRETE FACILITIES MAINTENANCE**					
1000	Patching concrete					
1010	Floors, 1/4" thick, small areas, regular grout	1 Cefi	1 Cement Finisher	170	.047	S.F.
1015	Epoxy grout	"	"	100	.080	S.F.
1020	Walls, including chipping, cleaning and epoxy grout					
1025	Minimum	1 Cefi	1 Cement Finisher	65	.123	S.F.
1030	Average			50	.160	S.F.
1035	Maximum	↓	↓	40	.200	S.F.
1037	Stair cleaning, sweep	1 Clab	1 Building Laborer	50	.160	Flight
1039	Mop or scrub			5	1.600	Flight
1080	Sweep and damp mop concrete floor	↓	↓	20	.400	M.S.F.
040	**MASONRY FACILITIES MAINTENANCE**					
0040	Caulking masonry, no staging included					
0050	Re-caulk only, oil base	1 Bric	1 Bricklayer	225	.036	L.F.
0060	Butyl			205	.039	L.F.
0070	Poly sulfide			200	.040	L.F.
0080	Silicone			195	.041	L.F.
0100	Cut out and re-caulk, oil base			145	.055	L.F.
0110	Butyl			130	.062	L.F.
0120	Polysulfide			125	.064	L.F.
0130	Silicone	↓	↓	125	.064	L.F.
0800	Cleaning masonry, no staging included					
0850	Chemical cleaning, brush and wash, minimum cost	D-1	1 Bricklayer 1 Bricklayer Helper	800	.020	S.F.
0860	Average cost			400	.040	S.F.
0870	Maximum cost	↓	↓	330	.048	S.F.
0880	High pressure water only, minimum cost	B-9	1 Labor Foreman (outside) 4 Building Laborers 1 Air Compr., 250 C.F.M. Air Tools & Accessories 2-50 Ft. Air Hoses, 1.5" Dia.	2,000	.020	S.F.
0900	Average cost			1,500	.027	S.F.
0910	Maximum cost			1,000	.040	S.F.
0920	High pressure water and chemical, minimum cost			1,800	.022	S.F.
0930	Average cost			1,200	.033	S.F.
0940	Maximum cost			800	.050	S.F.
0950	Sandblast, wet system, minimum cost			1,750	.023	S.F.
0960	Average cost			1,100	.036	S.F.
0970	Maximum cost			700	.057	S.F.
0980	Dry system, minimum cost			2,500	.016	S.F.
0990	Average cost			1,750	.023	S.F.
1000	Maximum cost			1,000	.040	S.F.
1030	Steam cleaning, minimum cost			3,000	.013	S.F.
1040	Average cost			2,500	.016	S.F.
1050	Maximum cost	↓	↓	1,500	.027	S.F.
3000	Pointing masonry					
3030	Cut and repoint brick, hard mortar, running bond	1 Bric	1 Bricklayer	80	.100	S.F.
3040	Common bond			77	.104	S.F.
3050	Flemish bond			70	.114	S.F.
3060	English bond			65	.123	S.F.
3070	Soft old mortar, running bond			100	.080	S.F.
3080	Common bond			96	.083	S.F.
3090	Flemish bond			90	.089	S.F.
3100	English bond			82	.098	S.F.
3110	Stonework, hard mortar			140	.057	L.F.
3120	Soft old mortar			160	.050	L.F.
3130	Repoint, mask and grout method, running bond			95	.084	S.F.
3140	Common bond	↓	↓	90	.089	S.F.

			CREW	MAKEUP	DAILY OUTPUT	MAN-HOURS	UNIT
018 000		**Facilities Maintenance**					
040	3151	Repoint, mask and grout method, flemish bond	1 Bric	1 Bricklayer	86	.093	S.F.
	3160	English bond			77	.104	S.F.
	3170	Scrub coat, sand grout on walls, minimum			120	.067	S.F.
	3180	Maximum	↓	↓	98	.082	S.F.
	070	MOISTURE-THERMAL CONTROL FACILITIES MAINTENANCE					
	0110	Caulking around exterior doors and windows	1 Carp	1 Carpenter	400	.020	L.F.
	080	DOOR & WINDOW FACILITIES MAINTENANCE					
	0250	Cylinder dead bolt lock set, repair	1 Skwk	1 Skilled Worker	11	.727	Ea.
	0500	Door closer, overhaul			5	1.600	Ea.
	0510	Repair concealed door check or closer			4	2.000	Ea.
	0520	Adjust	↓	↓	26	.308	Ea.
	1500	Remove and reset window, minimum cost (labor)	1 Carp	1 Carpenter	4	2.000	Ea.
	1510	Average cost			2	4.000	Ea.
	1520	Maximum cost	↓	↓	1.33	6.020	Ea.
	1900	Washing door, 3' x 7', damp wipe	1 Clab	1 Building Laborer	145	.055	Ea.
	2000	Washing windows, at ground level w/ladder, sponge & squeegee					
	2010	Both sides, 4' x 7' 2 pane	1 Clab	1 Building Laborer	60	.133	Ea.
	2020	4' x 6', 4 pane			55	.145	Ea.
	2030	3.5' x 5.5', 8 pane			45	.178	Ea.
	2040	2.5' x 5.7', 12 pane			40	.200	Ea.
	2050	4' x 6', 16 pane			35	.229	Ea.
	2060	4' x 7', industrial, 20 pane			30	.267	Ea.
	2070	6' x 7', austral casement, 6 pane			35	.229	Ea.
	2080	Clear glass partition, 8 sq. ft. per unit			3	2.670	M.S.F.
	2090	Opaque, 20 sq. ft. per unit	↓	↓	3	2.670	M.S.F.
	2100	Alternate pricing method by window area to be washed					
	2110	Minimum productivity	1 Clab	1 Building Laborer	1	8.000	M.S.F.
	2120	Average productivity			2.50	3.200	M.S.F.
	2130	Maximum productivity	↓	↓	4	2.000	M.S.F.
	090	FINISHES, FACILITIES MAINTENANCE					
	0400	Floor maintenance					
	0530	Carpet cleaning, vacuum, dry pick-up					
	0540	Unobstructed	1 Clab	1 Building Laborer	30	.267	M.S.F.
	0550	Unobstructed			22	.364	M.S.F.
	0560	Wet pick-up, unobstructed			21	.381	M.S.F.
	0570	Obstructed			14	.571	M.S.F.
	0580	Steam clean, minimum			9,760	.001	S.F.
	0590	Maximum cost	↓	↓	3,250	.002	S.F.
	0700	Composition, resilient or wood flooring					
	0720	Dust mop, unobstructed	1 Clab	1 Building Laborer	60	.133	M.S.F.
	0730	Obstructed			35	.229	M.S.F.
	0740	Damp mop, unobstructed			26	.308	M.S.F.
	0750	Obstructed			16	.500	M.S.F.
	0780	Hand scrub, unobstructed			1.80	4.440	M.S.F.
	0790	Obstructed			1.30	6.150	M.S.F.
	0800	Machine scrub, unobstructed			17	.471	M.S.F.
	0810	Obstructed			12	.667	M.S.F.
	0820	Machine polish, unobstructed			28	.286	M.S.F.
	0830	Obstructed	↓	↓	14	.571	M.S.F.
	0850	Refinish old wood floors, minimum	1 Carp	1 Carpenter	400	.020	S.F.
	0860	Maximum cost	"	"	130	.062	S.F.
	0870	Strip & rewax/polish, unobstructed	1 Clab	1 Building Laborer	4	2.000	M.S.F.
	0880	Obstructed			3	2.670	M.S.F.
	0890	Sweeping, unobstructed			47	.170	M.S.F.
	0900	Obstructed	↓	↓	35	.229	M.S.F.
	2000	Wall maintenance					
	2400	Washing enamel finish walls with mild cleanser	1 Clab	1 Building Laborer	16	.500	M.S.F.

018 000 | Facilities Maintenance

		CREW	MAKEUP	DAILY OUTPUT	MAN-HOURS	UNIT
100	**SPECIALTIES, FACILITIES MAINTENANCE**					
0100	Bathroom accessories					
0150	Clean mirror, 36" x 24"	1 Clab	1 Building Laborer	840	.010	Ea.
0160	48" x 24"			630	.013	Ea.
0170	72" x 24"	↓	↓	420	.019	Ea.
0200	General cleaning of fixtures (basins, water closets, urinals)					
0210	Including shelves, partitions and dispenser servicing	1 Clab	1 Building Laborer	80	.100	Fixture
110	**ARCHITECTURAL EQUIPMENT, FACILITIES MAINTENANCE**					
0100	Bird control needle strips					
0110	Anchor clip mounted	2 Clab	2 Building Laborers	500	.032	L.F.
0120	Adhesive mounted	"	"	550	.029	L.F.
0500	Laundry equipment repair and maintenance					
0520	Dryer, domestic, remove or reinstall basket	1 Skwk	1 Skilled Worker	6	1.330	Ea.
0530	Commercial, disassemble, clean & reassemble			2	4.000	Ea.
0550	Extractor, replace belts (2)			6	1.330	Ea.
0560	Replace pressure pad			2	4.000	Ea.
0570	Flatwork ironer, replace feed ribbons			2	4.000	Ea.
0580	Press, overhaul air system			4	2.000	Ea.
0590	Tumbler, extractor, replace bearings and seal			2	4.000	Ea.
0600	Washer, domestic, replace bearings and seal			3	2.670	Ea.
0610	Remove or reinstall tub	↓	↓	4	2.000	Ea.
0700	Medical and ward equipment repair and maintenance					
0710	Aspirator-overhaul	1 Skwk	1 Skilled Worker	6	1.330	Ea.
0720	Autoclave-overhaul			4	2.000	Ea.
0730	Bed rails, assemble or repair			10	.800	Pr.
0770	Cart, medication, ice, etc. - replace wheels			6	1.330	Carton
0780	Replace rubber bumper			6	1.330	Carton
0800	Centrifuge, repair or replace timer or switch			11	.727	Ea.
0850	Litter, attach safety belt			16	.500	Ea.
0880	Operating table, overhaul and lubricate			6	1.330	Ea.
0900	Oxygen tent apparatus, overhaul			2	4.000	Ea.
0950	Still, clean			3	2.670	Ea.
0970	Striker saw, overhaul			5	1.600	Ea.
1100	Wheelchair, complete overhaul			3	2.670	Ea.
1110	Replace wheel	↓	↓	11	.727	Ea.
2000	Other equipment repair and maintenance					
2040	Cart or dolly, assemble or disassemble axles and wheels	1 Skwk	1 Skilled Worker	6	1.330	Carton
2090	Forge and harden tool			13	.615	Ea.
3100	Office furniture, repair			7	1.140	Ea.
3120	Portable power tool, assemble or disassemble			6	1.330	Ea.
3130	Repair or replace part			6	1.330	Ea.
3180	Replace tool handle			16	.500	Ea.
3200	Sharpen hand tool	↓	↓	16	.500	Ea.
120	**FURNISHINGS FACILITIES MAINTENANCE**					
1000	Reupholster, side chair	1 Skwk	1 Skilled Worker	2.50	3.200	Ea.
1040	Tubular frame chair seat and back			3	2.670	Ea.
1080	Sofa	↓	↓	2	4.000	Ea.
1540	Vacuum, large divan	1 Clab	1 Building Laborer	80	.100	Ea.
140	**CONVEYING SYSTEMS FACILITIES MAINTENANCE**					
0900	Elevator, general cleaning, vacuum, dust, mop, polish	1 Clab	1 Building Laborer	16	.500	Ea.
0920	Motor generator set, service	1 Elec	1 Electrician	8	1.000	Ea.
0930	Repair, minor			2	4.000	Ea.
0940	Limit switch, repair	↓	↓	11	.727	Ea.
0950	Troubleshoot, main control panel	2 Elec	2 Electricians	2.50	6.400	Ea.
1000	Escalator cleaning, dusting, polishing	1 Clab	1 Building Laborer	20	.400	Flight
1500	Vehicle maintenance, grease, light vehicle	1 Skwk	1 Skilled Worker	20	.400	Ea.
1510	Heavy vehicle			7	1.140	Ea.
1520	Wash, light vehicle	↓	↓	8	1.000	Ea.

		018 000 | Facilities Maintenance	CREW	MAKEUP	DAILY OUTPUT	MAN-HOURS	UNIT
140	1531	Vehicle maintenance, wash, heavy vehicle	1 Skwk	1 Skilled Worker	6	1.330	Ea.
	1540	Change oil and filter, light vehicle			10	.800	Ea.
	1570	Rotate tires, light vehicle	↓	↓	18	.444	Ea.
	150	**MECHANICAL FACILITIES MAINTENANCE**					
	0100	Air conditioning system maintenance					
	0130	Belt, replace	1 Stpi	1 Steamfitter	15	.533	Ea.
	0160	Duct work, clean			375	.021	L.F.
	0170	Fan, clean			16	.500	Ea.
	0180	Filter, remove, clean, replace			12	.667	Ea.
	0190	Flexible coupling alignment, inspect			40	.200	Ea.
	0200	Gas leak locate and repair			4	2.000	Ea.
	0250	Pump packing gland, remove and replace			11	.727	Ea.
	0270	Tighten			32	.250	Ea.
	0290	Pump disassemble and assemble	↓	↓	4	2.000	Ea.
	0300	Air pressure regulator, disassemble, clean, assemble	1 Skwk	1 Skilled Worker	4	2.000	Ea.
	0310	Repair or replace part	"	"	6	1.330	Ea.
	0320	Purging system	1 Stpi	1 Steamfitter	16	.500	Ea.
	0350	Replenish gas refrigerant from cylinder	"	"	3	2.670	Ea.
	0400	Compressor, air, remove or install fan wheel	1 Skwk	1 Skilled Worker	20	.400	Ea.
	0410	Disassemble or assemble 2 cylinder, 2 stage			4	2.000	Ea.
	0420	4 cylinder, 4 stage			1	8.000	Ea.
	0430	Repair or replace part	↓	↓	2	4.000	Ea.
	1000	Expansion joint, vacuum breaker, not screwed, install or remove	1 Stpi	1 Steamfitter	3	2.670	Ea.
	1010	Repack	"	"	6	1.330	Ea.
	1200	Fire protection equipment					
	1220	Fire hydrant, replace	Q-1	1 Plumber / 1 Plumber Apprentice	3	5.330	Ea.
	1230	Service, lubricate, inspect, flush, clean	1 Plum	1 Plumber	7	1.140	Ea.
	1240	Test	"	"	11	.727	Ea.
	1310	Inspect valves, pressure, nozzle, lubricate	1 Spri	1 Sprinkler Installer	4	2.000	System
	1801	Plumbing fixtures					
	1840	Open drain with snake	1 Plum	1 Plumber	13	.615	Ea.
	1850	Open drain with toilet auger			16	.500	Ea.
	1860	Grease trap, clean			2	4.000	Ea.
	1870	Plaster trap, clean	↓	↓	6	1.330	Ea.
	1900	Relief valve, test and adjust	1 Stpi	1 Steamfitter	20	.400	Ea.
	2000	Repair or replace-steam trap			8	1.000	Ea.
	2020	Y-type or bell strainer or screen			6	1.330	Ea.
	2040	Water trap or vacuum breaker, screwed joints	↓	↓	13	.615	Ea.
	2100	Steam specialties, clean					
	2120	Air separator with automatic trap, 1" fittings	1 Stpi	1 Steamfitter	12	.667	Ea.
	2130	Bucket trap, 2" pipe			7	1.140	Ea.
	2150	Drip leg, 2" fitting			45	.178	Ea.
	2200	Thermodynamic trap, 1" fittings			50	.160	Ea.
	2210	Thermostatic			65	.123	Ea.
	2240	Screen and seat in y-type strainer			25	.320	Ea.
	2500	Valve, replace broken handwheel	↓	↓	24	.333	Ea.
	3000	Valve, overhaul, regulator, relief, flushometer, mixing					
	3040	Cold water, gas	1 Stpi	1 Steamfitter	5	1.600	Ea.
	3050	Hot water, steam			3	2.670	Ea.
	3080	Globe, gate, check up to 4" cold water, gas			10	.800	Ea.
	3090	Hot water, steam			5	1.600	Ea.
	3100	Over 4" ID hot or cold line	↓	↓	1	5.710	Ea.
	3120	Remove and replace, gate, globe or check up to 4"	Q-5	1 Steamfitter / 1 Steamfitter Apprentice	6	2.670	Ea.
	3130	Over 4"	"	"	2	8.000	Ea.
	3150	Repack up to 4"	1 Stpi	1 Steamfitter	13	.615	Ea.
	3160	Over 4"	"	"	4	2.000	Ea.

018 000	Facilities Maintenance	CREW	MAKEUP	DAILY OUTPUT	MAN-HOURS	UNIT
160	**ELECTRICAL FACILITIES MAINTENANCE**					
0700	Cathodic protection systems					
0720	Check and adjust reading on rectifier	1 Elec	1 Electrician	20	.400	Ea.
0730	Check pipe to soil potential			20	.400	Ea.
0740	Replace lead connection			4	2.000	Ea.
0800	Control device, install			5.70	1.400	Ea.
0810	Disassemble, clean and reinstall			7	1.140	Ea.
0820	Replace			10.70	.748	Ea.
0830	Trouble shoot			10	.800	Ea.
1000	Distribution systems and equipment install or repair a breaker					
1010	In power panels up to 200 amps	1 Elec	1 Electrician	7	1.140	Ea.
1020	Over 200 amps			2	4.000	Ea.
1030	Reset breaker or replace fuse			20	.400	Ea.
1100	Megger test MCC (each stack)			4	2.000	Ea.
1110	MCC vacuum and clean (each stack)			5.30	1.510	Ea.
2500	Lighting equipment, replace road light			3	2.670	Ea.
2510	Fluorescent fixture			7	1.140	Ea.
2515	Relamp (flour.) facility area ea. tube			60	.133	Ea.
2518	Fluorescent fixture, clean (area)			44	.182	Ea.
2520	Incandescent fixture			11	.727	Ea.
2530	Lamp (incadescent or flourescent)			60	.133	Ea.
2535	Replace cord in socket lamp			13	.615	Ea.
2540	Ballast			6	1.330	Ea.
2541	Starter			30	.267	Ea.
2545	Replace other lighting parts			11	.727	Ea.
2550	Switch			11	.727	Ea.
2555	Receptacle			11	.727	Ea.
2560	Floodlight			4	2.000	Ea.
2570	Christmas lighting, indoor, per string			16	.500	Ea.
2580	Outdoor			13	.615	Ea.
2590	Test battery operated emergency lights			40	.200	Ea.
2600	Repair/replace component in communication system			6	1.330	Ea.
2700	Repair misc. appliances (incl. clocks, vent fan, blower, etc.)			6	1.330	Ea.
2710	Reset clocks & timers			50	.160	Ea.
2720	Adjust time delay relays			16	.500	Ea.
2730	Test specific gravity of lead-acid batteries			80	.100	Ea.
3000	Motors and generators					
3020	Disassemble, clean and reinstall motor, up to 1/4 HP	1 Elec	1 Electrician	4	2.000	Ea.
3030	Up to 3/4 HP			3	2.670	Ea.
3040	Up to 10 HP			2	4.000	Ea.
3050	Replace part, up to 1/4 HP			6	1.330	Ea.
3060	Up to 3/4 HP			4	2.000	Ea.
3070	Up to 10 HP			3	2.670	Ea.
3080	Megger test motor windings			5.33	1.500	Ea.
3082	Motor vibration check			16	.500	Ea.
3084	Oil motor bearings			25	.320	Ea.
3086	Run test emergency generator for 30 minutes			11	.727	Ea.
3090	Rewind motor, up to 1/4 HP			3	2.670	Ea.
3100	Up to 3/4 HP			2	4.000	Ea.
3110	Up to 10 HP			1.50	5.330	Ea.
3150	Generator, repair or replace part			4	2.000	Ea.
3160	Repair DC generator			2	4.000	Ea.
4000	Stub pole, install or remove			3	2.670	Ea.
4500	Transformer maintenance up to 15KVA			2.70	2.960	Ea.

DIVISION 2 SITE WORK

DIVISION 2 SITE WORK

Site work is comprised of many categories of work, from cleaning to landscaping. In this division, the choice of either equipment or hand labor can have a great effect on productivity. For this reason, carefully examine the makeup of each crew selected when working with man-hour figures for site work.

Productivity during any clearing operation is directly related to both the size and condition of the site. Generally, the smaller the project, the more labor-intensive it becomes. For instance, clearing a site smaller than two acres involves much more hand labor per acre than clearing one hundred acres. In order to justify employing heavy equipment, however, mobilization costs must be offset by the economics of the scale of the project.

The end product of the clearing operation can also influence the number of man-hours required. Equipment can be used to do the major portion of cutting, stacking, and hauling trees, but hand labor must be used to perform work such as chipping or burning.

Demolition work of any scale is labor-intensive because of its controlled limit, disposal requirements, and the need to protect the surroundings.

Access to the site is another important factor. When movement or access is restricted, earthwork operations cannot be accomplished with heavy equipment, and there is a corresponding increase in the amount of work that must be performed by laborers. This concept is illustrated through a comparison of different compaction operations. The compaction and fill of a road base can be easily handled with a road roller. The same operation for a utility trench, however, involves hand labor and a gas engine compactor.

Installation of caissons and piles involves a large amount of equipment, with the exception of work done on splices, points, and cutoffs which are done by hand with a corresponding increase in the number of man-hours involved.

Site utility work includes mostly piping with the addition of some underground conduits, manholes, and vaults. Although this work is very labor-intensive, some equipment is needed to handle piping larger than six inches. Small precast structures require even more equipment.

The heavy equipment used in paving operations requires much more labor support than earthwork operations. Curbing and guardrail installations increase total man-hour figures due to the amount of hand work involved. The same is true for masonry paving done for sidewalks and plazas.

Site improvements, such as fencing and site furnishings, are generally small jobs that require little special equipment. Retaining structures are the only improvements in which equipment plays a significant role.

Landscaping is a good example of the general rule that larger projects depend on the use of heavy equipment to accomplish the best level of productivity. Small areas can be done exclusively by hand using small tools. Large areas require special equipment. Some equipment, such as the hydraulic spreader used for seeding and mulching, is so much more efficient than other forms of labor (such as a hand spreader) that contractors readily accept mobilization costs even for small areas. However, it should be noted that planting in prepared beds is best accomplished by hand.

020 120	Std Penetration Tests	CREW	MAKEUP	DAILY OUTPUT	MAN-HOURS	UNIT
123	**BORINGS** Initial field stake out and determination of elevations	A-6	1 Chief Of Party	1	16.000	Day
			1 Instrument Man			
0300	Mobilization and demobilization, minimum	B-55	2 Building Laborers	4	6.000	Total
			1 Truck Driver (light)			
			1 Flatbed Truck w/Auger			
			1 Truck, 3 Ton			
0350	For over 100 miles, per added mile			450	.053	Mile
0600	Auger holes in earth, no samples, 2-1/2" diameter			78.60	.305	L.F.
0650	4" diameter			67.50	.356	L.F.
0800	Cased borings in earth, with samples, 2-1/2" diameter			55.50	.432	L.F.
0850	4" diameter	▼	▼	32.60	.736	L.F.
1000	Drilling in rock, "BX" core, no sampling	B-56	1 Building Laborer	34.90	.458	L.F.
			1 Equip. Oper. (light)			
			1 Crawler Type Drill, 4"			
			1 Air Compr., 600 C.F.M.			
			1-50 Ft. Air Hose, 3" dia			
1050	With casing & sampling			31.70	.505	L.F.
1200	"NX" core, no sampling			25.92	.617	L.F.
1250	With casing and sampling	▼	▼	25	.640	L.F.
1400	Drill rig and crew with light duty rig	B-55	2 Building Laborers	1	24.000	Day
			1 Truck Driver (light)			
			1 Flatbed Truck w/Auger			
			1 Truck, 3 Ton			
1450	With heavy duty rig	B-56	1 Building Laborer	1	16.000	Day
			1 Equip. Oper. (light)			
			1 Crawler Type Drill, 4"			
			1 Air Compr., 600 C.F.M.			
			1-50 Ft. Air Hose, 3" dia			
125	**DRILLING, CORE** Reinforced concrete slab, up to 6" thick slab					
0020	Including layout and set up					
0100	1" diameter core	B-89A	1 Equip. Oper. (light)	48	.333	Ea.
			1 Truck Driver (light)			
			1 Truck, Stake Body, 3 Ton			
			1 Concrete Saw			
			1 Water Tank, 65 Gal			
			1 Skilled Worker			
			1 Laborer			
			1 Core Drill (large)			
0150	Each added inch thick, add			400	.040	Ea.
0300	3" diameter core			40	.400	Ea.
0350	Each added inch thick, add			267	.060	Ea.
0500	4" diameter core			37	.432	Ea.
0550	Each added inch thick, add			242	.066	Ea.
0700	6" diameter core			29	.552	Ea.
0750	Each added inch thick, add			200	.080	Ea.
0900	8" diameter core			21	.762	Ea.
0950	Each added inch thick, add	▼	▼	133	.120	Ea.
1100	10" diameter core	A-1	1 Building Laborer	19	.421	Ea.
			1 Gas Eng. Power Tool			
1150	Each added inch thick, add			114	.070	Ea.
1300	12" diameter core			16	.500	Ea.
1350	Each added inch thick, add			96	.083	Ea.
1500	14" diameter core			13.80	.580	Ea.
1550	Each added inch thick, add			80	.100	Ea.
1700	18" diameter core			6.80	1.180	Ea.
1750	Each added inch thick, add	▼	▼	40	.200	Ea.
1771						

020 120 | Std Penetration Tests

		CREW	MAKEUP	DAILY OUTPUT	MAN-HOURS	UNIT
125	1781	Prestressed hollow core plank, 6" thick, 1" dia. core	B-89A	1 Equip. Oper. (light)	65	.246	Ea.
				1 Truck Driver (light)			
				1 Truck, Stake Body, 3 Ton			
				1 Concrete Saw			
				1 Water Tank, 65 Gal			
				1 Skilled Worker			
				1 Laborer			
				1 Core Drill (large)			
	1790	Each added inch thick, add			432	.037	Ea.
	1800	3" diameter core			66	.242	Ea.
	1810	Each added inch thick, add			296	.054	Ea.
	1820	4" diameter core			63	.254	Ea.
	1830	Each added inch thick, add			271	.059	Ea.
	1840	6" diameter core			52	.308	Ea.
	1850	Each added inch thick, add			222	.072	Ea.
	1860	8" diameter core			37	.432	Ea.
	1870	Each added inch thick, add	↓	↓	147	.109	Ea.
	1880	10" diameter core	A-1	1 Building Laborer	32	.250	Ea.
				1 Gas Eng. Power Tool			
	1890	Each added inch thick, add			124	.065	Ea.
	1900	12" diameter core			28	.286	Ea.
	1910	Each added inch thick, add	↓	↓	107	.075	Ea.
	1950	Minimum charge for above, 3" diameter core	B-89A	1 Equip. Oper. (light)	7.45	2.150	Ea.
				1 Truck Driver (light)			
				1 Truck, Stake Body, 3 Ton			
				1 Concrete Saw			
				1 Water Tank, 65 Gal			
				1 Skilled Worker			
				1 Laborer			
				1 Core Drill (large)			
	2000	4" diameter core			7.15	2.240	Ea.
	2050	6" diameter core			6.40	2.500	Ea.
	2100	8" diameter core			5.80	2.760	Ea.
	2150	10" diameter core			5	3.200	Ea.
	2200	12" diameter core			4.10	3.900	Ea.
	2250	14" diameter core			3.55	4.510	Ea.
	2300	18" diameter core	↓	↓	3.30	4.850	Ea.
	128	TEST PITS Hand digging, light soil	1 Clab	1 Building Laborer	4.50	1.780	C.Y.
	0100	Heavy soil	"	"	2.50	3.200	C.Y.
	0120	Loader-backhoe, light soil	B-11M	1 Equipment Oper. (med.)	28	.571	C.Y.
				1 Building Laborer			
				1 Backhoe Loader, 80 H.P.			
	0130	Heavy soil	"	"	20	.800	C.Y.

020 550 | Site Demolition

		CREW	MAKEUP	DAILY OUTPUT	MAN-HOURS	UNIT
554	SITE DEMOLITION No hauling, abandon catch basin or manhole	B-6	2 Building Laborers	7	3.430	Ea.
			1 Equip. Oper. (light)			
			1 Backhoe Loader, 48 H.P.			
0020	Remove existing catch basin or manhole			4	6.000	Ea.
0030	Catch basin or manhole frames and covers stored			13	1.850	Ea.
0040	Remove and reset	↓	↓	7	3.430	Ea.
0600	Fencing, barbed wire, 3 strand	2 Clab	2 Building Laborers	430	.037	L.F.
0650	5 strand			280	.057	L.F.
0700	Chain link, remove only			310	.052	L.F.
0750	Remove and reset			50	.320	L.F.
0800	Guide rail, remove only			85	.188	L.F.
0850	Remove and reset	↓	↓	35	.457	L.F.
0900	Hydrants, fire, remove only	2 Plum	2 Plumbers	4.70	3.400	Ea.

020 | Subsurface Investigation and Demolition

020 550 | Site Demolition

			CREW	MAKEUP	DAILY OUTPUT	MAN-HOURS	UNIT
554	0952	Hydrants, fire, remove and reset	2 Plum	2 Plumbers	1.40	11.430	Ea.
	1000	Remove masonry walls, block or tile, solid	B-5	1 Labor Foreman (outside)	1,800	.036	C.F.
				4 Building Laborers			
				2 Equip. Oper. (med.)			
				1 Mechanic			
				1 Air Compr., 250 C.F.M.			
				Air Tools & Accessories			
				2-50 Ft. Air Hoses, 1.5" Dia.			
				F.E. Loader, T.M., 2.5 C.Y.			
	1100	Cavity			2,200	.029	C.F.
	1200	Brick, solid			900	.071	C.F.
	1300	With block			1,130	.057	C.F.
	1400	Stone, with mortar			900	.071	C.F.
	1500	Dry set	↓	↓	1,500	.043	C.F.
	1800	Bituminous driveways	B-38	1 Labor Foreman (outside)	680	.059	S.Y.
				2 Building Laborers			
				1 Equip. Oper. (light)			
				1 Equip. Oper. (medium)			
				1 Backhoe Loader, 48 H.P.			
				1 Demol. Hammer, Hyd. (1000 lb)			
				1 F.E. Loader (170 H.P.)			
				1 Pavt. Rem. Bucket			
	1900	Concrete to 6" thick, mesh reinforced			255	.157	S.Y.
	2000	Rod reinforced			200	.200	S.Y.
	2100	Concrete 7" to 24" thick, plain			13.10	3.050	C.Y.
	2200	Reinforced	↓	↓	9.50	4.210	C.Y.
	2300	With hand held air equipment, bituminous	B-39	1 Labor Foreman (outside)	1,900	.025	S.F.
				4 Building Laborers			
				1 Equipment Oper. (light)			
				1 Air Compr., 250 C.F.M.			
				Air Tools & Accessories			
				2-50 Ft. Air Hoses, 1.5" Dia			
	2320	Concrete to 6" thick, no reinforcing			1,200	.040	S.F.
	2340	Mesh reinforced			830	.058	S.F.
	2360	Rod reinforced	↓	↓	765	.063	S.F.
	2400	Curbs, concrete, plain	B-6	2 Building Laborers	325	.074	L.F.
				1 Equip. Oper. (light)			
				1 Backhoe Loader, 48 H.P.			
	2500	Reinforced			220	.109	L.F.
	2600	Granite curbs			355	.068	L.F.
	2700	Bituminous curbs			830	.029	L.F.
	2900	Pipe removal, concrete, no excavation, 12" diameter			175	.137	L.F.
	2930	15" diameter			150	.160	L.F.
	2960	24" diameter			120	.200	L.F.
	3000	36" diameter			90	.267	L.F.
	3200	Steel, welded connections, 4" diameter			160	.150	L.F.
	3300	10" diameter	↓	↓	80	.300	L.F.
	3500	Railroad track removal, ties and track	B-14	1 Labor Foreman (outside)	110	.436	L.F.
				4 Building Laborers			
				1 Equip. Oper. (light)			
				1 Backhoe Loader, 48 H.P.			
	3600	Ballast			500	.096	C.Y.
	3700	Remove and re-install ties & track using new bolts & spikes			50	.960	L.F.
	3800	Turnouts using new bolts and spikes	↓	↓	1	48.000	Ea.
	4000	Sidewalk removal, bituminous, 2-1/2" thick	B-6	2 Building Laborers	325	.074	S.Y.
				1 Equip. Oper. (light)			
				1 Backhoe Loader, 48 H.P.			
	4050	Brick, set in mortar	"	"	185	.130	S.Y.

020 | Subsurface Investigation Demolition

020 550 | Site Demolition

		CREW	MAKEUP	DAILY OUTPUT	MAN-HOURS	UNIT
554	4101	Sidewalk removal, concrete, plain	B-6	2 Building Laborers	160	.150	S.Y.
				1 Equip. Oper. (light)			
				1 Backhoe Loader, 48 H.P.			
	4200	Mesh reinforced	"	"	150	.160	S.Y.

020 600 | Building Demolition

		CREW	MAKEUP	DAILY OUTPUT	MAN-HOURS	UNIT
604	BUILDING DEMOLITION Large urban projects, incl. disposal, steel	B-8	1 Labor Foreman (outside)	21,500	.003	C.F.
			2 Building Laborers			
			2 Equip. Oper. (med.)			
			1 Equip. Oper. Oiler			
			2 Truck Drivers (heavy)			
			1 Hyd. Crane, 25 Ton			
			F.E. Loader, T.M., 2.5 C.Y.			
			2 Dump Trucks, 16 Ton			
0050	Concrete			15,300	.004	C.F.
0080	Masonry			20,100	.003	C.F.
0100	Mixture of types, average			20,100	.003	C.F.
0500	Small bldgs, or single bldgs, no salvage included, steel	B-3	1 Labor Foreman (outside)	14,800	.003	C.F.
			2 Building Laborers			
			1 Equip. Oper. (med.)			
			2 Truck Drivers (heavy)			
			F.E. Loader, T.M., 2.5 C.Y.			
			2 Dump Trucks, 16 Ton			
0600	Concrete			11,300	.004	C.F.
0650	Masonry			14,800	.003	C.F.
0700	Wood			14,800	.003	C.F.
608 0020	DISPOSAL ONLY Urban buildings with salvage value allowed / Including loading and 5 mile haul to dump					
0200	Steel frame	B-3	1 Labor Foreman (outside)	430	.112	C.Y.
			2 Building Laborers			
			1 Equip. Oper. (med.)			
			2 Truck Drivers (heavy)			
			F.E. Loader, T.M., 2.5 C.Y.			
			2 Dump Trucks, 16 Ton			
0300	Concrete frame			365	.132	C.Y.
0400	Masonry construction			445	.108	C.Y.
0500	Wood frame			247	.194	C.Y.
620 0020	RUBBISH HANDLING The following are to be added to the / demolition prices					
0400	Chute, circular, prefabricated steel, 18" diameter	B-1	1 Labor Foreman (outside)	40	.600	L.F.
			2 Building Laborers			
0440	30" diameter	"	"	30	.800	L.F.
1000	Dust partition, 6 mil polyethylene, 4' x 8' panels, 1" x 3" frame	2 Carp	2 Carpenters	2,000	.008	S.F.
1080	2" x 4" frame	"	"	2,000	.008	S.F.
2000	Load, haul to chute & dumping into chute, 50' haul	2 Clab	2 Building Laborers	21.50	.744	C.Y.
2040	100' haul			16.50	.970	C.Y.
2080	Over 100' haul, add per 100 L.F.			35.50	.451	C.Y.
2120	In elevators, per 10 floors, add			140	.114	C.Y.
3000	Loading & trucking, including 2 mile haul, chute loaded	B-16	1 Labor Foreman (outside)	32	1.000	C.Y.
			2 Building Laborers			
			1 Truck Driver (heavy)			
			1 Dump Truck, 16 Ton			
3040	Hand loaded, 50' haul	2 Clab	2 Building Laborers	30	.533	C.Y.
3080	Machine loaded	B-6	2 Building Laborers	60	.400	C.Y.
			1 Equip. Oper. (light)			
			1 Backhoe Loader, 48 H.P.			
3120	Wheeled 50' and ramp dump loaded	2 Clab	2 Building Laborers	24	.667	C.Y.

020 600 | Building Demolition

		CREW	MAKEUP	DAILY OUTPUT	MAN-HOURS	UNIT
620 5001	Rubbish handling, haul, per mile, up to 8 C.Y. truck	B-34B	1 Truck Driver (heavy)	1,165	.007	C.Y.
			1 Dump Truck, 16 Ton			
5100	Over 8 C.Y. truck	"	"	1,550	.005	C.Y.

020 700 | Selective Demolition

		CREW	MAKEUP	DAILY OUTPUT	MAN-HOURS	UNIT
702	CEILING DEMOLITION					
0200	Drywall, on wood frame	2 Clab	2 Building Laborers	800	.020	S.F.
0220	On metal frame			760	.021	S.F.
0240	On suspension system, including system			720	.022	S.F.
1000	Plaster, lime and horse hair, on wood lath, incl. lath			700	.023	S.F.
1020	On metal lath			570	.028	S.F.
1100	Gypsum, on gypsum lath			720	.022	S.F.
1120	On metal lath			500	.032	S.F.
1500	Tile, wood fiber, 12" x 12", glued			900	.018	S.F.
1540	Stapled			1,000	.016	S.F.
1580	On suspension system, incl. system			760	.021	S.F.
2000	Wood, tongue and groove, 1" x 4"			1,000	.016	S.F.
2040	1" x 8"			1,100	.015	S.F.
2400	Plywood or wood fiberboard, 4' x 8' sheets	↓	↓	1,200	.013	S.F.
704	CUTOUT DEMOLITION Conc., elev. slab, light reinf., under 6 C.F.	B-9	1 Labor Foreman (outside)	65	.615	C.F.
			4 Building Laborers			
			1 Air Compr., 250 C.F.M.			
			Air Tools & Accessories			
			2-50 Ft. Air Hoses, 1.5" Dia.			
0050	Light reinforcing, over 6 C.F.			75	.533	C.F.
0200	Slab on grade to 6" thick, not reinforced, under 8 S.F.			85	.471	S.F.
0250	Not reinforced, over 8 S.F.			175	.229	S.F.
0600	Walls, not reinforced, under 6 C.F.			60	.667	C.F.
0650	Not reinforced, over 6 C.F.			65	.615	C.F.
1000	Concrete, elevated slab, bar reinforced, under 6 C.F.			45	.889	C.F.
1050	Bar reinforced, over 6 C.F.			50	.800	C.F.
1200	Slab on grade to 6" thick, bar reinforced, under 8 S.F.			75	.533	S.F.
1250	Bar reinforced, over 8 S.F.			105	.381	S.F.
1400	Walls, bar reinforced, under 6 C.F.			50	.800	C.F.
1450	Bar reinforced, over 6 C.F.	↓	↓	55	.727	C.F.
2000	Brick, to 4 S.F. opening, not including toothing					
2040	4" thick	B-9	1 Labor Foreman (outside)	30	1.330	Ea.
			4 Building Laborers			
			1 Air Compr., 250 C.F.M.			
			Air Tools & Accessories			
			2-50 Ft. Air Hoses, 1.5" Dia.			
2060	8" thick			18	2.220	Ea.
2080	12" thick			10	4.000	Ea.
2400	Concrete block, to 4 S.F. opening, 2" thick			35	1.140	Ea.
2420	4" thick			30	1.330	Ea.
2440	8" thick			27	1.480	Ea.
2460	12" thick			24	1.670	Ea.
2600	Gypsum block, to 4 S.F. opening, 2" thick			80	.500	Ea.
2620	4" thick			70	.571	Ea.
2640	8" thick			55	.727	Ea.
2800	Terra cotta, to 4 S.F. opening, 4" thick			70	.571	Ea.
2840	8" thick			65	.615	Ea.
2880	12" thick	↓	↓	50	.800	Ea.
6000	Walls, interior, not including re-framing,					
6010	openings to 5 S.F.					
6100	Drywall to 5/8" thick	A-1	1 Building Laborer	24	.333	Ea.
			1 Gas Eng. Power Tool			
6200	Paneling to 3/4" thick	"	"	20	.400	Ea.

020 700 | Selective Demolition

		Description	CREW	MAKEUP	DAILY OUTPUT	MAN-HOURS	UNIT
704	6301	Cutout demolition, walls, plaster, on gypsum lath	A-1	1 Building Laborer 1 Gas Eng. Power Tool	20	.400	Ea.
	6340	On wire lath	"	"	14	.571	Ea.
	7000	Wood frame, not including re-framing, openings to 5 S.F.					
	7200	Floors, sheathing and flooring to 2" thick	A-1	1 Building Laborer 1 Gas Eng. Power Tool	5	1.600	Ea.
	7310	Roofs, sheathing to 1" thick, not including roofing	↓	↓	6	1.330	Ea.
	7410	Walls, sheathing to 1" thick, not including siding			7	1.140	Ea.
706		**DOOR DEMOLITION**					
	0200	Doors, exterior, 1-3/4" thick, single, 3' x 7' high	1 Clab	1 Building Laborer	16	.500	Ea.
	0220	Double, 6' x 7' high			12	.667	Ea.
	0500	Interior, 1-3/8" thick, single, 3' x 7' high			20	.400	Ea.
	0520	Double, 6' x 7' high			16	.500	Ea.
	0700	Bi-folding, 3' x 6'-8" high			20	.400	Ea.
	0720	6' x 6'-8" high			18	.444	Ea.
	0900	Bi-passing, 3' x 6'-8" high			16	.500	Ea.
	0940	6' x 6'-8" high	↓	↓	14	.571	Ea.
	1500	Remove and reset, minimum	1 Carp	1 Carpenter	8	1.000	Ea.
	1520	Maximum	"	"	6	1.330	Ea.
	2000	Frames, including trim, metal	A-1	1 Building Laborer 1 Gas Eng. Power Tool	8	1.000	Ea.
	2200	Wood			14	.571	Ea.
	2201	Alternate pricing method	↓	↓	200	.040	L.F.
	3000	Special doors, counter doors	F-2	2 Carpenters Power Tools	6	2.670	Ea.
	3100	Double acting			10	1.600	Ea.
	3200	Floor door (trap type)			8	2.000	Ea.
	3300	Glass, sliding, including frames			12	1.330	Ea.
	3400	Overhead, commercial, 12' x 12' high			4	4.000	Ea.
	3440	20' x 16' high			3	5.330	Ea.
	3500	Residential, 9' x 7' high			8	2.000	Ea.
	3540	16' x 7' high			7	2.290	Ea.
	3600	Remove and reset, minimum			4	4.000	Ea.
	3620	Maximum			2	6.400	Ea.
	3700	Roll-up grille			5	3.200	Ea.
	3800	Revolving door			2	8.000	Ea.
	3900	Swing door	↓	↓	3	5.330	Ea.
708		**ELECTRICAL DEMOLITION**					
	0020	Conduit to 15' high, including fittings & hangers					
	0100	Rigid galvanized steel, 1/2" to 1" diameter	1 Elec	1 Electrician	242	.033	L.F.
	0120	1-1/4" to 2"			200	.040	L.F.
	0140	2" to 4"			151	.053	L.F.
	0160	4" to 6"			57	.140	L.F.
	0200	Electric metallic tubing (EMT) 1/2" to 1"			394	.020	L.F.
	0220	1-1/4" to 1-1/2"			326	.025	L.F.
	0240	2" to 3"			236	.034	L.F.
	0260	3-1/2" to 4"	↓	↓	95	.084	L.F.
	0270	Armored cable, (BX) ave. 50' runs					
	0280	#14, 2 wire	1 Elec	1 Electrician	690	.012	L.F.
	0290	#14, 3 wire			571	.014	L.F.
	0300	#12, 2 wire			605	.013	L.F.
	0310	#12, 3 wire			514	.016	L.F.
	0320	#10, 2 wire			514	.016	L.F.
	0330	#10, 3 wire			425	.019	L.F.
	0340	#8, 3 wire	↓	↓	342	.023	L.F.
	0350	Non metallic sheathed cable (Romex)					
	0360	#14, 2 wire	1 Elec	1 Electrician	720	.011	L.F.
	0370	#14, 3 wire	"	"	657	.012	L.F.

		020 700	Selective Demolition	CREW	MAKEUP	DAILY OUTPUT	MAN-HOURS	UNIT
708	0381	Elec. demolition, non metallic sheathed cable, #12, 2 wire		1 Elec	1 Electrician	629	.013	L.F.
	0390	#10, 3 wire		"	"	450	.018	L.F.
	0400	Wiremold raceway, including fittings & hangers						
	0420	No. 3000		1 Elec	1 Electrician	250	.032	L.F.
	0440	No. 4000				217	.037	L.F.
	0460	No. 6000		↓	↓	166	.048	L.F.
	0500	Channels, steel, including fittings & hangers						
	0520	3/4" x 1-1/2"		1 Elec	1 Electrician	308	.026	L.F.
	0540	1-1/2" x 1-1/2"				269	.030	L.F.
	0560	1-1/2" x 1-7/8"		↓	↓	229	.035	L.F.
	0600	Copper bus duct, indoor, 3 ph, incl. removal of						
	0610	hangers & supports						
	0620	225 amp		1 Elec	1 Electrician	67	.119	L.F.
	0640	400 amp				53	.151	L.F.
	0660	600 amp				43	.186	L.F.
	0680	1000 amp				30	.267	L.F.
	0700	1600 amp				20	.400	L.F.
	0720	3000 amp		↓	↓	10	.800	L.F.
	0800	Plug-in switches, 600V 3 ph, incl. disconnecting						
	0820	wire, pipe terminations, 30 amp		1 Elec	1 Electrician	15.50	.516	Ea.
	0840	60 amp				13.90	.576	Ea.
	0850	100 amp				10.40	.769	Ea.
	0860	200 amp				6.20	1.290	Ea.
	0880	400 amp				2.70	2.960	Ea.
	0900	600 amp				1.70	4.710	Ea.
	0920	800 amp				1.30	6.150	Ea.
	0940	1200 amp				1	8.000	Ea.
	0960	1600 amp		↓	↓	.85	9.410	Ea.
	1000	Safety switches, 250 or 600V, incl. disconnection						
	1050	of wire & pipe terminations						
	1100	30 amp		1 Elec	1 Electrician	12.30	.650	Ea.
	1120	60 amp				8.80	.909	Ea.
	1140	100 amp				7.30	1.100	Ea.
	1160	200 amp				5	1.600	Ea.
	1180	400 amp				3.40	2.350	Ea.
	1200	600 amp		↓	↓	2.30	3.480	Ea.
	1210	Panel boards, incl. removal of all breakers,						
	1220	pipe terminations & wire connections						
	1230	3 wire, 120/240V, 100A, to 20 circuits		1 Elec	1 Electrician	2.60	3.080	Ea.
	1240	200 amps, to 42 circuits				1.30	6.150	Ea.
	1250	400 amps, to 42 circuits				1.10	7.270	Ea.
	1260	4 wire, 120/208V, 125A, to 20 circuits				2.40	3.330	Ea.
	1270	200 amps, to 42 circuits				1.20	6.670	Ea.
	1280	400 amps, to 42 circuits		↓	↓	.96	8.330	Ea.
	1300	Transformer, dry type, 1 ph, incl. removal of						
	1320	supports, wire & pipe terminations						
	1340	1 KVA		1 Elec	1 Electrician	7.70	1.040	Ea.
	1360	5 KVA				4.70	1.700	Ea.
	1380	10 KVA				3.60	2.220	Ea.
	1400	37.5 KVA				1.50	5.330	Ea.
	1420	75 KVA		↓	↓	1.25	6.400	Ea.
	1440	3 Phase to 600V, primary						
	1460	3 KVA		1 Elec	1 Electrician	3.85	2.080	Ea.
	1480	15 KVA				2.10	3.810	Ea.
	1500	30 KVA				1.74	4.600	Ea.
	1510	45 KVA				1.53	5.230	Ea.
	1520	75 KVA				1.35	5.930	Ea.
	1530	112.5 KVA		↓	↓	1.16	6.900	Ea.

020 700 | Selective Demolition

		CREW	MAKEUP	DAILY OUTPUT	MAN-HOURS	UNIT
708 1541	Elec. demolition, transformer, 3 ph, to 600V, 150 KVA	1 Elec	1 Electrician	1.09	7.340	Ea.
1560	500 KVA			.58	13.790	Ea.
1570	750 KVA	↓	↓	.45	17.780	Ea.
1600	Pull boxes & cabinets, sheet metal, incl. removal					
1620	of supports and pipe terminations					
1640	6" x 6" x 4"	1 Elec	1 Electrician	31.10	.257	Ea.
1660	12" x 12" x 4"			23.30	.343	Ea.
1680	24" x 24" x 6"			12.30	.650	Ea.
1700	36" x 36" x 8"			7.70	1.040	Ea.
1720	Junction boxes, 4" sq. & oct.			80	.100	Ea.
1740	Handy box			107	.075	Ea.
1760	Switch box			107	.075	Ea.
1780	Receptacle & switch plates			257	.031	Ea.
1790	Receptacles & switches, 15 to 30 amp	↓	↓	135	.059	Ea.
1800	Wire, THW-THWN-THHN, removed from					
1810	in place conduit, to 15' high					
1830	#14	1 Elec	1 Electrician	65	.123	C.L.F.
1840	#12			55	.145	C.L.F.
1850	#10			45.50	.176	C.L.F.
1860	#8			40.40	.198	C.L.F.
1870	#6			32.60	.245	C.L.F.
1880	#4			26.50	.302	C.L.F.
1890	#3			25	.320	C.L.F.
1900	#2			22.30	.359	C.L.F.
1910	1/0			16.60	.482	C.L.F.
1920	2/0			14.60	.548	C.L.F.
1930	3/0			12.50	.640	C.L.F.
1940	4/0			11	.727	C.L.F.
1950	250 MCM			10	.800	C.L.F.
1960	300 MCM			9.50	.842	C.L.F.
1970	350 MCM			9	.889	C.L.F.
1980	400 MCM			8.50	.941	C.L.F.
1990	500 MCM	↓	↓	8.10	.988	C.L.F.
2000	Interior fluorescent fixtures, incl. supports					
2010	& whips, to 15' high					
2100	Recessed drop-in 2' x 2', 2 lamp	2 Elec	2 Electricians	35	.457	Ea.
2120	2' x 4', 2 lamp			33	.485	Ea.
2140	2' x 4', 4 lamp			30	.533	Ea.
2160	4' x 4', 4 lamp	↓	↓	20	.800	Ea.
2180	Surface mount, acrylic lens & hinged frame					
2200	1' x 4', 2 lamp	2 Elec	2 Electricians	44	.364	Ea.
2220	2' x 2', 2 lamp			44	.364	Ea.
2260	2' x 4', 4 lamp			33	.485	Ea.
2280	4' x 4', 4 lamp	↓	↓	23	.696	Ea.
2300	Strip fixtures, surface mount					
2320	4' long, 1 lamp	2 Elec	2 Electricians	53	.302	Ea.
2340	4' long, 2 lamp			50	.320	Ea.
2360	8' long, 1 lamp			42	.381	Ea.
2380	8' long, 2 lamp	↓	↓	40	.400	Ea.
2400	Pendant mount, industrial, incl. removal					
2410	of chain or rod hangers, to 15' high					
2420	4' long, 2 lamp	2 Elec	2 Electricians	35	.457	Ea.
2440	8' long, 2 lamp	"	"	27	.593	Ea.
2460	Interior incandescent, surface, ceiling					
2470	or wall mount, to 12' high					
2480	Metal cylinder type, 75 Watt	2 Elec	2 Electricians	62	.258	Ea.
2500	150 Watt	"	"	62	.258	Ea.
2501						

020 | Subsurface Investigation Demolition

020 700 | Selective Demolition

		CREW	MAKEUP	DAILY OUTPUT	MAN-HOURS	UNIT
708 2541	Elec. demolition, interior metal halide, high bay, 400 watt	2 Elec	2 Electricians	15	1.070	Ea.
2560	1000 Watt	↓	↓	12	1.330	Ea.
2580	150 Watt, low bay			20	.800	Ea.
2600	Exterior fixtures, incandescent, wall mount					
2620	100 Watt	2 Elec	2 Electricians	50	.320	Ea.
2640	Quartz, 500 Watt	↓	↓	33	.485	Ea.
2660	1500 Watt			27	.593	Ea.
2680	Wall pack, mercury vapor					
2700	175 Watt	2 Elec	2 Electricians	25	.640	Ea.
2720	250 Watt	"	"	25	.640	Ea.
712	**FLOORING DEMOLITION**					
0200	Brick with mortar	A-1	1 Building Laborer	300	.027	S.F.
			1 Gas Eng. Power Tool			
0400	Carpet, bonded, including surface scraping	2 Clab	2 Building Laborers	2,000	.008	S.F.
0480	Tackless	"	"	9,000	.002	S.F.
0600	Composition	A-1	1 Building Laborer	200	.040	S.F.
			1 Gas Eng. Power Tool			
0800	Resilient, sheet goods (linoleum)	2 Clab	2 Building Laborers	1,400	.011	S.F.
0820	For gym floors	↓	↓	900	.018	S.F.
0900	Tile, 12" x 12"			1,000	.016	S.F.
2000	Tile, ceramic, thin set	A-1	1 Building Laborer	400	.020	S.F.
2020	Mud set		1 Gas Eng. Power Tool	350	.023	S.F.
2200	Marble, slate, thin set			400	.020	S.F.
2220	Mud set			350	.023	S.F.
2600	Terrazzo, thin set			250	.032	S.F.
2620	Mud set			225	.036	S.F.
2640	Cast in place			175	.046	S.F.
3000	Wood, block, on end			400	.020	S.F.
3200	Parquet			450	.018	S.F.
3400	Strip flooring, interior, 2-1/4" x 25/32" thick			325	.025	S.F.
3500	Exterior, porch flooring, 1" x 4"			220	.036	S.F.
3800	Subfloor, tongue and groove, 1" x 6"			325	.025	S.F.
3820	1" x 8"			430	.019	S.F.
3840	1" x 10"			520	.015	S.F.
4000	Plywood, nailed			600	.013	S.F.
4100	Glued and nailed	↓	↓	400	.020	S.F.
714	**FRAMING DEMOLITION**					
1020	Concrete, average reinforcing, beams, 8" x 10"	B-9	1 Labor Foreman (outside)	120	.333	L.F.
			4 Building Laborers			
			1 Air Compr., 250 C.F.M.			
			Air Tools & Accessories			
			2-50 Ft. Air Hoses, 1.5" Dia.			
1040	10" x 12"			110	.364	L.F.
1060	12" x 14"			90	.444	L.F.
1200	Columns, 8" x 8"			120	.333	L.F.
1240	10" x 10"			120	.333	L.F.
1280	12" x 12"			110	.364	L.F.
1320	14" x 14"			100	.400	L.F.
1400	Girders, 14" x 16"			55	.727	L.F.
1440	16" x 18"			40	1.000	L.F.
1600	Slabs, elevated, 6" thick			600	.067	S.F.
1640	8" thick			450	.089	S.F.
1680	10" thick	↓	↓	360	.111	S.F.

020 700 | Selective Demolition

		Description	CREW	MAKEUP	DAILY OUTPUT	MAN-HOURS	UNIT
714	2001	Framing demolition, steel, beams, 4" x 6"	B-13	1 Labor Foreman (outside)	500	.112	L.F.
				4 Building Laborers			
				1 Equip. Oper. (crane)			
				1 Equip. Oper. Oiler			
				1 Hyd. Crane, 25 Ton			
	2020	4" x 8"			400	.140	L.F.
	2080	8" x 12"			250	.224	L.F.
	2200	Columns, 6" x 6"			400	.140	L.F.
	2240	8" x 8"			350	.160	L.F.
	2280	10" x 10"			320	.175	L.F.
	2400	Girders, 10" x 12"			225	.249	L.F.
	2440	10" x 14"			200	.280	L.F.
	2480	10" x 16"			165	.339	L.F.
	2520	10" x 24"	↓	↓	125	.448	L.F.
	3000	Wood framing, beams, 6" x 8"	B-2	1 Labor Foreman (outside)	275	.145	L.F.
				4 Building Laborers			
	3040	6" x 10"			220	.182	L.F.
	3080	6" x 12"			185	.216	L.F.
	3120	8" x 12"			140	.286	L.F.
	3160	10" x 12"	↓	↓	110	.364	L.F.
	3400	Fascia boards, 1" x 6"	1 Clab	1 Building Laborer	500	.016	L.F.
	3440	1" x 8"			450	.018	L.F.
	3480	1" x 10"			400	.020	L.F.
	3800	Headers over openings, 2 @ 2" x 6"			110	.073	L.F.
	3840	2 @ 2" x 8"			100	.080	L.F.
	3880	2 @ 2" x 10"	↓	↓	90	.089	L.F.
	4230	Joists, 2" x 6"	2 Clab	2 Building Laborers	970	.016	L.F.
	4240	2" x 8"			940	.017	L.F.
	4250	2" x 10"			910	.018	L.F.
	4280	2" x 12"			880	.018	L.F.
	5400	Posts, 4" x 4"			800	.020	L.F.
	5440	6" x 6"			400	.040	L.F.
	5480	8" x 8"			300	.053	L.F.
	5500	10" x 10"			240	.067	L.F.
	5800	Rafters, ordinary, 2" x 6"			850	.019	L.F.
	5840	2" x 8"			720	.022	L.F.
	5900	Hip & valley, 2" x 6"			500	.032	L.F.
	5940	2" x 8"			420	.038	L.F.
	6200	Stairs and stringers, minimum			40	.400	Riser
	6240	Maximum			26	.615	Riser
	6600	Studs, 2" x 4"			2,000	.008	L.F.
	6640	2" x 6"	↓	↓	1,600	.010	L.F.
716		**GUTTING** Building interior, including disposal					
	0500	Residential building					
	0560	Minimum	B-16	1 Labor Foreman (outside)	400	.080	SF Flr.
				2 Building Laborers			
				1 Truck Driver (heavy)			
				1 Dump Truck, 16 Ton			
	0580	Maximum			360	.089	SF Flr.
	1000	Commercial building, minimum			350	.091	SF Flr.
	1020	Maximum	↓	↓	250	.128	SF Flr.
718		**HVAC DEMOLITION**					
	0100	Air conditioner, split unit, 3 ton	Q-5	1 Steamfitter	2	8.000	Ea.
				1 Steamfitter Apprentice			
	0150	Package unit, 3 ton	Q-6	2 Steamfitters	3	8.000	Ea.
				1 Steamfitter Apprentice			

020 | Subsurface Investigation and Demolition

020 700 | Selective Demolition

		Description	CREW	MAKEUP	DAILY OUTPUT	MAN-HOURS	UNIT
718	0301	HVAC demolition, boiler, electric	Q-19	1 Steamfitter	2	12.000	Ea.
				1 Steamfitter Apprentice			
				1 Electrician			
	0340	Gas or oil, steel, under 150 MBH	Q-6	2 Steamfitters	3	8.000	Ea.
				1 Steamfitter Apprentice			
	0380	Over 150 MBH	"	"	2	12.000	Ea.
	1000	Ductwork, 4" high, 8" wide	1 Clab	1 Building Laborer	200	.040	L.F.
	1020	10" wide			190	.042	L.F.
	1040	14" wide			180	.044	L.F.
	1100	6" high, 8" wide			165	.048	L.F.
	1120	12" wide			150	.053	L.F.
	1140	18" wide			135	.059	L.F.
	1200	10" high, 12" wide			125	.064	L.F.
	1220	18" wide			115	.070	L.F.
	1240	24" wide			110	.073	L.F.
	1300	12" high, 18" wide			85	.094	L.F.
	1320	24" wide			75	.107	L.F.
	1340	48" wide			71	.113	L.F.
	1400	18" high, 24" wide			67	.119	L.F.
	1420	36" wide			63	.127	L.F.
	1440	48" wide			59	.136	L.F.
	1500	30" high, 36" wide			56	.143	L.F.
	1520	48" wide			53	.151	L.F.
	1540	72" wide	↓	↓	50	.160	L.F.
	1550	Duct heater, electric strip	1 Elec	1 Electrician	8	1.000	Ea.
	2200	Furnace, electric	Q-20	1 Sheet Metal Worker	2	10.000	Ea.
				1 Sheet Metal Apprentice			
				.5 Electrician			
	2300	Gas or oil, under 120 MBH	Q-9	1 Sheet Metal Worker	4	4.000	Ea.
				1 Sheet Metal Apprentice			
	2340	Over 120 MBH	"	"	3	5.330	Ea.
	2800	Heat pump, package unit, 3 ton	Q-5	1 Steamfitter	2.40	6.670	Ea.
				1 Steamfitter Apprentice			
	2840	Split unit, 3 ton			2	8.000	Ea.
	3000	Mechanical equipment, light items			.90	17.780	Ton
	3600	Heavy items	↓	↓	1.10	14.550	Ton
	720	**MILLWORK AND TRIM DEMOLITION**					
	1000	Cabinets, wood, base cabinets	2 Clab	2 Building Laborers	80	.200	L.F.
	1020	Wall cabinets	"	"	80	.200	L.F.
	1060	Remove and reset, base cabinets	2 Carp	2 Carpenters	18	.889	Ea.
	1070	Wall cabinets	"	"	20	.800	Ea.
	1100	Steel, painted, base cabinets	2 Clab	2 Building Laborers	60	.267	L.F.
	1120	Wall cabinets			60	.267	L.F.
	1200	Casework, large area			320	.050	S.F.
	1220	Selective			200	.080	S.F.
	1500	Counter top, minimum			200	.080	L.F.
	1510	Maximum	↓	↓	120	.133	L.F.
	1550	Remove and reset, minimum	2 Carp	2 Carpenters	50	.320	L.F.
	1560	Maximum	"	"	40	.400	L.F.
	2000	Paneling, 4' x 8' sheets, 1/4" thick	2 Clab	2 Building Laborers	1,000	.016	S.F.
	2100	Boards, 1" x 4"			700	.023	S.F.
	2120	1" x 6"			750	.021	S.F.
	2140	1" x 8"			800	.020	S.F.
	3000	Trim, baseboard, to 6" wide			1,200	.013	L.F.
	3040	12" wide	↓	↓	1,000	.016	L.F.
	3080	Remove and reset, minimum	2 Carp	2 Carpenters	400	.040	L.F.
	3090	Maximum	"	"	300	.053	L.F.
	3100	Ceiling trim	2 Clab	2 Building Laborers	1,000	.016	L.F.

020 700	Selective Demolition	CREW	MAKEUP	DAILY OUTPUT	MAN-HOURS	UNIT
720 3121	Trim demolition, chair rail	2 Clab	2 Building Laborers	1,200	.013	L.F.
3140	Railings with balusters	↓	↓	240	.067	L.F.
3160	Wainscoting			700	.023	S.F.
722 0020	**MOVING EQUIPMENT**, Remove and reset, 100' distance, No obstructions, no assembly or leveling					
0100	Annealing furnace, 24' overall	B-67	1 Millwright	4	4.000	Ea.
			1 Equip. Oper. (light)			
			1 Forklift			
0200	Annealing oven, small			14	1.140	Ea.
0240	Very large			1	16.000	Ea.
0400	Band saw, small			12	1.330	Ea.
0440	Large			8	2.000	Ea.
0500	Blue print copy machine			7	2.290	Ea.
0600	Bonding mill, 6"			7	2.290	Ea.
0620	12"			6	2.670	Ea.
0640	18"			4	4.000	Ea.
0660	24"	↓	↓	2	8.000	Ea.
0700	Boring machine (jig)	B-68	2 Millwrights	7	3.430	Ea.
			1 Equip. Oper. (light)			
			1 Forklift			
0800	Bridgeport mill, standard	B-67	1 Millwright	14	1.140	Ea.
			1 Equip. Oper. (light)			
			1 Forklift			
1000	Calibrator, 6 unit	"	"	14	1.140	Ea.
1100	Comparitor, bench top	2 Clab	2 Building Laborers	14	1.140	Ea.
1140	Floor mounted	B-67	1 Millwright	7	2.290	Ea.
			1 Equip. Oper. (light)			
			1 Forklift			
1200	Computer, desk top	2 Clab	2 Building Laborers	25	.640	Ea.
1300	Copy machine	"	"	25	.640	Ea.
1500	Deflasher	B-67	1 Millwright	14	1.140	Ea.
			1 Equip. Oper. (light)			
			1 Forklift			
1600	Degreaser, small	↓	↓	14	1.140	Ea.
1640	Large 24' overall			1	16.000	Ea.
1700	Desk with chair	2 Clab	2 Building Laborers	25	.640	Ea.
1800	Dial press	B-67	1 Millwright	7	2.290	Ea.
			1 Equip. Oper. (light)			
			1 Forklift			
1900	Drafting table	2 Clab	2 Building Laborers	14	1.140	Ea.
2000	Drill press, bench top	"	"	14	1.140	Ea.
2040	Floor mounted	B-67	1 Millwright	14	1.140	Ea.
			1 Equip. Oper. (light)			
			1 Forklift			
2080	Industrial radial	"	"	7	2.290	Ea.
2100	Dust collector, portable	2 Clab	2 Building Laborers	25	.640	Ea.
2140	Stationary, small	B-67	1 Millwright	7	2.290	Ea.
			1 Equip. Oper. (light)			
			1 Forklift			
2180	Stationary, large	"	"	2	8.000	Ea.
2300	Electric discharge machine	B-68	2 Millwrights	7	3.430	Ea.
			1 Equip. Oper. (light)			
			1 Forklift			
2400	Environmental chamber walls	4 Clab	4 Building Laborers	18	1.780	L.F.
2600	File cabinet	2 Clab	2 Building Laborers	25	.640	Ea.
2800	Grinder/sander, pedestal mount	B-67	1 Millwright	14	1.140	Ea.
			1 Equip. Oper. (light)			
			1 Forklift			

020 700 | Selective Demolition

			Description	CREW	MAKEUP	DAILY OUTPUT	MAN-HOURS	UNIT
722	3001		Remove and reset, hack saw, power	2 Clab	2 Building Laborers	24	.667	Ea.
	3100		Hydraulic press	B-67	1 Millwright	14	1.140	Ea.
					1 Equip. Oper. (light)			
					1 Forklift			
	3500		Laminar flow tables	"	"	14	1.140	Ea.
	3600		Lathe, bench	2 Clab	2 Building Laborers	14	1.140	Ea.
	3640		6"	B-67	1 Millwright	14	1.140	Ea.
					1 Equip. Oper. (light)			
					1 Forklift			
	3680		10"			13	1.230	Ea.
	3720		12"			12	1.330	Ea.
	4000		Milling machine			8	2.000	Ea.
	4100		Molding press, 25 ton			5	3.200	Ea.
	4140		60 ton			4	4.000	Ea.
	4180		100 ton			2	8.000	Ea.
	4220		150 ton			1.50	10.670	Ea.
	4260		200 ton			1	16.000	Ea.
	4300		300 ton			.75	21.330	Ea.
	4700		Oil pot stand			14	1.140	Ea.
	5000		Press, 10 ton			14	1.140	Ea.
	5040		15 ton			12	1.330	Ea.
	5080		20 ton			10	1.600	Ea.
	5120		30 ton			8	2.000	Ea.
	5160		45 ton			6	2.670	Ea.
	5200		60 ton			4	4.000	Ea.
	5240		75 ton			2.50	6.400	Ea.
	5280		100 ton	↓	↓	2	8.000	Ea.
	5500		Raised floor	2 Carp	2 Carpenters	250	.064	S.F.
	5600		Rolling mill, 6"	B-67	1 Millwright	7	2.290	Ea.
					1 Equip. Oper. (light)			
					1 Forklift			
	5640		9"			6	2.670	Ea.
	5680		12"			4	4.000	Ea.
	5720		13"			3.50	4.570	Ea.
	5760		18"			2	8.000	Ea.
	5800		25"			1	16.000	Ea.
	6000		Sander, floor stand			14	1.140	Ea.
	6100		Screw machine			7	2.290	Ea.
	6200		Shaper, 16"			14	1.140	Ea.
	6300		Shear, power assist			4	4.000	Ea.
	6400		Slitter, 6"			14	1.140	Ea.
	6440		8"			13	1.230	Ea.
	6480		10"			12	1.330	Ea.
	6520		12"			11	1.450	Ea.
	6560		16"			10	1.600	Ea.
	6600		20"			8	2.000	Ea.
	6640		24"			6	2.670	Ea.
	6800		Snag and tap machine			7	2.290	Ea.
	6900		Solder machine (auto)	↓	↓	7	2.290	Ea.
	7000		Storage cabinet metal, small	2 Clab	2 Building Laborers	36	.444	Ea.
	7040		Large			25	.640	Ea.
	7100		Storage rack open, small			14	1.140	Ea.
	7140		Large	↓	↓	7	2.290	Ea.
	7200		Surface bench, small	B-67	1 Millwright	14	1.140	Ea.
					1 Equip. Oper. (light)			
					1 Forklift			
	7240		Large	"	"	5	3.200	Ea.

		020 700	Selective Demolition	CREW	MAKEUP	DAILY OUTPUT	MAN-HOURS	UNIT
722	7301		Remove and reset, surface grinder, large wet	B-68	2 Millwrights	5	4.800	Ea.
					1 Equip. Oper. (light)			
					1 Forklift			
	7500		Time check machine	2 Clab	2 Building Laborers	14	1.140	Ea.
	8000		Welder, 30 KVA (bench)	↓	↓	14	1.140	Ea.
	8100		Work bench with chair			25	.640	Ea.
	724	**PLUMBING DEMOLITION**						
	1020		Fixtures, including 10' piping					
	1100		Bath tubs, cast iron	1 Plum	1 Plumber	4	2.000	Ea.
	1120		Fiberglass			6	1.330	Ea.
	1140		Steel			5	1.600	Ea.
	1200		Lavatory, wall hung			10	.800	Ea.
	1220		Counter top			8	1.000	Ea.
	1300		Sink, steel or cast iron, single			8	1.000	Ea.
	1320		Double			7	1.140	Ea.
	1400		Water closet, floor mounted			8	1.000	Ea.
	1420		Wall mounted			7	1.140	Ea.
	1500		Urinal, floor mounted			4	2.000	Ea.
	1520		Wall mounted			7	1.140	Ea.
	1600		Water fountains, free standing			8	1.000	Ea.
	1620		Recessed			6	1.330	Ea.
	2000		Piping, metal, to 2" diameter			200	.040	L.F.
	2050		To 4" diameter	↓	↓	150	.053	L.F.
	2100		To 8" diameter	2 Plum	2 Plumbers	100	.160	L.F.
	2150		To 16" diameter	"	"	60	.267	L.F.
	2250		Water heater, 40 gal.	1 Plum	1 Plumber	6	1.330	Ea.
	6000		Remove and reset fixtures, minimum			6	1.330	Ea.
	6100		Maximum	↓	↓	4	2.000	Ea.
	726	**ROOFING AND SIDING DEMOLITION**						
	1000		Deck, roof, concrete plank	B-13	1 Labor Foreman (outside)	1,680	.033	S.F.
					4 Building Laborers			
					1 Equip. Oper. (crane)			
					1 Equip. Oper. Oiler			
					1 Hyd. Crane, 25 Ton			
	1100		Gypsum plank	↓	↓	3,900	.014	S.F.
	1150		Metal decking			3,500	.016	S.F.
	1200		Wood, boards, tongue and groove, 2" x 6"	2 Clab	2 Building Laborers	960	.017	S.F.
	1220		2" x 10"			1,040	.015	S.F.
	1280		Standard planks, 1" x 6"			1,080	.015	S.F.
	1320		1" x 8"			1,160	.014	S.F.
	1340		1" x 12"	↓	↓	1,200	.013	S.F.
	2000		Gutters, aluminum or wood, edge hung	1 Clab	1 Building Laborer	200	.040	L.F.
	2100		Built-in			100	.080	L.F.
	2500		Roof accessories, plumbing vent flashing			14	.571	Ea.
	2600		Adjustable metal chimney flashing	↓	↓	9	.889	Ea.
	3000		Roofing, built-up, 5 ply roof, no gravel	B-2	1 Labor Foreman (outside)	1,600	.025	S.F.
					4 Building Laborers			
	3001		Including gravel			890	.045	S.F.
	3100		Gravel removal, minimum			5,000	.008	S.F.
	3120		Maximum			2,000	.020	S.F.
	3400		Roof insulation board			3,900	.010	S.F.
	4000		Shingles, asphalt strip			3,500	.011	S.F.
	4100		Slate			2,500	.016	S.F.
	4300		Wood	↓	↓	2,200	.018	S.F.
	4500		Skylight to 10 S.F.	1 Clab	1 Building Laborer	4	2.000	Ea.
	5000		Siding, metal, horizontal			300	.027	S.F.
	5020		Vertical			280	.029	S.F.
	5200		Wood, boards, vertical	↓	↓	280	.029	S.F.

		CREW	MAKEUP	DAILY OUTPUT	MAN-HOURS	UNIT
726 5221	Siding demolition, clapboards, horizontal	1 Clab	1 Building Laborer	260	.031	S.F.
5240	Shingles	↓	↓	250	.032	S.F.
5260	Textured plywood	↓	↓	500	.016	S.F.
728	**SAW CUTTING** Asphalt over 1000 L.F., 3" deep	B-89	1 Equip. Oper. (light)	775	.021	L.F.
			1 Truck Driver (light)			
			1 Truck, Stake Body, 3 Ton			
			1 Concrete Saw			
			1 Water Tank, 65 Gal			
0020	Each additional inch of depth			1,250	.013	L.F.
0400	Concrete slabs, mesh reinforcing, per inch of depth			960	.017	L.F.
0420	Rod reinforcing, per inch of depth	↓	↓	550	.029	L.F.
0800	Concrete walls, plain, per inch of depth	A-1A	1 Laborer	100	.080	L.F.
			1 Power Equipment			
0820	Rod reinforcing, per inch of depth			60	.133	L.F.
1200	Masonry walls, brick, per inch of depth			146	.055	L.F.
1220	Block walls, solid, per inch of depth	↓	↓	122	.066	L.F.
5000	Wood sheathing to 1" thick, on walls	1 Carp	1 Carpenter	200	.040	L.F.
5020	On roof	"	"	250	.032	L.F.
730	**TORCH CUTTING** Steel, 1" thick plate	A-1A	1 Laborer	95	.084	L.F.
			1 Power Equipment			
0040	1" diameter bar	"	"	210	.038	Ea.
1000	Oxygen lance cutting, reinforced concrete walls					
1040	12" to 16" thick walls	A-1A	1 Laborer	10	.800	L.F.
			1 Power Equipment			
1080	24" thick walls	"	"	6	1.330	L.F.
732	**WALLS AND PARTITIONS DEMOLITION**					
0100	Brick, 4" to 12" thick	B-9	1 Labor Foreman (outside)	220	.182	C.F.
			4 Building Laborers			
			1 Air Compr., 250 C.F.M.			
			Air Tools & Accessories			
			2-50 Ft. Air Hoses, 1.5" Dia.			
0200	Concrete block, 4" thick	↓	↓	1,000	.040	S.F.
0280	8" thick	↓	↓	810	.049	S.F.
1000	Drywall, nailed	1 Clab	1 Building Laborer	1,000	.008	S.F.
1020	Glued and nailed			900	.009	S.F.
1500	Fiberboard, nailed			900	.009	S.F.
1520	Glued and nailed			800	.010	S.F.
2000	Movable walls, metal, 5' high			300	.027	S.F.
2020	8' high	↓	↓	400	.020	S.F.
2200	Metal or wood studs, finish 2 sides, fiberboard	B-1	1 Labor Foreman (outside)	520	.046	S.F.
			2 Building Laborers			
2250	Lath and plaster			260	.092	S.F.
2300	Plasterboard (drywall)			520	.046	S.F.
2350	Plywood	↓	↓	450	.053	S.F.
3000	Plaster, lime and horsehair, on wood lath	1 Clab	1 Building Laborer	400	.020	S.F.
3020	On metal lath			335	.024	S.F.
3400	Gypsum or perlite, on gypsum lath			410	.020	S.F.
3420	On metal lath	↓	↓	300	.027	S.F.
3750	Terra cotta block and plaster, to 6" thick	B-1	1 Labor Foreman (outside)	175	.137	S.F.
			2 Building Laborers			
3800	Toilet partitions, slate or marble	1 Clab	1 Building Laborer	5	1.600	Ea.
3820	Hollow metal	"	"	8	1.000	Ea.
734	**WINDOW DEMOLITION**					
0200	Aluminum, including trim, to 12 S.F.	A-1A	1 Laborer	12	.667	Ea.
			1 Power Equipment			
0240	To 25 S.F.			8	1.000	Ea.
0280	To 50 S.F.			4	2.000	Ea.
0320	Storm windows, to 12 S.F.	↓	↓	20	.400	Ea.

020 700 | Selective Demolition

		Description	CREW	MAKEUP	DAILY OUTPUT	MAN-HOURS	UNIT
734	0361	Storm window demolition, aluminum, to 25 S.F.	A-1A	1 Laborer	16	.500	Ea.
				1 Power Equipment			
	0400	To 50 S.F.	"	"	12	.667	Ea.
	0600	Glass, minimum	1 Clab	1 Building Laborer	200	.040	S.F.
	0620	Maximum	"	"	150	.053	S.F.
	1000	Steel, including trim, to 12 S.F.	A-1A	1 Laborer	10	.800	Ea.
				1 Power Equipment			
	1020	To 25 S.F.	↓	↓	7	1.140	Ea.
	1040	To 50 S.F.			3	2.670	Ea.
	2000	Wood, including trim, to 12 S.F.	1 Clab	1 Building Laborer	16	.500	Ea.
	2020	To 25 S.F.	↓	↓	12	.667	Ea.
	2060	To 50 S.F.			6	1.330	Ea.
	5020	Remove and reset window, minimum	1 Carp	1 Carpenter	6	1.330	Ea.
	5040	Average	↓	↓	4	2.000	Ea.
	5080	Maximum			2	4.000	Ea.

020 750 | Concrete Removal

		Description	CREW	MAKEUP	DAILY OUTPUT	MAN-HOURS	UNIT
754		**FOOTINGS AND FOUNDATIONS DEMOLITION**					
	0200	Floors, concrete slab on grade,					
	0240	4" thick, plain concrete	B-9	1 Labor Foreman (outside)	500	.080	S.F.
				4 Building Laborers			
				1 Air Compr., 250 C.F.M.			
				Air Tools & Accessories			
				2-50 Ft. Air Hoses, 1.5" Dia.			
	0280	Reinforced, wire mesh			470	.085	S.F.
	0300	Rods			400	.100	S.F.
	0400	6" thick, plain concrete			375	.107	S.F.
	0420	Reinforced, wire mesh			340	.118	S.F.
	0440	Rods	↓	↓	300	.133	S.F.
	1000	Footings, concrete, 1' thick, 2' wide	B-5	1 Labor Foreman (outside)	300	.213	L.F.
				4 Building Laborers			
				2 Equip. Oper. (med.)			
				1 Mechanic			
				1 Air Compr., 250 C.F.M.			
				Air Tools & Accessories			
				2-50 Ft. Air Hoses, 1.5" Dia.			
				F.E. Loader, T.M., 2.5 C.Y.			
	1080	1'-6" thick, 2' wide			250	.256	L.F.
	1120	3' wide			200	.320	L.F.
	1140	2' thick, 3' wide	↓	↓	175	.366	L.F.
	2000	Walls, block, 4" thick	A-1	1 Building Laborer	200	.040	S.F.
				1 Gas Eng. Power Tool			
	2040	6" thick			190	.042	S.F.
	2080	8" thick			180	.044	S.F.
	2100	12" thick	↓	↓	175	.046	S.F.
	2400	Concrete, plain concrete, 6" thick	B-9	1 Labor Foreman (outside)	160	.250	S.F.
				4 Building Laborers			
				1 Air Compr., 250 C.F.M.			
				Air Tools & Accessories			
				2-50 Ft. Air Hoses, 1.5" Dia.			
	2420	8" thick			140	.286	S.F.
	2440	10" thick			120	.333	S.F.
	2500	12" thick	↓	↓	100	.400	S.F.

020 | Subsurface Investigation Demolition

020 750 | Concrete Removal

		CREW	MAKEUP	DAILY OUTPUT	MAN-HOURS	UNIT
758	**MASONRY DEMOLITION**					
1000	Chimney, 16" x 16", soft old mortar	A-1	1 Building Laborer 1 Gas Eng. Power Tool	24	.333	V.L.F.
1020	Hard mortar			18	.444	V.L.F.
1080	20" x 20", soft old mortar			12	.667	V.L.F.
1100	Hard mortar			10	.800	V.L.F.
1140	20" x 32", soft old mortar			10	.800	V.L.F.
1160	Hard mortar			8	1.000	V.L.F.
1200	48" x 48", soft old mortar			5	1.600	V.L.F.
1220	Hard mortar			4	2.000	V.L.F.
2000	Columns, 8" x 8", soft old mortar			48	.167	V.L.F.
2020	Hard mortar			40	.200	V.L.F.
2060	16" x 16", soft old mortar			16	.500	V.L.F.
2100	Hard mortar			14	.571	V.L.F.
2140	24" x 24", soft old mortar			8	1.000	V.L.F.
2160	Hard mortar			6	1.330	V.L.F.
2200	36" x 36", soft old mortar			4	2.000	V.L.F.
2220	Hard mortar	↓	↓	3	2.670	V.L.F.
3000	Copings, precast or masonry, to 8" wide					
3020	Soft old mortar	A-1	1 Building Laborer 1 Gas Eng. Power Tool	180	.044	L.F.
3040	Hard mortar	"	"	160	.050	L.F.
3100	To 12" wide					
3120	Soft old mortar	A-1	1 Building Laborer 1 Gas Eng. Power Tool	160	.050	L.F.
3140	Hard mortar	"	"	140	.057	L.F.
4000	Fireplace, brick, 30" x 24" opening					
4020	Soft old mortar	A-1	1 Building Laborer 1 Gas Eng. Power Tool	2	4.000	Ea.
4040	Hard mortar			1.25	6.400	Ea.
4100	Stone, soft old mortar			1.50	5.330	Ea.
4120	Hard mortar			1	8.000	Ea.
5000	Veneers, brick, soft old mortar			140	.057	S.F.
5020	Hard mortar			125	.064	S.F.
5100	Granite and marble, 2" thick			180	.044	S.F.
5120	4" thick			170	.047	S.F.
5140	Stone, 4" thick			180	.044	S.F.
5160	8" thick			175	.046	S.F.
5400	Alternate pricing method, stone, 4" thick			60	.133	C.F.
5420	8" thick	↓	↓	85	.094	C.F.

020 800 | Asbestos Removal

		CREW	MAKEUP	DAILY OUTPUT	MAN-HOURS	UNIT
804	**ASBESTOS CONTROL METHODS**					
0100	Removal, including cleanup, disposable clothing & respirators					
0200	Beams, W10 x 19	B-1	1 Labor Foreman (outside) 2 Building Laborers	88	.273	L.F.
0300	W12 x 22			78	.308	L.F.
0400	W14 x 26			67	.358	L.F.
0500	W16 x 31			60	.400	L.F.
0600	W18 x 40			53	.453	L.F.
0700	W24 x 55			42	.571	L.F.
0800	W30 x 108			32	.750	L.F.
1000	Ceilings, fluted			220	.109	S.F.
1100	Smooth			240	.100	S.F.
1200	Wire lath, complete, leaving lath			220	.109	S.F.
2000	Columns, W6 x 12			106	.226	L.F.
2100	W8 x 31			62	.387	L.F.
2200	W10 x 49	↓	↓	50	.480	L.F.

020 | Subsurface Investigation and Demolition

020 800 | Asbestos Removal

		Description	CREW	MAKEUP	DAILY OUTPUT	MAN-HOURS	UNIT
804	2301	Asbestos removal, columns, W12 x 40	B-1	1 Labor Foreman (outside)	53	.453	L.F.
				2 Building Laborers			
	3000	Encapsulation, with sealants					
	3100	Ceilings and walls, minimum	B-1	1 Labor Foreman (outside)	8,000	.003	S.F.
				2 Building Laborers			
	3200	Maximum			4,000	.006	S.F.
	3300	Columns and beams, minimum			5,000	.005	S.F.
	3400	Maximum			2,000	.012	S.F.
	3500	Pipes, 12" diam. or less, minor repairs minimum			300	.080	L.F.
	3600	Maximum	↓	↓	150	.160	L.F.
	4000	Dust protection, polyethylene sheeting, 6 mil thick, 4" duct tape	2 Carp	2 Carpenters	1,600	.010	S.F.

021 | Site Preparation

021 100 | Site Clearing

	Description	CREW	MAKEUP	DAILY OUTPUT	MAN-HOURS	UNIT
104	**CLEAR AND GRUB** Light, trees to 6" diam., cut & chip	B-7	1 Labor Foreman (outside)	1	48.000	Acre
			4 Building Laborers			
			1 Equip. Oper. (med.)			
			1 Chipping Machine			
			F.E. Loader, T.M., 2.5 C.Y.			
			2 Chain Saws			
0150	Grub stumps and remove	B-30	1 Equip. Oper. (med.)	2	12.000	Acre
			2 Truck Drivers (heavy)			
			1 Hyd. Excavator, 1.5 C.Y.			
			2 Dump Trucks, 16 Ton			
0200	Medium, trees to 12" diam., cut & chip	B-7	1 Labor Foreman (outside)	.70	68.570	Acre
			4 Building Laborers			
			1 Equip. Oper. (med.)			
			1 Chipping Machine			
			F.E. Loader, T.M., 2.5 C.Y.			
			2 Chain Saws			
0250	Grub stumps and remove	B-30	1 Equip. Oper. (med.)	1	24.000	Acre
			2 Truck Drivers (heavy)			
			1 Hyd. Excavator, 1.5 C.Y.			
			2 Dump Trucks, 16 Ton			
0300	Heavy, trees to 24" diam., cut & chip	B-7	1 Labor Foreman (outside)	.30	160.000	Acre
			4 Building Laborers			
			1 Equip. Oper. (med.)			
			1 Chipping Machine			
			F.E. Loader, T.M., 2.5 C.Y.			
			2 Chain Saws			
0350	Grub stumps and remove	B-30	1 Equip. Oper. (med.)	.50	48.000	Acre
			2 Truck Drivers (heavy)			
			1 Hyd. Excavator, 1.5 C.Y.			
			2 Dump Trucks, 16 Ton			
3000	Chipping stumps, to 18" deep, 12" diam.	B-86	1 Equip. Oper. (med.)	20	.400	Ea.
			1 Stump Chipper, S.P.			
3040	18" diameter			16	.500	Ea.
3080	24" diameter			14	.571	Ea.
3100	30" diameter			12	.667	Ea.
3120	36" diameter			10	.800	Ea.
3160	48" diameter	↓	↓	8	1.000	Ea.

021 | Site Preparation

021 100 | Site Clearing

		CREW	MAKEUP	DAILY OUTPUT	MAN-HOURS	UNIT
104 5000	Tree thinning, feller buncher, conifer					
5080	Up to 8" diameter	B-93	1 Equip. Oper. (med.)	240	.033	Ea.
			1 Feller Buncher, 50 H.P.			
5120	12" diameter			160	.050	Ea.
5240	Hardwood, up to 4" diameter			240	.033	Ea.
5280	8" diameter	↓	↓	180	.044	Ea.
5320	12" diameter			120	.067	Ea.
7000	Tree removal, congested area, aerial lift truck					
7040	8" diameter	B-85	3 Highway Laborers	7	5.710	Ea.
			1 Equip. Oper. (med.)			
			1 Truck Driver (heavy)			
			1 Aerial Lift Truck			
			1 Brush Chipper, 130 H.P.			
			1 Pruning Saw, Rotary			
7080	12" diameter			6	6.670	Ea.
7120	18" diameter			5	8.000	Ea.
7160	24" diameter			4	10.000	Ea.
7240	36" diameter			3	13.330	Ea.
7280	48" diameter	↓	↓	2	20.000	Ea.
116	**FELLING TREES & PILING** With tractor, large tract, firm					
0020	level terrain, no boulders, less than 12" diam. trees					
0300	300 HP dozer, up to 400 trees/acre, 0 to 25% hardwoods	B-10M	1 Equip. Oper. (med.)	.75	16.000	Acre
			.5 Building Laborer			
			1 Dozer, 300 H.P.			
0340	25% to 50% hardwoods			.60	20.000	Acre
0370	75% to 100% hardwoods			.45	26.670	Acre
0400	500 trees/acre, 0% to 25% hardwoods			.60	20.000	Acre
0440	25% to 50% hardwoods			.48	25.000	Acre
0470	75% to 100% hardwoods			.36	33.330	Acre
0500	More than 600 trees/acre, 0 to 25% hardwoods			.52	23.080	Acre
0540	25% to 50% hardwoods			.42	28.570	Acre
0570	75% to 100% hardwoods	↓	↓	.31	38.710	Acre
0900	Large tract clearing per tree					
1500	300 HP dozer, to 12" diameter, softwood	B-10M	1 Equip. Oper. (med.)	320	.038	Ea.
			.5 Building Laborer			
			1 Dozer, 300 H.P.			
1550	Hardwood			100	.120	Ea.
1600	12" to 24" diameter, softwood			200	.060	Ea.
1650	Hardwood			80	.150	Ea.
1700	24" to 36" diameter, softwood			100	.120	Ea.
1750	Hardwood			50	.240	Ea.
1800	36" to 48" diameter, softwood	↓	↓	70	.171	Ea.
1850	Hardwood			35	.343	Ea.

021 140 | Stripping

		CREW	MAKEUP	DAILY OUTPUT	MAN-HOURS	UNIT
144	**STRIPPING** Topsoil, and stockpiling, sandy loam					
0020	200 H.P. dozer, ideal conditions	B-10B	1 Equip. Oper. (med.)	2,300	.005	C.Y.
			.5 Building Laborer			
			1 Dozer, 200 H.P.			
0100	Adverse conditions	"	"	1,150	.010	C.Y.
0200	300 HP dozer, ideal conditions	B-10M	1 Equip. Oper. (med.)	3,000	.004	C.Y.
			.5 Building Laborer			
			1 Dozer, 300 H.P.			
0300	Adverse conditions	"	"	1,650	.007	C.Y.
0400	400 HP dozer, ideal conditions	B-10X	1 Equip. Oper. (med.)	3,900	.003	C.Y.
			.5 Building Laborer			
			1 Dozer, 410 H.P.			
0500	Adverse conditions	"	"	2,000	.006	C.Y.

021 140 | Stripping

		CREW	MAKEUP	DAILY OUTPUT	MAN-HOURS	UNIT
144 0601	Strip topsoil, clay, dry & soft, 200 HP dozer, ideal conditions	B-10B	1 Equip. Oper. (med.)	1,600	.008	C.Y.
			.5 Building Laborer			
			1 Dozer, 200 H.P.			
0700	Adverse conditions	"	"	800	.015	C.Y.
1000	Medium hard, 300 HP dozer, ideal conditions	B-10M	1 Equip. Oper. (med.)	2,000	.006	C.Y.
			.5 Building Laborer			
			1 Dozer, 300 H.P.			
1100	Adverse conditions	"	"	1,100	.011	C.Y.
1200	Very hard, 400 HP dozer, ideal conditions	B-10X	1 Equip. Oper. (med.)	2,600	.005	C.Y.
			.5 Building Laborer			
			1 Dozer, 410 H.P.			
1300	Adverse conditions	"	"	1,340	.009	C.Y.
1301						

021 150 | Selective Clearing

		CREW	MAKEUP	DAILY OUTPUT	MAN-HOURS	UNIT
154	SELECTIVE CLEARING					
1000	Stump removal on site by hydraulic backhoe, 1-1/2 C.Y.					
1050	8" to 12" diameter	B-30	1 Equip. Oper. (med.)	33	.727	Ea.
			2 Truck Drivers (heavy)			
			1 Hyd. Excavator, 1.5 C.Y.			
			2 Dump Trucks, 16 Ton			
1100	14" to 24" diameter	↓	↓	25	.960	Ea.
1150	26" to 36" diameter			16	1.500	Ea.
2000	Remove selective trees, on site using chain saws and chipper,					
2050	not incl. stumps, up to 6" diameter	B-7	1 Labor Foreman (outside)	18	2.670	Ea.
			4 Building Laborers			
			1 Equip. Oper. (med.)			
			1 Chipping Machine			
			F.E. Loader, T.M., 2.5 C.Y.			
			2 Chain Saws			
2100	8" to 12" diameter	↓	↓	12	4.000	Ea.
2150	14" to 24" diameter			10	4.800	Ea.
2200	26" to 36" diameter	↓	↓	8	6.000	Ea.

021 200 | Structure Moving

		CREW	MAKEUP	DAILY OUTPUT	MAN-HOURS	UNIT
204	MOVING BUILDINGS One day move, up to 24' wide					
0020	Reset on new foundation, patch & hook-up, average move					Total
0040	Wood or steel frame bldg., based on ground floor area	B-4	1 Labor Foreman (outside)	185	.259	S.F.
			4 Building Laborers			
			1 Truck Driver (heavy)			
			1 Tractor, 4 x 2, 195 H.P.			
			1 Platform Trailer			
0060	Masonry bldg., based on ground floor area	↓	↓	137	.350	S.F.
0220	For each additional day on road, add			1	48.000	Day
0240	Construct new basement, move building, 1 day					
0300	move, patch & hook-up, based on ground floor area	B-3	1 Labor Foreman (outside)	155	.310	S.F.
			2 Building Laborers			
			1 Equip. Oper. (med.)			
			2 Truck Drivers (heavy)			
			F.E. Loader, T.M., 2.5 C.Y.			
			2 Dump Trucks, 16 Ton			

021 400	Dewatering	CREW	MAKEUP	DAILY OUTPUT	MAN-HOURS	UNIT
404	404	**DEWATERING** Excavate drainage trench, 2' wide, 2' deep	B-11C	1 Equipment Oper. (med.)	90	.178	C.Y.
				1 Building Laborer			
				1 Backhoe Loader, 48 H.P.			
	0100	2' wide, 3' deep, with backhoe loader	"	"	135	.119	C.Y.
	0200	Excavate sump pits by hand, light soil	1 Clab	1 Building Laborer	7.10	1.130	C.Y.
	0300	Heavy soil	"	"	3.50	2.290	C.Y.
	0500	Pumping 8 hr., attended 2 hrs. per day, including 20 L.F.					
	0550	of suction hose & 100 L.F. discharge hose					
	0600	2" diaphragm pump used for 8 hours	B-10H	1 Equip. Oper. (med.)	4	3.000	Day
				.5 Building Laborer			
				1 Diaphr. Water Pump, 2"			
				1-20 Ft. Suction Hose, 2"			
				2-50 Ft. Disch. Hoses, 2"			
	0650	4" diaphragm pump used for 8 hours	B-10I	1 Equip. Oper. (med.)	4	3.000	Day
				.5 Building Laborer			
				1 Diaphr. Water Pump, 4"			
				1-20 Ft. Suction Hose, 4"			
				2-50 Ft. Disch. Hoses, 4"			
	0800	8 hrs. attended, 2" diaphragm pump	B-10H	1 Equip. Oper. (med.)	1	12.000	Day
				.5 Building Laborer			
				1 Diaphr. Water Pump, 2"			
				1-20 Ft. Suction Hose, 2"			
				2-50 Ft. Disch. Hoses, 2"			
	0900	3" centrifugal pump	B-10J	1 Equip. Oper. (med.)	1	12.000	Day
				.5 Building Laborer			
				1 Centr. Water Pump, 3"			
				1-20 Ft. Suction Hose, 3"			
				2-50 Ft. Disch. Hoses, 3"			
	1000	4" diaphragm pump	B-10I	1 Equip. Oper. (med.)	1	12.000	Day
				.5 Building Laborer			
				1 Diaphr. Water Pump, 4"			
				1-20 Ft. Suction Hose, 4"			
				2-50 Ft. Disch. Hoses, 4"			
	1100	6" centrifugal pump	B-10K	1 Equip. Oper. (med.)	1	12.000	Day
				.5 Building Laborer			
				1 Centr. Water Pump, 6"			
				1-20 Ft. Suction Hose, 6"			
				2-50 Ft. Disch. Hoses, 6"			
	1300	Re-lay CMP, incl. excavation 3' deep, 12" diameter	B-6	2 Building Laborers	115	.209	L.F.
				1 Equip. Oper. (light)			
				1 Backhoe Loader, 48 H.P.			
	1400	18" diameter			100	.240	L.F.
	1600	Sump hole construction, incl. excavation and gravel, pit			1,250	.019	C.F.
	1700	With 12" gravel collar, 12" pipe, corrugated, 16 ga.			70	.343	L.F.
	1800	15" pipe, corrugated, 16 ga.			55	.436	L.F.
	1900	18" pipe, corrugated, 16 ga.			50	.480	L.F.
	2000	24" pipe, corrugated, 14 ga.			40	.600	L.F.
	2200	Wood lining, up to 4' x 4', add	↓	↓	300	.080	SFCA

021 440	Wellpoints	CREW	MAKEUP	DAILY OUTPUT	MAN-HOURS	UNIT
444	**WELLPOINTS**					
0100	Installation and removal of single stage system					
0110	Labor only, .75 man-hours per L.F., minimum	1 Clab	1 Building Laborer	10.70	.748	LF Hdr
0200	2.0 man-hours per L.F., maximum	"	"	4	2.000	LF Hdr
0400	Pump operation, 4 @ 6 hr. shifts					
0410	Per 24 hour day	4 Eqlt	4 Equipment Oper. (light)	1.27	25.200	Day
0500	Per 168 hour week, 160 hr. straight, 8 hr. double time	↓	↓	.18	178.000	Week
0550	Per 4.3 week month			.04	800.000	Month

021 | Site Preparation

021 440 | Wellpoints

		CREW	MAKEUP	DAILY OUTPUT	MAN-HOURS	UNIT
444 0600	Complete installation, operation, equipment rental, fuel &					
0610	removal of system with 2" wellpoints 5' O.C.					
0700	100' long header, 6" diameter, first month	4 Eqlt	4 Equipment Oper. (light)	3.23	9.910	LF Hdr
0800	Thereafter, per month			4.13	7.750	LF Hdr
1000	200' long header, 8" diameter, first month			6	5.330	LF Hdr
1100	Thereafter, per month			8.39	3.810	LF Hdr
1300	500' long header, 8" diameter, first month			10.63	3.010	LF Hdr
1400	Thereafter, per month			20.91	1.530	LF Hdr
1600	1,000' long header, 10" diameter, first month			11.62	2.750	LF Hdr
1700	Thereafter, per month	↓	↓	41.81	.765	LF Hdr
1900	Note: above figures include pumping 168 hrs. per week					
1910	and include the pump operator and one stand-by pump.					

021 480 | Relief Wells

		CREW	MAKEUP	DAILY OUTPUT	MAN-HOURS	UNIT
484	WELLS For dewatering 10' to 20' deep, 2' diameter					
0020	with steel casing, minimum	B-6	2 Building Laborers	165	.145	V.L.F.
			1 Equip. Oper. (light)			
			1 Backhoe Loader, 48 H.P.			
0050	Average	↓	↓	98	.245	V.L.F.
0100	Maximum			49	.490	V.L.F.

021 520 | Shores

		CREW	MAKEUP	DAILY OUTPUT	MAN-HOURS	UNIT
524	SHORING Existing building, with timber, no salvage allowance	B-51	1 Labor Foreman (outside)	2.20	21.820	M.B.F.
			4 Building Laborers			
			1 Truck Driver (light)			
			1 Light Truck, 1.5 Ton			
1000	With 35 ton screw jacks, per box and jack	"	"	3.60	13.330	Jack

021 560 | Underpinning

		CREW	MAKEUP	DAILY OUTPUT	MAN-HOURS	UNIT
564	UNDERPINNING FOUNDATIONS Including excavation,					
0020	forming, reinforcing, concrete and equipment					
0100	5' to 16' below grade, 100 to 500 C.Y.	B-52	1 Carpenter Foreman	2.30	24.350	C.Y.
			1 Carpenter			
			3 Building Laborers			
			1 Cement Finisher			
			.5 Rodman (reinf.)			
			.5 Equip. Oper. (med.)			
			.5 F.E. Ldr., T.M., 2.5 C.Y.			
0200	Over 1000 C.Y.			2.50	22.400	C.Y.
0400	16' to 25' below grade, 100 to 500 C.Y.			2	28.000	C.Y.
0500	Over 1000 C.Y.			2.10	26.670	C.Y.
0700	26' to 40' below grade, 100 to 500 C.Y.			1.60	35.000	C.Y.
0800	Over 1000 C.Y.	↓	↓	1.80	31.110	C.Y.

021 610 | Sheet Piling

		CREW	MAKEUP	DAILY OUTPUT	MAN-HOURS	UNIT
614	SHEET PILING Steel, not incl. wales, 22 psf, 15' excav., left in place	B-40	1 Pile Driver Foreman	10.81	5.920	Ton
			4 Pile Drivers			
			2 Equip. Oper. (crane)			
			1 Equip. Oper. Oiler			
			1 Crane, 40 Ton			
			Vibratory Hammer & Gen.			
0100	Pull & salvage			7.22	8.860	Ton
0300	20' deep excavation, 27 psf, left in place			12.95	4.940	Ton
0400	Pull & salvage			8.65	7.400	Ton
0600	25' deep excavation, 38 psf, left in place			19	3.370	Ton
0700	Pull & salvage			12.75	5.020	Ton
0900	40' deep excavation, 38 psf, left in place			21.20	3.020	Ton
1000	Pull & salvage	↓	↓	14.20	4.510	Ton

021 610 | Sheet Piling

		Description	CREW	MAKEUP	DAILY OUTPUT	MAN-HOURS	UNIT
614	1201	Sheet piling, steel, 15' deep excavation, 22 psf, left in place	B-40	1 Pile Driver Foreman	983	.065	S.F.
				4 Pile Drivers			
				2 Equip. Oper. (crane)			
				1 Equip. Oper. Oiler			
				1 Crane, 40 Ton			
				Vibratory Hammer & Gen.			
	1300	Pull & salvage			656	.098	S.F.
	1500	20' deep excavation, 27 psf, left in place			960	.067	S.F.
	1600	Pull & salvage			640	.100	S.F.
	1800	25' deep excavation, 38 psf, left in place			1,000	.064	S.F.
	1900	Pull & salvage	↓	↓	670	.096	S.F.
	3900	Wood, solid sheeting, incl. wales, braces and spacers,					
	3910	pull & salvage, 8' deep excavation	B-31	1 Labor Foreman (outside)	330	.121	S.F.
				3 Building Laborers			
				1 Carpenter			
				1 Air Compr., 250 C.F.M.			
				1 Sheeting Driver			
				2-50 Ft Air Hoses, 1.5" Dia.			
	4000	10' deep, 50 S.F./hr. in & 150 S.F./hr. out			300	.133	S.F.
	4100	12' deep, 45 S.F./hr. in & 135 S.F./hr. out			270	.148	S.F.
	4200	14' deep, 42 S.F./hr. in & 126 S.F./hr. out			250	.160	S.F.
	4300	16' deep, 40 S.F./hr. in & 120 S.F./hr. out			240	.167	S.F.
	4400	18' deep, 38 S.F./hr. in & 114 S.F./hr. out			230	.174	S.F.
	4500	20' deep, 35 S.F./hr. in & 105 S.F./hr. out			210	.190	S.F.
	4520	Left in place, 8' deep, 55 S.F./hr.			440	.091	S.F.
	4540	10' deep, 50 S.F./hr.			400	.100	S.F.
	4560	12' deep, 45 S.F./hr.			360	.111	S.F.
	4570	16' deep, 40 S.F./hr.			320	.125	S.F.
	4580	18' deep, 38 S.F./hr.			305	.131	S.F.
	4590	20' deep, 35 S.F./hr.			280	.143	S.F.
	4700	Alternate pricing, left in place, 8' deep			1.76	22.730	M.B.F.
	4800	Pull and salvage, 8' deep	↓	↓	1.32	30.300	M.B.F.

021 620 | Cribbing And Walers

		Description	CREW	MAKEUP	DAILY OUTPUT	MAN-HOURS	UNIT
624		**SOLDIER BEAMS & LAGGING** H piles with 3" wood sheeting					
	0020	Horizontal between piles, including removal of wales & braces					
	0100	No hydrostatic head, 15' deep, 1 line of braces , minimum	B-50	2 Pile Driver Foremen	545	.206	S.F.
				6 Pile Drivers			
				2 Equip. Oper. (crane)			
				1 Equip. Oper. Oiler			
				3 Building Laborers			
				1 Crane, 40 Ton			
				60 L.F. Leads, 15K Ft. Lbs.			
				1 Hammer, 15K Ft. Lbs.			
				1 Air Compr., 600 C.F.M.			
				2-50 Ft. Air Hoses, 3" Dia			
				1 Chain Saw, 36" Long			
	0200	Maximum			495	.226	S.F.
	0400	15' to 22' deep with 2 lines of braces, 10" H, minimum			360	.311	S.F.
	0500	Maximum			330	.339	S.F.
	0700	23' to 35' deep with 3 lines of braces, 12" H, minimum			325	.345	S.F.
	0800	Maximum			295	.380	S.F.
	1000	36' to 45' deep with 4 lines of braces, 14" H, minimum			290	.386	S.F.
	1100	Maximum			265	.423	S.F.
	1300	No hydrostatic head, left in place, 15' dp., 1 line of braces, min.			635	.176	S.F.
	1400	Maximum			575	.195	S.F.
	1600	15' to 22' deep with 2 lines of braces, minimum			455	.246	S.F.
	1700	Maximum	↓	↓	415	.270	S.F.

021 620 | Cribbing And Walers

		Description	CREW	MAKEUP	DAILY OUTPUT	MAN-HOURS	UNIT
624	1901	Soldier beams, 23'-35' deep w/3 lines of braces, minimum	B-50	2 Pile Driver Foremen	420	.267	S.F.
				6 Pile Drivers			
				2 Equip. Oper. (crane)			
				1 Equip. Oper. Oiler			
				3 Building Laborers			
				1 Crane, 40 Ton			
				60 L.F. Leads, 15K Ft. Lbs.			
				1 Hammer, 15K Ft. Lbs.			
				1 Air Compr., 600 C.F.M.			
				2-50 Ft. Air Hoses, 3" Dia			
				1 Chain Saw, 36" Long			
	2000	Maximum			380	.295	S.F.
	2200	36' to 45' deep with 4 lines of braces, minimum			385	.291	S.F.
	2300	Maximum	↓	↓	350	.320	S.F.
	2350	Lagging only, 3" thick wood between piles 8' O.C., minimum	B-46	1 Pile Driver Foreman	400	.120	S.F.
				2 Pile Drivers			
				3 Building Laborers			
				1 Chain Saw, 36" Long			
	2370	Maximum			250	.192	S.F.
	2400	Open sheeting no bracing, for trenches to 10' deep, min.			1,736	.028	S.F.
	2450	Maximum			1,510	.032	S.F.
	2700	Tie-backs only, based on tie-backs total length, minimum			86.80	.553	L.F.
	2750	Maximum			38.50	1.250	L.F.
	3500	Tie-backs only, typical average, 25' long			2	24.000	Ea.
	3600	35' long	↓	↓	1.58	30.380	Ea.
	5200	Wood sheeting, in trench, jacks at 4' O.C., 8' deep	B-1	1 Labor Foreman (outside)	800	.030	S.F.
				2 Building Laborers			
	5250	12' deep			700	.034	S.F.
	5300	15' deep	↓	↓	600	.040	S.F.

021 680 | Slurry Wall

		Description	CREW	MAKEUP	DAILY OUTPUT	MAN-HOURS	UNIT
684	0020	**SLURRY TRENCH** Excavated slurry trench in wet soils backfilled with 3000 psi concrete, no reinforcing steel					
	0050	Minimum	C-7	1 Labor Foreman (outside)	333	.192	C.F.
				5 Building Laborers			
				1 Cement Finisher			
				1 Equip. Oper. (med.)			
				2 Gas Engine Vibrators			
				1 Concrete Bucket, 1 C.Y.			
				1 Hyd. Crane, 55 Ton			
	0100	Maximum			200	.320	C.F.
	0200	Alternate pricing method, minimum			150	.427	S.F.
	0300	Maximum	↓	↓	120	.533	S.F.
	0500	Reinforced slurry trench, minimum	B-48	1 Labor Foreman (outside)	177	.316	S.F.
				3 Building Laborers			
				1 Equip. Oper. (crane)			
				1 Equip. Oper. Oiler			
				1 Equip. Oper. (light)			
				1 Centr. Water Pump, 6"			
				1-20 Ft. Suction Hose, 6"			
				1-50 Ft. Disch. Hose, 6"			
				1 Drill Rig & Augers			
	0600	Maximum	"	"	69	.812	S.F.
	0800	Haul for disposal, 2 mile haul, excavated material, add	B-34B	1 Truck Driver (heavy)	99	.081	C.Y.
				1 Dump Truck, 16 Ton			
	0900	Haul bentonite castings for disposal, add	"	"	40	.200	C.Y.

022 200	Excavation, Backfill, Compact	CREW	MAKEUP	DAILY OUTPUT	MAN-HOURS	UNIT
204	**BACKFILL** By hand, no compaction, light soil	1 Clab	1 Building Laborer	14	.571	C.Y.
0100	Heavy soil			11	.727	C.Y.
0300	Compaction in 6" layers, hand tamp, add to above	↓	↓	20.60	.388	C.Y.
0400	Roller compaction operator walking, add	B-10A	1 Equip. Oper. (med.) .5 Building Laborer 1 Roll. Compact., 2K Lbs.	100	.120	C.Y.
0500	Air tamp, add	B-9	1 Labor Foreman (outside) 4 Building Laborers 1 Air Compr., 250 C.F.M. Air Tools & Accessories 2-50 Ft. Air Hoses, 1.5" Dia.	190	.211	C.Y.
0600	Vibrating plate, add	A-1	1 Building Laborer 1 Gas Eng. Power Tool	60	.133	C.Y.
0800	Compaction in 12" layers, hand tamp, add to above	1 Clab	1 Building Laborer	34	.235	C.Y.
0900	Roller compaction operator walking, add	B-10A	1 Equip. Oper. (med.) .5 Building Laborer 1 Roll. Compact., 2K Lbs.	150	.080	C.Y.
1000	Air tamp, add	B-9	1 Labor Foreman (outside) 4 Building Laborers 1 Air Compr., 250 C.F.M. Air Tools & Accessories 2-50 Ft. Air Hoses, 1.5" Dia.	285	.140	C.Y.
1100	Vibrating plate, add	A-1	1 Building Laborer 1 Gas Eng. Power Tool	90	.089	C.Y.
208	**BACKFILL, STRUCTURAL** Dozer or F.E. loader					
0020	From existing stockpile, no compaction					
2000	75 H.P., 50' haul, sand & gravel	B-10L	1 Equip. Oper. (med.) .5 Building Laborer 1 Dozer, 75 H.P.	1,100	.011	C.Y.
2020	Common earth			975	.012	C.Y.
2040	Clay			850	.014	C.Y.
2200	150' haul, sand & gravel			550	.022	C.Y.
2220	Common earth			490	.024	C.Y.
2240	Clay			425	.028	C.Y.
2400	300' haul, sand & gravel			370	.032	C.Y.
2420	Common earth			330	.036	C.Y.
2440	Clay	↓	↓	290	.041	C.Y.
3000	105 H.P., 50' haul, sand & gravel	B-10W	1 Equip. Oper. (med.) .5 Building Laborer 1 Dozer, 105 H.P.	1,350	.009	C.Y.
3020	Common earth			1,225	.010	C.Y.
3040	Clay			1,100	.011	C.Y.
3200	150' haul, sand & gravel			670	.018	C.Y.
3220	Common earth			610	.020	C.Y.
3240	Clay			550	.022	C.Y.
3300	300' haul, sand & gravel			465	.026	C.Y.
3320	Common earth			415	.029	C.Y.
3340	Clay	↓	↓	370	.032	C.Y.
4000	200 H.P., 50' haul, sand & gravel	B-10B	1 Equip. Oper. (med.) .5 Building Laborer 1 Dozer, 200 H.P.	2,500	.005	C.Y.
4020	Common earth			2,200	.005	C.Y.
4040	Clay			1,950	.006	C.Y.
4200	150' haul, sand & gravel			1,225	.010	C.Y.
4220	Common earth			1,100	.011	C.Y.
4240	Clay			975	.012	C.Y.
4400	300' haul, sand & gravel			805	.015	C.Y.
4420	Common earth	↓	↓	735	.016	C.Y.

022 200 | Excavation, Backfill, Compact

		CREW	MAKEUP	DAILY OUTPUT	MAN-HOURS	UNIT
208	4441 Backfill, 200 H.P. dozer, 300' haul, clay	B-10B	1 Equip. Oper. (med.)	660	.018	C.Y.
			.5 Building Laborer			
			1 Dozer, 200 H.P.			
	5000 300 H.P., 50' haul, sand & gravel	B-10M	1 Equip. Oper. (med.)	3,170	.004	C.Y.
			.5 Building Laborer			
			1 Dozer, 300 H.P.			
	5020 Common earth			2,900	.004	C.Y.
	5040 Clay			2,700	.004	C.Y.
	5200 150' haul, sand & gravel			2,200	.005	C.Y.
	5220 Common earth			1,950	.006	C.Y.
	5240 Clay			1,700	.007	C.Y.
	5400 300' haul, sand & gravel			1,500	.008	C.Y.
	5420 Common earth			1,350	.009	C.Y.
	5440 Clay	↓	↓	1,225	.010	C.Y.
216	**BORROW** Buy and load at pit, no haul included,					
	0500 Machine spread, 200 H.P. dozer, bank run gravel	B-15	1 Equipment Oper. (med)	1,100	.025	Ton
			.5 Building Laborer			
			2 Truck Drivers (heavy)			
			2 Dump Trucks, 16 Ton			
			1 Dozer, 200 H.P.			
	0540 Crushed stone, 1-1/2" to 3/4" size			1,150	.024	Ton
	0560 3/8" size			1,150	.024	Ton
	0600 Sand, bank, damp	↓	↓	1,000	.028	Ton
	1000 Hand spread, bank run gravel	A-5	2 Building Laborers	33	.545	Ton
			.25 Truck Driver (light)			
			.25 Light Truck, 1.5 Ton			
	1040 Crushed stone, 1-1/2" to 3/4" size			38	.474	Ton
	1060 3/8" size			40	.450	Ton
	1100 Sand, bank, damp	↓	↓	33	.545	Ton
	2500 Machine spread, 200 H.P. dozer, bank measure	B-15	1 Equipment Oper. (med)	600	.047	C.Y.
			.5 Building Laborer			
			2 Truck Drivers (heavy)			
			2 Dump Trucks, 16 Ton			
			1 Dozer, 200 H.P.			
	3000 Hand spread, bank measure	A-5	2 Building Laborers	20	.900	C.Y.
			.25 Truck Driver (light)			
			.25 Light Truck, 1.5 Ton			
	3800 Delivery charge, minimum 12 c.y., 1 hr round trip, add	B-34B	1 Truck Driver (heavy)	84	.095	C.Y.
			1 Dump Truck, 16 Ton			
	3820 1-1/2 hr round trip			60	.133	C.Y.
	3840 2 hr round trip	↓	↓	42	.190	C.Y.
222	**COMPACTION** Steel wheel tandem roller, 5 tons	B-10E	1 Equip. Oper. (med.)	8	1.500	Hr.
			.5 Building Laborer			
			1 Tandem Roller, 5 Ton			
	0500 Terra Probe, deep sand, vibrating 30,000 C.Y., minimum	B-43	1 Labor Foreman (outside)	1,800	.027	C.Y.
			3 Building Laborers			
			1 Equip. Oper. (crane)			
			1 Equip. Oper. Oiler			
			1 Drill Rig & Augers			
	0520 Maximum	"	"	1,100	.044	C.Y.
	0540 Mobilization and demobilization, minimum	B-8	1 Labor Foreman (outside)	.63	102.000	Total
			2 Building Laborers			
			2 Equip. Oper. (med.)			
			1 Equip. Oper. Oiler			
			2 Truck Drivers (heavy)			
			1 Hyd. Crane, 25 Ton			
			F.E. Loader, T.M., 2.5 C.Y.			
			2 Dump Trucks, 16 Ton			

		022 200	Excavation, Backfill, Compact	CREW	MAKEUP	DAILY OUTPUT	MAN-HOURS	UNIT
222	0561		Steel wheel tandem roller, mobil. & demobil., maximum	B-8	1 Labor Foreman (outside)	.48	133.000	Total
					2 Building Laborers			
					2 Equip. Oper. (med.)			
					1 Equip. Oper. Oiler			
					2 Truck Drivers (heavy)			
					1 Hyd. Crane, 25 Ton			
					F.E. Loader, T.M., 2.5 C.Y.			
					2 Dump Trucks, 16 Ton			
	226		COMPACTION					
	5000		Riding, vibrating roller, 6" lifts, 2 passes	B-10Y	1 Equip. Oper. (med.)	2,600	.005	C.Y.
					.5 Building Laborer			
					1 Vibratory Drum Roller			
	5020		3 passes			1,950	.006	C.Y.
	5040		4 passes			1,300	.009	C.Y.
	5060		12" lifts, 2 passes			5,200	.002	C.Y.
	5080		3 passes			3,900	.003	C.Y.
	5100		4 passes	▼	▼	2,600	.005	C.Y.
	5600		Sheepsfoot or wobbly wheel roller, 6" lifts, 2 passes	B-10G	1 Equip. Oper. (med.)	2,600	.005	C.Y.
					.5 Building Laborer			
					1 Sheepsft. Roll., 130 H.P.			
	5620		3 passes			1,950	.006	C.Y.
	5640		4 passes			1,300	.009	C.Y.
	5680		12" lifts, 2 passes			5,200	.002	C.Y.
	5700		3 passes			3,900	.003	C.Y.
	5720		4 passes	▼	▼	2,600	.005	C.Y.
	7000		Walk behind, vibrating plate 18" wide, 6" lifts, 2 passes	A-1	1 Building Laborer	280	.029	C.Y.
					1 Gas Eng. Power Tool			
	7020		3 passes			210	.038	C.Y.
	7040		4 passes			140	.057	C.Y.
	7200		12" lifts, 2 passes			560	.014	C.Y.
	7220		3 passes			320	.025	C.Y.
	7240		4 passes	▼	▼	280	.029	C.Y.
	7500		Vibrating roller 24" wide, 6" lifts, 2 passes	B-10A	1 Equip. Oper. (med.)	420	.029	C.Y.
					.5 Building Laborer			
					1 Roll. Compact., 2K Lbs.			
	7520		3 passes			315	.038	C.Y.
	7540		4 passes			210	.057	C.Y.
	7600		12" lifts, 2 passes			840	.014	C.Y.
	7620		3 passes			630	.019	C.Y.
	7640		4 passes	▼	▼	420	.029	C.Y.
	8000		Rammer tamper, 11" x 13", 4" lifts, 2 passes	A-1	1 Building Laborer	130	.062	C.Y.
					1 Gas Eng. Power Tool			
	8050		3 passes			97	.082	C.Y.
	8100		4 passes			65	.123	C.Y.
	8200		8" lifts, 2 passes			260	.031	C.Y.
	8250		3 passes			195	.041	C.Y.
	8300		4 passes			130	.062	C.Y.
	8400		18" x 35", 4" lifts, 2 passes			390	.021	C.Y.
	8450		3 passes			290	.028	C.Y.
	8500		4 passes			195	.041	C.Y.
	8600		8" lifts, 2 passes			780	.010	C.Y.
	8650		3 passes			585	.014	C.Y.
	8700		4 passes	▼	▼	390	.021	C.Y.

022 200	Excavation, Backfill, Compact	CREW	MAKEUP	DAILY OUTPUT	MAN-HOURS	UNIT
230	**DRILLING ONLY** 2" hole for rock bolts, average	B-47	1 Blast Foreman	395	.061	L.F.
			1 Driller			
			1 Equip. Oper. (light)			
			1 Crawler Type Drill, 4"			
			1 Air Compr., 600 C.F.M.			
			2-50 Ft. Air Hoses, 3" Dia			
0800	2-1/2" hole for pre-splitting, average			540	.044	L.F.
1600	Quarry operations, 2-1/2" to 3-1/2" diameter			715	.034	L.F.
234	**DRILLING AND BLASTING** Only, rock, open face, under 1500 C.Y.			225	.107	C.Y.
0100	Over 1500 C.Y.			300	.080	C.Y.
1300	Deep hole method, up to 1500 C.Y.			50	.480	C.Y.
1400	Over 1500 C.Y.			66	.364	C.Y.
1900	Restricted areas, up to 1500 C.Y.			13	1.850	C.Y.
2000	Over 1500 C.Y.			20	1.200	C.Y.
2200	Trenches, up to 1500 C.Y.			22	1.090	C.Y.
2300	Over 1500 C.Y.			26	.923	C.Y.
2500	Pier holes, up to 1500 C.Y.			22	1.090	C.Y.
2600	Over 1500 C.Y.	↓	↓	31	.774	C.Y.
2800	Boulders under 1/2 cy, loaded on truck, no hauling	B-100	1 Equip. Oper. (med.)	80	.150	C.Y.
			.5 Building Laborer			
			F.E. Loader, T.M., 2.25 C.Y.			
2900	Drilled, blasted and loaded on truck, no hauling	B-47	1 Blast Foreman	30	.800	C.Y.
			1 Driller			
			1 Equip. Oper. (light)			
			1 Crawler Type Drill, 4"			
			1 Air Compr., 600 C.F.M.			
			2-50 Ft. Air Hoses, 3" Dia			
3100	Jackhammer operators with foreman compressor, air tools	B-9	1 Labor Foreman (outside)	1	40.000	Day
			4 Building Laborers			
			1 Air Compr., 250 C.F.M.			
			Air Tools & Accessories			
			2-50 Ft. Air Hoses, 1.5" Dia.			
3300	Track drill, compressor, operator and foreman	B-47	1 Blast Foreman	1	24.000	Day
			1 Driller			
			1 Equip. Oper. (light)			
			1 Crawler Type Drill, 4"			
			1 Air Compr., 600 C.F.M.			
			2-50 Ft. Air Hoses, 3" Dia			
4200	Preblast survey for 6 room house, individual lot, minimum	A-6	1 Chief Of Party	2.40	6.670	Ea.
			1 Instrument Man			
4300	Maximum	"	"	1.35	11.850	Ea.
4500	City block within zone of influence, minimum	A-8	1 Chief Of Party	25,200	.001	S.F.
			1 Instrument Man			
			2 Rodmen/Chainmen			
4600	Maximum	"	"	15,100	.002	S.F.
5000	Excavate and load boulders, less than 0.5 C.Y.	B-10T	1 Equip. Oper. (med.)	80	.150	C.Y.
			.5 Building Laborer			
			F.E. Loader, W.M., 2.5 C.Y.			
5020	0.5 C.Y. to 1 C.Y.	B-10U	1 Equip. Oper. (med.)	100	.120	C.Y.
			.5 Building Laborer			
			F.E. Loader, W.M., 5.5 C.Y.			
5200	Excavate and load blasted rock, 3 C.Y. power shovel	B-12T	1 Equip. Oper. (crane)	1,530	.010	C.Y.
			1 Equip. Oper. Oiler			
			1 Crawler Crane, 75 Ton			
			1 F.E. Attachment, 3 C.Y.			
5400	Haul boulders, 25 Ton off-highway dump, 1 mile round trip	B-34E	1 Truck Driver (heavy)	330	.024	C.Y.
			1 Truck, Off Highway, 25 Ton			
5420	2 mile round trip	"	"	275	.029	C.Y.

230

			CREW	MAKEUP	DAILY OUTPUT	MAN-HOURS	UNIT
022 200	**Excavation, Backfill, Compact**						
234	5621	Bury boulders, under .5 C.Y., 300 H.P. dozer, 150' haul	B-10M	1 Equip. Oper. (med.)	310	.039	C.Y.
				.5 Building Laborer			
				1 Dozer, 300 H.P.			
	5640	300' haul			210	.057	C.Y.
	5800	0.5 to 1 C.Y., 300 H.P. dozer, 150' haul			300	.040	C.Y.
	5820	300' haul	↓	↓	200	.060	C.Y.
	238	**EXCAVATING, BULK BANK MEASURE** Common earth piled					
	0200	Backhoe, hydraulic, crawler mtd., 1 C.Y. cap. = 75 C.Y./hr.	B-12A	1 Equip. Oper. (crane)	600	.027	C.Y.
				1 Equip. Oper. Oiler			
				1 Hyd. Excavator, 1 C.Y.			
	0250	1-1/2 C.Y. cap. = 100 C.Y./hr.	B-12B	1 Equip. Oper. (crane)	800	.020	C.Y.
				1 Equip. Oper. Oiler			
				1 Hyd. Excavator, 1.5 C.Y.			
	0260	2 C.Y. cap. = 130 C.Y./hr.	B-12C	1 Equip. Oper. (crane)	1,040	.015	C.Y.
				1 Equip. Oper. Oiler			
				1 Hyd. Excavator, 2 C.Y.			
	0300	3 C.Y. cap. = 160 C.Y./hr.	B-12D	1 Equip. Oper. (crane)	1,620	.010	C.Y.
				1 Equip. Oper. Oiler			
				1 Hyd. Excavator, 3.5 C.Y.			
	0310	Wheel mounted, 1/2 C.Y. cap. = 30 C.Y./hr.	B-12E	1 Equip. Oper. (crane)	240	.067	C.Y.
				1 Equip. Oper. Oiler			
				1 Hyd. Excavator, .5 C.Y.			
	0360	3/4 C.Y. cap. = 45 C.Y./hr.	B-12F	1 Equip. Oper. (crane)	360	.044	C.Y.
				1 Equip. Oper. Oiler			
				1 Hyd. Excavator, .75 C.Y.			
	0500	Clamshell, 1/2 C.Y. cap. = 20 C.Y./hr.	B-12G	1 Equip. Oper. (crane)	160	.100	C.Y.
				1 Equip. Oper. Oiler			
				1 Power Shovel, .5 C.Y.			
				1 Clamshell Bucket, .5 C.Y			
	0550	1 C.Y. cap. = 35 C.Y./hr.	B-12H	1 Equip. Oper. (crane)	280	.057	C.Y.
				1 Equip. Oper. Oiler			
				1 Power Shovel, 1 C.Y.			
				1 Clamshell Bucket, 1 C.Y.			
	0950	Dragline, 1/2 C.Y. cap. = 30 C.Y./hr.	B-12I	1 Equip. Oper. (crane)	240	.067	C.Y.
				1 Equip. Oper. Oiler			
				1 Power Shovel, .75 C.Y.			
				1 Dragline Bucket, .75 C.Y.			
	1000	Dragline, 3/4 C.Y. cap. = 35 C.Y./hr.	"	"	280	.057	C.Y.
	1050	1-1/2 C.Y. cap. = 65 C.Y./hr.	B-12P	1 Equip. Oper. (crane)	520	.031	C.Y.
				1 Equip. Oper. Oiler			
				1 Crawler Crane, 40 Ton			
				1 Dragline Bucket, 1.5 C.Y.			
	1100	3 C.Y. cap. = 112 C.Y./hr.	B-12V	1 Equip. Oper. (crane)	900	.018	C.Y.
				1 Equip. Oper. Oiler			
				1 Crawler Crane, 75 Ton			
				1 Dragline Bucket, 3 C.Y.			
	1200	Front end loader, track mtd., 1-1/2 C.Y. cap. = 70 C.Y./hr.	B-10N	1 Equip. Oper. (med.)	560	.021	C.Y.
				.5 Building Laborer			
				F.E. Loader, T.M., 1.5 C.Y			
	1250	2-1/2 C.Y. cap. = 95 C.Y./hr.	B-10O	1 Equip. Oper. (med.)	760	.016	C.Y.
				.5 Building Laborer			
				F.E. Loader, T.M., 2.25 C.Y.			
	1300	3 C.Y. cap. = 130 C.Y./hr.	B-10P	1 Equip. Oper. (med.)	1,040	.012	C.Y.
				.5 Building Laborer			
				F.E. Loader, T.M., 2.5 C.Y.			
	1350	5 C.Y. cap. = 160 C.Y./hr.	B-10Q	1 Equip. Oper. (med.)	1,620	.007	C.Y.
				.5 Building Laborer			
				F.E. Loader, T.M., 5 C.Y.			

022 200	Excavation, Backfill, Compact	CREW	MAKEUP	DAILY OUTPUT	MAN-HOURS	UNIT
238 1501	Excav., F.E. Loader, wheel mtd., 3/4 C.Y. cap., = 45 C.Y./hr.	B-10R	1 Equip. Oper. (med.) .5 Building Laborer F.E. Loader, W.M., 1 C.Y.	360	.033	C.Y.
1550	1-1/2 C.Y. cap. = 80 C.Y./hr.	B-10S	1 Equip. Oper. (med.) .5 Building Laborer F.E. Loader, W.M., 1.5 C.Y.	640	.019	C.Y.
1601	3 C.Y. cap. = 100 C.Y./hr.	B-10T	1 Equip. Oper. (med.) .5 Building Laborer F.E. Loader, W.M., 2.5 C.Y.	1,100	.011	C.Y.
1650	5 C.Y. cap. = 185 C.Y./hr.	B-10U	1 Equip. Oper. (med.) .5 Building Laborer F.E. Loader, W.M., 5.5 C.Y.	1,480	.008	C.Y.
1800	Hydraulic excavator, truck mtd, 1/2 C.Y. = 30 C.Y./hr.	B-12J	1 Equip. Oper. (crane) 1 Equip. Oper. Oiler 1 Gradall, 3 Ton, .5 C.Y.	240	.067	C.Y.
1850	48 inch bucket, 1 C.Y. = 45 C.Y./hr.	B-12K	1 Equip. Oper. (crane) 1 Equip. Oper. Oiler 1 Gradall, 3 Ton, 1 C.Y.	360	.044	C.Y.
3700	Shovel, 1/2 C.Y. capacity = 55 C.Y./hr.	B-12L	1 Equip. Oper. (crane) 1 Equip. Oper. Oiler 1 Power Shovel, .5 C.Y. 1 F.E. Attachment, .5 C.Y.	440	.036	C.Y.
3750	3/4 C.Y. capacity = 85 C.Y./hr.	B-12M	1 Equip. Oper. (crane) 1 Equip. Oper. Oiler 1 Power Shovel, .75 1 F.E. Attachment, .75 C.Y.	680	.024	C.Y.
3800	1 C.Y. capacity = 120 C.Y./hr.	B-12N	1 Equip. Oper. (crane) 1 Equip. Oper. Oiler 1 Power Shovel, 1 C.Y. 1 F.E. Attachment, 1 C.Y.	960	.017	C.Y.
3850	1-1/2 C.Y. capacity = 160 C.Y./hr.	B-120	1 Equip. Oper. (crane) 1 Equip. Oper. Oiler 1 Power Shovel, 1.5 C.Y. 1 F.E. Attachment, 1.5 C.Y.	1,280	.013	C.Y.
3900	3 C.Y. cap. = 250 C.Y./hr.	B-12T	1 Equip. Oper. (crane) 1 Equip. Oper. Oiler 1 Crawler Crane, 75 Ton 1 F.E. Attachment, 3 C.Y.	2,000	.008	C.Y.
4400	Clamshell in sheeting or cofferdam, minimum	B-12H	1 Equip. Oper. (crane) 1 Equip. Oper. Oiler 1 Power Shovel, 1 C.Y. 1 Clamshell Bucket, 1 C.Y.	160	.100	C.Y.
4450	Maximum	"	"	60	.267	C.Y.
242	**EXCAVATING, BULK, DOZER** Open site					
2000	75 H.P., 50' haul, sand & gravel	B-10L	1 Equip. Oper. (med.) .5 Building Laborer 1 Dozer, 75 H.P.	460	.026	C.Y.
2020	Common earth			400	.030	C.Y.
2040	Clay			250	.048	C.Y.
2200	150' haul, sand & gravel			230	.052	C.Y.
2220	Common earth			200	.060	C.Y.
2240	Clay			125	.096	C.Y.
2400	300' haul, sand & gravel			120	.100	C.Y.
2420	Common earth			100	.120	C.Y.
2440	Clay			65	.185	C.Y.
3000	105 H.P., 50' haul, sand & gravel	B-10W	1 Equip. Oper. (med.) .5 Building Laborer 1 Dozer, 105 H.P.	700	.017	C.Y.

022 200	Excavation, Backfill, Compact	CREW	MAKEUP	DAILY OUTPUT	MAN-HOURS	UNIT
242 3021	Excav., 105 H.P. dozer, 50' haul, common earth	B-10W	1 Equip. Oper. (med.)	610	.020	C.Y.
			.5 Building Laborer			
			1 Dozer, 105 H.P.			
3040	Clay			385	.031	C.Y.
3200	150' haul, sand & gravel			310	.039	C.Y.
3220	Common earth			270	.044	C.Y.
3240	Clay			170	.071	C.Y.
3300	300' haul, sand & gravel			140	.086	C.Y.
3320	Common earth			120	.100	C.Y.
3340	Clay	↓	↓	100	.120	C.Y.
4000	200 H.P., 50' haul, sand & gravel	B-10B	1 Equip. Oper. (med.)	1,400	.009	C.Y.
			.5 Building Laborer			
			1 Dozer, 200 H.P.			
4020	Common earth			1,230	.010	C.Y.
4040	Clay			770	.016	C.Y.
4200	150' haul, sand & gravel			595	.020	C.Y.
4220	Common earth			516	.023	C.Y.
4240	Clay			325	.037	C.Y.
4400	300' haul, sand & gravel			310	.039	C.Y.
4420	Common earth			270	.044	C.Y.
4440	Clay	↓	↓	170	.071	C.Y.
5000	300 H.P., 50' haul, sand & gravel	B-10M	1 Equip. Oper. (med.)	1,900	.006	C.Y.
			.5 Building Laborer			
			1 Dozer, 300 H.P.			
5020	Common earth			1,650	.007	C.Y.
5040	Clay			1,025	.012	C.Y.
5200	150' haul, sand & gravel			920	.013	C.Y.
5220	Common earth			800	.015	C.Y.
5240	Clay			500	.024	C.Y.
5400	300' haul, sand & gravel			470	.026	C.Y.
5420	Common earth			410	.029	C.Y.
5440	Clay	↓	↓	250	.048	C.Y.
246	**EXCAVATION, BULK, SCRAPERS**					
0100	Elevating scraper 11 C.Y., sand & gravel 1500' haul	B-33F	1 Equip. Oper. (med.)	690	.020	C.Y.
			.5 Building Laborer			
			.25 Equip. Oper. (med.)			
			1 Elev. Scraper, 11 C.Y.			
			.25 Dozer, 300 H.P.			
0150	3000' haul			610	.023	C.Y.
0200	5000' haul			505	.028	C.Y.
0300	Common earth, 1500' haul			600	.023	C.Y.
0350	3000' haul			530	.026	C.Y.
0400	5000' haul			440	.032	C.Y.
0500	Clay, 1500' haul			375	.037	C.Y.
0550	3000' haul			330	.042	C.Y.
0600	5000' haul	↓	↓	275	.051	C.Y.
1000	Self propelled scraper, 14 C.Y. 1/4 push dozer, sand					
1050	and gravel, 1500' haul	B-33D	1 Equip. Oper. (med.)	920	.015	C.Y.
			.5 Building Laborer			
			.25 Equip. Oper. (med.)			
			1 S.P. Scraper, 14 C.Y.			
			.25 Dozer, 300 H.P.			
1100	3000' haul			805	.017	C.Y.
1200	5000' haul			645	.022	C.Y.
1300	Common earth, 1500' haul			800	.018	C.Y.
1350	3000' haul			700	.020	C.Y.
1400	5000' haul			560	.025	C.Y.
1500	Clay, 1500' haul	↓	↓	500	.028	C.Y.

022 200 | **Excavation, Backfill, Compact**	CREW	MAKEUP	DAILY OUTPUT	MAN-HOURS	UNIT
246 **1551** Excav., self-propelled scraper, clay, 3000' haul	B-33D	1 Equip. Oper. (med.)	440	.032	C.Y.
		.5 Building Laborer			
		.25 Equip. Oper. (med.)			
		1 S.P. Scraper, 14 C.Y.			
		.25 Dozer, 300 H.P.			
1600 5000' haul	"	"	350	.040	C.Y.
2000 21 C.Y., 1/4 push dozer, sand & gravel, 1500' haul	B-33E	1 Equip. Oper. (med.)	1,180	.012	C.Y.
		.5 Building Laborer			
		.25 Equip. Oper. (med.)			
		1 S.P. Scraper, 24 C.Y.			
		.25 Dozer, 300 H.P.			
2100 3000' haul			910	.015	C.Y.
2200 5000' haul			750	.019	C.Y.
2300 Common earth, 1500' haul			1,030	.014	C.Y.
2350 3000' haul			790	.018	C.Y.
2400 5000' haul			650	.022	C.Y.
2500 Clay, 1500' haul			645	.022	C.Y.
2550 3000' haul			495	.028	C.Y.
2600 5000' haul			405	.035	C.Y.
2700 Towed, 10 C.Y., 1/4 push dozer, sand & gravel, 1500' haul	B-33B	1 Equip. Oper. (med.)	560	.025	C.Y.
		.5 Building Laborer			
		.25 Equip. Oper. (med.)			
		1 Scraper, Towed, 10 C.Y.			
		1 Dozer, 300 H.P.			
		.25 Dozer, 300 H.P.			
2720 3000' haul			450	.031	C.Y.
2730 5000' haul			365	.038	C.Y.
2750 Common earth, 1500' haul			420	.033	C.Y.
2770 3000' haul			400	.035	C.Y.
2780 5000' haul			310	.045	C.Y.
2800 Clay, 1500' haul			315	.044	C.Y.
2820 3000' haul			300	.047	C.Y.
2840 5000' haul			225	.062	C.Y.
2900 15 C.Y., 1/4 push dozer, sand & gravel, 1500' haul	B-33C	1 Equip. Oper. (med.)	800	.018	C.Y.
		.5 Building Laborer			
		.25 Equip. Oper. (med.)			
		1 Scraper, Towed, 12 C.Y.			
		1 Dozer, 300 H.P.			
		.25 Dozer, 300 H.P.			
2920 3000' haul			640	.022	C.Y.
2940 5000' haul			520	.027	C.Y.
2960 Common earth, 1500' haul			600	.023	C.Y.
2980 3000' haul			560	.025	C.Y.
3000 5000' haul			440	.032	C.Y.
3020 Clay, 1500' haul			450	.031	C.Y.
3040 3000' haul			420	.033	C.Y.
3060 5000' haul			320	.044	C.Y.
250 **EXCAVATING, STRUCTURAL** Hand, pits to 6' deep, sandy soil	1 Clab	1 Building Laborer	8	1.000	C.Y.
0100 Heavy soil or clay			4	2.000	C.Y.
0300 Pits 6' to 12' deep, sandy soil			5	1.600	C.Y.
0500 Heavy soil or clay			3	2.670	C.Y.
0700 Pits 12' to 18' deep, sandy soil			4	2.000	C.Y.
0900 Heavy soil or clay			2	4.000	C.Y.
1100 Hand loading trucks from stock pile, sandy soil			12	.667	C.Y.
1300 Heavy soil or clay			8	1.000	C.Y.

022 200 | Excavation, Backfill, Compact

			CREW	MAKEUP	DAILY OUTPUT	MAN-HOURS	UNIT
250	1550	Excavation rock by hand/air tool	B-9	1 Labor Foreman (outside)	3.40	11.760	C.Y.
				4 Building Laborers			
				1 Air Compr., 250 C.F.M.			
				Air Tools & Accessories			
				2-50 Ft. Air Hoses, 1.5" Dia.			
	254	**EXCAVATING, TRENCH** or continuous footing, common earth					
	0020	No sheeting or dewatering included					
	0050	1' to 4' deep, 3/8 C.Y. tractor loader/backhoe	B-11C	1 Equipment Oper. (med.)	150	.107	C.Y.
				1 Building Laborer			
				1 Backhoe Loader, 48 H.P.			
	0060	1/2 C.Y. tractor loader/backhoe	B-11M	1 Equipment Oper. (med.)	200	.080	C.Y.
				1 Building Laborer			
				1 Backhoe Loader, 80 H.P.			
	0090	4' to 6' deep, 1/2 C.Y. tractor loader/backhoe	"	"	200	.080	C.Y.
	0100	5/8 C.Y. hydraulic backhoe	B-12Q	1 Equip. Oper. (crane)	250	.064	C.Y.
				1 Equip. Oper. Oiler			
				1 Hyd. Excavator, 5/8 C.Y.			
	0300	1/2 C.Y. hydraulic excavator, truck mounted	B-12J	1 Equip. Oper. (crane)	200	.080	C.Y.
				1 Equip. Oper. Oiler			
				1 Gradall, 3 Ton, .5 C.Y.			
	0500	6' to 10' deep, 3/4 C.Y. hydraulic backhoe	B-12F	1 Equip. Oper. (crane)	225	.071	C.Y.
				1 Equip. Oper. Oiler			
				1 Hyd. Excavator, .75 C.Y.			
	0600	1 C.Y. hydraulic excavator, truck mounted	B-12K	1 Equip. Oper. (crane)	400	.040	C.Y.
				1 Equip. Oper. Oiler			
				1 Gradall, 3 Ton, 1 C.Y.			
	0900	10' to 14' deep, 3/4 C.Y. hydraulic backhoe	B-12F	1 Equip. Oper. (crane)	200	.080	C.Y.
				1 Equip. Oper. Oiler			
				1 Hyd. Excavator, .75 C.Y.			
	1000	1-1/2 C.Y. hydraulic backhoe	B-12B	1 Equip. Oper. (crane)	540	.030	C.Y.
				1 Equip. Oper. Oiler			
				1 Hyd. Excavator, 1.5 C.Y.			
	1300	14' to 20' deep, 1 C.Y. hydraulic backhoe	B-12A	1 Equip. Oper. (crane)	320	.050	C.Y.
				1 Equip. Oper. Oiler			
				1 Hyd. Excavator, 1 C.Y.			
	1400	By hand with pick and shovel to 6' deep, light soil	1 Clab	1 Building Laborer	8	1.000	C.Y.
	1500	Heavy soil	"	"	4	2.000	C.Y.
	1700	For tamping backfilled trenches, air tamp, add	A-1	1 Building Laborer	100	.080	C.Y.
				1 Gas Eng. Power Tool			
	1900	Vibrating plate, add		↓	90	.089	C.Y.
	2100	Trim sides and bottom for concrete pours, common earth		↓	600	.013	S.F.
	2300	Hardpan	↓	↓	180	.044	S.F.
	3000	Backfill trench, F.E. loader, wheel mtd., 1 C.Y. bucket					
	3020	Minimal haul	B-10R	1 Equip. Oper. (med.)	400	.030	C.Y.
				.5 Building Laborer			
				F.E. Loader, W.M., 1 C.Y.			
	3040	100' haul		↓	200	.060	C.Y.
	3060	200' haul	↓	↓	100	.120	C.Y.
	258	**EXCAVATING, UTILITY TRENCH** Common earth					
	0050	Trenching with chain trencher, 12 H.P., operator walking					
	0100	4" wide trench, 12" deep	B-53	1 Equip. Oper. (light)	800	.010	L.F.
				1 Trencher, Chain, 12 H.P.			
	0150	18" deep		↓	750	.011	L.F.
	0200	24" deep		↓	700	.011	L.F.
	0300	6" wide trench, 12" deep			650	.012	L.F.
	0350	18" deep			600	.013	L.F.
	0400	24" deep		↓	550	.015	L.F.
	0450	36" deep	↓	↓	450	.018	L.F.

022 200 | Excavation, Backfill, Compact

			CREW	MAKEUP	DAILY OUTPUT	MAN-HOURS	UNIT
258	0601	Excav., w/chain trencher, 8" wide trench, 12" deep	B-53	1 Equip. Oper. (light)	475	.017	L.F.
				1 Trencher, Chain, 12 H.P.			
	0650	18" deep			400	.020	L.F.
	0700	24" deep			350	.023	L.F.
	0750	36" deep	↓	↓	300	.027	L.F.
	1050	4" wide trench, 12" deep	A-1	1 Building Laborer	800	.010	L.F.
				1 Gas Eng. Power Tool			
	1100	18" deep			530	.015	L.F.
	1150	24" deep			400	.020	L.F.
	1300	6" wide trench, 12" deep			540	.015	L.F.
	1350	18" deep			405	.020	L.F.
	1400	24" deep			270	.030	L.F.
	1450	36" deep			180	.044	L.F.
	1600	8" wide trench, 12" deep			400	.020	L.F.
	1650	18" deep			265	.030	L.F.
	1700	24" deep			200	.040	L.F.
	1750	36" deep	↓	↓	135	.059	L.F.
	2000	Chain trencher, 40 H.P. operator riding					
	2050	6" wide trench and backfill, 12" deep	B-54	1 Equip. Oper. (light)	1,200	.007	L.F.
				1 Trencher, Chain, 40 H.P.			
	2100	18" deep			1,000	.008	L.F.
	2150	24" deep			975	.008	L.F.
	2200	36" deep			900	.009	L.F.
	2250	48" deep			750	.011	L.F.
	2300	60" deep			650	.012	L.F.
	2400	8" wide trench and backfill, 12" deep			1,000	.008	L.F.
	2450	18" deep			950	.008	L.F.
	2500	24" deep			900	.009	L.F.
	2550	36" deep			800	.010	L.F.
	2600	48" deep			650	.012	L.F.
	2700	12" wide trench and backfill, 12" deep			975	.008	L.F.
	2750	18" deep			860	.009	L.F.
	2800	24" deep			800	.010	L.F.
	2850	36" deep			725	.011	L.F.
	3000	16" wide trench and backfill, 12" deep			835	.010	L.F.
	3050	18" deep			750	.011	L.F.
	3100	24" deep	↓	↓	700	.011	L.F.
	262	FILL Spread dumped material, by dozer, no compaction	B-10B	1 Equip. Oper. (med.)	1,000	.012	C.Y.
				.5 Building Laborer			
				1 Dozer, 200 H.P.			
	0100	By hand	1 Clab	1 Building Laborer	12	.667	C.Y.
	0150	Spread fill, from stockpile with 2-1/2 C.Y. F.E. loader					
	0170	130 H.P. 300' haul	B-10P	1 Equip. Oper. (med.)	600	.020	C.Y.
				.5 Building Laborer			
				F.E. Loader, T.M., 2.5 C.Y.			
	0190	With dozer 300 H.P. 300' haul	B-10M	1 Equip. Oper. (med.)	600	.020	C.Y.
				.5 Building Laborer			
				1 Dozer, 300 H.P.			
	0500	Gravel fill, compacted, under floor slabs, 4" deep	B-37	1 Labor Foreman (outside)	10,000	.005	S.F.
				4 Building Laborers			
				1 Equip. Oper. (light)			
				1 Tandem Roller, 5 Ton			
	0600	6" deep			8,600	.006	S.F.
	0700	9" deep			7,200	.007	S.F.
	0800	12" deep			6,000	.008	S.F.
	1000	Alternate pricing method, 4" deep			120	.400	C.Y.
	1100	6" deep			160	.300	C.Y.
	1200	9" deep	↓	↓	200	.240	C.Y.

022 200 | Excavation, Backfill, Compact

		CREW	MAKEUP	DAILY OUTPUT	MAN-HOURS	UNIT
262 1301	Gravel fill, compacted under floor slabs, 12" deep	B-37	1 Labor Foreman (outside)	220	.218	C.Y.
			4 Building Laborers			
			1 Equip. Oper. (light)			
			1 Tandem Roller, 5 Ton			
266	**HAULING** Earth 6 C.Y. dump truck, 1/4 mile round trip, 5.0 loads/hr.	B-34A	1 Truck Driver (heavy)	240	.033	C.Y.
			1 Dump Truck, 12 Ton			
0030	1/2 mile round trip, 4.1 loads/hr.			197	.041	C.Y.
0040	1 mile round trip, 3.3 loads/hr.			160	.050	C.Y.
0100	2 mile round trip, 2.6 loads/hr.			125	.064	C.Y.
0150	3 mile round trip, 2.1 loads/hr.			100	.080	C.Y.
0200	4 mile round trip, 1.8 loads/hr.	↓	↓	85	.094	C.Y.
0310	12 C.Y. dump truck, 1/4 mile round trip 3.7 loads/hr.	B-34B	1 Truck Driver (heavy)	356	.022	C.Y.
			1 Dump Truck, 16 Ton			
0320	1/2 mile round trip, 3.2 loads/hr.			308	.026	C.Y.
0330	1 mile round trip 2.7 loads/hr.			260	.031	C.Y.
0400	2 mile round trip, 2.2 loads/hr.			210	.038	C.Y.
0450	3 mile round trip, 1.9 loads/hr.			180	.044	C.Y.
0500	4 mile round trip, 1.6 loads/hr.			150	.053	C.Y.
0540	5 mile round trip, 1 load/hr.			98	.082	C.Y.
0550	10 mile round trip, .75 load/hr.			49	.163	C.Y.
0560	20 mile round trip, .5 load/hr.	↓	↓	32	.250	C.Y.
0600	16.5 C.Y. dump trailer, 1 mile round trip, 2.6 loads/hr.	B-34C	1 Truck Driver (heavy)	340	.024	C.Y.
			1 Truck Tractor, 40 Ton			
			1 Dump Trailer, 16.5 C.Y.			
0700	2 mile round trip, 2.1 loads/hr.			275	.029	C.Y.
1000	3 mile round trip, 1.8 loads/hr.			235	.034	C.Y.
1100	4 mile round trip, 1.6 loads/hr.			210	.038	C.Y.
1110	5 mile round trip, 1 load/hr.			132	.061	C.Y.
1120	10 mile round trip, .75 load/hr.			100	.080	C.Y.
1130	20 mile round trip, .5 load/hr.	↓	↓	66	.121	C.Y.
1150	20 C.Y. dump trailer, 1 mile round trip, 2.5 loads/hr.	B-34D	1 Truck Driver (heavy)	400	.020	C.Y.
			1 Truck Tractor, 40 Ton			
			1 Dump Trailer, 20 C.Y.			
1200	2 mile round trip, 2 loads/hr.			320	.025	C.Y.
1220	3 mile round trip, 1.7 loads/hr.			270	.030	C.Y.
1240	4 mile round trip, 1.5 loads/hr.			240	.033	C.Y.
1245	5 mile round trip, 1.1 load/hr.			172	.047	C.Y.
1250	10 mile round trip, .85 load/hr.			136	.059	C.Y.
1255	20 mile round trip, .6 load/hr.	↓	↓	96	.083	C.Y.
1600	Grading at dump, or embankment if required, by dozer	B-10B	1 Equip. Oper. (med.)	1,000	.012	C.Y.
			.5 Building Laborer			
			1 Dozer, 200 H.P.			
1800	Spotter at fill or cut, if required	1 Clab	1 Building Laborer	8	1.000	Hr.
270 0020	**HORIZONTAL BORING** Casing only, 100' minimum, not incl. jacking pits or dewatering					
0100	Roadwork, 1/2" thick wall, 24" diameter casing	B-42	1 Labor Foreman (outside)	10	6.400	L.F.
			4 Building Laborers			
			1 Equip. Oper. (crane)			
			1 Equip. Oper. Oiler			
			1 Welder			
			1 Hyd. Crane, 25 Ton			
			1 Gas Welding Machine			
			1 Horz. Boring Csg. Mch.			
0200	36" diameter			9.50	6.740	L.F.
0300	48" diameter			9	7.110	L.F.
0500	Railroad work, 24" diameter			7	9.140	L.F.
0600	36" diameter			6.50	9.850	L.F.
0700	48" diameter	↓	↓	6	10.670	L.F.

022 200 | Excavation, Backfill, Compact

			CREW	MAKEUP	DAILY OUTPUT	MAN-HOURS	UNIT
270	1000	Small diameter boring, 3", sandy soil	B-82	1 Highway Laborer	1,050	.015	L.F.
				1 Equip. Oper. (light)			
				1 Horiz. Borer, 6 H.P.			
	1040	Rocky soil	"	"	550	.029	L.F.
274		**MOBILIZATION AND DEMOBILIZATION** Up to 25 miles	B-34K	1 Truck Driver (heavy)	4	2.000	Ea.
				1 Truck Tractor, 240 H.P.			
				1 Low Bed Trailer			
	0020	Dozer or loader, 105 H.P.			4	2.000	Ea.
	0100	300 H.P.			3.80	2.110	Ea.
	0300	Scraper, towed type (incl. tractor), 6 C.Y. capacity			3.50	2.290	Ea.
	0400	10 C.Y.			3.20	2.500	Ea.
	0600	Self-propelled scraper, 15 C.Y.			3.10	2.580	Ea.
	0700	24 C.Y.			3	2.670	Ea.
	0900	Shovel, backhoe or dragline, 3/4 C.Y.			3.60	2.220	Ea.
	1000	1-1/2 C.Y.			3	2.670	Ea.
	1200	Tractor shovel or front end loader, 1 C.Y.			4.50	1.780	Ea.
	1300	2-1/4 C.Y.	↓	↓	4	2.000	Ea.
278		**RIPPING** Trap rock, soft, 200 HP dozer, ideal conditions	B-10B	1 Equip. Oper. (med.)	710	.017	C.Y.
				.5 Building Laborer			
				1 Dozer, 200 H.P.			
	1500	Adverse conditions	"	"	660	.018	C.Y.
	1600	Medium hard, 300 HP dozer, ideal conditons	B-10M	1 Equip. Oper. (med.)	600	.020	C.Y.
				.5 Building Laborer			
				1 Dozer, 300 H.P.			
	1700	Adverse conditions	"	"	540	.022	C.Y.
	2000	Very hard, 460 HP dozer, ideal conditions	B-10X	1 Equip. Oper. (med.)	300	.040	C.Y.
				.5 Building Laborer			
				1 Dozer, 410 H.P.			
	2100	Adverse conditions	"	"	270	.044	C.Y.
	2200	Shale, soft, 200 HP dozer, ideal conditons	B-10B	1 Equip. Oper. (med.)	850	.014	C.Y.
				.5 Building Laborer			
				1 Dozer, 200 H.P.			
	2300	Adverse conditions	"	"	790	.015	C.Y.
	2400	Medium hard, 300 HP dozer, ideal conditons	B-10M	1 Equip. Oper. (med.)	720	.017	C.Y.
				.5 Building Laborer			
				1 Dozer, 300 H.P.			
	2500	Adverse conditions	"	"	650	.018	C.Y.
	2600	Very hard, 460 HP dozer, ideal conditons	B-10X	1 Equip. Oper. (med.)	360	.033	C.Y.
				.5 Building Laborer			
				1 Dozer, 410 H.P.			
	2700	Adverse conditions	"	"	320	.038	C.Y.
	3000	Dozing ripped material, 200 HP, 100' haul	B-10B	1 Equip. Oper. (med.)	700	.017	C.Y.
				.5 Building Laborer			
				1 Dozer, 200 H.P.			
	3050	300' haul	"	"	250	.048	C.Y.
	3200	300 HP, 100' haul	B-10M	1 Equip. Oper. (med.)	1,150	.010	C.Y.
				.5 Building Laborer			
				1 Dozer, 300 H.P.			
	3250	300' haul	"	"	400	.030	C.Y.
	3400	460 HP, 100' haul	B-10X	1 Equip. Oper. (med.)	1,680	.007	C.Y.
				.5 Building Laborer			
				1 Dozer, 410 H.P.			
	3450	300' haul	"	"	600	.020	C.Y.

022 | Earthwork

022 200 | Excavation, Backfill, Compact

			CREW	MAKEUP	DAILY OUTPUT	MAN-HOURS	UNIT
282	282	**FILL** Borrow, load, 1 mile haul, compact and shape					
	0020	for embankments	B-15	1 Equipment Oper. (med)	1,200	.023	C.Y.
				.5 Building Laborer			
				2 Truck Drivers (heavy)			
				2 Dump Trucks, 16 Ton			
				1 Dozer, 200 H.P.			
	0100	Select fill for shoulders & embankments	" "		1,200	.023	C.Y.

022 300 | Paving

		CREW	MAKEUP	DAILY OUTPUT	MAN-HOURS	UNIT
304	**BASE** Prepare and roll sub-base, small areas to 2500 S.Y.	B-32A	1 Highway Laborer	1,500	.016	S.Y.
			3 Equip. Oper. (med.)			
			1 Grader, 30,000 lbs.			
			1 Tandem Roller, 10 Ton			
			1 Dozer, 200 H.P.			
			1 Laborer			
			2 Equip. Oper. (medium)			
			1 Grader, 30,000 lbs			
			1 Roller, Vibratory, 29,000 lbs			
0100	Large areas over 2500 S.Y.	B-32	1 Highway Laborer	3,700	.009	S.Y.
			3 Equip. Oper. (med.)			
			1 Grader, 30,000 lbs.			
			1 Tandem Roller, 10 Ton			
			1 Dozer, 200 H.P.			
308	**BASE COURSE** For roadways and large paved areas					
0050	3/4" stone compacted to 3" deep	B-36	1 Labor Foreman (outside)	4,000	.010	S.Y.
			2 Highway Laborers			
			2 Equip. Oper. (med.)			
			1 Dozer, 200 H.P.			
			1 Aggregate Spreader			
			1 Tandem Roller, 10 Ton			
0100	6" deep			3,900	.010	S.Y.
0200	9" deep			2,875	.014	S.Y.
0300	12" deep			2,350	.017	S.Y.
0301	Crushed 1-1/2" stone base, compacted to 4" deep			5,225	.008	S.Y.
0302	6" deep			3,900	.010	S.Y.
0303	8" deep			3,000	.013	S.Y.
0304	12" deep	↓	↓	1,800	.022	S.Y.
0350	Bank run gravel, spread and compacted					
0370	6" deep	B-32	1 Highway Laborer	6,000	.005	S.Y.
			3 Equip. Oper. (med.)			
			1 Grader, 30,000 lbs.			
			1 Tandem Roller, 10 Ton			
			1 Dozer, 200 H.P.			
0390	9" deep	↓	↓	44,000	.001	S.Y.
0400	12" deep			3,600	.009	S.Y.
0500	Bituminous concrete, 4" thick	B-25	1 Labor Foreman	4,545	.019	S.Y.
			7 Laborers			
			3 Equip. Oper. (med.)			
			1 Asphalt Paver, 130 H.P			
			1 Tandem Roller, 10 Ton			
			1 Roller, Pneumatic Wheel			
0550	6" thick			3,700	.024	S.Y.
0560	8" thick			3,000	.029	S.Y.
0570	10" thick	↓	↓	2,545	.035	S.Y.
0601						

			CREW	MAKEUP	DAILY OUTPUT	MAN-HOURS	UNIT
022	**300**	**Paving**					
308	0701	Cold laid, liquid application to gravel base, asphalt emulsion	B-45	1 Equip. Oper. (med.)	6,000	.003	Gal.
				1 Truck Driver (heavy)			
				1 Dist. Tank Truck, 3K Gal.			
				1 Tractor, 4 x 2, 250 H.P.			
	0800	Prime and seal, cut back asphalt			6,000	.003	Gal.
	1000	Macadam penetration crushed stone, 2 gal. per S.Y., 4" thick			6,000	.003	S.Y.
	1100	6" thick, 3 gal. per S.Y.			4,000	.004	S.Y.
	1200	8" thick, 4 gal. per S.Y.	↓	↓	3,000	.005	S.Y.
	1500	Alternate method to figure base course					
	1510	Crushed stone, 3/4" maximum size, 3" deep	B-36	1 Labor Foreman (outside)	435	.092	C.Y.
				2 Highway Laborers			
				2 Equip. Oper. (med.)			
				1 Dozer, 200 H.P.			
				1 Aggregate Spreader			
				1 Tandem Roller, 10 Ton			
	1511	6" deep			1,305	.031	C.Y.
	1512	9" deep			1,435	.028	C.Y.
	1513	12" deep			1,565	.026	C.Y.
	1520	Crushed stone, 1-1/2" maximum size, 4" deep			580	.069	C.Y.
	1521	6" deep			650	.062	C.Y.
	1522	8" deep			665	.060	C.Y.
	1523	12" deep	↓	↓	785	.051	C.Y.
	1530	Gravel, bank run, 6" deep	B-32A	1 Highway Laborer	650	.037	C.Y.
				3 Equip. Oper. (med.)			
				1 Grader, 30,000 lbs.			
				1 Tandem Roller, 10 Ton			
				1 Dozer, 200 H.P.			
				1 Laborer			
				2 Equip. Oper. (medium)			
				1 Grader, 30,000 lbs			
				1 Roller, Vibratory, 29,000 lbs			
	1531	9" deep			720	.033	C.Y.
	1532	12" deep	↓	↓	785	.031	C.Y.
	2000	Alternate method to figure base course					
	2005	Bituminous concrete, 4" thick	B-25	1 Labor Foreman	1,000	.088	Ton
				7 Laborers			
				3 Equip. Oper. (med.)			
				1 Asphalt Paver, 130 H.P			
				1 Tandem Roller, 10 Ton			
				1 Roller, Pneumatic Wheel			
	2006	6" thick			1,220	.072	Ton
	2007	8" thick			1,320	.067	Ton
	2008	10" thick	↓	↓	1,400	.063	Ton
	2010	Crushed stone, 3/4" maximum size, 3" deep	B-36	1 Labor Foreman (outside)	540	.074	Ton
				2 Highway Laborers			
				2 Equip. Oper. (med.)			
				1 Dozer, 200 H.P.			
				1 Aggregate Spreader			
				1 Tandem Roller, 10 Ton			
	2011	6" deep			1,625	.025	Ton
	2012	9" deep			1,785	.022	Ton
	2013	12" deep			1,950	.021	Ton
	2020	Crushed stone, 1-1/2" maximum size, 4" deep			720	.056	Ton
	2021	6" deep			815	.049	Ton
	2022	8" deep			835	.048	Ton
	2023	12" deep	↓	↓	975	.041	Ton

022 300 | Paving

		Description	CREW	MAKEUP	DAILY OUTPUT	MAN-HOURS	UNIT
308	2029	Base course, bank run gravel, 6" deep	B-32A	1 Highway Laborer	875	.027	Ton
				3 Equip. Oper. (med.)			
				1 Grader, 30,000 lbs.			
				1 Tandem Roller, 10 Ton			
				1 Dozer, 200 H.P.			
				1 Laborer			
				2 Equip. Oper. (medium)			
				1 Grader, 30,000 lbs			
				1 Roller, Vibratory, 29,000 lbs			
	2031	9" deep	↓	↓	970	.025	Ton
	2032	12" deep			1,060	.023	Ton
	6000	Stabilization fabric, polypropylene, 6 oz./S.Y.	B-6	2 Building Laborers	10,000	.002	S.Y.
				1 Equip. Oper. (light)			
				1 Backhoe Loader, 48 H.P.			

022 400 | Soil Stabilization

		Description	CREW	MAKEUP	DAILY OUTPUT	MAN-HOURS	UNIT
408		GROUTING, PRESSURE Cement and sand, 1:1 mix, minimum	B-61	1 Labor Foreman (outside)	124	.323	Bag
				3 Building Laborers			
				1 Equip. Oper. (light)			
				1 Cement Mixer, 2 C.Y.			
				1 Air Compr., 160 C.F.M.			
	0100	Maximum		↓	51	.784	Bag
	0200	Cement and sand, 1:1 mix, minimum			250	.160	C.F.
	0300	Maximum			100	.400	C.F.
	0400	Cement grout, minimum (1 bag = 1 C.F.)			137	.292	C.F.
	0500	Maximum	↓	↓	57	.702	C.F.
	0700	Alternate pricing method: (Add for materials)					
	0710	5 man crew and equipment	B-61	1 Labor Foreman (outside)	1	40.000	Day
				3 Building Laborers			
				1 Equip. Oper. (light)			
				1 Cement Mixer, 2 C.Y.			
				1 Air Compr., 160 C.F.M.			
412		SOIL STABILIZATION Including scarifying and compaction					
	0020	Asphalt, 1-1/2" deep, 1/2 gal/S.Y.	B-75	1 Labor Foreman (outside)	4,000	.014	S.Y.
				1 Highway Laborer			
				4 Equip. Oper. (med.)			
				1 Truck Driver (heavy)			
				1 Motor Grader, 30,000 Lb.			
				1 Grader Attach., Ripper			
				2 Stabilizers, 310 H.P.			
				1 Dist. Truck, 3000 Gal.			
				1 Vibr. Roller, 29,000 Lb.			
	0040	3/4 gal/S.Y.			4,000	.014	S.Y.
	0100	3" deep, 1 gal/S.Y.			3,500	.016	S.Y.
	0140	1-1/2 gal/S.Y.			3,500	.016	S.Y.
	0200	6" deep, 2 gal/S.Y.			3,000	.019	S.Y.
	0240	3 gal/S.Y.			3,000	.019	S.Y.
	0300	8" deep, 2-2/3 gal/S.Y.			2,800	.020	S.Y.
	0340	4 gal/S.Y.			2,800	.020	S.Y.
	0500	12" deep, 4 gal/S.Y.			5,000	.011	S.Y.
	0540	6 gal/S.Y.	↓	↓	2,600	.022	S.Y.

022 | Earthwork

022 400 | Soil Stabilization

		Description	CREW	MAKEUP	DAILY OUTPUT	MAN-HOURS	UNIT
412	1021	Soil stabilization, cement, 4% mix, by volume, 6" deep	B-74	1 Labor Foreman (outside)	1,100	.058	S.Y.
				1 Highway Laborer			
				4 Equip. Oper. (med.)			
				2 Truck Drivers (heavy)			
				1 Motor Grader, 30,000 Lb.			
				1 Grader Attach., Ripper			
				2 Stabilizers, 310 H.P.			
				1 Flatbed Truck, 3 Ton			
				1 Chem. Spreader, Towed			
				1 Vibr. Roller, 29,000 Lb.			
				1 water tank 5000 gal.			
				1 truck, 30 ton			
	1030	8" deep			1,050	.061	S.Y.
	1060	12" deep			960	.067	S.Y.
	1100	6% mix, 6" deep			1,100	.058	S.Y.
	1120	8" deep			1,050	.061	S.Y.
	1160	12" deep			960	.067	S.Y.
	1200	9% mix, 6" deep			1,100	.058	S.Y.
	1220	8" deep			1,050	.061	S.Y.
	1260	12" deep			960	.067	S.Y.
	1300	12% mix, 6" deep			1,100	.058	S.Y.
	1320	8" deep			1,050	.061	S.Y.
	1360	12" deep			960	.067	S.Y.
	2020	Hydrated lime, for base, 2% mix by weight, 6" deep			1,800	.036	S.Y.
	2030	8" deep			1,700	.038	S.Y.
	2060	12" deep			1,550	.041	S.Y.
	2100	4% mix, 6" deep			1,800	.036	S.Y.
	2120	8" deep			1,700	.038	S.Y.
	2160	12" deep			1,550	.041	S.Y.
	2200	6% mix, 6" deep			1,800	.036	S.Y.
	2220	8" deep			1,700	.038	S.Y.
	2260	12" deep	↓	↓	1,550	.041	S.Y.

022 500 | Vibroflotation

		Description	CREW	MAKEUP	DAILY OUTPUT	MAN-HOURS	UNIT
	504	**VIBROFLOTATION**					
	0900	Vibroflotation compacted sand cylinder, minimum	B-60	1 Labor Foreman (outside)	750	.075	V.L.F.
				2 Building Laborers			
				1 Equip. Oper. (crane)			
				2 Equip. Oper. (light)			
				1 Equip. Oper. Oiler			
				1 Crawler Crane, 40 Ton			
				45 L.F. Leads, 15K Ft. Lbs.			
				1 Backhoe Loader, 48 H.P.			
	0950	Maximum			325	.172	V.L.F.
	1100	Vibro replacement compacted stone cylinder, minimum			500	.112	V.L.F.
	1150	Maximum			250	.224	V.L.F.
	1300	Mobilization and demobilization, minimum			.47	119.000	Total
	1400	Maximum	↓	↓	.14	400.000	Total

022 700 | Slope/Erosion Control

		Description	CREW	MAKEUP	DAILY OUTPUT	MAN-HOURS	UNIT
	704	**EROSION CONTROL** Jute mesh, 100 S.Y. per roll, 4' wide, stapled	B-1	1 Labor Foreman (outside)	2,500	.010	S.Y.
				2 Building Laborers			
	0100	Plastic netting, stapled, 2" x 1" mesh, 20 mil			2,500	.010	S.Y.
	0200	Polypropylene mesh, stapled, 6.5 oz./S.Y.			2,500	.010	S.Y.
	0300	Tobacco netting, or jute mesh #2, stapled	↓	↓	2,500	.010	S.Y.
	1000	Silt fence, polypropylene, ideal conditions	2 Clab	2 Building Laborers	1,600	.010	L.F.
	1100	Adverse conditions	"	"	950	.017	L.F.

58

022 700 | Slope/Erosion Control

			CREW	MAKEUP	DAILY OUTPUT	MAN-HOURS	UNIT
708	708	**RETAINING WALLS** Asbestos bonded steel bin, excavation					
	0020	and backfill not included, 10' wide					
	0100	4' high, design A, 5.5' deep	E-2	1 Struc. Steel Foreman	650	.086	S.F.
				4 Struc. Steel Workers			
				1 Equip. Oper. (crane)			
				1 Equip. Oper. Oiler			
				1 Crane, 90 Ton			
	0200	8' high, design A, 5.5' deep			615	.091	S.F.
	0300	10' high, design B, 7.7' deep			580	.097	S.F.
	0400	12' high, design B, 7.7' deep			530	.106	S.F.
	0500	16' high, design B, 7.7' deep			515	.109	S.F.
	0600	16' high, design C, 9.9' deep			500	.112	S.F.
	0700	20' high, design C, 9.9' deep			470	.119	S.F.
	0800	20' high, design D, 12.1' deep			460	.122	S.F.
	0900	24' high, design D, 12.1' deep			455	.123	S.F.
	1000	24' high, design E, 14.3' deep			450	.124	S.F.
	1100	28' high, design E, 14.3' deep	↓	↓	440	.127	S.F.
	1800	Gravity concrete with vertical face including					
	1850	excavation and backfill, no reinforcing					
	1900	6' high, level embankment	C-17C	2 Skilled Worker Foremen	36	2.310	L.F.
				8 Skilled Workers			
				.375 Equip. Oper. (crane)			
				.375 Crane, 80 Ton & Tools			
				.375 Hand held power tools			
				.375 Walk behind power tools			
	2000	33° slope embankment			32	2.590	L.F.
	2200	8' high, no surcharge			27	3.070	L.F.
	2300	33° slope embankment			24	3.460	L.F.
	2500	10' high, level embankment			19	4.370	L.F.
	2600	33° slope embankment	↓	↓	18	4.610	L.F.
	2800	Reinforced concrete cantilever, incl. excavation, backfill & reinf.					
	2900	6' high, 33° slope embankment	C-17C	2 Skilled Worker Foremen	35	2.370	L.F.
				8 Skilled Workers			
				.375 Equip. Oper. (crane)			
				.375 Crane, 80 Ton & Tools			
				.375 Hand held power tools			
				.375 Walk behind power tools			
	3000	8' high, 33° slope embankment			29	2.860	L.F.
	3100	10' high, 33° slope embankment			20	4.150	L.F.
	3200	20' high, 500 lb. per L.F. surcharge	↓	↓	7.50	11.070	L.F.
	3500	Concrete cribbing, incl. excavation and backfill					
	3700	12' high, open face	B-13	1 Labor Foreman (outside)	210	.267	S.F.
				4 Building Laborers			
				1 Equip. Oper. (crane)			
				1 Equip. Oper. Oiler			
				1 Hyd. Crane, 25 Ton			
	3900	Closed face	"	"	210	.267	S.F.
	4300	Stone filled gabions, not incl. excavation,					
	4310	stone @ $6.50 per ton delivered, 3' deep					
	4340	Galvanized, 6' long, 1' high	B-13	1 Labor Foreman (outside)	200	.280	Ea.
				4 Building Laborers			
				1 Equip. Oper. (crane)			
				1 Equip. Oper. Oiler			
				1 Hyd. Crane, 25 Ton			
	4400	1'-6" high			130	.431	Ea.
	4490	3'-0" high			55	1.020	Ea.
	4590	9' long, 1' high			130	.431	Ea.
	4650	1'-6" high	↓	↓	87	.644	Ea.

022 700	Slope/Erosion Control	CREW	MAKEUP	DAILY OUTPUT	MAN-HOURS	UNIT
708 4691	Retaining walls, stone filled gabions, galv., 9' long, 3' high	B-13	1 Labor Foreman (outside)	37	1.510	Ea.
			4 Building Laborers			
			1 Equip. Oper. (crane)			
			1 Equip. Oper. Oiler			
			1 Hyd. Crane, 25 Ton			
4890	12' long, 1' high			100	.560	Ea.
4950	1'-6" high			55	1.020	Ea.
4990	3'-0" high			25	2.240	Ea.
5200	PVC coated, 6' long, 1' high			200	.280	Ea.
5250	1'-6" high			130	.431	Ea.
5300	3' high			55	1.020	Ea.
5500	9' long, 1' high			130	.431	Ea.
5550	1'-6" high			87	.644	Ea.
5600	3' high			37	1.510	Ea.
5800	12' long, 1' high			100	.560	Ea.
5850	1'-6" high			55	1.020	Ea.
5900	3' high	↓	↓	25	2.240	Ea.
712	RIP-RAP Random, broken stone					
0100	Machine placed for slope protection	B-12G	1 Equip. Oper. (crane)	62	.258	C.Y.
			1 Equip. Oper. Oiler			
			1 Power Shovel, .5 C.Y.			
			1 Clamshell Bucket, .5 C.Y			
0110	3/8 to 1/4 C.Y. pieces, grouted	B-13	1 Labor Foreman (outside)	80	.700	S.Y.
			4 Building Laborers			
			1 Equip. Oper. (crane)			
			1 Equip. Oper. Oiler			
			1 Hyd. Crane, 25 Ton			
0200	18" minimum thickness, not grouted			53	1.060	S.Y.
0400	Gabions, galvanized steel mesh boxes, stone filled, 6" deep			190	.295	S.Y.
0500	9" deep			163	.344	S.Y.
0600	12" deep			153	.366	S.Y.
0700	18" deep			102	.549	S.Y.
0800	36" deep	↓	↓	60	.933	S.Y.
716 0020	STONE WALL Including excavation, concrete footing and stone 3' below grade. Price is exposed face area.					
0200	Decorative random stone, to 6' high, 1'-6" thick, dry set	D-1	1 Bricklayer	35	.457	S.F.
			1 Bricklayer Helper			
0300	Mortar set			40	.400	S.F.
0500	Cut stone, to 6' high, 1'-6" thick, dry set			35	.457	S.F.
0600	Mortar set			40	.400	S.F.
0800	Retaining wall, random stone, 6' to 10' high, 2' thick, dry set			45	.356	S.F.
0900	Mortar set			50	.320	S.F.
1100	Cut stone, 6' to 10' high, 2' thick, dry set			45	.356	S.F.
1200	Mortar set			50	.320	S.F.
5100	Setting stone, dry			100	.160	C.F.
5600	With mortar	↓	↓	120	.133	C.F.

022 800	Soil Treatment	CREW	MAKEUP	DAILY OUTPUT	MAN-HOURS	UNIT
804	TERMITE PRETREATMENT					
0020	Slab and walls, residential	1 Skwk	1 Skilled Worker	1,508	.005	SF Flr.
0100	Commercial, minimum			2,496	.003	SF Flr.
0200	Maximum			1,645	.005	SF Flr.
0400	Insecticides for termite control, minimum			14.20	.563	Gal.
0500	Maximum	↓	↓	11	.727	Gal.

		023 550 | **Pile Driving**	CREW	MAKEUP	DAILY OUTPUT	MAN-HOURS	UNIT
554	554	**MOBILIZATION** Set up & remove, air compressor, 600 C.F.M.	A-5	2 Building Laborers	3.30	5.450	Ea.
				.25 Truck Driver (light)			
				.25 Light Truck, 1.5 Ton			
	0100	1200 C.F.M.	"	"	2.20	8.180	Ea.
	0200	Crane, with pile leads and pile hammer, 75 ton	B-19	1 Pile Driver Foreman	.60	107.000	Ea.
				4 Pile Drivers			
				2 Equip. Oper. (crane)			
				1 Equip. Oper. Oiler			
				1 Crane, 40 Ton & Access.			
				60 L.F. Leads, 15K Ft. Lbs.			
				1 Hammer, 15K Ft. Lbs.			
				1 Air Compr., 600 C.F.M.			
				2-50 Ft. Air Hoses, 3" Dia.			
	0300	150 ton	"	"	.36	178.000	Ea.
	0500	Drill rig, for caissons, to 36", minimum	B-43	1 Labor Foreman (outside)	2	24.000	Ea.
				3 Building Laborers			
				1 Equip. Oper. (crane)			
				1 Equip. Oper. Oiler			
				1 Drill Rig & Augers			
	0520	Maximum	↓	↓	.50	96.000	Ea.
	0600	Up to 84"			1	48.000	Ea.
	0800	Auxiliary boiler, for steam small	A-5	2 Building Laborers	1.66	10.840	Ea.
				.25 Truck Driver (light)			
				.25 Light Truck, 1.5 Ton			
	0900	Large	"	"	.83	21.690	Ea.
	1100	Rule of thumb: complete pile driving set up, small	B-19	1 Pile Driver Foreman	.45	142.000	Ea.
				4 Pile Drivers			
				2 Equip. Oper. (crane)			
				1 Equip. Oper. Oiler			
				1 Crane, 40 Ton & Access.			
				60 L.F. Leads, 15K Ft. Lbs.			
				1 Hammer, 15K Ft. Lbs.			
				1 Air Compr., 600 C.F.M.			
				2-50 Ft. Air Hoses, 3" Dia.			
	1200	Large	"	"	.27	237.000	Ea.
	558	**PILING SPECIAL COSTS**					
	0100	Concrete pile cap for pile groups, 40 to 80 ton capacity					
	0150	2 pile cap	C-17B	2 Skilled Worker Foremen	15	5.470	Ea.
				8 Skilled Workers			
				.25 Equip. Oper. (crane)			
				.25 Crane, 80 Ton, & Tools			
				.25 Hand held power tools			
				.25 Walk behind power tools			
	0200	3 pile cap			15	5.470	Ea.
	0250	4 pile cap			11	7.450	Ea.
	0300	5 pile cap			8	10.250	Ea.
	0350	6 pile cap			6.70	12.240	Ea.
	0400	7 pile cap	↓	↓	5.30	15.470	Ea.
	0500	Cutoffs, concrete piles, plain	1 Pile	1 Pile Driver	5.50	1.450	Ea.
	0600	With steel thin shell			38	.211	Ea.
	0700	Steel pile or "H" piles			19	.421	Ea.
	0800	Wood piles	↓	↓	38	.211	Ea.
	0900	Pre-augering up to 30' deep, average soil, 24" diameter	B-43	1 Labor Foreman (outside)	180	.267	L.F.
				3 Building Laborers			
				1 Equip. Oper. (crane)			
				1 Equip. Oper. Oiler			
				1 Drill Rig & Augers			
	0920	36" diameter	"	"	115	.417	L.F.

023 550	Pile Driving	CREW	MAKEUP	DAILY OUTPUT	MAN-HOURS	UNIT
558 0961	Piling, pre-augering to 30' deep, avg. soil, 48" diameter	B-43	1 Labor Foreman (outside)	70	.686	L.F.
			3 Building Laborers			
			1 Equip. Oper. (crane)			
			1 Equip. Oper. Oiler			
			1 Drill Rig & Augers			
0980	60" diameter	"	"	50	.960	L.F.

023 600	Driven Piles	CREW	MAKEUP	DAILY OUTPUT	MAN-HOURS	UNIT
604	PILES, CONCRETE 200 piles, 60' long					
0020	unless specified otherwise, not incl. pile caps or mobilization					
0100	Cast in place, thin wall shell pile, straight sided,					
0110	not incl. reinforcing, 8" diam., 16 ga., 5.8 lb./L.F.	B-19	1 Pile Driver Foreman	700	.091	V.L.F.
			4 Pile Drivers			
			2 Equip. Oper. (crane)			
			1 Equip. Oper. Oiler			
			1 Crane, 40 Ton & Access.			
			60 L.F. Leads, 15K Ft. Lbs.			
			1 Hammer, 15K Ft. Lbs.			
			1 Air Compr., 600 C.F.M.			
			2-50 Ft. Air Hoses, 3" Dia.			
0200	10" diameter, 16 ga. corrugated, 7.3 lb./L.F.			650	.098	V.L.F.
0300	12" diameter, 16 ga. corrugated, 8.7 lb./L.F.			600	.107	V.L.F.
0400	14" diameter, 16 ga. corrugated, 10.0 lb./L.F.			550	.116	V.L.F.
0500	16" diameter, 16 ga. corrugated, 11.6 lb./L.F.			500	.128	V.L.F.
0800	Cast in place friction pile, 50' long, fluted,					
0810	tapered steel, 4000 psi concrete, no reinforcing					
0900	12" diameter, 7 ga.	B-19	1 Pile Driver Foreman	600	.107	V.L.F.
			4 Pile Drivers			
			2 Equip. Oper. (crane)			
			1 Equip. Oper. Oiler			
			1 Crane, 40 Ton & Access.			
			60 L.F. Leads, 15K Ft. Lbs.			
			1 Hammer, 15K Ft. Lbs.			
			1 Air Compr., 600 C.F.M.			
			2-50 Ft. Air Hoses, 3" Dia.			
1000	14" diameter, 7 ga.			560	.114	V.L.F.
1100	16" diameter, 7 ga.			520	.123	V.L.F.
1200	18" diameter, 7 ga.			480	.133	V.L.F.
1300	End bearing, fluted, constant diameter,					
1320	4000 psi concrete, no reinforcing					
1340	12" diameter, 7 ga.	B-19	1 Pile Driver Foreman	600	.107	V.L.F.
			4 Pile Drivers			
			2 Equip. Oper. (crane)			
			1 Equip. Oper. Oiler			
			1 Crane, 40 Ton & Access.			
			60 L.F. Leads, 15K Ft. Lbs.			
			1 Hammer, 15K Ft. Lbs.			
			1 Air Compr., 600 C.F.M.			
			2-50 Ft. Air Hoses, 3" Dia.			
1360	14" diameter, 7 ga.			560	.114	V.L.F.
1380	16" diameter, 7 ga.			520	.123	V.L.F.
1400	18" diameter, 7 ga.			480	.133	V.L.F.
1700	For ball or pedestal end, add			11	5.820	C.Y.
1900	For lengths above 60', concrete, add			11	5.820	C.Y.
2200	Precast, prestressed, straight cylinder, 12" diam., 2-3/8" wall			720	.089	V.L.F.
2300	14" diameter, 2-1/2" wall			680	.094	V.L.F.
2500	16" diameter, 3" wall			640	.100	V.L.F.
2600	18" diameter, 3" wall			600	.107	V.L.F.

023 | Tunneling, Piles and Caissons

023 600 | Driven Piles

		Description	CREW	MAKEUP	DAILY OUTPUT	MAN-HOURS	UNIT
604	2801	Piles, straight cylinder, 20" diameter, 3-1/2" wall	B-19	1 Pile Driver Foreman	560	.114	V.L.F.
				4 Pile Drivers			
				2 Equip. Oper. (crane)			
				1 Equip. Oper. Oiler			
				1 Crane, 40 Ton & Access.			
				60 L.F. Leads, 15K Ft. Lbs.			
				1 Hammer, 15K Ft. Lbs.			
				1 Air Compr., 600 C.F.M.			
				2-50 Ft. Air Hoses, 3" Dia.			
	2900	24" diameter, 3-1/2" wall			520	.123	V.L.F.
	2920	36" diameter, 4-1/2" wall			400	.160	V.L.F.
	2940	54" diameter, 5" wall			340	.188	V.L.F.
	2960	66" diameter, 6" wall			220	.291	V.L.F.
	3100	Precast, prestressed, 40' long, 10" thick, square			700	.091	V.L.F.
	3200	12" thick, square			680	.094	V.L.F.
	3400	14" thick, square			600	.107	V.L.F.
	3500	Octagonal			640	.100	V.L.F.
	3700	16" thick, square			560	.114	V.L.F.
	3800	Octagonal			600	.107	V.L.F.
	4000	18" thick, square			520	.123	V.L.F.
	4100	Octagonal			560	.114	V.L.F.
	4300	20" thick, square			480	.133	V.L.F.
	4400	Octagonal			520	.123	V.L.F.
	4600	24" thick, square			440	.145	V.L.F.
	4700	Octagonal			480	.133	V.L.F.
	4750	Mobilization for 10,000 L.F. pile job, add			3,300	.019	V.L.F.
	4800	25,000 L.F. pile job, add	↓	↓	8,500	.008	V.L.F.
	5000	Pressure grouted pin pile, 5" diam., cased, up to 50 ton,					
	5040	End bearing, less than 20'	B-48	1 Labor Foreman (outside)	90	.622	V.L.F.
				3 Building Laborers			
				1 Equip. Oper. (crane)			
				1 Equip. Oper. Oiler			
				1 Equip. Oper. (light)			
				1 Centr. Water Pump, 6"			
				1-20 Ft. Suction Hose, 6"			
				1-50 Ft. Disch. Hose, 6"			
				1 Drill Rig & Augers			
	5080	More than 40'			135	.415	V.L.F.
	5120	Friction, loose sand and gravel			107	.523	V.L.F.
	5160	Dense sand and gravel			135	.415	V.L.F.
	5200	Uncased, up to 10 ton capacity, 20'	↓	↓	135	.415	V.L.F.
	608	**PILES, STEEL** Not including mobilization or demobilization					
	0100	Step tapered, round, concrete filled					
	0110	8" tip, 60 ton capacity, 30' depth	B-19	1 Pile Driver Foreman	760	.084	V.L.F.
				4 Pile Drivers			
				2 Equip. Oper. (crane)			
				1 Equip. Oper. Oiler			
				1 Crane, 40 Ton & Access.			
				60 L.F. Leads, 15K Ft. Lbs.			
				1 Hammer, 15K Ft. Lbs.			
				1 Air Compr., 600 C.F.M.			
				2-50 Ft. Air Hoses, 3" Dia.			
	0120	60' depth			740	.086	V.L.F.
	0130	80' depth			700	.091	V.L.F.
	0150	10" tip, 90 ton capacity, 30' depth			700	.091	V.L.F.
	0160	60' depth			690	.093	V.L.F.
	0170	80' depth			670	.096	V.L.F.
	0190	12" tip, 120 ton capacity, 30' depth	↓	↓	660	.097	V.L.F.

023 600 | Driven Piles

		Description	CREW	MAKEUP	DAILY OUTPUT	MAN-HOURS	UNIT
608	0201	Piles, conc. filled steel, 12" tip, 120 ton cap., 60' depth	B-19	1 Pile Driver Foreman	630	.102	V.L.F.
				4 Pile Drivers			
				2 Equip. Oper. (crane)			
				1 Equip. Oper. Oiler			
				1 Crane, 40 Ton & Access.			
				60 L.F. Leads, 15K Ft. Lbs.			
				1 Hammer, 15K Ft. Lbs.			
				1 Air Compr., 600 C.F.M.			
				2-50 Ft. Air Hoses, 3" Dia.			
	0210	80' depth			590	.108	V.L.F.
	0250	"H" Sections, 8" x 8", 36 lb. per L.F.			640	.100	V.L.F.
	0400	10" x 10", 42 lb. per L.F.			610	.105	V.L.F.
	0500	57 lb. per L.F.			610	.105	V.L.F.
	0700	12" x 12", 53 lb. per L.F.			590	.108	V.L.F.
	0800	74 lb. per L.F.			590	.108	V.L.F.
	1000	14" x 14", 73 lb. per L.F.			540	.119	V.L.F.
	1100	89 lb. per L.F.			540	.119	V.L.F.
	1300	14" x 14", 102 lb. per L.F.			510	.125	V.L.F.
	1400	117 lb. per L.F.	↓	↓	510	.125	V.L.F.
	1600	Splice or standard points, not in leads, 8" or 10"	1 Sswl	1 Welder	5	1.600	Ea.
	1700	12" or 14"			4	2.000	Ea.
	1900	Heavy duty points, not in leads, 10" wide			4	2.000	Ea.
	2100	14" wide	↓	↓	3.50	2.290	Ea.
	2600	Pipe piles, 8" diameter, 29 lb. per L.F., no concrete	B-19	1 Pile Driver Foreman	500	.128	V.L.F.
				4 Pile Drivers			
				2 Equip. Oper. (crane)			
				1 Equip. Oper. Oiler			
				1 Crane, 40 Ton & Access.			
				60 L.F. Leads, 15K Ft. Lbs.			
				1 Hammer, 15K Ft. Lbs.			
				1 Air Compr., 600 C.F.M.			
				2-50 Ft. Air Hoses, 3" Dia.			
	2700	Concrete filled			460	.139	V.L.F.
	2900	10" diameter, 34 lb. per L.F., no concrete			500	.128	V.L.F.
	3000	Concrete filled			450	.142	V.L.F.
	3200	12" diameter, 44 lb. per L.F., no concrete			475	.135	V.L.F.
	3300	Concrete filled			415	.154	V.L.F.
	3500	14" diameter, 46 lb. per L.F., no concrete			430	.149	V.L.F.
	3600	Concrete filled			355	.180	V.L.F.
	3800	16" diameter, 52 lb. per L.F., no concrete			385	.166	V.L.F.
	3900	Concrete filled			335	.191	V.L.F.
	4100	18" diameter, 59 lb. per L.F., no concrete			355	.180	V.L.F.
	4200	Concrete filled	↓	↓	310	.206	V.L.F.
	4400	Splices for pipe piles, not in leads 8" or 10" diam.	1 Sswl	1 Welder	4.67	1.710	Ea.
	4500	12" or 14" diameter			3.79	2.110	Ea.
	4600	16" diameter			3.03	2.640	Ea.
	4650	18" diameter			4.50	1.780	Ea.
	4800	Standard points, 8" or 10" diameter			4.61	1.740	Ea.
	4900	12" or 14" diameter			4.05	1.980	Ea.
	5000	16" diameter			3.37	2.370	Ea.
	5050	18" diameter			5	1.600	Ea.
	5200	Heavy duty points, 10" or 12" diameter			2.89	2.770	Ea.
	5300	14" or 16" diameter			2.02	3.960	Ea.
	5500	For reinforcing steel, add			1,150	.007	Lb.
	6020	Steel pipe pile end plates, 8" diameter			14	.571	Ea.
	6050	10" diameter			14	.571	Ea.
	6100	12" diameter			12	.667	Ea.
	6150	14" diameter	↓	↓	10	.800	Ea.

023 600 | Driven Piles

		Description	CREW	MAKEUP	DAILY OUTPUT	MAN-HOURS	UNIT
608	6201	Steel pipe pile end plates, 16" diameter	1 Sswl	1 Welder	9	.889	Ea.
	6250	18" diameter			8	1.000	Ea.
	6300	Steel pipe pile shoes, 8" diameter			12	.667	Ea.
	6350	10" diameter			12	.667	Ea.
	6400	12" diameter			10	.800	Ea.
	6450	14" diameter			9	.889	Ea.
	6500	16" diameter			8	1.000	Ea.
	6550	18" diameter	↓	↓	6	1.330	Ea.
	612	**PILES, WOOD** Untreated, friction or end bearing, not including					
	0050	mobilization or demobilization					
	0100	Up to 30' long, 12" butts, 8" points	B-19	1 Pile Driver Foreman 4 Pile Drivers 2 Equip. Oper. (crane) 1 Equip. Oper. Oiler 1 Crane, 40 Ton & Access. 60 L.F. Leads, 15K Ft. Lbs. 1 Hammer, 15K Ft. Lbs. 1 Air Compr., 600 C.F.M. 2-50 Ft. Air Hoses, 3" Dia.	625	.102	V.L.F.
	0200	30' to 39' long, 12" butts, 8" points			700	.091	V.L.F.
	0300	40' to 49' long, 12" butts, 7" points			720	.089	V.L.F.
	0400	50' to 59' long, 13" butts, 7" points			800	.080	V.L.F.
	0500	60' to 69' long, 13" butts, 7" points			840	.076	V.L.F.
	0600	70' to 80' long, 13" butts, 6" points	↓	↓	840	.076	V.L.F.
	0800	Treated piles, 12 lb. creosote per C.F.,					
	0810	friction or end bearing, ASTM class B					
	1000	Up to 30' long, 12" butts, 8" points	B-19	1 Pile Driver Foreman 4 Pile Drivers 2 Equip. Oper. (crane) 1 Equip. Oper. Oiler 1 Crane, 40 Ton & Access. 60 L.F. Leads, 15K Ft. Lbs. 1 Hammer, 15K Ft. Lbs. 1 Air Compr., 600 C.F.M. 2-50 Ft. Air Hoses, 3" Dia.	625	.102	V.L.F.
	1100	30' to 39' long, 12" butts, 8" points			700	.091	V.L.F.
	1200	40' to 49' long, 12" butts, 7" points			720	.089	V.L.F.
	1300	50' to 59' long, 13" butts, 7" points			800	.080	V.L.F.
	1400	60' to 69' long, 13" butts, 6" points			840	.076	V.L.F.
	1500	70' to 80' long, 13" butts, 6" points	↓	↓	840	.076	V.L.F.
	1700	Boot for pile tip, minimum	1 Pile	1 Pile Driver	27	.296	Ea.
	1800	Maximum			21	.381	Ea.
	2000	Point for pile tip, minimum			20	.400	Ea.
	2100	Maximum	↓	↓	15	.533	Ea.
	2300	Splice for piles over 50' long, minimum	B-46	1 Pile Driver Foreman 2 Pile Drivers 3 Building Laborers 1 Chain Saw, 36" Long	35	1.370	Ea.
	2400	Maximum	↓	↓	20	2.400	Ea.
	2600	Concrete encasement with wire mesh and tube			331	.145	V.L.F.

023 600 | Driven Piles

			CREW	MAKEUP	DAILY OUTPUT	MAN-HOURS	UNIT
612	2700	Mobilization for 10,000 L.F. pile job, add	B-19	1 Pile Driver Foreman	3,300	.019	V.L.F.
				4 Pile Drivers			
				2 Equip. Oper. (crane)			
				1 Equip. Oper. Oiler			
				1 Crane, 40 Ton & Access.			
				60 L.F. Leads, 15K Ft. Lbs.			
				1 Hammer, 15K Ft. Lbs.			
				1 Air Compr., 600 C.F.M.			
				2-50 Ft. Air Hoses, 3" Dia.			
	2800	25,000 L.F. pile job, add	"	"	8,500	.008	V.L.F.

023 700 | Bored/Augered Piles

			CREW	MAKEUP	DAILY OUTPUT	MAN-HOURS	UNIT
704	0100	PRESSURE INJECTED FOOTINGS or Displacement Caissons, incl. mobilization and demobilization, up to 50 miles					
	0200	Uncased shafts, 30 to 80 tons cap., 17" diam., 10' depth	B-44	1 Pile Driver Foreman	88	.727	V.L.F.
				4 Pile Drivers			
				2 Equip. Oper. (crane)			
				1 Building Laborer			
				1 Crane, 40 Ton, & Access.			
				45 L.F. Leads, 15K Ft. Lbs.			
	0300	25' depth			165	.388	V.L.F.
	0400	80-150 ton capacity, 22" diameter, 10' depth			80	.800	V.L.F.
	0500	20' depth			130	.492	V.L.F.
	0700	Cased shafts, 10 to 30 ton capacity, 10-5/8" diam., 20' depth			175	.366	V.L.F.
	0800	30' depth			240	.267	V.L.F.
	0850	30 to 60 ton capacity, 12" diameter, 20' depth			160	.400	V.L.F.
	0900	40' depth			230	.278	V.L.F.
	1000	80 to 100 ton capacity, 16" diameter, 20' depth			160	.400	V.L.F.
	1100	40' depth			230	.278	V.L.F.
	1200	110 to 140 ton capacity, 17-5/8" diameter, 20' depth			160	.400	V.L.F.
	1300	40' depth			230	.278	V.L.F.
	1400	140 to 175 ton capacity, 19" diameter, 20' depth			130	.492	V.L.F.
	1500	40' depth	↓	↓	210	.305	V.L.F.

023 800 | Caissons

			CREW	MAKEUP	DAILY OUTPUT	MAN-HOURS	UNIT
804	0020	CAISSONS Incl. excav., concrete, 50 lbs. reinf. per C.Y., but not incl. mobilization, boulder removal, disposal or pre-drilling					
	0100	Open style, machine drilled, to 50' diam., .065 C.Y./L.F.					
	0110	casings or ground water, 18" diam., .065 C.Y./L.F.	B-43	1 Labor Foreman (outside)	200	.240	V.L.F.
				3 Building Laborers			
				1 Equip. Oper. (crane)			
				1 Equip. Oper. Oiler			
				1 Drill Rig & Augers			
	0200	24" diameter, .116 C.Y./L.F.			190	.253	V.L.F.
	0300	30" diameter, .182 C.Y./L.F.			150	.320	V.L.F.
	0400	36" diameter, .262 C.Y./L.F.			125	.384	V.L.F.
	0500	48" diameter, .465 C.Y./L.F.			100	.480	V.L.F.
	0600	60" diameter, .727 C.Y./L.F.			90	.533	V.L.F.
	0700	72" diameter, 1.05 C.Y./L.F.			80	.600	V.L.F.
	0800	84" diameter, 1.43 C.Y./L.F.	↓	↓	75	.640	V.L.F.
	1000	For bell excavation and concrete, add					
	1020	4' bell diameter, 24" shaft, .444 C.Y.	B-43	1 Labor Foreman (outside)	20	2.400	Ea.
				3 Building Laborers			
				1 Equip. Oper. (crane)			
				1 Equip. Oper. Oiler			
				1 Drill Rig & Augers			
	1040	6' bell diameter, 30" shaft, 1.57 C.Y.			5.70	8.420	Ea.
	1060	8' bell diameter, 36" shaft, 3.72 C.Y.	↓	↓	2.40	20.000	Ea.

023 800 | Caissons

		Description	CREW	MAKEUP	DAILY OUTPUT	MAN-HOURS	UNIT
804	1081	Bell excav. & conc., 9' bell dia., 48" shaft, 4.48 C.Y., add	B-43	1 Labor Foreman (outside)	2	24.000	Ea.
				3 Building Laborers			
				1 Equip. Oper. (crane)			
				1 Equip. Oper. Oiler			
				1 Drill Rig & Augers			
	1100	10' bell diameter, 60" shaft, 5.24 C.Y.			1.70	28.240	Ea.
	1120	12' bell diameter, 72" shaft, 8.74 C.Y.			1	48.000	Ea.
	1140	14' bell diameter, 84" shaft, 13.6 C.Y.	↓	↓	.70	68.570	Ea.
	1200	Open style, machine drilled, to 50' deep, in wet ground, pulled					
	1300	casing and pumping, 18" diameter, .065 C.Y./L.F.	B-48	1 Labor Foreman (outside)	160	.350	V.L.F.
				3 Building Laborers			
				1 Equip. Oper. (crane)			
				1 Equip. Oper. Oiler			
				1 Equip. Oper. (light)			
				1 Centr. Water Pump, 6"			
				1-20 Ft. Suction Hose, 6"			
				1-50 Ft. Disch. Hose, 6"			
				1 Drill Rig & Augers			
	1400	24" diameter, .116 C.Y./L.F.			125	.448	V.L.F.
	1500	30" diameter, .182 C.Y./L.F.			85	.659	V.L.F.
	1600	36" diameter, .262 C.Y./L.F.	↓	↓	60	.933	V.L.F.
	1700	48" diameter, .465 C.Y./L.F.	B-49	1 Labor Foreman (outside)	55	1.600	V.L.F.
				3 Building Laborers			
				2 Equip. Oper. (crane)			
				2 Equip. Oper. Oilers			
				1 Equip. Oper. (light)			
				2 Pile Drivers			
				1 Hyd. Crane, 25 Ton			
				1 Centr. Water Pump, 6"			
				1-20 Ft. Suction Hose, 6"			
				1-50 Ft. Disch. Hose, 6"			
				1 Drill Rig & Augers			
	1800	60" diameter, .727 C.Y./L.F.			35	2.510	V.L.F.
	1900	72" diameter, 1.05 C.Y./L.F.			30	2.930	V.L.F.
	2000	84" diameter, 1.43 C.Y./L.F.	↓	↓	25	3.520	V.L.F.
	2100	For bell excavation and concrete, add					
	2120	4' bell diameter, 24" shaft, .444 C.Y.	B-48	1 Labor Foreman (outside)	19.80	2.830	Ea.
				3 Building Laborers			
				1 Equip. Oper. (crane)			
				1 Equip. Oper. Oiler			
				1 Equip. Oper. (light)			
				1 Centr. Water Pump, 6"			
				1-20 Ft. Suction Hose, 6"			
				1-50 Ft. Disch. Hose, 6"			
				1 Drill Rig & Augers			
	2140	6' bell diameter, 30" shaft, 1.57 C.Y.	↓	↓	5.70	9.820	Ea.
	2160	8' bell diameter, 36" shaft, 3.72 C.Y.			2.40	23.330	Ea.
	2180	9' bell diameter, 48" shaft, 4.48 C.Y.	B-49	1 Labor Foreman (outside)	3.30	26.670	Ea.
				3 Building Laborers			
				2 Equip. Oper. (crane)			
				2 Equip. Oper. Oilers			
				1 Equip. Oper. (light)			
				2 Pile Drivers			
				1 Hyd. Crane, 25 Ton			
				1 Centr. Water Pump, 6"			
				1-20 Ft. Suction Hose, 6"			
				1-50 Ft. Disch. Hose, 6"			
				1 Drill Rig & Augers			

023 800 | Caissons

			CREW	MAKEUP	DAILY OUTPUT	MAN-HOURS	UNIT
804	2201	Bell excav. & conc., 10' bell dia., 60" shaft, 5.24 C.Y., add	B-49	1 Labor Foreman (outside)	2.80	31.430	Ea.
				3 Building Laborers			
				2 Equip. Oper. (crane)			
				2 Equip. Oper. Oilers			
				1 Equip. Oper. (light)			
				2 Pile Drivers			
				1 Hyd. Crane, 25 Ton			
				1 Centr. Water Pump, 6"			
				1-20 Ft. Suction Hose, 6"			
				1-50 Ft. Disch. Hose, 6"			
				1 Drill Rig & Augers			
	2220	12' bell diameter, 72" shaft, 8.74 C.Y.	↓	↓	1.60	55.000	Ea.
	2240	14' bell diameter, 84" shaft, 13.6 C.Y.			1	88.000	Ea.
	2300	Open style, machine drilled, to 50' deep, in soft rocks and					
	2400	medium hard shales, 18" diameter, .065 C.Y./L.F.	B-49	1 Labor Foreman (outside)	50	1.760	V.L.F.
				3 Building Laborers			
				2 Equip. Oper. (crane)			
				2 Equip. Oper. Oilers			
				1 Equip. Oper. (light)			
				2 Pile Drivers			
				1 Hyd. Crane, 25 Ton			
				1 Centr. Water Pump, 6"			
				1-20 Ft. Suction Hose, 6"			
				1-50 Ft. Disch. Hose, 6"			
				1 Drill Rig & Augers			
	2500	24" diameter, .116 C.Y./L.F.			30	2.930	V.L.F.
	2600	30" diameter, .182 C.Y./L.F.			20	4.400	V.L.F.
	2700	36" diameter, .262 C.Y./L.F.			15	5.870	V.L.F.
	2800	48" diameter, .465 C.Y./L.F.			10	8.800	V.L.F.
	2900	60" diameter, .727 C.Y./L.F.			7	12.570	V.L.F.
	3000	72" diameter, 1.05 C.Y./L.F.			6	14.670	V.L.F.
	3100	84" diameter, 1.43 C.Y./L.F.	↓	↓	5	17.600	V.L.F.
	3200	For bell excavation and concrete, add					
	3220	4' bell diameter, 24" shaft, .444 C.Y.	B-49	1 Labor Foreman (outside)	10.90	8.070	Ea.
				3 Building Laborers			
				2 Equip. Oper. (crane)			
				2 Equip. Oper. Oilers			
				1 Equip. Oper. (light)			
				2 Pile Drivers			
				1 Hyd. Crane, 25 Ton			
				1 Centr. Water Pump, 6"			
				1-20 Ft. Suction Hose, 6"			
				1-50 Ft. Disch. Hose, 6"			
				1 Drill Rig & Augers			
	3240	6' bell diameter, 30" shaft, 1.57 C.Y.			3.10	28.390	Ea.
	3260	8' bell diameter, 36" shaft, 3.72 C.Y.			1.30	67.690	Ea.
	3280	9' bell diameter, 48" shaft, 4.48 C.Y.			1.10	80.000	Ea.
	3300	10' bell diameter, 60" shaft, 5.24 C.Y.			.90	97.780	Ea.
	3320	12' bell diameter, 72" shaft, 8.74 C.Y.			.60	147.000	Ea.
	3340	14' bell diameter, 84" shaft, 13.6 C.Y.			.40	220.000	Ea.
	3600	for rock excavation, sockets, add, minimum			120	.733	C.F.
	3650	Average			95	.926	C.F.
	3700	Maximum			48	1.830	C.F.
	4400	For steel "I" beam cores, add	↓	↓	8.30	10.600	Ton
	4500	Load and haul excess excavation, 2 miles	B-34B	1 Truck Driver (heavy)	178	.045	C.Y.
				1 Dump Truck, 16 Ton			

024 520	Railroad Trackwork	CREW	MAKEUP	DAILY OUTPUT	MAN-HOURS	UNIT
524 524	**RAILROAD** Car bumpers, standard	B-14	1 Labor Foreman (outside)	2	24.000	Ea.
			4 Building Laborers			
			1 Equip. Oper. (light)			
			1 Backhoe Loader, 48 H.P.			
0100	Heavy duty			2	24.000	Ea.
0200	Derails hand throw (sliding)			10	4.800	Ea.
0300	Hand throw with standard timbers, open stand & target			5.50	8.730	Ea.
0400	Resurface and realign existing track			200	.240	L.F.
0600	For crushed stone ballast, add	↓	↓	500	.096	L.F.
0800	Siding, yard spur, level grade,					
0810	100 lb. rail, new material on wood ties	B-14	1 Labor Foreman (outside)	57	.842	L.F.
			4 Building Laborers			
			1 Equip. Oper. (light)			
			1 Backhoe Loader, 48 H.P.			
1000	Steel ties in concrete w/100# rail, fasteners & plates			22	2.180	L.F.
1200	Switch timber, for a #8 switch, creosoted			3.70	12.970	M.B.F.
1300	Complete set of timbers, 3.7 M.B.F. for #8 switch			1	48.000	Total
1400	Ties, concrete, 8'-6" long, 30" O.C.			80	.600	Ea.
1600	Wood, creosoted, 6" x 8" x 8'-6", C.L. lots			90	.533	Ea.
1700	L.C.L. lots			90	.533	Ea.
1900	Heavy duty, 7" x 9" x 8'-6", C.L. lots			70	.686	Ea.
2000	L.C.L. lots	↓	↓	70	.686	Ea.
2200	Turnouts, #8, incl. 100 lb. rails, plates, bars, frog, switch points,					
2300	timbers and ballast 6" below bottom of tie	B-14	1 Labor Foreman (outside)	.50	96.000	Ea.
			4 Building Laborers			
			1 Equip. Oper. (light)			
			1 Backhoe Loader, 48 H.P.			
2400	Wheel stops, fixed	↓	↓	14	3.430	Pr.
2450	Hinged			14	3.430	Pr.

024 820	Dredging	CREW	MAKEUP	DAILY OUTPUT	MAN-HOURS	UNIT
824	**DREDGING** Mobilization and demobilization., add to below, minimum	B-8	1 Labor Foreman (outside)	.53	121.000	Total
			2 Building Laborers			
			2 Equip. Oper. (med.)			
			1 Equip. Oper. Oiler			
			2 Truck Drivers (heavy)			
			1 Hyd. Crane, 25 Ton			
			F.E. Loader, T.M., 2.5 C.Y.			
			2 Dump Trucks, 16 Ton			
0100	Maximum	"	"	.10	640.000	Total
0300	Barge mounted clamshell excavation into scows,					
0310	Dumped 20 miles at sea, minimum	B-57	1 Labor Foreman (outside)	310	.155	C.Y.
			2 Building Laborers			
			1 Equip. Oper. (crane)			
			1 Equip. Oper. (light)			
			1 Equip. Oper. Oiler			
			1 Power Shovel, 1 C.Y.			
			1 Clamshell Bucket, 1 C.Y.			
			1 Centr. Water Pump, 6"			
			1-20 Ft. Suction Hose, 6"			
			20-50 Ft. Disch. Hoses, 6"			
0400	Maximum	"	"	213	.225	C.Y.
0501						

024 820 | Dredging

		CREW	MAKEUP	DAILY OUTPUT	MAN-HOURS	UNIT
824	0511	Dredge, barge mtd dragline, pumped 1000' to shore dump, min.	B-57	1 Labor Foreman (outside)	340	.141	C.Y.
				2 Building Laborers			
				1 Equip. Oper. (crane)			
				1 Equip. Oper. (light)			
				1 Equip. Oper. Oiler			
				1 Power Shovel, 1 C.Y.			
				1 Clamshell Bucket, 1 C.Y.			
				1 Centr. Water Pump, 6"			
				1-20 Ft. Suction Hose, 6"			
				20-50 Ft. Disch. Hoses, 6"			
	0600	Maximum			243	.198	C.Y.
	1000	Hydraulic method, pumped 1000' to shore dump, minimum			460	.104	C.Y.
	1100	Maximum			310	.155	C.Y.
	1400	Into scows dumped 20 miles, minimum			425	.113	C.Y.
	1500	Maximum			243	.198	C.Y.

024 840 | Seawall & Bulkheads

		CREW	MAKEUP	DAILY OUTPUT	MAN-HOURS	UNIT
844	**BULKHEADS** Reinforced concrete, include footing and tie-backs					
0060	Maximum	C-17C	2 Skilled Worker Foremen	24.25	3.420	L.F.
			8 Skilled Workers			
			.375 Equip. Oper. (crane)			
			.375 Crane, 80 Ton & Tools			
			.375 Hand held power tools			
			.375 Walk behind power tools			
0100	12' high, minimum			20	4.150	L.F.
0160	Maximum			18.50	4.490	L.F.
0200	Steel sheeting, w/4' x 4' x 8" concrete deadmen, @ 10' O.C.					
0210	12' high, shore driven	B-40	1 Pile Driver Foreman	27	2.370	L.F.
			4 Pile Drivers			
			2 Equip. Oper. (crane)			
			1 Equip. Oper. Oiler			
			1 Crane, 40 Ton			
			Vibratory Hammer & Gen.			
0260	Barge driven	B-76	1 Dock Builder Foreman	15	4.800	L.F.
			5 Dock Builders			
			2 Equip. Oper. (crane)			
			1 Equip. Oper. Oiler			
			1 Crawler Crane, 50 Ton			
			1 Barge, 400 Ton			
			1 Hammer, 15K. Ft. Lbs.			
			60 L.F. Leads, 15K. Ft. Lbs.			
			1 Air Compr., 600 C.F.M.			
			2-50 Ft. Air Hoses, 3" Dia.			

024 | Railroad and Marine Work

024 880 | Docks And Facilities

882			CREW	MAKEUP	DAILY OUTPUT	MAN-HOURS	UNIT
882		**DOCKS** Floating, recreational, prefabricated aluminum or					
	0020	concrete over polystyrene, no pilings included	F-3	4 Carpenters	330	.121	S.F.
				1 Equip. Oper. (crane)			
				1 Hyd. Crane, 12 Ton			
				Power Tools			
	0200	Pile supported, shore constructed, bare, 3" decking			130	.308	S.F.
	0250	4" decking			120	.333	S.F.
	0400	Floating, small boat, prefab, no shore facilities, minimum			250	.160	S.F.
	0500	Maximum			150	.267	S.F.
	0700	Per slip, minimum (180 S.F. each)			1.59	25.160	Ea.
	0800	Maximum	↓	↓	1.40	28.570	Ea.

025 | Paving and Surfacing

025 100 | Walk/Rd/Parking Paving

			CREW	MAKEUP	DAILY OUTPUT	MAN-HOURS	UNIT
104		**BITUMINOUS CONCRETE PAVEMENT** for highways					
0020		and large paved areas					
0080		Binder course, 1-1/2" thick	B-25	1 Labor Foreman	3,050	.029	S.Y.
				7 Laborers			
				3 Equip. Oper. (med.)			
				1 Asphalt Paver, 130 H.P			
				1 Tandem Roller, 10 Ton			
				1 Roller, Pneumatic Wheel			
0120		2" thick			3,390	.026	S.Y.
0160		3" thick			4,850	.018	S.Y.
0200		4" thick	↓	↓	4,500	.020	S.Y.
0300		Wearing course, 1" thick	B-25B	1 Labor Foreman	10,500	.009	S.Y.
				7 Laborers			
				3 Equip. Oper. (med.)			
				1 Asphalt Paver, 130 H.P			
				1 Tandem Roller, 10 Ton			
				1 Roller, Pneumatic Wheel			
				1 Labor Foreman			
				7 Laborers			
				4 Equip. Oper. (medium)			
				1 Asphalt Paver, 130 H.P.			
				2 Rollers, Steel Wheel			
				1 Roller, Pneumatic Wheel			
0340		1-1/2" thick			7,635	.013	S.Y.
0380		2" thick			6,270	.015	S.Y.
0420		2-1/2" thick			5,420	.018	S.Y.
0460		3" thick	↓	↓	4,900	.020	S.Y.
0800		Alternate method of figuring paving costs					
0810		Binder course, 1-1/2" thick	B-25	1 Labor Foreman	630	.140	Ton
				7 Laborers			
				3 Equip. Oper. (med.)			
				1 Asphalt Paver, 130 H.P			
				1 Tandem Roller, 10 Ton			
				1 Roller, Pneumatic Wheel			
0811		2" thick			690	.128	Ton
0812		3" thick			800	.110	Ton
0813		4" thick	↓	↓	1,080	.081	Ton

025 100	Walk/Rd/Parking Paving		CREW	MAKEUP	DAILY OUTPUT	MAN-HOURS	UNIT
104	0849	Bituminous concrete pavement, wearing course, 1" thick	B-25B	1 Labor Foreman	575	.167	Ton
				7 Laborers			
				3 Equip. Oper. (med.)			
				1 Asphalt Paver, 130 H.P			
				1 Tandem Roller, 10 Ton			
				1 Roller, Pneumatic Wheel			
				1 Labor Foreman			
				7 Laborers			
				4 Equip. Oper. (medium)			
				1 Asphalt Paver, 130 H.P.			
				2 Rollers, Steel Wheel			
				1 Roller, Pneumatic Wheel			
	0851	1-1/2" thick			630	.152	Ton
	0852	2" thick			690	.139	Ton
	0853	2-1/2" thick			745	.129	Ton
	0854	3" deep	↓	↓	800	.120	Ton
	120	**CONCRETE PAVEMENT** Including joints, finishing, and curing					
	0020	Fixed form, 12' pass, unreinforced, 6" thick	B-26	1 Labor Foreman (outside)	3,000	.029	S.Y.
				6 Building Laborers			
				2 Equip. Oper. (med.)			
				1 Rodman (reinf.)			
				1 Cement Finisher			
				1 Grader, 30,000 Lbs.			
				1 Paving Mach. & Equip.			
	0030	7" thick			2,850	.031	S.Y.
	0100	8" thick			2,700	.033	S.Y.
	0200	9" thick			2,900	.030	S.Y.
	0300	10" thick			2,100	.042	S.Y.
	0400	12" thick	↓	↓	1,800	.049	S.Y.
	0500	15" thick			1,500	.059	S.Y.
	0700	Finishing, broom finish small areas	2 Cefi	2 Cement Finishers	135	.119	S.Y.
	0710	Transverse joint support dowels	C-1	3 Carpenters	350	.091	Ea.
				1 Building Laborer			
				Power Tools			
	0720	Transverse contraction joints, saw cut & grind	A-1	1 Building Laborer	120	.067	L.F.
				1 Gas Eng. Power Tool			
	0730	Transverse expansion joints, incl. premolded bit. jt. filler	C-1	3 Carpenters	150	.213	L.F.
				1 Building Laborer			
				Power Tools			
	0740	Transverse construction joint using bulkhead	"	"	73	.438	L.F.
	0750	Longitudinal joint tie bars, grouted	B-23	1 Labor Foreman (outside)	70	.571	Ea.
				4 Building Laborers			
				1 Drill Rig			
				1 Light Truck, 3 Ton			
	1000	Curing, with sprayed membrane by hand	2 Clab	2 Building Laborers	1,500	.011	S.Y.
	3000	Cold planing incl. cleaning, 1-1/2" thick	B-32	1 Highway Laborer	170	.188	S.Y.
				3 Equip. Oper. (med.)			
				1 Grader, 30,000 lbs.			
				1 Tandem Roller, 10 Ton			
				1 Dozer, 200 H.P.			
	122	**FINE GRADE** Area to be paved with grader, small area	B-11L	1 Equipment Oper. (med.)	800	.020	S.Y.
				1 Building Laborer			
				1 Grader, 30,000 Lbs.			
	0100	Large area	"	"	2,000	.008	S.Y.

025 100	Walk/Rd/Parking Paving	CREW	MAKEUP	DAILY OUTPUT	MAN-HOURS	UNIT
128	SIDEWALKS Bituminous, no base included, 2" thick	B-37	1 Labor Foreman (outside)	720	.067	S.Y.
			4 Building Laborers			
			1 Equip. Oper. (light)			
			1 Tandem Roller, 5 Ton			
0100	2-1/2" thick	"	"	660	.073	S.Y.
0110	Bedding for brick or stone, mortar, 1" thick	D-1	1 Bricklayer	300	.053	S.F.
			1 Bricklayer Helper			
0120	2" thick	"	"	200	.080	S.F.
0130	Sand, 2" thick	B-18	1 Labor Foreman (outside)	8,000	.003	S.F.
			2 Building Laborers			
			1 Vibrating Compactor			
0140	4" thick	"	"	4,000	.006	S.F.
0300	Concrete, 3000 psi, cast in place with 6 x 6 - #10/10 mesh,					
0310	broomed finish, no base, 4" thick	B-24	1 Cement Finisher	600	.040	S.F.
			1 Building Laborer			
			1 Carpenter			
0350	5" thick	↓	↓	545	.044	S.F.
0400	6" thick			510	.047	S.F.
0450	For bank run gravel base, 4" thick, add	B-18	1 Labor Foreman (outside)	2,500	.010	S.F.
			2 Building Laborers			
			1 Vibrating Compactor			
0520	8" thick, add	"	"	1,600	.015	S.F.
0550	Exposed aggregate finish, add to above, minimum	B-24	1 Cement Finisher	1,875	.013	S.F.
			1 Building Laborer			
			1 Carpenter			
0600	Maximum	"	"	455	.053	S.F.
0910	Paving stone, interlocking, 2-1/2" thick	D-1	1 Bricklayer	240	.067	S.F.
			1 Bricklayer Helper			
0920	3-1/4" thick	"	"	240	.067	S.F.
0950	Tree grate	B-6	2 Building Laborers	25	.960	Ea.
			1 Equip. Oper. (light)			
			1 Backhoe Loader, 48 H.P.			
0960	Cast iron tree grate with frame, 2 piece, round, 5' diameter	↓	↓	25	.960	Ea.
0980	Square, 5' side			25	.960	Ea.
1000	Crushed stone, 1" thick, white marble	2 Clab	2 Building Laborers	1,700	.009	S.F.
1050	Bluestone	↓	↓	1,700	.009	S.F.
1070	Granite chips			1,700	.009	S.F.
1660	Limestone pavers, 3" thick	D-1	1 Bricklayer	72	.222	S.F.
			1 Bricklayer Helper			
1670	4" thick	↓	↓	70	.229	S.F.
1680	5" thick			68	.235	S.F.
1700	Redwood, prefabricated, 4' x 4' sections	F-2	2 Carpenters	316	.051	S.F.
			Power Tools			
1750	Redwood planks, 1" thick, on sleepers	"	"	240	.067	S.F.
1830	1-1/2" thick	B-28	2 Carpenters	167	.144	S.F.
			1 Building Laborer			
1840	2" thick			167	.144	S.F.
1850	3" thick			150	.160	S.F.
1860	4" thick	↓	↓	150	.160	S.F.
1870	5" thick			150	.160	S.F.
2100	River or beach stone, stock	B-1	1 Labor Foreman (outside)	18	1.330	Ton
			2 Building Laborers			
2150	Quarried	"	"	18	1.330	Ton
2170	Shale paver, 2-1/4" thick	D-1	1 Bricklayer	200	.080	S.F.
			1 Bricklayer Helper			
2200	Stone dust, 2" thick	B-62	2 Building Laborers	1,350	.018	S.Y.
			1 Equip. Oper. (light)			
			1 Loader, Skid Steer			

025 150 | Unit Pavers

		Description	CREW	MAKEUP	DAILY OUTPUT	MAN-HOURS	UNIT
154	154	ASPHALT BLOCKS Premold, 6"x12"x1-1/4", w/bed & neopr. adhesive	D-1	1 Bricklayer	135	.119	S.F.
				1 Bricklayer Helper			
	0100	3" thick			130	.123	S.F.
	0300	Hexagonal tile, 8" wide, 1-1/4" thick			135	.119	S.F.
	0400	2" thick			130	.123	S.F.
	0500	Square, 8" x 8", 1-1/4" thick			135	.119	S.F.
	0600	2" thick			130	.123	S.F.
	158	BRICK PAVING 4" x 8" x 1-1/2", without joints (4.5 brick/S.F.)			110	.145	S.F.
	0100	Grouted, 3/8" joint (3.9 brick/S.F.)			90	.178	S.F.
	0200	4" x 8" x 2-1/4", without joints (4.5 bricks/S.F.)			110	.145	S.F.
	0300	Grouted, 3/8" joint (3.9 brick/S.F.)	↓	↓	90	.178	S.F.
	0500	Bedding, asphalt, 3/4" thick	B-25	1 Labor Foreman	5,130	.017	S.F.
				7 Laborers			
				3 Equip. Oper. (med.)			
				1 Asphalt Paver, 130 H.P			
				1 Tandem Roller, 10 Ton			
				1 Roller, Pneumatic Wheel			
	0540	Brick sand, 1" thick	B-18	1 Labor Foreman (outside)	5,000	.005	S.F.
				2 Building Laborers			
				1 Vibrating Compactor			
	0550	Sand, 2" thick			4,800	.005	S.F.
	0555	4" thick	↓	↓	4,000	.006	S.F.
	0580	Mortar, 1" thick	D-1	1 Bricklayer	300	.053	S.F.
				1 Bricklayer Helper			
	0620	2" thick			200	.080	S.F.
	1600	Brick pavers, 4.15 per S.F., 1-3/4" thick			240	.067	S.F.
	1700	2-1/4" thick			240	.067	S.F.
	2000	Laid on edge, 7.2 per S.F.			70	.229	S.F.
	2500	For 4" thick concrete bed and joints, add	↓	↓	595	.027	S.F.
	2800	For steam cleaning, add	A-1	1 Building Laborer	950	.008	S.F.
				1 Gas Eng. Power Tool			
	162	CONCRETE BLOCK PAVERS					
	0710	Precast concrete patio blocks, 2" thick, colors, 8" x 16"	D-1	1 Bricklayer	265	.060	S.F.
				1 Bricklayer Helper			
	0720	16" x 16"			335	.048	S.F.
	0730	24" x 24"			510	.031	S.F.
	0740	Green, 8" x 16"			265	.060	S.F.
	0750	Exposed local aggregate, natural			265	.060	S.F.
	0800	Colors			265	.060	S.F.
	0850	Exposed granite or limestone aggregate			265	.060	S.F.
	0900	Exposed white tumblestone aggregate	↓	↓	265	.060	S.F.
	166	STONE PAVERS					
	1100	Flagging, bluestone, irregular, 1" thick,	D-1	1 Bricklayer	81	.198	S.F.
				1 Bricklayer Helper			
	1110	1-1/2" thick			90	.178	S.F.
	1120	Pavers, 1/2" thick			110	.145	S.F.
	1130	3/4" thick			95	.168	S.F.
	1140	1" thick			81	.198	S.F.
	1150	Snapped random rectangular, 1" thick			92	.174	S.F.
	1200	1-1/2" thick			85	.188	S.F.
	1250	2" thick			83	.193	S.F.
	1300	Slate, natural cleft, irregular, 3/4" thick			92	.174	S.F.
	1310	1" thick			85	.188	S.F.
	1350	Random rectangular, gauged, 1/2" thick			105	.152	S.F.
	1400	Random rectangular, butt joint, gauged, 1/4" thick			150	.107	S.F.
	1550	Granite blocks, 3-1/2" x 3-1/2" x 3-1/2"			92	.174	S.F.
	1560	4" x 4" x 4"			95	.168	S.F.
	1600	4" to 12" long, 3" to 5" wide, 3" to 5" thick	↓	↓	98	.163	S.F.

025 | Paving and Surfacing

025 250 | Curbs

		CREW	MAKEUP	DAILY OUTPUT	MAN-HOURS	UNIT
254	**CURBS** Bituminous, machine formed, 8" wide, 6" high, 40 L.F./ton	B-27	1 Labor Foreman (outside)	1,000	.032	L.F.
			3 Building Laborers			
			1 Berm Machine			
0100	8" wide, 8" high, 30 L.F. per ton			900	.036	L.F.
0150	Bitum. berm, 12"W, 3" to 6"H, 35 L.F./ton, before pavement			700	.046	L.F.
0200	12"W, 1-1/2"to 4" H, 60 L.F. per ton, laid with pavement	B-2	1 Labor Foreman (outside)	1,050	.038	L.F.
			4 Building Laborers			
0300	Concrete, 6" x 18", wood forms, straight	C-2	1 Carpenter Foreman (out)	500	.096	L.F.
			4 Carpenters			
			1 Building Laborer			
			Power Tools			
0400	6" x 18", radius	"	"	200	.240	L.F.
0421	Curb and gutter, straight					
0422	with 6" high curb and 6" thick gutter, wood forms					
0430	24" wide, .055 C.Y. per L.F.	C-2	1 Carpenter Foreman (out)	375	.128	L.F.
			4 Carpenters			
			1 Building Laborer			
			Power Tools			
0435	30" wide, .066 C.Y. per L.F.	"	"	340	.141	L.F.
0550	Precast, 6" x 18", straight	B-29	1 Labor Foreman (outside)	700	.080	L.F.
			4 Building Laborers			
			1 Equip. Oper. (crane)			
			1 Equip. Oper. Oiler			
			1 Gradall, 3 Ton, 1/2 C.Y.			
0600	6" x 18", radius			325	.172	L.F.
1000	Granite, split face, straight, 5" x 16"			500	.112	L.F.
1300	Radius curbing, 6" x 18", over 10' radius			260	.215	L.F.
1400	Corners, 2' radius			80	.700	Ea.
1600	Edging, 4-1/2" x 12", straight			300	.187	L.F.
1800	Curb inlets, (guttermouth) straight			41	1.370	Ea.
258	**EDGING**					
0100	Brick, set horizontally, 1-1/2 per L.F.	D-1	1 Bricklayer	370	.043	L.F.
			1 Bricklayer Helper			
0150	Set vertically, 3 per L.F.	"	"	135	.119	L.F.
0200	Corrugated aluminum, 4" wide	F-1	1 Carpenter	650	.012	L.F.
			Power Tools			
0250	6" wide	"	"	550	.015	L.F.
0350	Granite, 4-1/2" x 12", straight	B-29	1 Labor Foreman (outside)	300	.187	L.F.
			4 Building Laborers			
			1 Equip. Oper. (crane)			
			1 Equip. Oper. Oiler			
			1 Gradall, 3 Ton, 1/2 C.Y.			
0400	Polyethylene grass barrier, 5" x 1/8"	D-1	1 Bricklayer	400	.040	L.F.
			1 Bricklayer Helper			
0500	Precast scallops, green, 2" x 8" x 16"			400	.040	L.F.
0550	Other colors			400	.040	L.F.
0600	Railroad ties, 6" x 8"	F-2	2 Carpenters	170	.094	L.F.
			Power Tools			
0650	7" x 9"			136	.118	L.F.
0700	Redwood, 1" x 4"			500	.032	L.F.
0750	2" x 4"			330	.048	L.F.
0800	Steel edge strips, 1/4" x 5", incl. stakes			330	.048	L.F.
0850	3/16" x 4"			330	.048	L.F.
0900	Hardwood, pressure creosoted, 4" x 6"			250	.064	L.F.
0940	6" x 6"			200	.080	L.F.
0980	6" x 8"			170	.094	L.F.

025 | Paving and Surfacing

025 250 | Curbs

		CREW	MAKEUP	DAILY OUTPUT	MAN-HOURS	UNIT
258 1000	Edging, hardwood, pressure treated pine, 1" x 4"	F-2	2 Carpenters	500	.032	L.F.
1040	2" x 4"		Power Tools	330	.048	L.F.
1081	4" x 6"			250	.064	L.F.
1100	6" x 6"			200	.080	L.F.
1140	6" x 8"			170	.094	L.F.

025 300 | Athletic Pave/Surfacing

		CREW	MAKEUP	DAILY OUTPUT	MAN-HOURS	UNIT
304	RUNNING TRACK Gravel and cinders over stone base	B-36	1 Labor Foreman (outside)	127	.315	S.Y.
			2 Highway Laborers			
			2 Equip. Oper. (med.)			
			1 Dozer, 200 H.P.			
			1 Aggregate Spreader			
			1 Tandem Roller, 10 Ton			
0100	Rubber-vermiculite asphalt pavement, 1" thick	B-25	1 Labor Foreman	1,350	.065	S.Y.
			7 Laborers			
			3 Equip. Oper. (med.)			
			1 Asphalt Paver, 130 H.P			
			1 Tandem Roller, 10 Ton			
			1 Roller, Pneumatic Wheel			
0300	Colored rubberized asphalt	"	"	1,350	.065	S.Y.
0400	Artificial resilient mat over asphalt	B-2	1 Labor Foreman (outside)	101	.396	S.Y.
			4 Building Laborers			
308	TENNIS COURT Bituminous, incl. base, 2-1/2" thick, single court	B-37	1 Labor Foreman (outside)	450	.107	S.Y.
			4 Building Laborers			
			1 Equip. Oper. (light)			
			1 Tandem Roller, 5 Ton			
0200	Double court			675	.071	S.Y.
0300	Clay courts			360	.133	S.Y.
0400	Pulverized natural greenstone with 4" base, fast dry			250	.192	S.Y.
0800	Rubber-acrylic base resilient pavement			600	.080	S.Y.
1000	Colored sealer, acrylic emulsion, 3 coats	2 Clab	2 Building Laborers	800	.020	S.Y.
1100	2 color seal coating	"	"	800	.020	S.Y.
1200	For preparing old courts, add	1 Clab	1 Building Laborer	825	.010	S.Y.
1400	Posts for nets, 3-1/2" diameter with eye bolts	B-1	1 Labor Foreman (outside)	3.40	7.060	Pr.
			2 Building Laborers			
1500	With pulley & reel			3.40	7.060	Pr.
1700	Net, 42' long, nylon thread with binder			50	.480	Ea.
1800	All metal			6.50	3.690	Ea.
2000	Paint markings on asphalt, 2 coats	1 Pord	1 Painter, Ordinary	2.50	3.200	Court
2200	Complete court with fence, etc., bituminous, minimum	B-37	1 Labor Foreman (outside)	.20	240.000	Court
			4 Building Laborers			
			1 Equip. Oper. (light)			
			1 Tandem Roller, 5 Ton			
2300	Maximum			.16	300.000	Court
2800	Clay courts, minimum			.20	240.000	Court
2900	Maximum			.16	300.000	Court

025 400 | Synthetic Surfacing

		CREW	MAKEUP	DAILY OUTPUT	MAN-HOURS	UNIT
404 0020	TURF, ARTIFICIAL Not including asphalt base or drainage, but including cushion pad, over 50,000 S.F.					
0200	1/2" pile and 5/16" cushion pad, standard	C-17	2 Skilled Worker Foremen	3,200	.025	S.F.
			8 Skilled Workers			
0300	Deluxe			2,560	.031	S.F.
0500	1/2" pile and 5/8" cushion pad, standard			2,844	.028	S.F.
0600	Deluxe			2,327	.034	S.F.
0801						

025 400 | Synthetic Surfacing

		CREW	MAKEUP	DAILY OUTPUT	MAN-HOURS	UNIT
404 0901	Artificial turf, 2-1/2" bitum. base, w/6" crushed stone, add	B-25	1 Labor Foreman	16,000	.006	S.F.
			7 Laborers			
			3 Equip. Oper. (med.)			
			1 Asphalt Paver, 130 H.P			
			1 Tandem Roller, 10 Ton			
			1 Roller, Pneumatic Wheel			

025 450 | Surfacing

		CREW	MAKEUP	DAILY OUTPUT	MAN-HOURS	UNIT
454	**SURFACE TREATMENT**					
3000	Pavement overlay, polypropylene (including tack coat)					
3040	6 oz. per S.Y., ideal conditions	B-63	4 Building Laborers	10,000	.004	S.Y.
			1 Equip. Oper. (light)			
			1 Loader, Skid Steer			
3080	Adverse conditions			1,000	.040	S.Y.
3120	4 oz. per S.Y., ideal conditions			10,000	.004	S.Y.
3160	Adverse conditions	↓	↓	1,000	.040	S.Y.
3200	Tack coat, emulsion, .05 gal per S.Y., 1000 S.Y	B-45	1 Equip. Oper. (med.)	2,500	.006	S.Y.
			1 Truck Driver (heavy)			
			1 Dist. Tank Truck, 3K Gal.			
			1 Tractor, 4 x 2, 250 H.P.			
3240	10,000 S.Y.			10,000	.002	S.Y.
3280	.15 gal per S.Y., 1000 S.Y.			2,500	.006	S.Y.
3320	10,000 S.Y.	↓	↓	10,000	.002	S.Y.
5000	Reclamation, pulverizing and blending with existing base					
5040	Aggregate base, 4" thick pavement, over 15,000 S.Y.	B-73	1 Labor Foreman (outside)	2,400	.027	S.Y.
			2 Highway Laborers			
			5 Equip. Oper. (med.)			
			1 Road Mixer, 310 H.P.			
			1 Roller, Tandem, 12 Ton			
			1 Hammermill, 250 H.P.			
			1 Motor Grader, 30,000 Lb.			
			.5 F.E. Loader, 1-3/4 C.Y.			
			.5 Truck, 30 ton			
			.5 Water tank 5000 gal.			
5080	5,000 to 15,000 S.Y.			2,200	.029	S.Y.
5120	8" thick pavement, over 15,000 S.Y.			2,200	.029	S.Y.
5160	5,000 to 15,000 S.Y.	↓	↓	2,000	.032	S.Y.
5200	Cold planing & cleaning, 1"-3" asphalt pavmt., over 25,000 S.Y.	B-71	1 Labor Foreman (outside)	6,000	.009	S.Y.
			3 Highway Laborers			
			3 Equip. Oper. (med.)			
			1 Pvmt. Profiler, 450 H.P.			
			1 Road Sweeper, S.P.			
			1 F.E. Loader, 1-3/4 C.Y.			
5280	5,000 to 10,000 S.Y.	"	"	4,000	.014	S.Y.
5300	Asphalt pavement removal from conc. base, no haul					
5320	Rip, load & sweep 1" to 3"	B-70	1 Labor Foreman (outside)	8,000	.007	S.Y.
			3 Highway Laborers			
			3 Equip. Oper. (med.)			
			1 Motor Grader, 30,000 Lb.			
			1 Grader Attach., Ripper			
			1 Road Sweeper, S.P.			
			1 F.E. Loader, 1-3/4 C.Y.			
5330	3" to 6" deep	"	"	5,000	.011	S.Y.

025 450 | Surfacing

			CREW	MAKEUP	DAILY OUTPUT	MAN-HOURS	UNIT
454	5341	Surface treatment, profile, asphalt pvmnt, load/sweep, 1" deep	B-71	1 Labor Foreman (outside)	12,500	.004	S.Y.
				3 Highway Laborers			
				3 Equip. Oper. (med.)			
				1 Pvmt. Profiler, 450 H.P.			
				1 Road Sweeper, S.P.			
				1 F.E. Loader, 1-3/4 C.Y.			
	5350	3" deep	↓	↓	9,000	.006	S.Y.
	5360	6" deep			5,000	.011	S.Y.
	5520	Remove, rejuvenate and spread 4" deep	B-72	1 Labor Foreman (outside)	2,500	.026	S.Y.
				3 Highway Laborers			
				4 Equip. Oper. (med.)			
				1 Pvmt. Profiler, 450 H.P.			
				1 Hammermill, 250 H.P.			
				1 Windrow Loader			
				1 Mix Paver 165 H.P.			
				1 Roller, Pneu. Tire, 12 T.			
	5521	6" deep	"	"	2,000	.032	S.Y.
458		**SEALCOATING** 2 coat tar pitch emulsion over 10,000 S.Y.	B-45	1 Equip. Oper. (med.)	5,000	.003	S.Y.
				1 Truck Driver (heavy)			
				1 Dist. Tank Truck, 3K Gal.			
				1 Tractor, 4 x 2, 250 H.P.			
	0100	Under 1000 S.Y.	B-1	1 Labor Foreman (outside)	1,050	.023	S.Y.
				2 Building Laborers			
	0300	Petroleum resistant, over 10,000 S.Y.	B-45	1 Equip. Oper. (med.)	5,000	.003	S.Y.
				1 Truck Driver (heavy)			
				1 Dist. Tank Truck, 3K Gal.			
				1 Tractor, 4 x 2, 250 H.P.			
	0400	Under 1000 S.Y.	B-1	1 Labor Foreman (outside)	1,050	.023	S.Y.
				2 Building Laborers			
	0600	Non-skid pavement renewal, over 10,000 S.Y.	B-45	1 Equip. Oper. (med.)	5,000	.003	S.Y.
				1 Truck Driver (heavy)			
				1 Dist. Tank Truck, 3K Gal.			
				1 Tractor, 4 x 2, 250 H.P.			
	0700	Under 1000 S.Y.	B-1	1 Labor Foreman (outside)	1,050	.023	S.Y.
				2 Building Laborers			
	0800	Prepare and clean surface for above	A-2	2 Building Laborers	8,545	.003	S.Y.
				1 Truck Driver (light)			
				1 Light Truck, 1.5 Ton			
	1000	Hand seal bituminous curbing	B-1	1 Labor Foreman (outside)	4,420	.005	L.F.
				2 Building Laborers			
	1900	Bituminous surface treatment, single course, small area					
	1901	0.30 gal/S.Y. bituminous material, 20#/S.Y. aggregate	B-91	1 Labor Foreman (outside)	5,000	.013	S.Y.
				2 Highway Laborers			
				4 Equip. Oper. (med.)			
				1 Truck Driver (heavy)			
				1 Dist. Truck, 3000 Gal.			
				1 Aggreg. Spreader, S.P.			
				1 Roller, Pneu. Tire, 12 Ton			
				1 Roller, Steel, 10 Ton			
	1910	Roadway or large area			10,000	.006	S.Y.
	1950	Bituminous surface treatment, dbl. course for small area			3,000	.021	S.Y.
	1960	Roadway or large area			6,000	.011	S.Y.
	1980	Bituminous surface treatment, single course, for shoulders			7,500	.009	S.Y.
	2080	Sand sealing, sharp sand, asphalt emulsion, small area			10,000	.006	S.Y.
	2120	Roadway or large area	↓	↓	20,000	.003	S.Y.

025 450 | Surfacing

		CREW	MAKEUP	DAILY OUTPUT	MAN-HOURS	UNIT
458 2201	Sealcoating, slurry sealing, 1 coat, small area	B-90	1 Labor Foreman (outside)	3,000	.021	S.Y.
			3 Highway Laborers			
			2 Equip. Oper. (light)			
			2 Truck Drivers (heavy)			
			1 Road Mixer, 310 H.P.			
			1 Dist. Truck, 2000 Gal.			
2240	Large area			16,000	.004	S.Y.
2300	2 coats, small area			2,000	.032	S.Y.
2340	Large area	↓	↓	11,000	.006	S.Y.
3000	Sealing random cracks, min 1/2" wide, 1,000 L.F.	B-77	1 Labor Foreman	4,800	.008	L.F.
			3 Laborers			
			1 Truck Driver (light)			
			1 Crack Cleaner, 25 H.P.			
			1 Crack Filler, Trailer Mtd.			
			1 Flatbed Truck, 3 Ton			
3040	10,000 L.F.			7,800	.005	L.F.
3080	Alternate method, 1,000 L.F.			200	.200	Gal.
3120	10,000 L.F.	↓	↓	325	.123	Gal.
3200	Multi-cracks (flooding), 1 coat, small area	B-92	1 Labor Foreman (outside)	460	.070	S.Y.
			3 Highway Laborers			
			1 Crack Cleaner, 25 H.P.			
			1 Air Compressor			
			1 Tar Kettle, T.M.			
			1 Flatbed Truck, 3 Ton			
3240	Large area			2,850	.011	S.Y.
3280	2 coat, small area			230	.139	S.Y.
3320	Large area			1,425	.022	S.Y.
3360	Alternate method, small area			115	.278	Gal.
3400	Large area	↓	↓	715	.045	Gal.
3600	Waterproofing, membrane, tar and fabric, small area	B-63	4 Building Laborers	233	.172	S.Y.
			1 Equip. Oper. (light)			
			1 Loader, Skid Steer			
3640	Large area			1,435	.028	S.Y.
3680	Preformed rubberized asphalt, small area			100	.400	S.Y.
3720	Large area	↓	↓	367	.109	S.Y.

025 500 | Highway Paving

		CREW	MAKEUP	DAILY OUTPUT	MAN-HOURS	UNIT
504 0020	**BRIDGES** Pedestrian, spans over streams, roadways, etc. including erection, not including foundations					
0050	Precast concrete, complete in place, 8' wide, 60' span	E-2	1 Struc. Steel Foreman	215	.260	S.F.
			4 Struc. Steel Workers			
			1 Equip. Oper. (crane)			
			1 Equip. Oper. Oiler			
			1 Crane, 90 Ton			
0100	100' span			185	.303	S.F.
0150	120' span			160	.350	S.F.
0200	150' span			145	.386	S.F.
0300	Steel, trussed or arch spans, compl. in place, 8' wide, 40' span			320	.175	S.F.
0400	50' span			395	.142	S.F.
0500	60' span			465	.120	S.F.
0600	80' span			570	.098	S.F.
0700	100' span			465	.120	S.F.
0800	120' span			365	.153	S.F.
0900	150' span			310	.181	S.F.
1000	160' span			255	.220	S.F.
1100	10' wide, 80' span			640	.088	S.F.
1200	120' span	↓	↓	415	.135	S.F.
1300	150' span			445	.126	S.F.

025 | Paving and Surfacing

025 500 | Highway Paving

		CREW	MAKEUP	DAILY OUTPUT	MAN-HOURS	UNIT
504 **1401**	Pedestrian bridge, steel, trussed/arch spans, 10' wide, 200' span	E-2	1 Struc. Steel Foreman	205	.273	S.F.
			4 Struc. Steel Workers			
			1 Equip. Oper. (crane)			
			1 Equip. Oper. Oiler			
			1 Crane, 90 Ton			
1600	Wood, laminated type, complete in place, 80' span	C-12	1 Carpenter Foreman (out)	203	.236	S.F.
			3 Carpenters			
			1 Building Laborer			
			1 Equip. Oper. (crane)			
			1 Hyd. Crane, 12 Ton			
1700	130' span	"	"	153	.314	S.F.

025 800 | Pavement Marking

		CREW	MAKEUP	DAILY OUTPUT	MAN-HOURS	UNIT
804	**PAINTING LINES** On pavement, reflectorized white or yellow, 4" wide	B-78	1 Labor Foreman	20,000	.002	L.F.
			4 Laborers			
			1 Truck Driver (light)			
			1 Paint Striper, S.P.			
			1 Flatbed Truck, 3 Ton			
			1 Pickup Truck, 3/4 Ton			
0200	6" wide			11,000	.004	L.F.
0500	8" wide			10,000	.005	L.F.
0600	12" wide			4,000	.012	L.F.
0620	Arrows or gore lines			2,300	.021	S.F.
0640	Temporary paint, white or yellow	↓	↓	15,000	.003	L.F.
0660	Removal	A-1	1 Building Laborer	360	.022	L.F.
			1 Gas Eng. Power Tool			
0680	Temporary tape, white			776	.010	L.F.
0700	Yellow	↓	↓	679	.012	L.F.
0710	Thermoplastic, white or yellow, 4" wide	B-79	1 Labor Foreman	15,000	.003	L.F.
			3 Laborers			
			1 Truck Driver (light)			
			1 Thermo. Striper, T.M.			
			1 Flatbed Truck, 3 Ton			
			2 Pickup Trucks, 3/4 Ton			
0730	6" wide			14,000	.003	L.F.
0740	8" wide			12,000	.003	L.F.
0750	12" wide			6,000	.007	L.F.
0760	Arrows			660	.061	S.F.
0770	Gore lines			2,500	.016	S.F.
0780	Letters	↓	↓	660	.061	S.F.
0790	Layout of pavement marking	A-2	2 Building Laborers	25,000	.001	L.F.
			1 Truck Driver (light)			
			1 Light Truck, 1.5 Ton			
0800	Parking stall, paint, white	B-78	1 Labor Foreman	860	.056	Stall
			4 Laborers			
			1 Truck Driver (light)			
			1 Paint Striper, S.P.			
			1 Flatbed Truck, 3 Ton			
			1 Pickup Truck, 3/4 Ton			
1000	Street letters and numbers	"	"	1,600	.030	S.F.

026 | Piped Utilities

026 010 | Piped Utility

			CREW	MAKEUP	DAILY OUTPUT	MAN-HOURS	UNIT
012	012	**BEDDING** For pipe and conduit, not incl. compaction					
	0050	Crushed or screened bank run gravel	B-6	2 Building Laborers	150	.160	C.Y.
				1 Equip. Oper. (light)			
				1 Backhoe Loader, 48 H.P.			
	0100	Crushed stone 3/4" to 1/2"	↓	↓	150	.160	C.Y.
	0200	Sand, dead or bank,			150	.160	C.Y.
	0500	Compacting bedding in trench	A-1	1 Building Laborer	90	.089	C.Y.
				1 Gas Eng. Power Tool			
	014	**EXCAVATION AND BACKFILL**					
	0100	Hand excavate and trim for pipe bells after trench excavation					
	0200	8" pipe	1 Clab	1 Building Laborer	155	.052	L.F.
	0300	18" pipe	"	"	130	.062	L.F.

026 050 | Manholes And Cleanouts

			CREW	MAKEUP	DAILY OUTPUT	MAN-HOURS	UNIT
	054	**UTILITY VAULTS** Precast concrete, 6" thick					
	0040	4' x 6' x 6' high, I.D.	B-13	1 Labor Foreman (outside)	2	28.000	Ea.
				4 Building Laborers			
				1 Equip. Oper. (crane)			
				1 Equip. Oper. Oiler			
				1 Hyd. Crane, 25 Ton			
	0050	5' x 10' x 6' high, I.D.			2	28.000	Ea.
	0100	6' x 10' x 6' high, I.D.			2	28.000	Ea.
	0150	5' x 12' x 6' high, I.D.			2	28.000	Ea.
	0200	6' x 12' x 6' high, I.D.			1.80	31.110	Ea.
	0250	6' x 13' x 6' high, I.D.			1.50	37.330	Ea.
	0300	8' x 14' x 7' high, I.D.	↓	↓	1	56.000	Ea.
	0350	Hand hole, precast concrete, 1-1/2" thick					
	0400	1'-4" x 2'-4" x 1'-3", I.D., light duty	B-1	1 Labor Foreman (outside)	4	6.000	Ea.
				2 Building Laborers			
	0450	4'-6" x 5'-10" x 2'-7", O.D., heavy duty	B-6	2 Building Laborers	3	8.000	Ea.
				1 Equip. Oper. (light)			
				1 Backhoe Loader, 48 H.P.			
	0460	Meter pit, 4' x 4', 4' deep			2	12.000	Ea.
	0470	6' deep			1.60	15.000	Ea.
	0480	8' deep			1.40	17.140	Ea.
	0490	10' deep			1.20	20.000	Ea.
	0500	15' deep			1	24.000	Ea.
	0510	6' x 6', 4' deep			1.40	17.140	Ea.
	0520	6' deep			1.20	20.000	Ea.
	0530	8' deep			1	24.000	Ea.
	0540	10' deep			.80	30.000	Ea.
	0550	15' deep	↓	↓	.60	40.000	Ea.

026 100 | Pipe And Fittings

			CREW	MAKEUP	DAILY OUTPUT	MAN-HOURS	UNIT
	104	**PIPE INSULATION**					
	0100	Calcium silicate, 1" thick, 4" diameter	Q-14	1 Asbestos Worker	150	.107	L.F.
				1 Asbestos Apprentice			
	0120	5" diameter			145	.110	L.F.
	0140	6" diameter			140	.114	L.F.
	0160	1-1/2" thick, 8" diameter			130	.123	L.F.
	0180	10" diameter			125	.128	L.F.
	0200	12" diameter			120	.133	L.F.
	0240	16" diameter			100	.160	L.F.
	0400	2" thick, 4" diameter			125	.128	L.F.
	0440	6" diameter			115	.139	L.F.
	0480	10" diameter			95	.168	L.F.
	0500	12" diameter			90	.178	L.F.
	0540	16" diameter	↓	↓	80	.200	L.F.

026 | Piped Utilities

026 100 | Pipe And Fittings

		CREW	MAKEUP	DAILY OUTPUT	MAN-HOURS	UNIT
104 0601	Pipe insulation, calcium silicate, 2" thick, 24" diameter	Q-14	1 Asbestos Worker	55	.291	L.F.
			1 Asbestos Apprentice			
0700	3" thick, 4" diameter			95	.168	L.F.
0740	6" diameter			90	.178	L.F.
0760	8" diameter			85	.188	L.F.
0780	10" diameter			75	.213	L.F.
0800	12" diameter			70	.229	L.F.
0840	16" diameter			60	.267	L.F.
0900	24" diameter			40	.400	L.F.
1020	Fiberglass, 1" thick, 4" diameter			150	.107	L.F.
1060	6" diameter			120	.133	L.F.
1080	8" diameter			100	.160	L.F.
1100	10" diameter			90	.178	L.F.
1120	12" diameter			80	.200	L.F.
1160	16" diameter			70	.229	L.F.
1220	24" diameter			60	.267	L.F.
1300	1-1/2" thick, 4" diameter			130	.123	L.F.
1340	6" diameter			100	.160	L.F.
1360	8" diameter			80	.200	L.F.
1380	10" diameter			70	.229	L.F.
1400	12" diameter			65	.246	L.F.
1440	16" diameter			55	.291	L.F.
1500	24" diameter			40	.400	L.F.
1600	2" thick, 4" diameter			110	.145	L.F.
1640	6" diameter			80	.200	L.F.
1660	8" diameter			60	.267	L.F.
1680	10" diameter			55	.291	L.F.
1700	12" diameter			50	.320	L.F.
1740	16" diameter			40	.400	L.F.
1760	18" diameter			35	.457	L.F.
1800	24" diameter	↓	↓	25	.640	L.F.
1810						

026 400 | Valves And Cocks

		CREW	MAKEUP	DAILY OUTPUT	MAN-HOURS	UNIT
404	PIPING VALVES Water distribution					
0020	Not including excavation or backfill					
0400	Ball, valve PVC, socket or threaded, single union					
0540	1/2" size	1 Plum	1 Plumber	26	.308	Ea.
0580	3/4" size			25	.320	Ea.
0700	1" size			23	.348	Ea.
0740	1-1/4" size			21	.381	Ea.
0780	1-1/2" size			20	.400	Ea.
0900	2" size	↓	↓	17	.471	Ea.
0940	3" size	2 Plum	2 Plumbers	24	.667	Ea.
0980	4" size	"	"	20	.800	Ea.
1500	Ball check, PVC, socket or threaded					
1600	1/2" size	1 Plum	1 Plumber	26	.308	Ea.
1640	3/4" size			25	.320	Ea.
1680	1" size			23	.348	Ea.
1700	1-1/4" size			21	.381	Ea.
1740	1-1/2" size			20	.400	Ea.
1800	2" size	↓	↓	17	.471	Ea.
1840	3" size	2 Plum	2 Plumbers	24	.667	Ea.
1900	4" size	"	"	20	.800	Ea.
2400	Bronze, ball, 125 lb. solder or thread					
2440	1-1/2" diameter	1 Plum	1 Plumber	13	.615	Ea.
2480	2" diameter			11	.727	Ea.
2500	2-1/2" diameter	↓	↓	9	.889	Ea.

026 400 | Valves And Cocks

		CREW	MAKEUP	DAILY OUTPUT	MAN-HOURS	UNIT
404 2541	Piping, valves, bronze, ball, 125 lb. solder/thread, 3" diameter	1 Plum	1 Plumber	8	1.000	Ea.
2640	Check, swing, 125 lb., regrinding disk					
2680	1-1/2" diameter	1 Plum	1 Plumber	13	.615	Ea.
2800	2" diameter			11	.727	Ea.
2840	2-1/2" diameter			9	.889	Ea.
2880	3" diameter	↓	↓	8	1.000	Ea.
3000	Butterfly valves with boxes, cast iron					
3100	4" diameter	B-20	1 Labor Foreman (out) 1 Skilled worker 1 Building Laborer	6	4.000	Ea.
3180	8" diameter	B-21	1 Labor Foreman (out) 1 Skilled worker 1 Building Laborer .5 Equip. Oper. (crane) .5 S.P. Crane, 5 Ton	4	7.000	Ea.
3340	12" diameter			3	9.330	Ea.
3400	14" diameter			2	14.000	Ea.
3460	18" diameter			1.50	18.670	Ea.
3480	20" diameter			1	28.000	Ea.
3500	24" diameter	↓	↓	.50	56.000	Ea.
3600	With lever operator					
3610	4" diameter	B-20	1 Labor Foreman (out) 1 Skilled worker 1 Building Laborer	6	4.000	Ea.
3616	8" diameter	B-21	1 Labor Foreman (out) 1 Skilled worker 1 Building Laborer .5 Equip. Oper. (crane) .5 S.P. Crane, 5 Ton	4	7.000	Ea.
3620	12" diameter			3	9.330	Ea.
3624	18" diameter			2	14.000	Ea.
3630	24" diameter	↓	↓	.50	56.000	Ea.
3700	Check valves, flanged					
3710	4" diameter	B-20	1 Labor Foreman (out) 1 Skilled worker 1 Building Laborer	6	4.000	Ea.
3714	6" diameter	"	"	5	4.800	Ea.
3716	8" diameter	B-21	1 Labor Foreman (out) 1 Skilled worker 1 Building Laborer .5 Equip. Oper. (crane) .5 S.P. Crane, 5 Ton	4	7.000	Ea.
3720	12" diameter			3	9.330	Ea.
3724	16" diameter			2	14.000	Ea.
3726	18" diameter			1.50	18.670	Ea.
3730	24" diameter	↓	↓	.50	56.000	Ea.
3800	Gate valves, flanged					
3810	4" diameter	B-20	1 Labor Foreman (out) 1 Skilled worker 1 Building Laborer	6	4.000	Ea.
3814	6" diameter	"	"	5	4.800	Ea.
3816	8" diameter	B-21	1 Labor Foreman (out) 1 Skilled worker 1 Building Laborer .5 Equip. Oper. (crane) .5 S.P. Crane, 5 Ton	4	7.000	Ea.
3820	12" diameter			3	9.330	Ea.
3824	16" diameter	↓	↓	1	28.000	Ea.

026 | Piped Utilities

026 400 | Valves And Cocks

		CREW	MAKEUP	DAILY OUTPUT	MAN-HOURS	UNIT
404	3829	Piping, gate valves, flanged, 20" diameter	B-21	1 Labor Foreman (out)	.80	35.000	Ea.
				1 Skilled worker			
				1 Building Laborer			
				.5 Equip. Oper. (crane)			
				.5 S.P. Crane, 5 Ton			
	3830	24" diameter	"	"	.50	56.000	Ea.
	3840	With boxes					
	3842	4" diameter	B-20	1 Labor Foreman (out)	5	4.800	Ea.
				1 Skilled worker			
				1 Building Laborer			
	3846	8" diameter	B-21	1 Labor Foreman (out)	3.50	8.000	Ea.
				1 Skilled worker			
				1 Building Laborer			
				.5 Equip. Oper. (crane)			
				.5 S.P. Crane, 5 Ton			
	3848	10" diameter			3	9.330	Ea.
	3850	12" diameter			3	9.330	Ea.
	3854	16" diameter			2	14.000	Ea.
	3858	20" diameter			1	28.000	Ea.
	3860	24" diameter			.50	56.000	Ea.
	3900	Globe valves, flanged					
	3910	4" diameter	B-20	1 Labor Foreman (out)	10	2.400	Ea.
				1 Skilled worker			
				1 Building Laborer			
	3914	6" diameter	"	"	9	2.670	Ea.
	3916	8" diameter	B-21	1 Labor Foreman (out)	6	4.670	Ea.
				1 Skilled worker			
				1 Building Laborer			
				.5 Equip. Oper. (crane)			
				.5 S.P. Crane, 5 Ton			
	3920	12" diameter			4	7.000	Ea.
	3924	16" diameter			2	14.000	Ea.
	3928	20" diameter			.60	46.670	Ea.
	3930	24" diameter			.50	56.000	Ea.

026 450 | Hydrants

		CREW	MAKEUP	DAILY OUTPUT	MAN-HOURS	UNIT
454 1000	**PIPING, WATER DISTRIBUTION** Mech. joints unless noted Fire hydrants, two way; excavation and backfill not incl.					
1100	4-1/2" valve size, depth 2'-0"	B-21	1 Labor Foreman (out)	10	2.800	Ea.
			1 Skilled worker			
			1 Building Laborer			
			.5 Equip. Oper. (crane)			
			.5 S.P. Crane, 5 Ton			
1200	4'-6"			9	3.110	Ea.
1260	6'-0"			7	4.000	Ea.
1340	8'-0"			6	4.670	Ea.
1420	10'-0"			5	5.600	Ea.
2000	5-1/4" valve size, depth 2'-0"			10	2.800	Ea.
2080	4'-0"			9	3.110	Ea.
2160	6'-0"			7	4.000	Ea.
2240	8'-0"			6	4.670	Ea.
2320	10'-0"			5	5.600	Ea.
2400	Lower barrel extensions with stems, 1'-0"	B-20	1 Labor Foreman (out)	14	1.710	Ea.
			1 Skilled worker			
			1 Building Laborer			
2440	2'-0"			13	1.850	Ea.
2480	3'-0"			12	2.000	Ea.
2520	4'-0"			10	2.400	Ea.

026 | Piped Utilities

026 450 | Hydrants

		CREW	MAKEUP	DAILY OUTPUT	MAN-HOURS	UNIT
454 3041	Piping, wall hydrant, bronze, non-freeze, 3/4" dia. for 12" wall	2 Plum	2 Plumbers	11	1.450	Ea.
3140	For 18" wall			10.50	1.520	Ea.
3180	For 24" wall			10	1.600	Ea.
3200	Post type, non freeze, 4' depth of bury, 3/4" conn.	↓	↓	4	4.000	Ea.
4000	1" connection	1 Plum	1 Plumber	8	1.000	Ea.
4020	1-1/4" connection			8	1.000	Ea.
4040	1-1/2" connection			7	1.140	Ea.
4060	2" connection	↓	↓	7	1.140	Ea.
5000	Indicator post					
5020	Adjustable, valve size 4" to 14", 4' bury	B-21	1 Labor Foreman (out)	10	2.800	Ea.
			1 Skilled worker			
			1 Building Laborer			
			.5 Equip. Oper. (crane)			
			.5 S.P. Crane, 5 Ton			
5060	8' bury			8	3.500	Ea.
5080	10' bury			8	3.500	Ea.
5100	12' bury			6	4.670	Ea.
5500	Non-adjustable, valve size 4" to 14", 3' bury	↓	↓	10	2.800	Ea.

026 650 | Water Systems

		CREW	MAKEUP	DAILY OUTPUT	MAN-HOURS	UNIT
654	PIPING, WATER DISTRIBUTION, ASBESTOS CEMENT					
0020	Not including excavation or backfill					
2000	Pipe, 150 psi, 4" diameter	B-20	1 Labor Foreman (out)	300	.080	L.F.
			1 Skilled worker			
			1 Building Laborer			
2020	6" diameter	"	"	290	.083	L.F.
2040	8" diameter	B-21	1 Labor Foreman (out)	290	.097	L.F.
			1 Skilled worker			
			1 Building Laborer			
			.5 Equip. Oper. (crane)			
			.5 S.P. Crane, 5 Ton			
2060	10" diameter			270	.104	L.F.
2080	12" diameter			250	.112	L.F.
2100	14" diameter			200	.140	L.F.
2120	16" diameter			180	.156	L.F.
2140	18" diameter			150	.187	L.F.
2160	20" diameter			125	.224	L.F.
2180	24" diameter	↓	↓	95	.295	L.F.
8006	Fittings, 150 psi, elbows, 4" diameter	B-20	1 Labor Foreman (out)	37	.649	Ea.
			1 Skilled worker			
			1 Building Laborer			
8020	6" diameter			30	.800	Ea.
8040	8" diameter			28	.857	Ea.
8060	10" diameter			25	.960	Ea.
8080	12" diameter			20	1.200	Ea.
8100	14" diameter			20	1.200	Ea.
8120	16" diameter	↓	↓	18	1.330	Ea.
8140	18" diameter	B-21	1 Labor Foreman (out)	18	1.560	Ea.
			1 Skilled worker			
			1 Building Laborer			
			.5 Equip. Oper. (crane)			
			.5 S.P. Crane, 5 Ton			
8160	20" diameter			15	1.870	Ea.
8180	24" diameter	↓	↓	12	2.330	Ea.

026 650	Water Systems	CREW	MAKEUP	DAILY OUTPUT	MAN-HOURS	UNIT
658	**PIPING, WATER DISTRIBUTION, CONCRETE**					
0020	Not including excavation or backfill					
2000	R.C.P. class 150, 10" diameter	B-21	1 Labor Foreman (out)	270	.104	L.F.
			1 Skilled worker			
			1 Building Laborer			
			.5 Equip. Oper. (crane)			
			.5 S.P. Crane, 5 Ton			
2010	12" diameter			250	.112	L.F.
2030	16" diameter			180	.156	L.F.
2060	24" diameter			90	.311	L.F.
8010	Bends or elbows, 12" diameter			24	1.170	Ea.
8030	16" diameter			18	1.560	Ea.
8050	20" diameter			10	2.800	Ea.
8060	24" diameter			6	4.670	Ea.
9000	Wyes or tees, 10" diameter			20	1.400	Ea.
9010	12" diameter			18	1.560	Ea.
9030	16" diameter			10	2.800	Ea.
9060	24" diameter	▼	▼	4	7.000	Ea.
662	**PIPING, WATER DISTRIBUTION, COPPER**					
0020	Not including excavation or backfill					
2000	Tubing, type K, 20' joints, 3/4" diameter	1 Plum	1 Plumber	150	.053	L.F.
2200	1" diameter			136	.059	L.F.
3000	1-1/2" diameter			120	.067	L.F.
3020	2" diameter	▼	▼	105	.076	L.F.
3040	2-1/2" diameter	Q-1	1 Plumber	146	.110	L.F.
			1 Plumber Apprentice			
3060	3" diameter			134	.119	L.F.
4012	4" diameter	▼	▼	105	.152	L.F.
4016	6" diameter	Q-2	2 Plumbers	24	1.000	L.F.
			1 Plumber Apprentice			
5000	Tubing, type L					
5108	95/5 solder, 2" diameter	1 Plum	1 Plumber	106	.075	L.F.
6010	3" diameter	Q-1	1 Plumber	140	.114	L.F.
			1 Plumber Apprentice			
6012	4" diameter	"	"	105	.152	L.F.
6016	6" diameter	Q-2	2 Plumbers	24	1.000	L.F.
			1 Plumber Apprentice			
7020	Fittings, brass, corporation stops, 3/4" diameter	1 Plum	1 Plumber	19	.421	Ea.
7040	1" diameter			16	.500	Ea.
7060	1-1/2" diameter			13	.615	Ea.
7080	2" diameter			11	.727	Ea.
7100	Curb stops, 3/4" diameter			19	.421	Ea.
7120	1" diameter			16	.500	Ea.
7140	1-1/2" diameter			13	.615	Ea.
7160	2" diameter			11	.727	Ea.
7180	Curb box, cast iron, 3/4" diameter			12	.667	Ea.
7200	2" diameter			8	1.000	Ea.
8010	Fittings, copper 90° elbow, 3/4" diameter			19	.421	Ea.
8040	1" diameter			16	.500	Ea.
8222	2" diameter	▼	▼	11	.727	Ea.
8224	3" diameter	Q-1	1 Plumber	11	1.450	Ea.
			1 Plumber Apprentice			
8226	4" diameter	"	"	9	1.780	Ea.
8230	6" diameter	Q-2	2 Plumbers	9	2.670	Ea.
			1 Plumber Apprentice			
8240	Tees, 3/4" diameter	1 Plum	1 Plumber	12	.667	Ea.
8241	1" diameter			12	.667	Ea.
8242	2" diameter	▼	▼	7	1.140	Ea.

026 650 | Water Systems

		Description	CREW	MAKEUP	DAILY OUTPUT	MAN-HOURS	UNIT
662	8245	Piping, fittings, copper tees, 3" diameter	Q-1	1 Plumber	7	2.290	Ea.
				1 Plumber Apprentice			
	8246	4" diameter	"	"	5	3.200	Ea.
	8250	6" diameter	Q-2	2 Plumbers	6	4.000	Ea.
				1 Plumber Apprentice			
	666	**PIPING, WATER DISTRIBUTION, DUCTILE IRON**					
	0020	Not including excavation or backfill					
	2000	Pipe, class 250 water piping, 18' lengths					
	2020	Mechanical joint, 4" diameter	B-20	1 Labor Foreman (out)	144	.167	L.F.
				1 Skilled worker			
				1 Building Laborer			
	2040	6" diameter	"	"	126	.190	L.F.
	2060	8" diameter	B-21	1 Labor Foreman (out)	108	.259	L.F.
				1 Skilled worker			
				1 Building Laborer			
				.5 Equip. Oper. (crane)			
				.5 S.P. Crane, 5 Ton			
	2080	10" diameter			90	.311	L.F.
	2100	12" diameter			72	.389	L.F.
	2120	14" diameter			54	.519	L.F.
	2140	16" diameter			46	.609	L.F.
	2160	18" diameter	B-22	1 Labor Foreman (out)	38	.789	L.F.
				1 Skilled worker			
				1 Building Laborer			
				.75 Equip. Oper. (crane)			
				.75 S.P. Crane, 5 Ton			
	2170	20" diameter			37	.811	L.F.
	2180	24" diameter			36	.833	L.F.
	3000	Tyton joint, 4" diameter	B-20	1 Labor Foreman (out)	158	.152	L.F.
				1 Skilled worker			
				1 Building Laborer			
	3020	6" diameter	"	"	138	.174	L.F.
	3040	8" diameter	B-21	1 Labor Foreman (out)	118	.237	L.F.
				1 Skilled worker			
				1 Building Laborer			
				.5 Equip. Oper. (crane)			
				.5 S.P. Crane, 5 Ton			
	3060	10" diameter			100	.280	L.F.
	3080	12" diameter			80	.350	L.F.
	3100	14" diameter			60	.467	L.F.
	3120	16" diameter			54	.519	L.F.
	3140	18" diameter	B-22	1 Labor Foreman (out)	44	.682	L.F.
				1 Skilled worker			
				1 Building Laborer			
				.75 Equip. Oper. (crane)			
				.75 S.P. Crane, 5 Ton			
	3160	20" diameter			42	.714	L.F.
	3180	24" diameter			40	.750	L.F.
	4000	Drill and tap pressurized main (labor only)					
	4100	6" main, 1" to 2" service	Q-1	1 Plumber	3	5.330	Ea.
				1 Plumber Apprentice			
	4150	8" main, 1" to 2" service	"	"	2.75	5.820	Ea.
	4500	Tap and insert gate valve					
	4600	8" main, 4" branch	B-21	1 Labor Foreman (out)	3.20	8.750	Ea.
				1 Skilled worker			
				1 Building Laborer			
				.5 Equip. Oper. (crane)			
				.5 S.P. Crane, 5 Ton			

026 650 | Water Systems

			CREW	MAKEUP	DAILY OUTPUT	MAN-HOURS	UNIT
666	4651	Piping, drill, tap & insert gate valve, 8" main, 6" branch	B-21	1 Labor Foreman (out)	2.70	10.370	Ea.
				1 Skilled worker			
				1 Building Laborer			
				.5 Equip. Oper. (crane)			
				.5 S.P. Crane, 5 Ton			
	4700	10" main, 4" branch			2.70	10.370	Ea.
	4750	6" branch			2.35	11.910	Ea.
	4800	12" main, 6" branch			2.35	11.910	Ea.
	4850	8" branch	↓	↓	2.35	11.910	Ea.
	8000	Fittings					
	8006	Mechanical joint, 90° bend or elbows, 4" diameter	B-20	1 Labor Foreman (out)	37	.649	Ea.
				1 Skilled worker			
				1 Building Laborer			
	8020	6" diameter	↓	↓	25	.960	Ea.
	8040	8" diameter			21	1.140	Ea.
	8060	10" diameter	B-21	1 Labor Foreman (out)	21	1.330	Ea.
				1 Skilled worker			
				1 Building Laborer			
				.5 Equip. Oper. (crane)			
				.5 S.P. Crane, 5 Ton			
	8080	12" diameter			18	1.560	Ea.
	8100	14" diameter			16	1.750	Ea.
	8120	16" diameter			14	2.000	Ea.
	8140	18" diameter			10	2.800	Ea.
	8160	20" diameter	↓	↓	8	3.500	Ea.
	8180	24" diameter			6	4.670	Ea.
	8200	Wye or tee, 4" diameter	B-20	1 Labor Foreman (out)	25	.960	Ea.
				1 Skilled worker			
				1 Building Laborer			
	8220	6" diameter	↓	↓	17	1.410	Ea.
	8240	8" diameter			14	1.710	Ea.
	8260	10" diameter	B-21	1 Labor Foreman (out)	14	2.000	Ea.
				1 Skilled worker			
				1 Building Laborer			
				.5 Equip. Oper. (crane)			
				.5 S.P. Crane, 5 Ton			
	8280	12" diameter			12	2.330	Ea.
	8300	14" diameter			10	2.800	Ea.
	8320	16" diameter			8	3.500	Ea.
	8340	18" diameter			6	4.670	Ea.
	8360	20" diameter	↓	↓	4	7.000	Ea.
	8380	24" diameter			3	9.330	Ea.
	8400	45° bends, 6" diameter	B-20	1 Labor Foreman (out)	24	1.000	Ea.
				1 Skilled worker			
				1 Building Laborer			
	8410	12" diameter	"	"	16	1.500	Ea.
	8420	16" diameter	B-21	1 Labor Foreman (out)	12	2.330	Ea.
				1 Skilled worker			
				1 Building Laborer			
				.5 Equip. Oper. (crane)			
				.5 S.P. Crane, 5 Ton			
	8430	20" diameter	↓	↓	6	4.670	Ea.
	8440	24" diameter			4	7.000	Ea.
	8450	Increaser, 4" x 6" diameter	B-20	1 Labor Foreman (out)	12	2.000	Ea.
				1 Skilled worker			
				1 Building Laborer			
	8460	6" x 8" diameter	↓	↓	10	2.400	Ea.
	8470	6" x 10" diameter			9	2.670	Ea.

026 650 | Water Systems

		Description	CREW	MAKEUP	DAILY OUTPUT	MAN-HOURS	UNIT
666	8481	Piping, fittings, increaser, 6" x 12" diameter	B-20	1 Labor Foreman (out)	8	3.000	Ea.
				1 Skilled worker			
				1 Building Laborer			
	8490	6" x 16" diameter	B-21	1 Labor Foreman (out)	6	4.670	Ea.
				1 Skilled worker			
				1 Building Laborer			
				.5 Equip. Oper. (crane)			
				.5 S.P. Crane, 5 Ton			
	8500	6" x 20" diameter	↓	↓	5	5.600	Ea.
	8510	6" x 24" diameter			4	7.000	Ea.
	8610	Blind flanges, 150 lbs., 4" diameter	Q-1	1 Plumber	10	1.600	Ea.
				1 Plumber Apprentice			
	8630	6" diameter	Q-2	2 Plumbers	10	2.400	Ea.
				1 Plumber Apprentice			
	8640	8" diameter			8	3.000	Ea.
	8660	12" diameter			6	4.000	Ea.
	8680	16" diameter			5	4.800	Ea.
	8700	20" diameter			3	8.000	Ea.
	8710	24" diameter	↓	↓	2	12.000	Ea.
	8720	300 lbs., 4" diameter	Q-1	1 Plumber	6	2.670	Ea.
				1 Plumber Apprentice			
	8750	8" diameter	Q-2	2 Plumbers	4	6.000	Ea.
				1 Plumber Apprentice			
	8770	12" diameter			2.80	8.570	Ea.
	8790	16" diameter			2	12.000	Ea.
	8810	20" diameter			1.50	16.000	Ea.
	8820	24" diameter	↓	↓	1	24.000	Ea.
	8900	Companion flanges, standard, 4" diameter	Q-1	1 Plumber	10	1.600	Ea.
				1 Plumber Apprentice			
	8930	8" diameter	Q-2	2 Plumbers	8	3.000	Ea.
				1 Plumber Apprentice			
	8950	12" diameter	"	"	6	4.000	Ea.
	8960	Extra heavy, 4" diameter	Q-1	1 Plumber	8	2.000	Ea.
				1 Plumber Apprentice			
	8990	8" diameter	Q-2	2 Plumbers	7	3.430	Ea.
				1 Plumber Apprentice			
	9010	12" diameter	"	"	5	4.800	Ea.
	9020	Slip on weld flanges, 150#, 4" diameter	Q-15	1 Plumber	6	2.670	Ea.
				1 Plumber Apprentice			
				1 Electric Welding Mach.			
	9050	8" diameter	Q-16	2 Plumbers	5	4.800	Ea.
				1 Plumber Apprentice			
				1 Electric Welding Mach.			
	9070	12" diameter			3	8.000	Ea.
	9090	16" diameter			2	12.000	Ea.
	9110	20" diameter			1	24.000	Ea.
	9120	24" diameter	↓	↓	1	24.000	Ea.
	9130	300 lbs., 4" diameter	Q-15	1 Plumber	6	2.670	Ea.
				1 Plumber Apprentice			
				1 Electric Welding Mach.			
	9160	8" diameter	Q-16	2 Plumbers	4	6.000	Ea.
				1 Plumber Apprentice			
				1 Electric Welding Mach.			
	9180	12" diameter			2.80	8.570	Ea.
	9200	16" diameter			2	12.000	Ea.
	9220	20" diameter			1.50	16.000	Ea.
	9230	24" diameter	↓	↓	1	24.000	Ea.

026 650 | Water Systems

		Description	CREW	MAKEUP	DAILY OUTPUT	MAN-HOURS	UNIT
666	9301	Piping, weld neck flanges, 150 lbs., 4" diameter	Q-15	1 Plumber 1 Plumber Apprentice 1 Electric Welding Mach.	10	1.600	Ea.
	9330	8" diameter	Q-16	2 Plumbers 1 Plumber Apprentice 1 Electric Welding Mach.	7	3.430	Ea.
	9350	12" diameter			5	4.800	Ea.
	9370	16" diameter			4	6.000	Ea.
	9390	20" diameter			3	8.000	Ea.
	9400	24" diameter			2	12.000	Ea.
	9410	300 lbs., 4" diameter	Q-15	1 Plumber 1 Plumber Apprentice 1 Electric Welding Mach.	8	2.000	Ea.
	9440	8" diameter	Q-16	2 Plumbers 1 Plumber Apprentice 1 Electric Welding Mach.	8	3.000	Ea.
	9460	12" diameter			7	3.430	Ea.
	9480	16" diameter			5	4.800	Ea.
	9500	20" diameter			3	8.000	Ea.
	9510	24" diameter			2	12.000	Ea.
	9600	Steel sleeve and tap, 4" diameter	B-20	1 Labor Foreman (out) 1 Skilled worker 1 Building Laborer	3	8.000	Ea.
	9630	8" diameter			2	12.000	Ea.
	9650	12" diameter			1.70	14.120	Ea.
	9670	16" diameter			1.50	16.000	Ea.
	9690	20" diameter			1.30	18.460	Ea.
	9700	24" diameter			1.20	20.000	Ea.
670		**PIPING, WATER DISTRIBUTION, PLASTIC**					
	0020	Not including excavation or backfill					
	1100	Reinforced plastic pipe, general strength, 18" diameter	B-21	1 Labor Foreman (out) 1 Skilled worker 1 Building Laborer .5 Equip. Oper. (crane) .5 S.P. Crane, 5 Ton	90	.311	L.F.
	1120	21" diameter			80	.350	L.F.
	1130	24" diameter			70	.400	L.F.
	1140	27" diameter			60	.467	L.F.
	1160	30" diameter			50	.560	L.F.
	1180	36" diameter			40	.700	L.F.
674		**PIPING, WATER DISTRIBUTION, POLYETHYLENE**					
	0020	Not including excavation or backfill					
	1000	Piping, 160 P.S.I., 3/4" diameter	B-20	1 Labor Foreman (out) 1 Skilled worker 1 Building Laborer	525	.046	L.F.
	1120	1" diameter			485	.049	L.F.
	1140	1-1/2" diameter			450	.053	L.F.
	1160	2" diameter			365	.066	L.F.
678		**PIPING, WATER DISTRIBUTION, POLYVINYL CHLORIDE**					
	0020	Not including excavation or backfill					
	2100	Class 160, S.D.R. 26, 1-1/2" diameter	B-20	1 Labor Foreman (out) 1 Skilled worker 1 Building Laborer	300	.080	L.F.
	2120	2" diameter			250	.096	L.F.
	2140	2-1/2" diameter			250	.096	L.F.
	2160	3" diameter			200	.120	L.F.
	2180	4" diameter			200	.120	L.F.
	2200	6" diameter			180	.133	L.F.

026 650 | Water Systems

			CREW	MAKEUP	DAILY OUTPUT	MAN-HOURS	UNIT
678	8007	Piping, fittings, class 160, bends or elbows, 4" diameter	B-20	1 Labor Foreman (out)	100	.240	Ea.
				1 Skilled worker			
				1 Building Laborer			
	8020	6" diameter			90	.267	Ea.
	8040	8" diameter			80	.300	Ea.
	8060	10" diameter			50	.480	Ea.
	8080	12" diameter			30	.800	Ea.
	8100	Wye or tee, 4" diameter			90	.267	Ea.
	8120	6" diameter			80	.300	Ea.
	8140	8" diameter			70	.343	Ea.
	8160	10" diameter			40	.600	Ea.
	8180	12" diameter	↓	↓	20	1.200	Ea.
690		**DISTRIBUTION CONNECTION**					
	7000	Tapping crosses, sleeves, valves; with duck tip gaskets					
	7020	Crosses, 4" x 4"	B-21	1 Labor Foreman (out)	37	.757	Ea.
				1 Skilled worker			
				1 Building Laborer			
				.5 Equip. Oper. (crane)			
				.5 S.P. Crane, 5 Ton			
	7060	8" x 6"			21	1.330	Ea.
	7080	8" x 8"			21	1.330	Ea.
	7100	10" x 6"			21	1.330	Ea.
	7160	12" x 12"			18	1.560	Ea.
	7180	14" x 6"			16	1.750	Ea.
	7240	16" x 10"			14	2.000	Ea.
	7280	18" x 6"			10	2.800	Ea.
	7320	18" x 18"			10	2.800	Ea.
	7340	20" x 6"			8	3.500	Ea.
	7360	20" x 12"			8	3.500	Ea.
	7420	24" x 12"			6	4.670	Ea.
	7440	24" x 18"			6	4.670	Ea.
	7600	Cut-in sleeves with duck tip gaskets, 4"			18	1.560	Ea.
	7640	8"			10	2.800	Ea.
	7680	12"			9	3.110	Ea.
	7800	Cut-in valves with duck tip gaskets, 4"			18	1.560	Ea.
	7840	8"			10	2.800	Ea.
	7880	12"			9	3.110	Ea.
	8000	Sleeves with duck tip gaskets, 4" x 4"			37	.757	Ea.
	8040	8" x 6"			21	1.330	Ea.
	8060	8" x 8"			21	1.330	Ea.
	8080	10" x 6"			21	1.330	Ea.
	8140	12" x 12"			18	1.560	Ea.
	8160	14" x 6"			16	1.750	Ea.
	8220	16" x 10"			14	2.000	Ea.
	8260	18" x 6"			10	2.800	Ea.
	8300	18" x 18"			10	2.800	Ea.
	8320	20" x 6"			8	3.500	Ea.
	8340	20" x 12"			8	3.500	Ea.
	8400	24" x 12"			6	4.670	Ea.
	8420	24" x 18"	↓	↓	6	4.670	Ea.
	8800	Curb box, 6' long	B-20	1 Labor Foreman (out)	20	1.200	Ea.
				1 Skilled worker			
				1 Building Laborer			
	8820	8' long	"	"	18	1.330	Ea.
	8821						

026 650 | Water Systems

		CREW	MAKEUP	DAILY OUTPUT	MAN-HOURS	UNIT
690 9001	Distribution connection, gate valve, N.R.S. post type, 4" dia.	B-21	1 Labor Foreman (out)	32	.875	Ea.
			1 Skilled worker			
			1 Building Laborer			
			.5 Equip. Oper. (crane)			
			.5 S.P. Crane, 5 Ton			
9040	8" diameter			16	1.750	Ea.
9080	12" diameter			13	2.150	Ea.
9120	O.S.&Y., 4" diameter			32	.875	Ea.
9160	8" diameter			16	1.750	Ea.
9200	12" diameter			13	2.150	Ea.
9220	14" diameter	↓	↓	11	2.550	Ea.
9400	Check valves, rubber disc, 2-1/2" diameter	B-20	1 Labor Foreman (out)	44	.545	Ea.
			1 Skilled worker			
			1 Building Laborer			
9440	4" diameter	B-21	1 Labor Foreman (out)	32	.875	Ea.
			1 Skilled worker			
			1 Building Laborer			
			.5 Equip. Oper. (crane)			
			.5 S.P. Crane, 5 Ton			
9500	8" diameter			16	1.750	Ea.
9540	12" diameter			13	2.150	Ea.
9700	Detector check valves, red, 4" diameter			32	.875	Ea.
9740	8" diameter			16	1.750	Ea.
9800	Galvanized, 4" diameter			32	.875	Ea.
9840	8" diameter	↓	↓	16	1.750	Ea.

026 700 | Water Wells

		CREW	MAKEUP	DAILY OUTPUT	MAN-HOURS	UNIT
704	**WELLS** Domestic water, drilled and cased, including casing					
0100	4" to 6" diameter	B-23	1 Labor Foreman (outside)	160	.250	V.L.F.
			4 Building Laborers			
			1 Drill Rig			
			1 Light Truck, 3 Ton			
0200	8" diameter	"	"	127	.315	V.L.F.
0400	Gravel pack well, 40' deep, incl. gravel & casing, complete					
0500	24" diameter casing x 18" diameter screen	B-23	1 Labor Foreman (outside)	.13	308.000	Total
			4 Building Laborers			
			1 Drill Rig			
			1 Light Truck, 3 Ton			
0600	36" diameter casing x 18" diameter screen			.12	333.000	Total
0800	Observation wells, 1-1/4" riser pipe	↓	↓	163	.245	V.L.F.
0900	For flush Buffalo roadway box, add	1 Skwk	1 Skilled Worker	16.60	.482	Ea.
1200	Test well, 2-1/2" diameter, up to 50' deep (15 to 50 GPM)	B-23	1 Labor Foreman (outside)	1.51	26.490	Ea.
			4 Building Laborers			
			1 Drill Rig			
			1 Light Truck, 3 Ton			
1300	Over 50' deep, add	"	"	121.80	.328	L.F.
1500	Pumps, installed in wells to 100' deep, 4" submersible					
1510	1/2 H.P.	B-21	1 Labor Foreman (out)	1.80	15.560	Ea.
			1 Skilled worker			
			1 Building Laborer			
			.5 Equip. Oper. (crane)			
			.5 S.P. Crane, 5 Ton			
1520	3/4 H.P.			1.65	16.970	Ea.
1600	1 H.P.			1.10	25.450	Ea.
1700	1-1/2 H.P.			1	28.000	Ea.
1800	2 H.P.			1	28.000	Ea.
1900	3 H.P.			.90	31.110	Ea.
2000	5 H.P.	↓	↓	.90	31.110	Ea.

026 700	Water Wells	CREW	MAKEUP	DAILY OUTPUT	MAN-HOURS	UNIT
704 3001	Well pump, 6" submersible, 25'-150' deep, 25 H.P., 249-297 GPM	B-21	1 Labor Foreman (out)	.70	40.000	Ea.
			1 Skilled worker			
			1 Building Laborer			
			.5 Equip. Oper. (crane)			
			.5 S.P. Crane, 5 Ton			
3100	25' to 500' deep, 30 H.P., 100 to 300 GPM	"	"	.50	56.000	Ea.

026 850	Gas Distribution System	CREW	MAKEUP	DAILY OUTPUT	MAN-HOURS	UNIT
854	PIPING, GAS SERVICE & DISTRIBUTION, POLYETHYLENE					
0020	not including excavation or backfill					
1000	60 psi coils, 1/2" diameter, SDR 7	B-20	1 Labor Foreman (out)	450	.053	L.F.
			1 Skilled worker			
			1 Building Laborer			
1040	1-1/4" diameter, SDR 10			400	.060	L.F.
1100	2" diameter, SDR 11			360	.067	L.F.
1160	3" diameter, SDR 11.5	↓	↓	300	.080	L.F.
1500	40' joints with coupling, 3" diameter, SDR 11.5	B-21	1 Labor Foreman (out)	300	.093	L.F.
			1 Skilled worker			
			1 Building Laborer			
			.5 Equip. Oper. (crane)			
			.5 S.P. Crane, 5 Ton			
1540	4" diameter, SDR 11			260	.108	L.F.
1600	6" diameter, SDR 21			240	.117	L.F.
1640	8" diameter, SDR 21	↓	↓	200	.140	L.F.
856	PIPING, GAS SERVICE & DISTRIBUTION, STEEL					
0020	not including excavation or backfill, tar coated and wrapped					
4000	Schedule 40, plain end					
4040	1" diameter	Q-4	1 Plumber Foreman (ins)	300	.107	L.F.
			1 Plumber			
			1 Welder (plumber)			
			1 Plumber Apprentice			
			1 Electric Welding Mach.			
4080	2" diameter			280	.114	L.F.
4120	3" diameter	↓	↓	260	.123	L.F.
4160	4" diameter	B-35	1 Laborer Foreman (out)	255	.188	L.F.
			1 Skilled worker			
			1 Welder (plumber)			
			1 Laborer			
			1 Equip. Oper. (crane)			
			1 Equip. Oper. Oiler			
			1 Electric Welding Mach.			
			1 Hyd. Excavator, .75 C.Y.			
4200	5" diameter			220	.218	L.F.
4240	6" diameter			180	.267	L.F.
4280	8" diameter	↓	↓	140	.343	L.F.
4320	10" diameter	B-21	1 Labor Foreman (out)	100	.280	L.F.
			1 Skilled worker			
			1 Building Laborer			
			.5 Equip. Oper. (crane)			
			.5 S.P. Crane, 5 Ton			
4360	12" diameter			80	.350	L.F.
4400	14" diameter			75	.373	L.F.
4440	16" diameter	↓	↓	70	.400	L.F.
4480	18" diameter	B-22	1 Labor Foreman (out)	65	.462	L.F.
			1 Skilled worker			
			1 Building Laborer			
			.75 Equip. Oper. (crane)			
			.75 S.P. Crane, 5 Ton			

026 850	Gas Distribution System	CREW	MAKEUP	DAILY OUTPUT	MAN-HOURS	UNIT
856 4521	Piping, gas, schedule 40, plain end, 20" diameter	B-22	1 Labor Foreman (out)	60	.500	L.F.
			1 Skilled worker			
			1 Building Laborer			
			.75 Equip. Oper. (crane)			
			.75 S.P. Crane, 5 Ton			
4560	24" diameter	"	"	50	.600	L.F.
5000	Threaded and coupled					
5002	4" diameter	B-20	1 Labor Foreman (out)	144	.167	L.F.
			1 Skilled worker			
			1 Building Laborer			
5008	8" diameter	B-21	1 Labor Foreman (out)	108	.259	L.F.
			1 Skilled worker			
			1 Building Laborer			
			.5 Equip. Oper. (crane)			
			.5 S.P. Crane, 5 Ton			
5012	12" diameter	"	"	72	.389	L.F.
6000	Schedule 80, plain end					
6002	4" diameter	B-20	1 Labor Foreman (out)	144	.167	L.F.
			1 Skilled worker			
			1 Building Laborer			
6006	6" diameter	B-21	1 Labor Foreman (out)	126	.222	L.F.
			1 Skilled worker			
			1 Building Laborer			
			.5 Equip. Oper. (crane)			
			.5 S.P. Crane, 5 Ton			
6008	8" diameter			108	.259	L.F.
6012	12" diameter			72	.389	L.F.
6016	16" diameter, 1/2" wall			48	.583	L.F.
6020	20" diameter, 1/2" wall	B-22	1 Labor Foreman (out)	38	.789	L.F.
			1 Skilled worker			
			1 Building Laborer			
			.75 Equip. Oper. (crane)			
			.75 S.P. Crane, 5 Ton			
6022	24" diameter, 1/2" wall	"	"	36	.833	L.F.
8008	Elbow, weld joint, standard weight					
8020	4" diameter	Q-16	2 Plumbers	6.80	3.530	Ea.
			1 Plumber Apprentice			
			1 Electric Welding Mach.			
8026	8" diameter			3.40	7.060	Ea.
8030	12" diameter			2.30	10.430	Ea.
8034	16" diameter			1.50	16.000	Ea.
8038	20" diameter			1.20	20.000	Ea.
8040	24" diameter			1.02	23.530	Ea.
8100	Extra heavy					
8102	4" diameter	Q-16	2 Plumbers	5.30	4.530	Ea.
			1 Plumber Apprentice			
			1 Electric Welding Mach.			
8108	8" diameter			2.60	9.230	Ea.
8112	12" diameter			1.80	13.330	Ea.
8116	16" diameter			1.20	20.000	Ea.
8120	20" diameter			.94	25.530	Ea.
8122	24" diameter			.80	30.000	Ea.
8200	Malleable, standard weight					
8202	4" diameter	B-20	1 Labor Foreman (out)	12	2.000	Ea.
			1 Skilled worker			
			1 Building Laborer			
8208	8" diameter			6	4.000	Ea.
8212	12" diameter			4	6.000	Ea.

026 | Piped Utilities

026 850 | Gas Distribution System

		Description	CREW	MAKEUP	DAILY OUTPUT	MAN-HOURS	UNIT
856	8303	Piping, gas, elbow, malleable, extra heavy, 4" diameter	B-20	1 Labor Foreman (out)	12	2.000	Ea.
				1 Skilled worker			
				1 Building Laborer			
	8308	8" diameter	B-21	1 Labor Foreman (out)	6	4.670	Ea.
				1 Skilled worker			
				1 Building Laborer			
				.5 Equip. Oper. (crane)			
				.5 S.P. Crane, 5 Ton			
	8312	12" diameter	"	"	4	7.000	Ea.
	8500	Tee weld, standard weight					
	8510	4" diameter	Q-16	2 Plumbers	4.50	5.330	Ea.
				1 Plumber Apprentice			
				1 Electric Welding Mach.			
	8514	6" diameter			3	8.000	Ea.
	8516	8" diameter			2.30	10.430	Ea.
	8520	12" diameter			1.50	16.000	Ea.
	8524	16" diameter			1	24.000	Ea.
	8528	20" diameter			.80	30.000	Ea.
	8530	24" diameter			.70	34.290	Ea.
	8810	Malleable, standard weight					
	8812	4" diameter	B-20	1 Labor Foreman (out)	8	3.000	Ea.
				1 Skilled worker			
				1 Building Laborer			
	8818	8" diameter	B-21	1 Labor Foreman (out)	4	7.000	Ea.
				1 Skilled worker			
				1 Building Laborer			
				.5 Equip. Oper. (crane)			
				.5 S.P. Crane, 5 Ton			
	8822	12" diameter	"	"	2.70	10.370	Ea.
	8900	Extra heavy					
	8902	4" diameter	B-20	1 Labor Foreman (out)	8	3.000	Ea.
				1 Skilled worker			
				1 Building Laborer			
	8908	8" diameter	B-21	1 Labor Foreman (out)	4	7.000	Ea.
				1 Skilled worker			
				1 Building Laborer			
				.5 Equip. Oper. (crane)			
				.5 S.P. Crane, 5 Ton			
	8912	12" diameter	"	"	2.70	10.370	Ea.
858		**PIPING, VALVES, GAS DISTRIBUTION**					
	0020	not including excavation or backfill					
	0100	Gas stops, with or without checks					
	0140	1-1/4" size	1 Plum	1 Plumber	12	.667	Ea.
	0180	1-1/2" size			10	.800	Ea.
	0200	2" size jx gas valve			8	1.000	Ea.
	0600	Pressure reducing valves iron and bronze					
	0640	1-1/2" diameter	1 Plum	1 Plumber	5	1.600	Ea.
	0680	2" diameter			4.50	1.780	Ea.
	0700	3" diameter			3.50	2.290	Ea.
	0740	4" diameter			2.50	3.200	Ea.
	0780	6" diameter	Q-1	1 Plumber	2	8.000	Ea.
				1 Plumber Apprentice			
	0800	8" diameter			1.50	10.670	Ea.
	0840	10" diameter			1	16.000	Ea.
	2000	Lubricated semi-steel plug valve					
	2040	3/4" diameter	1 Plum	1 Plumber	16	.500	Ea.
	2080	1" diameter			14	.571	Ea.
	2100	1-1/4" diameter			12	.667	Ea.

026 | Piped Utilities

026 850 | Gas Distribution System

		CREW	MAKEUP	DAILY OUTPUT	MAN-HOURS	UNIT
858	2141	Piping, lubricated semi-steel plug valve, 1-1/2" diameter	1 Plum	1 Plumber	11	.727	Ea.
	2180	2" diameter	"	"	8	1.000	Ea.
	2300	2-1/2" diameter	Q-1	1 Plumber	5	3.200	Ea.
				1 Plumber Apprentice			
	2340	3" diameter	"	"	4.50	3.560	Ea.

027 | Sewerage & Drainage

027 050 | Drainage

		CREW	MAKEUP	DAILY OUTPUT	MAN-HOURS	UNIT
054	DRAINAGE , geotextiles					
0100	Fabric, laid in trench, polypropylene, ideal conditions	2 Clab	2 Building Laborers	2,400	.007	S.Y.
0110	Adverse conditions			1,600	.010	S.Y.
0170	Fabric ply bonded to 3 dimen. nylon mat, .4" thk, ideal conditions			2,000	.008	S.F.
0180	Adverse conditions			1,200	.013	S.F.
0190	0.8" thick, ideal conditions			2,400	.007	S.F.
0200	Adverse conditions	↓	↓	1,600	.010	S.F.
0300	Drainage material, 3/4" stone	B-6	2 Building Laborers	260	.092	C.Y.
			1 Equip. Oper. (light)			
			1 Backhoe Loader, 48 H.P.			
0400	Pea stone	"	"	260	.092	C.Y.

027 100 | Subdrainage Systems

		CREW	MAKEUP	DAILY OUTPUT	MAN-HOURS	UNIT
104	PIPING, SUBDRAINAGE, ASBESTOS CEMENT					
0021	Not including excavation and backfill					
2000	Class 4000 underdrain, perforated					
2040	4" diameter	B-20	1 Labor Foreman (out)	390	.062	L.F.
			1 Skilled worker			
			1 Building Laborer			
2080	6" diameter	"	"	380	.063	L.F.
2120	8" diameter	B-21	1 Labor Foreman (out)	370	.076	L.F.
			1 Skilled worker			
			1 Building Laborer			
			.5 Equip. Oper. (crane)			
			.5 S.P. Crane, 5 Ton			
2160	10" diameter	↓	↓	365	.077	L.F.
2200	12" diameter			360	.078	L.F.
2800	Unperforated, 4" diameter	B-20	1 Labor Foreman (out)	390	.062	L.F.
			1 Skilled worker			
			1 Building Laborer			
2840	6" diameter	"	"	380	.063	L.F.
2860	8" diameter	B-21	1 Labor Foreman (out)	370	.076	L.F.
			1 Skilled worker			
			1 Building Laborer			
			.5 Equip. Oper. (crane)			
			.5 S.P. Crane, 5 Ton			
2880	10" diameter	↓	↓	365	.077	L.F.
2900	12" diameter			360	.078	L.F.
8000	45 degree elbow, 4" diameter	B-20	1 Labor Foreman (out)	35	.686	Ea.
			1 Skilled worker			
			1 Building Laborer			
8020	6" diameter			30	.800	Ea.
8040	8" diameter	↓	↓	28	.857	Ea.

027 100 | Subdrainage Systems

		Description	CREW	MAKEUP	DAILY OUTPUT	MAN-HOURS	UNIT
104	8061	Piping, asbestos cement, 45 degree elbow, 10" diameter	B-20	1 Labor Foreman (out) 1 Skilled worker 1 Building Laborer	25	.960	Ea.
	8080	12" diameter			20	1.200	Ea.
	8100	Tees,			30	.800	Ea.
	8120	6" diameter			27	.889	Ea.
	8140	8" diameter			25	.960	Ea.
	8160	10" diameter			21	1.140	Ea.
	8180	12" diameter			18	1.330	Ea.
	106	PIPING, SUBDRAINAGE, BITUMINOUS					
	0021	Not including excavation and backfill					
	2000	Perforated underdrain, 3" diameter	B-20	1 Labor Foreman (out) 1 Skilled worker 1 Building Laborer	800	.030	L.F.
	2020	4" diameter			760	.032	L.F.
	2040	5" diameter			720	.033	L.F.
	2060	6" diameter			680	.035	L.F.
	108	PIPING, SUBDRAINAGE, CONCRETE					
	0021	Not including excavation and backfill					
	3000	Porous wall concrete underdrain, std. strength, 4" diameter	B-20	1 Labor Foreman (out) 1 Skilled worker 1 Building Laborer	335	.072	L.F.
	3020	6" diameter	"	"	315	.076	L.F.
	3040	8" diameter	B-21	1 Labor Foreman (out) 1 Skilled worker 1 Building Laborer .5 Equip. Oper. (crane) .5 S.P. Crane, 5 Ton	310	.090	L.F.
	3060	12" diameter			285	.098	L.F.
	3080	15" diameter			230	.122	L.F.
	3100	18" diameter			165	.170	L.F.
	4000	Extra strength, 6" diameter	B-20	1 Labor Foreman (out) 1 Skilled worker 1 Building Laborer	315	.076	L.F.
	4020	8" diameter	B-21	1 Labor Foreman (out) 1 Skilled worker 1 Building Laborer .5 Equip. Oper. (crane) .5 S.P. Crane, 5 Ton	310	.090	L.F.
	4040	10" diameter			285	.098	L.F.
	4060	12" diameter			230	.122	L.F.
	4080	15" diameter			200	.140	L.F.
	4100	18" diameter			165	.170	L.F.
	110	PIPING, SUBDRAINAGE, CORRUGATED METAL					
	0021	Not including excavation and backfill					
	2010	Aluminum or steel, perforated, asphalt coated					
	2020	6" diameter, 18 ga.	B-20	1 Labor Foreman (out) 1 Skilled worker 1 Building Laborer	380	.063	L.F.
	2200	8" diameter, 16 ga.	"	"	370	.065	L.F.
	2220	10" diameter, 16 ga.	B-21	1 Labor Foreman (out) 1 Skilled worker 1 Building Laborer .5 Equip. Oper. (crane) .5 S.P. Crane, 5 Ton	360	.078	L.F.
	2240	12" diameter, 16 ga.			285	.098	L.F.
	2260	18" diameter, 16 ga.			205	.137	L.F.
	3001						

027 100 | Subdrainage Systems

		CREW	MAKEUP	DAILY OUTPUT	MAN-HOURS	UNIT
110 3021	Piping, aluminum or steel, uncoated, 6" dia., 18 ga.	B-20	1 Labor Foreman (out)	380	.063	L.F.
			1 Skilled worker			
			1 Building Laborer			
3200	8" diameter, 16 ga.	"	"	370	.065	L.F.
3220	10" diameter, 16 ga.	B-21	1 Labor Foreman (out)	360	.078	L.F.
			1 Skilled worker			
			1 Building Laborer			
			.5 Equip. Oper. (crane)			
			.5 S.P. Crane, 5 Ton			
3240	12" diameter, 16 ga.	↓	↓	285	.098	L.F.
3260	18" diameter, 16 ga.			205	.137	L.F.
112	PIPING, SUBDRAINAGE, VITRIFIED CLAY					
0020	Not including excavation and backfill					
3000	Perforated, 6' lengths, C700, 4" diameter	B-20	1 Labor Foreman (out)	400	.060	L.F.
			1 Skilled worker			
			1 Building Laborer			
3020	6" diameter	↓	↓	315	.076	L.F.
3040	8" diameter			290	.083	L.F.
3050	10" diameter	B-21	1 Labor Foreman (out)	320	.088	L.F.
			1 Skilled worker			
			1 Building Laborer			
			.5 Equip. Oper. (crane)			
			.5 S.P. Crane, 5 Ton			
3060	12" diameter	"	"	275	.102	L.F.
4000	Channel pipe, 4" diameter	B-20	1 Labor Foreman (out)	430	.056	L.F.
			1 Skilled worker			
			1 Building Laborer			
4020	6" diameter	↓	↓	335	.072	L.F.
4060	8" diameter			295	.081	L.F.
4080	12" diameter	B-21	1 Labor Foreman (out)	280	.100	L.F.
			1 Skilled worker			
			1 Building Laborer			
			.5 Equip. Oper. (crane)			
			.5 S.P. Crane, 5 Ton			
7998	Fittings					
8000	Elbows, 4" diameter	B-20	1 Labor Foreman (out)	35	.686	Ea.
			1 Skilled worker			
			1 Building Laborer			
8020	6" diameter			30	.800	Ea.
8040	8" diameter			28	.857	Ea.
8060	10" diameter			25	.960	Ea.
8080	12" diameter			20	1.200	Ea.
8100	Tees, 4" diameter			30	.800	Ea.
8120	6" diameter			27	.889	Ea.
8140	8" diameter			25	.960	Ea.
8160	10" diameter			21	1.140	Ea.
8180	12" diameter	↓	↓	18	1.330	Ea.

027 150 | Sewage Systems

		CREW	MAKEUP	DAILY OUTPUT	MAN-HOURS	UNIT
152	CATCH BASINS OR MANHOLES Including footing & excavation,					
0020	not including frame and cover					
0050	Brick, 4' inside diameter, 4' deep	D-1	1 Bricklayer	1	16.000	Ea.
			1 Bricklayer Helper			
0100	6' deep			.70	22.860	Ea.
0150	8' deep			.50	32.000	Ea.
0200	For depths over 8', add			4	4.000	V.L.F.
0400	Concrete blocks (radial), 4' I.D., 4' deep			1.50	10.670	Ea.
0500	6' deep	↓	↓	1	16.000	Ea.

027 150	Sewage Systems	CREW	MAKEUP	DAILY OUTPUT	MAN-HOURS	UNIT
152 0601	Catch basin or manhole, concrete block, 4' I.D., 8' deep	D-1	1 Bricklayer	.70	22.860	Ea.
			1 Bricklayer Helper			
0700	For depths over 8', add	"	"	5.50	2.910	V.L.F.
0800	Concrete, cast in place, 4' x 4', 8" thick, 4' deep	B-6	2 Building Laborers	2	12.000	Ea.
			1 Equip. Oper. (light)			
			1 Backhoe Loader, 48 H.P.			
0900	6' deep			1.50	16.000	Ea.
1000	8' deep			1	24.000	Ea.
1100	For depths over 8', add			8	3.000	V.L.F.
1110	Precast, 4' I.D., 4' deep			4.10	5.850	Ea.
1120	6' deep			3	8.000	Ea.
1130	8' deep			2	12.000	Ea.
1140	For depths over 8', add			16	1.500	V.L.F.
1150	5' I.D., 4' deep			3	8.000	Ea.
1160	6' deep			2	12.000	Ea.
1170	8' deep			1.50	16.000	Ea.
1180	For depths over 8', add			12	2.000	V.L.F.
1190	6' I.D., 4' deep			2	12.000	Ea.
1200	6' deep			1.50	16.000	Ea.
1210	8' deep			1	24.000	Ea.
1220	For depths over 8', add	↓	↓	8	3.000	V.L.F.
1250	Slab tops, precast, 8" thick					
1300	4' diameter manhole	B-6	2 Building Laborers	8	3.000	Ea.
			1 Equip. Oper. (light)			
			1 Backhoe Loader, 48 H.P.			
1400	5' diameter manhole			7.50	3.200	Ea.
1500	6' diameter manhole			7	3.430	Ea.
1600	Frames and covers, C.I., 24" square, 500 lb.			7.80	3.080	Ea.
1700	26" D shape, 600 lb.			7	3.430	Ea.
1800	Light traffic, 18" diameter, 100 lb.			10	2.400	Ea.
1900	24" diameter, 300 lb.			8.70	2.760	Ea.
2000	36" diameter, 900 lb.			5.80	4.140	Ea.
2100	Heavy traffic, 24" diameter, 400 lb.			7.80	3.080	Ea.
2200	36" diameter, 1150 lb.			3	8.000	Ea.
2300	Mass. State standard, 26" diameter, 475 lb.			7	3.430	Ea.
2400	30" diameter, 620 lb.			7	3.430	Ea.
2500	Watertight, 24" diameter, 350 lb.			7.80	3.080	Ea.
2600	26" diameter, 500 lb.			7	3.430	Ea.
2700	32" diameter, 575 lb.	↓	↓	6	4.000	Ea.
2800	3 piece cover & frame, 10" deep,					
2900	1200 lbs., for heavy equipment	B-6	2 Building Laborers	3	8.000	Ea.
			1 Equip. Oper. (light)			
			1 Backhoe Loader, 48 H.P.			
3000	Raised for paving 1-1/4" to 2" high,					
3100	4 piece expansion ring					
3200	20" to 26" diameter	1 Clab	1 Building Laborer	3	2.670	Ea.
3300	30" to 36" diameter	"	"	3	2.670	Ea.
3320	Frames and covers, existing, raised for paving 2", including					
3340	row of brick, concrete collar, up to 12" wide frame	B-9	1 Labor Foreman (outside)	18	2.220	Ea.
			4 Building Laborers			
			1 Air Compr., 250 C.F.M.			
			Air Tools & Accessories			
			2-50 Ft. Air Hoses, 1.5" Dia.			
3360	20" to 26" wide frame			11	3.640	Ea.
3380	30" to 36" wide frame	↓	↓	9	4.440	Ea.
3400	Inverts, single channel brick	D-1	1 Bricklayer	3	5.330	Ea.
			1 Bricklayer Helper			
3500	Concrete	"	"	5	3.200	Ea.

027 150 | Sewage Systems

		Description	CREW	MAKEUP	DAILY OUTPUT	MAN-HOURS	UNIT
152	3601	Catch basin or manhole, inverts, triple channel, brick	D-1	1 Bricklayer	2	8.000	Ea.
				1 Bricklayer Helper			
	3700	Concrete	"	"	3	5.330	Ea.
	3800	Steps, heavyweight cast iron, 7" x 9"	1 Bric	1 Bricklayer	40	.200	Ea.
	3900	8" x 9"			40	.200	Ea.
	4000	Standard sizes, galvanized steel			40	.200	Ea.
	4100	Aluminum	↓	↓	40	.200	Ea.
155		**MANHOLE COVERS** and frames					
	0200	Aluminum, plain cover, lightweight, 12" x 12" opening	1 Sswk	1 Struc. Steel Worker	9	.889	Ea.
	0300	18" x 18" opening			8	1.000	Ea.
	0400	24" x 24" opening			7	1.140	Ea.
	0600	Heavyweight, 24" x 24" opening	↓	↓	6	1.330	Ea.
158		**PIPING, DRAINAGE & SEWAGE, ASBESTOS CEMENT**					
	0020	Not including excavation or backfill					
	2000	Class 2400, 6" diameter	B-20	1 Labor Foreman (out)	330	.073	L.F.
				1 Skilled worker			
				1 Building Laborer			
	2040	8" diameter	B-21	1 Labor Foreman (out)	380	.074	L.F.
				1 Skilled worker			
				1 Building Laborer			
				.5 Equip. Oper. (crane)			
				.5 S.P. Crane, 5 Ton			
	2080	10" diameter			330	.085	L.F.
	2120	12" diameter			280	.100	L.F.
	2160	14" diameter			245	.114	L.F.
	2200	16" diameter			210	.133	L.F.
	3000	Class 4000, truckload lots, 10" diameter			320	.088	L.F.
	3040	12" diameter			265	.106	L.F.
	3080	14" diameter			235	.119	L.F.
	3120	16" diameter			200	.140	L.F.
	3200	18" diameter	↓	↓	150	.187	L.F.
	3240	24" diameter	B-22	1 Labor Foreman (out)	115	.261	L.F.
				1 Skilled worker			
				1 Building Laborer			
				.75 Equip. Oper. (crane)			
				.75 S.P. Crane, 5 Ton			
	3280	30" diameter			80	.375	L.F.
	3320	36" diameter	↓	↓	65	.462	L.F.
160		**PIPING, DRAINAGE & SEWAGE, BITUMINOUS FIBER**					
	0020	Not including excavation or backfill					
	2000	Plain, 2" diameter	2 Clab	2 Building Laborers	400	.040	L.F.
	2040	3" diameter			400	.040	L.F.
	2080	4" diameter			380	.042	L.F.
	2120	5" diameter			360	.044	L.F.
	2200	6" diameter			340	.047	L.F.
	2240	8" diameter	↓	↓	300	.053	L.F.
162		**PIPING, DRAINAGE & SEWAGE, CONCRETE**					
	0020	Not including excavation or backfill					
	0100	Box culvert, precast, base price, 8' long, 6' x 3'	B-69	1 Labor Foreman (outside)	140	.343	L.F.
				3 Highway Laborers			
				1 Equip Oper. (crane)			
				1 Equip Oper. Oiler			
				1 Truck Crane, 80 Ton			
	0150	6' x 7'			125	.384	L.F.
	0200	8' x 3'			133	.361	L.F.
	0250	8' x 8'			100	.480	L.F.
	0300	10' x 3'			110	.436	L.F.
	0350	10' x 8'	↓	↓	80	.600	L.F.

027 150 | Sewage Systems

		CREW	MAKEUP	DAILY OUTPUT	MAN-HOURS	UNIT
162 0401	Piping, precast concrete, box culvert, 8' long, 12' x 3'	B-69	1 Labor Foreman (outside)	100	.480	L.F.
			3 Highway Laborers			
			1 Equip Oper. (crane)			
			1 Equip Oper. Oiler			
			1 Truck Crane, 80 Ton			
0450	12' x 8'	"	"	67	.716	L.F.
1000	Non-reinforced pipe, extra strength, B&S or T&G joints					
1010	6" diameter	B-20	1 Labor Foreman (out)	150	.160	L.F.
			1 Skilled worker			
			1 Building Laborer			
1020	8" diameter	B-21	1 Labor Foreman (out)	200	.140	L.F.
			1 Skilled worker			
			1 Building Laborer			
			.5 Equip. Oper. (crane)			
			.5 S.P. Crane, 5 Ton			
1030	10" diameter			173	.162	L.F.
1040	12" diameter			173	.162	L.F.
1050	15" diameter			167	.168	L.F.
1060	18" diameter			167	.168	L.F.
1070	21" diameter			153	.183	L.F.
1080	24" diameter	↓	↓	153	.183	L.F.
1560	Reinforced culvert, class 2, no gaskets					
1590	27" diameter	B-21	1 Labor Foreman (out)	145	.193	L.F.
			1 Skilled worker			
			1 Building Laborer			
			.5 Equip. Oper. (crane)			
			.5 S.P. Crane, 5 Ton			
1592	30" diameter			132	.212	L.F.
1594	36" diameter	↓	↓	112	.250	L.F.
2000	Reinforced culvert, class 3, no gaskets					
2010	12" diameter	B-21	1 Labor Foreman (out)	190	.147	L.F.
			1 Skilled worker			
			1 Building Laborer			
			.5 Equip. Oper. (crane)			
			.5 S.P. Crane, 5 Ton			
2020	15" diameter			155	.181	L.F.
2030	18" diameter			122	.230	L.F.
2035	21" diameter			105	.267	L.F.
2040	24" diameter			88	.318	L.F.
2045	27" diameter	↓	↓	84	.333	L.F.
2050	30" diameter	B-13	1 Labor Foreman (outside)	80	.700	L.F.
			4 Building Laborers			
			1 Equip. Oper. (crane)			
			1 Equip. Oper. Oiler			
			1 Hyd. Crane, 25 Ton			
2060	36" diameter			60	.933	L.F.
2070	42" diameter			55	1.020	L.F.
2080	48" diameter			50	1.120	L.F.
2090	60" diameter			35	1.600	L.F.
2100	72" diameter			30	1.870	L.F.
2120	84" diameter			24	2.330	L.F.
2140	96" diameter	↓	↓	20	2.800	L.F.
2200	With gaskets, class 3, 12" diameter	B-21	1 Labor Foreman (out)	210	.133	L.F.
			1 Skilled worker			
			1 Building Laborer			
			.5 Equip. Oper. (crane)			
			.5 S.P. Crane, 5 Ton			
2220	15" diameter	"	"	175	.160	L.F.

027 150	Sewage Systems	CREW	MAKEUP	DAILY OUTPUT	MAN-HOURS	UNIT
162 2231	Piping, concrete, reinforced culvert w/gaskets, class 3, 18" dia.	B-21	1 Labor Foreman (out)	150	.187	L.F.
			1 Skilled worker			
			1 Building Laborer			
			.5 Equip. Oper. (crane)			
			.5 S.P. Crane, 5 Ton			
2240	24" diameter	" "	"	100	.280	L.F.
2260	30" diameter	B-13	1 Labor Foreman (outside)	85	.659	L.F.
			4 Building Laborers			
			1 Equip. Oper. (crane)			
			1 Equip. Oper. Oiler			
			1 Hyd. Crane, 25 Ton			
2270	36" diameter		.	70	.800	L.F.
2290	48" diameter			58	.966	L.F.
2310	72" diameter	↓	↓	38	1.470	L.F.
2330	Flared ends, 6'-1" long, 12" diameter	B-21	1 Labor Foreman (out)	190	.147	Ea.
			1 Skilled worker			
			1 Building Laborer			
			.5 Equip. Oper. (crane)			
			.5 S.P. Crane, 5 Ton			
2340	15" diameter			155	.181	Ea.
2400	6'-2" long, 18" diameter			122	.230	Ea.
2420	24" diameter	↓	↓	88	.318	Ea.
2430	30" diameter	B-13	1 Labor Foreman (outside)	80	.700	Ea.
			4 Building Laborers			
			1 Equip. Oper. (crane)			
			1 Equip. Oper. Oiler			
			1 Hyd. Crane, 25 Ton			
2440	36" diameter	"	"	60	.933	Ea.
2500	Class 4					
2510	12" diameter	B-21	1 Labor Foreman (out)	173	.162	L.F.
			1 Skilled worker			
			1 Building Laborer			
			.5 Equip. Oper. (crane)			
			.5 S.P. Crane, 5 Ton			
2512	15" diameter			167	.168	L.F.
2514	18" diameter			167	.168	L.F.
2516	21" diameter			153	.183	L.F.
2518	24" diameter			153	.183	L.F.
2520	27" diameter			145	.193	L.F.
2522	30" diameter			132	.212	L.F.
2524	36" diameter	↓	↓	112	.250	L.F.
2600	Class 5					
2610	12" diameter	B-21	1 Labor Foreman (out)	173	.162	L.F.
			1 Skilled worker			
			1 Building Laborer			
			.5 Equip. Oper. (crane)			
			.5 S.P. Crane, 5 Ton			
2612	15" diameter			167	.168	L.F.
2614	18" diameter			167	.168	L.F.
2616	21" diameter			153	.183	L.F.
2618	24" diameter			153	.183	L.F.
2620	27" diameter			145	.193	L.F.
2622	30" diameter			132	.212	L.F.
2624	36" diameter	↓	↓	112	.250	L.F.

027 150	Sewage Systems	CREW	MAKEUP	DAILY OUTPUT	MAN-HOURS	UNIT
164	**PIPING, DRAINAGE & SEWAGE, CORRUGATED METAL**					
0020	Not including excavation or backfill					
2000	Corrugated Metal Pipe, galv. or aluminum,					
2020	Bituminous coated with paved invert, 20' to 30' lengths					
2040	8" diameter 16 ga.	B-20	1 Labor Foreman (out)	330	.073	L.F.
			1 Skilled worker			
			1 Building Laborer			
2060	10" diameter 16 ga.			260	.092	L.F.
2080	12" diameter 16 ga.	↓	↓	210	.114	L.F.
2100	15" diameter 16 ga.	B-21	1 Labor Foreman (out)	210	.133	L.F.
			1 Skilled worker			
			1 Building Laborer			
			.5 Equip. Oper. (crane)			
			.5 S.P. Crane, 5 Ton			
2120	18" diameter 16 ga.			190	.147	L.F.
2140	24" diameter 14 ga.			160	.175	L.F.
2160	30" diameter 14 ga.			120	.233	L.F.
2180	36" diameter 12 ga.	↓	↓	100	.280	L.F.
2200	48" diameter 12 ga.	B-13	1 Labor Foreman (outside)	100	.560	L.F.
			4 Building Laborers			
			1 Equip. Oper. (crane)			
			1 Equip. Oper. Oiler			
			1 Hyd. Crane, 25 Ton			
2220	60" diameter 10 ga.	↓	↓	75	.747	L.F.
2240	72" diameter 8 ga.	↓	↓	45	1.240	L.F.
2300	Bends or elbows, 8" diameter	B-20	1 Labor Foreman (out)	28	.857	Ea.
			1 Skilled worker			
			1 Building Laborer			
2320	10" diameter			25	.960	Ea.
2340	12" diameter			20	1.200	Ea.
2360	Wyes or tees, 8" diameter			25	.960	Ea.
2380	10" diameter			21	1.140	Ea.
2400	12" diameter	↓	↓	18	1.330	Ea.
2500	Plain, 20' to 30' lengths					
2520	8" diameter 16 ga.	B-20	1 Labor Foreman (out)	355	.068	L.F.
			1 Skilled worker			
			1 Building Laborer			
2540	10" diameter 16 ga.			280	.086	L.F.
2560	12" diameter 16 ga.	↓	↓	220	.109	L.F.
2580	15" diameter 16 ga.	B-21	1 Labor Foreman (out)	220	.127	L.F.
			1 Skilled worker			
			1 Building Laborer			
			.5 Equip. Oper. (crane)			
			.5 S.P. Crane, 5 Ton			
2600	18" diameter 16 ga.			205	.137	L.F.
2620	24" diameter 14 ga.			175	.160	L.F.
2640	30" diameter 14 ga.	↓	↓	130	.215	L.F.
2660	36" diameter 12 ga.	B-13	1 Labor Foreman (outside)	130	.431	L.F.
			4 Building Laborers			
			1 Equip. Oper. (crane)			
			1 Equip. Oper. Oiler			
			1 Hyd. Crane, 25 Ton			
2680	48" diameter 12 ga.	↓	↓	110	.509	L.F.
2700	60" diameter 10 ga.	↓	↓	78	.718	L.F.

		CREW	MAKEUP	DAILY OUTPUT	MAN-HOURS	UNIT
**027 150	Sewage Systems**						
164 2801	Piping, corrugated metal, plain, end sections, 18" diameter	B-21	1 Labor Foreman (out)	16	1.750	Ea.
			1 Skilled worker			
			1 Building Laborer			
			.5 Equip. Oper. (crane)			
			.5 S.P. Crane, 5 Ton			
2820	30" diameter	"	"	12	2.330	Ea.
3000	Corrugated steel or alum. oval arch culverts, coated & paved					
3020	17" x 11" 16 ga., 15" equivalent	B-22	1 Labor Foreman (out)	200	.150	L.F.
			1 Skilled worker			
			1 Building Laborer			
			.75 Equip. Oper. (crane)			
			.75 S.P. Crane, 5 Ton			
3040	21" x 15" 16 ga., 18" equivalent			150	.200	L.F.
3060	28" x 20" 14 ga., 24" equivalent			125	.240	L.F.
3080	35" x 24" 14 ga., 30" equivalent			100	.300	L.F.
3100	42" x 29" 12 ga., 36" equivalent	B-13	1 Labor Foreman (outside)	100	.560	L.F.
			4 Building Laborers			
			1 Equip. Oper. (crane)			
			1 Equip. Oper. Oiler			
			1 Hyd. Crane, 25 Ton			
3120	49" x 33" 12 ga., 42" equivalent			90	.622	L.F.
3140	57" x 38" 12 ga., 48" equivalent			70	.800	L.F.
3160	Steel or alum. oval arch culverts, plain					
3180	17" x 13" 16 ga., 15" equivalent	B-22	1 Labor Foreman (out)	225	.133	L.F.
			1 Skilled worker			
			1 Building Laborer			
			.75 Equip. Oper. (crane)			
			.75 S.P. Crane, 5 Ton			
3200	21" x 15" 16 ga., 18" equivalent			175	.171	L.F.
3220	28" x 20" 14 ga., 24" equivalent			150	.200	L.F.
3240	35" x 24" 14 ga., 30" equivalent			108	.278	L.F.
3260	42" x 29" 12 ga., 36" equivalent	B-13	1 Labor Foreman (outside)	108	.519	L.F.
			4 Building Laborers			
			1 Equip. Oper. (crane)			
			1 Equip. Oper. Oiler			
			1 Hyd. Crane, 25 Ton			
3280	49" x 33" 12 ga., 42" equivalent			92	.609	L.F.
3300	57" x 38" 12 ga., 48" equivalent			75	.747	L.F.
3320	End sections, 18" x 11"			22	2.550	Ea.
3340	43" x 27"			17	3.290	Ea.
3360	Multi-plate arch, steel	B-20	1 Labor Foreman (out)	1,690	.014	Lb.
			1 Skilled worker			
			1 Building Laborer			
166 0020	**PIPING, DRAINAGE & SEWAGE, PLASTIC**					
	Not including excavation & backfill					
1000	Reinforced plastic pipe, general strength, 4" diameter	B-20	1 Labor Foreman (out)	190	.126	L.F.
			1 Skilled worker			
			1 Building Laborer			
1020	8" diameter	B-21	1 Labor Foreman (out)	160	.175	L.F.
			1 Skilled worker			
			1 Building Laborer			
			.5 Equip. Oper. (crane)			
			.5 S.P. Crane, 5 Ton			
1040	12" diameter	"	"	100	.280	L.F.
5000	High strength, 4" diameter	B-20	1 Labor Foreman (out)	190	.126	L.F.
			1 Skilled worker			
			1 Building Laborer			

027 150 | Sewage Systems

		Description	CREW	MAKEUP	DAILY OUTPUT	MAN-HOURS	UNIT
166	5021	Piping, reinforced plastic, high strength, 8" diameter	B-21	1 Labor Foreman (out)	160	.175	L.F.
				1 Skilled worker			
				1 Building Laborer			
				.5 Equip. Oper. (crane)			
				.5 S.P. Crane, 5 Ton			
	5040	12" diameter	"	"	100	.280	L.F.
	9100	Bends and elbows, general strength, 4" diameter	B-20	1 Labor Foreman (out)	19	1.260	Ea.
				1 Skilled worker			
				1 Building Laborer			
	9120	8" diameter			11	2.180	Ea.
	9140	12" diameter			6	4.000	Ea.
	9210	High strength, 4" diameter			19	1.260	Ea.
	9230	8" diameter			11	2.180	Ea.
	9250	12" diameter			6	4.000	Ea.
	9610	Wyes and tees, general strength, 4" diameter			12	2.000	Ea.
	9630	8" diameter			7	3.430	Ea.
	9650	12" diameter			5	4.800	Ea.
	9710	High strength, 4" diameter			12	2.000	Ea.
	9730	8" diameter			7	3.430	Ea.
	9750	12" diameter	↓	↓	5	4.800	Ea.
168		**PIPING, DRAINAGE & SEWAGE, POLYVINYL CHLORIDE**					
	0020	Not including excavation or backfill					
	2000	10' lengths, S.D.R. 35, 4" diameter	B-20	1 Labor Foreman (out)	375	.064	L.F.
				1 Skilled worker			
				1 Building Laborer			
	2040	6" diameter	↓		350	.069	L.F.
	2080	8" diameter	↓	↓	335	.072	L.F.
	2120	10" diameter	B-21	1 Labor Foreman (out)	330	.085	L.F.
				1 Skilled worker			
				1 Building Laborer			
				.5 Equip. Oper. (crane)			
				.5 S.P. Crane, 5 Ton			
	2160	12" diameter	↓		320	.088	L.F.
	2200	15" diameter	↓	↓	190	.147	L.F.
	3040	Fittings, bends or elbows, 4" diameter	B-20	1 Labor Foreman (out)	19	1.260	Ea.
				1 Skilled worker			
				1 Building Laborer			
	3080	6" diameter			15	1.600	Ea.
	3120	Tees, 4" diameter			12	2.000	Ea.
	3160	6" diameter			10	2.400	Ea.
	3200	Wyes, 4" diameter			12	2.000	Ea.
	3240	6" diameter	↓	↓	10	2.400	Ea.
170		**PIPING, DRAINAGE & SEWAGE, SEWAGE VENT CAST IRON**					
	0020	Not including excavation or backfill					
	2022	Sewage vent cast iron, B & S, 4" diameter	Q-1	1 Plumber	44	.364	L.F.
				1 Plumber Apprentice			
	2024	5" diameter	Q-2	2 Plumbers	62	.387	L.F.
				1 Plumber Apprentice			
	2026	6" diameter	"	"	59	.407	L.F.
	2028	8" diameter	Q-3	1 Plumber Foreman (ins)	49	.653	L.F.
				2 Plumbers			
				1 Plumber Apprentice			
	2030	10" diameter			45	.711	L.F.
	2032	12" diameter			39	.821	L.F.
	2034	15" diameter	↓	↓	35	.914	L.F.
	8001	Fittings, bends and elbows					
	8110	4" diameter	Q-1	1 Plumber	13	1.230	Ea.
				1 Plumber Apprentice			

027 150 | Sewage Systems

		Description	CREW	MAKEUP	DAILY OUTPUT	MAN-HOURS	UNIT
170	8113	Piping, sewage vent cast iron, bend & elbows, 5" diameter	Q-2	2 Plumbers	18	1.330	Ea.
				1 Plumber Apprentice			
	8114	6" diameter	"	"	17	1.410	Ea.
	8116	8" diameter	Q-3	1 Plumber Foreman (ins)	11	2.910	Ea.
				2 Plumbers			
				1 Plumber Apprentice			
	8118	10" diameter			10	3.200	Ea.
	8120	12" diameter			9	3.560	Ea.
	8122	15" diameter	↓	↓	7	4.570	Ea.
	8500	Wyes and tees					
	8510	4" diameter	Q-1	1 Plumber	8	2.000	Ea.
				1 Plumber Apprentice			
	8512	5" diameter	Q-2	2 Plumbers	12	2.000	Ea.
				1 Plumber Apprentice			
	8514	6" diameter	"	"	11	2.180	Ea.
	8516	8" diameter	Q-3	1 Plumber Foreman (ins)	7	4.570	Ea.
				2 Plumbers			
				1 Plumber Apprentice			
	8518	10" diameter			6	5.330	Ea.
	8520	12" diameter			4	8.000	Ea.
	8522	15" diameter	↓	↓	3	10.670	Ea.
	172	**PIPING, DRAINAGE & SEWAGE, VITRIFIED CLAY, C700**					
	0020	Not including excavation or backfill, 4' & 5' lengths					
	4030	Extra strength, compression joints, C425					
	5000	4" diameter	B-20	1 Labor Foreman (out)	265	.091	L.F.
				1 Skilled worker			
				1 Building Laborer			
	5010	5" diameter			265	.091	L.F.
	5020	6" diameter	↓	↓	200	.120	L.F.
	5040	8" diameter	B-21	1 Labor Foreman (out)	200	.140	L.F.
				1 Skilled worker			
				1 Building Laborer			
				.5 Equip. Oper. (crane)			
				.5 S.P. Crane, 5 Ton			
	5060	10" diameter			190	.147	L.F.
	5080	12" diameter			150	.187	L.F.
	5100	15" diameter			110	.255	L.F.
	5120	18" diameter			88	.318	L.F.
	5140	24" diameter	↓	↓	45	.622	L.F.
	5160	30" diameter	B-22	1 Labor Foreman (out)	31	.968	L.F.
				1 Skilled worker			
				1 Building Laborer			
				.75 Equip. Oper. (crane)			
				.75 S.P. Crane, 5 Ton			
	5180	36" diameter	"	"	20	1.500	L.F.
	7010	Plain joints, 4" diameter	B-20	1 Labor Foreman (out)	380	.063	L.F.
				1 Skilled worker			
				1 Building Laborer			
	7012	5" diameter			350	.069	L.F.
	7014	6" diameter	↓	↓	340	.071	L.F.
	7016	8" diameter	B-21	1 Labor Foreman (out)	300	.093	L.F.
				1 Skilled worker			
				1 Building Laborer			
				.5 Equip. Oper. (crane)			
				.5 S.P. Crane, 5 Ton			
	7018	10" diameter			240	.117	L.F.
	7020	12" diameter			190	.147	L.F.
	7022	15" diameter	↓	↓	155	.181	L.F.

027 150 | Sewage Systems

		Description	CREW	MAKEUP	DAILY OUTPUT	MAN-HOURS	UNIT
172	7025	Piping, vitrified clay, extra strength, plain joint, 18" dia.	B-21	1 Labor Foreman (out)	122	.230	L.F.
				1 Skilled worker			
				1 Building Laborer			
				.5 Equip. Oper. (crane)			
				.5 S.P. Crane, 5 Ton			
	7026	21" diameter			108	.259	L.F.
	7028	24" diameter	↓	↓	88	.318	L.F.
	7032	30" diameter	B-22	1 Labor Foreman (out)	40	.750	L.F.
				1 Skilled worker			
				1 Building Laborer			
				.75 Equip. Oper. (crane)			
				.75 S.P. Crane, 5 Ton			
	7034	36" diameter	"	"	30	1.000	L.F.
	8300	Bends and elbows, extra strength, C700					
	8312	Plain joints, 4" diameter	B-20	1 Labor Foreman (out)	50	.480	Ea.
				1 Skilled worker			
				1 Building Laborer			
	8314	5" diameter			48	.500	Ea.
	8316	6" diameter			46	.522	Ea.
	8318	8" diameter			38	.632	Ea.
	8320	10" diameter			32	.750	Ea.
	8322	12" diameter			28	.857	Ea.
	8324	15" diameter	↓	↓	18	1.330	Ea.
	8326	18" diameter	B-21	1 Labor Foreman (out)	8	3.500	Ea.
				1 Skilled worker			
				1 Building Laborer			
				.5 Equip. Oper. (crane)			
				.5 S.P. Crane, 5 Ton			
	8328	21" diameter			7	4.000	Ea.
	8330	24" diameter			6	4.670	Ea.
	8332	27" diameter			5	5.600	Ea.
	8334	30" diameter			4	7.000	Ea.
	8336	36" diameter	↓	↓	3	9.330	Ea.
	8350	Compression joints, C425, 4" diameter	B-20	1 Labor Foreman (out)	60	.400	Ea.
				1 Skilled worker			
				1 Building Laborer			
	8352	5" diameter			58	.414	Ea.
	8354	6" diameter			56	.429	Ea.
	8356	8" diameter			48	.500	Ea.
	8358	10" diameter			42	.571	Ea.
	8360	12" diameter			38	.632	Ea.
	8362	15" diameter	↓	↓	28	.857	Ea.
	8364	18" diameter	B-21	1 Labor Foreman (out)	18	1.560	Ea.
				1 Skilled worker			
				1 Building Laborer			
				.5 Equip. Oper. (crane)			
				.5 S.P. Crane, 5 Ton			
	8366	21" diameter			17	1.650	Ea.
	8368	24" diameter			16	1.750	Ea.
	8372	30" diameter			14	2.000	Ea.
	8374	36" diameter	↓	↓	13	2.150	Ea.
	8400	Wyes and tees, extra strength, C700					
	8410	Plain joints, 4" diameter	B-20	1 Labor Foreman (out)	43	.558	Ea.
				1 Skilled worker			
				1 Building Laborer			
	8412	5" diameter			41	.585	Ea.
	8414	6" diameter			39	.615	Ea.
	8416	8" diameter	↓	↓	31	.774	Ea.

027 150 | Sewage Systems

		CREW	MAKEUP	DAILY OUTPUT	MAN-HOURS	UNIT
172	8419	Piping, vitrified clay, extra strength, wyes & tees, 10" dia.	B-20	1 Labor Foreman (out)	25	.960	Ea.
				1 Skilled worker			
				1 Building Laborer			
	8420	12" diameter	↓	↓	21	1.140	Ea.
	8422	15" diameter			11	2.180	Ea.
	8424	18" diameter	B-21	1 Labor Foreman (out)	4	7.000	Ea.
				1 Skilled worker			
				1 Building Laborer			
				.5 Equip. Oper. (crane)			
				.5 S.P. Crane, 5 Ton			
	8426	21" diameter			2	14.000	Ea.
	8428	24" diameter			1	28.000	Ea.
	8430	27" diameter			.80	35.000	Ea.
	8432	30" diameter			.50	56.000	Ea.
	8434	36" diameter	↓	↓	.40	70.000	Ea.
	8450	Compression joints, C425, 4" diameter	B-20	1 Labor Foreman (out)	53	.453	Ea.
				1 Skilled worker			
				1 Building Laborer			
	8452	5" diameter			51	.471	Ea.
	8454	6" diameter			49	.490	Ea.
	8456	8" diameter			41	.585	Ea.
	8458	10" diameter			35	.686	Ea.
	8460	12" diameter			31	.774	Ea.
	8462	15" diameter	↓	↓	21	1.140	Ea.
	8464	18" diameter	B-21	1 Labor Foreman (out)	14	2.000	Ea.
				1 Skilled worker			
				1 Building Laborer			
				.5 Equip. Oper. (crane)			
				.5 S.P. Crane, 5 Ton			
	8466	21" diameter			12	2.330	Ea.
	8468	24" diameter			11	2.550	Ea.
	8472	30" diameter			5	5.600	Ea.
	8474	36" diameter	↓	↓	4	7.000	Ea.
174		SEWAGE PUMPING STATIONS Prefabricated steel, concrete					
	0020	or fiberglass, 200 GPM	C-17D	2 Skilled Worker Foremen	.17	494.000	Total
				8 Skilled Workers			
				.5 Equip. Oper. (crane)			
				.5 Crane, 80 Ton & Tools			
				.5 Hand held power tools			
				.5 Walk behind power tools			
	0200	1,000 GPM			.07	1200.000	Total
	0500	Add for generator unit, 200 GPM, steel			.34	247.000	Total
	0600	Concrete			.51	165.000	Total
	1000	Add for generator unit, 1,000 GPM, steel			.30	280.000	Total
	1200	Concrete	↓	↓	.38	221.000	Total
	1500	For wet well, if required, add	B-23	1 Labor Foreman (outside)	.50	80.000	Total
				4 Building Laborers			
				1 Drill Rig			
				1 Light Truck, 3 Ton			
176		SEWAGE TREATMENT					
	2000	Holding tank system, not incl. excavation or backfill					
	2010	Recirculating chemical water closet	2 Plum	2 Plumbers	4	4.000	Ea.
	2100	For voltage converter, add	"	"	16	1.000	Ea.
	2200	For high level alarm, add	1 Plum	1 Plumber	7.80	1.030	Ea.

027 | Sewerage & Drainage

027 350 | Wastewater System

			CREW	MAKEUP	DAILY OUTPUT	MAN-HOURS	UNIT
354	354	WASTEWATER TREATMENT SYSTEM Fiberglass, 1,000 gallon	B-21	1 Labor Foreman (out)	1.29	21.710	Ea.
				1 Skilled worker			
				1 Building Laborer			
				.5 Equip. Oper. (crane)			
				.5 S.P. Crane, 5 Ton			
	0100	1,500 gallon	"	"	1.03	27.180	Ea.

027 400 | Septic Systems

		CREW	MAKEUP	DAILY OUTPUT	MAN-HOURS	UNIT
404	SEPTIC TANKS Not incl. excav. or piping, precast, 1,000 gallon	B-21	1 Labor Foreman (out)	8	3.500	Ea.
			1 Skilled worker			
			1 Building Laborer			
			.5 Equip. Oper. (crane)			
			.5 S.P. Crane, 5 Ton			
0020	1250 gallon			8	3.500	Ea.
0060	1500 gallon			7	4.000	Ea.
0100	2,000 gallon			5	5.600	Ea.
0140	2500 gallon			5	5.600	Ea.
0180	4000 gallon			4	7.000	Ea.
0220	5000 gal., 4 piece	↓	↓	3	9.330	Ea.
0300	15,000 gallon	B-13	1 Labor Foreman (outside)	1.30	43.080	Ea.
			4 Building Laborers			
			1 Equip. Oper. (crane)			
			1 Equip. Oper. Oiler			
			1 Hyd. Crane, 25 Ton			
0400	25,000 gallon	↓	↓	.80	70.000	Ea.
0500	40,000 gallon	↓	↓	.60	93.330	Ea.
0600	Fiberglass, 1,000 gallon	B-21	1 Labor Foreman (out)	6	4.670	Ea.
			1 Skilled worker			
			1 Building Laborer			
			.5 Equip. Oper. (crane)			
			.5 S.P. Crane, 5 Ton			
0700	1,500 gallon	↓	↓	4	7.000	Ea.
0900	Galley, 4' x 4' x 4'	↓	↓	16	1.750	Ea.
1000	Distribution boxes, concrete, 5 outlets	2 Clab	2 Building Laborers	16	1.000	Ea.
1100	12 outlets	"	"	8	2.000	Ea.
1150	Leaching field chambers, 13' x 3'-7" x 1'-4", standard	B-13	1 Labor Foreman (outside)	16	3.500	Ea.
			4 Building Laborers			
			1 Equip. Oper. (crane)			
			1 Equip. Oper. Oiler			
			1 Hyd. Crane, 25 Ton			
1200	Heavy duty, 8' x 4' x 1'-6"			14	4.000	Ea.
1300	13' x 3'-9" x 1'-6"			12	4.670	Ea.
1350	20' x 4' x 1'-6"	↓	↓	5	11.200	Ea.
1600	Leaching pit, 6'-6 diameter, 6' deep	B-21	1 Labor Foreman (out)	5	5.600	Ea.
			1 Skilled worker			
			1 Building Laborer			
			.5 Equip. Oper. (crane)			
			.5 S.P. Crane, 5 Ton			
1620	8' deep			4	7.000	Ea.
1700	8' diameter, H-20 load, 6' deep			4	7.000	Ea.
1720	8' deep			3	9.330	Ea.
2000	Velocity reducing pit, precast conc., 6' diameter, 3' deep	↓	↓	4.70	5.960	Ea.
2200	Excavation for septic tank, 3/4 C.Y. backhoe	B-12F	1 Equip. Oper. (crane)	145	.110	C.Y.
			1 Equip. Oper. Oiler			
			1 Hyd. Excavator, .75 C.Y.			
2400	4' trench for disposal field, 3/4 C.Y. backhoe	"	"	335	.048	L.F.

027 | Sewerage & Drainage

027 400 | Septic Systems

		CREW	MAKEUP	DAILY OUTPUT	MAN-HOURS	UNIT
404	2601	Septic tanks, gravel fill, run of bank	B-6	2 Building Laborers	150	.160	C.Y.
				1 Equip. Oper. (light)			
				1 Backhoe Loader, 48 H.P.			
	2800	Crushed stone, 3/4"	"	"	150	.160	C.Y.

027 660 | Relining Existing Pipelines

		CREW	MAKEUP	DAILY OUTPUT	MAN-HOURS	UNIT
664	**LINING PIPE** with cement, incl. bypass and cleaning					
0020	Less than 10,000 L.F., urban, 6" to 10"	C-17E	2 Skilled Worker Foremen	130	.615	L.F.
			8 Skilled Workers			
			1 Hyd. Jack with Rods			
0050	10" to 12"			125	.640	L.F.
0070	12" to 16"			115	.696	L.F.
0100	16" to 20"			95	.842	L.F.
0200	24" to 36"			90	.889	L.F.
0300	48" to 72"			80	1.000	L.F.
0500	Rural, 6" to 10"			180	.444	L.F.
0550	10" to 12"			175	.457	L.F.
0570	12" to 16"			160	.500	L.F.
0600	16" to 20"			135	.593	L.F.
0700	24" to 36"			125	.640	L.F.
0800	48" to 72"			100	.800	L.F.
1000	Greater than 10,000 L.F., urban, 6" to 10"			160	.500	L.F.
1050	10" to 12"			155	.516	L.F.
1070	12" to 16"			140	.571	L.F.
1100	16" to 20"			120	.667	L.F.
1200	24" to 36"			115	.696	L.F.
1300	48" to 72"			95	.842	L.F.
1500	Rural, 6" to 10"			215	.372	L.F.
1550	10" to 12"			210	.381	L.F.
1570	12" to 16"			185	.432	L.F.
1600	16" to 20"			150	.533	L.F.
1700	24" to 36"			140	.571	L.F.
1800	48" to 72"			120	.667	L.F.

028 | Site Improvements

028 100 | Irrigation Systems

		CREW	MAKEUP	DAILY OUTPUT	MAN-HOURS	UNIT
104	**SPRINKLER IRRIGATION SYSTEM** For lawns					
0100	Golf courses with fully automatic system	C-17	2 Skilled Worker Foremen	.05	600.000	9 Holes
			8 Skilled Workers			
0200	24' diam. head at 15' O.C incl. piping, minimum	B-20	1 Labor Foreman (out)	70	.343	Head
			1 Skilled worker			
			1 Building Laborer			
0300	Maximum			40	.600	Head
0500	60' diameter head, automatic operation, minimum			28	.857	Head
0600	Maximum			23	1.040	Head
0800	Residential system, custom, 1" supply			2,619	.009	S.F.
0900	1-1/2" supply			2,311	.010	S.F.
1000	Sprinkler heads					
2000	Pop-up spray, head & nozzle, low/medium volume, plastic	1 Skwk	1 Skilled Worker	30	.267	Ea.
2200	Brass, economy			30	.267	Ea.
2400	Heavy duty			30	.267	Ea.

028 | Site Improvements

028 100 | Irrigation Systems

			CREW	MAKEUP	DAILY OUTPUT	MAN-HOURS	UNIT
104	3001	Sprinkler head, riser mtd spray, low/med volume, plastic	1 Skwk	1 Skilled Worker	30	.267	Ea.
	3200	Brass			30	.267	Ea.
	4000	Pop-up impact sprinkler, body & case, plastic low/medium volume			30	.267	Ea.
	4200	Brass, high/medium volume			30	.267	Ea.
	4400	High volume			30	.267	Ea.
	5000	Quick coupling valve and key, brass, thread type			25	.320	Ea.
	5200	Lug type			25	.320	Ea.
	5400	Pop-up gear drive sprinkler, nozzle & case plastic, medium volume	↓	↓	30	.267	Ea.
	6000	Riser mounted gear drive sprinkler, nozzle and case					
	6200	Plastic, medium volume	1 Skwk	1 Skilled Worker	30	.267	Ea.
	7000	Riser mounted impact sprinkler, body, part or					
	7200	Full circle plastic, low/medium volume	1 Skwk	1 Skilled Worker	25	.320	Ea.
	7400	Brass, low/medium volume			25	.320	Ea.
	7600	Medium volume			25	.320	Ea.
	7800	Female thread	↓	↓	25	.320	Ea.
	8000	Riser mounted impact sprinkler, body, full circle only					
	8200	Plastic, low/medium volume	1 Skwk	1 Skilled Worker	25	.320	Ea.
	8400	Brass, low/medium volume			25	.320	Ea.
	8600	High volume			25	.320	Ea.
	8800	Very high volume	↓	↓	25	.320	Ea.

028 200 | Fountains

			CREW	MAKEUP	DAILY OUTPUT	MAN-HOURS	UNIT
	204	FOUNTAINS Incl. fiberglass pools, pumps, piping and lights					
	0200	4' diameter pool, 18" diameter spray ring	Q-1	1 Plumber	2	8.000	Ea.
				1 Plumber Apprentice			
	0300	6' diameter pool, 24" diameter spray ring			1.50	10.670	Ea.
	0400	7.5' diameter pool, 48" diameter spray ring			1	16.000	Ea.
	0500	Rain curtains, 3' rain bar, 2' x 4' x 1' pool			2	8.000	Ea.
	0600	7' rain bar, 2' x 8' x 1' pool	↓	↓	1	16.000	Ea.

028 300 | Fences And Gates

			CREW	MAKEUP	DAILY OUTPUT	MAN-HOURS	UNIT
	308	FENCE, CHAIN LINK INDUSTRIAL 6' high plus 3 strands					
	0020	barbed wire, 2" line post @ 10' O.C., 1-5/8" top rail					
	0200	9 ga. wire, galv. steel	B-80	1 Labor Foreman	250	.128	L.F.
				1 Laborer			
				1 Truck Driver (light)			
				1 Equip. Oper. (light)			
				1 Flatbed Truck, 3 Ton			
				1 Post Driver, T.M.			
	0300	Aluminized steel			250	.128	L.F.
	0500	6 ga. wire, galv. steel			250	.128	L.F.
	0600	Aluminized steel			250	.128	L.F.
	0800	6 ga. wire, 6' high but omit barbed wire, galv. steel			260	.123	L.F.
	0900	Aluminized steel			260	.123	L.F.
	1100	Add for corner posts, 3" diam., galv. steel			40	.800	Ea.
	1200	Aluminized steel			40	.800	Ea.
	1300	Add for braces, galv. steel			80	.400	Ea.
	1350	Aluminized steel			80	.400	Ea.
	1400	Gate for 6' high fence, 1-5/8" frame, 3' wide, galv. steel			10	3.200	Ea.
	1500	Aluminized steel	↓	↓	10	3.200	Ea.
	2000	5'-0" high fence, 9 ga., no barbed wire, 2" line post,					
	2010	10' O.C., 1-5/8" top rail					
	2100	Galvanized steel	B-80	1 Labor Foreman	315	.102	L.F.
				1 Laborer			
				1 Truck Driver (light)			
				1 Equip. Oper. (light)			
				1 Flatbed Truck, 3 Ton			
				1 Post Driver, T.M.			

028 300 | Fences And Gates

			Description	CREW	MAKEUP	DAILY OUTPUT	MAN-HOURS	UNIT
308	2201		Fence, chain link, 5' high, 9 ga., aluminized steel	B-80	1 Labor Foreman	315	.102	L.F.
					1 Laborer			
					1 Truck Driver (light)			
					1 Equip. Oper. (light)			
					1 Flatbed Truck, 3 Ton			
					1 Post Driver, T.M.			
	2400		Gate, 4' wide, 5' high, 2" frame, galv. steel	↓	↓	10	3.200	Ea.
	2500		Aluminized steel			10	3.200	Ea.
	2700	Motor operator for gates, not including gates or							
	2710		electrical wiring, for swinging gate 15' wide	B-80	1 Labor Foreman	2	16.000	Opng.
					1 Laborer			
					1 Truck Driver (light)			
					1 Equip. Oper. (light)			
					1 Flatbed Truck, 3 Ton			
					1 Post Driver, T.M.			
	2800		For swinging gate up to 30' wide (pair)	↓	↓	2	16.000	Opng.
	2900		For sliding gate up to 45' long (pair)			2	16.000	Opng.
	3100		Overhead slide gate, chain link, 6' high, to 18' wide			38	.842	L.F.
	3110		Cantilever type	↓	↓	48	.667	L.F.
	312	**FENCE, CHAIN LINK RESIDENTIAL** 11 ga. wire, 1-5/8" post,							
	0020		10' O.C., 1-3/8" top rail, 2" corner post, galv. stl. 3' high	B-1	1 Labor Foreman (outside)	500	.048	L.F.
					2 Building Laborers			
	0050		4' high			400	.060	L.F.
	0100		6' high			200	.120	L.F.
	0150		Add for gate 3' wide, 1-3/8" frame, 3' high			12	2.000	Ea.
	0170		4' high			10	2.400	Ea.
	0190		6' high			10	2.400	Ea.
	0200		Add for gate 4' wide, 1-3/8" frame, 3' high			9	2.670	Ea.
	0220		4' high			9	2.670	Ea.
	0240		6' high			8	3.000	Ea.
	0350		Aluminized steel, 11 ga. wire, 3' high			500	.048	L.F.
	0380		4' high			400	.060	L.F.
	0400		6' high			200	.120	L.F.
	0450		Add for gate 3' wide, 1-3/8" frame, 3' high			12	2.000	Ea.
	0470		4' high			10	2.400	Ea.
	0490		6' high			10	2.400	Ea.
	0500		Add for gate 4' wide, 1-3/8" frame, 3' high			10	2.400	Ea.
	0520		4' high			9	2.670	Ea.
	0540		6' high			8	3.000	Ea.
	0620		Vinyl covered, 9 ga. wire, 3' high			500	.048	L.F.
	0640		4' high			400	.060	L.F.
	0660		6' high			200	.120	L.F.
	0720		Add for gate 3' wide, 1-3/8" frame, 3' high			12	2.000	Ea.
	0740		4' high			10	2.400	Ea.
	0760		6' high			10	2.400	Ea.
	0780		Add for gate 4' wide, 1-3/8" frame, 3' high			10	2.400	Ea.
	0800		4' high			9	2.670	Ea.
	0820		6' high	↓	↓	8	3.000	Ea.
	0860		Tennis courts, 11 ga. wire, 2 1/2" post 10' O.C., 1-5/8" top rail						
	0900		10' high	B-1	1 Labor Foreman (outside)	155	.155	L.F.
					2 Building Laborers			
	0920		12' high			130	.185	L.F.
	1000		Add for gate 4' wide, 1-5/8" frame 7' high			10	2.400	Ea.
	1040		Aluminized steel, 11 ga. wire 10' high			155	.155	L.F.
	1100		12' high			130	.185	L.F.
	1250		Vinyl covered, 9 ga. wire, 10' high			155	.155	L.F.
	1300		12' high			130	.185	L.F.
	1400		Add for gate 4' wide, 1-5/8" frame, 7' high	↓	↓	10	2.400	Ea.

028 300 | Fences And Gates

		Description	CREW	MAKEUP	DAILY OUTPUT	MAN-HOURS	UNIT
320	320	**FENCE, MISC. METAL** Chicken wire, posts @ 4', 1" mesh, 4' high	B-80	1 Labor Foreman	410	.078	L.F.
				1 Laborer			
				1 Truck Driver (light)			
				1 Equip. Oper. (light)			
				1 Flatbed Truck, 3 Ton			
				1 Post Driver, T.M.			
	0100	2" mesh, 6' high			350	.091	L.F.
	0200	Galv. steel, 12 ga., 2" x 4" mesh, posts 5' O.C., 3' high			300	.107	L.F.
	0300	5' high			300	.107	L.F.
	0400	14 ga., 1" x 2" mesh, 3' high			300	.107	L.F.
	0500	5' high	↓	↓	300	.107	L.F.
	1000	Kennel fencing, 1-1/2" mesh, 6' long, 3'-6" wide, 6'-2" high	2 Clab	2 Building Laborers	4	4.000	Ea.
	1050	12' long			4	4.000	Ea.
	1200	Top covers, 1-1/2" mesh, 6' long			15	1.070	Ea.
	1250	12' long	↓	↓	12	1.330	Ea.
	4500	Security fence, prison grade, set in concrete, 12' high	B-80	1 Labor Foreman	25	1.280	L.F.
				1 Laborer			
				1 Truck Driver (light)			
				1 Equip. Oper. (light)			
				1 Flatbed Truck, 3 Ton			
				1 Post Driver, T.M.			
	4600	16' high	"	"	20	1.600	L.F.
	4800	Snow fence on steel posts 10' O.C., 4' high	B-1	1 Labor Foreman (outside)	500	.048	L.F.
				2 Building Laborers			
	5300	Tubular picket, steel, 6' sections, 1-9/16" posts, 4' high	B-80	1 Labor Foreman	300	.107	L.F.
				1 Laborer			
				1 Truck Driver (light)			
				1 Equip. Oper. (light)			
				1 Flatbed Truck, 3 Ton			
				1 Post Driver, T.M.			
	5400	2" posts, 5' high			240	.133	L.F.
	5600	2" posts, 6' high			200	.160	L.F.
	5700	Staggered picket 1-9/16" posts, 4' high			300	.107	L.F.
	5800	2" posts, 5' high			240	.133	L.F.
	5900	2" posts, 6' high	↓	↓	200	.160	L.F.
	6200	Gates, 4' high, 3' wide	B-1	1 Labor Foreman (outside)	10	2.400	Ea.
				2 Building Laborers			
	6300	5' high, 3' wide			10	2.400	Ea.
	6400	6' high, 3' wide			10	2.400	Ea.
	6500	4' wide	↓	↓	10	2.400	Ea.
	328	**FENCE, WOOD** Basket weave, 3/8" x 4" boards, 2" x 4"					
	0020	stringers on spreaders, 4" x 4" posts					
	0050	No. 1 cedar, 6' high	B-1	1 Labor Foreman (outside)	160	.150	L.F.
				2 Building Laborers			
	0070	Treated pine, 6' high	"	"	150	.160	L.F.
	0200	Board fence, 1" x 4" boards, 2" x 4" rails, 4" x 4" post					
	0220	Preservative treated, 2 rail, 3' high	B-1	1 Labor Foreman (outside)	145	.166	L.F.
				2 Building Laborers			
	0240	4' high			135	.178	L.F.
	0260	3 rail, 5' high			130	.185	L.F.
	0300	6' high			125	.192	L.F.
	0320	No. 2 grade western cedar, 2 rail, 3' high			145	.166	L.F.
	0340	4' high			135	.178	L.F.
	0360	3 rail, 5' high			130	.185	L.F.
	0400	6' high			125	.192	L.F.
	0420	No. 1 grade cedar, 2 rail, 3' high			145	.166	L.F.
	0440	4' high			135	.178	L.F.
	0460	3 rail, 5' high	↓	↓	130	.185	L.F.

028 300 | Fences And Gates

		CREW	MAKEUP	DAILY OUTPUT	MAN-HOURS	UNIT
328 0510	Fence, 1" x 4" boards, No. 1 grade cedar, 3 rail, 6' high	B-1	1 Labor Foreman (outside) 2 Building Laborers	125	.192	L.F.
0540	Shadow box, 1' x 6" board, 2" x 4" rail, 4" x 4"post					
0560	Pine, pressure treated, 3 rail, 6' high	B-1	1 Labor Foreman (outside) 2 Building Laborers	160	.150	L.F.
0600	Gate, 3'-6" wide			8	3.000	Ea.
0620	No. 1 cedar, 3 rail, 4' high			135	.178	L.F.
0640	6' high			130	.185	L.F.
0860	Open rail fence, split rails, 2 rail 3' high, no. 1 cedar			160	.150	L.F.
0870	No. 2 cedar			160	.150	L.F.
0880	3 rail, 4' high, no. 1 cedar			150	.160	L.F.
0890	No. 2 cedar			150	.160	L.F.
0920	Rustic rails, 2 rail 3' high, no. 1 cedar			160	.150	L.F.
0930	No. 2 cedar			160	.150	L.F.
0940	3 rail, 4' high			150	.160	L.F.
0950	No. 2 cedar	▼	▼	150	.160	L.F.
0960	Picket fence, gothic, pressure treated pine					
1000	2 rail, 3' high	B-1	1 Labor Foreman (outside) 2 Building Laborers	140	.171	L.F.
1020	3 rail, 4' high			130	.185	L.F.
1040	Gate, 3'-6" wide			9	2.670	Ea.
1060	No. 2 cedar, 2 rail, 3' high			140	.171	L.F.
1100	3 rail, 4' high			130	.185	L.F.
1120	Gate, 3'-6" wide			9	2.670	Ea.
1140	No. 1 cedar, 2 rail 3' high			140	.171	L.F.
1160	3 rail, 4' high			130	.185	L.F.
1170	Gate, 3'-6" wide			9	2.670	Ea.
1200	Rustic picket, molded pine, 2 rail, 3' high			140	.171	L.F.
1220	No. 1 cedar, 2 rail, 3' high			140	.171	L.F.
1240	Stockade fence, no. 1 cedar, 3-1/4" rails, 6' high			160	.150	L.F.
1260	8' high			155	.155	L.F.
1300	No. 2 cedar, treated wood rails, 6' high			160	.150	L.F.
1320	Gate, 3'-6" wide			8	3.000	Ea.
1360	Treated pine, treated rails, 6' high			160	.150	Ea.
1400	8' high	▼	▼	150	.160	Ea.

028 400 | Walk/Road/Parkg Appurt

		CREW	MAKEUP	DAILY OUTPUT	MAN-HOURS	UNIT
404	**GUIDE RAIL** Corrugated steel, galv. steel posts, 6'-3" O.C.	B-80	1 Labor Foreman 1 Laborer 1 Truck Driver (light) 1 Equip. Oper. (light) 1 Flatbed Truck, 3 Ton 1 Post Driver, T.M.	850	.038	L.F.
0200	End sections, galvanized, flared			50	.640	Ea.
0300	Wrap around end			50	.640	Ea.
0400	Timber guide rail, 4" x 8" with 6" x 8" wood posts, treated			960	.033	L.F.
0600	Cable guide rail, 3 at 3/4" cables, steel posts			900	.036	L.F.
0700	Wood posts			950	.034	L.F.
0900	Guide rail, steel box beam, 6" x 6"			120	.267	L.F.
1100	Median barrier, steel box beam, 6" x 8"	▼	▼	215	.149	L.F.
1200	Impact barrier, barrel type	B-16	1 Labor Foreman (outside) 2 Building Laborers 1 Truck Driver (heavy) 1 Dump Truck, 16 Ton	30	1.070	Ea.
1400	Resilient guide fence and light shield, 6' high	B-2	1 Labor Foreman (outside) 4 Building Laborers	130	.308	L.F.

114

028 | Site Improvements

			CREW	MAKEUP	DAILY OUTPUT	MAN-HOURS	UNIT
404	1501	Guide rail, concrete posts, individual, 6'-5", triangular	B-80	1 Labor Foreman	110	.291	Ea.
				1 Laborer			
				1 Truck Driver (light)			
				1 Equip. Oper. (light)			
				1 Flatbed Truck, 3 Ton			
				1 Post Driver, T.M.			
	1550	Square	"	"	110	.291	Ea.
	2000	Median, barrier, precast concrete, 3'-6" high, single face,	B-29	1 Labor Foreman (outside)	380	.147	L.F.
				4 Building Laborers			
				1 Equip. Oper. (crane)			
				1 Equip. Oper. Oiler			
				1 Gradall, 3 Ton, 1/2 C.Y.			
	2200	Double face, 2'-0" wide	"	"	340	.165	L.F.
408		**PARKING BARRIERS** Timber with saddles, treated type					
	0100	4" x 4" for cars	B-2	1 Labor Foreman (outside)	520	.077	L.F.
				4 Building Laborers			
	0200	6" x 6" for trucks			520	.077	L.F.
	0400	Folding with individual padlocks			50	.800	Ea.
	0600	Flexible fixed stanchion, 2' high, 3" diameter			100	.400	Ea.
	1000	Precast concrete wheel stops, incl. dowels, 6" x 10" x 6'-0"			120	.333	Ea.
	1100	8" x 13" x 6'-0"	↓	↓	120	.333	Ea.
412		**SIGNS** Stock, 24" x 24", no posts, .080" alum. reflectorized	B-80	1 Labor Foreman	70	.457	Ea.
				1 Laborer			
				1 Truck Driver (light)			
				1 Equip. Oper. (light)			
				1 Flatbed Truck, 3 Ton			
				1 Post Driver, T.M.			
	0100	High intensity			70	.457	Ea.
	0300	30" x 30", reflectorized			70	.457	Ea.
	0400	High intensity			70	.457	Ea.
	0600	Guide and directional signs, 12" x 18", reflectorized			70	.457	Ea.
	0700	High intensity			70	.457	Ea.
	0900	18" x 24", stock signs, reflectorized			70	.457	Ea.
	1000	High intensity			70	.457	Ea.
	1200	24" x 24", stock signs, reflectorized			70	.457	Ea.
	1300	High intensity			70	.457	Ea.
	1500	Add to above for steel posts, galvanized, 10'-0" upright, bolted			200	.160	Ea.
	1600	12'-0" upright, bolted			140	.229	Ea.
	1800	Highway road signs, aluminum, over 20 S. F., reflectorized			350	.091	S.F.
	2000	High intensity			350	.091	S.F.
	2200	Highway, suspended over road, 80 S.F. min., reflectorized			165	.194	S.F.
	2300	High intensity	↓	↓	165	.194	S.F.
416		**STEPS** Incl. excav., borrow & concrete base, where applicable					
	0100	Bricks	B-24	1 Cement Finisher	35	.686	LF Rsr
				1 Building Laborer			
				1 Carpenter			
	0200	Railroad ties	2 Clab	2 Building Laborers	25	.640	LF Rsr
	0300	Bluestone treads, 12" x 2" or 12" x 1-1/2"	B-24	1 Cement Finisher	30	.800	LF Rsr
				1 Building Laborer			
				1 Carpenter			
424		**TRAFFIC SIGNALS** Mid block pedestrian crosswalk,					
	0020	with pushbutton and mast arms	R-2	1 Electrician Foreman	.30	187.000	Total
				3 Electricians			
				2 Helpers			
				1 Equip. Oper. (crane)			
				1 S.P. Crane, 5 Ton			
	0100	Intersection, 8 signals (2 each direction), programmed	"	"	.15	373.000	Total

028 400 | Walk/Road/Parkg Appurt

		CREW	MAKEUP	DAILY OUTPUT	MAN-HOURS	UNIT
424 0121	Traffic signals, for each additional traffic phase controller, add	L-9	1 Labor Foreman (inside)	1.20	30.000	Total
			2 Building Laborers			
			1 Struc. Steel Worker			
			.5 Electrician			
0200	Semi-actuated, detectors in side street only, add			.81	44.440	Total
0300	Fully-actuated, detectors in all streets, add			.49	73.470	Total
0400	For pedestrian pushbutton, add			.70	51.430	Total
0500	Optically programmed signal only, add			1.64	21.950	Total
0600	School flashing system, programmed	↓	↓	.41	87.800	Signal

028 600 | Playfields & Equipment

		CREW	MAKEUP	DAILY OUTPUT	MAN-HOURS	UNIT
604	BACKSTOPS Baseball, prefabricated, 30' wide, 12' high & 1 overhang	B-1	1 Labor Foreman (outside)	1	24.000	Ea.
			2 Building Laborers			
0100	40' wide, 12' high & 2 overhangs			.75	32.000	Ea.
0300	Basketball, steel, single pole			8	3.000	Ea.
0400	Double pole	↓	↓	6	4.000	Ea.
0600	Tennis, wire mesh with pair of ends	B-80	1 Labor Foreman	4	8.000	Set
			1 Laborer			
			1 Truck Driver (light)			
			1 Equip. Oper. (light)			
			1 Flatbed Truck, 3 Ton			
			1 Post Driver, T.M.			
0700	Enclosed court	"	"	1.30	24.620	Ea.
0900	Handball or squash court, outdoor, wood	2 Carp	2 Carpenters	.50	32.000	Ea.
1000	Masonry	D-1	1 Bricklayer	.30	53.330	Ea.
			1 Bricklayer Helper			
608	GOAL POSTS Steel, football, double post	B-1	1 Labor Foreman (outside)	1.50	16.000	Pr.
			2 Building Laborers			
0100	Deluxe, single post			1.50	16.000	Pr.
0300	Football, convertible to soccer			1.50	16.000	Pr.
0500	Soccer, regulation	↓	↓	2	12.000	Pr.
612	PLAYGROUND EQUIPMENT See also individual items					
0200	Bike rack, 10' long, permanent	B-1	1 Labor Foreman (outside)	12	2.000	Ea.
			2 Building Laborers			
0240	Climber, arch, 6' high			4	6.000	Ea.
0260	Fitness trail, with signs, 9 to 10 stations, treated pine, minimum			.25	96.000	Ea.
0270	Maximum			.17	141.000	Ea.
0280	Metal, minimum			.25	96.000	Ea.
0285	Maximum			.17	141.000	Ea.
0300	Redwood, minimum			.25	96.000	Ea.
0310	Maximum			.17	141.000	Ea.
0320	16 to 20 station, treated pine, minimum			.17	141.000	Ea.
0330	Maximum			.13	185.000	Ea.
0340	Metal, minimum			.17	141.000	Ea.
0350	Maximum			.13	185.000	Ea.
0360	Redwood, minimum			.17	141.000	Ea.
0370	Maximum			.13	185.000	Ea.
0400	Horizontal monkey ladder, 14' long			4	6.000	Ea.
0505	Modular playground, platform, 1 level, treated pine/metal, 10'x12'			1	24.000	Ea.
0510	Redwood			1	24.000	Ea.
0520	Two levels, treated pine or metal			.70	34.290	Ea.
0530	Redwood			.70	34.290	Ea.
0540	Six levels, treated pine or metal			.50	48.000	Ea.
0550	Redwood			.70	34.290	Ea.
0560	Component, attached to platform average			2.70	8.890	Ea.
0580	Component, linked between platforms, average			5	4.800	Ea.
0590	Parallel bars, 10' long			4	6.000	Ea.
0600	Posts, tether ball set, 2-3/8" O.D.	↓	↓	8	3.000	Ea.

028 600 | Playfields & Equipment

		CREW	MAKEUP	DAILY OUTPUT	MAN-HOURS	UNIT
612 0801	Playground equipment, poles, multiple purpose, 10'-6" long	B-1	1 Labor Foreman (outside)	4	6.000	Pr.
			2 Building Laborers			
1000	Ground socket for movable posts, 2-3/8" post			4	6.000	Pr.
1100	3-1/2" post			4	6.000	Pr.
1300	See-saw, steel, 2 units			6	4.000	Ea.
1400	4 units			4	6.000	Ea.
1500	6 units			3	8.000	Ea.
1700	Shelter, fiberglass golf tee, 3 person, turnable			4.60	5.220	Ea.
1900	Slides, stainless steel bed, 12' long, 6' high			3	8.000	Ea.
2000	20' long, 10' high			2	12.000	Ea.
2200	Swings, 8' high, plain seats, 4 seats			2	12.000	Ea.
2300	8 seats			1.30	18.460	Ea.
2500	12' high, 4 seats			2	12.000	Ea.
2600	8 seats			1.30	18.460	Ea.
2800	Whirlers, 8' diameter			3	8.000	Ea.
2900	10' diameter			3	8.000	Ea.
616	MODULAR PLAYGROUND Platform, 1 level, treated pine/metal, 10' x 12'			1	24.000	Ea.
0510	Redwood			1	24.000	Ea.
0520	Two levels, treated pine or metal			.70	34.290	Ea.
0530	Redwood			.70	34.290	Ea.
0540	Six levels, treated pine or metal			.50	48.000	Ea.
0550	Redwood			.70	34.290	Ea.
0560	Component, attached to platform average			2.70	8.890	Ea.
0580	Component, linked between platforms, average	↓	↓	5	4.800	Ea.
620	PLATFORM PADDLE TENNIS COURT Complete with lighting, etc.					
0100	Aluminum slat deck with aluminum frame	B-1	1 Labor Foreman (outside)	.08	300.000	Court
			2 Building Laborers			
0500	Aluminum slat deck and wood frame	C-1	3 Carpenters	.12	267.000	Court
			1 Building Laborer			
			Power Tools			
0800	Aluminum deck heater, add	B-1	1 Labor Foreman (outside)	1.18	20.340	Court
			2 Building Laborers			
0900	Douglas fir planking and wood frame 2" x 6" x 30'	C-1	3 Carpenters	.12	267.000	Court
			1 Building Laborer			
			Power Tools			
1000	Plywood deck with steel frame	↓	↓	.12	267.000	Court
1100	Steel slat deck with wood frame			.12	267.000	Court

028 700 | Site/Street Furnishings

		CREW	MAKEUP	DAILY OUTPUT	MAN-HOURS	UNIT
704	BENCHES Park, precast concrete, w/backs, wood rails, 4' long	2 Clab	2 Building Laborers	5	3.200	Ea.
0100	8' long			4	4.000	Ea.
0300	Fiberglass, backless, one piece, 4' long			10	1.600	Ea.
0400	8' long			7	2.290	Ea.
0500	Steel barstock pedestals w/backs, 2" x 3" wood rails, 4' long			10	1.600	Ea.
0510	8' long			7	2.290	Ea.
0520	3" x 8" wood plank, 4' long			10	1.600	Ea.
0530	8' long			7	2.290	Ea.
0540	Backless, 4" x 4" wood plank, 4' square			10	1.600	Ea.
0550	8' long			7	2.290	Ea.
0600	Aluminum pedestals, with backs, aluminum slats, 8' long			8	2.000	Ea.
0610	15' long			5	3.200	Ea.
0620	Portable, aluminum slats, 8' long			8	2.000	Ea.
0630	15' long			5	3.200	Ea.
0800	Cast iron pedestals, back & arms, wood slats, 4' long			8	2.000	Ea.
0820	8' long			5	3.200	Ea.
0840	Backless, wood slats, 4' long			8	2.000	Ea.
0860	8' long			5	3.200	Ea.
1700	Steel frame, fir seat, 10' long	↓	↓	10	1.600	Ea.

028 700 | Site/Street Furnishings

			CREW	MAKEUP	DAILY OUTPUT	MAN-HOURS	UNIT
708	708	**BLEACHERS** Outdoor, portable, 3 to 5 tiers, to 300' long, min.	2 Sswk	2 Struc. Steel Workers	120	.133	Seat
	0100	Maximum, less than 15' long, prefabricated			80	.200	Seat
	0200	6 to 20 tiers, minimum, up to 300' long			120	.133	Seat
	0300	Max., under 15', (highly prefabricated, on wheels)	↓	↓	800	.020	Seat
	0500	Permanent grandstands, wood seat, steel frame, 24" row					
	0600	3 to 15 tiers, minimum	2 Sswk	2 Struc. Steel Workers	60	.267	Seat
	0700	Maximum			48	.333	Seat
	0900	16 to 30 tiers, minimum			60	.267	Seat
	0950	Average			55	.291	Seat
	1000	Maximum			48	.333	Seat
	1200	Seat backs only, 30" row, fiberglass			160	.100	Seat
	1300	Steel and wood	↓	↓	160	.100	Seat
	1500	Seat renewal, cover with fiberglass on wood, with backs	2 Carp	2 Carpenters	100	.160	Seat
	1600	Plain bench, no backs	"	"	200	.080	Seat
712	712	**PLANTER BLOCKS** Precast concrete, interlocking					
	0020	"V" blocks for retaining soil	D-1	1 Bricklayer 1 Bricklayer Helper	205	.078	S.F.
716	716	**PLANTERS** Concrete, sandblasted, precast, 48" diameter, 24" high	2 Clab	2 Building Laborers	15	1.070	Ea.
	0100	Fluted, precast, 7' diameter, 36" high			10	1.600	Ea.
	0300	Fiberglass, circular, 36" diameter, 24" high			15	1.070	Ea.
	0400	60" diameter, 24" high			10	1.600	Ea.
	0600	Square, 24" side, 36" high			15	1.070	Ea.
	0700	48" side, 36" high			15	1.070	Ea.
	0900	Planter/bench, 72" square, 36" high			5	3.200	Ea.
	1000	96" square, 27" high			5	3.200	Ea.
	1200	Wood, square, 48" side, 24" high			15	1.070	Ea.
	1300	Circular, 48" diameter, 30" high			10	1.600	Ea.
	1500	72" diameter, 30" high			10	1.600	Ea.
	1600	Planter/bench, 72"	↓	↓	5	3.200	Ea.
720	720	**TRASH CLOSURE** Steel with pullover cover					
	0020	2'-3" wide, 4'-7" high, 6'-2" long	2 Clab	2 Building Laborers	5	3.200	Ea.
	0100	10'-1" long			4	4.000	Ea.
	0300	Wood, 10' wide, 6' high, 10' long			1.20	13.330	Ea.
724	724	**TRASH RECEPTACLE** Fiberglass, 2' square, 18" high			30	.533	Ea.
	0100	2' square, 2'-6" high			30	.533	Ea.
	0300	Circular , 2' diameter, 18" high			30	.533	Ea.
	0400	2' diameter, 2'-6" high	↓	↓	30	.533	Ea.
	1000	Alum. frame, hardboard panels, steel drum base,					
	1020	30 gal. capacity, silk screen on plastic finish	2 Clab	2 Building Laborers	25	.640	Ea.
	1040	Aggregate finish			25	.640	Ea.
	1100	50 gal. capacity, silk screen on plastic finish			20	.800	Ea.
	1140	Aggregate finish			20	.800	Ea.
	1200	Formed plastic liner, 14 gal., silk screen on plastic finish			40	.400	Ea.
	1240	Aggregate finish			40	.400	Ea.
	1300	30 gal. capacity, silk screen on plastic finish			35	.457	Ea.
	1340	Aggregate finish	↓	↓	35	.457	Ea.
	1400	Redwood slats, plastic liner, leg base, 14 gal. capacity,					
	1420	Varnish w/routed message	2 Clab	2 Building Laborers	40	.400	Ea.
	2000	Concrete, precast, 2' to 2-1/2' wide, 3' high, sandblasted	"	"	15	1.070	Ea.
	3000	Galv. steel frame and panels, leg base, poly bag retainer,					
	3020	40 gal. capacity, silk screen on enamel finish	2 Clab	2 Building Laborers	25	.640	Ea.
	3040	Aggregate finish			25	.640	Ea.
	3200	Formed plastic liner, 50 gal., silk screen on enamel finish			20	.800	Ea.
	3240	Aggregate finish			20	.800	Ea.
	4000	Perforated steel, pole mounted, 12" diam., 10 gal., painted			25	.640	Ea.
	4040	Redwood slats			25	.640	Ea.
	4100	22 gal. capacity, painted			25	.640	Ea.
	4140	Redwood slats	↓	↓	25	.640	Ea.

028 | Site Improvements

028 700	Site/Street Furnishings	CREW	MAKEUP	DAILY OUTPUT	MAN-HOURS	UNIT
4400	Trash receptacle					
4501	Galv. steel street basket, 52 gal. cap., unpainted	2 Clab	2 Building Laborers	40	.400	Ea.

029 | Landscaping

029 100	Shrub/Tree Transplanting	CREW	MAKEUP	DAILY OUTPUT	MAN-HOURS	UNIT
104	**TREE GUYING** Including stakes, guy wire and wrap					
0100	Less than 3" caliper, 2 stakes	2 Clab	2 Building Laborers	35	.457	Ea.
0200	3" to 4" caliper, 3 stakes	"	"	21	.762	Ea.
1000	Including arrowhead anchor, cable, turnbuckles and wrap					
1100	Less than 3" caliper, 3" anchors	2 Clab	2 Building Laborers	20	.800	Ea.
1200	3" to 6" caliper, 4" anchors			15	1.070	Ea.
1300	6" caliper, 6" anchors	↓	↓	12	1.330	Ea.
1400	8" caliper, 8" anchors			9	1.780	Ea.
108	**TREE REMOVAL**					
0100	Dig & lace, shrubs, broadleaf evergreen, 18"-24"	B-1	1 Labor Foreman (outside) 2 Building Laborers	55	.436	Ea.
0200	2'-3'	"	"	35	.686	Ea.
0300	3'-4'	B-6	2 Building Laborers 1 Equip. Oper. (light) 1 Backhoe Loader, 48 H.P.	30	.800	Ea.
0400	4'-5'	"	"	20	1.200	Ea.
1000	Deciduous, 12"-15"	B-1	1 Labor Foreman (outside) 2 Building Laborers	110	.218	Ea.
1100	18"-24"			65	.369	Ea.
1200	2'-3'	↓	↓	55	.436	Ea.
1300	3'-4'	B-6	2 Building Laborers 1 Equip. Oper. (light) 1 Backhoe Loader, 48 H.P.	50	.480	Ea.
2000	Evergreeen, 18"-24"	B-1	1 Labor Foreman (outside) 2 Building Laborers	55	.436	Ea.
2100	2'-0" to 2'-6"			50	.480	Ea.
2200	2'-6" to 3'-0"			35	.686	Ea.
2300	3'-0" to 3'-6"	↓	↓	20	1.200	Ea.
3000	Trees, deciduous, small, 2'-3'			55	.436	Ea.
3100	3'-4'	B-6	2 Building Laborers 1 Equip. Oper. (light) 1 Backhoe Loader, 48 H.P.	50	.480	Ea.
3200	4'-5'			35	.686	Ea.
3300	5'-6'			30	.800	Ea.
4000	Shade, 5'-6'			50	.480	Ea.
4100	6'-8'			35	.686	Ea.
4200	8'-10'			25	.960	Ea.
4300	2" caliper			12	2.000	Ea.
5000	Evergreen, 4'-5'			35	.686	Ea.
5100	5'-6'			25	.960	Ea.
5200	6'-7'			19	1.260	Ea.
5300	7'-8'			15	1.600	Ea.
5400	8'-10'	↓	↓	11	2.180	Ea.

029 200 | Soil Preparation

		CREW	MAKEUP	DAILY OUTPUT	MAN-HOURS	UNIT
204	**LAWN BED PREPARATION**					
0100	Rake topsoil, site material, harley rock rake, ideal	B-6	2 Building Laborers	33	.727	M.S.F.
			1 Equip. Oper. (light)			
			1 Backhoe Loader, 48 H.P.			
0200	Adverse	"	"	7	3.430	M.S.F.
0300	Screened loam, york rake and finish, ideal	B-62	2 Building Laborers	24	1.000	M.S.F.
			1 Equip. Oper. (light)			
			1 Loader, Skid Steer			
0400	Adverse	"	"	20	1.200	M.S.F.
1000	Remove topsoil & stock pile on site, 75 HP dozer, 6" deep, 50' haul	B-10L	1 Equip. Oper. (med.)	30	.400	M.S.F.
			.5 Building Laborer			
			1 Dozer, 75 H.P.			
1050	300' haul			6.10	1.970	M.S.F.
1100	12" deep, 50' haul			15.50	.774	M.S.F.
1150	300' haul	↓	↓	3.10	3.870	M.S.F.
1200	200 HP dozer, 6" deep, 50' haul	B-10B	1 Equip. Oper. (med.)	125	.096	M.S.F.
			.5 Building Laborer			
			1 Dozer, 200 H.P.			
1250	300' haul			30.70	.391	M.S.F.
1300	12" deep, 50' haul			62	.194	M.S.F.
1350	300' haul	↓	↓	15.40	.779	M.S.F.
1400	Alternate method, 75 HP dozer, 50' haul	B-10L	1 Equip. Oper. (med.)	860	.014	C.Y.
			.5 Building Laborer			
			1 Dozer, 75 H.P.			
1450	300' haul	"	"	114	.105	C.Y.
1500	200 HP dozer, 50' haul	B-10B	1 Equip. Oper. (med.)	2,660	.005	C.Y.
			.5 Building Laborer			
			1 Dozer, 200 H.P.			
1600	300' haul	"	"	570	.021	C.Y.
1800	Rolling topsoil, hand push roller	1 Clab	1 Building Laborer	3,555	.002	C.Y.
1850	Tractor drawn roller	B-66	1 Equip. Oper. (light)	210	.038	C.Y.
			1 Backhoe Ldr. w/Attchmt.			
2000	Root raking and loading, residential, no boulders	B-6	2 Building Laborers	53.30	.450	M.S.F.
			1 Equip. Oper. (light)			
			1 Backhoe Loader, 48 H.P.			
2100	With boulders			32	.750	M.S.F.
2200	Municipal, no boulders			200	.120	M.S.F.
2300	With boulders	↓	↓	120	.200	M.S.F.
2400	Large commercial, no boulders	B-10B	1 Equip. Oper. (med.)	400	.030	M.S.F.
			.5 Building Laborer			
			1 Dozer, 200 H.P.			
2500	With boulders	"	"	240	.050	M.S.F.
3000	Scarify subsoil, residential, skid steer loader w/scarifiers, 50 HP	B-66	1 Equip. Oper. (light)	32	.250	M.S.F.
			1 Backhoe Ldr. w/Attchmt.			
3050	Municipal, skid steer loader w/scarifiers, 50 HP	"	"	120	.067	M.S.F.
3100	Large commercial, 75 HP, dozer w/ripper	B-10L	1 Equip. Oper. (med.)	240	.050	M.S.F.
			.5 Building Laborer			
			1 Dozer, 75 H.P.			
3500	Screen topsoil from stockpile, vibrating screen, wet material (organic)	B-10P	1 Equip. Oper. (med.)	200	.060	C.Y.
			.5 Building Laborer			
			F.E. Loader, T.M., 2.5 C.Y.			
3550	Dry material	"	"	300	.040	C.Y.
3600	Mixing with conditioners, manure and peat	B-10R	1 Equip. Oper. (med.)	550	.022	C.Y.
			.5 Building Laborer			
			F.E. Loader, W.M., 1 C.Y.			
3650	Mobilization add for 2 days or less operation	B-34K	1 Truck Driver (heavy)	3	2.670	Job
			1 Truck Tractor, 240 H.P.			
			1 Low Bed Trailer			

029 200 | Soil Preparation

		CREW	MAKEUP	DAILY OUTPUT	MAN-HOURS	UNIT
204	3800	Spread conditioned topsoil, 6" deep, by hand	B-1	1 Labor Foreman (outside)	360	.067	S.Y.
				2 Building Laborers			
	3850	300 HP dozer	B-38	1 Labor Foreman (outside)	27	1.480	M.S.F.
				2 Building Laborers			
				1 Equip. Oper. (light)			
				1 Equip. Oper. (medium)			
				1 Backhoe Loader, 48 H.P.			
				1 Demol. Hammer, Hyd. (1000 lb)			
				1 F.E. Loader (170 H.P.)			
				1 Pavt. Rem. Bucket			
	4000	Spread soil conditioners, alum. sulfate, 1#/S.Y., hand push spreader	A-1	1 Building Laborer	17,500		S.Y.
				1 Gas Eng. Power Tool			
	4050	Tractor spreader	B-66	1 Equip. Oper. (light)	700	.011	M.S.F.
				1 Backhoe Ldr. w/Attchmt.			
	4100	Fertilizer, 0.2#/S.Y., push spreader	A-1	1 Building Laborer	17,500		S.Y.
				1 Gas Eng. Power Tool			
	4150	Tractor spreader	B-66	1 Equip. Oper. (light)	700	.011	M.S.F.
				1 Backhoe Ldr. w/Attchmt.			
	4200	Ground limestone, 1#/S.Y., push spreader	A-1	1 Building Laborer	17,500		S.Y.
				1 Gas Eng. Power Tool			
	4250	Tractor spreader	B-66	1 Equip. Oper. (light)	700	.011	M.S.F.
				1 Backhoe Ldr. w/Attchmt.			
	4300	Lusoil, 3#/S.Y., push spreader	A-1	1 Building Laborer	17,500		S.Y.
				1 Gas Eng. Power Tool			
	4350	Tractor spreader	B-66	1 Equip. Oper. (light)	700	.011	M.S.F.
				1 Backhoe Ldr. w/Attchmt.			
	4400	Manure, 18.#/S.Y., push spreader	A-1	1 Building Laborer	2,500	.003	S.Y.
				1 Gas Eng. Power Tool			
	4450	Tractor spreader	B-66	1 Equip. Oper. (light)	280	.029	M.S.F.
				1 Backhoe Ldr. w/Attchmt.			
	4500	Perlite, 1" deep, push spreader	A-1	1 Building Laborer	17,500		S.Y.
				1 Gas Eng. Power Tool			
	4550	Tractor spreader	B-66	1 Equip. Oper. (light)	700	.011	M.S.F.
				1 Backhoe Ldr. w/Attchmt.			
	4600	Vermiculite, push spreader	A-1	1 Building Laborer	17,500		S.Y.
				1 Gas Eng. Power Tool			
	4650	Tractor spreader	B-66	1 Equip. Oper. (light)	700	.011	M.S.F.
				1 Backhoe Ldr. w/Attchmt.			
	5000	Spread topsoil, skid steer loader and hand dress	B-62	2 Building Laborers	270	.089	C.Y.
				1 Equip. Oper. (light)			
				1 Loader, Skid Steer			
	5100	Articulated loader and hand dress	B-100	1 Equip. Oper. (med.)	320	.038	C.Y.
				.5 Building Laborer			
				F.E. Loader, T.M., 2.25 C.Y.			
	5200	Articulated loader, 75 HP dozer	B-38	1 Labor Foreman (outside)	500	.080	C.Y.
				2 Building Laborers			
				1 Equip. Oper. (light)			
				1 Equip. Oper. (medium)			
				1 Backhoe Loader, 48 H.P.			
				1 Demol. Hammer, Hyd. (1000 lb)			
				1 F.E. Loader (170 H.P.)			
				1 Pavt. Rem. Bucket			
	5300	Road grader and hand dress	B-11L	1 Equipment Oper. (med.)	1,000	.016	C.Y.
				1 Building Laborer			
				1 Grader, 30,000 Lbs.			
	6000	Tilling topsoil, 20 HP tractor, disk harrow, 2" deep	B-66	1 Equip. Oper. (light)	50,000		S.Y.
				1 Backhoe Ldr. w/Attchmt.			
	6050	4" deep	"	"	40,000		S.Y.

029 200 | Soil Preparation

		CREW	MAKEUP	DAILY OUTPUT	MAN-HOURS	UNIT
204 6101	Tilling topsoil, 20 HP tractor, disk harrow, 6″ deep	B-66	1 Equip. Oper. (light)	30,000		S.Y.
			1 Backhoe Ldr. w/Attchmt.			
6150	26″ rototiller, 2″ deep	A-1	1 Building Laborer	1,250	.006	S.Y.
			1 Gas Eng. Power Tool			
6200	4″ deep	↓	↓	1,000	.008	S.Y.
6250	6″ deep			750	.011	S.Y.
208	**PLANT BED PREPARATION**					
0100	Backfill planting pit, by hand, on site topsoil	2 Clab	2 Building Laborers	18	.889	C.Y.
0200	Prepared planting mix	"	"	24	.667	C.Y.
0300	Skid steer loader, on site topsoil	B-62	2 Building Laborers	340	.071	C.Y.
			1 Equip. Oper. (light)			
			1 Loader, Skid Steer			
0400	Prepared planting mix	"	"	410	.059	C.Y.
1000	Excavate planting pit, by hand, sandy soil	2 Clab	2 Building Laborers	16	1.000	C.Y.
1100	Heavy soil or clay	"	"	8	2.000	C.Y.
1200	1/2 C.Y. backhoe, sandy soil	B-11C	1 Equipment Oper. (med.)	150	.107	C.Y.
			1 Building Laborer			
			1 Backhoe Loader, 48 H.P.			
1300	Heavy soil or clay	"	"	115	.139	C.Y.
2000	Mix planting soil, incl. loam, manure, peat, by hand	2 Clab	2 Building Laborers	60	.267	C.Y.
2100	Skid steer loader	B-62	2 Building Laborers	150	.160	C.Y.
			1 Equip. Oper. (light)			
			1 Loader, Skid Steer			
3000	Pile sod, skid steer loader	"	"	2,800	.009	S.Y.
3100	By hand	2 Clab	2 Building Laborers	400	.040	S.Y.
4000	Remove sod, F.E. loader	B-10S	1 Equip. Oper. (med.)	2,000	.006	S.Y.
			.5 Building Laborer			
			F.E. Loader, W.M., 1.5 C.Y.			
4100	Sod cutter	B-12K	1 Equip. Oper. (crane)	3,200	.005	S.Y.
			1 Equip. Oper. Oiler			
			1 Gradall, 3 Ton, 1 C.Y.			
4200	By hand	2 Clab	2 Building Laborers	240	.067	S.Y.

029 300 | Lawns & Grasses

		CREW	MAKEUP	DAILY OUTPUT	MAN-HOURS	UNIT
308	**SEEDING** Athletic field mix, 8#/M.S.F., push spreader	A-1	1 Building Laborer	10	.800	M.S.F.
			1 Gas Eng. Power Tool			
0100	Tractor spreader	B-66	1 Equip. Oper. (light)	52	.154	M.S.F.
			1 Backhoe Ldr. w/Attchmt.			
0200	Hydraulic or air seeding, with mulch & fertil.	B-81	1 Laborer	80	.300	M.S.F.
			1 Equip. Oper. (med.)			
			1 Truck Driver (heavy)			
			1 Hydromulcher, T.M.			
			1 Tractor Truck, 4x2			
0400	Birds foot trefoil, .45#/M.S.F., push spreader	A-1	1 Building Laborer	10	.800	M.S.F.
			1 Gas Eng. Power Tool			
0500	Tractor spreader	B-66	1 Equip. Oper. (light)	52	.154	M.S.F.
			1 Backhoe Ldr. w/Attchmt.			
0600	Hydraulic or air seeding, with mulch & fertil.	B-81	1 Laborer	80	.300	M.S.F.
			1 Equip. Oper. (med.)			
			1 Truck Driver (heavy)			
			1 Hydromulcher, T.M.			
			1 Tractor Truck, 4x2			
0800	Bluegrass, 4#/M.S.F., common, push spreader	A-1	1 Building Laborer	10	.800	M.S.F.
			1 Gas Eng. Power Tool			
0900	Tractor spreader	B-66	1 Equip. Oper. (light)	52	.154	M.S.F.
			1 Backhoe Ldr. w/Attchmt.			

		Description	CREW	MAKEUP	DAILY OUTPUT	MAN-HOURS	UNIT
308	1001	Bluegrass, hydraulic or air seeding, w/mulch & fertil.	B-81	1 Laborer	80	.300	M.S.F.
				1 Equip. Oper. (med.)			
				1 Truck Driver (heavy)			
				1 Hydromulcher, T.M.			
				1 Tractor Truck, 4x2			
	1100	Baron, push spreader	A-1	1 Building Laborer	10	.800	M.S.F.
				1 Gas Eng. Power Tool			
	1200	Tractor spreader	B-66	1 Equip. Oper. (light)	26	.308	M.S.F.
				1 Backhoe Ldr. w/Attchmt.			
	1300	Hydraulic or air seeding, with mulch & fertil.	B-81	1 Laborer	80	.300	M.S.F.
				1 Equip. Oper. (med.)			
				1 Truck Driver (heavy)			
				1 Hydromulcher, T.M.			
				1 Tractor Truck, 4x2			
	1500	Clover, 0.67#/M.S.F., white, push spreader	A-1	1 Building Laborer	10	.800	M.S.F.
				1 Gas Eng. Power Tool			
	1600	Tractor spreader	B-66	1 Equip. Oper. (light)	52	.154	M.S.F.
				1 Backhoe Ldr. w/Attchmt.			
	1700	Hydraulic or air seeding, with mulch and fertil.	B-81	1 Laborer	80	.300	M.S.F.
				1 Equip. Oper. (med.)			
				1 Truck Driver (heavy)			
				1 Hydromulcher, T.M.			
				1 Tractor Truck, 4x2			
	1800	Ladino, push spreader	A-1	1 Building Laborer	10	.800	M.S.F.
				1 Gas Eng. Power Tool			
	1900	Tractor spreader	B-66	1 Equip. Oper. (light)	52	.154	M.S.F.
				1 Backhoe Ldr. w/Attchmt.			
	2000	Hydraulic or air seeding, with mulch and fertil.	B-81	1 Laborer	80	.300	M.S.F.
				1 Equip. Oper. (med.)			
				1 Truck Driver (heavy)			
				1 Hydromulcher, T.M.			
				1 Tractor Truck, 4x2			
	2200	Fescue 5.5#/M.S.F., tall, push spreader	A-1	1 Building Laborer	10	.800	M.S.F.
				1 Gas Eng. Power Tool			
	2300	Tractor spreader	B-66	1 Equip. Oper. (light)	26	.308	M.S.F.
				1 Backhoe Ldr. w/Attchmt.			
	2400	Hydraulic or air seeding, with mulch and fertil.	B-81	1 Laborer	80	.300	M.S.F.
				1 Equip. Oper. (med.)			
				1 Truck Driver (heavy)			
				1 Hydromulcher, T.M.			
				1 Tractor Truck, 4x2			
	2500	Chewing, push spreader	A-1	1 Building Laborer	10	.800	M.S.F.
				1 Gas Eng. Power Tool			
	2600	Tractor spreader	B-66	1 Equip. Oper. (light)	26	.308	M.S.F.
				1 Backhoe Ldr. w/Attchmt.			
	2700	Hydraulic or air seeding, with mulch and fertil.	B-81	1 Laborer	80	.300	M.S.F.
				1 Equip. Oper. (med.)			
				1 Truck Driver (heavy)			
				1 Hydromulcher, T.M.			
				1 Tractor Truck, 4x2			
	2900	Crown vetch, 4#/M.S.F., push spreader	A-1	1 Building Laborer	10	.800	M.S.F.
				1 Gas Eng. Power Tool			
	3000	Tractor spreader	B-66	1 Equip. Oper. (light)	52	.154	M.S.F.
				1 Backhoe Ldr. w/Attchmt.			

029 300 | Lawns & Grasses

		Description	CREW	MAKEUP	DAILY OUTPUT	MAN-HOURS	UNIT
308	3101	Crown Vetch, hydraulic or air seeding, w/mulch & fertil.	B-81	1 Laborer	80	.300	M.S.F.
				1 Equip. Oper. (med.)			
				1 Truck Driver (heavy)			
				1 Hydromulcher, T.M.			
				1 Tractor Truck, 4x2			
	3300	Rye, 10#/M.S.F., annual, push spreader	A-1	1 Building Laborer	10	.800	M.S.F.
				1 Gas Eng. Power Tool			
	3400	Tractor spreader	B-66	1 Equip. Oper. (light)	26	.308	M.S.F.
				1 Backhoe Ldr. w/Attchmt.			
	3500	Hydraulic or air seeding, with mulch and fertil.	B-81	1 Laborer	80	.300	M.S.F.
				1 Equip. Oper. (med.)			
				1 Truck Driver (heavy)			
				1 Hydromulcher, T.M.			
				1 Tractor Truck, 4x2			
	3600	Fine textured, push spreader	A-1	1 Building Laborer	10	.800	M.S.F.
				1 Gas Eng. Power Tool			
	3700	Tractor spreader	B-66	1 Equip. Oper. (light)	26	.308	M.S.F.
				1 Backhoe Ldr. w/Attchmt.			
	3800	Hydraulic or air seeding, with mulch and fertil.	B-81	1 Laborer	80	.300	M.S.F.
				1 Equip. Oper. (med.)			
				1 Truck Driver (heavy)			
				1 Hydromulcher, T.M.			
				1 Tractor Truck, 4x2			
	4000	Shade mix, 6#/M.S.F., push spreader	A-1	1 Building Laborer	10	.800	M.S.F.
				1 Gas Eng. Power Tool			
	4100	Tractor spreader	B-66	1 Equip. Oper. (light)	26	.308	M.S.F.
				1 Backhoe Ldr. w/Attchmt.			
	4200	Hydraulic or air seeding, with mulch and fertil.	B-81	1 Laborer	80	.300	M.S.F.
				1 Equip. Oper. (med.)			
				1 Truck Driver (heavy)			
				1 Hydromulcher, T.M.			
				1 Tractor Truck, 4x2			
	4400	Slope mix, 6#/M.S.F., push spreader	A-1	1 Building Laborer	10	.800	M.S.F.
				1 Gas Eng. Power Tool			
	4500	Tractor spreader	B-66	1 Equip. Oper. (light)	26	.308	M.S.F.
				1 Backhoe Ldr. w/Attchmt.			
	4600	Hydraulic or air seeding, with mulch and fertil.	B-81	1 Laborer	80	.300	M.S.F.
				1 Equip. Oper. (med.)			
				1 Truck Driver (heavy)			
				1 Hydromulcher, T.M.			
				1 Tractor Truck, 4x2			
	4800	Turf mix, 4#/M.S.F., push spreader	A-1	1 Building Laborer	10	.800	M.S.F.
				1 Gas Eng. Power Tool			
	4900	Tractor spreader	B-66	1 Equip. Oper. (light)	26	.308	M.S.F.
				1 Backhoe Ldr. w/Attchmt.			
	5000	Hydraulic or air seeding, with mulch and fertil.	B-81	1 Laborer	80	.300	M.S.F.
				1 Equip. Oper. (med.)			
				1 Truck Driver (heavy)			
				1 Hydromulcher, T.M.			
				1 Tractor Truck, 4x2			
	5200	Utility mix, 7#/M.S.F., push spreader	A-1	1 Building Laborer	10	.800	M.S.F.
				1 Gas Eng. Power Tool			
	5300	Tractor spreader	B-66	1 Equip. Oper. (light)	26	.308	M.S.F.
				1 Backhoe Ldr. w/Attchmt.			

029 300 | Lawns & Grasses

			CREW	MAKEUP	DAILY OUTPUT	MAN-HOURS	UNIT
308	5401	Utility mix, hydraulic or air seeding, w/mulch & fertil.	B-81	1 Laborer	80	.300	M.S.F.
				1 Equip. Oper. (med.)			
				1 Truck Driver (heavy)			
				1 Hydromulcher, T.M.			
				1 Tractor Truck, 4x2			
	5600	Wildflower, .10#/M.S.F., push spreader	A-1	1 Building Laborer	10	.800	M.S.F.
				1 Gas Eng. Power Tool			
	5700	Tractor spreader	B-66	1 Equip. Oper. (light)	52	.154	M.S.F.
				1 Backhoe Ldr. w/Attchmt.			
	5800	Hydraulic or air seeding, with mulch and fertil.	B-81	1 Laborer	80	.300	M.S.F.
				1 Equip. Oper. (med.)			
				1 Truck Driver (heavy)			
				1 Hydromulcher, T.M.			
				1 Tractor Truck, 4x2			
	316	SODDING, 1" deep, blue grass sod, on level ground, over 8 M.S.F.	B-63	4 Building Laborers	8	5.000	M.S.F.
				1 Equip. Oper. (light)			
				1 Loader, Skid Steer			
	0200	4 M.S.F.			7	5.710	M.S.F.
	0300	1000 S.F.			6	6.670	M.S.F.
	0500	Sloped ground, over 8 M.S.F.			6	6.670	M.S.F.
	0600	4 M.S.F.			5	8.000	M.S.F.
	0700	1000 S.F.			4	10.000	M.S.F.
	1000	Bent grass sod, on level ground, over 6 M.S.F.			20	2.000	M.S.F.
	1100	3 M.S.F.			18	2.220	M.S.F.
	1200	1000 S.F.			16	2.500	M.S.F.
	1500	Sloped ground, over 6 M.S.F.			15	2.670	M.S.F.
	1600	3 M.S.F.			13.50	2.960	M.S.F.
	1700	1000 S.F.	↓	↓	12	3.330	M.S.F.

029 500 | Trees/Plants/Grnd Cover

			CREW	MAKEUP	DAILY OUTPUT	MAN-HOURS	UNIT
	508	GROUND COVER AND VINES planting only, no preparation					
	0100	Ajuga, 1 year, bare root	B-1	1 Labor Foreman (outside)	9	2.670	C
				2 Building Laborers			
	0150	Potted, 2 year			6	4.000	C
	0200	Bearberry, potted, 2 year			6	4.000	C
	0250	Cotoneaster, 15"-18", shady areas, B & B			.60	40.000	C
	0300	Boston ivy, on bank, 1 year, bare root			6	4.000	C
	0350	Potted, 2 year			6	4.000	C
	0400	English ivy, 1 year, bare root			9	2.670	C
	0450	Potted, 2 year			6	4.000	C
	0500	Halls honeysuckle, 1 year, bare root			5	4.800	C
	0550	Potted, 2 year			4	6.000	C
	0600	Memorial rose, 9"-12", 1 gallon container			3	8.000	C
	0650	Potted, 2 gallon container			2	12.000	C
	0700	Pachysandra, 1 year, bare root			10	2.400	C
	0750	Potted, 2 year			6	4.000	C
	0800	Vinca minor, 1 year, bare root			10	2.400	C
	0850	Potted, 2 year			6	4.000	C
	0900	Woodbine, on bank, 1/2 year, bare root			6	4.000	C
	0950	Potted, 2 year	↓	↓	4	6.000	C
	2000	Alternate method of figuring					
	2100	Ajuga, field division, 4000/M.S.F.	B-1	1 Labor Foreman (outside)	.23	104.000	M.S.F.
				2 Building Laborers			
	2300	Boston ivy, 1 year, 60/M.S.F.			10	2.400	M.S.F.
	2400	English ivy, 1 yr., 500/M.S.F.			1.80	13.330	M.S.F.
	2500	Halls honeysuckle, 1 yr., 333/M.S.F.			1.50	16.000	M.S.F.
	2600	Memorial rose, 9"-12", 1 gal., 333/M.S.F.			.90	26.670	M.S.F.
	2700	Pachysandra, 1 yr., 4000/M.S.F.	↓	↓	.25	96.000	M.S.F.

029 500 | Trees/Plants/Grnd Cover

			CREW	MAKEUP	DAILY OUTPUT	MAN-HOURS	UNIT
508	2801	Planting, Vinca Minor, rooted cutting, 2000/M.S.F.	B-1	1 Labor Foreman (outside)	1	24.000	M.S.F.
				2 Building Laborers			
	2900	Woodbine, 1 yr., 60/M.S.F.	"	"	10	2.400	M.S.F.
	516	**MULCH**					
	0100	Aged barks, 3" deep, hand spread	1 Clab	1 Building Laborer	100	.080	S.Y.
	0150	Skid steer loader	B-63	4 Building Laborers	13.50	2.960	M.S.F.
				1 Equip. Oper. (light)			
				1 Loader, Skid Steer			
	0200	Hay, 1" deep, hand spread	1 Clab	1 Building Laborer	475	.017	S.Y.
	0250	Power mulcher, small	B-64	1 Building Laborer	180	.089	M.S.F.
				1 Truck Driver (light)			
				1 Power Mulcher (small)			
				1 Light Truck, 1.5 Ton			
	0350	Large	B-65	1 Building Laborer	530	.030	M.S.F.
				1 Truck Driver (light)			
				1 Power Mulcher (large)			
				1 Light Truck, 1.5 Ton			
	0400	Humus peat, 1" deep, hand spread	1 Clab	1 Building Laborer	700	.011	S.Y.
	0450	Push spreader	A-1	1 Building Laborer	2,500	.003	S.Y.
				1 Gas Eng. Power Tool			
	0550	Tractor spreader	B-66	1 Equip. Oper. (light)	700	.011	M.S.F.
				1 Backhoe Ldr. w/Attchmt.			
	0600	Oat straw, 1" deep, hand spread	1 Clab	1 Building Laborer	475	.017	S.Y.
	0650	Power mulcher, small	B-64	1 Building Laborer	180	.089	M.S.F.
				1 Truck Driver (light)			
				1 Power Mulcher (small)			
				1 Light Truck, 1.5 Ton			
	0700	Large	B-65	1 Building Laborer	530	.030	M.S.F.
				1 Truck Driver (light)			
				1 Power Mulcher (large)			
				1 Light Truck, 1.5 Ton			
	0750	Add for asphaltic emulsion	B-45	1 Equip. Oper. (med.)	1,770	.009	Gal.
				1 Truck Driver (heavy)			
				1 Dist. Tank Truck, 3K Gal.			
				1 Tractor, 4 x 2, 250 H.P.			
	0800	Peat moss, 1" deep, hand spread	1 Clab	1 Building Laborer	900	.009	S.Y.
	0850	Push spreader	A-1	1 Building Laborer	2,500	.003	S.Y.
				1 Gas Eng. Power Tool			
	0950	Tractor spreader	B-66	1 Equip. Oper. (light)	700	.011	M.S.F.
				1 Backhoe Ldr. w/Attchmt.			
	1000	Polyethylene film, 6 mil.	2 Clab	2 Building Laborers	2,000	.008	S.Y.
	1100	Redwood nuggets, 3" deep, hand spread	1 Clab	1 Building Laborer	150	.053	S.Y.
	1150	Skid steer loader	B-63	4 Building Laborers	13.50	2.960	M.S.F.
				1 Equip. Oper. (light)			
				1 Loader, Skid Steer			
	1200	Stone mulch, hand spread, ceramic chips, economy	B-14	1 Labor Foreman (outside)	125	.384	S.Y.
				4 Building Laborers			
				1 Equip. Oper. (light)			
				1 Backhoe Loader, 48 H.P.			
	1250	Deluxe	"	"	95	.505	S.Y.
	1300	Granite chips	B-1	1 Labor Foreman (outside)	10	2.400	C.Y.
				2 Building Laborers			
	1400	Marble chips			10	2.400	C.Y.
	1500	Onyx gemstone			10	2.400	C.Y.
	1600	Pea gravel	↓	↓	28	.857	C.Y.
	1700	Quartz			10	2.400	C.Y.
	1800	Tar paper, 15 Lb. felt	1 Clab	1 Building Laborer	800	.010	S.Y.
	1900	Wood chips, 2" deep, hand spread	"	"	220	.036	S.Y.

029 500 | Trees/Plants/Grnd Cover

		Item	CREW	MAKEUP	DAILY OUTPUT	MAN-HOURS	UNIT
516	1951	Wood chips, 2" deep, skid steer loader	B-63	4 Building Laborers	20.30	1.970	M.S.F.
				1 Equip. Oper. (light)			
				1 Loader, Skid Steer			
	520	**PLANTING** Moving shrubs on site, 12" ball	B-1	1 Labor Foreman (outside)	28	.857	Ea.
				2 Building Laborers			
	0100	24" ball	"	"	22	1.090	Ea.
	0300	Moving trees on site, 36" ball	B-6	2 Building Laborers	3.75	6.400	Ea.
				1 Equip. Oper. (light)			
				1 Backhoe Loader, 48 H.P.			
	0400	60" ball	"	"	1	24.000	Ea.
	524	**SHRUBS** Broadleaf evergreen, planted in prepared beds					
	0100	Andromeda, 15"-18", container	B-1	1 Labor Foreman (outside)	96	.250	Ea.
				2 Building Laborers			
	0200	Azalea, 15"-18", container			96	.250	Ea.
	0300	Barberry, 9"-12", container			130	.185	Ea.
	0400	Boxwood, 15"-18", B & B			96	.250	Ea.
	0500	Euonymus, emerald gaiety, 12" to 15", container			115	.209	Ea.
	0600	Holly, 15"-18", B & B			96	.250	Ea.
	0700	Leucothoe, 15"-18", container			96	.250	Ea.
	0800	Mahonia, 18"-24", container			80	.300	Ea.
	0900	Mount laurel, 18"-24", B & B			80	.300	Ea.
	1000	Privet, 18" to 24" high			130	.185	Ea.
	1100	Rhododendron, 18"-24", container			48	.500	Ea.
	1200	Rosemary, 1 gal container			600	.040	Ea.
	2000	Deciduous, amelanchier, 2'-3', B & B			57	.421	Ea.
	2100	Azalea, 15"-18", B & B			96	.250	Ea.
	2200	Barberry, 2'-3', B & B			57	.421	Ea.
	2300	Bayberry, 2'-3', B & B			57	.421	Ea.
	2400	Boston ivy, 2 year, container	↓	↓	600	.040	Ea.
	2500	Corylus, 3'-4', B & B	B-17	2 Building Laborers	75	.427	Ea.
				1 Equip. Oper. (light)			
				1 Truck Driver (heavy)			
				1 Backhoe Loader, 48 H.P.			
				1 Dump Truck, 12 Ton			
	2600	Cotoneaster, 15"-18", B & B	B-1	1 Labor Foreman (outside)	80	.300	Ea.
				2 Building Laborers			
	2700	Deutzia, 12"-15", B & B	"	"	96	.250	Ea.
	2800	Dogwood, 3'-4', B & B	B-17	2 Building Laborers	40	.800	Ea.
				1 Equip. Oper. (light)			
				1 Truck Driver (heavy)			
				1 Backhoe Loader, 48 H.P.			
				1 Dump Truck, 12 Ton			
	2900	Euonymus, alatus compacta, 15" to 18", container	B-1	1 Labor Foreman (outside)	80	.300	Ea.
				2 Building Laborers			
	3000	Flowering almond, 2'-3', container	"	"	36	.667	Ea.
	3100	Flowering currant, 3'-4', container	B-17	2 Building Laborers	75	.427	Ea.
				1 Equip. Oper. (light)			
				1 Truck Driver (heavy)			
				1 Backhoe Loader, 48 H.P.			
				1 Dump Truck, 12 Ton			
	3200	Forsythia, 2'-3', container	B-1	1 Labor Foreman (outside)	60	.400	Ea.
				2 Building Laborers			
	3300	Hibiscus, 3'-4', B & B	B-17	2 Building Laborers	75	.427	Ea.
				1 Equip. Oper. (light)			
				1 Truck Driver (heavy)			
				1 Backhoe Loader, 48 H.P.			
				1 Dump Truck, 12 Ton			

029 500 | Trees/Plants/Grnd Cover

		Description	CREW	MAKEUP	DAILY OUTPUT	MAN-HOURS	UNIT
524	3401	Shrub planting, Honeysuckle, 3'-4', b & b	B-1	1 Labor Foreman (outside) 2 Building Laborers	60	.400	Ea.
	3500	Hydrangea, 2'-3', B & B	"	"	57	.421	Ea.
	3600	Lilac, 3'-4', B & B	B-17	2 Building Laborers 1 Equip. Oper. (light) 1 Truck Driver (heavy) 1 Backhoe Loader, 48 H.P. 1 Dump Truck, 12 Ton	40	.800	Ea.
	3700	Mockorange, 3'-4', B & B	B-1	1 Labor Foreman (outside) 2 Building Laborers	36	.667	Ea.
	3800	Osier willow, 2'-3', B & B			57	.421	Ea.
	3900	Privet, bare root, 18"-24"			80	.300	Ea.
	4000	Pyracantha, 2'-3', container			80	.300	Ea.
	4100	Quince, 2'-3', B & B	↓	↓	57	.421	Ea.
	4200	Russian olive, 3'-4', B & B	B-17	2 Building Laborers 1 Equip. Oper. (light) 1 Truck Driver (heavy) 1 Backhoe Loader, 48 H.P. 1 Dump Truck, 12 Ton	75	.427	Ea.
	4300	Snowberry, 2'-3', B & B	B-1	1 Labor Foreman (outside) 2 Building Laborers	57	.421	Ea.
	4400	Spirea, 3'-4', B & B	"	"	70	.343	Ea.
	4500	Viburnum, 3'-4', B & B	B-17	2 Building Laborers 1 Equip. Oper. (light) 1 Truck Driver (heavy) 1 Backhoe Loader, 48 H.P. 1 Dump Truck, 12 Ton	40	.800	Ea.
	4600	Weigela, 3'-4', B & B	B-1	1 Labor Foreman (outside) 2 Building Laborers	70	.343	Ea.
	528	**SHRUBS AND TREES** Evergreen, in prepared beds, B & B					
	0100	Arborvitae pyramidal, 4'-5'	B-17	2 Building Laborers 1 Equip. Oper. (light) 1 Truck Driver (heavy) 1 Backhoe Loader, 48 H.P. 1 Dump Truck, 12 Ton	30	1.070	Ea.
	0150	Globe, 12"-15"	B-1	1 Labor Foreman (outside) 2 Building Laborers	96	.250	Ea.
	0200	Balsam, fraser, 6'-7'	B-17	2 Building Laborers 1 Equip. Oper. (light) 1 Truck Driver (heavy) 1 Backhoe Loader, 48 H.P. 1 Dump Truck, 12 Ton	30	1.070	Ea.
	0300	Cedar, blue, 8'-10'			18	1.780	Ea.
	0350	Japanese, 4'-5'	↓	↓	55	.582	Ea.
	0400	Cypress, hinoki, 15"-18"	B-1	1 Labor Foreman (outside) 2 Building Laborers	80	.300	Ea.
	0500	Hemlock, canadian, 2-1/2'-3'			36	.667	Ea.
	0600	Juniper, andora, 18"-24"			80	.300	Ea.
	0620	Wiltoni, 15"-18"	↓	↓	80	.300	Ea.
	0640	Skyrocket, 4-1/2'-5'	B-17	2 Building Laborers 1 Equip. Oper. (light) 1 Truck Driver (heavy) 1 Backhoe Loader, 48 H.P. 1 Dump Truck, 12 Ton	55	.582	Ea.
	0660	Blue pfitzer, 2'-2-1/2'	B-1	1 Labor Foreman (outside) 2 Building Laborers	44	.545	Ea.
	0680	Ketleerie, 2-1/2'-3'			50	.480	Ea.
	0700	Pine, black, 2-1/2'-3'	↓	↓	50	.480	Ea.

029 500 | Trees/Plants/Grnd Cover

		Item	CREW	MAKEUP	DAILY OUTPUT	MAN-HOURS	UNIT
528	0721	Shrub & tree planting, pine, Mugo, 18"-24"	B-1	1 Labor Foreman (outside)	60	.400	Ea.
				2 Building Laborers			
	0740	White, 4'-5'	B-17	2 Building Laborers	75	.427	Ea.
				1 Equip. Oper. (light)			
				1 Truck Driver (heavy)			
				1 Backhoe Loader, 48 H.P.			
				1 Dump Truck, 12 Ton			
	0800	Spruce, blue, 18"-24"	B-1	1 Labor Foreman (outside)	60	.400	Ea.
				2 Building Laborers			
	0820	Dwarf alberta, 18"-24"	"	"	60	.400	Ea.
	0840	Norway, 4'-5'	B-17	2 Building Laborers	75	.427	Ea.
				1 Equip. Oper. (light)			
				1 Truck Driver (heavy)			
				1 Backhoe Loader, 48 H.P.			
				1 Dump Truck, 12 Ton			
	0900	Yew, denisforma, 12"-15"	B-1	1 Labor Foreman (outside)	60	.400	Ea.
				2 Building Laborers			
	1000	Capitata, 18"-24"	↓	↓	30	.800	Ea.
	1100	Hicksi, 2'-2-1/2'			30	.800	Ea.
536		**TREES** Deciduous, in prep. beds, balled & burlapped (B&B)					
	0100	2" caliper	B-17	2 Building Laborers	8	4.000	Ea.
				1 Equip. Oper. (light)			
				1 Truck Driver (heavy)			
				1 Backhoe Loader, 48 H.P.			
				1 Dump Truck, 12 Ton			
	0200	Beech, 5'-6'			50	.640	Ea.
	0300	Birch, 6'-8', 3 stems			20	1.600	Ea.
	0400	Cherry, 6'-8', 1" caliper			24	1.330	Ea.
	0500	Crabapple, 6'-8'			20	1.600	Ea.
	0600	Dogwood, 4'-5'			40	.800	Ea.
	0700	Eastern redbud 4'-5'			40	.800	Ea.
	0800	Elm, 8'-10'			20	1.600	Ea.
	0900	Ginkgo, 6'-7'			24	1.330	Ea.
	1000	Hawthorn, 8'-10', 1" caliper			20	1.600	Ea.
	1100	Honeylocust, 10'-12', 1-1/2" caliper			10	3.200	Ea.
	1200	Laburnum, 6'-8', 1" caliper			24	1.330	Ea.
	1300	Larch, 8'			32	1.000	Ea.
	1400	Linden, 8'-10', 1" caliper			20	1.600	Ea.
	1500	Magnolia, 4'-5'			20	1.600	Ea.
	1600	Maple, red, 8'-10', 1-1/2" caliper			10	3.200	Ea.
	1700	Mountain ash, 8'-10', 1" caliper			16	2.000	Ea.
	1800	Oak, 2-1/2"-3" caliper			3	10.670	Ea.
	1900	Pagoda, 6'-8'			20	1.600	Ea.
	2000	Pear, 6'-8', 1" caliper			20	1.600	Ea.
	2100	Planetree, 9'-11', 1-1/4" caliper			10	3.200	Ea.
	2200	Plum, 6'-8', 1" caliper			20	1.600	Ea.
	2300	Poplar, 9'-11', 1-1/4" caliper			10	3.200	Ea.
	2400	Shadbush, 4'-5'			60	.533	Ea.
	2500	Sumac, 2'-3'			75	.427	Ea.
	2600	Tupelo, 5'-6'			40	.800	Ea.
	2700	Tulip, 5'-6'			40	.800	Ea.
	2800	Willow, 6'-8', 1" caliper	↓	↓	20	1.600	Ea.

3

DIVISION 3

CONCRETE

DIVISION 3 CONCRETE

Subdivisions in the Concrete Division include: Formwork and Expansion Joints, Reinforcing Steel, Cast in Place Concrete, Precast Concrete, and Cementitous Decks.

The most important element affecting productivity in concrete construction is advance planning. Many of the factors that normally add time to a job can be avoided with careful scheduling and adequate supervision. Close coordination and cooperation with all other trades is a prerequisite since work in concrete is somewhat irreversible. For the project manager, this is a matter of forethought and exact scheduling of important steps such as the forming sequence, placing of reinforcing steel, concrete delivery and placement, as well as form stripping, finishing, and curing.

A major portion of any concrete job falls under the "Formwork" classification. Productivity in formwork is dependent on site conditions and material access, the height of work, and the type of forming system employed. Specialty jobs involve a higher number of man-hours. Productivity decreases when special finishes are required or when there is an increase in the complexity of the form geometry.

Special attention must be paid to weather conditions. Concrete can be placed at higher or lower temperatures than normal, but there are added costs and time involved due to additives and special protection required during the curing process.

When estimating the duration of a concrete pour, it is important to know how close trucks will be able to get to the pour. If it is not possible to use a direct chute for the truck, alternate concrete placement methods must be analyzed ahead of time. Each method of placement — concrete pump, conveyor belt, crane and bucket, wheelbarrow, and buggy — has its own particular productivity level.

By design, reinforcing steel has a regimented method of placement and requires planning and scheduling to ensure that equipment is available for sorting, lifting, and placing final elements. Special connections and splices, as well as complex forms, field bends, and installation in restricted work areas greatly affect productivity. Reinforcing steel is more difficult to install when the placement and dimension of the reinforcement are out of the ordinary.

031 100	Struct C.I.P. Formwork	CREW	MAKEUP	DAILY OUTPUT	MAN-HOURS	UNIT
132	**EXPANSION JOINT** Keyed cold joint, 24 ga., incl. stakes, 3-1/2" high	1 Carp	1 Carpenter	200	.040	L.F.
0050	4-1/2" high			200	.040	L.F.
0100	5-1/2" high			195	.041	L.F.
0150	7-1/2" high			190	.042	L.F.
0300	Poured asphalt, plain, 1/2" x 1"	1 Clab	1 Building Laborer	450	.018	L.F.
0350	1" x 2"			400	.020	L.F.
0500	Neoprene, liquid, cold applied, 1/2" x 1"			450	.018	L.F.
0550	1" x 2"			400	.020	L.F.
0700	Polyurethane, 1 part, 1/2" x 1"			400	.020	L.F.
0750	1" x 2"			350	.023	L.F.
0900	Rubberized asphalt, hot or cold applied, 1/2" x 1"			450	.018	L.F.
0950	1" x 2"			400	.020	L.F.
1100	Hot applied, fuel resistant, 1/2" x 1"			450	.018	L.F.
1150	1" x 2"			400	.020	L.F.
2000	Premolded, bituminous fiber, 1/2" x 6"	1 Carp	1 Carpenter	375	.021	L.F.
2050	1" x 12"			300	.027	L.F.
2250	Cork with resin binder, 1/2" x 6"			375	.021	L.F.
2300	1" x 12"			300	.027	L.F.
2500	Neoprene sponge, closed cell, 1/2" x 6"			375	.021	L.F.
2550	1" x 12"			300	.027	L.F.
2750	Polyethylene foam, 1/2" x 6"			375	.021	L.F.
2800	1" x 12"			300	.027	L.F.
3000	Polyethylene backer rod, 3/8" diameter			500	.016	L.F.
3050	3/4" diameter			495	.016	L.F.
3100	1" diameter			490	.016	L.F.
3500	Polyurethane foam, with polybutylene, 1/2" x 1/2"			475	.017	L.F.
3550	1" x 1"			450	.018	L.F.
3750	Polyurethane foam, regular, closed cell, 1/2" x 6"			375	.021	L.F.
3800	1" x 12"			300	.027	L.F.
4000	Polyvinyl chloride foam, closed cell, 1/2" x 6"			375	.021	L.F.
4050	1" x 12"			300	.027	L.F.
4250	Rubber, gray sponge, 1/2" x 6"			375	.021	L.F.
4300	1" x 12"			300	.027	L.F.
138	**FORMS IN PLACE, BEAMS AND GIRDERS**					
0504	Beam and Girder, exterior spandrel, 12" wide, 1 use	C-2	1 Carpenter Foreman (out) 4 Carpenters 1 Building Laborer Power Tools	225	.213	SFCA
0550	2 use			275	.175	SFCA
0604	3 use			295	.163	SFCA
0650	4 use			310	.155	SFCA
1004	Exterior spandrel, 18" wide, 1 use			250	.192	SFCA
1050	2 use			275	.175	SFCA
1100	3 use			305	.157	SFCA
1150	4 use			315	.152	SFCA
1500	Exterior spandrel, 24" wide, 1 use			265	.181	SFCA
1550	2 use			290	.166	SFCA
1600	3 use			315	.152	SFCA
1650	4 use			325	.148	SFCA
2000	Interior beams, 12" wide, 1 use			300	.160	SFCA
2050	2 use			340	.141	SFCA
2100	3 use			364	.132	SFCA
2150	4 use			377	.127	SFCA
2500	Interior beams, 24" wide, 1 use			320	.150	SFCA
2550	2 use			365	.132	SFCA
2600	3 use			385	.125	SFCA
2650	4 use			395	.122	SFCA
3000	Beam and Girder, encasing steel frame, hung, 1 use			325	.148	SFCA

031 100 | Struct C.I.P. Formwork

		CREW	MAKEUP	DAILY OUTPUT	MAN-HOURS	UNIT
138 3051	Forms in place, beam & girder, encase stl frame, hung, 2 use	C-2	1 Carpenter Foreman (out)	390	.123	SFCA
			4 Carpenters			
			1 Building Laborer			
			Power Tools			
3100	3 use			415	.116	SFCA
3150	4 use			430	.112	SFCA
3500	Beam bottoms only, 24" wide, 1 use			230	.209	SFCA
3550	2 use			265	.181	SFCA
3600	3 use			280	.171	SFCA
3650	4 use			290	.166	SFCA
4000	Beam sides only, vertical, 36" high, 1 use			335	.143	SFCA
4050	2 use			405	.119	SFCA
4100	3 use			430	.112	SFCA
4150	4 use			445	.108	SFCA
4500	Sloped sides, 36" high, 1 use			305	.157	SFCA
4550	2 use			370	.130	SFCA
4600	3 use			405	.119	SFCA
4650	4 use			425	.113	SFCA
5000	Upstanding beams, 36" high, 1 use			225	.213	SFCA
5050	2 use			255	.188	SFCA
5100	3 use			275	.175	SFCA
5150	4 use	↓	↓	280	.171	SFCA
142	**FORMS IN PLACE, COLUMNS**					
0500	Round fiberglass, 4 use per mo., rent, 12" diameter	C-1	3 Carpenters	160	.200	L.F.
			1 Building Laborer			
			Power Tools			
0550	16" diameter			150	.213	L.F.
0600	18" diameter			140	.229	L.F.
0650	24" diameter			135	.237	L.F.
0700	28" diameter			130	.246	L.F.
0800	30" diameter			125	.256	L.F.
0850	36" diameter			120	.267	L.F.
1500	Round fiber tube, 1 use, 8" diameter			155	.206	L.F.
1550	10" diameter			155	.206	L.F.
1600	12" diameter			150	.213	L.F.
1650	14" diameter			145	.221	L.F.
1700	16" diameter			140	.229	L.F.
1750	20" diameter			135	.237	L.F.
1800	24" diameter			130	.246	L.F.
1850	30" diameter			125	.256	L.F.
1900	36" diameter			115	.278	L.F.
1950	42" diameter			100	.320	L.F.
2000	48" diameter			85	.376	L.F.
3000	Round, steel, 4 use per mo., rent, regular duty, 12" diam.			145	.221	L.F.
3050	16" diameter			125	.256	L.F.
3100	Heavy duty, 20" diameter			105	.305	L.F.
3150	24" diameter			85	.376	L.F.
3200	30" diameter			70	.457	L.F.
3250	36" diameter			60	.533	L.F.
3300	48" diameter			50	.640	L.F.
3350	60" diameter			45	.711	L.F.
4000	Column capitals, 4 use per mo., 24" col, 4' cap diameter			12	2.670	Ea.
4050	5' cap diameter			11	2.910	Ea.
4100	6' cap diameter			10	3.200	Ea.
4150	7' cap diameter			9	3.560	Ea.
5004	Plywood, 8" x 8" columns, 1 use			165	.194	SFCA
5050	2 use			195	.164	SFCA
5104	3 use	↓	↓	210	.152	SFCA

031 100 | Struct C.I.P. Formwork

		Description	CREW	MAKEUP		DAILY OUTPUT	MAN-HOURS	UNIT
142	5151	Forms in place, 8" x 8" plywood columns, 4 use	C-1	3 Carpenters		215	.149	SFCA
				1 Building Laborer				
				Power Tools				
	5500	12" x 12" plywood columns, 1 use				180	.178	SFCA
	5550	2 use				210	.152	SFCA
	5600	3 use				220	.145	SFCA
	5650	4 use				225	.142	SFCA
	6000	16" x 16" plywood columns, 1 use				185	.173	SFCA
	6050	2 use				215	.149	SFCA
	6100	3 use				230	.139	SFCA
	6150	4 use				235	.136	SFCA
	6500	24" x 24" plywood columns, 1 use				190	.168	SFCA
	6550	2 use				216	.148	SFCA
	6600	3 use				230	.139	SFCA
	6650	4 use				238	.134	SFCA
	7000	36" x 36" plywood columns, 1 use				200	.160	SFCA
	7050	2 use				230	.139	SFCA
	7100	3 use				245	.131	SFCA
	7150	4 use				250	.128	SFCA
	7500	Steel framed plywood, 4 use per mo., rent, 8" x 8"				290	.110	SFCA
	7550	10" x 10"				300	.107	SFCA
	7600	12" x 12"				310	.103	SFCA
	7650	16" x 16"				335	.096	SFCA
	7700	20" x 20"				350	.091	SFCA
	7750	24" x 24"				365	.088	SFCA
	146	**FORMS IN PLACE, CULVERT** 5' to 8' square or rectangular, 1 use				170	.188	SFCA
	0050	2 use				180	.178	SFCA
	0104	3 use				190	.168	SFCA
	0150	4 use	↓	↓		200	.160	SFCA
	150	**FORMS IN PLACE, ELEVATED SLABS**						
	1000	Flat plate to 15' high, 1 use	C-2	1 Carpenter Foreman (out)		470	.102	S.F.
				4 Carpenters				
				1 Building Laborer				
				Power Tools				
	1050	2 use				520	.092	S.F.
	1100	3 use				545	.088	S.F.
	1150	4 use				560	.086	S.F.
	1500	15' to 20' high ceilings, 4 use				495	.097	S.F.
	1600	21' to 35' high ceilings, 4 use				450	.107	S.F.
	2000	Flat slab with drop panels, to 15' high, 1 use				449	.107	S.F.
	2050	2 use				509	.094	S.F.
	2100	3 use				532	.090	S.F.
	2150	4 use				544	.088	S.F.
	2250	15' to 20' high ceilings, 4 use				480	.100	S.F.
	2350	21' to 35' high ceilings, 4 use				435	.110	S.F.
	3000	Floor slab hung from steel beams, 1 use				485	.099	S.F.
	3050	2 use				535	.090	S.F.
	3100	3 use				550	.087	S.F.
	3150	4 use				565	.085	S.F.
	3510	Floor slab, with 20" metal pans, 1 use				415	.116	S.F.
	3550	2 use				445	.108	S.F.
	3600	3 use				475	.101	S.F.
	3650	4 use				500	.096	S.F.
	3700	Floor slab with 30" metal pans, 1 use				418	.115	S.F.
	3720	2 use				455	.105	S.F.
	3740	3 use				470	.102	S.F.
	3760	4 use				480	.100	S.F.
	4004	Floor slab with 19" metal domes, 1 use	↓	↓		405	.119	S.F.

031 100 | Struct C.I.P. Formwork

		CREW	MAKEUP	DAILY OUTPUT	MAN-HOURS	UNIT
150 4051	Forms in place, floor slab w/19" metal domes, 2 use	C-2	1 Carpenter Foreman (out)	435	.110	S.F.
			4 Carpenters			
			1 Building Laborer			
			Power Tools			
4100	3 use			465	.103	S.F.
4150	4 use			495	.097	S.F.
5000	Box out for slab openings, over 16" deep, 1 use			190	.253	SFCA
5050	2 use			240	.200	SFCA
5500	Shallow slab box outs, to 10 S.F.			42	1.140	Ea.
5550	Over 10 S.F. (use perimeter)			400	.120	L.F.
6000	Bulkhead forms for slab, with keyway, 1 use, 2 piece			500	.096	L.F.
6100	3 piece	↓	↓	460	.104	L.F.
6500	Curb forms, wood, 6" to 12" high, on elevated slabs, 1 use	C-1	3 Carpenters	180	.178	SFCA
			1 Building Laborer			
			Power Tools			
6550	2 use			205	.156	SFCA
6600	3 use			220	.145	SFCA
6650	4 use			225	.142	SFCA
7000	Edge forms to 6" high, on elevated slab, 4 use			500	.064	L.F.
7070	7" to 12" high, 1 use			162	.198	SFCA
7080	2 use			198	.162	SFCA
7090	3 use			222	.144	SFCA
7101	4 use			350	.091	SFCA
7500	Depressed area forms to 12" high, 4 use			300	.107	L.F.
7550	12" to 24" high, 4 use			175	.183	L.F.
8000	Perimeter deck and rail for elevated slabs, straight			90	.356	L.F.
8050	Curved			65	.492	L.F.
8500	Void forms, round fiber, 3" diameter			450	.071	L.F.
8550	4" diameter, void			425	.075	L.F.
8600	6" diameter, void			400	.080	L.F.
8650	8" diameter, void			375	.085	L.F.
8700	10" diameter, void			350	.091	L.F.
8750	12" diameter, void	↓	↓	300	.107	L.F.
154	**FORMS IN PLACE, EQUIPMENT FOUNDATIONS** 1 use	C-2	1 Carpenter Foreman (out)	160	.300	SFCA
			4 Carpenters			
			1 Building Laborer			
			Power Tools			
0050	2 use			190	.253	SFCA
0100	3 use			200	.240	SFCA
0150	4 use	↓	↓	205	.234	SFCA
158	**FORMS IN PLACE, FOOTINGS** Continuous wall, 1 use	C-1	3 Carpenters	375	.085	SFCA
			1 Building Laborer			
			Power Tools			
0050	2 use			440	.073	SFCA
0100	3 use			470	.068	SFCA
0150	4 use			485	.066	SFCA
0500	Dowel supports for footings or beams, 1 use			500	.064	L.F.
1000	Integral starter wall, to 4" high, 1 use	↓	↓	400	.080	L.F.
1500	Keyway, 4 uses, tapered wood, 2" x 4"	1 Carp	1 Carpenter	530	.015	L.F.
1550	2" x 6"			500	.016	L.F.
2000	Tapered plastic, 2" x 3"			530	.015	L.F.
2050	2" x 4"			500	.016	L.F.
2250	For keyway hung from supports, add	↓	↓	150	.053	L.F.
3004	Pile cap, square or rectangular, 1 use	C-1	3 Carpenters	291	.110	SFCA
			1 Building Laborer			
			Power Tools			
3050	2 use			346	.092	SFCA
3100	3 use	↓	↓	371	.086	SFCA

031 100 | Struct C.I.P. Formwork

		Description	CREW	MAKEUP	DAILY OUTPUT	MAN-HOURS	UNIT
158	3151	Forms in place, pile cap, square or rectangular, 4 use	C-1	3 Carpenters	383	.084	SFCA
				1 Building Laborer			
				Power Tools			
	4000	Triangular or hexagonal caps, 1 use			225	.142	SFCA
	4050	2 use			280	.114	SFCA
	4100	3 use			305	.105	SFCA
	4150	4 use			315	.102	SFCA
	5004	Spread footings, 1 use			306	.105	SFCA
	5050	2 use			371	.086	SFCA
	5100	3 use			401	.080	SFCA
	5150	4 use			414	.077	SFCA
	6000	Supports for dowels, plinths or templates, 2' x 2'			25	1.280	Ea.
	6050	4' x 4' footing			22	1.450	Ea.
	6100	8' x 8' footing			20	1.600	Ea.
	6150	12' x 12' footing			17	1.880	Ea.
	7000	Plinths, 1 use			250	.128	SFCA
	7100	4 use	↓	↓	270	.119	SFCA
162		FORMS IN PLACE, GRADE BEAM 1 use	C-2	1 Carpenter Foreman (out)	530	.091	SFCA
				4 Carpenters			
				1 Building Laborer			
				Power Tools			
	0050	2 use			580	.083	SFCA
	0100	3 use			600	.080	SFCA
	0150	4 use			605	.079	SFCA
166		FORMS IN PLACE, MAT FOUNDATION 1 use			290	.166	SFCA
	0050	2 use			310	.155	SFCA
	0100	3 use			330	.145	SFCA
	0120	4 use	↓	↓	350	.137	SFCA
170		FORMS IN PLACE, SLAB ON GRADE					
	1000	Bulkhead forms with keyway, 1 use, 2 piece	C-1	3 Carpenters	510	.063	L.F.
				1 Building Laborer			
				Power Tools			
	1050	3 piece (see also edge forms)			400	.080	L.F.
	1100	4 piece			350	.091	L.F.
	2000	Curb forms, wood, 6" to 12" high, on grade, 1 use			215	.149	SFCA
	2050	2 use			250	.128	SFCA
	2100	3 use			265	.121	SFCA
	2150	4 use			275	.116	SFCA
	3000	Edge forms, to 6" high, 4 use, on grade			600	.053	L.F.
	3050	7" to 12" high, 4 use, on grade			435	.074	SFCA
	3500	For depressed slabs, 4 use, to 12" high			300	.107	L.F.
	3550	To 24" high			175	.183	L.F.
	4000	For slab blockouts, 1 use to 12" high			200	.160	L.F.
	4050	To 24" high	↓	↓	120	.267	L.F.
	5001	Screed, 24 ga. metal key joint, see Division 031-132					
	5020	Wood, incl. wood stakes, 1" x 3"	C-1	3 Carpenters	900	.036	L.F.
				1 Building Laborer			
				Power Tools			
	5050	2" x 4"			900	.036	L.F.
	6000	Trench forms in floor, 1 use			160	.200	SFCA
	6050	2 use			175	.183	SFCA
	6100	3 use			180	.178	SFCA
	6150	4 use	↓	↓	185	.173	SFCA

031 | Concrete Formwork

031 100 | Struct C.I.P. Formwork

			CREW	MAKEUP	DAILY OUTPUT	MAN-HOURS	UNIT
174	174	FORMS IN PLACE, STAIRS (Slant length x width), 1 use	C-2	1 Carpenter Foreman (out)	165	.291	S.F.
				4 Carpenters			
				1 Building Laborer			
				Power Tools			
	0050	2 use			170	.282	S.F.
	0100	3 use			180	.267	S.F.
	0150	4 use			190	.253	S.F.
	1000	Alternate pricing method (0.7 L.F./S.F.), 1 use			100	.480	LF Rsr
	1050	2 use			105	.457	LF Rsr
	1100	3 use			110	.436	LF Rsr
	1150	4 use			115	.417	LF Rsr
	2000	Stairs, cast on sloping ground (length x width), 1 use			220	.218	S.F.
	2100	4 use	↓	↓	240	.200	S.F.
	182	FORMS IN PLACE, WALLS					
	0100	Box out for wall openings, to 16" thick, to 10 S.F.	C-2	1 Carpenter Foreman (out)	24	2.000	Ea.
				4 Carpenters			
				1 Building Laborer			
				Power Tools			
	0150	Over 10 S.F. (use perimeter)	"	"	280	.171	L.F.
	0250	Brick shelf, 4" wide, add to wall forms, use wall area					
	0260	above shelf, 1 use	C-2	1 Carpenter Foreman (out)	240	.200	SFCA
				4 Carpenters			
				1 Building Laborer			
				Power Tools			
	0300	2 use			275	.175	SFCA
	0350	4 use			300	.160	SFCA
	0500	Bulkhead forms for walls, with keyway, 1 use, 2 piece			265	.181	L.F.
	0550	3 piece			175	.274	L.F.
	0700	Buttress forms, to 8' high, 1 use			350	.137	SFCA
	0750	2 use			430	.112	SFCA
	0800	3 use			460	.104	SFCA
	0850	4 use			480	.100	SFCA
	1000	Corbel (haunch) forms, up to 12" wide, add to wall forms, 1 use			150	.320	L.F.
	1050	2 use			170	.282	L.F.
	1100	3 use			175	.274	L.F.
	1150	4 use			180	.267	L.F.
	2000	Job built plyform wall forms, to 8' high, 1 use			370	.130	SFCA
	2050	2 use			435	.110	SFCA
	2104	3 use			495	.097	SFCA
	2150	4 use			505	.095	SFCA
	2400	Over 8' to 16' high, 1 use			280	.171	SFCA
	2450	2 use			345	.139	SFCA
	2500	3 use			375	.128	SFCA
	2550	4 use			395	.122	SFCA
	2700	Over 16' high, 1 use			235	.204	SFCA
	2750	2 use			290	.166	SFCA
	2800	3 use			315	.152	SFCA
	2850	4 use			330	.145	SFCA
	3000	For architectural finish, add			1,820	.026	SFCA
	4000	Radial wall forms, smooth curved, 1 use			245	.196	SFCA
	4050	2 use			300	.160	SFCA
	4100	3 use			325	.148	SFCA
	4150	4 use			335	.143	SFCA
	4300	Curved, with 2' chords, 1 use			290	.166	SFCA
	4350	2 use			355	.135	SFCA
	4400	3 use			385	.125	SFCA
	4450	4 use	↓	↓	400	.120	SFCA
	4601						

031 100 | Struct C.I.P. Formwork

		CREW	MAKEUP	DAILY OUTPUT	MAN-HOURS	UNIT
182 4901	Forms in place, retaining walls, 8' to 16' high, 1 use	C-2	1 Carpenter Foreman (out)	240	.200	SFCA
			4 Carpenters			
			1 Building Laborer			
			Power Tools			
4950	2 use			295	.163	SFCA
5000	3 use			305	.157	SFCA
5050	4 use	↓	↓	320	.150	SFCA
5750	Liners for forms (add to wall forms), A.B.S. plastic					
5800	Aged wood, 4" wide, 1 use	1 Carp	1 Carpenter	250	.032	SFCA
5820	2 use			400	.020	SFCA
5840	4 use			750	.011	SFCA
5900	Fractured rope rib, 1 use			250	.032	SFCA
6000	4 use			750	.011	SFCA
6100	Ribbed look, 1/2" & 3/4" deep, 1 use			300	.027	SFCA
6200	4 use			800	.010	SFCA
6300	Rustic brick pattern, 1 use			250	.032	SFCA
6400	4 use			750	.011	SFCA
6500	Striated, random, 3/8" x 3/8" deep, 1 use			300	.027	SFCA
6600	4 use	↓	↓	800	.010	SFCA
6800	Rustication strips, A.B.S. plastic, 2 piece snap-on					
6850	1" deep x 1-3/8" wide, 1 use	C-2	1 Carpenter Foreman (out)	400	.120	L.F.
			4 Carpenters			
			1 Building Laborer			
			Power Tools			
6900	2 use			600	.080	L.F.
6950	4 use			800	.060	L.F.
7050	Wood, beveled edge, 3/4" deep, 1 use			600	.080	L.F.
7100	1" deep, 1 use			450	.107	L.F.
7200	For solid board finish, uniform, 1 use, add to wall forms			300	.160	SFCA
7300	Non-uniform finish, 1 use, add to wall forms	↓	↓	250	.192	SFCA
7500	Lintel or sill forms, 1 use	1 Carp	1 Carpenter	30	.267	SFCA
7520	2 use			34	.235	SFCA
7540	3 use			36	.222	SFCA
7560	4 use	↓	↓	37	.216	SFCA
7804	Modular prefabricated plywood, to 8' high, 1 use per month	C-2	1 Carpenter Foreman (out)	910	.053	SFCA
			4 Carpenters			
			1 Building Laborer			
			Power Tools			
7820	2 use per month			930	.052	SFCA
7840	3 use per month			950	.051	SFCA
7860	4 use per month			970	.049	SFCA
8000	To 16' high, 1 use per month			550	.087	SFCA
8020	2 use per month			570	.084	SFCA
8040	3 use per month			590	.081	SFCA
8060	4 use per month			610	.079	SFCA
8600	Pilasters, 1 use			270	.178	SFCA
8620	2 use			330	.145	SFCA
8640	3 use			370	.130	SFCA
8660	4 use			385	.125	SFCA
9004	Steel framed plywood, to 8' high, 1 use per month			600	.080	SFCA
9020	2 use per month			640	.075	SFCA
9040	3 use per month			655	.073	SFCA
9060	4 use per month			665	.072	SFCA
9200	Over 8' to 16' high, 1 use per month			455	.105	SFCA
9220	2 use per month			505	.095	SFCA
9240	3 use per month			525	.091	SFCA
9260	4 use per month			530	.091	SFCA
9400	Over 16' to 20' high, 1 use per month	↓	↓	425	.113	SFCA

031 | Concrete Formwork

031 100 | Struct C.I.P. Formwork

		Description	CREW	MAKEUP	DAILY OUTPUT	MAN-HOURS	UNIT
182	9421	Forms in place, steel framed plywood, 16'-20' high, 2 use/ mo.	C-2	1 Carpenter Foreman (out)	435	.110	SFCA
				4 Carpenters			
				1 Building Laborer			
				Power Tools			
	9440	3 use per month	↓	↓	455	.105	SFCA
	9460	4 use per month			465	.103	SFCA
	186	GAS STATION FORMS Curb fascia, with template,					
	0050	12 ga. steel, left in place, 9" high	1 Carp	1 Carpenter	50	.160	L.F.
	1000	Sign or light bases, 18" diameter, 9" high	↓	↓	9	.889	Ea.
	1050	30" diameter, 13" high			8	1.000	Ea.
	2000	Island forms, 10' long, 9" high, 3'- 6" wide	C-1	3 Carpenters	10	3.200	Ea.
				1 Building Laborer			
				Power Tools			
	2050	4' wide			9	3.560	Ea.
	2500	20' long, 9" high, 4' wide			6	5.330	Ea.
	2550	5' wide	↓	↓	5	6.400	Ea.
	192	SHORES Erect and strip, by hand, horizontal members					
	0500	Aluminum joists and stringers	2 Carp	2 Carpenters	60	.267	Ea.
	0600	Steel, adjustable beams			45	.356	Ea.
	0700	Wood joists			50	.320	Ea.
	0800	Wood stringers			30	.533	Ea.
	1000	Vertical members to 10' high			55	.291	Ea.
	1050	To 13' high			50	.320	Ea.
	1100	To 16' high			45	.356	Ea.
	1500	Reshoring	↓	↓	1,400	.011	S.F.
	1600	Flying truss system	C-17D	2 Skilled Worker Foremen	9,600	.009	SFCA
				8 Skilled Workers			
				.5 Equip. Oper. (crane)			
				.5 Crane, 80 Ton & Tools			
				.5 Hand held power tools			
				.5 Walk behind power tools			
	196	SLIPFORMS Silos, minimum	C-17E	2 Skilled Worker Foremen	3,885	.021	SFCA
				8 Skilled Workers			
				1 Hyd. Jack with Rods			
	0050	Maximum			1,095	.073	SFCA
	1004	Buildings, minimum			3,660	.022	SFCA
	1050	Maximum	↓	↓	875	.091	SFCA
	198	WATERSTOP Polyvinyl chloride, ribbed 3/16" thick, 4" wide	1 Carp	1 Carpenter	155	.052	L.F.
	0050	3/16" thick, 6" wide			145	.055	L.F.
	0500	Ribbed, PVC, with center bulb, 3/16" thick, 9" wide			135	.059	L.F.
	0550	3/8" thick			130	.062	L.F.
	0800	Dumbbell type, PVC, 6" wide, 3/16" thick			150	.053	L.F.
	0850	3/8" thick			145	.055	L.F.
	1000	9" wide, 3/8" thick, PVC, plain			130	.062	L.F.
	1050	Center bulb			130	.062	L.F.
	1250	Split PVC, 3/8" thick, 6" wide			145	.055	L.F.
	1300	9" wide			130	.062	L.F.
	2000	Rubber, flat dumbbell, 3/8" thick, 6" wide			145	.055	L.F.
	2050	9" wide			135	.059	L.F.
	2500	Flat dumbbell split, 3/8" thick, 6" wide			145	.055	L.F.
	2550	9" wide			135	.059	L.F.
	3000	Center bulb, 1/4" thick, 6" wide			145	.055	L.F.
	3050	9" wide			135	.059	L.F.
	3500	Center bulb split, 3/8" thick, 6" wide			145	.055	L.F.
	3550	9" wide	↓	↓	135	.059	L.F.
	5000	Waterstop fittings, rubber, flat					
	5010	Dumbbell or center bulb, 3/8" thick,					
	5200	Field Union, 6" wide	1 Carp	1 Carpenter	50	.160	Ea.

141

031 | Concrete Formwork

031 100 | Struct C.I.P. Formwork

		CREW	MAKEUP	DAILY OUTPUT	MAN-HOURS	UNIT
198 5251	Waterstop fittings, rubber, 3/8" thick, 9" wide	1 Carp	1 Carpenter	50	.160	Ea.
5500	Flat Cross, 6" wide			30	.267	Ea.
5550	9" wide			30	.267	Ea.
6000	Flat Tee, 6" wide			30	.267	Ea.
6050	9" wide			30	.267	Ea.
6500	Flat Ell, 6" wide			40	.200	Ea.
6550	9" wide			40	.200	Ea.
7000	Vertical Tee, 6" wide			25	.320	Ea.
7050	9" wide			25	.320	Ea.
7500	Vertical Ell, 6" wide			35	.229	Ea.
7550	9" wide	↓	↓	35	.229	Ea.

032 | Concrete Reinforcement

032 100 | Reinforcing Steel

		CREW	MAKEUP	DAILY OUTPUT	MAN-HOURS	UNIT
107	**REINFORCING IN PLACE** A615 Grade 60					
0100	Beams & Girders, #3 to #7	4 Rodm	4 Rodman, (Reinf.)	1.60	20.000	Ton
0150	#8 to #14			2.70	11.850	Ton
0200	Columns, #3 to #7			1.50	21.330	Ton
0250	#8 to #14			2.30	13.910	Ton
0300	Spirals, hot rolled, 8" to 15" diameter			2.20	14.550	Ton
0320	15" to 24" diameter			2.20	14.550	Ton
0330	24" to 36" diameter			2.30	13.910	Ton
0340	36" to 48" diameter			2.40	13.330	Ton
0360	48" to 64" diameter			2.50	12.800	Ton
0380	64" to 84" diameter			2.60	12.310	Ton
0390	84" to 96" diameter			2.70	11.850	Ton
0400	Elevated slabs, #4 to #7			2.90	11.030	Ton
0500	Footings, #4 to #7			2.10	15.240	Ton
0550	#8 to #14			3.60	8.890	Ton
0600	Slab on grade, #3 to #7			2.30	13.910	Ton
0700	Walls, #3 to #7			3	10.670	Ton
0750	#8 to #14			4	8.000	Ton
1000	Typical in place, 10 ton lots, average			1.70	18.820	Ton
1100	Over 50 ton lots, average	↓	↓	2.30	13.910	Ton
2000	Unloading & sorting, add to above	C-5	1 Rodman Foreman	100	.560	Ton
			4 Rodmen (reinf.)			
			1 Equip. Oper. (crane)			
			1 Equip. Oper. Oiler			
			1 Hyd. Crane, 25 Ton			
2200	Crane cost for handling, add to above, minimum			135	.415	Ton
2210	Average			92	.609	Ton
2220	Maximum	↓	↓	35	1.600	Ton
2400	Dowels, 2 feet long, deformed, #3 bar	2 Rodm	2 Rodman, (Reinf.)	140	.114	Ea.
2410	#4 bar			125	.128	Ea.
2420	#5 bar			110	.145	Ea.
2430	#6 bar			105	.152	Ea.
2450	Longer and heavier dowels			450	.036	Lb.
2500	Smooth dowels, 12" long, 1/4" or 3/8" diameter			140	.114	Ea.
2520	5/8" diameter			125	.128	Ea.
2530	3/4" diameter			110	.145	Ea.
2700	Dowel caps, 5" long, 1/2" to 3/4" diameter	↓	↓	800	.020	Ea.

032 100 | Reinforcing Steel

		Description	CREW	MAKEUP	DAILY OUTPUT	MAN-HOURS	UNIT
107	2721	Reinforcing, dowel caps, 5" long, 1-1/4" diameter	2 Rodm	2 Rodman, (Reinf.)	750	.021	Ea.
	109	**SPLICING REINFORCING BARS** Incl. holding bars in					
	0020	place while splicing					
	0100	Butt weld columns #4 bars	C-5	1 Rodman Foreman	190	.295	Ea.
				4 Rodmen (reinf.)			
				1 Equip. Oper. (crane)			
				1 Equip. Oper. Oiler			
				1 Hyd. Crane, 25 Ton			
	0110	#6 bars			150	.373	Ea.
	0130	#10 bars			95	.589	Ea.
	0150	#14 bars	↓	↓	65	.862	Ea.
	0280	Column splice clamps, sleeve & wedge, or end bearing					
	0300	#7 or #8 bars	C-5	1 Rodman Foreman	190	.295	Ea.
				4 Rodmen (reinf.)			
				1 Equip. Oper. (crane)			
				1 Equip. Oper. Oiler			
				1 Hyd. Crane, 25 Ton			
	0310	#9 or #10 bars			170	.329	Ea.
	0320	#11 bars			160	.350	Ea.
	0330	#14 bars			150	.373	Ea.
	0340	#18 bars	↓	↓	140	.400	Ea.
	0800	Mechanical butt splice, sleeve type with filler metal, compression					
	0810	only, all grades, columns only #11 bars	C-5	1 Rodman Foreman	68	.824	Ea.
				4 Rodmen (reinf.)			
				1 Equip. Oper. (crane)			
				1 Equip. Oper. Oiler			
				1 Hyd. Crane, 25 Ton			
	0900	#14 bars			62	.903	Ea.
	0920	#18 bars			62	.903	Ea.
	1000	125% yield point, grade 60, columns only, #6 bars			68	.824	Ea.
	1020	#7 or #8 bars			68	.824	Ea.
	1030	#9 bars			68	.824	Ea.
	1040	#10 bars			68	.824	Ea.
	1050	#11 bars			68	.824	Ea.
	1060	#14 bars			62	.903	Ea.
	1070	#18 bars	↓	↓	62	.903	Ea.
	1200	Full tension, grade 60 steel, columns,					
	1220	Slabs or beams, #6, #7, #8 bars	C-5	1 Rodman Foreman	68	.824	Ea.
				4 Rodmen (reinf.)			
				1 Equip. Oper. (crane)			
				1 Equip. Oper. Oiler			
				1 Hyd. Crane, 25 Ton			
	1230	#9 bars			68	.824	Ea.
	1240	#10 bars			68	.824	Ea.
	1250	#11 bars			68	.824	Ea.
	1260	#14 bars			62	.903	Ea.
	1270	#18 bars	↓	↓	62	.903	Ea.
	1600	Mechanical threaded type, bar threading not included,					
	1700	Straight bars, #10 & #11	C-5	1 Rodman Foreman	190	.295	Ea.
				4 Rodmen (reinf.)			
				1 Equip. Oper. (crane)			
				1 Equip. Oper. Oiler			
				1 Hyd. Crane, 25 Ton			
	1750	#14 bars			170	.329	Ea.
	1800	#18 bars			100	.560	Ea.
	2100	#11 to #18 & #14 to #18 transition			100	.560	Ea.
	2400	Bent bars, #10 & #11			140	.400	Ea.
	2500	#14	↓	↓	120	.467	Ea.

143

032 | Concrete Reinforcement

032 100 | Reinforcing Steel

		CREW	MAKEUP	DAILY OUTPUT	MAN-HOURS	UNIT
2601	Splicing reinf. bars, mech. threaded type, bent bars, #18	C-5	1 Rodman Foreman	90	.622	Ea.
			4 Rodmen (reinf.)			
			1 Equip. Oper. (crane)			
			1 Equip. Oper. Oiler			
			1 Hyd. Crane, 25 Ton			
2800	#11 to #14 transition	↓	↓	100	.560	Ea.
2900	#11 to #18 & #14 to #18 transition			90	.622	Ea.

032 200 | Welded Wire Fabric

		CREW	MAKEUP	DAILY OUTPUT	MAN-HOURS	UNIT
207	**WELDED WIRE FABRIC** Rolls, 6 x 6 #10/10 (W1.4/W1.4) 21 lb.	2 Rodm	2 Rodman, (Reinf.)	35	.457	C.S.F.
0200	6 x 6 - #8/8 (W2.1/W2.1) 30 lb. per C.S.F.			31	.516	C.S.F.
0300	6 x 6 - #6/6 (W2.9/W2.9) 42 lb. per C.S.F.			29	.552	C.S.F.
0400	6 x 6 - #4/4 (W4/W4) 58 lb. per C.S.F.			27	.593	C.S.F.
0500	4 x 4 - #10/10 (W1.4/W1.4) 31 lb. per C.S.F.			31	.516	C.S.F.
0600	4 x 4 - #8/8 (W2.1/W2.1) 44 lb. per C.S.F.			29	.552	C.S.F.
0650	4 x 4 - #6/6 (W2.9/W2.9) 61 lb. per C.S.F.			27	.593	C.S.F.
0700	4 x 4 - #4/4 (W4/W4) 85 lb. per C.S.F.			25	.640	C.S.F.
0800	2 x 2 - #14 galv. @ 21 lb., beam & column wrap			6.50	2.460	C.S.F.
0900	2 x 2 - #12 galv. for gunite reinforcing	↓	↓	6.50	2.460	C.S.F.
1000	Specially fabricated heavier gauges in sheets	4 Rodm	4 Rodman, (Reinf.)	50	.640	C.S.F.

032 300 | Stressing Tendons

		CREW	MAKEUP	DAILY OUTPUT	MAN-HOURS	UNIT
307	**PRESTRESSING STEEL** Post-tensioned in field					
0100	Grouted strand, 50' span, 100 kip	C-3	1 Rodman Foreman	1,200	.053	Lb.
			4 Rodmen (reinf.)			
			1 Equip. Oper. (light)			
			2 Building Laborers			
			Stressing Equipment			
			Grouting Equipment			
0150	300 kip			2,700	.024	Lb.
0300	100' span, grouted, 100 kip			1,700	.038	Lb.
0350	300 kip			3,200	.020	Lb.
0500	200' span, grouted, 100 kip			2,700	.024	Lb.
0550	300 kip			3,500	.018	Lb.
0800	Grouted bars, 50' span, 42 kip			2,600	.025	Lb.
0850	143 kip			3,200	.020	Lb.
1000	75' span, grouted, 42 kip			3,200	.020	Lb.
1050	143 kip	↓	↓	4,200	.015	Lb.
1200	Ungrouted strand, 50' span, 100 kip	C-4	1 Rodman Foreman	1,275	.025	Lb.
			3 Rodmen (reinf.)			
			Stressing Equipment			
1250	200 kip			1,475	.022	Lb.
1400	100' span, ungrouted, 100 kip			1,500	.021	Lb.
1450	200 kip			1,650	.019	Lb.
1600	200' span, ungrouted, 100 kip			1,500	.021	Lb.
1650	200 kip			1,700	.019	Lb.
1800	Ungrouted bars, 50' span, 42 kip			1,400	.023	Lb.
1850	143 kip			1,700	.019	Lb.
2000	75' span, ungrouted, 42 kip			1,800	.018	Lb.
2050	143 kip			2,200	.015	Lb.
2220	Ungrouted single strand, 100' slab, 25 kip			1,200	.027	Lb.
2250	35 kip	↓	↓	1,475	.022	Lb.

033 100	Structural Concrete	CREW	MAKEUP	DAILY OUTPUT	MAN-HOURS	UNIT
130	**CONCRETE IN PLACE** Including forms (4 uses), reinforcing					
0050	steel, including finishing unless otherwise indicated					
0100	Average for concrete framed building,					
0110	including finishing	C-17B	2 Skilled Worker Foremen	15.75	5.210	C.Y.
			8 Skilled Workers			
			.25 Equip. Oper. (crane)			
			.25 Crane, 80 Ton, & Tools			
			.25 Hand held power tools			
			.25 Walk behind power tools			
0130	Average for substructure only, simple design, incl. finishing	↓	↓	29.07	2.820	C.Y.
0150	Average for superstructure only, including finishing			13.42	6.110	C.Y.
0200	Base, granolithic, 1" x 5" high, straight	C-10	1 Building Laborer	175	.137	L.F.
			2 Cement Finishers			
			2 Gas Finishing Mach.			
0220	Cove	"	"	140	.171	L.F.
0300	Beams, 5 kip per L.F., 10' span	C-17A	2 Skilled Worker Foremen	6.28	12.900	C.Y.
			8 Skilled Workers			
			.125 Equip. Oper. (crane)			
			.125 Crane, 80 Ton, & Tools			
			.125 Hand held power tools			
			.125 Walk behind power tools			
0350	25' span			7.40	10.950	C.Y.
0500	Chimney foundations, minimum			26.70	3.030	C.Y.
0510	Maximum			19.70	4.110	C.Y.
0700	Columns, square, 12" x 12", minimum reinforcing			4.60	17.610	C.Y.
0720	Average reinforcing	↓	↓	4.10	19.760	C.Y.
0740	Maximum reinforcing	C-17B	2 Skilled Worker Foremen	3.84	21.350	C.Y.
			8 Skilled Workers			
			.25 Equip. Oper. (crane)			
			.25 Crane, 80 Ton, & Tools			
			.25 Hand held power tools			
			.25 Walk behind power tools			
0800	16" x 16", minimum reinforcing	C-17A	2 Skilled Worker Foremen	6.25	12.960	C.Y.
			8 Skilled Workers			
			.125 Equip. Oper. (crane)			
			.125 Crane, 80 Ton, & Tools			
			.125 Hand held power tools			
			.125 Walk behind power tools			
0820	Average reinforcing	"	"	4.93	16.430	C.Y.
0840	Maximum reinforcing	C-17B	2 Skilled Worker Foremen	4.34	18.890	C.Y.
			8 Skilled Workers			
			.25 Equip. Oper. (crane)			
			.25 Crane, 80 Ton, & Tools			
			.25 Hand held power tools			
			.25 Walk behind power tools			
0900	24" x 24", minimum reinforcing	C-17A	2 Skilled Worker Foremen	9.08	8.920	C.Y.
			8 Skilled Workers			
			.125 Equip. Oper. (crane)			
			.125 Crane, 80 Ton, & Tools			
			.125 Hand held power tools			
			.125 Walk behind power tools			
0920	Average reinforcing	↓	↓	6.90	11.740	C.Y.
0940	Maximum reinforcing			5.65	14.340	C.Y.

033 100	Structural Concrete	CREW	MAKEUP	DAILY OUTPUT	MAN-HOURS	UNIT
130	1002	Concrete in place, columns, square, 36" x 36", min. reinforcing	C-17B	2 Skilled Worker Foremen 8 Skilled Workers .25 Equip. Oper. (crane) .25 Crane, 80 Ton, & Tools .25 Hand held power tools .25 Walk behind power tools	13.39	6.120	C.Y.
	1020	Average reinforcing			9.61	8.530	C.Y.
	1040	Maximum reinforcing			7.50	10.930	C.Y.
	1200	Columns, round, tied, 16" diameter, minimum reinforcing			13.02	6.300	C.Y.
	1220	Average reinforcing			8.30	9.880	C.Y.
	1240	Maximum reinforcing			6.05	13.550	C.Y.
	1300	20" diameter, minimum reinforcing			17.35	4.730	C.Y.
	1320	Average reinforcing			10.43	7.860	C.Y.
	1340	Maximum reinforcing			7.47	10.980	C.Y.
	1400	24" diameter, minimum reinforcing			22.18	3.700	C.Y.
	1420	Average reinforcing			11.86	6.910	C.Y.
	1440	Maximum reinforcing			8.10	10.120	C.Y.
	1500	36" diameter, minimum reinforcing			32.40	2.530	C.Y.
	1520	Average reinforcing	↓	↓	16.57	4.950	C.Y.
	1540	Maximum reinforcing			11.15	7.350	C.Y.
	1900	Elevated slabs, flat slab, 125 psf Sup. Load, 20' span	C-17A	2 Skilled Worker Foremen 8 Skilled Workers .125 Equip. Oper. (crane) .125 Crane, 80 Ton, & Tools .125 Hand held power tools .125 Walk behind power tools	13.36	6.060	C.Y.
	1950	30' span	C-17B	2 Skilled Worker Foremen 8 Skilled Workers .25 Equip. Oper. (crane) .25 Crane, 80 Ton, & Tools .25 Hand held power tools .25 Walk behind power tools	18.25	4.490	C.Y.
	2100	Flat plate, 125 psf Sup. Load, 15' span	C-17A	2 Skilled Worker Foremen 8 Skilled Workers .125 Equip. Oper. (crane) .125 Crane, 80 Ton, & Tools .125 Hand held power tools .125 Walk behind power tools	10.28	7.880	C.Y.
	2150	25' span	C-17B	2 Skilled Worker Foremen 8 Skilled Workers .25 Equip. Oper. (crane) .25 Crane, 80 Ton, & Tools .25 Hand held power tools .25 Walk behind power tools	17.01	4.820	C.Y.
	2300	Waffle const., 30" domes, 125 psf Sup. Load, 20' span	↓	↓	14.10	5.820	C.Y.
	2350	30' span			17.02	4.820	C.Y.

			CREW	MAKEUP	DAILY OUTPUT	MAN-HOURS	UNIT
130	2502	Conc. in place, 1 way jsts, 30" pans, 125 psf Sup. Load, 15' span	C-17A	2 Skilled Worker Foremen	11.07	7.320	C.Y.
				8 Skilled Workers			
				.125 Equip. Oper. (crane)			
				.125 Crane, 80 Ton, & Tools			
				.125 Hand held power tools			
				.125 Walk behind power tools			
	2550	25' span			11.04	7.340	C.Y.
	2700	One way beam & slab, 125 psf Sup. Load, 15' span			7.49	10.810	C.Y.
	2750	25' span			10.15	7.980	C.Y.
	2900	Two way beam & slab, 125 psf Sup. Load, 15' span	↓	↓	8.22	9.850	C.Y.
	2950	25' span	C-17B	2 Skilled Worker Foremen	12.23	6.700	C.Y.
				8 Skilled Workers			
				.25 Equip. Oper. (crane)			
				.25 Crane, 80 Ton, & Tools			
				.25 Hand held power tools			
				.25 Walk behind power tools			
	3100	Elevated slabs including					
	3110	including forms or reinforcing					
	3150	Regular concrete, 4" slab	C-8	1 Labor Foreman (outside)	2,685	.021	S.F.
				3 Building Laborers			
				2 Cement Finishers			
				1 Equip. Oper. (med.)			
				1 Concrete Pump (small)			
	3200	6" slab			2,585	.022	S.F.
	3250	2-1/2" thick floor fill			2,685	.021	S.F.
	3300	Lightweight, 110# per C.F., 2-1/2" thick floor fill			2,585	.022	S.F.
	3400	Cellular concrete, 1-5/8" fill, under 5000 S.F.			2,000	.028	S.F.
	3450	Over 10,000 S.F.			2,200	.025	S.F.
	3500	Add per floor for 3 to 6 stories high			31,800	.002	S.F.
	3520	For 7 to 20 stories high	↓	↓	21,200	.003	S.F.
	3800	Footings, spread under 1 C.Y.	C-17B	2 Skilled Worker Foremen	31.82	2.580	C.Y.
				8 Skilled Workers			
				.25 Equip. Oper. (crane)			
				.25 Crane, 80 Ton, & Tools			
				.25 Hand held power tools			
				.25 Walk behind power tools			
	3850	Over 5 C.Y.	C-17C	2 Skilled Worker Foremen	70.45	1.180	C.Y.
				8 Skilled Workers			
				.375 Equip. Oper. (crane)			
				.375 Crane, 80 Ton & Tools			
				.375 Hand held power tools			
				.375 Walk behind power tools			
	3900	Footings, strip, 18" x 9", plain	C-17B	2 Skilled Worker Foremen	34.22	2.400	C.Y.
				8 Skilled Workers			
				.25 Equip. Oper. (crane)			
				.25 Crane, 80 Ton, & Tools			
				.25 Hand held power tools			
				.25 Walk behind power tools			
	3950	36" x 12", reinforced			49.07	1.670	C.Y.
	4000	Foundation mat, under 10 C.Y.			32.32	2.540	C.Y.
	4050	Over 20 C.Y.	↓	↓	47.37	1.730	C.Y.
	4200	Grade walls, 8" thick, 8' high	C-17A	2 Skilled Worker Foremen	10.16	7.970	C.Y.
				8 Skilled Workers			
				.125 Equip. Oper. (crane)			
				.125 Crane, 80 Ton, & Tools			
				.125 Hand held power tools			
				.125 Walk behind power tools			

033 100	Structural Concrete	CREW	MAKEUP	DAILY OUTPUT	MAN-HOURS	UNIT
130 4252	Concrete in place, grade walls, 8" thick, 14' high	C-20	1 Labor Foreman (outside)	7.30	8.770	C.Y.
			5 Building Laborers			
			1 Cement Finisher			
			1 Equip. Oper. (med.)			
			2 Gas Engine Vibrators			
			1 Concrete Pump (small)			
4260	12" thick, 8' high	C-17A	2 Skilled Worker Foremen	13.50	6.000	C.Y.
			8 Skilled Workers			
			.125 Equip. Oper. (crane)			
			.125 Crane, 80 Ton, & Tools			
			.125 Hand held power tools			
			.125 Walk behind power tools			
4270	14' high	C-20	1 Labor Foreman (outside)	11.60	5.520	C.Y.
			5 Building Laborers			
			1 Cement Finisher			
			1 Equip. Oper. (med.)			
			2 Gas Engine Vibrators			
			1 Concrete Pump (small)			
4300	15" thick, 8' high	C-17B	2 Skilled Worker Foremen	20.01	4.100	C.Y.
			8 Skilled Workers			
			.25 Equip. Oper. (crane)			
			.25 Crane, 80 Ton, & Tools			
			.25 Hand held power tools			
			.25 Walk behind power tools			
4350	12' high	C-20	1 Labor Foreman (outside)	14.80	4.320	C.Y.
			5 Building Laborers			
			1 Cement Finisher			
			1 Equip. Oper. (med.)			
			2 Gas Engine Vibrators			
			1 Concrete Pump (small)			
4500	18' high	"	"	12	5.330	C.Y.
4650	Ground slab, not including finish, 4" thick	C-17C	2 Skilled Worker Foremen	75.28	1.100	C.Y.
			8 Skilled Workers			
			.375 Equip. Oper. (crane)			
			.375 Crane, 80 Ton & Tools			
			.375 Hand held power tools			
			.375 Walk behind power tools			
4700	6" thick	"	"	113.47	.731	C.Y.
4750	Ground slab, incl. troweled finish, not incl. forms					
4760	or reinforcing, over 10,000 S.F., 4" thick slab	C-8	1 Labor Foreman (outside)	3,520	.016	S.F.
			3 Building Laborers			
			2 Cement Finishers			
			1 Equip. Oper. (med.)			
			1 Concrete Pump (small)			
4820	6" thick slab			3,610	.016	S.F.
4840	8" thick slab			3,275	.017	S.F.
4900	12" thick slab			2,875	.019	S.F.
4950	15" thick slab			2,560	.022	S.F.
5200	Lift slab in place above the foundation, incl. forms,					
5210	reinforcing, concrete and columns, minimum	C-17E	2 Skilled Worker Foremen	745	.107	S.F.
			8 Skilled Workers			
			1 Hyd. Jack with Rods			
	Average			675	.119	S.F.
	Maximum			430	.186	S.F.

033 100	Structural Concrete	CREW	MAKEUP	DAILY OUTPUT	MAN-HOURS	UNIT
130 5540	Concrete, lightweight, ready mix, incl. screed finish, no forms					
5550	1:4 for structural roof decks	C-8	1 Labor Foreman (outside)	80	.700	C.Y.
			3 Building Laborers			
			2 Cement Finishers			
			1 Equip. Oper. (med.)			
			1 Concrete Pump (small)			
5600	1:6 for ground slab with radiant heat			90	.622	C.Y.
5650	1:3:2 with sand aggregate, roof deck	↓	↓	80	.700	C.Y.
5900	Pile caps, incl. forms and reinf., sq. or rect., under 5 C.Y.	C-17C	2 Skilled Worker Foremen	47.26	1.760	C.Y.
			8 Skilled Workers			
			.375 Equip. Oper. (crane)			
			.375 Crane, 80 Ton & Tools			
			.375 Hand held power tools			
			.375 Walk behind power tools			
5950	Over 10 C.Y.			76.47	1.090	C.Y.
6000	Triangular or hexagonal, under 5 C.Y.			47.95	1.730	C.Y.
6050	Over 10 C.Y.	↓	↓	77.85	1.070	C.Y.
6201	Retaining walls, gravity, 4' high	C-17B	2 Skilled Worker Foremen	19.10	4.290	C.Y.
			8 Skilled Workers			
			.25 Equip. Oper. (crane)			
			.25 Crane, 80 Ton, & Tools			
			.25 Hand held power tools			
			.25 Walk behind power tools			
6250	10' high			27.10	3.030	C.Y.
6300	Cantilever, level backfill loading, 8' high			16.30	5.030	C.Y.
6350	16' high	↓	↓	17	4.820	C.Y.
6800	Stairs, not including safety treads, free standing	C-15	1 Carpenter Foreman (out)	120	.600	LF Nose
			2 Carpenters			
			3 Building Laborers			
			2 Cement Finishers			
			1 Rodman (reinf.)			
			Power Tools			
			1 Gas Finishing Mach.			
6850	Cast on ground			180	.400	LF Nose
7000	Stair landings, free standing			285	.253	S.F.
7050	Cast on ground	↓	↓	685	.105	S.F.
134	CURING With burlap, 4 uses assumed, 7.5 oz.	2 Clab	2 Building Laborers	55	.291	C.S.F.
0100	12 oz.			55	.291	C.S.F.
0200	With waterproof curing paper, 2 ply, reinforced			70	.229	C.S.F.
0300	With sprayed membrane curing compound	↓	↓	95	.168	C.S.F.
156	GROUT Column & machine bases, non-shrink, metallic grout, 1" deep	1 Cefi	1 Cement Finisher	35	.229	S.F.
0050	2" deep			25	.320	S.F.
0300	Non-shrink, non-metallic grout, 1" deep			35	.229	S.F.
0350	2" deep	↓	↓	25	.320	S.F.
160	GUNITE					
0020	Applied in 1" layers, no mesh included	C-8	1 Labor Foreman (outside)	1,550	.036	S.F.
			3 Building Laborers			
			2 Cement Finishers			
			1 Equip. Oper. (med.)			
			1 Concrete Pump (small)			
0100	Mesh for gunite 2 x 2, #12, to 3" thick	2 Rodm	2 Rodman, (Reinf.)	600	.027	S.F.
0150	Over 3" thick	"	"	400	.040	S.F.
0300	Typical in place, including mesh, 2" thick, minimum	C-16	1 Labor Foreman (outside)	665	.108	S.F.
			3 Building Laborers			
			2 Cement Finishers			
			1 Equip. Oper. (med.)			
			2 Rodmen (reinf.)			
			1 Concrete Pump (small)			

			CREW	MAKEUP	DAILY OUTPUT	MAN-HOURS	UNIT
033 100 Structural Concrete							
160	0351	Gunite, typical in place, incl. mesh, 2" thick, maximum	C-16	1 Labor Foreman (outside)	395	.182	S.F.
				3 Building Laborers			
				2 Cement Finishers			
				1 Equip. Oper. (med.)			
				2 Rodmen (reinf.)			
				1 Concrete Pump (small)			
	0500	4" thick, minimum	↓	↓	595	.121	S.F.
	0550	Maximum			275	.262	S.F.
	0900	Prepare old walls, no scaffolding, minimum	C-10	1 Building Laborer	1,000	.024	S.F.
				2 Cement Finishers			
				2 Gas Finishing Mach.			
	0950	Maximum	"	"	275	.087	S.F.
172	**PLACING CONCRETE** and vibrating, including labor & equipment						
	0050	Beams, elevated, small beams, pumped	C-20	1 Labor Foreman (outside)	40	1.600	C.Y.
				5 Building Laborers			
				1 Cement Finisher			
				1 Equip. Oper. (med.)			
				2 Gas Engine Vibrators			
				1 Concrete Pump (small)			
	0100	With crane and bucket	C-7	1 Labor Foreman (outside)	45	1.420	C.Y.
				5 Building Laborers			
				1 Cement Finisher			
				1 Equip. Oper. (med.)			
				2 Gas Engine Vibrators			
				1 Concrete Bucket, 1 C.Y.			
				1 Hyd. Crane, 55 Ton			
	0200	Large beams, pumped	C-20	1 Labor Foreman (outside)	60	1.070	C.Y.
				5 Building Laborers			
				1 Cement Finisher			
				1 Equip. Oper. (med.)			
				2 Gas Engine Vibrators			
				1 Concrete Pump (small)			
	0250	With crane and bucket	C-7	1 Labor Foreman (outside)	65	.985	C.Y.
				5 Building Laborers			
				1 Cement Finisher			
				1 Equip. Oper. (med.)			
				2 Gas Engine Vibrators			
				1 Concrete Bucket, 1 C.Y.			
				1 Hyd. Crane, 55 Ton			
	0400	Columns, square or round, 12" thick, pumped	C-20	1 Labor Foreman (outside)	45	1.420	C.Y.
				5 Building Laborers			
				1 Cement Finisher			
				1 Equip. Oper. (med.)			
				2 Gas Engine Vibrators			
				1 Concrete Pump (small)			
	0450	With crane and bucket	C-7	1 Labor Foreman (outside)	40	1.600	C.Y.
				5 Building Laborers			
				1 Cement Finisher			
				1 Equip. Oper. (med.)			
				2 Gas Engine Vibrators			
				1 Concrete Bucket, 1 C.Y.			
				1 Hyd. Crane, 55 Ton			
	0600	18" thick, pumped	C-20	1 Labor Foreman (outside)	60	1.070	C.Y.
				5 Building Laborers			
				1 Cement Finisher			
				1 Equip. Oper. (med.)			
				2 Gas Engine Vibrators			
				1 Concrete Pump (small)			

033 100 | Structural Concrete

		Description	CREW	MAKEUP	DAILY OUTPUT	MAN-HOURS	UNIT
172	0651	Placing concrete, columns, 18" thick, with crane and bucket	C-7	1 Labor Foreman (outside) 5 Building Laborers 1 Cement Finisher 1 Equip. Oper. (med.) 2 Gas Engine Vibrators 1 Concrete Bucket, 1 C.Y. 1 Hyd. Crane, 55 Ton	55	1.160	C.Y.
	0800	24" thick, pumped	C-20	1 Labor Foreman (outside) 5 Building Laborers 1 Cement Finisher 1 Equip. Oper. (med.) 2 Gas Engine Vibrators 1 Concrete Pump (small)	92	.696	C.Y.
	0850	With crane and bucket	C-7	1 Labor Foreman (outside) 5 Building Laborers 1 Cement Finisher 1 Equip. Oper. (med.) 2 Gas Engine Vibrators 1 Concrete Bucket, 1 C.Y. 1 Hyd. Crane, 55 Ton	70	.914	C.Y.
	1000	36" thick, pumped	C-20	1 Labor Foreman (outside) 5 Building Laborers 1 Cement Finisher 1 Equip. Oper. (med.) 2 Gas Engine Vibrators 1 Concrete Pump (small)	140	.457	C.Y.
	1050	With crane and bucket	C-7	1 Labor Foreman (outside) 5 Building Laborers 1 Cement Finisher 1 Equip. Oper. (med.) 2 Gas Engine Vibrators 1 Concrete Bucket, 1 C.Y. 1 Hyd. Crane, 55 Ton	100	.640	C.Y.
	1400	Elevated slabs, less than 6" thick, pumped	C-20	1 Labor Foreman (outside) 5 Building Laborers 1 Cement Finisher 1 Equip. Oper. (med.) 2 Gas Engine Vibrators 1 Concrete Pump (small)	110	.582	C.Y.
	1450	With crane and bucket	C-7	1 Labor Foreman (outside) 5 Building Laborers 1 Cement Finisher 1 Equip. Oper. (med.) 2 Gas Engine Vibrators 1 Concrete Bucket, 1 C.Y. 1 Hyd. Crane, 55 Ton	95	.674	C.Y.
	1500	6" to 10" thick, pumped	C-20	1 Labor Foreman (outside) 5 Building Laborers 1 Cement Finisher 1 Equip. Oper. (med.) 2 Gas Engine Vibrators 1 Concrete Pump (small)	130	.492	C.Y.

033 100 | Structural Concrete

		Description	CREW	MAKEUP	DAILY OUTPUT	MAN-HOURS	UNIT
172	1551	Placing concrete, elev. slabs, 6"-10" thick, w/crane & bucket	C-7	1 Labor Foreman (outside) 5 Building Laborers 1 Cement Finisher 1 Equip. Oper. (med.) 2 Gas Engine Vibrators 1 Concrete Bucket, 1 C.Y. 1 Hyd. Crane, 55 Ton	110	.582	C.Y.
	1600	Slabs over 10" thick, pumped	C-20	1 Labor Foreman (outside) 5 Building Laborers 1 Cement Finisher 1 Equip. Oper. (med.) 2 Gas Engine Vibrators 1 Concrete Pump (small)	150	.427	C.Y.
	1650	With crane and bucket	C-7	1 Labor Foreman (outside) 5 Building Laborers 1 Cement Finisher 1 Equip. Oper. (med.) 2 Gas Engine Vibrators 1 Concrete Bucket, 1 C.Y. 1 Hyd. Crane, 55 Ton	130	.492	C.Y.
	1900	Footings, continuous, shallow, direct chute	C-6	1 Labor Foreman (outside) 4 Building Laborers 1 Cement Finisher 2 Gas Engine Vibrators	120	.400	C.Y.
	1950	Pumped	C-20	1 Labor Foreman (outside) 5 Building Laborers 1 Cement Finisher 1 Equip. Oper. (med.) 2 Gas Engine Vibrators 1 Concrete Pump (small)	100	.640	C.Y.
	2000	With crane and bucket	C-7	1 Labor Foreman (outside) 5 Building Laborers 1 Cement Finisher 1 Equip. Oper. (med.) 2 Gas Engine Vibrators 1 Concrete Bucket, 1 C.Y. 1 Hyd. Crane, 55 Ton	90	.711	C.Y.
	2100	Deep continuous footings, direct chute	C-6	1 Labor Foreman (outside) 4 Building Laborers 1 Cement Finisher 2 Gas Engine Vibrators	155	.310	C.Y.
	2150	Pumped	C-20	1 Labor Foreman (outside) 5 Building Laborers 1 Cement Finisher 1 Equip. Oper. (med.) 2 Gas Engine Vibrators 1 Concrete Pump (small)	120	.533	C.Y.
	2200	With crane and bucket	C-7	1 Labor Foreman (outside) 5 Building Laborers 1 Cement Finisher 1 Equip. Oper. (med.) 2 Gas Engine Vibrators 1 Concrete Bucket, 1 C.Y. 1 Hyd. Crane, 55 Ton	110	.582	C.Y.
	2400	Footings, spread, under 1 C.Y., direct chute	C-6	1 Labor Foreman (outside) 4 Building Laborers 1 Cement Finisher 2 Gas Engine Vibrators	55	.873	C.Y.

033 100	Structural Concrete	CREW	MAKEUP	DAILY OUTPUT	MAN-HOURS	UNIT
172 2451	Placing concrete, footings, spread, under 1 C.Y., pumped	C-20	1 Labor Foreman (outside)	50	1.280	C.Y.
			5 Building Laborers			
			1 Cement Finisher			
			1 Equip. Oper. (med.)			
			2 Gas Engine Vibrators			
			1 Concrete Pump (small)			
2500	With crane and bucket	C-7	1 Labor Foreman (outside)	45	1.420	C.Y.
			5 Building Laborers			
			1 Cement Finisher			
			1 Equip. Oper. (med.)			
			2 Gas Engine Vibrators			
			1 Concrete Bucket, 1 C.Y.			
			1 Hyd. Crane, 55 Ton			
2600	Spread footings, over 5 C.Y., direct chute	C-6	1 Labor Foreman (outside)	110	.436	C.Y.
			4 Building Laborers			
			1 Cement Finisher			
			2 Gas Engine Vibrators			
2650	Pumped	C-20	1 Labor Foreman (outside)	105	.610	C.Y.
			5 Building Laborers			
			1 Cement Finisher			
			1 Equip. Oper. (med.)			
			2 Gas Engine Vibrators			
			1 Concrete Pump (small)			
2700	With crane and bucket	C-7	1 Labor Foreman (outside)	100	.640	C.Y.
			5 Building Laborers			
			1 Cement Finisher			
			1 Equip. Oper. (med.)			
			2 Gas Engine Vibrators			
			1 Concrete Bucket, 1 C.Y.			
			1 Hyd. Crane, 55 Ton			
2900	Foundation mats, over 20 C.Y., direct chute	C-6	1 Labor Foreman (outside)	350	.137	C.Y.
			4 Building Laborers			
			1 Cement Finisher			
			2 Gas Engine Vibrators			
2950	Pumped	C-20	1 Labor Foreman (outside)	325	.197	C.Y.
			5 Building Laborers			
			1 Cement Finisher			
			1 Equip. Oper. (med.)			
			2 Gas Engine Vibrators			
			1 Concrete Pump (small)			
3000	With crane and bucket	C-7	1 Labor Foreman (outside)	300	.213	C.Y.
			5 Building Laborers			
			1 Cement Finisher			
			1 Equip. Oper. (med.)			
			2 Gas Engine Vibrators			
			1 Concrete Bucket, 1 C.Y.			
			1 Hyd. Crane, 55 Ton			
3200	Grade beams, direct chute	C-6	1 Labor Foreman (outside)	150	.320	C.Y.
			4 Building Laborers			
			1 Cement Finisher			
			2 Gas Engine Vibrators			
3250	Pumped	C-20	1 Labor Foreman (outside)	130	.492	C.Y.
			5 Building Laborers			
			1 Cement Finisher			
			1 Equip. Oper. (med.)			
			2 Gas Engine Vibrators			
			1 Concrete Pump (small)			

		Description	CREW	MAKEUP	DAILY OUTPUT	MAN-HOURS	UNIT
033 100	**Structural Concrete**						
172	3301	Placing concrete, grade beams, with crane and bucket	C-7	1 Labor Foreman (outside)	120	.533	C.Y.
				5 Building Laborers			
				1 Cement Finisher			
				1 Equip. Oper. (med.)			
				2 Gas Engine Vibrators			
				1 Concrete Bucket, 1 C.Y.			
				1 Hyd. Crane, 55 Ton			
	3500	High rise, for more than 5 stories, pumped, add per story	C-20	1 Labor Foreman (outside)	2,100	.030	C.Y.
				5 Building Laborers			
				1 Cement Finisher			
				1 Equip. Oper. (med.)			
				2 Gas Engine Vibrators			
				1 Concrete Pump (small)			
	3510	With crane and bucket, add per story	C-7	1 Labor Foreman (outside)	2,100	.030	C.Y.
				5 Building Laborers			
				1 Cement Finisher			
				1 Equip. Oper. (med.)			
				2 Gas Engine Vibrators			
				1 Concrete Bucket, 1 C.Y.			
				1 Hyd. Crane, 55 Ton			
	3700	Pile caps, under 5 C.Y., direct chute	C-6	1 Labor Foreman (outside)	90	.533	C.Y.
				4 Building Laborers			
				1 Cement Finisher			
				2 Gas Engine Vibrators			
	3750	Pumped	C-20	1 Labor Foreman (outside)	85	.753	C.Y.
				5 Building Laborers			
				1 Cement Finisher			
				1 Equip. Oper. (med.)			
				2 Gas Engine Vibrators			
				1 Concrete Pump (small)			
	3800	With crane and bucket	C-7	1 Labor Foreman (outside)	80	.800	C.Y.
				5 Building Laborers			
				1 Cement Finisher			
				1 Equip. Oper. (med.)			
				2 Gas Engine Vibrators			
				1 Concrete Bucket, 1 C.Y.			
				1 Hyd. Crane, 55 Ton			
	3850	Pile cap, 5 C.Y. to 10 C.Y., direct chute	C-6	1 Labor Foreman (outside)	175	.274	C.Y.
				4 Building Laborers			
				1 Cement Finisher			
				2 Gas Engine Vibrators			
	3900	Pumped	C-20	1 Labor Foreman (outside)	160	.400	C.Y.
				5 Building Laborers			
				1 Cement Finisher			
				1 Equip. Oper. (med.)			
				2 Gas Engine Vibrators			
				1 Concrete Pump (small)			
	3950	With crane and bucket	C-7	1 Labor Foreman (outside)	150	.427	C.Y.
				5 Building Laborers			
				1 Cement Finisher			
				1 Equip. Oper. (med.)			
				2 Gas Engine Vibrators			
				1 Concrete Bucket, 1 C.Y.			
				1 Hyd. Crane, 55 Ton			
	4000	Pile cap, over 10 C.Y., direct chute	C-6	1 Labor Foreman (outside)	215	.223	C.Y.
				4 Building Laborers			
				1 Cement Finisher			
				2 Gas Engine Vibrators			

033 100 | Structural Concrete

		CREW	MAKEUP	DAILY OUTPUT	MAN-HOURS	UNIT
172 4051	Placing concrete, pile cap, over 10 C.Y., pumped	C-20	1 Labor Foreman (outside) 5 Building Laborers 1 Cement Finisher 1 Equip. Oper. (med.) 2 Gas Engine Vibrators 1 Concrete Pump (small)	195	.328	C.Y.
4100	With crane and bucket	C-7	1 Labor Foreman (outside) 5 Building Laborers 1 Cement Finisher 1 Equip. Oper. (med.) 2 Gas Engine Vibrators 1 Concrete Bucket, 1 C.Y. 1 Hyd. Crane, 55 Ton	185	.346	C.Y.
4300	Slab on grade, 4" thick, direct chute	C-6	1 Labor Foreman (outside) 4 Building Laborers 1 Cement Finisher 2 Gas Engine Vibrators	110	.436	C.Y.
4350	Pumped	C-20	1 Labor Foreman (outside) 5 Building Laborers 1 Cement Finisher 1 Equip. Oper. (med.) 2 Gas Engine Vibrators 1 Concrete Pump (small)	120	.533	C.Y.
4400	With crane and bucket	C-7	1 Labor Foreman (outside) 5 Building Laborers 1 Cement Finisher 1 Equip. Oper. (med.) 2 Gas Engine Vibrators 1 Concrete Bucket, 1 C.Y. 1 Hyd. Crane, 55 Ton	110	.582	C.Y.
4600	Slab over 6" thick, direct chute	C-6	1 Labor Foreman (outside) 4 Building Laborers 1 Cement Finisher 2 Gas Engine Vibrators	165	.291	C.Y.
4650	Pumped	C-20	1 Labor Foreman (outside) 5 Building Laborers 1 Cement Finisher 1 Equip. Oper. (med.) 2 Gas Engine Vibrators 1 Concrete Pump (small)	165	.388	C.Y.
4700	With crane and bucket	C-7	1 Labor Foreman (outside) 5 Building Laborers 1 Cement Finisher 1 Equip. Oper. (med.) 2 Gas Engine Vibrators 1 Concrete Bucket, 1 C.Y. 1 Hyd. Crane, 55 Ton	145	.441	C.Y.
4900	Walls, 8" thick, direct chute	C-6	1 Labor Foreman (outside) 4 Building Laborers 1 Cement Finisher 2 Gas Engine Vibrators	90	.533	C.Y.
4950	Pumped	C-20	1 Labor Foreman (outside) 5 Building Laborers 1 Cement Finisher 1 Equip. Oper. (med.) 2 Gas Engine Vibrators 1 Concrete Pump (small)	85	.753	C.Y.

033 100	Structural Concrete	CREW	MAKEUP	DAILY OUTPUT	MAN-HOURS	UNIT
172 5001	Placing concrete, walls, 8" thick, with crane and bucket	C-7	1 Labor Foreman (outside)	80	.800	C.Y.
			5 Building Laborers			
			1 Cement Finisher			
			1 Equip. Oper. (med.)			
			2 Gas Engine Vibrators			
			1 Concrete Bucket, 1 C.Y.			
			1 Hyd. Crane, 55 Ton			
5050	12" thick, direct chute	C-6	1 Labor Foreman (outside)	100	.480	C.Y.
			4 Building Laborers			
			1 Cement Finisher			
			2 Gas Engine Vibrators			
5100	Pumped	C-20	1 Labor Foreman (outside)	95	.674	C.Y.
			5 Building Laborers			
			1 Cement Finisher			
			1 Equip. Oper. (med.)			
			2 Gas Engine Vibrators			
			1 Concrete Pump (small)			
5200	With crane and bucket	C-7	1 Labor Foreman (outside)	90	.711	C.Y.
			5 Building Laborers			
			1 Cement Finisher			
			1 Equip. Oper. (med.)			
			2 Gas Engine Vibrators			
			1 Concrete Bucket, 1 C.Y.			
			1 Hyd. Crane, 55 Ton			
5300	15" thick, direct chute	C-6	1 Labor Foreman (outside)	105	.457	C.Y.
			4 Building Laborers			
			1 Cement Finisher			
			2 Gas Engine Vibrators			
5350	Pumped	C-20	1 Labor Foreman (outside)	100	.640	C.Y.
			5 Building Laborers			
			1 Cement Finisher			
			1 Equip. Oper. (med.)			
			2 Gas Engine Vibrators			
			1 Concrete Pump (small)			
5400	With crane and bucket	C-7	1 Labor Foreman (outside)	95	.674	C.Y.
			5 Building Laborers			
			1 Cement Finisher			
			1 Equip. Oper. (med.)			
			2 Gas Engine Vibrators			
			1 Concrete Bucket, 1 C.Y.			
			1 Hyd. Crane, 55 Ton			
5600	Wheeled concrete dumping, add to placing costs above					
5610	Walking cart, 50' haul, add	C-18	.125 Labor Foreman (out)	32	.281	C.Y.
			1 Building Laborer			
			1 Concrete Cart, 10 C.F.			
5620	150' haul, add	↓	↓	24	.375	C.Y.
5700	250' haul, add			18	.500	C.Y.
5800	Riding cart, 50' haul, add	C-19	.125 Labor Foreman (out)	80	.113	C.Y.
			1 Building Laborer			
			1 Concrete Cart, 18 C.F.			
5810	150' haul, add	↓	↓	60	.150	C.Y.
5900	250' haul, add			45	.200	C.Y.
5901						

033 100 | Structural Concrete

		CREW	MAKEUP	DAILY OUTPUT	MAN-HOURS	UNIT
176	**PRESTRESSED CONCRETE** Tensioned in place, small job	C-17B	2 Skilled Worker Foremen	8.50	9.650	C.Y.
			8 Skilled Workers			
			.25 Equip. Oper. (crane)			
			.25 Crane, 80 Ton, & Tools			
			.25 Hand held power tools			
			.25 Walk behind power tools			
0200	Large job	"	"	10	8.200	C.Y.
184	**STAIR TREAD INSERTS** Cast iron, abrasive, 3" wide	1 Carp	1 Carpenter	90	.089	L.F.
0020	4" wide			80	.100	L.F.
0040	6" wide			75	.107	L.F.
0050	9" wide			70	.114	L.F.
0100	12" wide			65	.123	L.F.
0500	Extruded aluminum safety tread, 3" wide			75	.107	L.F.
0550	4" wide			75	.107	L.F.
0600	6" wide			75	.107	L.F.
0650	9" wide to resurface stairs	↓	↓	70	.114	L.F.
1700	Cement filled pan type, plain	1 Cefi	1 Cement Finisher	115	.070	S.F.
1750	Non-slip	"	"	100	.080	S.F.

033 450 | Concrete Finishing

		CREW	MAKEUP	DAILY OUTPUT	MAN-HOURS	UNIT
454	**FINISHING FLOORS** Monolithic, screed finish	1 Cefi	1 Cement Finisher	900	.009	S.F.
0050	Darby finish	"	"	750	.011	S.F.
0100	Float finish	C-9	1 Cement Finisher	725	.011	S.F.
			1 Gas Finishing Mach.			
0150	Broom finish			675	.012	S.F.
0200	Steel trowel finish, for resilient tile			625	.013	S.F.
0250	For finish floor	↓	↓	550	.015	S.F.
0400	Integral topping and finish, using 1:1:2 mix, 3/16" thick	C-10	1 Building Laborer	1,000	.024	S.F.
			2 Cement Finishers			
			2 Gas Finishing Mach.			
0450	1/2" thick			950	.025	S.F.
0500	3/4" thick			850	.028	S.F.
0600	1" thick			750	.032	S.F.
0800	Granolithic topping, laid after, 1:1:1-1/2 mix, 1/2" thick			590	.041	S.F.
0820	3/4" thick			580	.041	S.F.
0850	1" thick			575	.042	S.F.
0950	2" thick			500	.048	S.F.
1200	Heavy duty, 1:1:2, 3/4" thick, preshrunk, gray, 20 MSF			320	.075	S.F.
1300	100 MSF			380	.063	S.F.
1350	For colors, .50 psf, add, minimum			1,650	.015	S.F.
1400	Maximum	↓	↓	1,500	.016	S.F.
1600	Exposed local aggregate finish, minimum	1 Cefi	1 Cement Finisher	625	.013	S.F.
1650	Maximum	"	"	465	.017	S.F.
1800	Floor abrasives, .25 psf, add to above, aluminum oxide	C-9	1 Cement Finisher	850	.009	S.F.
			1 Gas Finishing Mach.			
1850	Silicon carbide			850	.009	S.F.
2000	Floor hardeners, metallic, light service, .50 psf, add			850	.009	S.F.
2050	Medium service, .75 psf, add			750	.011	S.F.
2100	Heavy service, 1.0 psf, add			650	.012	S.F.
2150	Extra heavy, 1.5 psf, add			575	.014	S.F.
2300	Non-metallic, add to above, light service, .50 psf add			850	.009	S.F.
2350	Medium service, .75 psf, add			750	.011	S.F.
2400	Heavy service, 1.00 psf, add			650	.012	S.F.
2450	Extra heavy, 1.50 psf, add	↓	↓	575	.014	S.F.
2800	Trap rock wearing surface for monolithic floors					
2810	2.0 psf, add to above	C-10	1 Building Laborer	1,250	.019	S.F.
			2 Cement Finishers			
			2 Gas Finishing Mach.			

033 | Cast-In-Place Concrete

033 450 | Concrete Finishing

			CREW	MAKEUP	DAILY OUTPUT	MAN-HOURS	UNIT
454	3001	Floor finishing, coloring, dusted on, .5 psf/S.F., add, min.	C-9	1 Cement Finisher	1,300	.006	S.F.
				1 Gas Finishing Mach.			
	3050	Maximum	"	"	625	.013	S.F.
	3600	1/2" topping using 5 lb. per bag, regular colors	C-10	1 Building Laborer	590	.041	S.F.
				2 Cement Finishers			
				2 Gas Finishing Mach.			
	3650	Blue or green	"	"	590	.041	S.F.
	3800	Dustproofing, silicate liquids, 1 coat	1 Cefi	1 Cement Finisher	1,900	.004	S.F.
	3850	2 coats			1,300	.006	S.F.
	4000	Epoxy coating, 1 coat, clear			1,500	.005	S.F.
	4050	Colors			1,500	.005	S.F.
	4400	Stair finish, float			275	.029	S.F.
	4500	Steel trowel finish			200	.040	S.F.
	4600	Silicon carbide finish, .25 psf			150	.053	S.F.
458		FINISHING WALLS Break ties and patch voids			540	.015	S.F.
	0050	Burlap rub with grout			450	.018	S.F.
	0100	Carborundum rub, dry			270	.030	S.F.
	0150	Wet rub			175	.046	S.F.
	0300	Bush hammer, green concrete			170	.047	S.F.
	0350	Cured concrete			110	.073	S.F.
	0600	Float finish, 1/16" thick	↓	↓	300	.027	S.F.
	0700	Sandblast, light penetration	C-10	1 Building Laborer	1,100	.022	S.F.
				2 Cement Finishers			
				2 Gas Finishing Mach.			
	0750	Heavy penetration	"	"	375	.064	S.F.

034 | Precast Concrete

034 100 | Structural Precast

			CREW	MAKEUP	DAILY OUTPUT	MAN-HOURS	UNIT
104		BEAMS Rectangular, to 20' spans, small beams	C-11	1 Struc. Steel Foreman	320	.225	L.F.
				6 Struc. Steel Workers			
				1 Equip. Oper. (crane)			
				1 Equip. Oper. Oiler			
				1 Truck Crane, 150 Ton			
	0050	Large beams			240	.300	L.F.
	0300	30' spans, small beams			480	.150	L.F.
	0350	Large beams			360	.200	L.F.
	0600	40' spans, small beams			640	.113	L.F.
	0650	Large beams			480	.150	L.F.
	1200	Rectangular, 20' span, 12" x 20"			32	2.250	Ea.
	1300	24" x 44"			22	3.270	Ea.
	1600	40' span, 12" x 52"			20	3.600	Ea.
	2000	"T" shaped, 20' span, 12" x 20"			32	2.250	Ea.
	2100	24" x 44"			22	3.270	Ea.
	2500	40' span, 12" x 52"			20	3.600	Ea.
112		COLUMNS Rectangular to 12' high, small columns			120	.600	L.F.
	0050	Large columns			96	.750	L.F.
	0300	24' high, small columns			192	.375	L.F.
	0350	Large columns			144	.500	L.F.
	0700	24' high, 1 haunch, 12" x 12"			32	2.250	Ea.
	0800	20" x 20"	↓	↓	28	2.570	Ea.

034 100 | Structural Precast

		Description	CREW	MAKEUP	DAILY OUTPUT	MAN-HOURS	UNIT
128	128	JOISTS 40 psf L.L., 6" deep for 12' spans	C-12	1 Carpenter Foreman (out)	600	.080	L.F.
				3 Carpenters			
				1 Building Laborer			
				1 Equip. Oper. (crane)			
				1 Hyd. Crane, 12 Ton			
	0050	8" deep for 16' spans			575	.083	L.F.
	0100	10" deep for 20' spans			550	.087	L.F.
	0150	12" deep for 24' spans	↓	↓	525	.091	L.F.
	136	PRESTRESSED ROOF AND FLOOR MEMBERS, GROUTED, 4" DEEP	C-11	1 Struc. Steel Foreman	4,875	.015	S.F.
				6 Struc. Steel Workers			
				1 Equip. Oper. (crane)			
				1 Equip. Oper. Oiler			
				1 Truck Crane, 150 Ton			
	0050	6" deep			5,850	.012	S.F.
	0100	8" deep			7,200	.010	S.F.
	0150	10" deep			8,800	.008	S.F.
	0200	12" deep			9,500	.008	S.F.
	140	TEES Prestressed quad tee, short spans, roof			7,200	.010	S.F.
	0050	Floor			7,200	.010	S.F.
	0200	Double tee, floor members, 60' span			8,400	.009	S.F.
	0250	80' span			8,000	.009	S.F.
	0300	Roof members, 30' span			4,800	.015	S.F.
	0350	50' span			6,400	.011	S.F.
	0400	Wall members, up to 55' high			3,600	.020	S.F.
	0500	Single tee roof members, 40' span			3,200	.023	S.F.
	0550	80' span			5,120	.014	S.F.
	0600	100' span			6,000	.012	S.F.
	0650	120' span	↓	↓	6,000	.012	S.F.
	1000	Double tees, floor members					
	1100	Lightweight, 20" x 8' wide, 45' span	C-11	1 Struc. Steel Foreman	20	3.600	Ea.
				6 Struc. Steel Workers			
				1 Equip. Oper. (crane)			
				1 Equip. Oper. Oiler			
				1 Truck Crane, 150 Ton			
	1150	24" x 8' wide, 50' span			18	4.000	Ea.
	1200	32" x 10' wide, 60' span			16	4.500	Ea.
	1250	Standard weight, 12" x 8' wide, 20' span			22	3.270	Ea.
	1300	16" x 8' wide, 25' span			20	3.600	Ea.
	1350	18" x 8' wide, 30' span			20	3.600	Ea.
	1400	20" x 8' wide, 45' span			18	4.000	Ea.
	1450	24" x 8' wide, 50' span			16	4.500	Ea.
	1500	32" x 10' wide, 60' span	↓	↓	14	5.140	Ea.
	2000	Roof members					
	2050	Lightweight, 20" x 8' wide, 40' span	C-11	1 Struc. Steel Foreman	20	3.600	Ea.
				6 Struc. Steel Workers			
				1 Equip. Oper. (crane)			
				1 Equip. Oper. Oiler			
				1 Truck Crane, 150 Ton			
	2100	24" x 8' wide, 50' span			18	4.000	Ea.
	2150	32" x 10' wide, 60' span			16	4.500	Ea.
	2200	Standard weight, 12" x 8' wide, 30' span			22	3.270	Ea.
	2250	16" x 8' wide, 30' span			20	3.600	Ea.
	2300	18" x 8' wide, 30' span			20	3.600	Ea.
	2350	20" x 8' wide, 40' span			18	4.000	Ea.
	2400	24" x 8' wide, 50' span			16	4.500	Ea.
	2450	32" x 10' wide, 60' span	↓	↓	14	5.140	Ea.

034 | Precast Concrete

034 500 | Architectural Precast

		CREW	MAKEUP	DAILY OUTPUT	MAN-HOURS	UNIT
504	**WALL PANELS** High rise, 4' x 8', 4" thick, smooth gray	C-11	1 Struc. Steel Foreman	256	.281	S.F.
			6 Struc. Steel Workers			
			1 Equip. Oper. (crane)			
			1 Equip. Oper. Oiler			
			1 Truck Crane, 150 Ton			
0100	Exposed aggregate			256	.281	S.F.
0400	8' x 8', 4" thick, smooth gray			576	.125	S.F.
0500	Exposed aggregate			576	.125	S.F.
1000	20' x 10', 6" thick, smooth gray			1,800	.040	S.F.
1100	Exposed aggregate			1,800	.040	S.F.
1500	30' x 10', 6" thick, smooth gray			2,100	.034	S.F.
1600	White face	↓	↓	2,100	.034	S.F.

034 700 | Tilt Up Precast

		CREW	MAKEUP	DAILY OUTPUT	MAN-HOURS	UNIT
704	**TILT-UP** Wall panel construction, walls only, 5-1/2" thick	C-14	1 Carpenter Foreman (out)	2,515	.057	S.F.
			5 Carpenters			
			4 Building Laborers			
			4 Rodmen (reinf.)			
			2 Cement Finishers			
			1 Equip. Oper. (crane)			
			1 Equip. Oper. Oiler			
			1 Crane, 80 Ton, & Tools			
			Power Tools			
			2 Gas Finishing Mach.			
0100	Walls only, 7-1/2" thick			2,115	.068	S.F.
0500	walls and columns, 5-1/2" thick walls, 12" x 12" columns			1,565	.092	S.F.
0550	7-1/2" thick wall, 12" x 12" columns			1,370	.105	S.F.
0800	Columns only, site precast, minimum			200	.720	L.F.
0850	Maximum	↓	↓	105	1.370	L.F.

034 800 | Precast Specialties

		CREW	MAKEUP	DAILY OUTPUT	MAN-HOURS	UNIT
802	**LINTELS**					
0800	Precast concrete, 4" x 8", stock units to 5' long	D-1	1 Bricklayer	175	.091	L.F.
			1 Bricklayer Helper			
0850	To 12' long	D-4	1 Bricklayer	190	.168	L.F.
			2 Bricklayer Helpers			
			1 Equip. Oper. (light)			
			1 Grout Pump			
			1 Hoses & Hopper			
			1 Accessories			
1000	6" wide, 8" high, solid, stock units to 5' long			185	.173	L.F.
1050	To 12' long			190	.168	L.F.
1200	8" wide, 8" high, stock units to 5' long			185	.173	L.F.
1250	To 12' long			190	.168	L.F.
1400	10" wide, 8" high, stock units to 14' long			180	.178	L.F.
1450	12" wide, 8" high, stock units to 19' long	↓	↓	185	.173	L.F.
804	**STAIRS** Concrete treads on steel stringers, 3' wide	C-12	1 Carpenter Foreman (out)	75	.640	Riser
			3 Carpenters			
			1 Building Laborer			
			1 Equip. Oper. (crane)			
			1 Hyd. Crane, 12 Ton			
0050	Building stairs, 3'-4" wide, 9' high, straight	C-11	1 Struc. Steel Foreman	7	10.290	Flight
			6 Struc. Steel Workers			
			1 Equip. Oper. (crane)			
			1 Equip. Oper. Oiler			
			1 Truck Crane, 150 Ton			
0100	Dogleg type with divider wall, 8' x 15'	"	"	5	14.400	Flight

034 | Precast Concrete

034 800 | Precast Specialties

		CREW	MAKEUP	DAILY OUTPUT	MAN-HOURS	UNIT
804	0303	Stairs, concrete, front entrance, 5' wide w/48" platform, 2 risers	C-12	1 Carpenter Foreman (out)	16	3.000	Flight
				3 Carpenters			
				1 Building Laborer			
				1 Equip. Oper. (crane)			
				1 Hyd. Crane, 12 Ton			
	0350	5 risers			12	4.000	Flight
	0500	6' wide, 2 risers			15	3.200	Flight
	0550	5 risers			11	4.360	Flight
	0700	7' wide, 2 risers			14	3.430	Flight
	0750	5 risers	↓	↓	10	4.800	Flight
	1200	Basement entrance stairs, steel bulkhead doors, minimum	B-51	1 Labor Foreman (outside)	22	2.180	Flight
				4 Building Laborers			
				1 Truck Driver (light)			
				1 Light Truck, 1.5 Ton			
	1250	Maximum	"	"	11	4.360	Flight

035 | Cementitious Decks

035 200 | Lightweight Concrete

		CREW	MAKEUP	DAILY OUTPUT	MAN-HOURS	UNIT
204	**CONCRETE CHANNEL SLABS** 2-3/4" or 3-1/2" thick, straight	C-12	1 Carpenter Foreman (out)	1,575	.030	S.F.
			3 Carpenters			
			1 Building Laborer			
			1 Equip. Oper. (crane)			
			1 Hyd. Crane, 12 Ton			
0050	Chopped up			785	.061	S.F.
0200	6" thick, span to 20'			1,300	.037	S.F.
0300	8" thick, span to 24'			1,100	.044	S.F.
208	**CONCRETE PLANK** Lightweight, nailable, T&G, 2" thick			1,800	.027	S.F.
0050	2-3/4" thick			1,575	.030	S.F.
0100	3-3/4" thick	↓	↓	1,375	.035	S.F.
212	**INSULATING** Lightweight cellular concrete roof fill					
0020	Portland cement and foaming agent	C-8	1 Labor Foreman (outside)	50	1.120	C.Y.
			3 Building Laborers			
			2 Cement Finishers			
			1 Equip. Oper. (med.)			
			1 Concrete Pump (small)			
0100	Poured vermiculite or perlite, field mix,					
0110	1:6 roof fill, add formboards above	C-8	1 Labor Foreman (outside)	50	1.120	C.Y.
			3 Building Laborers			
			2 Cement Finishers			
			1 Equip. Oper. (med.)			
			1 Concrete Pump (small)			
0200	Ready mix, 1:6 mix, roof fill, 2" thick	↓	↓	10,000	.006	S.F.
0250	3" thick			7,700	.007	S.F.
0400	Expanded volcanic glass rock, with binder, minimum	2 Carp	2 Carpenters	1,500	.011	S.F.
0450	Maximum	"	"	1,200	.013	S.F.

035 | Cementitious Decks

035 300 | Wood Fiber Systems

		Description	CREW	MAKEUP	DAILY OUTPUT	MAN-HOURS	UNIT
304	304	**FORMBOARD** Including subpurlins					
	0050	Non-asbestos fiber cement, 1/8" thick	C-13	1 Struc. Steel Worker	2,950	.008	S.F.
				1 Welder			
				1 Carpenter			
				1 Gas Welding Machine			
	0070	1/4" thick	↓	↓	2,950	.008	S.F.
	0100	Fiberglass, 1" thick, economy			2,700	.009	S.F.
	1000	Poured gypsum, 2" thick, add to formboard above	C-8	1 Labor Foreman (outside)	6,000	.009	S.F.
				3 Building Laborers			
				2 Cement Finishers			
				1 Equip. Oper. (med.)			
				1 Concrete Pump (small)			
	1100	3" thick	"	"	4,800	.012	S.F.
	306	**WOOD FIBER** Lightweight cement T&G planks, 1" thick	2 Carp	2 Carpenters	1,000	.016	S.F.
	0100	2" thick			950	.017	S.F.
	0150	2-1/2" thick			925	.017	S.F.
	0200	3" thick			900	.018	S.F.
	0400	Long span plank, 2" thick			950	.017	S.F.
	0450	3" thick	↓	↓	900	.018	S.F.
	1000	Add for bulb tees, subpurlins and grout, 6' span	E-1	1 Welder Foreman	5,000	.005	S.F.
				1 Welder			
				1 Equip. Oper. (light)			
				1 Gas Welding Machine			
	1100	8' span	"	"	4,200	.006	S.F.

4

DIVISION 4

MASONRY

DIVISION 4

MASONRY

Most masonry projects are fairly straightforward. However, there are factors that affect both the cost of placing materials and the rate at which the work can be done. Experience shows that a straight wall with few openings is more quickly constructed than a wall with openings such as doors and windows. Because no two masonry jobs are alike, the exact man-hour adjustment for different phases of work can only be determined by the estimator through past experience and judgement.

One of the most important considerations in planning the man-hours for masonry jobs is to allow for the initial layout of the project by the mason supervising the job. This is a time-consuming first step in any project which, if performed correctly, can actually increase productivity in the long run.

There are many other factors related to the job site that are just as important to consider. These include: the height of the wall being built, type of material used, the method used to handle materials, the type of scaffolding used, and the weight of material being placed. Also examine the work conditions at the job site. Man-hour figures can be seriously affected by the number of floors in a building, the amount of overhead work, and crew sizes.

Weather conditions, particularly the time of the year and location of the project, must be considered. Masonry should not be placed when the temperature drops below 40 degrees Fahrenheit. It is possible to "close in" and heat the work area; though this procedure increases the man-hours involved in preparation.

There are always specific applications that require some judgement on the part of the estimator to adjust productivity. For instance, when working with glazed tile, it is important to add a time allowance if stack bond is required.

Man-hour listings for brick, block, and stone work include the time needed to mix and handle mortar. Time is also allowed for repointing, repairs if needed, and clean-up at the end of each day. Modern mechanized equipment for brick handling can reduce the need for one laborer on a typical crew. Such devices are now in wide use in masonry construction.

041 | Mortar and Masonry Accessories

041 000 | Mortar

		CREW	MAKEUP	DAILY OUTPUT	MAN-HOURS	UNIT
016	**GROUTING** Bond bms. & lintels, 8" dp., pumped, not incl. block					
0020	8" thick, 0.2 C.F. per L.F.	D-4	1 Bricklayer	1,750	.018	L.F.
			2 Bricklayer Helpers			
			1 Equip. Oper. (light)			
			1 Grout Pump			
			1 Hoses & Hopper			
			1 Accessories			
0054	10" thick, 0.25 C.F. per L.F.	↓	↓	1,500	.021	L.F.
0060	12" thick, 0.3 C.F. per L.F.			1,300	.025	L.F.
0204	Concrete block cores, solid, 4" thk., by hand, .067 C.F./S.F.	D-8	3 Bricklayers	1,200	.033	S.F.
			2 Bricklayer Helpers			
0250	8" thick, pumped .258 C.F. per S.F.	D-4	1 Bricklayer	850	.038	S.F.
			2 Bricklayer Helpers			
			1 Equip. Oper. (light)			
			1 Grout Pump			
			1 Hoses & Hopper			
			1 Accessories			
0300	10" thick, .340 C.F. per S.F.			825	.039	S.F.
0350	12" thick, .422 C.F. per S.F.			800	.040	S.F.
0500	Cavity walls, 2" space, pumped, .167 C.F. per S.F.			2,000	.016	S.F.
0550	3" space, shoring not incl., .250 C.F. per S.F.			1,500	.021	S.F.
0600	4" space, .333 C.F. per S.F.			1,250	.026	S.F.
0700	6" space, .500 C.F. per S.F.			950	.034	S.F.
0800	Door frames, 3' x 7' opening, 2.5 C.F. per opening	↓	↓	60	.533	Opng.
0850	6' x 7' opening, 3.5 C.F. per opening			45	.711	Opng.
036	**SURFACE BONDING** Block walls with fiberglass mortar,					
0020	gray or white colors, not incl. block work	1 Bric	1 Bricklayer	540	.015	S.F.

041 500 | Masonry Accessories

		CREW	MAKEUP	DAILY OUTPUT	MAN-HOURS	UNIT
504	**ANCHOR BOLTS** Hooked type with nut, 1/2" diam., 8" long	1 Bric	1 Bricklayer	200	.040	Ea.
0030	12" long			190	.042	Ea.
0040	5/8" diameter, 8" long			180	.044	Ea.
0050	12" long			170	.047	Ea.
0060	3/4" diameter, 8" long			160	.050	Ea.
0070	12" long			150	.053	Ea.
508	**CONTROL JOINT** Rubber, 4" and wider wall			600	.013	L.F.
0050	PVC, 4" wall			600	.013	L.F.
0100	Rubber, 6" wall only			500	.016	L.F.
0120	PVC, 6" wall			500	.016	L.F.
0140	Rubber, 8" and wider wall			400	.020	L.F.
0160	PVC, 8" wall			400	.020	L.F.
0180	PVC, 12" wall			300	.027	L.F.
0300	Boxboard, asphalt impregnated, 1/4" thick			500	.016	S.F.
512	**JOINT REINFORCING** Steel bars, placed horizontal, #3 & #4 bars			450	.018	Lb.
0020	#5 & #6 bars			800	.010	Lb.
0050	Placed vertical, #3 & #4 bars			350	.023	Lb.
0060	#5 & #6 bars	↓	↓	650	.012	Lb.
0500	Wire strips, ladder type, galvanized					
0600	8 ga. sides, 9 ga. ties, 4" wall	1 Bric	1 Bricklayer	30	.267	C.L.F.
0650	6" wall			30	.267	C.L.F.
0700	8" wall			25	.320	C.L.F.
0750	10" wall			20	.400	C.L.F.
0800	12" wall	↓	↓	20	.400	C.L.F.
1000	Wire strips, truss type, galvanized					
1100	9 ga. sides, 9 ga. ties, 4" wall	1 Bric	1 Bricklayer	30	.267	C.L.F.
1150	6" wall			30	.267	C.L.F.
1200	8" wall			25	.320	C.L.F.
1250	10" wall	↓	↓	20	.400	C.L.F.

		041 500 Masonry Accessories	CREW	MAKEUP	DAILY OUTPUT	MAN-HOURS	UNIT
512	1301	Joint reinf., truss, galv., 9 ga. sides/ties, 12" wall	1 Bric	1 Bricklayer	20	.400	C.L.F.
	1500	3/16" sides 9 ga. ties 4" wall			30	.267	C.L.F.
	1550	6" wall			30	.267	C.L.F.
	1600	8" wall			25	.320	C.L.F.
	1650	10" wall			20	.400	C.L.F.
	1700	12" wall			20	.400	C.L.F.
	2000	3/16" sides 3/16" ties 4" wall			30	.267	C.L.F.
	2050	6" wall			30	.267	C.L.F.
	2100	8" wall			25	.320	C.L.F.
	2150	10" wall			20	.400	C.L.F.
	2200	12" wall	↓	↓	20	.400	C.L.F.
	2500	Wire strips cavity truss type, galvanized					
	2600	9 ga. sides 9 ga. ties 4" wall	1 Bric	1 Bricklayer	25	.320	C.L.F.
	2650	6" wall			25	.320	C.L.F.
	2700	8" wall			20	.400	C.L.F.
	2750	10" wall			15	.533	C.L.F.
	2800	12" wall			15	.533	C.L.F.
	3000	3/16" sides 9 ga. ties 4" wall			25	.320	C.L.F.
	3050	6" wall			25	.320	C.L.F.
	3100	8" wall			20	.400	C.L.F.
	3150	10" wall			15	.533	C.L.F.
	3200	12" wall			15	.533	C.L.F.
	518	WALL PLUGS For nailing to brickwork, 26 ga., galvanized, plain			10.50	.762	C
	0050	Wood filled			10.50	.762	C
	520	WALL TIES To brick veneer, galv., corrugated, 7/8" x 7", 24 gauge			10.50	.762	C
	0100	24 gauge			10.50	.762	C
	0150	16 gauge	↓	↓	10.50	.762	C
	0300	Buck anchors, galvanized					
	0350	16 gauge	1 Bric	1 Bricklayer	10.50	.762	C
	0400	14 gauge	"	"	10.50	.762	C
	0500	Cavity wall tie, adj., corrugated, with anchor					
	0520	Double type wall tie	1 Bric	1 Bricklayer	10.50	.762	C
	0550	Single type wall tie			10.50	.762	C
	0700	"Z" type, 6" long, 1/8" dia.			10.50	.762	C
	0750	3/16" dia.			10.50	.762	C
	0900	"Z" type, 8" long, 3/16" dia., galv.			10.50	.762	C
	0950	Copper weld			10.50	.762	C
	1100	Rectangular type, 3/16" dia., galv., 2" x 6"			10.50	.762	C
	1150	2" x 8"			10.50	.762	C
	1300	Stainless, 2" x 8" or 4" x 6"			10.50	.762	C
	1350	Copper weld	↓	↓	10.50	.762	C
	1600	Stone anchors					
	1650	"L" type, plain, 6" x 1" x 1/8" - 3/4" bend	1 Bric	1 Bricklayer	10.50	.762	C
	1700	Electro-galvanized			10.50	.762	C
	1750	Stainless			10.50	.762	C
	2300	"U" type, plain, 6" x 1" x 1/8" - 3/4" bend			10.50	.762	C
	2350	Electro-galvanized			10.50	.762	C
	2400	Stainless			10.50	.762	C
	2600	Split-bend, plain, 6" x 1" x 1/8" - 3/4" bend			10.50	.762	C
	2650	Electro-galvanized			10.50	.762	C
	2700	Stainless			10.50	.762	C
	2800	Twisted type, plain, 7-3/8" x 1" x 1/8" - 3/4" bend			10.50	.762	C
	2850	Electro-galvanized			10.50	.762	C
	2900	Stainless	↓	↓	10.50	.762	C
	3000	Granite anchors					
	3100	"L" type rod, 1/8" x 1" x 2" strap 3/4" bend					
	3110	welded to 1/4" dia x 2" long corrugated rod	1 Bric	1 Bricklayer	10.50	.762	C
	3111						

041 | Mortar and Masonry Accessories

041 500 | Masonry Accessories

		CREW	MAKEUP	DAILY OUTPUT	MAN-HOURS	UNIT
520 3300	Plate rod, 16 ga. 1-1/2" x 2-1/2" plate, welded to 3/16"					
3310	diam. x 6" long rod, corrugated, stainless	1 Bric	1 Bricklayer	10.50	.762	C
3500	"T" type rod, 1" x 2" x 1/8" strap & cross piece, welded					
3510	to 3/16" x 6" long rod, corrugated, stainless	1 Bric	1 Bricklayer	10.50	.762	C
4000	Stone pin anchors					
4100	Flat type, 6" x 1" x 1/8" with 1/2" dia. x 2" pin					
4150	Galvanized	1 Bric	1 Bricklayer	10.50	.762	C
4200	Stainless	"	"	10.50	.762	C
4300	"L" type, 6" x 1" x 1/8", 3/4" bend, 1/2" dia. x 2" pin					
4350	Galvanized	1 Bric	1 Bricklayer	10.50	.762	C
4400	Stainless	"	"	10.50	.762	C
4500	Split-bend, 6" x 1" x 1/8" - 3/4" bend, 1/2" dia. x 2" pin					
4550	Galvanized	1 Bric	1 Bricklayer	10.50	.762	C
4600	Stainless	"	"	10.50	.762	C
4700	Flange-hook, 6"x1"x1/8" - 3/4" bend, 1/2" dia. x 2" pin					
4750	Galvanized	1 Bric	1 Bricklayer	10.50	.762	C
4800	Stainless			10.50	.762	C
524	**VENT BOX** Extruded aluminum, 4" deep, 8" x 2-1/2"			30	.267	Ea.
0050	8" x 5"			25	.320	Ea.
0100	16" x 2-1/2"			25	.320	Ea.
0150	16" x 8"			22	.364	Ea.
0200	24" x 5"			22	.364	Ea.
0250	24" x 8"			20	.400	Ea.
1000	Stainless steel ventilators, 6" x 6"			25	.320	Ea.
1050	8" x 8"			24	.333	Ea.
1100	12" x 12"			23	.348	Ea.
1150	12" x 6"			24	.333	Ea.
1200	Foundation vent, galv., 1-1/4" thick, 8"H, 16"L, no damper			30	.267	Ea.

042 | Unit Masonry

042 050 | Chimneys

		CREW	MAKEUP	DAILY OUTPUT	MAN-HOURS	UNIT
054	**CHIMNEY** For foundation, add to prices below, see div 033-130-0500					
0100	Brick @ $230/M, 16" x 16", 8" flue, scaff. not incl.	D-1	1 Bricklayer 1 Bricklayer Helper	18.20	.879	V.L.F.
0150	16" x 20" with one 8" x 12" flue			16	1.000	V.L.F.
0200	16" x 24" with two 8" x 8" flues			14	1.140	V.L.F.
0250	20" x 20" with one 12" x 12" flue			13.70	1.170	V.L.F.
0300	20" x 24" with two 8" x 12" flues			12	1.330	V.L.F.
0350	20" x 32" with two 12" x 12" flues			10	1.600	V.L.F.
1800	Metal, steel, guyed, 2' diameter, 1/4" thick shell	E-2	1 Struc. Steel Foreman 4 Struc. Steel Workers 1 Equip. Oper. (crane) 1 Equip. Oper. Oiler 1 Crane, 90 Ton	65	.862	V.L.F.
1900	5' diameter, 1/2" thick shell	"	"	30	1.870	V.L.F.

042 100 | Brick Masonry

			CREW	MAKEUP	DAILY OUTPUT	MAN-HOURS	UNIT
108	108	**COLUMNS** Brick @ $230 per M, 8" x 8", 9 brick, scaff. not incl.	D-1	1 Bricklayer 1 Bricklayer Helper	56	.286	V.L.F.
	0100	12" x 8", 13.5 brick			37	.432	V.L.F.
	0200	12" x 12", 20.3 brick			25	.640	V.L.F.
	0300	16" x 12", 27 brick			19	.842	V.L.F.
	0400	16" x 16", 36 brick			14	1.140	V.L.F.
	0500	20" x 16", 45 brick			11	1.450	V.L.F.
	0600	20" x 20", 56.3 brick			9	1.780	V.L.F.
	0700	24" x 20", 67.5 brick			7	2.290	V.L.F.
	0800	24" x 24", 81 brick			6	2.670	V.L.F.
	1000	36" x 36", 182.3 brick			3	5.330	V.L.F.
	116	**COPING** For 12" wall, stock units, aluminum			80	.200	L.F.
	0050	Precast concrete, stock units, 6" wide			100	.160	L.F.
	0100	10" wide			90	.178	L.F.
	0110	12" wide			85	.188	L.F.
	0150	14" wide			80	.200	L.F.
	0300	Limestone for 12" wall, 4" thick			90	.178	L.F.
	0350	6" thick			80	.200	L.F.
	0500	Marble to 4" thick, no wash, 9" wide			90	.178	L.F.
	0550	12" wide			80	.200	L.F.
	0700	Terra cotta, 9" wide			90	.178	L.F.
	0750	12" wide	↓	↓	80	.200	L.F.
	162	**SIMULATED BRICK** Aluminum, baked on colors	1 Carp	1 Carpenter	200	.040	S.F.
	0050	Fiberglass panels			200	.040	S.F.
	0100	Urethane pieces cemented in mastic			150	.053	S.F.
	0150	Vinyl siding panels	↓	↓	200	.040	S.F.
	0160	Cement base, brick, incl. mastic	D-1	1 Bricklayer 1 Bricklayer Helper	100	.160	S.F.
	0170	Corner			50	.320	V.L.F.
	0180	Stone face, incl. mastic			100	.160	S.F.
	0190	Corner			50	.320	V.L.F.
	170	**STEPS** With select common at $230 per M	↓	↓	.30	53.330	M
	184	**WALLS** Brick purchased in truck lots					
	0060	Includes a 3% brick waste factor and 25% mortar waste					
	0140	Common, 8" x 2-2/3" x 4", $197/M, 4" wall, face brick	D-8	3 Bricklayers 2 Bricklayer Helpers	1.45	27.590	M
	0150	4" thick as back-up			1.45	27.590	M
	0204	8" thick wall, 13.50 bricks per S.F.			1.80	22.220	M
	0250	12" thick wall, 20.25 bricks per S.F.			1.90	21.050	M
	0304	16" thick wall, 27.00 bricks per S.F.			2	20.000	M
	0500	Reinf., straight hard, 8" x 2-2/3" x 4" at $230 per M 4" wall			1.40	28.570	M
	0550	8" thick wall, 13.50 bricks per S.F.			1.75	22.860	M
	0600	12" thick wall, 20.25 bricks per S.F.			1.85	21.620	M
	0650	16" thick wall, 27.00 bricks per S.F.	↓	↓	1.95	20.510	M
	0790	Alternate method of figuring by square foot					
	0800	Common 8" x 2-2/3" x 4" at $197/M, 4" wall, as face brick	D-8	3 Bricklayers 2 Bricklayer Helpers	215	.186	S.F.
	0850	4" thick, as back up			240	.167	S.F.
	0900	8" thick wall, 13.50 brick per S.F.			135	.296	S.F.
	1000	12" thick wall, 20.25 bricks per S.F.			95	.421	S.F.
	1050	16" thick wall, 27.00 bricks per S.F.			75	.533	S.F.
	1200	Reinf., straight hard, 8" x 2-2/3" x 4" at $230/M, 4" wall			205	.195	S.F.
	1250	8" thick wall, 13.50 brick per S.F.			130	.308	S.F.
	1300	12" thick wall, 20.25 bricks per S.F.			90	.444	S.F.
	1350	16" thick wall, 27.00 bricks per S.F.	↓	↓	70	.571	S.F.

042 100 | Brick Masonry

		Description	CREW	MAKEUP	DAILY OUTPUT	MAN-HOURS	UNIT
194	194	WINDOW SILL Bluestone, natural cleft, 12" wide, 1-1/2" thick	D-1	1 Bricklayer 1 Bricklayer Helper	85	.188	S.F.
	0050	2" thick			75	.213	S.F.
	0100	Cut stone, 5" x 8" plain			48	.333	L.F.
	0200	Face brick on edge, brick @ $250 per M, 8" wide			80	.200	L.F.
	0400	Marble, 12" wide, 1" thick			85	.188	L.F.
	0600	Precast concrete, stock sections, 6" wide			70	.229	L.F.
	0650	10" wide			60	.267	L.F.
	0700	14" wide			50	.320	L.F.
	0900	Slate, colored, unfading, 12" wide, 1" thick			85	.188	L.F.
	0950	2" thick			70	.229	L.F.
	1200	Stainless steel, stock			125	.128	L.F.
	1250	Custom	↓	↓	125	.128	L.F.

042 200 | Concrete Unit Masonry

		Description	CREW	MAKEUP	DAILY OUTPUT	MAN-HOURS	UNIT
216		CONCRETE BLOCK, BACK-UP, Scaffolding not included					
0020		Sand aggregate, tooled joint 1 side					
0050		Not-reinforced, 8" x 16", 2" thick, 2000 psi	D-8	3 Bricklayers 2 Bricklayer Helpers	475	.084	S.F.
0200		Regular block, 4" thick			440	.091	S.F.
0300		6" thick			420	.095	S.F.
0350		8" thick			400	.100	S.F.
0400		10" thick	↓	↓	390	.103	S.F.
0450		12" thick	D-9	3 Bricklayers 3 Bricklayer Helpers	370	.130	S.F.
1000		Reinforced, alternate courses, 4" thick	D-8	3 Bricklayers 2 Bricklayer Helpers	435	.092	S.F.
1100		6" thick			415	.096	S.F.
1150		8" thick			395	.101	S.F.
1200		10" thick	↓	↓	385	.104	S.F.
1250		12" thick	D-9	3 Bricklayers 3 Bricklayer Helpers	365	.132	S.F.
2000		Lightweight, not reinforced, 4" thick	D-8	3 Bricklayers 2 Bricklayer Helpers	445	.090	S.F.
2100		6" thick			425	.094	S.F.
2150		8" thick			405	.099	S.F.
2200		10" thick	↓	↓	395	.101	S.F.
2250		12" thick	D-9	3 Bricklayers 3 Bricklayer Helpers	375	.128	S.F.
3000		Lightweight, reinforced, 4" thick	D-8	3 Bricklayers 2 Bricklayer Helpers	440	.091	S.F.
3100		6" thick			420	.095	S.F.
3150		8" thick			400	.100	S.F.
3200		10" thick	↓	↓	390	.103	S.F.
3250		12" thick	D-9	3 Bricklayers 3 Bricklayer Helpers	370	.130	S.F.
220		CONCRETE BLOCK, DECORATIVE Scaffolding not included					
0020		Embossed, simulated brick face, not reinforced					
0100		8" x 16" units, 4" thick	D-8	3 Bricklayers 2 Bricklayer Helpers	400	.100	S.F.
0200		8" thick			340	.118	S.F.
0250		12" thick	↓	↓	300	.133	S.F.
0400		Embossed both sides					
0500		8" thick	D-8	3 Bricklayers 2 Bricklayer Helpers	300	.133	S.F.
0550		12" thick	"	"	275	.145	S.F.
1001							

042 200 | Concrete Unit Masonry

		Description	CREW	MAKEUP	DAILY OUTPUT	MAN-HOURS	UNIT
220	1151	Concrete block, high strength, flutes 2 sides, 8" x 16" x 4" thick	D-8	3 Bricklayers 2 Bricklayer Helpers	335	.119	S.F.
	1200	8" thick	"	"	300	.133	S.F.
	1400	Deep grooved, smooth face					
	1450	8" x 16" x 4" thick	D-8	3 Bricklayers 2 Bricklayer Helpers	345	.116	S.F.
	1500	8" thick	"	"	300	.133	S.F.
	2000	Formbloc, incl. inserts & reinforcing					
	2100	8" x 16" x 8" thick	D-8	3 Bricklayers 2 Bricklayer Helpers	345	.116	S.F.
	2150	12" thick	"	"	310	.129	S.F.
	2500	Ground face					
	2600	8" x 16" x 4" thick	D-8	3 Bricklayers 2 Bricklayer Helpers	345	.116	S.F.
	2650	6" thick			310	.129	S.F.
	2700	8" thick	↓	↓	290	.138	S.F.
	2750	12" thick	D-9	3 Bricklayers 3 Bricklayer Helpers	265	.181	S.F.
	4000	Slump block					
	4100	4" face height x 16" x 4" thick	D-1	1 Bricklayer 1 Bricklayer Helper	165	.097	S.F.
	4150	6" thick			160	.100	S.F.
	4200	8" thick			155	.103	S.F.
	4250	10" thick			140	.114	S.F.
	4300	12" thick			130	.123	S.F.
	4400	6" face height x 16" x 6" thick			155	.103	S.F.
	4450	8" thick			150	.107	S.F.
	4500	10" thick			130	.123	S.F.
	4550	12" thick	↓	↓	120	.133	S.F.
	5000	Split rib profile units, 1" deep ribs, 8 ribs					
	5100	8" x 16" x 4" thick	D-8	3 Bricklayers 2 Bricklayer Helpers	345	.116	S.F.
	5150	6" thick			325	.123	S.F.
	5200	8" thick	↓	↓	305	.131	S.F.
	5250	12" thick	D-9	3 Bricklayers 3 Bricklayer Helpers	275	.175	S.F.
	6000	Split face or scored split face					
	6100	8" x 16" x 4" thick	D-8	3 Bricklayers 2 Bricklayer Helpers	350	.114	S.F.
	6150	6" thick			315	.127	S.F.
	6200	8" thick	↓	↓	295	.136	S.F.
	6250	12" thick	D-9	3 Bricklayers 3 Bricklayer Helpers	270	.178	S.F.
	7000	Scored ground face, 2 to 5 scores					
	7100	8" x 16" x 4" thick	D-8	3 Bricklayers 2 Bricklayer Helpers	345	.116	S.F.
	7150	6" thick			310	.129	S.F.
	7200	8" thick	↓	↓	290	.138	S.F.
	7250	12" thick	D-9	3 Bricklayers 3 Bricklayer Helpers	265	.181	S.F.
	8000	Hexagonal face profile units, 8" x 16" units					
	8100	4" thick, hollow	D-8	3 Bricklayers 2 Bricklayer Helpers	345	.116	S.F.
	8200	Solid			345	.116	S.F.
	8300	6" thick, hollow			310	.129	S.F.
	8350	8" thick, hollow			290	.138	S.F.
	8500	For stacked bond, add			4.20	9.520	M.S.F.
	8550	For high rise construction, add per story	↓	↓	67.80	.590	M.S.F.

042 200 | Concrete Unit Masonry

		Description	CREW	MAKEUP	DAILY OUTPUT	MAN-HOURS	UNIT
224	224	**CONCRETE BLOCK, INTERLOCKING** Scaffolding not included					
	0100	Not including grout or reinforcing					
	0200	8" x 16" units, 8" thick, 2000 psi	D-1	1 Bricklayer	245	.065	S.F.
				1 Bricklayer Helper			
	0300	12" thick	↓	↓	220	.073	S.F.
	0350	16" thick			185	.086	S.F.
	0400	Including grout & reinforcing, 8" thick	D-4	1 Bricklayer	245	.131	S.F.
				2 Bricklayer Helpers			
				1 Equip. Oper. (light)			
				1 Grout Pump			
				1 Hoses & Hopper			
				1 Accessories			
	0450	12" thick	↓	↓	220	.145	S.F.
	0500	16" thick			185	.173	S.F.
228		**CONCRETE BLOCK, LEAD LINED** Scaffolding not included					
	0200	12" x 12" x 4" thick, 1/16" core	D-9	3 Bricklayers	165	.291	S.F.
				3 Bricklayer Helpers			
	0300	1/4" core	"	"	100	.480	S.F.
232		**CONCRETE BLOCK, PARTITIONS** Scaffolding not included					
	0100	Acoustical slotted block					
	0200	N.R.C., .50 type A, 4" thick	D-8	3 Bricklayers	315	.127	S.F.
				2 Bricklayer Helpers			
	0210	N.R.C., .65 type R, 4" thick			315	.127	S.F.
	0250	N.R.C., .50 type A, 6" thick			290	.138	S.F.
	0260	N.R.C., .65 type R, 6" thick			290	.138	S.F.
	0400	N.R.C., .45 type A-1, 8" thick			265	.151	S.F.
	0410	N.R.C., .55 type Q, 8" thick			265	.151	S.F.
	0500	N.R.C., .60 type R, 8" thick			265	.151	S.F.
	0600	N.R.C., .65 type RR, 8" thick			265	.151	S.F.
	0700	N.R.C., .65 type RSR, 8" thick			265	.151	S.F.
	0710	N.R.C., .70 type R, 12" thick	↓	↓	245	.163	S.F.
	1000	Lightweight block, tooled joints, 2 sides, hollow					
	1100	Not reinforced, 8" x 16" x 4" thick	D-8	3 Bricklayers	435	.092	S.F.
				2 Bricklayer Helpers			
	1150	6" thick			405	.099	S.F.
	1200	8" thick			380	.105	S.F.
	1250	10" thick	↓	↓	365	.110	S.F.
	1300	12" thick	D-9	3 Bricklayers	345	.139	S.F.
				3 Bricklayer Helpers			
	1500	Reinforced, 4" thick	D-8	3 Bricklayers	444	.090	S.F.
				2 Bricklayer Helpers			
	1600	6" thick			421	.095	S.F.
	1650	8" thick			400	.100	S.F.
	1700	10" thick	↓	↓	390	.103	S.F.
	1750	12" thick	D-9	3 Bricklayers	370	.130	S.F.
				3 Bricklayer Helpers			
	2000	Not reinforced, 8" x 24" x 4" thick, hollow			460	.104	S.F.
	2100	6" thick			440	.109	S.F.
	2150	8" thick			415	.116	S.F.
	2200	10" thick			385	.125	S.F.
	2250	12" thick			365	.132	S.F.
	2400	Reinforced, 4" thick			460	.104	S.F.
	2500	6" thick			440	.109	S.F.
	2550	8" thick			415	.116	S.F.
	2600	10" thick			385	.125	S.F.
	2650	12" thick	↓	↓	365	.132	S.F.
	2800	Solid, not reinforced, 8" x 16" x 2" thick	D-8	3 Bricklayers	440	.091	S.F.
				2 Bricklayer Helpers			

042 200	Concrete Unit Masonry	CREW	MAKEUP	DAILY OUTPUT	MAN-HOURS	UNIT
2901	Concrete block partitions, lightweight, solid, 8" x 16" x 4" thick	D-8	3 Bricklayers	420	.095	S.F.
			2 Bricklayer Helpers			
2950	6" thick			390	.103	S.F.
3000	8" thick			365	.110	S.F.
3050	10" thick	↓	↓	350	.114	S.F.
3100	12" thick	D-9	3 Bricklayers	330	.145	S.F.
			3 Bricklayer Helpers			
3300	Solid, reinforced, 4" thick	D-8	3 Bricklayers	415	.096	S.F.
			2 Bricklayer Helpers			
3400	6" thick			385	.104	S.F.
3450	8" thick			360	.111	S.F.
3500	10" thick	↓	↓	345	.116	S.F.
3550	12" thick	D-9	3 Bricklayers	325	.148	S.F.
			3 Bricklayer Helpers			
4000	Regular block, tooled joints, 2 sides, hollow					
4100	Not reinforced, 8" x 16" x 4" thick	D-8	3 Bricklayers	430	.093	S.F.
			2 Bricklayer Helpers			
4150	6" thick			400	.100	S.F.
4200	8" thick			375	.107	S.F.
4250	10" thick	↓	↓	360	.111	S.F.
4300	12" thick	D-9	3 Bricklayers	340	.141	S.F.
			3 Bricklayer Helpers			
4500	Reinforced, 8" x 16" x 4" thick	D-8	3 Bricklayers	425	.094	S.F.
			2 Bricklayer Helpers			
4550	6" thick			395	.101	S.F.
4600	8" thick			370	.108	S.F.
4650	10" thick	↓	↓	355	.113	S.F.
4700	12" thick	D-9	3 Bricklayers	335	.143	S.F.
			3 Bricklayer Helpers			
4900	Solid, not reinforced, 2" thick	D-8	3 Bricklayers	435	.092	S.F.
			2 Bricklayer Helpers			
5000	3" thick			430	.093	S.F.
5050	4" thick			415	.096	S.F.
5100	6" thick			385	.104	S.F.
5150	8" thick	↓	↓	360	.111	S.F.
5200	12" thick	D-9	3 Bricklayers	325	.148	S.F.
			3 Bricklayer Helpers			
5500	Solid, reinforced, 4" thick	D-8	3 Bricklayers	420	.095	S.F.
			2 Bricklayer Helpers			
5550	6" thick			380	.105	S.F.
5600	8" thick	↓	↓	355	.113	S.F.
5650	12" thick	D-9	3 Bricklayers	320	.150	S.F.
			3 Bricklayer Helpers			
6000	Stud block, 8" x 16", 6" + 2", plain	D-8	3 Bricklayers	410	.098	S.F.
			2 Bricklayer Helpers			
6050	Embossed			390	.103	S.F.
6100	8" + 2", plain			390	.103	S.F.
6150	Embossed			370	.108	S.F.
6200	10" + 2", plain			370	.108	S.F.
6250	Embossed			350	.114	S.F.
6500	Stud block wall, 8" x 16" unit, 6" + 2" + 2"			350	.114	S.F.
6550	8" + 2" + 2"			340	.118	S.F.
6700	Special jamb block, 6" + 2"			390	.103	S.F.
6750	8" + 2"			370	.108	S.F.
6800	10" + 2"	↓	↓	350	.114	S.F.

232

042 200 | Concrete Unit Masonry

			CREW	MAKEUP	DAILY OUTPUT	MAN-HOURS	UNIT
236	**236**	**CHIMNEY BLOCK** Scaffolding not included					
	0220	1 piece, with 8" x 8" flue, 16" x 16"	D-1	1 Bricklayer	28	.571	V.L.F.
				1 Bricklayer Helper			
	0230	2 piece, 16" x 16"			26	.615	V.L.F.
	0240	2 piece, with 8" x 12" flue, 16" x 20"			24	.667	V.L.F.
	0250	With 12" x 12" flue, 20" x 20"	↓	↓	22	.727	V.L.F.
	240	**CONCRETE BLOCK, SOLAR SCREEN** Scaffolding not included					
	0200	4" thick, 6" x 6" units	D-8	3 Bricklayers	180	.222	S.F.
				2 Bricklayer Helpers			
	0300	8" x 8" units			270	.148	S.F.
	0350	12" x 12" units			300	.133	S.F.
	0500	8" thick, 8" x 16" units	↓	↓	330	.121	S.F.
	248	**GLAZED CONCRETE BLOCK** Scaffolding not included					
	0100	Not reinforced, 2" thick, solid	D-8	3 Bricklayers	360	.111	S.F.
				2 Bricklayer Helpers			
	0200	Hollow core, 8" x 16" units, 4" thick			345	.116	S.F.
	0250	6" thick			330	.121	S.F.
	0300	8" thick			310	.129	S.F.
	0350	10" thick	↓	↓	295	.136	S.F.
	0400	12" thick	D-9	3 Bricklayers	280	.171	S.F.
				3 Bricklayer Helpers			
	0700	Double face, 8" x 16" units, 4" thick	D-8	3 Bricklayers	310	.129	S.F.
				2 Bricklayer Helpers			
	0750	6" thick			290	.138	S.F.
	0800	8" thick			270	.148	S.F.
	1000	Corner, bullnose or square, 8" x 16" units, 2" thick			315	.127	Ea.
	1050	4" thick			285	.140	Ea.
	1200	Cap and sill, 8" x 16" units, 2" thick			420	.095	L.F.
	1250	4" thick			380	.105	L.F.
	1500	Cove base, 8" high, 2" thick			315	.127	L.F.
	1550	4" thick			285	.140	L.F.
	1600	6" thick			265	.151	L.F.
	1650	8" thick	↓	↓	245	.163	L.F.

042 300 | Reinforced Unit Masonry

		CREW	MAKEUP	DAILY OUTPUT	MAN-HOURS	UNIT
304	**CONCRETE BLOCK BOND BEAM** Scaffolding not included					
0020	Not including grout or reinforcing					
0100	Regular block, 8" high, 8" thick	D-8	3 Bricklayers	565	.071	L.F.
			2 Bricklayer Helpers			
0150	12" thick	D-9	3 Bricklayers	510	.094	L.F.
			3 Bricklayer Helpers			
0500	Lightweight, 8" high, 8" thick	D-8	3 Bricklayers	575	.070	L.F.
			2 Bricklayer Helpers			
0550	12" thick	D-9	3 Bricklayers	520	.092	L.F.
			3 Bricklayer Helpers			
2000	Including grout and 2 #5 bars					
2100	Regular block, 8" high, 8" thick	D-8	3 Bricklayers	300	.133	L.F.
			2 Bricklayer Helpers			
2150	12" thick	D-9	3 Bricklayers	250	.192	L.F.
			3 Bricklayer Helpers			
2500	Lightweight, 8" high, 8" thick	D-8	3 Bricklayers	305	.131	L.F.
			2 Bricklayer Helpers			
2550	12" thick	D-9	3 Bricklayers	255	.188	L.F.
			3 Bricklayer Helpers			

042 300	Reinforced Unit Masonry	CREW	MAKEUP	DAILY OUTPUT	MAN-HOURS	UNIT
310	**310** **CONCRETE BLOCK, EXTERIOR** Not including scaffolding					
	0020 Reinforced, tooled joints 2 sides, styrofoam inserts					
	0100 Regular, 8" x 16" x 6" thick	D-8	3 Bricklayers	390	.103	S.F.
			2 Bricklayer Helpers			
	0200 8" thick	↓	↓	365	.110	S.F.
	0250 10" thick			355	.113	S.F.
	0300 12" thick	D-9	3 Bricklayers	330	.145	S.F.
			3 Bricklayer Helpers			
	0500 Lightweight, 8" x 16" x 6" thick	D-8	3 Bricklayers	410	.098	S.F.
			2 Bricklayer Helpers			
	0600 8" thick	↓	↓	385	.104	S.F.
	0650 10" thick			370	.108	S.F.
	0700 12" thick	D-9	3 Bricklayers	350	.137	S.F.
			3 Bricklayer Helpers			
	320 **CONCRETE BLOCK FOUNDATION WALL** Scaffolding not included					
	0050 Sand aggregate, trowel cut joints, not reinf., parged 1/2" thick					
	0200 Regular, 8" x 16" x 6" thick	D-8	3 Bricklayers	450	.089	S.F.
			2 Bricklayer Helpers			
	0250 8" thick	↓	↓	430	.093	S.F.
	0300 10" thick			420	.095	S.F.
	0350 12" thick	D-9	3 Bricklayers	395	.122	S.F.
			3 Bricklayer Helpers			
	0500 Solid, 8" x 16" block, 6" thick	D-8	3 Bricklayers	440	.091	S.F.
			2 Bricklayer Helpers			
	0550 8" thick	"	"	415	.096	S.F.
	0600 12" thick	D-9	3 Bricklayers	380	.126	S.F.
			3 Bricklayer Helpers			
	1000 Reinforced					
	1100 Regular, 8" x 16" block, 6" thick	D-8	3 Bricklayers	445	.090	S.F.
			2 Bricklayer Helpers			
	1150 8" thick	↓	↓	425	.094	S.F.
	1200 10" thick			415	.096	S.F.
	1250 12" thick	D-9	3 Bricklayers	390	.123	S.F.
			3 Bricklayer Helpers			
	1500 Solid, 8" x 16" block, 6" thick	D-8	3 Bricklayers	435	.092	S.F.
			2 Bricklayer Helpers			
	1600 8" thick	"	"	410	.098	S.F.
	1650 12" thick	D-9	3 Bricklayers	375	.128	S.F.
			3 Bricklayer Helpers			
	325 **CONCRETE BLOCK, HIGH STRENGTH** Scaffolding not included					
	0050 Hollow, reinforced, 8" x 16" units					
	0200 3000 psi, 4" thick	D-8	3 Bricklayers	430	.093	S.F.
			2 Bricklayer Helpers			
	0250 6" thick	↓	↓	400	.100	S.F.
	0300 8" thick			375	.107	S.F.
	0350 12" thick	D-9	3 Bricklayers	340	.141	S.F.
			3 Bricklayer Helpers			
	0500 5000 psi, 4" thick	D-8	3 Bricklayers	430	.093	S.F.
			2 Bricklayer Helpers			
	0550 6" thick	↓	↓	400	.100	S.F.
	0600 8" thick			375	.107	S.F.
	0650 12" thick	D-9	3 Bricklayers	340	.141	S.F.
			3 Bricklayer Helpers			

042 | Unit Masonry

042 300 | Reinforced Unit Masonry

			CREW	MAKEUP	DAILY OUTPUT	MAN-HOURS	UNIT
330	330	**CONCRETE BLOCK, LINTELS** Scaffolding not included					
	0100	Including grout and reinforcing					
	0200	8" high, 6" thick, 1 #4 bar	D-4	1 Bricklayer	300	.107	L.F.
				2 Bricklayer Helpers			
				1 Equip. Oper. (light)			
				1 Grout Pump			
				1 Hoses & Hopper			
				1 Accessories			
	0250	2 #4 bars			295	.108	L.F.
	0400	16" high, 1 #4 bar			275	.116	L.F.
	0450	2 #4 bars			270	.119	L.F.
	1000	8" high, 8" thick, 1 #4 bar			275	.116	L.F.
	1100	2 #4 bars			270	.119	L.F.
	1150	2 #5 bars			270	.119	L.F.
	1200	2 #6 bars			265	.121	L.F.
	1500	16" high, 1 #4 bar			250	.128	L.F.
	1600	2 #3 bars			245	.131	L.F.
	1650	2 #4 bars			245	.131	L.F.
	1700	2 #5 bars	↓	↓	240	.133	L.F.
335		**COLUMN BLOCK** Pilaster incl. reinf. and grout. Scaffolding not incl.					
	0160	1 piece unit, 16" x 16"	D-1	1 Bricklayer	26	.615	V.L.F.
				1 Bricklayer Helper			
	0170	2 piece units, 16" x 20"			24	.667	V.L.F.
	0180	20" x 20"			22	.727	V.L.F.
	0190	22" x 24"			18	.889	V.L.F.
	0200	20" x 32"	↓	↓	14	1.140	V.L.F.

042 350 | Masonry Panels

			CREW	MAKEUP	DAILY OUTPUT	MAN-HOURS	UNIT
354		**WALL PANELS** Prefabricated, 4" thick, minimum	C-11	1 Struc. Steel Foreman	775	.093	S.F.
				6 Struc. Steel Workers			
				1 Equip. Oper. (crane)			
				1 Equip. Oper. Oiler			
				1 Truck Crane, 150 Ton			
	0100	Maximum	"	"	500	.144	S.F.

042 450 | Structural Facing Tile

			CREW	MAKEUP	DAILY OUTPUT	MAN-HOURS	UNIT
454		**STRUCTURAL FACING TILE** Scaffolding not incl., 6T, 5-1/3" x 12"					
	0020	Functional colors, 2.3 pieces per S.F., 2" thick, glazed 1 side	D-8	3 Bricklayers	225	.178	S.F.
				2 Bricklayer Helpers			
	0100	4" thick, glazed 1 side			220	.182	S.F.
	0150	Glazed 2 sides			195	.205	S.F.
	0250	6" thick, glazed 1 side			210	.190	S.F.
	0300	Glazed 2 sides			185	.216	S.F.
	0400	8" thick, glazed 1 side			180	.222	S.F.
	0500	6T special shapes, group 1			300	.133	Ea.
	0550	Group 2			275	.145	Ea.
	0600	Group 3			250	.160	Ea.
	0650	Group 4			225	.178	Ea.
	0700	Group 5			200	.200	Ea.
	0750	Group 6			190	.211	Ea.
	1000	6T fire rated, 4" thick, 1 hr. rating			210	.190	S.F.
	1050	6" thick, 2 hr. rating			200	.200	S.F.
	1300	6T acoustic, 4" thick	↓	↓	210	.190	S.F.
	2000	8W series, 8" x 16", grade S.S., 1.125 pieces per S.F.					
	2050	2" thick, glazed 1 side	D-8	3 Bricklayers	360	.111	S.F.
				2 Bricklayer Helpers			
	2100	4" thick, glazed 1 side			345	.116	S.F.
	2150	Glazed 2 sides	↓	↓	325	.123	S.F.

042 | Unit Masonry

042 450 | Structural Facing Tile

		CREW	MAKEUP	DAILY OUTPUT	MAN-HOURS	UNIT
454	2201	Structural facing tile, 8W series, 8" x 16" x 6", glazed 1 side	D-8	3 Bricklayers	330	.121	S.F.
				2 Bricklayer Helpers			
	2250	8" thick, glazed 1 side			310	.129	S.F.
	2500	8W special shapes, group 1			270	.148	Ea.
	2550	Group 2			260	.154	Ea.
	2600	Group 3			250	.160	Ea.
	2650	Group 4			240	.167	Ea.
	2700	Group 5			230	.174	Ea.
	2750	Group 6			220	.182	Ea.
	3000	8W fire rated, 4" thick, 1 hr.			345	.116	S.F.
	3100	8W acoustic, 4" thick	↓	↓	345	.116	S.F.

042 500 | Ceramic Veneer

		CREW	MAKEUP	DAILY OUTPUT	MAN-HOURS	UNIT
510	TERRA COTTA Coping, split type, not glazed, 9" wide	D-1	1 Bricklayer	90	.178	L.F.
			1 Bricklayer Helper			
0100	13" wide			80	.200	L.F.
0200	Split type, glazed, 9" wide			90	.178	L.F.
0250	13" wide	↓	↓	80	.200	L.F.
0500	Partition or back-up blocks, scored, in C.L. lots					
0600	Split furring tiles, 12" x 12", 2" thick	D-8	3 Bricklayers	600	.067	S.F.
			2 Bricklayer Helpers			
0700	Non-load bearing, 12" x 12", 3" thick			550	.073	S.F.
0750	4" thick			500	.080	S.F.
0800	6" thick			450	.089	S.F.
0850	8" thick			400	.100	S.F.
1000	Load bearing, 12" x 12", 4" thick, in walls			500	.080	S.F.
1050	In floors			750	.053	S.F.
1200	6" thick, in walls			450	.089	S.F.
1250	In floors			675	.059	S.F.
1400	8" thick, in walls			400	.100	S.F.
1450	In floors			575	.070	S.F.
1600	10" thick, in walls			350	.114	S.F.
1650	In floors			500	.080	S.F.
1800	12" thick, in walls			300	.133	S.F.
1850	In floors	↓	↓	450	.089	S.F.
512	TERRA COTTA TILE On walls, dry set, 1/2" thick					
0100	Square, hexagonal or lattice shapes, unglazed	1 Tilf	1 Tile Layer	135	.059	S.F.
0300	Glazed, plain colors			130	.062	S.F.
0400	Intense colors	↓	↓	125	.064	S.F.

042 550 | Masonry Veneer

		CREW	MAKEUP	DAILY OUTPUT	MAN-HOURS	UNIT
554	BRICK VENEER Scaffolding not included, truck load lots					
0020	4" thk., sel. common, 8" x 2-2/3" x 4" @ $230 per M (6.75/S.F.)	D-8	3 Bricklayers	1.50	26.670	M
			2 Bricklayer Helpers			
0050	Standard 8" x 2-2/3" x 4", running bond, red face, $250 per M			1.50	26.670	M
0100	Full header every 6th course (7.88/S.F.)			1.45	27.590	M
0150	English, full header every 2nd course (10.13/S.F.)			1.40	28.570	M
0200	Flemish, alternate header every course (9.00/S.F.)			1.40	28.570	M
0250	Flemish, alt. header every 6th course (7.13/S.F.)			1.45	27.590	M
0300	Full headers throughout (13.50/S.F.)			1.40	28.570	M
0350	Rowlock course (13.50/S.F.)			1.35	29.630	M
0400	Rowlock stretcher (4.50/S.F.)			1.40	28.570	M
0450	Soldier course (6.75/S.F.)			1.40	28.570	M
0500	Sailor course (4.50/S.F.)			1.30	30.770	M
0601	Running bond, buff or gray face, (6.75/S.F.) $290 per M			1.50	26.670	M
0700	Glazed face, 8" x 2-2/3" x 4" @ $775 per M, running bond			1.40	28.570	M
0750	Full header every 6th course (7.88/S.F.)			1.35	29.630	M
1000	Jumbo, 12" x 4" x 6" $975/M (3.00/S.F.)	↓	↓	1.30	30.770	M

042 | Unit Masonry

042 550 | Masonry Veneer

		CREW	MAKEUP	DAILY OUTPUT	MAN-HOURS	UNIT
554 1052	Brick veneer, Norman, 12" x 2-2/3" x 4", $430/M, (4.50/S.F.)	D-8	3 Bricklayers	1.45	27.590	M
			2 Bricklayer Helpers			
1100	Norwegian, 12" x 3-1/5" x 4" at $480 per M (3.75/S.F.)			1.40	28.570	M
1150	Economy, 8" x 4" x 4" at $400 per M (4.50 per S.F.)			1.40	28.570	M
1201	Engineer, 8" x 3-1/5" x 4", $290/M (5.63/S.F.)			1.45	27.590	M
1251	Roman, 12" x 2" x 4", $525/M (6.00/S.F.)			1.50	26.670	M
1300	S.C.R. 12" x 2-2/3" x 6" $600/M (4.50/S.F.)			1.40	28.570	M
1350	Utility, 12" x 4" x 4" $725/M (3.00/S.F.)	↓	↓	1.35	29.630	M
1999	Alternate method of figuring by square foot					
2000	Standard, sel. common, 8" x 2-2/3" x 4", $230 per M (6.75/S.F.)	D-8	3 Bricklayers	230	.174	S.F.
			2 Bricklayer Helpers			
2020	Stnd, 8" x 2-2/3" x 4", running bond, red, (6.75/S.F.), $250/M			220	.182	S.F.
2050	Full header every 6th course (7.88/S.F.)			185	.216	S.F.
2100	English, full header every 2nd course (10.13/S.F.)			140	.286	S.F.
2150	Flemish, alternate header every course (9.00/S.F.)			150	.267	S.F.
2200	Flemish, alt. header every 6th course (7.13/S.F.)			205	.195	S.F.
2250	Full headers throughout (13.50/S.F.)			105	.381	S.F.
2300	Rowlock course (13.50/S.F.)			100	.400	S.F.
2350	Rowlock stretcher (4.50/S.F.)			310	.129	S.F.
2400	Soldier course (6.75/S.F.)			200	.200	S.F.
2450	Sailor course (4.50/S.F.)			290	.138	S.F.
2600	Running bond, buff or gray face at $290 per M (6.75/S.F.)			220	.182	S.F.
2700	Glazed face, brick at $775 per M, running bond			210	.190	S.F.
2750	Full header every 6th course (7.88/S.F.)			170	.235	S.F.
3000	Jumbo, 12" x 4" x 6" running bond @ $975 per M (3.00/S.F.)			435	.092	S.F.
3050	Norman, 12" x 2-2/3" x 4" running bond, $430/M (4.50/S.F.)			320	.125	S.F.
3100	Norwegian, 12" x 3-1/5" x 4" at $480 per M (3.75/S.F.)			375	.107	S.F.
3150	Economy, 8" x 4" x 4" at $400 per M (4.50/S.F.)			310	.129	S.F.
3200	Engineer, 8" x 3-1/5" x 4" at $290 per M (5.63/S.F.)			260	.154	S.F.
3250	Roman, 12" x 2" x 4" at $525 per M (6.00/S.F.)			250	.160	S.F.
3300	SCR, 12" x 2-2/3" x 6" at $600 per M (4.50/S.F.)			310	.129	S.F.
3350	Utility, 12" x 4" x 4" at $725 per M (3.00/S.F.)	↓	↓	450	.089	S.F.

042 700 | Glass Unit Masonry

		CREW	MAKEUP	DAILY OUTPUT	MAN-HOURS	UNIT
704	GLASS BLOCK Scaffolding not included					
0100	4" thick, plain, under 1000 S.F., 6" x 6" block	D-8	3 Bricklayers	115	.348	S.F.
			2 Bricklayer Helpers			
0150	8" x 8" block			160	.250	S.F.
0300	Plain, 1000 to 5000 S.F., 6" x 6" block			135	.296	S.F.
0350	8" x 8" block			190	.211	S.F.
0400	12" x 12" block			215	.186	S.F.
0500	Plain, over 5000 S.F., 6" x 6" block			145	.276	S.F.
0550	8" x 8" block			215	.186	S.F.
0600	12" x 12" block			240	.167	S.F.
0800	Plain, 4" x 8" blocks, under 1000 S.F.			145	.276	S.F.
0850	Over 5000 S.F.			170	.235	S.F.
1000	3-1/8" thick thinline, plain, under 1000 S.F., 6" x 6" block			115	.348	S.F.
1050	8" x 8" block			160	.250	S.F.
1200	Plain, over 5000 S.F., 6" x 6" block	↓	↓	145	.276	S.F.

042 900 | Adobe Masonry

		CREW	MAKEUP	DAILY OUTPUT	MAN-HOURS	UNIT
904	ADOBE BRICK Unstabilized, with adobe mortar (Southwestern States)					
0060	Brick, 4" x 3" x 8" @ $300 per M (6.0 per S.F.)	D-8	3 Bricklayers	1.60	25.000	M
			2 Bricklayer Helpers			
0080	4" x 4" x 8" @ $380 per M (4.5 per S.F.)			1.50	26.670	M
0100	4" x 4" x 14" @ $450 per M (2.5 per S.F.)			1.35	29.630	M
0120	8" x 3" x 16" @ $480 per M (3.0 per S.F.)			1.40	28.570	M
0140	4" x 3" x 12" @ $350 per M (4.0 per S.F.)	↓	↓	1.45	27.590	M

042 | Unit Masonry

042 900 | Adobe Masonry

		CREW	MAKEUP	DAILY OUTPUT	MAN-HOURS	UNIT
904 0161	Adobe brick, 6" x 3" x 12" @ $380 per M (4.0 per S.F.)	D-8	3 Bricklayers	1.45	27.590	M
			2 Bricklayer Helpers			
0180	4" x 5" x 16" @ $420 per M (1.80 per S.F.)			1.35	29.630	M
0200	8" x 4" x 16" @ $525 per M (2.25 per S.F.)			1.30	30.770	M
0220	10" x 4" x 14" @ $550 per M (2.57 per S.F.)			1.25	32.000	M
0260	Brick, 4" x 3" x 8" @ $300 per M (6.0 per S.F.)			266	.150	S.F.
0280	4" x 4" x 8" @ $380 per M (4.5 per S.F.)			333	.120	S.F.
0300	4" x 4" x 14" @ $450 per M (2.5 per S.F.)			540	.074	S.F.
0320	8" x 3" x 16" @ $480 per M (3.0 per S.F.)			466	.086	S.F.
0340	4" x 3" x 12" @ $350 per M (4.0 per S.F.)			362	.110	S.F.
0360	6" x 3" x 12" @ $380 per M (4.0 per S.F.)			362	.110	S.F.
0380	4" x 5" x 16" @ $420 per M (1.80 per S.F.)			600	.067	S.F.
0400	8" x 4" x 16" @ $525 per M (2.25 per S.F.)			577	.069	S.F.
0420	10" x 4" x 14" @ $550 per M (2.57 per S.F.)	↓	↓	555	.072	S.F.

044 | Stone

044 100 | Rough Stone

		CREW	MAKEUP	DAILY OUTPUT	MAN-HOURS	UNIT
104	**ROUGH STONE WALL**					
0150	Over 18" thick	D-12	1 Bricklayer Foreman	63	.508	C.F.
			1 Bricklayer			
			2 Bricklayer Helpers			

044 200 | Cut Stone

		CREW	MAKEUP	DAILY OUTPUT	MAN-HOURS	UNIT
204	**BLUESTONE** Cut to size					
0100	Paving, natural cleft, to 3' x 4', 1" thick	D-8	3 Bricklayers	150	.267	S.F.
			2 Bricklayer Helpers			
0150	1-1/2" thick			145	.276	S.F.
0200	Smooth finish, 1" thick			150	.267	S.F.
0250	1-1/2" thick			145	.276	S.F.
0300	Thermal finish, 1" thick			150	.267	S.F.
0350	1-1/2" thick	↓	↓	145	.276	S.F.
0500	Sills, natural cleft, 10" wide to 6' long, 1-1/2" thick	D-11	1 Bricklayer Foreman	70	.343	L.F.
			1 Bricklayer			
			1 Bricklayer Helper			
0550	2" thick			63	.381	L.F.
0600	Smooth finish, 1-1/2" thick			70	.343	L.F.
0650	2" thick			63	.381	L.F.
0800	Thermal finish, 1-1/2" thick			70	.343	L.F.
0850	2" thick	↓	↓	63	.381	L.F.
1000	Stair treads, natural cleft, 12" wide, 6' long, 1-1/2" thick	D-10	1 Bricklayer Foreman	115	.348	L.F.
			1 Bricklayer			
			2 Bricklayer Helpers			
			1 Equip. Oper. (crane)			
			1 Truck Crane, 12.5 Ton			
1050	2" thick			105	.381	L.F.
1100	Smooth finish, 1-1/2" thick			115	.348	L.F.
1150	2" thick			105	.381	L.F.
1300	Thermal finish, 1-1/2" thick			115	.348	L.F.
1350	2" thick	↓	↓	105	.381	L.F.
2001						

044 | Stone

044 200 | Cut Stone

		CREW	MAKEUP	DAILY OUTPUT	MAN-HOURS	UNIT
2101	Bluestone, coping, finished, 12" to 6', natural cleft, 1-1/2" thick	D-10	1 Bricklayer Foreman 1 Bricklayer 2 Bricklayer Helpers 1 Equip. Oper. (crane) 1 Truck Crane, 12.5 Ton	115	.348	L.F.
2150	2" thick			105	.381	L.F.
2200	Smooth finish, 1-1/2" thick			115	.348	L.F.
2250	2" thick			105	.381	L.F.
2300	Thermal finish, 1-1/2" thick			115	.348	L.F.
2350	2" thick	↓	↓	105	.381	L.F.

(204)

044 300 | Simulated Stone

		CREW	MAKEUP	DAILY OUTPUT	MAN-HOURS	UNIT
304	**SIMULATED STONE**					
0100	Insulated fiberglass panels	L-4	2 Skilled Workers 1 Helper	200	.120	S.F.

044 500 | Stone Veneer

		CREW	MAKEUP	DAILY OUTPUT	MAN-HOURS	UNIT
504	**ASHLAR VENEER 4" + or - thick, random or random rectangular**					
0150	Sawn face, split joints, low priced stone	D-8	3 Bricklayers 2 Bricklayer Helpers	120	.333	S.F.
0200	Medium priced stone			130	.308	S.F.
0300	high priced stone			140	.286	S.F.
0600	Seam face, split joints, medium price stone			120	.333	S.F.
0700	High price stone			125	.320	S.F.
1000	Split or rock face, split joints, medium price stone			120	.333	S.F.
1100	High price stone	↓	↓	125	.320	S.F.
508	**LIGHTWEIGHT NATURAL STONE Lava type**					
0100	Veneer, rubble face, sawed back, irregular shapes	D-10	1 Bricklayer Foreman 1 Bricklayer 2 Bricklayer Helpers 1 Equip. Oper. (crane) 1 Truck Crane, 12.5 Ton	130	.308	S.F.
0200	Sawed face and back, irregular shapes	"	"	130	.308	S.F.

044 550 | Marble

		CREW	MAKEUP	DAILY OUTPUT	MAN-HOURS	UNIT
554	**MARBLE Ashlar, split face, 4" + or - thick, random**					
0040	lengths 1' to 4' & heights 2" to 7-1/2", average	D-8	3 Bricklayers 2 Bricklayer Helpers	175	.229	S.F.
0100	Base, polished, 3/4" or 7/8" thick, polished, 6" high	D-10	1 Bricklayer Foreman 1 Bricklayer 2 Bricklayer Helpers 1 Equip. Oper. (crane) 1 Truck Crane, 12.5 Ton	65	.615	L.F.
0300	Carvings or bas relief, from templates, average			80	.500	S.F.
0350	Maximum	↓	↓	80	.500	S.F.
0600	Columns, cornices, mouldings, etc.					
0650	Hand or special machine cut, average	D-10	1 Bricklayer Foreman 1 Bricklayer 2 Bricklayer Helpers 1 Equip. Oper. (crane) 1 Truck Crane, 12.5 Ton	35	1.140	C.F.
0700	Maximum	"	"	35	1.140	C.F.
1000	Facing, polished finish, cut to size, 3/4" to 7/8" thick					
1050	Average	D-10	1 Bricklayer Foreman 1 Bricklayer 2 Bricklayer Helpers 1 Equip. Oper. (crane) 1 Truck Crane, 12.5 Ton	130	.308	S.F.

044 550 | Marble

		CREW	MAKEUP	DAILY OUTPUT	MAN-HOURS	UNIT
554	1101	Marble ashlar, facing, polished, cut, 3/4" to 7/8" thick, maximum	D-10	1 Bricklayer Foreman 1 Bricklayer 2 Bricklayer Helpers 1 Equip. Oper. (crane) 1 Truck Crane, 12.5 Ton	130	.308	S.F.
	1300	1-1/4" thick, average	↓	↓	125	.320	S.F.
	1350	Maximum			125	.320	S.F.
	1500	2" thick, average			120	.333	S.F.
	1550	Maximum	↓	↓	120	.333	S.F.
	1700	Rubbed finish, cut to size, 4" thick					
	1740	Average	D-10	1 Bricklayer Foreman 1 Bricklayer 2 Bricklayer Helpers 1 Equip. Oper. (crane) 1 Truck Crane, 12.5 Ton	100	.400	S.F.
	1780	Maximum	"	"	100	.400	S.F.
	2500	Flooring, polished tiles, 12" x 12" x 3/8" thick					
	2510	Thin set, average	D-11	1 Bricklayer Foreman 1 Bricklayer 1 Bricklayer Helper	90	.267	S.F.
	2600	Maximum			90	.267	S.F.
	2700	Mortar bed, average			65	.369	S.F.
	2740	Maximum	↓	↓	65	.369	S.F.
	2780	Travertine, 1-1/4" thick, average	D-10	1 Bricklayer Foreman 1 Bricklayer 2 Bricklayer Helpers 1 Equip. Oper. (crane) 1 Truck Crane, 12.5 Ton	130	.308	S.F.
	2790	Maximum	"	"	130	.308	S.F.
	2800	Patio blocks, non-slip, 7/8" thick	D-11	1 Bricklayer Foreman 1 Bricklayer 1 Bricklayer Helper	75	.320	S.F.
	2900	Shower or toilet partitions, 7/8" thick partitions					
	3050	3/4" or 1-1/4" thick stiles, polished 2 sides, average	D-11	1 Bricklayer Foreman 1 Bricklayer 1 Bricklayer Helper	75	.320	S.F.
	3210	Stairs, risers, 7/8" thick x 6" high	D-10	1 Bricklayer Foreman 1 Bricklayer 2 Bricklayer Helpers 1 Equip. Oper. (crane) 1 Truck Crane, 12.5 Ton	115	.348	L.F.
	3360	Treads, 12" wide x 1-1/4" thick	"	"	115	.348	L.F.
	3500	Thresholds, 3' long, 7/8" thick, 4" to 5" wide, plain	D-12	1 Bricklayer Foreman 1 Bricklayer 2 Bricklayer Helpers	24	1.330	Ea.
	3550	Beveled	↓	↓	24	1.330	Ea.
	3700	Window stools, polished, 7/8" thick, 5" wide			85	.376	L.F.

044 600 | Limestone

		CREW	MAKEUP	DAILY OUTPUT	MAN-HOURS	UNIT
604	LIMESTONE, Cut to size					
0020	Veneer facing panels					
0100	Sawn finish, 2" thick, to 3' x 5' panels	D-10	1 Bricklayer Foreman 1 Bricklayer 2 Bricklayer Helpers 1 Equip. Oper. (crane) 1 Truck Crane, 12.5 Ton	130	.308	S.F.
0150	Smooth finish, 2" thick, to 3' x 5' panels	↓	↓	130	.308	S.F.
0300	3" thick, to 4' x 9' panels			225	.178	S.F.

044 600 | Limestone

		CREW	MAKEUP	DAILY OUTPUT	MAN-HOURS	UNIT
604 0351	Limestone, smooth finish, 4" thick, to 5' x 11' panels	D-10	1 Bricklayer Foreman	275	.145	S.F.
			1 Bricklayer			
			2 Bricklayer Helpers			
			1 Equip. Oper. (crane)			
			1 Truck Crane, 12.5 Ton			
0700	Light stick, textured finish, 4-1/2" thick to 5' x 12'			275	.145	S.F.
0750	5" thick, to 5' x 14' panels			275	.145	S.F.
1000	Medium ribbed, textured finish, 4-1/2" thick, to 5' x 12'			275	.145	S.F.
1050	5" thick, to 5' x 14' panels			275	.145	S.F.
1200	Deep ribbed, textured finish, 4-1/2" thick, to 5' x 10'			275	.145	S.F.
1250	5" thick, to 5' x 14' panels			275	.145	S.F.
1400	Sugar cube, textured finish, 4-1/2" thick, to 5' x 12'			275	.145	S.F.
1450	5" thick, to 5' x 14' panels			275	.145	S.F.
2000	Coping, smooth finish, top & 2 sides			30	1.330	C.F.
2100	Sills, lintels, jambs, smooth finish, average			20	2.000	C.F.
2150	Detailed			20	2.000	C.F.
2300	Steps, extra hard, 14" wide, 6" rise	↓	↓	50	.800	L.F.

044 650 | Granite

		CREW	MAKEUP	DAILY OUTPUT	MAN-HOURS	UNIT
651 0050	**GRANITE,** Cut to size, 3/4" to 1-1/2" thick, veneer, polished					
	Veneer, polished face, 3/4" to 1-1/2" thick					
0150	Low price, gray, light gray, etc.	D-10	1 Bricklayer Foreman	130	.308	S.F.
			1 Bricklayer			
			2 Bricklayer Helpers			
			1 Equip. Oper. (crane)			
			1 Truck Crane, 12.5 Ton			
0180	Medium price, pink, brown, etc.			130	.308	S.F.
0220	High price, red, black, etc.	↓	↓	130	.308	S.F.
0300	1-1/2" to 2-1/2" thick, veneer					
0350	Low price, gray, light gray, etc.	D-10	1 Bricklayer Foreman	130	.308	S.F.
			1 Bricklayer			
			2 Bricklayer Helpers			
			1 Equip. Oper. (crane)			
			1 Truck Crane, 12.5 Ton			
0500	Medium price, pink, brown, etc.			130	.308	S.F.
0550	High price, red, black, etc.	↓	↓	130	.308	S.F.
0700	2-1/2" to 4" thick, veneer					
0750	Low price, gray, light gray, etc.	D-10	1 Bricklayer Foreman	110	.364	S.F.
			1 Bricklayer			
			2 Bricklayer Helpers			
			1 Equip. Oper. (crane)			
			1 Truck Crane, 12.5 Ton			
0850	Medium price, pink, brown, etc.			110	.364	S.F.
0950	High price, red, black, etc.	↓	↓	110	.364	S.F.
1800	Carving or bas-relief, from templates or plaster molds					
1850	Minimum	D-10	1 Bricklayer Foreman	80	.500	C.F.
			1 Bricklayer			
			2 Bricklayer Helpers			
			1 Equip. Oper. (crane)			
			1 Truck Crane, 12.5 Ton			
1900	Maximum	"	"	80	.500	C.F.
2500	Steps, copings, etc., finished on more than one surface					
2550	Minimum	D-10	1 Bricklayer Foreman	50	.800	C.F.
			1 Bricklayer			
			2 Bricklayer Helpers			
			1 Equip. Oper. (crane)			
			1 Truck Crane, 12.5 Ton			
2600	Maximum	"	"	50	.800	C.F.

044 | Stone

044 650 | Granite

		CREW	MAKEUP	DAILY OUTPUT	MAN-HOURS	UNIT
651 2701	Granite pavers, Belgian block, 8"-13" long, 4"-6" wide, 4"-6" deep	D-11	1 Bricklayer Foreman 1 Bricklayer 1 Bricklayer Helper	120	.200	S.F.
2800	Pavers, 4" x 4" x 4" blocks, split face and joints					
2850	Minimum	D-11	1 Bricklayer Foreman 1 Bricklayer 1 Bricklayer Helper	80	.300	S.F.
2900	Maximum	"	"	80	.300	S.F.
3000	Pavers, 4" x 4" x 4", thermal face, sawn joints					
3050	Minimum	D-11	1 Bricklayer Foreman 1 Bricklayer 1 Bricklayer Helper	65	.369	S.F.
3100	Maximum	"	"	65	.369	S.F.
3500	Curbing, city street type, 6" x 18", split face,					
3510	sawn top, radius nosing, 4' to 7' lengths	D-10	1 Bricklayer Foreman 1 Bricklayer 2 Bricklayer Helpers 1 Equip. Oper. (crane) 1 Truck Crane, 12.5 Ton	75	.533	L.F.
3600	Highway type, 5" x 16", split face,					
3610	sawn top, 4' to 7' lengths	D-10	1 Bricklayer Foreman 1 Bricklayer 2 Bricklayer Helpers 1 Equip. Oper. (crane) 1 Truck Crane, 12.5 Ton	300	.133	L.F.
3700	Slope, 4-1/2" x 12", split face,					
3710	sawn top, 2' to 6' lengths	D-10	1 Bricklayer Foreman 1 Bricklayer 2 Bricklayer Helpers 1 Equip. Oper. (crane) 1 Truck Crane, 12.5 Ton	300	.133	L.F.
4000	Soffits, 2" thick, minimum	D-13	1 Bricklayer Foreman 1 Bricklayer 2 Bricklayer Helpers 1 Carpenter 1 Equip. Oper. (crane) 1 Truck Crane, 12.5 Ton	35	1.370	S.F.
4100	Maximum			35	1.370	S.F.
4200	4" thick, minimum			35	1.370	S.F.
4300	Maximum	↓	↓	35	1.370	S.F.

044 700 | Sandstone

		CREW	MAKEUP	DAILY OUTPUT	MAN-HOURS	UNIT
704	SANDSTONE OR BROWNSTONE					
0100	Sawed face veneer, 2-1/2" thick, to 2' x 4' panels	D-10	1 Bricklayer Foreman 1 Bricklayer 2 Bricklayer Helpers 1 Equip. Oper. (crane) 1 Truck Crane, 12.5 Ton	130	.308	S.F.
0150	4" thick, to 3'-6" x 8' panels	↓	↓	100	.400	S.F.
0300	Split face, random sizes			100	.400	S.F.
0350	Cut stone trim (sandstone)					
0360	Ribbon stone, 4" thick, 5' pieces	D-8	3 Bricklayers 2 Bricklayer Helpers	120	.333	Ea.
0370	Cove stone, 4" thick, 5' pieces			105	.381	Ea.
0380	Cornice stone, 10" to 12" wide			90	.444	Ea.
0390	Band stone, 4" thick, 5' pieces			145	.276	Ea.
0410	Window and door trim, 3" to 4" wide			160	.250	Ea.
0420	Key stone, 18" long	↓	↓	60	.667	Ea.

044 750 | Slate

			CREW	MAKEUP	DAILY OUTPUT	MAN-HOURS	UNIT
754	754	**SLATE** Pennsylvania, blue gray to gray black; Vermont,					
	0050	Unfading green, mottled green & purple, gray & purple					
	0100	Virginia, blue black					
	0200	Exterior paving, natural cleft, 1″ thick					
	0250	6″ x 6″ Pennsylvania	D-12	1 Bricklayer Foreman	100	.320	S.F.
				1 Bricklayer			
				2 Bricklayer Helpers			
	0300	Vermont			100	.320	S.F.
	0350	Virginia			100	.320	S.F.
	0500	24″ x 24″, Pennsylvania			120	.267	S.F.
	0550	Vermont			120	.267	S.F.
	0600	Virginia			120	.267	S.F.
	0700	18″ x 30″ Pennsylvania			120	.267	S.F.
	0750	Vermont			120	.267	S.F.
	0800	Virginia	↓	↓	120	.267	S.F.
	1000	Interior flooring, natural cleft, 1/2″ thick					
	1100	6″ x 6″ Pennsylvania	D-12	1 Bricklayer Foreman	100	.320	S.F.
				1 Bricklayer			
				2 Bricklayer Helpers			
	1150	Vermont			100	.320	S.F.
	1200	Virginia			100	.320	S.F.
	1300	24″ x 24″ Pennsylvania			120	.267	S.F.
	1350	Vermont			120	.267	S.F.
	1400	Virginia			120	.267	S.F.
	1500	18″ x 24″ Pennsylvania			120	.267	S.F.
	1550	Vermont			120	.267	S.F.
	1600	Virginia	↓	↓	120	.267	S.F.
	2000	Facing panels, 1-1/4″ thick, to 4′ x 6′ panels					
	2100	Natural cleft finish, Pennsylvania	D-10	1 Bricklayer Foreman	180	.222	S.F.
				1 Bricklayer			
				2 Bricklayer Helpers			
				1 Equip. Oper. (crane)			
				1 Truck Crane, 12.5 Ton			
	2110	Vermont			180	.222	S.F.
	2120	Virginia			180	.222	S.F.
	2500	Ribbon, natural cleft finish, 1″ thick, to 9 S.F.			80	.500	S.F.
	2550	Sand rubbed finish			80	.500	S.F.
	2600	Honed finish			80	.500	S.F.
	2700	1-1/2″ thick			78	.513	S.F.
	2750	Sand rubbed finish			78	.513	S.F.
	2800	Honed finish			78	.513	S.F.
	2850	2″ thick			76	.526	S.F.
	2900	Sand rubbed finish			76	.526	S.F.
	2950	Honed finish	↓	↓	76	.526	S.F.
	3500	Stair treads, sand finish, 1″ thick x 12″ wide					
	3550	Under 3 L.F.	D-10	1 Bricklayer Foreman	85	.471	L.F.
				1 Bricklayer			
				2 Bricklayer Helpers			
				1 Equip. Oper. (crane)			
				1 Truck Crane, 12.5 Ton			
	3600	3 L.F. to 6 L.F.	″	″	120	.333	L.F.
	3700	Ribbon, sand finish, 1″ thick x 12″ wide					
	3750	To 6 L.F.	D-10	1 Bricklayer Foreman	120	.333	L.F.
				1 Bricklayer			
				2 Bricklayer Helpers			
				1 Equip. Oper. (crane)			
				1 Truck Crane, 12.5 Ton			

044 | Stone

044 750 | Slate

		CREW	MAKEUP	DAILY OUTPUT	MAN-HOURS	UNIT
754 4000	Slate, stools or sills, sand finish, 1" thick, 6" wide	D-12	1 Bricklayer Foreman 1 Bricklayer 2 Bricklayer Helpers	160	.200	L.F.
4101	Honed finish, 1" thick, 6" wide			160	.200	L.F.
4200	10" wide			90	.356	L.F.
4250	Honed finish			90	.356	L.F.
4400	2" thick, 6" wide			140	.229	L.F.
4450	Honed finish			140	.229	L.F.
4600	10" wide			90	.356	L.F.
4650	Honed finish	↓	↓	90	.356	L.F.

045 | Masonry Restoration and Cleaning/Refractories

045 100 | Masonry Cleaning

		CREW	MAKEUP	DAILY OUTPUT	MAN-HOURS	UNIT
106	CLEAN AND POINT Smooth brick	1 Bric	1 Bricklayer	300	.027	S.F.
0100	Rough brick			265	.030	S.F.
108	WASHING BRICK Smooth brick			560	.014	S.F.
0050	Rough brick	↓	↓	400	.020	S.F.

045 200 | Masonry Restoration

		CREW	MAKEUP	DAILY OUTPUT	MAN-HOURS	UNIT
240	NEEDLE MASONRY Includes shoring					
0400	Block, concrete, 8" thick	B-9	1 Labor Foreman (outside) 4 Building Laborers 1 Air Compr., 250 C.F.M. Air Tools & Accessories 2-50 Ft. Air Hoses, 1.5" Dia.	7.10	5.630	Ea.
0420	12" thick			6.70	5.970	Ea.
0800	Brick, 4" thick with 8" backup block			5.70	7.020	Ea.
1000	Brick, solid, 8" thick			6.20	6.450	Ea.
1040	12" thick			4.90	8.160	Ea.
1080	16" thick	↓	↓	4.50	8.890	Ea.
2000	Add for additional floors of shoring	B-1	1 Labor Foreman (outside) 2 Building Laborers	6	4.000	Ea.
290	TOOTHING MASONRY					
0500	Brickwork, soft old mortar	1 Clab	1 Building Laborer	40	.200	V.L.F.
0520	Hard mortar			30	.267	V.L.F.
0700	Blockwork, soft old mortar			70	.114	V.L.F.
0720	Hard mortar	↓	↓	50	.160	V.L.F.

045 550 | Flue Liners

		CREW	MAKEUP	DAILY OUTPUT	MAN-HOURS	UNIT
554	FLUE LINING Square, including mortar joints, 8" x 8"	D-1	1 Bricklayer 1 Bricklayer Helper	125	.128	V.L.F.
0100	8" x 12"			103	.155	V.L.F.
0200	12" x 12"			93	.172	V.L.F.
0300	12" x 18"			84	.190	V.L.F.
0400	18" x 18"			75	.213	V.L.F.
0500	20" x 20"			66	.242	V.L.F.
0600	24" x 24"			56	.286	V.L.F.
1000	Round, 18" diameter			66	.242	V.L.F.
1100	24" diameter	↓	↓	47	.340	V.L.F.

045 650	Fire Brick	CREW	MAKEUP	DAILY OUTPUT	MAN-HOURS	UNIT
652	**FIRE BRICK** 9" x 2-1/2" x 4-1/2",	D-1	1 Bricklayer	.60	26.670	M
			1 Bricklayer Helper			
0050	High duty, 3000° F	"	"	.60	26.670	M
656	**FIREPLACE** For prefabricated fireplace, see div. 103-054					
0100	Brick fireplace, not incl. foundations or chimneys					
0110	30" x 24" opening, plain brickwork	D-1	1 Bricklayer	.40	40.000	Ea.
			1 Bricklayer Helper			
0200	Fireplace box only (110 brick)			2	8.000	Ea.
0300	Elaborate brickwork and details			.20	80.000	Ea.
0400	For hearth, brick & stone, add			2	8.000	Ea.
0600	Plain brickwork, incl. metal circulator			.50	32.000	Ea.
0800	Face brick only, standard size, 8" x 2-2/3" x 4"	↓	↓	.30	53.330	M

DIVISION
5
METALS

5

DIVISION 5 METALS

A reasonable guideline to use for the erection of structural steel is that a crane can sort and raise 35 to 60 pieces per day. That would make it safe to assume an average daily output of 40 lifts. Larger cranes usually raise faster due to the need for fewer moves or repositioning. Evaluate crane size requirements by height, reach, and location (or proximity to the area where erection is taking place). The proper choice of equipment is important.

Production rates for guy derricks, stiff leg derricks, and climbing cranes decrease as the building gets higher. Time must be allotted to jump or raise the derricks or climbing cranes.

Time for guying, plumbing, and performing high-strength bolting or welding must be added to the raising time to arrive at a total erection time.

Allow 20 bolts per ton for a 6-story office building, apartment house, or light industrial building. For 6 to 12 stories, allow 18 bolts per ton. Above 12 stories, allow 25 bolts per ton. On power stations, 20 to 25 bolts per ton are required. Bolted moment connections can add considerably to the bolt allowances shown above.

Full penetration welds for columns and girders, as well as for welded moment connections, may affect raising times. Carefully analyze each situation.

Hanging and adjustable lintels do not affect raising times, but add to erection time. Some lintels require readjustment as work on the building fascia progresses.

Short open web bar joists, lifted in bundles and hand-spread, can be raised at the rate of 75 to 90 per day. Individually picked longer-span joists can be raised at the rate of 50 pieces per day, and long span joists at 40 pieces per day. Time for welding joist seats and bridging must be added to the raising time to arrive at the total erection time. Bolted cross bridging may be erected at the rate of 35 sets per day using two structural steel workers. Welded cross bridging may be erected at the rate of 25 sets per day. Roof or opening frames should be included as a piece or lift when estimating raising time.

The floor or roof deck is usually lifted to the required area by crane and spread by hand. Raising time should be allotted as a lift per bundle of decking.

Codes require decking or planking to be spread every other floor or, in some cases, every floor for safety. Some high floor to ceiling buildings require safety nets which may slow erection.

Weather and site conditions, or congestion in the area of the project, are important considerations when determining the erection time.

050 | Metal Materials, Finishes and Fastenings

050 500 | Metal Fastening

			CREW	MAKEUP	DAILY OUTPUT	MAN-HOURS	UNIT
510	510	**CURB EDGING** Steel angle w/anchors, on forms, 1" x 1", 1.5#/L.F.	E-4	1 Struc. Steel Foreman	350	.091	L.F.
				3 Struc. Steel Workers			
				1 Gas Welding Machine			
	0100	2" x 2" angles, 3.5#/L.F.			330	.097	L.F.
	0200	3" x 3" angles, 6#/L.F.			300	.107	L.F.
	0300	4" x 4" angles, 8#/L.F.			275	.116	L.F.
	1000	6" x 4" angles, 12 #/L.F.			250	.128	L.F.
	1050	Steel channels with anchors, on forms, 3" channel, 5#/L.F.			290	.110	L.F.
	1100	4" channel, 6#/L.F.			270	.119	L.F.
	1200	6" channel, 9#/L.F.			255	.125	L.F.
	1300	8" channel, 12#/L.F.			225	.142	L.F.
	1400	10" channel, 16#/L.F.			180	.178	L.F.
	1500	12" channel, 22#/L.F.	↓	↓	140	.229	L.F.
	515	**DRILLING** And layout for anchors, per					
	0050	inch of depth, concrete or brick walls					
	0100	1/4" diameter	1 Carp	1 Carpenter	32	.250	Ea.
	0200	3/8" diameter			29	.276	Ea.
	0300	1/2" diameter			26	.308	Ea.
	0400	5/8" diameter			25	.320	Ea.
	0500	3/4" diameter			23	.348	Ea.
	0600	7/8" diameter			21	.381	Ea.
	0700	1" diameter			20	.400	Ea.
	0800	1-1/4" diameter			18	.444	Ea.
	0900	1-1/2" diameter	↓	↓	16	.500	Ea.
	1100	Drilling & layout for drywall or plaster walls					
	1200	Holes, 1/4" diameter	1 Carp	1 Carpenter	150	.053	Ea.
	1300	3/8" diameter			140	.057	Ea.
	1400	1/2" diameter			130	.062	Ea.
	1500	3/4" diameter			120	.067	Ea.
	1600	1" diameter			110	.073	Ea.
	1700	1-1/4" diameter			100	.080	Ea.
	1800	1-1/2" diameter	↓	↓	90	.089	Ea.
	520	**EXPANSION ANCHORS** Bolts & shields					
	0100	Bolt anchors for concrete, brick or stone, no layout and drilling					
	0200	Expansion shields, zinc, 1/4" diameter, 1" long, single	1 Carp	1 Carpenter	90	.089	Ea.
	0300	1-3/8" long, double			85	.094	Ea.
	0400	3/8" diameter, 2" long, single			85	.094	Ea.
	0500	2" long, double			80	.100	Ea.
	0600	1/2" diameter, 2-1/2" long, single			80	.100	Ea.
	0700	2-1/2" long, double			75	.107	Ea.
	0800	5/8" diameter, 2-5/8" long, single			75	.107	Ea.
	0900	3" long, double			70	.114	Ea.
	1000	3/4" diameter, 2-3/4" long, single			70	.114	Ea.
	1100	4" long, double			65	.123	Ea.
	1200	7/8" diameter, 5-1/2" long, double			65	.123	Ea.
	1300	1" diameter, 6" long, double			60	.133	Ea.
	1500	Self drilling, steel, 1/4" diameter bolt			26	.308	Ea.
	1600	3/8" diameter bolt			23	.348	Ea.
	1700	1/2" diameter bolt			20	.400	Ea.
	1800	5/8" diameter bolt			18	.444	Ea.
	1900	3/4" diameter bolt			16	.500	Ea.
	2000	7/8" diameter bolt			14	.571	Ea.
	3000	Toggle bolts, bright steel, 1/8" diameter, 2" long			85	.094	Ea.
	3100	4" long			80	.100	Ea.
	3200	3/16" diameter, 3" long			80	.100	Ea.
	3300	6" long			75	.107	Ea.
	3400	1/4" diameter, 3" long			75	.107	Ea.
	3500	6" long	↓	↓	70	.114	Ea.

050 500	Metal Fastening	CREW	MAKEUP	DAILY OUTPUT	MAN-HOURS	UNIT
520 3601	Self drilling, toggle bolts, bright steel, 3/8" dia., 3" long	1 Carp	1 Carpenter	70	.114	Ea.
3700	6" long			60	.133	Ea.
3800	1/2" diameter, 4" long			60	.133	Ea.
3900	6" long	↓	↓	50	.160	Ea.
8000	Wedge bolts, not including layout or drilling					
8050	Carbon steel, 1/4" diameter, 1-3/4" long	1 Carp	1 Carpenter	150	.053	Ea.
8100	3 1/4" long			145	.055	Ea.
8150	3/8" diameter, 2-1/4" long			150	.053	Ea.
8200	5" long			145	.055	Ea.
8250	1/2" diameter, 2-3/4" long			140	.057	Ea.
8300	7" long			130	.062	Ea.
8350	5/8" diameter, 3-1/2" long			130	.062	Ea.
8400	8-1/2" long			115	.070	Ea.
8450	3/4" diameter, 4-1/4" long			115	.070	Ea.
8500	10" long			100	.080	Ea.
8550	1" diameter, 6" long			100	.080	Ea.
8600	12" long			80	.100	Ea.
8650	1-1/4" diameter, 9" long			70	.114	Ea.
8700	12" long			60	.133	Ea.
530	LAG SCREWS Steel, 1/4" diameter, 2" long			140	.057	Ea.
0100	3/8" diameter, 3" long			105	.076	Ea.
0200	1/2" diameter, 3" long			95	.084	Ea.
0300	5/8" diameter, 3" long	↓	↓	85	.094	Ea.
560	WELDED SHEAR CONNECTORS 3/4" diameter, 3-3/16" long	E-10	1 Welder Foreman	1,030	.016	Ea.
			1 Welder			
			4 Gas Welding Machines			
			1 Truck, 3 Ton			
0020	3-3/8" long			1,030	.016	Ea.
0200	3-7/8" long			1,030	.016	Ea.
0300	4-3/16" long			1,030	.016	Ea.
0500	4-7/8" long			1,030	.016	Ea.
0600	5-3/16" long			1,030	.016	Ea.
0800	5-3/8" long			1,030	.016	Ea.
0900	6-3/16" long			1,000	.016	Ea.
1000	7-3/16" long			1,000	.016	Ea.
1100	8-3/16" long			1,000	.016	Ea.
1500	7/8" diameter, 3-11/16" long			1,030	.016	Ea.
1600	4-3/16" long			1,030	.016	Ea.
1700	5-3/16" long			1,030	.016	Ea.
1800	6-3/16" long			1,000	.016	Ea.
1900	7-3/16" long			1,000	.016	Ea.
2000	8-3/16" long			1,000	.016	Ea.
565	WELDED STUDS 1/4" diameter, 2-11/16" long			1,030	.016	Ea.
0100	4-1/8" long			1,030	.016	Ea.
0200	3/8" diameter, 4-1/8" long			1,030	.016	Ea.
0300	6-1/8" long			1,030	.016	Ea.
0400	1/2" diameter, 2-1/8" long			1,030	.016	Ea.
0500	3-1/8" long			1,030	.016	Ea.
0600	4-1/8" long			1,030	.016	Ea.
0700	5-5/16" long			1,030	.016	Ea.
0800	6-1/8" long			1,000	.016	Ea.
0900	8-1/8" long			1,000	.016	Ea.
1000	5/8" diameter, 2-11/16" long			1,030	.016	Ea.
1100	6-9/16" long			1,000	.016	Ea.
1200	8-3/16" long	↓	↓	1,000	.016	Ea.

050 | Metal Materials, Finishes and Fastenings

050 500 | Metal Fastening

			CREW	MAKEUP	DAILY OUTPUT	MAN-HOURS	UNIT
575	575	WELDING Field. Cost per welder, no operating engineer	E-14	1 Welder Foreman 1 Gas Welding Machine	8	1.000	Hr.
	0200	With 1/2 operating engineer	E-13	1 Welder Foreman .5 Equip. Oper. (light) 1 Gas Welding Machine	8	1.500	Hr.
	0300	With 1 operating engineer	E-12	1 Welder Foreman 1 Equip. Oper. (light) 1 Gas Welding Machine	8	2.000	Hr.
	0500	With no operating engineer, minimum	E-14	1 Welder Foreman 1 Gas Welding Machine	13.30	.602	Ton
	0600	Maximum	"	"	2.50	3.200	Ton
	0800	With one operating engineer per welder, minimum	E-12	1 Welder Foreman 1 Equip. Oper. (light) 1 Gas Welding Machine	13.30	1.200	Ton
	0900	Maximum	"	"	2.50	6.400	Ton
	1200	Continuous fillet, stick welding, incl. equipment					
	1300	Single pass, 1/8" thick, 0.1#/L.F.	E-14	1 Welder Foreman 1 Gas Welding Machine	240	.033	L.F.
	1400	3/16" thick, 0.2#/L.F.			120	.067	L.F.
	1500	1/4" thick, 0.3#/L.F.			80	.100	L.F.
	1610	5/16" thick, 0.4#/L.F.			60	.133	L.F.
	1800	3 passes, 3/8" thick, 0.5#/L.F.			48	.167	L.F.
	2010	4 passes, 1/2" thick, 0.7#/L.F.			34	.235	L.F.
	2200	5 to 6 passes, 3/4" thick, 1.3#/L.F.			19	.421	L.F.
	2400	8 to 11 passes, 1" thick, 2.4#/L.F.	↓	↓	10	.800	L.F.
	4000	Cleaning and welding plates, bars, or rods					
	4010	to existing beams, columns, or trusses	E-14	1 Welder Foreman 1 Gas Welding Machine	12	.667	L.F.

051 | Structural Metal Framing

051 100 | Bracing

		CREW	MAKEUP	DAILY OUTPUT	MAN-HOURS	UNIT
108	BRACING				5.330	
0300	Let-in, "T" shaped, 20 ga. galv. steel, studs at 16" O.C.	F-1	1 Carpenter Power Tools	5.80	1.380	C.L.F.
0400	Studs at 24" O.C.			6	1.330	C.L.F.
0500	16 ga. galv. steel straps, studs at 16" O.C.			6	1.330	C.L.F.
0600	Studs at 24" O.C.	↓	↓	6.20	1.290	C.L.F.
110	PIPE SUPPORT Framing, under 10#/L.F.	E-4	1 Struc. Steel Foreman 3 Struc. Steel Workers 1 Gas Welding Machine	3,900	.008	Lb.
0200	10.1 to 15#/L.F.			4,300	.007	Lb.
0400	15.1 to 20#/L.F.			4,800	.007	Lb.
0600	Over 20#/L.F.	↓	↓	5,400	.006	Lb.

051 200 | Structural Steel

		CREW	MAKEUP	DAILY OUTPUT	MAN-HOURS	UNIT
210	BULB TEE Subpurlins, 40 psf L.L., painted, 5' span	E-1	1 Welder Foreman 1 Welder 1 Equip. Oper. (light) 1 Gas Welding Machine	5,900	.004	S.F.
0100	8' span			4,200	.006	S.F.
0300	11' span	↓	↓	2,700	.009	S.F.

051 200 | **Structural Steel**

			CREW	MAKEUP	DAILY OUTPUT	MAN-HOURS	UNIT
212	212	**CANOPY FRAMING** 6" and 8" members	E-4	1 Struc. Steel Foreman	3,000	.011	Lb.
				3 Struc. Steel Workers			
				1 Gas Welding Machine			
	215	**CEILING SUPPORTS**					
	1000	Entrance door/folding partition supports	E-4	1 Struc. Steel Foreman	60	.533	L.F.
				3 Struc. Steel Workers			
				1 Gas Welding Machine			
	1100	Linear accelerator door supports			14	2.290	L.F.
	1200	Lintels or shelf angles, hung, exterior hot dipped galv.			267	.120	L.F.
	1250	Two coats primer paint instead of galv.			267	.120	L.F.
	1400	Monitor support, ceiling hung, expansion bolted			4	8.000	Ea.
	1450	Hung from pre-set inserts			6	5.330	Ea.
	1600	Motor supports for overhead doors			4	8.000	Ea.
	1700	Partition support for heavy folding partitions, without pocket			24	1.330	L.F.
	1750	Supports at pocket only			12	2.670	L.F.
	2000	Rolling grilles & fire door supports			34	.941	L.F.
	2100	Spider-leg light supports, expansion bolted to ceiling slab			8	4.000	Ea.
	2150	Hung from pre-set inserts			12	2.670	Ea.
	2400	Toilet partition support			36	.889	L.F.
	2500	X-ray travel gantry support			12	2.670	L.F.
	220	**COLUMNS** Aluminum, extruded, stock units, 6" diameter			240	.133	L.F.
	0100	8" diameter			170	.188	L.F.
	0200	10" diameter			150	.213	L.F.
	0300	12" diameter			140	.229	L.F.
	0400	15" diameter			120	.267	L.F.
	0600	Tubular aluminum			1,500	.021	Lb.
	0700	Residential, flat, 8' high, plain			20	1.600	Ea.
	0720	Fancy			20	1.600	Ea.
	0740	Corner type, plain			20	1.600	Ea.
	0760	Fancy	↓	↓	20	1.600	Ea.
	0800	Steel, concrete filled, extra strong pipe, 3-1/2" diameter	E-2	1 Struc. Steel Foreman	660	.085	L.F.
				4 Struc. Steel Workers			
				1 Equip. Oper. (crane)			
				1 Equip. Oper. Oiler			
				1 Crane, 90 Ton			
	0830	4" diameter			780	.072	L.F.
	0850	4-1/2" diameter			900	.062	L.F.
	0890	5" diameter			1,020	.055	L.F.
	0900	5-1/2" diameter			1,140	.049	L.F.
	0930	6-5/8" diameter			1,200	.047	L.F.
	1000	Lightweight units, 3-1/2" diameter			780	.072	L.F.
	1050	4" diameter	↓	↓	900	.062	L.F.
	1300	For web ties, angles, etc., add per added lb.	1 Sswk	1 Struc. Steel Worker	945	.008	Lb.
	1500	Steel pipe, extra strong, no concrete, 3" to 5" O.D.	E-2	1 Struc. Steel Foreman	12,960	.004	Lb.
				4 Struc. Steel Workers			
				1 Equip. Oper. (crane)			
				1 Equip. Oper. Oiler			
				1 Crane, 90 Ton			
	1600	6" to 12" O.D.			39,100	.001	Lb.
	1700	Steel pipe, extra strong, no concrete, 3" diameter x 12'-0"			60	.933	Ea.
	1750	4" diameter x 12'-0"			58	.966	Ea.
	1800	6" diameter x 12'-0"			54	1.040	Ea.
	1850	8" diameter x 14'-0"			50	1.120	Ea.
	1900	10" diameter x 16'-0"			48	1.170	Ea.
	1950	12" diameter x 18'-0"			45	1.240	Ea.
	3300	Square structural tubing, 4" to 6" square, light section			11,270	.005	Lb.
	3600	Heavy section			27,600	.002	Lb.
	4500	Square structural tubing, 4" x 4" x 1/4" x 12'-0"	↓	↓	58	.966	Ea.

051 | Structural Metal Framing

051 200 | Structural Steel

		Description	CREW	MAKEUP	DAILY OUTPUT	MAN-HOURS	UNIT
220	4551	Columns, square structural tubing, 6" x 6" x 1/4" x 12'-0"	E-2	1 Struc. Steel Foreman	54	1.040	Ea.
				4 Struc. Steel Workers			
				1 Equip. Oper. (crane)			
				1 Equip. Oper. Oiler			
				1 Crane, 90 Ton			
	4600	8" x 8" x 3/8" x 14'-0"			50	1.120	Ea.
	4650	10" x 10" x 1/2" x 16'-0"			48	1.170	Ea.
	5100	Rectangular structural tubing, 5" to 6" wide, light section			9,500	.006	Lb.
	5200	Heavy section			31,200	.002	Lb.
	5300	7" to 10" wide, light section			37,000	.002	Lb.
	5400	Heavy section			68,000	.001	Lb.
	5500	Rectangular structural tubing, 5" x 3" x 1/4" x 12'-0"			58	.966	Ea.
	5550	6" x 4" x 5/16" x 12'-0"			54	1.040	Ea.
	5600	8" x 4" x 3/8" x 12'-0"			54	1.040	Ea.
	5650	10" x 6" x 3/8" x 14'-0"			50	1.120	Ea.
	5700	12" x 8" x 1/2" x 16'-0"	↓	↓	48	1.170	Ea.
	6000	Prefabricated fireproof with steel jackets and one coat					
	6100	shop paint, 2 to 4 hour rated, minimum	E-2	1 Struc. Steel Foreman	27,000	.002	Lb.
				4 Struc. Steel Workers			
				1 Equip. Oper. (crane)			
				1 Equip. Oper. Oiler			
				1 Crane, 90 Ton			
	6200	Average			35,000	.002	Lb.
	6250	Maximum	↓	↓	43,000	.001	Lb.
	6400	Mild steel, flat, 9" wide, stock units, painted, plain	E-4	1 Struc. Steel Foreman	160	.200	L.F.
				3 Struc. Steel Workers			
				1 Gas Welding Machine			
	6450	Fancy			160	.200	L.F.
	6500	Corner columns, painted, plain			160	.200	L.F.
	6550	Fancy	↓	↓	160	.200	L.F.
	6800	Wide flange, A36 steel, 2 tier, W 8 x 24	E-2	1 Struc. Steel Foreman	1,080	.052	L.F.
				4 Struc. Steel Workers			
				1 Equip. Oper. (crane)			
				1 Equip. Oper. Oiler			
				1 Crane, 90 Ton			
	6850	W 8 x 31			1,080	.052	L.F.
	6900	W 8 x 48			1,032	.054	L.F.
	6950	W 8 x 67			984	.057	L.F.
	7000	W 10 x 45			1,032	.054	L.F.
	7050	W 10 x 68			984	.057	L.F.
	7100	W 10 x 112			960	.058	L.F.
	7150	W 12 x 50			1,032	.054	L.F.
	7200	W 12 x 87			984	.057	L.F.
	7250	W 12 x 120			960	.058	L.F.
	7300	W 12 x 190			912	.061	L.F.
	7350	W 14 x 74			984	.057	L.F.
	7400	W 14 x 120			960	.058	L.F.
	7450	W 14 x 176	↓	↓	912	.061	L.F.
	230	**LIGHTGAGE FRAMING**					
	0400	Angle framing, 4" and larger	E-4	1 Struc. Steel Foreman	3,000	.011	Lb.
				3 Struc. Steel Workers			
				1 Gas Welding Machine			
	0450	Less than 4" angles			1,800	.018	Lb.
	0600	Channel framing, 8" and larger			3,500	.009	Lb.
	0650	Less than 8" channels	↓	↓	2,000	.016	Lb.
	1000	Continuous slotted channel framing system, minimum	2 Sswk	2 Struc. Steel Workers	2,400	.007	Lb.
	1200	Maximum	"	"	1,600	.010	Lb.

			CREW	MAKEUP	DAILY OUTPUT	MAN-HOURS	UNIT
051 200		**Structural Steel**					
230	1302	Lightgage framing, cross bracing, rods, 3/4" diameter	E-3	1 Struc. Steel Foreman	700	.034	Lb.
				1 Struc. Steel Worker			
				1 Welder			
				1 Gas Welding Machine			
				1 Torch, Gas & Air			
	1310	7/8" diameter			700	.034	Lb.
	1320	1" diameter			700	.034	Lb.
	1330	Angle, 5" x 5" x 3/8"			2,800	.009	Lb.
	1350	Hanging lintels, average	↓	↓	850	.028	Lb.
	1380	Roof frames, 3'-0" square, 5' span	E-2	1 Struc. Steel Foreman	4,200	.013	Lb.
				4 Struc. Steel Workers			
				1 Equip. Oper. (crane)			
				1 Equip. Oper. Oiler			
				1 Crane, 90 Ton			
	1400	Tie rod, not upset, 1-1/2" to 4" diameter, with turnbuckle	2 Sswk	2 Struc. Steel Workers	800	.020	Lb.
	1420	No turnbuckle			700	.023	Lb.
	1500	Upset, 1-3/4" to 4" diameter, with turnbuckle			800	.020	Lb.
	1520	No turnbuckle			700	.023	Lb.
	1600	Tubular aluminum framing for window wall, minimum			600	.027	Lb.
	1800	Maximum	↓	↓	500	.032	Lb.
	232	**LINTELS** Plain steel angles, under 500 lb.	1 Bric	1 Bricklayer	500	.016	Lb.
	0100	500 to 1000 lb.			600	.013	Lb.
	0200	1000 to 2000 lb.			600	.013	Lb.
	0300	2000 to 4000 lb.			600	.013	Lb.
	2000	Steel angles, 3-1/2" x 3", 1/4" thick, 2'-6" long			50	.160	Ea.
	2100	4'-6" long			45	.178	Ea.
	2500	3-1/2" x 3-1/2" x 5/16", 5'-0" long			44	.182	Ea.
	2600	4" x 3-1/2", 1/4" thick, 5'-0" long			40	.200	Ea.
	2700	9'-0" long			35	.229	Ea.
	2800	4" x 3-1/2" x 5/16", 7'-0" long			38	.211	Ea.
	2900	5" x 3-1/2" x 5/16", 10'-0" long	↓	↓	35	.229	Ea.
	235	**PRE-ENGINEERED STEEL BUILDINGS** For Hangars see 131-211					
	0100	Building shell above the foundations with 26 ga. colored					
	0111	Roofing and siding, minimum	E-2	1 Struc. Steel Foreman	1,800	.031	SF Flr.
				4 Struc. Steel Workers			
				1 Equip. Oper. (crane)			
				1 Equip. Oper. Oiler			
				1 Crane, 90 Ton			
	0200	Maximum	"	"	1,000	.056	SF Flr.
	0800	Accessory items: add to the basic building cost above					
	1000	Eave overhang, 2' wide, 26 ga., with soffit	E-2	1 Struc. Steel Foreman	360	.156	L.F.
				4 Struc. Steel Workers			
				1 Equip. Oper. (crane)			
				1 Equip. Oper. Oiler			
				1 Crane, 90 Ton			
	1200	4' wide , without soffit			300	.187	L.F.
	1300	With soffit			250	.224	L.F.
	1500	6' wide , without soffit			250	.224	L.F.
	1600	With soffit			200	.280	L.F.
	1800	Entrance canopy, incl. frame, 4' x 4'			25	2.240	Ea.
	1900	4' x 8'			19	2.950	Ea.
	2100	End wall roof overhang, 4' wide , without soffit			850	.066	L.F.
	2200	With soffit	↓	↓	500	.112	L.F.
	2300	Doors, H.M. self-framing, incl. butts, lockset and trim					
	2350	Single leaf, 3070 (3' x 7'), economy	2 Sswk	2 Struc. Steel Workers	5	3.200	Opng.
	2400	Deluxe			4	4.000	Opng.
	2450	Glazed			4	4.000	Opng.
	2500	3670 (3'-6" x 7')	↓	↓	4	4.000	Opng.

051 200	Structural Steel	CREW	MAKEUP	DAILY OUTPUT	MAN-HOURS	UNIT
235	2551	Pre-engineered steel doors, single leaf, 4070 (4' x 7')	2 Sswk	2 Struc. Steel Workers	3	5.330	Opng.
	2600	Double leaf, 6070 (6' x 7')	↓	↓	2	8.000	Opng.
	2650	Glazed	↓	↓	2	8.000	Opng.
	2700	Framing only, for openings, 3' x 7'	E-2	1 Struc. Steel Foreman	25	2.240	Opng.
				4 Struc. Steel Workers			
				1 Equip. Oper. (crane)			
				1 Equip. Oper. Oiler			
				1 Crane, 90 Ton			
	2800	10' x 10'			21	2.670	Opng.
	3000	For windows below, 2020 (2' x 2')			25	2.240	Opng.
	3100	4030 (4' x 3')	↓	↓	22	2.550	Opng.
	3300	Flashings, 26 ga., corner or eave, painted	2 Sswk	2 Struc. Steel Workers	240	.067	L.F.
	3400	Galvanized			240	.067	L.F.
	3600	Rake flashing, painted			240	.067	L.F.
	3700	Galvanized			240	.067	L.F.
	4200	Ridge flashing, 18" wide, painted			240	.067	L.F.
	4300	Galvanized			240	.067	L.F.
	4500	Gutter, eave type, 26 ga., painted			320	.050	L.F.
	4700	Galvanized			320	.050	L.F.
	4900	Valley type, between buildings, painted			120	.133	L.F.
	5000	Galvanized	↓	↓	120	.133	L.F.
	5200	Insulation, rated .6 lb density, vinyl faced					
	5250	1-1/2" thick, R5	2 Carp	2 Carpenters	2,300	.007	S.F.
	5300	3" thick, R10			2,300	.007	S.F.
	5350	4" thick, R11			2,300	.007	S.F.
	5400	Foil faced, 1-1/2" thick, R5			2,300	.007	S.F.
	5450	2" thick, R6			2,300	.007	S.F.
	5500	3" thick, R10			2,300	.007	S.F.
	5550	4" thick, R13			2,300	.007	S.F.
	5600	Metalized polyester facing, 1-1/2" thick, R6			2,300	.007	S.F.
	5650	2" thick, R8			2,300	.007	S.F.
	5700	3" thick, R11			2,300	.007	S.F.
	5750	4" thick, R13			2,300	.007	S.F.
	5800	Vinyl, scrim foil (SD), 1-1/2" thick, R5			2,300	.007	S.F.
	5850	2" thick, R6			2,300	.007	S.F.
	5900	3" thick, R10			2,300	.007	S.F.
	5950	4" thick, R13	↓	↓	2,300	.007	S.F.
	6500	Sash, single slide, glazed, with screens, 2020 (2'x 2')	E-1	1 Welder Foreman	22	1.090	Opng.
				1 Welder			
				1 Equip. Oper. (light)			
				1 Gas Welding Machine			
	6550	3030 (3' x 3')			14	1.710	Opng.
	6700	4030 (4' x 3')			13	1.850	Opng.
	6750	6040 (6' x 4')			12	2.000	Opng.
	6800	Double slide sash, 3030 (3' x 3')			14	1.710	Opng.
	6900	6040 (6' x 4')			12	2.000	Opng.
	7100	Fixed glass, no screens, 3030 (3' x 3')			14	1.710	Opng.
	7200	6040 (6' x 4')			12	2.000	Opng.
	7400	Prefinished storm sash, 3030 (3' x 3')			70	.343	Opng.
	7600	6040 (6' x 4')			60	.400	Opng.
	7810	Skylight, fiberglass panels, to 30 S.F.			10	2.400	Ea.
	7820	Larger sizes, add for excess over 30 S.F.	↓	↓	300	.080	S.F.
	8000	Roof vents, circular with damper, birdscreen					
	8010	and operator hardware, painted					
	8100	26 ga., 12" diameter	1 Sswk	1 Struc. Steel Worker	4	2.000	Ea.
	8150	20" diameter			3	2.670	Ea.
	8200	24 ga., 24" diameter			2	4.000	Ea.
	8250	Galvanized	↓	↓	2	4.000	Ea.

		Description	CREW	MAKEUP	DAILY OUTPUT	MAN-HOURS	UNIT
		**051 200	Structural Steel**					
235	8301	Pre-eng. steel, roof vents, continuous, 26 ga., 10' long, 9" wide	2 Sswk	2 Struc. Steel Workers	4	4.000	Ea.
	8400	12" wide	"	"	4	4.000	Ea.
	238	**SPACE FRAME** Steel 4' modular, 40' to 70' spans, 5.5 psf, minimum	E-2	1 Struc. Steel Foreman	556	.101	S.F.
				4 Struc. Steel Workers			
				1 Equip. Oper. (crane)			
				1 Equip. Oper. Oiler			
				1 Crane, 90 Ton			
	0200	Maximum			365	.153	S.F.
	0400	5' modular, 4.5 psf minimum			585	.096	S.F.
	0500	Maximum			405	.138	S.F.
	245	**STRESSED SKIN** Roof and ceiling system, spans to 100', minimum			1,150	.049	S.F.
	0200	Maximum	↓	↓	760	.074	S.F.
	250	**STRUCTURAL STEEL MEMBERS** Common WF sizes, spans 10' to 45'					
	0020	including bolted connections and erection					
	0100	W 6 x 9	E-2	1 Struc. Steel Foreman	600	.093	L.F.
				4 Struc. Steel Workers			
				1 Equip. Oper. (crane)			
				1 Equip. Oper. Oiler			
				1 Crane, 90 Ton			
	0300	W 8 x 10			600	.093	L.F.
	0500	x 31			500	.112	L.F.
	0700	W 10 x 22			660	.085	L.F.
	0900	x 49			540	.104	L.F.
	1100	W 12 x 14			880	.064	L.F.
	1300	x 22			880	.064	L.F.
	1500	x 26			880	.064	L.F.
	1700	x 72			640	.088	L.F.
	1900	W 14 x 26			990	.057	L.F.
	2100	x 30			900	.062	L.F.
	2300	x 34			810	.069	L.F.
	2500	x 120			720	.078	L.F.
	2700	W 16 x 26			1,000	.056	L.F.
	2900	x 31			900	.062	L.F.
	3100	x 40	↓	↓	800	.070	L.F.
	3300	W 18 x 35	E-5	2 Struc. Steel Foremen	960	.083	L.F.
				5 Struc. Steel Workers			
				1 Equip. Oper. (crane)			
				1 Welder			
				1 Equip. Oper. Oiler			
				1 Crane, 90 Ton			
				1 Gas Welding Machine			
				1 Torch, Gas & Air			
	3500	x 40			960	.083	L.F.
	3700	x 50			912	.088	L.F.
	3900	x 55			912	.088	L.F.
	4100	W 21 x 44			1,064	.075	L.F.
	4300	x 50			1,064	.075	L.F.
	4500	x 62			1,036	.077	L.F.
	4700	x 68			1,036	.077	L.F.
	4900	W 24 x 55			1,110	.072	L.F.
	5100	x 62			1,110	.072	L.F.
	5300	x 68			1,110	.072	L.F.
	5500	x 76			1,110	.072	L.F.
	5700	x 84			1,080	.074	L.F.
	5900	W 27 x 94			1,190	.067	L.F.
	6100	W 30 x 99			1,200	.067	L.F.
	6300	x 108			1,200	.067	L.F.
	6500	x 116	↓	↓	1,160	.069	L.F.

051 200 | Structural Steel

			CREW	MAKEUP	DAILY OUTPUT	MAN-HOURS	UNIT
250	6702	Structural steel members, spans 10'-45', W 33 x 118	E-5	2 Struc. Steel Foremen	1,176	.068	L.F.
				5 Struc. Steel Workers			
				1 Equip. Oper. (crane)			
				1 Welder			
				1 Equip. Oper. Oiler			
				1 Crane, 90 Ton			
				1 Gas Welding Machine			
				1 Torch, Gas & Air			
	6900	x 130			1,134	.071	L.F.
	7100	x 141			1,134	.071	L.F.
	7300	W 36 x 135			1,170	.068	L.F.
	7500	x 150			1,170	.068	L.F.
	7700	x 194			1,125	.071	L.F.
	7900	x 230			1,125	.071	L.F.
	8100	x 300	↓	↓	1,035	.077	L.F.
255		**STRUCTURAL STEEL PROJECTS** Bolted, unless mentioned otherwise					
	0200	Apts., nursing homes, etc., steel bearing, 1 to 2 stories	E-5	2 Struc. Steel Foremen	10.30	7.770	Ton
				5 Struc. Steel Workers			
				1 Equip. Oper. (crane)			
				1 Welder			
				1 Equip. Oper. Oiler			
				1 Crane, 90 Ton			
				1 Gas Welding Machine			
				1 Torch, Gas & Air			
	0300	3 to 6 stories	"	"	10.10	7.920	Ton
	0400	7 to 15 stories	E-6	3 Struc. Steel Foreman	14.20	9.010	Ton
				9 Struc. Steel Workers			
				1 Equip. Oper. (crane)			
				1 Welder			
				1 Equip. Oper. Oiler			
				1 Equip. Oper. (light)			
				1 Crane, 90 Ton			
				1 Gas Welding Machine			
				1 Torch, Gas & air			
				1 Air Compr., 160 C.F.M.			
				2 Impact Wrenches			
	0500	Over 15 stories	"	"	13.90	9.210	Ton
	0700	Offices, hospitals, etc., steel bearing, 1 to 2 stories	E-5	2 Struc. Steel Foremen	10.30	7.770	Ton
				5 Struc. Steel Workers			
				1 Equip. Oper. (crane)			
				1 Welder			
				1 Equip. Oper. Oiler			
				1 Crane, 90 Ton			
				1 Gas Welding Machine			
				1 Torch, Gas & Air			
	0800	3 to 6 stories	E-6	3 Struc. Steel Foreman	14.40	8.890	Ton
				9 Struc. Steel Workers			
				1 Equip. Oper. (crane)			
				1 Welder			
				1 Equip. Oper. Oiler			
				1 Equip. Oper. (light)			
				1 Crane, 90 Ton			
				1 Gas Welding Machine			
				1 Torch, Gas & air			
				1 Air Compr., 160 C.F.M.			
				2 Impact Wrenches			
	0900	7 to 15 stories	↓	↓	14.20	9.010	Ton
	1000	Over 15 stories			13.90	9.210	Ton

051 200 | Structural Steel

		Description	CREW	MAKEUP	DAILY OUTPUT	MAN-HOURS	UNIT
255	1300	Industrial bldgs., 1 story, beams & girders, steel bearing	E-5	2 Struc. Steel Foremen	12.90	6.200	Ton
				5 Struc. Steel Workers			
				1 Equip. Oper. (crane)			
				1 Welder			
				1 Equip. Oper. Oiler			
				1 Crane, 90 Ton			
				1 Gas Welding Machine			
				1 Torch, Gas & Air			
	1400	Masonry bearing	"	"	10	8.000	Ton
	1500	Industrial bldgs., 1 story, under 10 tons,					
	1510	steel from warehouse, trucked	E-2	1 Struc. Steel Foreman	7.50	7.470	Ton
				4 Struc. Steel Workers			
				1 Equip. Oper. (crane)			
				1 Equip. Oper. Oiler			
				1 Crane, 90 Ton			
	1600	1 story with roof trusses, steel bearing	E-5	2 Struc. Steel Foremen	10.60	7.550	Ton
				5 Struc. Steel Workers			
				1 Equip. Oper. (crane)			
				1 Welder			
				1 Equip. Oper. Oiler			
				1 Crane, 90 Ton			
				1 Gas Welding Machine			
				1 Torch, Gas & Air			
	1700	Masonry bearing	"	"	8.30	9.640	Ton
	1900	Monumental structures, banks, stores, etc., minimum	E-6	3 Struc. Steel Foreman	13	9.850	Ton
				9 Struc. Steel Workers			
				1 Equip. Oper. (crane)			
				1 Welder			
				1 Equip. Oper. Oiler			
				1 Equip. Oper. (light)			
				1 Crane, 90 Ton			
				1 Gas Welding Machine			
				1 Torch, Gas & air			
				1 Air Compr., 160 C.F.M.			
				2 Impact Wrenches			
	2000	Maximum	"	"	9	14.220	Ton
	2200	Churches, minimum	E-5	2 Struc. Steel Foremen	11.60	6.900	Ton
				5 Struc. Steel Workers			
				1 Equip. Oper. (crane)			
				1 Welder			
				1 Equip. Oper. Oiler			
				1 Crane, 90 Ton			
				1 Gas Welding Machine			
				1 Torch, Gas & Air			
	2300	Maximum	"	"	5.20	15.380	Ton
	2800	Power stations, fossil fuels, minimum	E-6	3 Struc. Steel Foreman	11	11.640	Ton
				9 Struc. Steel Workers			
				1 Equip. Oper. (crane)			
				1 Welder			
				1 Equip. Oper. Oiler			
				1 Equip. Oper. (light)			
				1 Crane, 90 Ton			
				1 Gas Welding Machine			
				1 Torch, Gas & air			
				1 Air Compr., 160 C.F.M.			
				2 Impact Wrenches			
	2900	Maximum	↓	↓	5.70	22.460	Ton
	2950	Nuclear fuels, non-safety steel, minimum			7	18.290	Ton

			CREW	MAKEUP	DAILY OUTPUT	MAN-HOURS	UNIT
	051 200	**Structural Steel**					
255	3001	Power stations, nuclear fuels, non-safety steel, maximum	E-6	3 Struc. Steel Foreman	5.50	23.270	Ton
				9 Struc. Steel Workers			
				1 Equip. Oper. (crane)			
				1 Welder			
				1 Equip. Oper. Oiler			
				1 Equip. Oper. (light)			
				1 Crane, 90 Ton			
				1 Gas Welding Machine			
				1 Torch, Gas & air			
				1 Air Compr., 160 C.F.M.			
				2 Impact Wrenches			
	3040	Safety steel, minimum	↓	↓	2.50	51.200	Ton
	3070	Maximum			1.50	85.330	Ton
	3100	Roof trusses, minimum	E-5	2 Struc. Steel Foremen	13	6.150	Ton
				5 Struc. Steel Workers			
				1 Equip. Oper. (crane)			
				1 Welder			
				1 Equip. Oper. Oiler			
				1 Crane, 90 Ton			
				1 Gas Welding Machine			
				1 Torch, Gas & Air			
	3200	Maximum			8.30	9.640	Ton
	3210	Schools, minimum			14.50	5.520	Ton
	3220	Maximum	↓	↓	8.30	9.640	Ton
	3400	Welded construction, simple commercial bldgs., 1 to 2 stories	E-7	1 Struc. Steel Foreman	7.60	10.530	Ton
				4 Struc. Steel Workers			
				1 Equip. Oper. (crane)			
				1 Equip. Oper. Oiler			
				1 Welder Foreman			
				2 Welders			
				1 Crane, 90 Ton			
				2 Gas Welding Machines			
	3500	7 to 15 stories	E-9	2 Struc. Steel Foremen	8.30	15.420	Ton
				5 Struc. Steel Workers			
				1 Welder Foreman			
				5 Welders			
				1 Equip. Oper. (crane)			
				1 Equip. Oper. Oiler			
				1 Equip. Oper. (light)			
				1 Crane, 90 Ton			
				5 Gas Welding Machines			
				1 Torch, Gas & Air			
	3700	Welded rigid frame, 1 story, minimum	E-7	1 Struc. Steel Foreman	15.80	5.060	Ton
				4 Struc. Steel Workers			
				1 Equip. Oper. (crane)			
				1 Equip. Oper. Oiler			
				1 Welder Foreman			
				2 Welders			
				1 Crane, 90 Ton			
				2 Gas Welding Machines			
	3800	Maximum	"	"	5.50	14.550	Ton
	4300	Column base plates, light	2 Sswk	2 Struc. Steel Workers	2,000	.008	Lb.
	4400	Heavy plates	E-2	1 Struc. Steel Foreman	15,000	.004	Lb.
				4 Struc. Steel Workers			
				1 Equip. Oper. (crane)			
				1 Equip. Oper. Oiler			
				1 Crane, 90 Ton			
	4600	Castellated beams, light sections, to 50#/L.F., minimum	"	"	10.70	5.230	Ton

051 | Structural Metal Framing

051 200 | Structural Steel

		Item	CREW	MAKEUP	DAILY OUTPUT	MAN-HOURS	UNIT
255	4701	Castellated beams, light sections, to 50#/L.F., maximum	E-2	1 Struc. Steel Foreman	7	8.000	Ton
				4 Struc. Steel Workers			
				1 Equip. Oper. (crane)			
				1 Equip. Oper. Oiler			
				1 Crane, 90 Ton			
	4900	Heavy sections, over 50# per L.F., minimum	↓	↓	11.70	4.790	Ton
	5000	Maximum			7.80	7.180	Ton
	5200	High strength bolts in place, light reaming, 3/4" bolts, average	2 Sswk	2 Struc. Steel Workers	165	.097	Ea.
	5300	7/8" bolts, average	"	"	160	.100	Ea.
	6100	Cold galvanizing, brush	1 Psst	1 Painter, Structural Steel	1,100	.007	S.F.
	6120	Steel surface treatments, sand blast, on grade					
	6130	Brush off blast	E-11	2 Painters, Struc. Steel	2,250	.014	S.F.
				1 Building Laborer			
				1 Equip. Oper. (light)			
				1 Air compressor 250 cfm			
				1 Sand blaster			
				1 Sand blasting accessories			
	6140	Commercial			1,352	.024	S.F.
	6150	Near white			1,040	.031	S.F.
	6160	White	↓	↓	845	.038	S.F.
	6170	Wire brush, hand	1 Psst	1 Painter, Structural Steel	695	.012	S.F.
	6180	Power tool	"	"	533	.015	S.F.
	6510	Paints & protective coatings, sprayed					
	6520	Alkyds, primer	E-15	2 Painters, Struc. Steel	1,830	.009	S.F.
				1 Paint Sprayer, 17 C.F.M.			
	6540	Gloss topcoats			1,830	.009	S.F.
	6560	Silicone alkyd			1,830	.009	S.F.
	6610	Epoxy, primer			1,350	.012	S.F.
	6630	Intermediate or topcoat			1,350	.012	S.F.
	6650	Enamel coat			1,350	.012	S.F.
	6700	Epoxy ester, primer			1,350	.012	S.F.
	6720	Topcoats			1,350	.012	S.F.
	6810	Latex primer			1,830	.009	S.F.
	6830	Topcoats			1,830	.009	S.F.
	6910	Universal primers, one part, phenolic, modified alkyd			1,830	.009	S.F.
	6940	Two part, epoxy spray			1,350	.012	S.F.
	7000	Zinc rich primers, self cure, spray, inorganic,			890	.018	S.F.
	7010	Epoxy, spray, organic	↓	↓	890	.018	S.F.
275		**VIBRATION PADS**					
	0300	Laminated synthetic rubber impregnated cotton duck	2 Sswk	2 Struc. Steel Workers	20	.800	B.F.
	0600	Neoprene bearing pads, 1/2" thick			24	.667	S.F.
	0700	1" thick			20	.800	S.F.
	0900	Fabric reinforced neoprene, 5000 psi, 1/2" thick			24	.667	S.F.
	1000	1" thick			20	.800	S.F.
	1200	Felt surfaced vinyl pads, cork and sisal, 5/8" thick			24	.667	S.F.
	1300	1" thick			20	.800	S.F.
	1500	Teflon bonded to 10 ga. carbon steel, 1/32" layer			24	.667	S.F.
	1600	3/32" layer			24	.667	S.F.
	1800	Bonded to 10 ga. stainless steel, 1/32" layer			24	.667	S.F.
	1900	3/32" layer	↓	↓	24	.667	S.F.

051 400 | Structural Aluminum

		Item	CREW	MAKEUP	DAILY OUTPUT	MAN-HOURS	UNIT
	404	**ALUMINUM** Structural shapes, 1" to 10" members, under 1 ton	E-2	1 Struc. Steel Foreman	1,050	.053	Lb.
				4 Struc. Steel Workers			
				1 Equip. Oper. (crane)			
				1 Equip. Oper. Oiler			
				1 Crane, 90 Ton			
	0100	Over 5 tons	"	"	1,330	.042	Lb.

051 | Structural Metal Framing

051 400 | Structural Aluminum

		Description	CREW	MAKEUP	DAILY OUTPUT	MAN-HOURS	UNIT
404	0301	Aluminum extrusions, over 5 tons, stock shapes	E-2	1 Struc. Steel Foreman	1,330	.042	Lb.
				4 Struc. Steel Workers			
				1 Equip. Oper. (crane)			
				1 Equip. Oper. Oiler			
				1 Crane, 90 Ton			
	0400	Custom shapes	"	"	1,330	.042	Lb.

052 | Metal Joists

052 100 | Steel Joists

		Description	CREW	MAKEUP	DAILY OUTPUT	MAN-HOURS	UNIT
108		**LIGHTGAGE JOISTS**					
	0120	Punched, double nailable, 6" deep, 16 gauge, painted	E-4	1 Struc. Steel Foreman	1,800	.018	L.F.
				3 Struc. Steel Workers			
				1 Gas Welding Machine			
	0140	14 gauge			1,800	.018	L.F.
	0160	8" deep, 16 gauge			1,550	.021	L.F.
	0180	14 gauge			1,550	.021	L.F.
	0200	10" deep, 14 gauge			1,350	.024	L.F.
	0220	12 gauge			1,350	.024	L.F.
	0240	12" deep, 14 gauge			1,200	.027	L.F.
	0260	12 gauge	↓	↓	1,200	.027	L.F.
110		**OPEN WEB JOISTS** H or K series, horizontal bridging,					
	0020	truckload lots, span up to 30', minimum	E-7	1 Struc. Steel Foreman	15	5.330	Ton
				4 Struc. Steel Workers			
				1 Equip. Oper. (crane)			
				1 Equip. Oper. Oiler			
				1 Welder Foreman			
				2 Welders			
				1 Crane, 90 Ton			
				2 Gas Welding Machines			
	0031	Average	E-2	1 Struc. Steel Foreman	7.50	7.470	Ton
				4 Struc. Steel Workers			
				1 Equip. Oper. (crane)			
				1 Equip. Oper. Oiler			
				1 Crane, 90 Ton			
	0100	Maximum	E-7	1 Struc. Steel Foreman	9	8.890	Ton
				4 Struc. Steel Workers			
				1 Equip. Oper. (crane)			
				1 Equip. Oper. Oiler			
				1 Welder Foreman			
				2 Welders			
				1 Crane, 90 Ton			
				2 Gas Welding Machines			
	0300	Span 30' to 50', minimum	↓	↓	17	4.710	Ton
	0400	Maximum			10	8.000	Ton

052 | Metal Joists

052 100 | Steel Joists

		Description	CREW	MAKEUP	DAILY OUTPUT	MAN-HOURS	UNIT
110	0612	Open web joists, LH series, bolted, spans to 96', minimum	E-7	1 Struc. Steel Foreman	16	5.000	Ton
				4 Struc. Steel Workers			
				1 Equip. Oper. (crane)			
				1 Equip. Oper. Oiler			
				1 Welder Foreman			
				2 Welders			
				1 Crane, 90 Ton			
				2 Gas Welding Machines			
	0620	Average	↓	↓	13	6.150	Ton
	0700	Maximum			11	7.270	Ton
	0900	DLH series, bolted cross bridging					
	0910	Spans to 144' (shipped in 2 pieces), minimum	E-7	1 Struc. Steel Foreman	16	5.000	Ton
				4 Struc. Steel Workers			
				1 Equip. Oper. (crane)			
				1 Equip. Oper. Oiler			
				1 Welder Foreman			
				2 Welders			
				1 Crane, 90 Ton			
				2 Gas Welding Machines			
	0920	Average	↓	↓	13	6.150	Ton
	1000	Maximum			11	7.270	Ton
	3000	Joist girders, average	E-5	2 Struc. Steel Foremen	13	6.150	Ton
				5 Struc. Steel Workers			
				1 Equip. Oper. (crane)			
				1 Welder			
				1 Equip. Oper. Oiler			
				1 Crane, 90 Ton			
				1 Gas Welding Machine			
				1 Torch, Gas & Air			
	4000	Trusses, factory fabricated WT chords, average	"	"	11	7.270	Ton

053 | Metal Decking

053 100 | Steel Deck

		Description	CREW	MAKEUP	DAILY OUTPUT	MAN-HOURS	UNIT
	104	METAL DECKING Steel floor panels, over 15,000 S.F.					
	0200	Cellular units, galvanized, 2" deep, 20-20 gauge	E-4	1 Struc. Steel Foreman	1,460	.022	S.F.
				3 Struc. Steel Workers			
				1 Gas Welding Machine			
	0300	18-18 gauge			1,390	.023	S.F.
	0400	3" deep, galvanized, 20-20 gauge			1,375	.023	S.F.
	0500	18-20 gauge			1,350	.024	S.F.
	0600	18-18 gauge			1,290	.025	S.F.
	0700	16-18 gauge			1,230	.026	S.F.
	0800	16-16 gauge			1,150	.028	S.F.
	1000	4-1/2" deep, galvanized, 20-18 gauge			1,100	.029	S.F.
	1100	18-18 gauge			1,040	.031	S.F.
	1200	16-18 gauge			980	.033	S.F.
	1300	16-16 gauge			935	.034	S.F.
	2100	Open type, galv., 1-1/2" deep, 22 ga., under 50 square			4,500	.007	S.F.
	2400	Over 50 square			4,900	.007	S.F.
	2600	20 ga., under 50 square	↓	↓	3,865	.008	S.F.
	2700	Over 50 square			4,170	.008	S.F.

053 | Metal Decking

053 100 | Steel Deck

		CREW	MAKEUP	DAILY OUTPUT	MAN-HOURS	UNIT
104 2901	Metal decking, open type, galv., 18 ga., under 50 square	E-4	1 Struc. Steel Foreman	3,800	.008	S.F.
			3 Struc. Steel Workers			
			1 Gas Welding Machine			
3000	Over 50 square			4,100	.008	S.F.
3200	3″ deep, over 50 sq., 22 gauge			3,600	.009	S.F.
3300	20 gauge			3,400	.009	S.F.
3400	18 gauge			3,200	.010	S.F.
3500	16 gauge			3,000	.011	S.F.
3700	4-1/2″ deep, long span roof, 20 gauge			2,700	.012	S.F.
3800	18 gauge			2,460	.013	S.F.
3900	16 gauge			2,350	.014	S.F.
4100	6″ deep, long span, 18 gauge			2,000	.016	S.F.
4200	16 gauge			1,930	.017	S.F.
4300	14 gauge			1,860	.017	S.F.
4500	7-1/2″ deep, long span, 18 gauge			1,690	.019	S.F.
4600	16 gauge			1,590	.020	S.F.
5200	Non-cellular composite deck, galv., 2″ deep, 22 gauge			3,860	.008	S.F.
5300	20 gauge			3,600	.009	S.F.
5400	18 gauge			3,380	.009	S.F.
5500	16 gauge			3,200	.010	S.F.
5700	3″ deep, galv., 22 gauge			3,200	.010	S.F.
5800	20 gauge			3,000	.011	S.F.
5900	18 gauge			2,850	.011	S.F.
6000	16 gauge	↓	↓	2,700	.012	S.F.
6100	Slab form, steel 28 gauge, 9/16″ deep, uncoated	E-1	1 Welder Foreman	4,000	.006	S.F.
			1 Welder			
			1 Equip. Oper. (light)			
			1 Gas Welding Machine			
6200	Galvanized			4,000	.006	S.F.
6300	24 gauge, 1-5/16″ deep, uncoated			3,800	.006	S.F.
6400	Galvanized			3,800	.006	S.F.
6500	22 gauge, 1-5/16″ deep, uncoated			3,700	.006	S.F.
6600	Galvanized	↓	↓	3,700	.006	S.F.
7000	Sheet metal edge closure form, 12″ wide with 2 bends					
7100	18 gauge	E-14	1 Welder Foreman	360	.022	L.F.
			1 Gas Welding Machine			
7200	16 gauge	″	″	360	.022	L.F.
8000	Metal deck and trench, 2″ thick, 20 ga. combination,					
8010	60% cellular, 40% non-cellular, inserts and trench	R-4	1 Struc. Steel Foreman	1,100	.036	S.F.
			3 Struc. Steel Workers			
			1 Electrician			
			1 Gas Welding Machine			

055 | Metal Fabrications

055 100 | Metal Stairs

		CREW	MAKEUP	DAILY OUTPUT	MAN-HOURS	UNIT
104	STAIR Steel, 3′-6″ wide, grating tread, safety nosing, steel					
0020	stringers and pipe railing, stock units	E-4	1 Struc. Steel Foreman	35	.914	Riser
			3 Struc. Steel Workers			
			1 Gas Welding Machine			
0200	Cement fill metal pan and picket rail			35	.914	Riser
0400	Cast iron tread and pipe rail	↓	↓	35	.914	Riser

055 100 | Metal Stairs

		Description	CREW	MAKEUP	DAILY OUTPUT	MAN-HOURS	UNIT
104	0801	Stairs, 3'-6" wide, safety nosing, custom steel, minimum	E-4	1 Struc. Steel Foreman	35	.914	Riser
				3 Struc. Steel Workers			
				1 Gas Welding Machine			
	0810	Average			30	1.070	Riser
	0900	Maximum			20	1.600	Riser
	1500	Landing, steel pan, conventional			160	.200	S.F.
	1600	Pre-erected			255	.125	S.F.
	1700	Pre-erected, steel pan tread, 3'-6" wide, with flat bar rail			85	.376	Riser
	1800	With picket rail			17	1.880	Riser
	1810	Spiral aluminum, 5'-0" diameter, stock units			45	.711	Riser
	1820	Custom units			45	.711	Riser
	1830	Stock units, 4'-0" diameter, safety treads			50	.640	Riser
	1840	Oak treads			50	.640	Riser
	1850	5'-0" diameter, safety treads			45	.711	Riser
	1860	Oak treads			45	.711	Riser
	1870	6'-0" diameter, safety treads			40	.800	Riser
	1880	Oak treads			40	.800	Riser
	1900	Spiral, cast iron, 4'-0" diameter, ornamental, minimum			45	.711	Riser
	1920	Maximum			25	1.280	Riser
	2000	Spiral, steel, industrial checkered plate, 4' diameter			45	.711	Riser
	2200	Stock units, 6'-0" diameter			40	.800	Riser
	2400	Custom units, 4' to 6' diameter, minimum			45	.711	Riser
	2500	Maximum			25	1.280	Riser
	3900	Inclined ladder type, 3' wide, steel, 8' vertical rise	↓	↓	100	.320	V.L.F.
	4000	Aluminum			100	.320	V.L.F.
108		**STAIR TREADS** Aluminum grating, 3' long, 1" x 3/16" bars, 6" wide	1 Sswk	1 Struc. Steel Worker	24	.333	Ea.
	0100	12" wide			22	.364	Ea.
	0200	1-1/2" x 3/16" bars, 6" wide			24	.333	Ea.
	0300	12" wide	↓	↓	22	.364	Ea.
	0600	Treads, 12" x 3'-6", not incl. stringers. See also div. 033-184					
	0700	Cast aluminum, abrasive, 5/16" thick	1 Sswk	1 Struc. Steel Worker	15	.533	Ea.
	0800	3/8" thick			15	.533	Ea.
	0900	1/2" thick			15	.533	Ea.
	1000	Cast bronze, abrasive, 3/8" thick			8	1.000	Ea.
	1100	1/2" thick			8	1.000	Ea.
	1200	Cast iron, abrasive, 3/8" thick			15	.533	Ea.
	1300	1/2" thick	↓	↓	15	.533	Ea.
	1400	Fiberglass reinforced plastic with safety nosing,					
	1500	1-1/2" thick, 12" wide, 24" long	1 Sswk	1 Struc. Steel Worker	22	.364	Ea.
	1600	30" long			22	.364	Ea.
	1700	36" long	↓	↓	22	.364	Ea.
	2012	Steel grating, 3' long, painted,					
	2022	Plain, 3/4" x 1/8", 6" wide	1 Sswk	1 Struc. Steel Worker	17	.471	Ea.
	2024	12" wide			15	.533	Ea.
	2032	1-1/4" x 3/16", 6" wide			17	.471	Ea.
	2034	12" wide			15	.533	Ea.
	2062	Serrated, 3/4" x 1/8", 6" wide			17	.471	Ea.
	2064	12" wide			15	.533	Ea.
	2072	1-1/4" x 3/16", 6" wide			17	.471	Ea.
	2074	12" wide			15	.533	Ea.
	2500	Expanded steel, 2-1/2" deep, 9" x 3' long, 18 gauge			20	.400	Ea.
	2600	14 gauge	↓	↓	20	.400	Ea.

055 | Metal Fabrications

055 150 | Ladders

		CREW	MAKEUP	DAILY OUTPUT	MAN-HOURS	UNIT
154	**FIRE ESCAPE**					
0200	2' wide balcony, 1" x 1/4" bars 1-1/2" O.C.	1 Sswk	1 Struc. Steel Worker	5	1.600	L.F.
0400	1st story cantilever, standard	↓	↓	.09	88.890	Ea.
0700	Platform & stair, 36" x 40"			.17	47.060	Flight
158	**LADDER** Steel, bolted to concrete, with cage	E-4	1 Struc. Steel Foreman	50	.640	V.L.F.
			3 Struc. Steel Workers			
			1 Gas Welding Machine			
0100	Without cage			85	.376	V.L.F.
0300	Aluminum, bolted to concrete, with cage			50	.640	V.L.F.
0400	Without cage	↓	↓	85	.376	V.L.F.

055 200 | Handrails & Railings

		CREW	MAKEUP	DAILY OUTPUT	MAN-HOURS	UNIT
202	**BUMPER RAILS** For garages, 12 ga. rail, 6" wide, with steel					
0020	posts 12'-6" O.C., Minimum	E-4	1 Struc. Steel Foreman	190	.168	L.F.
			3 Struc. Steel Workers			
			1 Gas Welding Machine			
0030	Average			165	.194	L.F.
0100	Maximum			140	.229	L.F.
0300	12" channel rail, minimum			160	.200	L.F.
0400	Maximum			120	.267	L.F.
204	**RAILINGS, COMMERCIAL** Aluminum pipe rail, anodized			195	.164	L.F.
0900	Aluminum balcony rail, 1-1/2" posts, with pickets			195	.164	L.F.
1000	With expanded metal panels			195	.164	L.F.
1200	Hammered wire glass panel inserts			195	.164	L.F.
1300	Porcelain enamel panel inserts			195	.164	L.F.
1600	Mild steel, ornamental rounded top rail			195	.164	L.F.
1700	As above but flat top rail			195	.164	L.F.
1800	As above but pitch down stairs			175	.183	L.F.
1900	Residential, stock units, mild steel, deluxe			315	.102	L.F.
1910	Economy			315	.102	L.F.
2400	Steel pipe, welded, 1-1/2" round, painted			200	.160	L.F.
2500	Galvanized			200	.160	L.F.
2700	Steel pipe with 4" x 1/4" toe plate, painted			200	.160	L.F.
2800	Galvanized			200	.160	L.F.
3400	Wall rail, with returns, aluminum pipe			255	.125	L.F.
3500	Steel pipe			255	.125	L.F.
3600	Mild steel pipe			255	.125	L.F.
3700	Stainless steel pipe			255	.125	L.F.
4000	For gypsum stud wall mounted, add			340	.094	L.F.
206	**RAILINGS, INDUSTRIAL** Welded, 2 rail, 3'-6" high, 1-1/2" pipe			255	.125	L.F.
0100	2" angle rail	↓	↓	255	.125	L.F.
208	**RAILINGS, ORNAMENTAL** Aluminum, bronze or stainless, minimum	1 Sswk	1 Struc. Steel Worker	24	.333	L.F.
0100	Maximum			9	.889	L.F.
0200	Aluminum pipe rail, minimum			15	.533	L.F.
0300	Maximum			8	1.000	L.F.
0400	Hand-forged wrought iron, minimum			12	.667	L.F.
0500	Maximum			8	1.000	L.F.
0600	Composite metal and wood or glass, minimum			6	1.330	L.F.
0700	Maximum	↓	↓	5	1.600	L.F.

055 300 | Gratings & Floor Plates

		CREW	MAKEUP	DAILY OUTPUT	MAN-HOURS	UNIT
302	**CHECKERED PLATE** 1/4" & 3/8", 2000 to 5000 S.F., bolted	E-4	1 Struc. Steel Foreman	2,900	.011	Lb.
			3 Struc. Steel Workers			
			1 Gas Welding Machine			
0100	Welded			4,400	.007	Lb.
0300	Pit or trench cover and frame, 1/4" plate, 2' to 3' wide			100	.320	S.F.
0500	Platforms, 1/4" plate, no handrails included, rectangular			4,200	.008	Lb.
0600	Circular	↓	↓	2,500	.013	Lb.

055 300 | Gratings & Floor Plates

		CREW	MAKEUP	DAILY OUTPUT	MAN-HOURS	UNIT
304	**FLOOR GRATING, ALUMINUM**					
0104	Pressure-locked gratings					
0110	Bearing bars @ 1-3/16" O.C., cross bars @ 4" O.C.,					
0112	1" x 1/8" bar, up to 75 S.F.	E-4	1 Struc. Steel Foreman 3 Struc. Steel Workers 1 Gas Welding Machine	600	.053	S.F.
0114	Over 300 S.F.			1,000	.032	S.F.
0122	1-1/4" x 3/16", up o 75 S.F.			600	.053	S.F.
0124	Over 300 S.F.			1,000	.032	S.F.
0132	1-1/2" x 1/8", up to 75 S.F.			600	.053	S.F.
0134	Over 300 S.F.			1,000	.032	S.F.
0136	1-3/4" x 3/16", up to 75 S.F.			600	.053	S.F.
0138	Over 300 S.F.			1,000	.032	S.F.
0142	2-1/4" x 3/16", up to 75 S.F.			600	.053	S.F.
0144	Over 300 S.F.			1,000	.032	S.F.
0162	Cross bars @ 2" O.C., 1" x 1/8", up to 75 S.F.			600	.053	S.F.
0164	Over 300 S.F.			1,000	.032	S.F.
0172	1-1/4" x 3/16", up to 75 S.F.			600	.053	S.F.
0182	1-1/2" x 1/8", upt o 75 S.F.			600	.053	S.F.
0184	Over 300 S.F.			1,000	.032	S.F.
0186	1-3/4" x 3/16", up to 75 S.F.			600	.053	S.F.
0188	Over 300 S.F.			1,000	.032	S.F.
0212	Close mesh, 1" x 1/8", up to 75 S.F.			520	.062	S.F.
0214	Over 300 S.F.			920	.035	S.F.
0222	1-1/4" x 3/16", up to 75 S.F.			520	.062	S.F.
0224	Over 300 S.F.			920	.035	S.F.
0232	1-1/2" x 1/8", up to 75 S.F.			520	.062	S.F.
0234	Over 300 S.F.			920	.035	S.F.
1200	Expanded aluminum, .65# per S.F., on grade			1,050	.030	S.F.
1600	Heavy duty, all extruded panels, 3/4" deep, 1.7 # per S.F.			1,100	.029	S.F.
1700	1-1/4" deep, 2.5# per S.F.			1,000	.032	S.F.
1800	1-3/4" deep, 4.8# per S.F.			925	.035	S.F.
1900	2-1/4" deep, 6.1# per S.F.			875	.037	S.F.
2400	Close spaced aluminum grating with vinyl tread inserts			255	.125	S.F.
2600	For bottom drainage pan, add	↓	↓	510	.063	S.F.
308	**FLOOR GRATING, FIBERGLASS** Reinforced polyester, fire retardant					
0100	1" x 4" grid, 1" thick	E-4	1 Struc. Steel Foreman 3 Struc. Steel Workers 1 Gas Welding Machine	510	.063	S.F.
0200	1-1/2" thick			500	.064	S.F.
0300	Fiberglass reinforced epoxy, 1" x 4" grid, 1-1/2" thick	↓	↓	500	.064	S.F.
310	**FLOOR GRATING PLANKS** Aluminum, 9-1/2" wide					
0020	14 ga., 2" rib	E-4	1 Struc. Steel Foreman 3 Struc. Steel Workers 1 Gas Welding Machine	950	.034	L.F.
0200	Galvanized steel, 9-1/2" wide, 14 ga., 2-1/2" rib			950	.034	L.F.
0300	4" rib			950	.034	L.F.
0500	12 gauge, 2-1/2" rib			950	.034	L.F.
0600	3" rib			950	.034	L.F.
0800	Stainless steel, type 304, 16 ga., 2" rib			950	.034	L.F.
0900	Type 316			950	.034	L.F.
312	**FLOOR GRATING, STEEL** Labor for installing , on grade			845	.038	S.F.
0100	Elevated			460	.070	S.F.
0300	Platforms, to 12' high, rectangular			3,150	.010	Lb.
0400	Circular	↓	↓	2,300	.014	Lb.

055 300 | Gratings & Floor Plates

			CREW	MAKEUP	DAILY OUTPUT	MAN-HOURS	UNIT
312	0413	Floor grating, cross bars @ 4" O.C., 3/4" x 1/8", to 75 S.F.	E-2	1 Struc. Steel Foreman	500	.112	S.F.
				4 Struc. Steel Workers			
				1 Equip. Oper. (crane)			
				1 Equip. Oper. Oiler			
				1 Crane, 90 Ton			
	0414	Over 300 S.F.			750	.075	S.F.
	0422	1-1/4" x 3/16", up to 75 S.F.			400	.140	S.F.
	0432	1-1/2" x 1/8", up to 75 S.F.			400	.140	S.F.
	0436	1-3/4" x 3/16", up to 75 S.F.			400	.140	S.F.
	0462	Cross bars @ 2" O.C., 3/4" x 1/8", up to 75 S.F.			500	.112	S.F.
	0464	Over 300 S.F.			750	.075	S.F.
	0472	1-1/4" x 3/16", up to 75 S.F.			400	.140	S.F.
	0474	Over 300 S.F.			600	.093	S.F.
	0482	1-1/2" x 1/8", up to 75 S.F.			400	.140	S.F.
	0484	Over 300 S.F.			600	.093	S.F.
	0486	1-3/4" x 3/16", up to 75 S.F.			400	.140	S.F.
	0488	Over 300 S.F.			600	.093	S.F.
	0502	2-1/4" x 3/16", up to 75 S.F.			300	.187	S.F.
	0504	Over 300 S.F.	↓	↓	450	.124	S.F.
	0601	Painted bearing bars @ 15/16" O.C., cross bars @ 4" O.C.,					
	0612	Up to 75 S.F., 3/4" x 1/8"	E-2	1 Struc. Steel Foreman	500	.112	S.F.
				4 Struc. Steel Workers			
				1 Equip. Oper. (crane)			
				1 Equip. Oper. Oiler			
				1 Crane, 90 Ton			
	0622	1-1/4" x 3/16"			400	.140	S.F.
	0632	1-1/2" x 1/8"			400	.140	S.F.
	0636	1-3/4" x 3/16"			300	.187	S.F.
	0652	2-1/4" x 3/16"			300	.187	S.F.
	0662	Cross bars @ 2" O.C., up to 75 S.F., 3/4" x 1/8"			500	.112	S.F.
	0672	1-1/4" x 3/16"			400	.140	S.F.
	0682	1-1/2" x 1/8"			400	.140	S.F.
	0686	1-3/4" x 3/16"	↓	↓	300	.187	S.F.
	2000	Stainless steel gratings, close spaced, on grade	E-4	1 Struc. Steel Foreman	340	.094	S.F.
				3 Struc. Steel Workers			
				1 Gas Welding Machine			
	2100	Standard grating, 3.3# per S.F.			300	.107	S.F.
	2200	4.5# per S.F.			275	.116	S.F.
	2400	Expanded steel grating, on grade, 3.0# per S.F.			900	.036	S.F.
	2500	3.14# per S.F.			900	.036	S.F.
	2600	4.0# per S.F.			850	.038	S.F.
	2650	4.27# per S.F.			850	.038	S.F.
	2700	5.0# per S.F.			800	.040	S.F.
	2800	6.25# per S.F.			750	.043	S.F.
	2900	7.0# per S.F.	↓	↓	700	.046	S.F.
	314	**GRATING FRAME** Aluminum, for gratings 1" to 1-1/2" deep	1 Sswk	1 Struc. Steel Worker	70	.114	L.F.
	370	**TRENCH COVER** Steel gratings with bar stops and angle					
	0020	frame, to 18" wide	1 Sswk	1 Struc. Steel Worker	20	.400	L.F.
	0100	Frame only (both sides of trench), 1" grating			45	.178	L.F.
	0150	2" grating	↓	↓	35	.229	L.F.
	0200	Aluminum, stock units, including frames and					
	0210	3/8" plain cover plate, 2" opening	E-4	1 Struc. Steel Foreman	205	.156	L.F.
				3 Struc. Steel Workers			
				1 Gas Welding Machine			
	0300	6" opening			185	.173	L.F.
	0400	10" opening			170	.188	L.F.
	0500	16" opening	↓	↓	155	.206	L.F.

055 | Metal Fabrications

055 400 | Castings

		CREW	MAKEUP	DAILY OUTPUT	MAN-HOURS	UNIT
404	**CONSTRUCTION CASTINGS**					
0100	Column bases, cast iron, 16" x 16" x 2-1/2"	E-4	1 Struc. Steel Foreman	46	.696	Ea.
			3 Struc. Steel Workers			
			1 Gas Welding Machine			
0200	32" x 32" x 3-3/4"	"	"	23	1.390	Ea.
0400	Cast aluminum for wood columns, 8" x 8"	1 Carp	1 Carpenter	32	.250	Ea.
0500	12" x 12"	"	"	32	.250	Ea.
0600	Miscellaneous C.I. castings, light sections	E-4	1 Struc. Steel Foreman	3,200	.010	Lb.
			3 Struc. Steel Workers			
			1 Gas Welding Machine			
1100	Heavy sections	↓	↓	4,200	.008	Lb.
1300	Special low volume items			3,200	.010	Lb.

055 500 | Metal Specialties

		CREW	MAKEUP	DAILY OUTPUT	MAN-HOURS	UNIT
504	**LAMP POSTS** Only, 6' high, stock units, aluminum	1 Carp	1 Carpenter	16	.500	Ea.
0100	Mild steel, plain	"	"	16	.500	Ea.
508	**WINDOW GUARDS** Expanded metal, steel angle frame, permanent	E-4	1 Struc. Steel Foreman	350	.091	S.F.
			3 Struc. Steel Workers			
			1 Gas Welding Machine			
0020	Steel bars, 1/2" x 1/2", spaced 5" O.C.			290	.110	S.F.
0100	Mild steel, stock units, economy			405	.079	S.F.
0200	Deluxe			405	.079	S.F.
0400	Woven wire, stock units, 3/8" channel frame, 3' x 5' opening			40	.800	Opng.
0500	4' x 6' opening	↓	↓	38	.842	Opng.

057 | Ornamental Metal

057 250 | Ornamental Metal

		CREW	MAKEUP	DAILY OUTPUT	MAN-HOURS	UNIT
252	**WEATHERVANES** Residential types, minimum	1 Carp	1 Carpenter	8	1.000	Ea.
0100	Maximum	"	"	2	4.000	Ea.

058 | Expansion Controls

058 100 | Exp Cover Assemblies

		CREW	MAKEUP	DAILY OUTPUT	MAN-HOURS	UNIT
104	**EXPANSION JOINT ASSEMBLIES** Custom					
0200	Floor cover assemblies, 1" space, aluminum	1 Sswk	1 Struc. Steel Worker	38	.211	L.F.
0300	Bronze or stainless			38	.211	L.F.
0500	2" space, aluminum			38	.211	L.F.
0600	Bronze or stainless			38	.211	L.F.
0800	Wall and ceiling assemblies, 1" space, aluminum			38	.211	L.F.
0900	Bronze or stainless			38	.211	L.F.
1100	2" space, aluminum			38	.211	L.F.
1200	Bronze or stainless			38	.211	L.F.
1400	Floor to wall assemblies, 1" space, aluminum			38	.211	L.F.
1500	Bronze or stainless			38	.211	L.F.
1700	Gym floor angle covers, aluminum, 3" x 3" angle	↓	↓	46	.174	L.F.

058 | Expansion Control

058 100	Exp Cover Assemblies	CREW	MAKEUP	DAILY OUTPUT	MAN-HOURS	UNIT
104 1802	Gym floor angle covers, aluminum, 3" x 4" angles	1 Sswk	1 Struc. Steel Worker	46	.174	L.F.
2000	Roof closures, aluminum, 1" space, flat roof, low profile			57	.140	L.F.
2100	High profile			57	.140	L.F.
2300	Roof to wall, 1" space, low profile			57	.140	L.F.
2400	High profile	↓	↓	57	.140	L.F.

DIVISION 6

WOOD AND PLASTICS

6

DIVISION 6

WOOD AND PLASTICS

Because most installation in this division is done by carpenters, it is important to remember that the productivity levels of workers in this trade can vary greatly due to job location and quality of the labor force.

Framing productivity itself is directly related to the difficulty of the shape of the building, the steepness of the roof pitch, and all relevant job site conditions. The figures for installation of large members and trusses are based on the assumption that power equipment is used. Normal structural joists can be placed by hand on some residential projects. However, trusses and structural joists are more easily installed using power equipment when longer lengths are involved. Contractors readily accept the mobilization costs of the lifting equipment to realize an increase in productivity.

It is impossible to directly relate man-hours to the amount of materials used when analyzing framing productivity. In general, man-hour figures are based on longer lengths. Using shorter lengths in complex areas of a structure can add to the time needed to get the job done. The same basic idea applies to plywood and interior paneling. It is assumed that whole sheets are used. If workers are expected to install half-sheets, the man-hours per square foot involved increase significantly.

The type of wood used on a project has an obvious effect on overall efficiency. Treated lumber, for instance, is heavier than normal wood, making it harder to transport and install. It causes increased wear on equipment and adds to the installation time.

All pre-made items under finish carpentry — counter tops, cupolas, mantels, etc. — are assumed to be finished unless otherwise noted. The figures for moldings are based on longer lengths; the use of shorter lengths can slow a job down. Productivity figures for the installation of siding are always affected by the size of the exposed "lap". Smaller clapboards require more man-hours per square foot for installation.

Carefully examine ahead of time the unit of measure being used for each productivity figure, because certain items are often expressed in terms of two units of measure. All framing figures under "Rough Carpentry", for instance, are defined in terms of both thousand board feet and lineal feet. Be sure to check the unit designation whenever using this information, since each user has a preference. Units of measure must be consistent to make productivity data useful.

060 | Fasteners and Adhesives

060 500	Fasteners & Adhesives	CREW	MAKEUP	DAILY OUTPUT	MAN-HOURS	UNIT
512	**TIMBER CONNECTORS**					
0100	Connector plates, steel, with bolts, straight	2 Carp	2 Carpenters	75	.213	Ea.
0110	Tee	"	"	50	.320	Ea.
0200	Bolts, machine, sq. hd. with nut & washer, 1/2″ diameter, 4″ long	1 Carp	1 Carpenter	140	.057	Ea.
0300	7-1/2″ long			130	.062	Ea.
0500	3/4″ diameter, 7-1/2″ long			130	.062	Ea.
0600	15″ long			95	.084	Ea.
0800	Drilling bolt holes in timber, 1/2″ diameter			450	.018	Inch
0900	1″ diameter			350	.023	Inch
1100	Framing anchors, 2 or 3 dimensional, 10 gauge, no nails incl.			175	.046	Ea.
1300	Joist and beam hangers, 18 ga. galv., for 2″ x 4″ joist			175	.046	Ea.
1400	2″ x 6″ to 2″ x 10″ joist			165	.048	Ea.
1600	16 ga. galv., 3″ x 6″ to 3″ x 10″ joist			160	.050	Ea.
1700	3″ x 10″ to 3″ x 14″ joist			160	.050	Ea.
1800	4″ x 6″ to 4″ x 10″ joist			155	.052	Ea.
1900	4″ x 10″ to 4″ x 14″ joist			155	.052	Ea.
2000	2-2″ x 6″ to 2-2″ x 10″ joist			150	.053	Ea.
2100	2-2″ x 10″ to 2-2″ x 14″ joist			150	.053	Ea.
2300	3/16″ thick for 6″ x 8″ joist			145	.055	Ea.
2400	6″ x 10″ joist			140	.057	Ea.
2500	6″ x 12″ joist			135	.059	Ea.
2700	1/4″ thick, 6″ x 14″ joist			130	.062	Ea.
2800	Joist anchors, 1/4″ x 1-1/4″ x 18″			140	.057	Ea.
3200	Post framing, 16 ga. galv. for 4″ x 4″ base, 2 piece			130	.062	Ea.
3300	Cap			130	.062	Ea.
3500	Rafter anchors, 18 ga. galv., 1-1/2″ wide, 5-1/4″ long			145	.055	Ea.
3600	10-3/4″ long			145	.055	Ea.
3800	Shear plates, 2-5/8″ diameter			120	.067	Ea.
3900	4″ diameter			115	.070	Ea.
4000	Sill anchors, (embedded in concrete or block), 18-5/8″ long			115	.070	Ea.
4100	Spike grids, 4″ x 4″, flat or curved			120	.067	Ea.
4400	Split rings, 2-1/2″ diameter			120	.067	Ea.
4500	4″ diameter			110	.073	Ea.
4700	Strap ties, 16 ga., 1-3/8″ wide, 12″ long			180	.044	Ea.
4800	24″ long			160	.050	Ea.
5000	Toothed rings, 2-5/8″ or 4″ diameter			90	.089	Ea.
5200	Truss plates, nailed, 20 gauge, up to 32′ span	↓	↓	17	.471	Truss

061 | Rough Carpentry

061 100	Wood Framing	CREW	MAKEUP	DAILY OUTPUT	MAN-HOURS	UNIT
102	**BLOCKING**					
2600	Miscellaneous, to wood construction					
2620	2″ x 4″	F-1	1 Carpenter Power Tools	.17	47.060	M.B.F.
2660	2″ x 8″	"	"	.27	29.630	M.B.F.
2720	To steel construction					
2740	2″ x 4″	F-1	1 Carpenter Power Tools	.14	57.140	M.B.F.
2780	2″ x 8″	"	"	.21	38.100	M.B.F.

061 | Rough Carpentry

061 100 | Wood Framing

		Description	CREW	MAKEUP	DAILY OUTPUT	MAN-HOURS	UNIT
104	104	**BRACING** Let-in, with 1" x 6" boards, studs @ 16" O.C.	F-1	1 Carpenter Power Tools	1.50	5.330	C.L.F.
	0200	Studs @ 24" O.C.			2.30	3.480	C.L.F.
	106	**BRIDGING** Wood, for joists 16" O.C., 1" x 3"			1.30	6.150	C.Pr.
	0100	2" x 3" bridging	↓	↓	1.30	6.150	C.Pr.
	0300	Steel, galvanized, 18 ga., for 2" x 10" joists at 12" O.C.	1 Carp	1 Carpenter	1.30	6.150	C.Pr.
	0400	24" O.C.			1.40	5.710	C.Pr.
	0900	Compression type, 16" O.C., 2" x 8" joists			2	4.000	C.Pr.
	1000	2" x 12" joists	↓	↓	2	4.000	C.Pr.
	108	**FRAMING, LIGHT** Average for all light framing	F-2	2 Carpenters Power Tools	1.05	15.240	M.B.F.
	2300	Joists, fir, 2" x 4"			.85	18.820	M.B.F.
	3300	Mud sills, redwood, construction grade, 2" x 4"			.60	26.670	M.B.F.
	3400	Nailers, treated, 2" x 4" to 2" x 8" wood construction			.75	21.330	M.B.F.
	4300	Post, columns & girts, 4" x 4"			.52	30.770	M.B.F.
	5400	Roof cants, split 4" x 4"			6.50	2.460	C.L.F.
	5500	Split 6" x 6"			6	2.670	C.L.F.
	6100	Rough bucks, treated, for doors or windows, 2" x 6"			.40	40.000	M.B.F.
	6500	Sills, 4" x 4"			.78	20.510	M.B.F.
	6800	Sleepers on concrete, treated, 1" x 2"			.40	40.000	M.B.F.
	7300	Stair stringers, fir, 2" x 10"	↓	↓	.30	53.330	M.B.F.
	110	**FRAMING, BEAMS & GIRDERS**					
	1000	Single, 2" x 6"	F-2	2 Carpenters Power Tools	700	.023	L.F.
	1020	2" x 8"			650	.025	L.F.
	1040	2" x 10"			600	.027	L.F.
	1060	2" x 12"			550	.029	L.F.
	1080	2" x 14"			500	.032	L.F.
	1100	3" x 8"			550	.029	L.F.
	1120	3" x 10"			500	.032	L.F.
	1140	3" x 12"			450	.036	L.F.
	1160	3" x 14"	↓	↓	400	.040	L.F.
	1180	4" x 8"	F-3	4 Carpenters 1 Equip. Oper. (crane) 1 Hyd. Crane, 12 Ton Power Tools	1,000	.040	L.F.
	1200	4" x 10"			950	.042	L.F.
	1220	4" x 12"			900	.044	L.F.
	1240	4" x 14"	↓	↓	850	.047	L.F.
	2000	Double, 2" x 6"	F-2	2 Carpenters Power Tools	625	.026	L.F.
	2020	2" x 8"			600	.027	L.F.
	2040	2" x 10"			575	.028	L.F.
	2060	2" x 12"			550	.029	L.F.
	2080	2" x 14"		(	525	.030	L.F.
	3000	Triple, 2" x 6"			550	.029	L.F.
	3020	2" x 8"			525	.030	L.F.
	3040	2" x 10"			500	.032	L.F.
	3060	2" x 12"			475	.034	L.F.
	3080	2" x 14"	↓	↓	450	.036	L.F.
	112	**FRAMING, CEILINGS**					
	6000	Suspended, 2" x 3"	F-2	2 Carpenters Power Tools	1,000	.016	L.F.
	6050	2" x 4"			900	.018	L.F.
	6100	2" x 6"			800	.020	L.F.
	6150	2" x 8"	↓	↓	650	.025	L.F.

061 100	Wood Framing	CREW	MAKEUP	DAILY OUTPUT	MAN-HOURS	UNIT
114	**FRAMING, JOISTS**					
2000	Joists, 2″ x 4″	F-2	2 Carpenters / Power Tools	1,250	.013	L.F.
2100	2″ x 6″			1,250	.013	L.F.
2150	2″ x 8″			1,100	.015	L.F.
2200	2″ x 10″			900	.018	L.F.
2250	2″ x 12″			875	.018	L.F.
2300	2″ x 14″			770	.021	L.F.
2350	3″ x 6″			925	.017	L.F.
2400	3″ x 10″			780	.021	L.F.
2450	3″ x 12″			600	.027	L.F.
2500	4″ x 6″			800	.020	L.F.
2550	4″ x 10″			600	.027	L.F.
2600	4″ x 12″			450	.036	L.F.
2605	Sister joist, 2″ x 6″			800	.020	L.F.
2610	2″ x 8″			640	.025	L.F.
2615	2″ x 10″			535	.030	L.F.
2620	2″ x 12″	↓	↓	455	.035	L.F.
116	**FRAMING, MISCELLANEOUS**					
2000	Firestops, 2″ x 4″	F-2	2 Carpenters / Power Tools	780	.021	L.F.
2100	2″ x 6″			600	.027	L.F.
5000	Nailers, treated, wood construction, 2″ x 4″			800	.020	L.F.
5100	2″ x 6″			750	.021	L.F.
5120	2″ x 8″			700	.023	L.F.
5200	Steel construction, 2″ x 4″			750	.021	L.F.
5220	2″ x 6″			700	.023	L.F.
5240	2″ x 8″			650	.025	L.F.
7000	Rough bucks, treated, for doors or windows, 2″ x 6″			400	.040	L.F.
7100	2″ x 8″			380	.042	L.F.
8000	Stair stringers, 2″ x 10″			130	.123	L.F.
8100	2″ x 12″			130	.123	L.F.
8150	3″ x 10″			125	.128	L.F.
8200	3″ x 12″	↓	↓	125	.128	L.F.
118	**FRAMING, COLUMNS**					
0100	4″ x 4″	F-2	2 Carpenters / Power Tools	390	.041	L.F.
0150	4″ x 6″			275	.058	L.F.
0200	4″ x 8″			220	.073	L.F.
0250	6″ x 6″			215	.074	L.F.
0300	6″ x 8″			175	.091	L.F.
0350	6″ x 10″	↓	↓	150	.107	L.F.
120	**FRAMING, ROOFS**					
6070	Fascia boards, 2″ x 8″	F-2	2 Carpenters / Power Tools	.30	53.330	M.B.F.
6080	2″ x 10″			.30	53.330	M.B.F.
7000	Rafters, to 4 in 12 pitch, 2″ x 6″			1	16.000	M.B.F.
7060	2″ x 8″			1.26	12.700	M.B.F.
7300	Hip and valley rafters, 2″ x 6″			.76	21.050	M.B.F.
7360	2″ x 8″			.96	16.670	M.B.F.
7540	Hip and valley jacks, 2″ x 6″			.60	26.670	M.B.F.
7600	2″ x 8″			.65	24.620	M.B.F.
7800	Rafter tie, 1″ x 4″, #3			.27	59.260	M.B.F.
7820	Ridge board, #2 or better, 1″ x 6″			.30	53.330	M.B.F.
7840	1″ x 8″			.37	43.240	M.B.F.
7860	1″ x 10″			.42	38.100	M.B.F.
7880	2″ x 6″			.50	32.000	M.B.F.
7900	2″ x 8″	↓	↓	.60	26.670	M.B.F.

061 100	Wood Framing	CREW	MAKEUP	DAILY OUTPUT	MAN-HOURS	UNIT
120 7921	Framing roofs, ridge boards, #2 or better, 2" x 10"	F-2	2 Carpenters Power Tools	.66	24.240	M.B.F.
7940	Roof cants, split, 4" x 4"			.86	18.600	M.B.F.
7960	6" x 6"			1.80	8.890	M.B.F.
7980	Roof curbs, untreated, 2" x 6"			.52	30.770	M.B.F.
8000	2" x 12"			.80	20.000	M.B.F.
8020	Sister rafters, 2" x 6"			.80	20.000	M.B.F.
8040	2" x 8"			.85	18.820	M.B.F.
8060	2" x 10"			.89	17.980	M.B.F.
8080	2" x 12"	↓	↓	.91	17.580	M.B.F.
122	**FRAMING, SILLS**					
2000	Ledgers, nailed, 2" x 4"	F-2	2 Carpenters Power Tools	755	.021	L.F.
2050	2" x 6"			600	.027	L.F.
2100	Bolted, not including bolts, 3" x 6"			325	.049	L.F.
2150	3" x 12"			233	.069	L.F.
2600	Mud sills, redwood, construction grade, 2" x 4"			895	.018	L.F.
2620	2" x 6"			780	.021	L.F.
4000	Sills, 2" x 4"			600	.027	L.F.
4050	2" x 6"			550	.029	L.F.
4080	2" x 8"			500	.032	L.F.
4200	Treated, 2" x 4"			550	.029	L.F.
4220	2" x 6"			500	.032	L.F.
4240	2" x 8"			450	.036	L.F.
4400	4" x 4"			450	.036	L.F.
4420	4" x 6"			350	.046	L.F.
4460	4" x 8"			300	.053	L.F.
4480	4" x 10"	↓	↓	260	.062	L.F.
124	**FRAMING, SLEEPERS**					
0100	On concrete, treated, 1" x 2"	F-2	2 Carpenters Power Tools	2,350	.007	L.F.
0150	1" x 3"			2,000	.008	L.F.
0200	2" x 4"			1,500	.011	L.F.
0250	2" x 6"	↓	↓	1,300	.012	L.F.
126	**FRAMING, SOFFITS & CANOPIES**					
1000	Canopy or soffit framing , 1" x 4"	F-2	2 Carpenters Power Tools	900	.018	L.F.
1040	1" x 8"			750	.021	L.F.
1100	2" x 4"			620	.026	L.F.
1140	2" x 8"			500	.032	L.F.
1200	3" x 4"			500	.032	L.F.
1240	3" x 10"	↓	↓	300	.053	L.F.
128	**FRAMING, WALLS**					
2000	Headers over openings, 2" x 6"	F-2	2 Carpenters Power Tools	360	.044	L.F.
2050	2" x 8"			340	.047	L.F.
2110	2" x 10"			320	.050	L.F.
2150	2" x 12"			300	.053	L.F.
2200	4" x 12"			190	.084	L.F.
2250	6" x 12"			140	.114	L.F.
5000	Plates, untreated, 2" x 3"			850	.019	L.F.
5020	2" x 4"			800	.020	L.F.
5040	2" x 6"			750	.021	L.F.
5120	Studs, 8' high wall, 2" x 3"			1,200	.013	L.F.
5140	2" x 4"			1,100	.015	L.F.
5160	2" x 6"			1,000	.016	L.F.
5180	3" x 4"	↓	↓	800	.020	L.F.

061 | Rough Carpentry

061 100 | Wood Framing

		CREW	MAKEUP	DAILY OUTPUT	MAN-HOURS	UNIT
130	**FURRING** Wood strips, on walls, 1" x 2", on wood	1 Carp	1 Carpenter	550	.015	L.F.
0300	On masonry			495	.016	L.F.
0400	On concrete			260	.031	L.F.
0600	1" x 3", wood strips, on walls, on wood			550	.015	L.F.
0700	On masonry			495	.016	L.F.
0800	On concrete			260	.031	L.F.
0850	1" x 3", wood strips, on ceilings, on wood			350	.023	L.F.
0900	On masonry			320	.025	L.F.
0950	On concrete			210	.038	L.F.
132	**GROUNDS** For casework, 1" x 2" wood strips, on wood			330	.024	L.F.
0100	On masonry			285	.028	L.F.
0200	On concrete			250	.032	L.F.
0400	For plaster, 3/4" deep, on wood			450	.018	L.F.
0500	On masonry			225	.036	L.F.
0600	On concrete			175	.046	L.F.
0700	On metal lath	↓	↓	200	.040	L.F.
138	**PARTITIONS** Wood stud with single bottom plate and					
0020	double top plate, no waste, std. & better lumber					
0180	2" x 4" studs, 8' high, studs 12" O.C.	F-2	2 Carpenters Power Tools	80	.200	L.F.
0200	16" O.C.			100	.160	L.F.
0300	24" O.C.			125	.128	L.F.
0380	10' high, studs 12" O.C.			80	.200	L.F.
0400	16" O.C.			100	.160	L.F.
0500	24" O.C.			125	.128	L.F.
0580	12' high, studs 12" O.C.			65	.246	L.F.
0600	16" O.C.			80	.200	L.F.
0700	24" O.C.			100	.160	L.F.
0780	2" x 6" studs, 8' high, studs 12" O.C.			70	.229	L.F.
0800	16" O.C.			90	.178	L.F.
0900	24" O.C.			115	.139	L.F.
0980	10' high, studs 12" O.C.			70	.229	L.F.
1000	16" O.C.			90	.178	L.F.
1100	24" O.C.			115	.139	L.F.
1180	12' high, studs 12" O.C.			55	.291	L.F.
1200	16" O.C.			70	.229	L.F.
1300	24" O.C.			90	.178	L.F.
1400	For horizontal blocking, 2" x 4", add			600	.027	L.F.
1500	2" x 6", add			600	.027	L.F.
1600	For openings, add	↓	↓	250	.064	L.F.

061 150 | Sheathing

		CREW	MAKEUP	DAILY OUTPUT	MAN-HOURS	UNIT
154	**SHEATHING** Plywood on roof, CDX					
0030	5/16" thick	F-2	2 Carpenters Power Tools	1,600	.010	S.F.
0050	3/8" thick			1,525	.010	S.F.
0100	1/2" thick			1,400	.011	S.F.
0200	5/8" thick			1,300	.012	S.F.
0300	3/4" thick			1,200	.013	S.F.
0500	Plywood on walls with exterior CDX, 3/8" thick			1,200	.013	S.F.
0600	1/2" thick			1,125	.014	S.F.
0700	5/8" thick			1,050	.015	S.F.
0800	3/4" thick			975	.016	S.F.
1400	With boards, on roof 1" x 6" boards, laid horizontal			725	.022	S.F.
1500	Laid diagonal			650	.025	S.F.
1700	1" x 8" boards, laid horizontal			875	.018	S.F.
1800	Laid diagonal			725	.022	S.F.
2400	Boards on walls, 1" x 6" boards, laid regular	↓	↓	650	.025	S.F.

130

220

061 150 | Sheathing

			CREW	MAKEUP	DAILY OUTPUT	MAN-HOURS	UNIT
154	2501	Sheathing, boards on walls, 1" x 6" boards, laid diagonal	F-2	2 Carpenters Power Tools	585	.027	S.F.
	2700	1" x 8" boards, laid regular			765	.021	S.F.
	2800	Laid diagonal			650	.025	S.F.
	2850	Gypsum, weatherproof, 1/2" thick			1,050	.015	S.F.
	2900	Sealed, 4/10" thick			1,100	.015	S.F.
	3000	Wood fiber, regular, no vapor barrier, 1/2" thick			1,200	.013	S.F.
	3100	5/8" thick			1,200	.013	S.F.
	3300	No vapor barrier, in colors, 1/2" thick			1,200	.013	S.F.
	3400	5/8" thick			1,200	.013	S.F.
	3600	With vapor barrier one side, white, 1/2" thick			1,200	.013	S.F.
	3700	Vapor barrier 2 sides			1,200	.013	S.F.
	3800	Asphalt impregnated, 25/32" thick			1,200	.013	S.F.
	3850	Intermediate, 1/2" thick	↓	↓	1,200	.013	S.F.

061 160 | Subfloor

			CREW	MAKEUP	DAILY OUTPUT	MAN-HOURS	UNIT
164		SUBFLOOR Plywood, CDX, 1/2" thick	F-2	2 Carpenters Power Tools	1,500	.011	SF Flr.
	0100	5/8" thick			1,350	.012	SF Flr.
	0200	3/4" thick			1,250	.013	SF Flr.
	0300	1-1/8" thick, 2-4-1 including underlayment			1,050	.015	SF Flr.
	0500	With boards, 1" x 10" S4S, laid regular			1,100	.015	SF Flr.
	0600	Laid diagonal			900	.018	SF Flr.
	0800	1" x 8" S4S, laid regular			1,000	.016	SF Flr.
	0900	Laid diagonal			850	.019	SF Flr.
	1100	Wood fiber, T&G, 2' x 8' planks, 1" thick			1,000	.016	SF Flr.
	1200	1-3/8" thick			900	.018	SF Flr.
168		UNDERLAYMENT Plywood, underlayment grade, 3/8" thick			1,500	.011	SF Flr.
	0100	1/2" thick			1,450	.011	SF Flr.
	0200	5/8" thick			1,400	.011	SF Flr.
	0300	3/4" thick			1,300	.012	SF Flr.
	0500	Particle board, 3/8" thick			1,500	.011	SF Flr.
	0600	1/2" thick			1,450	.011	SF Flr.
	0800	5/8" thick			1,400	.011	SF Flr.
	0900	3/4" thick			1,300	.012	SF Flr.
	1100	Hardboard, underlayment grade, 4' x 4', .215" thick	↓	↓	1,500	.011	SF Flr.

061 200 | Structural Panels

			CREW	MAKEUP	DAILY OUTPUT	MAN-HOURS	UNIT
208		STRESSED SKIN PLYWOOD ROOF PANELS 3/8" group 1 top					
	0020	skin, 3/8" exterior AD bottom skin					
	0030	1150f stringers, 4' x 8' panels					
	0100	4-1/4" deep	F-3	4 Carpenters 1 Equip. Oper. (crane) 1 Hyd. Crane, 12 Ton Power Tools	2,075	.019	S.F.Roof
	0200	6-1/8" deep			1,725	.023	S.F.Roof
	0300	8-1/8" deep			1,475	.027	S.F.Roof
	0500	3/8" top skin, no bottom skin, 5-3/4" deep			1,725	.023	S.F.Roof
	0600	7-3/4" deep	↓	↓	1,475	.027	S.F.Roof
	2000	Curved roof panels, 3/8" structural 1 top skin,					
	2010	3/8" exterior AC bottom skin, laminated ribs					
	2200	8' radius, 2-1/4" deep, tie rods not req'd.	F-3	4 Carpenters 1 Equip. Oper. (crane) 1 Hyd. Crane, 12 Ton Power Tools	1,150	.035	SF Flr.
	2400	10' radius, 1-1/2" deep, tie rods are included			950	.042	SF Flr.
	2600	10' radius, 3-3/8" deep, tie rods not req'd.			1,150	.035	SF Flr.
	2800	12' radius, 2" deep, tie rods are included	↓	↓	950	.042	SF Flr.

061 200 | Structural Panels

		CREW	MAKEUP	DAILY OUTPUT	MAN-HOURS	UNIT
208 3001	Curved roof panels, 12' radius, 4-1/2" deep, no tie rods	F-3	4 Carpenters 1 Equip. Oper. (crane) 1 Hyd. Crane, 12 Ton Power Tools	1,150	.035	SF Flr.
4000 4010	Folded plate roofs, structural 1 top skin with intermediate rafters and end chord. Cost of tie rods included					
4200	Slope 7 in 12, 4' fold, 2" thick, 32' span	F-3	4 Carpenters 1 Equip. Oper. (crane) 1 Hyd. Crane, 12 Ton Power Tools	850	.047	SF Flr.
4400	Slope 8-1/2 in 12, 5' fold, 4" thick, 56' span			950	.042	SF Flr.
4600	Slope 10 in 12, 8' fold, 4" thick, 52' span			950	.042	SF Flr.
4800	Slope 10 in 12, 8' fold, 4" thick, 72' span	↓	↓	1,025	.039	SF Flr.
6000	Box beams, structural 1 web					
6200	24" deep, 2-2" x 4" flanges, 2 webs @ 3/8"	F-3	4 Carpenters 1 Equip. Oper. (crane) 1 Hyd. Crane, 12 Ton Power Tools	295	.136	L.F.
6400	24" deep, 3-2" x 4" flanges, 2 webs @ 1/2"			260	.154	L.F.
6600	48" deep, 3-2" x 6" flanges, 2 webs @ 3/4"	↓	↓	140	.286	L.F.
6800	48" deep, 6-2" x 6" flanges, 4 webs @ 3/8",					
6810	including 2 interior webs	F-3	4 Carpenters 1 Equip. Oper. (crane) 1 Hyd. Crane, 12 Ton Power Tools	115	.348	L.F.

061 250 | Wood Decking

		CREW	MAKEUP	DAILY OUTPUT	MAN-HOURS	UNIT
258	ROOF DECKS For laminated decks, see division 061-808					
0400	Cedar planks, 3.65 B.F. per S.F., 3" thick	F-2	2 Carpenters Power Tools	320	.050	S.F.
0500	4.65 B.F. per S.F., 4" thick			250	.064	S.F.
0700	Douglas fir, 3" thick			320	.050	S.F.
0800	4" thick			250	.064	S.F.
1000	Hemlock, 3" thick			320	.050	S.F.
1100	4" thick			250	.064	S.F.
1300	Western white spruce, 3" thick			320	.050	S.F.
1400	4" thick	↓	↓	250	.064	S.F.

061 280 | Mineral Fbr Cem Panel

		CREW	MAKEUP	DAILY OUTPUT	MAN-HOURS	UNIT
281 0100	MINERAL FIBER CEMENT PANELS Including panels, fasteners, accessories, trim & sealant					
0130	Architectural, textured finish, 1/8" thick, minimum	G-3	2 Sheet Metal Workers 2 Building Laborers Power Tools	500	.064	S.F.
0140	Maximum			500	.064	S.F.
0150	1/4" thick, minimum			500	.064	S.F.
0200	Maximum			500	.064	S.F.
0250	3/8" thick, minimum			500	.064	S.F.
0300	Maximum			500	.064	S.F.
0350	5/8" thick, minimum			300	.107	S.F.
0400	Maximum			300	.107	S.F.
2000	Flat sheets, 1/8" thick			1,200	.027	S.F.
2100	1/4" thick			1,020	.031	S.F.
2200	3/8" thick			885	.036	S.F.
2300	5/8" thick			795	.040	S.F.
3000	Glasweld, mineral enamel coating, 1/8" thick			600	.053	S.F.
3100	1/4" thick	↓	↓	322	.099	S.F.
4001						

061 | Rough Carpentry

061 280 | Mineral Fbr Cem Panel

		CREW	MAKEUP	DAILY OUTPUT	MAN-HOURS	UNIT
281 4101	Sandwich panel, Glasweld face & back, 1" thick perlite core	G-3	2 Sheet Metal Workers	322	.099	S.F.
			2 Building Laborers			
			Power Tools			
4200	Polyurethane core			322	.099	S.F.
4500	2" thick, perlite core			322	.099	S.F.
4600	Polyurethane core	↓	↓	322	.099	S.F.

061 300 | Heavy Timber Const

		CREW	MAKEUP	DAILY OUTPUT	MAN-HOURS	UNIT
304	FRAMING, HEAVY Mill timber, beams, single 6" x 10"	F-2	2 Carpenters	1.10	14.550	M.B.F.
			Power Tools			
0100	Single 8" x 16"			1.20	13.330	M.B.F.
0200	Built from 2" lumber, multiple 2" x 14"			.90	17.780	M.B.F.
0210	Built from 3" lumber, multiple 3" x 6"			.70	22.860	M.B.F.
0220	Multiple 3" x 8"			.80	20.000	M.B.F.
0230	Multiple 3" x 10"			.90	17.780	M.B.F.
0240	Multiple 3" x 12"			1	16.000	M.B.F.
0250	Built from 4" lumber, multiple 4" x 6"			.80	20.000	M.B.F.
0260	Multiple 4" x 8"			.90	17.780	M.B.F.
0270	Multiple 4" x 10"			1	16.000	M.B.F.
0280	Multiple 4" x 12"			1.10	14.550	M.B.F.
0290	Columns, structural grade, 1500f, 4" x 4"			.60	26.670	M.B.F.
0300	6" x 6"			.65	24.620	M.B.F.
0400	8" x 8"			.70	22.860	M.B.F.
0500	10" x 10"			.75	21.330	M.B.F.
0600	12" x 12"			.80	20.000	M.B.F.
0800	Floor planks, 2" thick, T & G, 2" x 6"			1.05	15.240	M.B.F.
0900	2" x 10"			1.10	14.550	M.B.F.
1100	3" thick, 3" x 6"			1.05	15.240	M.B.F.
1200	3" x 10"			1.10	14.550	M.B.F.
1400	Girders, structural grade, 12" x 12"			.80	20.000	M.B.F.
1500	10" x 16"			1	16.000	M.B.F.
2300	Roof purlins, 4" thick, structural grade			1.05	15.240	M.B.F.
2500	Roof trusses, add timber connectors, division 060-512	↓	↓	.45	35.560	M.B.F.

061 500 | Wood/Metal Systems

		CREW	MAKEUP	DAILY OUTPUT	MAN-HOURS	UNIT
508 0100	STRUCTURAL JOISTS Fabricated "I" joists with wood flanges, Plywood webs, incl. bridging & blocking, panels 24" O.C.					
1200	15' to 24' span, 50 psf live load	F-5	1 Carpenter Foreman	2,400	.013	SF Flr.
			3 Carpenters			
			Power Tools			
1300	55 psf live load			2,250	.014	SF Flr.
1400	24' to 30' span, 45 psf live load			2,600	.012	SF Flr.
1500	55 psf live load	↓	↓	2,400	.013	SF Flr.
1600	Tubular steel open webs, 45 psf, 24" O.C., 40' span	F-3	4 Carpenters	6,250	.006	SF Flr.
			1 Equip. Oper. (crane)			
			1 Hyd. Crane, 12 Ton			
			Power Tools			
1700	55' span			5,150	.008	SF Flr.
1800	70' span			9,250	.004	SF Flr.
1900	85 psf live load, 26' span	↓	↓	2,300	.017	SF Flr.

061 800 | Glued Laminated Const

		CREW	MAKEUP	DAILY OUTPUT	MAN-HOURS	UNIT
804	LAMINATED FRAMING Not including decking					
0200	Roof beams, 20' clear span, beams 8' O.C.	F-3	4 Carpenters	2,560	.016	SF Flr.
			1 Equip. Oper. (crane)			
			1 Hyd. Crane, 12 Ton			
			Power Tools			
0300	Beams 16' O.C.	"	"	3,200	.013	SF Flr.

061 800 | Glued Laminated Const

		CREW	MAKEUP	DAILY OUTPUT	MAN-HOURS	UNIT
804	0501	Laminated framing, roof beams, 40' clear span, beams 8' O.C.	F-3	4 Carpenters 1 Equip. Oper. (crane) 1 Hyd. Crane, 12 Ton Power Tools	3,200	.013	SF Flr.
0600	Beams 16' O.C.	"	"	3,840	.010	SF Flr.
0800	60' clear span, beams 8' O.C.	F-4	4 Carpenters 1 Equip. Oper. (crane) 1 Equip. Oper. Oiler 1 Hyd. Crane, 55 Ton Power Tools	2,880	.017	SF Flr.
0900	Beams 16' O.C.	"	"	3,840	.013	SF Flr.
1100	Tudor arches, 30' to 40' clear span, frames 8' O.C.	F-3	4 Carpenters 1 Equip. Oper. (crane) 1 Hyd. Crane, 12 Ton Power Tools	1,680	.024	SF Flr.
1200	Frames 16' O.C.	"	"	2,240	.018	SF Flr.
1400	50' to 60' clear span, frames 8' O.C.	F-4	4 Carpenters 1 Equip. Oper. (crane) 1 Equip. Oper. Oiler 1 Hyd. Crane, 55 Ton Power Tools	2,200	.022	SF Flr.
1500	Frames 16' O.C.			2,640	.018	SF Flr.
1700	Radial arches, 60' clear span, frames 8' O.C.			1,920	.025	SF Flr.
1800	Frames 16' O.C.			2,880	.017	SF Flr.
2000	100' clear span, frames 8' O.C.			1,600	.030	SF Flr.
2100	Frames 16' O.C.			2,400	.020	SF Flr.
2300	120' clear span, frames 8' O.C.			1,440	.033	SF Flr.
2400	Frames 16' O.C.	↓	↓	1,920	.025	SF Flr.
2600	Bowstring trusses, 20' O.C., 40' clear span	F-3	4 Carpenters 1 Equip. Oper. (crane) 1 Hyd. Crane, 12 Ton Power Tools	2,400	.017	SF Flr.
2700	60' clear span	F-4	4 Carpenters 1 Equip. Oper. (crane) 1 Equip. Oper. Oiler 1 Hyd. Crane, 55 Ton Power Tools	3,600	.013	SF Flr.
2800	100' clear span			4,000	.012	SF Flr.
2900	120' clear span	↓	↓	3,600	.013	SF Flr.
4300	Alternate pricing method: (use nominal footage of					
4310	components). Straight beams, camber less than 6"	F-3	4 Carpenters 1 Equip. Oper. (crane) 1 Hyd. Crane, 12 Ton Power Tools	3.50	11.430	M.B.F.
4400	Columns, including hardware			2	20.000	M.B.F.
4600	Curved members, radius over 32'			2.50	16.000	M.B.F.
4700	Radius 10' to 32'	↓	↓	3	13.330	M.B.F.
808	**LAMINATED ROOF DECK** Pine or hemlock, 3" thick	F-2	2 Carpenters Power Tools	425	.038	S.F.
0100	4" thick			325	.049	S.F.
0300	Cedar, 3" thick			425	.038	S.F.
0400	4" thick			325	.049	S.F.
0600	Fir, 3" thick			425	.038	S.F.
0700	4" thick	↓	↓	325	.049	S.F.

061 | Rough Carpentry

061 900 | Wood Trusses

		Description	CREW	MAKEUP	DAILY OUTPUT	MAN-HOURS	UNIT
908	908	ROOF TRUSSES For timber connectors, see div. 060-512					
	0100	Fink (W) or King post type, 2'-0" O.C.					
	0200	Metal plate connected, 4 in 12 slope					
	0210	24' to 29' span	F-3	4 Carpenters	3,000	.013	SF Flr.
				1 Equip. Oper. (crane)			
				1 Hyd. Crane, 12 Ton			
				Power Tools			
	0300	30' to 43' span			3,000	.013	SF Flr.
	0400	44' to 60' span			3,000	.013	SF Flr.
	0800	Flat wood truss 16' to 29' span	↓	↓	3,000	.013	SF Flr.

062 | Finish Carpentry

062 200 | Millwork Moldings

	Description	CREW	MAKEUP	DAILY OUTPUT	MAN-HOURS	UNIT
208	MOLDINGS, BASE					
0500	Base, stock pine, 9/16" x 3-1/2"	1 Carp	1 Carpenter	240	.033	L.F.
0550	9/16" x 4-1/2"	"	"	200	.040	L.F.
212	MOLDINGS, CASINGS					
0090	Apron, stock pine, 5/8" x 2"	1 Carp	1 Carpenter	250	.032	L.F.
0110	5/8" x 3-1/2"			220	.036	L.F.
0300	Band, stock pine, 11/16" x 1-1/8"			270	.030	L.F.
0350	11/16" x 1-3/4"			250	.032	L.F.
0700	Casing, stock pine, 11/16" x 2-1/2"			240	.033	L.F.
0750	11/16" x 3-1/2"	↓	↓	215	.037	L.F.
216	MOLDINGS, CEILINGS					
0600	Bed, stock pine, 9/16" x 1-3/4"	1 Carp	1 Carpenter	270	.030	L.F.
0650	9/16" x 2"			240	.033	L.F.
1200	Cornice molding, stock pine, 9/16" x 1-3/4"			330	.024	L.F.
1300	9/16" x 2-1/4"			300	.027	L.F.
2400	Cove scotia, stock pine, 9/16" x 1-3/4"			270	.030	L.F.
2500	11/16" x 2-3/4"			255	.031	L.F.
2600	Crown, stock pine, 9/16" x 3-5/8"			250	.032	L.F.
2700	11/16" x 4-5/8"	↓	↓	220	.036	L.F.
220	MOLDINGS, EXTERIOR					
1500	Cornice, boards, pine, 1" x 2"	1 Carp	1 Carpenter	330	.024	L.F.
1600	1" x 4"			250	.032	L.F.
1700	1" x 6"			200	.040	L.F.
1800	1" x 8"			200	.040	L.F.
1900	1" x 10"			180	.044	L.F.
2000	1" x 12"			180	.044	L.F.
2200	Three piece, built-up, pine, minimum			80	.100	L.F.
2300	Maximum			65	.123	L.F.
3000	Trim, exterior, sterling pine, corner board, 1" x 4"			200	.040	L.F.
3100	1" x 6"			200	.040	L.F.
3200	2" x 6"			165	.048	L.F.
3300	2" x 8"			165	.048	L.F.
3350	Fascia, 1" x 6"			250	.032	L.F.
3370	1" x 8"			225	.036	L.F.
3400	Moldings, back band			250	.032	L.F.
3500	Casing			250	.032	L.F.
3600	Crown			250	.032	L.F.
3700	Porch rail with balusters	↓	↓	22	.364	L.F.

062 200 | Millwork Moldings

		Description	CREW	MAKEUP	DAILY OUTPUT	MAN-HOURS	UNIT
220	3801	Moldings, trim, sterling pine, screen	1 Carp	1 Carpenter	395	.020	L.F.
	4100	Verge board, sterling pine, 1″ x 4″			200	.040	L.F.
	4200	1″ x 6″			200	.040	L.F.
	4300	2″ x 6″			165	.048	L.F.
	4400	2″ x 8″	↓	↓	165	.048	L.F.
224		**MOLDINGS, TRIM**					
	0200	Astragal, stock pine, 11/16″ x 1-3/4″	1 Carp	1 Carpenter	255	.031	L.F.
	0250	1-5/16″ x 2-3/16″			240	.033	L.F.
	0800	Chair rail, stock pine, 5/8″ x 2-1/2″			270	.030	L.F.
	0900	5/8″ x 3-1/2″			240	.033	L.F.
	1000	Closet pole, stock pine, 1-1/8″ diameter			200	.040	L.F.
	1100	Fir, 1-5/8″ diameter			200	.040	L.F.
	3300	Half round, stock pine, 1/4″ x 1/2″			270	.030	L.F.
	3350	1/2″ x 1″	↓	↓	255	.031	L.F.
	3400	Handrail, fir, single piece, stock, hardware not included					
	3450	1-1/2″ x 1-3/4″	1 Carp	1 Carpenter	80	.100	L.F.
	3470	Pine, 1-1/2″ x 1-3/4″			80	.100	L.F.
	3500	1-1/2″ x 2-1/2″			76	.105	L.F.
	3600	Lattice, stock pine, 1/4″ x 1-1/8″			270	.030	L.F.
	3700	1/4″ x 1-3/4″			250	.032	L.F.
	3800	Miscellaneous, custom, pine or cedar, 1″ x 1″			270	.030	L.F.
	3900	Nominal 1″ x 3″			240	.033	L.F.
	4100	Birch or oak, custom, nominal 1″ x 1″			240	.033	L.F.
	4200	Nominal 1″ x 3″			215	.037	L.F.
	4400	Walnut, custom, nominal 1″ x 1″			215	.037	L.F.
	4500	Nominal 1″ x 3″			200	.040	L.F.
	4700	Teak, custom, nominal 1″ x 1″			215	.037	L.F.
	4800	Nominal 1″ x 3″			200	.040	L.F.
	4900	Quarter round, stock pine, 1/4″ x 1/4″			275	.029	L.F.
	4950	3/4″ x 3/4″			255	.031	L.F.
	5600	Wainscot moldings, 1-1/8″ x 9/16″, 2′ high, minimum			76	.105	S.F.
	5700	Maximum	↓	↓	65	.123	S.F.
228		**MOLDINGS, WINDOW AND DOOR**					
	2800	Door moldings, stock, decorative, 1-1/8″ wide, plain	1 Carp	1 Carpenter	17	.471	Set
	2900	Detailed	″	″	17	.471	Set
	3100	Door trim, interior, including headers,					
	3150	stops and casings, 2 sides, pine, 2-1/2″ wide	1 Carp	1 Carpenter	5.90	1.360	Opng.
	3170	4-1/2″ wide			5.30	1.510	Opng.
	3200	Glass beads, stock pine, 1/4″ x 11/16″			285	.028	L.F.
	3250	3/8″ x 1/2″			275	.029	L.F.
	3270	3/8″ x 7/8″			270	.030	L.F.
	4850	Parting bead, stock pine, 3/8″ x 3/4″			275	.029	L.F.
	4870	1/2″ x 3/4″			255	.031	L.F.
	5000	Stool caps, stock pine, 11/16″ x 3-1/2″			200	.040	L.F.
	5100	1-1/16″ x 3-1/4″			150	.053	L.F.
	5300	Threshold, oak, 3′ long, inside, 5/8″ x 3-5/8″			32	.250	Ea.
	5400	Outside, 1-1/2″ x 7-5/8″	↓	↓	16	.500	Ea.
	5900	Window trim sets , including casings, header, stops,					
	5910	stool and apron, 2-1/2″ wide, minimum	1 Carp	1 Carpenter	13	.615	Opng.
	5950	Average			10	.800	Opng.
	6000	Maximum	↓	↓	6	1.330	Opng.

062 | Finish Carpentry

062 300 | Shelving

		Description	CREW	MAKEUP	DAILY OUTPUT	MAN-HOURS	UNIT
304	304	SHELVING Pine, clear grade, no edge band, 1" x 8"	F-1	1 Carpenter Power Tools	115	.070	L.F.
	0100	1" x 10"			110	.073	L.F.
	0200	1" x 12"			105	.076	L.F.
	0600	Plywood, 3/4" thick with lumber edge, 12" wide			75	.107	L.F.
	0700	24" wide			70	.114	L.F.
	0900	Bookcase, pine, clear grade, 8" shelves, 12" O.C.			70	.114	S.F.
	1000	12" wide shelves			65	.123	S.F.
	1200	Adjustable closet rod and shelf, 12" wide, 3' long			20	.400	Ea.
	1300	8' long			15	.533	Ea.
	1500	Prefinished shelves with supports, stock, 8" wide			75	.107	L.F.
	1600	10" wide			70	.114	L.F.

062 400 | Plastic Laminate

	Description	CREW	MAKEUP	DAILY OUTPUT	MAN-HOURS	UNIT
404	CONVECTOR COVERS Laminated plastic on 3/4"					
0020	thick particle board, 12" wide, minimum	1 Carp	1 Carpenter	16	.500	L.F.
0050	Average			14	.571	L.F.
0100	Maximum			12	.667	L.F.
0300	Add to above for grille, minimum			150	.053	S.F.
0400	Maximum			75	.107	S.F.
412	TOPS Counter and table, plastic laminate					
1000	Counter top, 24" wide, 1-1/2" thick edging					
1500	Plastic laminate edging, minimum	1 Carp	1 Carpenter	25	.320	L.F.
1520	Average			24	.333	L.F.
1540	Maximum			22	.364	L.F.
2500	Hardwood edging, minimum			20	.400	L.F.
2520	Average			18	.444	L.F.
2540	Maximum			16	.500	L.F.
2600	Backsplash, add to above, minimum			36	.222	L.F.
2620	Average			35	.229	L.F.
2640	Maximum			34	.235	L.F.
2900	Postformed backsplash, add to above					
2920	Minimum	1 Carp	1 Carpenter	21	.381	L.F.
2940	Average			20	.400	L.F.
2960	Maximum			19	.421	L.F.
3500	Well openings (for typewriters etc.)			2.50	3.200	Ea.
3900	Cutouts for sinks, lavatories			12	.667	Ea.
5000	Table tops, 1-1/2" thick, plastic laminate edge					
5200	24" x 24", minimum	1 Carp	1 Carpenter	15	.533	Ea.
5220	Maximum			14	.571	Ea.
5240	24" x 48" minimum			8	1.000	Ea.
5260	Maximum			7.50	1.070	Ea.
5500	30" x 30" minimum			10	.800	Ea.
5520	Maximum			9	.889	Ea.
5540	30" x 48", minimum			8	1.000	Ea.
5560	Maximum			7.50	1.070	Ea.
5580	30" x 60", minimum			7	1.140	Ea.
5600	Maximum			6.50	1.230	Ea.
5700	30" x 72", minimum			6	1.330	Ea.
5720	Maximum			5.50	1.450	Ea.
6000	Table tops, 1-1/2" thick, hardwood edging					
6200	24" x 24", minimum	1 Carp	1 Carpenter	13.50	.593	Ea.
6220	Maximum			12.50	.640	Ea.
6300	24" x 48", minimum			7	1.140	Ea.
6320	Maximum			6.50	1.230	Ea.
6800	30" x 30", minimum			8.80	.909	Ea.
6820	Maximum			7.80	1.030	Ea.
6900	30" x 48", minimum			7	1.140	Ea.

062 | Finish Carpentry

062 400 | Plastic Laminate

		CREW	MAKEUP	DAILY OUTPUT	MAN-HOURS	UNIT
412 6921	Table tops, 1-1/2" thick, hardboard edging, 30" x 48", maximum	1 Carp	1 Carpenter	6.50	1.230	Ea.
7000	30" x 60", minimum			6	1.330	Ea.
7020	Maximum			5.50	1.450	Ea.
7100	30" x 72", minimum			5.20	1.540	Ea.
7120	Maximum	↓	↓	5	1.600	Ea.

062 500 | Prefin Wood Paneling

		CREW	MAKEUP	DAILY OUTPUT	MAN-HOURS	UNIT
504	PANELING, PLYWOOD					
2400	Plywood, prefinished, 1/4" thick, 4' x 8' sheets					
2410	with vertical grooves. Birch faced, minimum	F-2	2 Carpenters Power Tools	500	.032	S.F.
2420	Average			420	.038	S.F.
2430	Maximum			350	.046	S.F.
2600	Mahogany, African			400	.040	S.F.
2700	Philippine (Lauan)			500	.032	S.F.
2900	Oak or Cherry, minimum			500	.032	S.F.
3000	Maximum			400	.040	S.F.
3200	Rosewood			320	.050	S.F.
3400	Teak			400	.040	S.F.
3600	Chestnut			375	.043	S.F.
3800	Pecan			400	.040	S.F.
3900	Walnut, minimum			500	.032	S.F.
3950	Maximum			400	.040	S.F.
4000	Plywood, prefinished, 3/4" thick, stock grades, minimum			320	.050	S.F.
4100	Maximum			224	.071	S.F.
4300	Architectural grade, minimum			224	.071	S.F.
4400	Maximum			160	.100	S.F.
4600	Plywood, "A" face, birch, V.C., 1/2" thick, natural			450	.036	S.F.
4700	Select			450	.036	S.F.
4900	Veneer core, 3/4" thick, natural			320	.050	S.F.
5000	Select			320	.050	S.F.
5200	Lumber core, 3/4" thick, natural			320	.050	S.F.
5500	Plywood, knotty pine, 1/4" thick, A2 grade			450	.036	S.F.
5600	A3 grade			450	.036	S.F.
5800	3/4" thick, veneer core, A2 grade			320	.050	S.F.
5900	A3 grade			320	.050	S.F.
6100	Aromatic cedar, 1/4" thick, plywood			400	.040	S.F.
6200	1/4" thick, particle board	↓	↓	400	.040	S.F.

062 550 | Prefin Hardboard Panel

		CREW	MAKEUP	DAILY OUTPUT	MAN-HOURS	UNIT
554	PANELING, HARDBOARD					
0050	Not incl. furring or trim, hardboard, tempered, 1/8" thick	F-2	2 Carpenters Power Tools	500	.032	S.F.
0100	1/4" thick			500	.032	S.F.
0300	Tempered pegboard, 1/8" thick			500	.032	S.F.
0400	1/4" thick			500	.032	S.F.
0600	Untempered hardboard, natural finish, 1/8" thick			500	.032	S.F.
0700	1/4" thick			500	.032	S.F.
0900	Untempered pegboard, 1/8" thick			500	.032	S.F.
1000	1/4" thick			500	.032	S.F.
1200	Plastic faced hardboard, 1/8" thick			500	.032	S.F.
1300	1/4" thick			500	.032	S.F.
1500	Plastic faced pegboard, 1/8" thick			500	.032	S.F.
1600	1/4" thick			500	.032	S.F.
1800	Wood grained, plain or grooved, 1/4" thick, minimum			500	.032	S.F.
1900	Maximum			425	.038	S.F.
2100	Moldings for hardboard, wood or aluminum, minimum			500	.032	L.F.
2200	Maximum	↓	↓	425	.038	L.F.

062 | Finish Carpentry

062 600 | Board Paneling

604

		CREW	MAKEUP	DAILY OUTPUT	MAN-HOURS	UNIT
604	PANELING, BOARDS					
6400	Wood board paneling, 3/4" thick, knotty pine	F-2	2 Carpenters Power Tools	300	.053	S.F.
6500	Rough sawn cedar			300	.053	S.F.
6700	Redwood, clear, 1" x 4" boards			300	.053	S.F.
6900	Aromatic cedar, closet lining, boards			275	.058	S.F.

062 700 | Misc Finish Carpentry

		CREW	MAKEUP	DAILY OUTPUT	MAN-HOURS	UNIT
704	**BEAMS, DECORATIVE** Rough sawn cedar, non-load bearing, 4" x 4"	2 Carp	2 Carpenters	180	.089	L.F.
0100	4" x 6"			170	.094	L.F.
0200	4" x 8"			160	.100	L.F.
0300	4" x 10"			150	.107	L.F.
0400	4" x 12"			140	.114	L.F.
0500	8" x 8"			130	.123	L.F.
720	**MANTEL BEAMS** Rough texture wood, 4" x 8"	1 Carp	1 Carpenter	36	.222	L.F.
0100	4" x 10"			35	.229	L.F.
0300	Laminated hardwood, 2-1/4" x 10-1/2" wide, 6' long			5	1.600	Ea.
0400	8' long			5	1.600	Ea.
0600	Brackets for above, rough sawn			12	.667	Pr.
0700	Laminated			12	.667	Pr.
725	**FIREPLACE MANTELS** 6" molding, 6' x 3'-6" opening, minimum			5.50	1.450	Opng.
0100	Maximum			4.50	1.780	Opng.
0300	Prefabricated pine, colonial type, stock, deluxe			2	4.000	Opng.
0400	Economy			3	2.670	Opng.
730	**GRILLES** and Panels, hardwood, sanded					
0020	2' x 4' to 4' x 8', custom designs, unfinished, minimum	1 Carp	1 Carpenter	38	.211	S.F.
0050	Average			30	.267	S.F.
0100	Maximum			19	.421	S.F.
0300	As above, but prefinished, minimum			38	.211	S.F.
0400	Maximum			19	.421	S.F.
740	**LOUVERS** Redwood, 2'-0" opening, full circle			16	.500	Ea.
0100	Half circle, 2'-0" diameter			16	.500	Ea.
0200	Octagonal, 2'-0" diameter			16	.500	Ea.
0300	Triangular, 5/12 pitch, 5'-0" at base			16	.500	Ea.
760	**SHUTTERS, EXTERIOR** Aluminum, louvered, 1'-4" wide, 3'-0" long			10	.800	Pr.
0200	4'-0" long			10	.800	Pr.
0300	5'-4" long			10	.800	Pr.
0400	6'-8" long			9	.889	Pr.
1000	Pine, louvered, primed, each 1'-2" wide, 3'-3" long			10	.800	Pr.
1100	4'-7" long			10	.800	Pr.
1250	Each 1'-4" wide, 3'-0" long			10	.800	Pr.
1350	5'-3" long			10	.800	Pr.
1500	Each 1'-6" wide, 3'-3" long			10	.800	Pr.
1600	4'-7" long			10	.800	Pr.
1620	Hemlock, louvered, 1'-2" wide, 5'-7" long			10	.800	Pr.
1630	Each 1'-4" wide, 2'-2" long			10	.800	Pr.
1640	3'-0" long			10	.800	Pr.
1650	3'-3" long			10	.800	Pr.
1660	3'-11" long			10	.800	Pr.
1670	4'-3" long			10	.800	Pr.
1680	5'-3" long			10	.800	Pr.
1690	5'-11" long			10	.800	Pr.
1700	Door blinds, 6'-9" long, each 1'-3" wide			9	.889	Pr.
1710	1'-6" wide			9	.889	Pr.
1720	Hemlock, solid raised panel, each 1'-4" wide, 3'-3" long			10	.800	Pr.
1730	3'-11" long			10	.800	Pr.
1740	4'-3" long			10	.800	Pr.
1750	4'-7" long			10	.800	Pr.

062 | Finish Carpentry

062 700 | Misc Finish Carpentry

			CREW	MAKEUP	DAILY OUTPUT	MAN-HOURS	UNIT
760	1760	Shutters, hemlock, solid raised, 1'-4" wide, 4'-11" long	1 Carp	1 Carpenter	10	.800	Pr.
	1770	5'-11" long			10	.800	Pr.
	1801	Door blinds, hemlock, 6'-9" long, each 1'-3" wide			9	.889	Pr.
	1900	1'-6" wide			9	.889	Pr.
	2500	Polystyrene, solid raised panel, each 1'-4" wide, 3'-3" long			10	.800	Pr.
	2600	3'-11" long			10	.800	Pr.
	2700	4'-7" long			10	.800	Pr.
	2800	5'-3" long			10	.800	Pr.
	2900	6'-8" long			9	.889	Pr.
	4500	Polystyrene, louvered, each 1'-2" wide, 3'-3" long			10	.800	Pr.
	4600	4'-7" long			10	.800	Pr.
	4750	5'-3" long			10	.800	Pr.
	4850	6'-8" long			9	.889	Pr.
	6000	Vinyl, louvered, each 1'-2" x 4'-7" long			10	.800	Pr.
	6200	Each 1'-4" x 6'-8" long	↓	↓	9	.889	Pr.
775		**SOFFITS** Wood fiber, no vapor barrier, 15/32" thick	F-2	2 Carpenters Power Tools	525	.030	S.F.
	0100	5/8" thick			525	.030	S.F.
	0300	As above, 5/8" thick, with factory finish			525	.030	S.F.
	0500	Hardboard, 3/8" thick, slotted			525	.030	S.F.
	1000	Exterior AC plywood, 1/4" thick			420	.038	S.F.
	1100	1/2" thick	↓	↓	420	.038	S.F.

064 | Architectural Woodwork

064 100 | Custom Casework

			CREW	MAKEUP	DAILY OUTPUT	MAN-HOURS	UNIT
102		**CABINETS** Corner china cabinets, stock pine,					
	0020	80" high, unfinished, minimum	2 Carp	2 Carpenters	6.60	2.420	Ea.
	0100	Maximum	"	"	4.40	3.640	Ea.
	0700	Kitchen base cabinets, hardwood, not incl. counter tops,					
	0710	24" deep, 35" high, prefinished					
	0800	One top drawer, one door below, 12" wide	2 Carp	2 Carpenters	24.80	.645	Ea.
	0820	15" wide			24	.667	Ea.
	0840	18" wide			23.30	.687	Ea.
	0860	21" wide			22.70	.705	Ea.
	0880	24" wide			22.30	.717	Ea.
	1000	Four drawers, 12" wide			24.80	.645	Ea.
	1020	15" wide			24	.667	Ea.
	1040	18" wide			23.30	.687	Ea.
	1060	24" wide			22.30	.717	Ea.
	1200	Two top drawers, two doors below, 27" wide			22	.727	Ea.
	1220	30" wide			21.40	.748	Ea.
	1240	33" wide			20.90	.766	Ea.
	1260	36" wide			20.30	.788	Ea.
	1280	42" wide			19.80	.808	Ea.
	1300	48" wide			18.90	.847	Ea.
	1500	Range or sink base, two doors below, 30" wide			21.40	.748	Ea.
	1520	33" wide			20.90	.766	Ea.
	1540	36" wide			20.30	.788	Ea.
	1560	42" wide			19.80	.808	Ea.
	1580	48" wide			18.90	.847	Ea.
	2000	Corner base cabinets, 36" wide, standard			18	.889	Ea.
	2100	Lazy Susan with revolving door	↓	↓	16.50	.970	Ea.

064 | Architectural Woodwork

064 100 | Custom Casework

		CREW	MAKEUP	DAILY OUTPUT	MAN-HOURS	UNIT
102 **4000**	Kitchen wall cabinets, hardwood, 12" deep with two doors					
4050	12" high, 30" wide	2 Carp	2 Carpenters	24.80	.645	Ea.
4100	36" wide			24	.667	Ea.
4400	15" high, 30" wide			24	.667	Ea.
4420	33" wide			23.30	.687	Ea.
4440	36" wide			22.70	.705	Ea.
4450	42" wide			22.70	.705	Ea.
4700	24" high, 30" wide			23.30	.687	Ea.
4720	36" wide			22.70	.705	Ea.
4740	42" wide			22.30	.717	Ea.
5000	30" high, one door, 12" wide			22	.727	Ea.
5020	15" wide			21.40	.748	Ea.
5040	18" wide			20.90	.766	Ea.
5060	24" wide			20.30	.788	Ea.
5300	Two doors, 27" wide			19.80	.808	Ea.
5320	30" wide			19.30	.829	Ea.
5340	36" wide			18.80	.851	Ea.
5360	42" wide			18.50	.865	Ea.
6000	Corner wall, 30" high, 24" wide			18	.889	Ea.
6050	30" wide			17.20	.930	Ea.
6100	36" wide			16.50	.970	Ea.
6500	Revolving Lazy Susan			15.20	1.050	Ea.
7000	Broom cabinet, 84" high, 24" deep, 18" wide			10	1.600	Ea.
7500	Oven cabinets, 84" high, 24" deep, 27" wide			8	2.000	Ea.
7750	Valance board trim	↓	↓	396	.040	L.F.
9550	Rule of thumb, kitchen cabinets not including					
9560	appliances & counter top, minimum	2 Carp	2 Carpenters	30	.533	L.F.
9600	Maximum	"	"	25	.640	L.F.
104	**CASEWORK, FRAMES**					
0050	Base cabinets, counter storage, 36" high, one bay					
0100	18" wide	1 Carp	1 Carpenter	2.70	2.960	Ea.
0200	24" wide			2.50	3.200	Ea.
0300	36" wide			2.30	3.480	Ea.
0400	Two bay, 36" wide			2.20	3.640	Ea.
1000	48" wide			2	4.000	Ea.
1050	72" wide			1.80	4.440	Ea.
1100	Three bay, 54" wide			1.50	5.330	Ea.
1200	72" wide			1.30	6.150	Ea.
1800	108" wide			1.10	7.270	Ea.
2000	Four bay, 72" wide			1.10	7.270	Ea.
2100	96" wide			1	8.000	Ea.
2500	144" wide			.90	8.890	Ea.
2800	Book cases, one bay, 7' high, 18" wide			2.40	3.330	Ea.
3000	24" wide			2.30	3.480	Ea.
3100	36" wide			2.20	3.640	Ea.
3500	Two bay, 36" wide			1.60	5.000	Ea.
3800	48" wide			1.50	5.330	Ea.
4000	72" wide			1.40	5.710	Ea.
4100	Three bay, 54" wide			1.20	6.670	Ea.
4200	72" wide			1.10	7.270	Ea.
4500	108" wide			1	8.000	Ea.
4600	Four bay, 72" wide			.95	8.420	Ea.
4700	96" wide			.90	8.890	Ea.
5000	144" wide			.85	9.410	Ea.
5100	Coat racks, one bay, 7' high, 24" wide			4.50	1.780	Ea.
5200	36" wide			4.30	1.860	Ea.
5300	Two bay, 48" wide			2.75	2.910	Ea.
5600	72" wide	↓	↓	2.50	3.200	Ea.

064 100 | Custom Casework

		CREW	MAKEUP	DAILY OUTPUT	MAN-HOURS	UNIT
104 5801	Coat racks, three bay, 72" wide	1 Carp	1 Carpenter	2.10	3.810	Ea.
6000	108" wide			1.90	4.210	Ea.
6100	Wall mounted cabinet, one bay, 24" high, 18" wide			3.60	2.220	Ea.
6400	24" wide			3.50	2.290	Ea.
6600	36" wide			3.40	2.350	Ea.
6800	Two bay, 36" wide			2.20	3.640	Ea.
7000	48" wide			2.10	3.810	Ea.
7200	72" wide			2	4.000	Ea.
7400	Three bay, 54" wide			1.70	4.710	Ea.
7600	72" wide			1.60	5.000	Ea.
7800	108" wide			1.50	5.330	Ea.
8000	Four bay, 72" wide			1.40	5.710	Ea.
8100	96" wide			1.30	6.150	Ea.
8200	144" wide			1.20	6.670	Ea.
8400	30" high, one bay, 18" wide			3.60	2.220	Ea.
8600	24" wide			3.40	2.350	Ea.
8800	36" wide			3.20	2.500	Ea.
9000	Two bay, 36" wide			2.15	3.720	Ea.
9100	48" wide			2	4.000	Ea.
9200	72" wide			1.85	4.320	Ea.
9400	Three bay, 54" wide			1.60	5.000	Ea.
9600	72" wide			1.50	5.330	Ea.
9650	108" wide			1.40	5.710	Ea.
9700	Four bay, 72" wide			1.30	6.150	Ea.
9750	96" wide			1.22	6.560	Ea.
9780	144" wide			1.15	6.960	Ea.
9800	Wardrobe, 7' high, single, 24" wide			2.70	2.960	Ea.
9850	36" wide			2.50	3.200	Ea.
9880	Partition & adjustable shelves, 48" wide			1.70	4.710	Ea.
9890	72" wide			1.55	5.160	Ea.
9950	Partition, adjustable shelves & drawers, 48" wide			1.40	5.710	Ea.
9960	72" wide	↓	↓	1.25	6.400	Ea.
106	**CABINET DOORS**					
2000	Glass panel, hardwood frame					
2200	12" wide, 18" high	1 Carp	1 Carpenter	34	.235	Ea.
2400	24" high			33	.242	Ea.
2600	30" high			32	.250	Ea.
2800	36" high			30	.267	Ea.
3000	48" high			23	.348	Ea.
3200	60" high			17	.471	Ea.
3400	72" high			15	.533	Ea.
3600	15" wide x 18" high			33	.242	Ea.
3800	24" high			32	.250	Ea.
4000	30" high			30	.267	Ea.
4250	36" high			28	.286	Ea.
4300	48" high			22	.364	Ea.
4350	60" high			16	.500	Ea.
4400	72" high			14	.571	Ea.
4450	18" wide, 18" high			32	.250	Ea.
4500	24" high			30	.267	Ea.
4550	30" high			29	.276	Ea.
4600	36" high			27	.296	Ea.
4650	48" high			21	.381	Ea.
4700	60" high			15	.533	Ea.
4750	72" high	↓	↓	13	.615	Ea.
5000	Hardwood, raised panel					
5100	12" wide, 18" high	1 Carp	1 Carpenter	16	.500	Ea.
5150	24" high	"	"	15.50	.516	Ea.

	064 100	Custom Casework	CREW	MAKEUP	DAILY OUTPUT	MAN-HOURS	UNIT
106	5201	Cabinet doors, hardwood, raised panel, 12" wide, 30" high	1 Carp	1 Carpenter	15	.533	Ea.
	5250	36" high			14	.571	Ea.
	5300	48" high			11	.727	Ea.
	5320	60" high			8	1.000	Ea.
	5340	72" high			7	1.140	Ea.
	5360	15" wide x 18" high			15.50	.516	Ea.
	5380	24" high			15	.533	Ea.
	5400	30" high			14.50	.552	Ea.
	5420	36" high			13.50	.593	Ea.
	5440	48" high			10.50	.762	Ea.
	5460	60" high			7.50	1.070	Ea.
	5480	72" high			6.50	1.230	Ea.
	5500	18" wide, 18" high			15	.533	Ea.
	5550	24" high			14.50	.552	Ea.
	5600	30" high			14	.571	Ea.
	5650	36" high			13	.615	Ea.
	5700	48" high			10	.800	Ea.
	5750	60" high			7	1.140	Ea.
	5800	72" high	↓	↓	6	1.330	Ea.
	6000	Plastic laminate on particle board					
	6100	12" wide, 18" high	1 Carp	1 Carpenter	25	.320	Ea.
	6120	24" high			24	.333	Ea.
	6140	30" high			23	.348	Ea.
	6160	36" high			21	.381	Ea.
	6200	48" high			16	.500	Ea.
	6250	60" high			13	.615	Ea.
	6300	72" high			12	.667	Ea.
	6320	15" wide x 18" high			24.50	.327	Ea.
	6340	24" high			23.50	.340	Ea.
	6360	30" high			22.50	.356	Ea.
	6380	36" high			20.50	.390	Ea.
	6400	48" high			15.50	.516	Ea.
	6450	60" high			12.50	.640	Ea.
	6480	72" high			11.50	.696	Ea.
	6500	18" wide, 18" high			24	.333	Ea.
	6550	24" high			23	.348	Ea.
	6600	30" high			22	.364	Ea.
	6650	36" high			20	.400	Ea.
	6700	48" high			15	.533	Ea.
	6750	60" high			12	.667	Ea.
	6800	72" high	↓	↓	11	.727	Ea.
	7000	Plywood, with edge band					
	7010	12" wide, 18" high	1 Carp	1 Carpenter	27	.296	Ea.
	7100	24" high			26	.308	Ea.
	7120	30" high			25	.320	Ea.
	7140	36" high			23	.348	Ea.
	7180	48" high			18	.444	Ea.
	7200	60" high			15	.533	Ea.
	7250	72" high			14	.571	Ea.
	7300	15" wide x 18" high			26.50	.302	Ea.
	7350	24" high			25.50	.314	Ea.
	7400	30" high			24.50	.327	Ea.
	7450	36" high			22.50	.356	Ea.
	7500	48" high			17.50	.457	Ea.
	7550	60" high			14.50	.552	Ea.
	7600	72" high			13.50	.593	Ea.
	7650	18" wide, 18" high			26	.308	Ea.
	7700	24" high	↓	↓	25	.320	Ea.

064 100 | Custom Casework

		CREW	MAKEUP	DAILY OUTPUT	MAN-HOURS	UNIT
106 7751	Cabinet doors, plywood, w/edge band, 18" wide, 30" high	1 Carp	1 Carpenter	24	.333	Ea.
7800	36" high			22	.364	Ea.
7850	48" high			17	.471	Ea.
7900	60" high			14	.571	Ea.
7950	72" high	↓	↓	13	.615	Ea.
108	**CABINET HARDWARE**					
1000	Catches, minimum	1 Carp	1 Carpenter	235	.034	Ea.
1020	Average			119.40	.067	Ea.
1040	Maximum	↓	↓	80	.100	Ea.
2000	Door/drawer pulls, handles					
2200	Handles and pulls, projecting, metal, minimum	1 Carp	1 Carpenter	160	.050	Ea.
2220	Average			95.24	.084	Ea.
2240	Maximum			68	.118	Ea.
2300	Wood, minimum			160	.050	Ea.
2320	Average			95.24	.084	Ea.
2340	Maximum			68	.118	Ea.
2600	Flush, metal, minimum			160	.050	Ea.
2620	Average			95.24	.084	Ea.
2640	Maximum			68	.118	Ea.
3000	Drawer tracks/glides, minimum			48	.167	Pr.
3020	Average			32	.250	Pr.
3040	Maximum			24	.333	Pr.
4000	Cabinet hinges, minimum			160	.050	Pr.
4020	Average			95.24	.084	Pr.
4040	Maximum			68	.118	Ea.
5000	Cabinet locks, minimum			47.90	.167	Ea.
5020	Average			23.95	.334	Ea.
5040	Maximum	↓	↓	16	.500	Ea.
110	**DRAWERS**					
0100	Solid hardwood front					
1000	4" high, 12" wide	1 Carp	1 Carpenter	17	.471	Ea.
1200	18" wide			16	.500	Ea.
1400	24" wide			15	.533	Ea.
1600	6" high x 12" wide			16	.500	Ea.
1800	18" wide			15	.533	Ea.
2000	24" wide			14	.571	Ea.
2200	9" high x 12" wide			15	.533	Ea.
2400	18" wide			14	.571	Ea.
2600	24" wide	↓	↓	13	.615	Ea.
2800	Plastic laminate on particle board front					
3000	4" high, 12" wide	1 Carp	1 Carpenter	17	.471	Ea.
3200	18" wide			16	.500	Ea.
3600	24" wide			15	.533	Ea.
3800	6" high, x 12" wide			16	.500	Ea.
4000	18" wide			15	.533	Ea.
4500	24" wide			14	.571	Ea.
4800	9" high x 12" wide			15	.533	Ea.
5000	18" wide			14	.571	Ea.
5200	24" wide	↓	↓	13	.615	Ea.
5400	Plywood, flush panel front					
6000	4" high, 12" wide	1 Carp	1 Carpenter	17	.471	Ea.
6200	18" wide			16	.500	Ea.
6400	24" wide			15	.533	Ea.
6600	6" high x 12" wide			16	.500	Ea.
7000	18" wide			15	.533	Ea.
7500	24" wide			14	.571	Ea.
8000	9" high x 12" wide			15	.533	Ea.
8500	18" wide	↓	↓	14	.571	Ea.

064 | Architectural Woodwork

064 100 | Custom Casework

140	VANITIES	CREW	MAKEUP	DAILY OUTPUT	MAN-HOURS	UNIT
8000	Vanity bases, 2 doors, 30" high, 21" deep, 24" wide	2 Carp	2 Carpenters	11	1.450	Ea.
8050	30" wide			9.80	1.630	Ea.
8100	36" wide			8	2.000	Ea.
8150	48" wide	↓	↓	6.60	2.420	Ea.

064 300 | Stairwork & Handrails

		CREW	MAKEUP	DAILY OUTPUT	MAN-HOURS	UNIT
306	STAIRS, PREFABRICATED					
0100	Box stairs, prefabricated, 3'-0" wide					
0110	Oak treads, no handrails, 2' high	2 Carp	2 Carpenters	5	3.200	Flight
0200	4' high			4	4.000	Flight
0300	6' high			3.50	4.570	Flight
0400	8' high			3	5.330	Flight
0600	With pine treads for carpet, 2' high			5	3.200	Flight
0700	4' high			4	4.000	Flight
0800	6' high			3.50	4.570	Flight
0900	8' high			3	5.330	Flight
1500	Prefabricated stair rail with balusters,	↓	↓	15	1.070	Ea.
1700	Basement stairs, prefabricated, soft wood,					
1710	open risers, 3' wide, 8' high	2 Carp	2 Carpenters	4	4.000	Flight
1900	Open stairs, prefabricated prefinished poplar, metal stringers,					
1910	treads 3'-6" wide, no railings					
2000	3' high	2 Carp	2 Carpenters	5	3.200	Flight
2100	4' high			4	4.000	Flight
2200	6' high			3.50	4.570	Flight
2300	8' high	↓	↓	3	5.330	Flight
2500	For prefab. 3 piece wood railings & balusters, add for					
2600	3' high stairs	2 Carp	2 Carpenters	15	1.070	Ea.
2700	4' high stairs			14	1.140	Ea.
2800	6' high stairs			13	1.230	Ea.
2900	8' high stairs			12	1.330	Ea.
3100	For 3'-6" x 3'-6" platform, add	↓	↓	4	4.000	Ea.
3300	Curved stairways, 3'-3" wide, prefabricated, oak, unfinished,					
3310	incl. curved balustrade system, open one side					
3400	9' high	2 Carp	2 Carpenters	.70	22.860	Flight
3500	10' high			.70	22.860	Flight
3700	Open two sides, 9' high			.50	32.000	Flight
3800	10' high			.50	32.000	Flight
4000	Residential, wood, oak treads, prefabricated			1.50	10.670	Flight
4200	Built in place	↓	↓	.44	36.360	Flight
4400	Spiral, oak, 4'-6" diameter, unfinished, prefabricated,					
4500	incl. railing, 9' high	2 Carp	2 Carpenters	1.50	10.670	Flight
308	STAIR PARTS Balusters, turned, 30" high, pine, minimum	1 Carp	1 Carpenter	28	.286	Ea.
0100	Maximum			26	.308	Ea.
0300	30" high birch balusters, minimum			28	.286	Ea.
0400	Maximum			26	.308	Ea.
0600	42" high, pine balusters, minimum			27	.296	Ea.
0700	Maximum			25	.320	Ea.
0900	42" high birch balusters, minimum			27	.296	Ea.
1000	Maximum			25	.320	Ea.
1050	Baluster, stock pine, 1-1/16" x 1-1/16"			240	.033	L.F.
1100	1-5/8" x 1-5/8"			220	.036	L.F.
1200	Newels, 3-1/4" wide, starting, minimum			7	1.140	Ea.
1300	Maximum			6	1.330	Ea.
1500	Landing, minimum			5	1.600	Ea.
1600	Maximum			4	2.000	Ea.
1800	Railings, oak, built-up, minimum			60	.133	L.F.
1900	Maximum	↓	↓	55	.145	L.F.

064 300 | Stairwork & Handrails

		CREW	MAKEUP	DAILY OUTPUT	MAN-HOURS	UNIT
308 2300	Risers, Beech, 3/4" x 7-1/2" high	1 Carp	1 Carpenter	64	.125	L.F.
2400	Fir, 3/4" x 7-1/2" high			64	.125	L.F.
2600	Oak, 3/4" x 7-1/2" high			64	.125	L.F.
2800	Pine, 3/4" x 7-1/2" high			66	.121	L.F.
2850	Skirt board, pine, 1" x 10"			55	.145	L.F.
2900	1" x 12"			52	.154	L.F.
3000	Treads, oak, 1-1/16" x 9-1/2" wide, 3' long			18	.444	Ea.
3100	4' long			17	.471	Ea.
3300	1-1/16" x 11-1/2" wide, 3' long			18	.444	Ea.
3400	6' long			14	.571	Ea.
310	**RAILING** Custom design, architectural grade, hardwood, minimum			38	.211	L.F.
0100	Maximum			30	.267	L.F.
0300	Stock interior railing with spindles 6" O.C., 4' long			40	.200	L.F.
0400	8' long	↓	↓	48	.167	L.F.

064 400 | Misc Ornamental Items

		CREW	MAKEUP	DAILY OUTPUT	MAN-HOURS	UNIT
402	**COLUMNS**					
0050	Aluminum, round colonial, 6" diameter	2 Carp	2 Carpenters	80	.200	V.L.F.
0100	8" diameter			62.25	.257	V.L.F.
0200	10" diameter			55	.291	V.L.F.
0250	Fir, stock units, hollow round, 6" diameter			80	.200	V.L.F.
0300	8" diameter			80	.200	V.L.F.
0350	10" diameter			70	.229	V.L.F.
0400	Solid turned, to 8' high, 3-1/2" diameter			80	.200	V.L.F.
0500	4-1/2" diameter			75	.213	V.L.F.
0600	5-1/2" diameter			70	.229	V.L.F.
0800	Square columns, built-up, 5" x 5"			65	.246	V.L.F.
0900	Solid, 3-1/2" x 3-1/2"			130	.123	V.L.F.
1600	Hemlock, tapered, T & G, 12" diam, 10' high			100	.160	V.L.F.
1700	16' high			65	.246	V.L.F.
1900	10' high, 14" diameter			100	.160	V.L.F.
2000	18' high			65	.246	V.L.F.
2200	18" diameter, 12' high			65	.246	V.L.F.
2300	20' high			50	.320	V.L.F.
2500	20" diameter, 14' high			40	.400	V.L.F.
2600	20' high			35	.457	V.L.F.
4000	Rough sawn cedar posts, 4" x 4"			250	.064	V.L.F.
4100	4" x 6"			235	.068	V.L.F.
4200	6" x 6"			220	.073	V.L.F.
4300	8" x 8"	↓	↓	200	.080	V.L.F.

DIVISION 7

MOISTURE-THERMAL CONTROL

7

DIVISION 7

MOISTURE-THERMAL CONTROL

This division includes all the materials necessary to keep moisture out of a building and keep heat (or cooled air) inside. The principle concern is to determine the most probable location of these materials in or on the building. After that, it becomes a problem of determining the most practical method of installing the items. Many times in the construction sequence, the installation of items in this division will hinge on the completion of other building elements or the cooperation of the trades. Not all buildings are alike, so on occasion the man-hour figures in the listings here will vary. Productivity data is based on new construction. If the numbers are to be used for remodeling work, some adjustment must be made based on the experience of the estimator.

Waterproofing is used in construction to keep moisture from entering the building through materials and joints of differing types. The materials are typically applied by hand using various tools. In almost all situations the materials are being applied by trades other than those who constructed the building. Also, sufficient time for the materials to dry or cure must be provided before other work continues, to prevent any damage to the membrane.

Insulation includes those materials in, on, and around the building which are used to maintain interior thermal comfort or control. The materials are often installed by different trades, such as: carpenters, bricklayers, roofers, and common laborers. As such, the productivity realized may vary from trade to trade.

Materials found in the ''Shingles'' subdivision are those which mechanically shed water from the top or sides of buildings. These materials are usually installed by carpenters or roofers.

''Roofing'' and ''Siding'' involves panels which are larger than the small items in the shingles subdivision. Items included can easily be broken down into two significant groups: Panelized Systems and Membrane Systems. The most important factors to be realized here are the roof shape (rectangular, round, H-shaped, T-shaped, etc.), number and size of penetrations, and height above ground.

239

"Sheet Metal Work" includes metal roofing and those items necessary to waterproof the discontinuities in buildings and carry away storm water from the roof. Also included are those items necessary to ventilate attic spaces. This subdivision does not include the materials used in mechanical or electrical work.

"Roof Accessories" are those unique items such as hatches, skylights, skyroofs, ventilators, etc. Installation may be done by any number of trades, but generally is performed by carpenters, sheet metal workers, or roofers.

The "Moisture Protection" subdivision is heavily affected by the outside weather. With the ideal working conditions being 75 degrees Fahrenheit and 60 percent Relative Humidity, any changes in either variable will cause the productivity figures in this section to be reduced. Therefore, some adjustments must be made in response to the expected changes in the construction weather conditions.

071 | Waterproofing and Dampproofing

071 100 | Sheet Waterproofing

		CREW	MAKEUP	DAILY OUTPUT	MAN-HOURS	UNIT
102	**ELASTOMERIC WATERPROOFING** EPDM, plain, 1/32" thick	2 Rofc	2 Roofers, Composition	580	.028	S.F.
0100	1/16" thick			570	.028	S.F.
0300	Nylon reinforced sheets, 1/32" thick			580	.028	S.F.
0400	1/16" thick			570	.028	S.F.
1200	Neoprene sheets, plain, 1/32" thick			580	.028	S.F.
1300	1/16" thick			570	.028	S.F.
1500	Nylon reinforced, 1/32" thick			580	.028	S.F.
1600	1/16" thick			570	.028	S.F.
1800	1/8" thick			500	.032	S.F.
2100	Fiberglass reinforced, fluid applied, 1/8" thick			500	.032	S.F.
2200	Polyethylene and rubberized asphalt sheets, 1/8" thick			550	.029	S.F.
2400	Polyvinyl chloride sheets, plain, 10 mils thick			580	.028	S.F.
2500	20 mils thick			570	.028	S.F.
2700	30 mils thick			560	.029	S.F.
2800	Mineral fiber back PVC, 45 mils thick			550	.029	S.F.
3300	Bitumen modified polyurethane, fluid applied, 55 mils thick			665	.024	S.F.
3600	Vinyl plastic, sprayed on, 25 to 40 mils thick	↓	↓	475	.034	S.F.
104	**MEMBRANE WATERPROOFING** On slabs, 1 ply, felt	G-1	1 Roofer Foreman 4 Roofers, Composition 2 Roofer Helpers Application Equipment	3,000	.019	S.F.
0100	Fabric			2,100	.027	S.F.
0300	2 ply, felt			2,500	.022	S.F.
0400	Fabric			11,650	.005	S.F.
0600	3 ply, felt			2,100	.027	S.F.
0700	Fabric	↓	↓	1,550	.036	S.F.
1000	For 1/4" backer board, add	2 Rofc	2 Roofers, Composition	3,500	.005	S.F.
1050	For protector board, 3/8" thick, add			3,500	.005	S.F.
1060	1/2" thick, add			3,500	.005	S.F.
1070	Fiberglass fabric, black, 20/10 mesh			116	.138	Sq.
1080	White, 20/10 mesh			116	.138	Sq.
1100	Fluid neoprene, 4 coats, 50 mil			200	.080	S.F.
1200	90 mil			120	.133	S.F.
1300	Fluid elastomeric copolymer compound, 32 mils thick	↓	↓	4,400	.004	S.F.

071 300 | Bentonite Waterproofing

		CREW	MAKEUP	DAILY OUTPUT	MAN-HOURS	UNIT
301	**BENTONITE** Panels, 4' x 4', for walls, 3/16" thick	1 Rofc	1 Roofer, Composition	625	.013	S.F.
0100	Under slabs, 5/8" thick			900	.009	S.F.
0401	Granular bentonite, 3/8" thick, troweled on	↓	↓	475	.017	S.F.
0500	Drain board, expanded polystyrene, binder encapsulated, 1" thick	1 Rohe	1 Roofer, Helper	1,600	.005	S.F.
0510	2" thick			1,600	.005	S.F.
0520	3" thick			1,600	.005	S.F.
0530	4" thick	↓	↓	1,600	.005	S.F.

071 450 | Cement Waterproofing

		CREW	MAKEUP	DAILY OUTPUT	MAN-HOURS	UNIT
452	**CEMENTITIOUS WATERPROOFING** One coat cement base					
0020	1/8" application, sprayed on	G-2	1 Plasterer 1 Plasterer Helper 1 Building Laborer Grouting Equipment	1,000	.024	S.F.

071 | Waterproofing and Dampproofing

071 600 | Bitum Dampproofing

			CREW	MAKEUP	DAILY OUTPUT	MAN-HOURS	UNIT
602	602	**BITUMINOUS ASPHALT COATING** For foundation					
	0030	Brushed on, below grade, 1 coat	1 Rofc	1 Roofer, Composition	665	.012	S.F.
	0100	2 coat			500	.016	S.F.
	0300	Sprayed on, below grade, 1 coat, 25.6 S.F./gal.			830	.010	S.F.
	0400	2 coat, 20.5 S.F./gal.			500	.016	S.F.
	0600	Troweled on, asphalt with fibers, 1/16" thick			500	.016	S.F.
	0700	1/8" thick			400	.020	S.F.
	1000	1/2" thick			350	.023	S.F.
	4000	Protective board, asphalt coated, in mastic, 1/4" thick	↓	↓	450	.018	S.F.

071 750 | Water Repellent Coat

		CREW	MAKEUP	DAILY OUTPUT	MAN-HOURS	UNIT
754	**RUBBER COATING** Water base liquid, roller applied	2 Rofc	2 Roofers, Composition	7,000	.002	S.F.
0200	Silicone or stearate, sprayed on masonry, 1 coat	1 Rofc	1 Roofer, Composition	4,000	.002	S.F.
0300	2 coats	"	"	2,000	.004	S.F.

071 800 | Cementitious Dampprfng

		CREW	MAKEUP	DAILY OUTPUT	MAN-HOURS	UNIT
802	**CEMENT PARGING** 2 coats, 1/2" thick, regular P.C.	D-1	1 Bricklayer	250	.064	S.F.
			1 Bricklayer Helper			
0100	Waterproofed portland cement	"	"	250	.064	S.F.

071 920 | Vapor Retarders

		CREW	MAKEUP	DAILY OUTPUT	MAN-HOURS	UNIT
922	**BUILDING PAPER** Aluminum and kraft laminated, foil 1 side	1 Carp	1 Carpenter	19	.421	Sq.
0100	Foil 2 sides			19	.421	Sq.
0300	Asphalt, two ply, 30#, for subfloors			37	.216	Sq.
0400	Asphalt felt sheathing paper, 15#			37	.216	Sq.
0600	Polyethylene vapor barrier, standard, .002" thick			37	.216	Sq.
0700	.004" thick			37	.216	Sq.
0900	.006" thick			37	.216	Sq.
1000	.008" thick			37	.216	Sq.
1200	.010" thick			37	.216	Sq.
1300	Clear reinforced, fire retardant, .008" thick			37	.216	Sq.
1350	Cross laminated type, .003" thick			37	.216	Sq.
1400	.004" thick			37	.216	Sq.
1500	Red rosin paper, 5 sq. rolls, 4 lbs. per square			37	.216	Sq.
1600	5 lbs. per square			37	.216	Sq.
1800	Reinf. waterproof, .002" polyethylene backing, 1 side			37	.216	Sq.
1900	2 sides	↓	↓	37	.216	Sq.
2100	Roof deck vapor barrier, class 1 metal decks	1 Rofc	1 Roofer, Composition	37	.216	Sq.
2200	For all other decks	"	"	37	.216	Sq.
2400	Waterproofed kraft with sisal or fiberglass fibers, minimum	1 Carp	1 Carpenter	37	.216	Sq.
2500	Maximum	"	"	37	.216	Sq.

072 | Insulation

072 100 | Building Insulation

		CREW	MAKEUP	DAILY OUTPUT	MAN-HOURS	UNIT
101	**BLOWN-IN INSULATION** Ceilings, with open access					
0020	Cellulose, 3-1/2" thick, R13	G-4	1 Labor Foreman (outside)	3,000	.008	S.F.
			2 Building Laborers			
			1 Light Truck, 1.5 Ton			
			1 Air Compr., 160 C.F.M.			
0030	5-3/16" thick, R19	↓	↓	1,900	.013	S.F.
0050	6-1/2" thick, R22			1,500	.016	S.F.

072 100 | Building Insulation

			CREW	MAKEUP	DAILY OUTPUT	MAN-HOURS	UNIT
101	0101	Blown-in insulation, ceilings, cellulose, 8-11/16" thick, R30	G-4	1 Labor Foreman (outside)	1,300	.018	S.F.
				2 Building Laborers			
				1 Light Truck, 1.5 Ton			
				1 Air Compr., 160 C.F.M.			
	0120	10-7/8" thick, R38			900	.027	S.F.
	1000	Fiberglass, 5" thick, R11			1,900	.013	S.F.
	1050	6" thick, R13			1,500	.016	S.F.
	1100	8-1/2" thick, R19			1,100	.022	S.F.
	1200	10" thick, R23			900	.027	S.F.
	1300	12" thick, R26			750	.032	S.F.
	2000	Mineral wool, 4" thick, R12			2,200	.011	S.F.
	2050	6" thick, R17			1,500	.016	S.F.
	2100	9" thick, R23	↓	↓	1,000	.024	S.F.
	2500	Wall installation, incl. drilling & patching from outside, two 1"					
	2510	diam. holes @ 16" O.C., top & mid-point of wall					
	2700	For masonry	G-4	1 Labor Foreman (outside)	415	.058	S.F.
				2 Building Laborers			
				1 Light Truck, 1.5 Ton			
				1 Air Compr., 160 C.F.M.			
	2800	For wood siding			840	.029	S.F.
	2900	For stucco/plaster	↓	↓	665	.036	S.F.
108		**MASONRY INSULATION** Vermiculite or perlite, poured					
	0100	In cores of concrete block, 4" thick wall, .115 C.F./S.F.	D-1	1 Bricklayer	4,800	.003	S.F.
				1 Bricklayer Helper			
	0200	6" thick wall, .175 C.F./S.F.			3,000	.005	S.F.
	0300	8" thick wall, .258 C.F./S.F.			2,400	.007	S.F.
	0400	10" thick wall, .340 C.F./S.F.			1,850	.009	S.F.
	0500	12" thick wall, .422 C.F./S.F.			1,200	.013	S.F.
	0600	Poured cavity wall, vermiculite or perlite, water repellant	↓	↓	250	.064	C.F.
	0700	Foamed in place, urethane in 2-5/8" cavity	G-2	1 Plasterer	1,035	.023	S.F.
				1 Plasterer Helper			
				1 Building Laborer			
				Grouting Equipment			
	0800	For each 1" added thickness, add	"	"	2,372	.010	S.F.
109		**PERIMETER INSULATION** Asphalt impregnated cork, 1/2" thick, R1.12	1 Carp	1 Carpenter	690	.012	S.F.
	0100	1" thick, R2.24			680	.012	S.F.
	0600	Polystyrene, molded bead board, 1" thick, R4			680	.012	S.F.
	0700	2" thick, R8			675	.012	S.F.
110		**POURED INSULATION** Cellulose fiber, R3.8 per inch			200	.040	C.F.
	0040	Ceramic type (perlite), R3.2 per inch			200	.040	C.F.
	0080	Fiberglass wool, R4 per inch			200	.040	C.F.
	0100	Mineral wool, R3 per inch			200	.040	C.F.
	0300	Polystyrene, R4 per inch			200	.040	C.F.
	0400	Vermiculite or perlite, R2.7 per inch			200	.040	C.F.
	0700	Wood fiber, R3.85 per inch			200	.040	C.F.
111		**REFLECTIVE** Aluminum foil on 40 lb. kraft, foil 1 side, R9			19	.421	C.S.F.
	0100	Multilayered with air spaces, 2 ply, R14			19	.421	C.S.F.
	0500	3 ply, R17			15	.533	C.S.F.
	0600	5 ply, R22	↓	↓	15	.533	C.S.F.
115		**SPRAYED** Fibrous/cementitious, finished wall, 1" thick, R3.7	G-2	1 Plasterer	2,050	.012	S.F.
				1 Plasterer Helper			
				1 Building Laborer			
				Grouting Equipment			
	0100	Attic, 5.2" thick, R19	"	"	1,550	.015	S.F.

072 100	Building Insulation	CREW	MAKEUP	DAILY OUTPUT	MAN-HOURS	UNIT
115 0601	Foam type sprayed urethane, 3 lb./C.F., 1" thick, R7.7	G-2	1 Plasterer	770	.031	S.F.
			1 Plasterer Helper			
			1 Building Laborer			
			Grouting Equipment			
0700	2" thick, R15.4	"	"	475	.051	S.F.
116	**WALL INSULATION, RIGID**					
0040	Fiberglass, 1.5#/C.F., unfaced, 1" thick, R4.1	1 Carp	1 Carpenter	1,000	.008	S.F.
0060	1-1/2" thick, R6.2			1,000	.008	S.F.
0080	2" thick, R8.3			1,000	.008	S.F.
0120	3" thick, R12.4			800	.010	S.F.
0370	3#/C.F., unfaced, 1" thick, R4.3			1,000	.008	S.F.
0390	1-1/2" thick, R6.5			1,000	.008	S.F.
0400	2" thick, R8.7			890	.009	S.F.
0420	2-1/2" thick, R10.9			800	.010	S.F.
0440	3" thick, R13			800	.010	S.F.
0520	Foil faced, 1" thick, R4.3			1,000	.008	S.F.
0540	1-1/2" thick, R6.5			1,000	.008	S.F.
0560	2" thick, R8.7			890	.009	S.F.
0580	2-1/2" thick, R10.9			800	.010	S.F.
0600	3" thick, R13			800	.010	S.F.
0670	6#/C.F., unfaced, 1" thick, R4.3			1,000	.008	S.F.
0690	1-1/2" thick, R6.5			890	.009	S.F.
0700	2" thick, R8.7			800	.010	S.F.
0721	2-1/2" thick, R10.9			800	.010	S.F.
0741	3" thick, R13			730	.011	S.F.
0821	Foil faced, 1" thick, R4.3			1,000	.008	S.F.
0840	1-1/2" thick, R6.5			890	.009	S.F.
0850	2" thick, R8.7			800	.010	S.F.
0880	2-1/2" thick, R10.9			800	.010	S.F.
0900	3" thick, R13			730	.011	S.F.
1500	Foamglass, 1-1/2" thick, R2.64			800	.010	S.F.
1550	2" thick, R5.26			730	.011	S.F.
1700	Perlite, 1" thick, R2.77			800	.010	S.F.
1750	2" thick, R5.55			730	.011	S.F.
1900	Polystyrene, extruded blue, 2.2#/C.F., 3/4" thick, R4			800	.010	S.F.
1940	1-1/2" thick, R8.1			730	.011	S.F.
1960	2" thick, R10.8			730	.011	S.F.
2100	Molded bead board, white, 1" thick, R3.85			800	.010	S.F.
2120	1-1/2" thick, R5.6			730	.011	S.F.
2140	2" thick, R7.7			730	.011	S.F.
2350	Sheathing, insulating foil faced fiberboard, 3/8" thick			670	.012	S.F.
2510	Urethane, no paper backing, 1/2" thick, R2.9			800	.010	S.F.
2520	1" thick, R5.8			800	.010	S.F.
2540	1-1/2" thick, R8.7			730	.011	S.F.
2560	2" thick, R11.7			730	.011	S.F.
2710	Fire resistant, 1/2" thick, R2.9			800	.010	S.F.
2720	1" thick, R5.8			800	.010	S.F.
2740	1-1/2" thick, R8.7			730	.011	S.F.
2760	2" thick, R11.7	↓	↓	730	.011	S.F.
118	**WALL OR CEILING INSUL., NON-RIGID**					
0040	Fiberglass, kraft faced, batts or blankets					
0060	3-1/2" thick, R11, 11" wide	1 Carp	1 Carpenter	1,150	.007	S.F.
0080	15" wide			1,600	.005	S.F.
0100	23" wide			1,600	.005	S.F.
0140	6" thick, R19, 11" wide			1,000	.008	S.F.
0160	15" wide			1,350	.006	S.F.
0180	23" wide			1,600	.005	S.F.
0200	9" thick, R30, 15" wide	↓	↓	1,150	.007	S.F.

072 | Insulation

072 100 | Building Insulation

		CREW	MAKEUP	DAILY OUTPUT	MAN-HOURS	UNIT
0221	Fiberglass insul., batts/blankets, 9" thick, R30, 23" wide	1 Carp	1 Carpenter	1,350	.006	S.F.
0240	12" thick, R38, 15" wide			1,000	.008	S.F.
0260	23" wide	↓	↓	1,350	.006	S.F.
0400	Fiberglass, foil faced, batts or blankets					
0420	3-1/2" thick, R11, 15" wide	1 Carp	1 Carpenter	1,600	.005	S.F.
0440	23" wide			1,600	.005	S.F.
0460	6" thick, R19, 15" wide			1,350	.006	S.F.
0480	23" wide			1,600	.005	S.F.
0500	9" thick, R30, 15" wide			1,150	.007	S.F.
0550	23" wide	↓	↓	1,350	.006	S.F.
0800	Fiberglass, unfaced, batts or blankets					
0820	3-1/2" thick, R11, 15" wide	1 Carp	1 Carpenter	1,350	.006	S.F.
0830	23" wide			1,600	.005	S.F.
0860	6" thick, R19, 15" wide			1,150	.007	S.F.
0880	23" wide			1,350	.006	S.F.
0900	9" thick, R30, 15" wide			1,000	.008	S.F.
0920	23" wide			1,150	.007	S.F.
0940	12" thick, R38, 15" wide			1,000	.008	S.F.
0960	23" wide	↓	↓	1,150	.007	S.F.
1300	Mineral fiber batts, kraft faced					
1320	3-1/2" thick, R13	1 Carp	1 Carpenter	1,600	.005	S.F.
1340	6" thick, R19			1,600	.005	S.F.
1380	10" thick, R30	↓	↓	1,350	.006	S.F.

072 200 | Roof & Deck Insulation

		CREW	MAKEUP	DAILY OUTPUT	MAN-HOURS	UNIT
203	ROOF DECK INSULATION					
0030	Fiberboard, mineral, 1" thick, R2.78	1 Rofc	1 Roofer, Composition	800	.010	S.F.
0080	1-1/2" thick, R4			800	.010	S.F.
0100	2" thick, R5.26	↓	↓	800	.010	S.F.
0300	Fiberglass, in 3' x 4' or 4' x 8' sheets					
0400	15/16" thick, R3.3	1 Rofc	1 Roofer, Composition	1,000	.008	S.F.
0460	1-1/16" thick, R3.8			1,000	.008	S.F.
0600	1-5/16" thick, R5.3			1,000	.008	S.F.
0650	1-5/8" thick, R5.7			1,000	.008	S.F.
0700	1-7/8" thick, R7.7			1,000	.008	S.F.
0800	2-1/4" thick, R8	↓	↓	800	.010	S.F.
0900	Fiberglass and urethane composite, 3' x 4' sheets					
1000	1-11/16" thick, R11.1	1 Rofc	1 Roofer, Composition	1,000	.008	S.F.
1200	2" thick, R14.3			800	.010	S.F.
1300	2-5/8" thick, R18.2	↓	↓	800	.010	S.F.
1500	Foamglass, 2' x 4' sheets, rectangular					
1510	1-1/2" thick R3.95	1 Rofc	1 Roofer, Composition	800	.010	S.F.
1520	2" thick R5.26			800	.010	S.F.
1530	3" thick R7.89			700	.011	S.F.
1540	4" thick R10.53			700	.011	S.F.
1600	Tapered 1/16", 1/8" or 1/4" per foot	↓	↓	600	.013	B.F.
1650	Perlite, 2' x 4' sheets					
1655	3/4" thick, R2.08	1 Rofc	1 Roofer, Composition	800	.010	S.F.
1660	1" thick, R2.78			800	.010	S.F.
1670	1-1/2" thick, R4.17			800	.010	S.F.
1680	2" thick, R5.26	↓	↓	700	.011	S.F.
1700	Perlite/urethane composite					
1711	1-1/4" thick, R5.88	1 Rofc	1 Roofer, Composition	1,000	.008	S.F.
1721	1-1/2" thick, R7.2			1,000	.008	S.F.
1730	1-3/4" thick, R10			1,000	.008	S.F.
1740	2" thick, R12.5			800	.010	S.F.
1750	2-1/2" thick, R14.3			750	.011	S.F.
1760	3" thick, R20	↓	↓	700	.011	S.F.

118

245

072 | Insulation

072 200 | Roof & Deck Insulation

		Description	CREW	MAKEUP	DAILY OUTPUT	MAN-HOURS	UNIT
203	1801	Roof deck insulation, phenolic foam, 4' x 8' sheets					
	1810	1-3/16" thick, R10	1 Rofc	1 Roofer, Composition	1,000	.008	S.F.
	1820	1-1/2" thick, R12.5			1,000	.008	S.F.
	1830	1-3/4" thick, R14.6			1,000	.008	S.F.
	1840	2" thick, R16.7			800	.010	S.F.
	1850	2-1/2" thick, R20			800	.010	S.F.
	1860	3" thick, R25	↓	↓	800	.010	S.F.
	1900	Polystyrene					
	1910	Extruded, 2.3#/C.F., 1" thick, R5.26	1 Rofc	1 Roofer, Composition	1,500	.005	S.F.
	1920	2" thick, R10			1,250	.006	S.F.
	1930	3" thick, R15			1,000	.008	S.F.
	2010	Expanded bead board, 1" thick, R3.57			1,500	.005	S.F.
	2100	2" thick, R7.14	↓	↓	1,250	.006	S.F.
	2200	Urethane, felt both sides					
	2210	1" thick, R6.7	1 Rofc	1 Roofer, Composition	1,000	.008	S.F.
	2220	1-1/2" thick, R11.11			1,000	.008	S.F.
	2230	2" thick, R14.3			800	.010	S.F.
	2240	2-1/2" thick, R20			800	.010	S.F.
	2250	3" thick, R25	↓	↓	800	.010	S.F.
	2300	Urethane and gypsum board composite					
	2310	1-5/8" thick, R7.7	1 Rofc	1 Roofer, Composition	1,000	.008	S.F.
	2320	2" thick, R10			800	.010	S.F.
	2330	2-1/2" thick, R14.3			800	.010	S.F.
	2340	3" thick, R18.2	↓	↓	800	.010	S.F.

072 400 | Exterior Insulation

		Description	CREW	MAKEUP	DAILY OUTPUT	MAN-HOURS	UNIT
	402	INTEGRATED SIDING Fabric reinforced synthetic exterior					
	0020	finish, on 1" polystyrene insulation board					
	0100	Minimum	J-1	3 Plasterers	380	.105	S.F.
				2 Plasterer Helpers			
				1 Mixing Machine, 6 C.F.			
	0200	Maximum	"	"	270	.148	S.F.
	0300	For insulation, 2" polystyrene, add	1 Plas	1 Plasterer	725	.011	S.F.

072 550 | Cement Fireproofing

		Description	CREW	MAKEUP	DAILY OUTPUT	MAN-HOURS	UNIT
	554	SPRAYED Mineral fiber or cementitious for fireproofing,					
	0050	not incl. tamping or canvas protection					
	0100	1" thick, on flat plate steel	G-2	1 Plasterer	3,000	.008	S.F.
				1 Plasterer Helper			
				1 Building Laborer			
				Grouting Equipment			
	0200	Flat decking			2,400	.010	S.F.
	0400	Beams			1,500	.016	S.F.
	0500	Corrugated or fluted decks			1,250	.019	S.F.
	0700	Columns, 1-1/8" thick			1,100	.022	S.F.
	0800	2-3/16" thick			700	.034	S.F.
	0900	For canvas protection, add			5,000	.005	S.F.
	1000	Acoustical sprayed, 1" thick, finished, straight work, minimum			520	.046	S.F.
	1100	Maximum			200	.120	S.F.
	1300	Difficult access, minimum			225	.107	S.F.
	1400	Maximum	↓	↓	130	.185	S.F.
	1500	Intumescent epoxy fireproofing on wire mesh, 3/16" thick					
	1550	1 hour rating, exterior use	G-2	1 Plasterer	136	.176	S.F.
				1 Plasterer Helper			
				1 Building Laborer			
				Grouting Equipment			
	1600	Magnesium oxychloride, 35# to 40# density, 1/4" thick			3,000	.008	S.F.
	1650	1/2" thick	↓	↓	2,000	.012	S.F.

072 | Insulation

072 550	Cement Fireproofing	CREW	MAKEUP	DAILY OUTPUT	MAN-HOURS	UNIT
554	1701	Sprayed, magnesium chloride, 60# to 70# density, 1/4" thick	G-2	1 Plasterer	3,000	.008	S.F.
				1 Plasterer Helper			
				1 Building Laborer			
				Grouting Equipment			
	1750	1/2" thick			2,000	.012	S.F.
	2000	Vermiculite cement, troweled or sprayed, 1/4" thick			3,000	.008	S.F.
	2050	1/2" thick	↓	↓	2,000	.012	S.F.

073 | Shingles and Roofing Tiles

073 100	Shingles	CREW	MAKEUP	DAILY OUTPUT	MAN-HOURS	UNIT
101	ALUMINUM Shingles, mill finish, .020" thick	1 Carp	1 Carpenter	2.50	3.200	Sq.
0100	.030" thick			2.50	3.200	Sq.
0600	Ridge cap, .020" thick			170	.047	L.F.
0700	.030" thick			170	.047	L.F.
0900	Valley section for above, .020" thick			170	.047	L.F.
1000	.030" thick			170	.047	L.F.
103	MINERAL FIBER Strip shingles, 14" x 30", 325 lb. per square			4	2.000	Sq.
0100	12" x 24", 167 lb. per square			3.50	2.290	Sq.
0200	Shakes, 9.35" x 16", 500 lb. per square (siding)			2.20	3.640	Sq.
0300	Hip & ridge shingles, 5-3/8" x 14"			1	8.000	C.L.F.
0400	Hexagonal shape, 16" x 16"			3	2.670	Sq.
0500	Square, 16" x 16"	↓	↓	3	2.670	Sq.
104	ASPHALT SHINGLES					
0100	Standard strip shingles					
0150	Inorganic, class A, 210-235 lb./square, 3 bundles/square	1 Rofc	1 Roofer, Composition	5.50	1.450	Sq.
0200	Organic, class C, 235-240 lb./square, 3 bundles/square	"	"	5	1.600	Sq.
0250	Standard, laminated multi-layered shingles					
0300	Class A, 240-260 lb./square, 3 bundles/square	1 Rofc	1 Roofer, Composition	4.50	1.780	Sq.
0350	Class C, 260-300 lb./square, 4 bundles/square	"	"	4	2.000	Sq.
0400	Premium, laminated multi-layered shingles					
0450	Class A, 260-300 lb./square, 4 bundles/square	1 Rofc	1 Roofer, Composition	3.50	2.290	Sq.
0500	Class C, 300-385 lb./square, 5 bundles/square			3	2.670	Sq.
0700	Hip and ridge roll			400	.020	L.F.
0900	Ridge shingles	↓	↓	330	.024	L.F.
105	PORCELAIN ENAMEL 22 ga., 10" x 10", 225 lb. per sq., minimum	1 Rots	1 Roofer, Tile & Slate	1.30	6.150	Sq.
0100	Maximum	"	"	1	8.000	Sq.
106	SLATE Including felt underlay & nails, Buckingham, Virginia, black					
0100	3/16" thick	1 Rots	1 Roofer, Tile & Slate	1.75	4.570	Sq.
0200	1/4" thick			1.75	4.570	Sq.
0904	Pennsylvania black, Bangor, #1 clear			1.75	4.570	Sq.
1200	Vermont, unfading colors, green, mottled green			1.75	4.570	Sq.
1300	Semi-weathering green & gray			1.75	4.570	Sq.
1400	Purple			1.75	4.570	Sq.
1500	Black or gray			1.75	4.570	Sq.
107	STEEL Shingles, galvanized, 26 gauge			2.20	3.640	Sq.
0200	24 gauge	↓	↓	2.20	3.640	Sq.

073 | Shingles and Roofing Tiles

073 100 | Shingles

		CREW	MAKEUP	DAILY OUTPUT	MAN-HOURS	UNIT
108	**WOOD** 16" No. 1 red cedar shingles, 5X, 5" exposure, on roof	1 Carp	1 Carpenter	2.50	3.200	Sq.
0200	7-1/2" exposure, on walls			2.05	3.900	Sq.
0300	18" No. 1 red cedar perfections, 5-1/2" exposure, on roof			2.75	2.910	Sq.
0600	Resquared, and rebutted, 5-1/2" exposure, on roof			3	2.670	Sq.
0900	7-1/2" exposure, on walls			2.45	3.270	Sq.
1100	Hand-split red cedar shakes, on walls, 24" long, 10" exposure			2.50	3.200	Sq.
1200	18" long, 8-1/2" exposure			2	4.000	Sq.
2000	White cedar shingles, 16" long, extras, 5" exposure, on roof			2.40	3.330	Sq.
2100	7-1/2" exposure, on walls			2	4.000	Sq.
2300	For #15 organic felt underlayment on roof, 1 layer, add	↓	↓	64	.125	Sq.
2400	2 layers, add			32	.250	Sq.
2700	Panelized systems, No.1 cedar shingles on 5/16" CDX plywood					
2800	On walls, 8' strips, 7" or 14" exposure	F-2	2 Carpenters Power Tools	700	.023	S.F.
2900	Matching flush corners	"	"	400	.040	L.F.
3500	On roofs, 8' strips, 7" or 14" exposure	1 Carp	1 Carpenter	3	2.670	Sq.
3600	Matching lap corners			200	.040	L.F.
3700	Matching rake corners			200	.040	L.F.
3800	Matching valley sheets	↓	↓	200	.040	L.F.

073 200 | Roofing Tile

		CREW	MAKEUP	DAILY OUTPUT	MAN-HOURS	UNIT
201	**ALUMINUM** Tiles, .019" thick, mission tile	1 Carp	1 Carpenter	2.50	3.200	Sq.
0200	Spanish tiles	"	"	3	2.670	Sq.
202	**CLAY TILE**					
0200	Lanai tile or Classic tile, 158 pcs. per sq.	1 Rots	1 Roofer, Tile & Slate	1.65	4.850	Sq.
0300	Americana, 158 pcs. per sq., most colors			1.65	4.850	Sq.
0350	Green, gray or brown			1.65	4.850	Sq.
0400	Blue			1.65	4.850	Sq.
0600	Spanish tile, 171 pcs. per sq., red			1.80	4.440	Sq.
0800	Buff, green, gray, brown			1.80	4.440	Sq.
0900	Blue			1.80	4.440	Sq.
1100	Mission tile, 166 pcs. per sq., machine scored finish, red			1.15	6.960	Sq.
1700	French tile, 133 pcs. per sq., smooth finish, red			1.35	5.930	Sq.
1750	Blue or green			1.35	5.930	Sq.
1800	Norman tile, 317 pcs. per sq.			1	8.000	Sq.
2200	Williamsburg tile, 158 pcs. per sq., aged cedar			1.35	5.930	Sq.
2250	Gray or green	↓	↓	1.35	5.930	Sq.
204	**CONCRETE TILE** Including installation of accessories					
0050	Earthtone colors, nailed to wood deck	1 Rots	1 Roofer, Tile & Slate	1.35	5.930	Sq.
0150	Custom blues			1.35	5.930	Sq.
0200	Custom greens	↓	↓	1.35	5.930	Sq.
0500	Shakes, 13" x 16-1/2", 90 per sq., 950 lb. per sq.					
0600	All colors, nailed to wood deck	1 Rots	1 Roofer, Tile & Slate	1.50	5.330	Sq.

074 | Preformed Roofing and Siding

074 100 | Preformed Panels

			CREW	MAKEUP	DAILY OUTPUT	MAN-HOURS	UNIT
101	101	**ALUMINUM ROOFING** Corrugated or ribbed, .0175" thick, natural	G-3	2 Sheet Metal Workers	1,000	.032	S.F.
				2 Building Laborers			
				Power Tools			
	0300	Painted			1,000	.032	S.F.
	0400	Corrugated, .0215" thick, on steel frame, natural finish			1,000	.032	S.F.
	0600	Painted			1,000	.032	S.F.
	0700	Corrugated, on steel frame, natural, .024" thick			1,000	.032	S.F.
	0900	.032" thick			1,000	.032	S.F.
	1000	Painted, .024" thick			1,000	.032	S.F.
	1200	.032" thick			1,000	.032	S.F.
	1300	V-Beam, on steel frame construction, .032" thick, natural			1,000	.032	S.F.
	1500	Painted			1,000	.032	S.F.
	1600	.040" thick, natural			1,000	.032	S.F.
	1800	Painted			1,000	.032	S.F.
	1900	.050" thick, natural			1,000	.032	S.F.
	2100	Painted			1,000	.032	S.F.
	2200	For roofing on wood frame, deduct			4,600	.007	S.F.
	2400	Ridge cap, .032" thick, natural	↓	↓	800	.040	L.F.
	102	**ASPHALT PANELS** Corrugated, 1/8" thick, smooth surface	1 Rofc	1 Roofer, Composition	335	.024	S.F.
	0100	Granulated surface			335	.024	S.F.
	0200	Ridge pieces, 1/8" thick, smooth			400	.020	L.F.
	0300	Granulated			400	.020	L.F.
	0500	PVC skylight sheets, 28" x 96"	↓	↓	12.50	.640	Ea.
	104	**FIBERGLASS** Corrugated panels, roofing, 6 oz. per S.F.	G-3	2 Sheet Metal Workers	1,000	.032	S.F.
				2 Building Laborers			
				Power Tools			
	0100	8 oz. per S.F.			1,000	.032	S.F.
	0300	Corrugated siding, 4 oz. per S.F.			880	.036	S.F.
	0400	5 oz. per S.F.			880	.036	S.F.
	0600	8 oz. siding, textured			880	.036	S.F.
	0700	Fire retardant			880	.036	S.F.
	0900	Flat panels, 6 oz. per S.F., clear or colors			880	.036	S.F.
	1100	Fire retardant, class A			880	.036	S.F.
	1300	8 oz. per S.F., clear or colors			880	.036	S.F.
	1700	Sandwich panels, fiberglass, 1-9/16" thick, panels to 20 S.F.			180	.178	S.F.
	1900	As above, but 2-3/4" thick, panels to 100 S.F.	↓	↓	265	.121	S.F.
	105	**PROTECTED METAL** Roofing, metallic adhesive,					
	0300	Box rib, colored, 24 gauge	G-3	2 Sheet Metal Workers	495	.065	S.F.
				2 Building Laborers			
				Power Tools			
	0400	22 gauge			495	.065	S.F.
	0600	Corrugated, colored, 24 gauge			495	.065	S.F.
	0700	22 gauge			495	.065	S.F.
	0900	Deep rib, 4" deep, colored, 24 gauge			495	.065	S.F.
	1000	22 gauge			420	.076	S.F.
	1200	Siding, box rib, colored, 24 gauge			420	.076	S.F.
	1300	22 gauge			420	.076	S.F.
	1500	Corrugated, colored, 24 gauge			420	.076	S.F.
	1600	22 gauge			420	.076	S.F.
	107	**STEEL ROOFING** Galv., corrugated or ribbed, on steel frame, 30 ga.			1,100	.029	S.F.
	0100	28 gauge			1,050	.030	S.F.
	0300	26 gauge			1,000	.032	S.F.
	0400	24 gauge			950	.034	S.F.
	0600	Colored, corrugated or ribbed, on steel frame, 28 gauge			1,050	.030	S.F.
	0700	26 gauge			1,000	.032	S.F.
	0900	Factory insulated, 26 gauge with 1" polystyrene, galvanized			800	.040	S.F.
	1000	Colored			800	.040	S.F.
	1200	Ridge, galvanized, 10" wide	↓	↓	800	.040	L.F.

074 | Preformed Roofing and Siding

074 100 | Preformed Panels

		CREW	MAKEUP	DAILY OUTPUT	MAN-HOURS	UNIT
107 1211	Steel roofing, ridge, galvanized, 20" wide	G-3	2 Sheet Metal Workers 2 Building Laborers Power Tools	750	.043	L.F.

074 200 | Composite Panels

		CREW	MAKEUP	DAILY OUTPUT	MAN-HOURS	UNIT
201	EXPOSED AGGREGATE PANELS					
0200	Polymer concrete matrix, 1/4" thick					
0300	Small size aggregate	F-3	4 Carpenters 1 Equip. Oper. (crane) 1 Hyd. Crane, 12 Ton Power Tools	445	.090	S.F.
0500	Large size aggregate	↓	↓	445	.090	S.F.
1100	Solid polyester panels, up to 5' x 14', 3/4" thick			335	.119	S.F.
1300	Polystyrene panels, aggregate face, 2' x 2' x 2-1/4", R8.4					
1400	Straight panels, minimum	D-1	1 Bricklayer 1 Bricklayer Helper	325	.049	S.F.
1500	Maximum			600	.027	S.F.
1600	Corners, angles, returns, etc., minimum			225	.071	S.F.
1700	Maximum	↓	↓	450	.036	S.F.
202	METAL FACING PANELS Field assembled, insulated sandwich					
0100	wall panels, over 5000 S.F.					
0300	16 ga. aluminum exterior, 1-1/2" fiberglass and					
0400	18 ga. galvanized steel interior	G-3	2 Sheet Metal Workers 2 Building Laborers Power Tools	195	.164	S.F.
0600	18 ga. galvanized steel both sides			195	.164	S.F.
0700	20 ga. stainless steel exterior face			195	.164	S.F.
0900	20 ga. protected metal or baked enamel exterior			195	.164	S.F.
1000	16 ga. porcelain on aluminum exterior	↓	↓	195	.164	S.F.
1200	Factory made sandwich wall panels, acryl. coated, 10 mil alum.					
1300	face on 5/16" plywood core, with foil back	G-3	2 Sheet Metal Workers 2 Building Laborers Power Tools	375	.085	S.F.
1400	28 ga. porcelain enamel face, insulated cores, hardboard					
1500	stabilizer and galvanized back, 1" thick	G-3	2 Sheet Metal Workers 2 Building Laborers Power Tools	375	.085	S.F.
1600	2" thick			375	.085	S.F.
1800	As above, but hardboard back, 1" thick			375	.085	S.F.
1900	2" thick			375	.085	S.F.
2100	As above, but porcelain enamel both sides, 1" thick			375	.085	S.F.
2200	2" thick			375	.085	S.F.
2400	Porcelain enamel both sides, 2' or 4' wide			375	.085	S.F.
2500	2" thick, fire rated, 3' wide	↓	↓	375	.085	S.F.
2700	Porcelain enamel on steel, 2 faces, laminated to hardboard core					
2800	1/4" thick	G-3	2 Sheet Metal Workers 2 Building Laborers Power Tools	375	.085	S.F.
3000	Interior, galvanized steel	"	"	375	.085	S.F.
3100	Porcelain enamel 2 sides, 1/4" thick, mineral fiber core	G-3	2 Sheet Metal Workers 2 Building Laborers Power Tools	375	.085	S.F.
3300	Porcelain enameled steel on 3/8" plywood	"	"	375	.085	S.F.

074 | Preformed Roofing and Siding

074 600 | Cladding/Siding

			CREW	MAKEUP	DAILY OUTPUT	MAN-HOURS	UNIT
602	602	ALUMINUM SIDING .019" thick, on steel construction, natural	G-3	2 Sheet Metal Workers	775	.041	S.F.
				2 Building Laborers			
				Power Tools			
	0100	Painted			775	.041	S.F.
	0400	Farm type, .021" thick on steel frame, natural			775	.041	S.F.
	0600	Painted			775	.041	S.F.
	0700	Industrial type, corrugated, .024" thick, on steel, natural			775	.041	S.F.
	0900	Painted			775	.041	S.F.
	1000	.032" thick, natural			775	.041	S.F.
	1200	Painted			775	.041	S.F.
	1300	V-Beam, on steel frame, .032" thick, natural			775	.041	S.F.
	1500	Painted			775	.041	S.F.
	1600	.040" thick, natural			775	.041	S.F.
	1800	Painted			775	.041	S.F.
	1900	.050" thick, natural			775	.041	S.F.
	2100	Painted			775	.041	S.F.
	2200	Ribbed, 4" profile, on steel frame, .032" thick, natural			775	.041	S.F.
	2400	Painted			775	.041	S.F.
	2500	.040" thick, natural			775	.041	S.F.
	2700	Painted			775	.041	S.F.
	2750	.050" thick, natural			775	.041	S.F.
	2760	Painted			775	.041	S.F.
	3100	Perforated, corrugated, 14% openings, .024" thick, natural			775	.041	S.F.
	3150	Painted			775	.041	S.F.
	3300	For siding on wood frame, deduct from above			2,800	.011	S.F.
	3630	Flashing, sidewall, .032" thick			800	.040	L.F.
	3650	End wall, .040" thick			800	.040	L.F.
	3670	Closure strips, corrugated, .032" thick			800	.040	L.F.
	3680	Ribbed, 4" or 8", .032" thick			800	.040	L.F.
	3690	V-beam, .040" thick	↓	↓	800	.040	L.F.
	3800	Horizontal, colored clapboard, 8" or 10" wide, plain	1 Carp	1 Carpenter	255	.031	S.F.
	3900	Insulated			255	.031	S.F.
	4000	Vertical board & batten, colored, non-insulated			255	.031	S.F.
	4300	Corners for above, outside			255	.031	V.L.F.
	4500	Inside corners	↓	↓	255	.031	V.L.F.
	4600	Sandwich panels, 1" insulation , single story	G-3	2 Sheet Metal Workers	395	.081	S.F.
				2 Building Laborers			
				Power Tools			
	4900	Multi-story	"	"	345	.093	S.F.
	606	STEEL SIDING Beveled, vinyl coated, 8" wide	1 Carp	1 Carpenter	265	.030	S.F.
	0050	10" wide	"	"	275	.029	S.F.
	0080	Galv. corrugated or ribbed, on steel frame, 30 gauge	G-3	2 Sheet Metal Workers	800	.040	S.F.
				2 Building Laborers			
				Power Tools			
	0100	28 gauge			795	.040	S.F.
	0300	26 gauge			790	.041	S.F.
	0400	24 gauge			785	.041	S.F.
	0600	22 gauge			770	.042	S.F.
	0700	Colored, corrugated/ribbed, on steel frame, 10 yr. fin., 28 ga.			800	.040	S.F.
	0900	26 gauge			795	.040	S.F.
	1000	24 gauge			790	.041	S.F.
	1200	Factory sandwich panel, 26 ga., 1" insulation, galvanized			380	.084	S.F.
	1300	Colored 1 side			380	.084	S.F.
	1500	Galvanized 2 sides			380	.084	S.F.
	1600	Colored 2 sides			380	.084	S.F.
	1800	Acrylic paint face, regular paint liner			380	.084	S.F.
	2000	22 ga., galv., 2" insulation, baked enamel exterior			360	.089	S.F.
	2100	P.V.F. exterior finish	↓	↓	360	.089	S.F.

074 600 | Cladding/Siding

		Description	CREW	MAKEUP	DAILY OUTPUT	MAN-HOURS	UNIT
607	607	**VINYL SIDING** Solid PVC panels, 8" to 10" wide, plain	1 Carp	1 Carpenter	255	.031	S.F.
	0100	Insulated			255	.031	S.F.
	0200	Soffit and fascia			205	.039	S.F.
	0300	Window and door trim moldings			185	.043	L.F.
	0500	Corner posts, outside corner			205	.039	L.F.
	0600	Inside corner			205	.039	L.F.
	0800	Corrugated vinyl sheets, .090" thick			235	.034	S.F.
	0900	.120" thick			225	.036	S.F.
	1100	Flat sheets with fibers, colored, 1/16" thick			235	.034	S.F.
	1200	1/8" thick			225	.036	S.F.
	1400	Insulated sandwich panels with 1/16" skin, 1" thick			180	.044	S.F.
	1500	1-1/2" thick	↓	↓	190	.042	S.F.
	609	**WOOD SIDING, BOARDS**					
	3200	Wood, cedar bevel, short lengths, A grade, 1/2" x 6"	1 Carp	1 Carpenter	250	.032	S.F.
	3300	1/2" x 8"			275	.029	S.F.
	3500	3/4" x 10", clear grade, 3' to 16'			300	.027	S.F.
	3600	"B" grade			300	.027	S.F.
	3800	Cedar, rough sawn, 1" x 4", B & Btr., natural			240	.033	S.F.
	3900	Stained			240	.033	S.F.
	4100	1" x 12", board & batten, #3 & Btr., natural			260	.031	S.F.
	4200	Stained			260	.031	S.F.
	4400	1" x 8" channel siding, #3 & Btr., natural			250	.032	S.F.
	4500	Stained			250	.032	S.F.
	4700	Redwood, clear, beveled, vertical grain, 1/2" x 4"			200	.040	S.F.
	4800	1/2" x 8"			250	.032	S.F.
	5000	3/4" x 10"			300	.027	S.F.
	5200	Channel siding, 1" x 10", clear	↓	↓	285	.028	S.F.
	5250	Redwood, T&G boards, clear, 1" x 4"	F-2	2 Carpenters Power Tools	300	.053	S.F.
	5270	1" x 8"	"	"	375	.043	S.F.
	5400	White pine, rough sawn, 1" x 8", natural	1 Carp	1 Carpenter	275	.029	S.F.
	5500	Stained	"	"	275	.029	S.F.
	611	**WOOD SIDING, SHEETS**					
	0030	Siding, hardboard, 7/16" thick, prime painted, lap,					
	0050	plain or grooved finish	F-2	2 Carpenters Power Tools	750	.021	S.F.
	0100	Board finish, 7/16" thick, lap or grooved, primed			750	.021	S.F.
	0200	Stained			750	.021	S.F.
	0700	Particle board, overlaid, 3/8" thick			750	.021	S.F.
	0900	Plywood, medium density overlaid, 3/8" thick			750	.021	S.F.
	1000	1/2" thick			700	.023	S.F.
	1100	3/4" thick			650	.025	S.F.
	1600	Texture 1-11, cedar, 5/8" thick, natural			675	.024	S.F.
	1700	Factory stained			675	.024	S.F.
	1900	Texture 1-11, fir, 5/8" thick, natural			675	.024	S.F.
	2000	Factory stained			675	.024	S.F.
	2050	Texture 1-11, S.Y.P., 5/8" thick, natural			675	.024	S.F.
	2100	Factory stained			675	.024	S.F.
	2200	Rough sawn cedar, 3/8" thick, natural			675	.024	S.F.
	2300	Factory stained			675	.024	S.F.
	2500	Rough sawn fir, 3/8" thick, natural			675	.024	S.F.
	2600	Factory stained			675	.024	S.F.
	2800	Redwood, textured siding, 5/8" thick			675	.024	S.F.
	3000	Polyvinyl chloride coated, 3/8" thick	↓	↓	750	.021	S.F.

075 | Membrane Roofing

075 100 | Built-Up Roofing

			CREW	MAKEUP	DAILY OUTPUT	MAN-HOURS	UNIT
101	101	**ASPHALT** Coated felt, #30, 2 sq. per roll, not mopped	1 Rofc	1 Roofer, Composition	58	.138	Sq.
	0200	#15, 4 sq. per roll, plain or perforated, not mopped			58	.138	Sq.
	0300	Roll roofing, smooth, #65			15	.533	Sq.
	0500	#90			15	.533	Sq.
	0520	Mineralized			15	.533	Sq.
	0540	D.C. (Double coverage), 19" selvage edge	↓	↓	10	.800	Sq.
	102	**BUILT-UP ROOFING**					
	0120	Asphalt flood coat with gravel/slag surfacing, not including					
	0140	Insulation, flashing or wood nailers					
	0200	Asphalt base sheet, 3 plies #15 asphalt felt, mopped	G-1	1 Roofer Foreman 4 Roofers, Composition 2 Roofer Helpers Application Equipment	22	2.550	Sq.
	0350	On nailable decks			21	2.670	Sq.
	0500	4 plies #15 asphalt felt, mopped			20	2.800	Sq.
	0550	On nailable decks			19	2.950	Sq.
	0700	Coated glass base sheet, 2 plies glass (type IV), mopped			22	2.550	Sq.
	0850	3 plies glass, mopped			20	2.800	Sq.
	0950	On nailable decks			19	2.950	Sq.
	1000	3 plies glass fiber felt (type IV), mopped			22	2.550	Sq.
	1050	On nailable decks			21	2.670	Sq.
	1100	4 plies glass fiber felt (type IV), mopped			20	2.800	Sq.
	1150	On nailable decks			19	2.950	Sq.
	1200	Organic base sheet, 3 plies #15 organic felt, mopped			20	2.800	Sq.
	1250	On nailable decks			19	2.950	Sq.
	1300	4 plies #15 organic felt, mopped	↓	↓	22	2.550	Sq.
	2000	Asphalt flood coat, smooth surface					
	2200	Asphalt base sheet & 3 plies #15 asphalt felt, mopped	G-1	1 Roofer Foreman 4 Roofers, Composition 2 Roofer Helpers Application Equipment	24	2.330	Sq.
	2400	On nailable decks			23	2.430	Sq.
	2600	4 plies #15 asphalt felt, mopped			24	2.330	Sq.
	2700	On nailable decks	↓	↓	23	2.430	Sq.
	2900	Coated glass fiber base sheet, mopped, and 2 plies of					
	2910	glass fiber felt (type IV)	G-1	1 Roofer Foreman 4 Roofers, Composition 2 Roofer Helpers Application Equipment	25	2.240	Sq.
	3100	On nailable decks			24	2.330	Sq.
	3200	3 plies, mopped			23	2.430	Sq.
	3300	On nailable decks			22	2.550	Sq.
	3500	3 plies glass fiber felt (type IV), mopped			25	2.240	Sq.
	3600	On nailable decks			24	2.330	Sq.
	3800	4 plies glass fiber felt (type IV), mopped			23	2.430	Sq.
	3900	On nailable decks			22	2.550	Sq.
	4000	Organic base sheet & 3 plies #15 organic felt, mopped			24	2.330	Sq.
	4200	On nailable decks			23	2.430	Sq.
	4300	4 plies #15 organic felt, mopped	↓	↓	22	2.550	Sq.
	4500	Coal tar pitch with gravel/slag surfacing					
	4600	4 plies #15 tarred felt, mopped	G-1	1 Roofer Foreman 4 Roofers, Composition 2 Roofer Helpers Application Equipment	21	2.670	Sq.
	4800	3 plies glass fiber felt (type IV), mopped	"	"	19	2.950	Sq.

075 100 | Built-Up Roofing

			Description	CREW	MAKEUP	DAILY OUTPUT	MAN-HOURS	UNIT
102	5011		Built-up roofing, glass fiber base & 2 plies felt, mopped	G-1	1 Roofer Foreman	19	2.950	Sq.
					4 Roofers, Composition			
					2 Roofer Helpers			
					Application Equipment			
	5300		On nailable decks			18	3.110	Sq.
	5400		On wood decks			18	3.110	Sq.
	5600		4 plies glass fiber felt (type IV), mopped			21	2.670	Sq.
	5800		On nailable decks			20	2.800	Sq.
	5900		On wood decks			20	2.800	Sq.
	6000		4 plies #15 tarred felt, mopped			21	2.670	Sq.
	103		CANTS 4" x 4" treated timber, cut diagonally	1 Rofc	1 Roofer, Composition	325	.025	L.F.
	0100		Foamglass			325	.025	L.F.
	0300		Mineral or fiber, trapezoidal, 1"x 4" x 48"			325	.025	L.F.
	0400		1-1/2" x 5-5/8" x 48"			325	.025	L.F.
	104		FELT Glass fibered, #15, no mopping			58	.138	Sq.
	0200		#43 base sheet			58	.138	Sq.
	0300		Base sheet, #45, channel vented			58	.138	Sq.
	0400		#50, coated			58	.138	Sq.
	0500		Cap, mineral surfaced			58	.138	Sq.
	0600		Flashing membrane, #65			16	.500	Sq.
	0800		Coal tar fibered, #15, no mopping			58	.138	Sq.
	0900		Asphalt felt, #15, 4 sq. per roll, no mopping			58	.138	Sq.
	1100		#30, 2 sq. per roll			58	.138	Sq.
	1200		Double coated, #33			58	.138	Sq.
	1400		#40, base sheet			58	.138	Sq.
	1500		Tarred felt, organic, #15, 4 sq. rolls			58	.138	Sq.
	1550		#30, 2 sq. roll			58	.138	Sq.
	1700		Add for mopping above felts, per ply, asphalt, 20 lbs. per sq.			28	.286	Sq.
	1800		Coal tar mopping, 30 lbs. per sq.			27	.296	Sq.
	1900		Flood coat, with asphalt, 60 lbs. per sq.	2 Rofc	2 Roofers, Composition	16.30	.982	Sq.
	2000		With coal tar, 75 lbs. per sq.	"	"	15.30	1.050	Sq.
	105		WALKWAY For built-up roofs, asphalt impregnated, 3' x 6' x 1/2" thk.	1 Rofc	1 Roofer, Composition	400	.020	S.F.
	0100		3' x 3' x 3/4" thick, hot application	"	"	400	.020	S.F.
	0300		Concrete patio blocks, 2" thick, natural	1 Clab	1 Building Laborer	115	.070	S.F.
	0400		Colors	"	"	115	.070	S.F.

075 200 | Prepared Roll Roofing

		Description	CREW	MAKEUP	DAILY OUTPUT	MAN-HOURS	UNIT
204		ROLL ROOFING					
0100		Asphalt, mineral surface					
0200		1 ply #15 organic felt, 1 ply mineral surfaced					
0300		selvage roofing, lap 19", nailed & mopped	G-1	1 Roofer Foreman	27	2.070	Sq.
				4 Roofers, Composition			
				2 Roofer Helpers			
				Application Equipment			
0400		3 plies glass fiber felt (type IV), 1 ply mineral surfaced					
0500		selvage roofing, lapped 19", mopped	G-1	1 Roofer Foreman	25	2.240	Sq.
				4 Roofers, Composition			
				2 Roofer Helpers			
				Application Equipment			
0600		Coated glass fiber base sheet, 2 plies of glass fiber					
0700		felt (type IV), 1 ply mineral surfaced selvage					
0800		roofing, lapped 19", mopped	G-1	1 Roofer Foreman	25	2.240	Sq.
				4 Roofers, Composition			
				2 Roofer Helpers			
				Application Equipment			
0900		On nailable decks	"	"	24	2.330	Sq.

075 200 | Prepared Roll Roofing

		CREW	MAKEUP	DAILY OUTPUT	MAN-HOURS	UNIT
204	1101 Roll roof, 3 ply glass fiber felt, 1 ply selvage, lap 19", mopped	G-1	1 Roofer Foreman 4 Roofers, Composition 2 Roofer Helpers Application Equipment	25	2.240	Sq.

075 300 | Elastomeric Roofing

		CREW	MAKEUP	DAILY OUTPUT	MAN-HOURS	UNIT
301	**ELASTOMERIC ROOFING**					
0300	Hypalon neoprene, fluid applied, 20 mil thick, not-reinforced	G-1	1 Roofer Foreman 4 Roofers, Composition 2 Roofer Helpers Application Equipment	1,135	.049	S.F.
0600	Non-woven polyester, reinforced			960	.058	S.F.
0700	5 coat neoprene deck, 60 mil thick, under 10,000 S.F.			325	.172	S.F.
0900	Over 10,000 S.F.			625	.090	S.F.
1000	Neoprene membrane, 1/16" thick			1,375	.041	S.F.
1300	Vinyl plastic traffic deck, sprayed, 2 to 4 mils thick			625	.090	S.F.
1500	Vinyl and neoprene membrane traffic deck	↓	↓	1,550	.036	S.F.
1600	Polyurethane spray-on with 20 mil silicone rubber coating applied					
1700	1" thick, R7, minimum	G-2	1 Plasterer 1 Plasterer Helper 1 Building Laborer Grouting Equipment	875	.027	S.F.
1800	Maximim			805	.030	S.F.
1900	2" thick, R14, minimum			685	.035	S.F.
2000	Maximum			575	.042	S.F.
2100	3" thick, R21, minimum			500	.048	S.F.
2200	Maximum	↓	↓	440	.055	S.F.
302	**SINGLE-PLY MEMBRANE**					
0200	Chlorinated polyethylene(CPE), 40 mils, 0.31 P.S.F.					
0300	Partially adhered with mechanical fasteners	G-5	1 Roofer Foreman 2 Roofers, Composition 2 Roofer Helpers Application Equipment	3,500	.011	S.F.
0800	Chlorosulfonated polyethylene-hypalon (CSPE), 35 mils,					
0900	0.25 P.S.F., fully adhered with neoprene latex	G-5	1 Roofer Foreman 2 Roofers, Composition 2 Roofer Helpers Application Equipment	2,600	.015	S.F.
1000	45 mils, 0.29 P.S.F.					
1100	Loose-laid & ballasted with stone (10 P.S.F.)	G-5	1 Roofer Foreman 2 Roofers, Composition 2 Roofer Helpers Application Equipment	5,100	.008	S.F.
1200	Partially adhered with fastening strips			3,500	.011	S.F.
1300	Plates with adhesive attachment	↓	↓	3,500	.011	S.F.
2000	Elastomer modified asphalt, 150 mils, 1.47 P.S.F.					
2500	Hot mopped with asphalt	G-5	1 Roofer Foreman 2 Roofers, Composition 2 Roofer Helpers Application Equipment	2,500	.016	S.F.
2700	Fully adhered-torched	"	"	2,000	.020	S.F.
3500	Ethylene propylene diene monomer (EPDM), 45 mils, 0.28 P.S.F.					
3600	Loose-laid & ballasted with stone (10 P.S.F.)	G-5	1 Roofer Foreman 2 Roofers, Composition 2 Roofer Helpers Application Equipment	5,100	.008	S.F.
3700	Partially adhered			3,500	.011	S.F.
3800	Fully adhered with adhesive	↓	↓	2,600	.015	S.F.

075 300 | Elastomeric Roofing

		CREW	MAKEUP	DAILY OUTPUT	MAN-HOURS	UNIT
302 4001	Single ply membrane, EPDM, 55 mils, 0.35 P.S.F.					
4100	Loose-laid & ballasted with stone, (10 P.S.F.)	G-5	1 Roofer Foreman	5,100	.008	S.F.
			2 Roofers, Composition			
			2 Roofer Helpers			
			Application Equipment			
4200	Partially adhered	↓	↓	3,500	.011	S.F.
4300	Fully adhered with adhesive	↓	↓	2,600	.015	S.F.
4500	60 mils, 0.40 P.S.F.					
4600	Loose-laid & ballasted with stone (10 P.S.F.)	G-5	1 Roofer Foreman	5,100	.008	S.F.
			2 Roofers, Composition			
			2 Roofer Helpers			
			Application Equipment			
4700	Partially adhered	↓	↓	3,500	.011	S.F.
4800	Fully adhered with adhesive	↓	↓	2,600	.015	S.F.
6800	Neoprene, 60 mils, 0.45 P.S.F.					
7000	Partially adhered with mechanical fasteners	G-5	1 Roofer Foreman	3,500	.011	S.F.
			2 Roofers, Composition			
			2 Roofer Helpers			
			Application Equipment			
7100	Fully adhered with contact adhesive	"	"	2,600	.015	S.F.
7110	Uncured neoprene, 60 mils, for flashing	1 Rofc	1 Roofer, Composition	600	.013	S.F.
7500	Polyisobutylene (PIB), 100 mils, 0.57 P.S.F.					
7600	Loose-laid & ballasted with stone/gravel (10 P.S.F.)	G-5	1 Roofer Foreman	5,100	.008	S.F.
			2 Roofers, Composition			
			2 Roofer Helpers			
			Application Equipment			
7700	Partially adhered with adhesive	↓	↓	3,500	.011	S.F.
7800	Hot asphalt attachment	↓	↓	3,500	.011	S.F.
7900	Fully adhered with contact cement	↓	↓	2,600	.015	S.F.
8200	Polyvinyl chloride (PVC)					
8250	45 mils, 0.30 P.S.F.					
8300	Loose-laid & ballasted with stone/gravel (10 P.S.F.)	G-5	1 Roofer Foreman	5,100	.008	S.F.
			2 Roofers, Composition			
			2 Roofer Helpers			
			Application Equipment			
8350	Partially adhered with mechanical fasteners	"	"	3,500	.011	S.F.
8400	48 mils, 0.33 to 0.38 P.S.F.					
8450	Loose-laid & ballasted with stone/gravel(10 P.S.F.)	G-5	1 Roofer Foreman	5,100	.008	S.F.
			2 Roofers, Composition			
			2 Roofer Helpers			
			Application Equipment			
8500	Partially adhered with mechanical & solvent weld			3,500	.011	S.F.
8550	Fully adhered with adhesive			2,600	.015	S.F.
8650	60 mils, 0.40#, partially adhered with PVC coated strips	↓	↓	3,500	.011	S.F.
8680	Uncured neoprene, 60 mils, for flashing	1 Rofc	1 Roofer, Composition	600	.013	S.F.
8690	Separator sheet	G-5	1 Roofer Foreman	4,000	.010	S.F.
			2 Roofers, Composition			
			2 Roofer Helpers			
			Application Equipment			
8700	Reinforced PVC, 48 mils, 0.33 P.S.F.					
8750	Loose-laid & ballasted with stone/gravel (12 P.S.F.)	G-5	1 Roofer Foreman	5,100	.008	S.F.
			2 Roofers, Composition			
			2 Roofer Helpers			
			Application Equipment			
8800	Partially adhered with mechanical fasteners	↓	↓	3,500	.011	S.F.
8850	Fully adhered with adhesive	↓	↓	2,600	.015	S.F.

075 350 | Modified Bit Roofing

		CREW	MAKEUP	DAILY OUTPUT	MAN-HOURS	UNIT
352	**MODIFIED BITUMEN**					
0100	120 mils, 0.92 P.S.F., fully adhered with torch welding	G-5	1 Roofer Foreman 2 Roofers, Composition 2 Roofer Helpers Application Equipment	2,800	.014	S.F.
0200	150 mils, 0.82 P.S.F.					
0300	Loose-laid & ballasted with gravel (4 P.S.F.)	G-5	1 Roofer Foreman 2 Roofers, Composition 2 Roofer Helpers Application Equipment	3,200	.013	S.F.
0400	Partially adhered with torch welding			2,500	.016	S.F.
0500	Fully adhered with torch welding			2,000	.020	S.F.
0600	Hot asphalt attachment	↓	↓	2,000	.020	S.F.
0700	160 mils, 0.78 to 1.2 P.S.F., with asphalt emulsion coating					
0800	Loose-laid & ballasted with stone/gravel (10 P.S.F.)	G-5	1 Roofer Foreman 2 Roofers, Composition 2 Roofer Helpers Application Equipment	3,200	.013	S.F.
0900	Partially adhered with torch welding			2,500	.016	S.F.
1000	Fully adhered with torch welding			2,000	.020	S.F.
1100	Hot asphalt attachment	↓	↓	2,000	.020	S.F.

076 100 | Sheet Metal Roofing

		CREW	MAKEUP	DAILY OUTPUT	MAN-HOURS	UNIT
101	**COPPER ROOFING** Batten seam, over 10 sq., 16 oz., 130 lb./sq.	1 Shee	1 Sheet Metal Worker	1.10	7.270	Sq.
0200	18 oz., 145 lb. per sq.			1	8.000	Sq.
0300	20 oz., 160 lb. per sq.			1	8.000	Sq.
0400	Standing seam, over 10 squares, 16 oz., 125 lb. per sq.			1.30	6.150	Sq.
0600	18 oz., 140 lb. per sq.			1.20	6.670	Sq.
0700	20 oz., 150 lb. per sq.			1.10	7.270	Sq.
0900	Flat seam, over 10 squares, 16 oz., 115 lb. per sq.			1.20	6.670	Sq.
1000	20 oz., 145 lb. per sq.			1.10	7.270	Sq.
102	**LEAD ROOFING** 3 lb. per S.F., batten seam			1.20	6.670	Sq.
0100	Flat seam			1.30	6.150	Sq.
103	**MONEL ROOFING** Batten seam, over 10 squares, .018" thick			1.20	6.670	Sq.
0100	.021" thick			1.15	6.960	Sq.
0300	Standing seam, .018" thick			1.35	5.930	Sq.
0400	.021" thick			1.30	6.150	Sq.
0600	Flat seam, .018" thick			1.30	6.150	Sq.
0700	.021" thick			1.20	6.670	Sq.
104	**STAINLESS STEEL ROOFING** Type 304, batten seam, 28 gauge			1.20	6.670	Sq.
0100	26 gauge			1.15	6.960	Sq.
105	**ZINC** Copper alloy roofing, batten seam, .020" thick			1.20	6.670	Sq.
0100	.027" thick			1.15	6.960	Sq.
0300	.032" thick			1.10	7.270	Sq.
0400	.040" thick	↓	↓	1.05	7.620	Sq.

076 200	Sheet Mtl Flash & Trim	CREW	MAKEUP	DAILY OUTPUT	MAN-HOURS	UNIT
201	**DOWNSPOUTS** Aluminum 2" x 3", .020" thick, embossed	1 Shee	1 Sheet Metal Worker	190	.042	L.F.
0100	Enameled			190	.042	L.F.
0300	Enameled, .024" thick, 2" x 3"			180	.044	L.F.
0400	3" x 4"			140	.057	L.F.
0600	Round, corrugated aluminum, 3" diameter, .020" thick			190	.042	L.F.
0700	4" diameter, .025" thick			140	.057	L.F.
0900	Wire strainer, round, 2" diameter			155	.052	Ea.
1000	4" diameter			155	.052	Ea.
1200	Rectangular, perforated, 2" x 3"			145	.055	Ea.
1300	3" x 4"			145	.055	Ea.
1500	Copper, round, 16 oz., stock, 2" diameter			190	.042	L.F.
1600	3" diameter			190	.042	L.F.
1800	4" diameter			145	.055	L.F.
1900	5" diameter			130	.062	L.F.
2100	Rectangular, corrugated copper, stock, 2" x 3"			190	.042	L.F.
2200	3" x 4"			145	.055	L.F.
2400	Rectangular, plain copper, stock, 2" x 3"			190	.042	L.F.
2500	3" x 4"			145	.055	L.F.
2700	Wire strainers, rectangular, 2" x 3"			145	.055	Ea.
2800	3" x 4"			145	.055	Ea.
3000	Round, 2" diameter			145	.055	Ea.
3100	3" diameter			145	.055	Ea.
3300	4" diameter			145	.055	Ea.
3400	5" diameter			115	.070	Ea.
3600	Lead-coated copper, round, stock, 2" diameter			190	.042	L.F.
3700	3" diameter			190	.042	L.F.
3900	4" diameter			145	.055	L.F.
4000	5" diameter, corrugated			130	.062	L.F.
4200	6" diameter, corrugated			105	.076	L.F.
4300	Rectangular, corrugated, stock, 2" x 3"			190	.042	L.F.
4500	Plain, stock, 2" x 3"			190	.042	L.F.
4600	3" x 4"			145	.055	L.F.
4800	Steel, galvanized, round, corrugated, 2" or 3" diam., 28 ga.			190	.042	L.F.
4900	4" diameter, 28 gauge			145	.055	L.F.
5100	5" diameter, 28 gauge			130	.062	L.F.
5200	26 gauge			130	.062	L.F.
5400	6" diameter, 28 gauge			105	.076	L.F.
5500	26 gauge			105	.076	L.F.
5700	Rectangular, corrugated, 28 gauge, 2" x 3"			190	.042	L.F.
5800	3" x 4"			145	.055	L.F.
6000	Rectangular, plain, 28 gauge, galvanized, 2" x 3"			190	.042	L.F.
6100	3" x 4"			145	.055	L.F.
6300	Epoxy painted, 24 gauge, corrugated, 2" x 3"			190	.042	L.F.
6400	3" x 4"			145	.055	L.F.
6600	Wire strainers, rectangular, 2" x 3"			145	.055	Ea.
6700	3" x 4"			145	.055	Ea.
6900	Round strainers, 2" or 3" diameter			145	.055	Ea.
7000	4" diameter			145	.055	Ea.
7200	5" diameter			145	.055	Ea.
7300	6" diameter			115	.070	Ea.
7500	Steel pipe, black, extra heavy, 4" diameter			20	.400	L.F.
7600	6" diameter			18	.444	L.F.
7800	Stainless steel tubing, schedule 5, 2" x 3" or 3" diameter			190	.042	L.F.
7900	3" x 4" or 4" diameter			145	.055	L.F.
8100	4" x 5" or 5" diameter			135	.059	L.F.
8200	Vinyl, rectangular, 2" x 3"			210	.038	L.F.
8300	Round, 2-1/2"	↓	↓	220	.036	L.F.

076 200 | Sheet Mtl Flash & Trim

		Description	CREW	MAKEUP	DAILY OUTPUT	MAN-HOURS	UNIT
202	202	**DRIP EDGE** Aluminum, .016" thick, 5" girth, mill finish	1 Carp	1 Carpenter	400	.020	L.F.
	0100	White finish			400	.020	L.F.
	0200	8" girth			400	.020	L.F.
	0300	28" girth			100	.080	L.F.
	0400	Galvanized, 5" girth			400	.020	L.F.
	0500	8" girth	↓	↓	400	.020	L.F.
	203	**ELBOWS** Aluminum, 2" x 3", embossed	1 Shee	1 Sheet Metal Worker	100	.080	Ea.
	0100	Enameled			100	.080	Ea.
	0200	3" x 4", .025" thick, embossed			100	.080	Ea.
	0300	Enameled			100	.080	Ea.
	0400	Round corrugated, 3", embossed, .020" thick			100	.080	Ea.
	0500	4", .025" thick			100	.080	Ea.
	0600	Copper, 16 oz. round, 2" diameter			100	.080	Ea.
	0700	3" diameter			100	.080	Ea.
	0800	4" diameter			100	.080	Ea.
	0900	5" diameter			100	.080	Ea.
	1000	2" x 3" corrugated			100	.080	Ea.
	1100	3" x 4" corrugated			100	.080	Ea.
	1300	Vinyl, 2-1/2" diameter, 45° or 75°			100	.080	Ea.
	1400	Tee Y junction			75	.107	Ea.
	204	**FLASHING** Aluminum, mill finish, .013" thick			145	.055	S.F.
	0030	.016" thick			145	.055	S.F.
	0060	.019" thick			145	.055	S.F.
	0100	.032" thick			145	.055	S.F.
	0200	.040" thick			145	.055	S.F.
	0300	.050" thick			145	.055	S.F.
	0500	Fabric-backed 2 sides, .004" thick			330	.024	S.F.
	0700	.016" thick			330	.024	S.F.
	0750	Mastic-backed, self adhesive			460	.017	S.F.
	0800	Mastic-coated 2 sides, .004" thick			330	.024	S.F.
	1000	.005" thick			330	.024	S.F.
	1100	.016" thick			330	.024	S.F.
	1600	Copper, 16 oz., sheets, under 6000 lbs.			115	.070	S.F.
	1700	Over 6000 lbs.			155	.052	S.F.
	1900	20 oz. sheets, under 6000 lbs.			110	.073	S.F.
	2000	Over 6000 lbs.			145	.055	S.F.
	2200	24 oz. sheets, under 6000 lbs.			105	.076	S.F.
	2300	Over 6000 lbs.			135	.059	S.F.
	2500	32 oz. sheets, under 6000 lbs.			100	.080	S.F.
	2600	Over 6000 lbs.			130	.062	S.F.
	2800	Copper, paperbacked 1 side, 2 oz.			330	.024	S.F.
	2900	3 oz.			330	.024	S.F.
	3100	Paperbacked 2 sides, copper, 2 oz.			330	.024	S.F.
	3150	3 oz.			330	.024	S.F.
	3200	5 oz.			330	.024	S.F.
	3250	7 oz.			330	.024	S.F.
	3400	Mastic-backed 2 sides, copper, 2 oz.			330	.024	S.F.
	3500	3 oz.			330	.024	S.F.
	3700	5 oz.			330	.024	S.F.
	3800	Fabric-backed 2 sides, copper, 2 oz.			330	.024	S.F.
	4000	3 oz.			330	.024	S.F.
	4100	5 oz.			330	.024	S.F.
	4300	Copper-clad stainless steel, .015" thick, under 500 lbs.			115	.070	S.F.
	4400	Over 2000 lbs.			155	.052	S.F.
	4600	.018" thick, under 500 lbs.			100	.080	S.F.
	4700	Over 2000 lbs.	↓	↓	145	.055	S.F.
	4900	Fabric, asphalt-saturated cotton, specification grade	1 Rofc	1 Roofer, Composition	35	.229	S.Y.
	5000	Utility grade	"	"	35	.229	S.Y.

076 200 | Sheet Mtl Flash & Trim

		Description	CREW	MAKEUP	DAILY OUTPUT	MAN-HOURS	UNIT
204	5201	Flashing, open-mesh fabric, saturated, 40 oz. per S.Y.	1 Rofc	1 Roofer, Composition	35	.229	S.Y.
	5300	Close-mesh fabric, saturated, 17 oz. per S.Y.			35	.229	S.Y.
	5500	Fiberglass, resin-coated			35	.229	S.Y.
	5600	Asphalt-coated, 40 oz. per S.Y.			35	.229	S.Y.
	5800	Lead, 2.5 lb. per S.F., up to 12" wide			135	.059	S.F.
	5900	Over 12" wide	▼	▼	135	.059	S.F.
	6100	Lead-coated copper, fabric-backed, 2 oz.	1 Shee	1 Sheet Metal Worker	330	.024	S.F.
	6200	5 oz.			330	.024	S.F.
	6400	Mastic-backed 2 sides, 2 oz.			330	.024	S.F.
	6500	5 oz.			330	.024	S.F.
	6700	Paperbacked 1 side, 2 oz.			330	.024	S.F.
	6800	3 oz.			330	.024	S.F.
	7000	Paperbacked 2 sides, 2 oz.			330	.024	S.F.
	7100	5 oz.	▼	▼	330	.024	S.F.
	7300	Polyvinyl chloride, black, .010" thick	1 Rofc	1 Roofer, Composition	285	.028	S.F.
	7400	.020" thick			285	.028	S.F.
	7600	.030" thick			285	.028	S.F.
	7700	.056" thick			285	.028	S.F.
	7900	Black or white for exposed roofs, .060" thick			285	.028	S.F.
	8000	Asbestos-backed for parking decks, .045" thick			285	.028	S.F.
	8050	PVC (19 mils) coated galv. steel (24 mils), 4' x 8' sheets			240	.033	S.F.
	8100	Rubber, butyl, 1/32" thick			285	.028	S.F.
	8200	1/16" thick			285	.028	S.F.
	8300	Neoprene, cured, 1/16" thick			285	.028	S.F.
	8400	1/8" thick	▼	▼	285	.028	S.F.
	8500	Shower pan, bituminous membrane, 7 oz.	1 Shee	1 Sheet Metal Worker	155	.052	S.F.
	8550	3 ply copper and fabric, 3 oz.			155	.052	S.F.
	8600	7 oz.			155	.052	S.F.
	8650	Copper, 16 oz.			100	.080	S.F.
	8700	Lead on copper and fabric, 5 oz.			155	.052	S.F.
	8800	7 oz.			155	.052	S.F.
	8850	Polyvinyl chloride, .030" thick			160	.050	S.F.
	8900	Stainless steel sheets, 32 ga., .010" thick			155	.052	S.F.
	9000	28 ga., .015" thick			155	.052	S.F.
	9100	26 ga., .018" thick			155	.052	S.F.
	9200	24 ga., .025" thick			155	.052	S.F.
	9300	Stainless steel, paperbacked 2 sides, .005" thick			330	.024	S.F.
	9400	Terne coated stainless steel, .015" thick, 28 ga.			155	.052	S.F.
	9500	.018" thick, 26 ga.			155	.052	S.F.
	9600	Zinc and copper alloy, .020" thick			155	.052	S.F.
	9700	.027" thick			155	.052	S.F.
	9800	.032" thick			155	.052	S.F.
	9900	.040" thick			155	.052	S.F.
	205	GUTTERS Aluminum, stock units, 5" box, .027" thick, plain			120	.067	L.F.
	0100	Enameled			120	.067	L.F.
	0300	5" box type, .032" thick, plain			120	.067	L.F.
	0400	Enameled			120	.067	L.F.
	0600	5" x 6" combination fascia & gutter, .032" thick, enameled			60	.133	L.F.
	0700	Copper, half round, 16 oz., stock units, 4" wide			120	.067	L.F.
	0900	5" wide			120	.067	L.F.
	1000	6" wide			115	.070	L.F.
	1200	K type copper gutter, stock, 4" wide			120	.067	L.F.
	1300	5" wide			120	.067	L.F.
	1500	Lead coated copper, half round, stock, 4" wide			120	.067	L.F.
	1600	6" wide			115	.070	L.F.
	1800	K type lead coated copper, stock, 4" wide			120	.067	L.F.
	1900	5" wide			120	.067	L.F.
	2100	Stainless steel, half round or box, stock, 4" wide	▼	▼	120	.067	L.F.

076 | Flashing and Sheet Metal

		076 200	Sheet Mtl Flash & Trim	CREW	MAKEUP	DAILY OUTPUT	MAN-HOURS	UNIT
205	2201		Gutters, stainless steel, half round or box, stock, 5" wide	1 Shee	1 Sheet Metal Worker	120	.067	L.F.
	2400		Steel, galv., half round or box, 28 ga., 5" wide, plain			120	.067	L.F.
	2500		Enameled			120	.067	L.F.
	2700		26 ga. galvanized steel, stock, 5" wide			120	.067	L.F.
	2800		6" wide	↓	↓	120	.067	L.F.
	3000		Vinyl, O.G., 4" wide	1 Carp	1 Carpenter	110	.073	L.F.
	3100		5" wide			110	.073	L.F.
	3200		4" half round, stock units			110	.073	L.F.
	3300		Wood, clear treated cedar, fir or hemlock, 3" x 4"			100	.080	L.F.
	3400		4" x 5"			100	.080	L.F.
	206		GUTTER GUARD 6" wide strip, aluminum mesh			500	.016	L.F.
	0100		Vinyl mesh	↓	↓	500	.016	L.F.
	207		MANSARD Colored aluminum, with battens, .032" thick					
	0600		Stock units, straight surfaces	1 Shee	1 Sheet Metal Worker	115	.070	S.F.
	0700		Concave or convex surfaces			75	.107	S.F.
	0800		For framing, to 5' high, add			115	.070	L.F.
	0900		Soffits, to 1' wide	↓	↓	125	.064	S.F.
	210		REGLET Aluminum, .025" thick, in concrete parapet	1 Carp	1 Carpenter	225	.036	L.F.
	0100		Copper, 10 oz.			225	.036	L.F.
	0300		16 oz.			225	.036	L.F.
	0400		Galvanized steel, 24 gauge			225	.036	L.F.
	0600		Stainless steel, .020" thick			225	.036	L.F.
	0700		Zinc and copper alloy, 20 oz.	↓	↓	225	.036	L.F.
	0900		Counter flashing for above, 12" wide, .032" aluminum	1 Shee	1 Sheet Metal Worker	150	.053	L.F.
	1000		Copper, 10 oz.			150	.053	L.F.
	1200		16 oz.			150	.053	L.F.
	1300		Galvanized steel, .020" thick			150	.053	L.F.
	1500		Stainless steel, .020" thick			150	.053	L.F.
	1600		Zinc and copper alloy, 20 oz.	↓	↓	150	.053	L.F.
	217		SOFFIT Aluminum, residential, stock units, .020" thick	1 Carp	1 Carpenter	210	.038	S.F.
	0100		Baked enamel on steel, 16 or 18 gauge			105	.076	S.F.
	0300		Polyvinyl chloride, white, solid			230	.035	S.F.
	0400		Perforated			230	.035	S.F.
	219		TERMITE Shields, zinc, 10" wide, .012" thick			350	.023	L.F.
	0100		.020" thick	↓	↓	350	.023	L.F.

077 | Roof Specialties and Accessories

	077 100	Prefab Roof Specialties	CREW	MAKEUP	DAILY OUTPUT	MAN-HOURS	UNIT
103		EXPANSION JOINT Butyl, 1/16" thick, 29" wide	1 Rofc	1 Roofer, Composition	165	.048	L.F.
0300		Butyl or neoprene center with foam insulation, metal flanges					
0400		Aluminum, .032" thick for openings to 2-1/2"	1 Rofc	1 Roofer, Composition	165	.048	L.F.
0600		For joint openings to 3-1/2"			165	.048	L.F.
0700		Copper, 16 oz. for openings to 2-1/2"			165	.048	L.F.
0900		For joint openings to 3-1/2"			165	.048	L.F.
1000		Galvanized steel, 26 ga. for openings to 2-1/2"			165	.048	L.F.
1200		For joint openings to 3-1/2"			165	.048	L.F.
1300		Lead-coated copper, 16 oz. for openings to 2-1/2"			165	.048	L.F.
1500		For joint openings to 3-1/2"			165	.048	L.F.
1600		Stainless steel, .018", for openings to 2-1/2"			165	.048	L.F.
1800		For joint openings to 3-1/2"			165	.048	L.F.
1900		Neoprene, double-seal type with thick center, 4-1/2" wide	↓	↓	125	.064	L.F.

077 100 | Prefab Roof Specialties

		Description	CREW	MAKEUP	DAILY OUTPUT	MAN-HOURS	UNIT
103	1951	Exp. joint, polyethylene bellows, w/galv. steel flat flanges	1 Rofc	1 Roofer, Composition	100	.080	L.F.
	1960	With galvanized angle flanges	"	"	100	.080	L.F.
	2000	Roof joint with extruded aluminum cover, 2"	1 Shee	1 Sheet Metal Worker	115	.070	L.F.
	2100	Roof joint, plastic curbs, foam center, standard	1 Rofc	1 Roofer, Composition	100	.080	L.F.
	2200	Large			100	.080	L.F.
	2300	Transitions, regular, minimum			10	.800	Ea.
	2350	Maximum			4	2.000	Ea.
	2400	Large, minimum			9	.889	Ea.
	2450	Maximum	↓	↓	3	2.670	Ea.
	2500	Roof to wall joint with extruded aluminum cover	1 Shee	1 Sheet Metal Worker	115	.070	L.F.
	2700	Wall joint, closed cell foam on PVC cover, 9" wide	1 Rofc	1 Roofer, Composition	125	.064	L.F.
	2800	12" wide	"	"	115	.070	L.F.
104		FASCIA Aluminum, reverse board and batten,					
	0100	.032" thick, colored, no furring included	1 Shee	1 Sheet Metal Worker	145	.055	S.F.
	0300	Steel, galv. and enameled, stock, no furring, long panels			145	.055	S.F.
	0600	Short panels			115	.070	S.F.
105		GRAVEL STOP Aluminum, .050" thick, 4" height, mill finish			145	.055	L.F.
	0080	Duranodic finish			145	.055	L.F.
	0100	Painted			145	.055	L.F.
	0300	6" face height, .050" thick, mill finish			135	.059	L.F.
	0350	Duranodic finish			135	.059	L.F.
	0400	Painted			135	.059	L.F.
	0600	8" face height, .050" thick, mill finish			125	.064	L.F.
	0650	Duranodic finish			125	.064	L.F.
	0700	Painted			125	.064	L.F.
	0900	12" face height, 2 piece, mill finish			100	.080	L.F.
	0950	Duranodic finish			100	.080	L.F.
	1000	Painted			100	.080	L.F.
	1200	Copper, 16 oz., 3" face height			145	.055	L.F.
	1300	6" face height			135	.059	L.F.
	1350	Galv. steel, 24 ga., 4" leg, plain, with continuous cleat, 4" face			145	.055	L.F.
	1360	6" face height			145	.055	L.F.
	1500	Polyvinyl chloride, 6" face height			135	.059	L.F.
	1600	9" face height			125	.064	L.F.
	1800	Stainless steel, 24 ga., 6" face height			135	.059	L.F.
	1900	12" face height			100	.080	L.F.
	2100	20 ga., 6" face height	↓	↓	135	.059	L.F.
	2200	12" face height			100	.080	L.F.

077 200 | Roof Accessories

		Description	CREW	MAKEUP	DAILY OUTPUT	MAN-HOURS	UNIT
204		CEILING HATCHES 2'-6" x 2'-6", single leaf, steel frame & cover	G-3	2 Sheet Metal Workers	11	2.910	Ea.
				2 Building Laborers			
				Power Tools			
	0100	Aluminum cover			11	2.910	Ea.
	0300	2'-6" x 3'-0", single leaf, steel frame & steel cover			11	2.910	Ea.
	0400	Aluminum cover	↓	↓	11	2.910	Ea.
206		ROOF HATCHES With curb, 1" fiberglass insulation, 2'-6" x 3'-0"					
	0500	Aluminum curb and cover	G-3	2 Sheet Metal Workers	10	3.200	Ea.
				2 Building Laborers			
				Power Tools			
	0520	Galvanized steel			10	3.200	Ea.
	0540	Plain steel, primed			10	3.200	Ea.
	0600	2'-6" x 4'-6", aluminum curb & cover			9	3.560	Ea.
	0800	Galvanized steel			9	3.560	Ea.
	0900	Plain steel, primed			9	3.560	Ea.
	1200	2'-6" x 8'-0", aluminum curb and cover			6.60	4.850	Ea.
	1400	Galvanized steel			6.60	4.850	Ea.
	1500	Plain steel, primed	↓	↓	6.60	4.850	Ea.

077 | Roof Specialties and Accessories

077 200 | Roof Accessories

		CREW	MAKEUP	DAILY OUTPUT	MAN-HOURS	UNIT
208	**SMOKE VENTS** Metal cover, heavy duty, low profile, 4' x 4'					
0100	Aluminum	G-3	2 Sheet Metal Workers 2 Building Laborers Power Tools	13	2.460	Ea.
0200	Galvanized steel			13	2.460	Ea.
0300	4' x 8' aluminum			8	4.000	Ea.
0400	Galvanized steel	↓	↓	8	4.000	Ea.
210	**ROOF VENTS** Mushroom for built-up roofs, aluminum	1 Rofc	1 Roofer, Composition	30	.267	Ea.
0100	PVC, 6" high			30	.267	Ea.
212	**VENTS, ONE-WAY** For insul. decks, 1 per M.S.F., plastic, min.			40	.200	Ea.
0100	Maximum			20	.400	Ea.
0300	Aluminum			30	.267	Ea.
0500	Copper	↓	↓	28	.286	Ea.
0800	Fiber board baffles, 12" wide for 16" O.C. rafter spacing	1 Carp	1 Carpenter	90	.089	Ea.
0900	For 24" O.C. rafter spacing	"	"	110	.073	Ea.

078 | Skylights

078 100 | Plastic Skylights

		CREW	MAKEUP	DAILY OUTPUT	MAN-HOURS	UNIT
101 0100	**SKYLIGHT** Plastic roof domes, flush or curb mounted, ten or more units, curb not included, "L" frames					
0300	Nominal size under 10 S.F., double	G-3	2 Sheet Metal Workers 2 Building Laborers Power Tools	130	.246	S.F.
0400	Single			160	.200	S.F.
0600	10 S.F. to 20 S.F., double			315	.102	S.F.
0700	Single			395	.081	S.F.
0900	20 S.F. to 30 S.F., double			395	.081	S.F.
1000	Single			465	.069	S.F.
1200	30 S.F. to 65 S.F., double			465	.069	S.F.
1300	Single	↓	↓	610	.052	S.F.
2120	Ventilating insulated plexiglass dome with					
2130	curb mounting, 36" x 36"	G-3	2 Sheet Metal Workers 2 Building Laborers Power Tools	12	2.670	Ea.
2150	52" x 52"			12	2.670	Ea.
2160	28" x 52"			10	3.200	Ea.
2170	36" x 52"			10	3.200	Ea.
2200	Field fabricated, factory type, aluminum and wire glass			120	.267	S.F.
2300	Insulated safety glass with aluminum frame			160	.200	S.F.
2400	Sandwich panels, fiberglass, for walls, 1-9/16" thick, to 250 S.F.			200	.160	S.F.
2500	250 S.F. and up			265	.121	S.F.
2700	As above, but for roofs, 2-3/4" thick, to 250 S.F.			295	.108	S.F.
2800	250 S.F. and up	↓	↓	330	.097	S.F.

078 200 | Metal Framed Skylights

		CREW	MAKEUP	DAILY OUTPUT	MAN-HOURS	UNIT
202	**SKYROOFS** Translucent panels, 2-3/4" thick, under 5000 S.F.	G-3	2 Sheet Metal Workers 2 Building Laborers Power Tools	395	.081	SF Hor.
0100	Over 5000 S.F.			465	.069	SF Hor.
0300	Continuous vaulted, semi-circular, to 8' wide, double glazed			145	.221	SF Hor.
0400	Single glazed	↓	↓	160	.200	SF Hor.

	078 200	Metal Framed Skylights	CREW	MAKEUP	DAILY OUTPUT	MAN-HOURS	UNIT
202	0601	Skyroof, continuous vaulted, semi-circ., to 20' wide, single glazed	G-3	2 Sheet Metal Workers 2 Building Laborers Power Tools	175	.183	SF Hor.
	0700	Over 20' wide, single glazed			200	.160	SF Hor.
	0900	Motorized opening type, single glazed, 1/3 opening			145	.221	SF Hor.
	1000	Full opening	↓	↓	130	.246	SF Hor.
	1200	Pyramid type units, self-supporting, to 30' clear opening,					
	1300	square or circular, single glazed, minimum	G-3	2 Sheet Metal Workers 2 Building Laborers Power Tools	200	.160	SF Hor.
	1310	Average			165	.194	SF Hor.
	1400	Maximum			130	.246	SF Hor.
	1500	Grid type, 4' to 10' modules, single glass glazed, minimum			200	.160	SF Hor.
	1550	Maximum			128	.250	SF Hor.
	1600	Preformed acrylic, minimum			300	.107	SF Hor.
	1650	Maximum	↓	↓	175	.183	SF Hor.
	1800	Dome type units, self-supporting, to 100' clear opening, circular ,					
	1900	rise to span ratio = 0.20					
	1920	Minimum	G-3	2 Sheet Metal Workers 2 Building Laborers Power Tools	197	.162	SF Hor.
	1950	Maximum			113	.283	SF Hor.
	2100	Rise to span ratio = 0.33, minimum			169	.189	SF Hor.
	2150	Maximum			101	.317	SF Hor.
	2200	Rise to span ratio = 0.50, minimum			148	.216	SF Hor.
	2250	Maximum			87	.368	SF Hor.
	2400	Ridge units, continuous, to 8' wide, double			130	.246	SF Hor.
	2500	Single			200	.160	SF Hor.
	2700	Ridge and furrow units, over 4' O.C., double, minimum			200	.160	SF Hor.
	2750	Maximum			120	.267	SF Hor.
	2800	Single, minimum			214	.150	SF Hor.
	2850	Maximum			153	.209	SF Hor.
	3000	Rolling roof, translucent panels, flat roof, residential, mininum			253	.126	S.F.
	3030	Maximum			160	.200	S.F.
	3100	Lean-to skyroof, long span, double, minimum			197	.162	S.F.
	3150	Maximum			101	.317	S.F.
	3300	Single, minimum			321	.100	S.F.
	3350	Maximum	↓	↓	160	.200	S.F.

	078 400	Glass Block Skylights	CREW	MAKEUP	DAILY OUTPUT	MAN-HOURS	UNIT
	402	PREFABRICATED Glass block with metal frame, min.	G-3	2 Sheet Metal Workers 2 Building Laborers Power Tools	265	.121	S.F.
	0100	Maximum	"	"	160	.200	S.F.
	0200	With precast concrete structural frame, minimum	C-11	1 Struc. Steel Foreman 6 Struc. Steel Workers 1 Equip. Oper. (crane) 1 Equip. Oper. Oiler 1 Truck Crane, 150 Ton	1,500	.048	S.F.
	0300	Maximum	"	"	1,000	.072	S.F.

079 204 | Sealants & Caulkings		CREW	MAKEUP	DAILY OUTPUT	MAN-HOURS	UNIT
204	204 CAULKING AND SEALANTS						
	0030	Backer rod, polyethylene, 1/4" diameter	1 Bric	1 Bricklayer	4.60	1.740	C.L.F.
	0050	1/2" diameter			4.60	1.740	C.L.F.
	0070	3/4" diameter			4.60	1.740	C.L.F.
	0090	1" diameter	↓	↓	4.60	1.740	C.L.F.
	0100	Caulking compound, oil base, bulk					
	0501	In place, 1/4" x 1/2", 154 L.F./gal.	1 Bric	1 Bricklayer	260	.031	L.F.
	0600	1/2" x 1/2", 77 L.F./gal.			250	.032	L.F.
	0800	3/4" x 3/4", 34 L.F./gal.			230	.035	L.F.
	0900	3/4" x 1", 26 L.F./gal.			200	.040	L.F.
	1000	1" x 1", 19 L.F./gal.	↓	↓	180	.044	L.F.
	1401	Butyl based					
	1700	Bulk, in place 1/4" x 1/2", 154 L.F./gal.	1 Bric	1 Bricklayer	230	.035	L.F.
	1800	1/2" x 1/2", 77 L.F./gal.	"	"	180	.044	L.F.
	2301	Polysulfide compounds					
	2600	1 or 2 component, in place, 1/4" x 1/4", 308 L.F./gal.	1 Bric	1 Bricklayer	145	.055	L.F.
	2700	1/2" x 1/4", 154 L.F./gal.			135	.059	L.F.
	2900	3/4" x 3/8", 68 L.F./gal.			130	.062	L.F.
	3000	1" x 1/2", 38 L.F./gal.	↓	↓	130	.062	L.F.
	3201	Polyurethane					
	3500	1 or 2 component, in place, 1/4" x 1/4", 308 L.F./gal.	1 Bric	1 Bricklayer	150	.053	L.F.
	3600	1/2" x 1/4", 154 L.F./gal.			145	.055	L.F.
	3800	3/4" x 3/8", 68 L.F./gal.			130	.062	L.F.
	3900	1" x 1/2", 38 L.F./gal.			110	.073	L.F.
	4400	Neoprene gaskets, closed cell, adhesive, 1/8" x 3/8"			240	.033	L.F.
	4500	1/4" x 3/4"			215	.037	L.F.
	4700	1/2" x 1"			200	.040	L.F.
	4800	3/4" x 1-1/2"	↓	↓	165	.048	L.F.

DOORS, WINDOWS AND GLASS

DIVISION 8

DOORS, WINDOWS AND GLASS

Subdivisions in the Doors, Windows, and Glass Division include: Metal Doors and Frames, Wood Doors and Frames, Special Doors, Entrances and Storefronts, Metal Windows, Wood Windows, Finish Hardware and Specialties, Glass and Glazing, plus Window and Curtain Walls.

As a rule, pre-hung and prefitted doors can be put in place very quickly. However, the heavier the door, the more difficult the delivery to the final point of installation, and the more man-hours for installation. Hollow-core doors are much lighter and easier to install than solid-core doors.

Some items in the "Special Doors" subdivision require a crew trained for the specific installation and have much higher man-hour figures than all common door types. For example, acoustical doors require a great deal of time to install. When installing doors, be certain that the architectural intent of the plans is being followed. In general, a great percentage of the work done on special doors is subcontracted.

When accumulating man-hours for door installation using this data, remember that the time required to install all hinges has been included in the figures. The man-hour requirements for installing locksets, however, have not been included. That information can be found under "Finish Hardware and Specialties" in Division 087.

The items included under "Metal Windows" are generally found in commercial work and are installed by structural steel workers. "Wood Windows" are generally installed by carpenters. In openings provided by others, it may be necessary to take the time for field measurements before windows are selected. This is particularly true in commercial applications such as the metal windows in storefronts.

Glass installation can be affected by weather conditions, particularly wind velocity. In addition, glazing cannot be done in cold weather. "Specialty Glass", as opposed to common plate glass, requires a considerable amount of time to install, since it involves small areas and expensive materials that require great care.

081 100	Steel Doors And Frames	CREW	MAKEUP	DAILY OUTPUT	MAN-HOURS	UNIT
103	**COMMERCIAL STEEL DOORS** Flush, full panel					
0020	Hollow core, 1-3/8" thick, 20 ga., 2'-0" x 6'-8"	F-2	2 Carpenters	20	.800	Ea.
			Power Tools			
0040	2'-6" x 6'-8"			18	.889	Ea.
0060	3'-0" x 6'-8"			17	.941	Ea.
0100	3'-0" x 7'-0"			17	.941	Ea.
0320	Half glass, 20 ga., 2'-0" x 6'-8"			20	.800	Ea.
0340	2'-6" x 6'-8"			18	.889	Ea.
0360	3'-0" x 6'-8"			17	.941	Ea.
0400	3'-0" x 7'-0"			17	.941	Ea.
1020	Hollow core, 1-3/4" thick, full panel, 20 ga., 2'-6" x 6'-8"			18	.889	Ea.
1040	3'-0" x 6'-8"			17	.941	Ea.
1060	3'-0" x 7'-0"			17	.941	Ea.
1080	4'-0" x 7'-0"			15	1.070	Ea.
1100	4'-0" x 8'-0"			13	1.230	Ea.
1120	18 ga., 2'-6" x 6'-8"			17	.941	Ea.
1140	3'-0" x 6'-8"			16	1.000	Ea.
1160	3'-0" x 7'-0"			16	1.000	Ea.
1180	4'-0" x 7'-0"			14	1.140	Ea.
1200	4'-0" x 8'-0"			14	1.140	Ea.
1220	Half glass, 20 ga., 2'-6" x 6'-8"			20	.800	Ea.
1240	3'-0" x 6'-8"			18	.889	Ea.
1260	3'-0" x 7'-0"			18	.889	Ea.
1280	4'-0" x 7'-0"			16	1.000	Ea.
1300	4'-0" x 8'-0"			13	1.230	Ea.
1320	18 ga., 2'-6" x 6'-8"			18	.889	Ea.
1340	3'-0" x 6'-8"			17	.941	Ea.
1360	3'-0" x 7'-0"			17	.941	Ea.
1380	4'-0" x 7'-0"			15	1.070	Ea.
1400	4'-0" x 8'-0"			14	1.140	Ea.
1720	Composite, 1-3/4" thick, full panel, 18 ga., 3'-0" x 6'-8"			15	1.070	Ea.
1740	2'-6" x 7'-0"			16	1.000	Ea.
1760	3'-0" x 7'-0"			15	1.070	Ea.
1800	4'-0" x 8'-0"			13	1.230	Ea.
1820	Half glass, 18 ga., 3'-0" x 6'-8"			16	1.000	Ea.
1840	2'-6" x 7'-0"			17	.941	Ea.
1860	3'-0" x 7'-0"			16	1.000	Ea.
1900	4'-0" x 8'-0"	↓	↓	14	1.140	Ea.
106	**DOOR FRAMES** Steel channels with anchors and bar stops					
0100	6" channel @ 8.2#/L.F., 3' x 7' door, weighs 200#	E-4	1 Struc. Steel Foreman	13	2.460	Ea.
			3 Struc. Steel Workers			
			1 Gas Welding Machine			
0200	8" channel @ 11.5#/L.F., 6' x 8' door, weighs 300#			9	3.560	Ea.
0300	8' x 12' door, weighs 450#			6.50	4.920	Ea.
0400	10" channel @ 15.3#/L.F., 10' x 10' door, weighs 525#			6	5.330	Ea.
0500	12' x 12' door, weighs 625#			5.50	5.820	Ea.
0600	12" channel @ 20.7#/L.F., 12' x 12' door, weighs 825#			4.50	7.110	Ea.
0700	12' x 16' door, weighs 1000#	↓	↓	4	8.000	Ea.
110	**FIRE DOOR** Steel, flush, "B" label, 90 minute					
0020	Full panel, 20 ga., 2'-0" x 6'-8"	F-2	2 Carpenters	20	.800	Ea.
			Power Tools			
0040	2'-6" x 6'-8"			18	.889	Ea.
0060	3'-0" x 6'-8"			17	.941	Ea.
0080	3'-0" x 7'-0"			17	.941	Ea.
0140	18 ga., 3'-0" x 6'-8"			16	1.000	Ea.
0160	2'-6" x 7'-0"			17	.941	Ea.
0180	3'-0" x 7'-0"			16	1.000	Ea.
0200	4'-0" x 7'-0"	↓	↓	15	1.070	Ea.

081 | Metal Doors and Frames

081 100 | Steel Doors And Frames

		CREW	MAKEUP	DAILY OUTPUT	MAN-HOURS	UNIT
110 0521	Fire door, flush, "B" label, 90 min., comp., 20 ga., 2' x 6'-8"	F-2	2 Carpenters Power Tools	18	.889	Ea.
0540	2'-6" x 6'-8"			17	.941	Ea.
0560	3'-0" x 6'-8"			16	1.000	Ea.
0580	3'-0" x 7'-0"			16	1.000	Ea.
0640	Flush, "A" label 3 hour, composite, 18 ga., 3'-0" x 6'-8"			15	1.070	Ea.
0660	2'-6" x 7'-0"			16	1.000	Ea.
0680	3'-0" x 7'-0"			15	1.070	Ea.
0700	4'-0" x 7'-0"			14	1.140	Ea.
114	**RESIDENTIAL DOOR** Steel, 24 ga., embos., full, 2'-8" x 6'-8"			16	1.000	Ea.
0040	3'-0" x 6'-8"			15	1.070	Ea.
0060	3'-0" x 7'-0"			15	1.070	Ea.
0220	Half glass, 2'-8" x 6'-8"			17	.941	Ea.
0240	3'-0" x 6'-8"			16	1.000	Ea.
0260	3'-0" x 7'-0"			16	1.000	Ea.
0720	Raised plastic face, full panel, 2'-8" x 6'-8"			16	1.000	Ea.
0740	3'-0" x 6'-8"			15	1.070	Ea.
0760	3'-0" x 7'-0"			15	1.070	Ea.
0820	Half glass, 2'-8" x 6'-8"			17	.941	Ea.
0840	3'-0" x 6'-8"			16	1.000	Ea.
0860	3'-0" x 7'-0"			16	1.000	Ea.
1320	Flush face, full panel, 2'-6" x 6'-8"			16	1.000	Ea.
1340	3'-0" x 6'-8"			15	1.070	Ea.
1360	3'-0" x 7'-0"			15	1.070	Ea.
1420	Half glass, 2'-8" x 6'-8"			17	.941	Ea.
1440	3'-0" x 6'-8"			16	1.000	Ea.
1460	3'-0" x 7'-0"			16	1.000	Ea.
2300	Interior, residential, closet, bi-fold, 6'-8" x 2'-0" wide			16	1.000	Ea.
2330	3'-0" wide			16	1.000	Ea.
2360	4'-0" wide			15	1.070	Ea.
2400	5'-0" wide			14	1.140	Ea.
2420	6'-0" wide	↓	↓	13	1.230	Ea.
118	**STEEL FRAMES, KNOCK DOWN** 18 ga., up to 5-3/4" deep					
0025	6'-8" high, 3'-0" wide, single	F-2	2 Carpenters Power Tools	16	1.000	Ea.
0040	6'-0" wide, double			14	1.140	Ea.
0100	7'-0" high, 3'-0" wide, single			16	1.000	Ea.
0140	6'-0" wide, double			14	1.140	Ea.
2800	18 ga. drywall, up to 4-7/8" deep, 7'-0" high, 3'-0" wide, single			16	1.000	Ea.
2840	6'-0" wide, double			14	1.140	Ea.
3600	16 ga., up to 5-3/4" deep, 7'-0" high, 4'-0" wide, single			15	1.070	Ea.
3640	8'-0" wide, double			12	1.330	Ea.
3700	8'-0" high, 4'-0" wide, single			15	1.070	Ea.
3740	8'-0" wide, double			12	1.330	Ea.
4000	6-3/4" deep, 7'-0" high, 4'-0" wide, single			15	1.070	Ea.
4040	8'-0" wide, double			12	1.330	Ea.
4100	8'-0" high, 4'-0" wide, single			15	1.070	Ea.
4140	8'-0" wide, double			12	1.330	Ea.
4400	8-3/4" deep, 7'-0" high, 4'-0" wide, single			15	1.070	Ea.
4440	8'-0" wide, double			12	1.330	Ea.
4500	8'-0" high, 4'-0" wide, single			15	1.070	Ea.
4540	8'-0" wide, double			12	1.330	Ea.
4800	16 ga. drywall, up to 3-7/8" deep, 7'-0" high, 3'-0" wide, single			16	1.000	Ea.
4840	6'-0" wide, double			14	1.140	Ea.
5400	16 ga. "B" label, up to 5-3/4" deep, 7'-0" high, 4'-0" wide, single			15	1.070	Ea.
5440	8'-0" wide, double			12	1.330	Ea.
5800	6-3/4" deep, 7'-0" high, 4'-0" wide, single			15	1.070	Ea.
5840	8'-0" wide, double	↓	↓	12	1.330	Ea.

081 | Metal Doors and Frames

081 100 | Steel Doors And Frames

		CREW	MAKEUP	DAILY OUTPUT	MAN-HOURS	UNIT
118 6201	Steel frame, 16 ga., 8-3/4" deep, 7' high, 4' wide, single	F-2	2 Carpenters Power Tools	15	1.070	Ea.
6240	8'-0" wide, double			12	1.330	Ea.
7900	Transom lite frames, fixed, add			155	.103	S.F.
8000	Movable, add	↓	↓	130	.123	S.F.

081 200 | Alum Doors And Frames

		CREW	MAKEUP	DAILY OUTPUT	MAN-HOURS	UNIT
204	**ALUMINUM FRAMES** Entrance, 3' x 7' opening, clear finish	2 Sswk	2 Struc. Steel Workers	7	2.290	Opng.
0100	Bronze finish			7	2.290	Opng.
0500	6' x 7' opening, clear finish			6	2.670	Opng.
0520	Bronze finish			6	2.670	Opng.
1000	With 3' high transoms, 3' x 10' opening, clear finish			6.50	2.460	Opng.
1050	Bronze finish			6.50	2.460	Opng.
1100	Black finish			6.50	2.460	Opng.
1500	With 3' high transoms, 6' x 10' opening, clear finish			5.50	2.910	Opng.
1550	Bronze finish			5.50	2.910	Opng.
1600	Black finish	↓	↓	5.50	2.910	Opng.
212	**ALUMINUM DOORS & FRAMES** Entrance, narrow stile, including					
0020	hardware & closer, clear finish, not incl. glass, 3' x 7' opening	2 Sswk	2 Struc. Steel Workers	2	8.000	Ea.
0100	3' x 10' opening, 3' high transom			1.80	8.890	Ea.
0200	3'-6" x 10' opening, 3' high transom			1.80	8.890	Ea.
0300	6' x 7' opening			1.30	12.310	Pr.
0400	6' x 10' opening, 3' high transom	↓	↓	1.10	14.550	Pr.

082 | Wood and Plastic Doors

082 050 | Wood And Plastic Doors

		CREW	MAKEUP	DAILY OUTPUT	MAN-HOURS	UNIT
054	**WOOD FRAMES**					
0400	Exterior frame, incl. ext. trim, pine, 5/4 x 4-9/16" deep	F-2	2 Carpenters Power Tools	375	.043	L.F.
0420	5-3/16" deep			375	.043	L.F.
0440	6-9/16" deep			375	.043	L.F.
0600	Oak, 5/4 x 4-9/16" deep			350	.046	L.F.
0620	5-3/16" deep			350	.046	L.F.
0640	6-9/16" deep			350	.046	L.F.
0800	Walnut, 5/4 x 4-9/16" deep			350	.046	L.F.
0820	5-3/16" deep			350	.046	L.F.
0840	6-9/16" deep			350	.046	L.F.
1000	Sills, 8/4 x 8" deep, oak, no horns			100	.160	L.F.
1020	2" horns			100	.160	L.F.
1040	3" horns			100	.160	L.F.
1100	8/4 x 10" deep, oak, no horns			90	.178	L.F.
1120	2" horns			90	.178	L.F.
1140	3" horns			90	.178	L.F.
2000	Exterior, colonial, frame & trim, 3' opng., in-swing, minimum			22	.727	Ea.
2020	Maximum			20	.800	Ea.
2100	5'-4" opening, in-swing, minimum			17	.941	Ea.
2120	Maximum			15	1.070	Ea.
2140	Out-swing, minimum			17	.941	Ea.
2160	Maximum			15	1.070	Ea.
2400	6'-0" opening, in-swing, minimum			16	1.000	Ea.
2420	Maximum	↓	↓	10	1.600	Ea.

082 | Wood and Plastic Doors

082 050 | Wood And Plastic Doors

		CREW	MAKEUP	DAILY OUTPUT	MAN-HOURS	UNIT
054 2461	Wood frame, exterior, colonial, 6' opening, out-swing, minimum	F-2	2 Carpenters Power Tools	16	1.000	Ea.
2480	Maximum			10	1.600	Ea.
2600	For two sidelights, add, minimum			30	.533	Opng.
2620	Maximum			20	.800	Opng.
2700	Custom birch frame, 3'-0" opening			16	1.000	Ea.
2750	6'-0" opening			16	1.000	Ea.
3000	Interior frame, pine, 11/16" x 3-5/8" deep			375	.043	L.F.
3020	4-9/16" deep			375	.043	L.F.
3040	5-3/16" deep			375	.043	L.F.
3200	Oak, 11/16" x 3-5/8" deep			350	.046	L.F.
3220	4-9/16" deep			350	.046	L.F.
3240	5-3/16" deep			350	.046	L.F.
3400	Walnut, 11/16" x 3-5/8" deep			350	.046	L.F.
3420	4-9/16" deep			350	.046	L.F.
3440	5-3/16" deep			350	.046	L.F.
3600	Pocket door frame			16	1.000	Ea.
3800	Threshold, oak, 5/8" x 3-5/8" deep			200	.080	L.F.
3820	4-5/8" deep			190	.084	L.F.
3840	5-5/8" deep	↓	↓	180	.089	L.F.
062	**WOOD DOOR, ARCHITECTURAL** Flush, interior, 7 ply, hollow core,					
0020	Lauan face, 2'-0" x 6'-8"	F-2	2 Carpenters Power Tools	17	.941	Ea.
0040	2'-6" x 6'-8"			17	.941	Ea.
0080	3'-0" x 6'-8"			17	.941	Ea.
0100	4'-0" x 6'-8"			16	1.000	Ea.
0120	Birch face, 2'-0" x 6'-8"			17	.941	Ea.
0140	2'-6" x 6'-8"			17	.941	Ea.
0180	3'-0" x 6'-8"			17	.941	Ea.
0200	4'-0" x 6'-8"			16	1.000	Ea.
0220	Oak face, 2'-0" x 6'-8"			17	.941	Ea.
0240	2'-6" x 6'-8"			17	.941	Ea.
0280	3'-0" x 6'-8"			17	.941	Ea.
0300	4'-0" x 6'-8"			16	1.000	Ea.
0320	Walnut face, 2'-0" x 6'-8"			17	.941	Ea.
0340	2'-6" x 6'-8"			17	.941	Ea.
0380	3'-0" x 6'-8"			17	.941	Ea.
0400	4'-0" x 6'-8"			16	1.000	Ea.
1320	M.D. overlay on hardboard, 2'-0" x 6'-8"			17	.941	Ea.
1340	2'-6" x 6'-8"			17	.941	Ea.
1380	3'-0" x 6'-8"			17	.941	Ea.
1400	4'-0" x 6'-8"			16	1.000	Ea.
1720	H.P. plastic laminate, 2'-0" x 6'-8"			16	1.000	Ea.
1740	2'-6" x 6'-8"			16	1.000	Ea.
1780	3'-0" x 6'-8"			15	1.070	Ea.
1800	4'-0" x 6'-8"			14	1.140	Ea.
2020	5 ply particle core, lauan face, 2'-6" x 6'-8"			15	1.070	Ea.
2040	3'-0" x 6'-8"			14	1.140	Ea.
2080	3'-0" x 7'-0"			13	1.230	Ea.
2100	4'-0" x 7'-0"			12	1.330	Ea.
2120	Birch face, 2'-6" x 6'-8"			15	1.070	Ea.
2140	3'-0" x 6'-8"			14	1.140	Ea.
2180	3'-0" x 7'-0"			13	1.230	Ea.
2200	4'-0" x 7'-0"			12	1.330	Ea.
2220	Oak face, 2'-6" x 6'-8"			15	1.070	Ea.
2240	3'-0" x 6'-8"			14	1.140	Ea.
2280	3'-0" x 7'-0"			13	1.230	Ea.
2300	4'-0" x 7'-0"	↓	↓	12	1.330	Ea.

082 050 | Wood And Plastic Doors

		Description	CREW	MAKEUP	DAILY OUTPUT	MAN-HOURS	UNIT
062	2321	Wood door, interior, 5 ply particle core, walnut face, 2' x 6'-8"	F-2	2 Carpenters Power Tools	15	1.070	Ea.
	2340	2'-6" x 6'-8"			14	1.140	Ea.
	2380	3'-0" x 6'-8"			13	1.230	Ea.
	2400	4'-0" x 6'-8"			12	1.330	Ea.
	3320	M.D. overlay on hardboard, 2'-6" x 6'-8"			14	1.140	Ea.
	3340	3'-0" x 6'-8"			13	1.230	Ea.
	3380	3'-0" x 7'-0"			12	1.330	Ea.
	3400	4'-0" x 7'-0"			10	1.600	Ea.
	3720	H.P. plastic laminate, 2'-6" x 6'-8"			13	1.230	Ea.
	3740	3'-0" x 6'-8"			12	1.330	Ea.
	3780	3'-0" x 7'-0"			11	1.450	Ea.
	3800	4'-0" x 7'-0"			8	2.000	Ea.
	4000	Exterior, flush, solid wood core, birch, 1-3/4" x 7'-0" x 2'-6"			15	1.070	Ea.
	4020	2'-8" wide			15	1.070	Ea.
	4040	3'-0" wide			14	1.140	Ea.
	4100	Oak faced 1-3/4" x 7'-0" x 2'-6" wide			15	1.070	Ea.
	4120	2'-8" wide			15	1.070	Ea.
	4140	3'-0" wide			14	1.140	Ea.
	4200	Walnut faced 1-3/4" x 7'-0" x 2'-6" wide			15	1.070	Ea.
	4220	2'-8" wide			15	1.070	Ea.
	4240	3'-0" wide	↓	↓	14	1.140	Ea.
066		**WOOD DOORS, DECORATOR**					
	4000	Hand carved door, mahogany, simple design					
	4020	1-3/4" x 7'-0" x 3'-0" wide	F-2	2 Carpenters Power Tools	14	1.140	Ea.
	4040	3'-6" wide			13	1.230	Ea.
	4200	Rosewood, 1-3/4" x 7'-0" x 3'-0" wide			14	1.140	Ea.
	4220	3'-6" wide			13	1.230	Ea.
	4600	Side panel, mahogany, simple design, 7'-0" x 1'-0" wide			21	.762	Ea.
	4620	1'-2" wide			20	.800	Ea.
	4640	1'-4" wide			19	.842	Ea.
	4800	Rosewood, simple design 7'-0" x 1'-0" wide			21	.762	Ea.
	4820	1'-2" wide			20	.800	Ea.
	4840	1'-4" wide			19	.842	Ea.
	6520	Interior cafe doors, 2'-6" opening, stock, panel pine			16	1.000	Ea.
	6540	3'-0" opening			16	1.000	Ea.
	6560	2'-6" opening			16	1.000	Ea.
	8000	3'-0" opening	↓	↓	16	1.000	Ea.
070		**WOOD FIRE DOORS** Mineral core, 3 ply stile, "B" label,					
	0040	1 hour, birch face, 2'-6" x 6'-8"	F-2	2 Carpenters Power Tools	14	1.140	Ea.
	0080	3'-0" x 6'-8"			13	1.230	Ea.
	0090	3'-0" x 7'-0"			12	1.330	Ea.
	0100	4'-0" x 7'-0"			12	1.330	Ea.
	0140	Oak face, 2'-6" x 6'-8"			14	1.140	Ea.
	0180	3'-0" x 6'-8"			13	1.230	Ea.
	0190	3'-0" x 7'-0"			12	1.330	Ea.
	0200	4'-0" x 7'-0"			12	1.330	Ea.
	0240	Walnut face, 2'-6" x 6'-8"			14	1.140	Ea.
	0280	3'-0" x 6'-8"			13	1.230	Ea.
	0290	3'-0" x 7'-0"			12	1.330	Ea.
	0300	4'-0" x 7'-0"			12	1.330	Ea.
	0440	M.D. overlay on hardboard, 2'-6" x 6'-8"			15	1.070	Ea.
	0480	3'-0" x 6'-8"			14	1.140	Ea.
	0490	3'-0" x 7'-0"			13	1.230	Ea.
	0500	4'-0" x 7'-0"	↓	↓	12	1.330	Ea.
	0540	H.P. plastic laminate, 2'-6" x 6'-8"			13	1.230	Ea.

082 050	Wood And Plastic Doors	CREW	MAKEUP	DAILY OUTPUT	MAN-HOURS	UNIT
070 0581	Wood fire door, 1 hour, H.P. plastic laminate, 3' x 6'-8"	F-2	2 Carpenters Power Tools	12	1.330	Ea.
0590	3'-0" x 7'-0"			11	1.450	Ea.
0600	4'-0" x 7'-0"			10	1.600	Ea.
0740	90 minutes, birch face, 2'-6" x 6'-8"			14	1.140	Ea.
0780	3'-0" x 6'-8"			13	1.230	Ea.
0790	3'-0" x 7'-0"			12	1.330	Ea.
0800	4'-0" x 7'-0"			12	1.330	Ea.
0840	Oak face, 2'-6" x 6'-8"			14	1.140	Ea.
0880	3'-0" x 6'-8"			13	1.230	Ea.
0890	3'-0" x 7'-0"			12	1.330	Ea.
0900	4'-0" x 7'-0"			12	1.330	Ea.
0940	Walnut face, 2'-6" x 6'-8"			14	1.140	Ea.
0980	3'-0" x 6'-8"			13	1.230	Ea.
0990	3'-0" x 7'-0"			12	1.330	Ea.
1000	4'-0" x 7'-0"			12	1.330	Ea.
1140	M.D. overlay on hardboard, 2'-6" x 6'-8"			15	1.070	Ea.
1180	3'-0" x 6'-8"			14	1.140	Ea.
1190	3'-0" x 7'-0"			13	1.230	Ea.
1200	4'-0" x 7'-0"			12	1.330	Ea.
1340	H.P. plastic laminate, 2'-6" x 6'-8"			13	1.230	Ea.
1380	3'-0" x 6'-8"			12	1.330	Ea.
1390	3'-0" x 7'-0"			11	1.450	Ea.
1400	4'-0" x 7'-0"	↓	↓	10	1.600	Ea.
2200	Custom architectural "B" label, flush, 1-3/4" thick, birch,					
2210	Solid core					
2220	2'-6" x 7'-0"	F-2	2 Carpenters Power Tools	15	1.070	Ea.
2260	3'-0" x 7'-0"			14	1.140	Ea.
2300	4'-0" x 7'-0"			13	1.230	Ea.
2420	4'-0" x 8'-0"	↓	↓	11	1.450	Ea.
074	**WOOD DOORS, PANELED** Interior, six panel, hollow core, 1-3/8" thick					
0040	Molded hardboard, 2'-0" x 6'-8"	F-2	2 Carpenters Power Tools	17	.941	Ea.
0060	2'-6" x 6'-8"			17	.941	Ea.
0080	3'-0" x 6'-8"			17	.941	Ea.
0140	Embossed print, molded hardboard, 2'-0" x 6'-8"			17	.941	Ea.
0160	2'-6" x 6'-8"			17	.941	Ea.
0180	3'-0" x 6'-8"			17	.941	Ea.
0540	Six panel, solid, 1-3/8" thick, pine, 2'-0" x 6'-8"			15	1.070	Ea.
0560	2'-6" x 6'-8"			14	1.140	Ea.
0580	3'-0" x 6'-8"			13	1.230	Ea.
1020	Two panel, bored rail, solid, 1-3/8" thick, pine, 1'-6" x 6'-8"			16	1.000	Ea.
1040	2'-0" x 6'-8"			15	1.070	Ea.
1060	2'-6" x 6'-8"			14	1.140	Ea.
1340	Two panel, solid, 1-3/8" thick, fir, 2'-0" x 6'-8"			15	1.070	Ea.
1360	2'-6" x 6'-8"			14	1.140	Ea.
1380	3'-0" x 6'-8"			13	1.230	Ea.
1740	Five panel, solid, 1-3/8" thick, fir, 2'-0" x 6'-8"			15	1.070	Ea.
1760	2'-6" x 6'-8"			14	1.140	Ea.
1780	3'-0" x 6'-8"	↓	↓	13	1.230	Ea.
078	**WOOD DOORS, RESIDENTIAL**					
0200	Exterior, combination storm & screen, pine					
0220	Cross buck, 6'-9" x 2'-6" wide	F-2	2 Carpenters Power Tools	11	1.450	Ea.
0260	2'-8" wide			10	1.600	Ea.
0280	3'-0" wide			9	1.780	Ea.
0300	7'-1" x 3'-0" wide	↓	↓	9	1.780	Ea.

		Wood And Plastic Doors	CREW	MAKEUP	DAILY OUTPUT	MAN-HOURS	UNIT
078	0401	Wood door, resi., exterior, full lite, 6'-9" x 2'-6" wide	F-2	2 Carpenters Power Tools	11	1.450	Ea.
	0420	2'-8" wide			10	1.600	Ea.
	0440	3'-0" wide			9	1.780	Ea.
	0500	7'-1" x 3'-0" wide			9	1.780	Ea.
	0700	Dutch door, pine, 1-3/4" x 6'-8" x 2'-8" wide, minimum			12	1.330	Ea.
	0720	Maximum			10	1.600	Ea.
	0800	3'-0" wide, minimum			12	1.330	Ea.
	0820	Maximum			10	1.600	Ea.
	1000	Entrance door, colonial, 1-3/4" x 6'-8" x 2'-8" wide			16	1.000	Ea.
	1020	6 panel pine, 3'-0" wide			15	1.070	Ea.
	1100	8 panel pine, 2'-8" wide			16	1.000	Ea.
	1120	3'-0" wide			15	1.070	Ea.
	1300	Flush, birch, solid core, 1-3/4" x 6'-8" x 2'-8" wide			16	1.000	Ea.
	1320	3'-0" wide			15	1.070	Ea.
	1340	7'-0" x 2'-8" wide			16	1.000	Ea.
	1360	3'-0" wide	▼	▼	15	1.070	Ea.
	2700	Interior closet, bi-fold, w/hardware, no frame or trim incl.					
	2720	Flush, birch, 6'-6" or 6'-8" x 2'-6" wide	F-2	2 Carpenters Power Tools	13	1.230	Ea.
	2740	3'-0" wide			13	1.230	Ea.
	2760	4'-0" wide			12	1.330	Ea.
	2780	5'-0" wide			11	1.450	Ea.
	2800	6'-0" wide			10	1.600	Ea.
	3000	Raised panel pine, 6'-6" or 6'-8" x 2'-6" wide			13	1.230	Ea.
	3020	3'-0" wide			13	1.230	Ea.
	3040	4'-0" wide			12	1.330	Ea.
	3060	5'-0" wide			11	1.450	Ea.
	3080	6'-0" wide			10	1.600	Ea.
	3200	Louvered, pine, 6'-6" or 6'-8" x 2'-6" wide			13	1.230	Ea.
	3220	3'-0" wide			13	1.230	Ea.
	3240	4'-0" wide			12	1.330	Ea.
	3260	5'-0" wide			11	1.450	Ea.
	3280	6'-0" wide	▼	▼	10	1.600	Ea.
	4400	Bi-passing closet, incl. hardware and frame, no trim incl.					
	4420	Flush, lauan, 6'-8" x 4'-0" wide	F-2	2 Carpenters Power Tools	12	1.330	Opng.
	4440	5'-0" wide			11	1.450	Opng.
	4460	6'-0" wide			10	1.600	Opng.
	4600	Flush, birch, 6'-8" x 4'-0" wide			12	1.330	Opng.
	4620	5'-0" wide			11	1.450	Opng.
	4640	6'-0" wide			10	1.600	Opng.
	4800	Louvered, pine, 6'-8" x 4'-0" wide			12	1.330	Opng.
	4820	5'-0" wide			11	1.450	Opng.
	4840	6'-0" wide			10	1.600	Opng.
	5000	Paneled, pine, 6'-8" x 4'-0" wide			12	1.330	Opng.
	5020	5'-0" wide			11	1.450	Opng.
	5040	6'-0" wide	▼	▼	10	1.600	Opng.
	6100	Folding accordion, closet, not including frame					
	6120	Vinyl, 2 layer, stock (see also division 106-552)	F-2	2 Carpenters Power Tools	400	.040	S.F.
	6140	Woven mahogany and vinyl, stock			400	.040	S.F.
	6160	Wood slats with vinyl overlay, stock			400	.040	S.F.
	6180	Economy vinyl, stock			400	.040	S.F.
	6200	Rigid PVC	▼	▼	400	.040	S.F.
	7400	Passage doors, flush, no frame included					
	7420	Lauan, hollow core, 1-3/8" x 6'-8" x 1'-6" wide	F-2	2 Carpenters Power Tools	19	.842	Ea.

082 | Wood and Plastic Doors

082 050 | Wood And Plastic Doors

		CREW	MAKEUP	DAILY OUTPUT	MAN-HOURS	UNIT
078 7441	Wood passage door, lauan hollow core, 1-3/8" x 6'-8" x 2' wide	F-2	2 Carpenters / Power Tools	18	.889	Ea.
7460	2'-6" wide			18	.889	Ea.
7480	2'-8" wide			18	.889	Ea.
7500	3'-0" wide			17	.941	Ea.
7700	Birch, hollow core, 1-3/8" x 6'-8" x 1'-6" wide			19	.842	Ea.
7720	2'-0" wide			18	.889	Ea.
7740	2'-6" wide			18	.889	Ea.
7760	2'-8" wide			18	.889	Ea.
7780	3'-0" wide			17	.941	Ea.
8000	Pine louvered, 1-3/8" x 6'-8" x 1'-6" wide			19	.842	Ea.
8020	2'-0" wide			18	.889	Ea.
8040	2'-6" wide			18	.889	Ea.
8060	2'-8" wide			18	.889	Ea.
8080	3'-0" wide			17	.941	Ea.
8300	Pine paneled, 1-3/8" x 6'-8" x 1'-6" wide			19	.842	Ea.
8320	2'-0" wide			18	.889	Ea.
8340	2'-6" wide			18	.889	Ea.
8360	2'-8" wide			18	.889	Ea.
8380	3'-0" wide	↓	↓	17	.941	Ea.
082	**PRE-HUNG DOORS**					
0300	Exterior, wood, combination storm & screen, 6'-9" x 2'-6" wide	F-2	2 Carpenters / Power Tools	15	1.070	Ea.
0320	2'-8" wide			15	1.070	Ea.
0340	3'-0" wide	↓	↓	15	1.070	Ea.
1600	Entrance door, flush, birch, solid core					
1620	4-5/8" solid jamb, 1-3/4" x 6'-8" x 2'-8" wide	F-2	2 Carpenters / Power Tools	16	1.000	Ea.
1640	3'-0" wide	"	"	16	1.000	Ea.
2000	Entrance door, colonial, 6 panel pine					
2020	4-5/8" solid jamb, 1-3/4" x 6'-8" x 2'-8" wide	F-2	2 Carpenters / Power Tools	16	1.000	Ea.
2040	3'-0" wide			16	1.000	Ea.
2300	French door, 6'-8" x 6'-0" wide, 1/2" insul. glass and grille	↓	↓	7	2.290	Pr.
4000	Interior, passage door, 4-5/8" solid jamb					
4400	Lauan, flush, solid core, 1-3/8" x 6'-8" x 2'-6" wide	F-2	2 Carpenters / Power Tools	20	.800	Ea.
4420	2'-8" wide			20	.800	Ea.
4440	3'-0" wide			19	.842	Ea.
4600	Hollow core, 1-3/8" x 6'-8" x 2'-6" wide			20	.800	Ea.
4620	2'-8" wide			20	.800	Ea.
4640	3'-0" wide			19	.842	Ea.
5000	Birch, flush, solid core, 1-3/8" x 6'-8" x 2'-6" wide			20	.800	Ea.
5020	2'-8" wide			20	.800	Ea.
5040	3'-0" wide			19	.842	Ea.
5200	Hollow core, 1-3/8" x 6'-8" x 2'-6" wide			20	.800	Ea.
5220	2'-8" wide			20	.800	Ea.
5240	3'-0" wide			19	.842	Ea.
5500	Pine louvered, 1-3/8" x 6'-8" x 2'-6" wide			20	.800	Ea.
5520	2'-8" wide			20	.800	Ea.
5540	3'-0" wide			19	.842	Ea.
6000	Paneled, 1-3/8" x 6'-8" x 2'-6" wide			20	.800	Ea.
6020	2'-8" wide			20	.800	Ea.
6040	3'-0" wide	↓	↓	19	.842	Ea.

083 | Special Doors

083 100 | Sliding Doors

		Description	CREW	MAKEUP	DAILY OUTPUT	MAN-HOURS	UNIT
102	102	**GLASS, SLIDING** Vinyl clad, 1" insulated glass, 6'-0" x 6'-10" high	2 Carp	2 Carpenters	4	4.000	Opng.
	0100	8'-0" x 6'-10" high			4	4.000	Opng.
	0500	3 leaf, 9'-0" x 6'-10" high			3	5.330	Opng.
	0600	12'-0" x 6'-10" high	▼	▼	3	5.330	Opng.
	108	**SLIDING** Steel, up to 50' x 18', electric, standard duty, minimum	L-5	1 Struc. Steel Foreman	360	.156	S.F.
				5 Struc. Steel Workers			
				1 Equip. Oper. (crane)			
				1 Hyd. Crane, 25 Ton			
	0100	Maximum			340	.165	S.F.
	0500	Heavy duty, minimum			297	.189	S.F.
	0600	Maximum	▼	▼	277	.202	S.F.

083 180 | Security Doors

	Description	CREW	MAKEUP	DAILY OUTPUT	MAN-HOURS	UNIT
184	**VAULT FRONT** Door and frame, 32" x 78", clear opening					
0100	1 hour test, weighs 750 lbs.	2 Sswk	2 Struc. Steel Workers	1.50	10.670	Opng.
0200	2 hour test, 32" door, weighs 950 lbs.			1.30	12.310	Opng.
0250	40" door, weighs 1130 lbs.			1	16.000	Opng.
0300	4 hour test, 32" door, weighs 1025 lbs.			1.20	13.330	Opng.
0350	40" door, weighs 1140 lbs.	▼	▼	.90	17.780	Opng.
0600	For time lock, two movement, add	1 Elec	1 Electrician	2	4.000	Ea.
0650	Three movement, add	"	"	2	4.000	Ea.
0800	Day gate, painted, steel, 32" wide	2 Sswk	2 Struc. Steel Workers	1.50	10.670	Ea.
0850	40" wide			1.40	11.430	Ea.
0900	Polished steel, 32" wide			1.50	10.670	Ea.
0950	40" wide			1.40	11.430	Ea.
2050	Security vault door, 3-1/2" thick, class 5R, minimum			.40	40.000	Opng.
2100	Maximum			.30	53.330	Opng.
2150	7" thick, class 9R, minimum			.40	40.000	Opng.
2200	Maximum	▼	▼	.30	53.330	Opng.

083 200 | Metal Clad Doors

	Description	CREW	MAKEUP	DAILY OUTPUT	MAN-HOURS	UNIT
202	**KALAMEIN** Interior, flush type, 3' x 7'	2 Carp	2 Carpenters	4.30	3.720	Opng.
204	**TIN CLAD** 3 ply, 6' x 7', double sliding, manual	"	"	1	16.000	Opng.
1000	For electric operator, add	1 Elec	1 Electrician	2	4.000	Opng.

083 250 | Cold Storage Doors

	Description	CREW	MAKEUP	DAILY OUTPUT	MAN-HOURS	UNIT
251	**COLD STORAGE** Single, galvanized steel					
0300	Horizontal sliding, 5' x 7', manual operation, 2" thick	F-2	2 Carpenters	2	8.000	Ea.
			Power Tools			
0400	4" thick			2	8.000	Ea.
0500	6" thick			2	8.000	Ea.
0800	Power operation, 2" thick			1.90	8.420	Ea.
0900	4" thick			1.90	8.420	Ea.
1000	6" thick			1.90	8.420	Ea.
1300	9' x 10', manual operation, 2" insulation			1.70	9.410	Ea.
1400	4" insulation			1.70	9.410	Ea.
1500	6" insulation			1.70	9.410	Ea.
1800	Power operation, 2" insulation			1.60	10.000	Ea.
1900	4" insulation			1.60	10.000	Ea.
2000	6" insulation	▼	▼	1.70	9.410	Ea.
3000	Hinged, lightweight, 3' x 6'-6", galvanized 1 face, 2" thick	2 Carp	2 Carpenters	2	8.000	Ea.
3050	4" thick			1.90	8.420	Ea.
3300	Aluminum doors, 3' x 6'-6", 4" thick			1.90	8.420	Ea.
3350	6" thick			1.40	11.430	Ea.
3600	Stainless steel, 3' x 6'-6", 4" thick			1.90	8.420	Ea.
3650	6" thick			1.40	11.430	Ea.
3900	Galvanized 2 face, 3' x 6'-6", 4" thick			1.90	8.420	Ea.
3950	6" thick	▼	▼	1.40	11.430	Ea.

083 | Special Doors

083 250 | Cold Storage Doors

		CREW	MAKEUP	DAILY OUTPUT	MAN-HOURS	UNIT
251 5001	Cold storage door, bi-parting, electric operated					
5010	6' x 8' opening, galvanized faces, for cooler	2 Carp	2 Carpenters	.80	20.000	Opng.
5050	For freezer			.80	20.000	Opng.
5300	For door buck framing and door protection, add			2.50	6.400	Opng.
6000	Galvanized batten door, galvanized hinges, 4' x 7'			2	8.000	Opng.
6050	6' x 8'			1.80	8.890	Opng.
6500	Fire door, 3 hr., 6' x 8', single slide			.80	20.000	Opng.
6550	Double, bi-parting	↓	↓	.70	22.860	Opng.

083 300 | Coiling Doors

		CREW	MAKEUP	DAILY OUTPUT	MAN-HOURS	UNIT
302	COUNTER DOORS 4' high roll-up, 6' long, galv. steel or aluminum	2 Carp	2 Carpenters	2	8.000	Opng.
0300	Galvanized steel, UL label			1.80	8.890	Opng.
0600	Stainless steel, 4' high roll-up, 6' long			2	8.000	Opng.
0700	10' long	↓	↓	1.80	8.890	Opng.

083 400 | Coiling Grilles

		CREW	MAKEUP	DAILY OUTPUT	MAN-HOURS	UNIT
402	ROLL UP GRILLE Aluminum, manual operated, mill finish	2 Sswk	2 Struc. Steel Workers	82	.195	S.F.
0100	Bronze anodized			82	.195	S.F.
0400	Steel, manual operated, 10' x 10' high			1	16.000	Opng.
0500	15' x 8' high			.80	20.000	Opng.
1100	For motor operation, add	↓	↓	5	3.200	Opng.
406	ROLLING GRILLE SUPPORTS Overhead framed	E-4	1 Struc. Steel Foreman	36	.889	L.F.
			3 Struc. Steel Workers			
			1 Gas Welding Machine			

083 550 | Flexible Doors

		CREW	MAKEUP	DAILY OUTPUT	MAN-HOURS	UNIT
551	FLEXIBLE TRANSPARENT STRIP ENTRANCE , 12" strip width					
0100	2/3 overlap	3 Shee	3 Sheet Metal Workers	135	.178	SF Surf
0200	Full overlap	"	"	115	.209	SF Surf

083 600 | Sectional Overhead Drs

		CREW	MAKEUP	DAILY OUTPUT	MAN-HOURS	UNIT
604	OVERHEAD, COMMERCIAL Frames not included					
1000	Stock, sectional, heavy duty, wood, 1-3/4" thick, 8' x 8' high	2 Carp	2 Carpenters	2	8.000	Ea.
1100	10' x 10' high			1.80	8.890	Ea.
1200	12' x 12' high			1.50	10.670	Ea.
1300	Chain hoist, 14' x 14' high			1.30	12.310	Ea.
1400	12' x 16' high			1	16.000	Ea.
1500	20' x 8' high			.80	20.000	Ea.
1600	20' x 16' high			.60	26.670	Ea.
1800	Center mullion openings, 8' high			4	4.000	Ea.
1900	20' high			2	8.000	Ea.
2300	Fiberglass and aluminum, heavy duty, sectional, 12' x 12' high			1.50	10.670	Ea.
2450	Chain hoist, 20' x 20' high			.50	32.000	Ea.
2600	Steel, 24 ga. sectional, manual, 8' x 8' high			2	8.000	Ea.
2650	10' x 10' high			1.80	8.890	Ea.
2700	12' x 12' high			1.50	10.670	Ea.
2800	Chain hoist, 20' x 14' high	↓	↓	.70	22.860	Ea.
2900	For electric trolley operator, to 14' x 14', add	1 Carp	1 Carpenter	2	4.000	Ea.
2950	Over 14' x 14', add	"	"	1	8.000	Ea.
606	RESIDENTIAL GARAGE DOORS Including hardware, no frame					
0050	Hinged, wood, custom, double door, 9' x 7'	2 Carp	2 Carpenters	3	5.330	Ea.
0070	16' x 7'			2	8.000	Ea.
0200	Overhead, sectional, incl. hardware, fiberglass, 9' x 7', standard			8	2.000	Ea.
0220	Deluxe			8	2.000	Ea.
0300	16' x 7', standard			6	2.670	Ea.
0320	Deluxe			6	2.670	Ea.
0500	Hardboard, 9' x 7', standard			8	2.000	Ea.
0520	Deluxe	↓	↓	8	2.000	Ea.

083 | Special Doors

		083 600	Sectional Overhead Drs	CREW	MAKEUP	DAILY OUTPUT	MAN-HOURS	UNIT
606	0602	Resi. overhead garage door, hardboard, 16' x 7', standard		2 Carp	2 Carpenters	6	2.670	Ea.
	0620	Deluxe				6	2.670	Ea.
	0700	Metal, 9' x 7', standard				8	2.000	Ea.
	0720	Deluxe				8	2.000	Ea.
	0800	16' x 7', standard				6	2.670	Ea.
	0820	Deluxe				6	2.670	Ea.
	0900	Wood, 9' x 7', standard				8	2.000	Ea.
	0920	Deluxe				8	2.000	Ea.
	1000	16' x 7', standard				6	2.670	Ea.
	1020	Deluxe		↓	↓	6	2.670	Ea.
	1800	Door hardware only, sectional		1 Carp	1 Carpenter	4	2.000	Ea.
	1820	One side only		"	"	7	1.140	Ea.
	3000	Swing-up, including hardware, fiberglass, 9' x 7', standard		2 Carp	2 Carpenters	8	2.000	Ea.
	3020	Deluxe				8	2.000	Ea.
	3100	16' x 7', standard				6	2.670	Ea.
	3120	Deluxe				6	2.670	Ea.
	3200	Hardboard, 9' x 7', standard				8	2.000	Ea.
	3220	Deluxe				8	2.000	Ea.
	3300	16' x 7', standard				6	2.670	Ea.
	3320	Deluxe				6	2.670	Ea.
	3400	Metal, 9' x 7', standard				8	2.000	Ea.
	3420	Deluxe				8	2.000	Ea.
	3500	16' x 7', standard				6	2.670	Ea.
	3520	Deluxe				6	2.670	Ea.
	3600	Wood, 9' x 7', standard				8	2.000	Ea.
	3620	Deluxe				8	2.000	Ea.
	3700	16' x 7', standard				6	2.670	Ea.
	3720	Deluxe		↓	↓	6	2.670	Ea.
	3900	Door hardware only, swing up		1 Carp	1 Carpenter	4	2.000	Ea.
	3920	One side only				7	1.140	Ea.
	4000	For electric operator, economy, add				8	1.000	Ea.
	4100	Deluxe, including remote control		↓	↓	8	1.000	Ea.

		083 650	Multileaf Vert Lift Drs	CREW	MAKEUP	DAILY OUTPUT	MAN-HOURS	UNIT
652		TELESCOPING STEEL DOORS Baked enamel finish,						
	1000	Overhead, .03" thick, electric operated, 10' x 10'		E-3	1 Struc. Steel Foreman	.80	30.000	Ea.
					1 Struc. Steel Worker			
					1 Welder			
					1 Gas Welding Machine			
					1 Torch, Gas & Air			
	2000	20' x 10'				.60	40.000	Ea.
	3000	20' x 16'				.40	60.000	Ea.
654		VERTICAL LIFT Doors, motor operator, incl. frame, 16' x 16' high		↓	↓	.50	48.000	Ea.
	0100	32' x 24' high		E-2	1 Struc. Steel Foreman	.75	74.670	Ea.
					4 Struc. Steel Workers			
					1 Equip. Oper. (crane)			
					1 Equip. Oper. Oiler			
					1 Crane, 90 Ton			

083 | Special Doors

083 700 | Hangar Doors

		CREW	MAKEUP	DAILY OUTPUT	MAN-HOURS	UNIT
701	**HANGAR DOOR** Bi-fold, ovhd.,20 PSF wind load, incl. elec. oper.					
0100	12' high	2 Sswk	2 Struc. Steel Workers	240	.067	S.F.
0200	16' high			230	.070	S.F.
0300	20' high	↓	↓	220	.073	S.F.

083 720 | Special Purpose Doors

		CREW	MAKEUP	DAILY OUTPUT	MAN-HOURS	UNIT
721	**BULKHEAD CELLAR DOORS** Steel, not incl. sides, minimum	1 Carp	1 Carpenter	5.50	1.450	Ea.
0100	Maximum			5.10	1.570	Ea.
0500	With sides and foundation plates, minimum			4.70	1.700	Ea.
0600	Maximum	↓	↓	4.30	1.860	Ea.
722	**AIR CURTAINS** Not incl. motor starters, transformers,					
0050	door switches or temperature controls					
0100	Shipping and receiving doors, unheated, minimal wind stoppage					
0150	8' high, multiples of 3' wide	2 Shee	2 Sheet Metal Workers	3.60	4.440	L.F.
0160	Multiples of 5' wide			3.60	4.440	L.F.
0210	10' high, multiples of 4' wide			3.60	4.440	L.F.
0250	12' high, 3'-6" wide			3.30	4.850	L.F.
0260	12' wide			3.30	4.850	L.F.
0350	16' high, 3'-6" wide			3.30	4.850	L.F.
0360	12' wide	↓	↓	3.30	4.850	L.F.
0500	Maximum wind stoppage					
0550	10' high, multiples of 4' wide	2 Shee	2 Sheet Metal Workers	3.60	4.440	L.F.
0650	14' high, multiples of 4' wide			3.25	4.920	L.F.
0750	20' high, multiples of 8' wide	↓	↓	3	5.330	L.F.
1100	Heated, maximum wind stoppage, steam heat					
1150	10' high, multiples of 4' wide	2 Shee	2 Sheet Metal Workers	3	5.330	L.F.
1250	14' high, multiples of 4' wide			2.80	5.710	L.F.
1350	20' high, multiples of 8' wide	↓	↓	2.60	6.150	L.F.
1500	Customer entrance doors, unheated, minimal wind stoppage					
1550	10' high, multiples of 3' wide	2 Shee	2 Sheet Metal Workers	3.60	4.440	L.F.
1560	Multiples of 5' wide			3.60	4.440	L.F.
1650	Maximum wind stoppage, 12' high, multiples of 4' wide	↓	↓	3.30	4.850	L.F.
1700	Heated, minimal wind stoppage, electric heat					
1750	8' high, multiples of 3' wide	2 Shee	2 Sheet Metal Workers	3.10	5.160	L.F.
1760	Multiples of 5' wide			3.10	5.160	L.F.
1850	10' high, multiples of 3' wide			3.10	5.160	L.F.
1860	Multiples of 5' wide	↓	↓	3.10	5.160	L.F.
1950	Maximum wind stoppage, steam heat					
1960	12' high, multiples of 4' wide	2 Shee	2 Sheet Metal Workers	2.80	5.710	L.F.
2000	Walk-in coolers and freezers, ambient air, minimal wind stoppage					
2050	8' high, multiples of 3' wide	2 Shee	2 Sheet Metal Workers	3.60	4.440	L.F.
2060	Multiples of 5' wide			3.60	4.440	L.F.
2250	Maximum wind stoppage, 12' high, multiples of 3' wide			3.30	4.850	L.F.
2450	Conveyor openings or service windows, unheated, 5' high			4	4.000	L.F.
2460	Heated, electric, 5' high, 2'-6" wide	↓	↓	3.30	4.850	L.F.
723	**FLOOR, COMMERCIAL** Alum. tile, steel frame, one leaf, 2'x2' opng.	2 Sswk	2 Struc. Steel Workers	3.50	4.570	Opng.
0050	3'-6" x 3'-6" opening			3.50	4.570	Opng.
0500	Double leaf, 4' x 4' opening			3	5.330	Opng.
0550	5' x 5' opening			3	5.330	Opng.
725	**FLOOR, INDUSTRIAL** Steel 300 psf L.L., single leaf, 2' x 2' opening			6	2.670	Opng.
0050	3' x 3' opening			5.50	2.910	Opng.
0300	Double leaf, 4' x 4' opening			5	3.200	Opng.
0350	5' x 5' opening			4.50	3.560	Opng.
1000	Aluminum, 300 psf L.L., single leaf, 2' x 2' opening			6	2.670	Opng.
1050	3' x 3' opening			5.50	2.910	Opng.
1500	Double leaf, 4' x 4' opening			5	3.200	Opng.
1550	5' x 5' opening			4.50	3.560	Opng.
2000	Aluminum, 150 psf L.L., single leaf, 2' x 2' opening	↓	↓	6	2.670	Opng.

083 | Special Doors

083 720 | Special Purpose Doors

		CREW	MAKEUP	DAILY OUTPUT	MAN-HOURS	UNIT
725 2052	Floor, alum., 150 psf L.L., single leaf, 3' x 3' opening	2 Sswk	2 Struc. Steel Workers	5.50	2.910	Opng.
2500	Double leaf, 4' x 4' opening			5	3.200	Opng.
2550	5' x 5' opening	↓	↓	4.50	3.560	Opng.
729	KENNEL 2 way, swinging type, 17" x 19" opening	2 Carp	2 Carpenters	11	1.450	Opng.
0100	17" x 24" opening	"	"	11	1.450	Opng.
732	ROLLING SERVICE DOORS Steel, manual, 20 ga., 8' x 8', std.	2 Sswk	2 Struc. Steel Workers	1.60	10.000	Ea.
0100	10' x 10' high			1.40	11.430	Ea.
0200	20' x 10' high			1	16.000	Ea.
0300	12' x 12' high			1.20	13.330	Ea.
0400	20' x 12' high			.90	17.780	Ea.
0500	14' x 14' high			.80	20.000	Ea.
0600	20' x 16' high			.60	26.670	Ea.
0700	10' x 20' high			.50	32.000	Ea.
1000	12' x 12', crank operated, crank on door side			.80	20.000	Ea.
1100	Crank thru wall			.70	22.860	Ea.
2000	Class A fire doors, manual, 20 ga., 8' x 8' high			1.40	11.430	Ea.
2100	10' x 10' high			1.10	14.550	Ea.
2200	20' x 10' high			.80	20.000	Ea.
2300	12' x 12' high			1	16.000	Ea.
2400	20' x 12' high			.80	20.000	Ea.
2500	14' x 14' high			.60	26.670	Ea.
2600	20' x 16' high			.50	32.000	Ea.
2700	10' x 20' high			.40	40.000	Ea.
4500	Motor operators, to 14' x 14' opening			5	3.200	Ea.
4600	Over 14' x 14', jack shaft type			5	3.200	Ea.
736	SHOCK ABSORBING Rigid, no frame, 1-1/2" thick, 5' x 7'			1.90	8.420	Opng.
0100	8' x 8'			1.80	8.890	Opng.
0500	Flexible, no frame, insulated, 1-13/16" thick, economy, 5' x 7'			2	8.000	Opng.
0600	Deluxe			1.90	8.420	Opng.
1000	8' x 8' opening, economy			2	8.000	Opng.
1100	Deluxe	↓	↓	1.90	8.420	Opng.

083 750 | Swing Doors

		CREW	MAKEUP	DAILY OUTPUT	MAN-HOURS	UNIT
752	DOUBLE ACTING With vision panel, incl. frame, closer & hardware					
1000	.063" aluminum, 7'-0" high, 4'-0" wide	2 Carp	2 Carpenters	4.20	3.810	Pr.
1050	6'-8" wide	"	"	4	4.000	Pr.
2000	Solid core wood, 3/4" thick, metal frame, stainless steel					
2010	base plate, 7' high opening, 4' wide	2 Carp	2 Carpenters	4	4.000	Pr.
2050	7' wide	"	"	3.80	4.210	Pr.
754	GLASS, SWING Tempered, 1/2" thick, incl. hardware, 3' x 7' opening	2 Glaz	2 Glaziers	2	8.000	Opng.
0100	6' x 7' opening	"	"	1.40	11.430	Opng.
756	SWING Tubular steel, 7' high, single, 3'-4" opening	2 Sswk	2 Struc. Steel Workers	2.50	6.400	Ea.
0100	Double, 6'-0" opening	"	"	2	8.000	Pr.

083 800 | Sound Retardant Doors

		CREW	MAKEUP	DAILY OUTPUT	MAN-HOURS	UNIT
804	ACOUSTICAL Incl. framed seals, 3' x 7', wood, 27 STC rating	F-2	2 Carpenters Power Tools	1.50	10.670	Ea.
0100	Steel, 40 STC rating			1.50	10.670	Ea.
0200	45 STC rating			1.50	10.670	Ea.
0300	48 STC rating			1.50	10.670	Ea.
0400	52 STC rating	↓	↓	1.50	10.670	Ea.

083 | Special Doors

083 900 | Screen And Storm Doors

		CREW	MAKEUP	DAILY OUTPUT	MAN-HOURS	UNIT
904	904	**STORM DOORS & FRAMES** Aluminum, residential,					
	0020	combination storm and screen					
	0400	Clear anodic coating, 6′-8″ x 2′-6″ wide	F-2	2 Carpenters Power Tools	15	1.070	Ea.
	0420	2′-8″ wide			14	1.140	Ea.
	0440	3′-0″ wide			14	1.140	Ea.
	1000	Mill finish, 6′-8″ x 2′-6″ wide			15	1.070	Ea.
	1020	2′-8″ wide			14	1.140	Ea.
	1040	3′-0″ wide			14	1.140	Ea.
	1500	White painted, 6′-8″ x 2′-6″ wide			15	1.070	Ea.
	1520	2′-8″ wide			14	1.140	Ea.
	1540	3′-0″ wide			14	1.140	Ea.

084 | Entrances and Storefronts

084 100 | Aluminum

		CREW	MAKEUP	DAILY OUTPUT	MAN-HOURS	UNIT
103	**BALANCED DOORS** Hdwre & frame, alum. & glass, 3′ x 7′, econ.	2 Sswk	2 Struc. Steel Workers	.90	17.780	Ea.
0150	Premium	″	″	.70	22.860	Ea.
105	**STOREFRONT SYSTEMS** Aluminum frame, clear 3/8″ plate glass,					
0020	incl. 3′ x 7′ door with hardware (400 sq. ft. max. wall)					
0500	Wall height to 12′ high, commercial grade	2 Glaz	2 Glaziers	150	.107	S.F.
0600	Institutional grade			130	.123	S.F.
0700	Monumental grade			115	.139	S.F.
1000	6′ x 7′ door with hardware, commercial grade			135	.119	S.F.
1100	Institutional grade			115	.139	S.F.
1200	Monumental grade			100	.160	S.F.
107	**SWING DOORS** Alum. entrance, 6′ x 7′, incl. hdwre & oper.	2 Sswk	2 Struc. Steel Workers	.70	22.860	Opng.

084 300 | Stainless Steel

		CREW	MAKEUP	DAILY OUTPUT	MAN-HOURS	UNIT
301	**STAINLESS STEEL AND GLASS** Entrance unit, narrow stiles					
0020	3′ x 7′ opening, including hardware, minimum	2 Sswk	2 Struc. Steel Workers	1.60	10.000	Opng.
0050	Average			1.40	11.430	Opng.
0100	Maximum			1.20	13.330	Opng.
2000	Balanced doors, 3′ x 7′, economy			.90	17.780	Ea.
2100	Premium			.70	22.860	Ea.

084 600 | Automatic Doors

		CREW	MAKEUP	DAILY OUTPUT	MAN-HOURS	UNIT
602	**SLIDING ENTRANCE** 12′ x 7′-6″ opng., 5′ x 7′ door, 2 way traf.,					
0020	mat activated, panic pushout, incl. operator & hardware,					
0030	not including glass or glazing	2 Glaz	2 Glaziers	.70	22.860	Opng.
604	**SLIDING PANEL** Mall fronts, aluminum & glass, 15′ x 9′ high			1.30	12.310	Opng.
0100	24′ x 9′ high			.70	22.860	Opng.
0200	48′ x 9′ high, with fixed panels			.90	17.780	Opng.

084 700 | Revolving Doors

		CREW	MAKEUP	DAILY OUTPUT	MAN-HOURS	UNIT
701	**REVOLVING DOORS** Aluminum, 6′-6″ to 7′-0″ diameter					
0020	6′-10″ to 7′ high, stock units, minimum	4 Sswk	4 Struc. Steel Workers	.75	42.670	Opng.
0050	Average			.60	53.330	Opng.
0100	Maximum			.45	71.110	Opng.
1000	Stainless steel			.30	107.000	Opng.
1500	For automatic controls, add	2 Elec	2 Electricians	2	8.000	Opng.

085 | Metal Windows

085 100 | Steel Windows

		CREW	MAKEUP	DAILY OUTPUT	MAN-HOURS	UNIT
102	**STEEL SASH** Custom units, glazing and trim not included,					
0100	Casement, 100% vented	2 Sswk	2 Struc. Steel Workers	200	.080	S.F.
0200	50% vented			200	.080	S.F.
0300	Fixed			200	.080	S.F.
1000	Projected, commercial, 40% vented			200	.080	S.F.
1100	Intermediate, 50% vented			200	.080	S.F.
1500	Industrial, horizontally pivoted			200	.080	S.F.
1600	Fixed			200	.080	S.F.
2000	Industrial security sash, 50% vented			200	.080	S.F.
2100	Fixed			200	.080	S.F.
2500	Picture window			200	.080	S.F.
3000	Double hung			200	.080	S.F.
5000	Mullions for above, open interior face			240	.067	L.F.
5100	With interior cover	↓	↓	240	.067	L.F.
104	**STEEL WINDOWS** Stock, including frame, trim and insulating glass					
1000	Custom units, double hung, 2'-8" x 4'-6" opening	2 Sswk	2 Struc. Steel Workers	12	1.330	Ea.
1100	2'-4" x 3'-9" opening			12	1.330	Ea.
1500	Commercial projected, 3'-9" x 5'-5" opening			10	1.600	Ea.
1600	6'-9" x 4'-1" opening			7	2.290	Ea.
2000	Intermediate projected, 2'-9" x 4'-1" opening			12	1.330	Ea.
2100	4'-1" x 5'-5" opening	↓	↓	10	1.600	Ea.

085 200 | Aluminum Windows

		CREW	MAKEUP	DAILY OUTPUT	MAN-HOURS	UNIT
202	**ALUMINUM SASH** Stock, grade c, glaze & trim not incl., casement	2 Sswk	2 Struc. Steel Workers	200	.080	S.F.
0050	Double hung			200	.080	S.F.
0100	Fixed casement			200	.080	S.F.
0150	Picture window			200	.080	S.F.
0200	Projected window			200	.080	S.F.
0250	Single hung			200	.080	S.F.
0300	Sliding			200	.080	S.F.
1000	Mullions for above, tubular			240	.067	L.F.
2000	Custom aluminum sash, grade hc, glazing not included, minimum			200	.080	S.F.
2100	Maximum	↓	↓	85	.188	S.F.
204	**ALUMINUM WINDOWS** Incl. frame and glazing, grade C					
1000	Stock units, casement, 3'-1" x 3'-2" opening	2 Sswk	2 Struc. Steel Workers	10	1.600	Ea.
1600	Projected, with screen, 3'-1" x 3'-2" opening			10	1.600	Ea.
2000	4'-5" x 5'-3" opening			8	2.000	Ea.
2500	Enamel finish windows, 3'-1" x 3'-2"			10	1.600	Ea.
2600	4'-5" x 5'-3"			8	2.000	Ea.
3000	Single hung, 2' x 3' opening, enameled, standard glazed			10	1.600	Ea.
3100	Insulating glass			10	1.600	Ea.
3300	2'-8" x 6'-8" opening, standard glazed			8	2.000	Ea.
3400	Insulating glass			8	2.000	Ea.
3700	3'-4" x 5'-0" opening, standard glazed			9	1.780	Ea.
3800	Insulating glass			9	1.780	Ea.
3890	Awning type, 3' x 3' opening standard glass			14	1.140	Ea.
3900	Insulating glass			14	1.140	Ea.
3910	3' x 4' opening, standard glass			10	1.600	Ea.
3920	Insulating glass			10	1.600	Ea.
3930	3' x 5'-4" opening, standard glass			10	1.600	Ea.
3940	Insulating glass			10	1.600	Ea.
3950	4' x 5'-4" opening, standard glass			9	1.780	Ea.
3960	Insulating glass			9	1.780	Ea.
4000	Sliding aluminum, 3' x 2' opening, standard glazed			10	1.600	Ea.
4100	Insulating glass			10	1.600	Ea.
4300	5' x 3' opening, standard glazed			9	1.780	Ea.
4400	Insulating glass			9	1.780	Ea.
4600	8' x 4' opening, standard glazed	↓	↓	6	2.670	Ea.

085 | Metal Windows

085 200 | Aluminum Windows

		CREW	MAKEUP	DAILY OUTPUT	MAN-HOURS	UNIT
204 4702	Aluminum windows, sliding, 8' x 4' opening, insulating glass	2 Sswk	2 Struc. Steel Workers	6	2.670	Ea.
5000	9' x 5' opening, standard glazed			4	4.000	Ea.
5100	Insulating glass			4	4.000	Ea.
5500	Sliding, with thermal barrier and screen, 6' x 4', 2 track			8	2.000	Ea.
5700	4 track	↓	↓	8	2.000	Ea.

085 500 | Metal Jalousie Windows

		CREW	MAKEUP	DAILY OUTPUT	MAN-HOURS	UNIT
502	JALOUSIES Aluminum incl. glazing & screens, stock, 1'-7" x 3'-2"	2 Sswk	2 Struc. Steel Workers	10	1.600	Ea.
0100	2'-3" x 4'-0"			10	1.600	Ea.
0200	3'-1" x 2'-0"			10	1.600	Ea.
0300	3'-1" x 5'-3"			10	1.600	Ea.
1000	Mullions for above, 2'-0" long			80	.200	Ea.
1100	5'-3" long	↓	↓	80	.200	Ea.

085 600 | Metal Storm Windows

		CREW	MAKEUP	DAILY OUTPUT	MAN-HOURS	UNIT
601	STORM WINDOWS Aluminum, residential					
0300	Basement, mill finish, incl. fiberglass screen					
0320	1'-10" x 1'-0" high	F-2	2 Carpenters / Power Tools	30	.533	Ea.
0340	2'-9" x 1'-6" high	"	"	30	.533	Ea.
1600	Double-hung, combination, storm & screen					
2000	Average quality, clear anodic coating, 2'-0" x 3'-5" high	F-2	2 Carpenters / Power Tools	30	.533	Ea.
2020	2'-6" x 5'-0" high			28	.571	Ea.
2040	4'-0" x 6'-0" high			25	.640	Ea.
2400	White painted, 2'-0" x 3'-5" high			30	.533	Ea.
2420	2'-6" x 5'-0" high			28	.571	Ea.
2440	4'-0" x 6'-0" high			25	.640	Ea.
2600	Mill finish, 2'-0" x 3'-5" high			30	.533	Ea.
2620	2'-6" x 5'-0" high			28	.571	Ea.
2640	4'-0" x 6-8" high	↓	↓	25	.640	Ea.

085 700 | Screens

		CREW	MAKEUP	DAILY OUTPUT	MAN-HOURS	UNIT
701	SCREENS For metal sash, aluminum or bronze mesh, flat screen	2 Sswk	2 Struc. Steel Workers	1,200	.013	S.F.
0500	Wicket screen, inside window			1,000	.016	S.F.
0800	Security screen, aluminum frame with stainless steel cloth			1,200	.013	S.F.
0900	Steel grate, painted, on steel frame			1,600	.010	S.F.
1000	For solar louvers, add	↓	↓	160	.100	S.F.

086 | Wood and Plastic Windows

086 100 | Wood Windows

		CREW	MAKEUP	DAILY OUTPUT	MAN-HOURS	UNIT
104	AWNING WINDOW Including frame, screen, and exterior trim					
0100	Average quality, builders model, 34" x 22", standard glazed	1 Carp	1 Carpenter	10	.800	Ea.
0200	Insulating glass			10	.800	Ea.
0300	40" x 28", standard glazed			9	.889	Ea.
0400	Insulating glass			9	.889	Ea.
0500	48" x 36", standard glazed			8	1.000	Ea.
0600	Insulating glass			8	1.000	Ea.
2000	Metal clad, deluxe, insulating glass, 34" x 22"			10	.800	Ea.
2100	40" x 22"			10	.800	Ea.
2200	36" x 28"	↓	↓	9	.889	Ea.

			086 100	Wood Windows	CREW	MAKEUP	DAILY OUTPUT	MAN-HOURS	UNIT
104	2301	Awning window, metal clad, deluxe, insulating glass, 40" x 28"	1 Carp	1 Carpenter	9	.889	Ea.
	2400	48" x 28"	↓	↓	8	1.000	Ea.
	2500	60" x 36"			8	1.000	Ea.
	108	BOW-BAY WINDOW Including frame, screen and exterior trim,					
	0020	end panels operable					
	1000	Awning type, builders model, 8' x 5' high, std. glazed, 4 panels	2 Carp	2 Carpenters	10	1.600	Ea.
	1050	Insulating glass			10	1.600	Ea.
	1100	10'-0" x 5'-0" high, standard glazed			6	2.670	Ea.
	1200	Insulating glass, 6 panels			6	2.670	Ea.
	1600	Metal clad, deluxe, insul. glass, 6'-0" x 4'-0" high, 3 panels			10	1.600	Ea.
	1640	9'-0" x 4'-0" high, 4 panels			8	2.000	Ea.
	1680	10'-0" x 5'-0" high, 5 panels			7	2.290	Ea.
	1720	12'-0" x 6'-0" high, 6 panels			6	2.670	Ea.
	2000	Casement, builders model, bow, 8' x 5' high, std. glazed, 4 panels			10	1.600	Ea.
	2050	Insulating glass			10	1.600	Ea.
	2100	12'-0" x 6'-0" high, 6 panels, standard glazed			6	2.670	Ea.
	2200	Insulating glass			6	2.670	Ea.
	2600	Metal clad, deluxe, insul. glass, 8'-0" x 5'-0" high, 4 panels			10	1.600	Ea.
	2640	10'-0" x 5'-0" high, 5 panels			8	2.000	Ea.
	2680	10'-0" x 6'-0" high, 5 panels			7	2.290	Ea.
	2720	12'-0" x 6'-0" high, 6 panels			6	2.670	Ea.
	3000	Double hung, bldrs. model, bay, 8' x 4' high, std. glazed			10	1.600	Ea.
	3050	Insulating glass			10	1.600	Ea.
	3100	9'-0" x 5'-0" high, standard glazed			6	2.670	Ea.
	3200	Insulating glass			6	2.670	Ea.
	3600	Metal clad, deluxe, insul. glass, 7'-0" x 4'-0" high			10	1.600	Ea.
	3640	8'-0" x 4'-0" high			8	2.000	Ea.
	3680	8'-0" x 5'-0" high			7	2.290	Ea.
	3720	9'-0" x 5'-0" high	↓	↓	6	2.670	Ea.
	120	CASEMENT WINDOW Including frame, screen, and exterior trim					
	0100	Average quality, bldrs. model, 2'-0" x 3'-0" high, standard glazed	1 Carp	1 Carpenter	10	.800	Ea.
	0150	Insulating glass			10	.800	Ea.
	0200	2'-0" x 4'-6" high, standard glazed			9	.889	Ea.
	0250	Insulating glass			9	.889	Ea.
	0300	2'-3" x 6'-0" high, standard glazed			8	1.000	Ea.
	0350	Insulating glass			8	1.000	Ea.
	2000	Metal clad, deluxe, insulating glass, 2'-0" x 3'-0" high			10	.800	Ea.
	2040	2'-0" x 4'-0" high			9	.889	Ea.
	2080	2'-0" x 5'-0" high			8	1.000	Ea.
	2120	2'-0" x 6'-0" high	↓	↓	8	1.000	Ea.
	124	DOUBLE HUNG Including frame, screen, and exterior trim					
	0100	Average quality, bldrs. model, 2'-0" x 3'-0" high, standard glazed	1 Carp	1 Carpenter	10	.800	Ea.
	0150	Insulating glass			10	.800	Ea.
	0200	3'-0" x 4'-0" high, standard glazed			9	.889	Ea.
	0250	Insulating glass			9	.889	Ea.
	0300	4'-0" x 4'-6" high, standard glazed			8	1.000	Ea.
	0350	Insulating glass			8	1.000	Ea.
	2000	Metal clad, deluxe, insulating glass, 2'-6" x 3'-0" high			10	.800	Ea.
	2100	3'-0" x 3'-6" high			10	.800	Ea.
	2200	3'-0" x 4'-0" high			9	.889	Ea.
	2300	3'-0" x 4'-6" high			9	.889	Ea.
	2400	3'-0" x 5'-0" high			8	1.000	Ea.
	2500	3'-6" x 6'-0" high	↓	↓	8	1.000	Ea.

086 100	Wood Windows	CREW	MAKEUP	DAILY OUTPUT	MAN-HOURS	UNIT
132	**PICTURE WINDOW** Including frame and exterior trim					
0100	Average quality, bldrs. model, 3'-6" x 4'-0" high, standard glazed	2 Carp	2 Carpenters	12	1.330	Ea.
0150	Insulating glass			12	1.330	Ea.
0200	4'-0" x 4'-6" high, standard glazed			11	1.450	Ea.
0250	Insulating glass			11	1.450	Ea.
0300	5'-0" x 4'-0" high, standard glazed			11	1.450	Ea.
0350	Insulating glass			11	1.450	Ea.
0400	6'-0" x 4'-6" high, standard glazed			10	1.600	Ea.
0450	Insulating glass			10	1.600	Ea.
2000	Metal clad, deluxe, insulating glass, 4'-0" x 4'-0" high			12	1.330	Ea.
2100	4'-0" x 6'-0" high			11	1.450	Ea.
2200	5'-0" x 6'-0" high			10	1.600	Ea.
2300	6'-0" x 6'-0" high	↓	↓	10	1.600	Ea.
140	**SLIDING WINDOW** Including frame, screen, and exterior trim					
0100	Average quality, bldrs. model, 3'-0" x 3'-0" high, standard glazed	1 Carp	1 Carpenter	10	.800	Ea.
0120	Insulating glass			10	.800	Ea.
0200	4'-0" x 3'-6" high, standard glazed			9	.889	Ea.
0220	Insulating glass			9	.889	Ea.
0300	6'-0" x 5'-0" high, standard glazed			8	1.000	Ea.
0320	Insulating glass			8	1.000	Ea.
2000	Metal clad, deluxe, insulating glass, 3'-0" x 3'-0" high			10	.800	Ea.
2050	4'-0" x 3'-6" high			9	.889	Ea.
2100	5'-0" x 4'-0" high			9	.889	Ea.
2150	6'-0" x 5'-0" high	↓	↓	8	1.000	Ea.
144	**WINDOW GRILLE OR MUNTIN** Snap-in type					
0020	Colonial or diamond pattern					
2000	Wood, awning window, glass size 28" x 16" high	1 Carp	1 Carpenter	30	.267	Ea.
2060	44" x 24" high			32	.250	Ea.
2100	Casement, glass size, 20" x 36" high			30	.267	Ea.
2180	20" x 56" high			32	.250	Ea.
2200	Double hung, glass size, 16" x 24" high			24	.333	Set
2280	32" x 32" high			34	.235	Set
2500	Picture, glass size, 48" x 48" high			30	.267	Ea.
2580	60" x 68" high			28	.286	Ea.
2600	Sliding, glass size, 14" x 36" high			24	.333	Set
2680	36" x 36" high	↓	↓	22	.364	Set
148	**WOOD SASH** Including glazing but not including trim					
0050	Custom, 5'-0" x 4'-0", 1" dbl. glazed, 3/16" thick lites	2 Carp	2 Carpenters	3.20	5.000	Ea.
0100	1/4" thick lites			5	3.200	Ea.
0200	1" thick, triple glazed			5	3.200	Ea.
0300	7'-0" x 4'-6" high, 1" double glazed, 3/16" thick lites			4.30	3.720	Ea.
0400	1/4" thick lites			4.30	3.720	Ea.
0500	1" thick, triple glazed			4.30	3.720	Ea.
0600	8'-6" x 5'-0" high, 1" double glazed, 3/16" thick lites			3.50	4.570	Ea.
0700	1/4" thick lites			3.50	4.570	Ea.
0800	1" thick, triple glazed	↓	↓	3.50	4.570	Ea.
3000	Replacement sash, double hung, double glazing, to 12 S.F.	1 Carp	1 Carpenter	64	.125	S.F.
3100	12 S.F. to 20 S.F.			94	.085	S.F.
3200	20 S.F. and over			106	.075	S.F.
7000	Sash, single lite, 2'-0" x 2'-0" high			20	.400	Ea.
7050	2'-6" x 2'-0" high			19	.421	Ea.
7100	2'-6" x 2'-6" high			18	.444	Ea.
7150	3'-0" x 2'-0" high	↓	↓	17	.471	Ea.

086 | Wood and Plastic Windows

086 100 | Wood Windows		CREW	MAKEUP	DAILY OUTPUT	MAN-HOURS	UNIT
152	152 WOOD SCREENS Over 3 S.F., 3/4" frames	2 Carp	2 Carpenters	375	.043	S.F.
	0100 1-1/8" frames	"	"	375	.043	S.F.

087 | Hardware

087 100 | Finish Hardware		CREW	MAKEUP	DAILY OUTPUT	MAN-HOURS	UNIT
103	BOLTS, FLUSH Standard, concealed	1 Carp	1 Carpenter	7	1.140	Ea.
0800	Automatic fire exit	"	"	5	1.600	Ea.
1600	For electric release, add	1 Elec	1 Electrician	3	2.670	Ea.
105	BUMPER PLATES 1-1/2" x 3/4" U channel	2 Carp	2 Carpenters	80	.200	L.F.
1000	Tear drop, spring-steel, 4" high			15	1.070	Ea.
1100	8" high			15	1.070	Ea.
1200	10" high	↓	↓	15	1.070	Ea.
108	DEADLOCKS Mortise, heavy duty, outside key	1 Carp	1 Carpenter	9	.889	Ea.
0020	Double cylinder			9	.889	Ea.
0100	Medium duty, outside key			10	.800	Ea.
0110	Double cylinder			10	.800	Ea.
1000	Tubular, standard duty, outside key			10	.800	Ea.
1010	Double cylinder			10	.800	Ea.
1200	Night latch, outside key			10	.800	Ea.
110	DOORSTOPS Holder and bumper, floor or wall			24	.333	Ea.
1300	Wall bumper			24	.333	Ea.
1600	Floor bumper, 1" high			24	.333	Ea.
1900	Plunger type, door mounted			24	.333	Ea.
112	ENTRANCE LOCKS Cylinder, grip handle, deadlocking latch			9	.889	Ea.
0020	Deadbolt			8	1.000	Ea.
0100	Push and pull plate, dead bolt			8	1.000	Ea.
0200	Push bar and pull, dead bolt, bronze			7	1.140	Ea.
0240	Push bar and pull bar, dead bolt, bronze			7	1.140	Ea.
114	FLOOR CHECKS For over 3' wide doors, single acting			2.50	3.200	Ea.
0500	Double acting			2.50	3.200	Ea.
118	KICK PLATE 6" high, for 3' door, aluminum			15	.533	Ea.
0500	Bronze	↓	↓	15	.533	Ea.
120	LOCKSET Standard duty, cylindrical, with sectional trim					
0020	Non-keyed, passage	1 Carp	1 Carpenter	12	.667	Ea.
0100	Privacy			12	.667	Ea.
0400	Keyed, single cylinder function			10	.800	Ea.
0420	Hotel			8	1.000	Ea.
1000	Heavy duty with sectional trim, non-keyed, passages			12	.667	Ea.
1100	Privacy			12	.667	Ea.
1400	Keyed, single cylinder function			10	.800	Ea.
1420	Hotel			8	1.000	Ea.
1600	Communicating			10	.800	Ea.
1700	Residential, interior door, minimum			16	.500	Ea.
1720	Maximum			8	1.000	Ea.
1800	Exterior, minimum			14	.571	Ea.
1820	Maximum	↓	↓	8	1.000	Ea.

		087 100 | **Finish Hardware**	CREW	MAKEUP	DAILY OUTPUT	MAN-HOURS	UNIT
125	125	**MORTISE LOCKSET** Comm., wrought knobs & full escutcheon trim					
	0020	Non-keyed, passage, minimum	1 Carp	1 Carpenter	9	.889	Ea.
	0030	Maximum			8	1.000	Ea.
	0040	Privacy, minimum			9	.889	Ea.
	0050	Maximum			8	1.000	Ea.
	0100	Keyed, office/entrance/apartment, minimum			8	1.000	Ea.
	0110	Maximum			7	1.140	Ea.
	0120	Single cylinder, typical, minimum			8	1.000	Ea.
	0130	Maximum			7	1.140	Ea.
	0200	Hotel, minimum			7	1.140	Ea.
	0210	Maximum			6	1.330	Ea.
	0300	Communication, double cylinder, minimum			8	1.000	Ea.
	0310	Maximum			7	1.140	Ea.
	1000	Wrought knobs and sectional trim, non-keyed, passage, minimum			10	.800	Ea.
	1010	Maximum			9	.889	Ea.
	1040	Privacy, minimum			10	.800	Ea.
	1050	Maximum			9	.889	Ea.
	1100	Keyed, entrance,office/apartment, minimum			9	.889	Ea.
	1110	Maximum			8	1.000	Ea.
	1120	Single cylinder, typical, minimum			9	.889	Ea.
	1130	Maximum	↓	↓	8	1.000	Ea.
	2000	Cast knobs and full escutcheon trim					
	2010	Non-keyed, passage, minimum	1 Carp	1 Carpenter	9	.889	Ea.
	2020	Maximum			8	1.000	Ea.
	2040	Privacy, minimum			9	.889	Ea.
	2050	Maximum			8	1.000	Ea.
	2120	Keyed, single cylinder, typical, minimum			8	1.000	Ea.
	2130	Maximum			7	1.140	Ea.
	2200	Hotel, minimum			7	1.140	Ea.
	2210	Maximum			6	1.330	Ea.
	3000	Cast knob and sectional trim, non-keyed, passage, minimum			10	.800	Ea.
	3010	Maximum			10	.800	Ea.
	3040	Privacy, minimum			10	.800	Ea.
	3050	Maximum			10	.800	Ea.
	3100	Keyed, office/entrance/apartment, minimum			9	.889	Ea.
	3110	Maximum			9	.889	Ea.
	3120	Single cylinder, typical, minimum			9	.889	Ea.
	3130	Maximum			9	.889	Ea.
	4000	Keyless, pushbutton type, with deadbolt, standard			9	.889	Ea.
	4100	Heavy duty			9	.889	Ea.
	127	**PANIC DEVICE** For rim locks, single door, exit only			6	1.330	Ea.
	0020	Outside key and pull			5	1.600	Ea.
	0200	Bar and vertical rod, exit only			5	1.600	Ea.
	0210	Outside key and pull			4	2.000	Ea.
	0400	Bar and concealed rod			4	2.000	Ea.
	0600	Touch bar, exit only			6	1.330	Ea.
	0610	Outside key and pull			5	1.600	Ea.
	0700	Touch bar and vertical rod, exit only			5	1.600	Ea.
	0710	Outside key and pull			4	2.000	Ea.
	0800	Touch bar, low profile, exit only			6	1.330	Ea.
	0810	Outside key and pull			5	1.600	Ea.
	0900	Touch bar and vertical rod, low profile, exit only			5	1.600	Ea.
	0910	Outside key and pull			4	2.000	Ea.
	1000	Mortise, bar, exit only			4	2.000	Ea.
	1600	Touch bar, exit only			4	2.000	Ea.
	2000	Narrow stile, rim mounted, bar, exit only			6	1.330	Ea.
	2010	Outside key and pull			5	1.600	Ea.
	2200	Bar and vertical rod, exit only	↓	↓	5	1.600	Ea.

087 100 | Finish Hardware

			CREW	MAKEUP	DAILY OUTPUT	MAN-HOURS	UNIT
127	2211	Panic device, narrow stile, rim mtd., outside key and pull	1 Carp	1 Carpenter	4	2.000	Ea.
	2400	Bar and concealed rod, exit only			3	2.670	Ea.
	3000	Mortise, bar, exit only			4	2.000	Ea.
	3600	Touch bar, exit only			4	2.000	Ea.
	6000	Trim, rim mounted, cylinder and pull			25	.320	Ea.
	6100	Cylinder, pull and thumb piece			20	.400	Ea.
	6200	Pull only			30	.267	Ea.
	6400	Mortise, cylinder and pull			25	.320	Ea.
	6500	Cylinder, pull and thumb piece			20	.400	Ea.
	6600	Pull only			30	.267	Ea.
	129	PUSH-PULL Push plate, pull plate, aluminum			12	.667	Ea.
	0500	Bronze			12	.667	Ea.
	1500	Pull handle and push bar, aluminum			11	.727	Ea.
	2000	Bronze			10	.800	Ea.
	3000	Push plate both sides, aluminum			14	.571	Ea.
	3500	Bronze			13	.615	Ea.
	4000	Door pull, designer style, cast aluminum, minimum			12	.667	Ea.
	5000	Maximum			8	1.000	Ea.
	6000	Cast bronze, minimum			12	.667	Ea.
	7000	Maximum			8	1.000	Ea.
	8000	Walnut, minimum			12	.667	Ea.
	9000	Maximum	↓	↓	8	1.000	Ea.

087 200 | Operators

			CREW	MAKEUP	DAILY OUTPUT	MAN-HOURS	UNIT
	202	AUTOMATIC OPENERS Swing doors, single	2 Skwk	2 Skilled Workers	.80	20.000	Ea.
	0100	Single operating pair			.50	32.000	Pr.
	0400	For double simultaneous doors, one way, add			1.20	13.330	Pr.
	0500	Two way, add			.90	17.780	Pr.
	1000	Sliding doors, 3′ wide, including track & hanger, single			.60	26.670	Opng.
	1300	Bi-parting			.50	32.000	Opng.
	1450	Activating carpet, single door, one way, add			2.20	7.270	Opng.
	1550	Two way, add	↓	↓	1.30	12.310	Opng.
	1750	Handicap opener, button operating	2 Carp	2 Carpenters	8	2.000	Ea.
	204	AUTOMATIC OPERATORS Industrial, sliding doors, to 6′ wide	2 Skwk	2 Skilled Workers	.60	26.670	Opng.
	0200	To 12′ wide			.40	40.000	Opng.
	1000	Swing doors, to 5′ wide			.80	20.000	Ea.
	1150	Add for controls, wall pushbutton, 3 button			4	4.000	Ea.
	1200	Ceiling pull cord	↓	↓	4.30	3.720	Ea.
	206	DOOR CLOSER Rack and pinion	1 Carp	1 Carpenter	6.50	1.230	Ea.
	0020	Adjustable backcheck, 3 way mount, all sizes, regular arm			6	1.330	Ea.
	0040	Hold open arm			6	1.330	Ea.
	0100	Fusible link			6.50	1.230	Ea.
	0200	Non sized, regular arm			6	1.330	Ea.
	0240	Hold open arm			6	1.330	Ea.
	0400	4 way mount, non sized, regular arm			6	1.330	Ea.
	0440	Hold open arm	↓	↓	6	1.330	Ea.
	2000	Backcheck and adjustable power, hinge face mount					
	2010	All sizes, regular arm	1 Carp	1 Carpenter	6.50	1.230	Ea.
	2040	Hold open arm			6.50	1.230	Ea.
	2400	Top jamb mount, all sizes, regular arm			6	1.330	Ea.
	2440	Hold open arm			6	1.330	Ea.
	2800	Top face mount, all sizes, regular arm			6.50	1.230	Ea.
	2840	Hold open arm			6.50	1.230	Ea.
	4000	Backcheck, overhead concealed, all sizes, regular arm			5.50	1.450	Ea.
	4040	Concealed arm			5	1.600	Ea.
	4400	Compact overhead, concealed, all sizes, regular arm			5.50	1.450	Ea.
	4440	Concealed arm			5	1.600	Ea.
	4800	Concealed in door, all sizes, regular arm	↓	↓	5.50	1.450	Ea.

087 | Hardware

087 200	Operators	CREW	MAKEUP	DAILY OUTPUT	MAN-HOURS	UNIT
206 4841	Door closer, concealed in door, all sizes, concealed arm	1 Carp	1 Carpenter	5	1.600	Ea.
4900	Floor concealed, all sizes, single acting			2.20	3.640	Ea.
4940	Double acting			2.20	3.640	Ea.
6000	Closer-holder, hinge face mount, all sizes, exposed arm			6.50	1.230	Ea.
7000	Electronic closer-holder, hinge facemount, concealed arm			5	1.600	Ea.
7400	With built-in detector	↓	↓	5	1.600	Ea.

087 300	Weatherstripping/Seals	CREW	MAKEUP	DAILY OUTPUT	MAN-HOURS	UNIT
302	**ASTRAGALS** One piece overlapping					
0400	Cadmium plated steel, flat, 3/16" x 2"	1 Carp	1 Carpenter	90	.089	L.F.
0600	Prime coated steel, flat, 1/8" x 3"			90	.089	L.F.
0800	Stainless steel, flat, 3/32" x 1-5/8"			90	.089	L.F.
1000	Aluminum, flat, 1/8" x 2"			90	.089	L.F.
1200	Nail on, "T" extrusion			120	.067	L.F.
1300	Vinyl bulb insert			105	.076	L.F.
1600	Screw on, "T" extrusion			90	.089	L.F.
1700	Vinyl insert			75	.107	L.F.
2000	"L" extrusion, neoprene bulbs			75	.107	L.F.
2100	Neoprene sponge insert			75	.107	L.F.
2200	Magnetic			75	.107	L.F.
2400	Spring hinged security seal, with cam			75	.107	L.F.
2600	Spring loaded locking bolt, vinyl insert			45	.178	L.F.
2800	Neoprene sponge strip, "Z" shaped, aluminum			60	.133	L.F.
2900	Solid neoprene strip, nail on aluminum strip	↓	↓	90	.089	L.F.
3000	One piece stile protection					
3020	Neoprene fabric loop, nail on aluminum strips	1 Carp	1 Carpenter	60	.133	L.F.
3110	Flush mounted aluminum extrusion, 1/2" x 1-1/4"			60	.133	L.F.
3140	3/4" x 1-3/8"			60	.133	L.F.
3160	1-1/8" x 1-3/4"			60	.133	L.F.
3300	Mortise, 9/16" x 3/4"			60	.133	L.F.
3320	13/16" x 1-3/8"			60	.133	L.F.
3600	Spring bronze strip, nail on type			105	.076	L.F.
3620	Screw on, with retainer			75	.107	L.F.
3800	Flexible stainless steel housing, pile insert, 1/2" door			105	.076	L.F.
3820	3/4" door			105	.076	L.F.
4000	Extruded aluminum retainer, flush mount, pile insert			105	.076	L.F.
4080	Mortise, felt insert			90	.089	L.F.
4160	Mortise with spring, pile insert			90	.089	L.F.
4400	Rigid vinyl retainer, mortise, pile insert			105	.076	L.F.
4600	Wool pile filler strip, aluminum backing	↓	↓	105	.076	L.F.
5000	Two piece overlapping astragal, extruded aluminum retainer					
5010	Pile insert	1 Carp	1 Carpenter	60	.133	L.F.
5020	Vinyl bulb insert			60	.133	L.F.
5040	Vinyl flap insert			60	.133	L.F.
5060	Solid neoprene flap insert			60	.133	L.F.
5080	Hypalon rubber flap insert			60	.133	L.F.
5090	Snap on cover, pile insert			60	.133	L.F.
5400	Magnetic aluminum, surface mounted			60	.133	L.F.
5500	Interlocking aluminum, 5/8" x 1" neoprene bulb insert			45	.178	L.F.
5600	Adjustable aluminum, 9/16" x 21/32", pile insert			45	.178	L.F.
5800	Magnetic, adjustable, 9/16" x 21/32"	↓	↓	45	.178	L.F.
6000	Two piece stile protection					
6010	Cloth backed rubber loop, 1" gap, nail on aluminum strips	1 Carp	1 Carpenter	45	.178	L.F.
6040	Screw on aluminum strips			45	.178	L.F.
6100	1-1/2" gap, screw on aluminum extrusion			45	.178	L.F.
6240	Vinyl fabric loop, slotted aluminum extrusion, 1" gap			45	.178	L.F.
6300	1-1/4" gap	↓	↓	45	.178	L.F.

087 | Hardware

087 300 | Weatherstripping/Seals

			CREW	MAKEUP	DAILY OUTPUT	MAN-HOURS	UNIT
304	304	**THRESHOLD** 3' long door saddles, aluminum, minimum	1 Carp	1 Carpenter	20	.400	Ea.
	0100	Maximum			12	.667	Ea.
	0500	Bronze, minimum			20	.400	Ea.
	0600	Maximum			12	.667	Ea.
	0700	Rubber, 1/2" thick, 5-1/2" wide			20	.400	Ea.
	0800	2-3/4" wide			20	.400	Ea.
	306	**WEATHERSTRIPPING** Window, double hung, 3' x 5', zinc			7.20	1.110	Opng.
	0100	Bronze			7.20	1.110	Opng.
	0500	As above but heavy duty, zinc			4.60	1.740	Opng.
	0600	Bronze			4.60	1.740	Opng.
	1000	Doors, wood frame, interlocking, for 3' x 7' door, zinc			3	2.670	Opng.
	1100	Bronze			3	2.670	Opng.
	1300	6' x 7' opening, zinc			2	4.000	Opng.
	1400	Bronze	↓	↓	2	4.000	Opng.
	1700	Wood frame, spring type, bronze					
	1800	3' x 7' door	1 Carp	1 Carpenter	7.60	1.050	Opng.
	1900	6' x 7' door	"	"	7	1.140	Opng.
	2200	Metal frame, spring type, bronze					
	2300	3' x 7' door	1 Carp	1 Carpenter	3	2.670	Opng.
	2400	6' x 7' door			2.50	3.200	Opng.
	2700	Metal frame, extruded sections, 3' x 7' door, aluminum			2	4.000	Opng.
	2800	Bronze			2	4.000	Opng.
	3100	6' x 7' door, aluminum			1.20	6.670	Opng.
	3200	Bronze	↓	↓	1.20	6.670	Opng.
	3500	Threshold weatherstripping					
	3650	Door sweep, flush mounted, aluminum	1 Carp	1 Carpenter	25	.320	Ea.
	3700	Vinyl			25	.320	Ea.
	5000	Garage door bottom weatherstrip, 12' aluminum, clear			14	.571	Ea.
	5010	Bronze			14	.571	Ea.
	5050	Bottom protection, 12' aluminum, clear			14	.571	Ea.
	5100	Bronze	↓	↓	14	.571	Ea.

087 500 | Door/Window Acces

			CREW	MAKEUP	DAILY OUTPUT	MAN-HOURS	UNIT
	501	**AREA WALL** Galvanized steel, 20 ga., 3'-2" wide, 1' deep	1 Sswk	1 Struc. Steel Worker	29	.276	Ea.
	0100	2' deep			23	.348	Ea.
	0300	16 ga., galv., 3'-2" wide, 1' deep			29	.276	Ea.
	0400	3' deep			23	.348	Ea.
	0600	Welded grating for above, 15 lbs., painted			45	.178	Ea.
	0700	Galvanized			45	.178	Ea.
	0900	Translucent plastic cap for above	↓	↓	60	.133	Ea.
	508	**DOOR PROTECTION** Acrylic and neoprene cover for door					
	0020	frame, high impact type	1 Carp	1 Carpenter	100	.080	L.F.

088 | Glazing

088 100 | Glass

			CREW	MAKEUP	DAILY OUTPUT	MAN-HOURS	UNIT
	104	**ACOUSTICAL GLASS UNITS** 1 lite at 3/8", 1 lite at 3/16", for 1" thick	2 Glaz	2 Glaziers	100	.160	S.F.
	0100	For 4" thick	"	"	80	.200	S.F.

088 | Glazing

		088 100	Glass	CREW	MAKEUP	DAILY OUTPUT	MAN-HOURS	UNIT
108	108	**BEVELED GLASS** With design patterns, 1/4" thick, 1/2" bevel, minimum	2 Glaz	2 Glaziers	150	.107	S.F.
	0050	Average			125	.128	S.F.
	0100	Maximum			100	.160	S.F.
	116	**FACETED** Color tinted glass, 3/4" thick, minimum			95	.168	S.F.
	0100	Maximum			75	.213	S.F.
	118	**FLOAT GLASS** 3/16" thick, clear, plain			130	.123	S.F.
	0100	Tinted			130	.123	S.F.
	0200	clear			130	.123	S.F.
	0300	Tinted			130	.123	S.F.
	0600	1/4" thick, clear, plain			120	.133	S.F.
	0700	Tinted			120	.133	S.F.
	0800	Tempered, clear			120	.133	S.F.
	0900	Tinted			120	.133	S.F.
	1200	5/16" thick, clear, plain			100	.160	S.F.
	1300	Tempered, clear			100	.160	S.F.
	1600	3/8" thick, clear, plain			75	.213	S.F.
	1700	Tinted			75	.213	S.F.
	1800	Tempered, clear			75	.213	S.F.
	1900	Tinted			75	.213	S.F.
	2200	1/2" thick, clear, plain			55	.291	S.F.
	2300	Tinted			55	.291	S.F.
	2400	Tempered, clear			55	.291	S.F.
	2500	Tinted			55	.291	S.F.
	2800	5/8" thick, clear, plain			45	.356	S.F.
	2900	Tempered, clear			45	.356	S.F.
	3200	3/4" thick, clear, plain			35	.457	S.F.
	3300	Tempered, clear			35	.457	S.F.
	3600	1" thick, clear, plain	↓	↓	30	.533	S.F.
	120	**FULL VISION** Window system with 3/4" glass mullions, 10' high	H-2	2 Glaziers 1 Building Laborer	130	.185	S.F.
	0100	10' to 20' high, minimum			110	.218	S.F.
	0150	Average			100	.240	S.F.
	0200	Maximum	↓	↓	80	.300	S.F.
	132	**INSULATING GLASS** 2 lites 1/8" float, 1/2" thk, under 15 S.F.					
	0020	Clear	2 Glaz	2 Glaziers	95	.168	S.F.
	0100	Tinted			95	.168	S.F.
	0200	2 lites 3/16" float, for 5/8" thk unit, 15 to 30 S.F., clear			90	.178	S.F.
	0300	Tinted			90	.178	S.F.
	0400	1" thick, double glazed, 1/4" float, 30 to 70 S.F., clear			75	.213	S.F.
	0500	Tinted			75	.213	S.F.
	0600	1" thick double glazed, 1/4" float, 1/4" wire			75	.213	S.F.
	0700	1/4" float, 1/4" tempered			75	.213	S.F.
	0800	1/4" wire, 1/4" tempered			75	.213	S.F.
	0900	Both lites, 1/4" wire			75	.213	S.F.
	2000	Both lites, light & heat reflective			85	.188	S.F.
	2500	Heat reflective, film inside, 1" thick unit, clear			85	.188	S.F.
	2600	Tinted			85	.188	S.F.
	3000	Film on weatherside, clear, 1/2" thick unit			95	.168	S.F.
	3100	5/8" thick unit			90	.178	S.F.
	3200	1" thick unit			85	.188	S.F.
	136	**LAMINATED GLASS** Clear float, .03" vinyl, 1/4" thick			90	.178	S.F.
	0100	3/8" thick			78	.205	S.F.
	0200	.06" vinyl, 1/2" thick			65	.246	S.F.
	1000	5/8" thick			90	.178	S.F.
	2000	Bullet-resisting, 1-3/16" thick, to 15 S.F.			16	1.000	S.F.
	2100	Over 15 S.F.			16	1.000	S.F.
	2500	2-1/4" thick, to 15 S.F.			12	1.330	S.F.
	2600	Over 15 S.F.	↓	↓	12	1.330	S.F.

088 | Glazing

088 100 | Glass

			Description	CREW	MAKEUP	DAILY OUTPUT	MAN-HOURS	UNIT
144	144		**MIRRORS** No frames, wall type, 1/4" plate glass, polished edge					
		0100	Up to 5 S.F.	2 Glaz	2 Glaziers	125	.128	S.F.
		0200	Over 15 S.F.			160	.100	S.F.
		0500	Door type, 1/4" plate glass, up to 12 S.F.			160	.100	S.F.
		1000	Float glass, up to 10 S.F., 1/8" thick			160	.100	S.F.
		1100	3/16" thick			150	.107	S.F.
		1500	12" x 12" wall tiles, square edge, clear			195	.082	S.F.
		1600	Veined			195	.082	S.F.
		2000	1/4" thick, stock sizes, one way transparent			125	.128	S.F.
		2010	Bathroom, unframed, laminated			160	.100	S.F.
		2500	Tempered			160	.100	S.F.
	148		**OBSCURE GLASS** 1/8" thick, minimum			140	.114	S.F.
		0100	Maximum			125	.128	S.F.
		0300	7/32" thick, minimum			120	.133	S.F.
		0400	Maximum			105	.152	S.F.
	152		**PATTERNED GLASS** Colored, 1/8" thick, minimum			140	.114	S.F.
		0100	Maximum			125	.128	S.F.
		0300	7/32" thick, minimum			120	.133	S.F.
		0400	Maximum			105	.152	S.F.
	160		**REFLECTIVE GLASS** 1/4" float with fused metallic oxide, tinted			115	.139	S.F.
		0500	1/4" float glass with reflective applied coating			115	.139	S.F.
		2000	Solar film on glass, not including glass, minimum			180	.089	S.F.
		2050	Maximum			225	.071	S.F.
	164		**SANDBLASTED GLASS** Float glass, 1/8" thick			160	.100	S.F.
		0100	3/16" thick			130	.123	S.F.
		0500	Plate glass, 1/4" thick			120	.133	S.F.
		0600	3/8" thick			75	.213	S.F.
	168		**SHEET GLASS** Gray, 1/8" thick			160	.100	S.F.
		0200	1/4" thick			130	.123	S.F.
	172		**SPANDREL GLASS** 1/4" thick, standard colors, over 2000 S.F.			110	.145	S.F.
		0200	Under 2000 S.F.			120	.133	S.F.
		2000	Panels, insulated, with aluminum backed fiberglass, 1" thick			120	.133	S.F.
		2100	2" thick			120	.133	S.F.
	176		**WINDOW GLASS** Clear float, stops, putty bed, 1/8" thick			480	.033	S.F.
		0500	3/16" thick, clear			480	.033	S.F.
		0600	Tinted			480	.033	S.F.
		0700	Tempered			480	.033	S.F.
	184		**WIRE GLASS** 1/4" thick, rough obscure (chicken wire)			135	.119	S.F.
		1000	Polished wire, 1/4" thick, diamond, clear			135	.119	S.F.
		1500	Pinstripe, obscure	↓	↓	135	.119	S.F.

088 400 | Plastic Glazing

		Description	CREW	MAKEUP	DAILY OUTPUT	MAN-HOURS	UNIT
404		**PLEXIGLASS ACRYLIC** Clear, masked, MCM, 1/8" thk, cut sheets	2 Glaz	2 Glaziers	170	.094	S.F.
	0200	Full sheets			195	.082	S.F.
	0500	1/4" thick, cut sheets			165	.097	S.F.
	0600	Full sheets			185	.086	S.F.
	0900	3/8" thick, cut sheets			155	.103	S.F.
	1000	Full sheets			180	.089	S.F.
	1300	1/2" thick, cut sheets			135	.119	S.F.
	1400	Full sheets			150	.107	S.F.
	1700	3/4" thick, cut sheets			115	.139	S.F.
	1800	Full sheets			130	.123	S.F.
	2100	1" thick, cut sheets			105	.152	S.F.
	2200	Full sheets			125	.128	S.F.
	3000	Colored, 1/8" thick, cut sheets			170	.094	S.F.
	3200	Full sheets			195	.082	S.F.
	3500	1/4" thick, cut sheets			165	.097	S.F.
	3600	Full sheets	↓	↓	185	.086	S.F.

088 | Glazing

088 400 | Plastic Glazing

		Description	CREW	MAKEUP	DAILY OUTPUT	MAN-HOURS	UNIT
404	4001	Plexiglass acrylic clear, mirrors, untinted, cut sheets, 1/8" thick	2 Glaz	2 Glaziers	185	.086	S.F.
	4200	1/4" thick			180	.089	S.F.
	408	POLYCARBONATE Clear, masked, cut sheets, 1/8" thick			170	.094	S.F.
	0500	3/16" thick			165	.097	S.F.
	1000	1/4" thick			155	.103	S.F.
	1500	3/8" thick			150	.107	S.F.
	412	VINYL GLASS Steel mesh reinforced, stock sizes, .090" thick			170	.094	S.F.
	0500	.120" thick			170	.094	S.F.
	1000	.250" thick	↓	↓	155	.103	S.F.

089 | Glazed Curtain Wall

089 200 | Glazed Curtain Wall

	Description	CREW	MAKEUP	DAILY OUTPUT	MAN-HOURS	UNIT
202	CURTAIN WALLS Aluminum, stock, including glazing, minimum	H-1	2 Glaziers	205	.156	S.F.
			2 Struc. Steel Workers			
0050	Average, single glazed			195	.164	S.F.
0150	Average, double glazed			180	.178	S.F.
0200	Maximum	↓	↓	160	.200	S.F.
204	TUBE FRAMING For window walls and store fronts, aluminum, stock					
0050	Plain tube frame, mill finish, 1-3/4" x 1-3/4"	2 Glaz	2 Glaziers	103	.155	L.F.
0150	1-3/4" x 4"			98	.163	L.F.
0200	1-3/4" x 4-1/2"			95	.168	L.F.
0250	2" x 6"			89	.180	L.F.
0350	4" x 4"			87	.184	L.F.
0400	4-1/2" x 4-1/2"			85	.188	L.F.
0450	Glass bead			240	.067	L.F.
1000	Flush tube frame, mill finish, 1/4" glass, 1-3/4" x 4", open header			80	.200	L.F.
1050	Open sill			82	.195	L.F.
1100	Closed back header			83	.193	L.F.
1150	Closed back sill			85	.188	L.F.
1200	Vertical mullion, one piece			75	.213	L.F.
1250	Two piece			73	.219	L.F.
1300	90° or 180° vertical corner post			75	.213	L.F.
1400	1-3/4" x 4-1/2", open header			80	.200	L.F.
1450	Open sill			82	.195	L.F.
1500	Closed back header			83	.193	L.F.
1550	Closed back sill			85	.188	L.F.
1600	Vertical mullion, one piece			75	.213	L.F.
1650	Two piece			73	.219	L.F.
1700	90° or 180° vertical corner post			75	.213	L.F.
2000	Flush tube frame, mill fin. for ins. glass, 2" x 4-1/2", open header			75	.213	L.F.
2050	Open sill			77	.208	L.F.
2100	Closed back header			78	.205	L.F.
2150	Closed back sill			80	.200	L.F.
2200	Vertical mullion, one piece			70	.229	L.F.
2250	Two piece			68	.235	L.F.
2300	90° or 180° vertical corner post			70	.229	L.F.
5000	Flush tube frame, mill fin., thermal brk., 2-1/4" x 4-1/2", open header			74	.216	L.F.
5050	Open sill			75	.213	L.F.
5100	Vertical mullion, one piece			69	.232	L.F.
5150	Two piece			67	.239	L.F.
5200	90° or 180° vertical corner post	↓	↓	69	.232	L.F.

089 200 | Glazed Curtain Wall

			CREW	MAKEUP	DAILY OUTPUT	MAN-HOURS	UNIT
206	206	**WINDOW WALLS** Aluminum, stock, including glazing, minimum	H-2	2 Glaziers	160	.150	S.F.
				1 Building Laborer			
	0050	Average	↓	↓	140	.171	S.F.
	0104	Maximum			110	.218	S.F.
	1200	Double glazed acoustical window wall for airports,					
	1220	including 1" thick glass with 2" x 4-1/2" tube frame	H-2	2 Glaziers	40	.600	S.F.
				1 Building Laborer			

DIVISION 9

FINISHES

DIVISION 9 FINISHES

Subdivisions in the Finishes Division include: Lath and Plaster, Drywall, Tile and Terrazzo, Acoustical Treatment, Flooring, Painting, and Wall Covering.

Productivity rates for applying finishes are based on workers who are trained craftsmen working in a reasonably comfortable environment without unnecessary space confinements. In actual practice, the expected productivity should be adjusted to make allowances for special conditions that enhance work conditions or slow it down due to unusual restrictions. The effects of special conditions are usually obvious. For example, drywall installation in an area where partitions are simple, consistent, and square is easier than in an area where partitions are irregular and curved.

Humidity and temperature can affect the properties of plaster, paints, and glues; and in large applications, these conditions can be a factor in the final productivity.

Man-hour figures in the listings have been developed for new construction only. For repair and remodeling work, substantial adjustments may be necessary to properly account for the unique nature of each project.

The "Lath and Plaster" subdivision includes productivity rates for the installation of various gypsum and metal laths and various plaster and stucco on walls and ceilings by lathers and plasterers. It also includes installation times for metal studs, furring, and accessories such as corner bead and expansion joints. Plaster is applied by hand and sufficient curing time must be allowed between applications of successive coats.

Ceiling applications add man-hours to all lath and plaster operations. Applications on beams and columns require even more time. Man-hours required for unloading, stacking, cutting, and handling materials are included in the listings for this work. When dealing with plaster, man-hour figures reflect the time needed to mix materials and erect scaffolding.

Listings for "Drywall" include stud and drywall accessories. The work in this subdivision is done by carpenters.

All work in the "Tile and Terrazzo" subdivision is done by tile layers and mosaic/terrazzo workers with some supplementary work by carpenters.

Installation of various types of flooring is done largely by tile layers and carpenters, with some work being done by cement finishers and laborers working with crews. The material installation covers carpeting, composition flooring, resilient flooring, and wood flooring.

Painting and installation of wall covering (including wall coatings and wallpaper) are done by painters, paperhangers, and, in some cases, carpenters.

091 | Metal Support Systems

091 300 | Suspension Systems

		CREW	MAKEUP	DAILY OUTPUT	MAN-HOURS	UNIT
304	304	**SUSPENSION SYSTEMS** For boards and tile				
	0050	Class A suspension system, T bar, 2' x 4' grid	1 Carp	1 Carpenter	800	.010	S.F.
	0300	2' x 2' grid			650	.012	S.F.
	0400	Concealed Z bar suspension system, 12" module			520	.015	S.F.
	0600	1-1/2" carrier channels, 4' O.C., add	↓	↓	470	.017	S.F.
	0700	Carrier channels for ceilings with					
	0900	recessed lighting fixtures, add	1 Carp	1 Carpenter	460	.017	S.F.
	1040	Hanging wire, 12 ga., 4' long			65	.123	C.S.F.
	1080	8' long	↓	↓	65	.123	C.S.F.

092 | Lath, Plaster and Gypsum Board

092 050 | Furring & Lathing

		CREW	MAKEUP	DAILY OUTPUT	MAN-HOURS	UNIT
052	**ACCESSORIES, PLASTER** Casing bead, expanded flange, galvanized	1 Lath	1 Lather	2.70	2.960	C.L.F.
0100	Zinc alloy			2.70	2.960	C.L.F.
1620	Corner bead, expanded bullnose, 3/4" radius, #10 galvanized			2.60	3.080	C.L.F.
1640	Zinc alloy			2.70	2.960	C.L.F.
1650	#1, galvanized			2.55	3.140	C.L.F.
1660	Zinc alloy			2.70	2.960	C.L.F.
1670	Expanded wing, 2-3/4" wide, galv. #1			2.65	3.020	C.L.F.
1680	Zinc alloy			2.70	2.960	C.L.F.
1700	Inside corner, (corner rite) 3" x 3", painted			2.60	3.080	C.L.F.
1750	Strip-ex, 4" wide, painted			2.55	3.140	C.L.F.
1800	Expansion joint, 3/4" grounds, limited expansion, galv., 1 piece			2.70	2.960	C.L.F.
1900	Zinc alloy			2.70	2.960	C.L.F.
2100	Extreme expansion, galvanized, 2 piece			2.60	3.080	C.L.F.
2300	Zinc alloy			2.70	2.960	C.L.F.
2500	Joist clips for lath, 2-1/2" flange			1.90	4.210	M
2600	4-1/2" flange			1.80	4.440	M
2800	Metal base, galvanized and painted, 2-1/2" high			2.40	3.330	C.L.F.
2900	Stud clips for gypsum lath, field clip			2.35	3.400	M
3100	Resilient			2.30	3.480	M
3200	Starter/finisher	↓	↓	2.20	3.640	M
054	**FURRING** Beams & columns, 3/4" galvanized channels,					
0030	12" O.C.	1 Lath	1 Lather	155	.052	S.F.
0050	16" O.C.			170	.047	S.F.
0070	24" O.C.			185	.043	S.F.
0100	Ceilings, on steel, 3/4" channels, galvanized, 12" O.C.			210	.038	S.F.
0300	16" O.C.			290	.028	S.F.
0400	24" O.C.			420	.019	S.F.
0600	1-1/2" channels, galvanized, 12" O.C.			190	.042	S.F.
0700	16" O.C.			260	.031	S.F.
0900	24" O.C.			390	.021	S.F.
1000	Walls, galvanized, 3/4" channels, 12" O.C.			235	.034	S.F.
1200	16" O.C.			265	.030	S.F.
1300	24" O.C.			350	.023	S.F.
1500	1-1/2" channels, galvanized, 12" O.C.,			210	.038	S.F.
1600	16" O.C.			240	.033	S.F.
1800	24" O.C.	↓	↓	305	.026	S.F.
8000	Suspended ceilings, including carriers					
8200	1-1/2" carriers, 24" O.C. with:					
8300	3/4" channels, 16" O.C.	1 Lath	1 Lather	165	.048	S.F.

		CREW	MAKEUP	DAILY OUTPUT	MAN-HOURS	UNIT
092 050	**Furring & Lathing**					
054 8321	Furring, susp. ceilings, 1-1/2" carrier, 3/4" channel, 24" O.C.	1 Lath	1 Lather	200	.040	S.F.
8400	1-1/2" channels, 16" O.C.			155	.052	S.F.
8420	24" O.C.	↓	↓	190	.042	S.F.
8600	2" carriers, 24" O.C. with:					
8700	3/4" channels, 16" O.C.	1 Lath	1 Lather	155	.052	S.F.
8720	24" O.C.			190	.042	S.F.
8800	1-1/2" channels, 16" O.C.			145	.055	S.F.
8820	24" O.C.			180	.044	S.F.
056	GYPSUM LATH Plain or perforated, nailed, 3/8" thick			85	.094	S.Y.
0100	1/2" thick, nailed			80	.100	S.Y.
0300	Clipped to steel studs, 3/8" thick			75	.107	S.Y.
0400	1/2" thick			70	.114	S.Y.
0600	Firestop gypsum base, to steel studs, 1/2" thick			70	.114	S.Y.
0700	5/8" thick			65	.123	S.Y.
0900	Moisture resistant, 4' x 8' sheets, 1/2" thick			75	.107	S.Y.
1000	5/8" thick			70	.114	S.Y.
1200	Laminated, 1" thick, to steel studs			65	.123	S.Y.
1500	For ceiling installations, add			198	.040	S.Y.
1600	For columns and beams, add	↓	↓	198	.040	S.Y.
058	METAL LATH					
3600	2.5 lb. diamond painted, on wood framing, on walls	1 Lath	1 Lather	85	.094	S.Y.
3700	On ceilings			75	.107	S.Y.
3900	3.4 lb. diamond painted, on wood framing, on walls			80	.100	S.Y.
4000	On ceilings			70	.114	S.Y.
4200	3.4 lb. diamond painted, wired to steel framing, on walls			75	.107	S.Y.
4300	On ceilings			60	.133	S.Y.
4600	Cornices, wired to steel			35	.229	S.Y.
4804	Screwed to steel studs, 2.5 lb.			80	.100	S.Y.
4900	3.4 lb.			75	.107	S.Y.
5100	Rib lath, painted, wired to steel, on walls, 2.75 lb.			75	.107	S.Y.
5200	3.4 lb.			70	.114	S.Y.
5400	4.0 lb.			65	.123	S.Y.
5700	Suspended ceiling system, incl. 3.4 lb. diamond lath, painted			15	.533	S.Y.
5800	Galvanized	↓	↓	15	.533	S.Y.
6000	Hollow metal stud partitions, 3.4 lb. painted lath both sides					
6010	Non-load bearing, 25 ga., w/rib lath 2-1/2" studs, 12" O.C.	1 Lath	1 Lather	20.30	.394	S.Y.
6300	16" O.C.			21.10	.379	S.Y.
6350	24" O.C.			22.70	.352	S.Y.
6400	3-5/8" studs, 16" O.C.			19.50	.410	S.Y.
6600	24" O.C.			20.40	.392	S.Y.
6700	4" studs, 16" O.C.			20.40	.392	S.Y.
6900	24" O.C.			21.60	.370	S.Y.
7000	6" studs, 16" O.C.			19.50	.410	S.Y.
7100	24" O.C.			21.10	.379	S.Y.
7200	L.B. partitions, 16 ga., w/rib lath, 2-1/2" studs, 16" O.C.			20	.400	S.Y.
7300	3-5/8" studs, 16 ga.			19.70	.406	S.Y.
7500	4" studs, 16 ga.			19.50	.410	S.Y.
7600	6" studs, 16 ga.	↓	↓	18.70	.428	S.Y.
7800	Solid 2" thick partition on 3/4" cold rolled channel, 3.4#					
7900	diamond painted metal lath, 1 side, no plaster	1 Lath	1 Lather	21.60	.370	S.Y.

		CREW	MAKEUP	DAILY OUTPUT	MAN-HOURS	UNIT
092 100	**Gypsum Plaster**					
108	GYPSUM PLASTER					
0300	2 coats, no lath included, on walls	J-1	3 Plasterers	105	.381	S.Y.
			2 Plasterer Helpers			
			1 Mixing Machine, 6 C.F.			
0400	On ceilings	"	"	92	.435	S.Y.

092 | Lath, Plaster and Gypsum Board

092 100 | Gypsum Plaster

		Description	CREW	MAKEUP	DAILY OUTPUT	MAN-HOURS	UNIT
108	0601	Gypsum plaster, 2 cts. on & incl. 3/8" gyp. lath on stl., on walls	J-2	3 Plasterers	97	.495	S.Y.
				2 Plasterer Helpers			
				1 Lather			
				1 Mixing Machine, 6 C.F.			
	0700	On ceilings	"	"	83	.578	S.Y.
	0900	3 coats, no lath included, on walls	J-1	3 Plasterers	87	.460	S.Y.
				2 Plasterer Helpers			
				1 Mixing Machine, 6 C.F.			
	1000	On ceilings	"	"	78	.513	S.Y.
	1200	3 coats on and including painted metal lath, on wood studs	J-2	3 Plasterers	86	.558	S.Y.
				2 Plasterer Helpers			
				1 Lather			
				1 Mixing Machine, 6 C.F.			
	1300	On ceilings	"	"	76.50	.627	S.Y.
112		KEENES CEMENT					
	0300	Finish only, add to plaster prices, standard	J-1	3 Plasterers	215	.186	S.Y.
				2 Plasterer Helpers			
				1 Mixing Machine, 6 C.F.			
	0400	High quality	"	"	144	.278	S.Y.
116		PERLITE OR VERMICULITE PLASTER					
	0300	2 coats, no lath included, on walls	J-1	3 Plasterers	92	.435	S.Y.
				2 Plasterer Helpers			
				1 Mixing Machine, 6 C.F.			
	0400	On ceilings	"	"	79	.506	S.Y.
	0600	2 coats, on and incl. 3/8" gypsum lath, on metal studs	J-2	3 Plasterers	84	.571	S.Y.
				2 Plasterer Helpers			
				1 Lather			
				1 Mixing Machine, 6 C.F.			
	0700	On ceilings	"	"	70	.686	S.Y.
	0900	3 coats, no lath included, on walls	J-1	3 Plasterers	74	.541	S.Y.
				2 Plasterer Helpers			
				1 Mixing Machine, 6 C.F.			
	1000	On ceilings	"	"	63	.635	S.Y.
	1200	3 coats, on and incl. painted metal lath, on metal studs	J-2	3 Plasterers	72	.667	S.Y.
				2 Plasterer Helpers			
				1 Lather			
				1 Mixing Machine, 6 C.F.			
	1300	On ceilings	↓	↓	61	.787	S.Y.
	1500	3 coats, on and incl. suspended metal lath ceiling			37	1.300	S.Y.
124		WOOD FIBER PLASTER On walls, no furring, 2 coats	J-1	3 Plasterers	72	.556	S.Y.
				2 Plasterer Helpers			
				1 Mixing Machine, 6 C.F.			
	0100	3 coats	"	"	57	.702	S.Y.

092 150 | Veneer Plaster

		Description	CREW	MAKEUP	DAILY OUTPUT	MAN-HOURS	UNIT
154		THIN COAT Plaster, 1 coat veneer, not incl. lath	J-1	3 Plasterers	360	.111	S.Y.
				2 Plasterer Helpers			
				1 Mixing Machine, 6 C.F.			

092 300 | Aggregate Coatings

		Description	CREW	MAKEUP	DAILY OUTPUT	MAN-HOURS	UNIT
304		STUCCO 3 coats 1" thick, float finish, on frame construction	J-2	3 Plasterers	52	.923	S.Y.
				2 Plasterer Helpers			
				1 Lather			
				1 Mixing Machine, 6 C.F.			
	0100	On masonry construction	J-1	3 Plasterers	55	.727	S.Y.
				2 Plasterer Helpers			
				1 Mixing Machine, 6 C.F.			
	0300	For trowel finish, add	1 Plas	1 Plasterer	170	.047	S.Y.

092 | Lath, Plaster and Gypsum Board

092 300 | Aggregate Coatings

		CREW	MAKEUP	DAILY OUTPUT	MAN-HOURS	UNIT
304 0401	Stucco, for 3/4" thick instead of 1", deduct	J-1	3 Plasterers	880	.045	S.Y.
			2 Plasterer Helpers			
			1 Mixing Machine, 6 C.F.			
0600	For coloring and special finish, add, minimum	↓	↓	685	.058	S.Y.
0700	Maximum			200	.200	S.Y.
0900	For soffits, add	J-2	3 Plasterers	155	.310	S.Y.
			2 Plasterer Helpers			
			1 Lather			
			1 Mixing Machine, 6 C.F.			
1000	Exterior plaster, with bonding agent, 1 coat, on walls	J-1	3 Plasterers	240	.167	S.Y.
			2 Plasterer Helpers			
			1 Mixing Machine, 6 C.F.			
1200	Ceilings	↓	↓	200	.200	S.Y.
1300	Beams			100	.400	S.Y.
1500	Columns	↓	↓	120	.333	S.Y.
1600	Mesh, painted, nailed to wood, 1.8 lb.	1 Lath	1 Lather	60	.133	S.Y.
1800	3.6 lb.			55	.145	S.Y.
1900	Wired to steel, painted, 1.8 lb.			53	.151	S.Y.
2100	3.6 lb.			50	.160	S.Y.
2200	Clinton cloth, on wood			60	.133	S.Y.
2400	On steel	↓	↓	53	.151	S.Y.

092 600 | Gypsum Board Systems

		CREW	MAKEUP	DAILY OUTPUT	MAN-HOURS	UNIT
604	**CEILINGS** Gypsum drywall, fire rated, finished					
0100	Screwed to grid, channel or joists, 1/2" thick	2 Carp	2 Carpenters	770	.021	S.F.
0200	5/8" thick			750	.021	S.F.
0300	Over 8' high, 1/2" thick			725	.022	S.F.
0400	5/8" thick	↓	↓	685	.023	S.F.
0600	Grid suspension system, direct hung					
0700	1-1/2" C.R.C., with 7/8" hi hat furring channel, 16" O.C.	2 Carp	2 Carpenters	600	.027	S.F.
0800	24" O.C.			900	.018	S.F.
0900	3-5/8" channel, 25 ga., with 7/8" hi hat furring channel			600	.027	S.F.
1000	24" O.C.	↓	↓	900	.018	S.F.
608 0100	**DRYWALL** Gypsum plasterboard, nailed or screwed to studs, unless otherwise noted					
0150	3/8" thick, on walls, standard, no finish included	2 Carp	2 Carpenters	2,000	.008	S.F.
0200	On ceilings, standard, no finish included			1,400	.011	S.F.
0250	On beams, columns, or soffits, no finish included			750	.021	S.F.
0300	1/2" thick, on walls, standard, no finish included			1,800	.009	S.F.
0350	Taped and finished			965	.017	S.F.
0400	Fire resistant, no finish included			1,800	.009	S.F.
0450	Taped and finished			965	.017	S.F.
0500	Water resistant, no finish included			1,800	.009	S.F.
0550	Taped and finished			965	.017	S.F.
0600	Prefinished, vinyl, clipped to studs			1,100	.015	S.F.
1000	On ceilings, standard, no finish included			1,265	.013	S.F.
1050	Taped and finished			765	.021	S.F.
1100	Fire resistant, no finish included			1,265	.013	S.F.
1150	Taped and finished			765	.021	S.F.
1200	Water resistant, no finish included			1,265	.013	S.F.
1250	Taped and finished			765	.021	S.F.
1500	On beams, columns, or soffits, standard, no finish included			675	.024	S.F.
1550	Taped and finished			475	.034	S.F.
1600	Fire resistant, no finish included			675	.024	S.F.
1650	Taped and finished			475	.034	S.F.
1700	Water resistant, no finish included			675	.024	S.F.
1750	Taped and finished			475	.034	S.F.
2000	5/8" thick, on walls, standard, no finish included	↓	↓	1,700	.009	S.F.

092 | Lath, Plaster and Gypsum Board

092 600	Gypsum Board Systems	CREW	MAKEUP	DAILY OUTPUT	MAN-HOURS	UNIT
608 2051	Drywall, 5/8" thick, on walls, standard, taped and finished	2 Carp	2 Carpenters	940	.017	S.F.
2100	Fire resistant, no finish included			1,700	.009	S.F.
2150	Taped and finished			940	.017	S.F.
2200	Water resistant, no finish included			1,700	.009	S.F.
2250	Taped and finished			940	.017	S.F.
2300	Prefinished, vinyl, clipped to studs			1,050	.015	S.F.
3000	On ceilings, standard, no finish included			1,175	.014	S.F.
3050	Taped and finished			730	.022	S.F.
3100	Fire resistant, no finish included			1,175	.014	S.F.
3150	Taped and finished			730	.022	S.F.
3200	Water resistant, no finish included			1,175	.014	S.F.
3250	Taped and finished			730	.022	S.F.
3500	On beams, columns, or soffits, standard, no finish included			650	.025	S.F.
3550	Taped and finished			450	.036	S.F.
3600	Fire resistant, no finish included			650	.025	S.F.
3650	Taped and finished			450	.036	S.F.
3700	Water resistant, no finish included			650	.025	S.F.
3750	Taped and finished			450	.036	S.F.
4000	Fireproofing, beams or columns, 2 layers, 1/2" thick, incl finish			330	.048	S.F.
4050	5/8" thick			300	.053	S.F.
4100	3 layers, 1/2" thick			225	.071	S.F.
4150	5/8" thick			210	.076	S.F.
4600	Blueboard, 1/2" thick, standard, not incl. skim coat			1,800	.009	S.F.
4650	Fireproof			1,800	.009	S.F.
4700	5/8" thick, fireproof			1,700	.009	S.F.
5050	For 1" thick coreboard on columns			480	.033	S.F.
5200	For high ceilings, over 8' high, add			3,060	.005	S.F.
5270	For textured spray, add			1,450	.011	S.F.
5300	For over 3 stories high, add per story	▼	▼	6,100	.003	S.F.
5400	For skim coat plaster, add	J-1	3 Plasterers	3,000	.013	S.F.
			2 Plasterer Helpers			
			1 Mixing Machine, 6 C.F.			
5500	For acoustical sealant, add per bead	1 Carp	1 Carpenter	500	.016	L.F.
5600	Sound deadening board, 1/4" gypsum	2 Carp	2 Carpenters	1,800	.009	S.F.
5650	1/2" wood fiber	"	"	1,800	.009	S.F.
612	**METAL STUDS, DRYWALL** Partitions, 10' high, with runners					
2000	Non-load bearing, galvanized, 25 ga. 1-5/8", 16" O.C.	1 Carp	1 Carpenter	420	.019	S.F.
2100	24" O.C.			500	.016	S.F.
2200	2-1/2" wide, 16" O.C.			410	.020	S.F.
2250	24" O.C.			490	.016	S.F.
2300	3-5/8" wide, 16" O.C.			400	.020	S.F.
2350	24" O.C.			480	.017	S.F.
2400	4" wide, 16" O.C.			390	.021	S.F.
2450	24" O.C.			450	.018	S.F.
2500	6" wide, 16" O.C.			360	.022	S.F.
2550	24" O.C.			440	.018	S.F.
2600	20 ga. studs, 1-5/8" wide, 16" O.C.			435	.018	S.F.
2650	24" O.C.			510	.016	S.F.
2700	2-1/2" wide, 16" O.C.			425	.019	S.F.
2750	24" O.C.			500	.016	S.F.
2800	3-5/8" wide, 16" O.C.			400	.020	S.F.
2850	24" O.C.			480	.017	S.F.
2900	4" wide, 16" O.C.			390	.021	S.F.
2950	24" O.C.			450	.018	S.F.
3000	6" wide, 16" O.C.			360	.022	S.F.
3050	24" O.C.			440	.018	S.F.
4000	LB studs, light ga. structural, galv., 18 ga., 2-1/2", 16" O.C.			425	.019	S.F.
4100	24" O.C.	▼	▼	500	.016	S.F.

092 600 | Gypsum Board Systems

		Description	CREW	MAKEUP	DAILY OUTPUT	MAN-HOURS	UNIT
612	4201	LB studs, galv., structural, 18 ga., 3-5/8" wide, 16" O.C.	1 Carp	1 Carpenter	400	.020	S.F.
	4250	24" O.C.			480	.017	S.F.
	4300	4" wide, 16" O.C.			390	.021	S.F.
	4350	24" O.C.			450	.018	S.F.
	4400	6" wide, 16" O.C.			360	.022	S.F.
	4450	24" O.C.			440	.018	S.F.
	4600	16 ga. studs, 2-1/2", 16" O.C.			400	.020	S.F.
	4650	24" O.C.			480	.017	S.F.
	4700	3-5/8" wide, 16" O.C.			390	.021	S.F.
	4750	24" O.C.			450	.018	S.F.
	4800	4" wide, 16" O.C.			380	.021	S.F.
	4850	24" O.C.			440	.018	S.F.
	4900	6" wide, 16" O.C.			340	.024	S.F.
	4950	24" O.C.	↓	↓	415	.019	S.F.
	620	**PARTITION WALL** Stud wall, 8' to 12' high					
	0050	1/2", interior, gypsum drywall, standard, taped both sides					
	0500	Installed on and incl., 2" x 4" wood studs, 16" O.C.	2 Carp	2 Carpenters	310	.052	S.F.
	1000	Metal studs, NLB, 25 ga., 16" O.C., 3-5/8" wide			350	.046	S.F.
	1200	6" wide			330	.048	S.F.
	1400	Water resistant, on 2" x 4" wood studs, 16" O.C.			310	.052	S.F.
	1600	Metal studs, NLB, 25 ga., 16" O.C., 3-5/8" wide			350	.046	S.F.
	1800	6" wide			330	.048	S.F.
	2000	Fire res.,2 layers,1-1/2 hr.,on 2" x 4" wood studs,16"O.C.			210	.076	S.F.
	2200	Metal studs, NLB, 25 ga., 16" O.C., 3-5/8" wide			250	.064	S.F.
	2400	6" wide			230	.070	S.F.
	2600	Fire & water res.,2 layers,1-1/2 hr., 2"x4" studs,16" O.C.			210	.076	S.F.
	2800	Metal studs, NLB, 25 ga., 16" O.C., 3-5/8" wide			250	.064	S.F.
	3000	6" wide	↓	↓	230	.070	S.F.
	3200	5/8", interior, gypsum drywall, standard, taped both sides					
	3400	Installed on and including 2" x 4" wood studs, 16" O.C.	2 Carp	2 Carpenters	300	.053	S.F.
	3600	24" O.C.			330	.048	S.F.
	3800	Metal studs, NLB, 25 ga., 16" O.C., 3-5/8" wide			340	.047	S.F.
	4000	6" wide			320	.050	S.F.
	4200	24" O.C., 3-5/8" wide			360	.044	S.F.
	4400	6" wide			340	.047	S.F.
	4800	Water resistant, on 2" x 4" wood studs, 16" O.C.			300	.053	S.F.
	5000	24" O.C.			330	.048	S.F.
	5200	Metal studs, NLB, 25 ga. 16" O.C., 3-5/8" wide			340	.047	S.F.
	5400	6" wide			320	.050	S.F.
	5600	24" O.C., 3-5/8" wide			360	.044	S.F.
	5800	6" wide			340	.047	S.F.
	6000	Fire res., 2 layers, 2 hr., on 2" x 4" wood studs, 16" O.C.			205	.078	S.F.
	6200	24" O.C.			235	.068	S.F.
	6400	Metal studs, NLB, 25 ga., 16" O.C., 3-5/8" wide			245	.065	S.F.
	6600	6" wide			225	.071	S.F.
	6800	24" O.C., 3-5/8" wide			265	.060	S.F.
	7000	6" wide			245	.065	S.F.
	7200	Fire & water res., 2 layers, 2 hr., 2" x 4" studs, 16" O.C.			205	.078	S.F.
	7400	24" O.C.			235	.068	S.F.
	7600	Metal studs, NLB, 25 ga., 16" O.C., 3-5/8" wide			245	.065	S.F.
	7800	6" wide			225	.071	S.F.
	8000	24" O.C., 3-5/8" wide			265	.060	S.F.
	8200	6" wide	↓	↓	245	.065	S.F.
	8600	1/2" blueboard, mesh tape both sides					
	8620	Installed on and including 2" x 4" wood studs, 16" O.C.	2 Carp	2 Carpenters	300	.053	S.F.
	8640	Metal studs, NLB, 25 ga., 16" O.C., 3-5/8" wide			340	.047	S.F.
	8660	6" wide	↓	↓	320	.050	S.F.

092 600 | Gypsum Board Systems

		CREW	MAKEUP	DAILY OUTPUT	MAN-HOURS	UNIT
620 9001	Stud wall, ext., 1/2" gyp. sheathing, 1/2" gyp. finished, interior,					
9100	including foil faced insulation, metal studs, 20 ga.					
9200	16" O.C., 3-5/8" wide	2 Carp	2 Carpenters	270	.059	S.F.
9400	6" wide	"	"	290	.055	S.F.
622	**PLASTER PARTITION WALL**					
0400	Stud walls, 3.4 lb. metal lath, 3 coat gypsum plaster, 2 sides					
0600	2" x 4" wood studs, 16" O.C.	J-2	3 Plasterers	315	.152	S.F.
			2 Plasterer Helpers			
			1 Lather			
			1 Mixing Machine, 6 C.F.			
0700	2-1/2" metal studs, 25 ga., 12" O.C.	↓	↓	325	.148	S.F.
0800	3-5/8" metal studs, 25 ga., 16" O.C.			320	.150	S.F.
0900	Gypsum lath, 2 coat vermiculite plaster, 2 sides					
1000	2" x 4" wood studs, 16" O.C.	J-2	3 Plasterers	355	.135	S.F.
			2 Plasterer Helpers			
			1 Lather			
			1 Mixing Machine, 6 C.F.			
1200	2-1/2" metal studs, 25 ga., 12" O.C.	↓	↓	365	.132	S.F.
1300	3-5/8" metal studs, 25 ga., 16" O.C.			360	.133	S.F.
624	**SHAFT WALL** Cavity type, 2-1/2", 25 ga. C-H studs, w/2 layers 1/2"					
0030	Gypsum board 1 side, 2 hour fire rating	2 Carp	2 Carpenters	165	.097	S.F.
0060	Laminated gypsum drywall, 2-1/2" solid or					
0100	3-3/4" core with steel H sections					
0300	24" wide units, to 10'-4" high	2 Carp	2 Carpenters	108	.148	S.F.
0400	16" wide units, to 11'-7" high	"	"	92	.174	S.F.
0600	Solid 2" thick, steel edge gypsum in channels with					
0700	1/2" fire resistant gypsum					
0800	1 side, 2 hour fire rating	2 Carp	2 Carpenters	150	.107	S.F.
0900	2 sides, 3 hour fire rating	"	"	135	.119	S.F.

092 800 | Drywall Accessories

		CREW	MAKEUP	DAILY OUTPUT	MAN-HOURS	UNIT
804	**ACCESSORIES, DRYWALL** Casing bead, galvanized steel	1 Carp	1 Carpenter	2.90	2.760	C.L.F.
0100	Vinyl			3	2.670	C.L.F.
0300	Corner bead, galvanized steel, 1" x 1"			2.90	2.760	C.L.F.
0400	1-1/4" x 1-1/4"			2.85	2.810	C.L.F.
0600	Vinyl corner bead			2.90	2.760	C.L.F.
0700	Door casing, vinyl, for 2" wall systems			2.50	3.200	C.L.F.
0900	Furring channel, galv. steel, 7/8" deep, standard			2.60	3.080	C.L.F.
1000	Resilient			2.55	3.140	C.L.F.
1100	J bead, galvanized steel, 1/2" wide			3	2.670	C.L.F.
1120	5/8" wide			2.95	2.710	C.L.F.
1140	L bead, galvanized			3	2.670	C.L.F.
1150	U bead, galvanized	↓	↓	2.95	2.710	C.L.F.
1200	Studs and runners for partitions, see also 051-230					
1500	Z bar, galvanized steel, 1-1/2" wide	1 Carp	1 Carpenter	2.60	3.080	C.L.F.
1600	2" wide	"	"	2.55	3.140	C.L.F.

093 | Tile

093 100 | Ceramic Tile

		CREW	MAKEUP	DAILY OUTPUT	MAN-HOURS	UNIT
102	**CERAMIC TILE** Base, using 1" x 1" tiles, 4" high, mud set	D-7	1 Tile Layer	82	.195	L.F.
			1 Tile Layer Helper			
0100	Thin set			128	.125	L.F.
0600	Cove base, 4-1/4" x 4-1/4" high, mud set			91	.176	L.F.
0700	Thin set			128	.125	L.F.
0900	6" x 4-1/4" high, mud set			100	.160	L.F.
1000	Thin set			137	.117	L.F.
1200	Sanitary cove base, 6" x 4-1/4" high, mud set			93	.172	L.F.
1300	Thin set			124	.129	L.F.
1500	6" x 6" high, mud set			84	.190	L.F.
1600	Thin set			117	.137	L.F.
1800	Bathroom accessories, average			82	.195	Ea.
1900	Bathtub, 5', recessed, modular wainscot, adhesive set, 6' high			4.30	3.720	Ea.
2100	7' high wainscot			4	4.000	Ea.
2200	8' high wainscot			3.80	4.210	Ea.
2400	Bullnose trim, 4-1/4" x 4-1/4", mud set			82	.195	L.F.
2500	Thin set			128	.125	L.F.
2700	6" x 4-1/4" bullnose trim, mud set			84	.190	L.F.
2800	Thin set			124	.129	L.F.
3000	Floors, natural clay, random or uniform, thin set, color group 1			183	.087	S.F.
3100	Color group 2			183	.087	S.F.
3300	Porcelain type, 1 color, color group 2, 1" x 1"			183	.087	S.F.
3400	2" x 2" or 2" x 1", thin set			190	.084	S.F.
4200	Conductive tile, 1" squares, black			109	.147	S.F.
4220	4" x 8" or 4" x 4", 3/8" thick			120	.133	S.F.
4240	Trim, bullnose, etc.			200	.080	L.F.
4300	Specialty tile, 3" x 6" x 1/2", decorator finish			183	.087	S.F.
4500	Add for epoxy grout, 1/16" joint, 1" x 1" tile			800	.020	S.F.
4600	2" x 2" tile	↓	↓	820	.020	S.F.
4800	Pregrouted sheets, walls, 4-1/4" x 4-1/4", 6" x 4-1/4"					
4810	and 8-1/2" x 4-1/4", 4 S.F. sheets, silicone grout	D-7	1 Tile Layer	240	.067	S.F.
			1 Tile Layer Helper			
5100	Floors, unglazed, 2 S.F. sheets,					
5110	urethane adhesive	D-7	1 Tile Layer	180	.089	S.F.
			1 Tile Layer Helper			
5400	Walls, interior, thin set, 4-1/4" x 4-1/4" tile			190	.084	S.F.
5500	6" x 4-1/4" tile			190	.084	S.F.
5700	8-1/2" x 4-1/4" tile			190	.084	S.F.
5800	6" x 6" tile			200	.080	S.F.
6000	Decorated wall tile, 4-1/4" x 4-1/4", minimum			870	.018	Ea.
6100	Maximum			580	.028	Ea.
6300	Exterior walls, frostproof, mud set, 4-1/4" x 4-1/4"			102	.157	S.F.
6400	1-3/8" x 1-3/8"			93	.172	S.F.
6600	Crystalline glazed, 4-1/4" x 4-1/4", mud set, plain			100	.160	S.F.
6700	4-1/4" x 4-1/4", scored tile			100	.160	S.F.
6900	1-3/8" squares			93	.172	S.F.
7000	For epoxy grout, 1/16" joints, 4-1/4" tile, add			800	.020	S.F.
7200	For tile set in dry mortar, add			1,735	.009	S.F.
7300	For tile set in portland cement mortar, add			290	.055	S.F.
104	**CERAMIC TILE PANELS** Insulated, over 1000 S.F., 1-1/2" thick			220	.073	S.F.
0100	2-1/2" thick	↓	↓	220	.073	S.F.

093 | Tile

093 300 | Quarry Tile

			CREW	MAKEUP	DAILY OUTPUT	MAN-HOURS	UNIT
304	304	QUARRY TILE Base, cove or sanitary, 2" or 5" high, mud set					
	0100	1/2" thick	D-7	1 Tile Layer	110	.145	L.F.
				1 Tile Layer Helper			
	0300	Bullnose trim, red, mud set, 6" x 6" x 1/2" thick			120	.133	L.F.
	0400	4" x 4" x 1/2" thick			110	.145	L.F.
	0600	4" x 8" x 1/2" thick, using 8" as edge			130	.123	L.F.
	0700	Floors, mud set, 1000 S.F. lots, red, 4" x 4" x 1/2" thick			120	.133	S.F.
	0900	6" x 6" x 1/2" thick			140	.114	S.F.
	1000	4" x 8" x 1/2" thick			130	.123	S.F.
	1800	Brown tile, imported, 6" x 6" x 7/8"			120	.133	S.F.
	1900	9" x 9" x 1-1/4"			110	.145	S.F.
	2100	For thin set mortar application, deduct			700	.023	S.F.
	2200	For epoxy grout & mortar, 6" x 6" x 1/2", add			350	.046	S.F.
	2700	Stair tread & riser, 6" x 6" x 3/4", plain			50	.320	S.F.
	2800	Abrasive			47	.340	S.F.
	3000	Wainscot, 6" x 6" x 1/2", thin set, red			105	.152	S.F.
	3100	Colors other than green			105	.152	S.F.
	3300	Window sill, 6" wide, 3/4" thick			90	.178	L.F.
	3400	Corners	↓	↓	80	.200	Ea.

093 500 | Glass Mosaics

			CREW	MAKEUP	DAILY OUTPUT	MAN-HOURS	UNIT
501		GLASS MOSAICS 3/4" tile on 12" sheets, color group 1 & 2, min.	D-7	1 Tile Layer	82	.195	S.F.
				1 Tile Layer Helper			
	0300	Maximum (latex set)			73	.219	S.F.
	0350	Color group 3			73	.219	S.F.
	0400	Color group 4			73	.219	S.F.
	0450	Color group 5			73	.219	S.F.
	0500	Color group 6			73	.219	S.F.
	0600	Color group 7			73	.219	S.F.
	0700	Color group 8, golds, silvers & specialties	↓	↓	64	.250	S.F.

093 600 | Plastic Tile

			CREW	MAKEUP	DAILY OUTPUT	MAN-HOURS	UNIT
604		PLASTIC TILE Walls, 4-1/4" x 4-1/4", .050" thick	1 Carp	1 Carpenter	125	.064	S.F.
	0100	.110" thick	"	"	120	.067	S.F.

093 700 | Metal Tile

			CREW	MAKEUP	DAILY OUTPUT	MAN-HOURS	UNIT
701		METAL TILE Cove base, standard colors, 4-1/4" square	1 Carp	1 Carpenter	150	.053	L.F.
	0200	4-1/8" x 8-1/2"			200	.040	L.F.
	0400	Wall tile, aluminum, 4-1/4" square, thin set, plain			80	.100	S.F.
	0500	Epoxy enameled			75	.107	S.F.
	0700	Leather on aluminum, colors			65	.123	S.F.
	0800	Stainless steel			75	.107	S.F.
	1000	Suede on aluminum	↓	↓	65	.123	S.F.

094 | Terrazzo

094 100 | Portland Cem Terrazzo

		CREW	MAKEUP	DAILY OUTPUT	MAN-HOURS	UNIT
104	**TERRAZZO, CAST IN PLACE** Cove base, 6" high	1 Mstz	1 Terrazzo Worker	23	.348	L.F.
0100	Curb, 6" high and 6" wide	"	"	15	.533	L.F.
1500	Floor, bonded to concrete, 1-3/4" thick, gray cement	J-3	1 Terrazzo Worker	130	.123	S.F.
			1 Terrazzo Helper			
			1 Terrazzo grinder, electric			
			1 Terrazzo mixer			
1600	White cement			125	.128	S.F.
1800	Not bonded, 3" total thickness, gray cement			100	.160	S.F.
1900	White cement			95	.168	S.F.
2400	Bonded conductive floor for hospitals			110	.145	S.F.
2500	Epoxy terrazzo, 1/4" thick, minimum			170	.094	S.F.
2550	Average			130	.123	S.F.
2600	Maximum	▼	▼	100	.160	S.F.
2700	Monolithic terrazzo, 5/8" thick, incl. 3-1/2" base slab,					
2710	10' panels, mesh and felt	J-3	1 Terrazzo Worker	230	.070	S.F.
			1 Terrazzo Helper			
			1 Terrazzo grinder, electric			
			1 Terrazzo mixer			
3000	Stairs, cast in place, pan filled treads			55	.291	L.F.
3100	Treads and risers			20	.800	L.F.
3300	Stair landings, add to floor prices			62	.258	S.F.
3400	Stair stringers and fascia			55	.291	S.F.
3600	For abrasive metal nosings on stairs, add			285	.056	L.F.
3700	For abrasive surface finish, add			600	.027	S.F.
3900	For flush abrasive strips, add			620	.026	L.F.
4000	Wainscot, bonded, 1-1/2" thick			40	.400	S.F.
4200	Epoxy terrazzo, 1/4" thick	▼	▼	70	.229	S.F.
108	**TILE OR TERRAZZO BASE** Scratch coat only	J-1	3 Plasterers	300	.133	S.Y.
			2 Plasterer Helpers			
			1 Mixing Machine, 6 C.F.			
0500	Scratch and brown coat only	"	"	115	.348	S.Y.

094 200 | Precast Terrazzo

		CREW	MAKEUP	DAILY OUTPUT	MAN-HOURS	UNIT
201	**TERRAZZO, PRECAST** Base, 6" high, straight	1 Mstz	1 Terrazzo Worker	120	.067	L.F.
0100	Cove			100	.080	L.F.
0300	8" high base, straight			110	.073	L.F.
0400	Cove			90	.089	L.F.
0900	Curbs, 4" x 4" high			55	.145	L.F.
1000	8" x 8" high	▼	▼	45	.178	L.F.
1200	Floor tiles, non-slip, 1" thick, 12" x 12"	D-1	1 Bricklayer	60	.267	S.F.
			1 Bricklayer Helper			
1300	1-1/4" thick, 12" x 12"			60	.267	S.F.
1500	16" x 16"			55	.291	S.F.
1600	1-1/2" thick, 16" x 16"	▼	▼	50	.320	S.F.
2100	Floor tiles, 12" x 12", 3/16" thick, 1/4" to 1/2" chips	1 Tilf	1 Tile Layer	130	.062	S.F.
2200	1/4" to 1" chips	"	"	130	.062	S.F.
2400	Stair treads, 1-1/2" thick, non-slip, diamond pattern	2 Mstz	2 Terrazzo Workers	95	.168	L.F.
2500	Line pattern			90	.178	L.F.
2700	2" thick treads, straight			90	.178	L.F.
2800	Curved			85	.188	L.F.
3000	Stair risers, 1" thick, to 6" high, straight sections			160	.100	L.F.
3100	Cove			150	.107	L.F.
3300	Curved, 1" thick, to 6" high, vertical			135	.119	L.F.
3400	Cove			130	.123	L.F.
3600	Stair tread and riser, single piece, straight, minimum			65	.246	L.F.
3700	Maximum			60	.267	L.F.
3900	Curved tread and riser, minimum			60	.267	L.F.
4000	Maximum	▼	▼	55	.291	L.F.

104

094 | Terrazzo

094 200 | Precast Terrazzo

		CREW	MAKEUP	DAILY OUTPUT	MAN-HOURS	UNIT
201 4202	Terrazzo, precast stair stringers, notched, 1" thick	2 Mstz	2 Terrazzo Workers	70	.229	L.F.
4300	2" thick			60	.267	L.F.
4500	Stair landings, structural, non-slip, 1-1/2" thick			105	.152	S.F.
4600	3" thick	↓	↓	95	.168	S.F.
4800	Wainscot, 12" x 12" x 1" tiles	1 Mstz	1 Terrazzo Worker	35	.229	S.F.
4900	16" x 16" x 1-1/2" tiles	"	"	30	.267	S.F.

095 | Acoustical Treatment and Wood Flooring

095 100 | Acoustical Ceilings

		CREW	MAKEUP	DAILY OUTPUT	MAN-HOURS	UNIT
102 0100	CEILING TILE Stapled, cemented or installed on suspension system, 12" x 12" or 12" x 24", not including furring					
0600	Mineral fiber, vinyl coated , 5/8" thick	1 Carp	1 Carpenter	200	.040	S.F.
0700	3/4" thick			200	.040	S.F.
0900	Fire rated, 3/4" thick, plain faced			200	.040	S.F.
1000	Plastic coated face			200	.040	S.F.
1200	Aluminum faced, 5/8" thick, plain	↓	↓	200	.040	S.F.
1500	Metal pan units, 24 ga. steel, not incl. pads, painted, 12" x 12"	1 Shee	1 Sheet Metal Worker	100	.080	S.F.
1600	12" x 36" or 12" x 24", 7% open area			100	.080	S.F.
1800	Aluminum, .025" thick, painted, 12" x 12"			100	.080	S.F.
1900	12" x 24"			100	.080	S.F.
2100	.032" thick, 12" x 12"			100	.080	S.F.
2200	12" x 24"			100	.080	S.F.
2400	Stainless steel, 12" x 24", 26 ga., solid			100	.080	S.F.
2500	5.2% open area	↓	↓	100	.080	S.F.
3700	Wall application of above, add	1 Carp	1 Carpenter	3,100	.003	S.F.
104 0100	SUSPENDED ACOUSTIC CEILING BOARDS Not including suspension system					
0300	Fiberglass boards, film faced, 2' x 2' or 2' x 4', 5/8" thick	1 Carp	1 Carpenter	675	.012	S.F.
0400	3/4" thick			500	.016	S.F.
0500	3" thick, thermal, R11			450	.018	S.F.
0600	Glass cloth faced fiberglass, 3/4" thick			500	.016	S.F.
0700	1" thick			485	.016	S.F.
0820	1-1/2" thick, nubby face			475	.017	S.F.
0900	Mineral fiber boards, 5/8" thick, aluminum faced, 24" x 24"			600	.013	S.F.
0930	24" x 48"			650	.012	S.F.
0960	Standard face			675	.012	S.F.
1000	Plastic coated face			400	.020	S.F.
1200	Mineral fiber, 2 hour rating, 5/8" thick			675	.012	S.F.
1300	Mirror faced panels, 15/16" thick			500	.016	S.F.
1900	Eggcrate, acrylic, 1/2" x 1/2" x 1/2" cubes			500	.016	S.F.
2100	Polystyrene eggcrate, 3/8" x 3/8" x 1/2" cubes			510	.016	S.F.
2200	1/2" x 1/2" x 1/2" cubes			500	.016	S.F.
2400	Luminous panels, prismatic, acrylic			400	.020	S.F.
2500	Polystyrene			400	.020	S.F.
2700	Flat white acrylic			400	.020	S.F.
2800	Polystyrene			400	.020	S.F.
3000	Drop pan, white, acrylic			400	.020	S.F.
3100	Polystyrene			400	.020	S.F.
3600	Perforated aluminum sheets, .024" thick, corrugated, painted			490	.016	S.F.
3700	Plain			500	.016	S.F.
3720	Mineral fiber, 24" x 24" or 48", reveal edge, painted, 5/8" thick	↓	↓	600	.013	S.F.

095 100 | Acoustical Ceilings

			CREW	MAKEUP	DAILY OUTPUT	MAN-HOURS	UNIT
104	3741	Susp. acoustic clng. board, mineral fbr, 2' x 2' or 4', 3/4" thick	1 Carp	1 Carpenter	575	.014	S.F.
	3750	Wood fiber in cementitious binder, 2' x 2' or 4', painted, 1" thick			600	.013	S.F.
	3760	2" thick			550	.015	S.F.
	3770	2-1/2" thick			500	.016	S.F.
	3780	3" thick			450	.018	S.F.
	3900	Access panels, metal, 12" x 12"			20	.400	Ea.
	4000	12" x 24"			15	.533	Ea.
	4100	18" x 18"			12	.667	Ea.
	4200	24" x 24"			10	.800	Ea.
	4300	24" x 36"			8	1.000	Ea.
	4400	Stainless steel, 12" x 12"			20	.400	Ea.
	4500	18" x 18"			12	.667	Ea.
	4600	24" x 24"			10	.800	Ea.
	4700	Fire rated, with lock, 12" x 12"			20	.400	Ea.
	4800	18" x 18"			12	.667	Ea.
	4900	24" x 24"			10	.800	Ea.
	5000	24" x 48"			8	1.000	Ea.
	5100	36" x 48"	↓	↓	6	1.330	Ea.
	106	**SUSPENDED CEILINGS, COMPLETE** Including standard					
	0100	suspension system but not incl. 1-1/2" carrier channels					
	0600	Ceiling board system, 2' x 4', plain faced, supermarkets	1 Carp	1 Carpenter	500	.016	S.F.
	0700	Offices			380	.021	S.F.
	0800	Wood fiber, cementitious binder, T bar susp. 2' x 2' x 1" board			345	.023	S.F.
	0810	2' x 4' x 1" board			380	.021	S.F.
	0900	Luminous panels, flat or ribbed, acrylic			255	.031	S.F.
	1000	Polystyrene			255	.031	S.F.
	1200	Metal pan with acoustic pad, steel			75	.107	S.F.
	1300	Painted aluminum			75	.107	S.F.
	1500	Aluminum, degreased finish			75	.107	S.F.
	1600	Stainless steel			75	.107	S.F.
	1800	Tile, Z bar suspension, 5/8" mineral fiber tile			150	.053	S.F.
	1900	3/4" mineral fiber tile	↓	↓	150	.053	S.F.
	2100	Reveal tile with drop, 2' x 2' grid					
	2200	with colored suspension system	1 Carp	1 Carpenter	250	.032	S.F.

095 250 | Acoustical Space Units

			CREW	MAKEUP	DAILY OUTPUT	MAN-HOURS	UNIT
	254	**SOUND ABSORBING PANELS** Perforated steel facing, painted with					
	0100	fiberglass or mineral filler, no backs, 2-1/4" thick, modular					
	0200	space units, ceiling or wall hung, white or colored	1 Carp	1 Carpenter	100	.080	S.F.
	0300	Fiberboard sound deadening panels, 1/2" thick	"	"	600	.013	S.F.
	0500	Fiberglass panels, 4' x 8' x 1" thick, with					
	0600	glass cloth face for walls, cemented	1 Carp	1 Carpenter	155	.052	S.F.
	0700	1-1/2" thick, dacron covered, inner aluminum frame,					
	0710	wall mounted	1 Carp	1 Carpenter	300	.027	S.F.
	0900	Mineral fiberboard panels, fabric covered, 30"x 108",					
	1000	3/4" thick, concealed spline, wall mounted	1 Carp	1 Carpenter	150	.053	S.F.

095 300 | Acoustical Insulation

			CREW	MAKEUP	DAILY OUTPUT	MAN-HOURS	UNIT
	304	**BARRIERS** Plenum, leaded vinyl, .48 lb. per S.F.	1 Carp	1 Carpenter	170	.047	S.F.
	0100	.87 lb. per S.F.			155	.052	S.F.
	0300	1.50 lb. per S.F.			140	.057	S.F.
	0400	3.0 lb. per S.F.			125	.064	S.F.
	0600	Aluminum foil, fiberglass reinf., parallel with joists			275	.029	S.F.
	0700	Perpendicular to joists			155	.052	S.F.
	0900	Aluminum mesh, kraft paperbacked			275	.029	S.F.
	0970	Fiberglass batts, kraft faced, 3-1/2" thick			1,400	.006	S.F.
	0980	6" thick			1,300	.006	S.F.
	1000	Sheet lead, 1 lb., 1/64" thick, perpendicular to joists	↓	↓	150	.053	S.F.

095 300 | Acoustical Insulation

		CREW	MAKEUP	DAILY OUTPUT	MAN-HOURS	UNIT
308	**SOUND ATTENUATION** Blanket, 1" thick	1 Carp	1 Carpenter	925	.009	S.F.
0500	1-1/2" thick			920	.009	S.F.
1000	2" thick			915	.009	S.F.
1500	3" thick			910	.009	S.F.
3000	Thermal or acoustical batt above ceiling, 2" thick			900	.009	S.F.
3100	3" thick			900	.009	S.F.
3200	4" thick	↓	↓	900	.009	S.F.
3400	Urethane plastic foam, open cell, on wall, 2" thick	2 Carp	2 Carpenters	2,050	.008	S.F.
3500	3" thick			1,550	.010	S.F.
3600	4" thick			1,050	.015	S.F.
3700	On ceiling, 2" thick			1,700	.009	S.F.
3800	3" thick			1,300	.012	S.F.
3900	4" thick	↓	↓	900	.018	S.F.
3901						
4000	Nylon matting 0.4" thick, with carbon black spinerette					
4010	plus polyester fabric, on floor	J-4	1 Tile Layer	4,000	.004	S.F.
			1 Tile Layer Helper			
4200	Fiberglass reinf. backer board underlayment, 7/16" thick, on floor	"	"	800	.020	S.F.

095 600 | Wood Strip Flooring

		CREW	MAKEUP	DAILY OUTPUT	MAN-HOURS	UNIT
604	**WOOD** Fir, vertical grain, 1" x 4", not incl. finish, B & better	1 Carp	1 Carpenter	255	.031	S.F.
0100	C grade & better	"	"	255	.031	S.F.
0600	Gym floor, in mastic, over 2 ply felt, #2 & better					
0700	25/32" thick maple, including finish	1 Carp	1 Carpenter	100	.080	S.F.
0900	33/32" thick maple, incl. finish			98	.082	S.F.
1000	For 1/2" corkboard underlayment, add	↓	↓	750	.011	S.F.
1600	Maple flooring, over sleepers,					
1700	finish, 25/32" thick	1 Carp	1 Carpenter	85	.094	S.F.
1900	33/32" thick			83	.096	S.F.
2200	For 3/4" subfloor, add			350	.023	S.F.
2300	With two 1/2" subfloors, 25/32" thick	↓	↓	69	.116	S.F.
2500	Maple, incl. finish, #2 & btr., 25/32" thick, on rubber					
2600	Sleepers, with two 1/2" subfloors	1 Carp	1 Carpenter	76	.105	S.F.
2800	With steel spline, double connection to channels			73	.110	S.F.
3700	Portable hardwood, prefinished panels			83	.096	S.F.
3720	Insulated with polystyrene, add			165	.048	S.F.
3750	Running tracks, Sitka spruce surface			62	.129	S.F.
3770	3/4" plywood surface			100	.080	S.F.
4000	Maple, strip, 25/32" x 2-1/4", not incl. finish, select			170	.047	S.F.
4100	#2 & better			170	.047	S.F.
4300	33/32" x 3-1/4", not incl. finish, #1 grade			170	.047	S.F.
4400	#2 & better	↓	↓	170	.047	S.F.
4600	Oak, white or red, 25/32" x 2-1/4", not incl. finish					
4700	Clear quartered	1 Carp	1 Carpenter	170	.047	S.F.
4900	Clear/select, 2-1/4" wide			170	.047	S.F.
5000	#1 common			185	.043	S.F.
5200	Parquetry, standard, 5/16" thick, not incl. finish, oak, minimum			160	.050	S.F.
5300	Maximum			100	.080	S.F.
5500	Teak, minimum			160	.050	S.F.
5600	Maximum			100	.080	S.F.
5650	13/16" thick, select grade oak, minimum			160	.050	S.F.
5700	Maximum			100	.080	S.F.
5800	Custom parquetry, including finish, minimum			100	.080	S.F.
5900	Maximum			50	.160	S.F.
6100	Prefinished white oak, prime grade, 2-1/4" wide			170	.047	S.F.
6200	3-1/4" wide			185	.043	S.F.
6400	Ranch plank			145	.055	S.F.
6500	Hardwood blocks, 9" x 9", 25/32" thick	↓	↓	160	.050	S.F.

095 | Acoustical Treatment and Wood Flooring

095 600 | Wood Strip Flooring

		CREW	MAKEUP	DAILY OUTPUT	MAN-HOURS	UNIT
6701	Wood flooring, parquetry, 5/16" thick, oak, minimum	1 Carp	1 Carpenter	160	.050	S.F.
6800	Maximum			100	.080	S.F.
7000	Walnut or teak, parquetry, minimum			160	.050	S.F.
7100	Maximum	↓	↓	100	.080	S.F.
7200	Acrylic wood parquet blocks, 12" x 12" x 5/16",					
7210	irradiated, set in epoxy	1 Carp	1 Carpenter	160	.050	S.F.
7400	Yellow pine, 3/4" x 3-1/8", T & G, C & better, not incl. finish			200	.040	S.F.
7800	Sanding and finishing, fill, shellac, wax	↓	↓	295	.027	S.F.

095 650 | Wood Block Flooring

		CREW	MAKEUP	DAILY OUTPUT	MAN-HOURS	UNIT
651	WOOD BLOCK FLOORING End grain flooring, creosoted, 2" thick	1 Carp	1 Carpenter	295	.027	S.F.
0400	Natural finish, 1" thick, fir			125	.064	S.F.
0600	1-1/2" thick, pine			125	.064	S.F.
0700	2" thick, pine	↓	↓	125	.064	S.F.

095 800 | Wood Comp Flooring

		CREW	MAKEUP	DAILY OUTPUT	MAN-HOURS	UNIT
801	WOOD COMPOSITION Gym floors					
0100	2-1/4" x 6-7/8" x 3/8", on 2" grout setting bed	D-7	1 Tile Layer	150	.107	S.F.
			1 Tile Layer Helper			
0200	Thin set, on concrete	"	"	250	.064	S.F.
0300	Sanding and finishing, add	1 Carp	1 Carpenter	200	.040	S.F.

096 | Flooring and Carpet

096 150 | Marble Flooring

		CREW	MAKEUP	DAILY OUTPUT	MAN-HOURS	UNIT
151	MARBLE Thin gauge tile, 12" x 6", 9/32", White Carara	D-7	1 Tile Layer	64	.250	S.F.
			1 Tile Layer Helper			
0100	Filled Travertine			64	.250	S.F.
0200	Synthetic tiles, 12" x 12" x 5/8", thin set, floors			64	.250	S.F.
0301	On walls	↓	↓	55	.291	S.F.

096 250 | Slate Flooring

		CREW	MAKEUP	DAILY OUTPUT	MAN-HOURS	UNIT
251	SLATE TILE Vermont, 6" x 6" x 1/4" thick, thin set	D-7	1 Tile Layer	180	.089	S.F.
			1 Tile Layer Helper			

096 350 | Brick Flooring

		CREW	MAKEUP	DAILY OUTPUT	MAN-HOURS	UNIT
354	FLOORING Acidproof shales, red, 8" x 3-3/4" x 1-1/4" thick	D-7	1 Tile Layer	.43	37.210	M
			1 Tile Layer Helper			
0050	2-1/4" thick	D-1	1 Bricklayer	.40	40.000	M
			1 Bricklayer Helper			
0200	Acid proof clay brick, 8" x 3-3/4" x 2-1/4" thick			.40	40.000	M
0250	9" x 4-1/2" x 3" thick	↓	↓	.37	43.240	M
0260	Cast ceramic, pressed, 4" x 8" x 1/2", unglazed	D-7	1 Tile Layer	100	.160	S.F.
			1 Tile Layer Helper			
0270	Glazed			100	.160	S.F.
0280	Hand molded flooring, 4" x 8" x 3/4", unglazed			95	.168	S.F.
0290	Glazed			95	.168	S.F.
0300	8" hexagonal, 3/4" thick, unglazed			85	.188	S.F.
0310	Glazed	↓	↓	85	.188	S.F.
0400	Heavy duty industrial, cement mortar bed	D-1	1 Bricklayer	80	.200	S.F.
			1 Bricklayer Helper			
0450	Acid proof joints	"	"	65	.246	S.F.

096 350 | Brick Flooring

		Description	CREW	MAKEUP	DAILY OUTPUT	MAN-HOURS	UNIT
354	0502	Flooring, pavers, 8" x 4", 1" to 1-1/4" thick, red	D-7	1 Tile Layer	95	.168	S.F.
				1 Tile Layer Helper			
	0510	Ironspot	D-1	1 Bricklayer	95	.168	S.F.
				1 Bricklayer Helper			
	0540	1-3/8" to 1-3/4" thick, red			95	.168	S.F.
	0560	Ironspot			95	.168	S.F.
	0580	2-1/4" thick, red			90	.178	S.F.
	0590	Ironspot			90	.178	S.F.
	0600	Sidewalk or patios, on sand bed, laid flat, no mortar, 4.5 per S.F.			110	.145	S.F.
	0650	Laid on edge, 7 per S.F.			70	.229	S.F.
	0860	For acid-resistant joints, add			2,100	.008	S.F.
	0870	For epoxy joints, add			600	.027	S.F.
	0880	For Furan underlayment, add	↓	↓	600	.027	S.F.
	0890	For waxed surface, steam cleaned, add	D-5	1 Bricklayer	1,000	.008	S.F.
				1 Power Tool			

096 600 | Resilient Tile Flooring

	Description	CREW	MAKEUP	DAILY OUTPUT	MAN-HOURS	UNIT
601	RESILIENT Asphalt tile, on concrete, 1/8" thick					
0050	Color group B	1 Tilf	1 Tile Layer	400	.020	S.F.
0100	Color group C & D			400	.020	S.F.
0500	For less than 500 S.F., add			500	.016	S.F.
0600	For over 5000 S.F., deduct	↓	↓	1,600	.005	S.F.
0800	Base, cove, rubber or vinyl, .080" thick					
1100	Standard colors, 2-1/2" high	1 Tilf	1 Tile Layer	315	.025	L.F.
1150	4" high			315	.025	L.F.
1200	6" high			315	.025	L.F.
1450	1/8" thick, standard colors, 2-1/2" high			315	.025	L.F.
1500	4" high			315	.025	L.F.
1550	6" high			315	.025	L.F.
1600	Corners, 2-1/2" high			315	.025	Ea.
1630	4" high			315	.025	Ea.
1660	6" high			315	.025	Ea.
1700	Conductive flooring, rubber tile, 1/8" thick			315	.025	S.F.
1800	Homogeneous vinyl tile, 1/8" thick			315	.025	S.F.
2200	Cork tile, standard finish, 1/8" thick			315	.025	S.F.
2250	3/16" thick			315	.025	S.F.
2300	5/16" thick			315	.025	S.F.
2350	1/2" thick			315	.025	S.F.
2500	Urethane finish, 1/8" thick			315	.025	S.F.
2550	3/16" thick			315	.025	S.F.
2600	5/16" thick			315	.025	S.F.
2650	1/2" thick			315	.025	S.F.
3700	Polyethylene, in rolls, no base incl., landscape surfaces			275	.029	S.F.
3800	Nylon action surface, 1/8" thick			275	.029	S.F.
3900	1/4" thick			275	.029	S.F.
4000	3/8" thick			275	.029	S.F.
4100	Golf tee surface with foam back			235	.034	S.F.
4200	Practice putting, knitted nylon surface	↓	↓	235	.034	S.F.
4400	Polyurethane, thermoset, prefabricated in place, indoor					
4500	3/8" thick for basketball, gyms, etc.	1 Tilf	1 Tile Layer	100	.080	S.F.
4600	1/2" thick for professional sports			95	.084	S.F.
4700	Outdoor, 1/4" thick, smooth, for tennis			100	.080	S.F.
4800	Rough, for track, 3/8" thick			95	.084	S.F.
5000	Poured in place, indoor, with finish, 1/4" thick			80	.100	S.F.
5050	3/8" thick			65	.123	S.F.
5100	1/2" thick			50	.160	S.F.
5500	Polyvinyl chloride, sheet goods for gyms, 1/4" thick			80	.100	S.F.
5600	3/8" thick	↓	↓	60	.133	S.F.

096 600 | Resilient Tile Flooring

		CREW	MAKEUP	DAILY OUTPUT	MAN-HOURS	UNIT
601 5901	Resilient flooring, rubber, sheet goods, 36" wide, 1/8" thick	1 Tilf	1 Tile Layer	210	.038	S.F.
5950	3/16" thick			210	.038	S.F.
6000	1/4" thick			200	.040	S.F.
6010	5/16" thick			185	.043	S.F.
6020	3/8" thick			170	.047	S.F.
6030	1/2" thick			160	.050	S.F.
6050	Tile, marbleized colors, 12" x 12", 1/8" thick			485	.016	S.F.
6100	3/16" thick			485	.016	S.F.
6150	1/4" thick			485	.016	S.F.
6300	Special tile, plain colors, 1/8" thick			485	.016	S.F.
6350	3/16" thick			485	.016	S.F.
6400	1/4" thick			485	.016	S.F.
6410	Raised, radial or square, minimum			485	.016	S.F.
6430	Maximum			485	.016	S.F.
6450	For golf course, skating rink, etc., 1/4" thick			275	.029	S.F.
6700	Synthetic turf, 3/8" thick	↓	↓	270	.030	S.F.
6750	Interlocking 2' x 2' squares, 1/2" thick, not					
6810	cemented, for playgrounds, minimum	1 Tilf	1 Tile Layer	485	.016	S.F.
6850	Maximum			400	.020	S.F.
7000	Vinyl composition tile, 12" x 12", 1/16" thick			315	.025	S.F.
7050	Embossed			315	.025	S.F.
7100	Marbleized			315	.025	S.F.
7150	Plain			315	.025	S.F.
7200	3/32" thick, embossed			315	.025	S.F.
7250	Marbleized			315	.025	S.F.
7300	Plain			315	.025	S.F.
7350	1/8" thick, marbleized			315	.025	S.F.
7400	Plain			315	.025	S.F.
7500	Vinyl tile, 12" x 12", .050" thick, minimum			315	.025	S.F.
7550	Maximum			315	.025	S.F.
7600	1/8" thick, minimum			315	.025	S.F.
7650	Solid colors			315	.025	S.F.
7700	Marbleized or Travertine pattern			315	.025	S.F.
7750	Florentine pattern			315	.025	S.F.
7800	Maximum			315	.025	S.F.
8000	Vinyl sheet goods, backed, .070" thick, minimum			230	.035	S.F.
8050	Maximum			230	.035	S.F.
8100	.093" thick, minimum			230	.035	S.F.
8150	Maximum			230	.035	S.F.
8200	.125" thick, minimum			230	.035	S.F.
8250	Maximum			230	.035	S.F.
8300	.250" thick, minimum			230	.035	S.F.
8350	Maximum	↓	↓	230	.035	S.F.

096 780 | Resilient Accessories

		CREW	MAKEUP	DAILY OUTPUT	MAN-HOURS	UNIT
781	STAIR TREADS AND RISERS See index for materials other					
0100	than rubber and vinyl					
0300	Rubber, molded tread, 12" wide, 5/16" thick, black	1 Tilf	1 Tile Layer	115	.070	L.F.
0400	Colors			115	.070	L.F.
0600	1/4" thick, black			115	.070	L.F.
0700	Colors			115	.070	L.F.
0900	Grip strip safety tread, colors, 5/16" thick			115	.070	L.F.
1000	3/16" thick			120	.067	L.F.
1200	Landings, smooth sheet rubber, 1/8" thick			275	.029	S.F.
1300	3/16" thick			270	.030	S.F.
1500	Nosings, 1-1/2" deep, 3" wide, residential			140	.057	L.F.
1600	Commercial			140	.057	L.F.
1800	Risers, 7" high, 1/8" thick, flat	↓	↓	175	.046	L.F.

096 | Flooring and Carpet

096 780 | Resilient Accessories

		CREW	MAKEUP	DAILY OUTPUT	MAN-HOURS	UNIT
781 1901	Stairs, rubber risers, 7" high, 1/8" thick, coved	1 Tilf	1 Tile Layer	175	.046	L.F.
2100	Vinyl, molded tread, 12" wide, colors, 1/8" thick			115	.070	L.F.
2200	1/4" thick			115	.070	L.F.
2300	Landing material, 1/8" thick			200	.040	S.F.
2400	Riser, 7" high, 1/8" thick, coved			175	.046	L.F.
2450	Threshold, 5-1/2" wide			100	.080	L.F.
2500	Tread and riser combined, 1/8" thick	↓	↓	80	.100	L.F.

096 850 | Sheet Carpet

		CREW	MAKEUP	DAILY OUTPUT	MAN-HOURS	UNIT
852	**CARPET** Commercial grades, cemented					
0700	Acrylic, 26 oz., light to medium traffic	1 Tilf	1 Tile Layer	57	.140	S.Y.
0900	28 oz., medium traffic			57	.140	S.Y.
1100	35 oz., medium to heavy traffic			57	.140	S.Y.
2100	Nylon, non anti-static, 15 oz., light traffic			57	.140	S.Y.
2800	Nylon, with anti-static, 17 oz., light to medium traffic			57	.140	S.Y.
2900	20 oz., medium traffic			57	.140	S.Y.
3000	22 oz., medium traffic			57	.140	S.Y.
3100	24 oz., medium to heavy traffic			57	.140	S.Y.
3200	26 oz., medium to heavy traffic			57	.140	S.Y.
3300	28 oz., heavy traffic			57	.140	S.Y.
3340	32 oz., heavy traffic			57	.140	S.Y.
3370	42 oz., heavy traffic			49	.163	S.Y.
3400	Needle bonded, 20 oz., no padding			57	.140	S.Y.
3500	Polypropylene, 15 oz., light traffic			57	.140	S.Y.
3650	22 oz., medium traffic			57	.140	S.Y.
3660	24 oz., medium to heavy traffic			57	.140	S.Y.
3670	26 oz., medium to heavy traffic			57	.140	S.Y.
3680	28 oz., heavy traffic			57	.140	S.Y.
3700	32 oz., heavy traffic			57	.140	S.Y.
3730	42 oz., heavy traffic			49	.163	S.Y.
3800	Scrim installed, nylon sponge back carpet, 20 oz.			57	.140	S.Y.
3850	60 oz.			57	.140	S.Y.
4000	Tile, foam-backed, needle punch			570	.014	S.F.
4100	Tufted loop or shag			570	.014	S.F.
4110	Wool, 30 oz., medium traffic			57	.140	S.Y.
4500	Wool, 36 oz., medium to heavy traffic			57	.140	S.Y.
4700	Sponge back, wool, 36 oz., medium to heavy traffic			57	.140	S.Y.
4900	42 oz., heavy traffic			49	.163	S.Y.
9000	Padding, sponge rubber cushion, minimum			150	.053	S.Y.
9100	Maximum			150	.053	S.Y.
9200	Felt, 32 oz. to 56 oz., minimum			150	.053	S.Y.
9300	Maximum			150	.053	S.Y.
9400	Bonded urethane, 3/8" thick, minimum			150	.053	S.Y.
9500	Maximum			150	.053	S.Y.
9600	Prime urethane, 1/4" thick, minimum			150	.053	S.Y.
9700	Maximum	↓	↓	150	.053	S.Y.

096 900 | Carpet Tile

		CREW	MAKEUP	DAILY OUTPUT	MAN-HOURS	UNIT
901	CARPET TILE					
1100	Fusion bonded, 18" x 18", 20 oz.	1 Tilf	1 Tile Layer	43	.186	S.Y.
1180	35 oz.			37	.216	S.Y.
5060	Tufted, 18" x 18", 26 oz.	↓	↓	40	.200	S.Y.

097 200	Epoxy Marble Flooring	CREW	MAKEUP	DAILY OUTPUT	MAN-HOURS	UNIT
201	**COMPOSITION FLOORING** Acrylic, 1/4" thick	C-6	1 Labor Foreman (outside)	520	.092	S.F.
			4 Building Laborers			
			1 Cement Finisher			
			2 Gas Engine Vibrators			
0100	3/8" thick			450	.107	S.F.
0300	Cupric oxychloride, on bond coat, minimum			480	.100	S.F.
0400	Maximum			420	.114	S.F.
0600	Epoxy, with colored quartz chips, broadcast, minimum			675	.071	S.F.
0700	Maximum			490	.098	S.F.
0900	Trowelled, minimum			560	.086	S.F.
1000	Maximum	↓	↓	480	.100	S.F.
1200	Heavy duty epoxy topping, 1/4" thick,					
1300	500 to 1,000 S.F.	C-6	1 Labor Foreman (outside)	420	.114	S.F.
			4 Building Laborers			
			1 Cement Finisher			
			2 Gas Engine Vibrators			
1500	1,000 to 2,000 S.F.			450	.107	S.F.
1600	Over 10,000 S.F.			480	.100	S.F.
1800	Epoxy terrazzo, 1/4" thick, chemical resistant, minimum			375	.128	S.F.
1900	Maximum			280	.171	S.F.
2100	Conductive, minimum			355	.135	S.F.
2200	Maximum			270	.178	S.F.
2400	Mastic, hot laid, 2 coat, 1-1/2" thick, standard, minimum			690	.070	S.F.
2500	Maximum			520	.092	S.F.
2700	Acidproof, minimum			605	.079	S.F.
2800	Maximum			350	.137	S.F.
3000	Neoprene, trowelled on, 1/4" thick, minimum			545	.088	S.F.
3100	Maximum			430	.112	S.F.
3150	Polyacrylate terrazzo, 1/4" thick, minimum			735	.065	S.F.
3170	Maximum			480	.100	S.F.
3200	3/8" thick, minimum			620	.077	S.F.
3220	Maximum			480	.100	S.F.
3300	Conductive terrazzo, 1/4" thick, minimum			450	.107	S.F.
3330	Maximum			305	.157	S.F.
3350	3/8" thick, minimum			365	.132	S.F.
3370	Maximum			255	.188	S.F.
3450	Granite, conductive, 1/4" thick, minimum			695	.069	S.F.
3470	Maximum			420	.114	S.F.
3500	3/8" thick, minimum			695	.069	S.F.
3520	Maximum			380	.126	S.F.
3600	Polyester, with colored quartz chips, 1/16" thick, minimum			1,065	.045	S.F.
3700	Maximum			560	.086	S.F.
3900	1/8" thick, minimum			810	.059	S.F.
4000	Maximum			675	.071	S.F.
4200	Polyester, heavy duty, compared to epoxy, add			2,590	.019	S.F.
4300	Polyurethane, with suspended vinyl chips, minimum			1,065	.045	S.F.
4500	Maximum	↓	↓	860	.056	S.F.

098 | Special Coatings

098 150 | Glazed Coatings

150			CREW	MAKEUP		DAILY OUTPUT	MAN-HOURS	UNIT
150		WALL COATINGS Acrylic glazed coatings, minimum	1 Pord	1 Painter, Ordinary		525	.015	S.F.
	0100	Maximum				305	.026	S.F.
	0300	Epoxy coatings, minimum				525	.015	S.F.
	0400	Maximum				170	.047	S.F.
	0600	Exposed aggregate, troweled on, 1/16" to 1/4", minimum				235	.034	S.F.
	0700	Maximum (epoxy or polyacrylate)				130	.062	S.F.
	0900	1/2" to 5/8" aggregate, minimum				130	.062	S.F.
	1000	Maximum				80	.100	S.F.
	1200	1" aggregate size, minimum				90	.089	S.F.
	1300	Maximum				55	.145	S.F.
	1500	Exposed aggregate, sprayed on, 1/8" aggregate, minimum				295	.027	S.F.
	1600	Maximum				145	.055	S.F.
	1802	High build epoxy, 50 mil, minimum				390	.021	S.F.
	1900	Maximum				95	.084	S.F.
	2100	Laminated epoxy with fiberglass, minimum				295	.027	S.F.
	2200	Maximum				145	.055	S.F.
	2400	Sprayed perlite or vermiculite, 1/16" thick, minimum				2,935	.003	S.F.
	2500	Maximum				640	.013	S.F.
	2700	Vinyl plastic wall coating, minimum				735	.011	S.F.
	2800	Maximum				240	.033	S.F.
	3000	Urethane on smooth surface, 2 coats, minimum				1,135	.007	S.F.
	3100	Maximum				665	.012	S.F.
	3300	3 coat, minimum				840	.010	S.F.
	3400	Maximum				470	.017	S.F.
	3600	Ceramic-like glazed coating, cementitious, minimum				440	.018	S.F.
	3700	Maximum				345	.023	S.F.
	3900	Resin base, minimum				640	.013	S.F.
	4000	Maximum	↓	↓		330	.024	S.F.

099 | Painting and Wall Coverings

099 100 | Exterior Painting

			CREW	MAKEUP		DAILY OUTPUT	MAN-HOURS	UNIT
106		SIDING Exterior						
	0021	Labor includes protection of adjacent items not painted						
	0100	Steel siding, oil base, primer or sealer coat, brushwork	2 Pord	2 Painters, Ordinary		1,700	.009	S.F.
	0500	Spray				3,200	.005	S.F.
	0800	Paint 2 coats, brushwork				1,350	.012	S.F.
	1000	Spray				2,600	.006	S.F.
	1200	Stucco, rough, oil base, paint 2 coats, brushwork				1,300	.012	S.F.
	1400	Roller				2,000	.008	S.F.
	1600	Spray				2,600	.006	S.F.
	1800	Texture 1-11 or clapboard, oil base, primer coat, brushwork				2,600	.006	S.F.
	2000	Spray				4,200	.004	S.F.
	2100	Paint 1 coat, brushwork				2,500	.006	S.F.
	2200	Spray				4,200	.004	S.F.
	2400	Paint 2 coats, brushwork				1,250	.013	S.F.
	2600	Spray				2,100	.008	S.F.
	3000	Stain 1 coat, brushwork				2,600	.006	S.F.
	3200	Spray				4,200	.004	S.F.
	3400	Stain 2 coats, brushwork				1,500	.011	S.F.
	4000	Spray				2,100	.008	S.F.
	4200	Wood shingles, oil base primer coat, brushwork	↓	↓		2,500	.006	S.F.

099 100 | Exterior Painting

		CREW	MAKEUP	DAILY OUTPUT	MAN-HOURS	UNIT
106 4401	Siding, ext. painting, wood shingles, oil base primer coat, spray	2 Pord	2 Painters, Ordinary	4,100	.004	S.F.
4600	Paint 1 coat, brushwork			2,400	.007	S.F.
4800	Spray			4,100	.004	S.F.
5000	Paint 2 coats, brushwork			1,400	.011	S.F.
5200	Spray			2,100	.008	S.F.
5800	Stain 1 coat, brushwork			2,500	.006	S.F.
6000	Spray			4,100	.004	S.F.
6500	Stain 2 coats, brushwork			1,400	.011	S.F.
7000	Spray	↓	↓	2,100	.008	S.F.

099 200 | Interior Painting

		CREW	MAKEUP	DAILY OUTPUT	MAN-HOURS	UNIT
204	CABINETS AND CASEWORK					
0021	Labor includes protection of adjacent items not painted					
1000	Primer coat, oil base, brushwork	1 Pord	1 Painter, Ordinary	400	.020	S.F.
2000	Paint, oil base, brushwork, 1 coat			380	.021	S.F.
2500	2 coats			200	.040	S.F.
3000	Stain, brushwork, wipe off			360	.022	S.F.
4000	Shellac, 1 coat, brushwork			380	.021	S.F.
4500	Varnish, 3 coats, brushwork			235	.034	S.F.
212	CORNER GUARDS Rubber, 3" wide, standard			135	.059	L.F.
0100	1/4" thick, 2-3/4" wide			135	.059	L.F.
0300	Bullnose			135	.059	L.F.
0400	Vinyl, 5/16" thick, 2-1/2" wide	↓	↓	135	.059	L.F.
216	DOORS AND WINDOWS					
0021	Labor includes protection of adjacent items not painted					
0500	Flush door and frame, per side, oil base, primer coat, brushwork	1 Pord	1 Painter, Ordinary	14	.571	Ea.
1000	Paint, 1 coat			13	.615	Ea.
1200	2 coats			7.50	1.070	Ea.
1220	3 coats			5.50	1.450	Ea.
1400	Stain, brushwork, wipe off			15	.533	Ea.
1600	Shellac, 1 coat, brushwork			12	.667	Ea.
1800	Varnish, 3 coats, brushwork			5	1.600	Ea.
2000	Panel door and frame, per side, oil base, primer coat, brushwork			10	.800	Ea.
2200	Paint, 1 coat			9	.889	Ea.
2400	2 coats			5	1.600	Ea.
2420	3 coats			3.50	2.290	Ea.
2600	Stain, brushwork, wipeoff			10	.800	Ea.
2800	Shellac, 1 coat, brushwork			9	.889	Ea.
3000	Varnish, 3 coats, brushwork	↓	↓	3.50	2.290	Ea.
4400	Windows, including frame and trim, per side					
4600	Colonial type, 2' x 3', oil base, primer coat, brushwork	1 Pord	1 Painter, Ordinary	24	.333	Ea.
5800	Paint, 1 coat			22	.364	Ea.
6000	2 coats			13	.615	Ea.
6010	3 coats			10	.800	Ea.
6200	3' x 5' opening, primer coat, brushwork			15	.533	Ea.
6400	Paint, 1 coat			13	.615	Ea.
6600	2 coats			8	1.000	Ea.
6610	3 coats			5.50	1.450	Ea.
6800	4' x 8' opening, primer coat, brushwork			12	.667	Ea.
7000	Paint, 1 coat			10	.800	Ea.
7200	2 coats			6	1.330	Ea.
7210	3 coats			4	2.000	Ea.
7500	Standard, 6 to 8 lites, 2' x 3', primer			26	.308	Ea.
7520	Paint 1 coat			24	.333	Ea.
7540	2 coats			14	.571	Ea.
7560	3 coats			10	.800	Ea.
7580	3' x 5', primer			17	.471	Ea.
7600	Paint 1 coat	↓	↓	15	.533	Ea.

099 200 | Interior Painting

		CREW	MAKEUP	DAILY OUTPUT	MAN-HOURS	UNIT
216 7621	Window painting, std., 6 to 8 lites, 3' x 5', paint 2 coats	1 Pord	1 Painter, Ordinary	9	.889	Ea.
7640	3 coats			6	1.330	Ea.
7660	4' x 8', primer			14	.571	Ea.
7680	Paint 1 coat			12	.667	Ea.
7700	2 coats			7	1.140	Ea.
7720	3 coats			5	1.600	Ea.
8000	Single lite type, 2' x 3', oil base, primer coat, brushwork			40	.200	Ea.
8200	Paint, 1 coat			37	.216	Ea.
8400	2 coats			21	.381	Ea.
8410	3 coats			15	.533	Ea.
8600	3' x 5' opening, primer coat, brushwork			27	.296	Ea.
8800	Paint, 1 coat			25	.320	Ea.
9000	2 coats			14	.571	Ea.
9010	3 coats			10	.800	Ea.
9200	4' x 8' opening, primer coat, brushwork			17	.471	Ea.
9400	Paint, 1 coat			15	.533	Ea.
9600	2 coats			10	.800	Ea.
9610	3 coats	↓	↓	8	1.000	Ea.
220	**MISCELLANEOUS**					
0021	Labor includes protection of adjacent items not painted					
0100	Blinds and shutters, oil base, 2 coats, brushwork	1 Pord	1 Painter, Ordinary	20	.400	Ea.
0700	Fence, chain link, per side, oil base, primer coat, brushwork	2 Pord	2 Painters, Ordinary	1,200	.013	S.F.
1000	Spray			1,600	.010	S.F.
1200	Paint 1 coat, brushwork			1,150	.014	S.F.
1400	Spray			1,600	.010	S.F.
1600	Picket, wood, one side, primer coat, brushwork			1,700	.009	S.F.
1800	Spray			3,400	.005	S.F.
2000	Paint 1 coat, brushwork			1,600	.010	S.F.
2200	Spray			3,200	.005	S.F.
2400	Floors, conc./wood, oil base, primer/sealer coat, brushwork			3,400	.005	S.F.
2450	Roller			3,800	.004	S.F.
2600	Spray			6,000	.003	S.F.
2650	Paint 1 coat, brushwork			3,200	.005	S.F.
2800	Roller			3,600	.004	S.F.
2850	Spray			6,000	.003	S.F.
3000	Stain, wood floor, brushwork			3,400	.005	S.F.
3200	Roller			3,800	.004	S.F.
3250	Spray			6,000	.003	S.F.
3400	Varnish, wood floor, brushwork			3,200	.005	S.F.
3450	Roller			3,400	.005	S.F.
3600	Spray	↓	↓	6,000	.003	S.F.
3800	Grilles, per side, oil base, primer coat, brushwork	1 Pord	1 Painter, Ordinary	400	.020	Ea.
3850	Spray			500	.016	Ea.
3880	Paint 1 coat, brushwork			370	.022	Ea.
3900	Spray			220	.036	Ea.
3920	Paint 2 coats, brushwork			220	.036	Ea.
3940	Spray	↓	↓	250	.032	Ea.
4200	Gutters and downspouts, oil base, primer coat, brushwork	2 Pord	2 Painters, Ordinary	650	.025	L.F.
4250	Paint 1 coat, brushwork			600	.027	L.F.
4300	Paint 2 coats, brushwork			325	.049	L.F.
5000	Pipe, to 4" diameter, primer or sealer coat, oil base, brushwork			800	.020	L.F.
5100	Spray			1,100	.015	L.F.
5200	Paint 1 coat, brushwork			750	.021	L.F.
5300	Spray			1,100	.015	L.F.
5350	Paint 2 coats, brushwork			440	.036	L.F.
5400	Spray			550	.029	L.F.
5450	To 8" diameter, primer or sealer coat, brushwork			400	.040	L.F.
5500	Spray	↓	↓	650	.025	L.F.

099 200	Interior Painting	CREW	MAKEUP	DAILY OUTPUT	MAN-HOURS	UNIT
220 5551	Pipe to 8" diameter, paint 1 coat, brushwork	2 Pord	2 Painters, Ordinary	350	.046	L.F.
5600	Spray			650	.025	L.F.
5650	Paint 2 coats, brushwork			205	.078	L.F.
5700	Spray			375	.043	L.F.
5750	To 12" diameter, primer or sealer coat, brushwork			240	.067	L.F.
5800	Spray			320	.050	L.F.
5850	Paint 1 coat, brushwork			220	.073	L.F.
6000	Spray			320	.050	L.F.
6200	Paint 2 coats, brushwork			120	.133	L.F.
6250	Spray			160	.100	L.F.
6300	To 16" diameter, primer or sealer coat, brushwork			192	.083	L.F.
6350	Spray			240	.067	L.F.
6400	Paint 1 coat, brushwork			180	.089	L.F.
6450	Spray			240	.067	L.F.
6500	Paint 2 coats, brushwork			100	.160	L.F.
6550	Spray	↓	↓	130	.123	L.F.
7000	Trim , wood, incl. puttying, under 6" wide					
7200	Primer coat, oil base, brushwork	1 Pord	1 Painter, Ordinary	900	.009	L.F.
7250	Paint, 1 coat, brushwork			875	.009	L.F.
7400	2 coats			520	.015	L.F.
7450	3 coats			370	.022	L.F.
7500	Over 6" wide, primer coat, brushwork			600	.013	L.F.
7550	Paint, 1 coat, brushwork			450	.018	L.F.
7600	2 coats			265	.030	L.F.
7650	3 coats			190	.042	L.F.
8000	Cornice, simple design, primer coat, oil base, brushwork			275	.029	S.F.
8250	Paint, 1 coat			250	.032	S.F.
8300	2 coats			150	.053	S.F.
8350	Ornate design, primer coat			150	.053	S.F.
8400	Paint, 1 coat			140	.057	S.F.
8450	2 coats			85	.094	S.F.
8600	Balustrades, per side, primer coat, oil base, brushwork			300	.027	S.F.
8650	Paint, 1 coat			285	.028	S.F.
8700	2 coats			170	.047	S.F.
8900	Trusses and wood frames, primer coat, oil base, brushwork			800	.010	S.F.
8950	Spray			1,200	.007	S.F.
9000	Paint 1 coat, brushwork			750	.011	S.F.
9200	Spray			1,200	.007	S.F.
9220	Paint 2 coats, brushwork			500	.016	S.F.
9240	Spray			600	.013	S.F.
9260	Stain, brushwork, wipe off			600	.013	S.F.
9280	Varnish, 3 coats, brushwork	↓	↓	275	.029	S.F.
224	**WALL AND CEILINGS**					
0021	Labor includes protection of adjacent items not painted					
0100	Concrete, dry wall or plaster, oil base, primer or sealer coat					
0200	Smooth finish, brushwork	1 Pord	1 Painter, Ordinary	1,900	.004	S.F.
0240	Roller			2,200	.004	S.F.
0300	Sand finish, brushwork			1,700	.005	S.F.
0340	Roller			2,100	.004	S.F.
0380	Spray			3,750	.002	S.F.
0400	Paint 1 coat, smooth finish, brushwork			1,800	.004	S.F.
0440	Roller			2,100	.004	S.F.
0480	Spray			3,750	.002	S.F.
0500	Sand finish, brushwork			1,600	.005	S.F.
0540	Roller			2,000	.004	S.F.
0580	Spray			3,750	.002	S.F.
0800	Paint 2 coats, smooth finish, brushwork			975	.008	S.F.
0840	Roller	↓	↓	1,125	.007	S.F.

099 | Painting and Wall Coverings

099 200 | Interior Painting

		CREW	MAKEUP	DAILY OUTPUT	MAN-HOURS	UNIT
0881	Wall & ceiling, paint 2 coats, smooth finish, spray	1 Pord	1 Painter, Ordinary	2,250	.004	S.F.
0900	Sand finish, brushwork			825	.010	S.F.
0940	Roller			1,050	.008	S.F.
0980	Spray			2,250	.004	S.F.
1200	Paint 3 coats, smooth finish, brushwork			675	.012	S.F.
1240	Roller			790	.010	S.F.
1280	Spray			1,500	.005	S.F.
1300	Sand finish, brushwork			560	.014	S.F.
1340	Roller			710	.011	S.F.
1380	Spray			1,500	.005	S.F.
1600	Glaze coating, 5 coats, spray, clear			900	.009	S.F.
1640	Multicolor	↓	↓	900	.009	S.F.
2000	Masonry or concrete block, oil base, primer or sealer coat					
2100	Smooth finish, brushwork	1 Pord	1 Painter, Ordinary	1,725	.005	S.F.
2180	Spray			3,750	.002	S.F.
2200	Sand finish, brushwork			1,400	.006	S.F.
2280	Spray			3,750	.002	S.F.
2400	Paint 1 coat, smooth finish, brushwork			1,550	.005	S.F.
2480	Spray			3,750	.002	S.F.
2500	Sand finish, brushwork			1,140	.007	S.F.
2580	Spray			3,750	.002	S.F.
2800	Paint 2 coats, smooth finish, brushwork			1,000	.008	S.F.
2880	Spray			2,250	.004	S.F.
2900	Sand finish, brushwork			666	.012	S.F.
2980	Spray			2,250	.004	S.F.
3200	Paint 3 coats, smooth finish, brushwork			727	.011	S.F.
3280	Spray			1,500	.005	S.F.
3300	Sand finish, brushwork			470	.017	S.F.
3380	Spray			1,500	.005	S.F.
3600	Glaze coating, 5 coats, spray, clear			900	.009	S.F.
3620	Multicolor			900	.009	S.F.
4000	Block filler, 1 coat, brushwork			1,350	.006	S.F.
4100	Silicone, water repellent, 2 coats, spray			900	.009	S.F.
228	VARNISH 1 coat + sealer, on wood trim, no sanding included			900	.009	S.F.
0100	Hardwood floors, 2 coats, no sanding included	↓	↓	800	.010	S.F.

099 700 | Wallpaper

		CREW	MAKEUP	DAILY OUTPUT	MAN-HOURS	UNIT
701	WALL COVERING					
0050	Aluminum foil	1 Pape	1 Paperhanger	275	.029	S.F.
0100	Copper sheets, .025" thick, vinyl backing			240	.033	S.F.
0300	Phenolic backing			240	.033	S.F.
0600	Cork tiles, light or dark, 12" x 12" x 3/16"			240	.033	S.F.
0700	5/16" thick			235	.034	S.F.
0900	1/4" basketweave			240	.033	S.F.
1000	1/2" natural, non-directional pattern			240	.033	S.F.
1200	Granular surface, 12" x 36", 1/2" thick			385	.021	S.F.
1300	1" thick			370	.022	S.F.
1500	Polyurethane coated, 12" x 12" x 3/16" thick			240	.033	S.F.
1600	5/16" thick			235	.034	S.F.
1800	Cork wallpaper, paperbacked, natural			480	.017	S.F.
1900	Colors			480	.017	S.F.
2100	Flexible wood veneer, 1/32" thick, plain woods			100	.080	S.F.
2200	Exotic woods	↓	↓	95	.084	S.F.
2400	Gypsum-based, fabric-backed, fire					
2500	resistant for masonry walls, minimum	1 Pape	1 Paperhanger	800	.010	S.F.
2600	Average			720	.011	S.F.
2700	Maximum	↓	↓	640	.013	S.F.
2750	Acrylic, modified, semi-rigid PVC, .028" thick	2 Carp	2 Carpenters	330	.048	S.F.

224

099 | Painting and Wall Coverings

099 700	Wallpaper	CREW	MAKEUP	DAILY OUTPUT	MAN-HOURS	UNIT
701 2801	Wallcovering, acrylic, modified, semi-rigid PVC, .040" thick	2 Carp	2 Carpenters	320	.050	S.F.
3000	Vinyl wall covering, fabric-backed, lightweight	1 Pape	1 Paperhanger	640	.013	S.F.
3300	Medium weight			480	.017	S.F.
3400	Heavy weight			435	.018	S.F.
3700	Wallpaper at $9.70 per double roll, average workmanship			640	.013	S.F.
3900	Paper at $20 per double roll, average workmanship			535	.015	S.F.
4000	Paper at $44 per double roll, quality workmanship			435	.018	S.F.
4200	Grass cloths with lining paper, minimum			400	.020	S.F.
4300	Maximum	▼	▼	350	.023	S.F.

099 900	Surface Preparation	CREW	MAKEUP	DAILY OUTPUT	MAN-HOURS	UNIT
902 0020	**REMOVAL** Existing lead paint, by chemicals, refinish with 2 coats of paint					
0050	Baseboard, to 6" wide	1 Pord	1 Painter, Ordinary	190	.042	L.F.
0070	To 12" wide			150	.053	L.F.
0200	Balustrades, one side			90	.089	S.F.
1400	Cabinets, simple design			85	.094	S.F.
1420	Ornate design			40	.200	S.F.
1600	Cornice, simple design			65	.123	S.F.
1620	Ornate design			35	.229	S.F.
2800	Doors, one side, flush			125	.064	S.F.
2820	Two panel			110	.073	S.F.
2840	Four panel			95	.084	S.F.
2880	For trim, one side, add			200	.040	L.F.
3000	Fence, picket, one side			80	.100	S.F.
3200	Grilles, one side, simple design			95	.084	S.F.
3220	Ornate design			45	.178	S.F.
4400	Pipes, to 4" diameter			200	.040	L.F.
4420	To 8" diameter			90	.089	L.F.
4440	To 12" diameter			65	.123	L.F.
4460	To 16" diameter			45	.178	L.F.
4500	For hangers, add			100	.080	Ea.
4800	Siding			170	.047	S.F.
5000	Trusses, open			75	.107	S.F.Face
6200	Windows, one side only, double hung, 1/1 light, 24" x 48" high			12	.667	Ea.
6220	30" x 60" high			9	.889	Ea.
6240	36" x 72" high			8	1.000	Ea.
6280	40" x 80" high			6	1.330	Ea.
6400	Colonial window, 6/6 light, 24" x 48" high			7	1.140	Ea.
6420	30" x 60" high			5	1.600	Ea.
6440	36" x 72" high			4	2.000	Ea.
6480	40" x 80" high			3.50	2.290	Ea.
6600	8/8 light, 24" x 48" high			6	1.330	Ea.
6620	40" x 80" high			3	2.670	Ea.
6800	12/12 light, 24" x 48" high			5	1.600	Ea.
6820	40" x 80" high			2.50	3.200	Ea.
6840	For frame & trim, add	▼	▼	150	.053	L.F.
906	**SCRAPE AFTER FIRE DAMAGE**					
0050	Boards, 1" x 4"	1 Pord	1 Painter, Ordinary	145	.055	L.F.
0060	1" x 6"			110	.073	L.F.
0070	1" x 8"			80	.100	L.F.
0080	1" x 10"			65	.123	L.F.
0500	Framing, 2" x 4"			110	.073	L.F.
0510	2" x 6"			90	.089	L.F.
0520	2" x 8"			70	.114	L.F.
0530	2" x 10"			60	.133	L.F.
0540	2" x 12"	▼	▼	50	.160	L.F.

099 | Painting and Wall Coverings

		099 900	Surface Preparation	CREW	MAKEUP	DAILY OUTPUT	MAN-HOURS	UNIT
906	1001	Scrape after fire damage, heavy framing, 3" x 4"	1 Pord	1 Painter, Ordinary	110	.073	L.F.
	1010	4" x 4"			90	.089	L.F.
	1020	4" x 6"			75	.107	L.F.
	1030	4" x 8"			60	.133	L.F.
	1040	4" x 10"			50	.160	L.F.
	1060	4" x 12"			45	.178	L.F.
	2900	For sealing, minimum			825	.010	S.F.
	2920	Maximum	↓	↓	460	.017	S.F.

DIVISION 10 SPECIALTIES

DIVISION
10
SPECIALTIES

The Specialties Division contains productivity rates for the installation of various special products that are commonly found in buildings. Examples include bathroom accessories, woodburning stoves, and moveable office partitions.

As a general rule, the products in this division are installed by the vendor as part of the purchase agreement. The installers are frequently specially trained for their task. The productivity rates in this division are based on the experience of properly trained craftsmen, but not necessarily specialists, working in a reasonably comfortable environment without unnecessary space confinements. In actual practice, the expected productivity should be adjusted to make allowances for either unusual productivity enhancing or restricting conditions.

The rates in this division represent new construction. For repair and remodeling work, substantial adjustments may be necessary for the unique nature of each project.

		101 100	Chalkboards	CREW	MAKEUP	DAILY OUTPUT	MAN-HOURS	UNIT
104	104	**CHALKBOARD** Cement asbestos, no frame, economy		2 Carp	2 Carpenters	270	.059	S.F.
	0100	Deluxe				260	.062	S.F.
	0300	Hardboard, tempered, no frame, 1/4" thick				270	.059	S.F.
	0400	1/2" thick				260	.062	S.F.
	0600	Hardboard, not tempered, no frame, 1/4" thick				270	.059	S.F.
	0700	1/2" thick		↓	↓	260	.062	S.F.
	0800	Porcelain enamel, 24 ga. steel, 4' high, with aluminum						
	0900	trim, alum. foil backing, with core materials as follows:						
	1000	3/8" gypsum core		2 Carp	2 Carpenters	260	.062	S.F.
	1100	1/4" hardboard core				270	.059	S.F.
	1200	7/16" hardboard core				255	.063	S.F.
	1300	3/8" honeycomb core				275	.058	S.F.
	1400	3/8" particleboard core				260	.062	S.F.
	1500	1/4" plywood core				270	.059	S.F.
	1550	3/8" plywood core				260	.062	S.F.
	2100	Slate, 3/8" thick, frame not included, to 4' wide				240	.067	S.F.
	2200	To 4'-6" wide				230	.070	S.F.
	2400	Over 4'-6" to 5'-0" wide				220	.073	S.F.
	2600	Treated plastic on plywood, no frame, 1/4" thick				240	.067	S.F.
	2800	1/2" thick				230	.070	S.F.
	3000	Frame for chalkboards, aluminum, chalk tray				290	.055	L.F.
	3100	Trim				385	.042	L.F.
	3300	Map and display rail, economy				385	.042	L.F.
	3400	Deluxe				350	.046	L.F.
	3600	Factory fabricated, tempered hardbd. w/wood frame, 3'-6" high				265	.060	S.F.
	3700	4' high				260	.062	S.F.
	3900	Aluminum frame, 3'-6" high				270	.059	S.F.
	4000	4' high				265	.060	S.F.
	4200	Porcelain steel, aluminum frame, 3' high				260	.062	S.F.
	4300	4' high				255	.063	S.F.
	4500	Magnetic swing leaf panels, 36" x 24", 4 panels				3	5.330	Total
	4600	5 panels				3	5.330	Total
	4700	6 panels				3	5.330	Total
	4800	8 panels				3	5.330	Total
	5000	Vertical sliding with tempered hardboard, manual				150	.107	S.F.
	5100	Electric				115	.139	S.F.
	5300	Horizontal sliding, 4' high, 10' long, 2 track				40	.400	S.F.
	5350	3 track				40	.400	S.F.
	5400	4 track				40	.400	S.F.
	5450	Horizontal sliding, 4' high, 20' long, 2 track				80	.200	S.F.
	5500	3 track				80	.200	S.F.
	5550	4 track		↓	↓	80	.200	S.F.
	602	**PARTITIONS, TOILET**						
	0100	Cubicles, ceiling hung, marble		2 Marb	2 Marble Setters	2	8.000	Ea.
	0200	Painted metal		2 Carp	2 Carpenters	4	4.000	Ea.
	0300	Plastic laminate on particle board				4	4.000	Ea.
	0400	Porcelain enamel				4	4.000	Ea.
	0500	Stainless steel		↓	↓	4	4.000	Ea.
	0800	Floor & ceiling anchored, marble		2 Marb	2 Marble Setters	2.50	6.400	Ea.
	1000	Painted metal		2 Carp	2 Carpenters	5	3.200	Ea.
	1100	Plastic laminate on particle board				5	3.200	Ea.
	1200	Porcelain enamel				5	3.200	Ea.
	1300	Stainless steel		↓	↓	5	3.200	Ea.
	1600	Floor mounted, marble		2 Marb	2 Marble Setters	3	5.330	Ea.
	1700	Painted metal		2 Carp	2 Carpenters	7	2.290	Ea.
	1800	Plastic laminate on particle board				7	2.290	Ea.
	1900	Porcelain enamel				7	2.290	Ea.
	2000	Stainless steel		↓	↓	7	2.290	Ea.

101 100 | Chalkboards

		Description	CREW	MAKEUP	DAILY OUTPUT	MAN-HOURS	UNIT
602	2402	Partitions, toilet, floor mtd., headrail braced, marble	2 Marb	2 Marble Setters	3	5.330	Ea.
	2500	Painted metal	2 Carp	2 Carpenters	6	2.670	Ea.
	2600	Plastic laminate on particle board			6	2.670	Ea.
	2700	Porcelain enamel			6	2.670	Ea.
	2800	Stainless steel			6	2.670	Ea.
	3000	Wall hung partitions, painted metal			7	2.290	Ea.
	3200	Porcelain enamel			7	2.290	Ea.
	3300	Stainless steel	↓	↓	7	2.290	Ea.
	4000	Screens, entrance, floor mounted, 54" high					
	4100	Marble	D-1	1 Bricklayer 1 Bricklayer Helper	35	.457	L.F.
	4200	Painted metal	2 Carp	2 Carpenters	60	.267	L.F.
	4300	Plastic laminate on particle board			60	.267	L.F.
	4400	Porcelain enamel			60	.267	L.F.
	4500	Stainless steel	↓	↓	60	.267	L.F.
	4600	Urinal screen, 18" wide, ceiling braced, marble	D-1	1 Bricklayer 1 Bricklayer Helper	6	2.670	Ea.
	4700	Painted metal	2 Carp	2 Carpenters	8	2.000	Ea.
	4800	Plastic laminate on particle board			8	2.000	Ea.
	4900	Porcelain enamel			8	2.000	Ea.
	5000	Stainless steel	↓	↓	8	2.000	Ea.
	5100	Floor mounted, head rail braced					
	5200	Marble	D-1	1 Bricklayer 1 Bricklayer Helper	6	2.670	Ea.
	5300	Painted metal	2 Carp	2 Carpenters	8	2.000	Ea.
	5400	Plastic laminate on particle board			8	2.000	Ea.
	5500	Porcelain enamel			8	2.000	Ea.
	5600	Stainless steel	↓	↓	8	2.000	Ea.
	5700	Pilaster, flush, marble	D-1	1 Bricklayer 1 Bricklayer Helper	9	1.780	Ea.
	5800	Painted metal	2 Carp	2 Carpenters	10	1.600	Ea.
	5900	Plastic laminate on particle board			10	1.600	Ea.
	6000	Porcelain enamel			10	1.600	Ea.
	6100	Stainless steel	↓	↓	10	1.600	Ea.
	6200	Post braced, marble	D-1	1 Bricklayer 1 Bricklayer Helper	9	1.780	Ea.
	6300	Painted metal	2 Carp	2 Carpenters	10	1.600	Ea.
	6400	Plastic laminate on particle board			10	1.600	Ea.
	6500	Porcelain enamel			10	1.600	Ea.
	6600	Stainless steel	↓	↓	10	1.600	Ea.
	6700	Wall hung, bracket supported					
	6800	Painted metal	2 Carp	2 Carpenters	10	1.600	Ea.
	6900	Plastic laminate on particle board			10	1.600	Ea.
	7000	Porcelain enamel			10	1.600	Ea.
	7100	Stainless steel			10	1.600	Ea.
	7400	Flange supported, painted metal			10	1.600	Ea.
	7500	Plastic laminate on particle board			10	1.600	Ea.
	7600	Porcelain enamel			10	1.600	Ea.
	7700	Stainless steel			10	1.600	Ea.
	7800	Wedge type, painted metal			10	1.600	Ea.
	8000	Porcelain enamel			10	1.600	Ea.
	8100	Stainless steel	↓	↓	10	1.600	Ea.

101 | Chalkboards, Compartments and Cubicles

101 850 | Shower Compartments

			CREW	MAKEUP	DAILY OUTPUT	MAN-HOURS	UNIT
852	852	**PARTITIONS, SHOWER** Economy, painted steel, steel					
	0100	base, no door or plumbing included	2 Shee	2 Sheet Metal Workers	5	3.200	Ea.
	0300	Square, 32" x 32", stock, with receptor & door, fiberglass			4.50	3.560	Ea.
	0600	Galvanized and painted steel	↓	↓	5	3.200	Ea.
	0700	Shower stall, double wall, incl. receptor but not including					
	0800	door or plumbing, enameled steel	2 Shee	2 Sheet Metal Workers	5	· 3.200	Ea.
	1100	Porcelain enameled steel			5	3.200	Ea.
	1200	Stainless steel			5	3.200	Ea.
	1500	Circular fiberglass, 36" diameter, no plumbing included			4	4.000	Ea.
	1700	One piece, 36" diameter, less door			4	4.000	Ea.
	1800	With door			3.50	4.570	Ea.
	2000	Curved shell shower, no door needed			3	5.330	Ea.
	2400	Glass stalls, with doors, no receptors, chrome on brass			3	5.330	Ea.
	2700	Anodized aluminum	↓	↓	4	4.000	Ea.
	2900	Marble shower stall, stock design, with shower door	2 Marb	2 Marble Setters	1.20	13.330	Ea.
	3000	With curtain			1.30	12.310	Ea.
	3200	Receptors, precast terrazzo, 32" x 32'			14	1.140	Ea.
	3300	48" x 34"			12	1.330	Ea.
	3500	Plastic, simulated terrazzo receptor, 32" x 32"			14	1.140	Ea.
	3600	32" x 48"			12	1.330	Ea.
	3800	Precast concrete, colors, 32" x 32"			14	1.140	Ea.
	3900	48" x 48"	↓	↓	12	1.330	Ea.
	4100	Shower doors, economy plastic, 24" wide	1 Shee	1 Sheet Metal Worker	9	.889	Ea.
	4200	Tempered glass door, economy			8	1.000	Ea.
	4400	Folding, tempered glass, aluminum frame			6	1.330	Ea.
	4500	Sliding, tempered glass, 48" opening			6	1.330	Ea.
	4700	Deluxe, tempered glass, chrome on brass frame, minimum			5	1.600	Ea.
	5000	Maximum			5	1.600	Ea.
	5300	On anodized aluminum frame, minimum			5	1.600	Ea.
	5400	Maximum			5	1.600	Ea.
	5600	Tub enclosure, plastic panels, economy, sliding panel			4	2.000	Ea.
	5700	Folding panel			4	2.000	Ea.
	5900	Deluxe, tempered glass, anodized alum. frame, minimum			2	4.000	Ea.
	6200	Maximum			1.50	5.330	Ea.
	6500	On chrome-plated brass frame, minimum			2	4.000	Ea.
	6600	Maximum	↓	↓	1.50	5.330	Ea.

102 | Louvers, Corner Protection and Access Flooring

102 100 | Metal Wall Louvers

			CREW	MAKEUP	DAILY OUTPUT	MAN-HOURS	UNIT
	104	**LOUVERS** Aluminum with screen, residential, 8" x 8"	1 Carp	1 Carpenter	38	.211	Ea.
	0100	12" x 12"			38	.211	Ea.
	0200	12" x 18"			35	.229	Ea.
	0250	14" x 24"			30	.267	Ea.
	0300	18" x 24"			27	.296	Ea.
	0500	30" x 24"			24	.333	Ea.
	0700	Triangle, adjustable, small			20	.400	Ea.
	0800	Large			15	.533	Ea.
	2100	Midget, aluminum, 3/4" deep, 1" diameter			85	.094	Ea.
	2150	3" diameter			60	.133	Ea.
	2200	4" diameter			50	.160	Ea.
	2250	6" diameter	↓	↓	30	.267	Ea.

102 | Louvers, Corner Protection and Access Flooring

102 100 | Metal Wall Louvers

		CREW	MAKEUP	DAILY OUTPUT	MAN-HOURS	UNIT
104 2301	Louvers, ridge vent strip, mill finish	1 Shee	1 Sheet Metal Worker	155	.052	L.F.
2330	Soffit vent, continuous, 3" wide, aluminum, mill finish	1 Carp	1 Carpenter	200	.040	L.F.
2340	Baked enamel finish			200	.040	L.F.
2400	Under eaves vent, aluminum, mill finish, 16" x 4"			75	.107	Ea.
2500	16" x 8"			75	.107	Ea.
7000	Vinyl wall louvers, 1-1/2" deep, 8" x 8"			38	.211	Ea.
7020	12" x 12"			38	.211	Ea.
7080	12" x 18"			35	.229	Ea.
7200	14" x 24"	↓	↓	30	.267	Ea.

102 600 | Wall & Corner Guards

		CREW	MAKEUP	DAILY OUTPUT	MAN-HOURS	UNIT
604	CORNER GUARDS Steel angle w/anchors, 1" x 1", 1.5#/L.F.	E-4	1 Struc. Steel Foreman	320	.100	L.F.
			3 Struc. Steel Workers			
			1 Gas Welding Machine			
0100	2" x 2" angles, 3.5#/L.F.			300	.107	L.F.
0200	3" x 3" angles, 6#/L.F.			275	.116	L.F.
0300	4" x 4" angles, 8#/L.F.			240	.133	L.F.
0500	Cast iron wheel guards , 3'-0" high			24	1.330	Ea.
0600	5'-0" high			19	1.680	Ea.
0800	Pipe bumper for truck doors, 8' long, 6" diameter			20	1.600	Ea.
0900	8" diameter	↓	↓	20	1.600	Ea.
608	CORNER PROTECTION					
0020	Acrylic and vinyl, high impact type, stainless frame	1 Sswk	1 Struc. Steel Worker	45	.178	L.F.
0030	Shock-absorbing water filled bumpers, corner, 26" long			14	.571	Ea.
0050	41" long			14	.571	Ea.
0070	Half round, 26" long			14	.571	Ea.
0090	40" long			14	.571	Ea.
0100	Stainless steel, 16 ga., with adhesive			80	.100	L.F.
0200	12 ga. stainless, with adhesive	↓	↓	80	.100	L.F.
0500	Vinyl adhesive type, 3-3/8" wide	1 Carp	1 Carpenter	128	.063	L.F.
612	WALLGUARD					
0500	Neoprene with aluminum fastening strip, 1-1/2" x 2"	1 Carp	1 Carpenter	110	.073	L.F.
1000	Trolley rail, PVC, clipped to wall, 5" high			185	.043	L.F.
1050	8" high			180	.044	L.F.
1200	Vinyl acrylic bed aligner and bumper, 37" long			10	.800	Ea.
1300	43" long	↓	↓	9	.889	Ea.

102 700 | Access Flooring

		CREW	MAKEUP	DAILY OUTPUT	MAN-HOURS	UNIT
705	PEDESTAL ACCESS FLOORS Computer room application, metal					
0020	Particle board or steel panels, no covering, under 6000 S. F.	2 Carp	2 Carpenters	1,000	.016	S.F.
0300	Metal covered, over 6000 S.F.			1,100	.015	S.F.
0400	Aluminum, 24" panels			500	.032	S.F.
0910	For snap on stringer system, add	↓	↓	1,000	.016	S.F.
0950	Office applications, to 8" high, steel panels,					
0960	no covering, over 6000 S.F.	2 Carp	2 Carpenters	400	.040	S.F.
1000	Machine cutouts after initial installation	1 Carp	1 Carpenter	10	.800	Ea.
1100	Air conditioning grilles, 4" x 12"			17	.471	Ea.
1150	6" x 18"	↓	↓	14	.571	Ea.
1200	Approach ramps, minimum	2 Carp	2 Carpenters	85	.188	S.F.
1300	Maximum	"	"	60	.267	S.F.
1500	Handrail, 2 rail aluminum	1 Carp	1 Carpenter	15	.533	L.F.

103 | Fireplaces, Ext. Specialties and Flagpoles

103 050 | Prefabricated Fireplaces

		CREW	MAKEUP		DAILY OUTPUT	MAN-HOURS	UNIT
054	**FIREPLACE, PREFABRICATED** Free standing or wall hung						
0100	with hood & screen, minimum	F-1	1 Carpenter		1.30	6.150	Ea.
			Power Tools				
0150	Average				1	8.000	Ea.
0200	Maximum				.90	8.890	Ea.
0500	Dbl wall for chimney heights over 8'-6", 7" diameter, add				33	.242	V.L.F.
0600	10" diameter, add				32	.250	V.L.F.
0700	12" diameter, add				31	.258	V.L.F.
0800	14" diameter, add				30	.267	V.L.F.
1000	Simulated brick chimney top, 4' high, 16" x 16"				10	.800	Ea.
1100	24" x 24"				7	1.140	Ea.
1500	Simulated logs, gas fired, 40,000 BTU, 2' long, minimum				7	1.140	Set
1600	Maximum				6	1.330	Set
1700	Electric, 1,500 BTU, 1'-6" long, minimum				7	1.140	Set
1800	11,500 BTU, maximum	↓	↓		6	1.330	Set

103 100 | Fireplace Accessories

		CREW	MAKEUP		DAILY OUTPUT	MAN-HOURS	UNIT
104	**FIREPLACE ACCESSORIES** Chimney screens, galv., 13" x 13" flue	1 Bric	1 Bricklayer		8	1.000	Ea.
0050	Galv., 24" x 24" flue				5	1.600	Ea.
0200	Stainless steel, 13" x 13" flue				8	1.000	Ea.
0250	20" x 20" flue				5	1.600	Ea.
0400	Cleanout doors and frames, cast iron, 8" x 8"				12	.667	Ea.
0450	12" x 12"				10	.800	Ea.
0500	18" x 24"				8	1.000	Ea.
0550	Cast iron frame, steel door, 24" x 30"				5	1.600	Ea.
0800	Damper, rotary control, steel, 30" opening				6	1.330	Ea.
0850	Cast iron, 30" opening				6	1.330	Ea.
0880	36" opening				6	1.330	Ea.
0900	48" opening				6	1.330	Ea.
0920	60" opening				6	1.330	Ea.
0950	72" opening				5	1.600	Ea.
1000	84" opening				5	1.600	Ea.
1050	96" opening				4	2.000	Ea.
1200	Steel plate, poker control, 60" opening				8	1.000	Ea.
1250	84" opening				5	1.600	Ea.
1400	"Universal" type, chain operated, 32" x 20" opening				8	1.000	Ea.
1450	48" x 24" opening				5	1.600	Ea.
1600	Dutch Oven door and frame, cast iron, 12" x 15" opening				13	.615	Ea.
1650	Copper plated, 12" x 15" opening				13	.615	Ea.
1800	Fireplace forms with registers, 25" opening				3	2.670	Ea.
1900	34" opening				2.50	3.200	Ea.
2000	48" opening				2	4.000	Ea.
2100	72" opening				1.50	5.330	Ea.
2400	Squirrel and bird screens, galvanized, 8" x 8" flue				16	.500	Ea.
2450	13" x 13" flue	↓	↓		12	.667	Ea.

103 200 | Stoves

		CREW	MAKEUP		DAILY OUTPUT	MAN-HOURS	UNIT
201	**WOODBURNING STOVES** Cast iron, minimum	F-2	2 Carpenters		1.30	12.310	Ea.
			Power Tools				
0020	Average				1	16.000	Ea.
0030	Maximum	↓	↓		.80	20.000	Ea.

103 520 | Ground Set Flagpoles

		Description	CREW	MAKEUP	DAILY OUTPUT	MAN-HOURS	UNIT
524	524	**FLAGPOLE** Not including base or foundation					
	0100	Aluminum, tapered, ground set 20' high	K-1	1 Carpenter	2	8.000	Ea.
				1 Truck Driver (light)			
				1 Truck w/Power Equip.			
	0200	25' high			1.70	9.410	Ea.
	0300	30' high			1.50	10.670	Ea.
	0400	35' high			1.40	11.430	Ea.
	0500	40' high			1.20	13.330	Ea.
	0600	50' high			1	16.000	Ea.
	0700	60' high			.90	17.780	Ea.
	0800	70' high			.80	20.000	Ea.
	0900	80' high			.70	22.860	Ea.
	1100	Counterbalanced, tapered, aluminum, 20' high			1.80	8.890	Ea.
	1200	30' high			1.50	10.670	Ea.
	1300	40' high			1.30	12.310	Ea.
	1400	50' high			1	16.000	Ea.
	2820	Aluminum, electronically operated, 30' high			1.40	11.430	Ea.
	2840	35' high			1.30	12.310	Ea.
	2860	40' high			1.10	14.550	Ea.
	2880	45' high			1	16.000	Ea.
	2900	50' high			.90	17.780	Ea.
	3000	Fiberglass, tapered, ground set, 25' high			2	8.000	Ea.
	3100	30' high			1.50	10.670	Ea.
	3200	35' high			1.40	11.430	Ea.
	3300	40' high			1.20	13.330	Ea.
	3400	50' high			1	16.000	Ea.
	3500	60' high			.90	17.780	Ea.
	4000	Yardarms and rigging for poles, 6' total length			1.90	8.420	Ea.
	4100	12' total length			1.80	8.890	Ea.
	4300	Steel, sectional, lightweight, ground set, 20' high			1.30	12.310	Ea.
	4400	25' high			1.20	13.330	Ea.
	4500	30' high			1.10	14.550	Ea.
	4600	35' high			1	16.000	Ea.
	4700	40' high			.90	17.780	Ea.
	4800	50' high			.80	20.000	Ea.
	5000	Tapered, heavyweight steel, ground set, 35' high			.80	20.000	Ea.
	5100	50' high			.70	22.860	Ea.
	5200	60' high			.70	22.860	Ea.
	5300	75' high	↓	↓	.60	26.670	Ea.
	5800	Bases, ornamental, minimum	1 Carp	1 Carpenter	6	1.330	Ea.
	5900	Average			4	2.000	Ea.
	6100	Maximum	↓	↓	2	4.000	Ea.
	6400	Wood poles, tapered, clear vertical grain fir with tilting					
	6410	base, not incl. foundation, 4" butt, 25' high	K-1	1 Carpenter	1.90	8.420	Ea.
				1 Truck Driver (light)			
				1 Truck w/Power Equip.			
	6800	6" butt, 30' high	"	"	1.30	12.310	Ea.
	7300	Foundations for flagpoles, including					
	7400	excavation and concrete, to 35' high poles	C-1	3 Carpenters	10	3.200	Ea.
				1 Building Laborer			
				Power Tools			
	7600	40' to 50' high	↓	↓	3.50	9.140	Ea.
	7700	Over 60' high			2	16.000	Ea.

103 | Fireplaces, Ext. Specialties and Flagpoles

103 540 | Wall Mounted Flagpoles

			CREW	MAKEUP	DAILY OUTPUT	MAN-HOURS	UNIT
544	544	FLAGPOLE Not including base or foundation, wall-mounted					
	0100	Aluminum, outrigger wall poles, including base					
	0200	10' long, minimum	K-1	1 Carpenter	1.70	9.410	Ea.
				1 Truck Driver (light)			
				1 Truck w/Power Equip.			
	0300	Maximum			1.40	11.430	Ea.
	0800	20' long outrigger, minimum			1.30	12.310	Ea.
	0900	Average			1.20	13.330	Ea.
	1000	Maximum			1	16.000	Ea.
	1300	Aluminum, vertical wall set, tapered, with base, 23' high			1.20	13.330	Ea.
	1400	28' high			1	16.000	Ea.
	2400	Outrigger poles with base, 12' long			1.30	12.310	Ea.
	2500	14' long	↓	↓	1	16.000	Ea.

104 | Identifying and Pedestrian Control Devices

104 100 | Directories

			CREW	MAKEUP	DAILY OUTPUT	MAN-HOURS	UNIT
104		DIRECTORY BOARDS Plastic, glass covered, 30" x 20"	2 Carp	2 Carpenters	3	5.330	Ea.
	0100	36" x 48"			2	8.000	Ea.
	0300	Grooved cork, 30" x 20"			3	5.330	Ea.
	0400	36" x 48"			2	8.000	Ea.
	0600	Black felt, 30" x 20"			3	5.330	Ea.
	0700	36" x 48"			2	8.000	Ea.
	0900	Outdoor, weatherproof, black plastic, 36" x 24"			2	8.000	Ea.
	1000	36" x 36"			1.50	10.670	Ea.
	1200	Grooved cork, 36" x 24"			2	8.000	Ea.
	1300	36" x 36"			1.50	10.670	Ea.
	1500	Vinyl plastic, 36" x 24"			2	8.000	Ea.
	1600	36" x 36"			1.50	10.670	Ea.
	1800	Indoor, economy, open face, 20" x 15"			7	2.290	Ea.
	1900	24" x 18"			7	2.290	Ea.
	2000	30" x 20"			6	2.670	Ea.
	2100	39" x 27"			6	2.670	Ea.
	2400	Building directory boards, alum., black felt panels, 24" x 18"			4	4.000	Ea.
	2500	39" x 22"			3.50	4.570	Ea.
	2600	48" x 32"			3	5.330	Ea.
	2700	36" x 48"			2.50	6.400	Ea.
	2800	48" x 60"			2	8.000	Ea.
	2900	48" x 72"	↓	↓	1	16.000	Ea.

104 150 | Bulletin Boards

			CREW	MAKEUP	DAILY OUTPUT	MAN-HOURS	UNIT
151		BULLETIN BOARD Cork sheets, unbacked, no frame, 1/8" thick	2 Carp	2 Carpenters	290	.055	S.F.
	0100	1/4" thick			290	.055	S.F.
	0300	Burlap-faced cork, no frame, 1/8" thick,			290	.055	S.F.
	0400	With 1/8" cork backing			290	.055	S.F.
	0600	With 1/4" cork backing			290	.055	S.F.
	0700	With 3/8" backboard			290	.055	S.F.
	0900	1/16" vinyl cork, on 3/8" fiber board, no frame			280	.057	S.F.
	1000	1/4" vinyl cork, on 7/16" backboard, no frame			280	.057	S.F.
	1200	1/4" vinyl cork, on 1/4" hardboard, no frame			280	.057	S.F.
	1300	No backing, no frame			280	.057	S.F.
	2000	For map and display rail, economy, add	↓	↓	385	.042	L.F.

104 150 | Bulletin Boards

		CREW	MAKEUP	DAILY OUTPUT	MAN-HOURS	UNIT
151 2101	Bulletin boards, for map & display rail, deluxe, add	2 Carp	2 Carpenters	350	.046	L.F.
2120	Prefabricated, 1/4" cork, 4' x 4' with aluminum frame			14	1.140	Ea.
2140	Aluminum frame with glass door			13	1.230	Ea.
2160	8' x 4' with aluminum frame			8	2.000	Ea.
2180	Aluminum frame with glass door			7	2.290	Ea.
2200	3' x 5' with wood frame			14	1.140	Ea.
2210	Wood frame with glass door			13	1.230	Ea.
2220	4' x 4' with wood frame			10	1.600	Ea.
2230	6' x 4' with wood frame			8	2.000	Ea.
2240	Prefabricated with vinyl covered cork, aluminum frame, 4' x 3'			12	1.330	Ea.
2250	Vinyl on 1/8" vinyl cork plus 3/8" fiberboard, 4' x 3'			11	1.450	Ea.
2260	Vinyl on 1/4" vinyl cork plus 1/4" hardboard, 8' x 4'			8	2.000	Ea.
2270	Vinyl on 3/8" fiberboard, aluminum frame, 8' x 4'			7	2.290	Ea.
2300	Prefabricated, sliding glass, enclosed, 3' x 4'			16	1.000	Ea.
2400	5' x 3'			12	1.330	Ea.
2500	5' x 4'			11	1.450	Ea.
2600	6' x 4'	↓	↓	7	2.290	Ea.
2900	For lights, add per cabinet	1 Elec	1 Electrician	13	.615	Ea.
3100	Horizontal sliding units with 2 sliders, 8' x 4'	2 Carp	2 Carpenters	3	5.330	Ea.
3200	12' x 4'			2	8.000	Ea.
3400	4 sliding units, 16' x 4'			2	8.000	Ea.
3500	24' x 4'			1.50	10.670	Ea.
155	CONTROL BOARDS Magnetic, porcelain finish, 24" x 18", framed			8	2.000	Ea.
0100	36" x 24"			7.50	2.130	Ea.
0200	48" x 36"			7	2.290	Ea.
0300	72" x 48"			6	2.670	Ea.
0400	96" x 48"			5	3.200	Ea.
1000	Roll type, 49" x 74" case, with 2 rollers, 8 to 60 S.F. sleeves			125	.128	S.F.
1200	49" x 95" case, with 4 rollers, 37 to 120 S.F. sleeves	↓	↓	130	.123	S.F.

104 300 | Signs

		CREW	MAKEUP	DAILY OUTPUT	MAN-HOURS	UNIT
304	SIGNS Letters, individual, 2" high, cast aluminum	1 Carp	1 Carpenter	32	.250	Ea.
0100	Cast bronze			32	.250	Ea.
0300	4" high, 5/8" deep, cast aluminum			24	.333	Ea.
0400	Cast bronze			24	.333	Ea.
0600	6" high, 1" deep, cast aluminum			20	.400	Ea.
0700	Cast bronze			20	.400	Ea.
0900	12" high, 1-1/4" deep, cast aluminum			18	.444	Ea.
1000	Cast bronze			18	.444	Ea.
1200	18" high, 1-1/4" deep, cast aluminum			12	.667	Ea.
1300	Cast bronze			12	.667	Ea.
1500	Fabricated aluminum, 12" high, 3" deep			18	.444	Ea.
1600	18" high, 3" deep			12	.667	Ea.
1800	Fabricated stainless steel, 6" high, 3" deep			20	.400	Ea.
1900	12" high, 3" deep			18	.444	Ea.
2100	18" high, 3" deep			12	.667	Ea.
2200	24" high, 4" deep			10	.800	Ea.
2400	Painted sheet steel, 12" high, 2" deep			18	.444	Ea.
2500	18" high, 3" deep			12	.667	Ea.
2700	Plastic, 6" high, 1" deep			20	.400	Ea.
2800	12" high, 2" deep			18	.444	Ea.
3000	Plastic face, alum. frame, 20" high, 15" wide			5	1.600	Ea.
3300	36" high, 24" deep			4	2.000	Ea.
3400	Stainless steel frame, 12" high, 6" deep			5	1.600	Ea.
3700	24" high, 8" deep	↓	↓	4	2.000	Ea.
3900	Plaques, 20" x 30", for up to 450 letters, cast aluminum	2 Carp	2 Carpenters	4	4.000	Ea.
4000	Cast bronze			4	4.000	Ea.
4200	30" x 40", up to 900 letters cast aluminum	↓	↓	3	5.330	Ea.

104 | Identifying and Pedestrian Control Devices

104 300 | Signs

		CREW	MAKEUP	DAILY OUTPUT	MAN-HOURS	UNIT
304	4301	Plaques, 30" x 40", for up to 900 letters, cast bronze	2 Carp	2 Carpenters	3	5.330	Ea.
	4500	36" x 48", for up to 1300 letters, cast bronze			2	8.000	Ea.
	4800	Signs, cast aluminum street signs, 2-way			30	.533	Ea.
	4900	4-way			30	.533	Ea.
	5100	Acrylic exit signs, 15" x 6", surface mounted, minimum			30	.533	Ea.
	5200	Maximum			20	.800	Ea.
	5400	Bracket mounted, double face, minimum			30	.533	Ea.
	5500	Maximum			20	.800	Ea.
	5700	Plexiglass, exterior, illuminated, single face			100	.160	S.F.
	5800	Double face			75	.213	S.F.
	6000	Interior, illuminated, single face			100	.160	S.F.
	6100	Double face			75	.213	S.F.
	6400	Painted plywood (MDO), over 4' x 8'			120	.133	S.F.
	6600	Under 4' x 8'	↓	↓	100	.160	S.F.

104 560 | Turnstiles

		CREW	MAKEUP	DAILY OUTPUT	MAN-HOURS	UNIT
561	TURNSTILES One way, 4 arm, 46" diameter, economy, manual	2 Carp	2 Carpenters	5	3.200	Ea.
0100	Electric			1.20	13.330	Ea.
0300	High security, galv., 5'-5" diameter, 7' high, manual			1	16.000	Ea.
0350	Electric			.60	26.670	Ea.
0420	Three arm, 24" opening, light duty, manual			2	8.000	Ea.
0450	Heavy duty			1.50	10.670	Ea.
0460	Manual, with registering & controls, light duty			2	8.000	Ea.
0470	Heavy duty			1.50	10.670	Ea.
0480	Electric, heavy duty	↓	↓	1.10	14.550	Ea.
1200	One way gate with horizontal bars, 5'-5" diameter					
1300	7' high, recreation or transit type	2 Carp	2 Carpenters	.80	20.000	Ea.

105 | Lockers, Protective Covers and Postal Specialties

105 050 | Metal Lockers

		CREW	MAKEUP	DAILY OUTPUT	MAN-HOURS	UNIT
054	LOCKERS Steel, baked enamel, 60" or 72", single tier, minimum	1 Shee	1 Sheet Metal Worker	14	.571	Opng.
0100	Maximum			12	.667	Opng.
0300	2 tier, 60" or 72" total height, minimum			26	.308	Opng.
0400	Maximum			20	.400	Opng.
0600	5 tier box lockers, minimum			30	.267	Opng.
0700	Maximum			24	.333	Opng.
0900	6 tier box lockers, minimum			36	.222	Opng.
1000	Maximum			30	.267	Opng.
1200	Basket rack with 32 baskets, 9" x 13" x 8" basket			50	.160	Basket
1300	24 baskets, 12" x 13" x 8" basket			50	.160	Basket
1500	Athletic, wire mesh, no lock, 18" x 18" x 72"	↓	↓	12	.667	Ea.
1600	Overhead locker baskets on chains, 14" x 14" baskets	3 Shee	3 Sheet Metal Workers	96	.250	Basket
1800	Overhead locker framing system, add			600	.040	Basket
1900	Locking rail and bench units, add	↓	↓	120	.200	Basket
2100	Locker bench, laminated maple, top only	1 Shee	1 Sheet Metal Worker	100	.080	L.F.
2200	Pedestals, steel pipe	"	"	25	.320	Ea.
2400	Teacher and pupil wardrobes, enameled					
2500	22" x 15" x 61" high, minimum	1 Shee	1 Sheet Metal Worker	10	.800	Ea.
2550	Average			9	.889	Ea.
2700	Maximum			8	1.000	Ea.
3000	Duplex lockers with 2 doors, 72" high, 15" x 15"	↓	↓	10	.800	Ea.

105 | Lockers, Protective Covers and Postal Specialties

105 050 | Metal Lockers

		CREW	MAKEUP	DAILY OUTPUT	MAN-HOURS	UNIT
054	3101	Lockers, steel, duplex, with 2 doors, 72" high, 15" x 21"	1 Shee	1 Sheet Metal Worker	10	.800	Ea.

105 380 | Canopies

		CREW	MAKEUP	DAILY OUTPUT	MAN-HOURS	UNIT
384	CANOPIES Wall hung, aluminum, prefinished, 8' x 10'	K-2	1 Struc. Steel Foreman	1.30	18.460	Ea.
			1 Struc. Steel Worker			
			1 Truck Driver (light)			
			1 Truck w/Power Equip.			
0300	8' x 20'			1.10	21.820	Ea.
0500	10' x 10'			1.30	18.460	Ea.
0700	10' x 20'			1.10	21.820	Ea.
1000	12' x 20'			1	24.000	Ea.
1360	12' x 30'			.80	30.000	Ea.
1700	12' x 40'	↓	↓	.60	40.000	Ea.
2300	Aluminum entrance canopies, flat soffit					
2500	3'-6" x 4'-0", clear anodized	2 Carp	2 Carpenters	4	4.000	Ea.
2700	Bronze anodized			4	4.000	Ea.
3000	Polyurethane painted			4	4.000	Ea.
3300	4'-6" x 10'-0", clear anodized			2	8.000	Ea.
3500	Bronze anodized			2	8.000	Ea.
3700	Polyurethane painted	↓	↓	2	8.000	Ea.
4000	Wall downspout, 10 L.F., clear anodized	1 Carp	1 Carpenter	7	1.140	Ea.
4300	Bronze anodized			7	1.140	Ea.
4500	Polyurethane painted	↓	↓	7	1.140	Ea.
4700	Canvas awnings, including canvas, frame & lettering					
5000	Minimum	2 Carp	2 Carpenters	100	.160	S.F.
5300	Average			90	.178	S.F.
5500	Maximum	↓	↓	80	.200	S.F.
7000	Carport, baked vinyl finish, 20' x 10', no foundations, minimum	K-2	1 Struc. Steel Foreman	4	6.000	Car
			1 Struc. Steel Worker			
			1 Truck Driver (light)			
			1 Truck w/Power Equip.			
7250	Maximum			2	12.000	Car
7500	Walkway cover, to 12' wide, stl., vinyl finish, no fndtns., min.			250	.096	S.F.
7750	Maximum	↓	↓	200	.120	S.F.

105 510 | Mail Chutes

		CREW	MAKEUP	DAILY OUTPUT	MAN-HOURS	UNIT
511	MAIL CHUTES Aluminum & glass, 14-1/4" wide, 4-5/8" deep	2 Shee	2 Sheet Metal Workers	4	4.000	Floor
0100	8-5/8" deep			3.80	4.210	Floor
0300	8-3/4" x 3-1/2", aluminum			5	3.200	Floor
0400	Bronze or stainless			4.50	3.560	Floor
0600	Lobby collection boxes, aluminum			5	3.200	Ea.
0700	Bronze or stainless	↓	↓	4.50	3.560	Ea.

105 520 | Mail Boxes

		CREW	MAKEUP	DAILY OUTPUT	MAN-HOURS	UNIT
521	MAIL BOXES Horiz., key lock, 5"H x 6"W x 15"D, alum., rear load	1 Carp	1 Carpenter	34	.235	Ea.
0100	Front loading			34	.235	Ea.
0200	Double, 5"H x 12"W x 15"D, rear loading			26	.308	Ea.
0300	Front loading			26	.308	Ea.
0500	Quadruple, 10"H x 12"W x 15"D, rear loading			20	.400	Ea.
0600	Front loading			20	.400	Ea.
0800	Vertical, front loading, 15"H x 5"W x 6"D, aluminum			34	.235	Ea.
0900	Bronze, duranodic finish			34	.235	Ea.
1000	Steel, enameled			34	.235	Ea.
1700	Alphabetical directories, 35 names			10	.800	Ea.
1800	Letter collection box			6	1.330	Ea.
1900	Letter slot, residential			20	.400	Ea.
2000	Post office type			8	1.000	Ea.
2200	Post office counter window, with grille	↓	↓	2	4.000	Ea.

105 | Lockers, Protective Covers and Postal Specialties

	105 520	Mail Boxes	CREW	MAKEUP	DAILY OUTPUT	MAN-HOURS	UNIT
521	2250	Key keeper, single key, aluminum	1 Carp	1 Carpenter	26	.308	Ea.
	2300	Steel, enameled	"	"	26	.308	Ea.

106 | Partitions and Storage Shelving

	106 040	Partition Supports	CREW	MAKEUP	DAILY OUTPUT	MAN-HOURS	UNIT
042		TOILET PARTITION SUPPORTS Overhead framing for ceiling					
	0020	hung partitions, 3' wide	E-4	1 Struc. Steel Foreman	16	2.000	Stall
				3 Struc. Steel Workers			
				1 Gas Welding Machine			

	106 050	Wire Mesh Partitions	CREW	MAKEUP	DAILY OUTPUT	MAN-HOURS	UNIT
052		PARTITIONS, WOVEN WIRE For tool or stockroom enclosures					
	0100	Channel frame, 1-1/2" diamond mesh, 10 ga. wire, painted					
	0300	Wall panels, 4'-0" wide, 7' high	2 Carp	2 Carpenters	25	.640	Ea.
	0400	8' high			23	.696	Ea.
	0600	10' high			18	.889	Ea.
	0900	Ceiling panels, 10' long, 2' wide			25	.640	Ea.
	1000	4' wide			15	1.070	Ea.
	1200	Panel with service window & shelf, 5' long, 7' high			20	.800	Ea.
	1300	10' high			15	1.070	Ea.
	1500	Sliding doors, 3' wide, 7' full height			6	2.670	Ea.
	1600	10' full height			5	3.200	Ea.
	1800	6' wide sliding door, 7' full height			5	3.200	Ea.
	1900	10' full height			4	4.000	Ea.
	2100	Swinging doors, 3' wide, 7' high, no transom			6	2.670	Ea.
	2200	7' high, 3' transom	↓	↓	5	3.200	Ea.

	106 100	Folding Gates	CREW	MAKEUP	DAILY OUTPUT	MAN-HOURS	UNIT
101		SECURITY GATES					
	0300	Scissors type folding gate, ptd. steel, single, 6' high, 51" wide	2 Sswk	2 Struc. Steel Workers	2.20	7.270	Opng.
	0350	75" wide			2	8.000	Opng.
	0400	99" wide			1.80	8.890	Opng.
	0600	Double gate, 92" wide			1.80	8.890	Opng.
	0650	124" wide			1.50	10.670	Opng.
	0700	156" wide			1.20	13.330	Opng.
	0750	172" wide	↓	↓	1	16.000	Opng.

	106 150	Demountable Partitions	CREW	MAKEUP	DAILY OUTPUT	MAN-HOURS	UNIT
152		PARTITIONS, MOVABLE OFFICE Demountable, add for doors					
	0100	Do not deduct door openings from total L.F.					
	0900	Asbestos cement, 1-3/4" thick, prefinished, low walls	2 Carp	2 Carpenters	80	.200	L.F.
	1000	Full height			40	.400	L.F.
	1500	Gypsum, laminated 2-1/4" thick, 9' high, unpainted			40	.400	L.F.
	1600	Painted			40	.400	L.F.
	1800	3" thick, acoustical, unpainted			40	.400	L.F.
	1900	Painted			40	.400	L.F.
	2350	Vinyl clad drywall on 2-1/2" metal studs, to 9' high			60	.267	L.F.
	2400	42" high, plus 10" glass			60	.267	L.F.
	2500	Vinyl clad gypsum with air space, 3" thick			60	.267	L.F.
	2510	Steel clad gypsum, as above			60	.267	L.F.
	2600	Hardboard, vinyl faced, 7' high, 1-9/16" thick	↓	↓	60	.267	L.F.

106 150 | Demountable Partitions

		Description	CREW	MAKEUP	DAILY OUTPUT	MAN-HOURS	UNIT
152	2801	Partitions, hardboard, vinyl faced, 7' high, 2-1/4" thick, painted	2 Carp	2 Carpenters	50	.320	L.F.
	2900	With 40" glass			40	.400	L.F.
	3100	10' high, vinyl faced, 1-9/16" thick			40	.400	L.F.
	3200	Enameled, 2-3/4" thick			30	.533	L.F.
	3400	Metal, to 9'-6" high, enameled steel, no glass			40	.400	L.F.
	3500	Steel frame, all glass			40	.400	L.F.
	3700	Vinyl covered, no glass			40	.400	L.F.
	3800	Steel frame with 52% glass			40	.400	L.F.
	4000	Free standing, 4'-6" high, steel with glass			100	.160	L.F.
	4100	Acoustical			100	.160	L.F.
	4300	Low rails, 3'-3" high, enameled steel			100	.160	L.F.
	4400	Vinyl covered			100	.160	L.F.
	4600	Plywood, prefin., 1-3/4" thick, rotary cut veneers, minimum			80	.200	L.F.
	4700	Maximum			80	.200	L.F.
	4900	Sliced veneers, book matched, minimum			80	.200	L.F.
	5000	Maximum			80	.200	L.F.
	5200	Sliced veneers, random matched, minimum			80	.200	L.F.
	5300	Maximum			80	.200	L.F.
	5310	Trackless wall, cork finish, semi-acoustic, 1-5/8" thick, minimum			325	.049	S.F.
	5320	Maximum			190	.084	S.F.
	5330	Acoustic, 2" thick, minimum			305	.052	S.F.
	5340	Maximum			225	.071	S.F.
	5700	For doors, not incl. hardware, hollow metal door, add			4.30	3.720	Ea.
	5800	Hardwood door, add			3.40	4.710	Ea.
	6000	Hardware for doors, not incl. closers, keyed			29	.552	Ea.
	6100	Non-keyed	↓	↓	29	.552	Ea.

106 300 | Portable Partitions

	Description	CREW	MAKEUP	DAILY OUTPUT	MAN-HOURS	UNIT
302	PARTITIONS, HOSPITAL Curtain track, box channel, ceiling mounted	1 Carp	1 Carpenter	135	.059	L.F.
0100	Suspended	"	"	100	.080	L.F.
0300	Curtains, 8' to 9', nylon mesh tops, fire resistant					
0310	Cotton, 2.85 lbs. per S.Y.	1 Carp	1 Carpenter	425	.019	L.F.
0500	Anti-bacterial, thermoplastic			425	.019	L.F.
0700	Fiberglass, 7 oz. per S.Y.	↓	↓	425	.019	L.F.
0800	I.V. track systems					
0820	I.V. track, 4'-0" x 7'-0" oval	1 Carp	1 Carpenter	135	.059	L.F.
0830	I.V. trolley			32	.250	Ea.
0840	I.V. pendent, (tree, 5 hook)	↓	↓	32	.250	Ea.
304	PARTITIONS, PORTABLE Divider walls, free standing, fiber core					
0020	Panels, 5' long, 4'-6" high					
0100	Burlap face, straight	2 Carp	2 Carpenters	160	.100	L.F.
0200	Curved			158	.101	L.F.
0500	Carpeted face, straight			160	.100	L.F.
0600	Curved			158	.101	L.F.
0900	Plastic laminated face, straight			160	.100	L.F.
1000	Curved			158	.101	L.F.
1500	5' high, burlap face, straight			150	.107	L.F.
1600	Curved			148	.108	L.F.
1800	Carpeted face, straight			150	.107	L.F.
1900	Curved			148	.108	L.F.
2200	Plastic laminated face, straight			150	.107	L.F.
2300	Curved			148	.108	L.F.
2600	6' high, burlap face, straight			125	.128	L.F.
2700	Curved			120	.133	L.F.
3000	Carpeted face, straight			125	.128	L.F.
3100	Curved			120	.133	L.F.
3400	Plastic laminated face, straight			125	.128	L.F.
3500	Curved	↓	↓	120	.133	L.F.

106 | Partitions and Storage Shelving

106 300 | Portable Partitions

		CREW	MAKEUP	DAILY OUTPUT	MAN-HOURS	UNIT
304	4001	Partitions, metal chalkboard, 6'-6" high, chalkboard 1 side	2 Carp	2 Carpenters	125	.128	L.F.
	4100	Metal chalkboard, 2 sides			120	.133	L.F.
	4200	Hardboard chalkboard, 1 side			125	.128	L.F.
	4300	Tackboard, both sides	↓	↓	123	.130	L.F.
	306	PARTITIONS, WORK STATIONS Incl. top cabinet & desk top					
	0200	Multi-station units, 1 to 3 person seating capacity					
	0250	Minimum per person	1 Carp	1 Carpenter	6	1.330	Ea.
	0260	Average per person			5	1.600	Ea.
	0270	Maximum per person	↓	↓	4	2.000	Ea.
	0280	4 to 6 person seating capacity					
	0290	Minimum per person	1 Carp	1 Carpenter	4	2.000	Ea.
	0300	Average per person			3	2.670	Ea.
	0320	Maximum per person	↓	↓	2	4.000	Ea.

106 520 | Panel Partitions

		CREW	MAKEUP	DAILY OUTPUT	MAN-HOURS	UNIT
522	PARTITIONS, FOLDING LEAF Acoustic, wood					
0100	Vinyl faced, to 18' high, 6 psf, minimum	2 Carp	2 Carpenters	60	.267	S.F.
0150	Average			45	.356	S.F.
0200	Maximum			30	.533	S.F.
0400	Formica or hardwood finish, minimum			60	.267	S.F.
0500	Maximum			30	.533	S.F.
0600	Wood, low acoustical type, 4.5 psf, to 14' high			50	.320	S.F.
1100	Steel, acoustical, 9 to 12 lb. per S.F., vinyl faced, minimum			60	.267	S.F.
1200	Maximum			30	.533	S.F.
1700	Aluminum framed, acoustical, to 12' high, 5.5 psf, minimum			60	.267	S.F.
1800	Maximum			30	.533	S.F.
2000	6.5 lb. per S.F., minimum			60	.267	S.F.
2100	Maximum			30	.533	S.F.
524	PARTITIONS, OPERABLE Acoustic air wall, 1-5/8" thick, minimum			375	.043	S.F.
0100	Maximum			365	.044	S.F.
0300	2-1/4" thick, minimum			360	.044	S.F.
0400	Maximum			330	.048	S.F.
0700	Overhead track type, acoustical, 3" thick, 11 psf, minimum			350	.046	S.F.
0800	Maximum	↓	↓	300	.053	S.F.

106 550 | Accordian Partitions

		CREW	MAKEUP	DAILY OUTPUT	MAN-HOURS	UNIT
552	PARTITIONS, FOLDING ACCORDION					
0100	Vinyl covered, over 150 S.F., frame not included					
0300	Residential, 1.25 lb. per S.F., 8' maximum height	2 Carp	2 Carpenters	300	.053	S.F.
0400	Commercial, 1.75 lb. per S.F., 8' maximum height			225	.071	S.F.
0600	2 lb. per S.F., 17' maximum height			150	.107	S.F.
0700	Industrial, 4 lb. per S.F., 27' maximum height			75	.213	S.F.
0900	Acoustical, 3 lb. per S.F., 17' maximum height			100	.160	S.F.
1200	5 lb. per S.F., 27' maximum height			95	.168	S.F.
1300	5.5 lb. per S.F., 17' maximum height			90	.178	S.F.
1400	Fire rated, 4.5 psf, 20' maximum height			160	.100	S.F.
1500	Vinyl clad wood or steel, electric operation, 5.0 psf			160	.100	S.F.
1900	Wood, non-acoustic, birch or mahogany, to 10' high	↓	↓	300	.053	S.F.

106 750 | Storage & Shelving

		CREW	MAKEUP	DAILY OUTPUT	MAN-HOURS	UNIT
752	PARTS BINS Metal, gray baked enamel finish					
0100	6'-3" high, 3' wide					
0300	12 bins, 18" wide x 12" high, 12" deep	2 Clab	2 Building Laborers	10	1.600	Ea.
0400	24" deep			10	1.600	Ea.
0600	72 bins, 6" wide x 6" high, 12" deep			8	2.000	Ea.
0700	24" deep	↓	↓	8	2.000	Ea.
1000	7'-3" high, 3' wide					
1200	14 bins, 18" wide x 12" high, 12" deep	2 Clab	2 Building Laborers	10	1.600	Ea.

106 | Partitions and Storage Shelving

106 750 | Storage & Shelving

		Description	CREW	MAKEUP	DAILY OUTPUT	MAN-HOURS	UNIT
752	1301	Parts bins, 7'-3" high, 14 bins, 18" wide x 12" high x 24" deep	2 Clab	2 Building Laborers	10	1.600	Ea.
	1500	84 bins, 6" wide x 6" high, 12" deep			8	2.000	Ea.
	1600	24" deep	↓	↓	8	2.000	Ea.
	754	SHELVING Metal, industrial, cross-braced, 3' wide, 12" deep	1 Sswk	1 Struc. Steel Worker	175	.046	SF Shlf
	0100	24" deep			330	.024	SF Shlf
	0300	4' wide, 12" deep			185	.043	SF Shlf
	0400	24" deep			380	.021	SF Shlf
	1200	Enclosed sides, cross-braced back, 3' wide, 12" deep			175	.046	SF Shlf
	1300	24" deep			290	.028	SF Shlf
	1500	Fully enclosed, sides and back, 3' wide, 12" deep			150	.053	SF Shlf
	1600	24" deep			255	.031	SF Shlf
	1800	4' wide, 12" deep			150	.053	SF Shlf
	1900	24" deep			290	.028	SF Shlf
	2200	Wide span, 1600 lb. capacity per shelf, 7' wide, 24" deep			380	.021	SF Shlf
	2400	36" deep			440	.018	SF Shlf
	2600	8' wide, 24" deep			440	.018	SF Shlf
	2800	36" deep	↓	↓	520	.015	SF Shlf
	4000	Pallet racks, steel frame 2500 lb. capacity, 7' long, 30" deep	2 Sswk	2 Struc. Steel Workers	450	.036	SF Shlf
	4200	36" deep			500	.032	SF Shlf
	4400	42" deep	↓	↓	520	.031	SF Shlf

107 | Telephone Specialties

107 550 | Telephone Enclosures

	Description	CREW	MAKEUP	DAILY OUTPUT	MAN-HOURS	UNIT
551	TELEPHONE ENCLOSURE Desk-top type	2 Carp	2 Carpenters	8	2.000	Ea.
0300	Shelf type, wall hung, minimum			5	3.200	Ea.
0400	Maximum			5	3.200	Ea.
0600	Booth type, painted steel, indoor or outdoor, minimum			1.50	10.670	Ea.
0700	Maximum (stainless steel)			1.50	10.670	Ea.
1300	Outdoor, acoustical, on post			3	5.330	Ea.
1400	Phone carousel, pedestal mounted with dividers			.60	26.670	Ea.
1900	Outdoor, drive-up type, wall mounted			4	4.000	Ea.
2000	Post mounted, stainless steel posts	↓	↓	3	5.330	Ea.
2200	Directory shelf, wall mounted, stainless steel					
2300	3 binders	2 Carp	2 Carpenters	8	2.000	Ea.
2500	4 binders			7	2.290	Ea.
2600	7 binders			6	2.670	Ea.
2800	Table type, stainless steel, 4 binders			8	2.000	Ea.
2900	7 binders	↓	↓	7	2.290	Ea.

108 200	Bath Accessories	CREW	MAKEUP	DAILY OUTPUT	MAN-HOURS	UNIT
204	**BATHROOM ACCESSORIES**					
0200	Curtain rod, stainless steel, 5' long, 1" diameter	1 Carp	1 Carpenter	13	.615	Ea.
0300	1-1/4" diameter	"	"	13	.615	Ea.
0500	Dispenser units, combined soap & towel dispensers,					
0510	mirror and shelf, flush mounted	1 Carp	1 Carpenter	10	.800	Ea.
0600	Towel dispenser and waste receptacle,					
0610	flush mounted	1 Carp	1 Carpenter	10	.800	Ea.
0800	Grab bar, straight, 1" diameter, stainless steel, 12" long			24	.333	Ea.
0900	18" long			23	.348	Ea.
1000	24" long			22	.364	Ea.
1100	36" long			20	.400	Ea.
1200	1-1/2" diameter, 18" long			23	.348	Ea.
1300	36" long			20	.400	Ea.
1500	Tub bar, 1" diameter, horizontal			14	.571	Ea.
1600	Plus vertical arm			12	.667	Ea.
1900	End tub bar, 1" diameter, 90° angle			12	.667	Ea.
2300	Hand dryer, surface mounted, electric, 110 volt			4	2.000	Ea.
2400	220 volt			4	2.000	Ea.
2600	Hat and coat strip, stainless steel, 4 hook, 36" long			24	.333	Ea.
2700	6 hook, 60" long			20	.400	Ea.
3000	Mirror with stainless steel, 3/4" square frame, 18" x 24"			20	.400	Ea.
3100	36" x 24"			15	.533	Ea.
3200	48" x 24"			10	.800	Ea.
3300	72" x 24"			6	1.330	Ea.
3500	Mirror with 5" stainless steel shelf, 3/4" sq. frame, 18" x 24"			20	.400	Ea.
3600	36" x 24"			15	.533	Ea.
3700	48" x 24"			10	.800	Ea.
3800	72" x 24"			6	1.330	Ea.
4100	Mop holder strip, stainless steel, 6 holders, 60" long			20	.400	Ea.
4200	Napkin/tampon dispenser, surface mounted			15	.533	Ea.
4300	Robe hook, single, regular			36	.222	Ea.
4400	Heavy duty, concealed mounting			36	.222	Ea.
4600	Soap dispenser, chrome, surface mounted, liquid			20	.400	Ea.
4700	Powder			20	.400	Ea.
5000	Recessed stainless steel, liquid			10	.800	Ea.
5100	Powder			10	.800	Ea.
5300	Soap tank, stainless steel, 1 gallon			10	.800	Ea.
5400	5 gallon			5	1.600	Ea.
5600	Shelf, stainless steel, 5" wide, 18 ga., 24" long			24	.333	Ea.
5700	72" long			16	.500	Ea.
5800	8" wide shelf, 18 ga., 24" long			22	.364	Ea.
5900	72" long			14	.571	Ea.
6000	Toilet seat cover dispenser, stainless steel, recessed			20	.400	Ea.
6050	Surface mounted			15	.533	Ea.
6100	Toilet tissue dispenser, surface mounted, S.S., single roll			30	.267	Ea.
6200	Double roll			24	.333	Ea.
6400	Towel bar, stainless steel, 18" long			23	.348	Ea.
6500	30" long			21	.381	Ea.
6700	Towel dispenser, stainless steel, surface mounted			16	.500	Ea.
6800	Flush mounted, recessed			10	.800	Ea.
7000	Towel holder, hotel type, 2 guest size			20	.400	Ea.
7200	Towel shelf, stainless steel, 24" long, 8" wide			20	.400	Ea.
7400	Tumbler holder, tumbler only			30	.267	Ea.
7500	Soap, tumbler & toothbrush			30	.267	Ea.
7700	Wall urn ash receiver, recessed, 14" long			12	.667	Ea.
7800	Surface, 8" long			18	.444	Ea.
8000	Waste receptacles, stainless steel, with top, 13 gallon			10	.800	Ea.
8100	36 gallon	▼	▼	8	1.000	Ea.

108 | Toilet and Bath Accessories and Scales

108 200 | Bath Accessories

		CREW	MAKEUP	DAILY OUTPUT	MAN-HOURS	UNIT
208	MEDICINE CABINETS With mirror, stock, 16" x 22", unlighted	1 Carp	1 Carpenter	14	.571	Ea.
0100	Lighted			6	1.330	Ea.
0300	Sliding mirror doors, 36" x 22", unlighted			7	1.140	Ea.
0400	Lighted			5	1.600	Ea.
0600	Center mirror, 2 end cabinets, unlighted, 48" long			7	1.140	Ea.
0700	72" long	▼	▼	5	1.600	Ea.
0900	For lighting, 48" long, add	1 Elec	1 Electrician	3.50	2.290	Ea.
1000	72" long, add	"	"	3	2.670	Ea.
1200	Hotel cabinets, stainless, with lower shelf, unlighted	1 Carp	1 Carpenter	10	.800	Ea.
1300	Lighted	"	"	5	1.600	Ea.

108 800 | Scales

		CREW	MAKEUP	DAILY OUTPUT	MAN-HOURS	UNIT
801	SCALES Built-in floor scale, not incl. foundations					
0100	Dial type, 5 ton capacity, 8' x 6' platform	3 Carp	3 Carpenters	.50	48.000	Ea.
0300	9' x 7' platform			.40	60.000	Ea.
0400	10 ton capacity, steel platform, 8' x 6' platform			.40	60.000	Ea.
0600	9' x 7' platform	▼	▼	.35	68.570	Ea.
0700	Truck scales, incl. steel weigh bridge,					
0800	not including foundations					
0900	Dial type, mech., 24' x 10' platform, 20 ton cap.	3 Carp	3 Carpenters	.30	80.000	Ea.
1000	30 ton capacity			.20	120.000	Ea.
1100	50 ton capacity, 50' x 10' platform			.14	171.000	Ea.
1200	70' x 10' platform			.12	200.000	Ea.
1400	60 ton capacity, 60' x 10' platform			.13	185.000	Ea.
1500	70' x 10' platform			.10	240.000	Ea.
1550	Digital, electronic, 30 ton capacity, 12' x 10' platform			.20	120.000	Ea.
1600	50 ton capacity, 40' x 10' platform			.14	171.000	Ea.
1640	60 ton capacity, 60' x 10' platform			.13	185.000	Ea.
1680	75' x 10' platform	▼	▼	.12	200.000	Ea.
2300	Concrete foundation pits for above, 8' x 6', 5 C.Y. required	C-1	3 Carpenters 1 Building Laborer Power Tools	.50	64.000	Ea.
2400	14' x 6' platform, 10 C.Y. required			.35	91.430	Ea.
2600	50' x 10' platform, 30 C.Y. required			.25	128.000	Ea.
2700	70' x 10' platform, 40 C.Y. required	▼	▼	.15	213.000	Ea.
2900	Low profile electronic warehouse scale,					
3000	not incl. printer, 4' x 6' platform, 6000 lb. capacity	2 Carp	2 Carpenters	.30	53.330	Ea.
3300	5' x 7' platform, 10,000 lb. capacity			.25	64.000	Ea.
3400	20,000 lb. capacity	▼	▼	.20	80.000	Ea.

109 | Wardrobe and Closet Specialties

109 010 | Coat Racks/Wardrobes

		CREW	MAKEUP	DAILY OUTPUT	MAN-HOURS	UNIT
011	COAT RACKS & WARDROBES Dormitory units, wood or metal					
0020	Stock units, 84" high, incl. door, minimum	1 Carp	1 Carpenter	10	.800	L.F.
0050	Average			7	1.140	L.F.
0100	Maximum			5	1.600	L.F.
0500	Hospital type, 84" high, plastic faced wood			5	1.600	L.F.
0650	Enameled steel			5	1.600	L.F.
0800	Stainless steel			5	1.600	L.F.
1500	Coat and hat rack, wall mounted, tubular steel, 1 shelf			70	.114	L.F.
1650	3 shelves	▼	▼	50	.160	L.F.

DIVISION 11 EQUIPMENT

DIVISION 11 EQUIPMENT

The Architectural Equipment Division contains productivity rates for the installation of various equipment commonly found in buildings. Examples include service windows for banks, dock levelers for warehouses, and scoreboards for gymnasiums.

As a general rule, the equipment in this division is installed by the vendor as part of the purchase agreement. The installers are frequently specially trained for their task. The productivity rates in this division are based on the experiences of properly trained craftsmen, but not necessarily specialists, working in a reasonable comfortable environment without unnecessary space confinements. In actual practice, the expected productivity should be adjusted to make allowances for either unusual productivity enhancing or restricting conditions.

The rates in this division represent new construction. For repair and remodeling work, substantial adjustments may be necessary to properly account for the unique nature of each project.

110 | Equipment

110 100 | Maintenance Equipment

		CREW	MAKEUP	DAILY OUTPUT	MAN-HOURS	UNIT
121	**VACUUM CLEANING** Central, 3 inlet, residential	1 Skwk	1 Skilled Worker	.90	8.890	Total
0200	Commercial			.70	11.430	Total
0400	5 inlet system, residential			.50	16.000	Total
0600	7 inlet system			.40	20.000	Total
0800	9 inlet system	↓	↓	.30	26.670	Total

110 300 | Teller And Service Equipment

		CREW	MAKEUP	DAILY OUTPUT	MAN-HOURS	UNIT
301	**BANK EQUIPMENT** Alarm system, police	2 Elec	2 Electricians	1.60	10.000	Ea.
0100	With vault alarm	"	"	.40	40.000	Ea.
0400	Bullet resistant teller window, 44" x 60"	1 Glaz	1 Glazier	.60	13.330	Ea.
0500	48" x 60"	"	"	.60	13.330	Ea.
3000	Counters for banks, frontal only	2 Carp	2 Carpenters	1	16.000	Station
3100	Complete with steel undercounter	"	"	.50	32.000	Station
4600	Door and frame, bullet-resistant, with vision panel, minimum	2 Sswk	2 Struc. Steel Workers	1.10	14.550	Ea.
4700	Maximum			1.10	14.550	Ea.
4800	Drive-up window, drawer & mike, not incl. glass, minimum			1	16.000	Ea.
4900	Maximum			.50	32.000	Ea.
5000	Night depository, with chest, minimum			1	16.000	Ea.
5100	Maximum			.50	32.000	Ea.
5200	Package receiver, painted			3.20	5.000	Ea.
5300	Stainless steel	↓	↓	3.20	5.000	Ea.
5400	Partitions, bullet-resistant, 1-3/16" glass, 8' high	2 Carp	2 Carpenters	10	1.600	L.F.
5450	Acrylic	"	"	10	1.600	L.F.
5500	Pneumatic tube systems, 2 lane drive-up, complete	L-3	1 Carpenter .5 Electrician .5 Sheet Metal Worker	.25	64.000	Total
5550	With T.V. viewer	"	"	.20	80.000	Total
5570	Safety deposit boxes, minimum	1 Sswk	1 Struc. Steel Worker	44	.182	Opng.
5580	Maximum, 10" x 15" opening			19	.421	Opng.
5590	Teller locker, average	↓	↓	15	.533	Opng.
5600	Pass thru, bullet-resist. window, painted steel, 24" x 36"	2 Sswk	2 Struc. Steel Workers	1.60	10.000	Ea.
5700	48" x 48"			1.20	13.330	Ea.
5800	72" x 40"	↓	↓	.80	20.000	Ea.
6000	Surveillance system, 16mm film camera, complete	2 Elec	2 Electricians	1	16.000	Ea.
6100	Surveillance system, video camera, complete	"	"	1	16.000	Ea.
6200	Twenty-four hour teller, single unit,					
6300	automated deposit, cash and memo	L-3	1 Carpenter .5 Electrician .5 Sheet Metal Worker	.25	64.000	Ea.

110 400 | Ecclesiastical Equipment

		CREW	MAKEUP	DAILY OUTPUT	MAN-HOURS	UNIT
401	**CHURCH EQUIPMENT** Altar, wood, custom design, plain	1 Carp	1 Carpenter	1.40	5.710	Ea.
0050	Deluxe	"	"	.20	40.000	Ea.
0070	Granite or marble, average	2 Marb	2 Marble Setters	.50	32.000	Ea.
0090	Deluxe	"	"	.20	80.000	Ea.
0100	Arks, prefabricated, plain	2 Carp	2 Carpenters	.80	20.000	Ea.
0130	Deluxe, maximum	"	"	.20	80.000	Ea.
0150	Baptistry, fiberglass, 3'-6" deep, x 13'-7" long,					
0160	steps at both ends, incl. plumbing, minimum	L-8	2 Carpenters .5 Plumber	1	20.000	Ea.
0200	Maximum	"	"	.70	28.570	Ea.
0500	Confessional, wood, prefabricated, single, plain	1 Carp	1 Carpenter	.60	13.330	Ea.
0550	Deluxe			.40	20.000	Ea.
0650	Double, plain			.40	20.000	Ea.
0700	Deluxe			.20	40.000	Ea.
1000	Lecterns, wood, plain			5	1.600	Ea.
1100	Deluxe			2	4.000	Ea.
1500	Pews, bench type, hardwood, minimum	↓	↓	20	.400	L.F.

110 400 | Ecclesiastical Equipment

		CREW	MAKEUP	DAILY OUTPUT	MAN-HOURS	UNIT
401 1551	Church equipment, pews, bench type, hardwood, maximum	1 Carp	1 Carpenter	15	.533	L.F.
2000	Pulpits, hardwood, prefabricated, plain			2	4.000	Ea.
2100	Deluxe			1.60	5.000	Ea.
2500	Railing, hardwood, average			25	.320	L.F.
3000	Seating, individual, oak, contour, laminated			21	.381	Person
3100	Cushion seat			21	.381	Person
3200	Fully upholstered			21	.381	Person
3300	Combination, self-rising	▼	▼	21	.381	Person
4000	Steeples, translucent fiberglass, 30" square, 15' high	F-3	4 Carpenters 1 Equip. Oper. (crane) 1 Hyd. Crane, 12 Ton Power Tools	2	20.000	Ea.
4150	25' high			1.80	22.220	Ea.
4350	Painted fiberglass, 24" square, 14' high			2	20.000	Ea.
4500	28' high			1.80	22.220	Ea.
4700	Porcelain enamel steeples, custom, 40' high			.50	80.000	Ea.
4800	60' high	▼	▼	.30	133.000	Ea.
5000	Wall cross, aluminum, extruded, 2" x 2" section	1 Carp	1 Carpenter	34	.235	L.F.
5150	4" x 4" section			29	.276	L.F.
5300	Bronze, extruded, 1" x 2" section			31	.258	L.F.
5350	2-1/2" x 2-1/2" section			34	.235	L.F.
5450	Solid bar stock, 1/2" x 3" section			29	.276	L.F.
5600	Fiberglass, stock			34	.235	L.F.
5700	Stainless steel, 4" deep, channel section			29	.276	L.F.
5800	4" deep box section	▼	▼	29	.276	L.F.

110 500 | Library Equipment

		CREW	MAKEUP	DAILY OUTPUT	MAN-HOURS	UNIT
501	**LIBRARY EQUIPMENT** Bookshelf, mtl, 90" high, 10" shelf, dbl face	1 Carp	1 Carpenter	12	.667	L.F.
0300	Single face			12	.667	L.F.
2500	Carrels, hardwood, 36" x 24", minimum			5	1.600	Ea.
2650	Maximum			4	2.000	Ea.
3500	Charging desk, built-in, with counter, plastic laminated top	▼	▼	7	1.140	L.F.

110 600 | Theater/Stage Equipment

		CREW	MAKEUP	DAILY OUTPUT	MAN-HOURS	UNIT
601	**STAGE EQUIPMENT** Control boards with dimmers & breakers					
0050	Minimum	1 Elec	1 Electrician	1	8.000	Ea.
0100	Average			.50	16.000	Ea.
0150	Maximum	▼	▼	.20	40.000	Ea.
0500	Curtain track, straight, light duty	2 Carp	2 Carpenters	20	.800	L.F.
0600	Heavy duty			18	.889	L.F.
0700	Curved sections			12	1.330	L.F.
1000	Curtains, velour, medium weight			600	.027	S.F.
1100	Asbestos			50	.320	S.F.
1150	Silica based yarn, fireproof	▼	▼	50	.320	S.F.
2000	Lights, border, quartz, reflector, vented,					
2100	colored or white	1 Elec	1 Electrician	20	.400	L.F.
2500	Spotlight, follow spot, with transformer, 2100 watt			4	2.000	Ea.
3000	Stationary spot, fresnel quartz, 6" lens			4	2.000	Ea.
3100	8" lens			4	2.000	Ea.
3500	Ellipsoidal quartz, 1000W, 6" lens			4	2.000	Ea.
3600	12" lens			4	2.000	Ea.
4000	Strobe light, 1 to 15 flashes per second, quartz			3	2.670	Ea.
4500	Color wheel, portable, five hole, motorized	▼	▼	4	2.000	Ea.
6000	Telescoping platforms, extruded alum., straight, minimum	4 Carp	4 Carpenters	157	.204	SF Stg.
6100	Maximum			77	.416	SF Stg.
6500	Pie-shaped, minimum			150	.213	SF Stg.
6600	Maximum			70	.457	SF Stg.
7000	Band risers, steel frame, plywood deck, minimum	▼	▼	275	.116	SF Stg.

110 | Equipment

110 600 | Theater/Stage Equipment

		CREW	MAKEUP	DAILY OUTPUT	MAN-HOURS	UNIT
601 7101	Stage equip., band risers, steel frame, plywood deck, maximum	4 Carp	4 Carpenters	138	.232	SF Stg.
7500	Chairs for above, self-storing, minimum	2 Carp	2 Carpenters	43	.372	Ea.
7600	Maximum	"	"	40	.400	Ea.
8000	Rule of thumb: total stage equipment, minimum	4 Carp	4 Carpenters	100	.320	SF Stg.
8100	Maximum	"	"	25	1.280	SF Stg.
604	**MOVIE EQUIPMENT**					
0800	Lamphouses, incl. rectifiers, xenon, 1000 watt	1 Elec	1 Electrician	2	4.000	Ea.
0900	1600 watt			2	4.000	Ea.
1000	2000 watt			1.50	5.330	Ea.
1100	4000 watt	↓	↓	1.50	5.330	Ea.
3000	Projection screens, rigid, in wall, acrylic, 1/4" thick	2 Glaz	2 Glaziers	195	.082	S.F.
3100	1/2" thick	"	"	130	.123	S.F.
3300	Electric operated, heavy duty, 400 S.F.	2 Carp	2 Carpenters	1	16.000	Ea.
3700	Sound systems, incl. amplifier, single system, minimum	1 Elec	1 Electrician	.90	8.890	Ea.
3800	Dolby/Super Sound, maximum			.40	20.000	Ea.
4100	Dual system, minimum			.70	11.430	Ea.
4200	Dolby/Super Sound, maximum			.40	20.000	Ea.
5300	Speakers, recessed behind screen, minimum			2	4.000	Ea.
5400	Maximum	↓	↓	1	8.000	Ea.
5700	Seating, painted steel, upholstered, minimum	2 Carp	2 Carpenters	35	.457	Ea.
5800	Maximum	"	"	28	.571	Ea.

111 | Mercantile, Commercial and Detention Equipment

111 020 | Barber Shop Equipment

		CREW	MAKEUP	DAILY OUTPUT	MAN-HOURS	UNIT
021	**BARBER EQUIPMENT** Chair, hydraulic, movable, minimum	1 Carp	1 Carpenter	24	.333	Ea.
0050	Maximum	"	"	16	.500	Ea.
0200	Wall hung styling station with mirrors, minimum	L-2	1 Carpenter 1 Helper	8	2.000	Ea.
0300	Maximum	"	"	4	4.000	Ea.
0500	Sink, hair washing basin, rough plumbing not incl.	1 Plum	1 Plumber	8	1.000	Ea.
1100	Total equipment, rule of thumb, per chair, minimum	L-8	2 Carpenters .5 Plumber	1	20.000	Ea.
1150	Maximum	"	"	1	20.000	Ea.

111 040 | Cash Register/Checking

		CREW	MAKEUP	DAILY OUTPUT	MAN-HOURS	UNIT
041	**CHECKOUT COUNTER** Supermarket conveyor, single belt	2 Clab	2 Building Laborers	10	1.600	Ea.
0100	Double belt			9	1.780	Ea.
0400	Power take-away			7	2.290	Ea.
0800	Warehouse or bulk type	↓	↓	6	2.670	Ea.

111 060 | Display Cases

		CREW	MAKEUP	DAILY OUTPUT	MAN-HOURS	UNIT
061	**REFRIGERATED FOOD CASES** Dairy, multi-deck, 12' long	Q-5	1 Steamfitter 1 Steamfitter Apprentice	3	5.330	Ea.
0200	Delicatessen case, service deli, 12' long, single deck			3.90	4.100	Ea.
0300	Multi-deck, 18 S.F. shelf display			3	5.330	Ea.
0400	Freezer, self-contained, chest-type, 30 C.F.			3.90	4.100	Ea.
0500	Glass door, upright, 78 C.F.			3.30	4.850	Ea.
0600	Frozen food, chest type, 12' long			3.30	4.850	Ea.
0700	Glass door, reach-in, 5 door			3	5.330	Ea.
0800	Island case, 12' long, single deck			3.30	4.850	Ea.
0900	Multi-deck	↓	↓	3	5.330	Ea.

111 | Mercantile, Commercial and Detention Equipment

111 060 | Display Cases

		Description	CREW	MAKEUP	DAILY OUTPUT	MAN-HOURS	UNIT
061	1000	Meat case, 12' long, single deck	Q-5	1 Steamfitter 1 Steamfitter Apprentice	3.30	4.850	Ea.
	1050	Multi-deck			3.10	5.160	Ea.
	1100	Produce, 12' long, single deck			3.30	4.850	Ea.
	1200	Multi-deck	↓	↓	3.10	5.160	Ea.

111 100 | Laundry/Dry Cleaning

		Description	CREW	MAKEUP	DAILY OUTPUT	MAN-HOURS	UNIT
101		LAUNDRY EQUIPMENT Not incl. rough-in.					
	0500	Residential, 16 lb. capacity, average	1 Plum	1 Plumber	3	2.670	Ea.
	1000	Commercial, 30 lb. capacity, coin operated, single			3	2.670	Ea.
	1100	Double stacked			2	4.000	Ea.
	1500	Industrial, 30 lb. capacity			2	4.000	Ea.
	1600	50 lb. capacity	↓	↓	1.70	4.710	Ea.
	2000	Dry cleaners, electric, 20 lb. capacity	L-1	1 Electrician 1 Plumber	.20	80.000	Ea.
	2050	25 lb. capacity			.17	94.120	Ea.
	2100	30 lb. capacity			.15	107.000	Ea.
	2150	60 lb. capacity	↓	↓	.09	178.000	Ea.
	3500	Folders, blankets & sheets, minimum	1 Elec	1 Electrician	.17	47.060	Ea.
	3700	King size with automatic stacker			.10	80.000	Ea.
	3800	For conveyor delivery, add			.45	17.780	Ea.
	4500	Ironers, institutional, 110", single roll	↓	↓	.20	40.000	Ea.
	4700	Lint collector, ductwork not included, 8,000 to 10,000 C.F.M.	Q-10	2 Sheet Metal Workers 1 Sheet Metal Apprentice	.30	80.000	Ea.
	5000	Washers, residential, 4 cycle, average	1 Plum	1 Plumber	3	2.670	Ea.
	5300	Commercial, coin operated, average	"	"	3	2.670	Ea.
	6000	Combination washer/extractor, 20 lb. capacity	L-6	1 Plumber .5 Electrician	1.50	8.000	Ea.
	6100	30 lb. capacity			.80	15.000	Ea.
	6200	50 lb. capacity			.68	17.650	Ea.
	6300	75 lb. capacity			.30	40.000	Ea.
	6350	125 lb. capacity	↓	↓	.16	75.000	Ea.

111 320 | Projection Screens

		Description	CREW	MAKEUP	DAILY OUTPUT	MAN-HOURS	UNIT
321		PROJECTION SCREENS Wall or ceiling hung, glass beaded					
	0100	Manually operated, economy	2 Carp	2 Carpenters	500	.032	S.F.
	0300	Intermediate			450	.036	S.F.
	0400	Deluxe			400	.040	S.F.
	0600	Electric operated, glass beaded, 25 S.F., economy			5	3.200	Ea.
	0700	Deluxe			4	4.000	Ea.
	0900	50 S.F., economy			3	5.330	Ea.
	1000	Deluxe			2	8.000	Ea.
	1200	Heavy duty, electric operated, 200 S.F.			1.50	10.670	Ea.
	1300	400 S.F.	↓	↓	1	16.000	Ea.
	1500	Rigid acrylic in wall, for rear projection, 1/4" thick	2 Glaz	2 Glaziers	195	.082	S.F.
	1600	1/2" thick (maximum size 10' x 20')	"	"	130	.123	S.F.

111 400 | Service Station Equipment

		Description	CREW	MAKEUP	DAILY OUTPUT	MAN-HOURS	UNIT
401		AUTOMOTIVE Compressors, electric, 1-1/2 H.P., standard controls	L-4	2 Skilled Workers 1 Helper	1.50	16.000	Ea.
	0550	Dual controls			1.50	16.000	Ea.
	0600	5 H.P., 115/230 volt, standard controls			1	24.000	Ea.
	0650	Dual controls			1	24.000	Ea.
	1000	Gasoline pumps, conventional, lighted, single			2.50	9.600	Ea.
	1010	Double			2	12.000	Ea.
	2200	Hoists, single post, 8000# capacity, swivel arms			.40	60.000	Ea.
	2400	Two posts, adjustable frames, 11,000# capacity			.25	96.000	Ea.
	2500	24,000# capacity	↓	↓	.15	160.000	Ea.

111 | Mercantile, Commercial and Detention Equipment

111 400 | Service Station Equipment

		CREW	MAKEUP	DAILY OUTPUT	MAN-HOURS	UNIT
401	2701	Automotive hoists, 7500# capacity, frame supports	L-4	2 Skilled Workers 1 Helper	.50	48.000	Ea.
2800	Four post, roll on ramp			.50	48.000	Ea.
3000	Lube equipment, 3 reel type, with pumps, not including piping			.50	48.000	Set
4000	Spray painting booth, 26' long, complete	↓	↓	.40	60.000	Ea.

111 500 | Parking Control Equipment

		CREW	MAKEUP	DAILY OUTPUT	MAN-HOURS	UNIT
501	PARKING EQUIPMENT Traffic, detectors, magnetic	2 Elec	2 Electricians	2.70	5.930	Ea.
0200	Single treadle			2.40	6.670	Ea.
0500	Automatic gates, 8' arm, one way			1.10	14.550	Ea.
0650	Two way			1.10	14.550	Ea.
1400	Fee indicator, 1" display			4.10	3.900	Ea.
3500	Ticket printer and dispenser, standard			1.40	11.430	Ea.
3700	Rate computing			1.40	11.430	Ea.
4000	Card control station, single period			4.10	3.900	Ea.
4200	4 period			4.10	3.900	Ea.
4500	Key station on pedestal			4.10	3.900	Ea.
4750	Coin station, multiple coins	↓	↓	4.10	3.900	Ea.

111 600 | Loading Dock Equipment

		CREW	MAKEUP	DAILY OUTPUT	MAN-HOURS	UNIT
601	LOADING DOCK Bumpers, rubber blocks 4-1/2" thk, 10" hg, 14" lg	1 Carp	1 Carpenter	26	.308	Ea.
0200	24" long			22	.364	Ea.
0300	36" long			17	.471	Ea.
0500	12" high, 14" long			25	.320	Ea.
0550	24" long			20	.400	Ea.
0600	36" long			15	.533	Ea.
0800	Rubber blocks 6" thick, 10" high, 14" long			22	.364	Ea.
0850	24" long			18	.444	Ea.
0900	36" long			13	.615	Ea.
0910	20" high, 11" long			13	.615	Ea.
0920	Extruded rubber bumpers, T section, 22" x 22" x 3" thick			41	.195	Ea.
0940	Molded rubber bumpers, 24" x 12" x 3" thick	↓	↓	20	.400	Ea.
1000	Welded installation of above bumpers	E-14	1 Welder Foreman 1 Gas Welding Machine	8	1.000	Ea.
1100	For drilled anchors, add per anchor	1 Carp	1 Carpenter	36	.222	Ea.
3600	Door seal for door perimeter, 12" x 12", vinyl covered	"	"	26	.308	L.F.
4500	Levelers, hinged for trucks, 10 ton capacity, 6' x 8'	L-4	2 Skilled Workers 1 Helper	1.90	12.630	Ea.
4650	7' x 8'			1.90	12.630	Ea.
4700	Hydraulic, 10 ton capacity, 6' x 8'			1.90	12.630	Ea.
4800	7' x 8'	↓	↓	1.90	12.630	Ea.
5000	Lights for loading docks, single arm, 24" long	1 Elec	1 Electrician	3.80	2.110	Ea.
5700	Double arm, 60" long	"	"	3.80	2.110	Ea.
6200	Shelters, fabric, for truck or train, scissor arms, minimum	1 Carp	1 Carpenter	1	8.000	Ea.
6300	Maximum	"	"	.50	16.000	Ea.
603	DOCK BUMPERS Bolts not included, 2" x 6" to 4" x 8", average	F-1	1 Carpenter Power Tools	.30	26.670	M.B.F.

111 700 | Waste Handling Equipment

		CREW	MAKEUP	DAILY OUTPUT	MAN-HOURS	UNIT
701	WASTE HANDLING Compactors, 115 volt, 250#/hr., chute fed	L-4	2 Skilled Workers 1 Helper	1	24.000	Ea.
0100	Hand fed			2.40	10.000	Ea.
0300	Multi-bag, hand or chute fed, 230 volt, 600#/hr.			1	24.000	Ea.
0500	Containerized, hand fed, 2 to 6 C.Y. containers, 250#/hr.			1	24.000	Ea.
0550	For chute fed, add per floor			1	24.000	Ea.
1000	Heavy duty industrial compactor, 0.5 C.Y. capacity			1.	24.000	Ea.
1050	1.0 C.Y. capacity			1	24.000	Ea.
1100	2.5 C.Y. capacity	↓	↓	.50	48.000	Ea.

111 700 | Waste Handling Equipment

		Description	CREW	MAKEUP	DAILY OUTPUT	MAN-HOURS	UNIT
701	1151	Compactor, heavy duty industrial, 5.0 C.Y. capacity	L-4	2 Skilled Workers	.50	48.000	Ea.
				1 Helper			
	1200	Combination shredder/compactor (5,000 lbs./hr.)	"	"	.50	48.000	Ea.
	1500	Crematory, not including building, 1 place	Q-3	1 Plumber Foreman (ins)	.20	160.000	Ea.
				2 Plumbers			
				1 Plumber Apprentice			
	1750	2 place	"	"	.10	320.000	Ea.
	3750	Incinerator, electric, 100 lb. per hr., minimum	L-9	1 Labor Foreman (inside)	.75	48.000	Ea.
				2 Building Laborers			
				1 Struc. Steel Worker			
				.5 Electrician			
	3850	Maximum			.70	51.430	Ea.
	4000	400 lb. per hr., minimum			.60	60.000	Ea.
	4100	Maximum			.50	72.000	Ea.
	4250	1000 lb. per hr., minimum			.25	144.000	Ea.
	4350	Maximum	↓	↓	.20	180.000	Ea.
	4400	Gas, not incl. chimney, elec. or pipe, 50#/hr., minimum	Q-3	1 Plumber Foreman (ins)	.80	40.000	Ea.
				2 Plumbers			
				1 Plumber Apprentice			
	4420	Maximum			.70	45.710	Ea.
	4440	200 lb. per hr., minimum (batch type)			.60	53.330	Ea.
	4460	Maximum (with feeder)			.50	64.000	Ea.
	4480	400 lb. per hr., minimum (batch type)			.30	107.000	Ea.
	4500	Maximum (with feeder)			.25	128.000	Ea.
	4520	800 lb. per hr., with feeder, minimum			.20	160.000	Ea.
	4540	Maximum			.17	188.000	Ea.
	4560	1200 lb. per hr., with feeder, minimum			.15	213.000	Ea.
	4580	Maximum			.11	291.000	Ea.
	4600	2000 lb. per hr., with feeder, minimum			.10	320.000	Ea.
	4620	Maximum			.05	640.000	Ea.
	4700	For heat recovery system, add, minimum			.25	128.000	Ea.
	4710	Add, maximum			.11	291.000	Ea.
	4720	For automatic ash conveyer, add			.50	64.000	Ea.
	4750	Large municipal incinerators, incl. stack, minimum			.25	128.000	Ton/Day
	4850	Maximum	↓	↓	.10	320.000	Ton/Day

111 900 | Detention Equipment

		Description	CREW	MAKEUP	DAILY OUTPUT	MAN-HOURS	UNIT
901		DETENTION EQUIPMENT Bar front, rolling, 7/8" bars,					
	0500	4" O.C., 7' high, 5' wide, with hardware	E-4	1 Struc. Steel Foreman	2	16.000	Ea.
				3 Struc. Steel Workers			
				1 Gas Welding Machine			
	1000	Doors & frames, 3' x 7', complete, with hardware, single plate	↓	↓	4	8.000	Ea.
	1650	Double plate			4	8.000	Ea.
	2000	Cells, prefab., 5' to 6' wide, 7' to 8' high, 7' to 8' deep,					
	2010	bar front, cot, not incl. plumbing	E-4	1 Struc. Steel Foreman	1.50	21.330	Ea.
				3 Struc. Steel Workers			
				1 Gas Welding Machine			
	2500	Cot, bolted, single, painted steel	↓	↓	20	1.600	Ea.
	2700	Stainless steel			20	1.600	Ea.
	3000	Toilet apparatus including wash basin, average	L-8	2 Carpenters	1.50	13.330	Ea.
				.5 Plumber			
	4000	Visitor cubicle, vision panel, no intercom	E-4	1 Struc. Steel Foreman	2	16.000	Ea.
				3 Struc. Steel Workers			
				1 Gas Welding Machine			

114 000 | Food Service Equipment

		Item	CREW	MAKEUP	DAILY OUTPUT	MAN-HOURS	UNIT
002	002	**APPLIANCES** Cooking range, 30" free standing, 1 oven, minimum	2 Clab	2 Building Laborers	10	1.600	Ea.
	0050	Maximum			4	4.000	Ea.
	0150	2 oven, minimum			10	1.600	Ea.
	0200	Maximum	↓	↓	4	4.000	Ea.
	0350	Built-in, 30" wide, 1 oven, minimum	2 Carp	2 Carpenters	4	4.000	Ea.
	0400	Maximum			2	8.000	Ea.
	0500	2 oven, minimum			4	4.000	Ea.
	0550	Maximum	↓	↓	2	8.000	Ea.
	0700	Free-standing, 21" wide range, 1 oven, minimum	2 Clab	2 Building Laborers	10	1.600	Ea.
	0750	Maximum	"	"	4	4.000	Ea.
	0900	Counter top cook tops, 4 burner, standard, minimum	1 Elec	1 Electrician	6	1.330	Ea.
	0950	Maximum			3	2.670	Ea.
	1050	As above, but with grille and griddle attachment, minimum			6	1.330	Ea.
	1100	Maximum			3	2.670	Ea.
	1200	Induction cooktop, 30" wide			3	2.670	Ea.
	1250	Microwave oven, minimum			4	2.000	Ea.
	1300	Maximum	↓	↓	2	4.000	Ea.
	1500	Combination range, refrigerator and sink, 30" wide, minimum	L-1	1 Electrician 1 Plumber	2	8.000	Ea.
	1550	Maximum			1	16.000	Ea.
	1570	60" wide, average			1.40	11.430	Ea.
	1590	72" wide, average			1.20	13.330	Ea.
	1600	Office model, 48" wide			2	8.000	Ea.
	1620	Refrigerator and sink only	↓	↓	2.40	6.670	Ea.
	1640	Combination range, refrigerator, sink, microwave					
	1660	oven and ice maker	L-1	1 Electrician 1 Plumber	.80	20.000	Ea.
	1750	Compactor, residential size, 4 to 1 compaction, minimum	1 Carp	1 Carpenter	5	1.600	Ea.
	1800	Maximum	"	"	3	2.670	Ea.
	2000	Deep freeze, 15 to 23 C.F., minimum	2 Clab	2 Building Laborers	10	1.600	Ea.
	2050	Maximum			5	3.200	Ea.
	2200	30 C.F., minimum			8	2.000	Ea.
	2250	Maximum	↓	↓	3	5.330	Ea.
	2750	Dishwasher, built-in, 2 cycles, minimum	L-1	1 Electrician 1 Plumber	4	4.000	Ea.
	2800	Maximum			2	8.000	Ea.
	2950	4 or more cycles, minimum			4	4.000	Ea.
	3000	Maximum	↓	↓	2	8.000	Ea.
	3200	Dryer, automatic, minimum	L-2	1 Carpenter 1 Helper	3	5.330	Ea.
	3250	Maximum	"	"	2	8.000	Ea.
	3300	Garbage disposer, sink type, minimum	L-1	1 Electrician 1 Plumber	5	3.200	Ea.
	3350	Maximum	"	"	3	5.330	Ea.
	3550	Heater, electric, built-in, 1250 watt, ceiling type, minimum	1 Elec	1 Electrician	4	2.000	Ea.
	3600	Maximum			3	2.670	Ea.
	3700	Wall type, minimum			4	2.000	Ea.
	3750	Maximum			3	2.670	Ea.
	3900	1500 watt wall type, with blower			4	2.000	Ea.
	3950	3000 watt	↓	↓	3	2.670	Ea.
	4150	Hood for range, 2 speed, vented, 30" wide, minimum	L-3	1 Carpenter .5 Electrician .5 Sheet Metal Worker	5	3.200	Ea.
	4200	Maximum			3	5.330	Ea.
	4300	42" wide, minimum			5	3.200	Ea.
	4350	Maximum	↓	↓	3	5.330	Ea.
	5200	Icemaker, automatic, 13 lb. per day	1 Plum	1 Plumber	7	1.140	Ea.
	5350	51 lb. per day	"	"	2	4.000	Ea.

114 000 | Food Service Equipment

		CREW	MAKEUP	DAILY OUTPUT	MAN-HOURS	UNIT
002 5500	Refrigerator, no frost, 10 C.F. to 12 C.F. minimum	2 Clab	2 Building Laborers	10	1.600	Ea.
5600	Maximum			6	2.670	Ea.
5750	14 C.F. to 16 C.F., minimum			9	1.780	Ea.
5800	Maximum			5	3.200	Ea.
5950	18 C.F. to 20 C.F., minimum			8	2.000	Ea.
6000	Maximum			4	4.000	Ea.
6150	21 C.F. to 29 C.F., minimum			7	2.290	Ea.
6200	Maximum	▼	▼	3	5.330	Ea.
6400	Sump pump cellar drainer, 1/3 H.P., minimum	1 Plum	1 Plumber	3	2.670	Ea.
6450	Maximum			2	4.000	Ea.
6650	Washing machine, automatic, minimum			3	2.670	Ea.
6700	Maximum	▼	▼	1	8.000	Ea.
6900	Water heater, electric, glass lined, 30 gallon, minimum	L-1	1 Electrician 1 Plumber	5	3.200	Ea.
6950	Maximum			3	5.330	Ea.
7100	80 gallon,			2	8.000	Ea.
7150	Maximum	▼	▼	1	16.000	Ea.
7180	Water heater, gas, glass lined, 30 gallon, minimum	2 Plum	2 Plumbers	5	3.200	Ea.
7220	Maximum			3	5.330	Ea.
7260	50 gallon, minimum			2.50	6.400	Ea.
7300	Maximum			1.50	10.670	Ea.
7350	Water softener, automatic, to 30 grains per gallon			5	3.200	Ea.
7400	To 75 grains per gallon	▼	▼	4	4.000	Ea.
7450	Vent kits for dryers	1 Carp	1 Carpenter	10	.800	Ea.
004	KITCHEN EQUIPMENT Bake oven, single deck	Q-1	1 Plumber 1 Plumber Apprentice	8	2.000	Ea.
0300	Double deck			7	2.290	Ea.
0600	Triple deck	▼	▼	6	2.670	Ea.
0900	Electric convection, 40" x 45" x 57"	L-7	2 Carpenters 1 Building Laborer .5 Electrician	4	7.000	Ea.
1300	Broiler, without oven, standard	Q-1	1 Plumber 1 Plumber Apprentice	8	2.000	Ea.
1550	Infra-red	L-7	2 Carpenters 1 Building Laborer .5 Electrician	4	7.000	Ea.
2350	Cooler, reach-in, beverage, 6' long	Q-1	1 Plumber 1 Plumber Apprentice	6	2.670	Ea.
2700	Dishwasher, commercial, rack type					
2720	10 to 12 racks per hour	Q-1	1 Plumber 1 Plumber Apprentice	3.20	5.000	Ea.
2750	Semi-automatic 38 to 50 racks per hour	"	"	1.30	12.310	Ea.
2800	Automatic 190 to 230 racks per hour	Q-2	2 Plumbers 1 Plumber Apprentice	.70	34.290	Ea.
2820	235 to 275 racks per hour			.50	48.000	Ea.
2840	8750 to 12,500 dishes per hour	▼	▼	.20	120.000	Ea.
3000	Fast food equipment, total package, minimum	6 Skwk	6 Skilled Workers	.08	600.000	Ea.
3100	Maximum	"	"	.07	686.000	Ea.
3800	Food mixers, 20 quarts	L-7	2 Carpenters 1 Building Laborer .5 Electrician	7	4.000	Ea.
4000	60 quarts	"	"	5	5.600	Ea.
4300	Freezers, reach-in, 44 C.F.	Q-1	1 Plumber 1 Plumber Apprentice	4	4.000	Ea.
4500	68 C.F.			3	5.330	Ea.
4750	Fryer, with submerger, single			7	2.290	Ea.
5000	Double			5	3.200	Ea.
5300	Griddle, 3' long	▼	▼	7	2.290	Ea.

114 000 | Food Service Equipment

		CREW	MAKEUP	DAILY OUTPUT	MAN-HOURS	UNIT
004 5551	Kitchen equipment, griddle, 4' long	Q-1	1 Plumber	6	2.670	Ea.
			1 Plumber Apprentice			
5800	Ice cube maker, 50 pounds per day			6	2.670	Ea.
6050	500 pounds per day	↓	↓	4	4.000	Ea.
6350	Kettles, steam-jacketed, 20 gallons	L-7	2 Carpenters	7	4.000	Ea.
			1 Building Laborer			
			.5 Electrician			
6600	60 gallons	"	"	6	4.670	Ea.
6900	Range, restaurant type, 6 burners and 1 oven, 36"	Q-1	1 Plumber	7	2.290	Ea.
			1 Plumber Apprentice			
7150	2 ovens, 60"			6	2.670	Ea.
7450	Heavy duty, single 34" oven, open top			5	3.200	Ea.
7700	Fry top			6	2.670	Ea.
7950	Hood fire protection system, minimum			3	5.330	Ea.
8050	Maximum			1	16.000	Ea.
8300	Refrigerators, reach-in type, 44 C.F.			5	3.200	Ea.
8550	With glass doors, 68 C.F.	↓	↓	4	4.000	Ea.
8850	Steamer, electric 27 KW	L-7	2 Carpenters	7	4.000	Ea.
			1 Building Laborer			
			.5 Electrician			
9100	Electric, 10 KW or gas 100,000	"	"	5	5.600	Ea.
9400	Rule of thumb: Equipment cost based					
9410	on kitchen work area					
9420	Office buildings, minimum	L-7	2 Carpenters	77	.364	S.F.
			1 Building Laborer			
			.5 Electrician			
9450	Maximum			58	.483	S.F.
9550	Public eating facilities, minimum			77	.364	S.F.
9600	Maximum			46	.609	S.F.
9750	Hospitals, minimum			58	.483	S.F.
9800	Maximum	↓	↓	39	.718	S.F.
008	WINE VAULT Redwood, air conditioned, walk-in type					
0020	6'-8" high, incl. racks, 2' x 4' for 156 bottles	2 Carp	2 Carpenters	2	8.000	Ea.
0200	4' x 6' for 614 bottles			1.50	10.670	Ea.
0400	6' x 12' for 1940 bottles	↓	↓	1	16.000	Ea.

114 580 | Disappearing Stairs

		CREW	MAKEUP	DAILY OUTPUT	MAN-HOURS	UNIT
581	DISAPPEARING STAIRWAY No trim included					
0100	Custom grade, pine, 8'-6" ceiling, minimum	1 Carp	1 Carpenter	4	2.000	Ea.
0150	Average			3.50	2.290	Ea.
0200	Maximum			3	2.670	Ea.
0500	Heavy duty, pivoted, 8'-6" ceiling			3	2.670	Ea.
0600	16'-0" ceiling			2	4.000	Ea.
0800	Economy folding, pine, 8'-6" ceiling			4	2.000	Ea.
0900	9'-6" ceiling	↓	↓	4	2.000	Ea.
1000	Fire escape, galvanized steel, 8'-0" to 10'-4" ceiling	2 Carp	2 Carpenters	1	16.000	Ea.
1010	10'-6" to 13'-6" ceiling			1	16.000	Ea.
1100	Automatic electric, aluminum, floor to floor height, 8' to 9'			1	16.000	Ea.
1400	11' to 12'			.90	17.780	Ea.
1700	14' to 15'	↓	↓	.70	22.860	Ea.

114 740 | Darkroom Processing

		CREW	MAKEUP	DAILY OUTPUT	MAN-HOURS	UNIT
741	DARKROOM EQUIPMENT Developing tanks, 5" deep, 24"x 48"	Q-1	1 Plumber	2	8.000	Ea.
			1 Plumber Apprentice			
0050	48" x 52"			1.70	9.410	Ea.
0200	10" deep, 24" x 48"			1.70	9.410	Ea.
0250	24" x 108"	↓	↓	1.50	10.670	Ea.

114 | Food Service, Residential, Darkroom, Athletic Equip.

114 740 | Darkroom Processing

		Description	CREW	MAKEUP	DAILY OUTPUT	MAN-HOURS	UNIT
741	0501	Darkroom equip., dryers, dehum. filtered air, 36" x 25" x 68" high	L-7	2 Carpenters	6	4.670	Ea.
				1 Building Laborer			
				.5 Electrician			
	0550	48" x 25" x 68" high			5	5.600	Ea.
	2000	Processors, automatic, color print, minimum			4	7.000	Ea.
	2050	Maximum			1	28.000	Ea.
	2300	Black and white print, minimum			4	7.000	Ea.
	2350	Maximum			1	28.000	Ea.
	2600	Manual processor, 16" x 20" maximum print size			4	7.000	Ea.
	2650	20" x 24" maximum print size			1	28.000	Ea.
	3000	Viewing lites, 20" x 24"			6	4.670	Ea.
	3100	20" x 24" with color correction	▼	▼	6	4.670	Ea.
	3500	Washers, round, maximum sheet 11" x 14"	Q-1	1 Plumber	2	8.000	Ea.
				1 Plumber Apprentice			
	3550	Maximum sheet			1	16.000	Ea.
	3800	Square, maximum sheet			1	16.000	Ea.
	3900	Maximum sheet	▼	▼	.80	20.000	Ea.
	4500	Combination tank sink, tray sink, washers, with					
	4510	dry side tables, average	Q-1	1 Plumber	1	16.000	Ea.
				1 Plumber Apprentice			

114 760 | Revolving Darkrm Doors

	Description	CREW	MAKEUP	DAILY OUTPUT	MAN-HOURS	UNIT
768	DARKROOM DOORS Revolving, standard, 2 way, 40" diameter	2 Carp	2 Carpenters	3.50	4.570	Opng.
0050	3 way, 50" diameter			3	5.330	Opng.
1000	4 way, 50" diameter			2	8.000	Opng.
2000	Hinged safety, 2 way, 40" diameter			3.20	5.000	Opng.
2500	3 way, 50" diameter			2.90	5.520	Opng.
3000	Pop out safety, 2 way, 40" diameter			3.10	5.160	Opng.
4000	3 way, 50" diameter	▼	▼	2.80	5.710	Opng.

114 800 | Athletic/Recreational

	Description	CREW	MAKEUP	DAILY OUTPUT	MAN-HOURS	UNIT
801	HEALTH CLUB EQUIPMENT					
0600	Circuit training apparatus, 12 machines minimum	2 Clab	2 Building Laborers	1.25	12.800	Set
0700	Average			1	16.000	Set
0800	Maximum			.75	21.330	Set
0900	Squat racks	▼	▼	5	3.200	Ea.
805	SCHOOL EQUIPMENT					
1000	Basketball backstops, wall mtd., 6' extended, fixed, minimum	L-2	1 Carpenter	1	16.000	Ea.
			1 Helper			
1100	Maximum			1	16.000	Ea.
1200	Swing up, minimum			1	16.000	Ea.
1250	Maximum			1	16.000	Ea.
1300	Portable, manual, heavy duty, hydraulic			1.90	8.420	Ea.
1400	Ceiling suspended, stationary, minimum			.78	20.510	Ea.
1450	Fold up, with accessories, maximum	▼	▼	1	16.000	Ea.
1600	For electrically operated, add	1 Elec	1 Electrician	1	8.000	Ea.
2000	Benches, folding, in wall, 14' table, 2 benches	L-4	2 Skilled Workers	2	12.000	Set
			1 Helper			
3000	Bleachers, telescoping, manual to 15 tier, minimum	F-5	1 Carpenter Foreman	65	.492	Seat
			3 Carpenters			
			Power Tools			
3100	Maximum			60	.533	Seat
3300	16 to 20 tier, minimum			60	.533	Seat
3400	Maximum			55	.582	Seat
3600	21 to 30 tier, minimum			50	.640	Seat
3700	Maximum	▼	▼	40	.800	Seat
3900	For integral power operation, add, minimum	2 Elec	2 Electricians	300	.053	Seat
4000	Maximum	"	"	250	.064	Seat

114 800 | Athletic/Recreational

		Item	CREW	MAKEUP	DAILY OUTPUT	MAN-HOURS	UNIT
805	4151	Exercise equipment					
	4180	Chinning bar, adjustable, wall mounted	1 Carp	1 Carpenter	5	1.600	Ea.
	4200	Exercise ladder, 16' x 1'-7", suspended	L-2	1 Carpenter	3	5.330	Ea.
				1 Helper			
	4210	High bar, floor plate attached	1 Carp	1 Carpenter	4	2.000	Ea.
	4240	Parallel bars, adjustable	↓	↓	4	2.000	Ea.
	4270	Uneven parallel bars, adjustable			4	2.000	Ea.
	4280	Wall mounted, adjustable	L-2	1 Carpenter	1.50	10.670	Set
				1 Helper			
	4300	Rope, ceiling mounted, 18' long	1 Carp	1 Carpenter	10	.800	Ea.
	4330	Side horse, vaulting	↓	↓	5	1.600	Ea.
	4360	Treadmill, motorized, deluxe, training type			5	1.600	Ea.
	4390	Weight lifting multi-station, minimum	2 Clab	2 Building Laborers	1	16.000	Ea.
	4450	Maximum	"	"	.50	32.000	Ea.
	7000	Scoreboards, baseball, minimum	R-3	1 Electrician Foreman	2.40	8.330	Ea.
				1 Electrician			
				.5 Equip. Oper. (crane)			
				.5 S.P. Crane, 5 Ton			
	7200	Maximum		↓	.05	400.000	Ea.
	7300	Football, minimum			1.20	16.670	Ea.
	7400	Maximum			.20	100.000	Ea.
	7500	Basketball (one side), minimum			2.40	8.330	Ea.
	7600	Maximum			.30	66.670	Ea.
	7700	Hockey-basketball (four sides), minimum			.25	80.000	Ea.
	7800	Maximum	↓	↓	.15	133.000	Ea.

114 880 | Bowling Alleys

		Item	CREW	MAKEUP	DAILY OUTPUT	MAN-HOURS	UNIT
	881	BOWLING ALLEYS Including alley, pinsetter, scorer,					
	0020	counters and misc. supplies, minimum	4 Carp	4 Carpenters	.20	160.000	Lane
	0150	Average	↓	↓	.19	168.000	Lane
	0300	Maximum			.18	178.000	Lane

114 960 | Shooting Ranges

		Item	CREW	MAKEUP	DAILY OUTPUT	MAN-HOURS	UNIT
	961	SHOOTING RANGE Incl. bullet traps, target provisions, controls,					
	0100	separators, ceiling system, etc. Not incl. structural shell					
	0200	Commercial	L-9	1 Labor Foreman (inside)	.85	42.350	Point
				2 Building Laborers			
				1 Struc. Steel Worker			
				.5 Electrician			
	0300	Law enforcement			.65	55.380	Point
	0400	National Guard armories			.71	50.700	Point
	0500	Reserve training centers			.85	42.350	Point
	0600	Schools and colleges			.75	48.000	Point
	0700	Major acadamies	↓	↓	.48	75.000	Point

115 | Industrial and Process Equipment

115 000 | Industrial Equipment

		CREW	MAKEUP	DAILY OUTPUT	MAN-HOURS	UNIT
005	005	EQUIPMENT INSTALLATION Industrial equipment, minimum	E-2	1 Struc. Steel Foreman	12	4.670	Ton
				4 Struc. Steel Workers			
				1 Equip. Oper. (crane)			
				1 Equip. Oper. Oiler			
				1 Crane, 90 Ton			
	0200	Maximum	"	"	2	28.000	Ton

115 010 | Specialized Equipment

		CREW	MAKEUP	DAILY OUTPUT	MAN-HOURS	UNIT
011	VOCATIONAL SHOP EQUIPMENT Benches, work, wood, average	2 Carp	2 Carpenters	5	3.200	Ea.
0100	Metal, average			5	3.200	Ea.
0400	Combination belt & disc sander, 6"			4	4.000	Ea.
0700	Drill press, floor mounted, 12", 1/2 H.P.			4	4.000	Ea.
0800	Dust collector, not incl. ductwork, 6' diameter	1 Shee	1 Sheet Metal Worker	1.10	7.270	Ea.
1000	Grinders, double wheel, 1/2 H.P.	2 Carp	2 Carpenters	5	3.200	Ea.
1300	Jointer, 4", 3/4 H.P.			4	4.000	Ea.
1600	Kilns, 16 C.F., to 2000°			4	4.000	Ea.
1900	Lathe, woodworking, 10", 1/2 H.P.			4	4.000	Ea.
2200	Planer, 13" x 6"			4	4.000	Ea.
2500	Potter's wheel, motorized			4	4.000	Ea.
2800	Saws, band, 14", 3/4 H.P.			4	4.000	Ea.
3100	Metal cutting band saw, 14"			4	4.000	Ea.
3400	Radial arm saw, 10", 2 H.P.			4	4.000	Ea.
3700	Scroll saw, 24"			4	4.000	Ea.
4000	Table saw, 10", 3 H.P.			4	4.000	Ea.
4300	Welder AC arc, 30 amp capacity			4	4.000	Ea.

116 | Laboratory, Planetarium, Observatory Equipment

116 000 | Laboratory Equipment

		CREW	MAKEUP	DAILY OUTPUT	MAN-HOURS	UNIT
001	LABORATORY EQUIPMENT Cabinets, base, door units, metal	2 Carp	2 Carpenters	18	.889	L.F.
0300	Drawer units			18	.889	L.F.
0700	Tall storage cabinets, open, 7' high			20	.800	L.F.
0900	With glazed doors			20	.800	L.F.
1300	Wall cabinets, metal, 12-1/2" deep, open			20	.800	L.F.
1500	With doors			20	.800	L.F.
1550	Counter tops, not incl. base cabinets, acidproof, minimum			82	.195	S.F.
1600	Maximum			70	.229	S.F.
1650	Stainless steel			82	.195	S.F.
2000	Fume hood, with countertop & base, not including HVAC					
2020	Simple, minimum	2 Carp	2 Carpenters	5.40	2.960	L.F.
2050	Complex, including fixtures			2.40	6.670	L.F.
2100	Special, maximum			1.70	9.410	L.F.
2200	Ductwork, minimum	2 Shee	2 Sheet Metal Workers	1	16.000	Hood
2250	Maximum	"	"	.50	32.000	Hood
2500	For sink assembly with hot and cold water, add	1 Plum	1 Plumber	1.40	5.710	Ea.
2550	Glassware washer, distilled water rinse, minimum	L-1	1 Electrician	1.80	8.890	Ea.
			1 Plumber			
2600	Maximum	"	"	1	16.000	Ea.
2800	Sink, one piece plastic, flask wash, hose, free standing	1 Plum	1 Plumber	1.60	5.000	Ea.
2850	Epoxy resin sink, 25" x 16" x 10"	"	"	2	4.000	Ea.
3000	Utility table, acid resistant top with drawers	2 Carp	2 Carpenters	30	.533	L.F.

117 | Medical Equipment

117 000 | Medical Equipment

		Item	CREW	MAKEUP	DAILY OUTPUT	MAN-HOURS	UNIT
001	001	**MEDICAL EQUIPMENT** Autopsy table, standard	1 Plum	1 Plumber	1	8.000	Ea.
	0200	Deluxe			.60	13.330	Ea.
	0700	Distiller, water, steam heated, 50 gal. capacity			1.40	5.710	Ea.
	6150	Automatic washer/sterilizer	↓	↓	2	4.000	Ea.
	6200	Steam generators, electric 10 KW to 180 KW					
	6250	Minimum	1 Elec	1 Electrician	3	2.670	Ea.
	6300	Maximum	"	"	.70	11.430	Ea.
	6500	Surgery table, minor minimum	1 Sswk	1 Struc. Steel Worker	.70	11.430	Ea.
	6520	Maximum			.50	16.000	Ea.
	6550	Major surgery table, minimum			.50	16.000	Ea.
	6570	Maximum	↓	↓	.50	16.000	Ea.
	6700	Surgical lights, single arm	2 Elec	2 Electricians	.90	17.780	Ea.
	6750	Dual arm	"	"	.30	53.330	Ea.
	7000	Tables, physical therapy, walk off, electric	2 Carp	2 Carpenters	3	5.330	Ea.
	7150	Standard, vinyl top with base cabinets, minimum			3	5.330	Ea.
	7200	Maximum	↓	↓	2	8.000	Ea.
	8100	Utensil washer-sanitizer	1 Plum	1 Plumber	2	4.000	Ea.

117 400 | Dental Equipment

	Item	CREW	MAKEUP	DAILY OUTPUT	MAN-HOURS	UNIT
401	**DENTAL EQUIPMENT** Central suction system, minimum	1 Plum	1 Plumber	1.20	6.670	Ea.
0100	Maximum	"	"	.90	8.890	Ea.
0300	Air compressor, minimum	1 Skwk	1 Skilled Worker	.80	10.000	Ea.
0400	Maximum			.50	16.000	Ea.
0600	Chair, electric or hydraulic, minimum			.50	16.000	Ea.
0700	Maximum			.25	32.000	Ea.
1000	Drill console with accessories, minimum			.50	16.000	Ea.
1100	Maximum			.33	24.240	Ea.
2000	Light, floor or ceiling mounted, minimum			3.60	2.220	Ea.
2100	Maximum			1.20	6.670	Ea.
3000	X-ray unit, wall			1.90	4.210	Ea.
3100	Panoramic unit			.60	13.330	Ea.
3500	Developers, X-ray, minimum			1	8.000	Ea.
3600	Maximum	↓	↓	1	8.000	Ea.

FURNISHINGS

DIVISION 12

FURNISHINGS

The Furnishings Division contains productivity rates for the installation of various products that are commonly found in buildings. Examples include exterior blinds, cabinets, and office furniture.

As a general rule the products in this division are installed by the vendor as part of the purchase agreement. The installers are frequently specially trained for their task. The productivity rates in this division are based on the experiences of properly trained craftsmen, but not necessarily specialists, working in a reasonably comfortable environment without unnecessary space confinements. In actual practice the expected productivity should be adjusted to make allowances for either unusual productivity-enhancing conditions or unusual productivity-restricting conditions.

The rates in this division represent new construction. For repair and remodeling work, substantial adjustments may be necessary to properly account for the unique nature of each project.

121 | Artwork

121 000	Artwork	CREW	MAKEUP	DAILY OUTPUT	MAN-HOURS	UNIT
005	005	**ART WORK** framed					
	1000	Photography, minimum	1 Carp	1 Carpenter	36	.222	Ea.
	1050	Maximum			30	.267	Ea.
	2000	Posters, minimum			36	.222	Ea.
	2050	Maximum			30	.267	Ea.
	3000	Reproductions, minimum			36	.222	Ea.
	3050	Maximum	↓	↓	30	.267	Ea.

123 | Manufactured Casework

123 010	Metal Casework	CREW	MAKEUP	DAILY OUTPUT	MAN-HOURS	UNIT
015	**KEY CABINETS** Wall mounted, 60 key capacity	1 Carp	1 Carpenter	20	.400	Ea.
0100	1200 key capacity	"	"	10	.800	Ea.
0200	Drawer type, 600 key capacity	1 Clab	1 Building Laborer	15	.533	Ea.
0300	2400 key capacity			20	.400	Ea.
0400	Tray type, 20 key capacity			50	.160	Ea.
0500	50 key capacity	↓	↓	40	.200	Ea.

123 500	Hospital Casework	CREW	MAKEUP	DAILY OUTPUT	MAN-HOURS	UNIT
501	**CABINETS**					
0500	Hospital, base cabinets, laminated plastic	2 Carp	2 Carpenters	10	1.600	L.F.
0700	Enameled steel			10	1.600	L.F.
1000	Stainless steel			10	1.600	L.F.
1300	Cabinet base trim, 4" high, enameled steel			200	.080	L.F.
1400	Stainless steel			200	.080	L.F.
1450	Counter top, laminated plastic, no backsplash			40	.400	L.F.
1650	With backsplash			40	.400	L.F.
1800	For sink cutout, add			12.20	1.310	Ea.
1900	Stainless steel counter top			40	.400	L.F.
2100	Nurses station, door type, laminated plastic			10	1.600	L.F.
2200	Enameled steel			10	1.600	L.F.
2300	Stainless steel			10	1.600	L.F.
2500	Wall cabinets, laminated plastic			15	1.070	L.F.
2600	Enameled steel			15	1.070	L.F.
2700	Stainless steel			15	1.070	L.F.
3500	Kitchen, base cabinets, metal, minimum			30	.533	L.F.
3600	Maximum			25	.640	L.F.
3700	Wall cabinets, metal, minimum			30	.533	L.F.
3800	Maximum			25	.640	L.F.
5000	School, 24" deep,			15	1.070	L.F.
5150	Counter height units			20	.800	L.F.
5450	Wood, custom fabricated, 32" high counter			20	.800	L.F.
5600	Add for counter top			56	.286	L.F.
5800	84" high wall units	↓	↓	15	1.070	L.F.

123 800	Display Casework	CREW	MAKEUP	DAILY OUTPUT	MAN-HOURS	UNIT
801	**DISPLAY CASES** Free standing, all glass					
0020	Aluminum frame, 42" high x 36" x 12" deep	2 Carp	2 Carpenters	8	2.000	Ea.
0100	70" high x 48" x 18" deep	"	"	6	2.670	Ea.
2000	Wall mounted, glass front, aluminum frame					
2010	Non-illuminated, one section 3' x 4' x 1'-4"	2 Carp	2 Carpenters	5	3.200	Ea.
2100	5' x 4' x 1'-4"	"	"	5	3.200	Ea.

123 | Manufactured Casework

123 800 | Display Casework

		CREW	MAKEUP	DAILY OUTPUT	MAN-HOURS	UNIT
801	2201	Display cases, wall mounted, one section, 6' x 4' x 1'-4"	2 Carp	2 Carpenters	4	4.000	Ea.
	2500	Two sections, 8' x 4' x 1'-4"			2	8.000	Ea.
	2600	10' x 4' x 1'-4"			2	8.000	Ea.
	3000	Three sections, 16' x 4' x 1'-4"			1.50	10.670	Ea.
	4000	Table exhibit cases, 2' wide, 3' high, 4' long, flat top			5	3.200	Ea.
	4100	3' wide, 3' high, 4' long, sloping top	↓	↓	3	5.330	Ea.

123 900 | Residential Casework

		CREW	MAKEUP	DAILY OUTPUT	MAN-HOURS	UNIT
905	IRONING CENTER Including cabinet, board & light, minimum	1 Carp	1 Carpenter	2	4.000	Ea.
0101	Maximum	"	"	1.50	5.330	Ea.

125 | Window Treatment

125 100 | Blinds

		CREW	MAKEUP	DAILY OUTPUT	MAN-HOURS	UNIT
103	BLINDS, INTERIOR Solid colors					
0090	Horizontal, 1" aluminum slats, custom, minimum	1 Carp	1 Carpenter	590	.014	S.F.
0100	Maximum			440	.018	S.F.
0250	2" aluminum slats, custom, minimum			590	.014	S.F.
0350	Maximum			440	.018	S.F.
0450	Stock, minimum			590	.014	S.F.
0500	Maximum			440	.018	S.F.
0600	2" steel slats, stock, minimum			590	.014	S.F.
0630	Maximum			440	.018	S.F.
0750	Custom, minimum			590	.014	S.F.
0850	Maximum	↓	↓	400	.020	S.F.
1000	Alternate method of figuring:					
1300	1" aluminum slats, 48" wide, 48" high	1 Carp	1 Carpenter	30	.267	Ea.
1320	72" high			29	.276	Ea.
1340	96" high			28	.286	Ea.
1400	72" wide, 72" high			25	.320	Ea.
1420	96" high			23	.348	Ea.
1480	96" wide, 96" high			20	.400	Ea.
1500	Vertical, 3" to 5" PVC or cloth strips, minimum			460	.017	S.F.
1600	Maximum			400	.020	S.F.
1800	4" aluminum slats, minimum			460	.017	S.F.
1900	Maximum			400	.020	S.F.
1950	Mylar mirror-finish strips, to 8" wide, minimum			460	.017	S.F.
1970	Maximum	↓	↓	400	.020	S.F.
1990	Alternate method of figuring:					
2000	2" aluminum slats, 48" wide, 48" high	1 Carp	1 Carpenter	30	.267	Ea.
2050	72" high			29	.276	Ea.
2100	96" high			28	.286	Ea.
2200	72" wide, 72" high			25	.320	Ea.
2250	96" high			23	.348	Ea.
2300	96" wide, 96" high			20	.400	Ea.
2500	Mirror finish, 48" wide, 48" high			30	.267	Ea.
2550	72" high			29	.276	Ea.
2600	96" high			28	.286	Ea.
2650	72" wide, 72" high			25	.320	Ea.
2700	96" high			23	.348	Ea.
2750	96" wide, 96" high			20	.400	Ea.
2800	Decorative printed finish, 48" wide, 48" high	↓	↓	30	.267	Ea.

125 | Window Treatment

125 100 | Blinds

		CREW	MAKEUP	DAILY OUTPUT	MAN-HOURS	UNIT
103 2851	Blinds, vertical, decorative printed finish, 48" wide, 72" high	1 Carp	1 Carpenter	29	.276	Ea.
2900	96" high			28	.286	Ea.
2950	72" wide, 72" high			25	.320	Ea.
2980	96" high			23	.348	Ea.
2990	96" wide, 96" high			20	.400	Ea.
3000	Wood folding panels with movable louvers, 7" x 20" each			17	.471	Pr.
3300	8" x 28" each			17	.471	Pr.
3450	9" x 36" each			17	.471	Pr.
3600	10" x 40" each			17	.471	Pr.
4000	Fixed louver type, stock units, 8" x 20" each			17	.471	Pr.
4150	10" x 28" each			17	.471	Pr.
4300	12" x 36" each			17	.471	Pr.
4450	18" x 40" each			17	.471	Pr.
5000	Insert panel type, stock, 7" x 20" each			17	.471	Pr.
5150	8" x 28" each			17	.471	Pr.
5300	9" x 36" each			17	.471	Pr.
5450	10" x 40" each			17	.471	Pr.
5600	Raised panel type, stock, 10" x 24" each			17	.471	Pr.
5650	12" x 26" each			17	.471	Pr.
5700	14" x 30" each			17	.471	Pr.
5750	16" x 36" each	↓	↓	17	.471	Pr.

125 200 | Shades

		CREW	MAKEUP	DAILY OUTPUT	MAN-HOURS	UNIT
201	SHADES Basswood, roll-up, stain finish, 3/8" slats	1 Carp	1 Carpenter	300	.027	S.F.
0200	7/8" slats			300	.027	S.F.
0300	Vertical side slide, stain finish, 3/8" slats			300	.027	S.F.
0400	7/8" slats			300	.027	S.F.
0500	For fire retardant finishes, add			300		S.F.
0600	For "B" rated finishes, add			300		S.F.
0900	Mylar, single layer, non-heat reflective			685	.012	S.F.
1000	Double layered, heat reflective			685	.012	S.F.
1100	Triple layered, heat reflective			685	.012	S.F.
1300	Vinyl coated cotton, standard			685	.012	S.F.
1400	Lightproof decorator shades			685	.012	S.F.
1500	Vinyl, lightweight, 4 gauge			685	.012	S.F.
1600	Heavyweight, 6 gauge			685	.012	S.F.
1700	Vinyl laminated fiberglass, 6 ga., translucent			685	.012	S.F.
1800	Lightproof			685	.012	S.F.
3000	Woven aluminum, 3/8" thick, lightproof and fireproof			350	.023	S.F.
5011	Insulative shades			125	.064	S.F.
6011	Solar screening, fiberglass	↓	↓	85	.094	S.F.
8011	Interior insulative shutter					
8111	Stock unit, 15" x 60"	1 Carp	1 Carpenter	17	.471	Pr.

125 300 | Drape/Curtain Hardware

		CREW	MAKEUP	DAILY OUTPUT	MAN-HOURS	UNIT
301	DRAPERY HARDWARE					
0030	Standard traverse, per foot, minimum	1 Carp	1 Carpenter	59	.136	L.F.
0100	Maximum			51	.157	L.F.
0200	Decorative traverse, 28"-48", minimum			22	.364	Ea.
0220	Maximum			21	.381	Ea.
0300	48"-84", minimum			20	.400	Ea.
0320	Maximum			19	.421	Ea.
0400	66"-120", minimum			18	.444	Ea.
0420	Maximum			17	.471	Ea.
0500	84"-156", minimum			16	.500	Ea.
0520	Maximum			15	.533	Ea.
0600	130"-240", minimum			14	.571	Ea.
0620	Maximum	↓	↓	13	.615	Ea.

125 | Window Treatment

125 300 | Drape/Curtain Hardware

			CREW	MAKEUP	DAILY OUTPUT	MAN-HOURS	UNIT
301	3001	Drapery hardware, ripplefold, snap-a-pleat sys., 3' or less, min.	1 Carp	1 Carpenter	15	.533	Ea.
	3020	Maximum			14	.571	Ea.
	4000	Traverse rods, adjustable, 28" to 48"			22	.364	Ea.
	4020	48" to 84"			20	.400	Ea.
	4040	66" to 120"			18	.444	Ea.
	4060	84" to 156"			16	.500	Ea.
	4080	120" to 220"			14	.571	Ea.
	4100	228" to 312"	↓	↓	13	.615	Ea.

125 400 | Draperies And Curtains

		CREW	MAKEUP	DAILY OUTPUT	MAN-HOURS	UNIT
401	DRAPERIES					
8800	Drapery installation, hardware & drapes,					
9000	Labor cost only, minimum	1 Clab	1 Building Laborer	75	.107	L.F.
9100	Maximum	"	"	20	.400	L.F.

126 | Furniture and Accessories

126 100 | Landscape Partitions

		CREW	MAKEUP	DAILY OUTPUT	MAN-HOURS	UNIT
105	PANELS & DIVIDERS Free standing					
0030	Fabric panel, class A fire rated					
0040	Minimum NRC .95, STC 28, fabric edged					
0200	40" high, 24" wide	2 Clab	2 Building Laborers	30	.533	Ea.
0220	36" wide			28	.571	Ea.
0240	48" wide			26	.615	Ea.
0260	60" wide			25	.640	Ea.
0400	50" high, 24" wide			30	.533	Ea.
0420	36" wide			28	.571	Ea.
0440	48" wide			26	.615	Ea.
0460	60" wide			25	.640	Ea.
0600	60" high, 24" wide			29	.552	Ea.
0620	36" wide			27	.593	Ea.
0640	48" wide			25	.640	Ea.
0660	60" wide			24	.667	Ea.
0800	72" high, 24" wide			29	.552	Ea.
1000	36" wide			27	.593	Ea.
1200	48" wide			25	.640	Ea.
1400	60" wide			24	.667	Ea.
2000	Hardwood edged, 40" high, 24" wide			30	.533	Ea.
2100	36" wide			28	.571	Ea.
2120	48" wide			26	.615	Ea.
2180	60" wide			25	.640	Ea.
2200	50" high, 24" wide			30	.533	Ea.
2220	36" wide			28	.571	Ea.
2240	48" wide			26	.615	Ea.
2300	60" wide			25	.640	Ea.
2400	60" high, 24" wide			29	.552	Ea.
2420	36" wide			27	.593	Ea.
2440	48" wide			25	.640	Ea.
2460	60" wide			24	.667	Ea.
2800	72" high, 24" wide			29	.552	Ea.
2820	36" wide	↓	↓	27	.593	Ea.
2840	48" wide			25	.640	Ea.

126 100	Landscape Partitions	CREW	MAKEUP	DAILY OUTPUT	MAN-HOURS	UNIT
105 2861	Panel, fabric, hardwood edged, 72" high, 60" wide	2 Clab	2 Building Laborers	24	.667	Ea.

126 200	Furniture	CREW	MAKEUP	DAILY OUTPUT	MAN-HOURS	UNIT
206	**FURNITURE, DORMITORY**					
1200	Desk top, built-in, laminated plastic, 24" deep, minimum	2 Carp	2 Carpenters	50	.320	L.F.
1300	Maximum			40	.400	L.F.
1450	30" deep, minimum			50	.320	L.F.
1550	Maximum			40	.400	L.F.
1750	Dressing unit, built-in, minimum			12	1.330	L.F.
1850	Maximum	↓	↓	8	2.000	L.F.
218	**FURNITURE, LIBRARY**					
0100	Attendant desk, 36" x 62" x 29" high	1 Carp	1 Carpenter	16	.500	Ea.
0200	Book display, "A" frame display, both sides			16	.500	Ea.
0220	Table with bulletin board	↓	↓	16	.500	Ea.
0300	Book trucks, descending platform,					
0320	Small, 14" x 30" x 35" high	1 Carp	1 Carpenter	16	.500	Ea.
0340	Large, 14" x 40" x 42" high			16	.500	Ea.
0800	Card catalogue, 30 tray unit			16	.500	Ea.
0840	60 tray unit	↓	↓	16	.500	Ea.
0880	72 tray unit	2 Carp	2 Carpenters	16	1.000	Ea.
0960	120 tray unit	"	"	16	1.000	Ea.
1000	Carrels, single face, initial unit	1 Carp	1 Carpenter	16	.500	Ea.
1050	Additional unit	"	"	16	.500	Ea.
1500	Double face, initial unit	2 Carp	2 Carpenters	16	1.000	Ea.
1550	Additional unit			16	1.000	Ea.
1600	Cloverleaf	↓	↓	11	1.450	Ea.
2000	Chairs, sled base, arms, minimum	1 Carp	1 Carpenter	24	.333	Ea.
2050	Maximum			16	.500	Ea.
2100	No arms, minimum			24	.333	Ea.
2150	Maximum			16	.500	Ea.
2500	Standard leg base, arms, minimum			24	.333	Ea.
2520	Maximum			16	.500	Ea.
2600	No arms, minimum			24	.333	Ea.
2620	Maximum	↓	↓	16	.500	Ea.
3000	Charge desk, modular unit, 35" x 27" x 39" high					
3020	Wood front and edges, plastic laminate tops					
3100	Book return	1 Carp	1 Carpenter	16	.500	Ea.
3150	Book truck port			16	.500	Ea.
3200	Card file drawer, 5 drawers			16	.500	Ea.
3250	10 drawers			16	.500	Ea.
3280	15 drawers			16	.500	Ea.
3300	Card & legal file			16	.500	Ea.
3350	Charging machine			16	.500	Ea.
3400	Corner			16	.500	Ea.
3450	Cupboard			16	.500	Ea.
3500	Detachable end panel			16	.500	Ea.
3550	Gate			16	.500	Ea.
3600	Knee space			16	.500	Ea.
3650	Open storage			16	.500	Ea.
3700	Station charge			16	.500	Ea.
3750	Work station			16	.500	Ea.
4000	Dictionary stand, stationary			16	.500	Ea.
4020	Revolving			16	.500	Ea.
4200	Exhibit case, table style, 60" x 28" x 36"			11	.727	Ea.
4500	Globe stand			16	.500	Ea.
4800	Magazine rack			16	.500	Ea.
5000	Newspaper rack			16	.500	Ea.
7000	Tables, card catalog reference, 24" x 60" x 42"	↓	↓	16	.500	Ea.

126 | Furniture and Accessories

126 200 | Furniture

		CREW	MAKEUP	DAILY OUTPUT	MAN-HOURS	UNIT
218 7051	Tables, card catalog reference, 24" x 60" x 72"	1 Carp	1 Carpenter	16	.500	Ea.
7100	Index, single tier, 48" x 72"	↓	↓	16	.500	Ea.
7150	Double tier, 48" x 72"	↓	↓	16	.500	Ea.
8000	Study, panel ends, plastic laminate surfaces 29" high, 36" x 60"	2 Carp	2 Carpenters	16	1.000	Ea.
8100	36" x 72"			16	1.000	Ea.
8150	36" x 90"			16	1.000	Ea.
8200	48" x 72"	↓	↓	16	1.000	Ea.
8500	Parsons table, 29" high, plastic lam. top, wood legs & edges					
8550	36" x 36"	2 Carp	2 Carpenters	16	1.000	Ea.
8600	36" x 60"			16	1.000	Ea.
8650	36" x 72"			16	1.000	Ea.
8700	36" x 84"			16	1.000	Ea.
8750	42" x 90"			16	1.000	Ea.
8800	48" x 72"			16	1.000	Ea.
8850	48" x 120"			16	1.000	Ea.
8900	Round, leg or pedestal base, 36" diameter			16	1.000	Ea.
8950	42" diameter			16	1.000	Ea.
9000	48" diameter			16	1.000	Ea.
9050	60" diameter	↓	↓	16	1.000	Ea.
226	FURNITURE, RESTAURANT Bars, built-in, front bar	1 Carp	1 Carpenter	5	1.600	L.F.
0200	Back bar	"	"	5	1.600	L.F.

126 500 | Furniture Accessories

		CREW	MAKEUP	DAILY OUTPUT	MAN-HOURS	UNIT
501	ASH/TRASH RECEIVERS					
1000	Ash urn, cylindrical metal					
1020	8" diameter, 20" high	1 Clab	1 Building Laborer	60	.133	Ea.
1040	8" dia., 25" high			60	.133	Ea.
1060	10" diameter, 26" high			60	.133	Ea.
1080	12" dia., 30" high	↓	↓	60	.133	Ea.
2000	Combination ash/trash urn, metal					
2020	8" diameter, 20" high	1 Clab	1 Building Laborer	60	.133	Ea.
2040	8" dia., 25" high			60	.133	Ea.
2050	10" diameter, 26" high			60	.133	Ea.
2060	12" dia., 30" high	↓	↓	60	.133	Ea.
4000	Trash receptacle, metal					
4020	8" diameter, 15" high	1 Clab	1 Building Laborer	60	.133	Ea.
4040	10" diameter, 18" high			60	.133	Ea.
4060	16" dia., 16" high			60	.133	Ea.
4100	18" dia., 32" high	↓	↓	60	.133	Ea.
5000	Trash receptacle, plastic, fire resistant					
5020	Rectangular 11" x 8" x 12" high	1 Clab	1 Building Laborer	60	.133	Ea.
5040	16" x 8" x 14" high	"	"	60	.133	Ea.
5500	Trash receptacle, plastic, with lid					
5520	35 gallon	1 Clab	1 Building Laborer	60	.133	Ea.
5540	45 gallon	"	"	60	.133	Ea.

126 900 | Floor Mats And Frames

		CREW	MAKEUP	DAILY OUTPUT	MAN-HOURS	UNIT
901	FLOOR MATS Recessed, in-laid black rubber, 3/8" thick, solid	1 Clab	1 Building Laborer	155	.052	S.F.
0050	Perforated			155	.052	S.F.
0100	1/2" thick, solid			155	.052	S.F.
0150	Perforated			155	.052	S.F.
0200	In colors, 3/8" thick, solid			155	.052	S.F.
0250	Perforated			155	.052	S.F.
0300	1/2" thick, solid			155	.052	S.F.
0350	Perforated			155	.052	S.F.
0500	Link mats, including nosings, aluminum, 3/8" thick			155	.052	S.F.
0550	Black rubber with galvanized tie rods			155	.052	S.F.
0600	Steel, galvanized, 3/8" thick	↓	↓	155	.052	S.F.

126 900 | Floor Mats And Frames

		CREW	MAKEUP	DAILY OUTPUT	MAN-HOURS	UNIT
901	0651	Floor link mats, vinyl, in colors	1 Clab	1 Building Laborer	155	.052	S.F.
	0850	Recess frames for above mats, aluminum	1 Carp	1 Carpenter	100	.080	L.F.
	0870	Bronze	"	"	100	.080	L.F.
	0900	Skate lock tile, 24" x 24" x 1/2" thick, rubber, black	1 Clab	1 Building Laborer	125	.064	S.F.
	0950	Color			125	.064	S.F.
	1000	12" x 24" border, black			75	.107	L.F.
	1100	Color			75	.107	L.F.
	1150	12" x 12" outside corner, black			100	.080	S.F.
	1200	Color			100	.080	S.F.
	1500	Duckboard, aluminum slats			155	.052	S.F.
	1700	Hardwood strips on rubber base, to 54" wide			155	.052	S.F.
	1800	Assembled with brass rods and vinyl spacers, to 48" wide			155	.052	S.F.
	1850	Tire fabric, 3/4" thick			155	.052	S.F.
	1900	Vinyl, 36" wide, in colors, hollow top & bottoms			155	.052	S.F.
	1950	Solid top & bottom members	↓	↓	155	.052	S.F.

127 100 | Miscellaneous Seating

		CREW	MAKEUP	DAILY OUTPUT	MAN-HOURS	UNIT
101	SEATING					
1000	Lecture hall, pedestal type, minimum	2 Carp	2 Carpenters	35	.457	Ea.
1200	Maximum			20	.800	Ea.
2000	Auditorium chair, all veneer construction			35	.457	Ea.
2200	Veneer back, padded seat			35	.457	Ea.
2350	Fully upholstered, spring seat	↓	↓	35	.457	Ea.

127 400 | Booths And Tables

		CREW	MAKEUP	DAILY OUTPUT	MAN-HOURS	UNIT
401	BOOTHS					
1000	Banquet, upholstered seat and back, custom					
1500	Straight, minimum	2 Carp	2 Carpenters	40	.400	L.F.
1520	Maximum			36	.444	L.F.
1600	"L" or "U" shape, minimum			35	.457	L.F.
1620	Maximum	↓	↓	30	.533	L.F.
1800	Upholstered outside finished backs for					
1810	single booths and custom banquets					
1820	Minimum	2 Carp	2 Carpenters	44	.364	L.F.
1840	Maximum	"	"	40	.400	L.F.
3000	Fixed seating, one piece plastic chair and					
3010	plastic laminate table top					
3100	Two seat, 24" x 24" table, minimum	F-7	2 Carpenters 2 Building Laborers Power Tools	30	1.070	Ea.
3120	Maximum			26	1.230	Ea.
3200	Four seat, 24" x 48" table, minimum			28	1.140	Ea.
3220	Maximum			24	1.330	Ea.
3300	Six seat, 24" x 76" table, minimum			26	1.230	Ea.
3320	Maximum			22	1.450	Ea.
3400	Eight seat, 24" x 102" table, minimum			20	1.600	Ea.
3420	Maximum	↓	↓	18	1.780	Ea.
4000	Free standing, wood fiber core with					
4010	plastic laminate face, single booth					
4100	24" wide	2 Carp	2 Carpenters	38	.421	Ea.
4150	48" wide			34	.471	Ea.
4200	60" wide			30	.533	Ea.
4300	Double booth, 24" wide			32	.500	Ea.
4350	48" wide			28	.571	Ea.
4400	60" wide	↓	↓	26	.615	Ea.
4600	Upholstered seat and back					
4650	Foursome, single booth, minimum	2 Carp	2 Carpenters	38	.421	Ea.
4700	Maximum	"	"	30	.533	Ea.

127 400 | Booths And Tables

		CREW	MAKEUP	DAILY OUTPUT	MAN-HOURS	UNIT
401	4801	Booths, free standing, upholstered seat & back, dbl. booth, min.	2 Carp	2 Carpenters	32	.500	Ea.
	4850	Maximum	"	"	26	.615	Ea.
	5000	Mount in floor, wood fiber core with					
	5010	plastic laminate face, single booth					
	5050	24" wide	F-7	2 Carpenters	30	1.070	Ea.
				2 Building Laborers			
				Power Tools			
	5100	48" wide			28	1.140	Ea.
	5150	60" wide			26	1.230	Ea.
	5200	Double booth, 24" wide			26	1.230	Ea.
	5250	48" wide			24	1.330	Ea.
	5300	60" wide	↓	↓	22	1.450	Ea.

DIVISION 13
SPECIAL CONSTRUCTION

DIVISION
13

SPECIAL CONSTRUCTION

The Special Construction Division contains productivity rates for the installation of various structures and products found in general construction. Examples include airplane hangars, greenhouses, and darkrooms.

As a general rule, the structures and products in this division are installed by the vendor as part of the purchase agreement. The installers are frequently specially trained for their task. The productivity rates in this division are based on the experiences of properly trained craftsmen, but not necessarily specialists, working in a reasonably comfortable environment without unnecessary space confinements. In actual practice, the expected productivity should be adjusted to make allowances for either unusual productivity-enhancing or restricting conditions.

The rates in this division represent new construction. For repair and remodeling work, substantial adjustments may be necessary to properly account for the unique nature of each project.

130 | Special Construction

130 100 | Air Supported Structures

			CREW	MAKEUP	DAILY OUTPUT	MAN-HOURS	UNIT
111		**AIR SUPPORTED STRUCTURES**					
	0020	Site preparation, incl. anchor placement and utilities	B-11B	1 Equipment Oper. (med.)	2,000	.008	SF Flr.
				1 Building Laborer			
				1 Dozer, 200 H.P.			
				1 Air Powered Tamper			
				1 Air Compr. 365 C.F.M.			
				2-50 Ft. Air Hoses, 1.5" Dia.			
	0050	Warehouse, polyester/vinyl fabric, 24 oz., over 10 yr. life, welded					
	0060	seams, tension cables, primary & auxiliary inflation system,					
	0070	airlock, personnel doors and liner					
	0100	5000 S.F.	4 Clab	4 Building Laborers	5,000	.006	SF Flr.
	0250	12,000 S.F.	"	"	6,000	.005	SF Flr.
	0400	24,000 S.F.	8 Clab	8 Building Laborers	12,000	.005	SF Flr.
	0500	50,000 S.F.	"	"	12,500	.005	SF Flr.
	0700	12 oz. reinforced vinyl fabric, 5 yr. life, sewn seams,					
	0710	accordian door, including liner					
	0750	3000 S.F.	4 Clab	4 Building Laborers	3,000	.011	SF Flr.
	0800	12,000 S.F.	"	"	6,000	.005	SF Flr.
	0850	24,000 S.F.	8 Clab	8 Building Laborers	12,000	.005	SF Flr.
	1250	Tedlar/vinyl fabric, 17 oz., with liner, over 10 yr. life,					
	1260	incl. overhead and personnel doors					
	1300	3000 S.F.	4 Clab	4 Building Laborers	3,000	.011	SF Flr.
	1450	12,000 S.F.	"	"	6,000	.005	SF Flr.
	1550	24,000 S.F.	8 Clab	8 Building Laborers	12,000	.005	SF Flr.
	2250	Greenhouse/shelter, woven polyethylene with liner, 2 yr. life,					
	2260	sewn seams, including doors					
	2300	3000 S.F.	4 Clab	4 Building Laborers	3,000	.011	SF Flr.
	2350	12,000 S.F.	"	"	6,000	.005	SF Flr.
	2450	24,000 S.F.	8 Clab	8 Building Laborers	12,000	.005	SF Flr.
	2600	Tennis/gymnasium, polyester/vinyl fabric, 24 oz., over 10 yr. life,					
	2610	including thermal liner, heat and lights					
	2650	7200 S.F.	4 Clab	4 Building Laborers	6,000	.005	SF Flr.
	2750	13,000 S.F.	"	"	6,500	.005	SF Flr.
	2850	Over 24,000 S.F.	8 Clab	8 Building Laborers	12,000	.005	SF Flr.
	3050	Stadium/convention center, teflon coated fiberglass, heavy weight,					
	3060	over 20 yr. life, incl. thermal liner and heating system					
	3100	Minimum	9 Clab	9 Building Laborers	26,000	.003	SF Flr.
	3110	Maximum	"	"	19,000	.004	SF Flr.
	3400	Doors, air lock, 15' long, 10' x 10'	2 Carp	2 Carpenters	.80	20.000	Ea.
	3600	15' x 15'	↓	↓	.50	32.000	Ea.
	3900	Revolving personnel door, 6' diameter, 6'-6" high			.80	20.000	Ea.
115	0100	**AIR SUPPORTED STORAGE TANK COVERS** Vinyl polyester scrim, double layer, with hardware, blower, standby & controls					
	0200	Round, 75' diameter	B-2	1 Labor Foreman (outside)	5,000	.008	S.F.
				4 Building Laborers			
	0300	100' diameter			6,000	.007	S.F.
	0400	150' diameter			6,000	.007	S.F.
	0500	Rectangular, 20' x 20'			6,000	.007	S.F.
	0600	30' x 40'			6,000	.007	S.F.
	0700	50' x 60'	↓	↓	6,000	.007	S.F.

130 250 | Integrated Ceilings

			CREW	MAKEUP	DAILY OUTPUT	MAN-HOURS	UNIT
251		**INTEGRATED CEILINGS** Lighting, ventilating & acoustical					
	0100	Luminaire, incl. HVAC & light., 5' x 5' modules, 50% lighted	L-3	1 Carpenter	90	.178	S.F.
				.5 Electrician			
				.5 Sheet Metal Worker			
	0200	100% lighted	↓	↓	50	.320	S.F.
	0701	Dimensionaire, 2' x 4' board system			50	.320	L.F.

130 250 | Integrated Ceilings

		CREW	MAKEUP	DAILY OUTPUT	MAN-HOURS	UNIT
0901	Integrated ceilings, dimensionaire, 2' x 4' tile system	1 Carp	1 Carpenter	250	.032	S.F.
1600	Grid sys. & ceil. tile only, flat profile, 5'x5' mod., 50% lghtd.					
1620	Mineral fiber panels	1 Carp	1 Carpenter	700	.011	S.F.
1630	Glass fiber panels			700	.011	S.F.
1660	For vaulted coffer, 5' x 5' modules, 50% lighted	↓	↓	500	.016	S.F.
4000	Radiant electric ceiling board, strapped between joists	1 Elec	1 Electrician	250	.032	S.F.
4100	2' x 4' heating panel for grid system, manila finish			25	.320	Ea.
4200	Textured epoxy finish			22	.364	Ea.
4300	Vinyl finish			19	.421	Ea.
4400	Hair cell, ABS plastic finish	↓	↓	13	.615	Ea.
4500	2' x 4' alternate blank panel, for use with above					
4600	Manila finish	1 Elec	1 Electrician	50	.160	Ea.
4700	Textured epoxy finish			45	.178	Ea.
4800	Vinyl finish			40	.200	Ea.
4900	Hair cell, ABS plastic finish	↓	↓	25	.320	Ea.

130 300 | Special Purpose Rooms

		CREW	MAKEUP	DAILY OUTPUT	MAN-HOURS	UNIT
305	DARKROOMS Shell, complete except for door, 64 S.F., 8' high	2 Carp	2 Carpenters	128	.125	SF Flr.
0100	12' high			64	.250	SF Flr.
0500	120 S.F. floor, 8' high			120	.133	SF Flr.
0600	12' high			60	.267	SF Flr.
0800	240 S.F. floor, 8' high			120	.133	SF Flr.
0900	12' high			60	.267	SF Flr.
1200	Mini-cylindrical, revolving, unlined, 4' diameter			3.50	4.570	Ea.
1400	5'-6" diameter	↓	↓	2.50	6.400	Ea.

130 320 | Athletic Rooms

		CREW	MAKEUP	DAILY OUTPUT	MAN-HOURS	UNIT
321	SPORT COURT					
0450	Rule of thumb for components:					
0470	Walls	3 Carp	3 Carpenters	.15	160.000	Court
0500	Floor	"	"	.25	96.000	Court
0550	Lighting	2 Elec	2 Electricians	.60	26.670	Court
0600	Handball, racquetball court in existing building, minimum	C-1	3 Carpenters 1 Building Laborer Power Tools	.20	160.000	Court
0800	Maximum	"	"	.10	320.000	Court
0900	Rule of thumb for components: walls	3 Carp	3 Carpenters	.12	200.000	Court
1000	Floor			.25	96.000	Court
1100	Ceiling	↓	↓	.33	72.730	Court
1200	Lighting	2 Elec	2 Electricians	.60	26.670	Court

130 340 | Audiometric Rooms

		CREW	MAKEUP	DAILY OUTPUT	MAN-HOURS	UNIT
341	AUDIOMETRIC ROOMS Under 500 S.F. surface	4 Carp	4 Carpenters	98	.327	SF Surf
0100	Over 500 S.F. surface	"	"	120	.267	SF Surf

130 380 | Cold Storage Rooms

		CREW	MAKEUP	DAILY OUTPUT	MAN-HOURS	UNIT
381	REFRIGERATORS Curbs, 12" high, 4" thick, concrete	2 Carp	2 Carpenters	58	.276	L.F.
2400	Finishes, 2 coat portland cement plaster, 1/2" thick	1 Plas	1 Plasterer	48	.167	S.F.
2500	For galvanized reinforcing mesh, add	1 Lath	1 Lather	335	.024	S.F.
2700	3/16" thick latex cement	1 Plas	1 Plasterer	88	.091	S.F.
2900	For glass cloth reinforced ceilings, add	"	"	450	.018	S.F.
3100	Fiberglass panels, 1/8" thick	1 Carp	1 Carpenter	149.45	.054	S.F.
3200	Polystyrene, plastic finish ceiling, 1" thick			274	.029	S.F.
3400	2" thick			274	.029	S.F.
3500	4" thick	↓	↓	219	.037	S.F.
3800	Floors, concrete, 4" thick	1 Cefi	1 Cement Finisher	93	.086	S.F.
3900	6" thick	"	"	85	.094	S.F.
4900	Partitions, galvanized sandwich panels, 4" thick, stock	2 Carp	2 Carpenters	219.20	.073	S.F.

.251

130 | Special Construction

130 380 | Cold Storage Rooms

		CREW	MAKEUP	DAILY OUTPUT	MAN-HOURS	UNIT
381 5001	Refrigerators, partitions, aluminum or fiberglass, 4" thick	2 Carp	2 Carpenters	219.20	.073	S.F.
5200	Prefab walk-in, 7'-6" high, aluminum, incl. door & floors,					
5210	not incl. partitions or refrigeration, 6' x 6' O.D. nominal	2 Carp	2 Carpenters	54.80	.292	SF Flr.
5500	10' x 10' O.D. nominal			82.20	.195	SF Flr.
5700	12' x 14' O.D. nominal			109.60	.146	SF Flr.
5800	12' x 20' O.D. nominal			109.60	.146	SF Flr.
6300	Rule of thumb for complete units, not incl. doors, cooler			146	.110	SF Flr.
6400	Freezer			109.60	.146	SF Flr.
6600	Shelving, plated or galvanized, steel wire type			360	.044	SF Hor.
6700	Slat shelf type			375	.043	SF Hor.
7000	Vapor barrier, on wood walls			1,644	.010	S.F.
7200	On masonry walls	↓	↓	1,315	.012	S.F.

130 520 | Saunas

		CREW	MAKEUP	DAILY OUTPUT	MAN-HOURS	UNIT
521	SAUNA Prefabricated, incl. heater & controls, 7' high, 6' x 4'	L-7	2 Carpenters 1 Building Laborer .5 Electrician	2.20	12.730	Ea.
0400	6' x 5'			2	14.000	Ea.
0600	6' x 6'			1.80	15.560	Ea.
0800	6' x 9'			1.60	17.500	Ea.
1000	8' x 12'			1.10	25.450	Ea.
1200	8' x 8'			1.40	20.000	Ea.
1400	8' x 10'			1.20	23.330	Ea.
1600	10' x 12'	↓	↓	1	28.000	Ea.
1700	Door only, with tempered insulated glass window	2 Carp	2 Carpenters	3.40	4.710	Ea.
1800	Prehung, incl. jambs, pulls & hardware	"	"	12	1.330	Ea.

130 540 | Steam Baths

		CREW	MAKEUP	DAILY OUTPUT	MAN-HOURS	UNIT
541	STEAM BATH Heater, timer & head, single, to 140 C.F.	1 Plum	1 Plumber	1.20	6.670	Ea.
0500	To 300 C.F.			1.10	7.270	Ea.
1000	Commercial size, to 800 C.F.			.90	8.890	Ea.
1500	To 2500 C.F.	↓	↓	.80	10.000	Ea.
2000	Multiple baths, motels, apartment, 2 baths	Q-1	1 Plumber 1 Plumber Apprentice	1.30	12.310	Ea.
2500	4 baths	"	"	.70	22.860	Ea.

130 810 | Acoustical Enclosures

		CREW	MAKEUP	DAILY OUTPUT	MAN-HOURS	UNIT
811	ACOUSTICAL Enclosure, 4" thick wall and ceiling panels					
0020	8# per S.F., up to 12' span	3 Carp	3 Carpenters	72	.333	SF Surf
0300	Better quality panels, 10.5# per S.F.			64	.375	SF Surf
0400	Reverb-chamber, 4" thick, parallel walls			60	.400	SF Surf
0600	Skewed wall, parallel roof, 4" thick panels			55	.436	SF Surf
0700	Skewed walls, skewed roof, 4" layers, 4" air space			48	.500	SF Surf
0900	Sound-absorbing panels, pntd mtl, 2'-6" x 8', under 1000 S.F.			215	.112	SF Surf
1100	Over 2400 S.F.			240	.100	SF Surf
1200	Fabric faced	↓	↓	240	.100	SF Surf
1500	Flexible transparent curtain, clear	3 Shee	3 Sheet Metal Workers	215	.112	SF Surf
1600	50% foam			215	.112	SF Surf
1700	75% foam			215	.112	SF Surf
1800	100% foam	↓	↓	215	.112	SF Surf
3100	Audio masking system, including speakers, amplification					
3110	and signal generator					
3200	Ceiling mounted, 5000 S.F.	2 Elec	2 Electricians	2,400	.007	S.F.
3300	10,000 S.F.			2,800	.006	S.F.
3400	Plenum mounted, 5000 S.F.			3,800	.004	S.F.
3500	10,000 S.F.	↓	↓	4,400	.004	S.F.

130 | Special Construction

130 810	Acoustical Enclosures	CREW	MAKEUP	DAILY OUTPUT	MAN-HOURS	UNIT
815	MUSIC Practice room, modular, perforated steel, under 500 S.F.	2 Carp	2 Carpenters	70	.229	SF Surf
0100	Over 500 S.F.	"	"	80	.200	SF Surf

130 910	Radiation Protection	CREW	MAKEUP	DAILY OUTPUT	MAN-HOURS	UNIT
911	SHIELDING LEAD					
0200	Lead lined door frame, not incl. steel frame					
0210	or hardware, 1/16" thick	1 Lath	1 Lather	2.40	3.330	Ea.
0300	Lead lath or sheets, 1/16" thick	2 Lath	2 Lathers	135	.119	S.F.
0400	1/8" thick			120	.133	S.F.
0600	Lead glass, 1/4" thick, 12" x 16"			13	1.230	Ea.
0700	24" x 36"			8	2.000	Ea.
0800	36" x 60"			2	8.000	Ea.
0850	Frame with 1/16" lead and voice passage, 36" x 60"			2	8.000	Ea.
0870	24" x 36" frame			8	2.000	Ea.
0900	Lead gypsum board, 5/8" thick with 1/16" lead			160	.100	S.F.
0910	1/8" lead			140	.114	S.F.
0930	1/32" lead			200	.080	S.F.
1000	Butt joints in 1/8" lead or thicker, lead strip, add	↓	↓	240	.067	S.F.
1200	X-ray protection, average radiography or fluoroscopy					
1210	room, up to 300 S.F. floor, 1/16" lead, minimum	2 Lath	2 Lathers	.25	64.000	Total
1500	Maximum, 7'-0" walls	"	"	.15	107.000	Total
1600	Deep therapy X-ray room, 250 KV capacity,					
1800	up to 300 S.F. floor, 1/4" lead, minimum	2 Lath	2 Lathers	.08	200.000	Total
1900	Maximum, 7'-0" walls	"	"	.06	267.000	Total
912	SHIELDING, RADIO FREQUENCY					
0020	Prefabricated or screen-type copper or steel, minimum	2 Carp	2 Carpenters	180	.089	SF Surf
0100	Average			155	.103	SF Surf
0150	Maximum	↓	↓	145	.110	SF Surf

131 | Pre-Eng. Structures, Pools and Ice Rinks

131 200	Pre-Eng Structures	CREW	MAKEUP	DAILY OUTPUT	MAN-HOURS	UNIT
202	DOMES Revolving aluminum, electric drive,					
0020	for astronomy observation, shell only, stock units					
0600	10'-0" diameter, 800#, dome	2 Carp	2 Carpenters	.25	64.000	Ea.
0700	Base			.67	23.880	Ea.
0900	18'-0" diameter, 2,500#, dome			.17	94.120	Ea.
1000	Base			.33	48.480	Ea.
1200	24'-0" diameter, 4,500#, dome			.08	200.000	Ea.
1300	Base	↓	↓	.25	64.000	Ea.
1500	Bulk storage, shell only, dual radius hemispher. arch, steel					
1600	framing, corrugated steel covering, 150' diameter	E-2	1 Struc. Steel Foreman 4 Struc. Steel Workers 1 Equip. Oper. (crane) 1 Equip. Oper. Oiler 1 Crane, 90 Ton	550	.102	SF Flr.
1700	400' diameter	"	"	720	.078	SF Flr.
1800	Wood framing, wood decking, to 400' diameter	F-4	4 Carpenters 1 Equip. Oper. (crane) 1 Equip. Oper. Oiler 1 Hyd. Crane, 55 Ton Power Tools	400	.120	SF Flr.

815

381

131 200	Pre-Eng Structures	CREW	MAKEUP	DAILY OUTPUT	MAN-HOURS	UNIT
202 1901	Domes, radial framed wood (2" x 6"), 1/2" thick					
2000	plywood, asphalt shingles, 50' diameter	F-3	4 Carpenters	2,000	.020	SF Flr.
			1 Equip. Oper. (crane)			
			1 Hyd. Crane, 12 Ton			
			Power Tools			
2100	60' diameter			1,900	.021	SF Flr.
2200	72' diameter			1,800	.022	SF Flr.
2300	116' diameter			1,730	.023	SF Flr.
2400	150' diameter			1,500	.027	SF Flr.
203	**GEODESIC DOME** Shell only, interlocking plywood panels					
0400	30' diameter	F-5	1 Carpenter Foreman	1.60	20.000	Ea.
			3 Carpenters			
			Power Tools			
0500	35' diameter			1.14	28.070	Ea.
0600	39' diameter			1	32.000	Ea.
0700	45' diameter			.90	35.560	Ea.
0800	60' diameter	F-3	4 Carpenters	.40	100.000	Ea.
			1 Equip. Oper. (crane)			
			1 Hyd. Crane, 12 Ton			
			Power Tools			
1100	Aluminum panel, stressed skin, with 1-1/2" insulation					
1200	82' diameter	L-5	1 Struc. Steel Foreman	900	.062	SF Flr.
			5 Struc. Steel Workers			
			1 Equip. Oper. (crane)			
			1 Hyd. Crane, 25 Ton			
1300	232' diameter	"	"	1,300	.043	SF Flr.
1600	Aluminum framed, plexiglass closure panels					
1700	40' diameter	K-2	1 Struc. Steel Foreman	250	.096	SF Flr.
			1 Struc. Steel Worker			
			1 Truck Driver (light)			
			1 Truck w/Power Equip.			
1800	200' diameter	L-5	1 Struc. Steel Foreman	1,000	.056	SF Flr.
			5 Struc. Steel Workers			
			1 Equip. Oper. (crane)			
			1 Hyd. Crane, 25 Ton			
2100	Aluminum framed, aluminum closure panels					
2200	40' diameter	K-2	1 Struc. Steel Foreman	500	.048	SF Flr.
			1 Struc. Steel Worker			
			1 Truck Driver (light)			
			1 Truck w/Power Equip.			
2300	320' diameter	C-17C	2 Skilled Worker Foremen	1,900	.044	SF Flr.
			8 Skilled Workers			
			.375 Equip. Oper. (crane)			
			.375 Crane, 80 Ton & Tools			
			.375 Hand held power tools			
			.375 Walk behind power tools			
2400	415' diameter	"	"	2,300	.036	SF Flr.
2700	Aluminum framed, fiberglass sandwich panel closure					
2800	6' diameter	F-2	2 Carpenters	150	.107	SF Flr.
			Power Tools			
2900	28' diameter	"	"	350	.046	SF Flr.
204	**GARAGES**					
0300	Residential, prefab shell, stock, wood, single car, minimum	F-2	2 Carpenters	1	16.000	Total
			Power Tools			
0350	Maximum			.67	23.880	Total
0400	Two car, minimum			.67	23.880	Total
0450	Maximum			.50	32.000	Total

131 | Pre-Eng. Structures, Pools and Ice Rinks

131 200 | Pre-Eng Structures

		CREW	MAKEUP	DAILY OUTPUT	MAN-HOURS	UNIT
205	**SILOS** Concrete stave industrial, not incl. foundations, conical or					
0100	sloping bottoms, 12' diameter, 35' high	D-8	3 Bricklayers	.11	364.000	Ea.
			2 Bricklayer Helpers			
0200	16' diameter, 45' high	↓	↓	.08	500.000	Ea.
0400	25' diameter, 75' high			.05	800.000	Ea.
0500	Steel, factory fab., 30,000 gallon cap., painted, minimum	L-5	1 Struc. Steel Foreman	1	56.000	Ea.
			5 Struc. Steel Workers			
			1 Equip. Oper. (crane)			
			1 Hyd. Crane, 25 Ton			
0700	Maximum			.50	112.000	Ea.
0800	Epoxy lined, minimum			1	56.000	Ea.
1000	Maximum	↓	↓	.50	112.000	Ea.
207	**TENSION STRUCTURES** Rigid steel frame, vinyl coated polyester					
0100	fabric shell, 72' clear span, not incl. foundations or floors					
0200	4,800 S.F.	B-41	1 Labor Foreman (outside)	1,000	.044	SF Flr.
			4 Building Laborers			
			.25 Equip. Oper. (crane)			
			.25 Equip. Oper. Oiler			
			.25 Crawler Crane, 40 Ton			
0300	12,000 S.F.	↓	↓	1,100	.040	SF Flr.
0400	20,600 S.F.			1,220	.036	SF Flr.
0410	124' clear span, 11,000 S.F.	L-5	1 Struc. Steel Foreman	2,175	.026	SF Flr.
			5 Struc. Steel Workers			
			1 Equip. Oper. (crane)			
			1 Hyd. Crane, 25 Ton			
0430	25,750 S.F.	↓	↓	2,300	.024	SF Flr.
0450	36,900 S.F.			2,500	.022	SF Flr.
0500	For roll-up door, 12' x 14', add	L-2	1 Carpenter	1	16.000	Ea.
			1 Helper			

131 210 | Pre-Engineered Buildings

		CREW	MAKEUP	DAILY OUTPUT	MAN-HOURS	UNIT
211	**HANGARS** Prefabricated steel T hangars, Galv. steel roof &					
0100	walls, incl. electric bi-folding doors, 4 or more units,					
0110	not including floors or foundations, minimum	E-2	1 Struc. Steel Foreman	1,275	.044	SF Flr.
			4 Struc. Steel Workers			
			1 Equip. Oper. (crane)			
			1 Equip. Oper. Oiler			
			1 Crane, 90 Ton			
0130	Maximum			1,063	.053	SF Flr.
0900	With bottom rolling doors, minimum			1,386	.040	SF Flr.
1000	Maximum	↓	↓	966	.058	SF Flr.
1200	Alternate pricing method:					
1300	Galv. roof and walls, electric bi-folding doors, minimum	E-2	1 Struc. Steel Foreman	1.06	52.830	Plane
			4 Struc. Steel Workers			
			1 Equip. Oper. (crane)			
			1 Equip. Oper. Oiler			
			1 Crane, 90 Ton			
1500	Maximum			.91	61.540	Plane
1600	With bottom rolling doors, minimum			1.25	44.800	Plane
1800	Maximum	↓	↓	.97	57.730	Plane
2000	Circular type, prefab., steel frame, plastic skin, electric					
2010	door, including foundations, 80' diameter,					
2020	for up to 5 light planes, minimum	E-2	1 Struc. Steel Foreman	.50	112.000	Total
			4 Struc. Steel Workers			
			1 Equip. Oper. (crane)			
			1 Equip. Oper. Oiler			
			1 Crane, 90 Ton			
2200	Maximum	"	"	.25	224.000	Total

131 | Pre-Eng. Structures, Pools and Ice Rinks

131 220 | Metal Building Systems

		CREW	MAKEUP	DAILY OUTPUT	MAN-HOURS	UNIT
221	**SHELTERS** Aluminum frame, acrylic glazing, 3' x 9' x 8' high	2 Sswk	2 Struc. Steel Workers	2	8.000	Ea.
0100	9' x 12' x 8' high			1	16.000	Ea.

131 230 | Greenhouses

		CREW	MAKEUP	DAILY OUTPUT	MAN-HOURS	UNIT
231	**GREENHOUSE** Shell only, stock units, not incl. 2' stub walls,					
0020	foundation, floors, heat or compartments					
0300	Residential type, free standing, 8'-6" long x 7'-6" wide	2 Carp	2 Carpenters	59	.271	SF Flr.
0400	10'-6" wide			85	.188	SF Flr.
0600	13'-6" wide			108	.148	SF Flr.
0700	17'-0" wide			160	.100	SF Flr.
0900	Lean-to type, 3'-10" wide			34	.471	SF Flr.
1000	6'-10" wide	↓	↓	58	.276	SF Flr.
6000	Geodesic hemisphere, 1/8" plexiglass glazing					
6050	8' diameter	2 Carp	2 Carpenters	2	8.000	Ea.
6150	24' diameter			.35	45.710	Ea.
6250	48' diameter	↓	↓	.20	80.000	Ea.

131 240 | Portable Buildings

		CREW	MAKEUP	DAILY OUTPUT	MAN-HOURS	UNIT
242	**COMFORT STATIONS** Prefab., stock, w/doors, windows & fixt.					
0100	Not incl. interior finish or electrical					
0400	Permanent, including concrete slab, minimum	B-12J	1 Equip. Oper. (crane)	50	.320	S.F.
			1 Equip. Oper. Oiler			
			1 Gradall, 3 Ton, .5 C.Y.			
0500	Maximum	"	"	43	.372	S.F.
244	**GARDEN HOUSE** Prefab wood, no floors or foundations					
0100	48 to 200 S.F., minimum	F-2	2 Carpenters	200	.080	SF Flr.
			Power Tools			
0300	Maximum	"	"	48	.333	SF Flr.

131 520 | Swimming Pools

		CREW	MAKEUP	DAILY OUTPUT	MAN-HOURS	UNIT
521	**SWIMMING POOL ENCLOSURE** Translucent, free standing,					
0020	not including foundations, heat or light					
0200	Economy, minimum	2 Carp	2 Carpenters	200	.080	SF Hor.
0300	Maximum			100	.160	SF Hor.
0400	Deluxe, minimum			100	.160	SF Hor.
0600	Maximum			70	.229	SF Hor.
523	**SWIMMING POOL EQUIPMENT** Diving stand, stainless steel, 3 meter			.40	40.000	Ea.
0300	1 meter			2.70	5.930	Ea.
0600	Diving boards, 16' long, aluminum			2.70	5.930	Ea.
0700	Fiberglass	↓	↓	2.70	5.930	Ea.
0900	Filter system, sand or diatomite type, incl. pump, 6000 gal./hr.	2 Plum	2 Plumbers	1.80	8.890	Total
1020	Add for chlorination system, 800 S.F. pool			3	5.330	Ea.
1040	5000 S.F. pool	↓	↓	3	5.330	Ea.
1100	Gutter system, stainless steel, with grating, stock,					
1110	contains supply and drainage system	E-1	1 Welder Foreman	20	1.200	L.F.
			1 Welder			
			1 Equip. Oper. (light)			
			1 Gas Welding Machine			
1120	Integral gutter and 5' high wall system, stainless steel	"	"	10	2.400	L.F.
1200	Ladders, heavy duty, stainless steel, 2 tread	2 Carp	2 Carpenters	7	2.290	Ea.
1500	4 tread			6	2.670	Ea.
1800	Lifeguard chair, stainless steel, fixed	↓	↓	2.70	5.930	Ea.
2100	Lights, underwater, 12 volt, with transformer, 300 watt	1 Elec	1 Electrician	.40	20.000	Ea.
2200	110 volt, 500 watt, standard			.40	20.000	Ea.
2400	Low water cutoff type	↓	↓	.40	20.000	Ea.
3300	Slides, fiberglass, aluminum handrails & ladder, 6'-0", straight	2 Carp	2 Carpenters	1.60	10.000	Ea.
3320	7'-6", curved			3	5.330	Ea.
3400	10'-6", curved	↓	↓	1	16.000	Ea.

131 | Pre-Eng. Structures, Pools and Ice Rinks

131 520 | Swimming Pools

		CREW	MAKEUP	DAILY OUTPUT	MAN-HOURS	UNIT
3420	Slides, fiberglass, 12'-0", straight with platform	2 Carp	2 Carpenters	1.20	13.330	Ea.
4500	Hydraulic lift, movable pool bottom, single ram					
4520	Under 1000 S.F. area	L-9	1 Labor Foreman (inside)	.03	200.000	Ea.
			2 Building Laborers			
			1 Struc. Steel Worker			
			.5 Electrician			
4600	Four ram lift, over 1000 S.F.	"	"	.02	800.000	Ea.
5000	Removable access ramp, stainless steel	2 Clab	2 Building Laborers	2	8.000	Ea.
5500	Removable stairs, stainless steel, collapsible	"	"	2	8.000	Ea.

131 600 | Ice Rinks

		CREW	MAKEUP	DAILY OUTPUT	MAN-HOURS	UNIT
601	ICE SKATING					
1000	Dasher boards, polyethylene coated plywood, 3' acrylic					
1020	screen at sides, 5' acrylic ends, 85' x 200'	F-5	1 Carpenter Foreman	.07	457.000	Ea.
			3 Carpenters			
			Power Tools			
1100	Fiberglass & aluminum construction, same sides and ends	"	"	.07	457.000	Ea.
1200	Subsoil heating system (recycled from compressor), 85' x 200'	Q-7	1 Steamfitter Foreman (ins)	.30	107.000	Ea.
			2 Steamfitters			
			1 Steamfitter Apprentice			
1300	Subsoil insulation, 2 lb. polystyrene with vapor barrier, 85' x 200'	F-2	2 Carpenters	.16	100.000	Ea.
			Power Tools			

132 | Tanks, Tank Covers, Filtration Equipment

132 050 | Ground Storage Tanks

		CREW	MAKEUP	DAILY OUTPUT	MAN-HOURS	UNIT
051	TANKS Not incl. pipe or pumps					
6000	Wood tanks, ground level, 2" cypress, 3,000 gallons	C-1	3 Carpenters	.19	168.000	Ea.
			1 Building Laborer			
			Power Tools			
6100	2-1/2" cypress, 10,000 gallons			.12	267.000	Ea.
6300	3" redwood or 3" fir, 20,000 gallons			.10	320.000	Ea.
6400	30,000 gallons			.08	400.000	Ea.
6600	45,000 gallons			.07	457.000	Ea.
7000	Vinyl coated fabric pillow tanks, freestanding, 5000 gallons	4 Clab	4 Building Laborers	4	8.000	Ea.
7100	Supporting embankment not included, 25,000 gallons	6 Clab	6 Building Laborers	2	24.000	Ea.
7200	50,000 gallons	8 Clab	8 Building Laborers	1.50	42.670	Ea.
7300	100,000 gallons	9 Clab	9 Building Laborers	.90	80.000	Ea.
7400	150,000 gallons			.50	144.000	Ea.
7500	200,000 gallons			.40	180.000	Ea.
7600	250,000 gallons			.30	240.000	Ea.

133 300	Power Control Systems	CREW	MAKEUP	DAILY OUTPUT	MAN-HOURS	UNIT
311	**311**	**RADIO TOWERS** Guyed, 50' high, 40 lb. section, wind load 30 psf	2 Sswk	2 Struc. Steel Workers	1	16.000	Ea.
	0100	Wind load 50 psf	"	"	1	16.000	Ea.
	0300	200' high, 40 lb. section, wind load 30 psf	K-2	1 Struc. Steel Foreman	.33	72.730	Ea.
				1 Struc. Steel Worker			
				1 Truck Driver (light)			
				1 Truck w/Power Equip.			
	0400	70 lb. section, wind load 50 psf			.33	72.730	Ea.
	0600	300' high, 70 lb. section, wind load 30 psf			.20	120.000	Ea.
	0700	90 lb. section, wind load 50 psf			.20	120.000	Ea.
	0800	400' high, 90 lb. section, 30 psf wind load			.14	171.000	Ea.
	0900	Self-supporting, 30 psf wind load, 60' high			.80	30.000	Ea.
	1000	120' high			.40	60.000	Ea.
	1200	200' high			.20	120.000	Ea.

DIVISION 14

CONVEYING SYSTEMS

DIVISION
14
CONVEYING SYSTEMS

The Conveying Systems Division contains productivity rates for the installation of various systems of this type that are commonly found in buildings. Examples include dumbwaiters, elevators, and escalators.

As a general rule, the products in this division are installed by the vendor as part of the purchase agreement. The installers are frequently specially trained for their task. The productivity rates in this division are based on the experiences of properly trained specialists, working in a reasonably comfortable environment without excessive space confinements. In actual practice, the expected productivity should be adjusted to make allowances for either unusual productivity-enhancing or restricting conditions.

The rates in this division represent new construction. For repair and remodeling work, substantial adjustments may be necessary to properly account for the unique nature of each project.

141 | Dumbwaiters

141 100 | Manual Dumbwaiters

		Description	CREW	MAKEUP	DAILY OUTPUT	MAN-HOURS	UNIT
101	101	DUMBWAITERS 2 stop, hand, minimum	2 Elev	2 Elevator Constructors	.23	69.570	Ea.
	0100	Maximum			.19	84.210	Ea.
	0300	For each additional stop, add	↓	↓	.60	26.670	Stop

141 200 | Electric Dumbwaiters

	Description	CREW	MAKEUP	DAILY OUTPUT	MAN-HOURS	UNIT
201	DUMBWAITERS 2 stop, electric, minimum	2 Elev	2 Elevator Constructors	.13	123.000	Ea.
0100	Maximum			.11	145.000	Ea.
0600	For each additional stop, add	↓	↓	.54	29.630	Stop

142 | Elevators

142 010 | Elevators

	Description	CREW	MAKEUP	DAILY OUTPUT	MAN-HOURS	UNIT
011	ELEVATORS					
0600	2 story, hydraulic, 4,000 lb. capacity, minimum	M-1	3 Elevator Constructors 1 Elevator Apprentice Hand Tools	.09	356.000	Ea.
0700	Maximum			.09	356.000	Ea.
0900	10,000 lb. capacity, minimum			.07	457.000	Ea.
1000	Maximum			.07	457.000	Ea.
1200	6 story hydraulic, 4,000 lb. capacity			.03	67.000	Ea.
1300	10,000 lb. capacity			.03	67.000	Ea.
1500	6 story geared electric 4,000 lb. capacity			.04	800.000	Ea.
1600	10,000 lb. capacity			.03	67.000	Ea.
1640	12 story gearless electric 4000 lb. capacity			.03	67.000	Ea.
1680	10,000 lb. capacity			.03	67.000	Ea.
1740	20 story gearless electric 4000 lb. capacity			.02	600.000	Ea.
1780	10,000 lb. capacity			.02	600.000	Ea.
2020	Passenger, 2 story hydraulic, 2000 lb. capacity			.07	457.000	Ea.
2040	5000 lb. capacity			.07	457.000	Ea.
2060	6 story hydraulic, 2000 lb. capacity			.03	67.000	Ea.
2080	5000 lb. capacity			.03	67.000	Ea.
2140	6 story geared electric, 2000 lb. capacity			.04	800.000	Ea.
2180	5000 lb. capacity			.04	800.000	Ea.
2240	12 story gearless electric, 2000 lb. capacity			.03	67.000	Ea.
2280	5000 lb. capacity			.03	67.000	Ea.
2340	20 story gearless electric, 2000 lb. capacity			.02	600.000	Ea.
2380	5000 lb. capacity			.02	600.000	Ea.
5000	Passenger, pre-engineered, 5 story, hydraulic, 2,500 lb. cap.			.04	800.000	Ea.
5100	For less than 5 stops, deduct			.29	110.000	Stop
5400	10 story, geared traction, 200 FPM, 2,500 lb. capacity			.02	600.000	Ea.
5500	For less than 10 stops, deduct			.34	94.120	Stop
5600	For 4,500 lb. capacity, general purpose			.02	600.000	Ea.
5700	For hospital	↓	↓	.02	600.000	Ea.
7000	Residential, cab type, 1 floor, 2 stop, minimum	2 Elev	2 Elevator Constructors	.20	80.000	Ea.
7100	Maximum			.10	160.000	Ea.
7200	2 floor, 3 stop, minimum			.12	133.000	Ea.
7300	Maximum			.06	267.000	Ea.
7700	Stair climber (chair lift), single seat, minimum			1	16.000	Ea.
7800	Maximum			.20	80.000	Ea.
8000	Wheelchair, porch lift, minimum			1	16.000	Ea.
8500	Maximum			.50	32.000	Ea.
8700	Stair lift, minimum	↓	↓	1	16.000	Ea.

142 | Elevators

	142 010	Elevators	CREW	MAKEUP	DAILY OUTPUT	MAN-HOURS	UNIT
011	8901	Elevators, residential wheelchair stair lift, maximum	2 Elev	2 Elevator Constructors	.20	80.000	Ea.

143 | Moving Stairs and Walks

	143 100	Escalators	CREW	MAKEUP	DAILY OUTPUT	MAN-HOURS	UNIT
	101	ESCALATORS Per single unit, minimum	M-1	3 Elevator Constructors	.06	533.000	Ea.
				1 Elevator Apprentice			
				Hand Tools			
	0300	Maximum	"	"	.04	800.000	Ea.

	143 200	Moving Walks	CREW	MAKEUP	DAILY OUTPUT	MAN-HOURS	UNIT
	201	MOVING RAMPS AND WALKS Walk, 24" tread width, minimum	M-1	3 Elevator Constructors	6.50	4.920	L.F.
				1 Elevator Apprentice			
				Hand Tools			
	0100	Maximum			4.43	7.220	L.F.
	0300	40" tread width walk, minimum			4.43	7.220	L.F.
	0400	Maximum			3.82	8.380	L.F.
	0600	Ramp, 12° incline, 32" tread width, minimum			5.27	6.070	L.F.
	0700	Maximum			3.82	8.380	L.F.
	0900	40" tread width, minimum			3.57	8.960	L.F.
	1000	Maximum	↓	↓	2.91	11.000	L.F.

144 | Lifts

	144 010	Lifts	CREW	MAKEUP	DAILY OUTPUT	MAN-HOURS	UNIT
	011	CORRESPONDENCE LIFT 1 floor 2 stop, 25 lb. capacity, electric	2 Elev	2 Elevator Constructors	.20	80.000	Ea.
	0100	Hand, 5 lb. capacity	"	"	.20	80.000	Ea.
	015	PARCEL LIFT 20" x 20", 100 lb. capacity, electric, per floor	2 Mill	2 Millwrights	.25	64.000	Ea.

145 | Material Handling Systems

	145 010	Mat Handling Systems	CREW	MAKEUP	DAILY OUTPUT	MAN-HOURS	UNIT
	011	MOTORIZED CAR Distribution systems, single track,					
	0100	20 lb. per car capacity, material handling					
	0200	Minimum	4 Mill	4 Millwrights	.19	168.000	Station
	0300	Maximum	"	"	.15	213.000	Station
	0400	Larger system, incl. hospital transport, track type,					
	0500	fully automated material handling system					
	0600	Minimum	4 Mill	4 Millwrights	.05	640.000	Station

145 | Material Handling Systems

145 010 | Mat Handling Systems

		Description	CREW	MAKEUP	DAILY OUTPUT	MAN-HOURS	UNIT
011	0701	Material handling system, track type, fully automated, maximum	E-6	3 Struc. Steel Foreman	.05	560.000	Station
				9 Struc. Steel Workers			
				1 Equip. Oper. (crane)			
				1 Welder			
				1 Equip. Oper. Oiler			
				1 Equip. Oper. (light)			
				1 Crane, 90 Ton			
				1 Gas Welding Machine			
				1 Torch, Gas & air			
				1 Air Compr., 160 C.F.M.			
				2 Impact Wrenches			

145 500 | Conveyors

	Description	CREW	MAKEUP	DAILY OUTPUT	MAN-HOURS	UNIT
501	**MATERIAL HANDLING** Conveyers, gravity type 2" rollers, 3" O.C.					
0350	Horizontal belt, center drive and takeup, 45 F.P.M.					
0400	16" belt, 26.5' length	M-2	2 Millwrights	.50	32.000	Ea.
			Power Tools			
0450	24" belt, 41.5' length	↓	↓	.40	40.000	Ea.
0500	61.5' length			.30	53.330	Ea.
0600	Inclined belt, 25° incline with horizontal loader and					
0620	end idler assembly, 34' length, 12" belt	M-2	2 Millwrights	.30	53.330	Ea.
			Power Tools			
0650	16" belt	↓	↓	.20	80.000	Ea.
0700	24" belt			.15	107.000	Ea.
1200	Conveyer, overhead, automatic powered					
1210	chain conveyer, 130 lb./L.F. capacity	M-2	2 Millwrights	17	.941	L.F.
			Power Tools			
3600	Monorail, overhead, manual, channel type					
3700	125 lb. per L.F.	1 Mill	1 Millwright	26	.308	L.F.
3900	500 lb. per L.F.	"	"	21	.381	L.F.
504	**VERTICAL CONVEYER** Automatic selective					
0100	central control, to 10 floors, base price	2 Mill	2 Millwrights	.04	400.000	Total
0200	For automatic service, any floor to any floor, add	"	"	1.15	13.910	Floor

145 600 | Chutes

	Description	CREW	MAKEUP	DAILY OUTPUT	MAN-HOURS	UNIT
601	**CHUTES** Linen or refuse, incl. sprinklers					
0050	Aluminized steel, 16 ga., 18" diameter	2 Shee	2 Sheet Metal Workers	3.50	4.570	Floor
0100	24" diameter			3.20	5.000	Floor
0200	30" diameter			3	5.330	Floor
0300	36" diameter			2.80	5.710	Floor
0400	Galvanized steel, 16 ga., 18" diameter			3.50	4.570	Floor
0500	24" diameter			3.20	5.000	Station
0600	30" diameter			3	5.330	Floor
0700	36" diameter			2.80	5.710	Floor
0800	Stainless steel, 18" diameter			3.50	4.570	Floor
0900	24" diameter			3.20	5.000	Floor
1000	30" diameter			3	5.330	Floor
1100	36" diameter			2.80	5.710	Floor
1200	Linen bottom collector, aluminized steel			4	4.000	Ea.
1300	Stainless steel			4	4.000	Ea.
1500	Refuse bottom hopper, aluminized steel, 18" diameter			3	5.330	Ea.
1600	24" diameter			3	5.330	Ea.
1800	36" diameter			3	5.330	Ea.
2900	Package chutes, spiral type, minimum			4.50	3.560	Floor
3000	Maximum	↓	↓	1.50	10.670	Floor

145 800 | **Tube Systems**	CREW	MAKEUP	DAILY OUTPUT	MAN-HOURS	UNIT
801 PNEUMATIC TUBE SYSTEM Single tube, 2 stations,					
0020 100' long, stock, economy,					
0100 3" diameter	2 Stpi	2 Steamfitters	.12	133.000	Total
0300 4" diameter	"	"	.09	178.000	Total
0400 Twin tube, two stations or more, conventional system					
0600 2-1/2" round	2 Stpi	2 Steamfitters	62.50	.256	L.F.
0700 3" round			46	.348	L.F.
0900 4" round			49.60	.323	L.F.
1000 4" x 7" oval			37.60	.426	L.F.
1050 Add for blower			2	8.000	System
1110 Plus for each round station, add			7.50	2.130	Ea.
1150 Plus for each oval station, add			7.50	2.130	Ea.
1200 Alternate pricing method: base cost, minimum			.75	21.330	Total
1300 Maximum			.25	64.000	Total
1500 Plus total system length, add, minimum			93.40	.171	L.F.
1600 Maximum			37.60	.426	L.F.
1800 Completely automatic system, 4" round, 15 to 50 stations			.29	55.170	Station
2200 51 to 144 stations			.32	50.000	Station
2400 6" round or 4" x 7" oval, 15 to 50 stations			.24	66.670	Station
2800 51 to 144 stations	↓	↓	.23	69.570	Station

DIVISION 15 MECHANICAL

DIVISION
15

MECHANICAL

Subdivisions in the Mechanical Division include: Pipe and Fittings, Plumbing Fixtures, Plumbing Appliances, Fire Extinguishing Systems, Heating, Air Conditioning, and Ventilating.

There are numerous factors that affect mechanical construction, but perhaps the most significant is job site conditions. The location of a mechanical installation varies to a great degree; therefore, the first task for developing productivity figures in this area is to evaluate the quality of access, height above floor, and routing of pipe or ducts. It is important to know exactly how many elevated installations are involved, how many straight runs, and how many complex runs there are in even the smallest portion of a job. All of these factors can add greatly to the time required to get the job done.

Since most tasks in this division are performed by specialists such as plumbers, steamfitters, and sheet metal workers, productivity is always directly tied to the level of expertise that these workers bring to the job. This varies with location and the quality of the labor force. The productivity figures in the listings assume that the mechanical craftsmen on the job are skilled, licensed workmen.

Weather may be a factor when installing mechanical items, since much of the work can only be done in a protected area within a reasonable temperature range.

Material storage methods must be evaluated, long trips up and down many stories for materials can add substantial man-hours to any project. This problem can be complicated by such factors as elevator access, general congestion at the job site, and competition with other trades for the work area.

The man-hours involved in assembling pipe or duct cannot always be directly tied to the number of fittings, since there are many different types of applications. Always take into consideration piping and ductwork that is prefabricated at the job site, as well as any other labor-saving procedures. A well organized schedule of prefabrication can improve productivity.

151 100	Miscellaneous Fittings	CREW	MAKEUP	DAILY OUTPUT	MAN-HOURS	UNIT
105 0020	**BACKFLOW PREVENTER** Includes gate valves, and four test cocks, corrosion resistant, automatic operation					
1000	Double check principle					
1080	Threaded					
1100	3/4" pipe size	1 Plum	1 Plumber	16	.500	Ea.
1120	1" pipe size			14	.571	Ea.
1140	1-1/2" pipe size			10	.800	Ea.
1160	2" pipe size	↓	↓	7	1.140	Ea.
1300	Flanged					
1380	3" pipe size	Q-1	1 Plumber / 1 Plumber Apprentice	4.50	3.560	Ea.
1400	4" pipe size	"	"	3	5.330	Ea.
1420	6" pipe size	Q-2	2 Plumbers / 1 Plumber Apprentice	3	8.000	Ea.
4000	Reduced pressure principle					
4100	Threaded					
4120	3/4" pipe size	1 Plum	1 Plumber	16	.500	Ea.
4140	1" pipe size			14	.571	Ea.
4150	1-1/4" pipe size			12	.667	Ea.
4160	1-1/2" pipe size			10	.800	Ea.
4180	2" pipe size	↓	↓	7	1.140	Ea.
5000	Flanged, bronze					
5060	2-1/2" pipe size	Q-1	1 Plumber / 1 Plumber Apprentice	5	3.200	Ea.
5080	3" pipe size	↓	↓	4.50	3.560	Ea.
5100	4" pipe size			3	5.330	Ea.
5120	6" pipe size	Q-2	2 Plumbers / 1 Plumber Apprentice	3	8.000	Ea.
5600	Flanged, iron					
5660	2-1/2" pipe size	Q-1	1 Plumber / 1 Plumber Apprentice	5	3.200	Ea.
5680	3" pipe size	↓	↓	4.50	3.560	Ea.
5700	4" pipe size			3	5.330	Ea.
5720	6" pipe size	Q-2	2 Plumbers / 1 Plumber Apprentice	3	8.000	Ea.
5740	8" pipe size	↓	↓	2	12.000	Ea.
5760	10" pipe size			1	24.000	Ea.
110 0060	**CLEANOUTS** Floor type					
0080	Round or square, scoriated nickel bronze top					
0100	2" pipe size	1 Plum	1 Plumber	10	.800	Ea.
0120	3" pipe size			8	1.000	Ea.
0140	4" pipe size			6	1.330	Ea.
0160	5" pipe size	↓	↓	4	2.000	Ea.
0180	6" pipe size	Q-1	1 Plumber / 1 Plumber Apprentice	6	2.670	Ea.
0200	8" pipe size	"	"	4	4.000	Ea.
0980	Round top, recessed for terrazzo					
1000	2"	1 Plum	1 Plumber	9	.889	Ea.
1080	3" pipe size			6	1.330	Ea.
1100	4" pipe size	↓	↓	4	2.000	Ea.
1120	5" pipe size	Q-1	1 Plumber / 1 Plumber Apprentice	6	2.670	Ea.
1140	6" pipe size	↓	↓	5	3.200	Ea.
1160	8" pipe size			4	4.000	Ea.
2000	Round scoriated nickel bronze top, extra heavy duty					
2060	2" pipe size	1 Plum	1 Plumber	9	.889	Ea.
2080	3" pipe size	"	"	6	1.330	Ea.

151 100 | Miscellaneous Fittings

		CREW	MAKEUP	DAILY OUTPUT	MAN-HOURS	UNIT
110 2101	Cleanouts, floor type, rd. scor. nickel brnz. top, 4" pipe size	1 Plum	1 Plumber	4	2.000	Ea.
2120	5" pipe size	Q-1	1 Plumber	6	2.670	Ea.
			1 Plumber Apprentice			
2140	6" pipe size	↓	↓	5	3.200	Ea.
2160	8" pipe size	↓	↓	4	4.000	Ea.
4000	Wall type, square smooth cover, over wall frame					
4060	2" pipe size	1 Plum	1 Plumber	14	.571	Ea.
4080	3" pipe size			12	.667	Ea.
4100	4" pipe size			10	.800	Ea.
4120	5" pipe size			9	.889	Ea.
4140	6" pipe size	↓	↓	8	1.000	Ea.
4160	8" pipe size	Q-1	1 Plumber	11	1.450	Ea.
			1 Plumber Apprentice			
5000	Extension, C.I.,bronze countersunk plug, 8" long					
5040	2" pipe size	1 Plum	1 Plumber	16	.500	Ea.
5060	3" pipe size			14	.571	Ea.
5080	4" pipe size			13	.615	Ea.
5100	5" pipe size			12	.667	Ea.
5120	6" pipe size	↓	↓	11	.727	Ea.
115	**CLEANOUT TEE** Cast iron with countersunk plug					
0200	2" pipe size	1 Plum	1 Plumber	4	2.000	Ea.
0220	3" pipe size			3.60	2.220	Ea.
0240	4" pipe size	↓	↓	3.30	2.420	Ea.
0260	5" pipe size	Q-1	1 Plumber	5.50	2.910	Ea.
			1 Plumber Apprentice			
0280	6" pipe size	"	"	5	3.200	Ea.
0300	8" pipe size	Q-3	1 Plumber Foreman (ins)	5	6.400	Ea.
			2 Plumbers			
			1 Plumber Apprentice			
120 0050	**CONNECTORS** Flexible, corrugated, 7/8" O.D., 1/2" I.D. Gas, seamless brass, steel fittings					
0200	12" long	1 Plum	1 Plumber	36	.222	Ea.
0220	18" long			36	.222	Ea.
0240	24" long			34	.235	Ea.
0260	30" long			34	.235	Ea.
0280	36" long			32	.250	Ea.
0320	48" long			30	.267	Ea.
0340	60" long			30	.267	Ea.
0360	72" long	↓	↓	30	.267	Ea.
2000	Water, copper tubing, dielectric separators					
2100	12" long	1 Plum	1 Plumber	36	.222	Ea.
2220	15" long			36	.222	Ea.
2240	18" long			36	.222	Ea.
2260	24" long	↓	↓	34	.235	Ea.
125 0140	**DRAINS** Cornice, C.I., 45° or 90° outlet					
0180	1-1/2" & 2" pipe size	Q-1	1 Plumber	14	1.140	Ea.
			1 Plumber Apprentice			
0200	3" and 4" pipe size	"	"	12	1.330	Ea.
0400	Deck, auto park, C.I., 13" top					
0440	3", 4", 5", and 6" pipe size	Q-1	1 Plumber	8	2.000	Ea.
			1 Plumber Apprentice			
0800	Promenade, heelproof grate, C.I., 14" top					
0840	2", 3", and 4" pipe size	Q-1	1 Plumber	10	1.600	Ea.
			1 Plumber Apprentice			
0860	5" and 6" pipe size	↓	↓	9	1.780	Ea.
0880	8" pipe size	↓	↓	8	2.000	Ea.
0890						

151 100 | Miscellaneous Fittings

			CREW	MAKEUP	DAILY OUTPUT	MAN-HOURS	UNIT
125	1201	Drains, deck, promenade, heelproof grate, C.I., lateral, 14" top					
	1240	2", 3" and 4" pipe size	Q-1	1 Plumber 1 Plumber Apprentice	10	1.600	Ea.
	1260	5" and 6" pipe size	↓	↓	9	1.780	Ea.
	1280	8" pipe size			8	2.000	Ea.
	1500	Promenade, slotted grate, C.I., 11" top					
	1540	2", 3", 4", 5", and 6" pipe size	Q-1	1 Plumber 1 Plumber Apprentice	12	1.330	Ea.
	2000	Floor, medium duty, C.I., deep flange, 7" top					
	2040	2" and 3" pipe size	Q-1	1 Plumber 1 Plumber Apprentice	12	1.330	Ea.
	2160	Heavy duty, C.I., 12" antitilt grate					
	2180	2", 3", 4", 5" and 6" pipe size	Q-1	1 Plumber 1 Plumber Apprentice	10	1.600	Ea.
	2300	X-Heavy duty, C.I., 15" antitilt grate					
	2320	4", 5", 6", and 8" pipe size	Q-1	1 Plumber 1 Plumber Apprentice	8	2.000	Ea.
	2400	Heavy duty, with sediment bucket, C.I., 12" loose grate					
	2420	3", 4", 5", and 6" pipe size	Q-1	1 Plumber 1 Plumber Apprentice	9	1.780	Ea.
	2500	Heavy duty, cleanout & trap w/bucket, C.I., 15" top					
	2540	2", 3", and 4" pipe size	Q-1	1 Plumber 1 Plumber Apprentice	6	2.670	Ea.
	2600	Medium duty, with perforated SS basket, C.I., body,					
	2610	18" top for refuse container washing area					
	2620	2" thru 6" pipe size	Q-1	1 Plumber 1 Plumber Apprentice	4	4.000	Ea.
	2630	Polyethylene, corrosion-resistant					
	2640	3" and 4" pipe size	Q-1	1 Plumber 1 Plumber Apprentice	16	1.000	Ea.
	2650	PVC or ABS thermoplastic					
	2660	3" and 4" pipe size	Q-1	1 Plumber 1 Plumber Apprentice	16	1.000	Ea.
	2680	Extra heavy duty, oil intercepting, gas seal cone,					
	2690	with cleanout, loose grate, C.I., body 16" top					
	2700	3" and 4" diameter outlet, 4" slab depth	Q-1	1 Plumber 1 Plumber Apprentice	4	4.000	Ea.
	2720	3" and 4" diameter outlet, 8" slab depth	↓	↓	3	5.330	Ea.
	2740	3" and 4" dia. outlet, 10"-12" slab depth			2	8.000	Ea.
	2780	Shower, with strainer, uniform diam. trap, bronze top					
	2800	1-1/2", 2" and 3" pipe size	Q-1	1 Plumber 1 Plumber Apprentice	8	2.000	Ea.
	2820	4" pipe size	"	"	7	2.290	Ea.
	2860	With strainer, backwater valve, drum trap					
	2880	1-1/2", 2", and 3" pipe size	Q-1	1 Plumber 1 Plumber Apprentice	8	2.000	Ea.
	2890	4" pipe size			7	2.290	Ea.
	2910	Prison cell, vandal-proof, 1-1/2", and 2" diam. pipe	↓	↓	12	1.330	Ea.
	2920	3" pipe size			10	1.600	Ea.
	2930	Trap drain, light duty, backwater valve C.I. top					
	2950	8" diameter top, 2" pipe size	Q-1	1 Plumber 1 Plumber Apprentice	12	1.330	Ea.
	2960	10" diameter top, 3" pipe size	↓	↓	10	1.600	Ea.
	2970	12" diameter top, 4" pipe size			8	2.000	Ea.
	2990	Pool main discharge, polished bronze top, C.I. body					
	3000	8" diam. grate, 2", 3" & 4" pipe size	Q-1	1 Plumber 1 Plumber Apprentice	8	2.000	Ea.
	3100	12" diam. grate, 4", 5" & 6" pipe size	"	"	8	2.000	Ea.

151 | Pipe and Fittings

151 100 | Miscellaneous Fittings

		CREW	MAKEUP	DAILY OUTPUT	MAN-HOURS	UNIT
125 3201	Drains, gutter, bronze body, polished bronze top					
3220	9" grate, 1-1/2" & 2" pipe size	Q-1	1 Plumber 1 Plumber Apprentice	8	2.000	Ea.
3240	12" grate, 2", 2-1/2" & 3" pipe size	"	"	7	2.290	Ea.
3380	Overflow, 5" dome & 6" high pipe polished bronze,					
3400	cast iron body, 2", 3", & 4" pipe size	Q-1	1 Plumber 1 Plumber Apprentice	10	1.600	Ea.
3580	Recirculating inlet, 6" sq face polished bronze,					
3600	C.I. body, 1-1/2", 2", 3" & 4" pipe size	Q-1	1 Plumber 1 Plumber Apprentice	10	1.600	Ea.
3860	Roof, flat metal deck, C.I. body, 10" aluminum dome					
3880	2" pipe size	Q-1	1 Plumber 1 Plumber Apprentice	15	1.070	Ea.
3890	3" pipe size			14	1.140	Ea.
3900	4" pipe size			13	1.230	Ea.
3910	5" pipe size			12	1.330	Ea.
3920	6" pipe size	↓	↓	10	1.600	Ea.
3980	Precast plank deck, C.I. body, aluminum dome					
4000	10" top, 2" pipe size	Q-1	1 Plumber 1 Plumber Apprentice	14	1.140	Ea.
4100	10" top, 3" pipe size			13	1.230	Ea.
4120	13" top, 4" pipe size			12	1.330	Ea.
4140	13" top, 5" pipe size			10	1.600	Ea.
4160	16" top, 6" pipe size			8	2.000	Ea.
4180	16" top, 8" pipe size	↓	↓	7	2.290	Ea.
4280	Integral expansion joint, C.I. body, 12" polypropylene dome					
4300	2" pipe size	Q-1	1 Plumber 1 Plumber Apprentice	8	2.000	Ea.
4320	3" pipe size			7	2.290	Ea.
4340	4" pipe size			6	2.670	Ea.
4360	5" pipe size			4	4.000	Ea.
4380	6" pipe size			3	5.330	Ea.
4400	8" pipe size	↓	↓	3	5.330	Ea.
4480	Flexible neoprene bellows, no-hub connection					
4500	3" and 4" pipe size	Q-1	1 Plumber 1 Plumber Apprentice	5	3.200	Ea.
4520	5" and 6" pipe size	"	"	4	4.000	Ea.
4620	Main, all aluminum, 12" low profile dome					
4640	2", 3" and 4" pipe size	Q-1	1 Plumber 1 Plumber Apprentice	14	1.140	Ea.
4660	5" and 6" pipe size			13	1.230	Ea.
4680	8" pipe size			10	1.600	Ea.
4690	Main, CI body, 12" polyprop. dome, 2", 3", & 4" pipe size			8	2.000	Ea.
4710	5" and 6" pipe size			6	2.670	Ea.
4720	8" pipe size			4	4.000	Ea.
4730	For underdeck clamp, add			22	.727	Ea.
4760	Main, PVC body and dome, 2" pipe size			14	1.140	Ea.
4780	3" pipe size			14	1.140	Ea.
4800	4" pipe size			14	1.140	Ea.
4820	For underdeck clamp, add	↓	↓	24	.667	Ea.
4900	Terrace planting area, with perforated overflow, C.I.					
4920	2", 3" and 4" pipe size	Q-1	1 Plumber 1 Plumber Apprentice	8	2.000	Ea.
4980	Scupper floor, oblique strainer, C.I.					
5000	6" x 7" top, 2", 3" and 4" pipe size	Q-1	1 Plumber 1 Plumber Apprentice	16	1.000	Ea.
5100	8" x 12" top, 5" and 6" pipe size	"	"	14	1.140	Ea.

151 100 | Miscellaneous Fittings

		CREW	MAKEUP	DAILY OUTPUT	MAN-HOURS	UNIT
125 5981	Drains, trench, floor, heavy duty, modular, C.I., 12" x 12" top					
6000	2", 3", 4", 5", & 6" pipe size	Q-1	1 Plumber 1 Plumber Apprentice	8	2.000	Ea.
6960	Backwater valve, in soil pipe, C.I. body					
6980	Bronze gate and automatic flapper valves					
7000	3" and 4" pipe size	Q-1	1 Plumber 1 Plumber Apprentice	13	1.230	Ea.
7100	5" and 6" pipe size	"	"	13	1.230	Ea.
7240	Bronze flapper valve, bolted cover					
7260	2" pipe size	Q-1	1 Plumber 1 Plumber Apprentice	16	1.000	Ea.
7280	3" pipe size	↓	↓	14.50	1.100	Ea.
7300	4" pipe size			13	1.230	Ea.
7320	5" pipe size	Q-2	2 Plumbers 1 Plumber Apprentice	18	1.330	Ea.
7340	6" pipe size	"	"	17	1.410	Ea.
7360	8" pipe size	Q-3	1 Plumber Foreman (ins) 2 Plumbers 1 Plumber Apprentice	10	3.200	Ea.
7380	10" pipe size	"	"	9	3.560	Ea.
9000	Sewer control system, valve unit, guardrail, leak detector					
9010	With fittings, monitor, 40' cable. No pit fabrication					
9020	4" pipe size	Q-2	2 Plumbers 1 Plumber Apprentice	.25	96.000	Ea.
9120	5" pipe size	"	"	.22	109.000	Ea.
130	**DIELECTRIC UNIONS** Standard gaskets for water and air					
0020	250 psi maximum pressure					
0281	Female IPT to sweat, brass pipe, or female IPT, straight					
0300	1/2" pipe size	1 Plum	1 Plumber	24	.333	Ea.
0340	3/4" pipe size			20	.400	Ea.
0360	1" pipe size			19	.421	Ea.
0380	1-1/4" pipe size			15	.533	Ea.
0400	1-1/2" pipe size			13	.615	Ea.
0420	2" pipe size	↓	↓	11	.727	Ea.
2000	175 psi maximum pressure, flanged					
2181	Female IPT to sweat, brass pipe, or female IPT					
2200	1-1/2" pipe size	1 Plum	1 Plumber	11	.727	Ea.
2240	2" pipe size	"	"	9	.889	Ea.
2260	2-1/2" pipe size	Q-1	1 Plumber 1 Plumber Apprentice	15	1.070	Ea.
2280	3" pipe size	↓	↓	14	1.140	Ea.
2300	4" pipe size			11	1.450	Ea.
2320	5" pipe size	Q-2	2 Plumbers 1 Plumber Apprentice	14	1.710	Ea.
2340	6" pipe size	↓	↓	12	2.000	Ea.
2360	8" pipe size			10	2.400	Ea.
3380	Copper to copper					
3400	1-1/2" pipe size	1 Plum	1 Plumber	11	.727	Ea.
3440	2" pipe size	"	"	9	.889	Ea.
3460	2-1/2" pipe size	Q-1	1 Plumber 1 Plumber Apprentice	15	1.070	Ea.
3480	3" pipe size	↓	↓	14	1.140	Ea.
3500	4" pipe size			11	1.450	Ea.
3520	5" pipe size	Q-2	2 Plumbers 1 Plumber Apprentice	14	1.710	Ea.
3540	6" pipe size	↓	↓	12	2.000	Ea.
3560	8" pipe size			10	2.400	Ea.

151 | Pipe and Fittings

151 100 | Miscellaneous Fittings

			CREW	MAKEUP	DAILY OUTPUT	MAN-HOURS	UNIT
141		**FAUCETS/FITTINGS**					
	0150	Bath, faucets, diverter spout combination, sweat	1 Plum	1 Plumber	8	1.000	Ea.
	0300	Three valve combinations, spout, head, arm, flange, sweat			6	1.330	Ea.
	0500	Drain, central lift, 1-1/2" IPS male			20	.400	Ea.
	0600	Trip lever, 1-1/2" IPS male			20	.400	Ea.
	0700	Pop up, 1-1/2" IPS male			18	.444	Ea.
	0800	Chain and stopper, 1-1/2" IPS male	↓	↓	24	.333	Ea.
	0840	Flush valves, with vacuum breaker					
	0850	Water closet					
	0860	Exposed, rear spud	1 Plum	1 Plumber	8	1.000	Ea.
	0870	Top spud			8	1.000	Ea.
	0880	Concealed, rear spud			8	1.000	Ea.
	0890	Top spud			8	1.000	Ea.
	0900	Wall hung	↓	↓	8	1.000	Ea.
	0920	Urinal					
	0930	Exposed, stall	1 Plum	1 Plumber	8	1.000	Ea.
	0940	Wall, (washout)			8	1.000	Ea.
	0950	Pedestal, top spud			8	1.000	Ea.
	0960	Concealed, stall			8	1.000	Ea.
	0970	Wall (washout)			8	1.000	Ea.
	1000	Kitchen sink faucets, top mount, cast spout			10	.800	Ea.
	1200	Wall type, swing tube spout			10	.800	Ea.
	2000	Laundry faucets, shelf type, IPS or copper unions			12	.667	Ea.
	2100	Lavatory faucet, centerset, without drain			10	.800	Ea.
	2400	Concealed, 12" centers			10	.800	Ea.
	2600	Shelfback, 4" to 6" centers, 17 Ga. tailpiece			10	.800	Ea.
	2800	Self-closing, center set			10	.800	Ea.
	3000	Service sink faucet, cast spout, pail hook, hose end			14	.571	Ea.
	4000	Shower by-pass valve with union			18	.444	Ea.
	4100	Shower arm with flange and head			22	.364	Ea.
	4200	Shower thermostatic mixing valve, concealed			8	1.000	Ea.
	5000	Sillcock, compact, brass, IPS or copper to hose	↓	↓	24	.333	Ea.
	6000	Stop and waste valves, bronze					
	6100	Angle, solder end 1/2"	1 Plum	1 Plumber	24	.333	Ea.
	6110	3/4"			20	.400	Ea.
	6301	Valves, straightway, solder end or threaded, 3/8"			24	.333	Ea.
	6310	1/2"			24	.333	Ea.
	6320	3/4"			20	.400	Ea.
	6330	1"	↓	↓	19	.421	Ea.
	8000	Water supply stops, polished chrome plate					
	8200	Angle, 3/8"	1 Plum	1 Plumber	24	.333	Ea.
	8300	1/2"			22	.364	Ea.
	8400	Straight, 3/8"			26	.308	Ea.
	8500	1/2"			24	.333	Ea.
	8600	Water closet, angle, w/flex riser, 3/8"	↓	↓	24	.333	Ea.
146		**FLOOR RECEPTORS** For connection to 2", 3" & 4" diameter pipe					
	0200	12-1/2" square top, 25 sq. in. open area	Q-1	1 Plumber / 1 Plumber Apprentice	10	1.600	Ea.
	2000	12-5/8" diameter top, 40 sq. in. open area			10	1.600	Ea.
	3000	8" x 4" rectangular top, 7.5 sq. in. open area			14	1.140	Ea.
	4000	24" x 16" rectangular top, 70 sq. in. open area	↓	↓	4	4.000	Ea.
156		**HYDRANTS**					
	0050	Wall type, moderate climate, bronze, encased					
	0200	3/4" IPS connection	1 Plum	1 Plumber	16	.500	Ea.
	0300	1" IPS connection	"	"	14	.571	Ea.
	1000	Non-freeze, bronze, exposed					
	1100	3/4" IPS connection, 4" to 9" thick wall	1 Plum	1 Plumber	14	.571	Ea.
	1120	10" to 14" thick wall	"	"	12	.667	Ea.

403

			CREW	MAKEUP	DAILY OUTPUT	MAN-HOURS	UNIT
	151 100	**Miscellaneous Fittings**					
156	1141	Hydrants, wall type, non-freeze, 3/4" IPS, 15"-19" thick wall	1 Plum	1 Plumber	12	.667	Ea.
	1160	20" to 24" thick wall	"	"	10	.800	Ea.
	2000	Non-freeze bronze, encased					
	2100	3/4" IPS connection, 5" to 9" thick wall	1 Plum	1 Plumber	14	.571	Ea.
	2120	10" to 14" thick wall			12	.667	Ea.
	2140	15" to 19" thick wall			12	.667	Ea.
	2160	20" to 24" thick wall	↓	↓	10	.800	Ea.
	3000	Ground box type, bronze frame, 3/4" IPS connection					
	3080	Non-freeze, all bronze, polished face, set flush					
	3100	2 feet depth of bury	1 Plum	1 Plumber	8	1.000	Ea.
	3120	3 feet depth of bury			8	1.000	Ea.
	3140	4 feet depth of bury			8	1.000	Ea.
	3160	5 feet depth of bury			7	1.140	Ea.
	3180	6 feet depth of bury			7	1.140	Ea.
	3200	7 feet depth of bury			6	1.330	Ea.
	3220	8 feet depth of bury			5	1.600	Ea.
	3240	9 feet depth of bury			4	2.000	Ea.
	3260	10 feet depth of bury	↓	↓	4	2.000	Ea.
	4000	Non-freeze, CI body, bronze frame & scoriated cover					
	4010	with hose storage					
	4100	2 feet depth of bury	1 Plum	1 Plumber	7	1.140	Ea.
	4120	3 feet depth of bury			7	1.140	Ea.
	4140	4 feet depth of bury			7	1.140	Ea.
	4160	5 feet depth of bury			6.50	1.230	Ea.
	4180	6 feet depth of bury			6	1.330	Ea.
	4200	7 feet depth of bury			5.50	1.450	Ea.
	4220	8 feet depth of bury			5	1.600	Ea.
	4240	9 feet depth of bury			4.50	1.780	Ea.
	4260	10 feet depth of bury	↓	↓	4	2.000	Ea.
	5000	Moderate climate, all bronze, polished face					
	5020	and scoriated cover, set flush					
	5100	3/4" IPS connection	1 Plum	1 Plumber	16	.500	Ea.
	5120	1" IPS connection	"	"	14	.571	Ea.
	6000	Ground post type, all non-freeze, all bronze, aluminum casing					
	6010	guard, exposed head, 3/4" IPS connection					
	6100	2 feet depth of bury	1 Plum	1 Plumber	8	1.000	Ea.
	6120	3 feet depth of bury			8	1.000	Ea.
	6140	4 feet depth of bury			8	1.000	Ea.
	6160	5 feet depth of bury			7	1.140	Ea.
	6180	6 feet depth of bury			7	1.140	Ea.
	6200	7 feet depth of bury			6	1.330	Ea.
	6220	8 feet depth of bury			5	1.600	Ea.
	6240	9 feet depth of bury			4	2.000	Ea.
	6260	10 feet depth of bury	↓	↓	4	2.000	Ea.
	165	**SHOCK ABSORBERS**					
	0500	3/4" male I.P.S. For 1 to 11 fixtures	1 Plum	1 Plumber	12	.667	Ea.
	0600	1" male I.P.S., For 12 to 32 fixtures			8	1.000	Ea.
	0700	For 33 to 60 fixtures			8	1.000	Ea.
	0800	For 61 to 113 fixtures			8	1.000	Ea.
	0900	For 114 to 154 fixtures			8	1.000	Ea.
	1000	For 155 to 330 fixtures	↓	↓	4	2.000	Ea.
	170	**SUPPORTS/CARRIERS** For plumbing fixtures					
	0500	Drinking fountain, wall mounted					
	0600	Plate type with studs, top back plate	1 Plum	1 Plumber	7	1.140	Ea.
	0700	Top front and back plate			7	1.140	Ea.
	0800	Top & bottom, front & back plates, w/bearing jacks	↓	↓	7	1.140	Ea.

		151 100 | Miscellaneous Fittings	CREW	MAKEUP	DAILY OUTPUT	MAN-HOURS	UNIT
170	3101	Supports, lavatory, floor mtd., single, high back fixture	1 Plum	1 Plumber	6	1.330	Ea.
	3200	Flat slab fixture			6	1.330	Ea.
	3220	Paraplegic	↓	↓	6	1.330	Ea.
	3250	Floor mounted, back to back					
	3300	High back fixtures	1 Plum	1 Plumber	5	1.600	Ea.
	3400	Flat slab fixtures			5	1.600	Ea.
	3430	Paraplegic	↓	↓	5	1.600	Ea.
	3500	Wall mounted, in stud or masonry					
	3600	High back fixture	1 Plum	1 Plumber	6	1.330	Ea.
	3700	Flat slab fixture	"	"	6	1.330	Ea.
	4000	Exposed arm type, floor mounted					
	4100	Single high back or flat slab fixture	1 Plum	1 Plumber	6	1.330	Ea.
	4200	Back to back, high back or flat slab fixtures			5	1.600	Ea.
	4300	Wall mounted, High back or flat slab lavatory	↓	↓	6	1.330	Ea.
	4600	Sink, floor mounted					
	4650	Exposed arm system					
	4700	Single heavy fixture	1 Plum	1 Plumber	5	1.600	Ea.
	4750	Single heavy sink with slab			5	1.600	Ea.
	4800	Back to back, standard fixtures			5	1.600	Ea.
	4850	Back to back, heavy fixtures			5	1.600	Ea.
	4900	Back to back, heavy sink with slab	↓	↓	5	1.600	Ea.
	4950	Exposed offset arm system					
	5000	Single heavy deep fixture	1 Plum	1 Plumber	5	1.600	Ea.
	5100	Plate type system					
	5200	With bearing jacks, single fixture	1 Plum	1 Plumber	5	1.600	Ea.
	5300	With exposed arms, single heavy fixture			5	1.600	Ea.
	5400	Wall mounted, exposed arms, single heavy fixture			5	1.600	Ea.
	6000	Urinal, floor mounted, 2" or 3" coupling, blowout type			6	1.330	Ea.
	6100	With fixture or hanger bolts, blowout or washout			6	1.330	Ea.
	6200	With bearing plate			6	1.330	Ea.
	6300	Wall mounted, plate type system	↓	↓	6	1.330	Ea.
	6980	Water closet, siphon jet					
	7000	Horizontal, adjustable, caulk					
	7040	Single, 4" pipe size	1 Plum	1 Plumber	6	1.330	Ea.
	7050	4" pipe size, paraplegic			6	1.330	Ea.
	7060	5" pipe size			6	1.330	Ea.
	7100	Double, 4" pipe size			5	1.600	Ea.
	7110	4" pipe size, paraplegic			5	1.600	Ea.
	7120	5" pipe size	↓	↓	5	1.600	Ea.
	7160	Horizontal, adjustable, extended, caulk					
	7180	Single, 4" pipe size	1 Plum	1 Plumber	6	1.330	Ea.
	7200	5" pipe size			6	1.330	Ea.
	7240	Double, 4" pipe size			5	1.600	Ea.
	7260	5" pipe size	↓	↓	5	1.600	Ea.
	7400	Vertical, adjustable, caulk or thread					
	7440	Single, 4" pipe size	1 Plum	1 Plumber	6	1.330	Ea.
	7460	5" pipe size			6	1.330	Ea.
	7480	6" pipe size			5	1.600	Ea.
	7520	Double, 4" pipe size			5	1.600	Ea.
	7540	5" pipe size			5	1.600	Ea.
	7560	6" pipe size	↓	↓	4	2.000	Ea.
	7600	Vertical, adjustable, extended, caulk					
	7620	Single, 4" pipe size	1 Plum	1 Plumber	6	1.330	Ea.
	7640	5" pipe size			6	1.330	Ea.
	7680	6" pipe size			5	1.600	Ea.
	7720	Double, 4" pipe size			5	1.600	Ea.
	7740	5" pipe size			5	1.600	Ea.
	7760	6" pipe size	↓	↓	4	2.000	Ea.

		151 100 | Miscellaneous Fittings	CREW	MAKEUP	DAILY OUTPUT	MAN-HOURS	UNIT
170	7781	Supports/carriers, water closet, blow out					
	7800	Vertical offset, caulk or thread					
	7820	Single, 4" pipe size	1 Plum	1 Plumber	6	1.330	Ea.
	7840	Double, 4" pipe size	"	"	5	1.600	Ea.
	7880	Vertical offset, extended, caulk					
	7900	Single, 4" pipe size	1 Plum	1 Plumber	6	1.330	Ea.
	7920	Double, 4" pipe size	"	"	5	1.600	Ea.
	7960	Vertical, for floor mounted back-outlet					
	7980	Single, 4" thread, 2" vent	1 Plum	1 Plumber	6	1.330	Ea.
	8000	Double, 4" thread, 2" vent	"	"	6	1.330	Ea.
	8040	Vertical, for floor mounted back-outlet, extended					
	8060	Single, 4" caulk, 2" vent	1 Plum	1 Plumber	6	1.330	Ea.
	8080	Double, 4" caulk, 2" vent	"	"	6	1.330	Ea.
	8200	Water closet, residential					
	8220	Vertical centerline, floor mount					
	8240	Single, 3" caulk, 2" or 3" vent	1 Plum	1 Plumber	6	1.330	Ea.
	8260	4" caulk, 2" or 4" vent			6	1.330	Ea.
	8280	3" copper sweat, 3" vent			6	1.330	Ea.
	8300	4" copper sweat, 4" vent	↓	↓	6	1.330	Ea.
	8400	Vertical offset, floor mount					
	8420	Single, 3" or 4" caulk, vent	1 Plum	1 Plumber	4	2.000	Ea.
	8440	3" or 4" copper sweat, vent			5	1.600	Ea.
	8460	Double, 3" or 4" caulk, vent			4	2.000	Ea.
	8480	3" or 4" copper sweat, vent	↓	↓	5	1.600	Ea.
	9000	Water cooler (electric), floor mounted					
	9100	Plate type with bearing plate, single	1 Plum	1 Plumber	6	1.330	Ea.
	9120	Plate type with bearing plate, double			4	2.000	Ea.
	9140	Plate type with bearing plate, back to back	↓	↓	4	2.000	Ea.
	181	**TRAPS**					
	0030	Cast iron, service weight					
	0050	Long P trap, 2" pipe size					
	1100	12" long	Q-1	1 Plumber 1 Plumber Apprentice	16	1.000	Ea.
	1140	18" long	"	"	16	1.000	Ea.
	1180	Running trap, single hub, with vent					
	2080	3" pipe size, 3" vent	Q-1	1 Plumber 1 Plumber Apprentice	14	1.140	Ea.
	2120	4" pipe size, 4" vent	"	"	13	1.230	Ea.
	2140	5" pipe size, 4" vent	Q-2	2 Plumbers 1 Plumber Apprentice	11	2.180	Ea.
	2160	6" pipe size, 4" vent			10	2.400	Ea.
	2180	6" pipe size, 6" vent	↓	↓	8	3.000	Ea.
	2200	8" pipe size, 4" vent	Q-3	1 Plumber Foreman (ins) 2 Plumbers 1 Plumber Apprentice	10	3.200	Ea.
	2220	8" pipe size, 6" vent	"	"	8	4.000	Ea.
	2800	S trap, extra heavy weight, 2" pipe size	Q-1	1 Plumber 1 Plumber Apprentice	15	1.070	Ea.
	2840	3" pipe size			14	1.140	Ea.
	2850	4" pipe size			13	1.230	Ea.
	3000	P trap, 2" pipe size			16	1.000	Ea.
	3040	3" pipe size			14	1.140	Ea.
	3060	4" pipe size	↓	↓	13	1.230	Ea.
	3080	5" pipe size	Q-2	2 Plumbers 1 Plumber Apprentice	18	1.330	Ea.
	3100	6" pipe size	"	"	17	1.410	Ea.

151 | Pipe and Fittings

151 100 | Miscellaneous Fittings

		CREW	MAKEUP	DAILY OUTPUT	MAN-HOURS	UNIT
181 3121	P trap, cast iron, 8" pipe size	Q-3	1 Plumber Foreman (ins)	11	2.910	Ea.
			2 Plumbers			
			1 Plumber Apprentice			
3130	10" pipe size	"	"	10	3.200	Ea.
3150	P trap, no hub, 1-1/2" pipe size	Q-1	1 Plumber	17	.941	Ea.
			1 Plumber Apprentice			
3160	2" pipe size			16	1.000	Ea.
3170	3" pipe size			14	1.140	Ea.
3180	4" pipe size	↓	↓	13	1.230	Ea.
3190	6" pipe size	Q-2	2 Plumbers	17	1.410	Ea.
			1 Plumber Apprentice			
3350	Deep seal trap					
3400	1-1/4" pipe size	Q-1	1 Plumber	14	1.140	Ea.
			1 Plumber Apprentice			
3410	1-1/2" pipe size			14	1.140	Ea.
3420	2" pipe size			14	1.140	Ea.
3440	3" pipe size	↓	↓	12	1.330	Ea.
3460	4" pipe size			11	1.450	Ea.
3800	Drum trap, 4" x 5", 1-1/2" tapping	Q-2	2 Plumbers	17	1.410	Ea.
			1 Plumber Apprentice			
3820	2" tapping	"	"	17	1.410	Ea.
4700	Copper, drainage, drum trap					
4800	3" x 5" solid, 1-1/2" pipe size	1 Plum	1 Plumber	16	.500	Ea.
4840	3" x 6" swivel, 1-1/2" pipe size			16	.500	Ea.
4900	4" x 8" swivel, 1-1/2" pipe size			13	.615	Ea.
4920	2" pipe size	↓	↓	13	.615	Ea.
5100	P trap, standard pattern					
5200	1-1/4" pipe size	1 Plum	1 Plumber	18	.444	Ea.
5240	1-1/2" pipe size			17	.471	Ea.
5260	2" pipe size			15	.533	Ea.
5280	3" pipe size	↓	↓	11	.727	Ea.
5340	With cleanout and slip joint					
5360	1-1/4" pipe size	1 Plum	1 Plumber	18	.444	Ea.
5400	1-1/2" pipe size			17	.471	Ea.
5420	2" pipe size	↓	↓	15	.533	Ea.
5751	Chromed brass, tubular, P or S trap, without cleanout, 20 Ga.					
5800	1-1/4" pipe size	1 Plum	1 Plumber	18	.444	Ea.
5840	1-1/2" pipe size	"	"	17	.471	Ea.
5900	With cleanout, 20 Ga.					
5940	1-1/4" pipe size	1 Plum	1 Plumber	18	.444	Ea.
6000	1-1/2" pipe size	"	"	17	.471	Ea.
6660	Corrosion resistant, glass, P trap, 1-1/2" pipe size	Q-1	1 Plumber	17	.941	Ea.
			1 Plumber Apprentice			
6670	2" pipe size			16	1.000	Ea.
6680	3" pipe size			14	1.140	Ea.
6690	4" pipe size	↓	↓	13	1.230	Ea.
6700	6" pipe size	Q-2	2 Plumbers	17	1.410	Ea.
			1 Plumber Apprentice			
6760	PP DWV, dilution trap, 1-1/2" pipe size	1 Plum	1 Plumber	16	.500	Ea.
6770	P trap, 1-1/2" pipe size			17	.471	Ea.
6830	S trap, 1-1/2" pipe size			16	.500	Ea.
6850	Universal trap, 1-1/2" pipe size			14	.571	Ea.
7000	Trap primer, flow through type, 1/2" diameter			24	.333	Ea.
7100	With sediment strainer	↓	↓	22	.364	Ea.
7450	Trap primer distribution unit					
7500	2 opening	1 Plum	1 Plumber	18	.444	Ea.
7540	3 opening			17	.471	Ea.
7560	4 opening	↓	↓	16	.500	Ea.

151 100 | Miscellaneous Fittings

		CREW	MAKEUP	DAILY OUTPUT	MAN-HOURS	UNIT
181 7850	Trap primer manifold					
7900	2 outlet	1 Plum	1 Plumber	18	.444	Ea.
7940	4 outlet			16	.500	Ea.
7960	6 outlet			15	.533	Ea.
7980	8 outlet	↓	↓	13	.615	Ea.
185	**VACUUM BREAKERS** Hot or cold water					
1030	Anti-siphon, brass					
1040	1/4" size	1 Plum	1 Plumber	24	.333	Ea.
1050	3/8" size			24	.333	Ea.
1060	1/2" size			24	.333	Ea.
1080	3/4" size			20	.400	Ea.
1100	1" size			19	.421	Ea.
1120	1-1/4" size			15	.533	Ea.
1140	1-1/2" size			13	.615	Ea.
1160	2" size			11	.727	Ea.
1180	2-1/2" size			9	.889	Ea.
1200	3" size	↓	↓	7	1.140	Ea.
1900	Vacuum relief, water service, bronze					
2000	1/2" size	1 Plum	1 Plumber	30	.267	Ea.
2040	3/4" size	"	"	28	.286	Ea.
195	**VENT FLASHING**					
1001	Aluminum, copper, or galvanized, with lead ring					
1020	1-1/4" pipe	1 Plum	1 Plumber	20	.400	Ea.
1030	1-1/2" pipe			20	.400	Ea.
1040	2" pipe			18	.444	Ea.
1050	3" pipe			17	.471	Ea.
1060	4" pipe	↓	↓	16	.500	Ea.
2980	Neoprene, one piece					
3000	1-1/4" pipe	1 Plum	1 Plumber	24	.333	Ea.
3030	1-1/2" pipe			24	.333	Ea.
3040	2" pipe			23	.348	Ea.
3050	3" pipe			21	.381	Ea.
3060	4" pipe	↓	↓	20	.400	Ea.

151 250 | Brass Pipe

		CREW	MAKEUP	DAILY OUTPUT	MAN-HOURS	UNIT
251	**PIPE, BRASS** Plain end,					
0900	Field threaded, coupling & clevis hanger 10' O.C.					
0920	Regular weight	↓	↓			
0980	1/8" diameter	1 Plum	1 Plumber	62	.129	L.F.
1000	1/4" diameter			57	.140	L.F.
1100	3/8" diameter			52	.154	L.F.
1120	1/2" diameter			48	.167	L.F.
1140	3/4" diameter			46	.174	L.F.
1160	1" diameter	↓	↓	43	.186	L.F.
1180	1-1/4" diameter	Q-1	1 Plumber 1 Plumber Apprentice	72	.222	L.F.
1200	1-1/2" diameter			65	.246	L.F.
1220	2" diameter			53	.302	L.F.
1240	2-1/2" diameter			41	.390	L.F.
1260	3" diameter	↓	↓	31	.516	L.F.
1280	3-1/2" diameter	Q-2	2 Plumbers 1 Plumber Apprentice	39	.615	L.F.
1300	4" diameter			37	.649	L.F.
1320	5" diameter			31	.774	L.F.
1340	6" diameter			24	1.000	L.F.
1360	8" diameter	↓	↓	20	1.200	L.F.
2000	Extra heavy weight					
2100	1/8" diameter	1 Plum	1 Plumber	58	.138	L.F.

151 | Pipe and Fittings

151 250 | Brass Pipe

		CREW	MAKEUP	DAILY OUTPUT	MAN-HOURS	UNIT
251 2121	Pipe, brass, plain end, extra heavy wt., 1/4" diameter	1 Plum	1 Plumber	55	.145	L.F.
2140	3/8" diameter			50	.160	L.F.
2160	1/2" diameter			46	.174	L.F.
2180	3/4" diameter			44	.182	L.F.
2200	1" diameter	↓	↓	41	.195	L.F.
2220	1-1/4" diameter	Q-1	1 Plumber 1 Plumber Apprentice	69	.232	L.F.
2240	1-1/2" diameter			62	.258	L.F.
2260	2" diameter			51	.314	L.F.
2280	2-1/2" diameter			39	.410	L.F.
2300	3" diameter	↓	↓	30	.533	L.F.
2320	3-1/2" diameter	Q-2	2 Plumbers 1 Plumber Apprentice	39	.615	L.F.
2340	4" diameter	"	"	35	.686	L.F.
258	**PIPE, BRASS, FITTINGS** Rough bronze, threaded					
1001	Standard wt., 45° or 90° Elbow					
1040	1/8"	1 Plum	1 Plumber	13	.615	Ea.
1060	1/4"			13	.615	Ea.
1080	3/8"			13	.615	Ea.
1100	1/2"			12	.667	Ea.
1120	3/4"			11	.727	Ea.
1140	1"	↓	↓	10	.800	Ea.
1160	1-1/4"	Q-1	1 Plumber 1 Plumber Apprentice	17	.941	Ea.
1180	1-1/2"			16	1.000	Ea.
1200	2"			14	1.140	Ea.
1220	2-1/2"			11	1.450	Ea.
1240	3"	↓	↓	8	2.000	Ea.
1260	4"	Q-2	2 Plumbers 1 Plumber Apprentice	11	2.180	Ea.
1280	5"			8	3.000	Ea.
1300	6"			7	3.430	Ea.
1320	8"	↓	↓	5	4.800	Ea.
2000	Tee, 1/8"	1 Plum	1 Plumber	9	.889	Ea.
2040	1/4"			9	.889	Ea.
2060	3/8"			9	.889	Ea.
2080	1/2"			8	1.000	Ea.
2100	3/4"			7	1.140	Ea.
2120	1"	↓	↓	6	1.330	Ea.
2140	1-1/4"	Q-1	1 Plumber 1 Plumber Apprentice	10	1.600	Ea.
2160	1-1/2"			9	1.780	Ea.
2180	2"			8	2.000	Ea.
2200	2-1/2"			7	2.290	Ea.
2220	3"	↓	↓	5	3.200	Ea.
2240	4"	Q-2	2 Plumbers 1 Plumber Apprentice	7	3.430	Ea.
2260	5"			5	4.800	Ea.
2280	6"	↓	↓	4	6.000	Ea.
2500	Coupling, 1/8"	1 Plum	1 Plumber	26	.308	Ea.
2540	1/4"			22	.364	Ea.
2560	3/8"			18	.444	Ea.
2580	1/2"			15	.533	Ea.
2600	3/4"			14	.571	Ea.
2620	1"	↓	↓	13	.615	Ea.
2640	1-1/4"	Q-1	1 Plumber 1 Plumber Apprentice	22	.727	Ea.
2660	1-1/2"	"	"	20	.800	Ea.

151 250 | Brass Pipe

			CREW	MAKEUP	DAILY OUTPUT	MAN-HOURS	UNIT
258	2681	Pipe, brass, standard weight, coupling, 2"	Q-1	1 Plumber 1 Plumber Apprentice	18	.889	Ea.
	2700	2-1/2"			14	1.140	Ea.
	2720	3"	↓	↓	10	1.600	Ea.
	2740	4"	Q-2	2 Plumbers 1 Plumber Apprentice	12	2.000	Ea.
	2760	5"			10	2.400	Ea.
	2780	6"			9	2.670	Ea.
	2790	8"	↓	↓	8	3.000	Ea.
	3000	Union, 150 lb					
	3020	1/8"	1 Plum	1 Plumber	12	.667	Ea.
	3040	1/4"			12	.667	Ea.
	3060	3/8"			12	.667	Ea.
	3080	1/2"			11	.727	Ea.
	3100	3/4"			10	.800	Ea.
	3120	1"	↓	↓	9	.889	Ea.
	3140	1-1/4"	Q-1	1 Plumber 1 Plumber Apprentice	16	1.000	Ea.
	3160	1-1/2"			15	1.070	Ea.
	3180	2"			13	1.230	Ea.
	3200	2-1/2"			10	1.600	Ea.
	3220	3"	↓	↓	7	2.290	Ea.
	3240	4"	Q-2	2 Plumbers 1 Plumber Apprentice	10	2.400	Ea.
	5001	Extra heavy, 45° or 90° Elbow					
	5040	1/8"	1 Plum	1 Plumber	13	.615	Ea.
	5060	1/4"			13	.615	Ea.
	5080	3/8"			13	.615	Ea.
	5100	1/2"			12	.667	Ea.
	5120	3/4"			11	.727	Ea.
	5140	1"	↓	↓	10	.800	Ea.
	5160	1-1/4"	Q-1	1 Plumber 1 Plumber Apprentice	17	.941	Ea.
	5180	1-1/2"			16	1.000	Ea.
	5200	2"			14	1.140	Ea.
	5220	2-1/2"			11	1.450	Ea.
	5240	3"	↓	↓	8	2.000	Ea.
	5260	4"	Q-2	2 Plumbers 1 Plumber Apprentice	11	2.180	Ea.
	6000	Tee, 1/8"	1 Plum	1 Plumber	9	.889	Ea.
	6040	1/4"			9	.889	Ea.
	6060	3/8"			9	.889	Ea.
	6080	1/2"			8	1.000	Ea.
	6100	3/4"			7	1.140	Ea.
	6120	1"	↓	↓	6	1.330	Ea.
	6140	1-1/4"	Q-1	1 Plumber 1 Plumber Apprentice	10	1.600	Ea.
	6160	1-1/2"			9	1.780	Ea.
	6180	2"			8	2.000	Ea.
	6200	2-1/2"			7	2.290	Ea.
	6220	3"	↓	↓	5	3.200	Ea.
	6240	4"	Q-2	2 Plumbers 1 Plumber Apprentice	7	3.430	Ea.
	6500	Coupling, 1/8"	1 Plum	1 Plumber	26	.308	Ea.
	6540	1/4"			22	.364	Ea.
	6560	3/8"			18	.444	Ea.
	6580	1/2"			15	.533	Ea.
	6600	3/4"	↓	↓	14	.571	Ea.

151 250 | Brass Pipe

		CREW	MAKEUP	DAILY OUTPUT	MAN-HOURS	UNIT
258 6621	Pipe, brass, extra heavy, coupling, 1"	1 Plum	1 Plumber	13	.615	Ea.
6640	1-1/4"	Q-1	1 Plumber	22	.727	Ea.
			1 Plumber Apprentice			
6660	1-1/2"			20	.800	Ea.
6680	2"			18	.889	Ea.
6700	2-1/2"			14	1.140	Ea.
6720	3"			10	1.600	Ea.
6730	3-1/2"	↓	↓	8	2.000	Ea.
6740	4"	Q-2	2 Plumbers	12	2.000	Ea.
			1 Plumber Apprentice			
7000	Union, 300 lb					
7020	1/8"	1 Plum	1 Plumber	12	.667	Ea.
7040	1/4"			12	.667	Ea.
7060	3/8"			12	.667	Ea.
7080	1/2"			11	.727	Ea.
7100	3/4"			10	.800	Ea.
7120	1"	↓	↓	9	.889	Ea.
7140	1-1/4"	Q-1	1 Plumber	16	1.000	Ea.
			1 Plumber Apprentice			
7160	1-1/2"			15	1.070	Ea.
7180	2"	↓	↓	13	1.230	Ea.

151 300 | Cast Iron Pipe

		CREW	MAKEUP	DAILY OUTPUT	MAN-HOURS	UNIT
301	PIPE, CAST IRON Soil, on hangers 5' O.C.					
0020	Single hub, service wt., lead & oakum joints 10' O.C.					
2120	2" diameter	Q-1	1 Plumber	63	.254	L.F.
			1 Plumber Apprentice			
2140	3" diameter			60	.267	L.F.
2160	4" diameter	↓	↓	55	.291	L.F.
2180	5" diameter	Q-2	2 Plumbers	76	.316	L.F.
			1 Plumber Apprentice			
2200	6" diameter	"	"	73	.329	L.F.
2220	8" diameter	Q-3	1 Plumber Foreman (ins)	59	.542	L.F.
			2 Plumbers			
			1 Plumber Apprentice			
2240	10" diameter			54	.593	L.F.
2260	12" diameter	↓	↓	48	.667	L.F.
3000	Single hub, service wt, push-on gasket joints 10' O.C.					
3010	2" diameter	Q-1	1 Plumber	66	.242	L.F.
			1 Plumber Apprentice			
3020	3" diameter			63	.254	L.F.
3030	4" diameter	↓	↓	57	.281	L.F.
3040	5" diameter	Q-2	2 Plumbers	79	.304	L.F.
			1 Plumber Apprentice			
3050	6" diameter	"	"	75	.320	L.F.
3060	8" diameter	Q-3	1 Plumber Foreman (ins)	62	.516	L.F.
			2 Plumbers			
			1 Plumber Apprentice			
3070	10" diameter			56	.571	L.F.
3080	12" diameter	↓	↓	49	.653	L.F.
4000	No hub, couplings 10' O.C.					
4100	1-1/2" diameter	Q-1	1 Plumber	71	.225	L.F.
			1 Plumber Apprentice			
4120	2" diameter			67	.239	L.F.
4140	3" diameter			64	.250	L.F.
4160	4" diameter	↓	↓	58	.276	L.F.
4180	5" diameter	Q-2	2 Plumbers	83	.289	L.F.
			1 Plumber Apprentice			

151 300 | Cast Iron Pipe

			CREW	MAKEUP	DAILY OUTPUT	MAN-HOURS	UNIT
301	4201	Pipe, cast iron soil, no hub, 6" diameter	Q-2	2 Plumbers	79	.304	L.F.
				1 Plumber Apprentice			
	4220	8" diameter	Q-3	1 Plumber Foreman (ins)	69	.464	L.F.
				2 Plumbers			
				1 Plumber Apprentice			
	4240	10" diameter	"	"	61	.525	L.F.
	320	**PIPE, CAST IRON, FITTINGS,** Soil					
	0040	Hub and spigot, service weight, lead & oakum joints					
	0080	1/4 Bend, 2"	Q-1	1 Plumber	16	1.000	Ea.
				1 Plumber Apprentice			
	0120	3"			14	1.140	Ea.
	0140	4"	↓	↓	13	1.230	Ea.
	0160	5"	Q-2	2 Plumbers	18	1.330	Ea.
				1 Plumber Apprentice			
	0180	6"	"	"	17	1.410	Ea.
	0200	8"	Q-3	1 Plumber Foreman (ins)	11	2.910	Ea.
				2 Plumbers			
				1 Plumber Apprentice			
	0220	10"			10	3.200	Ea.
	0240	12"	↓	↓	9	3.560	Ea.
	0250	Closet bend, 3" diameter with ring 10" x 16"	Q-1	1 Plumber	14	1.140	Ea.
				1 Plumber Apprentice			
	0260	16"x16"			12	1.330	Ea.
	0270	Closet bend, 4" diameter, 1" x 4" ring, 6" x 16"			13	1.230	Ea.
	0280	8" x 16"			13	1.230	Ea.
	0290	10" x 12"			12	1.330	Ea.
	0300	10" x 18"			11	1.450	Ea.
	0310	12" x 16"			11	1.450	Ea.
	0330	16" x 16"			10	1.600	Ea.
	0340	1/8 Bend, 2"			16	1.000	Ea.
	0350	3"			14	1.140	Ea.
	0360	4"	↓	↓	13	1.230	Ea.
	0380	5"	Q-2	2 Plumbers	18	1.330	Ea.
				1 Plumber Apprentice			
	0400	6"	"	"	17	1.410	Ea.
	0420	8"	Q-3	1 Plumber Foreman (ins)	11	2.910	Ea.
				2 Plumbers			
				1 Plumber Apprentice			
	0440	10"			10	3.200	Ea.
	0460	12"	↓	↓	9	3.560	Ea.
	0501	Tee and sanitary tee, 2"	Q-1	1 Plumber	10	1.600	Ea.
				1 Plumber Apprentice			
	0540	3"			9	1.780	Ea.
	0620	4"	↓	↓	8	2.000	Ea.
	0700	5"	Q-2	2 Plumbers	12	2.000	Ea.
				1 Plumber Apprentice			
	0800	6"	"	"	11	2.180	Ea.
	0880	8"	Q-3	1 Plumber Foreman (ins)	7	4.570	Ea.
				2 Plumbers			
				1 Plumber Apprentice			
	1400	Combination Y and 1/8 Bend					
	1420	2"	Q-1	1 Plumber	10	1.600	Ea.
				1 Plumber Apprentice			
	1460	3"			9	1.780	Ea.
	1520	4"	↓	↓	8	2.000	Ea.
	1540	5"	Q-2	2 Plumbers	12	2.000	Ea.
				1 Plumber Apprentice			
	1560	6"	"	"	11	2.180	Ea.

151 300 | Cast Iron Pipe

		Description	CREW	MAKEUP	DAILY OUTPUT	MAN-HOURS	UNIT
320	1581	Pipe, cast iron fittings, comb. Y and 1/8 bend, 8"	Q-2	2 Plumbers 1 Plumber Apprentice	7	3.430	Ea.
	1600	Double Y, 2"	Q-1	1 Plumber 1 Plumber Apprentice	8	2.000	Ea.
	1610	3"	↓	↓	7	2.290	Ea.
	1620	4"			6.50	2.460	Ea.
	1630	5"	Q-2	2 Plumbers 1 Plumber Apprentice	9	2.670	Ea.
	1640	6"	"	"	8	3.000	Ea.
	1650	8"	Q-3	1 Plumber Foreman (ins) 2 Plumbers 1 Plumber Apprentice	5.50	5.820	Ea.
	1660	10"	↓	↓	5	6.400	Ea.
	1670	12"			4.50	7.110	Ea.
	1740	Reducer, 3" x 2"	Q-1	1 Plumber 1 Plumber Apprentice	15	1.070	Ea.
	1750	4" x 2"			14.50	1.100	Ea.
	1760	4" x 3"			14	1.140	Ea.
	1770	5" x 2"			14	1.140	Ea.
	1780	5" x 3"			13.50	1.190	Ea.
	1790	5" x 4"			13	1.230	Ea.
	1800	6" x 2"			13.50	1.190	Ea.
	1810	6" x 3"			13	1.230	Ea.
	1840	6" x 5"	↓	↓	11	1.450	Ea.
	1860	8" x 2"	Q-2	2 Plumbers 1 Plumber Apprentice	14	1.710	Ea.
	1880	8" x 3"			13	1.850	Ea.
	1900	8" x 4"			13	1.850	Ea.
	1920	8" x 5"	↓	↓	12	2.000	Ea.
	1940	8" x 6"			12	2.000	Ea.
	1960	Increaser, 2" x 3"	Q-1	1 Plumber 1 Plumber Apprentice	15	1.070	Ea.
	1980	2" x 4"			14	1.140	Ea.
	2000	2" x 5"			13	1.230	Ea.
	2020	3" x 4"			13	1.230	Ea.
	2040	3" x 5"			13	1.230	Ea.
	2060	3" x 6"			12	1.330	Ea.
	2070	4" x 5"			13	1.230	Ea.
	2080	4" x 6"	↓	↓	12	1.330	Ea.
	2090	4" x 8"	Q-2	2 Plumbers 1 Plumber Apprentice	13	1.850	Ea.
	2100	5" x 6"	Q-1	1 Plumber 1 Plumber Apprentice	11	1.450	Ea.
	2110	5" x 8"	Q-2	2 Plumbers 1 Plumber Apprentice	12	2.000	Ea.
	2120	6" x 8"			12	2.000	Ea.
	2130	6" x 10"			8	3.000	Ea.
	2140	8" x 10"	↓	↓	6.50	3.690	Ea.
	2150	10" x 12"			5.50	4.360	Ea.
	2500	Y, 2"	Q-1	1 Plumber 1 Plumber Apprentice	10	1.600	Ea.
	2510	3"	↓	↓	9	1.780	Ea.
	2520	4"			8	2.000	Ea.
	2530	5"	Q-2	2 Plumbers 1 Plumber Apprentice	12	2.000	Ea.
	2540	6"	"	"	11	2.180	Ea.

151 300 | Cast Iron Pipe

		Description	CREW	MAKEUP	DAILY OUTPUT	MAN-HOURS	UNIT
320	2551	Pipe, cast iron fittings, Y, 8"	Q-3	1 Plumber Foreman (ins)	7	4.570	Ea.
				2 Plumbers			
				1 Plumber Apprentice			
	2560	10"	↓	↓	6	5.330	Ea.
	2570	12"			5	6.400	Ea.
	8000	Coupling, standard (by CISPI Mfrs.)					
	8020	1-1/2"	Q-1	1 Plumber	48	.333	Ea.
				1 Plumber Apprentice			
	8040	2"			44	.364	Ea.
	8080	3"			38	.421	Ea.
	8120	4"	↓	↓	33	.485	Ea.
	8160	5"	Q-2	2 Plumbers	44	.545	Ea.
				1 Plumber Apprentice			
	8180	6"	"	"	40	.600	Ea.
	8200	8"	Q-3	1 Plumber Foreman (ins)	33	.970	Ea.
				2 Plumbers			
				1 Plumber Apprentice			
	8220	10"	"	"	26	1.230	Ea.
	8300	Coupling, cast iron clamp & neoprene gasket (by MG)					
	8310	1-1/2"	Q-1	1 Plumber	48	.333	Ea.
				1 Plumber Apprentice			
	8320	2"			44	.364	Ea.
	8330	3"			38	.421	Ea.
	8340	4"	↓	↓	33	.485	Ea.
	8350	5"	Q-2	2 Plumbers	44	.545	Ea.
				1 Plumber Apprentice			
	8360	6"	"	"	40	.600	Ea.
	8380	8"	Q-3	1 Plumber Foreman (ins)	33	.970	Ea.
				2 Plumbers			
				1 Plumber Apprentice			
	8400	10"	"	"	26	1.230	Ea.
	8600	Coupling, Stainless steel, by Clamp-All Corp.					
	8620	1-1/2"	Q-1	1 Plumber	48	.333	Ea.
				1 Plumber Apprentice			
	8630	2"			44	.364	Ea.
	8640	2" x 1-1/2"			44	.364	Ea.
	8650	3"			38	.421	Ea.
	8660	4"			33	.485	Ea.
	8670	4" x 3"	↓	↓	33	.485	Ea.
	8680	5"	Q-2	2 Plumbers	44	.545	Ea.
				1 Plumber Apprentice			
	8690	6"	"	"	40	.600	Ea.
	8700	8"	Q-3	1 Plumber Foreman (ins)	33	.970	Ea.
				2 Plumbers			
				1 Plumber Apprentice			
	8710	10"	"	"	26	1.230	Ea.

151 400 | Copper Pipe & Tubing

		Description	CREW	MAKEUP	DAILY OUTPUT	MAN-HOURS	UNIT
	401	PIPE, COPPER Solder joints					
	0020	Type K tubing, couplings & clevis hangers 10' O.C.					
	1100	1/4" diameter	1 Plum	1 Plumber	55	.145	L.F.
	1120	3/8" diameter			54	.148	L.F.
	1140	1/2" diameter			50	.160	L.F.
	1160	5/8" diameter			47	.170	L.F.
	1180	3/4" diameter			42	.190	L.F.
	1200	1" diameter			34	.235	L.F.
	1220	1-1/4" diameter			28	.286	L.F.
	1240	1-1/2" diameter	↓	↓	26	.308	L.F.

151 400 | Copper Pipe & Tubing

		CREW	MAKEUP	DAILY OUTPUT	MAN-HOURS	UNIT
401 1261	Pipe, copper, solder joints, type K tubing, 2" diameter	1 Plum	1 Plumber	22	.364	L.F.
1280	2-1/2" diameter	Q-1	1 Plumber	31	.516	L.F.
			1 Plumber Apprentice			
1300	3" diameter			28	.571	L.F.
1320	3-1/2" diameter			24	.667	L.F.
1330	4" diameter			22	.727	L.F.
1340	5" diameter	↓	↓	18	.889	L.F.
1360	6" diameter	Q-2	2 Plumbers	23	1.040	L.F.
			1 Plumber Apprentice			
1380	8" diameter	"	"	20	1.200	L.F.
2000	Type L tubing, couplings & hangers 10' O.C.					
2100	1/4" diameter	1 Plum	1 Plumber	59	.136	L.F.
2120	3/8" diameter			56	.143	L.F.
2140	1/2" diameter			53	.151	L.F.
2160	5/8" diameter			49	.163	L.F.
2180	3/4" diameter			44	.182	L.F.
2200	1" diameter			36	.222	L.F.
2220	1-1/4" diameter			29	.276	L.F.
2240	1-1/2" diameter	↓	↓	27	.296	L.F.
2260	2" diameter			23	.348	L.F.
2280	2-1/2" diameter	Q-1	1 Plumber	33	.485	L.F.
			1 Plumber Apprentice			
2300	3" diameter			30	.533	L.F.
2320	3-1/2" diameter			25	.640	L.F.
2340	4" diameter			23	.696	L.F.
2360	5" diameter	↓	↓	19	.842	L.F.
2380	6" diameter	Q-2	2 Plumbers	24	1.000	L.F.
			1 Plumber Apprentice			
2400	8" diameter	"	"	21	1.140	L.F.
3000	Type M tubing, couplings & hangers 10' O.C.					
3100	1/4" diameter	1 Plum	1 Plumber	61	.131	L.F.
3120	3/8" diameter			59	.136	L.F.
3140	1/2" diameter			56	.143	L.F.
3160	5/8" diameter			51	.157	L.F.
3180	3/4" diameter			46	.174	L.F.
3200	1" diameter			37	.216	L.F.
3220	1-1/4" diameter			30	.267	L.F.
3240	1-1/2" diameter	↓	↓	28	.286	L.F.
3260	2" diameter			24	.333	L.F.
3280	2-1/2" diameter	Q-1	1 Plumber	35	.457	L.F.
			1 Plumber Apprentice			
3300	3" diameter			32	.500	L.F.
3320	3-1/2" diameter			27	.593	L.F.
3340	4" diameter			24	.667	L.F.
3360	5" diameter	↓	↓	20	.800	L.F.
3370	6" diameter	Q-2	2 Plumbers	25	.960	L.F.
			1 Plumber Apprentice			
3380	8" diameter	"	"	22	1.090	L.F.
4000	Type DWV tubing, couplings & hangers 10' O.C.					
4100	1-1/4" diameter	1 Plum	1 Plumber	30	.267	L.F.
4120	1-1/2" diameter	↓	↓	28	.286	L.F.
4140	2" diameter			24	.333	L.F.
4160	3" diameter	Q-1	1 Plumber	32	.500	L.F.
			1 Plumber Apprentice			
4180	4" diameter			24	.667	L.F.
4200	5" diameter	↓	↓	20	.800	L.F.
4220	6" diameter	Q-2	2 Plumbers	25	.960	L.F.
			1 Plumber Apprentice			

151 400 | Copper Pipe & Tubing

			CREW	MAKEUP	DAILY OUTPUT	MAN-HOURS	UNIT
401	4241	Pipe, copper, solder joints, type DWV tubing, 8" diameter	Q-2	2 Plumbers	20	1.200	L.F.
				1 Plumber Apprentice			
	430	PIPE, COPPER, FITTINGS, Wrought unless otherwise noted					
	0040	Solder joints, copper x copper					
	0071	45° or 90° Elbow, 1/4"	1 Plum	1 Plumber	22	.364	Ea.
	0090	3/8"			22	.364	Ea.
	0100	1/2"			20	.400	Ea.
	0110	5/8"			19	.421	Ea.
	0120	3/4"			19	.421	Ea.
	0130	1"			16	.500	Ea.
	0140	1-1/4"			15	.533	Ea.
	0150	1-1/2"			13	.615	Ea.
	0160	2"	↓	↓	11	.727	Ea.
	0170	2-1/2"	Q-1	1 Plumber	13	1.230	Ea.
				1 Plumber Apprentice			
	0180	3"			11	1.450	Ea.
	0190	3-1/2"			10	1.600	Ea.
	0200	4"			9	1.780	Ea.
	0210	5" cast brass	↓	↓	6	2.670	Ea.
	0220	6" cast brass	Q-2	2 Plumbers	9	2.670	Ea.
				1 Plumber Apprentice			
	0230	8" cast brass	"	"	8	3.000	Ea.
	0450	Tee, 1/4"	1 Plum	1 Plumber	14	.571	Ea.
	0470	3/8"			14	.571	Ea.
	0480	1/2"			13	.615	Ea.
	0490	5/8"			12	.667	Ea.
	0500	3/4"			12	.667	Ea.
	0510	1"			10	.800	Ea.
	0520	1-1/4"			9	.889	Ea.
	0530	1-1/2"			8	1.000	Ea.
	0540	2"	↓	↓	7	1.140	Ea.
	0550	2-1/2"	Q-1	1 Plumber	8	2.000	Ea.
				1 Plumber Apprentice			
	0560	3"			7	2.290	Ea.
	0570	3-1/2"			6	2.670	Ea.
	0580	4"			5	3.200	Ea.
	0590	5" cast brass	↓	↓	4	4.000	Ea.
	0600	6" cast brass	Q-2	2 Plumbers	6	4.000	Ea.
				1 Plumber Apprentice			
	0610	8" cast brass	"	"	5	4.800	Ea.
	0650	Coupling, 1/4"	1 Plum	1 Plumber	24	.333	Ea.
	0670	3/8"			24	.333	Ea.
	0680	1/2"			22	.364	Ea.
	0690	5/8"			21	.381	Ea.
	0700	3/4"			21	.381	Ea.
	0710	1"			18	.444	Ea.
	0720	1-1/4"			17	.471	Ea.
	0730	1-1/2"			15	.533	Ea.
	0740	2"	↓	↓	13	.615	Ea.
	0750	2-1/2"	Q-1	1 Plumber	15	1.070	Ea.
				1 Plumber Apprentice			
	0760	3"			13	1.230	Ea.
	0770	3-1/2"			8	2.000	Ea.
	0780	4"			7	2.290	Ea.
	0790	5"	↓	↓	6	2.670	Ea.
	0800	6"	Q-2	2 Plumbers	8	3.000	Ea.
				1 Plumber Apprentice			
	0810	8"	"	"	7	3.430	Ea.

151 400	Copper Pipe & Tubing	CREW	MAKEUP	DAILY OUTPUT	MAN-HOURS	UNIT
430 0851	Pipe, copper, fittings, unions, 1/4"	1 Plum	1 Plumber	21	.381	Ea.
0870	3/8"			21	.381	Ea.
0880	1/2"			19	.421	Ea.
0890	5/8"			18	.444	Ea.
0900	3/4"			18	.444	Ea.
0910	1"			15	.533	Ea.
0920	1-1/4"			14	.571	Ea.
0930	1-1/2"	↓	↓	12	.667	Ea.
0940	2"			10	.800	Ea.
0950	2-1/2" cast brass	Q-1	1 Plumber / 1 Plumber Apprentice	12	1.330	Ea.
0960	3" cast brass	"	"	10	1.600	Ea.
0980	Adapter, copper x male, 1/4" IPS	1 Plum	1 Plumber	24	.333	Ea.
0990	3/8" IPS			24	.333	Ea.
1000	1/2" IPS			22	.364	Ea.
1010	3/4" IPS			21	.381	Ea.
1020	1" IPS			18	.444	Ea.
1030	1-1/4" IPS			17	.471	Ea.
1040	1-1/2" IPS	↓	↓	15	.533	Ea.
1050	2" IPS			13	.615	Ea.
1060	2-1/2" IPS	Q-1	1 Plumber / 1 Plumber Apprentice	15	1.070	Ea.
1070	3" IPS			13	1.230	Ea.
1080	3-1/2" IPS			8	2.000	Ea.
1090	4" IPS			7	2.290	Ea.
1200	5" IPS	↓	↓	6	2.670	Ea.
1210	6" IPS	Q-2	2 Plumbers / 1 Plumber Apprentice	8	3.000	Ea.
1250	Cross, 1/2"	1 Plum	1 Plumber	10	.800	Ea.
1260	3/4"			9.50	.842	Ea.
1270	1"			8	1.000	Ea.
1280	1-1/4"			7.50	1.070	Ea.
1290	1-1/2"			6.50	1.230	Ea.
1300	2"	↓	↓	5.50	1.450	Ea.
1310	2-1/2"	Q-1	1 Plumber / 1 Plumber Apprentice	6.50	2.460	Ea.
1320	3"			5.50	2.910	Ea.
1340	4"			4.70	3.400	Ea.
1350	5"	↓	↓	3.20	5.000	Ea.
1360	6"	Q-2	2 Plumbers / 1 Plumber Apprentice	4.70	5.110	Ea.
1500	Tee, mechanically formed, 3/8"	1 Plum	1 Plumber	80	.100	Ea.
1520	1/2"			80	.100	Ea.
1530	3/4"			60	.133	Ea.
1540	1"			48	.167	Ea.
1550	1-1/4"			48	.167	Ea.
1560	1-1/2"			40	.200	Ea.
1570	2"	↓	↓	24	.333	Ea.
2000	DWV, solder joints, copper x copper					
2031	45° or 90° Elbow, 1-1/4"	1 Plum	1 Plumber	13	.615	Ea.
2050	1-1/2"			12	.667	Ea.
2070	2"	↓	↓	10	.800	Ea.
2090	3"	Q-1	1 Plumber / 1 Plumber Apprentice	10	1.600	Ea.
2100	4"	"	"	9	1.780	Ea.
2250	Tee, Sanitary, 1-1/4"	1 Plum	1 Plumber	9	.889	Ea.
2270	1-1/2"			8	1.000	Ea.
2290	2"	↓	↓	7	1.140	Ea.

151 | Pipe and Fittings

151 400 | Copper Pipe & Tubing

		CREW	MAKEUP	DAILY OUTPUT	MAN-HOURS	UNIT
430 2312	Pipe, copper, fittings, tee, sanitary, 3"	Q-1	1 Plumber 1 Plumber Apprentice	7	2.290	Ea.
2330	4"	"	"	6	2.670	Ea.
2400	Coupling, 1-1/4"	1 Plum	1 Plumber	14	.571	Ea.
2420	1-1/2"	↓	↓	13	.615	Ea.
2440	2"	↓	↓	11	.727	Ea.
2460	3"	Q-1	1 Plumber 1 Plumber Apprentice	11	1.450	Ea.
2480	4"	"	"	10	1.600	Ea.
3000	Refrigeration fittings, 90° Elbow					
3010	3/8" outside diameter	1 Plum	1 Plumber	22	.364	Ea.
3020	1/2" outside diameter			20	.400	Ea.
3030	5/8" outside diameter			19	.421	Ea.
3040	3/4" outside diameter			18	.444	Ea.
3050	7/8" outside diameter			17	.471	Ea.
3060	1-1/8" outside diameter			16	.500	Ea.
3070	1-3/8" outside diameter			15	.533	Ea.
3080	1-5/8" outside diameter			13	.615	Ea.
3090	2-1/8" outside diameter	↓	↓	11	.727	Ea.
3100	2-5/8" outside diameter	Q-1	1 Plumber 1 Plumber Apprentice	13	1.230	Ea.
3120	3-1/8" outside diameter			11	1.450	Ea.
3130	3-5/8" outside diameter			10	1.600	Ea.
3140	4-1/8" outside diameter	↓	↓	9	1.780	Ea.
6990	Polybutylene/polyethylene pipe, See 151-558-7990, plastic ftng.					
7000	Insert type Brass/copper, 100 psi @ 180°F, CTS					
7010	Adapter MPT 3/8" x 3/8" CTS	1 Plum	1 Plumber	29	.276	Ea.
7020	1/2" x 1/2"			26	.308	Ea.
7030	3/4" x 1/2"			26	.308	Ea.
7040	3/4" x 3/4"			25	.320	Ea.
7050	Adapter CTS 1/2" x 1/2" sweat			24	.333	Ea.
7060	3/4" x 3/4" sweat			22	.364	Ea.
7070	Coupler center set 3/8" CTS			25	.320	Ea.
7080	1/2" CTS			23	.348	Ea.
7090	3/4" CTS			22	.364	Ea.
7100	Elbow 90°, copper 3/8"			25	.320	Ea.
7110	1/2" CTS			23	.348	Ea.
7120	3/4" CTS			22	.364	Ea.
7130	Tee copper 3/8" CTS			17	.471	Ea.
7140	1/2" CTS			15	.533	Ea.
7150	3/4" CTS			14	.571	Ea.
7160	3/8" x 3/8" x 1/2"			16	.500	Ea.
7170	1/2" x 3/8" x 1/2"			15	.533	Ea.
7180	3/4" x 1/2" x 3/4"	↓	↓	14	.571	Ea.

151 450 | Corrosion Resistant Pipe

		CREW	MAKEUP	DAILY OUTPUT	MAN-HOURS	UNIT
451 0020	**PIPE, CORROSION RESISTANT** No couplings or hangers					
0020	Iron alloy, drain, mechanical joint					
1000	1-1/2" diameter	Q-1	1 Plumber 1 Plumber Apprentice	70	.229	L.F.
1100	2" diameter			66	.242	L.F.
1120	3" diameter			60	.267	L.F.
1140	4" diameter	↓	↓	52	.308	L.F.
1980	Iron alloy, drain, B&S joint					
2000	2" diameter	Q-1	1 Plumber 1 Plumber Apprentice	54	.296	L.F.
2100	3" diameter			52	.308	L.F.
2120	4" diameter	↓	↓	48	.333	L.F.

151 450 | Corrosion Resistant Pipe

		CREW	MAKEUP	DAILY OUTPUT	MAN-HOURS	UNIT
451 2141	Pipe, iron alloy, drain, B&S joint, 6" diameter	Q-2	2 Plumbers 1 Plumber Apprentice	59	.407	L.F.
2160	8" diameter	"	"	54	.444	L.F.
2981	Plastic, fiberglass filament wound, epoxy or polyester					
3000	2" diameter	Q-1	1 Plumber 1 Plumber Apprentice	62	.258	L.F.
3100	3" diameter			51	.314	L.F.
3120	4" diameter			45	.356	L.F.
3140	6" diameter	↓	↓	32	.500	L.F.
3160	8" diameter	Q-2	2 Plumbers 1 Plumber Apprentice	38	.632	L.F.
3180	10" diameter			32	.750	L.F.
3200	12" diameter	↓	↓	28	.857	L.F.
4981	Polypropylene or Proxylene, acid resistant, Schedule 40					
5000	1-1/2" diameter	Q-1	1 Plumber 1 Plumber Apprentice	68	.235	L.F.
5100	2" diameter			62	.258	L.F.
5120	3" diameter			51	.314	L.F.
5140	4" diameter			45	.356	L.F.
5160	6" diameter	↓	↓	32	.500	L.F.
6600	Polyvinylidene fluoride, Schedule 40					
6640	1/2" diameter	1 Plum	1 Plumber	44	.182	L.F.
6660	3/4" diameter			34	.235	L.F.
6680	1" diameter			31	.258	L.F.
6700	1-1/2" diameter			25	.320	L.F.
6720	2" diameter	↓	↓	22	.364	L.F.
7100	Steel pipe, plastic lined for temperature and chemical					
7120	resistance, flanged joints					
7140	Polypropylene lining for temperatures to 225°F.					
7160	1" diameter	Q-1	1 Plumber 1 Plumber Apprentice	76	.211	L.F.
7180	1-1/2" diameter			64	.250	L.F.
7200	2" diameter			51	.314	L.F.
7220	3" diameter			34	.471	L.F.
7240	4" diameter	↓	↓	29	.552	L.F.
7260	6" diameter	Q-2	2 Plumbers 1 Plumber Apprentice	26	.923	L.F.
7280	8" diameter			23	1.040	L.F.
7300	10" diameter	↓	↓	20	1.200	L.F.
7600	Fluorinated ethylene propylene lining					
7620	for temperatures to 300°F.					
7640	1" diameter	Q-1	1 Plumber 1 Plumber Apprentice	76	.211	L.F.
7660	1-1/2" diameter			64	.250	L.F.
7680	2" diameter			51	.314	L.F.
7700	3" diameter			34	.471	L.F.
7720	4" diameter	↓	↓	29	.552	L.F.
7740	6" diameter	Q-2	2 Plumbers 1 Plumber Apprentice	26	.923	L.F.
7760	8" diameter			23	1.040	L.F.
7780	10" diameter	↓	↓	20	1.200	L.F.
8000	Polytetrafluoroethylene lining					
8020	for temperatures to 500°F.					
8040	1" diameter	Q-1	1 Plumber 1 Plumber Apprentice	76	.211	L.F.
8060	1-1/2" diameter			64	.250	L.F.
8080	2" diameter			51	.314	L.F.
8100	3" diameter	↓	↓	34	.471	L.F.

151 450 | Corrosion Resistant Pipe

		Description	CREW	MAKEUP	DAILY OUTPUT	MAN-HOURS	UNIT
451	8121	Pipe, steel, polytetrafluoroethylene lining, 4" diameter	Q-1	1 Plumber 1 Plumber Apprentice	29	.552	L.F.
	8140	6" diameter	Q-2	2 Plumbers 1 Plumber Apprentice	26	.923	L.F.
	8160	8" diameter	↓	↓	23	1.040	L.F.
	8180	10" diameter			20	1.200	L.F.
454		PIPE, CORROSION RESISTANT, FITTINGS					
	0030	Iron alloy					
	0050	Mechanical joint					
	0061	1/8 or 1/4 Bend, 1-1/2"	Q-1	1 Plumber 1 Plumber Apprentice	12	1.330	Ea.
	0080	2"			10	1.600	Ea.
	0090	3"			9	1.780	Ea.
	0100	4"	↓	↓	8	2.000	Ea.
	0160	Tee and Y, sanitary, straight					
	0170	1-1/2"	Q-1	1 Plumber 1 Plumber Apprentice	8	2.000	Ea.
	0180	2"			7	2.290	Ea.
	0190	3"			6	2.670	Ea.
	0200	4"			5	3.200	Ea.
	0360	Coupling, 1-1/2"			14	1.140	Ea.
	0380	2"			12	1.330	Ea.
	0390	3"			11	1.450	Ea.
	0400	4"	↓	↓	10	1.600	Ea.
	0500	Bell & Spigot					
	0511	1/4, 1/8, or 1/16 Bend, 2"	Q-1	1 Plumber 1 Plumber Apprentice	16	1.000	Ea.
	0520	3"			14	1.140	Ea.
	0530	4"	↓	↓	13	1.230	Ea.
	0540	6"	Q-2	2 Plumbers 1 Plumber Apprentice	17	1.410	Ea.
	0550	8"	"	"	12	2.000	Ea.
	0701	Y and tee, sanitary, 2"	Q-1	1 Plumber 1 Plumber Apprentice	10	1.600	Ea.
	0710	3"			9	1.780	Ea.
	0720	4"	↓	↓	8	2.000	Ea.
	0730	6"	Q-2	2 Plumbers 1 Plumber Apprentice	11	2.180	Ea.
	0740	8"	"	"	8	3.000	Ea.
	3000	Epoxy, filament wound					
	3030	Quick-lock joint					
	3041	45° or 90° Elbow, 2"	Q-1	1 Plumber 1 Plumber Apprentice	28	.571	Ea.
	3060	3"			16	1.000	Ea.
	3070	4"			13	1.230	Ea.
	3080	6"	↓	↓	8	2.000	Ea.
	3090	8"	Q-2	2 Plumbers 1 Plumber Apprentice	9	2.670	Ea.
	3100	10"	"	"	7	3.430	Ea.
	3190	Tee, 2"	Q-1	1 Plumber 1 Plumber Apprentice	19	.842	Ea.
	3200	3"			11	1.450	Ea.
	3210	4"			9	1.780	Ea.
	3220	6"	↓	↓	5	3.200	Ea.
	3230	8"	Q-2	2 Plumbers 1 Plumber Apprentice	6	4.000	Ea.
	3240	10"			5	4.800	Ea.
	3250	12"	↓	↓	4	6.000	Ea.

			CREW	MAKEUP	DAILY OUTPUT	MAN-HOURS	UNIT
		**151 450	Corrosion Resistant Pipe**					
454	4001	Pipe fittings, polypropylene, acid resistant					
	4020	Non-pressure					
	4050	1/4 Bend, 1-1/2"	1 Plum	1 Plumber	16	.500	Ea.
	4060	2"	Q-1	1 Plumber	28	.571	Ea.
				1 Plumber Apprentice			
	4080	3"			17	.941	Ea.
	4090	4"			14	1.140	Ea.
	4110	6"	↓	↓	8	2.000	Ea.
	4250	1/8 Bend, 1-1/2"	1 Plum	1 Plumber	16	.500	Ea.
	4260	2"	Q-1	1 Plumber	28	.571	Ea.
				1 Plumber Apprentice			
	4280	3"			17	.941	Ea.
	4290	4"			14	1.140	Ea.
	4310	6"	↓	↓	8	2.000	Ea.
	4400	Tee, sanitary					
	4420	1-1/2"	1 Plum	1 Plumber	10	.800	Ea.
	4430	2"	Q-1	1 Plumber	17	.941	Ea.
				1 Plumber Apprentice			
	4450	3"			11	1.450	Ea.
	4460	4"			9	1.780	Ea.
	4480	6"	↓	↓	5	3.200	Ea.
	4500	Tee/wye, long turn					
	4520	1-1/2"	1 Plum	1 Plumber	10	.800	Ea.
	4530	2"	Q-1	1 Plumber	17	.941	Ea.
				1 Plumber Apprentice			
	4550	3"			11	1.450	Ea.
	4570	4"	↓	↓	9	1.780	Ea.
	4650	Wye 45°, 1-1/2"	1 Plum	1 Plumber	10	.800	Ea.
	4670	2"	Q-1	1 Plumber	17	.941	Ea.
				1 Plumber Apprentice			
	4680	3"			11	1.450	Ea.
	4700	4"			9	1.780	Ea.
	4720	6"	↓	↓	5	3.200	Ea.
	4800	Wye, double 45°					
	4820	1-1/2"	1 Plum	1 Plumber	8	1.000	Ea.
	4830	2"	Q-1	1 Plumber	14	1.140	Ea.
				1 Plumber Apprentice			
	4850	3"			9	1.780	Ea.
	4870	4"	↓	↓	4	4.000	Ea.

		**151 500	Glass Pipe**	CREW	MAKEUP	DAILY OUTPUT	MAN-HOURS	UNIT
	501	**PIPE, GLASS** Borosilicate, couplings & hangers 10' O.C.					
	0020	Drainage					
	1100	1-1/2" diameter	Q-1	1 Plumber	52	.308	L.F.
				1 Plumber Apprentice			
	1120	2" diameter			44	.364	L.F.
	1140	3" diameter			39	.410	L.F.
	1160	4" diameter			30	.533	L.F.
	1180	6" diameter	↓	↓	26	.615	L.F.
	2000	Process supply (pressure), beaded joints					
	2040	1/2" diameter	1 Plum	1 Plumber	36	.222	L.F.
	2060	3/4" diameter			31	.258	L.F.
	2080	1" diameter	↓	↓	27	.296	L.F.
	2100	1-1/2" diameter	Q-1	1 Plumber	47	.340	L.F.
				1 Plumber Apprentice			
	2120	2" diameter			39	.410	L.F.
	2140	3" diameter			34	.471	L.F.
	2160	4" diameter	↓	↓	25	.640	L.F.

151 | Pipe and Fittings

151 500 | Glass Pipe

		Description	CREW	MAKEUP	DAILY OUTPUT	MAN-HOURS	UNIT
501	2181	Pipe, glass borosilicate, process supply, beaded joints, 6" diam.	Q-1	1 Plumber 1 Plumber Apprentice	21	.762	L.F.
	3000	Beaded joint, armored, translucent					
	3040	1/2" diameter	1 Plum	1 Plumber	36	.222	L.F.
	3060	3/4" diameter			31	.258	L.F.
	3080	1" diameter	↓	↓	27	.296	L.F.
	3100	1-1/2" diameter	Q-1	1 Plumber 1 Plumber Apprentice	47	.340	L.F.
	3120	2" diameter			39	.410	L.F.
	3140	3" diameter			34	.471	L.F.
	3160	4" diameter			25	.640	L.F.
	3180	6" diameter	↓	↓	21	.762	L.F.
	3800	Conical joint, transparent					
	3880	1" diameter	1 Plum	1 Plumber	27	.296	L.F.
	3900	1-1/2" diameter	Q-1	1 Plumber 1 Plumber Apprentice	47	.340	L.F.
	3920	2" diameter			39	.410	L.F.
	3940	3" diameter			34	.471	L.F.
	3960	4" diameter			25	.640	L.F.
	3980	6" diameter	↓	↓	21	.762	L.F.
512		PIPE, GLASS, FITTINGS					
	0020	Drainage, beaded ends					
	0500	Coupling, stainless steel, TFE seal ring					
	0520	1-1/2"	Q-1	1 Plumber 1 Plumber Apprentice	32	.500	Ea.
	0530	2"			30	.533	Ea.
	0540	3"			25	.640	Ea.
	0550	4"			23	.696	Ea.
	0560	6"	↓	↓	20	.800	Ea.
	0600	Coupling, stainless steel, bead to plain end					
	0610	1-1/2"	Q-1	1 Plumber 1 Plumber Apprentice	36	.444	Ea.
	0620	2"			34	.471	Ea.
	0630	3"			29	.552	Ea.
	0640	4"			27	.593	Ea.
	0650	6"	↓	↓	24	.667	Ea.
	2000	Process supply (pressure), beaded ends					
	2350	Coupling, Hydrin liner, for temperatures to 300°F					
	2370	1/2"	Q-1	1 Plumber 1 Plumber Apprentice	40	.400	Ea.
	2380	3/4"			37	.432	Ea.
	2390	1"			35	.457	Ea.
	2400	1-1/2"			32	.500	Ea.
	2410	2"			30	.533	Ea.
	2420	3"			25	.640	Ea.
	2430	4"			23	.696	Ea.
	2440	6"	↓	↓	20	.800	Ea.

151 550 | Plastic Pipe

		Description	CREW	MAKEUP	DAILY OUTPUT	MAN-HOURS	UNIT
551		PIPE, PLASTIC See also division 151-451					
	0020	Fiberglass reinforced, couplings 10' O.C., hangers 3 per 10'					
	0080	General service					
	0120	2" diameter	Q-1	1 Plumber 1 Plumber Apprentice	59	.271	L.F.
	0140	3" diameter			52	.308	L.F.
	0150	4" diameter			48	.333	L.F.
	0160	6" diameter	↓	↓	39	.410	L.F.

151 | Pipe and Fittings

151 550 | Plastic Pipe

		CREW	MAKEUP	DAILY OUTPUT	MAN-HOURS	UNIT
551 0171	Pipe, plastic, fiberglass reinforced, gen. service, 8" diam.	Q-2	2 Plumbers 1 Plumber Apprentice	49	.490	L.F.
0180	10" diameter	↓	↓	41	.585	L.F.
0190	12" diameter			36	.667	L.F.
0200	High strength					
0240	2" diameter	Q-1	1 Plumber 1 Plumber Apprentice	58	.276	L.F.
0260	3" diameter			51	.314	L.F.
0280	4" diameter			47	.340	L.F.
0300	6" diameter	↓	↓	38	.421	L.F.
0320	8" diameter	Q-2	2 Plumbers 1 Plumber Apprentice	48	.500	L.F.
0340	10" diameter	↓	↓	40	.600	L.F.
0360	12" diameter			36	.667	L.F.
0600	PVC, high impact/pressure, cplgs. 10' O.C., hangers 3 per 10'					
0620	Schedule 40					
0670	1/2" diameter	1 Plum	1 Plumber	54	.148	L.F.
0680	3/4" diameter			51	.157	L.F.
0690	1" diameter			46	.174	L.F.
0700	1-1/4" diameter			42	.190	L.F.
0710	1-1/2" diameter	↓	↓	36	.222	L.F.
0720	2" diameter	Q-1	1 Plumber 1 Plumber Apprentice	59	.271	L.F.
0730	2-1/2" diameter			56	.286	L.F.
0740	3" diameter			53	.302	L.F.
0750	4" diameter			48	.333	L.F.
0760	5" diameter			43	.372	L.F.
0770	6" diameter	↓	↓	39	.410	L.F.
0780	8" diameter	Q-2	2 Plumbers 1 Plumber Apprentice	48	.500	L.F.
0790	10" diameter	↓	↓	43	.558	L.F.
0800	12" diameter			42	.571	L.F.
1020	Schedule 80					
1040	1/4" diameter	1 Plum	1 Plumber	58	.138	L.F.
1060	3/8" diameter			55	.145	L.F.
1070	1/2" diameter			50	.160	L.F.
1080	3/4" diameter			47	.170	L.F.
1090	1" diameter			43	.186	L.F.
1100	1-1/4" diameter			39	.205	L.F.
1110	1-1/2" diameter	↓	↓	34	.235	L.F.
1120	2" diameter	Q-1	1 Plumber 1 Plumber Apprentice	55	.291	L.F.
1130	2-1/2" diameter			52	.308	L.F.
1140	3" diameter			50	.320	L.F.
1150	4" diameter			46	.348	L.F.
1160	5" diameter			42	.381	L.F.
1170	6" diameter	↓	↓	38	.421	L.F.
1180	8" diameter	Q-2	2 Plumbers 1 Plumber Apprentice	47	.511	L.F.
1190	10" diameter	↓	↓	42	.571	L.F.
1200	12" diameter			38	.632	L.F.
1800	PVC, couplings 10' O.C., hangers 3 per 10'					
1820	Schedule 40					
1860	1/2" diameter	1 Plum	1 Plumber	54	.148	L.F.
1870	3/4" diameter			51	.157	L.F.
1880	1" diameter			46	.174	L.F.
1890	1-1/4" diameter			42	.190	L.F.
1900	1-1/2" diameter	↓	↓	36	.222	L.F.

151 550 | Plastic Pipe

			CREW	MAKEUP	DAILY OUTPUT	MAN-HOURS	UNIT
551	1911	Pipe, PVC, schedule 40, 2" diameter	Q-1	1 Plumber 1 Plumber Apprentice	59	.271	L.F.
	1920	2-1/2" diameter			56	.286	L.F.
	1930	3" diameter			53	.302	L.F.
	1940	4" diameter			48	.333	L.F.
	1950	5" diameter			43	.372	L.F.
	1960	6" diameter	↓	↓	39	.410	L.F.
	1970	8" diameter	Q-2	2 Plumbers 1 Plumber Apprentice	48	.500	L.F.
	1980	10" diameter			43	.558	L.F.
	1990	12" diameter			42	.571	L.F.
	2000	14" diameter			31	.774	L.F.
	2010	16" diameter	↓	↓	23	1.040	L.F.
	2420	Schedule 80					
	2440	1/4" diameter	1 Plum	1 Plumber	58	.138	L.F.
	2450	3/8" diameter			55	.145	L.F.
	2460	1/2" diameter			50	.160	L.F.
	2470	3/4" diameter			47	.170	L.F.
	2480	1" diameter			43	.186	L.F.
	2490	1-1/4" diameter			39	.205	L.F.
	2500	1-1/2" diameter	↓	↓	34	.235	L.F.
	2510	2" diameter	Q-1	1 Plumber 1 Plumber Apprentice	55	.291	L.F.
	2520	2-1/2" diameter			52	.308	L.F.
	2530	3" diameter			50	.320	L.F.
	2540	4" diameter			46	.348	L.F.
	2550	5" diameter			42	.381	L.F.
	2560	6" diameter	↓	↓	38	.421	L.F.
	2570	8" diameter	Q-2	2 Plumbers 1 Plumber Apprentice	47	.511	L.F.
	2580	10" diameter			42	.571	L.F.
	2590	12" diameter	↓	↓	38	.632	L.F.
	2900	Schedule 120					
	2910	1/2" diameter	1 Plum	1 Plumber	50	.160	L.F.
	2950	3/4" diameter			47	.170	L.F.
	2960	1" diameter			43	.186	L.F.
	2970	1-1/4" diameter			39	.205	L.F.
	2980	1-1/2" diameter	↓	↓	33	.242	L.F.
	2990	2" diameter	Q-1	1 Plumber 1 Plumber Apprentice	54	.296	L.F.
	3000	2-1/2" diameter			52	.308	L.F.
	3010	3" diameter			49	.327	L.F.
	3020	4" diameter			45	.356	L.F.
	3030	6" diameter	↓	↓	37	.432	L.F.
	3300	PVC, pressure, couplings 10' O.C., hangers 3 per 10'					
	3310	SDR 26, 160 psi					
	3350	1-1/4" diameter	1 Plum	1 Plumber	42	.190	L.F.
	3360	1-1/2" diameter	"	"	36	.222	L.F.
	3370	2" diameter	Q-1	1 Plumber 1 Plumber Apprentice	59	.271	L.F.
	3380	2-1/2" diameter			56	.286	L.F.
	3390	3" diameter			53	.302	L.F.
	3400	4" diameter			48	.333	L.F.
	3420	6" diameter	↓	↓	39	.410	L.F.
	3430	8" diameter	Q-2	2 Plumbers 1 Plumber Apprentice	48	.500	L.F.
	3720	SDR 21, 200 psi, 1/2" diameter	1 Plum	1 Plumber	54	.148	L.F.
	3740	3/4" diameter	"	"	51	.157	L.F.

151 550 | Plastic Pipe

		CREW	MAKEUP	DAILY OUTPUT	MAN-HOURS	UNIT
551	3751	Pipe, PVC, SDR 21, 200 psi, 1″ diameter	1 Plum	1 Plumber	46	.174	L.F.
	3760	1-1/4″ diameter			42	.190	L.F.
	3770	1-1/2″ diameter	↓	↓	36	.222	L.F.
	3780	2″ diameter	Q-1	1 Plumber	59	.271	L.F.
				1 Plumber Apprentice			
	3790	2-1/2″ diameter			56	.286	L.F.
	3800	3″ diameter			53	.302	L.F.
	3810	4″ diameter			48	.333	L.F.
	3830	6″ diameter	↓	↓	39	.410	L.F.
	3840	8″ diameter	Q-2	2 Plumbers	48	.500	L.F.
				1 Plumber Apprentice			
	4100	DWV type, schedule 40, couplings 10′ O.C., hangers 3 per 10′					
	4120	ABS					
	4140	1-1/4″ diameter	1 Plum	1 Plumber	42	.190	L.F.
	4150	1-1/2″ diameter	″	″	36	.222	L.F.
	4160	2″ diameter	Q-1	1 Plumber	59	.271	L.F.
				1 Plumber Apprentice			
	4170	3″ diameter			53	.302	L.F.
	4180	4″ diameter			48	.333	L.F.
	4190	6″ diameter	↓	↓	39	.410	L.F.
	4400	PVC					
	4410	1-1/4″ diameter	1 Plum	1 Plumber	42	.190	L.F.
	4420	1-1/2″ diameter	″	″	36	.222	L.F.
	4460	2″ diameter	Q-1	1 Plumber	59	.271	L.F.
				1 Plumber Apprentice			
	4470	3″ diameter			53	.302	L.F.
	4480	4″ diameter			48	.333	L.F.
	4490	6″ diameter	↓	↓	39	.410	L.F.
	4800	PVC, clear pipe, cplgs. 10′ O.C., hangers 3 per 10′, Sched. 40					
	4840	1/4″ diameter	1 Plum	1 Plumber	59	.136	L.F.
	4850	3/8″ diameter			56	.143	L.F.
	4860	1/2″ diameter			54	.148	L.F.
	4870	3/4″ diameter			51	.157	L.F.
	4880	1″ diameter			46	.174	L.F.
	4890	1-1/4″ diameter			42	.190	L.F.
	4900	1-1/2″ diameter	↓	↓	36	.222	L.F.
	4910	2″ diameter	Q-1	1 Plumber	59	.271	L.F.
				1 Plumber Apprentice			
	4920	2-1/2″ diameter			56	.286	L.F.
	4930	3″ diameter			53	.302	L.F.
	4940	3-1/2″ diameter			50	.320	L.F.
	4950	4″ diameter	↓	↓	48	.333	L.F.
	5360	CPVC, couplings 10′ O.C., hangers 3 per 10′					
	5380	Schedule 40					
	5460	1/2″ diameter	1 Plum	1 Plumber	54	.148	L.F.
	5470	3/4″ diameter			51	.157	L.F.
	5480	1″ diameter			46	.174	L.F.
	5490	1-1/4″ diameter			42	.190	L.F.
	5500	1-1/2″ diameter	↓	↓	36	.222	L.F.
	5510	2″ diameter	Q-1	1 Plumber	59	.271	L.F.
				1 Plumber Apprentice			
	5520	2-1/2″ diameter			56	.286	L.F.
	5530	3″ diameter			53	.302	L.F.
	5540	4″ diameter			48	.333	L.F.
	5550	6″ diameter	↓	↓	43	.372	L.F.
	5800	Schedule 80					
	5860	1/2″ diameter	1 Plum	1 Plumber	50	.160	L.F.
	5870	3/4″ diameter	″	″	47	.170	L.F.

151 550	Plastic Pipe	CREW	MAKEUP	DAILY OUTPUT	MAN-HOURS	UNIT
551 5881	Pipe, CPVC, schedule 80, 1" diameter	1 Plum	1 Plumber	43	.186	L.F.
5890	1-1/4" diameter			39	.205	L.F.
5900	1-1/2" diameter	↓	↓	34	.235	L.F.
5910	2" diameter	Q-1	1 Plumber	55	.291	L.F.
			1 Plumber Apprentice			
5920	2-1/2" diameter			52	.308	L.F.
5930	3" diameter			50	.320	L.F.
5940	4" diameter			46	.348	L.F.
5950	6" diameter	↓	↓	38	.421	L.F.
5960	8" diameter	Q-2	2 Plumbers	47	.511	L.F.
			1 Plumber Apprentice			
6240	CTS, 1/2" diameter	1 Plum	1 Plumber	54	.148	L.F.
6250	3/4" diameter			51	.157	L.F.
6260	1" diameter			46	.174	L.F.
6270	1 1/4"			42	.190	L.F.
6280	1 1/2" diameter	↓	↓	36	.222	L.F.
6290	2" diameter	Q-1	1 Plumber	59	.271	L.F.
			1 Plumber Apprentice			
6410	Polybutylene, flexible, no couplings or hangers, 100' coils					
6430	Cold water					
6440	SDR 13.5, 160 psi @ 73°F, 3/4" CTS	1 Plum	1 Plumber	250	.032	L.F.
6450	1" CTS			204	.039	L.F.
6460	1-1/4" CTS			151	.053	L.F.
6470	1-1/2" CTS			107	.075	L.F.
6480	2" CTS			87	.092	L.F.
6500	SDR 9, 250 psi @ 73°F, 3/4" CTS			250	.032	L.F.
6510	1" CTS			204	.039	L.F.
6520	1-1/4" CTS			151	.053	L.F.
6530	1-1/2" CTS			107	.075	L.F.
6540	2" CTS			87	.092	L.F.
6560	SDR 11.5, 160 psi @ 73°F, 3/4" IPS			239	.033	L.F.
6570	1" IPS			195	.041	L.F.
6580	1-1/4" IPS			143	.056	L.F.
6590	1-1/2" IPS			102	.078	L.F.
6600	2" IPS	↓	↓	83	.096	L.F.
6820	Hot and cold water					
6830	SDR 11, 100 psi @ 180°F, 1/8" CTS	1 Plum	1 Plumber	395	.020	L.F.
6840	1/4" CTS			390	.021	L.F.
6850	3/8" CTS			342	.023	L.F.
6860	1/2" CTS			294	.027	L.F.
6870	3/4" CTS			212	.038	L.F.
6900	SDR 11, 100 psi @ 180°F, fusion jts, 3/4" CTS			164	.049	L.F.
6910	1" CTS			157	.051	L.F.
6920	1-1/4" CTS			117	.068	L.F.
6930	1-1/2" CTS			83	.096	L.F.
6940	2" CTS			67	.119	L.F.
6950	3" CTS	↓	↓	61	.131	L.F.
558 0030	PIPE, PLASTIC, FITTINGS Epoxy resin, fiberglass reinforced, general service					
0090	Elbow, 90°, 2"	Q-1	1 Plumber	23	.696	Ea.
			1 Plumber Apprentice			
0100	3"			16	1.000	Ea.
0110	4"			13	1.230	Ea.
0120	6"	↓	↓	8	2.000	Ea.
0130	8"	Q-2	2 Plumbers	9	2.670	Ea.
			1 Plumber Apprentice			
0140	10"			7	3.430	Ea.
0150	12"	↓	↓	5	4.800	Ea.

151 550	Plastic Pipe	CREW	MAKEUP	DAILY OUTPUT	MAN-HOURS	UNIT
558 0161	Pipe, plastic, fittings, 45° elbow same as 90°					
0290	Tee, 2"	Q-1	1 Plumber	17	.941	Ea.
			1 Plumber Apprentice			
0300	3"			10	1.600	Ea.
0310	4"			8	2.000	Ea.
0320	6"	↓	↓	5	3.200	Ea.
0330	8"	Q-2	2 Plumbers	6	4.000	Ea.
			1 Plumber Apprentice			
0340	10"			5	4.800	Ea.
0350	12"	↓	↓	4	6.000	Ea.
0380	Couplings					
0410	2"	Q-1	1 Plumber	28	.571	Ea.
			1 Plumber Apprentice			
0420	3"			20	.800	Ea.
0430	4"			17	.941	Ea.
0440	6"	↓	↓	12	1.330	Ea.
0450	8"	Q-2	2 Plumbers	15	1.600	Ea.
			1 Plumber Apprentice			
0460	10"			11	2.180	Ea.
0470	12"	↓	↓	10	2.400	Ea.
0500	PVC, high impact/pressure, Schedule 40					
0531	45° or 90° Elbow, 1/2"	1 Plum	1 Plumber	20	.400	Ea.
0550	3/4"			19	.421	Ea.
0560	1"			16	.500	Ea.
0570	1-1/4"			15	.533	Ea.
0580	1-1/2"	↓	↓	14	.571	Ea.
0590	2"	Q-1	1 Plumber	23	.696	Ea.
			1 Plumber Apprentice			
0600	3"			16	1.000	Ea.
0610	4"			13	1.230	Ea.
0620	6"	↓	↓	8	2.000	Ea.
0630	8"	Q-2	2 Plumbers	9	2.670	Ea.
			1 Plumber Apprentice			
0800	Tee, 1/2"	1 Plum	1 Plumber	13	.615	Ea.
0820	3/4"			12	.667	Ea.
0830	1"			11	.727	Ea.
0840	1-1/4"			10	.800	Ea.
0850	1-1/2"	↓	↓	10	.800	Ea.
0860	2"	Q-1	1 Plumber	17	.941	Ea.
			1 Plumber Apprentice			
0870	3"			10	1.600	Ea.
0880	4"			8	2.000	Ea.
0890	6"	↓	↓	5	3.200	Ea.
0900	8"	Q-2	2 Plumbers	6	4.000	Ea.
			1 Plumber Apprentice			
0910	10"			4	6.000	Ea.
0920	12"	↓	↓	3	8.000	Ea.
1070	Coupling, 1/2"	1 Plum	1 Plumber	22	.364	Ea.
1080	3/4"			21	.381	Ea.
1090	1"			18	.444	Ea.
1100	1-1/4"			17	.471	Ea.
1110	1-1/2"	↓	↓	16	.500	Ea.
1120	2"	Q-1	1 Plumber	28	.571	Ea.
			1 Plumber Apprentice			
1130	2-1/2"			25	.640	Ea.
1140	3"			22	.727	Ea.
1150	3-1/2"			19	.842	Ea.
1160	4"	↓	↓	17	.941	Ea.

151 550 | Plastic Pipe

		Description	CREW	MAKEUP	DAILY OUTPUT	MAN-HOURS	UNIT
558	1171	Pipe, PVC fittings, schedule 40, coupling, 5"	Q-1	1 Plumber / 1 Plumber Apprentice	14	1.140	Ea.
	1180	6"	"	"	12	1.330	Ea.
	1190	8"	Q-2	2 Plumbers / 1 Plumber Apprentice	14	1.710	Ea.
	1200	10"			13	1.850	Ea.
	1210	12"			12	2.000	Ea.
	1220	14"			10	2.400	Ea.
	1230	16"	↓	↓	7	3.430	Ea.
	2100	Schedule 80					
	2111	45° or 90° Elbow, 1/2"	1 Plum	1 Plumber	18	.444	Ea.
	2130	3/4"			17	.471	Ea.
	2140	1"			15	.533	Ea.
	2150	1-1/4"			14	.571	Ea.
	2160	1-1/2"	↓	↓	13	.615	Ea.
	2170	2"	Q-1	1 Plumber / 1 Plumber Apprentice	22	.727	Ea.
	2180	3"			14	1.140	Ea.
	2190	4"			12	1.330	Ea.
	2200	6"	↓	↓	7	2.290	Ea.
	2210	8"	Q-2	2 Plumbers / 1 Plumber Apprentice	8	3.000	Ea.
	2400	Tee, 1/2"	1 Plum	1 Plumber	12	.667	Ea.
	2420	3/4"			11	.727	Ea.
	2430	1"			10	.800	Ea.
	2440	1-1/4"			9	.889	Ea.
	2450	1-1/2"	↓	↓	8	1.000	Ea.
	2460	2"	Q-1	1 Plumber / 1 Plumber Apprentice	14	1.140	Ea.
	2470	3"			9	1.780	Ea.
	2480	4"			8	2.000	Ea.
	2490	6"	↓	↓	5	3.200	Ea.
	2500	8"	Q-2	2 Plumbers / 1 Plumber Apprentice	6	4.000	Ea.
	2550	Coupling, 1/2"	1 Plum	1 Plumber	18	.444	Ea.
	2570	3/4"			17	.471	Ea.
	2580	1"			15	.533	Ea.
	2590	1-1/4"			14	.571	Ea.
	2600	1-1/2"	↓	↓	13	.615	Ea.
	2610	2"	Q-1	1 Plumber / 1 Plumber Apprentice	22	.727	Ea.
	2620	3"			19	.842	Ea.
	2630	4"			16	1.000	Ea.
	2640	6"	↓	↓	12	1.330	Ea.
	2650	8"	Q-2	2 Plumbers / 1 Plumber Apprentice	14	1.710	Ea.
	2660	10"			13	1.850	Ea.
	2670	12"	↓	↓	12	2.000	Ea.
	2700	PVC (white), Schedule 40, socket joints					
	2761	Elbow 45° or 90°, 1/2"	1 Plum	1 Plumber	22	.364	Ea.
	2770	3/4"			21	.381	Ea.
	2780	1"			18	.444	Ea.
	2790	1-1/4"			17	.471	Ea.
	2800	1-1/2"	↓	↓	16	.500	Ea.
	2810	2"	Q-1	1 Plumber / 1 Plumber Apprentice	28	.571	Ea.
	2820	2-1/2"			22	.727	Ea.
	2830	3"	↓	↓	17	.941	Ea.

151 550 | Plastic Pipe

		CREW	MAKEUP	DAILY OUTPUT	MAN-HOURS	UNIT
558 2841	Pipe, PVC, fittings, schedule 40, socket joints, elbow, 4"	Q-1	1 Plumber 1 Plumber Apprentice	14	1.140	Ea.
2850	5"			12	1.330	Ea.
2860	6"	↓	↓	8	2.000	Ea.
2870	8"	Q-2	2 Plumbers 1 Plumber Apprentice	10	2.400	Ea.
3180	Tee, 1/2"	1 Plum	1 Plumber	14	.571	Ea.
3190	3/4"			13	.615	Ea.
3200	1"			12	.667	Ea.
3210	1-1/4"			11	.727	Ea.
3220	1-1/2"	↓	↓	10	.800	Ea.
3230	2"	Q-1	1 Plumber 1 Plumber Apprentice	17	.941	Ea.
3240	2-1/2"			14	1.140	Ea.
3250	3"			11	1.450	Ea.
3260	4"			9	1.780	Ea.
3270	5"			8	2.000	Ea.
3280	6"	↓	↓	5	3.200	Ea.
3290	8"	Q-2	2 Plumbers 1 Plumber Apprentice	6	4.000	Ea.
3380	Coupling, 1/2"	1 Plum	1 Plumber	22	.364	Ea.
3390	3/4"			21	.381	Ea.
3400	1"			18	.444	Ea.
3410	1-1/4"			17	.471	Ea.
3420	1-1/2"	↓	↓	16	.500	Ea.
3430	2"	Q-1	1 Plumber 1 Plumber Apprentice	28	.571	Ea.
3440	2-1/2"			20	.800	Ea.
3450	3"			19	.842	Ea.
3460	4"			16	1.000	Ea.
3470	5"			14	1.140	Ea.
3480	6"	↓	↓	12	1.330	Ea.
3490	8"	Q-2	2 Plumbers 1 Plumber Apprentice	14	1.710	Ea.
4500	DWV, ABS, non pressure, socket joints					
4540	1/4 Bend, 1-1/4"	1 Plum	1 Plumber	17	.471	Ea.
4560	1-1/2"	"	"	16	.500	Ea.
4570	2"	Q-1	1 Plumber 1 Plumber Apprentice	28	.571	Ea.
4580	3"			17	.941	Ea.
4590	4"			14	1.140	Ea.
4600	6"	↓	↓	8	2.000	Ea.
4650	1/8 Bend, same as 1/4 Bend					
4800	Tee, sanitary					
4820	1-1/4"	1 Plum	1 Plumber	11	.727	Ea.
4830	1-1/2"	"	"	10	.800	Ea.
4840	2"	Q-1	1 Plumber 1 Plumber Apprentice	17	.941	Ea.
4850	3"			11	1.450	Ea.
4860	4"	↓	↓	9	1.780	Ea.
5000	PVC, Schedule 40, socket joints					
5041	1/4 or 1/8 Bend, 1-1/4"	1 Plum	1 Plumber	17	.471	Ea.
5060	1-1/2"	"	"	16	.500	Ea.
5070	2"	Q-1	1 Plumber 1 Plumber Apprentice	28	.571	Ea.
5080	3"			17	.941	Ea.
5090	4"			14	1.140	Ea.
5100	6"	↓	↓	8	2.000	Ea.

151 550	**Plastic Pipe**	CREW	MAKEUP	DAILY OUTPUT	MAN-HOURS	UNIT
558 5251	Pipe, DWV,, ABS fittings, PVC tee, sanitary, 1-1/4"	1 Plum	1 Plumber	11	.727	Ea.
5270	1-1/2"	"	"	10	.800	Ea.
5280	2"	Q-1	1 Plumber	17	.941	Ea.
			1 Plumber Apprentice			
5290	3"			11	1.450	Ea.
5300	4"			9	1.780	Ea.
5350	Coupling, 1-1/4"	1 Plum	1 Plumber	17	.471	Ea.
5360	1-1/2"	"	"	16	.500	Ea.
5370	2"	Q-1	1 Plumber	28	.571	Ea.
			1 Plumber Apprentice			
5380	3"			22	.727	Ea.
5390	4"			17	.941	Ea.
5400	6"			12	1.330	Ea.
5500	CPVC, Schedule 80, socket or threaded joints					
5540	90° Elbow, 1/4"	1 Plum	1 Plumber	20	.400	Ea.
5560	1/2"			18	.444	Ea.
5570	3/4"			17	.471	Ea.
5580	1"			15	.533	Ea.
5590	1-1/4"			14	.571	Ea.
5600	1-1/2"			13	.615	Ea.
5610	2"	Q-1	1 Plumber	22	.727	Ea.
			1 Plumber Apprentice			
5620	2-1/2"			18	.889	Ea.
5630	3"			14	1.140	Ea.
5640	4"			12	1.330	Ea.
5650	6"			7	2.290	Ea.
5700	45° Elbow same as 90° Elbow					
5850	Tee, 1/4"	1 Plum	1 Plumber	14	.571	Ea.
5870	1/2"			12	.667	Ea.
5880	3/4"			11	.727	Ea.
5890	1"			10	.800	Ea.
5900	1-1/4"			9	.889	Ea.
5910	1-1/2"			8	1.000	Ea.
5920	2"	Q-1	1 Plumber	14	1.140	Ea.
			1 Plumber Apprentice			
5930	2-1/2"			12	1.330	Ea.
5940	3"			9	1.780	Ea.
5950	4"			8	2.000	Ea.
5960	6"			5	3.200	Ea.
6000	Coupling, 1/4"	1 Plum	1 Plumber	20	.400	Ea.
6020	1/2"			18	.444	Ea.
6030	3/4"			17	.471	Ea.
6040	1"			15	.533	Ea.
6050	1-1/4"			14	.571	Ea.
6060	1-1/2"			13	.615	Ea.
6070	2"	Q-1	1 Plumber	22	.727	Ea.
			1 Plumber Apprentice			
6080	2-1/2"			20	.800	Ea.
6090	3"			19	.842	Ea.
6100	4"			16	1.000	Ea.
6110	6"			12	1.330	Ea.
6120	8"	Q-2	2 Plumbers	14	1.710	Ea.
			1 Plumber Apprentice			
6200	CTS, 100 psi at 180°F, hot and cold water					
6231	45° or 90° Elbow, 1/2"	1 Plum	1 Plumber	20	.400	Ea.
6250	3/4"			19	.421	Ea.
6251	1"			16	.500	Ea.
6252	1-1/4"			15	.533	Ea.

151 | Pipe and Fittings

151 550 | Plastic Pipe

		Description	CREW	MAKEUP	DAILY OUTPUT	MAN-HOURS	UNIT
558	6259	Pipe, PVC, fittings, CTS, elbow, 1-1/2"	1 Plum	1 Plumber	14	.571	Ea.
	6261	2"	Q-1	1 Plumber	23	.696	Ea.
				1 Plumber Apprentice			
	6290	Tee, 1/2"	1 Plum	1 Plumber	13	.615	Ea.
	6310	3/4"			12	.667	Ea.
	6311	1"			11	.727	Ea.
	6312	1-1/4"			10	.800	Ea.
	6313	1-1/2"	↓	↓	10	.800	Ea.
	6314	2"	Q-1	1 Plumber	17	.941	Ea.
				1 Plumber Apprentice			
	6320	Coupling, 1/2"	1 Plum	1 Plumber	22	.364	Ea.
	6340	3/4"			21	.381	Ea.
	6341	1"			18	.444	Ea.
	6342	1-1/4"			17	.471	Ea.
	6343	1-1/2"	↓	↓	16	.500	Ea.
	6344	2"	Q-1	1 Plumber	28	.571	Ea.
				1 Plumber Apprentice			
	7340	PVC flange, slip-on, 1/2"	1 Plum	1 Plumber	22	.364	Ea.
	7350	3/4"			21	.381	Ea.
	7360	1"			18	.444	Ea.
	7370	1-1/4"			17	.471	Ea.
	7380	1-1/2"	↓	↓	16	.500	Ea.
	7390	2"	Q-1	1 Plumber	26	.615	Ea.
				1 Plumber Apprentice			
	7400	2-1/2"			24	.667	Ea.
	7410	3"			18	.889	Ea.
	7420	4"			15	1.070	Ea.
	7430	6"	↓	↓	10	1.600	Ea.
	7440	8"	Q-2	2 Plumbers	11	2.180	Ea.
				1 Plumber Apprentice			
	7550	Union, sch 40, socket joints, 1/2"	1 Plum	1 Plumber	19	.421	Ea.
	7560	3/4"			18	.444	Ea.
	7570	1"			15	.533	Ea.
	7580	1-1/4"			14	.571	Ea.
	7590	1-1/2"	↓	↓	13	.615	Ea.
	7600	2"	Q-2	2 Plumbers	27	.889	Ea.
				1 Plumber Apprentice			

151 600 | Stainless Steel Pipe

		Description	CREW	MAKEUP	DAILY OUTPUT	MAN-HOURS	UNIT
	601	PIPE, STAINLESS STEEL					
	0020	Welded, with clevis type hangers 10' O.C.					
	0501	Schedule 5, type 304 and 316					
	0540	1/2" diameter	Q-15	1 Plumber	128	.125	L.F.
				1 Plumber Apprentice			
				1 Electric Welding Mach.			
	0550	3/4" diameter			116	.138	L.F.
	0560	1" diameter			103	.155	L.F.
	0570	1-1/4" diameter			93	.172	L.F.
	0580	1-1/2" diameter			85	.188	L.F.
	0590	2" diameter			69	.232	L.F.
	0600	2-1/2" diameter			53	.302	L.F.
	0610	3" diameter			48	.333	L.F.
	0620	4" diameter			44	.364	L.F.
	0630	5" diameter	↓	↓	36	.444	L.F.
	0640	6" diameter	Q-16	2 Plumbers	42	.571	L.F.
				1 Plumber Apprentice			
				1 Electric Welding Mach.			
	0650	8" diameter	"	"	34	.706	L.F.

151 600 | Stainless Steel Pipe

		Description	CREW	MAKEUP	DAILY OUTPUT	MAN-HOURS	UNIT
601	0661	Pipe, stainless steel, sched. 5, type 304 & 316, 10" diameter	Q-16	2 Plumbers	26	.923	L.F.
				1 Plumber Apprentice			
				1 Electric Welding Mach.			
	0670	12" diameter	"	"	21	1.140	L.F.
	2001	Schedule 10, type 304 and 316					
	2040	1/4" diameter	Q-15	1 Plumber	131	.122	L.F.
				1 Plumber Apprentice			
				1 Electric Welding Mach.			
	2050	3/8" diameter			128	.125	L.F.
	2060	1/2" diameter			125	.128	L.F.
	2070	3/4" diameter			113	.142	L.F.
	2080	1" diameter			100	.160	L.F.
	2090	1-1/4" diameter			91	.176	L.F.
	2100	1-1/2" diameter			83	.193	L.F.
	2110	2" diameter			67	.239	L.F.
	2120	2-1/2" diameter			51	.314	L.F.
	2130	3" diameter			46	.348	L.F.
	2140	4" diameter			42	.381	L.F.
	2150	5" diameter	↓	↓	35	.457	L.F.
	2160	6" diameter	Q-16	2 Plumbers	40	.600	L.F.
				1 Plumber Apprentice			
				1 Electric Welding Mach.			
	2170	8" diameter			33	.727	L.F.
	2180	10" diameter			25	.960	L.F.
	2190	12" diameter	↓	↓	21	1.140	L.F.
	3500	Threaded, couplings and hangers 10' O.C.					
	3521	Schedule 40, type 304 and 316					
	3540	1/4" diameter	1 Plum	1 Plumber	54	.148	L.F.
	3550	3/8" diameter			53	.151	L.F.
	3560	1/2" diameter			52	.154	L.F.
	3570	3/4" diameter			51	.157	L.F.
	3580	1" diameter	↓	↓	45	.178	L.F.
	3590	1-1/4" diameter	Q-1	1 Plumber	76	.211	L.F.
				1 Plumber Apprentice			
	3600	1-1/2" diameter			69	.232	L.F.
	3610	2" diameter			57	.281	L.F.
	3620	2-1/2" diameter			44	.364	L.F.
	3630	3"	↓	↓	38	.421	L.F.
	3640	4" diameter	Q-2	2 Plumbers	51	.471	L.F.
				1 Plumber Apprentice			
	5001	Schedule 80, type 304 and 316					
	5040	1/4" diameter	1 Plum	1 Plumber	53	.151	L.F.
	5050	3/8" diameter			52	.154	L.F.
	5060	1/2" diameter			51	.157	L.F.
	5070	3/4" diameter			48	.167	L.F.
	5080	1" diameter	↓	↓	43	.186	L.F.
	5090	1-1/4" diameter	Q-1	1 Plumber	73	.219	L.F.
				1 Plumber Apprentice			
	5100	1-1/2" diameter			67	.239	L.F.
	5110	2" diameter	↓	↓	54	.296	L.F.
	8000	Weld joints with clevis type hangers 10' O.C.					
	8011	Schedule 40, type 304 and 316					
	8050	1/8" pipe size	Q-15	1 Plumber	126	.127	L.F.
				1 Plumber Apprentice			
				1 Electric Welding Mach.			
	8060	1/4" pipe size			125	.128	L.F.
	8070	3/8" pipe size			122	.131	L.F.
	8080	1/2" pipe size	↓	↓	118	.136	L.F.

151 600 | Stainless Steel Pipe

			CREW	MAKEUP	DAILY OUTPUT	MAN-HOURS	UNIT
601	8091	Pipe, stainless steel, sched. 40, type 304 & 316, 3/4" pipe size	Q-15	1 Plumber	109	.147	L.F.
				1 Plumber Apprentice			
				1 Electric Welding Mach.			
	8100	1" pipe size			95	.168	L.F.
	8110	1-1/4" pipe size			86	.186	L.F.
	8120	1-1/2" pipe size			78	.205	L.F.
	8130	2" pipe size			62	.258	L.F.
	8140	2-1/2" pipe size			49	.327	L.F.
	8150	3" pipe size			44	.364	L.F.
	8160	3-1/2" pipe size			44	.364	L.F.
	8170	4" pipe size			39	.410	L.F.
	8180	5" pipe size	↓	↓	32	.500	L.F.
	8190	6" pipe size	Q-16	2 Plumbers	37	.649	L.F.
				1 Plumber Apprentice			
				1 Electric Welding Mach.			
	8200	8" pipe size			29	.828	L.F.
	8210	10" pipe size			24	1.000	L.F.
	8220	12" pipe size	↓	↓	20	1.200	L.F.
	8501	Schedule 80, type 304 and 316					
	8510	1/4" pipe size	Q-15	1 Plumber	110	.145	L.F.
				1 Plumber Apprentice			
				1 Electric Welding Mach.			
	8520	3/8" pipe size			109	.147	L.F.
	8530	1/2" pipe size			106	.151	L.F.
	8540	3/4" pipe size			96	.167	L.F.
	8550	1" pipe size			87	.184	L.F.
	8560	1-1/4" pipe size			81	.198	L.F.
	8570	1-1/2" pipe size			74	.216	L.F.
	8580	2" pipe size			58	.276	L.F.
	8590	2-1/2" pipe size			46	.348	L.F.
	8600	3" pipe size			41	.390	L.F.
	8610	4" pipe size	↓	↓	33	.485	L.F.
	8630	6" pipe size	Q-16	2 Plumbers	30	.800	L.F.
				1 Plumber Apprentice			
				1 Electric Welding Mach.			
	8790	Schedule 160, type 304					
	8800	1/2" pipe size	Q-15	1 Plumber	96	.167	L.F.
				1 Plumber Apprentice			
				1 Electric Welding Mach.			
	8810	3/4" pipe size			88	.182	L.F.
	8820	1" pipe size			80	.200	L.F.
	8840	1-1/2" pipe size			67	.239	L.F.
	8850	2" pipe size			53	.302	L.F.
	8870	3" pipe size	↓	↓	37	.432	L.F.
	8900	Schedule 160, type 316					
	8910	1/2" pipe size	Q-15	1 Plumber	96	.167	L.F.
				1 Plumber Apprentice			
				1 Electric Welding Mach.			
	8920	3/4" pipe size			88	.182	L.F.
	8930	1" pipe size			80	.200	L.F.
	8940	1-1/4" pipe size			73	.219	L.F.
	8950	1-1/2" pipe size			67	.239	L.F.
	8960	2" pipe size			53	.302	L.F.
	8990	4" pipe size	↓	↓	30	.533	L.F.

151 600 | Stainless Steel Pipe

		Description	CREW	MAKEUP	DAILY OUTPUT	MAN-HOURS	UNIT
601	9271	Welding labor per joint, st. st., sched. 5 & 10, 1/4" pipe size	Q-15	1 Plumber	36	.444	Ea.
				1 Plumber Apprentice			
				1 Electric Welding Mach.			
	9280	3/8" pipe size			35	.457	Ea.
	9290	1/2" pipe size			35	.457	Ea.
	9300	3/4" pipe size			28	.571	Ea.
	9310	1" pipe size			25	.640	Ea.
	9320	1-1/4" pipe size			22	.727	Ea.
	9330	1-1/2" pipe size			21	.762	Ea.
	9340	2" pipe size			18	.889	Ea.
	9350	2-1/2" pipe size			14	1.140	Ea.
	9360	3" pipe size			13	1.230	Ea.
	9370	4" pipe size			12	1.330	Ea.
	9380	5" pipe size			10	1.600	Ea.
	9390	6" pipe size			9	1.780	Ea.
	9400	8" pipe size			6	2.670	Ea.
	9410	10" pipe size			4	4.000	Ea.
	9420	12" pipe size	↓	↓	3	5.330	Ea.
	9500	Schedule 40					
	9510	1/4" pipe size	Q-15	1 Plumber	35	.457	Ea.
				1 Plumber Apprentice			
				1 Electric Welding Mach.			
	9520	3/8" pipe size			35	.457	Ea.
	9530	1/2" pipe size			34	.471	Ea.
	9540	3/4" pipe size			28	.571	Ea.
	9550	1" pipe size			24	.667	Ea.
	9560	1-1/4" pipe size			21	.762	Ea.
	9570	1-1/2" pipe size			20	.800	Ea.
	9580	2" pipe size			17	.941	Ea.
	9590	2-1/2" pipe size			14	1.140	Ea.
	9600	3" pipe size			13	1.230	Ea.
	9610	4" pipe size			11	1.450	Ea.
	9620	5" pipe size			9	1.780	Ea.
	9630	6" pipe size			8	2.000	Ea.
	9640	8" pipe size			5	3.200	Ea.
	9650	10" pipe size			4	4.000	Ea.
	9660	12" pipe size	↓	↓	3	5.330	Ea.
	9750	Schedule 80					
	9760	1/4" pipe size	Q-15	1 Plumber	28	.571	Ea.
				1 Plumber Apprentice			
				1 Electric Welding Mach.			
	9770	3/8" pipe size			28	.571	Ea.
	9780	1/2" pipe size			28	.571	Ea.
	9790	3/4" pipe size			24	.667	Ea.
	9800	1" pipe size			21	.762	Ea.
	9810	1-1/4" pipe size			20	.800	Ea.
	9820	1-1/2" pipe size			19	.842	Ea.
	9830	2" pipe size			16	1.000	Ea.
	9840	2-1/2" pipe size			13	1.230	Ea.
	9850	3" pipe size			12	1.330	Ea.
	9860	4" pipe size			8	2.000	Ea.
	9870	5" pipe size			6	2.670	Ea.
	9880	6" pipe size			5	3.200	Ea.
	9890	8" pipe size			3	5.330	Ea.
	9900	10" pipe size			2	8.000	Ea.
	9910	12" pipe size			1	16.000	Ea.
	9920	Schedule 160, 1/2" pipe size			25	.640	Ea.
	9930	3/4" pipe size	↓	↓	22	.727	Ea.

151 600 | Stainless Steel Pipe

		CREW	MAKEUP	DAILY OUTPUT	MAN-HOURS	UNIT
601 9941	Welding labor per joint, st. st., sched. 160, 1" pipe size	Q-15	1 Plumber 1 Plumber Apprentice 1 Electric Welding Mach.	19	.842	Ea.
9950	1-1/4" pipe size			18	.889	Ea.
9960	1-1/2" pipe size			17	.941	Ea.
9970	2" pipe size			14	1.140	Ea.
9980	3" pipe size			11	1.450	Ea.
9990	4" pipe size	↓	↓	7	2.290	Ea.
612	PIPE, STAINLESS STEEL, FITTINGS					
0100	Butt weld joint, schedule 5, type 304					
0121	45° or 90° Elbow, long, 1/2"	Q-15	1 Plumber 1 Plumber Apprentice 1 Electric Welding Mach.	16	1.000	Ea.
0140	1/2"			16	1.000	Ea.
0150	3/4"			16	1.000	Ea.
0160	1"			15	1.070	Ea.
0170	1-1/4"			14	1.140	Ea.
0180	1-1/2"			13	1.230	Ea.
0190	2"			11	1.450	Ea.
0200	2-1/2"			8	2.000	Ea.
0210	3"			6	2.670	Ea.
0220	3-1/2"			5	3.200	Ea.
0230	4"			4	4.000	Ea.
0240	5"			3	5.330	Ea.
0250	6"	Q-16	2 Plumbers 1 Plumber Apprentice 1 Electric Welding Mach.	4	6.000	Ea.
0260	8"			3	8.000	Ea.
0270	10"			2	12.000	Ea.
0280	12"	↓	↓	1.57	15.290	Ea.
1100	Tee, straight					
1130	1/2"	Q-15	1 Plumber 1 Plumber Apprentice 1 Electric Welding Mach.	10	1.600	Ea.
1140	3/4"			10	1.600	Ea.
1150	1"			10	1.600	Ea.
1160	1-1/4"			9	1.780	Ea.
1170	1-1/2"			8	2.000	Ea.
1180	2"			7	2.290	Ea.
1190	2-1/2"			5	3.200	Ea.
1200	3"			4	4.000	Ea.
1210	3-1/2"			3	5.330	Ea.
1220	4"			2	8.000	Ea.
1230	5"	↓	↓	2	8.000	Ea.
1240	6"	Q-16	2 Plumbers 1 Plumber Apprentice 1 Electric Welding Mach.	2.60	9.230	Ea.
1250	8"			2	12.000	Ea.
1260	10"			1.80	13.330	Ea.
1270	12"	↓	↓	1.40	17.140	Ea.
2000	Butt weld joint, schedule 10, type 304					
2021	45° or 90° Elbow, long					
2040	1/2"	Q-15	1 Plumber 1 Plumber Apprentice 1 Electric Welding Mach.	16	1.000	Ea.
2050	3/4"			16	1.000	Ea.
2060	1"			15	1.070	Ea.
2070	1-1/4"	↓	↓	14	1.140	Ea.

151 600 | Stainless Steel Pipe

			CREW	MAKEUP	DAILY OUTPUT	MAN-HOURS	UNIT
612	2081	St. st. butt weld jnt., sched. 10, type 304, elbow, 1-1/2"	Q-15	1 Plumber	13	1.230	Ea.
				1 Plumber Apprentice			
				1 Electric Welding Mach.			
	2090	2"			11	1.450	Ea.
	2100	2-1/2"			8	2.000	Ea.
	2110	3"			6	2.670	Ea.
	2120	3-1/2"			5	3.200	Ea.
	2130	4"			4	4.000	Ea.
	2140	5"	↓	↓	3	5.330	Ea.
	2150	6"	Q-16	2 Plumbers	4	6.000	Ea.
				1 Plumber Apprentice			
				1 Electric Welding Mach.			
	2160	8"			3	8.000	Ea.
	2170	10"			2	12.000	Ea.
	2180	12"	↓	↓	1.57	15.290	Ea.
	3250	Butt weld joint, schedule 40, type 304					
	3262	45° or 90° Elbow, long 1/2"	Q-15	1 Plumber	17	.941	Ea.
				1 Plumber Apprentice			
				1 Electric Welding Mach.			
	3270	3/4"			14	1.140	Ea.
	3280	1"			12	1.330	Ea.
	3290	1-1/4"			11	1.450	Ea.
	3300	1-1/2"			10	1.600	Ea.
	3310	2"			9	1.780	Ea.
	3320	2-1/2"			7	2.290	Ea.
	3330	3"			6	2.670	Ea.
	3340	3-1/2"			5.50	2.910	Ea.
	3350	4"			5	3.200	Ea.
	3360	5"	↓	↓	4	4.000	Ea.
	3370	6"	Q-16	2 Plumbers	6	4.000	Ea.
				1 Plumber Apprentice			
				1 Electric Welding Mach.			
	3380	8"			4	6.000	Ea.
	3390	10"			3	8.000	Ea.
	3400	12"	↓	↓	2	12.000	Ea.
	3660	Tee, straight 1/2"	Q-15	1 Plumber	11	1.450	Ea.
				1 Plumber Apprentice			
				1 Electric Welding Mach.			
	3670	3/4"			9	1.780	Ea.
	3680	1"			8	2.000	Ea.
	3690	1-1/4"			7	2.290	Ea.
	3700	1-1/2"			6.50	2.460	Ea.
	3710	2"			6	2.670	Ea.
	3720	2-1/2"			5	3.200	Ea.
	3730	3"			4	4.000	Ea.
	3740	3-1/2"			3.70	4.320	Ea.
	3750	4"			3.50	4.570	Ea.
	3760	5"	↓	↓	3	5.330	Ea.
	3770	6"	Q-16	2 Plumbers	4	6.000	Ea.
				1 Plumber Apprentice			
				1 Electric Welding Mach.			
	3780	8"			3	8.000	Ea.
	3790	10"			2	12.000	Ea.
	3800	12"	↓	↓	1.50	16.000	Ea.

151 600 | Stainless Steel Pipe

		CREW	MAKEUP	DAILY OUTPUT	MAN-HOURS	UNIT
612 4141	St. st. socket weld joint, 3000 lb., type 304, elbow, 1/4"	Q-15	1 Plumber 1 Plumber Apprentice 1 Electric Welding Mach.	20	.800	Ea.
4150	3/8"			18	.889	Ea.
4160	1/2"			17	.941	Ea.
4170	3/4"			16	1.000	Ea.
4180	1"			15	1.070	Ea.
4190	1-1/4"			14	1.140	Ea.
4200	1-1/2"			13	1.230	Ea.
4210	2"	↓	↓	11	1.450	Ea.
4500	Tee					
4540	1/4"	Q-15	1 Plumber 1 Plumber Apprentice 1 Electric Welding Mach.	13	1.230	Ea.
4550	3/8"			12	1.330	Ea.
4560	1/2"			12	1.330	Ea.
4570	3/4"			11	1.450	Ea.
4580	1"			10	1.600	Ea.
4590	1-1/4"			9	1.780	Ea.
4600	1-1/2"			8	2.000	Ea.
4610	2"	↓	↓	7	2.290	Ea.
5000	Socket weld joint, 3000 lb., type 316					
5101	45° or 90° Elbow					
5140	1/4"	Q-15	1 Plumber 1 Plumber Apprentice 1 Electric Welding Mach.	20	.800	Ea.
5150	3/8"			18	.889	Ea.
5160	1/2"			17	.941	Ea.
5170	3/4"			16	1.000	Ea.
5180	1"			15	1.070	Ea.
5190	1-1/4"			14	1.140	Ea.
5200	1-1/2"			13	1.230	Ea.
5210	2"	↓	↓	11	1.450	Ea.
5500	Tee					
5540	1/4"	Q-15	1 Plumber 1 Plumber Apprentice 1 Electric Welding Mach.	13	1.230	Ea.
5550	3/8"			12	1.330	Ea.
5560	1/2"			12	1.330	Ea.
5570	3/4"			11	1.450	Ea.
5580	1"			10	1.600	Ea.
5590	1-1/4"			9	1.780	Ea.
5600	1-1/2"			8	2.000	Ea.
5610	2"	↓	↓	7	2.290	Ea.
7000	Threaded joint, 150 lb., type 304					
7031	45° or 90° Elbow					
7040	1/8"	1 Plum	1 Plumber	13	.615	Ea.
7050	1/4"			13	.615	Ea.
7070	3/8"			13	.615	Ea.
7080	1/2"			12	.667	Ea.
7090	3/4"			11	.727	Ea.
7100	1"	↓	↓	10	.800	Ea.
7110	1-1/4"	Q-1	1 Plumber 1 Plumber Apprentice	17	.941	Ea.
7120	1-1/2"			16	1.000	Ea.
7130	2"			14	1.140	Ea.
7140	2-1/2"			11	1.450	Ea.
7150	3"	↓	↓	8	2.000	Ea.

				Stainless Steel Pipe	CREW	MAKEUP	DAILY OUTPUT	MAN-HOURS	UNIT
612	7161		St. st. threaded joint, 150 lb., type 304, elbow, 4"	Q-2	2 Plumbers 1 Plumber Apprentice	11	2.180	Ea.
	7320		Tee, straight					
	7330		1/8"	1 Plum	1 Plumber	9	.889	Ea.
	7340		1/4"			9	.889	Ea.
	7350		3/8"			9	.889	Ea.
	7360		1/2"			8	1.000	Ea.
	7370		3/4"			7	1.140	Ea.
	7380		1"	↓	↓	6.50	1.230	Ea.
	7390		1-1/4"	Q-1	1 Plumber 1 Plumber Apprentice	11	1.450	Ea.
	7400		1-1/2"			10	1.600	Ea.
	7410		2"			9	1.780	Ea.
	7420		2-1/2"			7	2.290	Ea.
	7430		3"	↓	↓	5	3.200	Ea.
	7440		4"	Q-2	2 Plumbers 1 Plumber Apprentice	7	3.430	Ea.
	7460		Coupling, straight					
	7470		1/8"	1 Plum	1 Plumber	19	.421	Ea.
	7480		1/4"			19	.421	Ea.
	7490		3/8"			19	.421	Ea.
	7500		1/2"			19	.421	Ea.
	7510		3/4"			18	.444	Ea.
	7520		1"	↓	↓	15	.533	Ea.
	7530		1-1/4"	Q-1	1 Plumber 1 Plumber Apprentice	26	.615	Ea.
	7540		1-1/2"			24	.667	Ea.
	7550		2"			21	.762	Ea.
	7560		2-1/2"			18	.889	Ea.
	7570		3"	↓	↓	14	1.140	Ea.
	7580		4"	Q-2	2 Plumbers 1 Plumber Apprentice	16	1.500	Ea.
	7710		Union					
	7720		1/8"	1 Plum	1 Plumber	12	.667	Ea.
	7730		1/4"			12	.667	Ea.
	7740		3/8"			12	.667	Ea.
	7750		1/2"			11	.727	Ea.
	7760		3/4"			10	.800	Ea.
	7770		1"	↓	↓	9	.889	Ea.
	7780		1-1/4"	Q-1	1 Plumber 1 Plumber Apprentice	16	1.000	Ea.
	7790		1-1/2"			15	1.070	Ea.
	7800		2"			13	1.230	Ea.
	7810		2-1/2"			10	1.600	Ea.
	7820		3"	↓	↓	7	2.290	Ea.
	7830		4"	Q-2	2 Plumbers 1 Plumber Apprentice	10	2.400	Ea.
	8750		Threaded joint, 2000 lb., type 304					
	8771		45° or 90° Elbow					
	8780		1/8"	1 Plum	1 Plumber	13	.615	Ea.
	8790		1/4"			13	.615	Ea.
	8800		3/8"			13	.615	Ea.
	8810		1/2"			12	.667	Ea.
	8820		3/4"			11	.727	Ea.
	8830		1"	↓	↓	10	.800	Ea.
	8840		1-1/4"	Q-1	1 Plumber 1 Plumber Apprentice	17	.941	Ea.
	8850		1-1/2"	"	"	16	1.000	Ea.

151 600 | Stainless Steel Pipe

		Description	CREW	MAKEUP	DAILY OUTPUT	MAN-HOURS	UNIT
612	8861	St. st. threaded joint, 2000 lb., type 304, elbow, 2"	Q-1	1 Plumber / 1 Plumber Apprentice	14	1.140	Ea.
	8990	Tee, straight					
	9000	1/8"	1 Plum	1 Plumber	9	.889	Ea.
	9010	1/4"			9	.889	Ea.
	9020	3/8"			9	.889	Ea.
	9030	1/2"			8	1.000	Ea.
	9040	3/4"			7	1.140	Ea.
	9050	1"	↓	↓	6.50	1.230	Ea.
	9060	1-1/4"	Q-1	1 Plumber / 1 Plumber Apprentice	11	1.450	Ea.
	9070	1-1/2"	↓	↓	10	1.600	Ea.
	9080	2"			9	1.780	Ea.
	9491	3000 lb., type 304 and 316					
	9510	Coupling					
	9520	1/8"	1 Plum	1 Plumber	19	.421	Ea.
	9530	1/4"			19	.421	Ea.
	9540	3/8"			19	.421	Ea.
	9550	1/2"			19	.421	Ea.
	9560	3/4"			18	.444	Ea.
	9570	1"	↓	↓	15	.533	Ea.
	9580	1-1/4"	Q-1	1 Plumber / 1 Plumber Apprentice	26	.615	Ea.
	9590	1-1/2"	↓	↓	24	.667	Ea.
	9600	2"			21	.762	Ea.
	9620	Union					
	9630	1/8"	1 Plum	1 Plumber	12	.667	Ea.
	9640	1/4"			12	.667	Ea.
	9650	3/8"			12	.667	Ea.
	9660	1/2"			11	.727	Ea.
	9670	3/4"			10	.800	Ea.
	9680	1"	↓	↓	9	.889	Ea.
	9690	1-1/4"	Q-1	1 Plumber / 1 Plumber Apprentice	16	1.000	Ea.
	9700	1-1/2"	↓	↓	15	1.070	Ea.
	9710	2"			13	1.230	Ea.

151 700 | Steel Pipe

		Description	CREW	MAKEUP	DAILY OUTPUT	MAN-HOURS	UNIT
	701	PIPE, STEEL					
	0050	Schedule 40, threaded, with couplings, and clevis type					
	0060	hangers sized for covering, 10' O.C.	↓	↓			
	0540	1/4" diameter	1 Plum	1 Plumber	66	.121	L.F.
	0550	3/8" diameter			65	.123	L.F.
	0560	1/2" diameter			63	.127	L.F.
	0570	3/4" diameter			61	.131	L.F.
	0580	1" diameter	↓	↓	53	.151	L.F.
	0590	1-1/4" diameter	Q-1	1 Plumber / 1 Plumber Apprentice	89	.180	L.F.
	0600	1-1/2" diameter			80	.200	L.F.
	0610	2" diameter			64	.250	L.F.
	0620	2-1/2" diameter			50	.320	L.F.
	0630	3" diameter			43	.372	L.F.
	0640	3-1/2" diameter			40	.400	L.F.
	0650	4" diameter			36	.444	L.F.
	0660	5" diameter	↓	↓	26	.615	L.F.
	0670	6" diameter	Q-2	2 Plumbers / 1 Plumber Apprentice	31	.774	L.F.
	0680	8" diameter	"	"	27	.889	L.F.

439

151 700	Steel Pipe	CREW	MAKEUP	DAILY OUTPUT	MAN-HOURS	UNIT
701 0691	Pipe, steel, black, schedule 40, 10" diameter	Q-2	2 Plumbers	23	1.040	L.F.
			1 Plumber Apprentice			
0700	12" diameter	"	"	18	1.330	L.F.
2000	Welded, sch. 40, on yoke & roll hangers					
2010	sized for covering, 10' O.C.					
2040	Black, 1" diameter	Q-15	1 Plumber	93	.172	L.F.
			1 Plumber Apprentice			
			1 Electric Welding Mach.			
2050	1-1/4" diameter			84	.190	L.F.
2060	1-1/2" diameter			76	.211	L.F.
2070	2" diameter			61	.262	L.F.
2080	2-1/2" diameter			47	.340	L.F.
2090	3" diameter			43	.372	L.F.
2100	3-1/2" diameter			39	.410	L.F.
2110	4" diameter			37	.432	L.F.
2120	5" diameter			32	.500	L.F.
2130	6" diameter	Q-16	2 Plumbers	36	.667	L.F.
			1 Plumber Apprentice			
			1 Electric Welding Mach.			
2140	8" diameter			29	.828	L.F.
2150	10" diameter			24	1.000	L.F.
2160	12" diameter			19	1.260	L.F.
3250	Flanged, 150 lb. weld neck, on yoke & roll hangers					
3260	size for covering, 10' O.C.					
3290	Black, 1" diameter	Q-15	1 Plumber	70	.229	L.F.
			1 Plumber Apprentice			
			1 Electric Welding Mach.			
3300	1-1/4" diameter			64	.250	L.F.
3310	1-1/2" diameter			58	.276	L.F.
3320	2" diameter			45	.356	L.F.
3330	2-1/2" diameter			36	.444	L.F.
3340	3" diameter			32	.500	L.F.
3350	3-1/2" diameter			29	.552	L.F.
3360	4" diameter			26	.615	L.F.
3370	5" diameter			21	.762	L.F.
3380	6" diameter	Q-16	2 Plumbers	25	.960	L.F.
			1 Plumber Apprentice			
			1 Electric Welding Mach.			
3390	8" diameter			19	1.260	L.F.
3400	10" diameter			16	1.500	L.F.
3410	12" diameter			14	1.710	L.F.
4750	Schedule 80, threaded, with couplings, and clevis type hangers					
4760	sized for covering, 10' O.C.					
4790	Black, 1/4" diameter	1 Plum	1 Plumber	54	.148	L.F.
4800	3/8" diameter			53	.151	L.F.
4810	1/2" diameter			52	.154	L.F.
4820	3/4" diameter			50	.160	L.F.
4830	1" diameter			45	.178	L.F.
4840	1-1/4" diameter	Q-1	1 Plumber	75	.213	L.F.
			1 Plumber Apprentice			
4850	1-1/2" diameter			69	.232	L.F.
4860	2" diameter			56	.286	L.F.
4870	2-1/2" diameter			44	.364	L.F.
4880	3" diameter			38	.421	L.F.
4890	3-1/2" diameter			35	.457	L.F.
4900	4" diameter			32	.500	L.F.
4910	5" diameter			23	.696	L.F.

151 700 | Steel Pipe

		Description	CREW	MAKEUP	DAILY OUTPUT	MAN-HOURS	UNIT
701	4921	Pipe, steel, black, schedule 80, 6" diameter	Q-2	2 Plumbers	28	.857	L.F.
				1 Plumber Apprentice			
	4930	8" diameter			23	1.040	L.F.
	4940	10" diameter			20	1.200	L.F.
	4950	12" diameter	↓	↓	15	1.600	L.F.
	6000	Welded, on yoke & roller hangers					
	6010	sized for covering, 10' O.C.					
	6040	Black, 1" diameter	Q-15	1 Plumber	85	.188	L.F.
				1 Plumber Apprentice			
				1 Electric Welding Mach.			
	6050	1-1/4" diameter			79	.203	L.F.
	6060	1-1/2" diameter			72	.222	L.F.
	6070	2" diameter			57	.281	L.F.
	6080	2-1/2" diameter			44	.364	L.F.
	6090	3" diameter			40	.400	L.F.
	6100	3-1/2" diameter			34	.471	L.F.
	6110	4" diameter			33	.485	L.F.
	6120	5" diameter	↓	↓	26	.615	L.F.
	6130	6" diameter	Q-16	2 Plumbers	30	.800	L.F.
				1 Plumber Apprentice			
				1 Electric Welding Mach.			
	6140	8" diameter			25	.960	L.F.
	6150	10" diameter			20	1.200	L.F.
	6160	12" diameter	↓	↓	15	1.600	L.F.
	7250	Flanged, 300 lb. weld neck, on yoke & roll hangers					
	7260	sized for covering, 10' O.C.					
	7290	Black, 1" diameter	Q-15	1 Plumber	66	.242	L.F.
				1 Plumber Apprentice			
				1 Electric Welding Mach.			
	7300	1-1/4" diameter			61	.262	L.F.
	7310	1-1/2" diameter			54	.296	L.F.
	7320	2" diameter			42	.381	L.F.
	7330	2-1/2" diameter			33	.485	L.F.
	7340	3" diameter			29	.552	L.F.
	7350	3-1/2" diameter			24	.667	L.F.
	7360	4" diameter			23	.696	L.F.
	7370	5" diameter	↓	↓	19	.842	L.F.
	7380	6" diameter	Q-16	2 Plumbers	23	1.040	L.F.
				1 Plumber Apprentice			
				1 Electric Welding Mach.			
	7390	8" diameter			17	1.410	L.F.
	7400	10" diameter			14	1.710	L.F.
	7410	12" diameter	↓	↓	12	2.000	L.F.
	9000	Threading pipe labor, one end, all schedules through 80					
	9010	1/4" through 3/4" pipe size	1 Plum	1 Plumber	80	.100	Ea.
	9020	1" through 2" pipe size			73	.110	Ea.
	9030	2-1/2" pipe size			53	.151	Ea.
	9040	3" pipe size	↓	↓	50	.160	Ea.
	9050	3-1/2" pipe size	Q-1	1 Plumber	89	.180	Ea.
				1 Plumber Apprentice			
	9060	4" pipe size			73	.219	Ea.
	9070	5" pipe size			53	.302	Ea.
	9080	6" pipe size			46	.348	Ea.
	9090	8" pipe size			29	.552	Ea.
	9100	10" pipe size			21	.762	Ea.
	9110	12" pipe size	↓	↓	13	1.230	Ea.

151 700 | Steel Pipe

		CREW	MAKEUP	DAILY OUTPUT	MAN-HOURS	UNIT
701	9231	Pipe, steel, welding labor per joint, sched. 40, 1/2" pipe size	Q-15	1 Plumber 1 Plumber Apprentice 1 Electric Welding Mach.	32	.500	Ea.
	9240	3/4" pipe size			27	.593	Ea.
	9250	1" pipe size			23	.696	Ea.
	9260	1-1/4" pipe size			20	.800	Ea.
	9270	1-1/2" pipe size			19	.842	Ea.
	9280	2" pipe size			16	1.000	Ea.
	9290	2-1/2" pipe size			13	1.230	Ea.
	9300	3" pipe size			12	1.330	Ea.
	9310	4" pipe size			10	1.600	Ea.
	9320	5" pipe size			9	1.780	Ea.
	9330	6" pipe size			8	2.000	Ea.
	9340	8" pipe size			5	3.200	Ea.
	9350	10" pipe size			4	4.000	Ea.
	9360	12" pipe size			3	5.330	Ea.
	9370	14" pipe size			2.60	6.150	Ea.
	9380	16" pipe size			2.20	7.270	Ea.
	9390	18" pipe size			2	8.000	Ea.
	9400	20" pipe size			1.80	8.890	Ea.
	9410	22" pipe size			1.70	9.410	Ea.
	9420	24" pipe size	↓	↓	1.50	10.670	Ea.
	9450	Schedule 80,					
	9460	1/2" pipe size	Q-15	1 Plumber 1 Plumber Apprentice 1 Electric Welding Mach.	27	.593	Ea.
	9470	3/4" pipe size			23	.696	Ea.
	9480	1" pipe size			20	.800	Ea.
	9490	1-1/4" pipe size			19	.842	Ea.
	9500	1-1/2" pipe size			18	.889	Ea.
	9510	2" pipe size			15	1.070	Ea.
	9520	2-1/2" pipe size			12	1.330	Ea.
	9530	3" pipe size			11	1.450	Ea.
	9540	4" pipe size			8	2.000	Ea.
	9550	5" pipe size			6	2.670	Ea.
	9560	6" pipe size			5	3.200	Ea.
	9570	8" pipe size			4	4.000	Ea.
	9580	10" pipe size			3	5.330	Ea.
	9590	12" pipe size	↓	↓	2	8.000	Ea.
	9600	14" pipe size	Q-16	2 Plumbers 1 Plumber Apprentice 1 Electric Welding Mach.	2.60	9.230	Ea.
	9610	16" pipe size			2.30	10.430	Ea.
	9620	18" pipe size			2	12.000	Ea.
	9630	20" pipe size			1.80	13.330	Ea.
	9640	22" pipe size			1.60	15.000	Ea.
	9650	24" pipe size	↓	↓	1.50	16.000	Ea.
	716	PIPE, STEEL, FITTINGS, Threaded					
	0020	Cast Iron,					
	0041	Standard weight, black or galvanized					
	0061	45° or 90° Elbow, straight					
	0070	1/4"	1 Plum	1 Plumber	16	.500	Ea.
	0080	3/8"			16	.500	Ea.
	0090	1/2"			15	.533	Ea.
	0100	3/4"			14	.571	Ea.
	0110	1"	↓	↓	13	.615	Ea.
	0120	1-1/4"	Q-1	1 Plumber 1 Plumber Apprentice	22	.727	Ea.

151 700 | Steel Pipe

			CREW	MAKEUP	DAILY OUTPUT	MAN-HOURS	UNIT
716	0131	Pipe, steel fittings, std. wt., elbow, straight, 1-1/2"	Q-1	1 Plumber 1 Plumber Apprentice	20	.800	Ea.
	0140	2"			18	.889	Ea.
	0150	2-1/2"			14	1.140	Ea.
	0160	3"			10	1.600	Ea.
	0170	3-1/2"			8	2.000	Ea.
	0180	4"			6	2.670	Ea.
	0190	5"			5	3.200	Ea.
	0200	6"	Q-2	2 Plumbers 1 Plumber Apprentice	7	3.430	Ea.
	0210	8"	"	"	6	4.000	Ea.
	0500	Tee, straight					
	0510	1/4"	1 Plum	1 Plumber	10	.800	Ea.
	0520	3/8"			10	.800	Ea.
	0530	1/2"			9	.889	Ea.
	0540	3/4"			9	.889	Ea.
	0550	1"			8	1.000	Ea.
	0560	1-1/4"	Q-1	1 Plumber 1 Plumber Apprentice	14	1.140	Ea.
	0570	1-1/2"			13	1.230	Ea.
	0580	2"			11	1.450	Ea.
	0590	2-1/2"			9	1.780	Ea.
	0600	3"			6	2.670	Ea.
	0610	3-1/2"			5	3.200	Ea.
	0620	4"			4	4.000	Ea.
	0630	5"			3	5.330	Ea.
	0640	6"	Q-2	2 Plumbers 1 Plumber Apprentice	4	6.000	Ea.
	0650	8"	"	"	3	8.000	Ea.
	1301	Extra heavy weight, black or galvanized					
	1310	Couplings, steel straight					
	1320	1/4"	1 Plum	1 Plumber	19	.421	Ea.
	1330	3/8"			19	.421	Ea.
	1340	1/2"			19	.421	Ea.
	1350	3/4"			18	.444	Ea.
	1360	1"			15	.533	Ea.
	1370	1-1/4"	Q-1	1 Plumber 1 Plumber Apprentice	26	.615	Ea.
	1380	1-1/2"			24	.667	Ea.
	1390	2"			21	.762	Ea.
	1400	2-1/2"			18	.889	Ea.
	1410	3"			14	1.140	Ea.
	1420	3-1/2"			12	1.330	Ea.
	1430	4"			10	1.600	Ea.
	1440	5"			6	2.670	Ea.
	1450	6"	Q-2	2 Plumbers 1 Plumber Apprentice	8	3.000	Ea.
	1460	8"			7	3.430	Ea.
	1470	10"			6	4.000	Ea.
	1480	12"			4	6.000	Ea.
	1511	45° or 90° Elbow, straight					
	1520	1/2"	1 Plum	1 Plumber	15	.533	Ea.
	1530	3/4"			14	.571	Ea.
	1540	1"			13	.615	Ea.
	1550	1-1/4"	Q-1	1 Plumber 1 Plumber Apprentice	22	.727	Ea.
	1560	1-1/2"			20	.800	Ea.
	1580	2"			18	.889	Ea.

			CREW	MAKEUP	DAILY OUTPUT	MAN-HOURS	UNIT
**151 700	Steel Pipe**						
716	1591	Pipe, steel fittings, extra hvy. wt., elbow, straight, 2-1/2"	Q-1	1 Plumber 1 Plumber Apprentice	14	1.140	Ea.
	1600	3"	↓	↓	10	1.600	Ea.
	1610	4"			6	2.670	Ea.
	1620	6"	Q-2	2 Plumbers 1 Plumber Apprentice	7	3.430	Ea.
	1800	Tee, straight					
	1810	1/2"	1 Plum	1 Plumber	9	.889	Ea.
	1820	3/4"			9	.889	Ea.
	1830	1"	↓	↓	8	1.000	Ea.
	1840	1-1/4"	Q-1	1 Plumber 1 Plumber Apprentice	14	1.140	Ea.
	1850	1-1/2"			13	1.230	Ea.
	1860	2"			11	1.450	Ea.
	1870	2-1/2"			9	1.780	Ea.
	1880	3"			6	2.670	Ea.
	1890	4"	↓	↓	4	4.000	Ea.
	1900	6"	Q-2	2 Plumbers 1 Plumber Apprentice	4	6.000	Ea.
	5001	Malleable iron, black or galvanized					
	5041	45° or 90° Elbow, straight					
	5060	1/4"	1 Plum	1 Plumber	16	.500	Ea.
	5070	3/8"			16	.500	Ea.
	5080	1/2"			15	.533	Ea.
	5090	3/4"			14	.571	Ea.
	5100	1"	↓	↓	13	.615	Ea.
	5110	1-1/4"	Q-1	1 Plumber 1 Plumber Apprentice	22	.727	Ea.
	5120	1-1/2"			20	.800	Ea.
	5130	2"			18	.889	Ea.
	5140	2-1/2"			14	1.140	Ea.
	5150	3"			10	1.600	Ea.
	5160	3-1/2"			8	2.000	Ea.
	5170	4"			6	2.670	Ea.
	5180	5"	↓	↓	5	3.200	Ea.
	5190	6"	Q-2	2 Plumbers 1 Plumber Apprentice	7	3.430	Ea.
	5450	Tee, straight					
	5470	1/4"	1 Plum	1 Plumber	10	.800	Ea.
	5480	3/8"			10	.800	Ea.
	5490	1/2"			9	.889	Ea.
	5500	3/4"			9	.889	Ea.
	5510	1"	↓	↓	8	1.000	Ea.
	5520	1-1/4"	Q-1	1 Plumber 1 Plumber Apprentice	14	1.140	Ea.
	5530	1-1/2"			13	1.230	Ea.
	5540	2"			11	1.450	Ea.
	5550	2-1/2"			9	1.780	Ea.
	5560	3"			6	2.670	Ea.
	5570	3-1/2"			5	3.200	Ea.
	5580	4"			4	4.000	Ea.
	5590	5"	↓	↓	3	5.330	Ea.
	5600	6"	Q-2	2 Plumbers 1 Plumber Apprentice	4	6.000	Ea.
	5650	Coupling, straight					
	5670	1/4"	1 Plum	1 Plumber	19	.421	Ea.
	5680	3/8"			19	.421	Ea.
	5690	1/2"	↓	↓	19	.421	Ea.

151 700 | Steel Pipe

		CREW	MAKEUP	DAILY OUTPUT	MAN-HOURS	UNIT
716 5701	Pipe, malleable iron fittings, coupling, straight, 3/4"	1 Plum	1 Plumber	18	.444	Ea.
5710	1"	"	"	15	.533	Ea.
5720	1-1/4"	Q-1	1 Plumber / 1 Plumber Apprentice	26	.615	Ea.
5730	1-1/2"			24	.667	Ea.
5740	2"			21	.762	Ea.
5750	2-1/2"			18	.889	Ea.
5760	3"			14	1.140	Ea.
5770	3-1/2"			12	1.330	Ea.
5780	4"			10	1.600	Ea.
5790	5"	↓	↓	6	2.670	Ea.
5800	6"	Q-2	2 Plumbers / 1 Plumber Apprentice	8	3.000	Ea.
5810	8"			7	3.430	Ea.
5820	10"			6	4.000	Ea.
5830	12"	↓	↓	4	6.000	Ea.
6077	Black					
7001	Union, with brass seat or all iron					
7010	1/4"	1 Plum	1 Plumber	15	.533	Ea.
7020	3/8"			15	.533	Ea.
7030	1/2"			14	.571	Ea.
7040	3/4"			13	.615	Ea.
7050	1"	↓	↓	12	.667	Ea.
7060	1-1/4"	Q-1	1 Plumber / 1 Plumber Apprentice	21	.762	Ea.
7070	1-1/2"			19	.842	Ea.
7080	2"			17	.941	Ea.
7090	2-1/2"			13	1.230	Ea.
7100	3"	↓	↓	9	1.780	Ea.
7501	Malleable iron, black or galvanized					
7541	45° or 90° Elbow, straight, 1/4"	1 Plum	1 Plumber	16	.500	Ea.
7560	3/8"			16	.500	Ea.
7570	1/2"			15	.533	Ea.
7580	3/4"			14	.571	Ea.
7590	1"	↓	↓	13	.615	Ea.
7600	1-1/4"	Q-1	1 Plumber / 1 Plumber Apprentice	22	.727	Ea.
7610	1-1/2"			20	.800	Ea.
7620	2"			18	.889	Ea.
7630	2-1/2"			14	1.140	Ea.
7640	3"			10	1.600	Ea.
7650	4"			6	2.670	Ea.
7660	5"	↓	↓	5	3.200	Ea.
7670	6"	Q-2	2 Plumbers / 1 Plumber Apprentice	7	3.430	Ea.
7680	8"	"	"	6	4.000	Ea.
7850	Tee, straight, 1/4"	1 Plum	1 Plumber	10	.800	Ea.
7870	3/8"			10	.800	Ea.
7880	1/2"			9	.889	Ea.
7890	3/4"			9	.889	Ea.
7900	1"	↓	↓	8	1.000	Ea.
7910	1-1/4"	Q-1	1 Plumber / 1 Plumber Apprentice	14	1.140	Ea.
7920	1-1/2"			13	1.230	Ea.
7930	2"			11	1.450	Ea.
7940	2-1/2"			9	1.780	Ea.
7950	3"			6	2.670	Ea.
7960	4"	↓	↓	4	4.000	Ea.

		Description	CREW	MAKEUP	DAILY OUTPUT	MAN-HOURS	UNIT
151 700		**Steel Pipe**					
716	7981	Pipe, malleable iron fittings, tee, straight, 6"	Q-2	2 Plumbers 1 Plumber Apprentice	4	6.000	Ea.
	7990	8"	"	"	3	8.000	Ea.
	8050	Couplings, straight, 1/4"	1 Plum	1 Plumber	19	.421	Ea.
	8070	3/8"			19	.421	Ea.
	8080	1/2"			19	.421	Ea.
	8090	3/4"			18	.444	Ea.
	8100	1"	↓	↓	15	.533	Ea.
	8110	1-1/4"	Q-1	1 Plumber 1 Plumber Apprentice	26	.615	Ea.
	8120	1-1/2"			24	.667	Ea.
	8130	2"			21	.762	Ea.
	8140	2-1/2"			18	.889	Ea.
	8150	3"	↓	↓	14	1.140	Ea.
	9501	Union with brass seat or all iron, 1/4"	1 Plum	1 Plumber	15	.533	Ea.
	9530	3/8"			15	.533	Ea.
	9540	1/2"			14	.571	Ea.
	9550	3/4"			13	.615	Ea.
	9560	1"	↓	↓	12	.667	Ea.
	9570	1-1/4"	Q-1	1 Plumber 1 Plumber Apprentice	21	.762	Ea.
	9580	1-1/2"			19	.842	Ea.
	9590	2"			17	.941	Ea.
	9600	2-1/2"			13	1.230	Ea.
	9610	3"			9	1.780	Ea.
	9620	4"	↓	↓	5	3.200	Ea.
	720	**PIPE, STEEL, FITTINGS** Flanged, welded and special type					
	0020	Flanged joints, C.I., standard weight, black. One gasket & bolt					
	0040	set required at each joint, not included (see line 0620)					
	0061	45° or 90° Elbow, straight, 1-1/2" pipe size	Q-1	1 Plumber 1 Plumber Apprentice	14	1.140	Ea.
	0080	2" pipe size			13	1.230	Ea.
	0090	2-1/2" pipe size			12	1.330	Ea.
	0100	3" pipe size			11	1.450	Ea.
	0110	4" pipe size			8	2.000	Ea.
	0120	5" pipe size	↓	↓	7	2.290	Ea.
	0130	6" pipe size	Q-2	2 Plumbers 1 Plumber Apprentice	9	2.670	Ea.
	0140	8" pipe size			8	3.000	Ea.
	0150	10" pipe size			7	3.430	Ea.
	0160	12" pipe size	↓	↓	6	4.000	Ea.
	0350	Tee, straight, 1-1/2" pipe size	Q-1	1 Plumber 1 Plumber Apprentice	10	1.600	Ea.
	0370	2" pipe size			9	1.780	Ea.
	0380	2-1/2" pipe size			8	2.000	Ea.
	0390	3" pipe size			7	2.290	Ea.
	0400	4" pipe size			5	3.200	Ea.
	0410	5" pipe size	↓	↓	4	4.000	Ea.
	0420	6" pipe size	Q-2	2 Plumbers 1 Plumber Apprentice	6	4.000	Ea.
	0430	8" pipe size			5	4.800	Ea.
	0440	10" pipe size			4	6.000	Ea.
	0450	12" pipe size	↓	↓	3	8.000	Ea.
	0620	Gasket and 4 to 20 bolt set, 1/2" thru 1-1/2" pipe size	1 Plum	1 Plumber	30	.267	Ea.
	0630	2" pipe size			30	.267	Ea.
	0640	2-1/2" pipe size			30	.267	Ea.
	0650	3" pipe size			30	.267	Ea.
	0660	3-1/2" pipe size	↓	↓	28	.286	Ea.

151 700 | Steel Pipe

		Description	CREW	MAKEUP	DAILY OUTPUT	MAN-HOURS	UNIT
720	0671	Steel flanged gasket & 4 to 20 bolt set, 4" pipe size	1 Plum	1 Plumber	27	.296	Ea.
	0680	5" pipe size			26	.308	Ea.
	0690	6" pipe size			24	.333	Ea.
	0700	8" pipe size			20	.400	Ea.
	0710	10" pipe size			18	.444	Ea.
	0720	12" pipe size			16	.500	Ea.
	0730	14" pipe size			14	.571	Ea.
	0740	16" pipe size			13	.615	Ea.
	0750	18" pipe size			12	.667	Ea.
	0760	20" pipe size			11	.727	Ea.
	0780	24" pipe size			10	.800	Ea.
	0790	26" pipe size			9	.889	Ea.
	0810	30" pipe size			8	1.000	Ea.
	0830	36" pipe size			7	1.140	Ea.
	2000	Unions, 125 lb., black, 1/2" pipe size			17	.471	Ea.
	2040	3/4" pipe size			17	.471	Ea.
	2050	1" pipe size	↓	↓	16	.500	Ea.
	2060	1-1/4" pipe size	Q-1	1 Plumber 1 Plumber Apprentice	28	.571	Ea.
	2070	1-1/2" pipe size			27	.593	Ea.
	2080	2" pipe size			26	.615	Ea.
	2090	2-1/2" pipe size			24	.667	Ea.
	2100	3"			22	.727	Ea.
	2110	3-1/2" pipe size			18	.889	Ea.
	2120	4" pipe size			16	1.000	Ea.
	2130	5" pipe size	↓	↓	14	1.140	Ea.
	2140	6" pipe size	Q-2	2 Plumbers 1 Plumber Apprentice	19	1.260	Ea.
	2150	8" pipe size	"	"	16	1.500	Ea.
	3000	Weld joint, butt, carbon steel, standard weight					
	3041	45° or 90° Elbow, long					
	3050	1/2" pipe size	Q-15	1 Plumber 1 Plumber Apprentice 1 Electric Welding Mach.	16	1.000	Ea.
	3060	3/4" pipe size			16	1.000	Ea.
	3070	1" pipe size			16	1.000	Ea.
	3080	1-1/4" pipe size			14	1.140	Ea.
	3090	1-1/2" pipe size			13	1.230	Ea.
	3100	2" pipe size			10	1.600	Ea.
	3110	2-1/2" pipe size			8	2.000	Ea.
	3120	3" pipe size			7	2.290	Ea.
	3130	4" pipe size	↓	↓	5	3.200	Ea.
	3140	6" pipe size	Q-16	2 Plumbers 1 Plumber Apprentice 1 Electric Welding Mach.	5	4.800	Ea.
	3150	8" pipe size			4	6.000	Ea.
	3160	10" pipe size			3	8.000	Ea.
	3170	12" pipe size			2.50	9.600	Ea.
	3180	14" pipe size			2	12.000	Ea.
	3190	16" pipe size			1.50	16.000	Ea.
	3191	18" pipe size			1.25	19.200	Ea.
	3192	20" pipe size			1.15	20.870	Ea.
	3194	24" pipe size			1.02	23.530	Ea.
	3195	26" pipe size			.85	28.240	Ea.
	3196	30" pipe size			.45	53.330	Ea.
	3198	36" pipe size	↓	↓	.38	63.160	Ea.
	3351						

151 700 | Steel Pipe

		CREW	MAKEUP	DAILY OUTPUT	MAN-HOURS	UNIT
720 3361	Steel flanged weld joint, std. wt., tee, straight, 1/2" pipe size	Q-15	1 Plumber	10	1.600	Ea.
			1 Plumber Apprentice			
			1 Electric Welding Mach.			
3370	3/4" pipe size			10	1.600	Ea.
3380	1" pipe size			10	1.600	Ea.
3390	1-1/4" pipe size			9	1.780	Ea.
3400	1-1/2" pipe size			8	2.000	Ea.
3410	2" pipe size			6	2.670	Ea.
3420	2-1/2" pipe size			5	3.200	Ea.
3430	3" pipe size			4	4.000	Ea.
3440	4" pipe size	↓	↓	3	5.330	Ea.
3450	6" pipe size	Q-16	2 Plumbers	3	8.000	Ea.
			1 Plumber Apprentice			
			1 Electric Welding Mach.			
3460	8" pipe size			2.50	9.600	Ea.
3470	10" pipe size			2	12.000	Ea.
3480	12" pipe size	↓	↓	1.60	15.000	Ea.
3517	Weld joint, butt, carbon steel, extra strong					
3518	45° or 90° Elbow, long					
3520	1/2" pipe size	Q-15	1 Plumber	16	1.000	Ea.
			1 Plumber Apprentice			
			1 Electric Welding Mach.			
3530	3/4" pipe size			16	1.000	Ea.
3540	1" pipe size			16	1.000	Ea.
3550	1-1/4" pipe size			14	1.140	Ea.
3560	1-1/2" pipe size			13	1.230	Ea.
3570	2" pipe size			10	1.600	Ea.
3580	2-1/2" pipe size			8	2.000	Ea.
3590	3" pipe size			7	2.290	Ea.
3600	4" pipe size	↓	↓	5	3.200	Ea.
3610	6" pipe size	Q-16	2 Plumbers	5	4.800	Ea.
			1 Plumber Apprentice			
			1 Electric Welding Mach.			
3620	8" pipe size			4	6.000	Ea.
3630	10" pipe size			3	8.000	Ea.
3640	12" pipe size	↓	↓	2.50	9.600	Ea.
3800	Tee, straight					
3810	1/2" pipe size	Q-15	1 Plumber	10	1.600	Ea.
			1 Plumber Apprentice			
			1 Electric Welding Mach.			
3820	3/4" pipe size			10	1.600	Ea.
3830	1" pipe size			10	1.600	Ea.
3840	1-1/4" pipe size			9	1.780	Ea.
3850	1-1/2" pipe size			8	2.000	Ea.
3860	2" pipe size			6	2.670	Ea.
3870	2-1/2" pipe size			5	3.200	Ea.
3880	3" pipe size			4	4.000	Ea.
3890	4" pipe size	↓	↓	3	5.330	Ea.
3900	6" pipe size	Q-16	2 Plumbers	3	8.000	Ea.
			1 Plumber Apprentice			
			1 Electric Welding Mach.			
3910	8" pipe size			2.50	9.600	Ea.
3920	10" pipe size			2	12.000	Ea.
3930	12" pipe size	↓	↓	1.60	15.000	Ea.

151 700	Steel Pipe	CREW	MAKEUP	DAILY OUTPUT	MAN-HOURS	UNIT
720 5061	Steel weld jnt, sched. 40, 45° or 90° elbow, strght, 1" pipe size	Q-15	1 Plumber	20	.800	Ea.
			1 Plumber Apprentice			
			1 Electric Welding Mach.			
5070	1-1/4" pipe size			18	.889	Ea.
5080	1-1/2" pipe size			16	1.000	Ea.
5090	2" pipe size			12	1.330	Ea.
5100	2-1/2" pipe size			10	1.600	Ea.
5110	3" pipe size			8	2.000	Ea.
5120	4" pipe size	↓	↓	6	2.670	Ea.
5250	Tee, straight					
5260	1" pipe size	Q-15	1 Plumber	13	1.230	Ea.
			1 Plumber Apprentice			
			1 Electric Welding Mach.			
5270	1-1/4" pipe size			12	1.330	Ea.
5280	1-1/2" pipe size			11	1.450	Ea.
5290	2" pipe size			8	2.000	Ea.
5300	2-1/2" pipe size			6	2.670	Ea.
5310	3" pipe size			5	3.200	Ea.
5320	4" pipe size	↓	↓	4	4.000	Ea.
5450	Couplings					
5460	1" pipe size	Q-15	1 Plumber	22	.727	Ea.
			1 Plumber Apprentice			
			1 Electric Welding Mach.			
5470	1-1/4" pipe size			20	.800	Ea.
5480	1-1/2" pipe size			18	.889	Ea.
5490	2" pipe size			14	1.140	Ea.
5500	2-1/2" pipe size			12	1.330	Ea.
5510	3" pipe size			9	1.780	Ea.
5520	4" pipe size	↓	↓	7	2.290	Ea.
6000	Weld-on flange, forged steel					
6020	Slip-on, 150 lb. flange, (welded front and back)					
6050	1/2" pipe size	Q-15	1 Plumber	18	.889	Ea.
			1 Plumber Apprentice			
			1 Electric Welding Mach.			
6060	3/4" pipe size			18	.889	Ea.
6070	1" pipe size			17	.941	Ea.
6080	1-1/4" pipe size			16	1.000	Ea.
6090	1-1/2" pipe size			15	1.070	Ea.
6100	2" pipe size			12	1.330	Ea.
6110	2-1/2" pipe size			10	1.600	Ea.
6120	3" pipe size			9	1.780	Ea.
6130	3-1/2" pipe size			7	2.290	Ea.
6140	4" pipe size			6	2.670	Ea.
6150	5" pipe size	↓	↓	5	3.200	Ea.
6160	6" pipe size	Q-16	2 Plumbers	6	4.000	Ea.
			1 Plumber Apprentice			
			1 Electric Welding Mach.			
6170	8" pipe size			5	4.800	Ea.
6180	10" pipe size			4	6.000	Ea.
6190	12" pipe size			3	8.000	Ea.
6191	14" pipe size			2.50	9.600	Ea.
6192	16" pipe size	↓	↓	1.80	13.330	Ea.
6200	300 lb. flange					
6210	1/2" pipe size	Q-15	1 Plumber	17	.941	Ea.
			1 Plumber Apprentice			
			1 Electric Welding Mach.			
6220	3/4" pipe size			17	.941	Ea.
6230	1" pipe size	↓	↓	16	1.000	Ea.

151 700 | Steel Pipe

			CREW	MAKEUP	DAILY OUTPUT	MAN-HOURS	UNIT
720	6241	Steel weld-on flange, slip-on, 300 lb., 1-1/4" pipe size	Q-15	1 Plumber	13	1.230	Ea.
				1 Plumber Apprentice			
				1 Electric Welding Mach.			
	6250	1-1/2" pipe size			12	1.330	Ea.
	6260	2" pipe size			11	1.450	Ea.
	6270	2-1/2" pipe size			9	1.780	Ea.
	6280	3" pipe size			7	2.290	Ea.
	6290	4" pipe size			6	2.670	Ea.
	6300	5" pipe size	↓	↓	4	4.000	Ea.
	6310	6" pipe size	Q-16	2 Plumbers	5	4.800	Ea.
				1 Plumber Apprentice			
				1 Electric Welding Mach.			
	6320	8" pipe size			4	6.000	Ea.
	6330	10" pipe size			3.40	7.060	Ea.
	6340	12" pipe size	↓	↓	2.80	8.570	Ea.
	6400	Welding neck, 150 lb. flange					
	6410	1/2" pipe size	Q-15	1 Plumber	40	.400	Ea.
				1 Plumber Apprentice			
				1 Electric Welding Mach.			
	6420	3/4" pipe size			36	.444	Ea.
	6430	1" pipe size			32	.500	Ea.
	6440	1-1/4" pipe size			29	.552	Ea.
	6450	1-1/2" pipe size			26	.615	Ea.
	6460	2" pipe size			20	.800	Ea.
	6470	2-1/2" pipe size			16	1.000	Ea.
	6480	3" pipe size			14	1.140	Ea.
	6490	3-1/2" pipe size			12	1.330	Ea.
	6500	4" pipe size			10	1.600	Ea.
	6510	5" pipe size	↓	↓	8	2.000	Ea.
	6520	6" pipe size	Q-16	2 Plumbers	10	2.400	Ea.
				1 Plumber Apprentice			
				1 Electric Welding Mach.			
	6530	8" pipe size			7	3.430	Ea.
	6540	10" pipe size			6	4.000	Ea.
	6550	12" pipe size	↓	↓	5	4.800	Ea.
	6560	300 lb. flange					
	6570	1/2" pipe size	Q-15	1 Plumber	36	.444	Ea.
				1 Plumber Apprentice			
				1 Electric Welding Mach.			
	6580	3/4" pipe size			34	.471	Ea.
	6590	1" pipe size			30	.533	Ea.
	6600	1-1/4" pipe size			28	.571	Ea.
	6610	1-1/2" pipe size			24	.667	Ea.
	6620	2" pipe size			18	.889	Ea.
	6630	2-1/2" pipe size			14	1.140	Ea.
	6640	3" pipe size			12	1.330	Ea.
	6650	4" pipe size			8	2.000	Ea.
	6660	5" pipe size	↓	↓	7	2.290	Ea.
	6670	6" pipe size	Q-16	2 Plumbers	9	2.670	Ea.
				1 Plumber Apprentice			
				1 Electric Welding Mach.			
	6680	8" pipe size			6	4.000	Ea.
	6690	10" pipe size			5	4.800	Ea.
	6700	12" pipe size	↓	↓	4	6.000	Ea.
	9180	Coupling, mechanical, plain end pipe to plain end pipe or fitting					
	9190	1"	Q-1	1 Plumber	29	.552	Ea.
				1 Plumber Apprentice			
	9200	1-1/2"	"	"	28	.571	Ea.

151 700 | Steel Pipe

			CREW	MAKEUP	DAILY OUTPUT	MAN-HOURS	UNIT
720	9211	Steel coupling, mechanical, 2"	Q-1	1 Plumber 1 Plumber Apprentice	27	.593	Ea.
	9220	2-1/2"			26	.615	Ea.
	9230	3"			25	.640	Ea.
	9240	3-1/2"			24	.667	Ea.
	9250	4"	↓	↓	22	.727	Ea.
	9260	5"	Q-2	2 Plumbers 1 Plumber Apprentice	28	.857	Ea.
	9270	6"			24	1.000	Ea.
	9280	8"			19	1.260	Ea.
	9290	10"			16	1.500	Ea.
	9300	12"	↓	↓	12	2.000	Ea.
	9400	Mechanical joint ends for plain end pipe					
	9410	Malleable iron, black					
	9420	90° Elbows, 1-1/4"	Q-1	1 Plumber 1 Plumber Apprentice	29	.552	Ea.
	9430	1-1/2"			27	.593	Ea.
	9440	2"	↓	↓	24	.667	Ea.
	9640	Tee, reducing run and outlet					
	9660	1-1/4" x 1" x 1/2"	Q-1	1 Plumber 1 Plumber Apprentice	18	.889	Ea.
	9670	1-1/4" x 1" x 3/4"			18	.889	Ea.
	9680	1-1/4" x 1" x 1"			18	.889	Ea.
	9690	1-1/2" x 1-1/4" x 1/2"			17	.941	Ea.
	9700	1-1/2" x 1-1/4" x 3/4"			17	.941	Ea.
	9710	1-1/2" x 1-1/4" x 1"			17	.941	Ea.
	9720	2" x 1-1/2" x 1/2"			15	1.070	Ea.
	9730	2" x 1-1/2" x 3/4"			15	1.070	Ea.
	9740	2" x 1-1/2" x 1"	↓	↓	15	1.070	Ea.
	9790	Tee, outlet					
	9810	3" x 1-1/4"	Q-1	1 Plumber 1 Plumber Apprentice	29	.552	Ea.
	9820	3" x 1-1/2"			28	.571	Ea.
	9830	3" x 2"			26	.615	Ea.
	9840	4" x 1-1/4"			28	.571	Ea.
	9850	4" x 1-1/2"			26	.615	Ea.
	9860	4" x 2"	↓	↓	24	.667	Ea.

151 800 | Grooved Joint Steel Pipe

			CREW	MAKEUP	DAILY OUTPUT	MAN-HOURS	UNIT
	801	**PIPE, GROOVED-JOINT STEEL FITTINGS & VALVES**					
	0020	Pipe includes coupling & clevis type hanger 10' O.C.					
	0500	Schedule 10, black					
	0550	2" diameter	1 Plum	1 Plumber	43	.186	L.F.
	0560	2-1/2" diameter	Q-1	1 Plumber 1 Plumber Apprentice	61	.262	L.F.
	0570	3" diameter			55	.291	L.F.
	0580	3-1/2" diameter			53	.302	L.F.
	0590	4" diameter	↓	↓	49	.327	L.F.
	0600	5" diameter			40	.400	L.F.
	0610	6" diameter	Q-2	2 Plumbers 1 Plumber Apprentice	46	.522	L.F.
	0620	8" diameter			41	.585	L.F.
	0630	10" diameter			34	.706	L.F.
	0640	12" diameter	↓	↓	30	.800	L.F.
	1001	Schedule 40, black or galvanized					
	1040	3/4" diameter	1 Plum	1 Plumber	71	.113	L.F.
	1050	1" diameter			63	.127	L.F.
	1060	1-1/4" diameter	↓	↓	58	.138	L.F.

	151 800 | Grooved Joint Steel Pipe	CREW	MAKEUP	DAILY OUTPUT	MAN-HOURS	UNIT
801 1071	Steel grooved joint fittings, schedule 40, 1-1/2" diameter	1 Plum	1 Plumber	51	.157	L.F.
1080	2" diameter	"	"	40	.200	L.F.
1090	2-1/2" diameter	Q-1	1 Plumber	57	.281	L.F.
			1 Plumber Apprentice			
1100	3" diameter			50	.320	L.F.
1110	4" diameter			45	.356	L.F.
1120	5" diameter	↓	↓	37	.432	L.F.
1130	6" diameter	Q-2	2 Plumbers	42	.571	L.F.
			1 Plumber Apprentice			
1140	8" diameter			37	.649	L.F.
1150	10" diameter			31	.774	L.F.
1160	12" diameter	↓	↓	27	.889	L.F.
2601	Schedule 80, black or galvanized					
2610	3/4" diameter	1 Plum	1 Plumber	65	.123	L.F.
2650	1" diameter			61	.131	L.F.
2660	1-1/4" diameter			55	.145	L.F.
2670	1-1/2" diameter	↓	↓	49	.163	L.F.
2680	2" diameter			38	.211	L.F.
2690	2-1/2" diameter	Q-1	1 Plumber	54	.296	L.F.
			1 Plumber Apprentice			
2700	3" diameter			48	.333	L.F.
2710	4" diameter			44	.364	L.F.
2720	5" diameter	↓	↓	35	.457	L.F.
2730	6" diameter	Q-2	2 Plumbers	40	.600	L.F.
			1 Plumber Apprentice			
2740	8" diameter			35	.686	L.F.
2750	10" diameter			29	.828	L.F.
2760	12" diameter	↓	↓	24	1.000	L.F.
4001	Elbows, 90° or 45°, steel, black or galvanized					
4030	3/4" diameter	1 Plum	1 Plumber	50	.160	Ea.
4040	1" diameter			50	.160	Ea.
4050	1-1/4" diameter			40	.200	Ea.
4060	1-1/2" diameter	↓	↓	33	.242	Ea.
4070	2" diameter			25	.320	Ea.
4080	2-1/2" diameter	Q-1	1 Plumber	40	.400	Ea.
			1 Plumber Apprentice			
4090	3" diameter			33	.485	Ea.
4100	4" diameter			25	.640	Ea.
4110	5" diameter	↓	↓	20	.800	Ea.
4120	6" diameter	Q-2	2 Plumbers	25	.960	Ea.
			1 Plumber Apprentice			
4130	8" diameter			21	1.140	Ea.
4140	10" diameter			18	1.330	Ea.
4150	12" diameter	↓	↓	15	1.600	Ea.
4691	Tees, steel, black or galvanized					
4700	3/4" diameter	1 Plum	1 Plumber	38	.211	Ea.
4740	1" diameter			33	.242	Ea.
4750	1-1/4" diameter			27	.296	Ea.
4760	1-1/2" diameter	↓	↓	22	.364	Ea.
4770	2" diameter			17	.471	Ea.
4780	2-1/2" diameter	Q-1	1 Plumber	27	.593	Ea.
			1 Plumber Apprentice			
4790	3" diameter			22	.727	Ea.
4800	4" diameter			17	.941	Ea.
4810	5" diameter	↓	↓	13	1.230	Ea.
4820	6" diameter	Q-2	2 Plumbers	17	1.410	Ea.
			1 Plumber Apprentice			
4830	8" diameter	"	"	14	1.710	Ea.

151 | Pipe and Fittings

151 800 | Grooved Joint Steel Pipe

		CREW	MAKEUP	DAILY OUTPUT	MAN-HOURS	UNIT
801 4841	Pipe, grooved joint steel, tees, 10" diameter	Q-2	2 Plumbers	12	2.000	Ea.
			1 Plumber Apprentice			
4850	12" diameter	"	"	10	2.400	Ea.
4941	Couplings, standard, steel, black or galvanized					
4950	3/4" diameter	1 Plum	1 Plumber	100	.080	Ea.
4960	1" diameter			100	.080	Ea.
4970	1-1/4" diameter			80	.100	Ea.
4980	1-1/2" diameter			67	.119	Ea.
4990	2" diameter			50	.160	Ea.
5000	2-1/2" diameter	Q-1	1 Plumber	80	.200	Ea.
			1 Plumber Apprentice			
5010	3" diameter			67	.239	Ea.
5020	3-1/2" diameter			57	.281	Ea.
5030	4" diameter			50	.320	Ea.
5040	5" diameter			40	.400	Ea.
5050	6" diameter	Q-2	2 Plumbers	50	.480	Ea.
			1 Plumber Apprentice			
5070	8" diameter			42	.571	Ea.
5090	10" diameter			35	.686	Ea.
5110	12" diameter			32	.750	Ea.
5750	Flange, w/groove gasket, black steel(see 151-720-0620, bolt sets)					
5780	2" pipe size	1 Plum	1 Plumber	23	.348	Ea.
5790	2-1/2" pipe size	Q-1	1 Plumber	37	.432	Ea.
			1 Plumber Apprentice			
5800	3" pipe size			31	.516	Ea.
5820	4" pipe size			23	.696	Ea.
5830	5" pipe size			19	.842	Ea.
5840	6" pipe size	Q-2	2 Plumbers	23	1.040	Ea.
			1 Plumber Apprentice			
5850	8" pipe size			17	1.410	Ea.
5860	10" pipe size			14	1.710	Ea.
5870	12" pipe size			12	2.000	Ea.
8001	Butterfly valve, with standard or stainless steel trim					
8010	1-1/2" pipe size	Q-1	1 Plumber	35	.457	Ea.
			1 Plumber Apprentice			
8020	2" pipe size			34	.471	Ea.
8030	3" pipe size			33	.485	Ea.
8050	4" pipe size			25	.640	Ea.
8070	6" pipe size	Q-2	2 Plumbers	25	.960	Ea.
			1 Plumber Apprentice			
8080	8" pipe size			21	1.140	Ea.
8090	10" pipe size			18	1.330	Ea.
9000	Cut one groove, labor					
9010	3/4" pipe size	Q-1	1 Plumber	152	.105	Ea.
			1 Plumber Apprentice			
9020	1" pipe size			140	.114	Ea.
9030	1-1/4" pipe size			124	.129	Ea.
9040	1-1/2" pipe size			114	.140	Ea.
9050	2" pipe size			104	.154	Ea.
9060	2-1/2" pipe size			96	.167	Ea.
9070	3" pipe size			88	.182	Ea.
9080	3-1/2" pipe size			83	.193	Ea.
9090	4" pipe size			78	.205	Ea.
9100	5" pipe size			72	.222	Ea.
9110	6" pipe size			70	.229	Ea.
9120	8" pipe size			54	.296	Ea.
9130	10" pipe size			38	.421	Ea.
9140	12" pipe size			30	.533	Ea.

151 | Pipe and Fittings

151 800 | Grooved Joint Steel Pipe

		CREW	MAKEUP	DAILY OUTPUT	MAN-HOURS	UNIT
801	9211	Pipe, grooved joint steel, roll one groove					
	9220	3/4" pipe size	Q-1	1 Plumber	266	.060	Ea.
				1 Plumber Apprentice			
	9230	1" pipe size			228	.070	Ea.
	9240	1-1/4" pipe size			200	.080	Ea.
	9250	1-1/2" pipe size			178	.090	Ea.
	9260	2" pipe size			116	.138	Ea.
	9270	2-1/2" pipe size			110	.145	Ea.
	9280	3" pipe size			100	.160	Ea.
	9290	3-1/2" pipe size			94	.170	Ea.
	9300	4" pipe size			86	.186	Ea.
	9310	5" pipe size			84	.190	Ea.
	9320	6" pipe size			80	.200	Ea.
	9330	8" pipe size			66	.242	Ea.
	9340	10" pipe size			58	.276	Ea.
	9350	12" pipe size	↓	↓	46	.348	Ea.

151 850 | Prefab Pipe Conduit

		CREW	MAKEUP	DAILY OUTPUT	MAN-HOURS	UNIT
851	PIPE CONDUIT, PREFABRICATED					
0020	Does not include trenching, hangers, fittings or crane.					
0580	Polyurethane insulated system, 250°F. max. temp.					
0620	Black steel service pipe, standard wt., 1/2" insulation	↓	↓			
0660	3/4" diam. pipe size	Q-17	1 Steamfitter	54	.296	L.F.
			1 Steamfitter Apprentice			
			1 Electric Welding Mach.			
0670	1" diam. pipe size			50	.320	L.F.
0680	1-1/4" diam. pipe size			47	.340	L.F.
0690	1-1/2" diam. pipe size			45	.356	L.F.
0700	2" diam. pipe size			42	.381	L.F.
0710	2-1/2" diam. pipe size			34	.471	L.F.
0720	3" diam. pipe size			28	.571	L.F.
0730	4" diam. pipe size			22	.727	L.F.
0740	5" diam. pipe size	↓	↓	18	.889	L.F.
0750	6" diam. pipe size	Q-18	2 Steamfitters	23	1.040	L.F.
			1 Steamfitter Apprentice			
			1 Electric Welding Mach.			
0760	8" diam. pipe size			19	1.260	L.F.
0770	10" diam. pipe size			16	1.500	L.F.
0780	12" diam. pipe size			13	1.850	L.F.
0790	14" diam. pipe size			11	2.180	L.F.
0800	16" diam. pipe size			10	2.400	L.F.
0810	18" diam. pipe size			8	3.000	L.F.
0820	20" diam. pipe size			7	3.430	L.F.
0830	24" diam. pipe size	↓	↓	6	4.000	L.F.
1500	Gland seal for system, 3/4" diam. pipe size	Q-17	1 Steamfitter	32	.500	Ea.
			1 Steamfitter Apprentice			
			1 Electric Welding Mach.			
1510	1" diam. pipe size			32	.500	Ea.
1540	1-1/4" diam. pipe size			30	.533	Ea.
1550	1-1/2" diam. pipe size			30	.533	Ea.
1560	2" diam. pipe size			28	.571	Ea.
1570	2-1/2" diam. pipe size			26	.615	Ea.
1580	3" diam. pipe size			24	.667	Ea.
1590	4" diam. pipe size			22	.727	Ea.
1600	5" diam. pipe size	↓	↓	19	.842	Ea.
1610	6" diam. pipe size	Q-18	2 Steamfitters	26	.923	Ea.
			1 Steamfitter Apprentice			
			1 Electric Welding Mach.			

151 | Pipe and Fittings

151 850 | Prefab Pipe Conduit

			CREW	MAKEUP	DAILY OUTPUT	MAN-HOURS	UNIT
851	1621	Pipe conduit, gland seal for system, 8" diam. pipe size	Q-18	2 Steamfitters	25	.960	Ea.
				1 Steamfitter Apprentice			
				1 Electric Welding Mach.			
	1630	10" diam. pipe size			23	1.040	Ea.
	1640	12" diam. pipe size			21	1.140	Ea.
	1650	14" diam. pipe size			19	1.260	Ea.
	1660	16" diam. pipe size			18	1.330	Ea.
	1670	18" diam. pipe size			16	1.500	Ea.
	1680	20" diam. pipe size			14	1.710	Ea.
	1690	24" diam. pipe size	↓	↓	12	2.000	Ea.
	2001	Elbow, 90° or 45°, for system					
	2020	3/4" diam. pipe size	Q-17	1 Steamfitter	14	1.140	Ea.
				1 Steamfitter Apprentice			
				1 Electric Welding Mach.			
	2040	1" diam. pipe size			13	1.230	Ea.
	2050	1-1/4" diam. pipe size			11	1.450	Ea.
	2060	1-1/2" diam. pipe size			9	1.780	Ea.
	2070	2" diam. pipe size			6	2.670	Ea.
	2080	2-1/2" diam. pipe size			4	4.000	Ea.
	2090	3" diam. pipe size			3.50	4.570	Ea.
	2100	4" diam. pipe size			3	5.330	Ea.
	2110	5" diam. pipe size	↓	↓	2.80	5.710	Ea.
	2120	6" diam. pipe size	Q-18	2 Steamfitters	4	6.000	Ea.
				1 Steamfitter Apprentice			
				1 Electric Welding Mach.			
	2130	8" diam. pipe size			3	8.000	Ea.
	2140	10" diam. pipe size			2.40	10.000	Ea.
	2150	12" diam. pipe size			2	12.000	Ea.
	2160	14" diam. pipe size			1.80	13.330	Ea.
	2170	16" diam. pipe size			1.60	15.000	Ea.
	2180	18" diam. pipe size			1.30	18.460	Ea.
	2190	20" diam. pipe size			1	24.000	Ea.
	2200	24" diam. pipe size	↓	↓	.70	34.290	Ea.
	2800	Calcium silicate insulated system, high temp. (1200°F)					
	2840	Steel casing with protective exterior coating					
	2850	6-5/8" diameter	Q-18	2 Steamfitters	52	.462	L.F.
				1 Steamfitter Apprentice			
				1 Electric Welding Mach.			
	2860	8-5/8" diameter			50	.480	L.F.
	2870	10-3/4" diameter			47	.511	L.F.
	2880	12-3/4" diameter			44	.545	L.F.
	2890	14" diameter			41	.585	L.F.
	2900	16" diameter			39	.615	L.F.
	2910	18" diameter			36	.667	L.F.
	2920	20" diameter			34	.706	L.F.
	2930	22" diameter			32	.750	L.F.
	2940	24" diameter			29	.828	L.F.
	2950	26" diameter			26	.923	L.F.
	2960	28" diameter			23	1.040	L.F.
	2970	30" diameter			21	1.140	L.F.
	2980	32" diameter			19	1.260	L.F.
	2990	34" diameter			18	1.330	L.F.
	3000	36" diameter	↓	↓	16	1.500	L.F.
	3400	Steel casing gland seal, single pipe					
	3420	6-5/8" diameter	Q-18	2 Steamfitters	25	.960	Ea.
				1 Steamfitter Apprentice			
				1 Electric Welding Mach.			
	3440	8-5/8" diameter	"	"	23	1.040	Ea.

151 850 | Prefab Pipe Conduit

			CREW	MAKEUP	DAILY OUTPUT	MAN-HOURS	UNIT
851	3451	Pipe conduit, stl. casing gland seal, single pipe, 10-3/4" diam.	Q-18	2 Steamfitters	21	1.140	Ea.
				1 Steamfitter Apprentice			
				1 Electric Welding Mach.			
	3460	12-3/4" diameter			19	1.260	Ea.
	3470	14" diameter			17	1.410	Ea.
	3480	16" diameter			16	1.500	Ea.
	3490	18" diameter			15	1.600	Ea.
	3500	20" diameter			13	1.850	Ea.
	3510	22" diameter			12	2.000	Ea.
	3520	24" diameter			11	2.180	Ea.
	3530	26" diameter			10	2.400	Ea.
	3540	28" diameter			9.50	2.530	Ea.
	3550	30" diameter			9	2.670	Ea.
	3560	32" diameter			8.50	2.820	Ea.
	3570	34" diameter			8	3.000	Ea.
	3580	36" diameter	↓	↓	7	3.430	Ea.
	4000	Steel casing anchors, single pipe					
	4020	6-5/8" diameter	Q-18	2 Steamfitters	8	3.000	Ea.
				1 Steamfitter Apprentice			
				1 Electric Welding Mach.			
	4040	8-5/8" diameter			7.50	3.200	Ea.
	4050	10-3/4" diameter			7	3.430	Ea.
	4060	12-3/4" diameter			6.50	3.690	Ea.
	4070	14" diameter			6	4.000	Ea.
	4080	16" diameter			5.50	4.360	Ea.
	4090	18" diameter			5	4.800	Ea.
	4100	20" diameter			4.50	5.330	Ea.
	4110	22" diameter			4	6.000	Ea.
	4120	24" diameter			3.50	6.860	Ea.
	4130	26" diameter			3	8.000	Ea.
	4140	28" diameter			2.50	9.600	Ea.
	4150	30" diameter			2	12.000	Ea.
	4160	32" diameter			1.50	16.000	Ea.
	4170	34" diameter			1	24.000	Ea.
	4180	36" diameter	↓	↓	1	24.000	Ea.
	4800	Steel casing elbow					
	4820	6-5/8" diameter	Q-18	2 Steamfitters	15	1.600	Ea.
				1 Steamfitter Apprentice			
				1 Electric Welding Mach.			
	4830	8-5/8" diameter			15	1.600	Ea.
	4850	10-3/4" diameter			14	1.710	Ea.
	4860	12-3/4" diameter			13	1.850	Ea.
	4870	14" diameter			12	2.000	Ea.
	4880	16" diameter			11	2.180	Ea.
	4890	18" diameter			10	2.400	Ea.
	4900	20" diameter			9	2.670	Ea.
	4910	22" diameter			8	3.000	Ea.
	4920	24" diameter			7	3.430	Ea.
	4930	26" diameter			6	4.000	Ea.
	4940	28" diameter			5	4.800	Ea.
	4950	30" diameter			4	6.000	Ea.
	4960	32" diameter			3	8.000	Ea.
	4970	34" diameter			2	12.000	Ea.
	4980	36" diameter	↓	↓	2	12.000	Ea.
	5501	Black steel service pipe, std. wt., 1" to 1-1/2" insulation					
	5510	3/4" diameter pipe size	Q-17	1 Steamfitter	54	.296	L.F.
				1 Steamfitter Apprentice			
				1 Electric Welding Mach.			

151 | Pipe and Fittings

151 850 | Prefab Pipe Conduit

			CREW	MAKEUP	DAILY OUTPUT	MAN-HOURS	UNIT
851	5541	Pipe conduit, blk. stl. svc. pipe, std. wt., 1" diam. pipe size	Q-17	1 Steamfitter 1 Steamfitter Apprentice 1 Electric Welding Mach.	50	.320	L.F.
	5550	1-1/4" diameter pipe size			47	.340	L.F.
	5560	1-1/2" diameter pipe size			45	.356	L.F.
	5570	2" diameter pipe size			42	.381	L.F.
	5580	2-1/2" diameter pipe size			34	.471	L.F.
	5590	3" diameter pipe size			28	.571	L.F.
	5600	4" diameter pipe size			22	.727	L.F.
	5610	5" diameter pipe size	↓	↓	18	.889	L.F.
	5620	6" diameter pipe size	Q-18	2 Steamfitters 1 Steamfitter Apprentice 1 Electric Welding Mach.	23	1.040	L.F.
	6801	Black steel service pipe, ex. hvy. wt., 1" to 1-1/2" insul.					
	6820	3/4" diameter pipe size	Q-17	1 Steamfitter 1 Steamfitter Apprentice 1 Electric Welding Mach.	50	.320	L.F.
	6840	1" diameter pipe size			47	.340	L.F.
	6850	1-1/4" diameter pipe size			44	.364	L.F.
	6860	1-1/2" diameter pipe size			42	.381	L.F.
	6870	2" diameter pipe size			40	.400	L.F.
	6880	2-1/2" diameter pipe size			31	.516	L.F.
	6890	3" diameter pipe size			27	.593	L.F.
	6900	4" diameter pipe size			21	.762	L.F.
	6910	5" diameter pipe size	↓	↓	17	.941	L.F.
	6920	6" diameter pipe size	Q-18	2 Steamfitters 1 Steamfitter Apprentice 1 Electric Welding Mach.	22	1.090	L.F.

151 900 | Pipe Supports/Hangers

		CREW	MAKEUP	DAILY OUTPUT	MAN-HOURS	UNIT
901	PIPE HANGERS AND SUPPORTS					
0050	Brackets					
0060	Beam side or wall, malleable iron					
0070	3/8" threaded rod size	1 Plum	1 Plumber	48	.167	Ea.
0080	1/2" threaded rod size			48	.167	Ea.
0090	5/8" threaded rod size			48	.167	Ea.
0100	3/4" threaded rod size			48	.167	Ea.
0110	7/8" threaded rod size	↓	↓	48	.167	Ea.
0150	Wall, welded steel					
0160	0 size, 12" wide, 18" deep	1 Plum	1 Plumber	34	.235	Ea.
0170	1 size, 18" wide 24" deep			34	.235	Ea.
0180	2 size, 24" wide, 30" deep	↓	↓	34	.235	Ea.
0300	Clamps					
0310	C-clamp, for mounting on steel beam flange, w/locknut					
0320	3/8" threaded rod size	1 Plum	1 Plumber	160	.050	Ea.
0330	1/2" threaded rod size			160	.050	Ea.
0340	5/8" threaded rod size			160	.050	Ea.
0350	3/4" threaded rod size	↓	↓	160	.050	Ea.
0400	High temperature to 1050°F, alloy steel					
0410	4" pipe size	Q-1	1 Plumber 1 Plumber Apprentice	106	.151	Ea.
0420	6" pipe size			106	.151	Ea.
0430	8" pipe size			97	.165	Ea.
0440	10" pipe size			84	.190	Ea.
0450	12" pipe size			72	.222	Ea.
0460	14" pipe size			64	.250	Ea.
0470	16" pipe size	↓	↓	56	.286	Ea.
0471						

151 | Pipe and Fittings

151 900 | Pipe Supports/Hangers

		Pipe Supports/Hangers	CREW	MAKEUP	DAILY OUTPUT	MAN-HOURS	UNIT
901	0501	Pipe clamps, I-beam, for mntg. on bottom flange, strap iron					
	0510	2" flange size	1 Plum	1 Plumber	96	.083	Ea.
	0520	3" flange size			95	.084	Ea.
	0530	4" flange size			93	.086	Ea.
	0540	5" flange size			92	.087	Ea.
	0550	6" flange size			90	.089	Ea.
	0560	7" flange size			88	.091	Ea.
	0570	8" flange size	↓	↓	86	.093	Ea.
	0600	One hole, vertical mounting, malleable iron					
	0610	1/2" pipe size	1 Plum	1 Plumber	160	.050	Ea.
	0620	3/4" pipe size			145	.055	Ea.
	0630	1" pipe size			136	.059	Ea.
	0640	1-1/4" pipe size			128	.063	Ea.
	0650	1-1/2" pipe size			120	.067	Ea.
	0660	2" pipe size			112	.071	Ea.
	0670	2-1/2" pipe size			104	.077	Ea.
	0680	3" pipe size			96	.083	Ea.
	0690	3-1/2" pipe size			90	.089	Ea.
	0700	4" pipe size	↓	↓	84	.095	Ea.
	0750	Riser or extension pipe, carbon steel					
	0760	3/4" pipe size	1 Plum	1 Plumber	48	.167	Ea.
	0770	1" pipe size			47	.170	Ea.
	0780	1-1/4" pipe size			46	.174	Ea.
	0790	1-1/2" pipe size			45	.178	Ea.
	0800	2" pipe size			43	.186	Ea.
	0810	2-1/2" pipe size			41	.195	Ea.
	0820	3" pipe size			40	.200	Ea.
	0830	3-1/2" pipe size			39	.205	Ea.
	0840	4" pipe size			38	.211	Ea.
	0850	5" pipe size			37	.216	Ea.
	0860	6" pipe size			36	.222	Ea.
	0870	8" pipe size			34	.235	Ea.
	0880	10" pipe size			32	.250	Ea.
	0890	12" pipe size	↓	↓	28	.286	Ea.
	0950	Two piece, complete, carbon steel, medium weight					
	0960	1/2" pipe size	Q-1	1 Plumber / 1 Plumber Apprentice	137	.117	Ea.
	0970	3/4" pipe size			134	.119	Ea.
	0980	1" pipe size			132	.121	Ea.
	0990	1-1/4" pipe size			130	.123	Ea.
	1000	1-1/2" pipe size			126	.127	Ea.
	1010	2" pipe size			124	.129	Ea.
	1020	2-1/2" pipe size			120	.133	Ea.
	1030	3" pipe size			117	.137	Ea.
	1040	3-1/2" pipe size			114	.140	Ea.
	1050	4" pipe size			110	.145	Ea.
	1060	5" pipe size			106	.151	Ea.
	1070	6" pipe size			104	.154	Ea.
	1080	8" pipe size			100	.160	Ea.
	1090	10" pipe size			96	.167	Ea.
	1100	12" pipe size			89	.180	Ea.
	1110	14" pipe size	↓	↓	82	.195	Ea.
	1150	Insert, concrete					
	1160	Wedge type, carbon steel body, malleable iron nut					
	1170	1/4" threaded rod size	1 Plum	1 Plumber	96	.083	Ea.
	1180	3/8" threaded rod size			96	.083	Ea.
	1190	1/2" threaded rod size			96	.083	Ea.
	1200	5/8" threaded rod size	↓	↓	96	.083	Ea.

151 | Pipe and Fittings

151 900 | Pipe Supports/Hangers

		CREW	MAKEUP	DAILY OUTPUT	MAN-HOURS	UNIT
901	1211	Insert, concrete, wedge type, 3/4" threaded rod size	1 Plum	1 Plumber	96	.083	Ea.
	1220	7/8" threaded rod size	"	"	96	.083	Ea.
	1250	Pipe guide sized for insulation					
	1260	No. 1, 1" pipe size, 1" thick insulation	1 Stpi	1 Steamfitter	26	.308	Ea.
	1270	No. 2, 1-1/4"-2" pipe size, 1" thick insulation			23	.348	Ea.
	1280	No. 3, 1-1/4"-2" pipe size, 1-1/2" thick insulation			21	.381	Ea.
	1290	No. 4, 2-1/2"-3-1/2" pipe size, 1-1/2" thick insulation	↓	↓	18	.444	Ea.
	1300	No. 5, 4"-5" pipe size, 1-1/2" thick insulation			16	.500	Ea.
	1310	No. 6, 5"-6" pipe size, 2" thick insulation	Q-5	1 Steamfitter	21	.762	Ea.
				1 Steamfitter Apprentice			
	1320	No. 7, 8" pipe size, 2" thick insulation			16	1.000	Ea.
	1330	No. 8, 10" pipe size, 2" thick insulation	↓	↓	12	1.330	Ea.
	1340	No. 9, 12" pipe size, 2" thick insulation	Q-6	2 Steamfitters	17	1.410	Ea.
				1 Steamfitter Apprentice			
	1350	No. 10, 12"-14" pipe size, 2-1/2" thick insulation			16	1.500	Ea.
	1360	No. 11, 16" pipe size, 2-1/2" thick insulation			10.50	2.290	Ea.
	1370	No. 12, 16"-18" pipe size, 3" thick insulation			9	2.670	Ea.
	1380	No. 13, 20" pipe size, 3" thick insulation			7.50	3.200	Ea.
	1390	No. 14, 24" pipe size, 3" thick insulation	↓	↓	7	3.430	Ea.
	1400	Rings					
	1410	Adjustable band, carbon steel, for non-insulated pipe					
	1420	1/2" pipe size	Q-1	1 Plumber	142	.113	Ea.
				1 Plumber Apprentice			
	1430	3/4" pipe size			140	.114	Ea.
	1440	1" pipe size			137	.117	Ea.
	1450	1-1/4" pipe size			134	.119	Ea.
	1460	1-1/2" pipe size			131	.122	Ea.
	1470	2" pipe size			129	.124	Ea.
	1480	2-1/2" pipe size			125	.128	Ea.
	1490	3" pipe size			122	.131	Ea.
	1500	3-1/2" pipe size			119	.134	Ea.
	1510	4" pipe size			114	.140	Ea.
	1520	5" pipe size			110	.145	Ea.
	1530	6" pipe size			108	.148	Ea.
	1540	8" pipe size	↓	↓	104	.154	Ea.
	1600	Adjusting nut malleable iron, steel band					
	1610	1/2" pipe size, galvanized band	Q-1	1 Plumber	137	.117	Ea.
				1 Plumber Apprentice			
	1620	3/4" pipe size, galvanized band			135	.119	Ea.
	1630	1" pipe size, gavanized band			132	.121	Ea.
	1640	1-1/4" pipe size, galvanized band			129	.124	Ea.
	1650	1-1/2" pipe size, galvanized band			126	.127	Ea.
	1660	2" pipe size, galvanized band			124	.129	Ea.
	1670	2-1/2" pipe size, galvanized band			120	.133	Ea.
	1680	3" pipe size, galvanized band			117	.137	Ea.
	1690	3-1/2" pipe size, galvanized band			114	.140	Ea.
	1700	4" pipe size, cadmium plated band			110	.145	Ea.
	1710	5" pipe size, cadmium plated band			106	.151	Ea.
	1720	6" pipe size, cadmium plated band			104	.154	Ea.
	1730	8" pipe size, cadmium plated band	↓	↓	100	.160	Ea.
	1800	Clevis, adjustable, carbon steel, for non-insulated pipe					
	1810	1/2" pipe size	Q-1	1 Plumber	137	.117	Ea.
				1 Plumber Apprentice			
	1820	3/4" pipe size			135	.119	Ea.
	1830	1" pipe size			132	.121	Ea.
	1840	1-1/4" pipe size			129	.124	Ea.
	1850	1-1/2" pipe size			126	.127	Ea.
	1860	2" pipe size	↓	↓	124	.129	Ea.

151 900 | Pipe Supports/Hangers

		Description	CREW	MAKEUP	DAILY OUTPUT	MAN-HOURS	UNIT
901	1871	Pipe hangers, clevis, adjustable, 2-1/2" pipe size	Q-1	1 Plumber	120	.133	Ea.
				1 Plumber Apprentice			
	1880	3" pipe size			117	.137	Ea.
	1890	3-1/2" pipe size			114	.140	Ea.
	1900	4" pipe size			110	.145	Ea.
	1910	5" pipe size			106	.151	Ea.
	1920	6" pipe size			104	.154	Ea.
	1930	8" pipe size			100	.160	Ea.
	1940	10" pipe size			96	.167	Ea.
	1950	12" pipe size			89	.180	Ea.
	1960	14" pipe size			82	.195	Ea.
	1970	16" pipe size	↓	↓	68	.235	Ea.
	2250	Split ring, malleable iron, for non-insulated pipe					
	2260	1/2" pipe size	Q-1	1 Plumber	137	.117	Ea.
				1 Plumber Apprentice			
	2270	3/4" pipe size			135	.119	Ea.
	2280	1" pipe size			132	.121	Ea.
	2290	1-1/4" pipe size			129	.124	Ea.
	2300	1-1/2" pipe size			126	.127	Ea.
	2310	2" pipe size			124	.129	Ea.
	2320	2-1/2" pipe size			120	.133	Ea.
	2330	3" pipe size			117	.137	Ea.
	2340	3-1/2" pipe size			114	.140	Ea.
	2350	4" pipe size			110	.145	Ea.
	2360	5" pipe size			106	.151	Ea.
	2370	6" pipe size			104	.154	Ea.
	2380	8" pipe size	↓	↓	100	.160	Ea.
	2650	Rods, carbon steel					
	2660	Continuous thread					
	2670	1/4" thread size	1 Plum	1 Plumber	144	.056	L.F.
	2680	3/8" thread size			144	.056	L.F.
	2690	1/2" thread size			144	.056	L.F.
	2700	5/8" thread size			144	.056	L.F.
	2710	3/4" thread size			144	.056	L.F.
	2720	7/8" thread size	↓	↓	144	.056	L.F.
	2750	Both ends machine threaded 18" length					
	2760	3/8" thread size	1 Plum	1 Plumber	240	.033	Ea.
	2770	1/2" thread size			240	.033	Ea.
	2780	5/8" thread size			240	.033	Ea.
	2790	3/4" thread size			240	.033	Ea.
	2800	7/8" thread size			240	.033	Ea.
	2810	1" thread size	↓	↓	240	.033	Ea.
	2900	Rolls					
	2910	Adjustable yoke, carbon steel with CI roll					
	2920	2-1/2" pipe size	Q-1	1 Plumber	137	.117	Ea.
				1 Plumber Apprentice			
	2930	3" pipe size			131	.122	Ea.
	2940	3-1/2" pipe size			124	.129	Ea.
	2950	4" pipe size			117	.137	Ea.
	2960	5" pipe size			110	.145	Ea.
	2970	6" pipe size			104	.154	Ea.
	2980	8" pipe size			96	.167	Ea.
	2990	10" pipe size			80	.200	Ea.
	3010	14" pipe size			56	.286	Ea.
	3020	16" pipe size	↓	↓	48	.333	Ea.
	3050	Chair, carbon steel with CI roll					
	3060	2" pipe size	1 Plum	1 Plumber	68	.118	Ea.
	3070	2-1/2" pipe size	"	"	65	.123	Ea.

151 900 | Pipe Supports/Hangers

		CREW	MAKEUP	DAILY OUTPUT	MAN-HOURS	UNIT
901 3081	Pipe hangers, rolls, chair, 3" pipe size	1 Plum	1 Plumber	62	.129	Ea.
3090	3-1/2" pipe size			60	.133	Ea.
3100	4" pipe size			58	.138	Ea.
3110	5" pipe size			56	.143	Ea.
3120	6" pipe size			53	.151	Ea.
3130	8" pipe size			50	.160	Ea.
3140	10" pipe size			48	.167	Ea.
3150	12" pipe size	↓	↓	46	.174	Ea.
3170	Trapeze w/roller, (see line 2650 for rods), 1" pipe size	Q-1	1 Plumber 1 Plumber Apprentice	137	.117	Ea.
3180	1-1/4" pipe size			131	.122	Ea.
3190	1-1/2" pipe size			129	.124	Ea.
3200	2" pipe size			124	.129	Ea.
3210	2-1/2" pipe size			118	.136	Ea.
3220	3" pipe size			115	.139	Ea.
3230	3-1/2" pipe size			113	.142	Ea.
3240	4" pipe size			112	.143	Ea.
3250	5" pipe size			110	.145	Ea.
3260	6" pipe size			101	.158	Ea.
3270	8" pipe size			90	.178	Ea.
3280	10" pipe size			80	.200	Ea.
3290	12" pipe size	↓	↓	68	.235	Ea.
3300	Saddles					
3310	Pipe support, complete, adjustable, CI saddle					
3320	2-1/2" pipe size	1 Plum	1 Plumber	96	.083	Ea.
3330	3" pipe size			88	.091	Ea.
3340	3-1/2" pipe size			79	.101	Ea.
3350	4" pipe size			68	.118	Ea.
3360	5" pipe size			64	.125	Ea.
3370	6" pipe size			59	.136	Ea.
3380	8" pipe size			53	.151	Ea.
3390	10" pipe size			50	.160	Ea.
3400	12" pipe size	↓	↓	48	.167	Ea.
3750	Covering protection					
3761	1" or 1-1/2" covering size					
3770	3/4" pipe size	1 Plum	1 Plumber	68	.118	Ea.
3780	1" pipe size			68	.118	Ea.
3790	1-1/4" pipe size			68	.118	Ea.
3800	1-1/2" pipe size			66	.121	Ea.
3810	2" pipe size			66	.121	Ea.
3820	2-1/2" pipe size			64	.125	Ea.
3830	3" pipe size			64	.125	Ea.
3840	3-1/2" pipe size			62	.129	Ea.
3850	4" pipe size			62	.129	Ea.
3860	5" pipe size			60	.133	Ea.
3870	6" pipe size	↓	↓	60	.133	Ea.
4200	Sockets					
4210	Rod end, malleable iron					
4220	1/4" thread size	1 Plum	1 Plumber	240	.033	Ea.
4230	3/8" thread size			240	.033	Ea.
4240	1/2" thread size			230	.035	Ea.
4250	5/8" thread size			225	.036	Ea.
4260	3/4" thread size			220	.036	Ea.
4270	7/8" thread size	↓	↓	210	.038	Ea.
4290	Strap, 1/2" pipe size	Q-1	1 Plumber 1 Plumber Apprentice	142	.113	Ea.
4300	3/4" pipe size			140	.114	Ea.
4310	1" pipe size	↓	↓	137	.117	Ea.

151 | Pipe and Fittings

151 900 | Pipe Supports/Hangers

		CREW	MAKEUP	DAILY OUTPUT	MAN-HOURS	UNIT
901 4321	Pipe hangers, strap, 1-1/4" pipe size	Q-1	1 Plumber	134	.119	Ea.
			1 Plumber Apprentice			
4330	1-1/2" pipe size			131	.122	Ea.
4340	2" pipe size			129	.124	Ea.
4350	2-1/2" pipe size			125	.128	Ea.
4360	3" pipe size			122	.131	Ea.
4370	3-1/2" pipe size			119	.134	Ea.
4380	4" pipe size	↓	↓	114	.140	Ea.
4400	U-bolt, carbon steel					
4410	Standard, with nuts					
4420	1/2" pipe size	1 Plum	1 Plumber	160	.050	Ea.
4430	3/4" pipe size			158	.051	Ea.
4450	1" pipe size			152	.053	Ea.
4460	1-1/4" pipe size			148	.054	Ea.
4470	1-1/2" pipe size			143	.056	Ea.
4480	2" pipe size			139	.058	Ea.
4490	2-1/2" pipe size			134	.060	Ea.
4500	3" pipe size			128	.063	Ea.
4510	3-1/2" pipe size			122	.066	Ea.
4520	4" pipe size			117	.068	Ea.
4530	5" pipe size			114	.070	Ea.
4540	6" pipe size			111	.072	Ea.
4550	8" pipe size			109	.073	Ea.
4560	10" pipe size			107	.075	Ea.
4570	12" pipe size	↓	↓	104	.077	Ea.
4700	U-hook, carbon steel, requires mounting screws or bolts					
4710	3/4" thru 2" pipe size					
4720	6" long	1 Plum	1 Plumber	96	.083	Ea.
4730	8" long			96	.083	Ea.
4740	10" long			96	.083	Ea.
4750	12" long	↓	↓	96	.083	Ea.

151 950 | Valves

		CREW	MAKEUP	DAILY OUTPUT	MAN-HOURS	UNIT
951	**VALVES, BRASS**					
0500	Gas stops, without checks					
0510	1/4" size	1 Plum	1 Plumber	26	.308	Ea.
0520	3/8" size			24	.333	Ea.
0530	1/2" size			24	.333	Ea.
0540	3/4" size			22	.364	Ea.
0550	1" size			19	.421	Ea.
0560	1-1/4" size			15	.533	Ea.
0570	1-1/2" size			13	.615	Ea.
0580	2" size	↓	↓	11	.727	Ea.
955	**VALVES, BRONZE**					
1020	Angle, 150 lb., rising stem, threaded					
1030	1/8" size	1 Plum	1 Plumber	24	.333	Ea.
1040	1/4" size			24	.333	Ea.
1050	3/8" size			24	.333	Ea.
1060	1/2" size			22	.364	Ea.
1070	3/4" size			20	.400	Ea.
1080	1" size			19	.421	Ea.
1090	1-1/4" size			15	.533	Ea.
1100	1-1/2" size			13	.615	Ea.
1110	2" size	↓	↓	11	.727	Ea.
1380	Ball, 150 psi, threaded					
1400	1/4" size	1 Plum	1 Plumber	24	.333	Ea.
1430	3/8" size			24	.333	Ea.
1450	1/2" size	↓	↓	22	.364	Ea.

151 950 | Valves

		CREW	MAKEUP	DAILY OUTPUT	MAN-HOURS	UNIT
955 1461	Valves, bronze, ball, 150 psi, threaded, 3/4" size	1 Plum	1 Plumber	20	.400	Ea.
1470	1" size			19	.421	Ea.
1480	1-1/4" size			15	.533	Ea.
1490	1-1/2" size	↓	↓	13	.615	Ea.
1500	2" size			11	.727	Ea.
1600	Butterfly, 175 psi, full port, solder or threaded ends					
1610	Stainless steel disc and stem					
1620	1/4" size	1 Plum	1 Plumber	24	.333	Ea.
1630	3/8" size			24	.333	Ea.
1640	1/2" size			22	.364	Ea.
1650	3/4" size			20	.400	Ea.
1660	1" size			19	.421	Ea.
1670	1-1/4" size			15	.533	Ea.
1680	1-1/2" size			13	.615	Ea.
1690	2" size	↓	↓	11	.727	Ea.
1750	Check, swing, class 150, regrinding disc, threaded					
1800	1/8" size	1 Plum	1 Plumber	24	.333	Ea.
1830	1/4" size			24	.333	Ea.
1840	3/8" size			24	.333	Ea.
1850	1/2" size			24	.333	Ea.
1860	3/4" size			20	.400	Ea.
1870	1" size			19	.421	Ea.
1880	1-1/4" size			15	.533	Ea.
1890	1-1/2" size			13	.615	Ea.
1900	2" size	↓	↓	11	.727	Ea.
1910	2-1/2" size	Q-1	1 Plumber 1 Plumber Apprentice	15	1.070	Ea.
1920	3" size	"	"	13	1.230	Ea.
2350	Check, lift, class 150, horizontal composition disc, threaded					
2400	1/8" size	1 Plum	1 Plumber	24	.333	Ea.
2430	1/4" size			24	.333	Ea.
2440	3/8" size			24	.333	Ea.
2450	1/2" size			24	.333	Ea.
2460	3/4" size			20	.400	Ea.
2470	1" size			19	.421	Ea.
2480	1-1/4" size			15	.533	Ea.
2490	1-1/2" size			13	.615	Ea.
2500	2" size	↓	↓	11	.727	Ea.
2850	Gate, N.R.S., soldered, 300 psi					
2900	3/8" size	1 Plum	1 Plumber	24	.333	Ea.
2920	1/2" size			24	.333	Ea.
2940	3/4" size			20	.400	Ea.
2950	1" size			19	.421	Ea.
2960	1-1/4" size			15	.533	Ea.
2970	1-1/2" size			13	.615	Ea.
2980	2" size	↓	↓	11	.727	Ea.
2990	2-1/2" size	Q-1	1 Plumber 1 Plumber Apprentice	15	1.070	Ea.
3000	3" size	"	"	13	1.230	Ea.
3350	Threaded, class 150					
3400	1/8" size	1 Plum	1 Plumber	24	.333	Ea.
3410	1/4" size			24	.333	Ea.
3420	3/8" size			24	.333	Ea.
3430	1/2" size			24	.333	Ea.
3440	3/4" size			20	.400	Ea.
3450	1" size			19	.421	Ea.
3460	1-1/4" size			15	.533	Ea.
3470	1-1/2" size	↓	↓	13	.615	Ea.

151 950 | Valves

		CREW	MAKEUP	DAILY OUTPUT	MAN-HOURS	UNIT
955	3481	Valves, bronze, gate, N.R.S., threaded, class 150, 2" size	1 Plum	1 Plumber	11	.727	Ea.
	3490	2-1/2" size	Q-1	1 Plumber	15	1.070	Ea.
				1 Plumber Apprentice			
	3500	3" size	"	"	13	1.230	Ea.
	3850	Rising stem, soldered, 300 psi					
	3900	3/8" size	1 Plum	1 Plumber	24	.333	Ea.
	3920	1/2" size			24	.333	Ea.
	3940	3/4" size			20	.400	Ea.
	3950	1" size			19	.421	Ea.
	3960	1-1/4" size			15	.533	Ea.
	3970	1-1/2" size			13	.615	Ea.
	3980	2" size	↓	↓	11	.727	Ea.
	3990	2-1/2" size	Q-1	1 Plumber	15	1.070	Ea.
				1 Plumber Apprentice			
	4000	3" size	"	"	13	1.230	Ea.
	4250	Threaded, class 150					
	4300	1/8" size	1 Plum	1 Plumber	24	.333	Ea.
	4310	1/4" size			24	.333	Ea.
	4320	3/8" size			24	.333	Ea.
	4330	1/2" size			24	.333	Ea.
	4340	3/4" size			20	.400	Ea.
	4350	1" size			19	.421	Ea.
	4360	1-1/4" size			15	.533	Ea.
	4370	1-1/2" size			13	.615	Ea.
	4380	2" size	↓	↓	11	.727	Ea.
	4390	2-1/2" size	Q-1	1 Plumber	15	1.070	Ea.
				1 Plumber Apprentice			
	4400	3" size	"	"	13	1.230	Ea.
	4850	Globe, class 150, rising stem, threaded					
	4900	1/8" size	1 Plum	1 Plumber	24	.333	Ea.
	4920	1/4" size			24	.333	Ea.
	4940	3/8" size			24	.333	Ea.
	4950	1/2" size			24	.333	Ea.
	4960	3/4" size			20	.400	Ea.
	4970	1" size			19	.421	Ea.
	4980	1-1/4" size			15	.533	Ea.
	4990	1-1/2" size			13	.615	Ea.
	5000	2" size	↓	↓	11	.727	Ea.
	5010	2-1/2" size	Q-1	1 Plumber	15	1.070	Ea.
				1 Plumber Apprentice			
	5020	3" size	"	"	13	1.230	Ea.
	5600	Relief, pressure & temperature, self-closing, ASME					
	5640	3/4" size	1 Plum	1 Plumber	28	.286	Ea.
	5650	1" size			24	.333	Ea.
	5660	1-1/4" size			20	.400	Ea.
	5670	1-1/2" size			18	.444	Ea.
	5680	2" size	↓	↓	16	.500	Ea.
	5950	Pressure, poppet type, threaded					
	6000	1/2" size	1 Plum	1 Plumber	30	.267	Ea.
	6040	3/4" size	"	"	28	.286	Ea.
	6400	Pressure, water, ASME, threaded					
	6440	3/4" size	1 Plum	1 Plumber	28	.286	Ea.
	6450	1" size			24	.333	Ea.
	6460	1-1/4" size			20	.400	Ea.
	6470	1-1/2" size			18	.444	Ea.
	6480	2" size	↓	↓	16	.500	Ea.
	6921						
	6922						

151 950 | Valves

		CREW	MAKEUP	DAILY OUTPUT	MAN-HOURS	UNIT
955 6941	Valves, bronze, reducing, 300 psi, threaded/sweat, 1/2" size	1 Plum	1 Plumber	24	.333	Ea.
6950	3/4" size			20	.400	Ea.
6960	1" size			19	.421	Ea.
6970	1-1/4" size			15	.533	Ea.
6980	1-1/2" size			13	.615	Ea.
6990	2" size	↓	↓	11	.727	Ea.
7700	High capacity, 250 psi to 25-75 psi, threaded					
7740	1/2" size	1 Plum	1 Plumber	24	.333	Ea.
7780	3/4" size			20	.400	Ea.
7790	1" size			19	.421	Ea.
7800	1-1/4" size			15	.533	Ea.
7810	1-1/2" size			13	.615	Ea.
7820	2" size			11	.727	Ea.
7830	2-1/2" size			9	.889	Ea.
7840	3" size	↓	↓	8	1.000	Ea.
7850	3" flanged (iron body)	Q-1	1 Plumber 1 Plumber Apprentice	10	1.600	Ea.
7860	4" flanged (iron body)	"	"	8	2.000	Ea.
8350	Tempering, water, sweat connections					
8400	1/2" size	1 Plum	1 Plumber	24	.333	Ea.
8440	3/4" size	"	"	20	.400	Ea.
8650	Threaded connections					
8700	1/2" size	1 Plum	1 Plumber	24	.333	Ea.
8740	3/4" size			20	.400	Ea.
8750	1" size			19	.421	Ea.
8760	1-1/4" size			15	.533	Ea.
8770	1-1/2" size			13	.615	Ea.
8780	2" size	↓	↓	11	.727	Ea.
960	**VALVES, IRON BODY**					
1021	Butterfly, wafer or lug type, lever actuator					
1030	2" size	1 Plum	1 Plumber	14	.571	Ea.
1040	2-1/2" size	Q-1	1 Plumber 1 Plumber Apprentice	9	1.780	Ea.
1050	3" size			8	2.000	Ea.
1060	4" size			5	3.200	Ea.
1070	5" size	Q-2	2 Plumbers 1 Plumber Apprentice	5	4.800	Ea.
1080	6" size			5	4.800	Ea.
1090	8" size			4.50	5.330	Ea.
1100	10" size			4	6.000	Ea.
1110	12" size	↓	↓	3	8.000	Ea.
1400	Diverter, 150 lb. flanged, bronze or iron plugs					
1440	2" pipe size	Q-1	1 Plumber 1 Plumber Apprentice	2	8.000	Ea.
1450	3" pipe size	"	"	1.50	10.670	Ea.
1650	Gate, 125 lb., N.R.S., threaded					
1700	2" size	1 Plum	1 Plumber	11	.727	Ea.
1740	2-1/2" size	Q-1	1 Plumber 1 Plumber Apprentice	15	1.070	Ea.
1760	3" size			13	1.230	Ea.
1780	4" size	↓	↓	10	1.600	Ea.
2150	Flanged					
2200	2" size	1 Plum	1 Plumber	5	1.600	Ea.
2240	2-1/2" size	Q-1	1 Plumber 1 Plumber Apprentice	5	3.200	Ea.
2260	3" size			4.50	3.560	Ea.
2280	4" size	↓	↓	3	5.330	Ea.

151 950 | Valves

			CREW	MAKEUP	DAILY OUTPUT	MAN-HOURS	UNIT
960	2291	Valves, iron body, gate, 125 lb., N.R.S., flanged, 5" size	Q-2	2 Plumbers	3.40	7.060	Ea.
				1 Plumber Apprentice			
	2300	6" size			3	8.000	Ea.
	2320	8" size			2.50	9.600	Ea.
	2340	10" size			2.20	10.910	Ea.
	2360	12" size			1.70	14.120	Ea.
	2370	14" size			1.30	18.460	Ea.
	2380	16" size	↓	↓	1	24.000	Ea.
	2950	OS&Y, threaded					
	2960	1/2" size	1 Plum	1 Plumber	24	.333	Ea.
	2970	3/4" size			20	.400	Ea.
	2980	1" size			19	.421	Ea.
	2990	1-1/2" size	↓	↓	13	.615	Ea.
	3000	2" size			11	.727	Ea.
	3060	2-1/2" size	Q-1	1 Plumber	15	1.070	Ea.
				1 Plumber Apprentice			
	3080	3" size			13	1.230	Ea.
	3100	4" size	↓	↓	10	1.600	Ea.
	3550	OS&Y, flanged					
	3600	2" size	1 Plum	1 Plumber	5	1.600	Ea.
	3640	2-1/2" size	Q-1	1 Plumber	5	3.200	Ea.
				1 Plumber Apprentice			
	3660	3" size			4.50	3.560	Ea.
	3670	3-1/2" size			3	5.330	Ea.
	3680	4" size	↓	↓	3	5.330	Ea.
	3690	5" size	Q-2	2 Plumbers	3.40	7.060	Ea.
				1 Plumber Apprentice			
	3700	6" size			3	8.000	Ea.
	3720	8" size			2.50	9.600	Ea.
	3740	10" size			2.20	10.910	Ea.
	3760	12" size	↓	↓	1.70	14.120	Ea.
	4350	Globe, OS&Y, class 125, threaded					
	4400	2" size	1 Plum	1 Plumber	11	.727	Ea.
	4440	2-1/2" size	Q-1	1 Plumber	15	1.070	Ea.
				1 Plumber Apprentice			
	4450	3" size			13	1.230	Ea.
	4460	4" size	↓	↓	10	1.600	Ea.
	4540	Class 125, flanged					
	4550	2" size	1 Plum	1 Plumber	5	1.600	Ea.
	4560	2-1/2" size	Q-1	1 Plumber	5	3.200	Ea.
				1 Plumber Apprentice			
	4570	3" size	↓	↓	4.50	3.560	Ea.
	4580	4" size			3	5.330	Ea.
	4590	5" size	Q-2	2 Plumbers	3.40	7.060	Ea.
				1 Plumber Apprentice			
	4600	6" size	↓	↓	3	8.000	Ea.
	4610	8" size			2.50	9.600	Ea.
	4850	Class 250, threaded					
	4940	2-1/2" size	Q-1	1 Plumber	13	1.230	Ea.
				1 Plumber Apprentice			
	5040	Class 250, flanged					
	5050	2" size	1 Plum	1 Plumber	4.50	1.780	Ea.
	5060	2-1/2" size	Q-1	1 Plumber	4.50	3.560	Ea.
				1 Plumber Apprentice			
	5070	3" size	↓	↓	4	4.000	Ea.
	5080	4" size			2.70	5.930	Ea.
	5090	5" size	Q-2	2 Plumbers	3	8.000	Ea.
				1 Plumber Apprentice			

		Description	CREW	MAKEUP	DAILY OUTPUT	MAN-HOURS	UNIT
151 950		**Valves**					
960	5101	Valves, iron body, globe, OS&Y, class 250, flanged, 6" size	Q-2	2 Plumbers	2.70	8.890	Ea.
				1 Plumber Apprentice			
	5110	8" size			2.20	10.910	Ea.
	5120	10" size			2	12.000	Ea.
	5130	12" size	↓	↓	1.60	15.000	Ea.
	5450	Swing check, 125 lb., threaded					
	5500	2" size	1 Plum	1 Plumber	11	.727	Ea.
	5540	2-1/2" size	Q-1	1 Plumber	15	1.070	Ea.
				1 Plumber Apprentice			
	5550	3" size			13	1.230	Ea.
	5560	4" size	↓	↓	10	1.600	Ea.
	5950	Flanged					
	6000	2" size	1 Plum	1 Plumber	5	1.600	Ea.
	6040	2-1/2" size	Q-1	1 Plumber	5	3.200	Ea.
				1 Plumber Apprentice			
	6050	3" size			4.50	3.560	Ea.
	6060	4" size	↓	↓	3	5.330	Ea.
	6070	6" size	Q-2	2 Plumbers	3	8.000	Ea.
				1 Plumber Apprentice			
	6080	8" size			2.50	9.600	Ea.
	6090	10" size			2.20	10.910	Ea.
	6100	12" size	↓	↓	1.70	14.120	Ea.
	6620	Wafer style, silent check or pump valve, 125 psi					
	6640	2" size	1 Plum	1 Plumber	9	.889	Ea.
	6650	2-1/2" size	Q-1	1 Plumber	9	1.780	Ea.
				1 Plumber Apprentice			
	6660	3" size			8	2.000	Ea.
	6670	4" size	↓	↓	5	3.200	Ea.
	6680	5" size	Q-2	2 Plumbers	6	4.000	Ea.
				1 Plumber Apprentice			
	6690	6" size			6	4.000	Ea.
	6700	8" size			4.50	5.330	Ea.
	6710	10" size			4	6.000	Ea.
	7100	Flanged, 12" size			2.50	9.600	Ea.
	7110	14" size			2.30	10.430	Ea.
	7120	16" size	↓	↓	1.75	13.710	Ea.
970		**VALVES, LINED, CORROSION RESISTANT/HIGH PURITY**					
	2000	Butterfly 150 lb. ductile iron,					
	2010	Wafer type					
	2030	FEP lined 3" lever handle	Q-1	1 Plumber	8	2.000	Ea.
				1 Plumber Apprentice			
	2050	4" lever handle	"	"	5	3.200	Ea.
	2070	6" gear operated	Q-2	2 Plumbers	4.50	5.330	Ea.
				1 Plumber Apprentice			
	2080	8" gear operated			4	6.000	Ea.
	2090	10" gear operated			3.50	6.860	Ea.
	2100	12" gear operated	↓	↓	2.50	9.600	Ea.
	3500	Check lift, 125 lb., cast iron flanged					
	3511	Horizontal or vertical PPL or SL lined					
	3530	1" size	1 Plum	1 Plumber	14	.571	Ea.
	3540	1-1/2" size			11	.727	Ea.
	3550	2" size	↓	↓	8	1.000	Ea.
	3560	2-1/2" size	Q-1	1 Plumber	5	3.200	Ea.
				1 Plumber Apprentice			
	3570	3" size			4.50	3.560	Ea.
	3590	4" size	↓	↓	3	5.330	Ea.
	3610	6" size	Q-2	2 Plumbers	3	8.000	Ea.
				1 Plumber Apprentice			

151 950 | Valves

		CREW	MAKEUP	DAILY OUTPUT	MAN-HOURS	UNIT
970	3621	Valves, cast iron, check lift, flanged, 8" size	Q-2	2 Plumbers 1 Plumber Apprentice	2.50	9.600	Ea.
	5000	Clamp type, ductile iron, 150 lb. flanged					
	5010	TFE lined					
	5030	1" size, lever handle	1 Plum	1 Plumber	9	.889	Ea.
	5050	1-1/2" size, lever handle	↓	↓	6	1.330	Ea.
	5060	2" size, lever handle			5	1.600	Ea.
	5080	3" size, lever handle	Q-1	1 Plumber 1 Plumber Apprentice	4.50	3.560	Ea.
	5100	4" size, gear operated	"	"	3	5.330	Ea.
	5120	6" size, gear operated	Q-2	2 Plumbers 1 Plumber Apprentice	3	8.000	Ea.
	5130	8" size, gear operated	"	"	2.50	9.600	Ea.
	6000	Diaphragm type, cast iron, 125 lb. flanged					
	6010	PPL or SL, lined					
	6030	1" size, handwheel operated	1 Plum	1 Plumber	9	.889	Ea.
	6050	1-1/2" size, handwheel operated	↓	↓	6	1.330	Ea.
	6060	2" size, handwheel operated			5	1.600	Ea.
	6070	2-1/2" size, handwheel operated	Q-1	1 Plumber 1 Plumber Apprentice	5	3.200	Ea.
	6080	3" size, handwheel operated	↓	↓	4.50	3.560	Ea.
	6100	4" size, handwheel operated			3	5.330	Ea.
	6120	6" size, handwheel operated	Q-2	2 Plumbers 1 Plumber Apprentice	3	8.000	Ea.
	6130	8" size, handwheel operated	"	"	2.50	9.600	Ea.
	8000	Plug, 150 lb. ductile iron flanged					
	8020	FEP lined 1" lever handle	1 Plum	1 Plumber	14	.571	Ea.
	8040	1-1/2" lever handle	↓	↓	11	.727	Ea.
	8050	2" lever handle			8	1.000	Ea.
	8070	3" lever handle	Q-1	1 Plumber 1 Plumber Apprentice	4.50	3.560	Ea.
	8090	4" lever handle	"	"	3	5.330	Ea.
	8110	6" gear operated	Q-2	2 Plumbers 1 Plumber Apprentice	3	8.000	Ea.
	8120	8" gear operated	"	"	2.50	9.600	Ea.
	975	VALVES, PLASTIC					
	1100	Angle, PVC, threaded					
	1110	1/4" size	1 Plum	1 Plumber	26	.308	Ea.
	1120	1/2" size			26	.308	Ea.
	1130	3/4" size			25	.320	Ea.
	1140	1" size	↓	↓	23	.348	Ea.
	1150	Ball, PVC, socket or threaded, single union					
	1200	1/4" size	1 Plum	1 Plumber	26	.308	Ea.
	1220	3/8" size			26	.308	Ea.
	1230	1/2" size			26	.308	Ea.
	1240	3/4" size			25	.320	Ea.
	1250	1" size			23	.348	Ea.
	1260	1-1/4" size			21	.381	Ea.
	1270	1-1/2" size			20	.400	Ea.
	1280	2" size	↓	↓	17	.471	Ea.
	1290	2-1/2" size	Q-1	1 Plumber 1 Plumber Apprentice	26	.615	Ea.
	1300	3" size	↓	↓	24	.667	Ea.
	1310	4" size			20	.800	Ea.
	1650	CPVC, socket or threaded, single union					
	1700	1/2" size	1 Plum	1 Plumber	26	.308	Ea.
	1720	3/4" size	↓	↓	25	.320	Ea.
	1730	1" size			23	.348	Ea.

151 950	Valves	CREW	MAKEUP	DAILY OUTPUT	MAN-HOURS	UNIT
975	1751	Valves, CPVC, ball, single union, 1-1/4" size	1 Plum	1 Plumber	21	.381	Ea.
	1760	1-1/2" size			20	.400	Ea.
	1770	2" size	↓	↓	17	.471	Ea.
	1780	3" size	Q-1	1 Plumber	24	.667	Ea.
				1 Plumber Apprentice			
	2050	Polypropylene, threaded					
	2100	1/4" size	1 Plum	1 Plumber	26	.308	Ea.
	2120	3/8" size			26	.308	Ea.
	2130	1/2" size			26	.308	Ea.
	2140	3/4" size			25	.320	Ea.
	2150	1" size			23	.348	Ea.
	2160	1-1/4" size			21	.381	Ea.
	2170	1-1/2" size			20	.400	Ea.
	2180	2" size	↓	↓	17	.471	Ea.
	2190	3" size	Q-1	1 Plumber	24	.667	Ea.
				1 Plumber Apprentice			
	2200	4" size	"	"	20	.800	Ea.
	2550	PVC, three way, socket or threaded					
	2600	1/2" size	1 Plum	1 Plumber	26	.308	Ea.
	2640	3/4" size			25	.320	Ea.
	2650	1" size			23	.348	Ea.
	2660	1-1/2" size			20	.400	Ea.
	2670	2" size	↓	↓	17	.471	Ea.
	2680	3" size	Q-1	1 Plumber	24	.667	Ea.
				1 Plumber Apprentice			
	3150	Ball check, PVC, socket or threaded					
	3200	1/4" size	1 Plum	1 Plumber	26	.308	Ea.
	3220	3/8" size			26	.308	Ea.
	3240	1/2" size			26	.308	Ea.
	3250	3/4" size			25	.320	Ea.
	3260	1" size			23	.348	Ea.
	3270	1-1/4" size			21	.381	Ea.
	3280	1-1/2" size			20	.400	Ea.
	3290	2" size	↓	↓	17	.471	Ea.
	3310	3" size	Q-1	1 Plumber	24	.667	Ea.
				1 Plumber Apprentice			
	3320	4" size	"	"	20	.800	Ea.
	3750	CPVC, socket or threaded					
	3800	1/2" size	1 Plum	1 Plumber	26	.308	Ea.
	3840	3/4" size			25	.320	Ea.
	3850	1" size			23	.348	Ea.
	3860	1-1/2" size			20	.400	Ea.
	3870	2" size	↓	↓	17	.471	Ea.
	3880	3" size	Q-1	1 Plumber	24	.667	Ea.
				1 Plumber Apprentice			
	3920	4" size	"	"	20	.800	Ea.
	4340	Polypropylene, threaded					
	4360	1/2" size	1 Plum	1 Plumber	26	.308	Ea.
	4400	3/4" size			25	.320	Ea.
	4440	1" size			23	.348	Ea.
	4450	1-1/2" size			20	.400	Ea.
	4460	2" size	↓	↓	17	.471	Ea.
	4851	Foot valve, PVC and CPVC, socket or threaded					
	4900	1/2" size	1 Plum	1 Plumber	34	.235	Ea.
	4930	3/4" size			32	.250	Ea.
	4940	1" size			28	.286	Ea.
	4950	1-1/4" size			27	.296	Ea.
	4960	1-1/2" size	↓	↓	26	.308	Ea.

			CREW	MAKEUP	DAILY OUTPUT	MAN-HOURS	UNIT
151 950		**Valves**					
975	4971	Valves, PVC and CPVC, foot valve, 2" size	1 Plum	1 Plumber	24	.333	Ea.
	4980	3" size			20	.400	Ea.
	4990	4" size	↓	↓	18	.444	Ea.
	5280	Needle valve, PVC, threaded					
	5300	1/4" size	1 Plum	1 Plumber	26	.308	Ea.
	5340	3/8" size			26	.308	Ea.
	5360	1/2" size	↓	↓	26	.308	Ea.
	5800	Y check, PVC, socket or threaded					
	5820	1/2" size	1 Plum	1 Plumber	26	.308	Ea.
	5840	3/4" size			25	.320	Ea.
	5850	1" size			23	.348	Ea.
	5860	1-1/4" size			21	.381	Ea.
	5870	1-1/2" size			20	.400	Ea.
	5880	2" size			17	.471	Ea.
	5890	2-1/2" size	↓	↓	15	.533	Ea.
	5900	3" size	Q-1	1 Plumber 1 Plumber Apprentice	24	.667	Ea.
	5910	4" size	"	"	20	.800	Ea.
	6350	Y sediment strainer, PVC, socket or threaded					
	6400	1/2" size	1 Plum	1 Plumber	26	.308	Ea.
	6440	3/4" size			24	.333	Ea.
	6450	1" size			23	.348	Ea.
	6460	1-1/4" size			21	.381	Ea.
	6470	1-1/2" size			20	.400	Ea.
	6480	2" size			17	.471	Ea.
	6490	2-1/2" size	↓	↓	15	.533	Ea.
	6500	3" size	Q-1	1 Plumber 1 Plumber Apprentice	24	.667	Ea.
	6510	4" size	"	"	20	.800	Ea.
	980	**VALVES, STEEL**					
	0801	Cast, angle or check valve, 150 lb., flanged					
	0830	2" size	1 Plum	1 Plumber	8	1.000	Ea.
	0840	2-1/2" size	Q-1	1 Plumber 1 Plumber Apprentice	5	3.200	Ea.
	0850	3" size			4.50	3.560	Ea.
	0860	4" size	↓	↓	3	5.330	Ea.
	0870	6" size	Q-2	2 Plumbers 1 Plumber Apprentice	3	8.000	Ea.
	0880	8" size			2.50	9.600	Ea.
	1596	10" size	↓	↓	2.10	11.430	Ea.
	1701	Diverter, 150 lb., flanged, bronze, iron, or stainless steel plugs					
	1720	1-1/2" pipe size	Q-1	1 Plumber 1 Plumber Apprentice	3	5.330	Ea.
	1730	2" pipe size			2	8.000	Ea.
	1740	3" pipe size			1.50	10.670	Ea.
	1750	4" pipe size	↓	↓	1	16.000	Ea.
	1760	6" pipe size	Q-2	2 Plumbers 1 Plumber Apprentice	1	24.000	Ea.
	1950	Gate valve, 150 lb., flanged					
	2000	2" size	1 Plum	1 Plumber	8	1.000	Ea.
	2040	2-1/2"size	Q-1	1 Plumber 1 Plumber Apprentice	5	3.200	Ea.
	2050	3" size			4.50	3.560	Ea.
	2060	4" size	↓	↓	3	5.330	Ea.
	2070	6" size	Q-2	2 Plumbers 1 Plumber Apprentice	3	8.000	Ea.
	2080	8" size			2.50	9.600	Ea.
	2090	10" size	↓	↓	2.20	10.910	Ea.

151 950 | Valves

		Description	CREW	MAKEUP	DAILY OUTPUT	MAN-HOURS	UNIT
980	2101	Valves, steel, gate , 150 lb., flanged, 12" size	Q-2	2 Plumbers	1.70	14.120	Ea.
				1 Plumber Apprentice			
	2110	14" size			1.30	18.460	Ea.
	2120	16" size			1	24.000	Ea.
	2130	18" size			.80	30.000	Ea.
	2140	20" size	↓	↓	.60	40.000	Ea.
	2650	300 lb., flanged					
	2700	2" size	1 Plum	1 Plumber	7.40	1.080	Ea.
	2740	2-1/2" size	Q-1	1 Plumber	4.20	3.810	Ea.
				1 Plumber Apprentice			
	2750	3" size			4	4.000	Ea.
	2760	4" size	↓	↓	2.80	5.710	Ea.
	2770	6" size	Q-2	2 Plumbers	2.90	8.280	Ea.
				1 Plumber Apprentice			
	2780	8" size			2.40	10.000	Ea.
	2790	10" size			2.10	11.430	Ea.
	2800	12" size			1.60	15.000	Ea.
	2810	14" size			1.20	20.000	Ea.
	2820	16" size			.90	26.670	Ea.
	2830	18" size			.70	34.290	Ea.
	2840	20" size	↓	↓	.50	48.000	Ea.
	3200	600 lb., flanged					
	3220	2" size	1 Plum	1 Plumber	7	1.140	Ea.
	3240	2-1/2" size	Q-1	1 Plumber	4	4.000	Ea.
				1 Plumber Apprentice			
	3250	3" size			3.60	4.440	Ea.
	3260	4" size	↓	↓	2.50	6.400	Ea.
	3270	6" size	Q-2	2 Plumbers	2.60	9.230	Ea.
				1 Plumber Apprentice			
	3280	8" size			2.10	11.430	Ea.
	3290	10" size			1.70	14.120	Ea.
	3300	12" size			1.20	20.000	Ea.
	3310	14" size			.80	30.000	Ea.
	3320	16" size			.60	40.000	Ea.
	3330	18" size			.50	48.000	Ea.
	3340	20" size	↓	↓	.40	60.000	Ea.
	3650	Globe valve, 150 lb., flanged					
	3700	2" size	1 Plum	1 Plumber	8	1.000	Ea.
	3740	2-1/2" size	Q-1	1 Plumber	5	3.200	Ea.
				1 Plumber Apprentice			
	3750	3" size			4.50	3.560	Ea.
	3760	4" size	↓	↓	3	5.330	Ea.
	3770	6" size	Q-2	2 Plumbers	3	8.000	Ea.
				1 Plumber Apprentice			
	3780	8" size			2.50	9.600	Ea.
	3790	10" size			2.20	10.910	Ea.
	3800	12" size			1.70	14.120	Ea.
	3810	14" size	↓	↓	1.30	18.460	Ea.
	4080	300 lb., flanged					
	4100	2" size	1 Plum	1 Plumber	7.40	1.080	Ea.
	4140	2-1/2" size	Q-1	1 Plumber	4.20	3.810	Ea.
				1 Plumber Apprentice			
	4150	3" size			4	4.000	Ea.
	4160	4" size	↓	↓	2.80	5.710	Ea.
	4170	6" size	Q-2	2 Plumbers	2.90	8.280	Ea.
				1 Plumber Apprentice			
	4180	8" size			2.40	10.000	Ea.
	4190	10" size	↓	↓	2.10	11.430	Ea.

151 950 | Valves

		CREW	MAKEUP	DAILY OUTPUT	MAN-HOURS	UNIT
980	4201	Valves, steel, globe, 300 lb., flanged, 12" size	Q-2	2 Plumbers	1.60	15.000	Ea.
				1 Plumber Apprentice			
	4680	600 lb., flanged					
	4700	2" size	1 Plum	1 Plumber	7	1.140	Ea.
	4740	2-1/2" size	Q-1	1 Plumber	4	4.000	Ea.
				1 Plumber Apprentice			
	4750	3" size			3.60	4.440	Ea.
	4760	4" size	↓	↓	2.50	6.400	Ea.
	4770	6" size	Q-2	2 Plumbers	2.60	9.230	Ea.
				1 Plumber Apprentice			
	4780	8" size	"	"	2.10	11.430	Ea.
	5150	Forged, angle, class 800, socket or threaded					
	5200	1/4" size	1 Plum	1 Plumber	24	.333	Ea.
	5220	3/8" size			24	.333	Ea.
	5230	1/2" size			24	.333	Ea.
	5240	3/4" size			20	.400	Ea.
	5250	1" size			19	.421	Ea.
	5260	1-1/4" size			15	.533	Ea.
	5270	1-1/2" size			13	.615	Ea.
	5280	2" size	↓	↓	11	.727	Ea.
	5650	Check valve, class 800, horizontal, socket or threaded					
	5700	1/4" size	1 Plum	1 Plumber	24	.333	Ea.
	5720	3/8" size			24	.333	Ea.
	5730	1/2" size			24	.333	Ea.
	5740	3/4" size			20	.400	Ea.
	5750	1" size			19	.421	Ea.
	5760	1-1/4" size			15	.533	Ea.
	5770	1-1/2" size			13	.615	Ea.
	5780	2" size	↓	↓	11	.727	Ea.
	6100	Gate, class 800, inside screw stem, socket or threaded					
	6120	3/8" size	1 Plum	1 Plumber	24	.333	Ea.
	6130	1/2" size			24	.333	Ea.
	6140	3/4" size			20	.400	Ea.
	6150	1" size			19	.421	Ea.
	6160	1-1/4" size			15	.533	Ea.
	6170	1-1/2" size			13	.615	Ea.
	6180	2" size	↓	↓	11	.727	Ea.
	6700	Globe, OS&Y, class 800, socket or threaded					
	6710	1/4" size	1 Plum	1 Plumber	24	.333	Ea.
	6720	3/8" size			24	.333	Ea.
	6730	1/2" size			24	.333	Ea.
	6740	3/4" size			20	.400	Ea.
	6750	1" size			19	.421	Ea.
	6760	1-1/4" size			15	.533	Ea.
	6770	1-1/2" size			13	.615	Ea.
	6780	2" size	↓	↓	11	.727	Ea.
985		**VALVES, STAINLESS STEEL**					
	1000	Butterfly, 175 lb., full port, threaded					
	1020	Type 316 stainless steel					
	1030	1/4" size	1 Plum	1 Plumber	24	.333	Ea.
	1040	3/8" size			24	.333	Ea.
	1050	1/2" size			22	.364	Ea.
	1060	3/4" size			20	.400	Ea.
	1070	1" size			19	.421	Ea.
	1080	1-1/4" size			15	.533	Ea.
	1090	1-1/2" size			13	.615	Ea.
	1100	2" size	↓	↓	11	.727	Ea.
	1610	Ball, threaded 1/4" size	1 Stpi	1 Steamfitter	24	.333	Ea.

151 950 | Valves

			CREW	MAKEUP	DAILY OUTPUT	MAN-HOURS	UNIT
985	1621	Valves, stainless steel, ball, threaded, 3/8" size	1 Stpi	1 Steamfitter	24	.333	Ea.
	1630	1/2" size			22	.364	Ea.
	1640	3/4" size			20	.400	Ea.
	1650	1" size			19	.421	Ea.
	1660	1-1/4 size			15	.533	Ea.
	1670	1-1/2" size			13	.615	Ea.
	1680	2" size	↓	↓	11	.727	Ea.
	1700	Check, 200 lb., threaded					
	1710	1/4" size	1 Plum	1 Plumber	24	.333	Ea.
	1720	1/2" size			22	.364	Ea.
	1730	3/4" size			20	.400	Ea.
	1750	1" size			19	.421	Ea.
	1760	1-1/2" size			13	.615	Ea.
	1770	2" size	↓	↓	11	.727	Ea.
	1800	150 lb., flanged					
	1810	2-1/2" size	Q-1	1 Plumber 1 Plumber Apprentice	5	3.200	Ea.
	1820	3" size			4.50	3.560	Ea.
	1830	4" size	↓	↓	3	5.330	Ea.
	1840	6" size	Q-2	2 Plumbers 1 Plumber Apprentice	3	8.000	Ea.
	1850	8" size	"	"	2.50	9.600	Ea.
	1900	Diverter, 150 lb. flanged, stainless steel plugs					
	1910	1-1/2" pipe size	Q-1	1 Plumber 1 Plumber Apprentice	3	5.330	Ea.
	1920	2" pipe size			2	8.000	Ea.
	1940	3" pipe size			1.50	10.670	Ea.
	1950	4" pipe size	↓	↓	1	16.000	Ea.
	2100	Gate, OS&Y, 150 lb., flanged					
	2120	1/2" size	1 Plum	1 Plumber	18	.444	Ea.
	2140	3/4" size			16	.500	Ea.
	2150	1" size			14	.571	Ea.
	2160	1-1/2" size			11	.727	Ea.
	2170	2" size	↓	↓	8	1.000	Ea.
	2180	2-1/2" size	Q-1	1 Plumber 1 Plumber Apprentice	5	3.200	Ea.
	2190	3" size			4.50	3.560	Ea.
	2200	4" size	↓	↓	3	5.330	Ea.
	2210	6" size	Q-2	2 Plumbers 1 Plumber Apprentice	3	8.000	Ea.
	2220	8" size	"	"	2.50	9.600	Ea.
	2600	600 lb., flanged					
	2620	1/2" size	1 Plum	1 Plumber	16	.500	Ea.
	2640	3/4" size			14	.571	Ea.
	2650	1" size			12	.667	Ea.
	2660	1-1/2" size			10	.800	Ea.
	2670	2" size	↓	↓	7	1.140	Ea.
	2680	2-1/2" size	Q-1	1 Plumber 1 Plumber Apprentice	4	4.000	Ea.
	2690	3" size			3.60	4.440	Ea.
	2700	4" size	↓	↓	2.50	6.400	Ea.
	2710	6" size	Q-2	2 Plumbers 1 Plumber Apprentice	2.60	9.230	Ea.
	2720	8" size			2.10	11.430	Ea.
	2730	10" size			1.70	14.120	Ea.
	2740	12" size	↓	↓	1.20	20.000	Ea.
	3100	Globe, OS&Y, 150 lb., flanged					
	3120	1/2" size	1 Plum	1 Plumber	18	.444	Ea.

151 | Pipe and Fittings

151 950 | Valves

		CREW	MAKEUP	DAILY OUTPUT	MAN-HOURS	UNIT
985 3141	Valves, stainless steel, globe, OS&Y, 150 lb., 3/4" size	1 Plum	1 Plumber	16	.500	Ea.
3150	1" size			14	.571	Ea.
3160	1-1/2" size			11	.727	Ea.
3170	2" size	↓	↓	8	1.000	Ea.
3180	2-1/2" size	Q-1	1 Plumber	5	3.200	Ea.
			1 Plumber Apprentice			
3190	3" size			4.50	3.560	Ea.
3200	4" size	↓	↓	3	5.330	Ea.
3210	6" size	Q-2	2 Plumbers	3	8.000	Ea.
			1 Plumber Apprentice			
990	VALVES, SEMI-STEEL					
1020	Lubricated plug valve, threaded					
1030	1/2" pipe size	1 Plum	1 Plumber	18	.444	Ea.
1040	3/4" pipe size			16	.500	Ea.
1050	1" pipe size			14	.571	Ea.
1060	1-1/4" pipe size			12	.667	Ea.
1070	1-1/2" pipe size			11	.727	Ea.
1080	2" pipe size	↓	↓	8	1.000	Ea.
1090	2-1/2" pipe size	Q-1	1 Plumber	5	3.200	Ea.
			1 Plumber Apprentice			
1100	3" pipe size	"	"	4.50	3.560	Ea.
6990	Flanged					
7000	2" pipe size	1 Plum	1 Plumber	8	1.000	Ea.
7010	2-1/2" pipe size	Q-1	1 Plumber	5	3.200	Ea.
			1 Plumber Apprentice			
7020	3" pipe size			4.50	3.560	Ea.
7030	4" pipe size	↓	↓	3	5.330	Ea.
7040	6" pipe size	Q-2	2 Plumbers	3	8.000	Ea.
			1 Plumber Apprentice			
7050	8" pipe size			2.50	9.600	Ea.
7060	10" pipe size			2.20	10.910	Ea.
7070	12" pipe size	↓	↓	1.70	14.120	Ea.

152 | Plumbing Fixtures

152 100 | Fixtures

		CREW	MAKEUP	DAILY OUTPUT	MAN-HOURS	UNIT
104	BATHS					
0100	Tubs, recessed porcelain enamel on cast iron, with trim					
0140	42" x 37"	Q-1	1 Plumber	5	3.200	Ea.
			1 Plumber Apprentice			
0180	48" x 42"			4	4.000	Ea.
0220	72" x 36"			3	5.330	Ea.
0300	Mat bottom, 4' long			5.50	2.910	Ea.
0340	4'-6" long			5	3.200	Ea.
0380	5' long			4.40	3.640	Ea.
0420	5'-6" long			4	4.000	Ea.
0480	Above floor drain, 5' long			4	4.000	Ea.
0560	Corner 48" x 44"			4.40	3.640	Ea.
2000	Enameled formed steel, 4'-6" long			5.80	2.760	Ea.
2200	5' long			5.50	2.910	Ea.
2300	Above floor drain, 5' long			5.50	2.910	Ea.
4000	Soaking, acrylic with pop-up drain, 40" x 40"	↓	↓	5.50	2.910	Ea.

152 100 | Fixtures

		CREW	MAKEUP	DAILY OUTPUT	MAN-HOURS	UNIT
104	4101	Baths, tubs, soaking, acrylic, 66" x 36" x 18-1/2" deep	Q-1	1 Plumber / 1 Plumber Apprentice	5	3.200	Ea.
	4200	72" x 44" x 18" deep	↓	↓	4.80	3.330	Ea.
	4300	72" x 60" x 20" deep			4.40	3.640	Ea.
	4600	Module tub & showerwall surround, molded fiberglass					
	4610	5' long x 34" wide x 76" high	Q-1	1 Plumber / 1 Plumber Apprentice	4	4.000	Ea.
	4750	Handicap with 1-1/2" OD grab bar, antiskid bottom					
	4760	60" x 32-3/4" x 72" high	Q-1	1 Plumber / 1 Plumber Apprentice	4	4.000	Ea.
	4770	75" x 40" x 76" high with molded seat	"	"	3.50	4.570	Ea.
	5000	Hospital type without trim (see 151-141)					
	5050	Bathing pool, porcelain enamel on cast iron, grab bars					
	5060	pop-up drain, 72" x 36"	Q-1	1 Plumber / 1 Plumber Apprentice	3	5.330	Ea.
	5100	Perineal (sitz), vitreous china			3	5.330	Ea.
	5120	Pedestal, vitreous china			8	2.000	Ea.
	5180	Pier tub, porcelain enamel on cast iron, 66-3/4" x 30"			3	5.330	Ea.
	5200	Base, porcelain enamel on cast iron			8	2.000	Ea.
	5300	Whirlpool, porcelain enamel on cast iron, 72" x 36"	↓	↓	1	16.000	Ea.
	6000	Whirlpool, bath with vented overflow, molded fiberglass					
	6100	56" x 46" x 23"	Q-1	1 Plumber / 1 Plumber Apprentice	1	16.000	Ea.
	6400	72" x 36" x 18"			1	16.000	Ea.
	6500	60" x 40-1/2" x 30"			1	16.000	Ea.
	6600	72" x 56" x 23"			1	16.000	Ea.
	6700	7' x 5-1/2'	↓	↓	.30	53.330	Ea.
	7000	Redwood tub system					
	7050	4' diameter x 4' deep	Q-1	1 Plumber / 1 Plumber Apprentice	1	16.000	Ea.
	7100	5' diameter x 4' deep			1	16.000	Ea.
	7150	6' diameter x 4' deep			.80	20.000	Ea.
	7200	8' diameter x 4' deep			.80	20.000	Ea.
	9600	Rough-in, supply, waste and vent, for all above tubs, add	↓	↓	1.73	9.250	Ea.
	108	**BIDET**					
	0180	Vitreous china, with trim on fixture	Q-1	1 Plumber / 1 Plumber Apprentice	5	3.200	Ea.
	0200	With trim for wall mounting			5	3.200	Ea.
	9600	For rough-in, supply, waste and vent, add	↓	↓	1.78	8.990	Ea.
	112	**DENTAL FOUNTAIN**					
	0020	Deck mounted, with cuspidor					
	0050	Stainless steel receptor	1 Plum	1 Plumber	4	2.000	Ea.
	0100	Enameled steel receptor			4	2.000	Ea.
	9600	For rough-in, supply and waste, add	↓	↓	1.16	6.900	Ea.
	116	**DRINKING FOUNTAIN** For connection to cold water supply					
	1000	Wall mounted, non-recessed					
	1200	Aluminum,					
	1280	bubbler type	1 Plum	1 Plumber	3.20	2.500	Ea.
	1400	Bronze, with no back			4	2.000	Ea.
	1600	Cast iron, enameled, low back, single bubbler			4	2.000	Ea.
	1640	Dual bubbler type			3.20	2.500	Ea.
	1680	Triple bubbler type			3.20	2.500	Ea.
	1800	Cast aluminum, enameled, for correctional institutions			4	2.000	Ea.
	2000	Fiberglass, 12" back, single bubbler unit			4	2.000	Ea.
	2040	Dual bubbler			3.20	2.500	Ea.
	2080	Triple bubbler			3.20	2.500	Ea.
	2200	Polymarble, no back, single bubbler			4	2.000	Ea.
	2240	Dual bubbler	↓	↓	3.20	2.500	Ea.

152 100 | Fixtures

			CREW	MAKEUP	DAILY OUTPUT	MAN-HOURS	UNIT
116	2281	Drinking fountain, wall mtd., polymarble, triple bubbler	1 Plum	1 Plumber	3.20	2.500	Ea.
	2400	Precast stone, no back			4	2.000	Ea.
	2700	Stainless steel, single bubbler, no back			4	2.000	Ea.
	2740	With back			4	2.000	Ea.
	2780	Dual handle & wheelchair projection type			4	2.000	Ea.
	2820	Dual level for handicapped type			3.20	2.500	Ea.
	2840	Vandal resistant type	↓	↓	4	2.000	Ea.
	3300	Vitreous china					
	3340	7" back	1 Plum	1 Plumber	4	2.000	Ea.
	3960	For freeze-proof valve system, add			2	4.000	Ea.
	3980	For rough-in, supply and waste, add	↓	↓	1.83	4.370	Ea.
	4000	Wall mounted, semi-recessed					
	4200	Poly-marble, single bubbler	1 Plum	1 Plumber	4	2.000	Ea.
	4300	Fountain and cuspidor combination			2	4.000	Ea.
	4600	Stainless steel, satin finish, single bubbler			4	2.000	Ea.
	4900	Vitreous china, single bubbler			4	2.000	Ea.
	5000	Fountain and cuspidor combination			2	4.000	Ea.
	5980	For rough-in, supply and waste, add	↓	↓	1.83	4.370	Ea.
	6000	Wall mounted, fully recessed					
	6400	Poly-marble, single bubbler	1 Plum	1 Plumber	4	2.000	Ea.
	6800	Stainless steel, single bubbler			4	2.000	Ea.
	6900	Fountain and cuspidor combination			2	4.000	Ea.
	7560	For freeze-proof valve system, add			2	4.000	Ea.
	7580	For rough-in, supply and waste, add	↓	↓	1.83	4.370	Ea.
	7600	Floor mounted, pedestal type					
	7700	Aluminum, architectural style, C.I. base	1 Plum	1 Plumber	2	4.000	Ea.
	7780	Wheelchair handicap unit			2	4.000	Ea.
	8000	Bronze, architectural style			2	4.000	Ea.
	8040	Enameled steel cylindrical column style			2	4.000	Ea.
	8200	Precast stone/concrete, cylindrical column			1	8.000	Ea.
	8240	Wheelchair handicap unit			1	8.000	Ea.
	8400	Stainless steel, architectural style			2	4.000	Ea.
	8600	Enameled iron, heavy duty service, 2 bubblers			2	4.000	Ea.
	8660	4 bubblers			2	4.000	Ea.
	8880	For freeze-proof valve system, add			2	4.000	Ea.
	8900	For rough-in, supply and waste, add	↓	↓	1.83	4.370	Ea.
	9100	Deck mounted					
	9500	Stainless steel, circular receptor	1 Plum	1 Plumber	4	2.000	Ea.
	9540	14" x 9" receptor			4	2.000	Ea.
	9580	25" x 17" deep receptor, with water glass filler			3	2.670	Ea.
	9760	White enameled steel, 14" x 9" receptor			4	2.000	Ea.
	9860	White enameled cast iron, 24" x 16" receptor			3	2.670	Ea.
	9980	For rough-in, supply and waste, add	↓	↓	1.83	4.370	Ea.
120		**HOT WATER DISPENSERS**					
	0160	Commercial, 100 cup, 11.3 amp	1 Plum	1 Plumber	14	.571	Ea.
	3180	Household, 60 cup	"	"	14	.571	Ea.
124		**INDUSTRIAL SAFETY FIXTURES** Rough-in not included					
	1000	Eye wash fountain					
	1400	Plastic bowl, pedestal mounted	Q-1	1 Plumber 1 Plumber Apprentice	4	4.000	Ea.
	1600	Unmounted			4	4.000	Ea.
	1800	Wall mounted			4	4.000	Ea.
	2000	Stainless steel, pedestal mounted			4	4.000	Ea.
	2200	Unmounted			4	4.000	Ea.
	2400	Wall mounted	↓	↓	4	4.000	Ea.
	4000	Eye and face wash, combination fountain					
	4200	Stainless steel, pedestal mounted	Q-1	1 Plumber 1 Plumber Apprentice	4	4.000	Ea.

			CREW	MAKEUP	DAILY OUTPUT	MAN-HOURS	UNIT
	152 100	**Fixtures**					
124	4401	Safety fixture, eye and face wash, stainless steel, unmounted	Q-1	1 Plumber	4	4.000	Ea.
				1 Plumber Apprentice			
	4600	Wall mounted			4	4.000	Ea.
	5000	Shower, single head, drench, ball valve, pull, freestanding			4	4.000	Ea.
	5200	Horizontal or vertical supply			4	4.000	Ea.
	6000	Multi-nozzle, eye/face wash combination			4	4.000	Ea.
	6400	Multi-nozzle, 12 spray, shower only			4	4.000	Ea.
	6600	For freeze-proof, add			6	2.670	Ea.
	8000	Walk-thru decontamination with eye-face wash			2	8.000	Ea.
	8200	For freeze proof, add	↓	↓	4	4.000	Ea.
	128	**INTERCEPTORS**					
	0150	Grease, cast iron, 4 GPM, 8 lb. fat capacity	1 Plum	1 Plumber	4	2.000	Ea.
	0200	7 GPM, 14 lb. fat capacity			4	2.000	Ea.
	1000	10 GPM, 20 lb. fat capacity			4	2.000	Ea.
	1040	15 GPM, 30 lb. fat capacity			4	2.000	Ea.
	1060	20 GPM, 40 lb. fat capacity	↓	↓	3	2.670	Ea.
	1080	25 GPM, 50 lb. fat capacity	Q-1	1 Plumber	3.50	4.570	Ea.
				1 Plumber Apprentice			
	1100	35 GPM, 70 lb. fat capacity			3	5.330	Ea.
	1120	Fabricated steel, 50 GPM, 100 lb. fat capacity			2	8.000	Ea.
	1140	75 GPM, 150 lb. fat capacity			2	8.000	Ea.
	1160	100 GPM, 200 lb. fat capacity			2	8.000	Ea.
	1180	150 GPM, 300 lb. fat capacity			2	8.000	Ea.
	1200	200 GPM, 400 lb. fat capacity			1.50	10.670	Ea.
	1220	250 GPM, 500 lb. fat capacity			1.30	12.310	Ea.
	1240	300 GPM, 600 lb. fat capacity	↓	↓	1	16.000	Ea.
	1260	400 GPM, 800 lb. fat capacity	Q-2	2 Plumbers	1.20	20.000	Ea.
				1 Plumber Apprentice			
	1280	500 GPM, 1000 lb. fat capacity	"	"	1	24.000	Ea.
	3000	Hair, cast iron, 1-1/4" and 1-1/2" pipe connection	1 Plum	1 Plumber	8	1.000	Ea.
	4000	Oil, fabricated steel, 10 GPM, 2" pipe size			4	2.000	Ea.
	4100	15 GPM, 2" or 3" pipe size			4	2.000	Ea.
	4120	20 GPM, 2" or 3" pipe size	↓	↓	3	2.670	Ea.
	4140	25 GPM, 2" or 3" pipe size	Q-1	1 Plumber	3.50	4.570	Ea.
				1 Plumber Apprentice			
	4160	35 GPM, 2", 3", or 4" pipe size			3	5.330	Ea.
	4180	50 GPM, 2", 3", or 4" pipe size			2	8.000	Ea.
	4200	75 GPM, 3" pipe size			2	8.000	Ea.
	4220	100 GPM, 3" pipe size			2	8.000	Ea.
	4240	150 GPM, 4" pipe size			2	8.000	Ea.
	4260	200 GPM, 4" pipe size			1.50	10.670	Ea.
	4280	250 GPM, 5" pipe size			1.30	12.310	Ea.
	4300	300 GPM, 5" pipe size	↓	↓	1	16.000	Ea.
	4320	400 GPM, 6" pipe size	Q-2	2 Plumbers	1.20	20.000	Ea.
				1 Plumber Apprentice			
	4340	500 GPM, 6" pipe size	"	"	1	24.000	Ea.
	6000	Solids, precious metals recovery, C.I., 1-1/4" to 2" pipe	1 Plum	1 Plumber	4	2.000	Ea.
	6100	Dental Lab., large, C.I., 1-1/2" to 2" pipe	"	"	3	2.670	Ea.
	132	**LABORATORY EQUIPMENT,** Corrosion resistant					
	7000	Tanks, covers included					
	7400	Halar E-CTFE, FRP casing, high chemical resistance					
	7410	Temperature range 110°F to 275°F					
	7420	7 gallon, 12" x 12" x 12"	Q-1	1 Plumber	20	.800	Ea.
				1 Plumber Apprentice			
	7430	15 gallon, 18" x 12" x 18"			17	.941	Ea.
	7440	30 gallon, 24" x 18" x 18"	↓	↓	12	1.330	Ea.

152 | Plumbing Fixtures

152 100 | Fixtures

		CREW	MAKEUP	DAILY OUTPUT	MAN-HOURS	UNIT
132 7501	Tanks, polyethylene, neutralization & dilution					
7510	Continuous use to 180°F, includes 4" inlet & outlet					
7550	55 gallon, upright cylinder	Q-1	1 Plumber	5	3.200	Ea.
			1 Plumber Apprentice			
7570	100 gallon, upright cylinder	↓	↓	4	4.000	Ea.
7590	250 gallon, upright cylinder	↓	↓	3	5.330	Ea.
7650	Polyethylene with ultra violet light inhibitor					
7660	Continuous use to 180°F, includes saddle & fittings					
7680	55 gallon 24" O.D. x 36" long	Q-1	1 Plumber	10	1.600	Ea.
			1 Plumber Apprentice			
7700	200 gallon 33" O.D. x 65" long			6	2.670	Ea.
7720	300 gallon 38" O.D. x 72" long			5	3.200	Ea.
7740	500 gallon 48" O.D. x 75" long	↓	↓	3	5.330	Ea.
7800	Polyethylene liner, fiberglass casing					
7810	Continuous service to 220°F					
7830	2 gallon, 8" x 8" x 8"	Q-1	1 Plumber	20	.800	Ea.
			1 Plumber Apprentice			
7850	7 gallon, 12" x 12" x 12"			20	.800	Ea.
7870	15 gallon, 24" x 12" x 12"			17	.941	Ea.
8010	30 gallon, 24" x 18" x 18"			12	1.330	Ea.
8070	45 gallon, 24" x 18" x 24"			10	1.600	Ea.
8080	90 gallon, 36" x 24" x 24"	↓	↓	8	2.000	Ea.
8150	Polyethylene, heavy duty walls					
8160	Continuous service to 180°F					
8180	5 gallon, 11" I.D. x 15" deep	Q-1	1 Plumber	20	.800	Ea.
			1 Plumber Apprentice			
8210	15 gallon, 14" I.D. x 27" deep			17	.941	Ea.
8230	55 gallon, 22" I.D. x 36" deep			10	1.600	Ea.
8250	100 gallon 28" I.D. x 42" deep			8	2.000	Ea.
8270	200 gallon 36" I.D. x 48" deep	↓	↓	6	2.670	Ea.
8350	With fiberglass casing					
8420	55 gallon tank size	Q-1	1 Plumber	20	.800	Ea.
			1 Plumber Apprentice			
8440	100 gallon tank size	↓	↓	16	1.000	Ea.
8460	200 gallon tank size	↓	↓	12	1.330	Ea.
136	**LAVATORIES** With trim, white unless noted otherwise					
0500	Vanity top, porcelain enamel on cast iron					
0600	20" x 18"	Q-1	1 Plumber	6.40	2.500	Ea.
			1 Plumber Apprentice			
0640	26" x 18" oval			6.40	2.500	Ea.
0680	19" x 16" oval			6.40	2.500	Ea.
0720	18" round			6.40	2.500	Ea.
0760	20" x 12" triangular bowl			6.40	2.500	Ea.
1000	Cultured marble, 19" x 17", single bowl			6.40	2.500	Ea.
1040	25" x 19", single bowl			6.40	2.500	Ea.
1080	31" x 19", single bowl			6.40	2.500	Ea.
1120	25" x 22", single bowl			6.40	2.500	Ea.
1160	37" x 22", single bowl			6.40	2.500	Ea.
1200	49" x 22", single bowl			6.40	2.500	Ea.
1240	61" x 22", single bowl			6.20	2.580	Ea.
1280	61" x 22", double bowl			4.80	3.330	Ea.
1320	73" x 22", double bowl			4.80	3.330	Ea.
1900	Stainless steel, self-rimming, 25" x 22", single bowl, ledge			6.40	2.500	Ea.
1960	17" x 22", single bowl			6.40	2.500	Ea.
2040	18-3/4" round			6.40	2.500	Ea.
2600	Steel, enameled, 20" x 17", single bowl			5.80	2.760	Ea.
2660	19" round			5.80	2.760	Ea.
2720	18" round	↓	↓	5.80	2.760	Ea.

		CREW	MAKEUP	DAILY OUTPUT	MAN-HOURS	UNIT
152 100	**Fixtures**					
136 2901	Lavatories, vanity top, vitreous china, 20" x 16", single bowl	Q-1	1 Plumber 1 Plumber Apprentice	5.40	2.960	Ea.
2960	20" x 17", single bowl			5.40	2.960	Ea.
3020	19" round, single bowl			5.40	2.960	Ea.
3080	19" x 16", single bowl			5.40	2.960	Ea.
3140	17" x 14", single bowl			5.40	2.960	Ea.
3200	22" x 13", single bowl			5.40	2.960	Ea.
3580	Rough-in, supply, waste and vent for all above lavatories	↓	↓	1.96	8.160	Ea.
4000	Wall hung					
4040	Porcelain enamel on cast iron, 16" x 14", single bowl	Q-1	1 Plumber 1 Plumber Apprentice	8	2.000	Ea.
4060	18" x 15" single bowl			8	2.000	Fa.
4120	19" x 17", single bowl			8	2.000	Ea.
4180	20" x 18", single bowl			8	2.000	Ea.
4240	22" x 19", single bowl			8	2.000	Ea.
6000	Vitreous china, 18" x 15", single bowl with backsplash			7	2.290	Ea.
6060	19" x 17", single bowl			7	2.290	Ea.
6120	24" x 20", single bowl			7	2.290	Ea.
6180	19" x 19", corner style			8	2.000	Ea.
6210	28" x 21", wheelchair type	↓	↓	7	2.290	Ea.
6700	Hospital type, without trim (see 151-141)					
6710	20" x 18", contoured splash shield	Q-1	1 Plumber 1 Plumber Apprentice	8	2.000	Ea.
6720	26" x 20", patient,corner,side deck & back			7	2.290	Ea.
6730	28" x 20", surgeon, side decks			8	2.000	Ea.
6740	28" x 22", surgeon scrub-up, deep bowl			8	2.000	Ea.
6750	20" x 27", patient, wheelchair			7	2.290	Ea.
6760	30" x 22", all purpose			7	2.290	Ea.
6770	30" x 22", plaster work			7	2.290	Ea.
6820	20" x 24" clinic service, liquid/solid waste			6	2.670	Ea.
6960	Rough-in, supply, waste and vent for above lavatories	↓	↓	1.66	9.640	Ea.
140	**LAUNDRY SINKS** With trim					
0020	Porcelain enamel on cast iron, black iron frame					
0050	24" x 20", single compartment	Q-1	1 Plumber 1 Plumber Apprentice	6	2.670	Ea.
0100	24" x 23", single compartment			6	2.670	Ea.
0200	48" x 20", double compartment	↓	↓	5	3.200	Ea.
2000	Molded stone, on wall hanger or legs					
2020	22" x 21", single compartment	Q-1	1 Plumber 1 Plumber Apprentice	6	2.670	Ea.
2100	45" x 21", double compartment	"	"	5	3.200	Ea.
3000	Plastic, on wall hanger or legs					
3020	18" x 23", single compartment	Q-1	1 Plumber 1 Plumber Apprentice	6.50	2.460	Ea.
3100	20" x 24", single compartment			6.50	2.460	Ea.
3200	36" x 23", double compartment			5.50	2.910	Ea.
3300	40" x 24", double compartment			5.50	2.910	Ea.
5000	Stainless steel, counter top, 22" x 17" single compartment			6	2.670	Ea.
5100	19" x 22", single compartment			6	2.670	Ea.
5200	33" x 22", double compartment			5	3.200	Ea.
9600	Rough-in, supply, waste and vent, for all laundry sinks	↓	↓	1.84	8.700	Ea.
144	**PRISON/INSTITUTION FIXTURES,** Stainless steel					
1000	Lavatory, wall hung, push button filler valve					
1100	Rectangular bowl	Q-1	1 Plumber 1 Plumber Apprentice	8	2.000	Ea.
1200	Oval bowl			8	2.000	Ea.
1240	Oval bowl, corner mount			8	2.000	Ea.
1300	For lavatory rough-in, supply, waste and vent	↓	↓	1.50	10.670	Ea.

152 100 | Fixtures

		CREW	MAKEUP	DAILY OUTPUT	MAN-HOURS	UNIT
144 **1700**	Service sink, with soap dish					
1740	24" x 19" size	Q-1	1 Plumber 1 Plumber Apprentice	3	5.330	Ea.
1790	For sink rough-in, supply, waste and vent	"	"	.89	17.980	Ea.
1800	Shower cabinet, unitized					
1840	36" x 36" x 88"	Q-1	1 Plumber 1 Plumber Apprentice	2.20	7.270	Ea.
1900	Shower package for built-in					
1940	Hot & cold valves, recessed soap dish	Q-1	1 Plumber 1 Plumber Apprentice	6	2.670	Ea.
2000	Urinal, back supply and flush					
2200	Wall hung	Q-1	1 Plumber 1 Plumber Apprentice	4	4.000	Ea.
2240	Stall	↓	↓	2.50	6.400	Ea.
2300	For urinal rough-in, supply, waste and vent			1.49	10.740	Ea.
3000	Water closet, integral seat, back supply and flush					
3300	Wall hung, wall outlet	Q-1	1 Plumber 1 Plumber Apprentice	5.80	2.760	Ea.
3400	Floor mount, wall outlet			5.80	2.760	Ea.
3440	Floor mount, floor outlet			5.80	2.760	Ea.
3500	For water closet rough-in, supply, waste and vent	↓	↓	1.19	13.450	Ea.
5000	Water closet and lavatory units, push button filler valves,					
5010	soap & paper holders, seat					
5300	Wall hung	Q-1	1 Plumber 1 Plumber Apprentice	5	3.200	Ea.
5400	Floor mount			5	3.200	Ea.
6300	For unit rough-in, supply, waste and vent	↓	↓	1	16.000	Ea.
148 **SHOWERS**						
1500	Stall, with door and trim					
1510	Baked enamel, molded stone receptor, 30" square	Q-1	1 Plumber 1 Plumber Apprentice	2	8.000	Ea.
1520	32" square			2	8.000	Ea.
1540	Terrazzo receptor, 32" square			2	8.000	Ea.
1560	36" square			1.80	8.890	Ea.
1580	36" corner angle			1.80	8.890	Ea.
3000	Fiberglass, one piece, with 3 walls, 32" x 32" square			2.40	6.670	Ea.
3100	36" x 36" square	↓	↓	2.40	6.670	Ea.
3200	Handicap, 1-1/2" O.D. grab bars, nonskid floor					
3210	48" x 34-1/2" x 72" corner seat	Q-1	1 Plumber 1 Plumber Apprentice	2.40	6.670	Ea.
3220	60" x 34-1/2" x 72" corner seat			2	8.000	Ea.
3230	36" x 34-1/2" x 72" fold up seat			2.20	7.270	Ea.
3250	64" x 65-3/4" x 81-1/2" fold. seat, whlchr.			1.80	8.890	Ea.
4000	Polypropylene, with molded-stone floor, 30" x 30"			2	8.000	Ea.
4100	32" x 32"			2	8.000	Ea.
4960	Rough-in, supply, waste and vent for above showers	↓	↓	1.71	9.360	Ea.
5000	Built-in, head, arm, 4 GPM	1 Plum	1 Plumber	4	2.000	Ea.
5200	Head, arm, by-pass, integral stops, handles			3.60	2.220	Ea.
5500	Head, water economizer, 3.0 GPM			24	.333	Ea.
5800	Mixing valve, Built-in			6	1.330	Ea.
5900	Exposed	↓	↓	6	1.330	Ea.
5950	Module, handicap, SS panel, fixed & hand held head, control					
5960	valves, grab bar, curtain & rod, folding seat	1 Plum	1 Plumber	4	2.000	Ea.
6000	Group, w/valve, rough-in and rigging not included					
6800	Column, 6 heads, no receptors, less partitions	Q-1	1 Plumber 1 Plumber Apprentice	3	5.330	Ea.
6900	With enameled partitions	↓	↓	1	16.000	Ea.
7600	5 heads, no receptors, less partitions			3	5.330	Ea.

152 100	Fixtures	CREW	MAKEUP	DAILY OUTPUT	MAN-HOURS	UNIT
148 7621	Showers, group, 4 heads (1 handicap), no recept., less partitions	Q-1	1 Plumber 1 Plumber Apprentice	3	5.330	Ea.
7700	With enameled partitions			1	16.000	Ea.
8000	Corner, 2 heads, no receptors, less partitions			4	4.000	Ea.
8100	With partitions	↓	↓	2	8.000	Ea.
152	**SINKS** With faucets and drain					
0050	Corrosion resistant					
1000	Polyethylene, single sink, bench mounted, with					
1020	plug & waste fitting with 1-1/2" straight threads					
1030	2 drainboards, backnut & strainer					
1050	18-1/2 " x 15-1/2" x 12-1/2" sink, 54" x 24" O.D.	Q-1	1 Plumber 1 Plumber Apprentice	3	5.330	Ea.
1100	Single drainboard, backnut & strainer					
1130	18-1/2" x 15-1/2" x 12-1/2" sink, 47" x 24" O.D.	Q-1	1 Plumber 1 Plumber Apprentice	3	5.330	Ea.
1150	18-1/2" x 15-1/2" x 12-1/2" sink, 70" x 24" O.D.	"	"	3	5.330	Ea.
1290	Flanged 1-1/4" wide, rectangular with strainer					
1300	plug & waste fitting, 1-1/2" straight threads					
1320	12" x 12" x 8" sink, 14-1/2" x 14-1/2" O.D.	Q-1	1 Plumber 1 Plumber Apprentice	4	4.000	Ea.
1340	16" x 16" x 8" sink, 18-1/2" x 18-1/2" O.D.			4	4.000	Ea.
1360	21" x 18" x 10" sink, 23-1/2" x 20-1/2" O.D.			4	4.000	Ea.
1490	For rough-in, supply, waste & vent, add	↓	↓	1.69	9.470	Ea.
1600	Polypropylene					
1620	Cup sink, oval, integral strainers					
1640	6" x 3" I.D., 7" x 4" O.D.	Q-1	1 Plumber 1 Plumber Apprentice	6	2.670	Ea.
1660	9" x 3" I.D., 10" x 4-1/2" O.D.			6	2.670	Ea.
1980	For rough-in, supply, waste & vent, add			1.70	9.410	Ea.
2000	Kitchen, counter top, P.E. on C.I., 24" x 21" single bowl			3.20	5.000	Ea.
2100	30" x 21" single bowl			3.20	5.000	Ea.
2200	32" x 21" double bowl			2.60	6.150	Ea.
2300	42" x 21" double bowl			2.60	6.150	Ea.
3000	Stainless steel, self rimming, 19" x 18" single bowl			3.20	5.000	Ea.
3100	25" x 22" single bowl			3.20	5.000	Ea.
3200	33" x 22" double bowl			2.60	6.150	Ea.
3300	43" x 22" double bowl			2.60	6.150	Ea.
3400	44" x 22" triple bowl			2.20	7.270	Ea.
3500	44" x 24" corner double bowl			2.60	6.150	Ea.
4000	Steel, enameled, with ledge, 24" x 21" single bowl			3.20	5.000	Ea.
4100	32" x 21" double bowl			2.60	6.150	Ea.
4980	For rough-in, supply, waste and vent, counter top sinks	↓	↓	1.85	8.650	Ea.
5000	Kitchen, raised deck, P.E. on C.I.					
5100	32" x 21", dual level, double bowl	Q-1	1 Plumber 1 Plumber Apprentice	1.60	10.000	Ea.
5200	42" x 21", double bowl & disposer well			1.20	13.330	Ea.
5790	For rough-in, supply, waste & vent, sinks			1.85	8.650	Ea.
6650	Service, floor, corner, P.E. on C.I., 28" x 28"			4	4.000	Ea.
6790	For rough-in, supply, waste & vent, floor service sinks			1.30	12.310	Ea.
7000	Service, wall, P.E. on C.I., roll rim, 22" x 18"			3	5.330	Ea.
7100	24" x 20"			3	5.330	Ea.
8600	Vitreous china, 22" x 20"			3	5.330	Ea.
8980	For rough-in, supply, waste & vent, wall service sinks	↓	↓	1.30	12.310	Ea.

152 100	Fixtures	CREW	MAKEUP	DAILY OUTPUT	MAN-HOURS	UNIT
160	**160** **SINK WASTE TREATMENT** System for commercial kitchens					
	0100 includes clock timer, & fittings					
	0200 System less chemical, wall mounted cabinet	1 Plum	1 Plumber	16	.500	Ea.
	164 **TOILET SEATS**					
	0100 Molded composition, white					
	0150 Industrial, w/o cover, open front, regular bowl	1 Plum	1 Plumber	24	.333	Ea.
	0200 With self-sustaining hinge			24	.333	Ea.
	0220 With self-sustaining check hinge			24	.333	Ea.
	0240 Extra heavy, with check hinge	↓	↓	24	.333	Ea.
	0400 Residential					
	0420 Regular bowl, w/cover, closed front	1 Plum	1 Plumber	24	.333	Ea.
	0440 Open front	"	"	24	.333	Ea.
	168 **URINALS**					
	3000 Wall hung, vitreous china, with hanger & self-closing valve	Q-1	1 Plumber 1 Plumber Apprentice	3	5.330	Ea.
	3300 Rough-in, supply, waste & vent			1.99	8.040	Ea.
	5000 Stall type, vitreous china, includes valve			2.50	6.400	Ea.
	5100 3" seam cover, add			12	1.330	Ea.
	5200 6" seam cover, add			12	1.330	Ea.
	6980 Rough-in, supply, waste and vent	↓	↓	1.99	8.040	Ea.
	172 **WASH CENTER** Prefabricated,stainless steel, semirecessed					
	0050 Lavatory, storage cabinet, mirror, light & switch, electric					
	0060 outlet, towel dispenser, waste receptacle & trim					
	0100 Foot water valve, cup & soap dispenser,16" W x 54-3/4" H	Q-1	1 Plumber 1 Plumber Apprentice	8	2.000	Ea.
	0200 Handicap, wrist blade handles, 17" W x 66-1/2" H			8	2.000	Ea.
	0220 20" W x 67-3/8" H	↓	↓	8	2.000	Ea.
	0300 Push button metering & thermostatic mixing valves					
	0320 Handicap 17" W x 27-1/2" H	Q-1	1 Plumber 1 Plumber Apprentice	8	2.000	Ea.
	0400 Rough-in, supply, waste and vent	"	"	2.10	7.620	Ea.
	176 **WASH FOUNTAINS** Rigging not included					
	1900 Group, foot control					
	2000 Precast terrazzo, circular, 36" diam., 5 or 6 persons	Q-2	2 Plumbers 1 Plumber Apprentice	3	8.000	Ea.
	2100 54" diameter for 8 or 10 persons			2.50	9.600	Ea.
	2400 Semi-circular, 36" diam. for 3 persons			3	8.000	Ea.
	2420 36" diam. for 3 persons in wheelchairs			3	8.000	Ea.
	2500 54" diam. for 4 or 5 persons			2.50	9.600	Ea.
	2520 54" diam. for 4 persons in wheelchairs			2.50	9.600	Ea.
	2700 Quarter circle (corner), 54" for 3 persons			3.50	6.860	Ea.
	2720 54" diam. for 3 persons in wheelchairs			3.50	6.860	Ea.
	3000 Stainless steel, circular, 36" diameter			3.50	6.860	Ea.
	3100 54" diameter			2.80	8.570	Ea.
	3400 Semi-circular, 36" diameter			3.50	6.860	Ea.
	3500 54" diameter			2.80	8.570	Ea.
	5000 Thermoplastic, circular, 36" diameter			3.50	6.860	Ea.
	5100 54" diameter			2.80	8.570	Ea.
	5400 Semi-circular, 36" diameter			3.50	6.860	Ea.
	5600 54" diameter	↓	↓	2.80	8.570	Ea.
	5700 Rough-in, supply, waste and vent for above wash fountains	Q-1	1 Plumber 1 Plumber Apprentice	1.38	11.590	Ea.
	6200 Duo for small washrooms, stainless steel			2	8.000	Ea.
	6400 Bowl with backsplash			2	8.000	Ea.
	6500 Rough-in, supply, waste & vent for duo fountains	↓	↓	2.02	7.920	Ea.

152 100 | Fixtures	CREW	MAKEUP	DAILY OUTPUT	MAN-HOURS	UNIT
180 WATER CLOSETS					
0150 Tank type, vitreous china, incl. seat, supply pipe w/stop					
0200 wall hung, one piece	Q-1	1 Plumber / 1 Plumber Apprentice	5.30	3.020	Ea.
0400 Two piece, close coupled			5.30	3.020	Ea.
0960 For rough-in, supply, waste, vent and carrier			2.24	7.140	Ea.
1000 Floor mounted, one piece			5.30	3.020	Ea.
1020 One piece, low profile			5.30	3.020	Ea.
1050 One piece combination			5.30	3.020	Ea.
1100 Two piece, close coupled, water saver			5.30	3.020	Ea.
1150 With wall outlet			5.30	3.020	Ea.
1200 With 18" high bowl			5.30	3.020	Ea.
1980 For rough-in, supply, waste and vent	↓	↓	1.94	8.250	Ea.
3000 Bowl only, with flush valve, seat					
3100 Wall hung	Q-1	1 Plumber / 1 Plumber Apprentice	5.80	2.760	Ea.
3150 Hospital type, slotted rim for bed pan					
3160 Elongated bowl	Q-1	1 Plumber / 1 Plumber Apprentice	5.80	2.760	Ea.
3200 For rough-in, supply, waste and vent, single WC			2.05	7.800	Ea.
3300 Floor mounted			5.80	2.760	Ea.
3350 With wall outlet	↓	↓	5.80	2.760	Ea.
3360 Hospital type, slotted rim for bed pan					
3370 Elongated bowl	Q-1	1 Plumber / 1 Plumber Apprentice	5	3.200	Ea.
3380 Elongated bowl, 18" high			5	3.200	Ea.
3400 For rough-in, supply, waste and vent, single WC	↓	↓	1.80	8.890	Ea.
3500 Gang side by side carrier system, rough-in, supply, waste & vent					
3510 For single hook-up	Q-1	1 Plumber / 1 Plumber Apprentice	1.54	10.390	Ea.
3520 For each additional hook-up, add	"	"	1.65	9.700	Ea.
3550 Gang back to back carrier system, rough-in, supply, waste & vent					
3560 For pair hook-up	Q-1	1 Plumber / 1 Plumber Apprentice	1.35	11.850	Pr.
3570 For each additional pair hook-up, add	"	"	1.40	11.430	Pr.
4000 Water conserving systems					
4100 2-1/2 gallon flush	Q-1	1 Plumber / 1 Plumber Apprentice	5.40	2.960	Ea.
4900 1 gallon flush			5.40	2.960	Ea.
4980 For rough-in, supply, waste and vent			1.94	8.250	Ea.
5100 2 quart flush			4.60	3.480	Ea.
5200 For remote valve, add			24	.667	Ea.
5300 For residential air compressor			6	2.670	Ea.
5400 For light industrial air compressor			4	4.000	Ea.
5500 For heavy duty industrial air compressor			1	16.000	Ea.
5600 For dual compressor alternator	↓	↓	20	.800	Ea.
184 WATER FILTERS Purification and treatment					
1000 Cartridge style, under sink, dirt and rust type	1 Plum	1 Plumber	12	.667	Ea.
1200 Replacement cartridge			32	.250	Ea.
1600 Taste and odor type			12	.667	Ea.
1700 Replacement cartridge			32	.250	Ea.
3000 Household unit, complete dwelling, 3 GPM			4	2.000	Ea.
3100 Replacement cartridge			20	.400	Ea.
3400 4 GPM			4	2.000	Ea.
3600 Replacement cartridge	↓	↓	20	.400	Ea.
4300 Oxidizing, removes iron, sulphur, manganese					
4400 5 GPM	1 Plum	1 Plumber	1	8.000	Ea.
4401					

180

152 100 | Fixtures

		CREW	MAKEUP	DAILY OUTPUT	MAN-HOURS	UNIT
184 5401	Water filters, neutralizing acid water, 5 GPM	1 Plum	1 Plumber	1	8.000	Ea.
6200	Sediment, removal of suspended particles					
6400	5 GPM	1 Plum	1 Plumber	1	8.000	Ea.
7200	Carbon filter, to remove taste & odor					
7400	5 GPM	1 Plum	1 Plumber	1	8.000	Ea.
8000	Commercial, fully automatic or push button automatic					
8200	Iron removal, 660 GPH, 1" pipe size	Q-1	1 Plumber / 1 Plumber Apprentice	1.50	10.670	Ea.
8240	1500 GPH, 1-1/4" pipe size			1	16.000	Ea.
8280	2340 GPH, 1-1/2" pipe size			.80	20.000	Ea.
8320	3420 GPH, 2" pipe size			.60	26.670	Ea.
8360	4620 GPH, 2-1/2" pipe size			.50	32.000	Ea.
8500	Neutralizer for acid water, 780 GPH, 1" pipe size			1.50	10.670	Ea.
8540	1140 GPH, 1" pipe size			1	16.000	Ea.
8580	1740 GPH, 1-1/4" pipe size			.80	20.000	Ea.
8620	2520 GPH, 2" pipe size			.60	26.670	Ea.
8660	3480 GPH, 2-1/2" pipe size			.50	32.000	Ea.
8800	Sediment removal, 780 GPH, 1" pipe size			1.50	10.670	Ea.
8840	1140 GPH, 1-1/4" pipe size			1	16.000	Ea.
8880	1740 GPH, 1-1/2" pipe size			.80	20.000	Ea.
8920	2520 GPH, 2" pipe size			.60	26.670	Ea.
8960	3480 GPH, 2-1/2" pipe size			.50	32.000	Ea.
9200	Taste and odor removal, 660 GPH, 1" pipe size			1.50	10.670	Ea.
9240	1500 GPH, 1-1/4" pipe size			1	16.000	Ea.
9280	2340 GPH, 1-1/2" pipe size			.80	20.000	Ea.
9320	3420 GPH, 2" pipe size			.60	26.670	Ea.
9360	4620 GPH, 2-1/2" pipe size	↓	↓	.50	32.000	Ea.

152 400 | Pumps

		CREW	MAKEUP	DAILY OUTPUT	MAN-HOURS	UNIT
410	**PUMPS, CIRCULATING** Heated or chilled water application					
0600	Bronze, sweat connections, 1/40 HP, in line					
0640	3/4" size	Q-1	1 Plumber / 1 Plumber Apprentice	16	1.000	Ea.
1000	Flange connection, 3/4" to 1-1/2" size					
1040	1/12 HP	Q-1	1 Plumber / 1 Plumber Apprentice	6	2.670	Ea.
1060	1/8 HP			6	2.670	Ea.
1100	1/3 HP			6	2.670	Ea.
1140	2" size, 1/6 HP			5	3.200	Ea.
1180	2-1/2" size, 1/4 HP			5	3.200	Ea.
1220	3" size, 1/4 HP			4	4.000	Ea.
1260	1/3 HP			4	4.000	Ea.
1300	1/2 HP			4	4.000	Ea.
1340	3/4 HP			4	4.000	Ea.
1380	1 HP	↓	↓	4	4.000	Ea.
2000	Cast iron, flange connection					
2040	3/4" to 1-1/2" size, in line, 1/12 HP	Q-1	1 Plumber / 1 Plumber Apprentice	6	2.670	Ea.
2060	1/8 HP			6	2.670	Ea.
2100	1/3 HP			6	2.670	Ea.
2140	2" size, 1/6 HP			5	3.200	Ea.
2180	2-1/2" size, 1/4 HP			5	3.200	Ea.
2220	3" size, 1/4 HP			4	4.000	Ea.
2260	1/3 HP			4	4.000	Ea.
2300	1/2 HP			4	4.000	Ea.
2340	3/4 HP			4	4.000	Ea.
2380	1 HP	↓	↓	4	4.000	Ea.
2381						

152 400 | Pumps

			CREW	MAKEUP	DAILY OUTPUT	MAN-HOURS	UNIT
410	3031	Pumps, circ., C.I., high head, bronze impeller, 1-1/2", 1/2 HP	Q-1	1 Plumber	5	3.200	Ea.
				1 Plumber Apprentice			
	3040	1-1/2" size 3/4 HP			5	3.200	Ea.
	3050	2" size 1 HP			4	4.000	Ea.
	3090	2" size 1-1/2 HP	↓	↓	4	4.000	Ea.
	4000	Close coupled, end suction, bronze impeller					
	4040	1-1/2" size, 1-1/2 HP, to 40 GPM	Q-1	1 Plumber	3	5.330	Ea.
				1 Plumber Apprentice			
	4090	2" size, 2 HP, to 50 GPM			3	5.330	Ea.
	4100	2" size, 3 HP, to 90 GPM			2.30	6.960	Ea.
	4190	2-1/2" size, 3 HP, to 150 GPM			2	8.000	Ea.
	4300	3" size, 5 HP, to 225 GPM			1.80	8.890	Ea.
	4410	4" size, 5 HP, to 350 GPM			1.60	10.000	Ea.
	4420	4" size, 7-1/2 HP, to 350 GPM	↓	↓	1.60	10.000	Ea.
	4520	5" size, 10 HP, to 600 GPM	Q-2	2 Plumbers	1.70	14.120	Ea.
				1 Plumber Apprentice			
	4530	5" size, 15 HP, to 1000 GPM			1.70	14.120	Ea.
	4610	6" size, 20 HP, to 1350 GPM			1.50	16.000	Ea.
	4620	6" size, 25 HP, to 1550 GPM	↓	↓	1.50	16.000	Ea.
	5000	Base mounted, bronze impeller, coupling guard					
	5040	1-1/2" size, 1-1/2 HP, to 40 GPM	Q-1	1 Plumber	2.30	6.960	Ea.
				1 Plumber Apprentice			
	5090	2" size, 2 HP, to 50 GPM			2.30	6.960	Ea.
	5100	2" size, 3 HP, to 90 GPM			2	8.000	Ea.
	5190	2-1/2" size, 3 HP, to 150 GPM			1.80	8.890	Ea.
	5300	3" size, 5 HP, to 225 GPM			1.60	10.000	Ea.
	5410	4" size, 5 HP, to 350 GPM			1.50	10.670	Ea.
	5420	4" size, 7-1/2 HP, to 350 GPM	↓	↓	1.50	10.670	Ea.
	5520	5" size, 10 HP, to 600 GPM	Q-2	2 Plumbers	1.60	15.000	Ea.
				1 Plumber Apprentice			
	5530	5" size, 15 HP, to 1000 GPM			1.60	15.000	Ea.
	5610	6" size, 20 HP, to 1350 GPM			1.40	17.140	Ea.
	5620	6" size, 25 HP, to 1550 GPM	↓	↓	1.40	17.140	Ea.
415		**PUMPS, CONDENSATE RETURN SYSTEM**					
	0200	Simplex, motor, float switch, controls, cast iron receiver	Q-1	1 Plumber	1	16.000	Ea.
				1 Plumber Apprentice			
	1000	Duplex, 2 pumps, motors, float switch,					
	1060	alternator asssembly, C.I. receiver	Q-1	1 Plumber	.50	32.000	Ea.
				1 Plumber Apprentice			
420		**PUMP FOOT VALVES** With strainer					
	0200	4" size	Q-2	2 Plumbers	2	12.000	Ea.
				1 Plumber Apprentice			
	0300	8" size	"	"	1.30	18.460	Ea.
	0400	12" size	Q-3	1 Plumber Foreman (ins)	1	32.000	Ea.
				2 Plumbers			
				1 Plumber Apprentice			
	0500	16" size	"	"	.60	53.330	Ea.
430		**PUMPS, GENERAL UTILITY** With motor, mounted on base					
	0200	Multi-stage, horizontal split, for boiler feed applications					
	0300	Two stage, 3" discharge x 4" suction, 75 HP	Q-7	1 Steamfitter Foreman (ins)	.30	107.000	Ea.
				2 Steamfitters			
				1 Steamfitter Apprentice			
	0340	Four stage, 3" discharge x 4" suction, 150 HP	"	"	.18	178.000	Ea.
	2000	Single stage					
	2060	End suction, 1"D. x 2"S., 3 HP	Q-1	1 Plumber	.50	32.000	Ea.
				1 Plumber Apprentice			
	2100	1-1/2"D. x 3"S., 10 HP	"	"	.40	40.000	Ea.

152 400 | Pumps

			CREW	MAKEUP	DAILY OUTPUT	MAN-HOURS	UNIT
430	2141	Pumps, gen. utility, sngl stg, end suction, 2"D. x 3" S., 15 HP	Q-2	2 Plumbers	.60	40.000	Ea.
				1 Plumber Apprentice			
	2180	3"D. x 4"S., 20 HP	↓	↓	.50	48.000	Ea.
	2220	4"D. x 6"S., 30 HP			.40	60.000	Ea.
	3000	Double suction, 2"D. x 2-1/2"S., 10 HP	Q-1	1 Plumber	.30	53.330	Ea.
				1 Plumber Apprentice			
	3060	3"D. x 4"S., 15 HP	Q-2	2 Plumbers	.46	52.170	Ea.
				1 Plumber Apprentice			
	3100	4"D. x 5"S., 30 HP	↓	↓	.40	60.000	Ea.
	3140	5"D. x 6"S., 50 HP			.33	72.730	Ea.
	3180	6"D. x 8"S., 60 HP	Q-3	1 Plumber Foreman (ins)	.30	107.000	Ea.
				2 Plumbers			
				1 Plumber Apprentice			
	8000	Vertical submerged, with non-submerged motor					
	8060	1"D., 3 HP	Q-1	1 Plumber	.50	32.000	Ea.
				1 Plumber Apprentice			
	8100	1-1/2"D., 10 HP	"	"	.30	53.330	Ea.
	8140	2"D., 15 HP	Q-2	2 Plumbers	.40	60.000	Ea.
				1 Plumber Apprentice			
	8180	3"D., 25 HP	↓	↓	.30	80.000	Ea.
	8220	4"D., 30 HP			.20	120.000	Ea.
	450	PUMPS, PRESSURE BOOSTER SYSTEM Constant speed					
	0200	2 pump system with hydrocumulator					
	0300	100 GPM	Q-2	2 Plumbers	.30	80.000	Ea.
				1 Plumber Apprentice			
	0400	300 GPM	"	"	.26	92.310	Ea.
	1000	3 pump system without hydrocumulator					
	1100	300 GPM	Q-2	2 Plumbers	.23	104.000	Ea.
				1 Plumber Apprentice			
	1200	1000 GPM	↓	↓	.12	200.000	Ea.
	1300	5000 GPM			.08	300.000	Ea.
	460	PUMPS, PEDESTAL SUMP With float control					
	0400	Molded base, 42 GPM	1 Plum	1 Plumber	5	1.600	Ea.
	0800	Iron base, 42 GPM	"	"	5	1.600	Ea.
	465	PUMPS, SEWAGE EJECTOR With operating and level controls					
	0100	Simplex, bitumastic coated steel tank, cover, 10' head, 230 volt					
	0600	Bronze pump					
	0640	70 GPM, 1/3 HP	Q-1	1 Plumber	3	5.330	Ea.
				1 Plumber Apprentice			
	0680	143 GPM, 1/2 HP	"	"	2.50	6.400	Ea.
	1040	Cast iron pump					
	1060	110 GPM, 1/2 HP	Q-1	1 Plumber	2.50	6.400	Ea.
				1 Plumber Apprentice			
	1080	173 GPM, 3/4 HP			2	8.000	Ea.
	1100	218 GPM, 1 HP			1.60	10.000	Ea.
	1120	285 GPM, 2 HP	↓	↓	1.30	12.310	Ea.
	1140	325 GPM, 3 HP	Q-2	2 Plumbers	1.40	17.140	Ea.
				1 Plumber Apprentice			
	1160	370 GPM, 5 HP	"	"	1	24.000	Ea.
	2000	Duplex, bitumastic coated steel tank, cover, 10' head, 230 volt					
	2640	Bronze pump					
	2660	70 GPM each pump, 1/3 HP	Q-1	1 Plumber	2.50	6.400	Ea.
				1 Plumber Apprentice			
	2700	143 GPM each pump, 1/2 HP	"	"	2	8.000	Ea.
	3040	Cast iron pump					
	3060	110 GPM each pump, 1/2 HP	Q-1	1 Plumber	2	8.000	Ea.
				1 Plumber Apprentice			
	3080	173 GPM each pump, 3/4 HP	"	"	1.60	10.000	Ea.

152 400 | Pumps

		CREW	MAKEUP	DAILY OUTPUT	MAN-HOURS	UNIT
465 3101	Pumps, sewage ejector, duplex, C.I., 218 GPM ea. pump, 1 HP	Q-2	2 Plumbers	1.20	20.000	Ea.
			1 Plumber Apprentice			
3120	285 GPM each pump, 2 HP			1	24.000	Ea.
3140	325 GPM each pump, 3 HP			.80	30.000	Ea.
3160	370 GPM each pump, 5 HP	↓	↓	.50	48.000	Ea.
470	**PUMPS, SPRINKLER** With check valve, steel base, 15' lift					
0100	37 GPM, 3/4 HP	1 Plum	1 Plumber	4	2.000	Ea.
0140	56 GPM, 1-1/2 HP	"	"	2	4.000	Ea.
0180	68 GPM, 2 H.P.	Q-1	1 Plumber	2	8.000	Ea.
			1 Plumber Apprentice			
480	**PUMPS, SUBMERSIBLE** Dewatering					
0020	Sand & sludge, 20' head, starter & level control					
0050	Cast iron					
0100	2" discharge, 10 GPM	1 Plum	1 Plumber	4	2.000	Ea.
0160	60 GPM			3	2.670	Ea.
0200	120 GPM	↓	↓	2	4.000	Ea.
1000	160 GPM	Q-1	1 Plumber	1.50	10.670	Ea.
			1 Plumber Apprentice			
1100	3" discharge, 220 GPM			1.20	13.330	Ea.
1200	300 GPM			1	16.000	Ea.
1360	4" discharge, 300 GPM	↓	↓	.90	17.780	Ea.
2000	Sewage & solids mixture, 8' head, automatic					
2020	Bronze, 1/2 HP					
2100	75 GPM, 1-1/4" or 1-1/2" NPT discharge	1 Plum	1 Plumber	8	1.000	Ea.
2140	120 GPM, 2" or 3" discharge	"	"	7	1.140	Ea.
2250	Cast iron					
2300	122 GPM, 1/2 HP, 2" or 3" discharge	1 Plum	1 Plumber	6	1.330	Ea.
3000	Sewage & Solids mixture, high capacity, 20' head, non-automatic					
3100	Cast iron, 3" flanged discharge					
3140	40 GPM, 3/4 HP	1 Plum	1 Plumber	4	2.000	Ea.
3160	100 GPM, 1 HP	"	"	3	2.670	Ea.
3180	175 GPM, 2 HP	Q-1	1 Plumber	4.50	3.560	Ea.
			1 Plumber Apprentice			
3200	240 GPM, 3 HP			4	4.000	Ea.
3220	310 GPM, 5 HP	↓	↓	3	5.330	Ea.
4000	Cast iron, 4" flanged discharge					
4100	10 GPM, 3/4 HP	1 Plum	1 Plumber	4	2.000	Ea.
4120	40 GPM, 1 HP	"	"	3	2.670	Ea.
4140	175 GPM, 2 HP	Q-1	1 Plumber	4.50	3.560	Ea.
			1 Plumber Apprentice			
4160	275 GPM, 3 HP			4	4.000	Ea.
4180	450 GPM, 5 HP	↓	↓	3	5.330	Ea.
5000	Sewage and solids, high head					
5100	Bronze, 45 GPM at 25', 1/2 HP	1 Plum	1 Plumber	6	1.330	Ea.
5140	28 GPM at 50', 1 HP			5	1.600	Ea.
5160	25 GPM at 75', 1-1/2 HP			4	2.000	Ea.
5180	18 GPM at 100', 1-1/2 HP			4	2.000	Ea.
5500	Cast iron, 45 GPM at 25', 1/2 HP			6	1.330	Ea.
5540	28 GPM at 50', 1 HP			5	1.600	Ea.
5560	25 GPM at 75', 1-1/2 HP	↓	↓	4	2.000	Ea.
7000	Sump pump, 10' head, automatic					
7100	Bronze, 22 GPM., 1/4 HP, 1-1/4" discharge	1 Plum	1 Plumber	6	1.330	Ea.
7140	68 GPM, 1/2 HP, 1-1/4" or 1-1/2" discharge			5	1.600	Ea.
7160	94 GPM, 1/2 HP, 1-1/4" or 1-1/2" discharge			5	1.600	Ea.
7180	105 GPM, 1/2 HP, 2" or 3" discharge			4	2.000	Ea.
7500	Cast iron, 23 GPM, 1/4 HP, 1-1/4" discharge			6	1.330	Ea.
7540	35 GPM, 1/3 HP, 1-1/4" discharge			6	1.330	Ea.
7560	68 GPM, 1/2 HP, 1-1/4" or 1-1/2" discharge	↓	↓	5	1.600	Ea.

152 | Plumbing Fixtures

152 400	Pumps	CREW	MAKEUP	DAILY OUTPUT	MAN-HOURS	UNIT
490 0100	**PUMPS, WELL** Water system, with pressure control					
1000	Deep well, multi-stage jet, 42 gal. tank					
1040	110' lift, 40 lb. discharge, 5 GPM, 3/4 HP	1 Plum	1 Plumber	.80	10.000	Ea.
2000	Shallow well, reciprocating, 25 gal. tank					
2040	25' lift, 5 GPM, 1/3 HP	1 Plum	1 Plumber	2	4.000	Ea.
3000	Shallow well, single stage jet, 42 gal. tank,					
3040	15' lift, 40 lb. discharge, 16 GPM, 3/4 HP	1 Plum	1 Plumber	2	4.000	Ea.

153 | Plumbing Appliances

153 100	Water Appliances	CREW	MAKEUP	DAILY OUTPUT	MAN-HOURS	UNIT
101	**WATER CHILLERS REMOTE** , 80°F inlet					
0100	Aircooled, 50°F outlet, 115V, 4.1 GPH	1 Plum	1 Plumber	6	1.330	Ea.
0200	5.7 GPH			5.50	1.450	Ea.
0300	8.0 GPH			5	1.600	Ea.
0400	10.3 GPH			4.50	1.780	Ea.
0500	13.4 GPH			4	2.000	Ea.
0600	19.5 GPH	↓	↓	3.60	2.220	Ea.
0700	29 GPH	Q-1	1 Plumber 1 Plumber Apprentice	5	3.200	Ea.
1000	230V, 32 GPH	"	"	5	3.200	Ea.
1200	For remote grill, add	1 Plum	1 Plumber	16	.500	Ea.
105	**WATER COOLER**					
0100	Wall mounted, non-recessed					
0140	4 GPH	Q-1	1 Plumber 1 Plumber Apprentice	4	4.000	Ea.
0180	8.2 GPH			4	4.000	Ea.
0220	14.3 GPH			4	4.000	Ea.
0260	16.1 GPH			4	4.000	Ea.
1000	Dual height, 8.2 GPH			3.80	4.210	Ea.
1040	14.3 GPH			3.80	4.210	Ea.
1080	16.1 GPH			3.80	4.210	Ea.
2600	Wheelchair type, 8 GPH			4	4.000	Ea.
3000	Simulated recessed, 8 GPH			4	4.000	Ea.
3040	11.5 GPH			4	4.000	Ea.
3300	Semi-recessed, 8.1 GPH			4	4.000	Ea.
3320	12 GPH			4	4.000	Ea.
3400	Full recessed, stainless steel, 8 GPH			3.50	4.570	Ea.
3420	11.5 GPH	↓	↓	3.50	4.570	Ea.
4600	Floor mounted, flush-to-wall					
4640	4 GPH	1 Plum	1 Plumber	3	2.670	Ea.
4680	8.2 GPH			3	2.670	Ea.
4720	14.3 GPH			3	2.670	Ea.
5000	Dual height, 8.2 GPH			2	4.000	Ea.
5040	14.3 GPH			2	4.000	Ea.
5080	19.5 GPH			2	4.000	Ea.
5600	Explosion Proof, 16 GPH			3	2.670	Ea.
6000	Refrigerator Compartment Type, 4.5 GPH			3	2.670	Ea.
6040	As above but hot and cold			3	2.670	Ea.
6100	Bottle Supply, cold only, 1.0 GPH			4	2.000	Ea.
6200	Hot and cold, 1.0 GPH	↓	↓	4	2.000	Ea.

		153 100	Water Appliances	CREW	MAKEUP	DAILY OUTPUT	MAN-HOURS	UNIT
105	6601	Water cooler, bottle supply type, 1.0 GPH		1 Plum	1 Plumber	4	2.000	Ea.
	6640	Hot and cold, 1.0 GPH		"	"	4	2.000	Ea.
	7700	Cafeteria type, dual glass fillers, 27 GPH		Q-1	1 Plumber	2.50	6.400	Ea.
					1 Plumber Apprentice			
	9800	For supply, waste & vent, all coolers		1 Plum	1 Plumber	1.24	6.450	Ea.
	110	**WATER HEATERS**						
	1000	Residential, electric, glass lined tank, 10 gal., single element		1 Plum	1 Plumber	2.30	3.480	Ea.
	1040	20 gallon, single element				2.20	3.640	Ea.
	1060	30 gallon, double element				2.20	3.640	Ea.
	1080	40 gallon, double element				2	4.000	Ea.
	1100	52 gallon, double element				2	4.000	Ea.
	1120	66 gallon, double element				1.80	4.440	Ea.
	1140	80 gallon, double element				1.60	5.000	Ea.
	1180	120 gallon, double element				1.40	5.710	Ea.
	2000	Gas fired, glass lined tank, vent not incl., 20 gallon				2.10	3.810	Ea.
	2040	30 gallon				2	4.000	Ea.
	2060	40 gallon				1.90	4.210	Ea.
	2080	50 gallon				1.80	4.440	Ea.
	2100	75 gallon				1.50	5.330	Ea.
	2120	100 gallon				1.30	6.150	Ea.
	3000	Oil fired, glass lined tank, vent not included, 30 gallon				2	4.000	Ea.
	3040	50 gallon				1.80	4.440	Ea.
	3060	70 gallon				1.50	5.330	Ea.
	3080	85 gallon		▼	▼	1.40	5.710	Ea.
	4000	Commercial, 100° rise. NOTE: for each size tank, a range of						
	4010	heaters between the ones shown are available						
	4020	Electric						
	4100	5 gal., 3 KW, 12 GPH		1 Plum	1 Plumber	2	4.000	Ea.
	4120	10 gal., 6 KW, 25 GPH				2	4.000	Ea.
	4140	50 gal., 9 KW, 37 GPH				1.80	4.440	Ea.
	4160	50 gal., 36 KW, 148 GPH				1.80	4.440	Ea.
	4180	80 gal., 12 KW, 49 GPH				1.50	5.330	Ea.
	4200	80 gal., 36 KW, 148 GPH				1.50	5.330	Ea.
	4220	100 gal., 36 KW, 148 GPH				1.20	6.670	Ea.
	4240	120 gal., 36 KW, 148 GPH				1.20	6.670	Ea.
	4260	150 gal., 15 KW , 61 GPH				1	8.000	Ea.
	4280	150 gal., 120 KW, 490 GPH		▼	▼	1	8.000	Ea.
	4300	200 gal., 15 KW, 61 GPH		Q-1	1 Plumber	1.70	9.410	Ea.
					1 Plumber Apprentice			
	4320	200 gal., 120 KW , 490 GPH				1.70	9.410	Ea.
	4340	250 gal., 15 KW, 61 GPH				1.50	10.670	Ea.
	4360	250 gal., 150 KW, 615 GPH				1.50	10.670	Ea.
	4380	300 gal., 30 KW, 123 GPH				1.30	12.310	Ea.
	4400	300 gal., 180 KW, 738 GPH				1.30	12.310	Ea.
	4420	350 gal., 30 KW, 123 GPH				1.10	14.550	Ea.
	4440	350 gal, 180 KW, 738 GPH				1.10	14.550	Ea.
	4460	400 gal., 30 KW, 123 GPH				1	16.000	Ea.
	4480	400 gal., 210 KW, 860 GPH				1	16.000	Ea.
	4500	500 gal., 30 KW, 123 GPH				.80	20.000	Ea.
	4520	500 gal., 240 KW, 984 GPH		▼	▼	.80	20.000	Ea.
	4540	600 gal., 30 KW, 123 GPH		Q-2	2 Plumbers	1.20	20.000	Ea.
					1 Plumber Apprentice			
	4560	600 gal., 300 KW, 1230 GPH				1.20	20.000	Ea.
	4580	700 gal., 30 KW, 123 GPH				1	24.000	Ea.
	4600	700 gal., 300 KW, 1230 GPH				1	24.000	Ea.
	4620	800 gal., 60 KW, 245 GPH				.90	26.670	Ea.
	4640	800 gal., 300 KW, 1230 GPH				.90	26.670	Ea.
	4660	1000 gal., 60 KW,		▼	▼	.70	34.290	Ea.

153 | Plumbing Appliances

153 100 | Water Appliances

		CREW	MAKEUP	DAILY OUTPUT	MAN-HOURS	UNIT
110 4681	Water heater, commercial, elec., 1000 gal., 480 KW, 1970 GPH	Q-2	2 Plumbers 1 Plumber Apprentice	.70	34.290	Ea.
4700	1250 gal., 60 KW, 245 GPH			.60	40.000	Ea.
4720	1250 gal., 480 KW, 1970 GPH			.60	40.000	Ea.
4740	1500 gal., 60 KW, 245 GPH			.50	48.000	Ea.
4760	1500 gal., 480 KW, 1970 GPH			.50	48.000	Ea.
4780	2000 gal., 60 KW, 245 GPH			.30	80.000	Ea.
4800	2000 gal., 480 KW, 1970 GPH	↓	↓	.30	80.000	Ea.
5400	Modulating step control, 2-5 steps	1 Elec	1 Electrician	5.30	1.510	Ea.
5440	6-10 steps			3.20	2.500	Ea.
5460	11-15 steps			2.70	2.960	Ea.
5480	16-20 steps			1.60	5.000	Ea.
5500	21-25 steps			.30	26.670	Ea.
5520	26-30 steps	↓	↓	.26	30.770	Ea.
6000	Gas fired, flush jacket, std. controls, vent not incl.					
6040	75 MBH input, 63 GPH	1 Plum	1 Plumber	1.40	5.710	Ea.
6060	96 MBH input, 81 GPH			1.40	5.710	Ea.
6080	120 MBH input, 101 GPH			1.20	6.670	Ea.
6100	115 MBH input, 110 GPH			1.10	7.270	Ea.
6120	135 MBH input, 130 GPH			1	8.000	Ea.
6140	155 MBH input, 150 GPH			.80	10.000	Ea.
6160	175 MBH input, 168 GPH			.70	11.430	Ea.
6180	200 MBH input, 192 GPH			.60	13.330	Ea.
6200	240 MBH input, 230 GPH	↓	↓	.50	16.000	Ea.
6220	295 MBH input, 278 GPH	Q-1	1 Plumber 1 Plumber Apprentice	.80	20.000	Ea.
6240	365 MBH input, 374 GPH			.80	20.000	Ea.
6260	500 MBH input, 480 GPH			.70	22.860	Ea.
6280	600 MBH input, 576 GPH			.60	26.670	Ea.
6300	800 MBH input, 768 GPH			.50	32.000	Ea.
6320	1000 MBH input, 960 GPH			.50	32.000	Ea.
6340	1200 MBH input, 1150 GPH	↓	↓	.40	40.000	Ea.
6360	1500 MBH input, 1440 GPH	Q-2	2 Plumbers 1 Plumber Apprentice	.60	40.000	Ea.
6380	1800 MBH input, 1730 GPH			.50	48.000	Ea.
6400	2450 MBH input, 2350 GPH			.40	60.000	Ea.
6420	3000 MBH input, 2880 GPH			.30	80.000	Ea.
6440	3750 MBH input, 3600 GPH	↓	↓	.30	80.000	Ea.
6900	For low water cutoff, add	1 Plum	1 Plumber	8	1.000	Ea.
6960	For bronze body hot water circulator, add	"	"	4	2.000	Ea.
8000	Oil fired, flush jacket, std. controls, vent not incl.					
8060	103 MBH gross output, 116 GPH	1 Plum	1 Plumber	1.10	7.270	Ea.
8080	122 MBH gross output, 141 GPH			1	8.000	Ea.
8100	137 MBH			.80	10.000	Ea.
8120	168 MBH gross output, 192 GPH			.60	13.330	Ea.
8140	195 MBH gross output, 224 GPH	↓	↓	.50	16.000	Ea.
8160	225 MBH gross output, 256 GPH	Q-1	1 Plumber 1 Plumber Apprentice	.80	20.000	Ea.
8180	262 MBH gross output, 315 GPH			.70	22.860	Ea.
8200	315 MBH gross output, 409 GPH			.70	22.860	Ea.
8220	420 MBH gross output, 504 GPH			.60	26.670	Ea.
8240	525 MBH gross output, 630 GPH			.50	32.000	Ea.
8260	630 MBH gross output, 756 GPH			.50	32.000	Ea.
8280	735 MBH gross output, 880 GPH			.40	40.000	Ea.
8300	840 MBH gross output, 1000 GPH	↓	↓	.40	40.000	Ea.
8320	1050 MBH gross output, 1260 GPH	Q-2	2 Plumbers 1 Plumber Apprentice	.60	40.000	Ea.
8340	1365 MBH gross output, 1640 GPH	"	"	.50	48.000	Ea.

153 | Plumbing Appliances

153 100 | Water Appliances

		Description	CREW	MAKEUP	DAILY OUTPUT	MAN-HOURS	UNIT
110	8361	Water heater, comm., oil fired, 1680 MBH gross output, 2000 GPH	Q-2	2 Plumbers 1 Plumber Apprentice	.40	60.000	Ea.
	8380	2310 MBH gross output, 2780 GPH			.30	80.000	Ea.
	8400	2835 MBH gross output, 3400 GPH			.30	80.000	Ea.
	8420	3150 MBH gross output, 3780 GPH	↓	↓	.20	120.000	Ea.
	8900	For low water cutoff, add	1 Plum	1 Plumber	8	1.000	Ea.
	8960	For bronze body hot water circulator, add	"	"	4	2.000	Ea.
120		**WATER HEATER PACKAGED SYSTEMS**					
	1000	Car wash package, continuous duty, high recovery, gas fired					
	1040	100° rise, 180 MBH input, 174 GPH	1 Plum	1 Plumber	3	2.670	Ea.
	1060	280 MBH input, 270 GPH			2.50	3.200	Ea.
	1080	400 MBH input, 386 GPH			2.50	3.200	Ea.
	1100	480 MBH input, 464 GPH			2	4.000	Ea.
	1120	605 MBH input, 584 GPH			1.50	5.330	Ea.
	1140	700 MBH input, 676 GPH	↓	↓	1	8.000	Ea.
	1160	1000 MBH input, 966 GPH	Q-1	1 Plumber 1 Plumber Apprentice	1.60	10.000	Ea.
	1180	1200 MBH input, 1159 GPH			1.40	11.430	Ea.
	1200	1400 MBH input, 1353 GPH	↓	↓	1.20	13.330	Ea.
	3000	Combination dishwasher & general purpose, 2 temp. gas fired					
	3040	124 GPH @ 140° rise; 434 GPH @ 40° rise	1 Plum	1 Plumber	2	4.000	Ea.
	3060	193 GPH @ 140° rise; 677 GPH @ 40° rise			1.60	5.000	Ea.
	3080	276 GPH @ 140° rise; 969 GPH @ 40° rise			1.40	5.710	Ea.
	3100	330 GPH @ 140° rise; 1160 GPH @ 40°rise			1.20	6.670	Ea.
	3120	417 GPH @ 140° rise; 1460 GPH @ 40°rise	↓	↓	1	8.000	Ea.
	3140	481 GPH @ 140° rise; 1685 GPH @ 40°rise	Q-1	1 Plumber 1 Plumber Apprentice	1.40	11.430	Ea.
	3160	688 GPH @ 140° rise; 2410 GPH @ 40°rise			1.20	13.330	Ea.
	3180	828 GPH @ 140° rise; 2790 GPH @ 40°rise			1	16.000	Ea.
	3200	965 GPH @ 140° rise; 3370 GPH @ 40°rise	↓	↓	.80	20.000	Ea.
	5000	Coin laundry units, gas fired, 100° rise					
	5020	Single heater,					
	5040	280 MBH input, 270 GPH	1 Plum	1 Plumber	1.60	5.000	Ea.
	5060	400 MBH input, 386 GPH			1.30	6.150	Ea.
	5080	480 MBH input, 464 GPH	↓	↓	1	8.000	Ea.
	5100	605 MBH input, 584 GPH	Q-1	1 Plumber 1 Plumber Apprentice	1.40	11.430	Ea.
	5120	700 MBH input, 676 GPH			1.20	13.330	Ea.
	5140	1000 MBH input, 966 GPH			1	16.000	Ea.
	5160	1200 MBH input, 1159 GPH			.90	17.780	Ea.
	5180	1400 MBH input, 1353 GPH	↓	↓	.70	22.860	Ea.
	6000	Multiple heater					
	6040	560 MBH input, 540 GPH	1 Plum	1 Plumber	1	8.000	Ea.
	6060	800 MBH input, 772 GPH	Q-1	1 Plumber 1 Plumber Apprentice	1.30	12.310	Ea.
	6080	960 MBH input, 928 GPH			1.20	13.330	Ea.
	6100	1210 MBH input, 1168 GPH			1	16.000	Ea.
	6120	1400 MBH input, 1352 GPH			1	16.000	Ea.
	6140	1700 MBH input, 1642 GPH			.80	20.000	Ea.
	6160	2000 MBH input, 1932 GPH			.70	22.860	Ea.
	6180	2400 MBH input, 2318 GPH	Q-2	2 Plumbers 1 Plumber Apprentice	.90	26.670	Ea.
	6200	2600 MBH input, 2512 GPH			.80	30.000	Ea.
	6220	2800 MBH input, 2706 GPH	↓	↓	.70	34.290	Ea.

153 100 | Water Appliances

		CREW	MAKEUP	DAILY OUTPUT	MAN-HOURS	UNIT
130	**WATER HEATER STORAGE TANKS**					
1000	Copper, lined, 190 gal., 30" diam x 66" LOA	1 Plum	1 Plumber	4	2.000	Ea.
1060	225 gal., 30" diam x 78" LOA	"	"	3	2.670	Ea.
1080	325 gal., 36" diam x 81" LOA	Q-1	1 Plumber	4	4.000	Ea.
			1 Plumber Apprentice			
1100	460 gal., 42" diam x 84" LOA			3	5.330	Ea.
1120	605 gal., 48" diam x 87" LOA			2.50	6.400	Ea.
1140	740 gal., 54" diam x 91" LOA			2	8.000	Ea.
1160	940 gal., 60" diam x 93" LOA			1.50	10.670	Ea.
1180	1505 gal., 66" diam x 119" LOA	↓	↓	1	16.000	Ea.
1200	1615 gal., 72" diam x 110" LOA	Q-2	2 Plumbers	1.50	16.000	Ea.
			1 Plumber Apprentice			
1220	2275 gal., 84" diam x 116" LOA	↓	↓	1	24.000	Ea.
1240	3815 gal., 96" diam x 145" LOA			1	24.000	Ea.
2000	Galvanized steel, 15 gal., 12" diam., 39" LOA	1 Plum	1 Plumber	12	.667	Ea.
2060	30 gal., 14" diam. x 40" LOA			11	.727	Ea.
2080	75 gal., 18" diam. x 72" LOA			9	.889	Ea.
2100	140 gal., 24" diam. x 75" LOA			6	1.330	Ea.
2120	225 gal., 30" diam. x 78" LOA			4	2.000	Ea.
2140	325 gal., 36" diam. x 81" LOA	↓	↓	3	2.670	Ea.
2160	460 gal., 36" diam. x 117" LOA	Q-1	1 Plumber	4	4.000	Ea.
			1 Plumber Apprentice			
2180	605 gal., 48" diam., x 87" LOA	"	"	3	5.330	Ea.
3000	Glass lined, P.E., 80 gal., 20" diam. x 60" LOA	1 Plum	1 Plumber	9	.889	Ea.
3060	140 gal., 24" diam. x 80" LOA			6	1.330	Ea.
3080	225 gal., 30" diam. x 78" LOA			4	2.000	Ea.
3100	325 gal., 36" diam. x 81" LOA	↓	↓	3	2.670	Ea.
3120	460 gal., 42" diam. x 84" LOA	Q-1	1 Plumber	4	4.000	Ea.
			1 Plumber Apprentice			
3140	605 gal., 48" diam. x 87" LOA			3	5.330	Ea.
3160	740 gal., 54" diam. x 91" LOA			3	5.330	Ea.
3180	940 gal., 60" diam. x 93" LOA			2.50	6.400	Ea.
3200	1330 gal., 66" diam. x 107" LOA			2	8.000	Ea.
3220	1615 gal., 72" diam. x 110" LOA			1.50	10.670	Ea.
3240	2275 gal., 84" diam. x 116" LOA	↓	↓	1	16.000	Ea.
3260	3815 gal., 96" diam. x 145" LOA	Q-2	2 Plumbers	1.50	16.000	Ea.
			1 Plumber Apprentice			
150	**WATER TREATMENT, POTABLE**					
2000	Chemical feeders, for chlorine, caustics, mild acids					
2600	Air-cooled, automatic, max. output 9 gal. per 24 hrs.	1 Plum	1 Plumber	8	1.000	Ea.
2700	30 gal. per 24 hrs			8	1.000	Ea.
4000	Oil cooled, automatic, max. output 4.3 gal. per 24 hrs.			8	1.000	Ea.
4100	14 gal. per 24 hrs.			8	1.000	Ea.
4200	28 gal. per 24 hrs.			8	1.000	Ea.
5400	Chemical solution tank for above feeders, 20 gallon	↓	↓	24	.333	Ea.
5800	Softener systems, automatic, intermediate sizes					
5820	available, may be used in multiples.					
6000	Hardness capacity between regenerations and flow					
6100	150,000 grains, 37 GPM cont., 51 GPM peak	Q-1	1 Plumber	1.20	13.330	Ea.
			1 Plumber Apprentice			
6200	300,000 grains, 81 GPM cont., 113 GPM peak			1	16.000	Ea.
6300	750,000 grains, 160			.80	20.000	Ea.
6400	900,000 grains, 185 GPM cont., 270 GPM	↓	↓	.70	22.860	Ea.

153 | Plumbing Appliances

153 100	Water Appliances	CREW	MAKEUP	DAILY OUTPUT	MAN-HOURS	UNIT
160	**WATER SUPPLY METERS**					
1000	Detector, serves dual systems such as fire and domestic or					
1020	process water, wide range cap., UL and FM approved					
1100	3" mainline x 2" by-pass, 400 GPM	Q-1	1 Plumber / 1 Plumber Apprentice	3.60	4.440	Ea.
1140	4" mainline x 2" by-pass, 700 GPM	"	"	2.50	6.400	Ea.
1180	6" mainline x 3" by-pass, 1600 GPM	Q-2	2 Plumbers / 1 Plumber Apprentice	2.60	9.230	Ea.
1220	8" mainline x 4" by-pass, 2800 GPM			2.10	11.430	Ea.
1260	10" mainline x 6" by-pass, 4400 GPM			2	12.000	Ea.
1300	10"x12" mainlines x 6" by-pass, 5400 GPM			1.70	14.120	Ea.
2000	Domestic/commercial, bronze					
2020	Threaded					
2060	5/8" diameter, to 20 GPM	1 Plum	1 Plumber	16	.500	Ea.
2080	3/4" diameter, to 30 GPM			14	.571	Ea.
2100	1" diameter, to 50 GPM			12	.667	Ea.
2300	Threaded/flanged					
2340	1-1/2" diameter, to 100 GPM	1 Plum	1 Plumber	8	1.000	Ea.
2360	2" diameter, to 160 GPM	"	"	6	1.330	Ea.
2600	Flanged, compound					
2640	3" diameter, 320 GPM	Q-1	1 Plumber / 1 Plumber Apprentice	3	5.330	Ea.
2660	4" diameter, to 500 GPM			1.50	10.670	Ea.
2680	6" diameter, to 1,000 GPM			1	16.000	Ea.
2700	8" diameter, to 1,800 GPM			.80	20.000	Ea.
7000	Turbine					
7260	Flanged					
7300	2" diameter, to 160 GPM	1 Plum	1 Plumber	7	1.140	Ea.
7320	3" diameter, to 450 GPM	Q-1	1 Plumber / 1 Plumber Apprentice	3.60	4.440	Ea.
7340	4" diameter, to 650 GPM	"	"	2.50	6.400	Ea.
7360	6" diameter, to 1800 GPM	Q-2	2 Plumbers / 1 Plumber Apprentice	2.60	9.230	Ea.
7380	8" diameter, to 2500 GPM			2.10	11.430	Ea.
7400	10" diameter, to 5500 GPM			1.70	14.120	Ea.

154 | Fire Extinguishing Systems

154 100	Fire Systems	CREW	MAKEUP	DAILY OUTPUT	MAN-HOURS	UNIT
101	**AUTOMATIC FIRE SUPPRESSION SYSTEMS**					
0100	Control panel, single zone with batteries (2 zones det., 1 suppr.)	1 Elec	1 Electrician	1	8.000	Ea.
0150	Multizone (4) with batteries (8 zones det., 4 suppr.)	"	"	.50	16.000	Ea.
1000	Dispersion nozzle, CO2, 3" x 5"	1 Plum	1 Plumber	18	.444	Ea.
1100	Halon, 1-1/2"	"	"	14	.571	Ea.
2000	Extinguisher, CO2 system, high pressure, 75 lb. cylinder	Q-1	1 Plumber / 1 Plumber Apprentice	6	2.670	Ea.
2100	100 lb. cylinder	"	"	5	3.200	Ea.
2400	Halon system, filled, with mounting bracket					
2460	26 lb. container	Q-1	1 Plumber / 1 Plumber Apprentice	8	2.000	Ea.
2480	44 lb. container			7	2.290	Ea.
2500	63 lb. container			6	2.670	Ea.

160

154 100	Fire Systems	CREW	MAKEUP	DAILY OUTPUT	MAN-HOURS	UNIT
101 2521	Fire extinguisher, halon system, 101 lb. container	Q-1	1 Plumber	5	3.200	Ea.
			1 Plumber Apprentice			
2540	196 lb. container	"	"	4	4.000	Ea.
3000	Electro/mechanical release	L-1	1 Electrician	4	4.000	Ea.
			1 Plumber			
3400	Manual pull station	1 Plum	1 Plumber	6	1.330	Ea.
4000	Pneumatic damper release	"	"	8	1.000	Ea.
115 0040	**FIRE EQUIPMENT CABINETS** Not equipped, 20 ga. steel box, recessed, D.S. glass in door, box size given					
1000	Portable extinguisher, single, 8" x 12" x 27", alum. door & frame	Q-12	1 Sprinkler Installer	8	2.000	Ea.
			1 Sprinkler Apprentice			
1100	Steel door and frame			8	2.000	Ea.
1200	Stainless steel door and frame			8	2.000	Ea.
2000	Portable extinguisher, large, 8" x 12" x 36", alum. door & frame			8	2.000	Ea.
2100	Steel door and frame			8	2.000	Ea.
2200	Stainless steel door and frame	↓	↓	8	2.000	Ea.
3000	Hose rack assy., 1-1/2" valve & 100' hose, 24" x 40" x 5-1/2"					
3100	Aluminum door and frame	Q-12	1 Sprinkler Installer	6	2.670	Ea.
			1 Sprinkler Apprentice			
3200	Steel door and frame			6	2.670	Ea.
3300	Stainless steel door and frame	↓	↓	6	2.670	Ea.
4000	Hose rack assy., 2-1/2" x 1-1/2" valve, 100' hose, 24" x 40" x 8"					
4100	Aluminum door and frame	Q-12	1 Sprinkler Installer	6	2.670	Ea.
			1 Sprinkler Apprentice			
4200	Steel door and frame			6	2.670	Ea.
4300	Stainless steel door and frame	↓	↓	6	2.670	Ea.
5000 5010	Hose rack assy., 2-1/2" x 1-1/2" valve, 100' hose and extinguisher, 30" x 40" x 8"					
5100	Aluminum door and frame	Q-12	1 Sprinkler Installer	5	3.200	Ea.
			1 Sprinkler Apprentice			
5200	Steel door and frame			5	3.200	Ea.
5300	Stainless steel door and frame	↓	↓	5	3.200	Ea.
6000 6010	Hose rack assy., 1-1/2" valve, 100' hose and 2-1/2" FD valve, 24" x 44" x 8"					
6100	Aluminum door and frame	Q-12	1 Sprinkler Installer	5	3.200	Ea.
			1 Sprinkler Apprentice			
6200	Steel door and frame			5	3.200	Ea.
6300	Stainless steel door and frame	↓	↓	5	3.200	Ea.
7000 7010	Hose rack assy., 1-1/2" valve & 100' hose, 2-1/2" FD valve and extinguisher, 30" x 44" x 8"					
7100	Aluminum door and frame	Q-12	1 Sprinkler Installer	5	3.200	Ea.
			1 Sprinkler Apprentice			
7200	Steel door and frame			5	3.200	Ea.
7300	Stainless steel door and frame	↓	↓	5	3.200	Ea.
8000	Valve cabinet for 2-1/2" FD angle valve, 18" x 18" x 8"					
8100	Aluminum door and frame	Q-12	1 Sprinkler Installer	12	1.330	Ea.
			1 Sprinkler Apprentice			
8200	Steel door and frame			12	1.330	Ea.
8300	Stainless steel door and frame	↓	↓	12	1.330	Ea.
125	**FIRE EXTINGUISHERS**					
9400	Installation of extinguishers, 12 or more, on wood	1 Carp	1 Carpenter	30	.267	Ea.
9420	On masonry or concrete	"	"	15	.533	Ea.
135 2600	**FIRE HOSE AND EQUIPMENT** Hose rack, swinging, for 1-1/2" diameter hose,					
2620	Enameled steel, 50' & 75' lengths of hose	Q-12	1 Sprinkler Installer	20	.800	Ea.
			1 Sprinkler Apprentice			
2640	100' and 125' lengths of hose			20	.800	Ea.
2680	Chrome plated, 50' and 75' lengths of hose	↓	↓	20	.800	Ea.

	154 100 Fire Systems	CREW	MAKEUP	DAILY OUTPUT	MAN-HOURS	UNIT
135	2701 Fire hose rack, chrome plated, 100' & 125' lengths of hose	Q-12	1 Sprinkler Installer 1 Sprinkler Apprentice	20	.800	Ea.
	2990 Hose reel, swinging, for 1-1/2" polyester neoprene lined hose					
	3000 50' long	Q-12	1 Sprinkler Installer 1 Sprinkler Apprentice	14	1.140	Ea.
	3020 100' long			14	1.140	Ea.
	3060 For 2-1/2" cotton rubber hose, 75' long			14	1.140	Ea.
	3100 150' long	↓	↓	14	1.140	Ea.
	3750 Hydrants, wall, w/caps, single, flush, polished brass					
	3800 2-1/2" x 2-1/2"	Q-12	1 Sprinkler Installer 1 Sprinkler Apprentice	5	3.200	Ea.
	3840 2-1/2" x 3"			5	3.200	Ea.
	3860 3" x 3"	↓	↓	4.80	3.330	Ea.
	3950 Double, flush, polished brass					
	4000 2-1/2" x 2-1/2" x 4"	Q-12	1 Sprinkler Installer 1 Sprinkler Apprentice	5	3.200	Ea.
	4040 2-1/2" x 2-1/2" x 6"			4.60	3.480	Ea.
	4080 3" x 3" x 4"			4.90	3.270	Ea.
	4120 3" x 3" x 6"	↓	↓	4.50	3.560	Ea.
	4350 Double, projecting, polished brass					
	4400 2-1/2" x 2-1/2" x 4"	Q-12	1 Sprinkler Installer 1 Sprinkler Apprentice	5	3.200	Ea.
	4450 2-1/2" x 2-1/2" x 6"	"	"	4.60	3.480	Ea.
	4460 Valve control, dbl. flush/projecting hydrant, cap &					
	4470 chain, ext. rod & cplg., escutcheon, polished brass	Q-12	1 Sprinkler Installer 1 Sprinkler Apprentice	8	2.000	Ea.
	4480 Four-way square, flush, polished brass					
	4540 2-1/2"(4) x 6"	Q-12	1 Sprinkler Installer 1 Sprinkler Apprentice	3.60	4.440	Ea.
	4600 Vertical, flush, cast brass					
	4620 Two-way, 2-1/2" x 2-1/2" x 4"	Q-12	1 Sprinkler Installer 1 Sprinkler Apprentice	5	3.200	Ea.
	4640 Three-way, 2-1/2" x 2-1/2" x 2-1/2" x 6"			4.60	3.480	Ea.
	4720 Four-way, 2-1/2"(4) x 6"	↓	↓	3.80	4.210	Ea.
	7140 Standpipe connections, wall, w/plugs & chains					
	7160 Single, flush, brass, 2-1/2" x 2-1/2"	Q-12	1 Sprinkler Installer 1 Sprinkler Apprentice	5	3.200	Ea.
	7180 2-1/2" x 3"	"	"	5	3.200	Ea.
	7280 Double, flush, polished brass					
	7300 2-1/2" x 2-1/2" x 4"	Q-12	1 Sprinkler Installer 1 Sprinkler Apprentice	5	3.200	Ea.
	7330 2-1/2" x 2-1/2" x 6"			4.60	3.480	Ea.
	7340 3" x 3" x 4"			4.90	3.270	Ea.
	7370 3" x 3" x 6"	↓	↓	4.50	3.560	Ea.
	7580 Double projecting, polished brass					
	7600 2-1/2" x 2-1/2" x 4"	Q-12	1 Sprinkler Installer 1 Sprinkler Apprentice	5	3.200	Ea.
	7630 2-1/2" x 2-1/2" x 6"	"	"	4.60	3.480	Ea.
	7900 Three way, flush, polished brass					
	7920 2-1/2" (3) x 4"	Q-12	1 Sprinkler Installer 1 Sprinkler Apprentice	4.80	3.330	Ea.
	7930 2-1/2" (3) x 6"	"	"	4.80	3.330	Ea.
	8020 Three way, projecting, polished brass					
	8040 2-1/2"(3) x 4"	Q-12	1 Sprinkler Installer 1 Sprinkler Apprentice	4.80	3.330	Ea.
	8070 2-1/2" (3) x 6"	"	"	4.60	3.480	Ea.

					DAILY	MAN-	
	154 100 | Fire Systems		CREW	MAKEUP	OUTPUT	HOURS	UNIT
135	8201	Fire standpipe conn., 4 way, sq., flush, polished brass,					
	8240	2-1/2"(4) x 6"	Q-12	1 Sprinkler Installer	3.60	4.440	Ea.
				1 Sprinkler Apprentice			
	8550	Wall, vertical, flush, cast brass					
	8600	Two way, 2-1/2" x 2-1/2" x 4"	Q-12	1 Sprinkler Installer	5	3.200	Ea.
				1 Sprinkler Apprentice			
	8660	Four way, 2-1/2"(4) x 6"	↓	↓	3.80	4.210	Ea.
	8680	Six way, 2-1/2"(6) x 6"			3.40	4.710	Ea.
	8800	Sidewalk siamese unit, polished brass, two way					
	8820	2-1/2" x 2-1/2" x 4"	Q-12	1 Sprinkler Installer	2.50	6.400	Ea.
				1 Sprinkler Apprentice			
	8850	2-1/2" x 2-1/2" x 6"	↓	↓	2	8.000	Ea.
	8860	3" x 3" x 4"			2.50	6.400	Ea.
	9100	Sidewalk siamese unit, polished brass, three way					
	9120	2-1/2" x 2-1/2" x 2-1/2" x 6"	Q-12	1 Sprinkler Installer	2	8.000	Ea.
				1 Sprinkler Apprentice			
	9340	Tools, crowbar and brackets	1 Carp	1 Carpenter	12	.667	Ea.
	9380	Fire axe and brackets					
	9400	6 lb.	1 Carp	1 Carpenter	12	.667	Ea.
	145	**FIRE PUMPS** Including controller, fittings and relief valve					
	0030	Diesel					
	0050	500 GPM, 50 psi, 40 HP, 4" pump	Q-13	1 Sprinkler Foreman (ins)	.64	50.000	Ea.
				2 Sprinkler Installers			
				1 Sprinkler Apprentice			
	0100	500 GPM, 100 psi, 68 HP, 4" pump			.60	53.330	Ea.
	0150	500 GPM, 125 psi, 103 HP, 4" pump			.56	57.140	Ea.
	0200	750 GPM, 50 psi, 40 HP, 5" pump			.60	53.330	Ea.
	0250	750 GPM, 100 psi, 99 HP, 5" pump			.56	57.140	Ea.
	0300	750 GPM, 165 psi, 188 HP, 5" pump			.52	61.540	Ea.
	0350	1000 GPM, 50 psi, 53 HP, 5" pump			.58	55.170	Ea.
	0400	1000 GPM, 100 psi, 99 HP, 5" pump			.56	57.140	Ea.
	0450	1000 GPM, 150 psi, 188 HP, 6" pump			.48	66.670	Ea.
	0470	1000 GPM, 200 psi, 238 HP, 6" pump			.40	80.000	Ea.
	0500	1500 GPM, 50 psi, 81 HP, 6" pump			.50	64.000	Ea.
	0550	1500 GPM, 100 psi, 188 HP, 6" pump			.46	69.570	Ea.
	0600	1500 GPM, 150 psi, 213 HP, 6" pump			.42	76.190	Ea.
	0650	1500 GPM, 200 psi, 288 HP, 6" pump			.38	84.210	Ea.
	0700	2000 GPM, 100 psi, 188 HP, 6" pump			.34	94.120	Ea.
	0750	2000 GPM, 150 psi, 292 HP, 6"pump			.30	107.000	Ea.
	0800	2500 GPM, 100 psi, 255 HP, 8" pump			.32	100.000	Ea.
	0820	2500 GPM, 150 psi, 427 HP, 8"pump			.26	123.000	Ea.
	0850	3000 GPM, 100 psi, 288 HP, 8"pump			.28	114.000	Ea.
	0900	3000 GPM, 150 psi, 534 HP, 10" pump			.20	160.000	Ea.
	0950	3500 GPM, 100 psi, 320 HP, 10" pump			.24	133.000	Ea.
	1000	3500 GPM, 150 psi, 534 HP, 10" pump	↓	↓	.20	160.000	Ea.
	3000	Electric					
	3100	250 GPM, 40 psi, 15 HP, 3550 RPM, 3" pump	Q-13	1 Sprinkler Foreman (ins)	.70	45.710	Ea.
				2 Sprinkler Installers			
				1 Sprinkler Apprentice			
	3200	500 GPM, 50 psi, 30 HP, 3550 RPM, 4" pump			.68	47.060	Ea.
	3250	500 GPM, 100 psi, 75 HP, 1770 RPM, 4" pump			.66	48.480	Ea.
	3300	500 GPM, 125 psi, 100 HP, 1770 RPM, 4" pump			.62	51.610	Ea.
	3350	750 GPM, 50 psi, 50 HP, 1770 RPM, 5" pump			.64	50.000	Ea.
	3400	750 GPM, 100 psi, 100 HP, 1770 RPM, 5" pump			.58	55.170	Ea.
	3450	750 GPM, 165 psi, 125 HP, 1770 RPM, 5" pump			.56	57.140	Ea.
	3500	1000 GPM, 50 psi, 50 HP 1770 RPM, 5" pump			.60	53.330	Ea.
	3550	1000 GPM, 100 psi, 125 HP, 1770 RPM, 5" pump			.54	59.260	Ea.
	3600	1000 GPM, 150 psi, 200 HP, 1770 RPM, 6" pump	↓	↓	.50	64.000	Ea.

154 100	Fire Systems	CREW	MAKEUP	DAILY OUTPUT	MAN-HOURS	UNIT
145 3651	Fire pumps, elec., 1000 GPM, 200 psi, 250 HP, 1770 RPM, 6" pump	Q-13	1 Sprinkler Foreman (ins)	.36	88.890	Ea.
			2 Sprinkler Installers			
			1 Sprinkler Apprentice			
3700	1500 GPM, 50 psi, 75 HP, 1770 RPM, 6" pump			.50	64.000	Ea.
3750	1500 GPM, 100 psi, 150 HP, 1770 RPM, 6" pump			.46	69.570	Ea.
3800	1500 GPM, 150 psi, 200 HP, 1770 RPM, 6" pump			.36	88.890	Ea.
3850	1500 GPM, 200 psi, 250 HP, 1770 RPM, 6" pump			.32	100.000	Ea.
3900	2000 GPM, 100 psi, 200 HP, 1770 RPM, 6" pump			.34	94.120	Ea.
3950	2000 GPM, 150 psi, 300 HP, 1770 RPM, 6" pump			.28	114.000	Ea.
4000	2500 GPM, 100 psi, 250 HP, 1770 RPM, 8" pump			.30	107.000	Ea.
4040	2500 GPM, 135 psi, 350 HP, 1770 RPM, 8" pump			.26	123.000	Ea.
4100	3000 GPM, 100 psi, 250 HP, 1770 RPM, 8" pump			.28	114.000	Ea.
4150	3000 GPM, 140 psi, 450 HP, 1770 RPM, 10" pump			.24	133.000	Ea.
4200	3500 GPM, 100 psi, 300 HP, 1770 RPM, 10" pump			.26	123.000	Ea.
4250	3500 GPM, 140 psi, 450 HP, 1770 RPM, 10" pump	↓	↓	.24	133.000	Ea.
5000	For jockey pump 1", 3 HP, add	Q-12	1 Sprinkler Installer	2	8.000	Ea.
			1 Sprinkler Apprentice			
160	**FIRE VALVES**					
0020	Angle, combination pressure adjustable/restricting, rough brass					
0030	1-1/2"	1 Spri	1 Sprinkler Installer	12	.667	Ea.
0040	2-1/2"			7	1.140	Ea.
0080	Wheel handle, 300 lb., 1-1/2"			12	.667	Ea.
0090	2-1/2"			7	1.140	Ea.
1000	Ball drip, automatic, rough brass, 1/2"			20	.400	Ea.
1010	3/4"	↓	↓	20	.400	Ea.
1100	Butterfly, 175 lb., sprinkler system, FM/UL, threaded, bronze					
1120	Slow close					
1150	1" size	1 Spri	1 Sprinkler Installer	19	.421	Ea.
1160	1-1/4" size			15	.533	Ea.
1170	1-1/2" size			13	.615	Ea.
1180	2" size	↓	↓	11	.727	Ea.
1190	2-1/2" size	Q-12	1 Sprinkler Installer	15	1.070	Ea.
			1 Sprinkler Apprentice			
1230	For supervisory switch kit, all sizes					
1240	One circuit, add	1 Spri	1 Sprinkler Installer	48	.167	Ea.
1250	Two circuits, add	"	"	40	.200	Ea.
1280	Quarter turn for trim					
1300	1/2" size	1 Spri	1 Sprinkler Installer	22	.364	Ea.
1310	3/4" size			20	.400	Ea.
1320	1" size			19	.421	Ea.
1330	1-1/4" size			15	.533	Ea.
1340	1-1/2" size			13	.615	Ea.
1350	2" size			11	.727	Ea.
3000	Gate, hose, wheel handle, N.R.S., rough brass, 1-1/2"			12	.667	Ea.
3040	2-1/2", 300 lb.	↓	↓	7	1.140	Ea.
3800	Hydrant, screw type, crank handle, brass					
3840	2-1/2" size	Q-12	1 Sprinkler Installer	11	1.450	Ea.
			1 Sprinkler Apprentice			
4200	Hydrolator, vent and draining, rough brass, 1-1/2"	1 Spri	1 Sprinkler Installer	12	.667	Ea.
4220	2-1/2"			7	1.140	Ea.
5000	Pressure restricting, adjustable rough brass, 1-1/2"			12	.667	Ea.
5020	2-1/2"	↓	↓	7	1.140	Ea.
6000	Roof manifold, horiz., brass, with valves & caps					
6040	2-1/2" x 2-1/2" x 4"	Q-12	1 Sprinkler Installer	4.80	3.330	Ea.
			1 Sprinkler Apprentice			
6060	2-1/2" x 2-1/2" x 6"			4.60	3.480	Ea.
6080	2-1/2" x 2-1/2" x 2-1/2" x 4"			4.60	3.480	Ea.
6090	2-1/2" x 2-1/2" x 2-1/2" x 6"	↓	↓	4.60	3.480	Ea.

154 100	Fire Systems	CREW	MAKEUP	DAILY OUTPUT	MAN-HOURS	UNIT
170	**170**	**SPRINKLER SYSTEM COMPONENTS**				
	0600	Accelerator	1 Spri	1 Sprinkler Installer	8	1.000	Ea.
	0800	Air compressor for dry pipe system, automatic, complete					
	0820	200 gal. system capacity, 1/3 HP	1 Spri	1 Sprinkler Installer	1.30	6.150	Ea.
	0840	350 gal. system capacity, 1/2 HP	↓	↓	1.30	6.150	Ea.
	0860	520 gal. system capacity, 1 HP			1.30	6.150	Ea.
	0900	Air compressor, with starting switch for manual operation					
	0910	200 gal. system capacity, 1/3 HP	1 Spri	1 Sprinkler Installer	1.30	6.150	Ea.
	0920	350 gal. system capacity, 1/2 HP			1.30	6.150	Ea.
	0930	520 gal. system capacity, 1 HP			1.30	6.150	Ea.
	0960	Air pressure maintenance control			24	.333	Ea.
	1100	Alarm, electric pressure switch (circuit closer)			26	.308	Ea.
	1140	For explosion proof, max 20 PSI, contacts close or open			26	.308	Ea.
	1220	Water motor, complete with gong			4	2.000	Ea.
	1400	Deluge system, pressured monitoring panel, 120V			18	.444	Ea.
	1420	Explosion proof panel, not incl. enclosure			16	.500	Ea.
	1600	Dehydrator package, incl. valves and nipples	↓	↓	12	.667	Ea.
	1800	Firecycle system, controls, includes panel,					
	1820	batteries, solenoid valves and pressure switches	Q-13	1 Sprinkler Foreman (ins)	1	32.000	Ea.
				2 Sprinkler Installers			
				1 Sprinkler Apprentice			
	1980	Detector	1 Spri	1 Sprinkler Installer	16	.500	Ea.
	2000	Release, emergency, manual, for hydraulic or pneumatic system			12	.667	Ea.
	2060	Release, thermostatic, for hydraulic or pneumatic release line			20	.400	Ea.
	2200	Sprinkler cabinets, 6 head capacity			16	.500	Ea.
	2260	12 head capacity			16	.500	Ea.
	2340	Sprinkler head escutcheons, standard, brass, 1" size			40	.200	Ea.
	2360	Chrome, 1" size			40	.200	Ea.
	2400	Recessed type, brass			40	.200	Ea.
	2440	Chrome or white enamel	↓	↓	40	.200	Ea.
	2600	Sprinkler heads, not including supply piping					
	2640	Dry, pendent, 1/2" orifice, 3/4" or 1" NPT					
	2660	1" to 4-3/4" length	1 Spri	1 Sprinkler Installer	14	.571	Ea.
	2670	5" to 6-3/4" length			14	.571	Ea.
	2680	7" to 8-3/4" length			14	.571	Ea.
	2690	9" to 10-3/4" length			14	.571	Ea.
	2700	11" to 12-3/4" length			14	.571	Ea.
	2710	13" to 14-3/4" length			13	.615	Ea.
	2720	15" to 16-3/4" length			13	.615	Ea.
	2730	17" to 18-3/4" length			13	.615	Ea.
	2740	19" to 20-3/4" length			13	.615	Ea.
	2750	21" to 22-3/4" length			13	.615	Ea.
	2760	23" to 24-3/4" length			13	.615	Ea.
	2780	25" to 26-3/4" length			12	.667	Ea.
	2790	27" to 28-3/4" length			12	.667	Ea.
	3600	Foam-water, pendent or upright, 1/2" NPT	↓	↓	12	.667	Ea.
	3630	On-off (automatic), 165°, 212°F					
	3640	Pendent, brass	1 Spri	1 Sprinkler Installer	12	.667	Ea.
	3650	Chrome			12	.667	Ea.
	3660	Flush, chrome or brass-	↓	↓	10	.800	Ea.
	3700	Standard spray, pendent or upright, brass, 135° to 286°F					
	3720	1/2" NPT, 3/8" orifice	1 Spri	1 Sprinkler Installer	16	.500	Ea.
	3730	1/2" NPT, 7/16" orifice			16	.500	Ea.
	3740	1/2" NPT, 1/2" orifice			16	.500	Ea.
	3760	1/2" NPT, 17/32" orifice			16	.500	Ea.
	3780	3/4" NPT, 17/32" orifice	↓	↓	16	.500	Ea.
	4200	Sidewall, vertical, brass, 135°-286°F					
	4220	1/2" NPT, 3/8" orifice	1 Spri	1 Sprinkler Installer	16	.500	Ea.

154 | Fire Extinguishing Systems

154 100 | Fire Systems

		CREW	MAKEUP	DAILY OUTPUT	MAN-HOURS	UNIT
170 4231	Sprinkler heads, sidewall, vert., brass, 1/2 NPT, 7/16" orifice	1 Spri	1 Sprinkler Installer	16	.500	Ea.
4240	1/2" NPT, 1/2" orifice			16	.500	Ea.
4260	1/2" NPT, 17/32" orifice			16	.500	Ea.
4280	3/4" NPT, 17/32" orifice	↓	↓	16	.500	Ea.
4500	Sidewall, horizontal, brass, 135° to 286°F					
4520	1/2" NPT, 1/2" orifice	1 Spri	1 Sprinkler Installer	16	.500	Ea.
4800	Recessed pendent, brass, 135° to 286°F					
4820	1/2" NPT, 3/8" orifice	1 Spri	1 Sprinkler Installer	10	.800	Ea.
4830	1/2" NPT, 7/16" orifice			10	.800	Ea.
4840	1/2" NPT, 1/2" orifice			10	.800	Ea.
4860	1/2" NPT, 17/32" orifice	↓	↓	10	.800	Ea.
5000	Recessed-vertical sidewall, brass, 135°-286°F					
5020	1/2" NPT, 3/8" orifice	1 Spri	1 Sprinkler Installer	10	.800	Ea.
5030	1/2" NPT, 7/16" orifice			10	.800	Ea.
5040	1/2" NPT, 1/2" orifice			10	.800	Ea.
5060	1/2" NPT, 17/32" orifice	↓	↓	10	.800	Ea.
5600	Concealed, complete with cover plate					
5620	1/2" NPT, 1/2" orifice, 135°F to 212°F	1 Spri	1 Sprinkler Installer	9	.889	Ea.
5800	Window, brass, 1/2" NPT, 1/4" orifice			16	.500	Ea.
5810	1/2" NPT, 5/16" orifice			16	.500	Ea.
5820	1/2" NPT, 3/8" orifice			16	.500	Ea.
5830	1/2" NPT, 7/16" orifice			16	.500	Ea.
5840	1/2" NPT, 1/2" orifice			16	.500	Ea.
5880	3/4" NPT, 5/8" orifice			16	.500	Ea.
5890	3/4 NPT, 3/4" orifice	↓	↓	16	.500	Ea.
6200	Valves					
6210	Alarm, includes					
6220	retard chamber, trim, gauges, alarm line strainer					
6260	2-1/2" size	Q-12	1 Sprinkler Installer	3	5.330	Ea.
			1 Sprinkler Apprentice			
6280	4" size	"	"	2	8.000	Ea.
6300	6" size	Q-13	1 Sprinkler Foreman (ins)	4	8.000	Ea.
			2 Sprinkler Installers			
			1 Sprinkler Apprentice			
6320	8" size	"	"	3	10.670	Ea.
6500	Check, swing, C.I. body, brass fittings, auto. ball drip					
6520	4" size	Q-12	1 Sprinkler Installer	3	5.330	Ea.
			1 Sprinkler Apprentice			
6540	6" size	Q-13	1 Sprinkler Foreman (ins)	4	8.000	Ea.
			2 Sprinkler Installers			
			1 Sprinkler Apprentice			
6580	8" size	"	"	3	10.670	Ea.
6800	Check, wafer, butterfly type, C.I. body, bronze fittings					
6820	4" size	Q-12	1 Sprinkler Installer	4	4.000	Ea.
			1 Sprinkler Apprentice			
6840	6" size	Q-13	1 Sprinkler Foreman (ins)	5.50	5.820	Ea.
			2 Sprinkler Installers			
			1 Sprinkler Apprentice			
6860	8" size			5	6.400	Ea.
6880	10" size			4.50	7.110	Ea.
6900	12" size	↓	↓	4	8.000	Ea.
7000	Deluge, assembly, incl. trim, pressure					
7020	operated relief, emergency release, gauges					
7040	2" size	Q-12	1 Sprinkler Installer	2	8.000	Ea.
			1 Sprinkler Apprentice			
7060	3" size	↓	↓	1.50	10.670	Ea.
7080	4" size			1	16.000	Ea.

154 100 | Fire Systems		CREW	MAKEUP	DAILY OUTPUT	MAN-HOURS	UNIT
170	7101	Sprinkler valves, deluge, assembly, 6" size	Q-13	1 Sprinkler Foreman (ins)	4	8.000	Ea.
				2 Sprinkler Installers			
				1 Sprinkler Apprentice			
	7300	Detector check, valve only, flanged,					
	7320	4" size, painted	Q-12	1 Sprinkler Installer	4	4.000	Ea.
				1 Sprinkler Apprentice			
	7340	6" size, painted	Q-13	1 Sprinkler Foreman (ins)	5.50	5.820	Ea.
				2 Sprinkler Installers			
				1 Sprinkler Apprentice			
	7360	8" size, painted	↓	↓	5	6.400	Ea.
	7380	10" size, painted			4.50	7.110	Ea.
	7400	4" size, galvanized	Q-12	1 Sprinkler Installer	4	4.000	Ea.
				1 Sprinkler Apprentice			
	7420	6" size, galvanized	Q-13	1 Sprinkler Foreman (ins)	5.50	5.820	Ea.
				2 Sprinkler Installers			
				1 Sprinkler Apprentice			
	7440	8" size, galvanized	↓	↓	5	6.400	Ea.
	7460	10" size, galvanized			4.50	7.110	Ea.
	7560	By-pass trim, not including meter					
	7580	For 5/8" meter	1 Spri	1 Sprinkler Installer	6	1.330	Ea.
	7600	For 1 meter			5.50	1.450	Ea.
	7620	For 1-1/2" meter			5	1.600	Ea.
	7640	For 2" meter	↓	↓	4.50	1.780	Ea.
	7800	Pneumatic actuator, bronze, required on all					
	7820	pneumatic release systems, any size deluge	1 Spri	1 Sprinkler Installer	18	.444	Ea.
	8000	Dry pipe air check valve, 3" size	Q-12	1 Sprinkler Installer	2	8.000	Ea.
				1 Sprinkler Apprentice			
	8200	Dry pipe valve, incl. trim and gauges, 3" size	↓	↓	2	8.000	Ea.
	8220	4" size			1	16.000	Ea.
	8240	6" size	Q-13	1 Sprinkler Foreman (ins)	2	16.000	Ea.
				2 Sprinkler Installers			
				1 Sprinkler Apprentice			
	8280	For accelerator trim with gauges, add	1 Spri	1 Sprinkler Installer	8	1.000	Ea.
	8400	Firecycle package, includes swing check					
	8420	and flow control valves with required trim					
	8440	2" size	Q-12	1 Sprinkler Installer	2	8.000	Ea.
				1 Sprinkler Apprentice			
	8460	3" size	↓	↓	1.50	10.670	Ea.
	8480	4" size			1	16.000	Ea.
	8500	6" size	Q-13	1 Sprinkler Foreman (ins)	1.40	22.860	Ea.
				2 Sprinkler Installers			
				1 Sprinkler Apprentice			
	8800	Flow control valve, includes trim and gauges, 2" size	Q-12	1 Sprinkler Installer	2	8.000	Ea.
				1 Sprinkler Apprentice			
	8820	3" size	"	"	1.50	10.670	Ea.
	8840	4" size	Q-13	1 Sprinkler Foreman (ins)	2.80	11.430	Ea.
				2 Sprinkler Installers			
				1 Sprinkler Apprentice			
	8860	6" size	"	"	2	16.000	Ea.
	9000	Magnetic by-pass valve, normally open circuit	1 Spri	1 Sprinkler Installer	16	.500	Ea.
	9040	Normally closed detection circuit			16	.500	Ea.
	9200	Pressure operated relief valve, brass body			18	.444	Ea.
	9300	Pressure regulating valve, brass body	↓	↓	20	.400	Ea.
	9600	Waterflow indicator, with recycling retard and					
	9610	two single pole retard switches, 2" thru 6" pipe size	1 Spri	1 Sprinkler Installer	8	1.000	Ea.

155 100 | Boilers

			CREW	MAKEUP	DAILY OUTPUT	MAN-HOURS	UNIT
110	110	**BOILERS, ELECTRIC, ASME** Standard controls and trim					
	1000	Steam, 6 KW, 20.5 MBH	Q-19	1 Steamfitter	1.20	20.000	Ea.
				1 Steamfitter Apprentice			
				1 Electrician			
	1020	9 KW, 30.7 MBH			1.20	20.000	Ea.
	1040	12 KW, 40.9 MBH			1.20	20.000	Ea.
	1060	18 KW, 61.4 MBH			1.20	20.000	Ea.
	1080	24 KW, 81.8 MBH			1.10	21.820	Ea.
	1100	30 KW, 102 MBH			1.10	21.820	Ea.
	1120	36 KW, 123 MBH			1.10	21.820	Ea.
	1140	45 KW, 153 MBH			1	24.000	Ea.
	1160	60 KW, 205 MBH			1	24.000	Ea.
	1180	75 KW, 256 MBH			.90	26.670	Ea.
	1200	105 KW, 358 MBH			.80	30.000	Ea.
	1220	120 KW, 409 MBH			.75	32.000	Ea.
	1240	150 KW, 512 MBH			.65	36.920	Ea.
	1260	180 KW, 614 MBH			.60	40.000	Ea.
	1280	210 KW, 716 MBH			.55	43.640	Ea.
	1300	240 KW, 819 MBH			.45	53.330	Ea.
	1320	300 KW, 1023 MBH			.40	60.000	Ea.
	1340	360 KW, 1228 MBH			.35	68.570	Ea.
	1360	420 KW, 1433 MBH	↓	↓	.30	80.000	Ea.
	1380	510 KW, 1740 MBH	Q-21	2 Steamfitters	.36	88.890	Ea.
				1 Steamfitter Apprentice			
				1 Electrician			
	1400	600 KW, 2047 MBH			.34	94.120	Ea.
	1420	720 KW, 2456 MBH			.32	100.000	Ea.
	1440	810 KW, 2764 MBH			.30	107.000	Ea.
	1460	900 KW, 3070 MBH			.28	114.000	Ea.
	1480	1080 KW, 3685 MBH			.25	128.000	Ea.
	1500	1260 KW, 4300 MBH			.22	145.000	Ea.
	1520	1620 KW, 5527 MBH			.20	160.000	Ea.
	1540	1800 KW, 6141 MBH			.19	168.000	Ea.
	1560	2070 KW, 7063 MBH			.18	178.000	Ea.
	1580	2250 KW, 7677 MBH			.17	188.000	Ea.
	1600	2340 KW, 7984 MBH			.16	200.000	Ea.
	1620	2430 KW, 8291 MBH			.14	229.000	Ea.
	1640	2520 KW, 8598 MBH	↓	↓	.12	267.000	Ea.
	2000	Hot water, 12 KW, 41 MBH	Q-19	1 Steamfitter	1.30	18.460	Ea.
				1 Steamfitter Apprentice			
				1 Electrician			
	2020	15 KW, 52 MBH			1.30	18.460	Ea.
	2040	24 KW, 82 MBH			1.20	20.000	Ea.
	2060	30 KW, 103 MBH			1.20	20.000	Ea.
	2070	36 KW, 123 MBH			1.20	20.000	Ea.
	2080	45 KW, 154 MBH			1.10	21.820	Ea.
	2100	60 KW, 205 MBH			1.10	21.820	Ea.
	2120	90 KW, 308 MBH			1	24.000	Ea.
	2140	120 KW, 410 MBH			.90	26.670	Ea.
	2160	150 KW, 510 MBH			.75	32.000	Ea.
	2180	180 KW, 615 MBH			.65	36.920	Ea.
	2200	210 KW, 716 MBH			.60	40.000	Ea.
	2220	240 KW, 820 MBH			.55	43.640	Ea.
	2240	270 KW, 922 MBH			.50	48.000	Ea.
	2260	300 KW, 1024 MBH			.45	53.330	Ea.
	2280	360 KW, 1228 MBH			.40	60.000	Ea.
	2300	420 KW, 1432 MBH	↓	↓	.35	68.570	Ea.

155 100 | Boilers

			CREW	MAKEUP	DAILY OUTPUT	MAN-HOURS	UNIT
110	2321	Boilers, hot water, 480 KW, 1636 MBH	Q-21	2 Steamfitters	.46	69.570	Ea.
				1 Steamfitter Apprentice			
				1 Electrician			
	2340	510 KW, 1739 MBH			.44	72.730	Ea.
	2360	570 KW, 1944 MBH			.43	74.420	Ea.
	2380	630 KW, 2148 MBH			.42	76.190	Ea.
	2400	690 KW, 2353 MBH			.40	80.000	Ea.
	2420	720 KW, 2452 MBH			.39	82.050	Ea.
	2440	810 KW, 2764 MBH			.38	84.210	Ea.
	2460	900 KW, 3071 MBH			.37	86.490	Ea.
	2480	1020 KW, 3480 MBH			.36	88.890	Ea.
	2500	1200 KW, 4095 MBH			.34	94.120	Ea.
	2520	1320 KW, 4505 MBH			.33	96.970	Ea.
	2540	1440 KW, 4915 MBH			.32	100.000	Ea.
	2560	1560 KW, 5323 MBH			.31	103.000	Ea.
	2580	1680 KW, 5733 MBH			.30	107.000	Ea.
	2600	1800 KW, 6143 MBH			.29	110.000	Ea.
	2620	1980 KW, 6757 MBH			.28	114.000	Ea.
	2640	2100 KW, 7167 MBH			.27	119.000	Ea.
	2660	2220 KW, 7576 MBH			.26	123.000	Ea.
	2680	2400 KW, 8191 MBH			.25	128.000	Ea.
	2700	2610 KW, 8905 MBH			.24	133.000	Ea.
	2720	2790 KW, 9519 MBH			.23	139.000	Ea.
	2740	2970 KW, 10133 MBH			.21	152.000	Ea.
	2760	3150 KW, 10748 MBH			.19	168.000	Ea.
	2780	3240 KW, 11055 MBH			.18	178.000	Ea.
	2800	3420 KW, 11669 MBH			.17	188.000	Ea.
	2820	3600 KW, 12,283 MBH	▼	▼	.16	200.000	Ea.
115		**BOILERS, GAS FIRED** Natural or propane, standard controls					
1000		Cast iron, with insulated jacket					
2000		Steam, gross output, 81 MBH	Q-7	1 Steamfitter Foreman (ins)	1.40	22.860	Ea.
				2 Steamfitters			
				1 Steamfitter Apprentice			
	2020	102 MBH			1.30	24.620	Ea.
	2040	122 MBH			1	32.000	Ea.
	2060	163 MBH			.90	35.560	Ea.
	2080	203 MBH			.90	35.560	Ea.
	2100	240 MBH			.85	37.650	Ea.
	2120	280 MBH			.80	40.000	Ea.
	2140	320 MBH			.70	45.710	Ea.
	2160	360 MBH			.65	49.230	Ea.
	2180	400 MBH			.60	53.330	Ea.
	2200	440 MBH			.55	58.180	Ea.
	2220	544 MBH			.50	64.000	Ea.
	2240	765 MBH			.45	71.110	Ea.
	2260	892 MBH			.40	80.000	Ea.
	2280	1275 MBH			.36	88.890	Ea.
	2300	1530 MBH			.31	103.000	Ea.
	2320	1875 MBH			.28	114.000	Ea.
	2340	2170 MBH			.26	123.000	Ea.
	2360	2675 MBH			.24	133.000	Ea.
	2380	3060 MBH			.23	139.000	Ea.
	2400	3570 MBH			.18	178.000	Ea.
	2420	4207 MBH			.16	200.000	Ea.
	2440	4720 MBH			.14	229.000	Ea.
	2460	5660 MBH			.13	246.000	Ea.
	2480	6100 MBH			.12	267.000	Ea.
	2500	6390 MBH	▼	▼	.10	320.000	Ea.

155 100 | Boilers

			CREW	MAKEUP	DAILY OUTPUT	MAN-HOURS	UNIT
115	2521	Boilers, gas fired, steam, gross output, 6680 MBH	Q-7	1 Steamfitter Foreman (ins)	.09	356.000	Ea.
				2 Steamfitters			
				1 Steamfitter Apprentice			
	2540	6970 MBH			.08	400.000	Ea.
	3000	Hot water, gross output, 80 MBH			1.46	21.920	Ea.
	3020	100 MBH			1.35	23.700	Ea.
	3040	122 MBH			1.10	29.090	Ea.
	3060	163 MBH			1	32.000	Ea.
	3080	203 MBH			1	32.000	Ea.
	3100	240 MBH			.95	33.680	Ea.
	3120	280 MBH			.90	35.560	Ea.
	3140	320 MBH			.80	40.000	Ea.
	3160	360 MBH			.75	42.670	Ea.
	3180	400 MBH			.70	45.710	Ea.
	3200	440 MBH			.65	49.230	Ea.
	3220	544 MBH			.60	53.330	Ea.
	3240	765 MBH			.55	58.180	Ea.
	3260	1088 MBH			.50	64.000	Ea.
	3280	1275 MBH			.46	69.570	Ea.
	3300	1530 MBH			.42	76.190	Ea.
	3320	2000 MBH			.38	84.210	Ea.
	3340	2312 MBH			.36	88.890	Ea.
	3360	2856 MBH			.33	96.970	Ea.
	3380	3264 MBH			.30	107.000	Ea.
	3400	3808 MBH			.26	123.000	Ea.
	3420	4488 MBH			.22	145.000	Ea.
	3440	4720 MBH			.18	178.000	Ea.
	3460	5520 MBH			.14	229.000	Ea.
	3480	6100 MBH			.12	267.000	Ea.
	3500	6390 MBH			.10	320.000	Ea.
	3520	6680 MBH			.09	356.000	Ea.
	3540	6970 MBH	↓	↓	.08	400.000	Ea.
	4000	Steel, insulating jacket					
	4500	Steam, not including burner, gross output					
	5500	1440 MBH	Q-6	2 Steamfitters	.35	68.570	Ea.
				1 Steamfitter Apprentice			
	5520	1630 MBH			.30	80.000	Ea.
	5540	1800 MBH			.26	92.310	Ea.
	5560	2520 MBH			.20	120.000	Ea.
	5580	3065 MBH			.18	133.000	Ea.
	5600	3600 MBH			.16	150.000	Ea.
	5620	5400 MBH	↓	↓	.14	171.000	Ea.
	5640	7200 MBH	Q-7	1 Steamfitter Foreman (ins)	.18	178.000	Ea.
				2 Steamfitters			
				1 Steamfitter Apprentice			
	5660	10,800 MBH			.17	188.000	Ea.
	5680	12,600 MBH			.15	213.000	Ea.
	5700	16,190 MBH			.12	267.000	Ea.
	5720	17,990 MBH	↓	↓	.10	320.000	Ea.
	6000	Hot water, including burner & one zone valve, gross output					
	6010	51.2 MBH	Q-6	2 Steamfitters	2	12.000	Ea.
				1 Steamfitter Apprentice			
	6020	72 MBH			2	12.000	Ea.
	6040	89 MBH			1.90	12.630	Ea.
	6060	105 MBH			1.80	13.330	Ea.
	6080	132 MBH			1.70	14.120	Ea.
	6100	155 MBH			1.50	16.000	Ea.
	6110	186 MBH	↓	↓	1.40	17.140	Ea.

155 100 | Boilers

			CREW	MAKEUP	DAILY OUTPUT	MAN-HOURS	UNIT
115	6121	Boilers, gas fired, hot water, gross output, 227 MBH	Q-6	2 Steamfitters	1.30	18.460	Ea.
				1 Steamfitter Apprentice			
	6140	292 MBH			1.20	20.000	Ea.
	6160	400 MBH			.80	30.000	Ea.
	6180	480 MBH			.70	34.290	Ea.
	6200	640 MBH			.60	40.000	Ea.
	6220	800 MBH			.50	48.000	Ea.
	6240	960 MBH			.45	53.330	Ea.
	6260	1200 MBH			.40	60.000	Ea.
	6280	1440 MBH			.35	68.570	Ea.
	6300	1960 MBH			.30	80.000	Ea.
	6320	2400 MBH			.20	120.000	Ea.
	6340	3000 MBH	↓	↓	.15	160.000	Ea.
	7990	Special feature gas fired boilers					
	8000	Pulse combustion 44,000 BTU	Q-5	1 Steamfitter	1.50	10.670	Ea.
				1 Steamfitter Apprentice			
	8050	88,000 BTU			1.40	11.430	Ea.
	8080	134,000 BTU	↓	↓	1.20	13.330	Ea.
	9000	Wall hung, C.I., sealed combustion, direct vent					
	9010	Packaged, net output					
	9020	44,400 BTUH	Q-6	2 Steamfitters	1.33	18.050	Ea.
				1 Steamfitter Apprentice			
	9030	53,100 BTUH			1.33	18.050	Ea.
	9040	64,500 BTUH	↓	↓	1.33	18.050	Ea.
	120	**BOILERS, OIL FIRED** Standard controls, flame retention burner					
	1000	Cast iron, with insulated flush jacket					
	2000	Steam, gross output, 109 MBH	Q-7	1 Steamfitter Foreman (ins)	1.20	26.670	Ea.
				2 Steamfitters			
				1 Steamfitter Apprentice			
	2020	144 MBH			1.10	29.090	Ea.
	2040	173 MBH			1	32.000	Ea.
	2060	207 MBH			.90	35.560	Ea.
	2080	236 MBH			.85	37.650	Ea.
	2100	336 MBH			.70	45.710	Ea.
	2120	480 MBH			.50	64.000	Ea.
	2140	625 MBH			.48	66.670	Ea.
	2160	794 MBH			.45	71.110	Ea.
	2180	1084 MBH			.42	76.190	Ea.
	2200	1360 MBH			.38	84.210	Ea.
	2220	1600 MBH			.31	103.000	Ea.
	2240	2175 MBH			.28	114.000	Ea.
	2260	2480 MBH			.25	128.000	Ea.
	2280	3000 MBH			.23	139.000	Ea.
	2300	3550 MBH			.22	145.000	Ea.
	2320	3820 MBH			.19	168.000	Ea.
	2340	4360 MBH			.17	188.000	Ea.
	2360	4940 MBH			.15	213.000	Ea.
	2380	5520 MBH			.13	246.000	Ea.
	2400	6100 MBH			.12	267.000	Ea.
	2420	6390 MBH			.10	320.000	Ea.
	2440	6680 MBH			.09	356.000	Ea.
	2460	6970 MBH	↓	↓	.08	400.000	Ea.
	5000	Steel, insulated jacket, burner					
	6000	Steam, full water leg construction, gross output					
	6020	144 MBH	Q-6	2 Steamfitters	1.60	15.000	Ea.
				1 Steamfitter Apprentice			
	6040	198 MBH			1.40	17.140	Ea.
	6060	252 MBH	↓	↓	1.30	18.460	Ea.

		Description	CREW	MAKEUP			DAILY OUTPUT	MAN-HOURS	UNIT
155 100		**Boilers**							
120	6081	Boilers, oil fired, stl. insul. jacket, steam, 324 MBH	Q-6	2 Steamfitters			1.20	20.000	Ea.
				1 Steamfitter Apprentice					
	6100	396 MBH					.90	26.670	Ea.
	6120	468 MBH					.80	30.000	Ea.
	6140	648 MBH					.60	40.000	Ea.
	6160	792 MBH					.50	48.000	Ea.
	6180	1008 MBH					.45	53.330	Ea.
	6200	1260 MBH					.40	60.000	Ea.
	6220	1512 MBH					.35	68.570	Ea.
	6240	1800 MBH					.33	72.730	Ea.
	6260	2100 MBH					.26	92.310	Ea.
	6280	2400 MBH					.22	109.000	Ea.
	7000	Hot water, gross output, 103 MBH					1.90	12.630	Ea.
	7020	122 MBH					1.80	13.330	Ea.
	7040	137 MBH					1.60	15.000	Ea.
	7060	168 MBH					1.50	16.000	Ea.
	7080	225 MBH					1.40	17.140	Ea.
	7100	315 MBH					1.10	21.820	Ea.
	7120	420 MBH					.80	30.000	Ea.
	7140	525 MBH					.65	36.920	Ea.
	7160	630 MBH					.60	40.000	Ea.
	7180	735 MBH					.55	43.640	Ea.
	7200	840 MBH					.50	48.000	Ea.
	7220	1050 MBH					.42	57.140	Ea.
	7240	1365 MBH					.37	64.860	Ea.
	7260	1680 MBH					.33	72.730	Ea.
	7280	2310 MBH					.24	100.000	Ea.
	7300	2835 MBH					.17	141.000	Ea.
	7320	3150 MBH	↓	↓			.13	185.000	Ea.
	125	**BOILERS, GAS/OIL** Combination with burners and controls							
	1000	Cast Iron with insulated jacket							
	2000	Steam, gross output, 720 MBH	Q-7	1 Steamfitter Foreman (ins)			.40	80.000	Ea.
				2 Steamfitters					
				1 Steamfitter Apprentice					
	2020	810 MBH					.37	86.490	Ea.
	2040	1084 MBH					.33	96.970	Ea.
	2060	1360 MBH					.30	107.000	Ea.
	2080	1600 MBH					.26	123.000	Ea.
	2100	2040 MBH					.23	139.000	Ea.
	2120	2450 MBH					.20	160.000	Ea.
	2140	2700 MBH					.19	168.000	Ea.
	2160	3000 MBH					.18	178.000	Ea.
	2180	3270 MBH					.17	188.000	Ea.
	2200	3770 MBH					.15	213.000	Ea.
	2220	4070 MBH					.14	229.000	Ea.
	2240	4650 MBH					.13	246.000	Ea.
	2260	5230 MBH					.11	291.000	Ea.
	2280	5520 MBH					.10	320.000	Ea.
	2300	5810 MBH					.09	356.000	Ea.
	2320	6100 MBH					.08	400.000	Ea.
	2340	6390 MBH					.07	457.000	Ea.
	2360	6680 MBH					.06	533.000	Ea.
	2380	6970 MBH					.05	640.000	Ea.
	3000	Hot water, gross output, 584 MBH					.54	59.260	Ea.
	3020	876 MBH					.50	64.000	Ea.
	3040	1168 MBH					.48	66.670	Ea.
	3060	1460 MBH					.45	71.110	Ea.
	3080	2044 MBH	↓	↓			.36	88.890	Ea.

			CREW	MAKEUP	DAILY OUTPUT	MAN-HOURS	UNIT
155 100	**Boilers**						
125	3101	Boilers, gas/oil, C.I. insul. jacket, hot water, 2628 MBH	Q-7	1 Steamfitter Foreman (ins)	.32	100.000	Ea.
				2 Steamfitters			
				1 Steamfitter Apprentice			
	3120	3210 MBH			.28	114.000	Ea.
	3140	3796 MBH			.24	133.000	Ea.
	3160	4088 MBH			.22	145.000	Ea.
	3180	4672 MBH			.18	178.000	Ea.
	3200	5256 MBH			.14	229.000	Ea.
	3220	6000 MBH, 179 BHP			.10	320.000	Ea.
	3240	7130 MBH, 213 BHP			.07	457.000	Ea.
	3260	9800 MBH, 286 BHP			.05	640.000	Ea.
	3280	10,900 MBH, 325.6 BHP			.04	800.000	Ea.
	3290	12,200 MBH, 364.5 BHP			.03	67.000	Ea.
	3300	13,500 MBH, 403.3 BHP	↓	↓	.02	600.000	Ea.
	4000	Steel, insulated jacket, skid base, tubeless					
	4100	Steam, 15 psi, gross output 517 MBH, 15 BHP	Q-6	2 Steamfitters	.81	29.630	Ea.
				1 Steamfitter Apprentice			
	4110	690 MBH, 20 BHP			.78	30.770	Ea.
	4120	862 MBH, 25 BHP			.61	39.340	Ea.
	4130	1004 MBH, 30 BHP			.59	40.680	Ea.
	4140	1340 MBH, 40 BHP			.52	46.150	Ea.
	4150	1675 MBH, 50 BHP			.48	50.000	Ea.
	4160	2175 MBH, 65 BHP			.42	57.140	Ea.
	4170	2510 MBH, 75 BHP			.34	70.590	Ea.
	4180	3015 MBH, 90 BHP	↓	↓	.28	85.710	Ea.
	4190	3350 MBH, 100 BHP	Q-7	1 Steamfitter Foreman (ins)	.32	100.000	Ea.
				2 Steamfitters			
				1 Steamfitter Apprentice			
	4200	3880 MBH, 116 BHP			.29	110.000	Ea.
	4210	4685 MBH, 140 BHP			.27	119.000	Ea.
	4220	5025 MBH, 150 BHP			.26	123.000	Ea.
	4230	5550 MBH, 166 BHP			.17	188.000	Ea.
	4240	6700 MBH, 200 BHP			.14	229.000	Ea.
	4250	7760 MBH, 232 BHP			.13	246.000	Ea.
	4260	8870 MBH, 265 BHP			.12	267.000	Ea.
	4270	11,100 MBH, 322 BHP			.09	356.000	Ea.
	4280	13,400 MBH, 400 BHP			.08	400.000	Ea.
	4290	17,750 MBH, 530 BHP			.06	533.000	Ea.
	4300	20,750 MBH, 620 BHP	↓	↓	.05	640.000	Ea.
	4500	Steam, 150 psi gross output, 335 MBH, 10 BHP	Q-6	2 Steamfitters	.65	36.920	Ea.
				1 Steamfitter Apprentice			
	4520	502 MBH, 15 BHP			.55	43.640	Ea.
	4560	670 MBH, 20 BHP			.45	53.330	Ea.
	4600	1005 MBH, 30 BHP			.36	66.670	Ea.
	4640	1339 MBH, 40 BHP			.28	85.710	Ea.
	4660	1674 MBH, 50 BHP			.24	100.000	Ea.
	4680	2009 MBH, 60 BHP			.21	114.000	Ea.
	4720	2511 MBH, 75 BHP			.17	141.000	Ea.
	5000	Hot water, gross output, 525 MBH			.60	40.000	Ea.
	5020	630 MBH			.55	43.640	Ea.
	5040	735 MBH			.50	48.000	Ea.
	5060	840 MBH			.45	53.330	Ea.
	5080	1050 MBH			.38	63.160	Ea.
	5100	1365 MBH			.33	72.730	Ea.
	5120	1680 MBH			.29	82.760	Ea.
	5140	2310 MBH			.20	120.000	Ea.
	5160	2835 MBH			.13	185.000	Ea.
	5180	3150 MBH	↓	↓	.09	267.000	Ea.

155 100 | Boilers

			CREW	MAKEUP	DAILY OUTPUT	MAN-HOURS	UNIT
130	130	**BOILERS, SOLID FUEL**					
	0020	Wood, coal, wood/paper waste, peat. Steel, 3" diam. horizontal					
	1000	Natural draft, gross output, 1445 MBH	Q-6	2 Steamfitters	.45	53.330	Ea.
				1 Steamfitter Apprentice			
	1050	1635 MBH			.43	55.810	Ea.
	1100	1805 MBH			.41	58.540	Ea.
	1150	2160 MBH			.38	63.160	Ea.
	1200	2520 MBH			.32	75.000	Ea.
	1250	3065 MBM	Q-7	1 Steamfitter Foreman (ins)	.40	80.000	Ea.
				2 Steamfitters			
				1 Steamfitter Apprentice			
	1300	3600 MBH			.38	84.210	Ea.
	1350	4500 MBH			.29	110.000	Ea.
	1400	5400 MBH			.26	123.000	Ea.
	1450	6295 MBH			.23	139.000	Ea.
	1500	7200 MBH			.21	152.000	Ea.
	1550	9000 MBH			.19	168.000	Ea.
	1600	10,800 MBH			.17	188.000	Ea.
	1650	12,600 MBH			.15	213.000	Ea.
	1700	14,390 MBH			.13	246.000	Ea.
	1750	16,190 MBH			.12	267.000	Ea.
	1800	17,990 MBH			.10	320.000	Ea.
	3000	Stoker fired (coal) cast iron with flush jacket and					
	3080	insulation, steam or water, gross output, 148 MBH	Q-6	2 Steamfitters	1.50	16.000	Ea.
				1 Steamfitter Apprentice			
	3100	200 MBH			1.30	18.460	Ea.
	3120	247 MBH			1.20	20.000	Ea.
	3140	300 MBH			1	24.000	Ea.
	3160	410 MBH			.96	25.000	Ea.
	3180	495 MBH			.88	27.270	Ea.
	3200	580 MBH			.80	30.000	Ea.
	3400	1280 MBH			.36	66.670	Ea.
	3420	1460 MBH			.30	80.000	Ea.
	3440	1640 MBH			.28	85.710	Ea.
	3460	1820 MBH			.26	92.310	Ea.
	3480	2000 MBH			.25	96.000	Ea.
	3500	2360 MBH			.23	104.000	Ea.
	3520	2540 MBH			.21	114.000	Ea.
	3540	2725 MBH			.20	120.000	Ea.
	3800	2950 MBH	Q-7	1 Steamfitter Foreman (ins)	.16	200.000	Ea.
				2 Steamfitters			
				1 Steamfitter Apprentice			
	3820	3210 MBH			.15	213.000	Ea.
	3840	3480 MBH			.14	229.000	Ea.
	3860	3745 MBH			.14	229.000	Ea.
	3880	4000 MBH			.13	246.000	Ea.
	3900	4200 MBH			.13	246.000	Ea.
	3920	4400 MBH			.12	267.000	Ea.
	3940	4600 MBH			.12	267.000	Ea.
	5000	Wood or coal and oil combination, circulator,					
	5050	mixing valve, controls					
	5100	Output (oil), 60 MBH, without burner	Q-5	1 Steamfitter	.84	19.050	Ea.
				1 Steamfitter Apprentice			
	5150	80 MBH, without burner			.80	20.000	Ea.
	5250	100 MBH, with burner			.73	21.920	Ea.
	5300	130 MBH, with burner			.69	23.190	Ea.
	5350	160 MBH, with burner			.65	24.620	Ea.

155 100	Boilers	CREW	MAKEUP	DAILY OUTPUT	MAN-HOURS	UNIT
135	**BOILERS, PACKAGED SCOTCH MARINE** Steam or hot water					
1000	Packaged fire tube, #2 oil, gross output					
1020	3348 MBH	Q-7	1 Steamfitter Foreman (ins)	.12	267.000	Ea.
			2 Steamfitters			
			1 Steamfitter Apprentice			
1040	6696 MBH			.08	400.000	Ea.
1060	10,044 MBH			.06	533.000	Ea.
1080	16,740 MBH			.04	800.000	Ea.
1100	23,435 MBH			.03	67.000	Ea.
1120	To fire #6, add			.83	38.550	Ea.
1140	To fire #6, and gas, add	↓	↓	.42	76.190	Ea.
1180	For duplex package feed system					
1200	To 3348 MBH boiler, add	Q-7	1 Steamfitter Foreman (ins)	.54	59.260	Ea.
			2 Steamfitters			
			1 Steamfitter Apprentice			
1220	To 6696 MBH boiler, add			.41	78.050	Ea.
1240	To 10,044 MBH boiler, add			.38	84.210	Ea.
1260	To 16,740 MBH boiler, add			.28	114.000	Ea.
1280	To 23,435 MBH boiler, add	↓	↓	.25	128.000	Ea.
2000	Packaged water tube, #2 oil, gross output					
2040	1200 MBH	Q-7	1 Steamfitter Foreman (ins)	.50	64.000	Ea.
			2 Steamfitters			
			1 Steamfitter Apprentice			
2060	1600 MBH			.40	80.000	Ea.
2080	2400 MBH			.30	107.000	Ea.
2100	3200 MBH			.25	128.000	Ea.
2120	4800 MBH			.20	160.000	Ea.
2140	For gas fired, add	↓	↓	.40	80.000	Ea.
150	**SWIMMING POOL HEATERS** Not including wiring, external					
0020	piping, base or pad,					
0060	Gas fired, gross output, 50 MBH	Q-6	2 Steamfitters	3	8.000	Ea.
			1 Steamfitter Apprentice			
0100	80 MBH			2	12.000	Ea.
0160	120 MBH			1.50	16.000	Ea.
0180	145 MBH			1.30	18.460	Ea.
0200	170 MBH			1	24.000	Ea.
0220	200 MBH			.70	34.290	Ea.
0240	280 MBH			.60	40.000	Ea.
0260	450 MBH			.50	48.000	Ea.
0280	500 MBH			.40	60.000	Ea.
0300	600 MBH			.35	68.570	Ea.
0320	750 MBH			.33	72.730	Ea.
0340	890 MBH			.26	92.310	Ea.
0360	965 MBH			.22	109.000	Ea.
0370	1080 MBH			.21	114.000	Ea.
0380	1312 MBH			.19	126.000	Ea.
0400	1600 MBH			.14	171.000	Ea.
0410	2100 MBH			.13	185.000	Ea.
0420	2450 MBH			.11	218.000	Ea.
0440	3000 MBH			.09	267.000	Ea.
1000	Oil fired, gross output, 97 MBH			1.70	14.120	Ea.
1020	118 MBH			1.70	14.120	Ea.
1040	134 MBH			1.60	15.000	Ea.
1060	161 MBH			1.30	18.460	Ea.
1080	187 MBH			1.20	20.000	Ea.
1100	214 MBH			1.10	21.820	Ea.
1120	262 MBH			.89	26.970	Ea.
1140	340 MBH	↓	↓	.68	35.290	Ea.

155 | Heating

155 100 | Boilers

		CREW	MAKEUP	DAILY OUTPUT	MAN-HOURS	UNIT
150	1161	Swimming pool heaters, oil fired, gross output, 420 MBH	Q-6	2 Steamfitters 1 Steamfitter Apprentice	.58	41.380	Ea.
	1180	525 MBH			.46	52.170	Ea.
	1200	630 MBH			.41	58.540	Ea.
	1220	735 MBH			.35	68.570	Ea.
	1240	840 MBH			.33	72.730	Ea.
	1260	1050 MBH			.27	88.890	Ea.
	1280	1365 MBH			.21	114.000	Ea.
	1300	1680 MBH			.18	133.000	Ea.
	1320	2310 MBH			.13	185.000	Ea.
	1340	2835 MBH			.11	218.000	Ea.
	1360	3150 MBH	↓	↓	.09	267.000	Ea.
	2000	Electric, 12 KW, 4800 gallon pool	Q-19	1 Steamfitter 1 Steamfitter Apprentice 1 Electrician	3	8.000	Ea.
	2020	18 KW, 7200 gallon pool			2.80	8.570	Ea.
	2040	24 KW, 9600 gallon pool			2.40	10.000	Ea.
	2060	30 KW, 12,000 gallon pool			2	12.000	Ea.
	2080	36 KW, 14,400 gallon pool			1.60	15.000	Ea.
	2100	54 KW, 24,000 gallon pool			1.20	20.000	Ea.
	2120	300 KW, 120,000 gallon pool			1	24.000	Ea.
	2140	600 KW, 240,000 gallon pool			.80	30.000	Ea.
	2160	1200 KW, 480,000 gallon pool	↓	↓	.60	40.000	Ea.

155 200 | Boiler Accessories

		CREW	MAKEUP	DAILY OUTPUT	MAN-HOURS	UNIT
220	**BOILER BLOWDOWN SYSTEMS**					
1010	Boiler blowdown, auto/manual to 2000 MBH	Q-5	1 Steamfitter 1 Steamfitter Apprentice	3.75	4.270	Ea.
1020	7300 MBH	"	"	3	5.330	Ea.
230	**BURNERS**					
0990	Residential, conversion, gas fired, LP or natural					
1000	Gun type, atmospheric input 35 to 180 MBH	Q-1	1 Plumber 1 Plumber Apprentice	2.50	6.400	Ea.
1020	50 to 240 MBH			2	8.000	Ea.
1040	200 to 400 MBH	↓	↓	1.70	9.410	Ea.
2000	Commercial and industrial, gun type, gas/oil, input					
2050	400 to 980 MBH	Q-1	1 Plumber 1 Plumber Apprentice	1.50	10.670	Ea.
2080	Oil side pilot, second redundant valve, add			35	.457	Ea.
2110	Low High Off firing, add			35	.457	Ea.
2140	750 to 2100 MBH			1.30	12.310	Ea.
2170	Low fire start, 2nd redund. valve Hi-low swtch, add			35	.457	Ea.
2200	1750 to 3080 MBH			1.20	13.330	Ea.
2230	Self check valve, 2nd redundant valve, add			35	.457	Ea.
2260	3000 to 4000 MBH			1.10	14.550	Ea.
2290	2nd red. valve,low fire start,self chk,add			35	.457	Ea.
2320	4000 to 6300 MBH			1	16.000	Ea.
2350	Low fire start, self check valve, gas firing	↓	↓	35	.457	Ea.
2500	Impinged jet, rectangular, burner only, 3-1/2" WC,					
2520	Gas fired, input, 420 to 640 MBH	Q-1	1 Plumber 1 Plumber Apprentice	2	8.000	Ea.
2540	560 to 860 MBH			2	8.000	Ea.
2560	630 to 950 MBH			1.90	8.420	Ea.
2580	950 to 1200 MBH			1.80	8.890	Ea.
2600	1120 to 1700 MBH			1.80	8.890	Ea.
2620	1700 to 1900 MBH			1.70	9.410	Ea.
2640	1400 to 2100 MBH			1.60	10.000	Ea.
2660	1600 to 2400 MBH	↓	↓	1.60	10.000	Ea.

155 200 | Boiler Accessories

			CREW	MAKEUP	DAILY OUTPUT	MAN-HOURS	UNIT
230	2681	Burners, comm., impinged jet, gas fired, input, 1700-2500 MBH	Q-1	1 Plumber	1.50	10.670	Ea.
				1 Plumber Apprentice			
	2700	1880 to 2880 MBH			1.40	11.430	Ea.
	2720	2260 to 3680 MBH			1.40	11.430	Ea.
	2740	2590 to 4320 MBH			1.30	12.310	Ea.
	2760	3020 to 5040 MBH			1.20	13.330	Ea.
	2780	3450 to 5760 MBH			1.20	13.330	Ea.
	2850	Burner pilot			50	.320	Ea.
	2860	Thermocouple			50	.320	Ea.
	2870	Thermcouple & pilot bracket	↓	↓	45	.356	Ea.
	3000	Flame retention oil fired assembly, input					
	3020	.50 to 2.25 GPH	Q-1	1 Plumber	2.40	6.670	Ea.
				1 Plumber Apprentice			
	3040	2.0 to 5.0 GPH			2	8.000	Ea.
	3060	3.0 to 7.0 GPH			1.80	8.890	Ea.
	3080	6.0 to 12.0 GPH	↓	↓	1.60	10.000	Ea.
	8020	Coal stoker, automatic, 1000 MBH boiler	Q-7	1 Steamfitter Foreman (ins)	1	32.000	Ea.
				2 Steamfitters			
				1 Steamfitter Apprentice			
	8040	2000 MBH boiler			.50	64.000	Ea.
	8060	7300 MBH boiler	↓	↓	.20	160.000	Ea.
240		DRAFT CONTROLS, BAROMETRIC					
	1000	Gas fired system only, 6" size for 5" and 6" pipes	1 Shee	1 Sheet Metal Worker	20	.400	Ea.
	1020	7" size, for 6" and 7" pipes			19	.421	Ea.
	1040	8" size, for 7" and 8" pipes			18	.444	Ea.
	1060	9" size, for 8" and 9" pipes	↓	↓	16	.500	Ea.
	2000	All fuel, oil, oil/gas, coal					
	2020	10" for 9" and 10" pipes	1 Shee	1 Sheet Metal Worker	15	.533	Ea.
	2040	12" for 11" and 12" pipes			15	.533	Ea.
	2060	14" for 13" and 14" pipes			14	.571	Ea.
	2080	16" for 15" and 16" pipes			13	.615	Ea.
	2100	18" for 17" and 18" pipes			12	.667	Ea.
	2120	20" for 19" and 21" pipes	↓	↓	10	.800	Ea.
	2140	24" for 22" and 25" pipes	Q-9	1 Sheet Metal Worker	12	1.330	Ea.
				1 Sheet Metal Apprentice			
	2160	28" for 26" and 30" pipes			10	1.600	Ea.
	2180	32" for 31" and 34" pipes	↓	↓	8	2.000	Ea.
	3260	For thermal switch for above, add	1 Shee	1 Sheet Metal Worker	24	.333	Ea.
	5000	Vent damper, bi-metal, gas, 3" diameter	Q-9	1 Sheet Metal Worker	24	.667	Ea.
				1 Sheet Metal Apprentice			
	5010	4" diameter			24	.667	Ea.
	5020	5" diameter			23	.696	Ea.
	5030	6" diameter			22	.727	Ea.
	5040	7" diameter			21	.762	Ea.
	5050	8" diameter			20	.800	Ea.
	5101	Electric, automatic, gas, 4" diameter			24	.667	Ea.
	5110	5" diameter			23	.696	Ea.
	5121	6" diameter			22	.727	Ea.
	5130	7" diameter			21	.762	Ea.
	5140	8" diameter			20	.800	Ea.
	5150	9" diameter			20	.800	Ea.
	5160	10" diameter			19	.842	Ea.
	5170	12" diameter			19	.842	Ea.
	5180	14" diameter			18	.889	Ea.
	5190	16" diameter			17	.941	Ea.
	5200	18" diameter			16	1.000	Ea.
	5250	Automatic, oil, 4" diameter			24	.667	Ea.
	5260	5" diameter	↓	↓	23	.696	Ea.

155 200	Boiler Accessories	CREW	MAKEUP	DAILY OUTPUT	MAN-HOURS	UNIT
240 5271	Vent damper, elec., automatic, oil, 6" diameter	Q-9	1 Sheet Metal Worker	22	.727	Ea.
			1 Sheet Metal Apprentice			
5280	7" diameter			21	.762	Ea.
5290	8" diameter			20	.800	Ea.
5300	9" diameter			20	.800	Ea.
5310	10" diameter			19	.842	Ea.
5320	12" diameter			19	.842	Ea.
5330	14" diameter			18	.889	Ea.
5340	16" diameter			17	.941	Ea.
5350	18" diameter	↓	↓	16	1.000	Ea.
250	FUEL OIL SPECIALTIES					
0020	Foot valve, single poppet, metal to metal construction,					
0040	bevel seat, 1/2" diameter	1 Stpi	1 Steamfitter	20	.400	Ea.
0060	3/4" diameter			18	.444	Ea.
0080	1" diameter			16	.500	Ea.
0100	1-1/4" diameter			15	.533	Ea.
0120	1-1/2" diameter			13	.615	Ea.
0140	2" diameter			11	.727	Ea.
1000	Oil filters, 3/8" IPT., 20 gal. per hour			20	.400	Ea.
1020	32 gal. per hour			18	.444	Ea.
1040	40 gal. per hour			16	.500	Ea.
1060	50 gal. per hour	↓	↓	14	.571	Ea.
1800	Pump and motor sets					
1810	Light fuel and diesel oils, 100 PSI					
1820	25 GPH 1/4 HP	Q-5	1 Steamfitter	6	2.670	Ea.
			1 Steamfitter Apprentice			
1830	45 GPH, 1/4 HP			6	2.670	Ea.
1840	90 GPH, 1/4 HP			5	3.200	Ea.
1850	160 GPH, 1/3 HP			4	4.000	Ea.
1860	325 GPH, 3/4 HP			4	4.000	Ea.
1870	700 GPH, 1-1/2 HP			3	5.330	Ea.
1880	1000 GPH, 2 HP			3	5.330	Ea.
1890	1800 GPH, 5 HP	↓	↓	1.80	8.890	Ea.
2000	Remote tank gauging system, self contained					
2020	30' transmission line					
2100	30" pointer travel	1 Stpi	1 Steamfitter	2	4.000	Ea.
2120	5" pointer travel			2.50	3.200	Ea.
3000	Valve, ball check, globe type, 3/8" diameter			24	.333	Ea.
3500	Fusible, 3/8" diameter			24	.333	Ea.
3600	1/2" diameter			24	.333	Ea.
3610	3/4" diameter			20	.400	Ea.
3620	1" diameter			19	.421	Ea.
4000	Nonfusible, 3/8" diameter	↓	↓	24	.333	Ea.
4500	Shutoff, gate type, lever handle, spring-fusible kit					
4520	1/4" diameter	1 Stpi	1 Steamfitter	14	.571	Ea.
4540	3/8" diameter			12	.667	Ea.
4560	1/2" diameter			10	.800	Ea.
4570	3/4" diameter	↓	↓	8	1.000	Ea.
4580	Lever handle, requires weight and fusible kit					
4600	1" diameter	1 Stpi	1 Steamfitter	9	.889	Ea.
4620	1-1/4" diameter			8	1.000	Ea.
4640	1-1/2" diameter			7	1.140	Ea.
5500	Vent protector/breather, 1-1/4" diameter			32	.250	Ea.
5520	1-1/2" diameter			32	.250	Ea.
5540	2" diameter			32	.250	Ea.
5560	3" diameter			28	.286	Ea.
5580	4" diameter	↓	↓	24	.333	Ea.
5581						

155 200	Boiler Accessories	CREW	MAKEUP	DAILY OUTPUT	MAN-HOURS	UNIT
250 8000	Fuel oil and tank heaters					
8020	Electric, capacity rated at 230 volts					
8040	Immersion element in steel manifold					
8060	96 GPH at 50°F rise	Q-5	1 Steamfitter	6.40	2.500	Ea.
			1 Steamfitter Apprentice			
8070	128 GPH at 50°F rise			6.20	2.580	Ea.
8080	160 GPH at 50°F rise			5.90	2.710	Ea.
8090	192 GPH at 50°F rise			5.50	2.910	Ea.
8100	240 GPH at 50°F rise			5.10	3.140	Ea.
8110	288 GPH at 50°F rise			4.60	3.480	Ea.
8120	384 GPH at 50°F rise			3.10	5.160	Ea.
8130	480 GPH at 50°F rise			2.30	6.960	Ea.
8140	576 GPH at 50°F rise	↓	↓	2.10	7.620	Ea.
8300	Suction stub, immersion type					
8320	75" long, 750 watts	1 Stpi	1 Steamfitter	14	.571	Ea.
8330	99" long, 2000 watts			12	.667	Ea.
8340	123" long, 3000 watts	↓	↓	10	.800	Ea.
8400	Electro/steam, electric capacity					
8420	rated at 230 volts/steam at 5 PSIG					
8440	28/50 GPH	Q-5	1 Steamfitter	3.50	4.570	Ea.
			1 Steamfitter Apprentice			
8450	64/135 GPH			3	5.330	Ea.
8460	80/257 GPH			2.50	6.400	Ea.
8470	96/303 GPH	↓	↓	2.10	7.620	Ea.
8480	120/384 GPH	Q-6	2 Steamfitters	3	8.000	Ea.
			1 Steamfitter Apprentice			
8490	144/720 GPH			1.80	13.330	Ea.
8500	192/800 GPH			1.60	15.000	Ea.
8510	240/1000 GPH	↓	↓	1.30	18.460	Ea.
8660	Steam, cross flow, rated at 5 PSIG					
8680	42 GPH	Q-5	1 Steamfitter	7	2.290	Ea.
			1 Steamfitter Apprentice			
8690	73 GPH			6.70	2.390	Ea.
8700	112 GPH			6.20	2.580	Ea.
8710	158 GPH			5.80	2.760	Ea.
8720	187 GPH			4	4.000	Ea.
8730	270 GPH	↓	↓	3.60	4.440	Ea.
8740	365 GPH	Q-6	2 Steamfitters	4.90	4.900	Ea.
			1 Steamfitter Apprentice			
8750	635 GPH			3.70	6.490	Ea.
8760	845 GPH			2.50	9.600	Ea.
8770	1420 GPH			1.60	15.000	Ea.
8780	2100 GPH	↓	↓	1.10	21.820	Ea.
8860	Steam or water, safety type					
8880	Water capacity at 180°F/steam at 5 PSIG					
8900	70/84 GPH	Q-5	1 Steamfitter	3.70	4.320	Ea.
			1 Steamfitter Apprentice			
8910	90/108 GPH			3.10	5.160	Ea.
8920	120/144 GPH			2.70	5.930	Ea.
8930	150/180 GPH			2.30	6.960	Ea.
8940	180/216 GPH			1.80	8.890	Ea.
8950	250/300 GPH	↓	↓	1.40	11.430	Ea.
8960	320/384 GPH	Q-6	2 Steamfitters	1.90	12.630	Ea.
			1 Steamfitter Apprentice			
8970	400/449 GPH			1.50	16.000	Ea.
8980	480/536 GPH			1.30	18.460	Ea.
8990	600/670 GPH	↓	↓	1.10	21.820	Ea.
8991						

155 200	Boiler Accessories	CREW	MAKEUP	DAILY OUTPUT	MAN-HOURS	UNIT
250 9101	Fuel oil and tank heaters, suction bell type					
9120	160 GPH, 17" high	Q-5	1 Steamfitter 1 Steamfitter Apprentice	8	2.000	Ea.
9140	240 GPH, 24" high	"	"	7	2.290	Ea.
9200	Tank heating coil					
9240	73" high by 15-3/8" diameter	Q-5	1 Steamfitter 1 Steamfitter Apprentice	5	3.200	Ea.
9280	Tank outlet heater (large capacity tank)					
9320	95/200 GPH	Q-5	1 Steamfitter 1 Steamfitter Apprentice	4	4.000	Ea.
9330	190/400 GPH	"	"	2.70	5.930	Ea.
9340	360/810 GPH	Q-6	2 Steamfitters 1 Steamfitter Apprentice	3.20	7.500	Ea.
9350	490/1070 GPH			2.60	9.230	Ea.
9360	830/1850 GPH			2	12.000	Ea.
9370	1000/2200 GPH			1.70	14.120	Ea.
9380	1310/2920 GPH			1.30	18.460	Ea.
9390	1500/3300 GPH			1.10	21.820	Ea.
9400	2280/5050 GPH			.83	28.920	Ea.
9410	2500/5550 GPH			.80	30.000	Ea.
9420	3000/6660 GPH			.72	33.330	Ea.
9430	4100/9150 GPH			.60	40.000	Ea.
9440	5450/12,100 GPH			.50	48.000	Ea.
9450	7000/15,500 GPH			.40	60.000	Ea.
9460	8700/19,300 GPH	↓	↓	.33	72.730	Ea.
260	**INDUCED DRAFT FANS**					
1000	Breeching installation					
1800	Hot gas, 600°F, variable pitch pulley and motor					
1840	6" diam. inlet, 1/4 H.P., 1 phase, 400 CFM	Q-9	1 Sheet Metal Worker 1 Sheet Metal Apprentice	6	2.670	Ea.
1850	7" diam. inlet, 1/4 H.P., 1 phase, 800 CFM			5	3.200	Ea.
1860	8" diam. inlet, 1/4 H.P., 1phase, 1120 CFM			4	4.000	Ea.
1870	9" diam. inlet, 3/4 H.P., 1 phase, 1440 CFM			3.60	4.440	Ea.
1880	10" diam. inlet, 3/4 H.P., 1 phase, 2000 CFM			3.30	4.850	Ea.
1900	12" diam. inlet, 3/4 H.P., 3 phase, 2960 CFM			3	5.330	Ea.
1910	14" diam. inlet, 1 H.P., 3 phase, 4160 CFM			2.60	6.150	Ea.
1920	16" diam. inlet, 2 H.P., 3 phase, 6720 CFM			2.30	6.960	Ea.
1940	18" diam. inlet, 3 H.P., 3 phase, 9120 CFM			2	8.000	Ea.
1950	20" diam. inlet, 3 H.P., 3 phase, 9760 CFM			1.50	10.670	Ea.
1960	22" diam. inlet, 5 H.P., 3 phase, 13,360 CFM			1	16.000	Ea.
1980	24" diam. inlet, 7-1/2 H.P., 3 phase, 17,760 CFM	↓	↓	.80	20.000	Ea.
3600	Chimneytop installation					
3700	6" size	1 Shee	1 Sheet Metal Worker	8	1.000	Ea.
3740	8" size			7	1.140	Ea.
3780	13" size	↓	↓	6	1.330	Ea.
5500	Flue shutter damper for draft control,					
5510	parallel blades					
5550	8" size	Q-9	1 Sheet Metal Worker 1 Sheet Metal Apprentice	8	2.000	Ea.
5560	9" size			7.50	2.130	Ea.
5570	10" size			7	2.290	Ea.
5580	12" size			6.50	2.460	Ea.
5590	14" size			6	2.670	Ea.
5600	16" size			5.50	2.910	Ea.
5610	18" size			5	3.200	Ea.
5620	20" size			4.50	3.560	Ea.
5630	22" size			4	4.000	Ea.
5640	24" size	↓	↓	3.50	4.570	Ea.

155 200 | Boiler Accessories

		CREW	MAKEUP	DAILY OUTPUT	MAN-HOURS	UNIT
260 5651	Flue shutter damper, parallel blades, 27" size	Q-9	1 Sheet Metal Worker	3	5.330	Ea.
			1 Sheet Metal Apprentice			
5660	30" size			2.50	6.400	Ea.
5670	32" size			2	8.000	Ea.
5680	36" size	↓	↓	1.50	10.670	Ea.

155 400 | Warm Air Systems

		CREW	MAKEUP	DAILY OUTPUT	MAN-HOURS	UNIT
401 0020	DUCT FURNACES Includes burner, controls, stainless steel heat exchanger. Gas fired, electric ignition					
0030	Indoor installation					
0080	100 MBH output	Q-5	1 Steamfitter	5	3.200	Ea.
			1 Steamfitter Apprentice			
0100	120 MBH output			4	4.000	Ea.
0130	200 MBH output			2.70	5.930	Ea.
0140	240 MBH output			2.30	6.960	Ea.
0160	280 MBH output			2	8.000	Ea.
0180	320 MBH output	↓	↓	1.60	10.000	Ea.
1000	Outdoor installation, with vent cap					
1020	75 MBH output	Q-5	1 Steamfitter	4	4.000	Ea.
			1 Steamfitter Apprentice			
1040	94 MBH output			4	4.000	Ea.
1060	120 MBH output			4	4.000	Ea.
1080	157 MBH output			3.50	4.570	Ea.
1100	187 MBH output			3	5.330	Ea.
1120	225 MBH output			2.50	6.400	Ea.
1140	300 MBH output			1.80	8.890	Ea.
1160	375 MBH output			1.60	10.000	Ea.
1180	450 MBH output			1.40	11.430	Ea.
1200	600 MBH output	↓	↓	1	16.000	Ea.
408 0020	DUCT HEATERS , Electric, 480 V, 3 ph Finned tubular insert, 500°F					
0100	8" wide x 6" high, 4.0KW	Q-20	1 Sheet Metal Worker	16	1.250	Ea.
			1 Sheet Metal Apprentice			
			.5 Electrician			
0120	12" high, 8.0KW			15	1.330	Ea.
0140	18" high, 12.0KW			14	1.430	Ea.
0160	24" high, 16.0KW			13	1.540	Ea.
0180	30" high, 20.0KW			12	1.670	Ea.
0300	12" wide x 6" high, 6.7KW			15	1.330	Ea.
0320	12" high, 13.3 KW			14	1.430	Ea.
0340	18" high, 20.0KW			13	1.540	Ea.
0360	24" high, 26.7KW			12	1.670	Ea.
0380	30" high, 33.3KW			11	1.820	Ea.
0500	18" wide x 6" high, 13.3KW			14	1.430	Ea.
0520	12" high, 26.7KW			13	1.540	Ea.
0540	18" high, 40.0KW			12	1.670	Ea.
0560	24" high, 53.3 KW			11	1.820	Ea.
0580	30" high, 66.7 KW			10	2.000	Ea.
0700	24" wide x 6" high, 17.8KW			13	1.540	Ea.
0720	12" high, 35.6KW			12	1.670	Ea.
0740	18" high, 53.3 KW			11	1.820	Ea.
0760	24" high, 71.1KW			10	2.000	Ea.
0780	30" high, 88.9KW			9	2.220	Ea.
0900	30" wide x 6" high, 22.2KW			12	1.670	Ea.
0920	12" high, 44.4KW			11	1.820	Ea.
0940	18" high, 66.7KW			10	2.000	Ea.
0960	24" high, 88.9KW			9	2.220	Ea.
0980	30" high, 111.0KW	↓	↓	8	2.500	Ea.

155 400 | Warm Air Systems

		CREW	MAKEUP	DAILY OUTPUT	MAN-HOURS	UNIT
408 2001	Duct heaters, finned tubular flange with insulated					
2020	terminal box, 500°F					
2100	12" wide x 36" high, 54KW	Q-20	1 Sheet Metal Worker	10	2.000	Ea.
			1 Sheet Metal Apprentice			
			.5 Electrician			
2120	40" high, 60KW			9	2.220	Ea.
2200	24" wide x 36" high, 118.8KW			9	2.220	Ea.
2220	40" high, 132KW			8	2.500	Ea.
2400	36" wide x 8" high, 40KW			11	1.820	Ea.
2420	16" high, 80KW			10	2.000	Ea.
2440	24" high, 120KW			9	2.220	Ea.
2460	32" high, 160KW			8	2.500	Ea.
2480	36" high, 180KW			7	2.860	Ea.
2500	40" high, 200KW			6	3.330	Ea.
2600	40" wide x 8" high, 45KW			11	1.820	Ea.
2620	16" high, 90KW			10	2.000	Ea.
2640	24" high, 135KW			9	2.220	Ea.
2660	32" high, 180KW			8	2.500	Ea.
2680	26" high, 202.5KW			7	2.860	Ea.
2700	40" high, 225KW			6	3.330	Ea.
2800	48" wide x 8" high, 54.8KW			10	2.000	Ea.
2820	16" high, 109.8KW			9	2.220	Ea.
2840	24" high, 164.4KW			8	2.500	Ea.
2860	32" high, 219.2KW			7	2.860	Ea.
2880	36" high, 246.6KW			6	3.330	Ea.
2900	40" high, 274KW			5	4.000	Ea.
3000	56" wide x 8" high, 64KW			9	2.220	Ea.
3020	16" high, 128KW			8	2.500	Ea.
3040	24" high, 192KW			7	2.860	Ea.
3060	32" high, 256KW			6	3.330	Ea.
3080	36" high, 288KW			5	4.000	Ea.
3100	40" high, 320KW			4	5.000	Ea.
3200	64" wide x 8" high, 74KW			8	2.500	Ea.
3220	16" high, 148KW			7	2.860	Ea.
3240	24" high, 222KW			6	3.330	Ea.
3260	32" high, 296KW			5	4.000	Ea.
3280	36" high, 333KW			4	5.000	Ea.
3300	40" high, 370KW	↓	↓	3	6.670	Ea.
5000	Duct heater modifications and accessories					
5120	T.C.O. limit auto or manual reset	Q-20	1 Sheet Metal Worker	42	.476	Ea.
			1 Sheet Metal Apprentice			
			.5 Electrician			
5140	Thermostat			28	.714	Ea.
5160	Overheat thermocouple (removable)			7	2.860	Ea.
5180	Fan interlock relay			18	1.110	Ea.
5200	Air flow switch			20	1.000	Ea.
5220	Split terminal box cover	↓	↓	100	.200	Ea.
420 0020	**FURNACES** Hot air heating, blowers, standard controls not including gas, oil or flue piping.					
1000	Electric, UL listed, heat staging, 240 volt					
1020	30 MBH	Q-20	1 Sheet Metal Worker	4	5.000	Ea.
			1 Sheet Metal Apprentice			
			.5 Electrician			
1040	47 MBH			4	5.000	Ea.
1060	61 MBH			3.80	5.260	Ea.
1080	76 MBH			3.60	5.560	Ea.
1100	91 MBH			3.40	5.880	Ea.
1120	112.7 MBH	↓	↓	3.20	6.250	Ea.

155 400	Warm Air Systems		CREW	MAKEUP	DAILY OUTPUT	MAN-HOURS	UNIT
420	1141	Furnaces, electric, 240 volt, 131.2 MBH	Q-20	1 Sheet Metal Worker	3.10	6.450	Ea.
				1 Sheet Metal Apprentice			
				.5 Electrician			
	1160	140.8 MBH	"	"	3	6.670	Ea.
	1500	For starter plenum, add	Q-9	1 Sheet Metal Worker	16	1.000	Ea.
				1 Sheet Metal Apprentice			
	2000	For external filter rack, add			16	1.000	Ea.
	2500	For electronic air filter, add	↓	↓	10	1.600	Ea.
	3000	Gas, AGA certified, direct drive models					
	3020	42 MBH output	Q-9	1 Sheet Metal Worker	4	4.000	Ea.
				1 Sheet Metal Apprentice			
	3040	63 MBH output			3.80	4.210	Ea.
	3060	79 MBH output			3.60	4.440	Ea.
	3080	84 MBH output			3.40	4.710	Ea.
	3100	105 MBH output			3.20	5.000	Ea.
	3120	126 MBH output			3	5.330	Ea.
	3130	160 MBH output			2.80	5.710	Ea.
	3140	200 MBH output			2.60	6.150	Ea.
	3160	300 MBH output			2.30	6.960	Ea.
	3180	400 MBH output			2	8.000	Ea.
	3290	For starter plenum, add			16	1.000	Ea.
	3300	For external filter rack, add			16	1.000	Ea.
	3310	For electronic air filter, add			10	1.600	Ea.
	3400	Pulse combustion 38 MBH output			4	4.000	Ea.
	3420	55 MBH output			3.80	4.210	Ea.
	3450	72 MBH output	↓	↓	3.60	4.440	Ea.
	6000	Oil, UL listed, atomizing gun type burner					
	6020	55 MBH output	Q-9	1 Sheet Metal Worker	3.60	4.440	Ea.
				1 Sheet Metal Apprentice			
	6030	84 MBH output			3.50	4.570	Ea.
	6040	99 MBH output			3.40	4.710	Ea.
	6060	125 MBH output			3.20	5.000	Ea.
	6080	152 MBH output			3	5.330	Ea.
	6100	200 MBH output			2.60	6.150	Ea.
	6120	300 MBH output			2.30	6.960	Ea.
	6140	400 MBH output			2	8.000	Ea.
	7500	For plenum, add			14	1.140	Ea.
	8000	For electronic air filter, add	↓	↓	10	1.600	Ea.
	8500	Wood, coal and oil combination complete with burner					
	8520	112 MBH output (oil)	Q-9	1 Sheet Metal Worker	3	5.330	Ea.
				1 Sheet Metal Apprentice			
	8540	140 MBH output (oil)			3	5.330	Ea.
	8560	150 MBH output (oil)			3	5.330	Ea.
	8580	170 MBH output (oil)	↓	↓	2.50	6.400	Ea.
430 0020		**FURNACES, COMBINATION SYSTEMS** Heating, cooling, electric air cleaner, humidification, dehumidification.					
	2000	Gas fired, 80 MBH heat output, 24 MBH cooling	Q-9	1 Sheet Metal Worker	1.20	13.330	Ea.
				1 Sheet Metal Apprentice			
	2020	80 MBH heat output, 36 MBH cooling			1.20	13.330	Ea.
	2040	100 MBH heat output, 29 MBH cooling			1	16.000	Ea.
	2060	100 MBH heat output, 36 MBH cooling			1	16.000	Ea.
	2080	100 MBH heat output, 47 MBH cooling	↓	↓	.90	17.780	Ea.
	2100	120 MBH heat output, 29 MBH cooling	Q-10	2 Sheet Metal Workers	1.30	18.460	Ea.
				1 Sheet Metal Apprentice			
	2120	120 MBH heat output, 42 MBH cooling			1.30	18.460	Ea.
	2140	120 MBH heat output, 47 MBH cooling			1.20	20.000	Ea.
	2160	120 MBH heat output, 55 MBH cooling			1.10	21.820	Ea.
	2180	144 MBH heat output, 42 MBH cooling	↓	↓	1.20	20.000	Ea.

155 400 | Warm Air Systems

		CREW	MAKEUP	DAILY OUTPUT	MAN-HOURS	UNIT
430 2201	Furnaces, gas fired, 144 MBH heat output, 47 MBH cooling	Q-10	2 Sheet Metal Workers 1 Sheet Metal Apprentice	1.20	20.000	Ea.
2220	144 MBH heat output, 58 MBH cooling	"	"	1	24.000	Ea.
3000	Oil fired, 84 MBH heat output, 24 MBH cooling	Q-9	1 Sheet Metal Worker 1 Sheet Metal Apprentice	1.20	13.330	Ea.
3020	84 MBH heat output, 36 MBH cooling			1.20	13.330	Ea.
3040	95.2 MBH heat output, 29 MBH cooling			1	16.000	Ea.
3060	95.2 MBH heat output, 36 MBH cooling			1	16.000	Ea.
3080	95.2 MBH heat output, 47 MBH cooling			.90	17.780	Ea.
3100	112 MBH heat output, 29 MBH cooling	Q-10	2 Sheet Metal Workers 1 Sheet Metal Apprentice	1.30	18.460	Ea.
3120	112 MBH heat output, 42 MBH cooling			1.30	18.460	Ea.
3140	112 MBH heat output, 47 MBH cooling			1.20	20.000	Ea.
3160	112 MBH heat output, 58 MBH cooling			1.10	21.820	Ea.
3180	151.2 MBH heat output, 42 MBH cooling			1.20	20.000	Ea.
3200	151.2 MBH heat output, 47 MBH cooling			1.20	20.000	Ea.
3240	151.2 MBH heat output, 58 MBH cooling			1	24.000	Ea.
440	**HEATING & VENTILATING UNITS** Classroom					
0020	Includes filter, heating/cooling coils, standard controls					
0080	750 CFM, 2 tons cooling	Q-6	2 Steamfitters 1 Steamfitter Apprentice	2	12.000	Ea.
0100	1000 CFM, 2-1/2 tons cooling			1.60	15.000	Ea.
0120	1250 CFM, 3 tons cooling			1.40	17.140	Ea.
0140	1500 CFM, 4 tons cooling			.80	30.000	Ea.
0160	2000 CFM 5 tons cooling			.50	48.000	Ea.
451	**INFRA-RED UNIT**					
0020	Gas fired, unvented, electric ignition, 100% shutoff. Piping and					
0030	wiring not included					
0060	Input, 15 MBH	Q-5	1 Steamfitter 1 Steamfitter Apprentice	7	2.290	Ea.
0100	30 MBH			6	2.670	Ea.
0120	45 MBH			5	3.200	Ea.
0140	50 MBH			4.50	3.560	Ea.
0160	60 MBH			4	4.000	Ea.
0180	75 MBH			3	5.330	Ea.
0200	90 MBH			2.50	6.400	Ea.
0220	105 MBH			2	8.000	Ea.
0240	120 MBH			2	8.000	Ea.
2000	Electric, single or three phase					
2050	6 KW, 20,478 BTU	1 Elec	1 Electrician	3	2.670	Ea.
2100	13.5 KW, 40,956 BTU			2.50	3.200	Ea.
2150	24 KW, 81,912 BTU			2	4.000	Ea.
3000	Oil fired, two stage pump, controls, solenoid valve, venter					
3050	117,000 BTU, one burner	Q-5	1 Steamfitter 1 Steamfitter Apprentice	2.50	6.400	Ea.
3080	234,000 BTU, two burner			2.25	7.110	Ea.
3110	351,000 BTU, three burner			2	8.000	Ea.
3140	468,000 BTU four burner			1.50	10.670	Ea.
461	**MAKE-UP AIR UNIT**					
0020	Indoor suspension, natural/LP gas, direct fired,					
0030	standard control. For flue see Division 155-680					
0040	70°F temperature rise, MBH is input					
0100	2000 CFM, 168 MBH	Q-6	2 Steamfitters 1 Steamfitter Apprentice	3	8.000	Ea.
0120	3000 CFM, 252 MBH			2	12.000	Ea.
0140	4000 CFM, 336 MBH			1.80	13.330	Ea.
0160	6000 CFM, 502 MBH			1.50	16.000	Ea.
0180	8000 CFM, 670 MBH			1.40	17.140	Ea.

155 400 | Warm Air Systems		CREW	MAKEUP	DAILY OUTPUT	MAN-HOURS	UNIT
461 0201	Make-up air unit, 10,000 CFM, 838 MBH	Q-6	2 Steamfitters	1.20	20.000	Ea.
			1 Steamfitter Apprentice			
0220	12,000 CFM, 1005 MBH			1	24.000	Ea.
0240	14,000 CFM, 1180 MBH			.94	25.530	Ea.
0260	18,000 CFM, 1340 MBH			.86	27.910	Ea.
0280	20,000 CFM, 1675 MBH	↓	↓	.76	31.580	Ea.
0300	24,000 CFM, 2007 MBH	Q-7	1 Steamfitter Foreman (ins)	1	32.000	Ea.
			2 Steamfitters			
			1 Steamfitter Apprentice			
0320	30,000 CFM, 2510 MBH			.96	33.330	Ea.
0340	35,000 CFM, 2930 MBH			.92	34.780	Ea.
0360	40,000 CFM, 3350 MBH			.88	36.360	Ea.
0380	45,000 CFM, 3770 MBH			.84	38.100	Ea.
0400	50,000 CFM, 4180 MBH			.80	40.000	Ea.
0420	55,000 CFM, 4600 MBH			.75	42.670	Ea.
0440	60,000 CFM, 5020 MBH			.70	45.710	Ea.
0460	65,000 CFM, 5435 MBH			.60	53.330	Ea.
0480	75,000 CFM, 6275 MBH	↓	↓	.50	64.000	Ea.
1000	Rooftop unit, natural gas, gravity vent, S.S. exchanger					
1010	70°F temperature rise, MBH is input					
1020	995 CFM, 75 MBH	Q-6	2 Steamfitters	4	6.000	Ea.
			1 Steamfitter Apprentice			
1040	1245 CFM, 95 MBH			3.60	6.670	Ea.
1060	1590 CFM, 120 MBH			3.30	7.270	Ea.
1080	2090 CFM, 159 MBH			3	8.000	Ea.
1100	2490 CFM, 190 MBH			2.60	9.230	Ea.
1120	2985 CFM, 225 MBH			2.30	10.430	Ea.
1140	3975 CFM, 300 MBH			1.90	12.630	Ea.
1160	4970 CFM, 375 MBH			1.40	17.140	Ea.
1180	5950 CFM, 450 MBH			1.20	20.000	Ea.
1200	7940 CFM, 600 MBH			1	24.000	Ea.
1220	9930 CFM, 750 MBH			.80	30.000	Ea.
1240	11,900 CFM, 900 MBH			.60	40.000	Ea.
1260	15,880 CFM, 1200 MBH	↓	↓	.30	80.000	Ea.
471 0500	**SOLAR ENERGY** Hot water, standard package, low temperature					
0540	2 collectors, circulator, fittings, no tank	Q-1	1 Plumber	.50	32.000	Ea.
			1 Plumber Apprentice			
0580	2 collectors, circulator, fittings, 120 gal. tank			.40	40.000	Ea.
0620	3 collectors, circulator, fittings, 120 gal. tank	↓	↓	.40	40.000	Ea.
0700	Medium temperature package					
0740	2 collectors, circulator, fittings, 80 gal. tank	Q-1	1 Plumber	.40	40.000	Ea.
			1 Plumber Apprentice			
0780	3 collectors, circulator, fittings, 120 gal. tank	"	"	.30	53.330	Ea.
0900	Commercial/process					
0940	10 med. temp. collectors, fittings, 120 gal. tank	Q-2	2 Plumbers	.15	160.000	Ea.
			1 Plumber Apprentice			
1300	Solar assist package, for space heating and domestic					
1340	hot water, 10 collectors, fittings	Q-2	2 Plumbers	.13	185.000	Ea.
			1 Plumber Apprentice			
1440	For heating, complete with heat pump, 9 collectors			.12	200.000	Ea.
1480	12 collectors			.10	240.000	Ea.
1540	18 collectors			.08	300.000	Ea.
2000	Seasonal pool heating package, fittings, 10 collectors	↓	↓	.30	80.000	Ea.
2250	Controller, liquid temperature	1 Plum	1 Plumber	5	1.600	Ea.

155 400 | Warm Air Systems

		CREW	MAKEUP	DAILY OUTPUT	MAN-HOURS	UNIT
471	2319	Solar energy circulators, air blowers					
	2320	30 to 100 S.F. system, 1/20 HP	Q-9	1 Sheet Metal Worker	16	1.000	Ea.
				1 Sheet Metal Apprentice			
	2330	100-300 S.F. system, 1/10 HP			16	1.000	Ea.
	2340	300-500 S.F. system, 1/5 HP			15	1.070	Ea.
	2350	Two speed, 100-300 S.F., 1/10 HP			14	1.140	Ea.
	2400	Reversible fan, 20" diameter, 2 speed			18	.889	Ea.
	2450	Room to room fan, 225 CFM			12	1.330	Ea.
	2480	Shutter mounted fan, 12" diameter, 650 CFM			14	1.140	Ea.
	2550	Booster fan 5" diameter, 70 CFM			16	1.000	Ea.
	2570	6" diameter, 90 CFM			16	1.000	Ea.
	2580	8" diameter, 150 CFM			16	1.000	Ea.
	2590	8" diameter, 250 CFM			14	1.140	Ea.
	2600	8" diameter, 310 CFM			14	1.140.	Ea.
	2650	Rheostat			32	.500	Ea.
	2660	Shutter/damper			12	1.330	Ea.
	2670	Shutter motor	↓	↓	16	1.000	Ea.
	2750	Circulators, liquid, 1/100 HP, 2 GPM	Q-1	1 Plumber	14	1.140	Ea.
				1 Plumber Apprentice			
	2770	1/100 HP, 3 GPM			14	1.140	Ea.
	2800	1/25 HP, 5.3 GPM			14	1.140	Ea.
	2820	1/20 HP, 17 GPM			12	1.330	Ea.
	2850	1/20 HP, 17 GPM, stainless steel			12	1.330	Ea.
	2870	1/12 HP, 30 GPM	↓	↓	10	1.600	Ea.
	3000	Collector panels, air with aluminum absorber plate					
	3010	Wall or roof mount					
	3040	Flat black, plastic glazing					
	3080	4' x 8'	Q-9	1 Sheet Metal Worker	6	2.670	Ea.
				1 Sheet Metal Apprentice			
	3100	5' x 9'			5	3.200	Ea.
	3200	Flush roof mount, 10' to 16' x 22" wide			96	.167	L.F.
	3210	Manifold, by L.F. width of collectors	↓	↓	160	.100	L.F.
	3300	Collector panels, liquid with copper absorber plate					
	3320	Black chrome, tempered glass glazing					
	3330	Alum. frame, 3' x 8', 5/32" single glazing	Q-1	1 Plumber	9.50	1.680	Ea.
				1 Plumber Apprentice			
	3360	Alum. frame, 3' x 8', 5/32" double glazing			9	1.780	Ea.
	3390	Alum. frame, 4' x 8', 3/16" single glazing	↓	↓	6	2.670	Ea.
	3440	Flat black					
	3450	Alum. frame, 3' x 8', 5/32" single glazing	Q-1	1 Plumber	9	1.780	Ea.
				1 Plumber Apprentice			
	3500	Alum. frame, 3' x 8', 5/32" double glazing			5.50	2.910	Ea.
	3520	Alum. frame, 3' x 10', plastic glazing			10	1.600	Ea.
	3540	Alum. frame, 3' x 8', 1/8" tempered glass	↓	↓	5	3.200	Ea.
	3550	Liquid with fin tube absorber plate					
	3560	Alum. frame 4' x 8' tempered glass	Q-1	1 Plumber	10	1.600	Ea.
				1 Plumber Apprentice			
	3580	Liquid with vacuum tubes, 4' x 6'-10"			9	1.780	Ea.
	3600	Liquid, full wetted, plastic, alum. frame, 3' x 10'			5	3.200	Ea.
	3650	Collector panel mounting, flat roof or ground rack			7	2.290	Ea.
	3670	Roof clamps	↓	↓	70	.229	Set
	3700	Roof strap, teflon	1 Plum	1 Plumber	205	.039	L.F.
	3900	Differential controller with two sensors					
	3930	Thermostat, hard wired	1 Plum	1 Plumber	8	1.000	Ea.
	3950	Line cord and receptacle			12	.667	Ea.
	4000	External adjustment			12	.667	Ea.
	4050	Pool valve system, 2" pipe size (plastic)			2.50	3.200	Ea.
	4070	1-1/2" pipe size (copper)	↓	↓	2	4.000	Ea.

155 400 | Warm Air Systems

		CREW	MAKEUP	DAILY OUTPUT	MAN-HOURS	UNIT
471 4081	Solar energy diff. controller, pool pump system, 2" pipe size	1 Plum	1 Plumber	6	1.330	Ea.
4100	Six station with digital read-out	"	"	3	2.670	Ea.
4150	Sensors					
4190	Brass plug, 1/4" MPT	1 Plum	1 Plumber	32	.250	Ea.
4200	Brass plug, 1/2" MPT			32	.250	Ea.
4210	Brass plug, reversed			32	.250	Ea.
4220	Freeze prevention			32	.250	Ea.
4240	Screw attached			32	.250	Ea.
4250	Brass, immersion	↓	↓	32	.250	Ea.
4300	Heat exchanger					
4310	Fluid to air coil					
4330	Up flow, 45 MBH	Q-1	1 Plumber 1 Plumber Apprentice	4	4.000	Ea.
4380	70 MBH			3.50	4.570	Ea.
4400	80 MBH			3	5.330	Ea.
4490	Horizontal, 110 MBH	↓	↓	2	8.000	Ea.
4580	Fluid to fluid package includes two circulating pumps					
4590	expansion tank, check valve, relief valve					
4600	controller, high temperature cutoff and sensors	Q-1	1 Plumber 1 Plumber Apprentice	2.50	6.400	Ea.
4650	Heat transfer fluid					
4700	Propylene glycol, inhibited anti-freeze	1 Plum	1 Plumber	28	.286	Gal.
4800	Solar storage tanks, knocked down					
4810	Air, galvanized steel clad, double wall, 4" fiberglass					
4820	insulation, 20 Mil PVC lining					
4860	4' high, 3' x 3', = 36 C.F./250 gallons	Q-9	1 Sheet Metal Worker 1 Sheet Metal Apprentice	2.60	6.150	Ea.
4870	4' x 4', = 64 C.F./480 gallons			2	8.000	Ea.
4880	5' x 5' = 100 C.F./750 gallons			1.50	10.670	Ea.
4890	6' x 6' = 144 C.F./1000 gallons			1.30	12.310	Ea.
4900	7' x 7' = 196 C.F./1450 gallons	↓	↓	1	16.000	Ea.
5010	6'-3" high, 7' x 7' = 306 C.F./2000 gallons	Q-10	2 Sheet Metal Workers 1 Sheet Metal Apprentice	1.20	20.000	Ea.
5020	7' x 10'-6" = 459 C.F./3000 gallons			.80	30.000	Ea.
5030	7' x 14' = 613 C.F./4000 gallons			.60	40.000	Ea.
5040	10'-6" x 10'-6" = 689 C.F./4500 gallons			.50	48.000	Ea.
5050	10'-6" x 14' = 919 C.F./6000 gallons	↓	↓	.40	60.000	Ea.
5120	30 Mil reinforced Chemflex lining,					
5130	4' high, 3' x 3' = 36 C.F./250 gallons	Q-9	1 Sheet Metal Worker 1 Sheet Metal Apprentice	2.60	6.150	Ea.
5140	4' x 4' = 64 C.F./480 gallons			2	8.000	Ea.
5150	5' x 5' = 100 C.F./750 gallons			1.50	10.670	Ea.
5160	6' x 6' = 144 C.F./1000 gallons			1.30	12.310	Ea.
5170	7' x 7' = 196 C.F./1450 gallons	↓	↓	1	16.000	Ea.
5190	6'-3" high, 7' x 7' = 306 C.F./2000 gallons	Q-10	2 Sheet Metal Workers 1 Sheet Metal Apprentice	1.20	20.000	Ea.
5200	7' x 10'-6" = 459 C.F./3000 gallons			.80	30.000	Ea.
5210	7' x 14' = 613 C.F./4000 gallons			.60	40.000	Ea.
5220	10'-6" x 10'-6" = 689 C.F./4500 gallons			.50	48.000	Ea.
5230	10'-6" x 14' = 919 C.F./6000 gallons			.40	60.000	Ea.
5240	14' x 14' = 1225 C.F./8000 gallons	Q-11	1 Sheet Metal Foreman (ins) 2 Sheet Metal Workers 1 Sheet Metal Apprentice	.40	80.000	Ea.
7000	Solar control valves and vents					
7050	Air purger, 1" pipe size	1 Plum	1 Plumber	12	.667	Ea.
7070	Air eliminator, automatic 3/4" size			32	.250	Ea.
7090	Air vent, automatic, 1/8" fitting			32	.250	Ea.
7100	Manual, 1/8" NPT	↓	↓	32	.250	Ea.

155 400 | Warm Air Systems

		CREW	MAKEUP	DAILY OUTPUT	MAN-HOURS	UNIT
471 7121	Solar control, backflow preventer, 1/2" pipe size	1 Plum	1 Plumber	16	.500	Ea.
7130	3/4" pipe size			16	.500	Ea.
7150	Balancing valve, 3/4" pipe size			20	.400	Ea.
7180	Draindown valve, 1/2" copper tube			9	.889	Ea.
7200	Flow control valve, 1/2" pipe size			22	.364	Ea.
7220	Expansion tank, up to 5 gal.			32	.250	Ea.
7250	Hydronic controller			8	1.000	Ea.
7400	Pressure gauge, 2" dial			32	.250	Ea.
7450	Relief valve, temp. and pressure 3/4" pipe size	↓	↓	30	.267	Ea.
7500	Solenoid valve, normally closed					
7520	Brass, 3/4" NPT, 24V	1 Plum	1 Plumber	9	.889	Ea.
7530	1" NPT, 24V			9	.889	Ea.
7550	1-1/2" NPT, 24V			8	1.000	Ea.
7560	2" NPT, 24V			7	1.140	Ea.
7600	Plastic 1-1/2" NPT, 24V			9	.889	Ea.
7610	2" NPT, 24V	↓	↓	8	1.000	Ea.
7650	Solenoid valve, normally open					
7670	Brass, 1-1/2" NPT, 24V	1 Plum	1 Plumber	7	1.140	Ea.
7680	2" NPT, 24V			6.50	1.230	Ea.
7700	Plastic, 1-1/2" NPT, 24V			9	.889	Ea.
7710	2" NPT, 24V			8	1.000	Ea.
7750	Vacuum relief valve, 3/4" pipe size			32	.250	Ea.
7770	Vent and vacuum breaker valve, 3/4" pipe size	↓	↓	32	.250	Ea.
7800	Thermometers					
7820	Digital temperature monitoring, 4 locations	1 Plum	1 Plumber	2.50	3.200	Ea.
7870	Indoor, outdoor			8	1.000	Ea.
7890	In line, dial, 1/2" NPT			8	1.000	Ea.
7900	Upright, 1/2" NPT			8	1.000	Ea.
7950	Maximum - minimum			16	.500	Ea.
7970	Remote probe, 2" dial			8	1.000	Ea.
7990	Stem, 2" dial, 9" stem	↓	↓	16	.500	Ea.
8250	Water storage tank with heat exchanger and electric element					
8260	66 gal. with 2" x 1/2 lb. density insulation	1 Plum	1 Plumber	1.60	5.000	Ea.
8270	66 gal. with 2" x 2 lb. density insulation			1.60	5.000	Ea.
8280	80 gal. with 2" x 1/2 lb. density insulation			1.60	5.000	Ea.
8300	80 gal. with 2" x 2 lb. density insulation			1.60	5.000	Ea.
8350	120 gal. with 2" x 1/2 lb. density insulation			1.40	5.710	Ea.
8380	120 gal. with 2" x 2 lb. density insulation			1.40	5.710	Ea.
8400	120 gal. with 2" x 2 lb. density insul., 40 S.F. heat coil	↓	↓	1.40	5.710	Ea.
8500	Water storage module, plastic					
8600	Tubular, 12" diameter, 4' high	1 Carp	1 Carpenter	48	.167	Ea.
8610	12" diameter, 8' high			40	.200	Ea.
8620	18" diameter, 5' high			38	.211	Ea.
8630	18" diameter, 10' high	↓	↓	32	.250	Ea.
8640	58" diameter, 5' high	F-2	2 Carpenters Power Tools	32	.500	Ea.
480 0020	**SPACE HEATERS** Cabinet, grilles, fan, controls, burner, thermostat, no piping. For flue see division 155-680					
1000	Gas fired, floor mounted					
1100	60 MBH output	Q-5	1 Steamfitter 1 Steamfitter Apprentice	10	1.600	Ea.
1120	80 MBH output			9	1.780	Ea.
1140	100 MBH output			8	2.000	Ea.
1160	120 MBH output			7	2.290	Ea.
1180	180 MBH output	↓	↓	6	2.670	Ea.
1500	Rooftop mounted, gravity vent, stainless steel exchanger					
1520	75 MBH output	Q-6	2 Steamfitters 1 Steamfitter Apprentice	4	6.000	Ea.

155 400 | Warm Air Systems

		CREW	MAKEUP	DAILY OUTPUT	MAN-HOURS	UNIT
480 1541	Space heaters, gas fired, rooftop mtd., 95 MBH output	Q-6	2 Steamfitters	3.60	6.670	Ea.
			1 Steamfitter Apprentice			
1560	120 MBH output			3.30	7.270	Ea.
1580	159 MBH output			3	8.000	Ea.
1600	190 MBH output			2.60	9.230	Ea.
1620	225 MBH output			2.30	10.430	Ea.
1640	300 MBH output			1.90	12.630	Ea.
1660	375 MBH output			1.40	17.140	Ea.
1680	450 MBH output			1.20	20.000	Ea.
1700	600 MBH output			1	24.000	Ea.
1720	750 MBH output			.80	30.000	Ea.
1740	900 MBH output			.60	40.000	Ea.
1760	1200 MBH output	↓	↓	.30	80.000	Ea.
2000	Suspension mounted, propeller fan, 36 MBH output	Q-5	1 Steamfitter	8	2.000	Ea.
			1 Steamfitter Apprentice			
2020	48 MBH output			7.50	2.130	Ea.
2040	60 MBH output			7	2.290	Ea.
2060	84 MBH output			6	2.670	Ea.
2080	100 MBH output			5.50	2.910	Ea.
2100	120 MBH output			5	3.200	Ea.
2120	140 MBH output			4.50	3.560	Ea.
2140	160 MBH output			4	4.000	Ea.
2160	180 MBH output			3.50	4.570	Ea.
2180	200 MBH output			3	5.330	Ea.
2200	240 MBH output			2.70	5.930	Ea.
2220	280 MBH output			2.30	6.960	Ea.
2240	320 MBH output			2	8.000	Ea.
3000	Suspension mounted, blower type, 40 MBH output			6.80	2.350	Ea.
3020	60 MBH output			6.60	2.420	Ea.
3040	84 MBH output			5.80	2.760	Ea.
3060	104 MBH output			5.20	3.080	Ea.
3080	140 MBH output			4.30	3.720	Ea.
3100	180 MBH output			3.30	4.850	Ea.
3120	240 MBH output			2.50	6.400	Ea.
3140	280 MBH output	↓	↓	2	8.000	Ea.
4000	Suspension mounted, sealed combustion system,					
4020	aluminized steel exchanger, powered vent					
4040	100 MBH output	Q-5	1 Steamfitter	5	3.200	Ea.
			1 Steamfitter Apprentice			
4060	120 MBH output			4.70	3.400	Ea.
4080	160 MBH output			3.70	4.320	Ea.
4100	200 MBH output			2.90	5.520	Ea.
4120	240 MBH output			2.50	6.400	Ea.
4140	320 MBH output			1.70	9.410	Ea.
5000	Wall furnace, 17.5 MBH			6	2.670	Ea.
5020	24 MBH output			5	3.200	Ea.
5040	35 MBH output			4	4.000	Ea.
6000	Oil fired, suspension mounted, 94 MBH output			4	4.000	Ea.
6040	140 MBH output			3	5.330	Ea.
6060	184 MBH output			3	5.330	Ea.
6080	250 MBH output	↓	↓	2	8.000	Ea.
6100	308 MBH output	Q-6	2 Steamfitters	2.60	9.230	Ea.
			1 Steamfitter Apprentice			

155 600	Heating System Access	CREW	MAKEUP	DAILY OUTPUT	MAN-HOURS	UNIT
601 0020	**HEAT EXCHANGERS** 4 pass, 3/4" O.D. copper tubes, C.I. heads, C.I. tube sheet, steel shell					
0100	Hot water 40°F to 180°F, by steam at 10 PSI					
0120	8 GPM	Q-5	1 Steamfitter	6	2.670	Ea.
			1 Steamfitter Apprentice			
0140	10 GPM			5	3.200	Ea.
0160	40 GPM			4	4.000	Ea.
0180	64 GPM			2	8.000	Ea.
0200	96 GPM	↓	↓	1	16.000	Ea.
0220	120 GPM	Q-6	2 Steamfitters	1.50	16.000	Ea.
			1 Steamfitter Apprentice			
0240	168 GPM			1	24.000	Ea.
0260	240 GPM	↓	↓	.80	30.000	Ea.
1000	Hot water 40°F to 140°F, by water at 200°F					
1020	7 GPM	Q-5	1 Steamfitter	6	2.670	Ea.
			1 Steamfitter Apprentice			
1040	16 GPM			5	3.200	Ea.
1060	34 GPM			4	4.000	Ea.
1080	55 GPM			3	5.330	Ea.
1100	74 GPM			1.50	10.670	Ea.
1120	86 GPM	↓	↓	1.40	11.430	Ea.
1140	112 GPM	Q-6	2 Steamfitters	2	12.000	Ea.
			1 Steamfitter Apprentice			
1160	126 GPM			1.80	13.330	Ea.
1180	152 GPM	↓	↓	1	24.000	Ea.
3000	Stainless plate heat exchanger 100 GPM	Q-5	1 Steamfitter	2	8.000	Ea.
			1 Steamfitter Apprentice			
3010	200 GPM	"	"	1.50	10.670	Ea.
3020	300 GPM	Q-6	2 Steamfitters	2	12.000	Ea.
			1 Steamfitter Apprentice			
3030	400 GPM			1.80	13.330	Ea.
3040	500 GPM	↓	↓	1.50	16.000	Ea.
4070	Unfired steam generator 5000 lbs hr.	Q-7	1 Steamfitter Foreman (ins)	.08	400.000	Ea.
			2 Steamfitters			
			1 Steamfitter Apprentice			
4080	7500 lbs hr.			.06	533.000	Ea.
4090	10m lbs hr.	↓	↓	.04	800.000	Ea.
610 0020	**HEAT TRANSFER PACKAGES** Complete, controls, expansion tank, converter, air separator					
1000	Hot water, 180°F enter, 200°F leaving, 15# steam					
1010	One pump system, 28 GPM	Q-6	2 Steamfitters	.75	32.000	Ea.
			1 Steamfitter Apprentice			
1020	35 GPM			.70	34.290	Ea.
1040	55 GPM			.65	36.920	Ea.
1060	130 GPM			.55	43.640	Ea.
1080	255 GPM			.40	60.000	Ea.
1100	550 GPM			.30	80.000	Ea.
1120	800 GPM			.25	96.000	Ea.
1220	Two pump system, 28 GPM			.70	34.290	Ea.
1240	35 GPM			.65	36.920	Ea.
1260	55 GPM			.60	40.000	Ea.
1280	130 GPM			.50	48.000	Ea.
1300	255 GPM			.35	68.570	Ea.
1320	550 GPM			.25	96.000	Ea.
1340	800 GPM	↓	↓	.20	120.000	Ea.

601

155 | Heating

	155 600	Heating System Access	CREW	MAKEUP	DAILY OUTPUT	MAN-HOURS	UNIT
620	620	**HEAT RECOVERY PACKAGES**					
	0100	Air to air					
	2000	Kitchen exhaust, commercial, heat pipe exchanger					
	2040	Combined supply/exhaust air volume					
	2080	2.5 to 6.0 MCFM	Q-10	2 Sheet Metal Workers 1 Sheet Metal Apprentice	2.80	8.570	MCFM
	2120	6 to 16 MCFM	↓	↓	5	4.800	MCFM
	2160	16 to 22 MCFM	↓	↓	6	4.000	MCFM
	4000	Enthalpy recovery wheel					
	4010	1000 max CFM	Q-9	1 Sheet Metal Worker 1 Sheet Metal Apprentice	1.20	13.330	Ea.
	4020	2000 max CFM	↓	↓	1	16.000	Ea.
	4030	4000 max CFM	↓	↓	.80	20.000	Ea.
	4040	6000 max CFM	↓	↓	.70	22.860	Ea.
	4050	8000 max CFM	Q-10	2 Sheet Metal Workers 1 Sheet Metal Apprentice	1	24.000	Ea.
	4060	10,000 max CFM	↓	↓	.90	26.670	Ea.
	4070	20,000 max CFM	↓	↓	.80	30.000	Ea.
	4080	25,000 max CFM	↓	↓	.70	34.290	Ea.
	4090	30,000 max CFM	↓	↓	.50	48.000	Ea.
	4100	40,000 max CFM	↓	↓	.45	53.330	Ea.
	4110	50,000 max CFM	↓	↓	.40	60.000	Ea.
	8000	Residential ventilation heat exchanger					
	8010	100 CFM exchanger	1 Shee	1 Sheet Metal Worker	12	.667	Ea.
	8020	200 CFM	↓	↓	10	.800	Ea.
	8030	400 CFM	↓	↓	8	1.000	Ea.
	630	**HYDRONIC HEATING** Terminal units, not incl. main supply pipe					
	1000	Radiation					
	1100	Panel, baseboard, C.I., including supports, no covers	Q-5	1 Steamfitter 1 Steamfitter Apprentice	46	.348	L.F.
	1150	Fin tube, wall hung, 14" slope top cover, with damper					
	1200	1-1/4" copper tube, 4-1/4" alum. fin	Q-5	1 Steamfitter 1 Steamfitter Apprentice	38	.421	L.F.
	1250	1-1/4" steel tube, 4-1/4" steel fin	↓	↓	36	.444	L.F.
	1300	2" steel tube, 4-1/4" steel fin	↓	↓	32	.500	L.F.
	1310	Baseboard, pkgd, 1/2" copper tube, alum. fin, 7" high	↓	↓	60	.267	L.F.
	1320	3/4" copper tube, alum. fin, 7" high	↓	↓	58	.276	L.F.
	1340	1" copper tube, alum. fin, 8-7/8" high	↓	↓	56	.286	L.F.
	1360	1-1/4" copper tube, alum. fin, 8-7/8" high	↓	↓	54	.296	L.F.
	1380	1-1/4" IPS steel tube with steel fins	↓	↓	52	.308	L.F.
	1990	Convector unit, floor recessed, flush, with trim					
	2000	for under large glass wall areas, no damper	Q-5	1 Steamfitter 1 Steamfitter Apprentice	20	.800	L.F.
	3000	Radiators, cast iron					
	3100	Free standing or wall hung, 6 tube, 25" high	Q-5	1 Steamfitter 1 Steamfitter Apprentice	96	.167	Section
	3150	4 tube 25" high	↓	↓	96	.167	Section
	3200	4 tube, 19" high	↓	↓	96	.167	Section
	3250	Adj. brackets, 2 per wall radiator up to 30 sections	1 Stpi	1 Steamfitter	32	.250	Ea.
	3500	Recessed, 20" high x 5" deep, without grille	Q-5	1 Steamfitter 1 Steamfitter Apprentice	60	.267	Section
	3950	Unit heaters, propeller, 1 speed, 200° EWT					
	4000	Horizontal, 14.7 MBH	Q-5	1 Steamfitter 1 Steamfitter Apprentice	12	1.330	Ea.
	4020	26.9 MBH	↓	↓	10	1.600	Ea.
	4040	33.5 MBH	↓	↓	8	2.000	Ea.
	4060	44.8 MBH	↓	↓	8	2.000	Ea.
	4080	55.4 MBH	↓	↓	7.50	2.130	Ea.

155 600 | Heating System Access

		CREW	MAKEUP	DAILY OUTPUT	MAN-HOURS	UNIT
630 4102	Hydronic unit heaters, 1 speed, horizontal, 72.7 MBH	Q-5	1 Steamfitter	7	2.290	Ea.
			1 Steamfitter Apprentice			
4120	88.3 MBH			6.50	2.460	Ea.
4140	106.4 MBH			6	2.670	Ea.
4160	143.7 MBH			5	3.200	Ea.
4180	160.9 MBH			4	4.000	Ea.
4200	207.3 MBH			3	5.330	Ea.
4220	254.5 MBH			2.50	6.400	Ea.
4240	292.5 MBH			2	8.000	Ea.
5000	Vertical flow, 52.4 MBH			11	1.450	Ea.
5020	71.4 MBH			8	2.000	Ea.
5040	88.4 MBH			7	2.290	Ea.
5060	123 MBH			6	2.670	Ea.
5080	140 MBH			4	4.000	Ea.
5100	177.4 MBH			3	5.330	Ea.
5120	220 MBH			2.20	7.270	Ea.
5140	296.7 MBH	↓	↓	2	8.000	Ea.
5160	408 MBH	Q-6	2 Steamfitters	1.80	13.330	Ea.
			1 Steamfitter Apprentice			
5180	520 MBH	"	"	1.40	17.140	Ea.
6000	Valance units, complete with 1/2" cooling coil, enclosure					
6020	2 tube	Q-5	1 Steamfitter	18	.889	L.F.
			1 Steamfitter Apprentice			
6040	3 tube			16	1.000	L.F.
6060	4 tube			16	1.000	L.F.
6080	5 tube			15	1.070	L.F.
6100	6 tube			15	1.070	L.F.
6120	8 tube	↓	↓	14	1.140	L.F.
640 0030	**HUMIDIFIERS** Centrifugal atomizing					
0050	5 lb. per hour	Q-5	1 Steamfitter	12	1.330	Ea.
			1 Steamfitter Apprentice			
0100	10 lb. per hour			10	1.600	Ea.
0120	24 lb. per hour	↓	↓	8	2.000	Ea.
0520	Steam, room or duct, filter, regulators, auto. controls, 220 V					
0540	10 lb. per hour	Q-5	1 Steamfitter	6	2.670	Ea.
			1 Steamfitter Apprentice			
0560	17 lb. per hour			5	3.200	Ea.
0580	30 lb. per hour			4	4.000	Ea.
0600	60 lb. per hour			4	4.000	Ea.
0620	90 lb. per hour			3	5.330	Ea.
0640	120 lb. per hour			2.50	6.400	Ea.
0660	180 lb. per hour			2	8.000	Ea.
0670	205 lb. per hour			2	8.000	Ea.
0680	365 lb. per hour			1.75	9.140	Ea.
0690	1040 lb. per hour	↓	↓	1.50	10.670	Ea.
0700	With blower					
0720	10 lb. per hour	Q-5	1 Steamfitter	5.50	2.910	Ea.
			1 Steamfitter Apprentice			
0740	17 lb. per hour			4.75	3.370	Ea.
0760	30 lb. per hour			3.75	4.270	Ea.
0780	60 lb. per hour			3.50	4.570	Ea.
0800	90 lb. per hour			2.75	5.820	Ea.
0820	120 lb. per hour			2	8.000	Ea.
0840	180 lb. per hour	↓	↓	1.50	10.670	Ea.

155 600	Heating System Access	CREW	MAKEUP	DAILY OUTPUT	MAN-HOURS	UNIT
651	**651** **INSULATION**					
1000	Boiler, 1-1/2" calcium silicate, 1/2" cement finish	Q-14	1 Asbestos Worker	50	.320	S.F.
			1 Asbestos Apprentice			
1020	2" fiberglass	"	"	80	.200	S.F.
2000	Breeching, 2" calcium silicate with 1/2" cement finish, no lath					
2020	Rectangular	Q-14	1 Asbestos Worker	50	.320	S.F.
			1 Asbestos Apprentice			
2040	Round	"	"	40	.400	S.F.
2300	Calcium silicate block, + 200° to + 1200°F					
2340	1" thick	Q-14	1 Asbestos Worker	30	.533	S.F.
			1 Asbestos Apprentice			
2360	1-1/2" thick			25	.640	S.F.
2380	2" thick			22	.727	S.F.
2400	3" thick	↓	↓	18	.889	S.F.
2900	Domestic water heater wrap kit					
2920	1-1/2" with vinyl jacket, 20-60 gal.	1 Plum	1 Plumber	8	1.000	Ea.
3000	Ductwork					
3020	Blanket type, fiberglass, flexible					
3030	Fire resistant liner, black coating one side					
3050	1/2" thick, 2 lb. density	Q-14	1 Asbestos Worker	380	.042	S.F.
			1 Asbestos Apprentice			
3060	1" thick, 1-1/2 lb. density			350	.046	S.F.
3070	1-1/2" thick, 1-1/2 lb. density			320	.050	S.F.
3080	2" thick, 1-1/2 lb. density	↓	↓	300	.053	S.F.
3140	FRK vapor barrier wrap, .75 lb. density					
3160	1" thick	Q-14	1 Asbestos Worker	350	.046	S.F.
			1 Asbestos Apprentice			
3170	1-1/2" thick			320	.050	S.F.
3180	2" thick			300	.053	S.F.
3190	3" thick	↓	↓	260	.062	S.F.
3280	Unfaced, 1 lb. density					
3310	1" thick	Q-14	1 Asbestos Worker	360	.044	S.F.
			1 Asbestos Apprentice			
3320	1-1/2" thick			330	.048	S.F.
3330	2" thick	↓	↓	310	.052	S.F.
3490	Board type, fiberglass, 3 lb. density					
3500	Fire resistant, black pigmented, 1 side					
3520	1" thick	Q-14	1 Asbestos Worker	150	.107	S.F.
			1 Asbestos Apprentice			
3540	1-1/2" thick			130	.123	S.F.
3560	2" thick	↓	↓	120	.133	S.F.
3600	FRK vapor barrier					
3620	1" thick	Q-14	1 Asbestos Worker	150	.107	S.F.
			1 Asbestos Apprentice			
3630	1-1/2" thick			130	.123	S.F.
3640	2" thick	↓	↓	120	.133	S.F.
3680	No finish					
3700	1" thick	Q-14	1 Asbestos Worker	170	.094	S.F.
			1 Asbestos Apprentice			
3710	1-1/2" thick			140	.114	S.F.
3720	2" thick	↓	↓	130	.123	S.F.
3750	Finishes					
3800	1/2" cement over 1" wire mesh, incl. corner bead	Q-14	1 Asbestos Worker	116	.138	S.F.
			1 Asbestos Apprentice			
3820	Canvas, 8 oz. pasted on			246	.065	S.F.
3900	Weatherproof, non-metallic, 2 lb. per S.F.	↓	↓	100	.160	S.F.

155 600	Heating System Access	CREW	MAKEUP	DAILY OUTPUT	MAN-HOURS	UNIT
651 4101	Pipe covering, air cell, w/cover, 3 ply, 1/2" iron pipe size	Q-14	1 Asbestos Worker 1 Asbestos Apprentice	145	.110	L.F.
4130	3/4" iron pipe size			145	.110	L.F.
4140	1" iron pipe size			145	.110	L.F.
4150	1-1/4" iron pipe size			140	.114	L.F.
4160	1-1/2" iron pipe size			140	.114	L.F.
4170	2" iron pipe size			135	.119	L.F.
4180	2-1/2" iron pipe size			135	.119	L.F.
4190	3" iron pipe size			130	.123	L.F.
4200	3-1/2" iron pipe size			130	.123	L.F.
4210	4" iron pipe size			125	.128	L.F.
4220	5" iron pipe size			120	.133	L.F.
4230	6" iron pipe size			115	.139	L.F.
4240	8" iron pipe size			105	.152	L.F.
4250	10" iron pipe size			95	.168	L.F.
4260	12" iron pipe size			90	.178	L.F.
4300	4 ply, 1/2" iron pipe size			115	.139	L.F.
4330	3/4" iron pipe size			115	.139	L.F.
4340	1" iron pipe size			115	.139	L.F.
4350	1-1/4" iron pipe size			110	.145	L.F.
4360	1-1/2" iron pipe size			110	.145	L.F.
4370	2" iron pipe size			105	.152	L.F.
4380	2-1/2" iron pipe size			105	.152	L.F.
4390	3" iron pipe size			100	.160	L.F.
4400	3-1/2" iron pipe size			100	.160	L.F.
4410	4" iron pipe size			95	.168	L.F.
4420	5" iron pipe size			90	.178	L.F.
4430	6" iron pipe size			90	.178	L.F.
4440	8" iron pipe size			85	.188	L.F.
4450	10" iron pipe size			75	.213	L.F.
4460	12" iron pipe size	↓	↓	70	.229	L.F.
4900	Calcium silicate, with cover					
5100	1" wall, 1/2" iron pipe size	Q-14	1 Asbestos Worker 1 Asbestos Apprentice	170	.094	L.F.
5130	3/4" iron pipe size			170	.094	L.F.
5140	1" iron pipe size			170	.094	L.F.
5150	1-1/4" iron pipe size			165	.097	L.F.
5160	1-1/2" iron pipe size			165	.097	L.F.
5170	2" iron pipe size			160	.100	L.F.
5180	2-1/2" iron pipe size			160	.100	L.F.
5190	3" iron pipe size			150	.107	L.F.
5200	4" iron pipe size			140	.114	L.F.
5210	5" iron pipe size			135	.119	L.F.
5220	6" iron pipe size			130	.123	L.F.
5280	1-1/2" wall, 1/2" iron pipe size			150	.107	L.F.
5310	3/4" iron pipe size			150	.107	L.F.
5320	1" iron pipe size			150	.107	L.F.
5330	1-1/4" iron pipe size			145	.110	L.F.
5340	1-1/2" iron pipe size			145	.110	L.F.
5350	2" iron pipe size			140	.114	L.F.
5360	2-1/2" iron pipe size			140	.114	L.F.
5370	3" iron pipe size			135	.119	L.F.
5380	4" iron pipe size			125	.128	L.F.
5390	5" iron pipe size			120	.133	L.F.
5400	6" iron pipe size			110	.145	L.F.
5460	2" wall, 1/2" iron pipe size			135	.119	L.F.
5490	3/4" iron pipe size			135	.119	L.F.
5500	1" iron pipe size	↓	↓	135	.119	L.F.

155 600	Heating System Access	CREW	MAKEUP	DAILY OUTPUT	MAN-HOURS	UNIT
651 5511	Pipe covering, calcium silicate, w/cover, 1-1/4" iron pipe size	Q-14	1 Asbestos Worker	130	.123	L.F.
			1 Asbestos Apprentice			
5520	1-1/2" iron pipe size			130	.123	L.F.
5530	2" iron pipe size			125	.128	L.F.
5540	2-1/2" iron pipe size			125	.128	L.F.
5550	3" iron pipe size			120	.133	L.F.
5560	4" iron pipe size			115	.139	L.F.
5570	5" iron pipe size			110	.145	L.F.
5580	6" iron pipe size	↓	↓	105	.152	L.F.
5600	Calcium silicate, no cover					
5720	1" wall, 1/2" iron pipe size	Q-14	1 Asbestos Worker	180	.089	L.F.
			1 Asbestos Apprentice			
5740	3/4" iron pipe size			180	.089	L.F.
5750	1" iron pipe size			180	.089	L.F.
5760	1-1/4" iron pipe size			175	.091	L.F.
5770	1-1/2" iron pipe size			175	.091	L.F.
5780	2" iron pipe size			170	.094	L.F.
5790	2-1/2" iron pipe size			170	.094	L.F.
5800	3" iron pipe size			160	.100	L.F.
5810	4" iron pipe size			150	.107	L.F.
5820	5" iron pipe size			145	.110	L.F.
5830	6" iron pipe size			140	.114	L.F.
5900	1-1/2" wall, 1/2" iron pipe size			160	.100	L.F.
5920	3/4" iron pipe size			160	.100	L.F.
5930	1" iron pipe size			160	.100	L.F.
5940	1-1/4" iron pipe size			155	.103	L.F.
5950	1-1/2" iron pipe size			155	.103	L.F.
5960	2" iron pipe size			150	.107	L.F.
5970	2-1/2" iron pipe size			150	.107	L.F.
5980	3" iron pipe size			145	.110	L.F.
5990	4" iron pipe size			135	.119	L.F.
6000	5" iron pipe size			130	.123	L.F.
6010	6" iron pipe size			120	.133	L.F.
6020	7" iron pipe size			115	.139	L.F.
6030	8" iron pipe size			105	.152	L.F.
6040	9" iron pipe size			100	.160	L.F.
6050	10" iron pipe size			95	.168	L.F.
6060	12" iron pipe size			90	.178	L.F.
6070	14" iron pipe size			85	.188	L.F.
6080	16" iron pipe size			80	.200	L.F.
6090	18" iron pipe size			75	.213	L.F.
6120	2" wall, 1/2" iron pipe size			145	.110	L.F.
6140	3/4" iron pipe size			145	.110	L.F.
6150	1" iron pipe size			145	.110	L.F.
6160	1-1/4" iron pipe size			140	.114	L.F.
6170	1-1/2" iron pipe size			140	.114	L.F.
6180	2" iron pipe size			135	.119	L.F.
6190	2-1/2" iron pipe size			135	.119	L.F.
6200	3" iron pipe size			130	.123	L.F.
6210	4" iron pipe size			125	.128	L.F.
6220	5" iron pipe size			120	.133	L.F.
6230	6" iron pipe size			115	.139	L.F.
6240	7" iron pipe size			110	.145	L.F.
6250	8" iron pipe size			105	.152	L.F.
6260	9" iron pipe size			100	.160	L.F.
6270	10" iron pipe size			95	.168	L.F.
6280	12" iron pipe size			90	.178	L.F.
6290	14" iron pipe size	↓	↓	85	.188	L.F.

		CREW	MAKEUP	DAILY OUTPUT	MAN-HOURS	UNIT
155 600	**Heating System Access**					
651 6301	Pipe covering, calcium silicate, no cover, 16" iron pipe size	Q-14	1 Asbestos Worker 1 Asbestos Apprentice	80	.200	L.F.
6310	18" iron pipe size			75	.213	L.F.
6320	20" iron pipe size			65	.246	L.F.
6330	22" iron pipe size			60	.267	L.F.
6340	24" iron pipe size			55	.291	L.F.
6360	3" wall, 1/2" iron pipe size			115	.139	L.F.
6380	3/4" iron pipe size			115	.139	L.F.
6390	1" iron pipe size			115	.139	L.F.
6400	1-1/4" iron pipe size			110	.145	L.F.
6410	1-1/2" iron pipe size			110	.145	L.F.
6420	2" iron pipe size			105	.152	L.F.
6430	2-1/2" iron pipe size			105	.152	L.F.
6440	3" iron pipe size			100	.160	L.F.
6450	4" iron pipe size			95	.168	L.F.
6460	5" iron pipe size			90	.178	L.F.
6470	6" iron pipe size			90	.178	L.F.
6480	7" iron pipe size			85	.188	L.F.
6490	8" iron pipe size			85	.188	L.F.
6500	9" iron pipe size			80	.200	L.F.
6510	10" iron pipe size			75	.213	L.F.
6520	12" iron pipe size			70	.229	L.F.
6530	14" iron pipe size			65	.246	L.F.
6540	16" iron pipe size			60	.267	L.F.
6550	18" iron pipe size			55	.291	L.F.
6560	20" iron pipe size			50	.320	L.F.
6570	22" iron pipe size			45	.356	L.F.
6580	24" iron pipe size	↓	↓	40	.400	L.F.
6600	Fiberglass, with all service jacket					
6640	1/2" wall, 1/2" iron pipe size	Q-14	1 Asbestos Worker 1 Asbestos Apprentice	250	.064	L.F.
6660	3/4" iron pipe size			240	.067	L.F.
6670	1" iron pipe size			230	.070	L.F.
6680	1-1/4" iron pipe size			220	.073	L.F.
6690	1-1/2" iron pipe size			220	.073	L.F.
6700	2" iron pipe size			210	.076	L.F.
6710	2-1/2" iron pipe size			200	.080	L.F.
6720	3" iron pipe size			190	.084	L.F.
6730	3-1/2" iron pipe size			180	.089	L.F.
6740	4" iron pipe size			160	.100	L.F.
6750	5" iron pipe size			150	.107	L.F.
6760	6" iron pipe size			120	.133	L.F.
6840	1" wall, 1/2" iron pipe size			240	.067	L.F.
6860	3/4" iron pipe size			230	.070	L.F.
6870	1" iron pipe size			220	.073	L.F.
6880	1-1/4" iron pipe size			210	.076	L.F.
6890	1-1/2" iron pipe size			210	.076	L.F.
6900	2" iron pipe size			200	.080	L.F.
6910	2-1/2" iron pipe size			190	.084	L.F.
6920	3" iron pipe size			180	.089	L.F.
6930	3-1/2" iron pipe size			170	.094	L.F.
6940	4" iron pipe size			150	.107	L.F.
6950	5" iron pipe size			140	.114	L.F.
6960	6" iron pipe size			120	.133	L.F.
6970	7" iron pipe size			110	.145	L.F.
6980	8" iron pipe size			100	.160	L.F.
6990	9" iron pipe size			90	.178	L.F.
7000	10" iron pipe size	↓	↓	90	.178	L.F.

155 600 | Heating System Access

		CREW	MAKEUP	DAILY OUTPUT	MAN-HOURS	UNIT
651 7011	Pipe covering, fiberglass, 1" wall, 12" iron pipe size	Q-14	1 Asbestos Worker	80	.200	L.F.
			1 Asbestos Apprentice			
7020	14" iron pipe size			80	.200	L.F.
7030	16" iron pipe size			70	.229	L.F.
7040	18" iron pipe size			70	.229	L.F.
7050	20" iron pipe size			60	.267	L.F.
7060	24" iron pipe size			60	.267	L.F.
7080	1-1/2" wall, 1/2" iron pipe size			230	.070	L.F.
7100	3/4" iron pipe size			220	.073	L.F.
7110	1" iron pipe size			210	.076	L.F.
7120	1-1/4" iron pipe size			200	.080	L.F.
7130	1-1/2" iron pipe size			200	.080	L.F.
7140	2" iron pipe size			190	.084	L.F.
7150	2-1/2" iron pipe size			180	.089	L.F.
7160	3" iron pipe size			170	.094	L.F.
7170	3-1/2" iron pipe size			160	.100	L.F.
7180	4" iron pipe size			140	.114	L.F.
7190	5" iron pipe size			130	.123	L.F.
7200	6" iron pipe size			110	.145	L.F.
7210	7" iron pipe size			100	.160	L.F.
7220	8" iron pipe size			90	.178	L.F.
7230	9" iron pipe size			85	.188	L.F.
7240	10" iron pipe size			80	.200	L.F.
7250	12" iron pipe size			75	.213	L.F.
7260	14" iron pipe size			70	.229	L.F.
7270	16" iron pipe size			65	.246	L.F.
7280	18" iron pipe size			60	.267	L.F.
7290	20" iron pipe size			55	.291	L.F.
7300	24" iron pipe size			50	.320	L.F.
7320	2" wall, 1/2" iron pipe size			220	.073	L.F.
7340	3/4" iron pipe size			210	.076	L.F.
7350	1" iron pipe size			200	.080	L.F.
7360	1-1/4" iron pipe size			190	.084	L.F.
7370	1-1/2" iron pipe size			190	.084	L.F.
7380	2" iron pipe size			180	.089	L.F.
7390	2-1/2" iron pipe size			170	.094	L.F.
7400	3" iron pipe size			160	.100	L.F.
7410	3-1/2" iron pipe size			150	.107	L.F.
7420	4" iron pipe size			130	.123	L.F.
7430	5" iron pipe size			120	.133	L.F.
7440	6" iron pipe size			100	.160	L.F.
7450	7" iron pipe size			90	.178	L.F.
7460	8" iron pipe size			80	.200	L.F.
7470	9" iron pipe size			75	.213	L.F.
7480	10" iron pipe size			70	.229	L.F.
7490	12" iron pipe size			65	.246	L.F.
7500	14" iron pipe size			60	.267	L.F.
7510	16" iron pipe size			55	.291	L.F.
7520	18" iron pipe size			50	.320	L.F.
7530	20" iron pipe size			45	.356	L.F.
7540	24" iron pipe size			40	.400	L.F.
7720	Finishes, for .010" aluminum jacket, add			120	.133	S.F.
7740	For .016" aluminum jacket, add			120	.133	S.F.
7760	For .010" stainless steel, add	↓	↓	100	.160	S.F.
7860	Rubber tubing, flexible closed cell foam					
7880	3/8" wall, 1/4" iron pipe size	1 Asbe	1 Asbestos Worker	120	.067	L.F.
7900	3/8" iron pipe size			120	.067	L.F.
7910	1/2" iron pipe size	↓	↓	115	.070	L.F.

155 600 | Heating System Access

		CREW	MAKEUP		DAILY OUTPUT	MAN-HOURS	UNIT
651	7921	Pipe covering, rubber tubing, 3/8" wall, 3/4" iron pipe size	1 Asbe	1 Asbestos Worker		115	.070	L.F.
	7930	1" iron pipe size				110	.073	L.F.
	7940	1-1/4" iron pipe size				110	.073	L.F.
	7950	1-1/2" iron pipe size				110	.073	L.F.
	7960	2" iron pipe size				105	.076	L.F.
	7970	2-1/2" iron pipe size				100	.080	L.F.
	7980	3" iron pipe size				100	.080	L.F.
	7990	3-1/2" iron pipe size				100	.080	L.F.
	8100	1/2" wall, 1/4" iron pipe size				90	.089	L.F.
	8120	3/8" iron pipe size				90	.089	L.F.
	8130	1/2" iron pipe size				89	.090	L.F.
	8140	3/4" iron pipe size				89	.090	L.F.
	8150	1" iron pipe size				88	.091	L.F.
	8160	1-1/4" iron pipe size				87	.092	L.F.
	8170	1-1/2" iron pipe size				87	.092	L.F.
	8180	2" iron pipe size				86	.093	L.F.
	8190	2-1/2" iron pipe size				86	.093	L.F.
	8200	3" iron pipe size				85	.094	L.F.
	8210	3-1/2" iron pipe size				85	.094	L.F.
	8220	4" iron pipe size				80	.100	L.F.
	8230	5" iron pipe size				80	.100	L.F.
	8300	3/4" wall, 1/4" iron pipe size				90	.089	L.F.
	8320	3/8" iron pipe size				90	.089	L.F.
	8330	1/2" iron pipe size				89	.090	L.F.
	8340	3/4" iron pipe size				89	.090	L.F.
	8350	1" iron pipe size				88	.091	L.F.
	8360	1-1/4" iron pipe size				87	.092	L.F.
	8370	1-1/2" iron pipe size				87	.092	L.F.
	8380	2" iron pipe size				86	.093	L.F.
	8390	2-1/2" iron pipe size				86	.093	L.F.
	8400	3" iron pipe size				85	.094	L.F.
	8410	3-1/2" iron pipe size				85	.094	L.F.
	8420	4" iron pipe size				80	.100	L.F.
	8430	5" iron pipe size				80	.100	L.F.
	8440	6" iron pipe size	↓	↓		80	.100	L.F.
	8800	Urethane, with ASJ, -60°F to +225°F						
	8960	1" wall, 1/2" iron pipe size	Q-14	1 Asbestos Worker	1 Asbestos Apprentice	240	.067	L.F.
	8980	3/4" iron pipe size				230	.070	L.F.
	8990	1" iron pipe size				220	.073	L.F.
	9000	1-1/4" iron pipe size				210	.076	L.F.
	9010	1-1/2" iron pipe size				210	.076	L.F.
	9020	2" iron pipe size				200	.080	L.F.
	9030	2-1/2" iron pipe size				190	.084	L.F.
	9040	3" iron pipe size				180	.089	L.F.
	9050	4" iron pipe size				150	.107	L.F.
	9060	5" iron pipe size				140	.114	L.F.
	9070	6" iron pipe size				120	.133	L.F.
	9120	1-1/2" wall, 1/2" iron pipe size				230	.070	L.F.
	9140	3/4" iron pipe size				220	.073	L.F.
	9150	1" iron pipe size				210	.076	L.F.
	9160	1-1/4" iron pipe size				200	.080	L.F.
	9170	1-1/2" iron pipe size				200	.080	L.F.
	9180	2" iron pipe size				190	.084	L.F.
	9190	2-1/2" iron pipe size				180	.089	L.F.
	9200	3" iron pipe size				170	.094	L.F.
	9210	4" iron pipe size				140	.114	L.F.
	9220	5" iron pipe size	↓	↓		130	.123	L.F.

155 600	Heating System Access	CREW	MAKEUP	DAILY OUTPUT	MAN-HOURS	UNIT
651 9231	Pipe covering, urethane w/ASJ, 1-1/2" wall, 8" iron pipe size	Q-14	1 Asbestos Worker	110	.145	L.F.
			1 Asbestos Apprentice			
9240	8" iron pipe size	"	"	90	.178	L.F.
9290	Urethane, with ultraviolet cover					
9310	1" wall, 1/2" pipe size	Q-14	1 Asbestos Worker	216	.074	L.F.
			1 Asbestos Apprentice			
9320	3/4" pipe size			207	.077	L.F.
9330	1" pipe size			198	.081	L.F.
9340	1-1/4" pipe size			189	.085	L.F.
9350	1-1/2" pipe size			185	.086	L.F.
9360	2" pipe size			180	.089	L.F.
9400	1-1/2" wall, 1/2" pipe size			207	.077	L.F.
9410	3/4" pipe size			198	.081	L.F.
9420	1" pipe size			189	.085	L.F.
9430	1-1/4" pipe size			180	.089	L.F.
9440	1-1/2" pipe size			175	.091	L.F.
9450	2" pipe size	↓	↓	171	.094	L.F.
9500	Urethane, with ultraviolet cover, fittings					
9510	90° & 45° elbows, 1" wall thickness					
9520	1/2" pipe size	Q-14	1 Asbestos Worker	108	.148	Ea.
			1 Asbestos Apprentice			
9530	3/4" pipe size			104	.154	Ea.
9540	1" pipe size			99	.162	Ea.
9550	1-1/4" pipe size			95	.168	Ea.
9560	1-1/2" pipe size			93	.172	Ea.
9570	2" pipe size	↓	↓	90	.178	Ea.
9650	90° & 45° elbows, 1-1/2" wall thickness					
9660	1/2" pipe size	Q-14	1 Asbestos Worker	104	.154	Ea.
			1 Asbestos Apprentice			
9670	3/4" pipe size			99	.162	Ea.
9680	1" pipe size			95	.168	Ea.
9690	1-1/4" pipe size			90	.178	Ea.
9700	1-1/2" pipe size			88	.182	Ea.
9710	2" pipe size	↓	↓	86	.186	Ea.
9800	Tees & valves, 1" wall thickness					
9820	1/2" pipe size	Q-14	1 Asbestos Worker	72	.222	Ea.
			1 Asbestos Apprentice			
9830	3/4" pipe size			69	.232	Ea.
9840	1" pipe size			66	.242	Ea.
9850	1-1/4" pipe size			63	.254	Ea.
9860	1-1/2" pipe size			62	.258	Ea.
9870	2" pipe size	↓	↓	60	.267	Ea.
9920	Tees & valves, 1-1/2" wall thickness					
9930	1/2" pipe size	Q-14	1 Asbestos Worker	69	.232	Ea.
			1 Asbestos Apprentice			
9940	3/4" pipe size			66	.242	Ea.
9950	1" pipe size			63	.254	Ea.
9960	1-1/4" pipe size			60	.267	Ea.
9970	1-1/2" pipe size			58	.276	Ea.
9980	2" pipe size	↓	↓	57	.281	Ea.
671 0020	**TANKS** Fiberglass, underground, U.L. listed, not including					
0030	manway or hold-down strap					
0040	550 gallon capacity	Q-6	2 Steamfitters	3	8.000	Ea.
			1 Steamfitter Apprentice			
0100	1000 gallon capacity	"	"	2	12.000	Ea.

155 600	Heating System Access	CREW	MAKEUP	DAILY OUTPUT	MAN-HOURS	UNIT
671	0141	Tanks, fiberglass, underground, 2000 gallon capacity	Q-7	1 Steamfitter Foreman (ins)	2	16.000	Ea.
				2 Steamfitters			
				1 Steamfitter Apprentice			
	0160	4000 gallon capacity			1.30	24.620	Ea.
	0180	6000 gallon capacity			1	32.000	Ea.
	0200	8000 gallon capacity			.80	40.000	Ea.
	0220	10,000 gallon capacity			.60	53.330	Ea.
	0240	12,000 gallon capacity			.50	64.000	Ea.
	0260	15,000 gallon capacity			.40	80.000	Ea.
	0280	20,000 gallon capacity			.30	107.000	Ea.
	0300	25,000 gallon capacity			.20	160.000	Ea.
	0320	30,000 gallon capacity			.20	160.000	Ea.
	0340	40,000 gallon capacity			.10	320.000	Ea.
	0360	48,000 gallon capacity	↓	↓	.10	320.000	Ea.
	1000	For helical heating coil, add	Q-5	1 Steamfitter	2.50	6.400	Ea.
				1 Steamfitter Apprentice			
	1020	Fiberglass, underground, double wall, U.L. listed,					
	1030	includes manways, not incl. hold-down straps					
	1040	550 gallon capacity	Q-6	2 Steamfitters	3	8.000	Ea.
				1 Steamfitter Apprentice			
	1050	1000 gallon capacity	"	"	2	12.000	Ea.
	1060	2000 gallon capacity	Q-7	1 Steamfitter Foreman (ins)	2	16.000	Ea.
				2 Steamfitters			
				1 Steamfitter Apprentice			
	1070	3000 gallon capacity			1.60	20.000	Ea.
	1080	4000 gallon capacity			1.30	24.620	Ea.
	1090	6000 gallon capacity			1	32.000	Ea.
	1100	8000 gallon capacity			.80	40.000	Ea.
	1110	10,000 gallon capacity			.60	53.330	Ea.
	1120	12,000 gallon capacity	↓	↓	.50	64.000	Ea.
	2000	Steel, liquid expansion, ASME, painted, 15 gallon capacity	Q-5	1 Steamfitter	17	.941	Ea.
				1 Steamfitter Apprentice			
	2020	24 gallon capacity			14	1.140	Ea.
	2040	30 gallon capacity			12	1.330	Ea.
	2060	40 gallon capacity			10	1.600	Ea.
	2080	60 gallon capacity			8	2.000	Ea.
	2100	80 gallon capacity			7	2.290	Ea.
	2120	100 gallon capacity			6	2.670	Ea.
	3000	Steel ASME expansion, rubber diaphragm, 19 gal. cap. accept.			12	1.330	Ea.
	3020	31 gallon capacity			8	2.000	Ea.
	3040	61 gallon capacity			6	2.670	Ea.
	3060	79 gallon capacity			5	3.200	Ea.
	3080	119 gallon capacity			4	4.000	Ea.
	3100	158 gallon capacity			3.80	4.210	Ea.
	3120	211 gallon capacity			3.30	4.850	Ea.
	3140	317 gallon capacity			2.80	5.710	Ea.
	3160	422 gallon capacity			2.60	6.150	Ea.
	3180	528 gallon capacity	↓	↓	2.40	6.670	Ea.
	4000	Steel, storage, above ground, including supports, coating,					
	4020	fittings, not including mat, pumps or piping					
	4040	275 gallon capacity	Q-5	1 Steamfitter	5	3.200	Ea.
				1 Steamfitter Apprentice			
	4060	550 gallon capacity	"	"	4	4.000	Ea.
	4080	1000 gallon capacity	Q-7	1 Steamfitter Foreman (ins)	4	8.000	Ea.
				2 Steamfitters			
				1 Steamfitter Apprentice			
	4100	1500 gallon capacity			3.70	8.650	Ea.
	4120	2000 gallon capacity	↓	↓	3	10.670	Ea.

155 600 | Heating System Access

		CREW	MAKEUP	DAILY OUTPUT	MAN-HOURS	UNIT
671 4141	Tanks, steel, storage, above ground, 5000 gal. capacity	Q-7	1 Steamfitter Foreman (ins)	1	32.000	Ea.
			2 Steamfitters			
			1 Steamfitter Apprentice			
5000	Steel underground, sti-P3, set in place, incl. hold-down bars.					
5500	Excavation, pad, pumps and piping not included					
5520	1000 gallon capacity, 7 gauge shell	Q-7	1 Steamfitter Foreman (ins)	4	8.000	Ea.
			2 Steamfitters			
			1 Steamfitter Apprentice			
5540	5000 gallon capacity, 1/4" thick shell			1	32.000	Ea.
5560	10,000 gallon capacity, 1/4" thick shell			.70	45.710	Ea.
5580	15,000 gallon capacity, 5/16" thick shell			.50	64.000	Ea.
5600	20,000 gallon capacity, 5/16" thick shell			.30	107.000	Ea.
5620	30,000 gallon capacity, 3/8" thick shell	▼	▼	.20	160.000	Ea.
6200	Steel, underground, double wall, U.L. listed,					
6240	not incl. manholes or hold-downs.					
6250	500 gallon capacity	Q-5	1 Steamfitter	5	3.200	Ea.
			1 Steamfitter Apprentice			
6260	1000 gallon capactiy	Q-7	1 Steamfitter Foreman (ins)	4	8.000	Ea.
			2 Steamfitters			
			1 Steamfitter Apprentice			
6270	2000 gallon capacity			3	10.670	Ea.
6280	3000 gallon capacity			2	16.000	Ea.
6290	4000 gallon capacity			1.50	21.330	Ea.
6300	5000 gallon capacity			1	32.000	Ea.
6310	6000 gallon capacity			.80	40.000	Ea.
6320	8000 gallon capacity			.70	45.710	Ea.
6330	10,000 gallon capacity			.60	53.330	Ea.
6340	12,000 gallon capacity			.50	64.000	Ea.
6350	15,000 gallon capacity			.40	80.000	Ea.
6360	20,000 gallon capacity			.30	107.000	Ea.
6400	For hold-downs 500-3000 gal, add			16	2.000	Set
6410	For hold-downs 4000-6000 gal, add			12	2.670	Set
6420	For hold-downs 8000-12,000 gal, add			11	2.910	Set
6430	For hold-downs 15,000 gal, add			9	3.560	Set
6440	For hold-downs 20,000 gal, add	▼	▼	8	4.000	Set
680	**VENT CHIMNEY** Prefab metal, U.L. listed					
0020	Gas, double wall, galvanized steel					
0080	3" diameter	Q-9	1 Sheet Metal Worker	72	.222	V.L.F.
			1 Sheet Metal Apprentice			
0100	4" diameter			68	.235	V.L.F.
0120	5" diameter			64	.250	V.L.F.
0140	6" diameter			60	.267	V.L.F.
0160	7" diameter			56	.286	V.L.F.
0180	8" diameter			52	.308	V.L.F.
0200	10" diameter			48	.333	V.L.F.
0220	12" diameter			44	.364	V.L.F.
0240	14" diameter			42	.381	V.L.F.
0260	16" diameter			40	.400	V.L.F.
0280	18" diameter	▼	▼	38	.421	V.L.F.
0300	20" diameter	Q-10	2 Sheet Metal Workers	36	.667	V.L.F.
			1 Sheet Metal Apprentice			
0320	22" diameter			34	.706	V.L.F.
0340	24" diameter			32	.750	V.L.F.
0360	26" diameter			31	.774	V.L.F.
0380	28" diameter			30	.800	V.L.F.
0400	30" diameter			28	.857	V.L.F.
0420	32" diameter			27	.889	V.L.F.
0440	34" diameter	▼	▼	26	.923	V.L.F.

155 | Heating

155 600	Heating System Access		CREW	MAKEUP	DAILY OUTPUT	MAN-HOURS	UNIT
680	0461	Vent chimney, gas, dbl. wall, galv. steel, 36" diameter	Q-10	2 Sheet Metal Workers	25	.960	V.L.F.
				1 Sheet Metal Apprentice			
	0480	38" diameter			24	1.000	V.L.F.
	0500	40" diameter			23	1.040	V.L.F.
	0520	42" diameter			22	1.090	V.L.F.
	0540	44" diameter			21	1.140	V.L.F.
	0560	46" diameter			20	1.200	V.L.F.
	0580	48" diameter	↓	↓	19	1.260	V.L.F.
	0650	Gas, double wall, galvanized steel, fittings					
	0660	Elbow 45°, 3" diameter	Q-9	1 Sheet Metal Worker	36	.444	Ea.
				1 Sheet Metal Apprentice			
	0670	4" diameter			34	.471	Ea.
	0680	5" diameter			32	.500	Ea.
	0690	6" diameter			30	.533	Ea.
	0700	7" diameter			28	.571	Ea.
	0710	8" diameter			26	.615	Ea.
	0720	10" diameter			24	.667	Ea.
	0730	12" diameter			22	.727	Ea.
	0740	14" diameter			21	.762	Ea.
	0750	16" diameter			20	.800	Ea.
	0760	18" diameter	↓	↓	19	.842	Ea.
	0770	20" diameter	Q-10	2 Sheet Metal Workers	18	1.330	Ea.
				1 Sheet Metal Apprentice			
	0780	22" diameter			17	1.410	Ea.
	0790	24" diameter			16	1.500	Ea.
	0800	26" diameter			16	1.500	Ea.
	0810	28" diameter			15	1.600	Ea.
	0820	30" diameter			14	1.710	Ea.
	0830	32" diameter			14	1.710	Ea.
	0840	34" diameter			13	1.850	Ea.
	0850	36" diameter			12	2.000	Ea.
	0860	38" diameter			12	2.000	Ea.
	0870	40" diameter			11	2.180	Ea.
	0880	42" diameter			11	2.180	Ea.
	0890	44" diameter			10	2.400	Ea.
	0900	46" diameter			10	2.400	Ea.
	0910	48" diameter	↓	↓	10	2.400	Ea.
	0950	Elbow 90°, adjustable, 3" diameter	Q-9	1 Sheet Metal Worker	36	.444	Ea.
				1 Sheet Metal Apprentice			
	0960	4" diameter			34	.471	Ea.
	0970	5" diameter			32	.500	Ea.
	0980	6" diameter			30	.533	Ea.
	0990	7" diameter			28	.571	Ea.
	1010	8" diameter			26	.615	Ea.
	1040	Roof flashing, 3" diameter			36	.444	Ea.
	1050	4" diameter			34	.471	Ea.
	1060	5" diameter			32	.500	Ea.
	1070	6" diameter			30	.533	Ea.
	1080	7" diameter			28	.571	Ea.
	1090	8" diameter			26	.615	Ea.
	1100	10" diameter			24	.667	Ea.
	1110	12" diameter			22	.727	Ea.
	1120	14" diameter			20	.800	Ea.
	1130	16" diameter			18	.889	Ea.
	1140	18" diameter	↓	↓	16	1.000	Ea.
	1150	20" diameter	Q-10	2 Sheet Metal Workers	18	1.330	Ea.
				1 Sheet Metal Apprentice			
	1160	22" diameter	"	"	14	1.710	Ea.

155 600 | Heating System Access

		Description	CREW	MAKEUP	DAILY OUTPUT	MAN-HOURS	UNIT
680	1171	Vent chimney, fittings, galv., roof flashing, 24" diameter	Q-10	2 Sheet Metal Workers 1 Sheet Metal Apprentice	12	2.000	Ea.
	1200	Tee, 3" diameter	Q-9	1 Sheet Metal Worker 1 Sheet Metal Apprentice	27	.593	Ea.
	1210	4" diameter			26	.615	Ea.
	1220	5" diameter			25	.640	Ea.
	1230	6" diameter			24	.667	Ea.
	1240	7" diameter			23	.696	Ea.
	1250	8" diameter			22	.727	Ea.
	1260	10" diameter			21	.762	Ea.
	1270	12" diameter			20	.800	Ea.
	1280	14" diameter			18	.889	Ea.
	1290	16" diameter			16	1.000	Ea.
	1300	18" diameter	↓	↓	14	1.140	Ea.
	1310	20" diameter	Q-10	2 Sheet Metal Workers 1 Sheet Metal Apprentice	17	1.410	Ea.
	1320	22" diameter			13	1.850	Ea.
	1330	24" diameter			12	2.000	Ea.
	1340	26" diameter			12	2.000	Ea.
	1350	28" diameter			11	2.180	Ea.
	1360	30" diameter			10	2.400	Ea.
	1370	32" diameter			10	2.400	Ea.
	1380	34" diameter			9	2.670	Ea.
	1390	36" diameter			9	2.670	Ea.
	1400	38" diameter			8	3.000	Ea.
	1410	40" diameter			7	3.430	Ea.
	1420	42" diameter			6	4.000	Ea.
	1430	44" diameter			5	4.800	Ea.
	1440	46" diameter			5	4.800	Ea.
	1450	48" diameter	↓	↓	5	4.800	Ea.
	1460	Tee cap, 3" diameter	Q-9	1 Sheet Metal Worker 1 Sheet Metal Apprentice	45	.356	Ea.
	1470	4" diameter			42	.381	Ea.
	1480	5" diameter			40	.400	Ea.
	1490	6" diameter			37	.432	Ea.
	1500	7" diameter			35	.457	Ea.
	1510	8" diameter			34	.471	Ea.
	1520	10" diameter			32	.500	Ea.
	1530	12" diameter			30	.533	Ea.
	1540	14" diameter			28	.571	Ea.
	1550	16" diameter			25	.640	Ea.
	1560	18" diameter	↓	↓	24	.667	Ea.
	1570	20" diameter	Q-10	2 Sheet Metal Workers 1 Sheet Metal Apprentice	27	.889	Ea.
	1580	22" diameter			22	1.090	Ea.
	1590	24" diameter			21	1.140	Ea.
	1600	26" diameter			20	1.200	Ea.
	1610	28" diameter			19	1.260	Ea.
	1620	30" diameter			18	1.330	Ea.
	1630	32" diameter			17	1.410	Ea.
	1640	34" diameter			16	1.500	Ea.
	1650	36" diameter			15	1.600	Ea.
	1660	38" diameter			14	1.710	Ea.
	1670	40" diameter			14	1.710	Ea.
	1680	42" diameter			13	1.850	Ea.
	1690	44" diameter			12	2.000	Ea.
	1700	46" diameter			12	2.000	Ea.
	1710	48" diameter	↓	↓	11	2.180	Ea.

155 600	Heating System Access	CREW	MAKEUP	DAILY OUTPUT	MAN-HOURS	UNIT
680 1751	Vent chimney, fittings, galv., top, 3" diameter	Q-9	1 Sheet Metal Worker 1 Sheet Metal Apprentice	46	.348	Ea.
1760	4" diameter			44	.364	Ea.
1770	5" diameter			42	.381	Ea.
1780	6" diameter			40	.400	Ea.
1790	7" diameter			38	.421	Ea.
1800	8" diameter			36	.444	Ea.
1810	10" diameter			34	.471	Ea.
1820	12" diameter			32	.500	Ea.
1830	14" diameter			30	.533	Ea.
1840	16" diameter			28	.571	Ea.
1850	18" diameter	↓	↓	26	.615	Ea.
1860	20" diameter	Q-10	2 Sheet Metal Workers 1 Sheet Metal Apprentice	28	.857	Ea.
1870	22" diameter			22	1.090	Ea.
1880	24" diameter	↓	↓	20	1.200	Ea.
3200	All fuel, pressure tight, double wall, U.L. listed, 1400°F.					
3210	304 stainless steel liner, aluminized steel outer jacket					
3220	6" diameter	Q-9	1 Sheet Metal Worker 1 Sheet Metal Apprentice	60	.267	L.F.
3221	8" diameter			52	.308	L.F.
3222	10" diameter			48	.333	L.F.
3223	12" diameter			44	.364	L.F.
3224	14" diameter			42	.381	L.F.
3225	16" diameter			40	.400	L.F.
3226	18" diameter	↓	↓	38	.421	L.F.
3227	20" diameter	Q-10	2 Sheet Metal Workers 1 Sheet Metal Apprentice	36	.667	L.F.
3228	24" diameter			32	.750	L.F.
3229	28" diameter			30	.800	L.F.
3230	32" diameter			27	.889	L.F.
3231	36" diameter			25	.960	L.F.
3232	42" diameter			22	1.090	L.F.
3233	48" diameter	↓	↓	19	1.260	L.F.
3280	All fuel, pressure tight, double wall fittings					
3284	304 stainless steel inner, aluminized steel jacket					
3288	Adjustable 18"/30" section					
3292	6" diameter	Q-9	1 Sheet Metal Worker 1 Sheet Metal Apprentice	30	.533	Ea.
3293	8" diameter			26	.615	Ea.
3294	10" diameter			24	.667	Ea.
3295	12" diameter			22	.727	Ea.
3296	14" diameter			21	.762	Ea.
3297	16" diameter			20	.800	Ea.
3298	18" diameter	↓	↓	19	.842	Ea.
3299	20" diameter	Q-10	2 Sheet Metal Workers 1 Sheet Metal Apprentice	18	1.330	Ea.
3300	24" diameter			16	1.500	Ea.
3301	28" diameter			15	1.600	Ea.
3302	32" diameter			14	1.710	Ea.
3303	36" diameter			12	2.000	Ea.
3304	42" diameter			11	2.180	Ea.
3305	48" diameter	↓	↓	10	2.400	Ea.
3310	Elbows, 15°, 30° and 45°					
3312	6" diameter	Q-9	1 Sheet Metal Worker 1 Sheet Metal Apprentice	30	.533	Ea.
3314	8" diameter			26	.615	Ea.
3316	10" diameter	↓	↓	24	.667	Ea.

			CREW	MAKEUP	DAILY OUTPUT	MAN-HOURS	UNIT
155 600	**Heating System Access**						
680	3320	Vent chimney, fittings, all fuel, elbows, 12" diameter	Q-9	1 Sheet Metal Worker 1 Sheet Metal Apprentice	22	.727	Ea.
	3358	14" diameter			21	.762	Ea.
	3359	16" diameter			20	.800	Ea.
	3360	18" diameter	↓	↓	19	.842	Ea.
	3361	20" diameter	Q-10	2 Sheet Metal Workers 1 Sheet Metal Apprentice	18	1.330	Ea.
	3362	24" diameter			16	1.500	Ea.
	3363	28" diameter			15	1.600	Ea.
	3364	32" diameter			14	1.710	Ea.
	3365	36" diameter			12	2.000	Ea.
	3366	42" diameter			11	2.180	Ea.
	3367	48" diameter	↓	↓	10	2.400	Ea.
	3450	Tee 90°					
	3454	6" diameter	Q-9	1 Sheet Metal Worker 1 Sheet Metal Apprentice	24	.667	Ea.
	3455	8" diameter			22	.727	Ea.
	3456	10" diameter			21	.762	Ea.
	3457	12" diameter			20	.800	Ea.
	3458	14" diameter			18	.889	Ea.
	3459	16" diameter			16	1.000	Ea.
	3460	18" diameter	↓	↓	14	1.140	Ea.
	3461	20" diameter	Q-10	2 Sheet Metal Workers 1 Sheet Metal Apprentice	17	1.410	Ea.
	3462	24" diameter			12	2.000	Ea.
	3463	28" diameter			11	2.180	Ea.
	3464	32" diameter			10	2.400	Ea.
	3465	36" diameter			9	2.670	Ea.
	3466	42" diameter			6	4.000	Ea.
	3467	48" diameter	↓	↓	5	4.800	Ea.
	3520	Plate support					
	3524	6" diameter	Q-9	1 Sheet Metal Worker 1 Sheet Metal Apprentice	26	.615	Ea.
	3525	8" diameter			22	.727	Ea.
	3526	10" diameter			20	.800	Ea.
	3527	12" diameter			18	.889	Ea.
	3528	14" diameter			17	.941	Ea.
	3529	16" diameter			16	1.000	Ea.
	3530	18" diameter	↓	↓	15	1.070	Ea.
	3531	20" diameter	Q-10	2 Sheet Metal Workers 1 Sheet Metal Apprentice	16	1.500	Ea.
	3532	24" diameter			14	1.710	Ea.
	3533	28" diameter			13	1.850	Ea.
	3534	32" diameter			12	2.000	Ea.
	3535	36" diameter			10	2.400	Ea.
	3536	42" diameter			9	2.670	Ea.
	3537	48" diameter	↓	↓	8	3.000	Ea.
	3570	Bellows, lined, 316 stainless steel only					
	3574	6" diameter	Q-9	1 Sheet Metal Worker 1 Sheet Metal Apprentice	30	.533	Ea.
	3575	8" diameter			26	.615	Ea.
	3576	10" diameter			24	.667	Ea.
	3577	12" diameter			22	.727	Ea.
	3578	14" diameter			21	.762	Ea.
	3579	16" diameter			20	.800	Ea.
	3580	18" diameter	↓	↓	19	.842	Ea.
	3581	20" diameter	Q-10	2 Sheet Metal Workers 1 Sheet Metal Apprentice	18	1.330	Ea.

155 600	Heating System Access	CREW	MAKEUP	DAILY OUTPUT	MAN-HOURS	UNIT
680 3590	Vent chimney, fittings, bellows, lined, 24" diameter	Q-10	2 Sheet Metal Workers 1 Sheet Metal Apprentice	16	1.500	Ea.
3591	28" diameter			15	1.600	Ea.
3592	32" diameter			14	1.710	Ea.
3594	36" diameter			12	2.000	Ea.
3596	42" diameter			11	2.180	Ea.
3598	48" diameter			10	2.400	Ea.
3600	Ventilated roof thimble, 304 stainless steel					
3620	6" diameter	Q-9	1 Sheet Metal Worker 1 Sheet Metal Apprentice	26	.615	Ea.
3624	8" diameter			22	.727	Ea.
3625	10" diameter			20	.800	Ea.
3626	12" diameter			18	.889	Ea.
3627	14" diameter			17	.941	Ea.
3628	16" diameter			16	1.000	Ea.
3629	18" diameter			15	1.070	Ea.
3630	20" diameter	Q-10	2 Sheet Metal Workers 1 Sheet Metal Apprentice	16	1.500	Ea.
3631	24" diameter			14	1.710	Ea.
3632	28" diameter			13	1.850	Ea.
3633	32" diameter			12	2.000	Ea.
3634	36" diameter			10	2.400	Ea.
3635	42" diameter			9	2.670	Ea.
3636	48" diameter			8	3.000	Ea.
3670	Exit cone, 316 stainless steel only					
3674	6" diameter	Q-9	1 Sheet Metal Worker 1 Sheet Metal Apprentice	46	.348	Ea.
3675	8" diameter			42	.381	Ea.
3676	10" diameter			40	.400	Ea.
3677	12" diameter			38	.421	Ea.
3678	14" diameter			37	.432	Ea.
3679	16" diameter			36	.444	Ea.
3680	18" diameter			35	.457	Ea.
3681	20" diameter	Q-10	2 Sheet Metal Workers 1 Sheet Metal Apprentice	28	.857	Ea.
3682	24" diameter			26	.923	Ea.
3683	28" diameter			25	.960	Ea.
3684	32" diameter			24	1.000	Ea.
3685	36" diameter			22	1.090	Ea.
3686	42" diameter			21	1.140	Ea.
3687	48" diameter			20	1.200	Ea.
3720	Roof support assy., incl. 30" pipe sect, 304 st. st.					
3724	6" diameter	Q-9	1 Sheet Metal Worker 1 Sheet Metal Apprentice	25	.640	Ea.
3725	8" diameter			21	.762	Ea.
3726	10" diameter			19	.842	Ea.
3727	12" diameter			17	.941	Ea.
3728	14" diameter			16	1.000	Ea.
3729	16" diameter			15	1.070	Ea.
3730	18" diameter			14	1.140	Ea.
3731	20" diameter	Q-10	2 Sheet Metal Workers 1 Sheet Metal Apprentice	15	1.600	Ea.
3732	24" diameter			13	1.850	Ea.
3733	28" diameter			12	2.000	Ea.
3734	32" diameter			11	2.180	Ea.
3735	36" diameter			9	2.670	Ea.
3736	42" diameter			8	3.000	Ea.
3737	48" diameter			7	3.430	Ea.

		CREW	MAKEUP	DAILY OUTPUT	MAN-HOURS	UNIT
155 600 | Heating System Access						
680 3771	Vent chimney, fittings, stack cap, 316 stainless steel only					
3774	6" diameter	Q-9	1 Sheet Metal Worker	46	.348	Ea.
			1 Sheet Metal Apprentice			
3775	8" diameter			42	.381	Ea.
3776	10" diameter			40	.400	Ea.
3777	12" diameter			38	.421	Ea.
3778	14" diameter			37	.432	Ea.
3779	16" diameter			36	.444	Ea.
3780	18" diameter	↓	↓	35	.457	Ea.
3781	20" diameter	Q-10	2 Sheet Metal Workers	28	.857	Ea.
			1 Sheet Metal Apprentice			
3782	24" diameter			26	.923	Ea.
3783	28" diameter			25	.960	Ea.
3784	32" diameter			24	1.000	Ea.
3785	36" diameter			22	1.090	Ea.
3786	42" diameter			21	1.140	Ea.
3787	48" diameter	↓	↓	20	1.200	Ea.
7800	All fuel, double wall, stainless steel, 6" diameter	Q-9	1 Sheet Metal Worker	60	.267	V.L.F.
			1 Sheet Metal Apprentice			
7802	7" diameter			56	.286	V.L.F.
7804	8" diameter			52	.308	V.L.F.
7806	10" diameter			48	.333	V.L.F.
7808	12" diameter			44	.364	V.L.F.
7810	14" diameter	↓	↓	42	.381	V.L.F.
8000	All fuel, double wall, stainless steel fittings					
8010	Roof support 6" diameter	Q-9	1 Sheet Metal Worker	30	.533	Ea.
			1 Sheet Metal Apprentice			
8020	7" diameter			28	.571	Ea.
8030	8" diameter			26	.615	Ea.
8040	10" diameter			24	.667	Ea.
8050	12" diameter			22	.727	Ea.
8060	14" diameter			21	.762	Ea.
8100	Elbow 15°, 6" diameter			30	.533	Ea.
8120	7" diameter			28	.571	Ea.
8140	8" diameter			26	.615	Ea.
8160	10" diameter			24	.667	Ea.
8180	12" diameter			22	.727	Ea.
8200	14" diameter			21	.762	Ea.
8300	Insulated tee with insulated tee cap, 6" diameter			30	.533	Ea.
8340	7" diameter			28	.571	Ea.
8360	8" diameter			26	.615	Ea.
8380	10" diameter			24	.667	Ea.
8400	12" diameter			22	.727	Ea.
8420	14" diameter			21	.762	Ea.
8500	Joist shield, 6" diameter			30	.533	Ea.
8510	7" diameter			28	.571	Ea.
8520	8" diameter			26	.615	Ea.
8530	10" diameter			24	.667	Ea.
8540	12" diameter			22	.727	Ea.
8550	14" diameter			21	.762	Ea.
8600	Round top, 6" diameter			30	.533	Ea.
8620	7" diameter			28	.571	Ea.
8640	8" diameter			26	.615	Ea.
8660	10" diameter			24	.667	Ea.
8680	12" diameter			22	.727	Ea.
8700	14" diameter			21	.762	Ea.
8800	Adjustable roof flashing, 6" diameter			30	.533	Ea.
8820	7" diameter	↓	↓	28	.571	Ea.

155 600 | Heating System Access

		CREW	MAKEUP	DAILY OUTPUT	MAN-HOURS	UNIT
680 8841	Vent chimney, fittings, adj. roof flashing, 8" diameter	Q-9	1 Sheet Metal Worker	26	.615	Ea.
			1 Sheet Metal Apprentice			
8860	10" diameter			24	.667	Ea.
8880	12" diameter			22	.727	Ea.
8900	14" diameter	↓	↓	21	.762	Ea.
9000	High temp. (2000° F), steel jacket, acid resist. refractory lining					
9010	11 ga. galvanized jacket, U.L. listed					
9020	Straight section, 48" long, 10" diameter	Q-10	2 Sheet Metal Workers	13.30	1.800	V.L.F.
			1 Sheet Metal Apprentice			
9030	12" diameter			11.20	2.140	V.L.F.
9040	18" diameter			7.40	3.240	V.L.F.
9050	24" diameter			4.60	5.220	V.L.F.
9060	30" diameter			3.70	6.490	V.L.F.
9070	36" diameter	↓	↓	2.70	8.890	V.L.F.
9080	42" diameter	Q-11	1 Sheet Metal Foreman (ins)	3.10	10.320	V.L.F.
			2 Sheet Metal Workers			
			1 Sheet Metal Apprentice			
9090	48" diameter			2.70	11.850	V.L.F.
9100	54" diameter			2.20	14.550	V.L.F.
9110	60" diameter	↓	↓	2	16.000	V.L.F.
9120	Tee section, 10" diameter	Q-10	2 Sheet Metal Workers	4.40	5.450	Ea.
			1 Sheet Metal Apprentice			
9130	12" diameter			3.70	6.490	Ea.
9140	18" diameter			2.40	10.000	Ea.
9150	24" diameter			1.50	16.000	Ea.
9160	30" diameter			1.20	20.000	Ea.
9170	36" diameter	↓	↓	.80	30.000	Ea.
9180	42" diameter	Q-11	1 Sheet Metal Foreman (ins)	1	32.000	Ea.
			2 Sheet Metal Workers			
			1 Sheet Metal Apprentice			
9190	48" diameter			.90	35.560	Ea.
9200	54" diameter			.70	45.710	Ea.
9210	60" diameter	↓	↓	.60	53.330	Ea.
9220	Cleanout pier section, 10" diameter	Q-10	2 Sheet Metal Workers	3.50	6.860	Ea.
			1 Sheet Metal Apprentice			
9230	12" diameter			2.50	9.600	Ea.
9240	18" diameter			1.90	12.630	Ea.
9250	24" diameter			1.30	18.460	Ea.
9260	30" diameter			1	24.000	Ea.
9270	36" diameter	↓	↓	.75	32.000	Ea.
9280	42" diameter	Q-11	1 Sheet Metal Foreman (ins)	.90	35.560	Ea.
			2 Sheet Metal Workers			
			1 Sheet Metal Apprentice			
9290	48" diameter			.75	42.670	Ea.
9300	54" diameter			.60	53.330	Ea.
9310	60" diameter	↓	↓	.50	64.000	Ea.
9330	Elbow, 30° and 45°, 10" diameter	Q-10	2 Sheet Metal Workers	6.60	3.640	Ea.
			1 Sheet Metal Apprentice			
9340	12" diameter			5.60	4.290	Ea.
9350	18" diameter			3.70	6.490	Ea.
9360	24" diameter			2.30	10.430	Ea.
9370	30" diameter			1.85	12.970	Ea.
9380	36" diameter	↓	↓	1.30	18.460	Ea.
9390	42" diameter	Q-11	1 Sheet Metal Foreman (ins)	1.60	20.000	Ea.
			2 Sheet Metal Workers			
			1 Sheet Metal Apprentice			
9400	48" diameter	↓	↓	1.35	23.700	Ea.
9410	54" diameter			1.10	29.090	Ea.

155 600	Heating System Access	CREW	MAKEUP	DAILY OUTPUT	MAN-HOURS	UNIT
680 9421	Vent chimney, fittings, high temp., elbow, 60" diameter	Q-11	1 Sheet Metal Foreman (ins) 2 Sheet Metal Workers 1 Sheet Metal Apprentice	1	32.000	Ea.
9440	End cap, 10" diameter	Q-10	2 Sheet Metal Workers 1 Sheet Metal Apprentice	26	.923	Ea.
9450	12" diameter			22	1.090	Ea.
9460	18" diameter			15	1.600	Ea.
9470	24" diameter			9	2.670	Ea.
9480	30" diameter			7.30	3.290	Ea.
9490	36" diameter	▼	▼	5	4.800	Ea.
9500	42" diameter	Q-11	1 Sheet Metal Foreman (ins) 2 Sheet Metal Workers 1 Sheet Metal Apprentice	6.30	5.080	Ea.
9510	48" diameter			5.30	6.040	Ea.
9520	54" diameter			4.40	7.270	Ea.
9530	60" diameter	▼	▼	3.90	8.210	Ea.
9540	Increaser (1 diameter), 10" diameter	Q-10	2 Sheet Metal Workers 1 Sheet Metal Apprentice	6.60	3.640	Ea.
9550	12" diameter			5.60	4.290	Ea.
9560	18" diameter			3.70	6.490	Ea.
9570	24" diameter			2.30	10.430	Ea.
9580	30" diameter			1.85	12.970	Ea.
9590	36" diameter	▼	▼	1.30	18.460	Ea.
9630	26 ga. aluminized jacket, straight section, 48" long					
9640	10" diameter	Q-10	2 Sheet Metal Workers 1 Sheet Metal Apprentice	15.30	1.570	V.L.F.
9650	12" diameter			12.90	1.860	V.L.F.
9660	18" diameter			8.50	2.820	V.L.F.
9670	24" diameter			5.30	4.530	V.L.F.
9680	30" diameter			4.30	5.580	V.L.F.
9690	36" diameter	▼	▼	3.10	7.740	V.L.F.
9700	Accessories (all models)					
9710	Guy band, 10" diameter	Q-10	2 Sheet Metal Workers 1 Sheet Metal Apprentice	32	.750	Ea.
9720	12" diameter			30	.800	Ea.
9730	18" diameter			26	.923	Ea.
9740	24" diameter			24	1.000	Ea.
9750	30" diameter			20	1.200	Ea.
9760	36" diameter	▼	▼	18	1.330	Ea.
9770	42" diameter	Q-11	1 Sheet Metal Foreman (ins) 2 Sheet Metal Workers 1 Sheet Metal Apprentice	22	1.450	Ea.
9780	48" diameter			20	1.600	Ea.
9790	54" diameter			16	2.000	Ea.
9800	60" diameter	▼	▼	12	2.670	Ea.
9810	Draw band, 11 gauge, 10" diameter	Q-10	2 Sheet Metal Workers 1 Sheet Metal Apprentice	32	.750	Ea.
9820	12" diameter			30	.800	Ea.
9830	18" diameter			26	.923	Ea.
9840	24" diameter			24	1.000	Ea.
9850	30" diameter			20	1.200	Ea.
9860	36" diameter	▼	▼	18	1.330	Ea.
9870	42" diameter	Q-11	1 Sheet Metal Foreman (ins) 2 Sheet Metal Workers 1 Sheet Metal Apprentice	22	1.450	Ea.
9880	48" diameter			20	1.600	Ea.
9890	54" diameter			16	2.000	Ea.
9900	60" diameter	▼	▼	12	2.670	Ea.

155 | Heating

155 600 | Heating System Access

		Description	CREW	MAKEUP	DAILY OUTPUT	MAN-HOURS	UNIT
680	9911	Vent chimney, fittings, accessories, draw band, 26 ga., 10" diam.	Q-10	2 Sheet Metal Workers 1 Sheet Metal Apprentice	32	.750	Ea.
	9920	12" diameter			30	.800	Ea.
	9930	18" diameter			26	.923	Ea.
	9940	24" diameter			24	1.000	Ea.
	9950	30" diameter			20	1.200	Ea.
	9960	36" diameter	↓	↓	15	1.600	Ea.

156 | HVAC Piping Specialties

156 200 | Heat/Cool Piping Misc

	Description	CREW	MAKEUP	DAILY OUTPUT	MAN-HOURS	UNIT
201	AUTOMATIC AIR VENT					
0020	Cast iron body, stainless steel internals					
0060	1/2" NPT inlet, 300 psi	1 Stpi	1 Steamfitter	12	.667	Ea.
0140	3/4" NPT inlet, 300 psi			12	.667	Ea.
0180	1/2" NPT inlet, 250 psi			10	.800	Ea.
0220	3/4" NPT inlet, 250 psi			10	.800	Ea.
0260	1" NPT inlet, 250 psi	↓	↓	10	.800	Ea.
0340	1-1/2" NPT inlet, 250 psi	Q-5	1 Steamfitter 1 Steamfitter Apprentice	12	1.330	Ea.
0380	2" NPT inlet, 250 psi	"	"	12	1.330	Ea.
0600	Forged steel body, stainless steel internals					
0640	1/2" NPT inlet, 750 psi	1 Stpi	1 Steamfitter	12	.667	Ea.
0680	3/4" NPT inlet, 750 psi			12	.667	Ea.
0760	3/4" NPT inlet, 1000 psi	↓	↓	10	.800	Ea.
0800	1" NPT inlet, 1000 psi	Q-5	1 Steamfitter 1 Steamfitter Apprentice	12	1.330	Ea.
0880	1-1/2" NPT inlet, 1000 psi	↓	↓	10	1.600	Ea.
0920	2" NPT inlet, 1000 psi	↓	↓	10	1.600	Ea.
1100	Formed steel body, non corrosive					
1110	1/8" NPT inlet 35 psi	1 Stpi	1 Steamfitter	32	.250	Ea.
1120	1/4" NPT inlet 150 psi			32	.250	Ea.
1130	3/4" NPT inlet 150 psi	↓	↓	32	.250	Ea.
1300	Chrome plated brass, automatic/manual, for radiators					
1310	1/8" NPT inlet, nickel plated brass	1 Stpi	1 Steamfitter	32	.250	Ea.
205	AIR CONTROL With strainer					
0040	2" diameter	Q-5	1 Steamfitter 1 Steamfitter Apprentice	6	2.670	Ea.
0080	2-1/2" diameter			5	3.200	Ea.
0100	3" diameter			4	4.000	Ea.
0120	4" diameter	↓	↓	3	5.330	Ea.
0140	6" diameter	Q-6	2 Steamfitters 1 Steamfitter Apprentice	3.40	7.060	Ea.
0160	8" diameter			3	8.000	Ea.
0180	10" diameter			2.20	10.910	Ea.
0200	12" diameter	↓	↓	1.70	14.120	Ea.
210	CIRCUIT SENSOR Flow meter,					
0060	2-1/2" pipe size	Q-5	1 Steamfitter 1 Steamfitter Apprentice	12	1.330	Ea.
0100	3" pipe size			11	1.450	Ea.
0140	4" pipe size			8	2.000	Ea.
0180	5" pipe size	↓	↓	7.30	2.190	Ea.

156 200	Heat/Cool Piping Misc		CREW	MAKEUP	DAILY OUTPUT	MAN-HOURS	UNIT
210	0221	Circuit sensor flow meter, 6" pipe size	Q-5	1 Steamfitter	6.40	2.500	Ea.
				1 Steamfitter Apprentice			
	0260	8" pipe size	Q-6	2 Steamfitters	5.30	4.530	Ea.
				1 Steamfitter Apprentice			
	0280	10" pipe size	↓	↓	4.60	5.220	Ea.
	0360	12" pipe size			4.20	5.710	Ea.
220		**CIRCUIT SETTER** Balance valve					
	0020	3/4" pipe size	1 Stpi	1 Steamfitter	20	.400	Ea.
	0040	1" pipe size			18	.444	Ea.
	0060	1-1/2" pipe size			12	.667	Ea.
	0080	2" pipe size	↓	↓	10	.800	Ea.
	0100	2-1/2" pipe size	Q-5	1 Steamfitter	15	1.070	Ea.
				1 Steamfitter Apprentice			
	0120	3" pipe size	↓	↓	10	1.600	Ea.
	0140	4" pipe size			3	5.330	Ea.
225		**EXPANSION JOINTS** Bellows type, neoprene cover, flanged spool					
	0100	6" face to face, 1/2" diameter	1 Stpi	1 Steamfitter	14	.571	Ea.
	0110	3/4" diameter			14	.571	Ea.
	0120	1" diameter			13	.615	Ea.
	0140	1-1/4" diameter			11	.727	Ea.
	0160	1-1/2" diameter	↓	↓	10.60	.755	Ea.
	0180	2" diameter	Q-5	1 Steamfitter	13.30	1.200	Ea.
				1 Steamfitter Apprentice			
	0200	3" diameter			11.40	1.400	Ea.
	0480	10" face to face, 2" diameter			13	1.230	Ea.
	0500	2-1/2" diameter			12	1.330	Ea.
	0520	3" diameter			11	1.450	Ea.
	0540	4" diameter			8	2.000	Ea.
	0560	5" diameter			7	2.290	Ea.
	0580	6" diameter			6	2.670	Ea.
	0600	8" diameter			5	3.200	Ea.
	0620	10" diameter			4.60	3.480	Ea.
	0640	12" diameter			4	4.000	Ea.
	0660	14" diameter	↓	↓	3.80	4.210	Ea.
230		**EXPANSION COUPLINGS** Hydronic					
	0100	Copper to copper, sweat					
	0120	3/4" diameter	1 Stpi	1 Steamfitter	20	.400	Ea.
	0140	1" diameter			19	.421	Ea.
	0160	1-1/4" diameter	↓	↓	15	.533	Ea.
	1000	Baseboard riser fitting, 5" stub by coupling 12" long					
	1020	1/2" diameter	1 Stpi	1 Steamfitter	24	.333	Ea.
	1040	3/4" diameter			20	.400	Ea.
	1060	1" diameter			19	.421	Ea.
	1080	1-1/4" diameter	↓	↓	15	.533	Ea.
	1180	9" Stub by tubing 8" long					
	1200	1/2" diameter	1 Stpi	1 Steamfitter	24	.333	Ea.
	1220	3/4" diameter			20	.400	Ea.
	1240	1" diameter			19	.421	Ea.
	1260	1-1/4" diameter	↓	↓	15	.533	Ea.
235		**FLEXIBLE METAL HOSE** Connectors, standard lengths					
	0100	Bronze braided, bronze ends					
	0120	3/8" diameter x 12"	1 Stpi	1 Steamfitter	26	.308	Ea.
	0140	1/2" diameter x 12"			24	.333	Ea.
	0160	3/4" diameter x 12"			20	.400	Ea.
	0180	1" diameter x 18"			19	.421	Ea.
	0200	1-1/2" diameter x 18"			13	.615	Ea.
	0220	2" diameter x 18"	↓	↓	11	.727	Ea.

156 | HVAC Piping Specialties

156 200	Heat/Cool Piping Misc	CREW	MAKEUP	DAILY OUTPUT	MAN-HOURS	UNIT
235 1021	Flex. hose conn., bronze braid, carbon stl. ends, 1/4" diam. x 12"	1 Stpi	1 Steamfitter	28	.286	Ea.
1040	3/8" diameter x 12"			26	.308	Ea.
1060	1/2" diameter x 12"			24	.333	Ea.
1080	1/2" diameter x 24"			24	.333	Ea.
1100	1/2" diameter x 36"			24	.333	Ea.
1120	3/4" diameter x 12"			20	.400	Ea.
1140	3/4" diameter x 24"			20	.400	Ea.
1160	3/4" diameter x 36"			20	.400	Ea.
1180	1" diameter x 18"			19	.421	Ea.
1200	1" diameter x 30"			19	.421	Ea.
1220	1" diameter x 36"			19	.421	Ea.
1240	1-1/4" diameter x 18"			15	.533	Ea.
1260	1-1/4" diameter x 36"			15	.533	Ea.
1280	1-1/2" diameter x 18"			13	.615	Ea.
1300	1-1/2" diameter x 36"			13	.615	Ea.
1320	2" diameter x 24"			11	.727	Ea.
1340	2" diameter x 36"			11	.727	Ea.
1360	2-1/2" diameter x 24"			9	.889	Ea.
1380	2-1/2" diameter x 36"			9	.889	Ea.
1400	3" diameter x 24"			7	1.140	Ea.
1420	3" diameter x 36"	↓	↓	7	1.140	Ea.
2000	Carbon steel braid, carbon steel solid ends					
2100	1/2" diameter x 12"	1 Stpi	1 Steamfitter	24	.333	Ea.
2120	3/4" diameter x 12"			20	.400	Ea.
2140	1" diameter x 12"			19	.421	Ea.
2160	1-1/4" diameter x 12"			15	.533	Ea.
2180	1-1/2" diameter x 12"	↓	↓	13	.615	Ea.
3000	Stainless steel braid, welded on carbon steel ends					
3100	1/2" diameter x 12"	1 Stpi	1 Steamfitter	24	.333	Ea.
3120	3/4" diameter x 12"			20	.400	Ea.
3140	3/4" diameter x 24"			20	.400	Ea.
3160	3/4" diameter x 36"			20	.400	Ea.
3180	1" diameter x 12"			19	.421	Ea.
3200	1" diameter x 24"			19	.421	Ea.
3220	1" diameter x 36"			19	.421	Ea.
3240	1-1/4" diameter x 12"			15	.533	Ea.
3260	1-1/4" diameter x 24"			15	.533	Ea.
3280	1-1/4" diameter x 36"			15	.533	Ea.
3300	1-1/2" diameter x 12"			13	.615	Ea.
3320	1-1/2" diameter x 24"			13	.615	Ea.
3340	1-1/2" diameter x 36"	↓	↓	13	.615	Ea.
240	**HEATING CONTROL VALVES**					
0050	Hot water, nonelectric, thermostatic					
0100	Radiator supply, 1/2" diameter	1 Stpi	1 Steamfitter	24	.333	Ea.
0120	3/4" diameter			20	.400	Ea.
0140	1" diameter			19	.421	Ea.
0160	1-1/4" diameter	↓	↓	15	.533	Ea.
1000	Manual, radiator supply					
1010	1/2" pipe size, angle union	1 Stpi	1 Steamfitter	24	.333	Ea.
1020	3/4" pipe size, angle union			20	.400	Ea.
1030	1" pipe size, angle union	↓	↓	19	.421	Ea.
1100	Radiator, balancing					
1110	1/2" pipe size, angle union	1 Stpi	1 Steamfitter	24	.333	Ea.
1120	3/4" pipe size, angle union			20	.400	Ea.
1130	1" pipe size, angle union			19	.421	Ea.
1140	Balance and stop valve 1/2" size			22	.364	Ea.
1150	3/4" size			20	.400	Ea.
1160	1" size	↓	↓	19	.421	Ea.

156 200 | Heat/Cool Piping Misc

			CREW	MAKEUP	DAILY OUTPUT	MAN-HOURS	UNIT
240	1171	Heating, balance and stop valve, 1-1/4" size	1 Stpi	1 Steamfitter	15	.533	Ea.
	1180	1-1/2" size			13	.615	Ea.
	1190	2" size	↓	↓	11	.727	Ea.
	1200	Steam, radiator, supply					
	1210	1/2" pipe size, angle union	1 Stpi	1 Steamfitter	24	.333	Ea.
	1220	3/4" pipe size, angle union			20	.400	Ea.
	1230	1" pipe size, angle union			19	.421	Ea.
	1240	1-1/4" pipe size, angle union	↓	↓	15	.533	Ea.
	8000	System balancing and shut-off					
	8020	Butterfly, quarter turn, calibrated, threaded or solder					
	8040	Bronze, -30° F to +350° F, pressure to 175 psi					
	8060	1/2" size	1 Stpi	1 Steamfitter	22	.364	Ea.
	8070	3/4" size			20	.400	Ea.
	8080	1" size			19	.421	Ea.
	8090	1-1/4" size			15	.533	Ea.
	8100	1-1/2" size			13	.615	Ea.
	8110	2" size	↓	↓	11	.727	Ea.
245		**MIXING VALVE** Automatic water tempering					
	0050	3/4" size	1 Stpi	1 Steamfitter	18	.444	Ea.
	0100	1" size			16	.500	Ea.
	0120	1-1/4" size			13	.615	Ea.
	0140	1-1/2" size			10	.800	Ea.
	0160	2" size			8	1.000	Ea.
	0180	3" size	↓	↓	4	2.000	Ea.
255		**PRESSURE REDUCING VALVE** Steam, pilot operated					
	0100	Threaded, iron body					
	0120	1/2" size	1 Stpi	1 Steamfitter	18	.444	Ea.
	0140	3/4" size			14	.571	Ea.
	0160	1" size			13	.615	Ea.
	0180	1-1/4" size			10	.800	Ea.
	0200	1-1/2" size			8	1.000	Ea.
	0220	2" size	↓	↓	5	1.600	Ea.
	1000	Flanged, iron body, 125 lb. flanges					
	1020	2" size	1 Stpi	1 Steamfitter	8	1.000	Ea.
	1040	2-1/2" size	"	"	4	2.000	Ea.
	1060	3" size	Q-5	1 Steamfitter	4.50	3.560	Ea.
				1 Steamfitter Apprentice			
	1080	4" size	"	"	3	5.330	Ea.
260		**PRESSURE REGULATOR**					
	0200	Oil, light, hot water, ordinary steam, threaded					
	0221	Bronze or iron body					
	0230	3/8" size	1 Stpi	1 Steamfitter	24	.333	Ea.
	0240	1/2" size			24	.333	Ea.
	0250	3/4" size			20	.400	Ea.
	0260	1" size			19	.421	Ea.
	0270	1-1/4" size			15	.533	Ea.
	0280	1-1/2" size			13	.615	Ea.
	0290	2" size	↓	↓	11	.727	Ea.
	0500	Oil, heavy, viscous fluids, threaded					
	0521	Bronze or iron body					
	0530	1/2" size	1 Stpi	1 Steamfitter	24	.333	Ea.
	0540	3/4" size			20	.400	Ea.
	0550	1" size			19	.421	Ea.
	0560	1-1/4" size			15	.533	Ea.
	0570	1-1/2" size	↓	↓	13	.615	Ea.
	0800	Process steam, wet or super heated, monel trim, threaded					
	0821	Bronze or iron body					
	0830	3/8" size	1 Stpi	1 Steamfitter	24	.333	Ea.

156 200 | Heat/Cool Piping Misc

		Description	CREW	MAKEUP	DAILY OUTPUT	MAN-HOURS	UNIT
260	0841	Pressure regul., process steam, bronze/iron body, 1/2" size	1 Stpi	1 Steamfitter	24	.333	Ea.
	0850	3/4" size			20	.400	Ea.
	0860	1" size			19	.421	Ea.
	0870	1-1/4" size			15	.533	Ea.
	0880	1-1/2" size			13	.615	Ea.
	0890	2" size	↓	↓	11	.727	Ea.
	3000	Steam, high capacity, bronze body, stainless steel trim					
	3020	Threaded, 1/2" diameter	1 Stpi	1 Steamfitter	24	.333	Ea.
	3030	3/4" diameter			24	.333	Ea.
	3040	1" diameter			19	.421	Ea.
	3060	1-1/4" diameter			15	.533	Ea.
	3080	1-1/2" diameter			13	.615	Ea.
	3100	2" diameter	↓	↓	11	.727	Ea.
	3120	2-1/2" diameter	Q-5	1 Steamfitter 1 Steamfitter Apprentice	12	1.330	Ea.
	3140	3" diameter	"	"	11	1.450	Ea.
	3500	Flanged connection, iron body, 125 lb. W.S.P.					
	3520	3" diameter	Q-5	1 Steamfitter 1 Steamfitter Apprentice	11	1.450	Ea.
	3540	4" diameter	"	"	5	3.200	Ea.
265		**SEPARATORS** Entrainment eliminator, steel body, 150 PSIG					
	0100	1/4" size	1 Stpi	1 Steamfitter	24	.333	Ea.
	0120	1/2" size			24	.333	Ea.
	0140	3/4" size			20	.400	Ea.
	0160	1" size			19	.421	Ea.
	0180	1-1/4" size			15	.533	Ea.
	0200	1-1/2" size			13	.615	Ea.
	0220	2" size	↓	↓	11	.727	Ea.
	0240	2-1/2" size	Q-5	1 Steamfitter 1 Steamfitter Apprentice	15	1.070	Ea.
	0260	3" size			13	1.230	Ea.
	0280	4" size			10	1.600	Ea.
	0300	5" size			6	2.670	Ea.
	0320	6" size	↓	↓	3	5.330	Ea.
	0340	8" size	Q-6	2 Steamfitters 1 Steamfitter Apprentice	4.40	5.450	Ea.
	0360	10" size			4	6.000	Ea.
	0380	12" size			3	8.000	Ea.
	0400	14" size	↓	↓	2	12.000	Ea.
270		**STEAM CONDENSATE METER**					
	0100	500 lb. per hour	1 Stpi	1 Steamfitter	14	.571	Ea.
	0140	1500 lb. per hour			7	1.140	Ea.
	0160	3000 lb. per hour	↓	↓	5	1.600	Ea.
	0200	12,000 lb. per hour	Q-5	1 Steamfitter 1 Steamfitter Apprentice	3.50	4.570	Ea.
272		**STEAM TRAP** Cast Iron					
	0040	Inverted bucket					
	0050	1/2" pipe size	1 Stpi	1 Steamfitter	12	.667	Ea.
	0070	3/4" pipe size			10	.800	Ea.
	0100	1" pipe size			9	.889	Ea.
	0120	1-1/4" pipe size	↓	↓	8	1.000	Ea.
	1000	Float & thermostatic, 15 psig					
	1010	3/4" pipe size	1 Stpi	1 Steamfitter	16	.500	Ea.
	1020	1" pipe size			15	.533	Ea.
	1030	1-1/4" pipe size			13	.615	Ea.
	1040	1-1/2" pipe size			9	.889	Ea.
	1060	2" pipe size	↓	↓	6	1.330	Ea.

156 200 | Heat/Cool Piping Misc

			CREW	MAKEUP	DAILY OUTPUT	MAN-HOURS	UNIT
272	1311	Steam trap, thermostatic, angle union, 15 psi, 1/2" pipe size	1 Stpi	1 Steamfitter	24	.333	Ea.
	1320	3/4" pipe size			20	.400	Ea.
	1330	1" pipe size	↓	↓	19	.421	Ea.
	275	**THERMOFLO INDICATOR** For balancing					
	1000	Sweat connections, 1-1/4" pipe size	1 Stpi	1 Steamfitter	12	.667	Ea.
	1020	1-1/2" pipe size			10	.800	Ea.
	1040	2" pipe size			8	1.000	Ea.
	1060	2-1/2" pipe size	↓	↓	7	1.140	Ea.
	2000	Flange connections, 3" pipe size	Q-5	1 Steamfitter 1 Steamfitter Apprentice	5	3.200	Ea.
	2020	4" pipe size			4	4.000	Ea.
	2030	5" pipe size			3.50	4.570	Ea.
	2040	6" pipe size			3	5.330	Ea.
	2060	8" pipe size	↓	↓	2	8.000	Ea.
	280	**VENTURI FLOW** Measuring device					
	0050	1/2" diameter	1 Stpi	1 Steamfitter	24	.333	Ea.
	0100	3/4" diameter			20	.400	Ea.
	0120	1" diameter			19	.421	Ea.
	0140	1-1/4" diameter			15	.533	Ea.
	0160	1-1/2" diameter			13	.615	Ea.
	0180	2" diameter	↓	↓	11	.727	Ea.
	0200	2-1/2" diameter	Q-5	1 Steamfitter 1 Steamfitter Apprentice	16	1.000	Ea.
	0220	3" diameter			14	1.140	Ea.
	0240	4" diameter	↓	↓	11	1.450	Ea.
	0260	5" diameter	Q-6	2 Steamfitters 1 Steamfitter Apprentice	4	6.000	Ea.
	0280	6" diameter			3.50	6.860	Ea.
	0300	8" diameter			3	8.000	Ea.
	0320	10" diameter	↓	↓	2	12.000	Ea.
	290	**WATER LEVEL CONTROLS**					
	1000	Electric water feeder	1 Stpi	1 Steamfitter	12	.667	Ea.
	2000	Feeder cut-off combination					
	2100	Steam system up to 5000 sq. ft.	1 Stpi	1 Steamfitter	12	.667	Ea.
	2200	Steam system above 5000 sq. ft.			12	.667	Ea.
	2300	Steam and hot water, high pressure	↓	↓	10	.800	Ea.
	3000	Low water cut-off for hot water boiler, 50 psi maximum					
	3100	1" top & bottom equalizing pipes, manual reset	1 Stpi	1 Steamfitter	14	.571	Ea.
	3200	1" top & bottom equalizing pipes			14	.571	Ea.
	3300	2-1/2" side connection for nipple-to-boiler	↓	↓	14	.571	Ea.
	4000	Low water cut-off for low pressure steam with quick hook-up ftgs.					
	4100	For installation in gauge glass tappings	1 Stpi	1 Steamfitter	16	.500	Ea.
	4200	Built-in type, 2-1/2" tap - 3-1/8" insertion			16	.500	Ea.
	4300	Built-in type, 2-1/2" tap - 1-3/4" insertion			16	.500	Ea.
	4400	Side connection to 2-1/2" tapping			16	.500	Ea.
	5000	Pump control, low water cut-off and alarm switch	↓	↓	14	.571	Ea.
	295	**WELD END BALL JOINTS** Steel					
	0050	2-1/2" diameter	Q-17	1 Steamfitter 1 Steamfitter Apprentice 1 Electric Welding Mach.	13	1.230	Ea.
	0100	3" diameter			12	1.330	Ea.
	0120	4" diameter	↓	↓	11	1.450	Ea.
	0140	5" diameter	Q-18	2 Steamfitters 1 Steamfitter Apprentice 1 Electric Welding Mach.	14	1.710	Ea.
	0160	6" diameter			12	2.000	Ea.
	0180	8" diameter			9	2.670	Ea.
	0200	10" diameter	↓	↓	8	3.000	Ea.

156 200 | Heat/Cool Piping Misc

		CREW	MAKEUP	DAILY OUTPUT	MAN-HOURS	UNIT
295 0221	Weld end ball joints, steel 12" diameter	Q-18	2 Steamfitters	6	4.000	Ea.
			1 Steamfitter Apprentice			
			1 Electric Welding Mach.			
0240	14" diameter	"	"	4	6.000	Ea.

156 600 | Strainers

		CREW	MAKEUP	DAILY OUTPUT	MAN-HOURS	UNIT
601	**STRAINERS, BASKET TYPE** Perforated stainless steel basket					
2000	Simplex style					
2301	Bronze or iron body	↓	↓			
2320	Screwed, 3/8" pipe size	1 Stpi	1 Steamfitter	22	.364	Ea.
2340	1/2" pipe size			20	.400	Ea.
2360	3/4" pipe size			17	.471	Ea.
2380	1" pipe size			15	.533	Ea.
2400	1-1/4" pipe size			13	.615	Ea.
2420	1-1/2" pipe size			12	.667	Ea.
2440	2" pipe size	↓	↓	10	.800	Ea.
2460	2-1/2" pipe size	Q-5	1 Steamfitter	15	1.070	Ea.
			1 Steamfitter Apprentice			
2480	3" pipe size	"	"	14	1.140	Ea.
2600	Flanged, 2" pipe size	1 Stpi	1 Steamfitter	6	1.330	Ea.
2620	2-1/2" pipe size	Q-5	1 Steamfitter	4.50	3.560	Ea.
			1 Steamfitter Apprentice			
2640	3" pipe size	↓	↓	3.50	4.570	Ea.
2660	4" pipe size			3	5.330	Ea.
2680	5" pipe size	Q-6	2 Steamfitters	3.40	7.060	Ea.
			1 Steamfitter Apprentice			
2700	6" pipe size	"	"	3	8.000	Ea.
6001	Cast steel or stainless steel body					
6400	Screwed, 1" pipe size	1 Stpi	1 Steamfitter	15	.533	Ea.
6420	1-1/2" pipe size			12	.667	Ea.
6440	2" pipe size	↓	↓	10	.800	Ea.
6460	2-1/2" pipe size	Q-5	1 Steamfitter	15	1.070	Ea.
			1 Steamfitter Apprentice			
6480	3" pipe size	"	"	14	1.140	Ea.
6560	Flanged, 2" pipe size	1 Stpi	1 Steamfitter	6	1.330	Ea.
6580	2-1/2" pipe size	Q-5	1 Steamfitter	4.50	3.560	Ea.
			1 Steamfitter Apprentice			
6600	3" pipe size	↓	↓	3.50	4.570	Ea.
6620	4" pipe size			3	5.330	Ea.
6640	6" pipe size	Q-6	2 Steamfitters	3	8.000	Ea.
			1 Steamfitter Apprentice			
6660	8" pipe size	"	"	2.50	9.600	Ea.
8100	Duplex style					
8201	Bronze or iron body					
8240	Screwed, 3/4" pipe size	1 Stpi	1 Steamfitter	16	.500	Ea.
8260	1" pipe size			14	.571	Ea.
8280	1-1/4" pipe size			12	.667	Ea.
8300	1-1/2" pipe size			11	.727	Ea.
8320	2" pipe size	↓	↓	9	.889	Ea.
8340	2-1/2" pipe size	Q-5	1 Steamfitter	14	1.140	Ea.
			1 Steamfitter Apprentice			
8420	Flanged, 2" pipe size	1 Stpi	1 Steamfitter	6	1.330	Ea.
8440	2-1/2" pipe size	Q-5	1 Steamfitter	4.50	3.560	Ea.
			1 Steamfitter Apprentice			
8460	3" pipe size	↓	↓	3.50	4.570	Ea.
8480	4" pipe size			3	5.330	Ea.
8500	5" pipe size	Q-6	2 Steamfitters	3.40	7.060	Ea.
			1 Steamfitter Apprentice			

156 600 | Strainers

			CREW	MAKEUP	DAILY OUTPUT	MAN-HOURS	UNIT
601	8521	Strainers, duplex style, bronze/iron body, flanged, 6" pipe size	Q-6	2 Steamfitters	3	8.000	Ea.
				1 Steamfitter Apprentice			
	9301	Cast steel or stainless steel body					
	9340	Screwed, 1" pipe size	1 Stpi	1 Steamfitter	14	.571	Ea.
	9360	1-1/2" pipe size			11	.727	Ea.
	9380	2" pipe size			9	.889	Ea.
	9460	Flanged, 2" pipe size	↓	↓	6	1.330	Ea.
	9480	2-1/2" pipe size	Q-5	1 Steamfitter	4.50	3.560	Ea.
				1 Steamfitter Apprentice			
	9500	3" pipe size			3.50	4.570	Ea.
	9520	4" pipe size	↓	↓	3	5.330	Ea.
	9540	6" pipe size	Q-6	2 Steamfitters	3	8.000	Ea.
				1 Steamfitter Apprentice			
	9560	8" pipe size	"	"	2.50	9.600	Ea.
608		**STRAINERS, Y TYPE** Bronze body					
	0050	Screwed, 150 lb., 1/4" pipe size	1 Stpi	1 Steamfitter	24	.333	Ea.
	0070	3/8" pipe size			24	.333	Ea.
	0100	1/2" pipe size			20	.400	Ea.
	0120	3/4" pipe size			19	.421	Ea.
	0140	1" pipe size			17	.471	Ea.
	0150	1-1/4" pipe size			15	.533	Ea.
	0160	1-1/2" pipe size			14	.571	Ea.
	0180	2" pipe size	↓	↓	13	.615	Ea.
	0200	2-1/2" pipe size	Q-5	1 Steamfitter	17	.941	Ea.
				1 Steamfitter Apprentice			
	0220	3" pipe size			16	1.000	Ea.
	0240	4" pipe size	↓	↓	15	1.070	Ea.
	1000	Flanged, 150 lb., 1-1/2" pipe size	1 Stpi	1 Steamfitter	11	.727	Ea.
	1020	2" pipe size	"	"	8	1.000	Ea.
	1040	3" pipe size	Q-5	1 Steamfitter	4.50	3.560	Ea.
				1 Steamfitter Apprentice			
	1060	4" pipe size	"	"	3	5.330	Ea.
	1080	5" pipe size	Q-6	2 Steamfitters	3.40	7.060	Ea.
				1 Steamfitter Apprentice			
	1100	6" pipe size			3	8.000	Ea.
	1120	8" pipe size	↓	↓	2.50	9.600	Ea.
612		**STRAINERS, Y TYPE** Iron body					
	0050	Screwed, 250 lb.,	1 Stpi	1 Steamfitter	20	.400	Ea.
	0070	3/8" pipe size			20	.400	Ea.
	0100	1/2" pipe size			20	.400	Ea.
	0120	3/4" pipe size			18	.444	Ea.
	0140	1" pipe size			16	.500	Ea.
	0150	1-1/4" pipe size			15	.533	Ea.
	0160	1-1/2" pipe size			12	.667	Ea.
	0180	2" pipe size	↓	↓	8	1.000	Ea.
	0200	2-1/2" pipe size	Q-5	1 Steamfitter	12	1.330	Ea.
				1 Steamfitter Apprentice			
	0220	3" pipe size			11	1.450	Ea.
	0240	4" pipe size	↓	↓	5	3.200	Ea.
	1000	Flanged, 125 lb.,	1 Stpi	1 Steamfitter	11	.727	Ea.
	1020	2" pipe size	"	"	8	1.000	Ea.
	1030	2-1/2" pipe size	Q-5	1 Steamfitter	5	3.200	Ea.
				1 Steamfitter Apprentice			
	1040	3" pipe size			4.50	3.560	Ea.
	1050	3-1/2" pipe size			4	4.000	Ea.
	1060	4" pipe size	↓	↓	3	5.330	Ea.
	1080	5" pipe size	Q-6	2 Steamfitters	3.40	7.060	Ea.
				1 Steamfitter Apprentice			

156 | HVAC Piping Specialties

		CREW	MAKEUP	DAILY OUTPUT	MAN-HOURS	UNIT
156 600 | Strainers						
612 1101	Strainers, Y type iron body, flanged, 6" pipe size	Q-6	2 Steamfitters	3	8.000	Ea.
			1 Steamfitter Apprentice			
1120	8" pipe size			2.50	9.600	Ea.
1140	10" pipe size			2	12.000	Ea.
1160	12" pipe size			1.70	14.120	Ea.
1170	14" pipe size			1.30	18.460	Ea.
1180	16" pipe size	↓	↓	1	24.000	Ea.

157 | Air Conditioning/Ventilating

		CREW	MAKEUP	DAILY OUTPUT	MAN-HOURS	UNIT
157 100 | AC & Vent Units						
110	**ABSORPTION COLD GENERATORS** Water chiller					
3000	Gas fired, air cooled					
3180	3 ton	Q-5	1 Steamfitter	1.30	12.310	Ea.
			1 Steamfitter Apprentice			
3200	4 ton			.90	17.780	Ea.
3220	5 ton			.60	26.670	Ea.
3250	8 ton			.50	32.000	Ea.
3270	10 ton	↓	↓	.40	40.000	Ea.
125	**CENTRAL STATION AIR-HANDLING UNIT** Chill water					
1000	Modular, capacity at 700 FPM face velocity					
1100	1300 CFM	Q-5	1 Steamfitter	1.20	13.330	Ea.
			1 Steamfitter Apprentice			
1200	1900 CFM			1.10	14.550	Ea.
1300	3200 CFM	↓	↓	.80	20.000	Ea.
1400	5400 CFM	Q-6	2 Steamfitters	.80	30.000	Ea.
			1 Steamfitter Apprentice			
1500	8000 CFM			.60	40.000	Ea.
1550	10,000 CFM			.54	44.440	Ea.
1600	12,000 CFM			.46	52.170	Ea.
1650	14,000 CFM			.42	57.140	Ea.
1670	16,000 CFM			.38	63.160	Ea.
1700	20,000 CFM			.31	77.420	Ea.
1800	23,000 CFM			.28	85.710	Ea.
1850	28,000 CFM			.24	100.000	Ea.
1900	33,500 CFM			.19	126.000	Ea.
1950	42,500 CFM	↓	↓	.15	160.000	Ea.
2000	52,500 CFM	Q-7	1 Steamfitter Foreman (ins)	.16	200.000	Ea.
			2 Steamfitters			
			1 Steamfitter Apprentice			
2100	63,000 CFM	"	"	.13	246.000	Ea.
3000	Packaged, 3000 CFM, 7.5 ton	Q-6	2 Steamfitters	1.70	14.120	Ea.
			1 Steamfitter Apprentice			
3050	3200 CFM, 8 ton			1.60	15.000	Ea.
3100	4000 CFM, 10 ton			1.40	17.140	Ea.
3150	4400 CFM, 11 ton			1.35	17.780	Ea.
3200	6000 CFM, 15 ton			1	24.000	Ea.
3250	7000 CFM, 17.5 ton			.90	26.670	Ea.
3300	10,000 CFM, 25 ton			.65	36.920	Ea.
3400	12,000 CFM, 30 ton	↓	↓	.50	48.000	Ea.

157 100	AC & Vent Units	CREW	MAKEUP	DAILY OUTPUT	MAN-HOURS	UNIT
130	**COMPUTER ROOM UNITS**					
1000	Air cooled, includes remote condenser but not					
1020	interconnecting tubing or refrigerant					
1080	3 ton	Q-5	1 Steamfitter	.50	32.000	Ea.
			1 Steamfitter Apprentice			
1120	5 ton			.45	35.560	Ea.
1160	6 ton			.30	53.330	Ea.
1200	8 ton			.27	59.260	Ea.
1240	10 ton			.25	64.000	Ea.
1280	15 ton	↓	↓	.22	72.730	Ea.
1320	20 ton	Q-6	2 Steamfitters	.29	82.760	Ea.
			1 Steamfitter Apprentice			
1360	23 ton	"	"	.28	85.710	Ea.
2200	Chilled water, for connection to					
2220	existing chiller system of adequate capacity					
2260	5 ton	Q-5	1 Steamfitter	.74	21.620	Ea.
			1 Steamfitter Apprentice			
2280	6 ton			.52	30.770	Ea.
2300	8 ton			.50	32.000	Ea.
2320	10 ton			.49	32.650	Ea.
2360	15 ton			.48	33.330	Ea.
2400	20 ton			.46	34.780	Ea.
2440	23 ton	↓	↓	.42	38.100	Ea.
4000	Glycol system, complete except for interconnecting tubing					
4060	3 ton	Q-5	1 Steamfitter	.40	40.000	Ea.
			1 Steamfitter Apprentice			
4100	5 ton			.38	42.110	Ea.
4120	6 ton			.25	64.000	Ea.
4140	8 ton			.23	69.570	Ea.
4160	10 ton	↓	↓	.21	76.190	Ea.
4200	15 ton	Q-6	2 Steamfitters	.26	92.310	Ea.
			1 Steamfitter Apprentice			
4240	20 ton			.24	100.000	Ea.
4280	23 ton	↓	↓	.22	109.000	Ea.
8000	Water cooled system, not including condenser,					
8020	water supply or cooling tower					
8060	3 ton	Q-5	1 Steamfitter	.62	25.810	Ea.
			1 Steamfitter Apprentice			
8100	5 ton			.54	29.630	Ea.
8120	6 ton			.35	45.710	Ea.
8140	8 ton			.33	48.480	Ea.
8160	10 ton			.31	51.610	Ea.
8200	15 ton	↓	↓	.27	59.260	Ea.
8240	20 ton	Q-6	2 Steamfitters	.38	63.160	Ea.
			1 Steamfitter Apprentice			
8280	23 ton	"	"	.34	70.590	Ea.
140	**DEHUMIDIFIERS**					
6000	Selfcontained with filters and standard controls					
6040	1 lb/hr	1 Plum	1 Plumber	8	1.000	Ea.
6060	3 lb/hr	Q-1	1 Plumber	12	1.330	Ea.
			1 Plumber Apprentice			
6070	12 lb/hr			5	3.200	Ea.
6080	3-40 lb/hr			4	4.000	Ea.
6090	10-60 lb/hr			3	5.330	Ea.
6100	20-120 lb/hr			2	8.000	Ea.
6110	40-300 lb/hr	↓	↓	1.50	10.670	Ea.
6120	100-750 lb/hr	Q-2	2 Plumbers	1.60	15.000	Ea.
			1 Plumber Apprentice			

157 | Air Conditioning/Ventilating

157 100 | AC & Vent Units

		Description	CREW	MAKEUP	DAILY OUTPUT	MAN-HOURS	UNIT
140	6131	Dehumidifiers, selfcontained, 130-1000 lb/hr	Q-2	2 Plumbers	1.40	17.140	Ea.
				1 Plumber Apprentice			
	6140	200-1500 lb/hr	↓	↓	1.20	20.000	Ea.
	6150	260-2000 lb/hr			1	24.000	Ea.
	145	**EVAPORATIVE COOLERS** Ducted, not incl. duct.					
	0100	Side draft style, capacities at .25" S.P.					
	0120	1785 CFM, 1/3 HP, 115 V	Q-9	1 Sheet Metal Worker	5	3.200	Ea.
				1 Sheet Metal Apprentice			
	0140	2740 CFM, 1/3 HP, 115 V			4.50	3.560	Ea.
	0160	3235 CFM, 1/2 HP, 115 V			4	4.000	Ea.
	0180	3615 CFM, 1/2 HP, 230 V			3.60	4.440	Ea.
	0200	4215 CFM, 3/4 HP, 230 V			3.20	5.000	Ea.
	0220	5255 CFM, 1 HP, 115/230 V			3	5.330	Ea.
	0240	6090 CFM, 1 HP, 230/460 V			2.80	5.710	Ea.
	0260	8300 CFM, 2 HP, 230/460 V			2.60	6.150	Ea.
	0280	8360 CFM, 1-1/2" HP, 230/460 V			2.20	7.270	Ea.
	0300	9725 CFM, 2 HP, 230/460 V			1.80	8.890	Ea.
	0320	11,715 CFM, 3 HP, 230/460 V			1 40	11.430	Ea.
	0340	14,410 CFM, 5 HP, 230/460 V	↓	↓	1	16.000	Ea.
	1000	High capacities at .4" S.P.					
	1040	12,100 CFM, 2 HP, 230/460 V	Q-9	1 Sheet Metal Worker	.54	29.630	Ea.
				1 Sheet Metal Apprentice			
	1080	16,000 CFM, 5HP, 230/460 V	"	"	.48	33.330	Ea.
	1100	24,000 CFM, 10 HP, 230/460 V	Q-10	2 Sheet Metal Workers	.54	44.440	Ea.
				1 Sheet Metal Apprentice			
	1140	29,500 CFM, 15 HP, 230/460 V			.46	52.170	Ea.
	1160	35,000 CFM, 15 HP, 230/460 V			.44	54.550	Ea.
	1180	40,000 CFM, 20 HP, 230/460 V	↓	↓	.42	57.140	Ea.
	150	**FAN COIL AIR CONDITIONING** Cabinet mounted, filters					
	0100	Chilled water, 1/2 ton cooling	Q-5	1 Steamfitter	8	2.000	Ea.
				1 Steamfitter Apprentice			
	0110	3/4 ton cooling			7	2.290	Ea.
	0120	1 ton cooling			6	2.670	Ea.
	0140	1.5 ton cooling			5.50	2.910	Ea.
	0150	2 ton cooling			5.25	3.050	Ea.
	0160	2.5 ton cooling			5	3.200	Ea.
	0180	3 ton cooling			4	4.000	Ea.
	0190	7.5 ton cooling			2.70	5.930	Ea.
	0195	8 ton cooling	↓	↓	2.20	7.270	Ea.
	0200	10 ton cooling	Q-6	2 Steamfitters	2.80	8.570	Ea.
				1 Steamfitter Apprentice			
	0210	12 ton cooling			2.20	10.910	Ea.
	0220	15 ton cooling			1.50	16.000	Ea.
	0240	20 ton cooling			.80	30.000	Ea.
	0250	25 ton cooling			.70	34.290	Ea.
	0260	30 ton cooling	↓	↓	.60	40.000	Ea.
	0940	Direct expansion, air cooled condensing, 1.5 ton cooling	Q-5	1 Steamfitter	5	3.200	Ea.
				1 Steamfitter Apprentice			
	0950	2 ton cooling			4.80	3.330	Ea.
	0960	2.5 ton cooling			4.40	3.640	Ea.
	0970	3 ton cooling			3.80	4.210	Ea.
	0980	3.5 ton cooling			3.60	4.440	Ea.
	0990	4 ton cooling			3.40	4.710	Ea.
	1000	5 ton cooling			3	5.330	Ea.
	1020	7.5 ton cooling	↓	↓	3	5.330	Ea.
	1040	10 ton cooling	Q-6	2 Steamfitters	2.60	9.230	Ea.
				1 Steamfitter Apprentice			
	1042	11 ton cooling	"	"	2.30	10.430	Ea.

157 100	AC & Vent Units	CREW	MAKEUP	DAILY OUTPUT	MAN-HOURS	UNIT
150 1051	Fan coil AC, direct expansion, 15 ton cooling	Q-6	2 Steamfitters	1.60	15.000	Ea.
			1 Steamfitter Apprentice			
1060	20 ton cooling			.70	34.290	Ea.
1070	25 ton cooling			.65	36.920	Ea.
1080	30 ton cooling			.60	40.000	Ea.
1100	40 ton cooling			.45	53.330	Ea.
1120	50 ton cooling	↓	↓	.38	63.160	Ea.
160	**HEAT PUMPS**					
1000	Air to air, split system, not including curbs or pads					
1015	1.5 ton cooling, 7 MBH heat @ 0°F	Q-5	1 Steamfitter	1.22	13.110	Ea.
			1 Steamfitter Apprentice			
1020	2 ton cooling, 8.5 MBH heat @ 0°F			1.20	13.330	Ea.
1030	2.5 ton cooling, 10 MBH heat @ 0°F			1	16.000	Ea.
1040	3 ton cooling, 13 MBH heat @ 0°F			.80	20.000	Ea.
1050	3.5 ton cooling, 18 MBH heat @ 0°F			.75	21.330	Ea.
1054	4 ton cooling, 24 MBH heat @ 0°F			.60	26.670	Ea.
1060	5 ton cooling, 27 MBH heat @ 0°F			.50	32.000	Ea.
1080	7.5 ton cooling, 33 MBH heat @ 0°F	↓	↓	.30	53.330	Ea.
1100	10 ton cooling, 50 MBH heat @ 0°F	Q-6	2 Steamfitters	.38	63.160	Ea.
			1 Steamfitter Apprentice			
1120	15 ton cooling, 64 MBH heat @ 0°F			.26	92.310	Ea.
1130	20 ton cooling, 85 MBH heat @ 0°F	↓	↓	.20	120.000	Ea.
1140	25 ton cooling, 119 MBH heat @ 0°F	Q-7	1 Steamfitter Foreman (ins)	.20	160.000	Ea.
			2 Steamfitters			
			1 Steamfitter Apprentice			
1160	30 ton cooling, 163 MBH heat @ 0°F			.17	188.000	Ea.
1180	40 ton cooling, 193 MBH heat @ 0°F			.12	267.000	Ea.
1200	50 ton cooling, 220 MBH heat @ 0°F	↓	↓	.10	320.000	Ea.
1500	Single package, not including curbs, pads, or plenums					
1510	1.5 ton cooling, 5 MBH heat @ 0°F	Q-5	1 Steamfitter	1.55	10.320	Ea.
			1 Steamfitter Apprentice			
1520	2 ton cooling, 6.5 MBH heat @ 0°F			1.50	10.670	Ea.
1540	2.5 ton cooling, 8 MBH heat @ 0°F			1.40	11.430	Ea.
1560	3 ton cooling, 10 MBH heat @ 0°F			1.20	13.330	Ea.
1570	3.5 ton cooling, 11 MBH heat @ 0°F			1	16.000	Ea.
1580	4 ton cooling, 13 MBH heat @ 0°F			.96	16.670	Ea.
1620	5 ton cooling, 27 MBH heat @ 0°F			.65	24.620	Ea.
1640	7.5 ton cooling, 35 MBH heat @ 0°F	↓	↓	.40	40.000	Ea.
1648	10 ton cooling, 45 MBH heat @ 0°F	Q-6	2 Steamfitters	.40	60.000	Ea.
			1 Steamfitter Apprentice			
1652	12 ton cooling, 50 MBH heat @ 0°F			.36	66.670	Ea.
1660	15 ton cooling, 56 MBH heat @ 0°F			.30	80.000	Ea.
1670	20 ton cooling, 100 MBH heat @ 0°F	↓	↓	.20	120.000	Ea.
1680	25 ton cooling, 120 MBH heat @ 0°F	Q-7	1 Steamfitter Foreman (ins)	.23	139.000	Ea.
			2 Steamfitters			
			1 Steamfitter Apprentice			
1690	30 ton cooling, 163 MBH heat @ 0°F	"	"	.19	168.000	Ea.
2000	Water source to air, single package					
2100	1 ton cooling, 13 MBH heat @ 75°F	Q-5	1 Steamfitter	2	8.000	Ea.
			1 Steamfitter Apprentice			
2120	1.5 ton cooling, 17 MBH heat @ 75°F			1.80	8.890	Ea.
2140	2 ton cooling, 19 MBH heat @ 75°F			1.70	9.410	Ea.
2160	2.5 ton cooling, 25 MBH heat @ 75°F			1.60	10.000	Ea.
2180	3 ton cooling, 27 MBH heat @ 75°F			1.40	11.430	Ea.
2190	3.5 ton cooling, 29 MBH heat @ 75°F			1.30	12.310	Ea.
2200	4 ton cooling, 31 MBH heat @ 75°F			1.20	13.330	Ea.
2220	5 ton cooling, 29 MBH heat @ 75°F			.90	17.780	Ea.
2240	7.5 ton cooling, 35 MBH heat @ 75°F	↓	↓	.60	26.670	Ea.

157 100 | AC & Vent Units

			CREW	MAKEUP	DAILY OUTPUT	MAN-HOURS	UNIT
160	2251	Heat pump, water to air, 8.5 ton cooling, 40 MBH heat @ 75°F.	Q-5	1 Steamfitter	.58	27.590	Ea.
				1 Steamfitter Apprentice			
	2260	10 ton cooling, 50 MBH heat @ 75°F	"	"	.53	30.190	Ea.
	2280	15 ton cooling, 64 MBH heat @ 75°F	Q-6	2 Steamfitters	.47	51.060	Ea.
				1 Steamfitter Apprentice			
	2300	20 ton cooling, 100 MBH heat @ 75°F	"	"	.41	58.540	Ea.
	170	**PACKAGED TERMINAL AIR CONDITIONER** Cabinet, wall sleeve,					
	0100	louver, electric heat, thermostat, manual changeover, 208 V					
	0200	6,000 BTUH cooling, 8800 BTU heat	Q-5	1 Steamfitter	6	2.670	Ea.
				1 Steamfitter Apprentice			
	0220	9,000 BTUH cooling, 13,900 BTU heat			5	3.200	Ea.
	0240	12,000 BTUH cooling, 13,900 BTU heat			4	4.000	Ea.
	0260	15,000 BTUH cooling, 13,900 BTU heat			3	5.330	Ea.
	0280	19,000 BTUH cooling, 28,000 BTU heat			2.40	6.670	Ea.
	0300	23,400 BTUH cooling, 28,000 BTU heat			1.90	8.420	Ea.
	0320	31,000 BTUH cooling, 35,000 BTU heat			1.40	11.430	Ea.
	0340	35,600 BTUH cooling, 35,000 BTU heat			1.25	12.800	Ea.
	0360	42,500 BTUH cooling, 36,000 BTU heat			1	16.000	Ea.
	0380	46,500 BTUH cooling, 54,000 BTU heat	↓	↓	.90	17.780	Ea.
	180	**ROOF TOP AIR CONDITIONERS** Standard controls, curb, economizer					
	1000	Single zone, electric cool, gas heat					
	1100	3 ton cooling, 60 MBH heating	Q-5	1 Steamfitter	1.30	12.310	Ea.
				1 Steamfitter Apprentice			
	1120	4 ton cooling, 95 MBH heating			1.10	14.550	Ea.
	1140	5 ton cooling, 112 MBH heating			.56	28.570	Ea.
	1145	6 ton cooling, 140 MBH heating			.52	30.770	Ea.
	1150	7.5 ton cooling, 170 MBH heating	↓	↓	.40	40.000	Ea.
	1160	10 ton cooling, 200 MBH heating	Q-6	2 Steamfitters	.46	52.170	Ea.
				1 Steamfitter Apprentice			
	1170	12.5 ton cooling, 230 MBH heating			.38	63.160	Ea.
	1180	15 ton cooling, 270 MBH heating			.31	77.420	Ea.
	1190	18 ton cooling, 330 MBH heating	↓	↓	.28	85.710	Ea.
	1200	20 ton cooling, 360 MBH heating	Q-7	1 Steamfitter Foreman (ins)	.32	100.000	Ea.
				2 Steamfitters			
				1 Steamfitter Apprentice			
	1210	25 ton cooling, 450 MBH heating			.27	119.000	Ea.
	1220	30 ton cooling, 540 MBH heating			.22	145.000	Ea.
	1240	40 ton cooling, 675 MBH heating			.16	200.000	Ea.
	1260	50 ton cooling, 810 MBH heating			.13	246.000	Ea.
	1265	60 ton cooling, 900 MBH heating			.11	291.000	Ea.
	1270	80 ton cooling, 1000 MBH heating			.09	356.000	Ea.
	1275	90 ton cooling, 1200 MBH heating			.08	400.000	Ea.
	1280	100 ton cooling, 1350 MBH heating	↓	↓	.07	457.000	Ea.
	1700	Gas cool, gas heat					
	1720	3 ton cooling, 90 MBH heating	Q-5	1 Steamfitter	1.40	11.430	Ea.
				1 Steamfitter Apprentice			
	1730	4 ton cooling, 112.5 MBH heating			1.10	14.550	Ea.
	1750	5 ton cooling, 135 MBH heating	↓	↓	.56	28.570	Ea.
	2000	Multizone, electric cool, gas heat, economizer					
	2100	15 ton cooling, 360 MBH heating	Q-7	1 Steamfitter Foreman (ins)	.22	145.000	Ea.
				2 Steamfitters			
				1 Steamfitter Apprentice			
	2120	20 ton cooling, 360 MBH heating			.21	152.000	Ea.
	2140	25 ton cooling, 450 MBH heating			.18	178.000	Ea.
	2160	28 ton cooling, 450 MBH heating			.16	200.000	Ea.
	2180	30 ton cooling, 540 MBH heating			.15	213.000	Ea.
	2190	33 ton cooling, 540 MBH heating			.14	229.000	Ea.
	2200	40 ton cooling, 540 MBH heating	↓	↓	.12	267.000	Ea.

			CREW	MAKEUP	DAILY OUTPUT	MAN-HOURS	UNIT
157 100		**AC & Vent Units**					
180	2221	Roof top AC, elec./gas, 70 ton cooling, 1500 MBH heating	Q-7	1 Steamfitter Foreman (ins)	356	.090	Ea.
				2 Steamfitters			
				1 Steamfitter Apprentice			
	2240	80 ton cooling, 1500 MBH heating			.08	400.000	Ea.
	2260	90 ton cooling, 1500 MBH heating			.07	457.000	Ea.
	2280	105 ton cooling, 1500 MBH heating	↓	↓	.06	533.000	Ea.
	5000	Single zone, electric cool only					
	5020	1.5 ton cooling	Q-5	1 Steamfitter	1.70	9.410	Ea.
				1 Steamfitter Apprentice			
	5030	2 ton cooling			1.60	10.000	Ea.
	5040	2.5 ton cooling			1.50	10.670	Ea.
	5050	3 ton cooling			1.40	11.430	Ea.
	5060	4 ton cooling			1.20	13.330	Ea.
	5070	5 ton cooling			.80	20.000	Ea.
	5080	6 ton cooling			.60	26.670	Ea.
	5090	7.5 ton cooling			.50	32.000	Ea.
	5100	8.5 ton cooling	↓	↓	.40	40.000	Ea.
	5110	10 ton cooling	Q-6	2 Steamfitters	.50	48.000	Ea.
				1 Steamfitter Apprentice			
	5120	12 ton cooling			.44	54.550	Ea.
	5130	15 ton cooling			.38	63.160	Ea.
	5140	18 ton cooling	↓	↓	.32	75.000	Ea.
	5150	20 ton cooling	Q-7	1 Steamfitter Foreman (ins)	.36	88.890	Ea.
				2 Steamfitters			
				1 Steamfitter Apprentice			
	5160	25 ton cooling			.32	100.000	Ea.
	5170	30 ton cooling			.28	114.000	Ea.
	5180	40 ton cooling			.22	145.000	Ea.
	5190	50 ton cooling			.18	178.000	Ea.
	5200	60 ton cooling	↓	↓	.14	229.000	Ea.
	6000	Single zone electric cooling with variable volume distribution					
	6020	20 ton cooling	Q-7	1 Steamfitter Foreman (ins)	.32	100.000	Ea.
				2 Steamfitters			
				1 Steamfitter Apprentice			
	6030	25 ton cooling			.27	119.000	Ea.
	6040	30 ton cooling			.22	145.000	Ea.
	6050	40 ton cooling			.16	200.000	Ea.
	6060	50 ton cooling			.14	229.000	Ea.
	6070	60 ton cooling	↓	↓	.12	267.000	Ea.
	7000	Multizone, cool/heat, variable volume distribution					
	7100	50 ton cooling	Q-7	1 Steamfitter Foreman (ins)	.13	246.000	Ea.
				2 Steamfitters			
				1 Steamfitter Apprentice			
	7110	70 ton cooling			.09	356.000	Ea.
	7120	90 ton cooling			.07	457.000	Ea.
	7130	105 ton cooling			.06	533.000	Ea.
	7140	120 ton cooling			.05	640.000	Ea.
	7150	140 ton cooling	↓	↓	.04	800.000	Ea.
185		**SELF-CONTAINED SINGLE PACKAGE**					
	0100	Air cooled, for free blow or duct, including remote condenser					
	0200	3 ton cooling	Q-5	1 Steamfitter	1	16.000	Ea.
				1 Steamfitter Apprentice			
	0210	4 ton cooling	"	"	.80	20.000	Ea.
	0220	5 ton cooling	Q-6	2 Steamfitters	1.20	20.000	Ea.
				1 Steamfitter Apprentice			
	0230	7.5 ton cooling	"	"	.90	26.670	Ea.

157 100 | AC & Vent Units

			CREW	MAKEUP	DAILY OUTPUT	MAN-HOURS	UNIT
185	0241	Self-contained single pkg., air cooled, 10 ton cooling	Q-7	1 Steamfitter Foreman (ins)	1	32.000	Ea.
				2 Steamfitters			
				1 Steamfitter Apprentice			
	0250	15 ton cooling			.95	33.680	Ea.
	0260	20 ton cooling			.90	35.560	Ea.
	0270	25 ton cooling			.85	37.650	Ea.
	0280	30 ton cooling			.80	40.000	Ea.
	0300	40 ton cooling			.60	53.330	Ea.
	0320	50 ton cooling			.50	64.000	Ea.
	0340	60 ton cooling	Q-8	1 Steamfitter Foreman (ins)	.40	80.000	Ea.
				1 Steamfitter			
				1 Welder (steamfitter)			
				1 Steamfitter Apprentice			
				1 Electric Welding Mach.			
	1000	Water cooled for free blow or duct, not including tower					
	1100	3 ton cooling	Q-6	2 Steamfitters	1	24.000	Ea.
				1 Steamfitter Apprentice			
	1120	5 ton cooling			1	24.000	Ea.
	1130	7.5 ton cooling			.80	30.000	Ea.
	1140	10 ton cooling	Q-7	1 Steamfitter Foreman (ins)	.90	35.560	Ea.
				2 Steamfitters			
				1 Steamfitter Apprentice			
	1150	15 ton cooling			.85	37.650	Ea.
	1160	20 ton cooling			.80	40.000	Ea.
	1170	25 ton cooling			.75	42.670	Ea.
	1180	30 ton cooling			.70	45.710	Ea.
	1200	40 ton cooling			.40	80.000	Ea.
	1220	50 ton cooling			.30	107.000	Ea.
	1240	60 ton cooling	Q-8	1 Steamfitter Foreman (ins)	.30	107.000	Ea.
				1 Steamfitter			
				1 Welder (steamfitter)			
				1 Steamfitter Apprentice			
				1 Electric Welding Mach.			
	190	WATER CHILLERS					
	0500	Reciprocating, air cooled, 20 ton cooling	Q-7	1 Steamfitter Foreman (ins)	.35	91.430	Ea.
				2 Steamfitters			
				1 Steamfitter Apprentice			
	0510	25 ton cooling			.32	100.000	Ea.
	0515	30 ton cooling			.29	110.000	Ea.
	0520	40 ton cooling			.24	133.000	Ea.
	0528	45 ton cooling			.22	145.000	Ea.
	0536	55 ton cooling			.18	178.000	Ea.
	0540	65 ton cooling			.14	229.000	Ea.
	0546	70 ton cooling			.13	246.000	Ea.
	0550	75 ton cooling			.12	267.000	Ea.
	0554	90 ton cooling			.11	291.000	Ea.
	0600	100 ton cooling			.10	320.000	Ea.
	0620	110 ton cooling	Q-8	1 Steamfitter Foreman (ins)	.09	356.000	Ea.
				1 Steamfitter			
				1 Welder (steamfitter)			
				1 Steamfitter Apprentice			
				1 Electric Welding Mach.			
	0630	125 ton cooling			.08	400.000	Ea.
	0640	150 ton cooling			.07	457.000	Ea.
	0650	175 ton cooling			.06	533.000	Ea.
	0660	200 ton cooling			.05	640.000	Ea.

	157 100 | **AC & Vent Units**	CREW	MAKEUP	DAILY OUTPUT	MAN-HOURS	UNIT
190 0701	Water chiller, water cooled, 1 compressor, 2 to 5 ton cooling	Q-5	1 Steamfitter	.44	36.360	Ea.
			1 Steamfitter Apprentice			
0720	6 ton cooling	↓	↓	.38	42.110	Ea.
0740	8 ton cooling			.27	59.260	Ea.
0760	10 ton cooling	Q-6	2 Steamfitters	.36	66.670	Ea.
			1 Steamfitter Apprentice			
0780	15 ton cooling	"	"	.33	72.730	Ea.
0800	20 ton cooling	Q-7	1 Steamfitter Foreman (ins)	.38	84.210	Ea.
			2 Steamfitters			
			1 Steamfitter Apprentice			
0820	30 ton cooling	↓	↓	.28	114.000	Ea.
0840	35 ton cooling			.27	119.000	Ea.
0980	Water cooled, multiple compressors, semi-hermetic					
1000	15 ton cooling	Q-6	2 Steamfitters	.30	80.000	Ea.
			1 Steamfitter Apprentice			
1020	20 ton cooling	Q-7	1 Steamfitter Foreman (ins)	.36	88.890	Ea.
			2 Steamfitters			
			1 Steamfitter Apprentice			
1040	25 ton cooling			.32	100.000	Ea.
1060	30 ton cooling			.27	119.000	Ea.
1080	40 ton cooling			.24	133.000	Ea.
1100	50 ton cooling			.21	152.000	Ea.
1120	60 ton cooling	↓	↓	.19	168.000	Ea.
1130	70 ton cooling			.16	200.000	Ea.
1140	80 ton cooling	Q-8	1 Steamfitter Foreman (ins)	.15	213.000	Ea.
			1 Steamfitter			
			1 Welder (steamfitter)			
			1 Steamfitter Apprentice			
			1 Electric Welding Mach.			
1150	90 ton cooling			.13	246.000	Ea.
1160	100 ton cooling			.12	267.000	Ea.
1170	110 ton cooling			.11	291.000	Ea.
1180	120 ton cooling			.10	320.000	Ea.
1200	140 ton cooling			.09	356.000	Ea.
1210	160 ton cooling	↓	↓	.08	400.000	Ea.
1300	Water cooled, single compressor, direct drive					
1320	40 ton cooling,	Q-8	1 Steamfitter Foreman (ins)	.19	168.000	Ea.
			1 Steamfitter			
			1 Welder (steamfitter)			
			1 Steamfitter Apprentice			
			1 Electric Welding Mach.			
1340	50 ton cooling			.16	200.000	Ea.
1360	60 ton cooling			.15	213.000	Ea.
1380	80 ton cooling	↓	↓	.12	267.000	Ea.
1450	Water cooled, dual compressors, direct drive					
1500	80 ton cooling	Q-8	1 Steamfitter Foreman (ins)	.10	320.000	Ea.
			1 Steamfitter			
			1 Welder (steamfitter)			
			1 Steamfitter Apprentice			
			1 Electric Welding Mach.			
1520	100 ton cooling			.09	356.000	Ea.
1540	120 ton cooling			.08	400.000	Ea.
1560	135 ton cooling			.07	457.000	Ea.
1580	150 ton cooling			.07	457.000	Ea.
1600	175 ton cooling			.06	533.000	Ea.
1620	200 ton cooling			.05	640.000	Ea.
1640	225 ton cooling	↓	↓	.05	640.000	Ea.
1660	250 ton cooling			.04	800.000	Ea.

			CREW	MAKEUP	DAILY OUTPUT	MAN-HOURS	UNIT
	157 100	**AC & Vent Units**					
190	2000	Packaged chiller, condenserless for remote condenser					
	2020	40 ton cooling	Q-7	1 Steamfitter Foreman (ins)	.27	119.000	Ea.
				2 Steamfitters			
				1 Steamfitter Apprentice			
	2040	60 ton cooling			.21	152.000	Ea.
	2060	80 ton cooling			.16	200.000	Ea.
	2080	100 ton cooling			.11	291.000	Ea.
	2100	120 ton cooling			.10	320.000	Ea.
	2120	160 ton cooling	↓	↓	.09	356.000	Ea.
	4000	Packaged chiller, with remote air cooled condensers					
	4020	15 ton cooling	Q-7	1 Steamfitter Foreman (ins)	.35	91.430	Ea.
				2 Steamfitters			
				1 Steamfitter Apprentice			
	4030	20 ton cooling			.32	100.000	Ea.
	4040	25 ton cooling			.30	107.000	Ea.
	4050	30 ton cooling			.27	119.000	Ea.
	4060	40 ton cooling			.22	145.000	Ea.
	4070	50 ton cooling			.18	178.000	Ea.
	4080	60 ton cooling			.14	229.000	Ea.
	4090	70 ton cooling			.12	267.000	Ea.
	4100	80 ton cooling			.11	291.000	Ea.
	4110	90 ton cooling			.10	320.000	Ea.
	4120	100 ton cooling	↓	↓	.09	356.000	Ea.
	4130	110 ton cooling	Q-8	1 Steamfitter Foreman (ins)	.08	400.000	Ea.
				1 Steamfitter			
				1 Welder (steamfitter)			
				1 Steamfitter Apprentice			
				1 Electric Welding Mach.			
	4140	120 ton cooling	↓	↓	.07	457.000	Ea.
	4150	140 ton cooling	↓	↓	.06	533.000	Ea.
	195	**WINDOW UNIT AIR CONDITIONERS**					
	4000	Portable, 15 amp 125V grounded receptacle required					
	4020	Standard models					
	4050	4000 BTUH, 1 speed fan	1 Carp	1 Carpenter	8	1.000	Ea.
	4060	4000 BTUH, 2 speed fan			8	1.000	Ea.
	4080	5000 BTUH, 2 speed fan	↓	↓	8	1.000	Ea.
	4250	Semi-permanent installation, 3 speed fan					
	4260	15 amp 125V grounded receptacle required					
	4280	Standard models, 2 way air direction					
	4320	5000 BTUH	1 Carp	1 Carpenter	8	1.000	Ea.
	4340	6000 BTUH	"	"	8	1.000	Ea.
	4400	High efficiency models					
	4450	5900 BTUH, 2 way air direction	1 Carp	1 Carpenter	8	1.000	Ea.
	4480	8000 BTUH, 4 way high thrust air			6	1.330	Ea.
	4500	10,000 BTUH, 4 way high thrust air	↓	↓	6	1.330	Ea.
	4520	12,000 BTUH, 4 way high thrust air	L-2	1 Carpenter	8	2.000	Ea.
				1 Helper			
	4540	14,000 BTUH, 4 way high thrust air	"	"	8	2.000	Ea.
	4600	15 amp 250V grounded receptacle required					
	4700	High efficiency, 4 way high thrust air					
	4740	15,000 BTUH	L-2	1 Carpenter	6	2.670	Ea.
				1 Helper			
	4780	18,000 BTUH	"	"	6	2.670	Ea.
	4820	20 amp 250V grounded receptacle required					
	4840	High efficiency, 4 way high thrust air					
	4860	21,000 BTUH	L-2	1 Carpenter	6	2.670	Ea.
				1 Helper			

157 100 | AC & Vent Units

		CREW	MAKEUP	DAILY OUTPUT	MAN-HOURS	UNIT
195	4901	Window unit AC, 30 amp 250 V grounded receptacle					
	4910	High efficiency, 4 way high thrust air					
	4940	25,000 BTUH	L-2	1 Carpenter	4	4.000	Ea.
				1 Helper			
	4960	29,000 BTUH	"	"	4	4.000	Ea.

157 200 | System Components

		CREW	MAKEUP	DAILY OUTPUT	MAN-HOURS	UNIT
201	COILS, FLANGED					
0500	Chilled water cooling, 6 rows, 24" x 48"	Q-5	1 Steamfitter	2	8.000	Ea.
			1 Steamfitter Apprentice			
1000	Direct expansion cooling, 6 rows, 24" x 48"			2	8.000	Ea.
1500	Hot water heating, 1 row, 24" x 48"			3	5.330	Ea.
2000	Steam heating, 1 row, 24" x 48"	↓	↓	3	5.330	Ea.
210	COMPRESSORS					
0100	Refrigeration, hermetic, switches and protective devices					
0110	Low & med. back pressure types for R-12					
0120	0.21 ton	1 Stpi	1 Steamfitter	4	2.000	Ea.
0130	0.28 ton			4	2.000	Ea.
0140	0.38 ton			4	2.000	Ea.
0150	0.53 ton	↓	↓	3	2.670	Ea.
0200	High back pressure types for R-22					
0210	1.25 ton	1 Stpi	1 Steamfitter	3	2.670	Ea.
0220	1.42 ton			3	2.670	Ea.
0230	1.68 ton			2.80	2.860	Ea.
0240	2.00 ton			2.60	3.080	Ea.
0250	2.37 ton			2.50	3.200	Ea.
0260	2.67 ton			2.40	3.330	Ea.
0270	3.53 ton			2.30	3.480	Ea.
0280	4.43 ton			2.20	3.640	Ea.
0290	5.08 ton			2.10	3.810	Ea.
0300	5.67 ton	↓	↓	2	4.000	Ea.
0310	7.31 ton	Q-5	1 Steamfitter	3	5.330	Ea.
			1 Steamfitter Apprentice			
0320	9.95 ton	"	"	2.60	6.150	Ea.
0990	Refrigeration, recip. hermetic, switches & protective devices					
1100	15 ton	Q-6	2 Steamfitters	.72	33.330	Ea.
			1 Steamfitter Apprentice			
1200	20 ton			.64	37.500	Ea.
1300	40 ton			.44	54.550	Ea.
1400	50 ton	↓	↓	.20	120.000	Ea.
1500	75 ton	Q-7	1 Steamfitter Foreman (ins)	.27	119.000	Ea.
			2 Steamfitters			
			1 Steamfitter Apprentice			
1600	130 ton	"	"	.21	152.000	Ea.
5000	Air, diaphragm, w/skid, motor, drive, valves, & protective devices					
5030	Single stage, 220 psig, 0.47 CFM	Q-5	1 Steamfitter	3.30	4.850	Ea.
			1 Steamfitter Apprentice			
5040	1.7 CFM			2	8.000	Ea.
5050	3.5 CFM			1.50	10.670	Ea.
5060	8.5 CFM	↓	↓	1	16.000	Ea.
5100	14 CFM	Q-6	2 Steamfitters	1	24.000	Ea.
			1 Steamfitter Apprentice			
5120	28 CFM			.60	40.000	Ea.
5130	56 CFM	↓	↓	.30	80.000	Ea.
5150	Two stage, 3600 psig, 0.47 CFM	Q-5	1 Steamfitter	2.50	6.400	Ea.
			1 Steamfitter Apprentice			
5160	1.7 CFM			1.50	10.670	Ea.
5170	3.5 CFM	↓	↓	1.10	14.550	Ea.

157 200	System Components	CREW	MAKEUP	DAILY OUTPUT	MAN-HOURS	UNIT
210 5181	Compressor, air diaphragm, 2 stage, 3600 psig, 8.5 CFM	Q-6	2 Steamfitters 1 Steamfitter Apprentice	1.10	21.820	Ea.
5190	14 CFM	↓	↓	.60	40.000	Ea.
5200	28 CFM			.30	80.000	Ea.
5250	Reciprocating air cooled heavy duty tank mounted					
5600	2 stage pkg. motor starter, duplex, control panel, drain					
5650	3.6 CFM at 90 psi 1 HP, 60 gal tank	Q-5	1 Steamfitter 1 Steamfitter Apprentice	3	5.330	Ea.
5670	11.5 CFM at 90 psi, 3 HP, 80 gal tank	↓	↓	1.50	10.670	Ea.
5680	43.2 CFM at 90 psi, 10 HP, 250 gal tank			.60	26.670	Ea.
5690	105 CFM at 90 psi, 25 HP, 250 gal tank	Q-6	2 Steamfitters 1 Steamfitter Apprentice	.60	40.000	Ea.
5800	Simplex, motor & starter, tank, drain					
5850	8 CFM at 90 psi, 2 HP, 80 gal tank	Q-6	2 Steamfitters 1 Steamfitter Apprentice	3.50	6.860	Ea.
5860	51.6 CFM at 90 psi, 10 HP, 250 gal tank	"	"	.90	26.670	Ea.
6000	Reciprocating water cooled heavy duty slow speed 100 psi					
6050	Lubricated, 73 CFM by 20 HP motor	Q-5	1 Steamfitter 1 Steamfitter Apprentice	.80	20.000	Ea.
6060	100 CFM by 25 HP motor			.60	26.670	Ea.
6070	132 CFM by 30 HP motor			.50	32.000	Ea.
6080	185 CFM by 40 HP motor	↓	↓	.40	40.000	Ea.
6090	210 CFM by 50 HP motor	Q-6	2 Steamfitters 1 Steamfitter Apprentice	.60	40.000	Ea.
6100	246 CFM by 50 HP motor			.50	48.000	Ea.
6110	330 CFM by 75 HP motor	↓	↓	.30	80.000	Ea.
6120	428 CFM by 100 HP motor	Q-7	1 Steamfitter Foreman (ins) 2 Steamfitters 1 Steamfitter Apprentice	.40	80.000	Ea.
6130	557 CFM by 125 HP motor	"	"	.30	107.000	Ea.
6200	Nonlubricated, 73 CFM by 20 HP motor	Q-5	1 Steamfitter 1 Steamfitter Apprentice	.80	20.000	Ea.
6210	100 CFM by 25 HP motor			.60	26.670	Ea.
6220	132 CFM by 30 HP motor			.50	32.000	Ea.
6230	185 CFM by 40 HP motor	↓	↓	.40	40.000	Ea.
6250	210 CFM by 50 HP motor	Q-6	2 Steamfitters 1 Steamfitter Apprentice	.60	40.000	Ea.
6260	246 CFM by 50 HP motor			.50	48.000	Ea.
6270	330 CFM by 75 HP motor	↓	↓	.30	80.000	Ea.
6280	428 CFM by 100 HP motor	Q-7	1 Steamfitter Foreman (ins) 2 Steamfitters 1 Steamfitter Apprentice	.40	80.000	Ea.
6290	557 CFM by 125 HP motor	"	"	.30	107.000	Ea.
6500	Rotary screw motor & starter aftercooler heavy duty,					
6550	Air cooled single stage, 100 CFM at 115 psi 25 HP	Q-5	1 Steamfitter 1 Steamfitter Apprentice	2.60	6.150	Ea.
6560	120 CFM at 115 psi 30 HP			2	8.000	Ea.
6570	160 CFM at 115 psi 40 HP			1.40	11.430	Ea.
6580	215 CFM at 115 psi 50 HP in enclosure			1	16.000	Ea.
6590	260 CFM at 115 psi 60 HP in enclosure	↓	↓	.80	20.000	Ea.
6600	330 CFM at 115 psi 75 HP in enclosure	Q-6	2 Steamfitters 1 Steamfitter Apprentice	1	24.000	Ea.
6610	490 CFM at 115 psi 100 HP			.90	26.670	Ea.
6620	600 CFM at 115 psi 125 HP			.80	30.000	Ea.
6630	710 CFM at 115 psi 150 HP	↓	↓	.60	40.000	Ea.
6640	950 CFM at 100 psi 200 HP	Q-7	1 Steamfitter Foreman (ins) 2 Steamfitters 1 Steamfitter Apprentice	.80	40.000	Ea.

157 200	System Components	CREW	MAKEUP	DAILY OUTPUT	MAN-HOURS	UNIT
210 6651	Compressor, air cooled, 1 stage, 1000 CFM at 115 psi 250 HP	Q-7	1 Steamfitter Foreman (ins)	.70	45.710	Ea.
			2 Steamfitters			
			1 Steamfitter Apprentice			
6660	1250 CFM at 115 psi 300 HP			.60	53.330	Ea.
6670	1500 CFM at 115 psi 350 HP			.50	64.000	Ea.
6680	2000 CFM at 100 psi 400 HP			.40	80.000	Ea.
6690	2000 CFM at 115 psi 450 HP	↓	↓	.30	107.000	Ea.
6800	Water cooled sngl stage, 100 CFM at 115 psi 25 HP	Q-5	1 Steamfitter	1.60	10.000	Ea.
			1 Steamfitter Apprentice			
6810	120 CFM at 115 psi 30 HP			1.40	11.430	Ea.
6820	180 CFM at 100 psi 40 HP in enclosure			1	16.000	Ea.
6830	235 CFM at 100 psi 50 HP in enclosure			.80	20.000	Ea.
6840	285 CFM at 100 psi 60 HP in enclosure	↓	↓	.60	26.670	Ea.
6850	355 CFM at 100 psi 75 HP in enclosure	Q-6	2 Steamfitters	1	24.000	Ea.
			1 Steamfitter Apprentice			
6860	515 CFM at 100 psi 100 HP			.80	30.000	Ea.
6870	640 CFM at 100 psi 125 HP			.70	34.290	Ea.
6880	750 CFM at 100 psi 150 HP	↓	↓	.60	40.000	Ea.
6900	950 CFM at 100 psi 200 HP	Q-7	1 Steamfitter Foreman (ins)	.60	53.330	Ea.
			2 Steamfitters			
			1 Steamfitter Apprentice			
6910	1000 CFM at 115 psi 250 HP			.50	64.000	Ea.
6920	1250 CFM at 115 psi 300 HP			.50	64.000	Ea.
6930	1500 CFM at 115 psi 350 HP			.40	80.000	Ea.
6940	2000 CFM at 100 psi 400 HP			.40	80.000	Ea.
6950	2000 CFM at 115 psi 450 HP	↓	↓	.30	107.000	Ea.
220	**COMPRESSOR ACCESSORIES**					
0100	Aftercooler					
0130	Air cooled, based on 100 psig and 250°F					
0140	Tank mounted single stage, 20 SCFM	Q-5	1 Steamfitter	7.50	2.130	Ea.
			1 Steamfitter Apprentice			
0150	46 SCFM			7	2.290	Ea.
0160	77 SCFM			6.50	2.460	Ea.
0170	Floor mounted horizontal draft, 36 SCFM			6.50	2.460	Ea.
0180	78 SCFM			6	2.670	Ea.
0190	190 SCFM			5.70	2.810	Ea.
0200	260 SCFM			5.20	3.080	Ea.
0210	440 SCFM			4	4.000	Ea.
0220	650 SCFM	↓	↓	3.50	4.570	Ea.
0300	Separator with automatic float trap					
0330	600 lb/hr drain cap. 125 psi 3/4" conn.	Q-5	1 Steamfitter	7.50	2.130	Ea.
			1 Steamfitter Apprentice			
0340	1200 lb/hr drain cap. 125 psi 1" conn.			7	2.290	Ea.
0350	1200 lb/hr drain cap. 125 psi 1-1/2" conn.			6	2.670	Ea.
0360	1200 lb/hr drain cap. 125 psi 2" conn.			5	3.200	Ea.
0370	1500 CFM at 200 psi 2-1/2" conn.			4	4.000	Ea.
0380	4000 CFM at 200 psi 4" conn.	↓	↓	3	5.330	Ea.
1250	Refrigeration, 50°F pressure dewpoint					
1280	20 CFM	Q-5	1 Steamfitter	7	2.290	Ea.
			1 Steamfitter Apprentice			
1290	60 CFM			6	2.670	Ea.
1300	130 CFM			5.50	2.910	Ea.
1310	150 CFM			5	3.200	Ea.
1320	200 CFM			4.50	3.560	Ea.
1330	280 CFM			4	4.000	Ea.
1340	350 CFM			3.50	4.570	Ea.
1350	450 CFM			3	5.330	Ea.
1360	520 CFM	↓	↓	2.80	5.710	Ea.

157 200 | System Components

		Description	CREW	MAKEUP	DAILY OUTPUT	MAN-HOURS	UNIT
220	1371	Compressor, aftercooler, refrigeration, 650 CFM	Q-5	1 Steamfitter	2.40	6.670	Ea.
				1 Steamfitter Apprentice			
	1380	800 CFM			2.20	7.270	Ea.
	1390	1000 CFM			2	8.000	Ea.
	1400	1400 CFM			1.50	10.670	Ea.
	1410	2000 CFM			1.20	13.330	Ea.
	1420	2400 CFM	↓	↓	1	16.000	Ea.
	1430	3000 CFM	Q-6	2 Steamfitters	1.30	18.460	Ea.
				1 Steamfitter Apprentice			
	1440	3600 CFM			1.20	20.000	Ea.
	1450	4800 CFM			1	24.000	Ea.
	1460	6000 CFM			.80	30.000	Ea.
	1470	7200 CFM	↓	↓	.50	48.000	Ea.
	3000	Filters Air					
	3100	Adsorptive, odors by glass fiber & carbon, 90 psi					
	3140	110 CFM	Q-5	1 Steamfitter	8	2.000	Ea.
				1 Steamfitter Apprentice			
	3150	190 CFM			7.50	2.130	Ea.
	3160	290 CFM			7	2.290	Ea.
	3170	380 CFM			6	2.670	Ea.
	3180	570 CFM			5	3.200	Ea.
	3190	870 CFM			4.50	3.560	Ea.
	3200	1160 CFM			4	4.000	Ea.
	3210	1450 CFM			3.50	4.570	Ea.
	3220	1740 CFM	↓	↓	3	5.330	Ea.
	225	**CONDENSERS** Ratings are for 30°F TD, R-22					
	0080	Air cooled, belt drive, propeller fan					
	0100	20 ton	Q-5	1 Steamfitter	1	16.000	Ea.
				1 Steamfitter Apprentice			
	0180	30 ton	"	"	.60	26.670	Ea.
	0200	37 ton	Q-6	2 Steamfitters	.60	40.000	Ea.
				1 Steamfitter Apprentice			
	0220	41 ton			.54	44.440	Ea.
	0240	48 ton			.48	50.000	Ea.
	0260	51 ton			.40	60.000	Ea.
	0280	60 ton			.32	75.000	Ea.
	0300	66 ton			.30	80.000	Ea.
	0320	72 ton			.29	82.760	Ea.
	0340	77 ton			.28	85.710	Ea.
	0360	82 ton			.27	88.890	Ea.
	0380	90 ton	↓	↓	.26	92.310	Ea.
	0400	100 ton	Q-7	1 Steamfitter Foreman (ins)	.30	107.000	Ea.
				2 Steamfitters			
				1 Steamfitter Apprentice			
	0500	157 ton			.20	160.000	Ea.
	0600	235 ton			.12	267.000	Ea.
	0700	314 ton			.09	356.000	Ea.
	0800	471 ton			.06	533.000	Ea.
	0900	630 ton			.05	640.000	Ea.
	1000	840 ton	↓	↓	.04	800.000	Ea.
	1550	Air cooled, direct drive, propeller fan					
	1600	1-1/2 ton	Q-5	1 Steamfitter	3.60	4.440	Ea.
				1 Steamfitter Apprentice			
	1620	2 ton			3.20	5.000	Ea.
	1630	3 ton			2.40	6.670	Ea.
	1640	5 ton			2	8.000	Ea.
	1650	8 ton			1.80	8.890	Ea.
	1660	10 ton	↓	↓	1.40	11.430	Ea.

157 200 | System Components

		CREW	MAKEUP	DAILY OUTPUT	MAN-HOURS	UNIT
225	1671	Condenser, air cooled, direct drive, 12 ton	Q-5	1 Steamfitter 1 Steamfitter Apprentice	1.30	12.310	Ea.
	1680	14 ton			1.20	13.330	Ea.
	1690	16 ton			1.10	14.550	Ea.
	1700	21 ton			1	16.000	Ea.
	1720	26 ton			.74	21.620	Ea.
	1740	30 ton	↓	↓	.60	26.670	Ea.
	1760	41 ton	Q-6	2 Steamfitters 1 Steamfitter Apprentice	.54	44.440	Ea.
	1780	52 ton			.40	60.000	Ea.
	1800	63 ton			.32	75.000	Ea.
	1820	76 ton			.28	85.710	Ea.
	1840	86 ton			.27	88.890	Ea.
	1860	97 ton	↓	↓	.25	96.000	Ea.
	1880	105 ton	Q-7	1 Steamfitter Foreman (ins) 2 Steamfitters 1 Steamfitter Apprentice	.30	107.000	Ea.
	2000	Centrifugal fan, integral receiver					
	2100	3 ton	Q-5	1 Steamfitter 1 Steamfitter Apprentice	1.40	11.430	Ea.
	2200	7.5 ton			.90	17.780	Ea.
	2300	10 ton			.70	22.860	Ea.
	2400	15 ton			.60	26.670	Ea.
	2500	20 ton	↓	↓	.50	32.000	Ea.
	2600	30 ton	Q-6	2 Steamfitters 1 Steamfitter Apprentice	.55	43.640	Ea.
	2700	40 ton			.28	85.710	Ea.
	2800	50 ton			.24	100.000	Ea.
	2900	60 ton	↓	↓	.21	114.000	Ea.
	3400	Evaporative, copper coil, pump, fan motor					
	3440	10 ton	Q-5	1 Steamfitter 1 Steamfitter Apprentice	.54	29.630	Ea.
	3460	15 ton			.50	32.000	Ea.
	3480	20 ton			.47	34.040	Ea.
	3500	25 ton			.45	35.560	Ea.
	3520	30 ton	↓	↓	.42	38.100	Ea.
	3540	40 ton	Q-6	2 Steamfitters 1 Steamfitter Apprentice	.49	48.980	Ea.
	3560	50 ton			.39	61.540	Ea.
	3580	65 ton			.35	68.570	Ea.
	3600	80 ton			.33	72.730	Ea.
	3620	90 ton	↓	↓	.29	82.760	Ea.
	3640	100 ton	Q-7	1 Steamfitter Foreman (ins) 2 Steamfitters 1 Steamfitter Apprentice	.36	88.890	Ea.
	3660	110 ton			.33	96.970	Ea.
	3680	125 ton			.30	107.000	Ea.
	3700	135 ton			.28	114.000	Ea.
	3720	150 ton			.25	128.000	Ea.
	3740	165 ton			.23	139.000	Ea.
	3760	185 ton	↓	↓	.22	145.000	Ea.
	3860	For fan damper control, add	Q-5	1 Steamfitter 1 Steamfitter Apprentice	2	8.000	Ea.

157 200	System Components	CREW	MAKEUP	DAILY OUTPUT	MAN-HOURS	UNIT
230	**230** **CONDENSING UNITS**					
	0030 Air cooled, compressor, standard controls					
	0050 1.5 ton	Q-5	1 Steamfitter	2.50	6.400	Ea.
			1 Steamfitter Apprentice			
	0100 2 ton			2.10	7.620	Ea.
	0200 2.5 ton			1.70	9.410	Ea.
	0300 3 ton			1.30	12.310	Ea.
	0350 3.5 ton			1.10	14.550	Ea.
	0400 4 ton			.90	17.780	Ea.
	0500 5 ton			.60	26.670	Ea.
	0550 7.5 ton			.55	29.090	Ea.
	0560 8.5 ton			.53	30.190	Ea.
	0600 10 ton			.50	32.000	Ea.
	0620 11 ton			.48	33.330	Ea.
	0650 15 ton	↓	↓	.40	40.000	Ea.
	0700 20 ton	Q-6	2 Steamfitters	.40	60.000	Ea.
			1 Steamfitter Apprentice			
	0720 25 ton			.35	68.570	Ea.
	0750 30 ton			.30	80.000	Ea.
	0800 40 ton			.20	120.000	Ea.
	0840 50 ton			.18	133.000	Ea.
	0860 60 ton			.16	150.000	Ea.
	0900 75 ton			.14	171.000	Ea.
	1000 80 ton			.12	200.000	Ea.
	1100 100 ton	↓	↓	.09	267.000	Ea.
	2000 Water cooled, compressor, heat exchanger, controls					
	2100 5 ton	Q-5	1 Steamfitter	.70	22.860	Ea.
			1 Steamfitter Apprentice			
	2200 15 ton	"	"	.50	32.000	Ea.
	2300 20 ton	Q-6	2 Steamfitters	.40	60.000	Ea.
			1 Steamfitter Apprentice			
	2400 40 ton	↓		.20	120.000	Ea.
	2500 100 ton	↓	↓	.11	218.000	Ea.
	240 **COOLING TOWERS** Packaged units					
	0080 Draw thru, single flow					
	0100 Belt drive, 60 tons	Q-6	2 Steamfitters	90	.267	Ton
			1 Steamfitter Apprentice			
	0150 90 tons	↓	↓	100	.240	Ton
	0200 100 tons			109	.220	Ton
	1500 Induced air, double flow					
	1800 Gear drive, 125 ton	Q-6	2 Steamfitters	120	.200	Ton
			1 Steamfitter Apprentice			
	1900 150 ton			126	.190	Ton
	2000 300 ton			129	.186	Ton
	2100 600 ton			132	.182	Ton
	2150 840 ton			142	.169	Ton
	2200 Up to 1000 tons			150	.160	Ton
	3500 For pumps and piping, add	↓	↓	38	.632	Ton
	250 **DUCTWORK**					
	0020 Fabricated rectangular, includes fittings, joints, supports,					
	0030 allowance for flexible connections, no insulation					
	0100 Aluminum, alloy 3003-H14, under 300 lb.	Q-10	2 Sheet Metal Workers	75	.320	Lb.
			1 Sheet Metal Apprentice			
	0110 300 to 500 lb.			80	.300	Lb.
	0120 500 to 1000 lb.			95	.253	Lb.
	0140 1000 to 2000 lb.			120	.200	Lb.
	0150 2000 to 4,000 lb.			130	.185	Lb.
	0155 4,000 to 10,000 lb.	↓	↓	140	.171	Lb.

		157 200 | **System Components**	CREW	MAKEUP	DAILY OUTPUT	MAN-HOURS	UNIT
250	0161	Ductwork, aluminum, over 10,000 lb.	Q-10	2 Sheet Metal Workers	145	.166	Lb.
				1 Sheet Metal Apprentice			
	0500	Galvanized steel, under 400 lb.			235	.102	Lb.
	0520	400 to 1000 lb.			255	.094	Lb.
	0540	1000 to 2000 lb.			265	.091	Lb.
	0560	2000 to 5000 lb.			275	.087	Lb.
	0570	5000 to 10,000 lb.			285	.084	Lb.
	0580	Over 10,000 lb.			300	.080	Lb.
	1000	Stainless steel, type 304, under 300 lb.			165	.145	Lb.
	1020	300 to 500 lb.			175	.137	Lb.
	1030	500 to 1,000 lb.			190	.126	Lb.
	1040	1000 to 2000 lb.			200	.120	Lb.
	1050	2000 to 5,000 lb.			225	.107	Lb.
	1055	5,000 to 10,000 lb.			230	.104	Lb.
	1060	Over 10,000 lb.	↓	↓	235	.102	Lb.
	1300	Flexible, coated fiberglass fabric on corr. resist. metal helix					
	1400	pressure to 12" (WG) UL-181					
	1500	Non-insulated, 3" diameter	Q-9	1 Sheet Metal Worker	400	.040	L.F.
				1 Sheet Metal Apprentice			
	1520	4" diameter			360	.044	L.F.
	1540	5" diameter			320	.050	L.F.
	1560	6" diameter			280	.057	L.F.
	1580	7" diameter			240	.067	L.F.
	1600	8" diameter			200	.080	L.F.
	1620	9" diameter			180	.089	L.F.
	1640	10" diameter			160	.100	L.F.
	1660	12" diameter			120	.133	L.F.
	1680	14" diameter			80	.200	L.F.
	1700	16" diameter			60	.267	L.F.
	1900	Insulated, 1" thick with 3/4 lb., PE jacket			340	.047	L.F.
	1920	5" diameter			300	.053	L.F.
	1940	6" diameter			260	.062	L.F.
	1960	7" diameter			220	.073	L.F.
	1980	8" diameter			180	.089	L.F.
	2000	9" diameter			160	.100	L.F.
	2020	10" diameter			140	.114	L.F.
	2040	12" diameter			100	.160	L.F.
	2060	14" diameter			80	.200	L.F.
	2080	16" diameter			60	.267	L.F.
	2100	18" diameter	↓	↓	45	.356	L.F.
	2120	20" diameter	Q-10	2 Sheet Metal Workers	65	.369	L.F.
				1 Sheet Metal Apprentice			
	2500	Insulated, heavy duty, coated fiberglass fabric					
	2520	4" diameter	Q-9	1 Sheet Metal Worker	340	.047	L.F.
				1 Sheet Metal Apprentice			
	2540	5" diameter			300	.053	L.F.
	2560	6" diameter			260	.062	L.F.
	2580	7" diameter			220	.073	L.F.
	2600	8" diameter			180	.089	L.F.
	2620	9" diameter			160	.100	L.F.
	2640	10" diameter			140	.114	L.F.
	2660	12" diameter			100	.160	L.F.
	2680	14" diameter			80	.200	L.F.
	2700	16" diameter			60	.267	L.F.
	2720	18" diameter	↓	↓	45	.356	L.F.
	3490	Rigid fiberglass duct board, foil reinf. kraft facing					
	3500	Rectangular, 1" thick, alum. faced, (FRK), std. weight	Q-10	2 Sheet Metal Workers	350	.069	SF Surf
				1 Sheet Metal Apprentice			

			CREW	MAKEUP	DAILY OUTPUT	MAN-HOURS	UNIT
	157 200	**System Components**					
250	3521	Rigid fiberglass duct board, rect., 1" thick, heavy weight	Q-10	2 Sheet Metal Workers 1 Sheet Metal Apprentice	350	.069	SF Surf
	4000	Rigid plastic, corrosive fume resistant PVC					
	4020	Straight, 6" diameter	Q-9	1 Sheet Metal Worker 1 Sheet Metal Apprentice	220	.073	L.F.
	4030	7" diameter			160	.100	L.F.
	4040	8" diameter			160	.100	L.F.
	4050	9" diameter			140	.114	L.F.
	4060	10" diameter			120	.133	L.F.
	4070	12" diameter			100	.160	L.F.
	4080	14" diameter			70	.229	L.F.
	4090	16" diameter			62	.258	L.F.
	4100	18" diameter	↓	↓	58	.276	L.F.
	4110	20" diameter	Q-10	2 Sheet Metal Workers 1 Sheet Metal Apprentice	75	.320	L.F.
	4120	22" diameter			60	.400	L.F.
	4130	24" diameter			55	.436	L.F.
	4140	26" diameter			42	.571	L.F.
	4150	28" diameter			35	.686	L.F.
	4160	30" diameter			28	.857	L.F.
	4170	36" diameter			23	1.040	L.F.
	4180	42" diameter			20	1.200	L.F.
	4200	48" diameter	↓	↓	18	1.330	L.F.
	4250	Coupling, 6" diameter	Q-9	1 Sheet Metal Worker 1 Sheet Metal Apprentice	88	.182	Ea.
	4260	7" diameter			82	.195	Ea.
	4270	8" diameter			78	.205	Ea.
	4280	9" diameter			74	.216	Ea.
	4290	10" diameter			70	.229	Ea.
	4300	12" diameter			55	.291	Ea.
	4310	14" diameter			44	.364	Ea.
	4320	16" diameter			40	.400	Ea.
	4330	18" diameter	↓	↓	38	.421	Ea.
	4340	20" diameter	Q-10	2 Sheet Metal Workers 1 Sheet Metal Apprentice	55	.436	Ea.
	4350	22" diameter			50	.480	Ea.
	4360	24" diameter			45	.533	Ea.
	4370	26" diameter			39	.615	Ea.
	4380	28" diameter			33	.727	Ea.
	4390	30" diameter			27	.889	Ea.
	4400	36" diameter			25	.960	Ea.
	4410	42" diameter			23	1.040	Ea.
	4420	48" diameter	↓	↓	21	1.140	Ea.
	4470	Elbow, 90°, 6" diameter	Q-9	1 Sheet Metal Worker 1 Sheet Metal Apprentice	44	.364	Ea.
	4480	7" diameter			36	.444	Ea.
	4490	8" diameter			28	.571	Ea.
	4500	9" diameter			22	.727	Ea.
	4510	10" diameter			18	.889	Ea.
	4520	12" diameter			15	1.070	Ea.
	4530	14" diameter			11	1.450	Ea.
	4540	16" diameter	↓	↓	10	1.600	Ea.
	4550	18" diameter	Q-10	2 Sheet Metal Workers 1 Sheet Metal Apprentice	15	1.600	Ea.
	4560	20" diameter			14	1.710	Ea.
	4570	22" diameter			13	1.850	Ea.
	4580	24" diameter			12	2.000	Ea.
	4590	26" diameter	↓	↓	11	2.180	Ea.

157 200 | System Components

		Description	CREW	MAKEUP	DAILY OUTPUT	MAN-HOURS	UNIT
250	4601	Ductwork, rigid plastic elbow, 90°, 28" diameter	Q-10	2 Sheet Metal Workers 1 Sheet Metal Apprentice	10	2.400	Ea.
	4610	30" diameter			9	2.670	Ea.
	4620	36" diameter			7	3.430	Ea.
	4630	42" diameter			5	4.800	Ea.
	4640	48" diameter	↓	↓	4	6.000	Ea.
	5040	Spiral preformed, aluminum, straight, 18 ga., 3" diameter	Q-9	1 Sheet Metal Worker 1 Sheet Metal Apprentice	400	.040	L.F.
	5050	4" diameter			360	.044	L.F.
	5060	5" diameter			320	.050	L.F.
	5070	6" diameter			280	.057	L.F.
	5080	7" diameter			240	.067	L.F.
	5090	8" diameter			200	.080	L.F.
	5100	9" diameter			180	.089	L.F.
	5110	10" diameter			160	.100	L.F.
	5120	12" diameter			120	.133	L.F.
	5130	14" diameter			80	.200	L.F.
	5140	16" diameter			60	.267	L.F.
	5150	18" diameter	↓	↓	45	.356	L.F.
	5160	20" diameter	Q-10	2 Sheet Metal Workers 1 Sheet Metal Apprentice	65	.369	L.F.
	5180	24" diameter			55	.436	L.F.
	5200	30" diameter			45	.533	L.F.
	5220	36" diameter			40	.600	L.F.
	5240	40" diameter			35	.686	L.F.
	5260	48" diameter	↓	↓	30	.800	L.F.
	5400	Steel, galvanized, straight lengths					
	5410	4" diameter, 26 ga.	Q-9	1 Sheet Metal Worker 1 Sheet Metal Apprentice	360	.044	L.F.
	5420	6" diameter, 26 ga.			280	.057	L.F.
	5430	8" diameter, 26 ga.			200	.080	L.F.
	5440	10" diameter, 24 ga.			160	.100	L.F.
	5450	12" diameter, 24 ga.			120	.133	L.F.
	5460	14" diameter, 24 ga.			80	.200	L.F.
	5480	16" diameter, 22 ga.	↓	↓	60	.267	L.F.
	5500	20" diameter, 22 ga.	Q-10	2 Sheet Metal Workers 1 Sheet Metal Apprentice	65	.369	L.F.
	5520	24" diameter, 20 ga.			55	.436	L.F.
	5540	30" diameter, 18 ga.			45	.533	L.F.
	5600	36" diameter, 18 ga.	↓	↓	40	.600	L.F.
	5800	Connector, 4" diameter	Q-9	1 Sheet Metal Worker 1 Sheet Metal Apprentice	100	.160	Ea.
	5820	6" diameter			88	.182	Ea.
	5840	8" diameter			78	.205	Ea.
	5860	10" diameter			70	.229	Ea.
	5880	12" diameter			50	.320	Ea.
	5900	14" diameter			44	.364	Ea.
	5920	16" diameter			40	.400	Ea.
	5940	20" diameter			34	.471	Ea.
	5960	24" diameter			28	.571	Ea.
	5980	30" diameter			22	.727	Ea.
	6000	36" diameter			18	.889	Ea.
	6300	Elbow, 45°, 4" diameter			60	.267	Ea.
	6320	6" diameter			44	.364	Ea.
	6340	8" diameter			28	.571	Ea.
	6360	10" diameter			18	.889	Ea.
	6380	12" diameter			13	1.230	Ea.
	6400	14" diameter	↓	↓	11	1.450	Ea.

157 200	System Components		CREW	MAKEUP	DAILY OUTPUT	MAN-HOURS	UNIT
250	6421	Ductwork, spiral preformed, steel, galv., elbow, 45°, 16" diameter	Q-9	1 Sheet Metal Worker 1 Sheet Metal Apprentice	10	1.600	Ea.
	6440	20" diameter	Q-10	2 Sheet Metal Workers 1 Sheet Metal Apprentice	14	1.710	Ea.
	6460	24" diameter			12	2.000	Ea.
	6480	30" diameter			9	2.670	Ea.
	6500	36" diameter	▼	▼	7	3.430	Ea.
	6800	Reducing coupling, 6" x 4"	Q-9	1 Sheet Metal Worker 1 Sheet Metal Apprentice	46	.348	Ea.
	6820	8" x 6"			40	.400	Ea.
	6840	10" x 8"			32	.500	Ea.
	6860	12" x 10"			24	.667	Ea.
	6880	14" x 12"			20	.800	Ea.
	6900	16" x 14"			18	.889	Ea.
	6920	18" x 16"	▼	▼	16	1.000	Ea.
	6940	20" x 18"	Q-10	2 Sheet Metal Workers 1 Sheet Metal Apprentice	24	1.000	Ea.
	6960	24" x 22"			22	1.090	Ea.
	6980	30" x 28"			18	1.330	Ea.
	7000	36" x 34"	▼	▼	16	1.500	Ea.
	7400	Steel, PVC coated both sides, straight lengths					
	7420	6" diameter, 26 ga.	Q-9	1 Sheet Metal Worker 1 Sheet Metal Apprentice	280	.057	L.F.
	7440	8" diameter, 26 ga.			200	.080	L.F.
	7460	10" diameter, 24 ga.			160	.100	L.F.
	7480	12" diameter, 24 ga.			120	.133	L.F.
	7500	14" diameter, 24 ga.			80	.200	L.F.
	7520	16" diameter, 22 ga.			60	.267	L.F.
	7540	18" diameter, 22 ga.	▼	▼	45	.356	L.F.
	7560	20" diameter, 22 ga.	Q-10	2 Sheet Metal Workers 1 Sheet Metal Apprentice	65	.369	L.F.
	7580	24" diameter, 20 ga.			55	.436	L.F.
	7600	30" diameter, 18 ga.			45	.533	L.F.
	7620	36" diameter, 18 ga.	▼	▼	40	.600	L.F.
	7900	Connector, 6" diameter	Q-9	1 Sheet Metal Worker 1 Sheet Metal Apprentice	88	.182	Ea.
	7920	8" diameter			78	.205	Ea.
	7940	10" diameter			70	.229	Ea.
	7960	12" diameter			50	.320	Ea.
	7980	14" diameter			44	.364	Ea.
	8000	16" diameter			40	.400	Ea.
	8020	18" diameter			37	.432	Ea.
	8040	20" diameter			34	.471	Ea.
	8060	24" diameter			28	.571	Ea.
	8080	30" diameter			22	.727	Ea.
	8100	36" diameter			18	.889	Ea.
	8400	Elbow, 45°, 6" diameter			44	.364	Ea.
	8420	8" diameter			28	.571	Ea.
	8440	10" diameter			18	.889	Ea.
	8460	12" diameter			13	1.230	Ea.
	8480	14" diameter			11	1.450	Ea.
	8500	16" diameter			10	1.600	Ea.
	8520	18" diameter	▼	▼	9	1.780	Ea.
	8540	20" diameter	Q-10	2 Sheet Metal Workers 1 Sheet Metal Apprentice	13	1.850	Ea.
	8560	24" diameter			11	2.180	Ea.
	8580	30" diameter			9	2.670	Ea.
	8600	36" diameter	▼	▼	7	3.430	Ea.

157 200	System Components	CREW	MAKEUP	DAILY OUTPUT	MAN-HOURS	UNIT
250	9001	Ductwork, steel, PVC coated, reducing coupling, tapered offset					
	9020	Diameter x any smaller diameter					
	9040	6" x	Q-9	1 Sheet Metal Worker	46	.348	Ea.
				1 Sheet Metal Apprentice			
	9060	8" x			40	.400	Ea.
	9080	10" x			32	.500	Ea.
	9100	12" x			24	.667	Ea.
	9120	14" x			20	.800	Ea.
	9140	16" x			18	.889	Ea.
	9160	18" x			16	1.000	Ea.
	9180	20" x	Q-10	2 Sheet Metal Workers	24	1.000	Ea.
				1 Sheet Metal Apprentice			
	9200	24" x			22	1.090	Ea.
	9220	30" x			18	1.330	Ea.
	9240	36" x			16	1.500	Ea.
	9400	Lateral 45°, straight barrel					
	9420	6" size	Q-9	1 Sheet Metal Worker	30	.533	Ea.
				1 Sheet Metal Apprentice			
	9440	8" size			19	.842	Ea.
	9460	10" size			12	1.330	Ea.
	9480	12" size			9	1.780	Ea.
	9500	14" size			7	2.290	Ea.
	9520	16" size			6.70	2.390	Ea.
	9540	18" size			6	2.670	Ea.
	9560	20" size	Q-10	2 Sheet Metal Workers	8.70	2.760	Ea.
				1 Sheet Metal Apprentice			
	9580	24" size			7	3.430	Ea.
	9600	30" size			6	4.000	Ea.
	9620	36" size			5	4.800	Ea.
	9700	Register boot, elbow or perimeter					
	9710	6" duct diameter	Q-9	1 Sheet Metal Worker	60	.267	Ea.
				1 Sheet Metal Apprentice			
	9720	8" duct diameter			56	.286	Ea.
	9730	10" duct diameter			45	.356	Ea.
	9740	12" duct diameter			36	.444	Ea.
	9800	Steel, stainless, straight lengths					
	9810	3" diameter	Q-9	1 Sheet Metal Worker	400	.040	L.F.
				1 Sheet Metal Apprentice			
	9820	4" diameter			360	.044	L.F.
	9830	5" diameter			320	.050	L.F.
	9840	6" diameter			280	.057	L.F.
	9850	7" diameter			240	.067	L.F.
	9860	8" diameter			200	.080	L.F.
	9870	9" diameter			180	.089	L.F.
	9880	10" diameter			160	.100	L.F.
	9890	12" diameter			120	.133	L.F.
	9900	14" diameter			80	.200	L.F.
	9910	16" diameter			60	.267	L.F.
	9920	18" diameter			45	.356	L.F.
	9930	20" diameter	Q-10	2 Sheet Metal Workers	65	.369	L.F.
				1 Sheet Metal Apprentice			
	9940	24" diameter			55	.436	L.F.
	9950	30" diameter			45	.533	L.F.
	9960	36" diameter			40	.600	L.F.
	9970	40" diameter			35	.686	L.F.

157 200 | System Components

		Description	CREW	MAKEUP	DAILY OUTPUT	MAN-HOURS	UNIT
270	270	EVAPORATORS DX coils, remote compressors not included					
	1000	Coolers, reach-in type, above freezing temperatures					
	1300	Shallow depth, wall mount, 7 fins per inch, air defrost					
	1310	600 BTUH, 8" fan, rust-proof core	Q-5	1 Steamfitter / 1 Steamfitter Apprentice	3.80	4.210	Ea.
	1320	900 BTUH, 8" fan, rust-proof core			3.30	4.850	Ea.
	1330	1200 BTUH, 8" fan, rust-proof core			3	5.330	Ea.
	1340	1800 BTUH, 8" fan, rust-proof core			2.40	6.670	Ea.
	1350	2500 BTUH, 10" fan, rust-proof core			2.20	7.270	Ea.
	1360	3500 BTUH, 10" fan			2	8.000	Ea.
	1370	4500 BTUH, 10" fan			1.90	8.420	Ea.
	1600	Undercounter refrigerators, ceiling or wall mount,					
	1610	8 fins per inch, air defrost, rust-proof core					
	1630	800 BTUH, one 6" fan	Q-5	1 Steamfitter / 1 Steamfitter Apprentice	5	3.200	Ea.
	1640	1300 BTUH, two 6" fans			4	4.000	Ea.
	1650	1700 BTUH, two 6" fans			3.60	4.440	Ea.
	2000	Coolers, reach-in and walk-in types, above freezing temperatures					
	2600	Two-way discharge, ceiling mount, 150-4100 CFM,					
	2610	above 34°F applications, air defrost					
	2630	900 BTUH, 7 fins per inch, 8" fan	Q-5	1 Steamfitter / 1 Steamfitter Apprentice	4	4.000	Ea.
	2660	2500 BTUH, 7 fins per inch, 10" fan			2.60	6.150	Ea.
	2690	5500 BTUH, 7 fins per inch, 12" fan			1.70	9.410	Ea.
	2720	8500 BTUH, 8 fins per inch, 16" fan			1.20	13.330	Ea.
	2750	15,000 BTUH, 7 fins per inch, 18" fan			1.10	14.550	Ea.
	2770	24,000 BTUH, 7 fins per inch, two 16" fans			1	16.000	Ea.
	2790	30,000 BTUH, 7 fins per inch, two 18" fans			.90	17.780	Ea.
	2850	Two-way discharge, low profile, ceiling mount,					
	2860	8 fins per inch, 200-570 CFM, air defrost					
	2880	800 BTUH, one 6" fan	Q-5	1 Steamfitter / 1 Steamfitter Apprentice	4	4.000	Ea.
	2890	1300 BTUH, two 6" fans			3.50	4.570	Ea.
	2900	1800 BTUH, two 6" fans			3.30	4.850	Ea.
	2910	2700 BTUH, three 6" fans			2.70	5.930	Ea.
	3000	Coolers, walk-in type, above freezing temperatures					
	3300	General use, ceiling mount, 108-2080 CFM					
	3320	600 BTUH, 7 fins per inch, 6" fan	Q-5	1 Steamfitter / 1 Steamfitter Apprentice	5.20	3.080	Ea.
	3340	1200 BTUH, 7 fins per inch, 8" fan			3.70	4.320	Ea.
	3360	1800 BTUH, 7 fins per inch, 10" fan			2.70	5.930	Ea.
	3380	3500 BTUH, 7 fins per inch, 12" fan			2.40	6.670	Ea.
	3400	5500 BTUH, 8 fins per inch, 12" fan			2	8.000	Ea.
	3430	8500 BTUH, 8 fins per inch, 16" fan			1.40	11.430	Ea.
	3460	15,000 BTUH, 7 fins per inch, two 16" fans			1.10	14.550	Ea.
	3640	Low velocity, high latent load, ceiling mount,					
	3650	1050-2420 CFM, air defrost, 6 fins per inch					
	3670	6700 BTUH, two 10" fans	Q-5	1 Steamfitter / 1 Steamfitter Apprentice	1.30	12.310	Ea.
	3680	10,000 BTUH, three 10" fans			1	16.000	Ea.
	3690	13,500 BTUH, three 10" fans			1	16.000	Ea.
	3700	18,000 BTUH, four 10" fans			1	16.000	Ea.
	3710	26,500 BTUH, four 10" fans			.80	20.000	Ea.
	5000	Freezers and coolers, reach-in type, above 34°F					
	5030	to sub-freezing temperature range, low latent load,					
	5050	air defrost, 7 fins per inch					
	5070	1200 BTUH, 8" fan, rustproof core	Q-5	1 Steamfitter / 1 Steamfitter Apprentice	4.40	3.640	Ea.

157 200 | **System Components**

		CREW	MAKEUP	DAILY OUTPUT	MAN-HOURS	UNIT
270 5081	Evaporators, air defrost, 1500 BTUH, 8" fan, rustproof core	Q-5	1 Steamfitter	4.20	3.810	Ea.
			1 Steamfitter Apprentice			
5090	1800 BTUH, 8" fan, rustproof core			3.70	4.320	Ea.
5100	2500 BTUH, 10" fan, rustproof core			2.90	5.520	Ea.
5110	3500 BTUH, 10" fan, rustproof core			2.50	6.400	Ea.
5120	4500 BTUH, 12" fan, rustproof core	↓	↓	2.10	7.620	Ea.
6000	Freezers and coolers, walk-in type					
6050	1960-18,000 CFM, medium profile					
6060	Standard motor, 4 fins per inch, to -30°F					
6080	10,500 BTUH, air defrost, one 18" fan	Q-5	1 Steamfitter	1.40	11.430	Ea.
			1 Steamfitter Apprentice			
6090	12,500 BTUH, air defrost, one 18" fan			1.40	11.430	Ea.
6100	15,000 BTUH, air defrost, one 20" fan			1.30	12.310	Ea.
6110	21,000 BTUH, air defrost, two 18" fans			1	16.000	Ea.
6120	25,000 BTUH, air defrost, two 18" fans	↓	↓	1	16.000	Ea.
6130	30,000 BTUH, air defrost, two 20" fans	Q-6	2 Steamfitters	1.30	18.460	Ea.
			1 Steamfitter Apprentice			
6140	37,300 BTUH, air defrost, two 18" fans			1.25	19.200	Ea.
6150	44,800 BTUH, air defrost, two 20" fans			1	24.000	Ea.
6160	60,700 BTUH, elec defrost, three 20" fans			1	24.000	Ea.
6170	91,000 BTUH, elec defrost, four 20" fans			.80	30.000	Ea.
6180	108,900 BTUH, elec defrost, four 24" fans	↓	↓	.60	40.000	Ea.
7000	580-3750 CFM, 10" fans					
7010	Four fins per inch					
7030	3400 BTUH, 1 fan	Q-5	1 Steamfitter	2.80	5.710	Ea.
			1 Steamfitter Apprentice			
7040	4000 BTUH, 2 fans			2.40	6.670	Ea.
7050	5300 BTUH, 2 fans			1.90	8.420	Ea.
7060	6800 BTUH, 2 fans			1.70	9.410	Ea.
7070	8000 BTUH, 3 fans			1.60	10.000	Ea.
7080	11,100 BTUH, 3 fans			1.40	11.430	Ea.
7090	13,600 BTUH, 4 fans			1.30	12.310	Ea.
7100	17,000 BTUH, 5 fans			1.20	13.330	Ea.
7110	20,400 BTUH, 6 fans	↓	↓	1	16.000	Ea.
8000	Freezers, pass-thru door uprights, walk-in storage					
8300	Low temperature, thin profile, electric defrost					
8310	138-1800 CFM, 5 fins per inch					
8320	900 BTUH, one 6" fan	Q-5	1 Steamfitter	3.30	4.850	Ea.
			1 Steamfitter Apprentice			
8340	1500 BTUH, two 6" fans			2.20	7.270	Ea.
8360	2600 BTUH, three 6" fans			1.90	8.420	Ea.
8370	3300 BTUH, four 6" fans			1.70	9.410	Ea.
8380	4400 BTUH, five 6" fans			1.40	11.430	Ea.
8400	7000 BTUH, three 10" fans			1.30	12.310	Ea.
8410	8700 BTUH, four 10" fans	↓	↓	1.10	14.550	Ea.
290 FANS						
0020	Air conditioning and process air handling					
0030	Axial flow, compact, low sound, 2.5" S.P.					
0050	3800 CFM, 5 HP	Q-20	1 Sheet Metal Worker	3.40	5.880	Ea.
			1 Sheet Metal Apprentice			
			.5 Electrician			
0080	6400 CFM, 5 HP			2.80	7.140	Ea.
0100	10,500 CFM, 7-1/2 HP			2.40	8.330	Ea.
0120	15,600 CFM, 10 HP			1.60	12.500	Ea.
0140	23,000 CFM, 15 HP			.70	28.570	Ea.
0160	28,000 CFM, 20 HP	↓	↓	.40	50.000	Ea.

157 200	System Components	CREW	MAKEUP	DAILY OUTPUT	MAN-HOURS	UNIT
290 0201	Fans, in-line centrifugal, supply/exhaust booster,					
0220	aluminum wheel/hub, disconnect switch, 1/4" S.P.					
0240	500 CFM, 10" diameter connection	Q-20	1 Sheet Metal Worker	3	6.670	Ea.
			1 Sheet Metal Apprentice			
			.5 Electrician			
0260	1380 CFM, 12" diameter connection			2	10.000	Ea.
0280	1520 CFM, 16" diameter connection			2	10.000	Ea.
0300	2560 CFM, 18" diameter connection			1	20.000	Ea.
0320	3480 CFM, 20" diameter connection			.80	25.000	Ea.
1500	Vaneaxial, low pressure, 2000 CFM, 1/2 HP			3.60	5.560	Ea.
1520	4000 CFM, 1 HP			3.20	6.250	Ea.
1540	8000 CFM, 2 HP			2.80	7.140	Ea.
1560	16,000 CFM, 5 HP			2.40	8.330	Ea.
2000	Blowers, direct drive with motor, complete					
2020	1030 CFM @ .5" S.P., 1/6 HP	Q-20	1 Sheet Metal Worker	18	1.110	Ea.
			1 Sheet Metal Apprentice			
			.5 Electrician			
2040	1150 CFM @ .5" S.P., 1/6 HP			18	1.110	Ea.
2060	1640 CFM @ 1.0" S.P., 1/3 HP			18	1.110	Ea.
2080	1720 CFM @ 1.0" S.P., 1/3 HP			18	1.110	Ea.
2090	4 speed					
2100	600 to 1160 CFM @ .5" S.P., 1/5 HP	Q-20	1 Sheet Metal Worker	16	1.250	Ea.
			1 Sheet Metal Apprentice			
			.5 Electrician			
2120	740 to 1700 CFM @ 1.0" S.P., 1/3 HP	"	"	14	1.430	Ea.
2500	Ceiling fan, right angle, extra quiet, 0.10" S.P.					
2520	95 CFM	Q-20	1 Sheet Metal Worker	20	1.000	Ea.
			1 Sheet Metal Apprentice			
			.5 Electrician			
2540	210 CFM			19	1.050	Ea.
2560	385 CFM			18	1.110	Ea.
2580	885 CFM			16	1.250	Ea.
2600	1650 CFM			13	1.540	Ea.
2620	2960 CFM			11	1.820	Ea.
2640	For wall or roof cap, add	1 Shee	1 Sheet Metal Worker	16	.500	Ea.
2680	For speed control switch, add	1 Elec	1 Electrician	16	.500	Ea.
3000	Paddle blade air circulator, 3 speed switch					
3020	36", 4000 CFM high, 3000 CFM low	Q-20	1 Sheet Metal Worker	6	3.330	Ea.
			1 Sheet Metal Apprentice			
			.5 Electrician			
3040	52", 7000 CFM high, 4000 CFM low	"	"	4	5.000	Ea.
3500	Centrifugal, airfoil, motor and drive, complete					
3520	1000 CFM, 1/2 HP	Q-20	1 Sheet Metal Worker	2.50	8.000	Ea.
			1 Sheet Metal Apprentice			
			.5 Electrician			
3540	2000 CFM, 1 HP			2	10.000	Ea.
3560	4000 CFM, 3 HP			1.80	11.110	Ea.
3580	8000 CFM, 7-1/2 HP			1.40	14.290	Ea.
3600	12,000 CFM, 10 HP			1	20.000	Ea.
4000	Single width, belt drive, not incl. motor, capacities					
4020	at 2000 FPM, 2.5" S.P. for indicated motor					
4040	6900 CFM, 5 HP	Q-9	1 Sheet Metal Worker	2.40	6.670	Ea.
			1 Sheet Metal Apprentice			
4060	10,340 CFM, 7-1/2" HP			2.20	7.270	Ea.
4080	15,320 CFM, 10 HP			2	8.000	Ea.
4100	22,780 CFM, 15 HP			1.80	8.890	Ea.
4120	33,840 CFM, 20 HP			1.60	10.000	Ea.
4140	41,400 CFM, 25 HP			1.40	11.430	Ea.

157 200 | System Components

		CREW	MAKEUP	DAILY OUTPUT	MAN-HOURS	UNIT
290 4201	Fans, centrifugal, dbl. width wheel, 12,420 CFM, 7.5 HP	Q-9	1 Sheet Metal Worker	2.20	7.270	Ea.
			1 Sheet Metal Apprentice			
4220	18,620 CFM, 15 HP			2	8.000	Ea.
4240	27,580 CFM, 20 HP			1.80	8.890	Ea.
4260	40,980 CFM, 25 HP			1.50	10.670	Ea.
4280	60,920 CFM, 40 HP			1	16.000	Ea.
4300	74,520 CFM, 50 HP			.80	20.000	Ea.
4320	90,160 CFM, 50 HP			.70	22.860	Ea.
4340	110,300 CFM, 60 HP			.50	32.000	Ea.
4360	134,960 CFM, 75 HP			.40	40.000	Ea.
4500	Corrosive fume resistant, plastic					
4600	roof ventilators, centrifugal, V belt drive, motor					
4620	1/4" S.P., 250 CFM, 1/4 HP	Q-20	1 Sheet Metal Worker	6	3.330	Ea.
			1 Sheet Metal Apprentice			
			.5 Electrician			
4640	895 CFM, 1/3 HP			5	4.000	Ea.
4660	1630 CFM, 1/2 HP			4	5.000	Ea.
4680	2240 CFM, 1 HP			3	6.670	Ea.
4700	3810 CFM, 2 HP			2	10.000	Ea.
4720	11760 CFM, 5 HP			1	20.000	Ea.
4740	18810 CFM, 10 HP			.70	28.570	Ea.
5000	Utility set, centrifugal, V belt drive, motor					
5020	1/4" S.P., 1900 CFM, 1/4 HP	Q-20	1 Sheet Metal Worker	6	3.330	Ea.
			1 Sheet Metal Apprentice			
			.5 Electrician			
5040	2170 CFM, 1/3 HP			5	4.000	Ea.
5060	2680 CFM, 1/2 HP			4	5.000	Ea.
5080	3020 CFM, 3/4 HP			3	6.670	Ea.
5100	1/2" S.P., 3195 CFM, 1 HP			2	10.000	Ea.
5120	3610 CFM, 1-1/2 HP			1.60	12.500	Ea.
5140	4120 CFM, 2 HP			1.40	14.290	Ea.
5160	7850 CFM, 5 HP			1.30	15.380	Ea.
5500	Industrial exhauster, for air which may contain granular material					
5520	1000 CFM, 1-1/2 HP	Q-20	1 Sheet Metal Worker	2.50	8.000	Ea.
			1 Sheet Metal Apprentice			
			.5 Electrician			
5540	2000 CFM, 3 HP			2	10.000	Ea.
5560	4000 CFM, 7-1/2 HP			1.80	11.110	Ea.
5580	8000 CFM, 15 HP			1.40	14.290	Ea.
5600	12,000 CFM, 30 HP			1	20.000	Ea.
6000	Propeller exhaust, wall shutter, 1/4" S.P.					
6020	Direct drive, two speed					
6100	375 CFM, 1/10 HP	Q-20	1 Sheet Metal Worker	10	2.000	Ea.
			1 Sheet Metal Apprentice			
			.5 Electrician			
6120	730 CFM, 1/7 HP			9	2.220	Ea.
6140	1000 CFM, 1/8 HP			8	2.500	Ea.
6160	1890 CFM, 1/4 HP			7	2.860	Ea.
6180	3275 CFM, 1/2 HP			6	3.330	Ea.
6200	4720 CFM, 1 HP			5	4.000	Ea.
6300	V-belt drive, 3 phase					
6320	6175 CFM, 3/4 HP	Q-20	1 Sheet Metal Worker	5	4.000	Ea.
			1 Sheet Metal Apprentice			
			.5 Electrician			
6340	7500 CFM, 3/4 HP			5	4.000	Ea.
6360	10,100 CFM, 1 HP			4.50	4.440	Ea.
6380	14,300 CFM, 1-1/2 HP			4	5.000	Ea.
6400	19,800 CFM, 2 HP			3	6.670	Ea.

		Description	CREW	MAKEUP	DAILY OUTPUT	MAN-HOURS	UNIT
		**157 200	System Components**					
290	6421	Fans, propeller exhaust, V-belt drive, 26,250 CFM, 3 HP	Q-20	1 Sheet Metal Worker / 1 Sheet Metal Apprentice / .5 Electrician	2.60	7.690	Ea.
	6440	38,500 CFM, 5 HP			2.20	9.090	Ea.
	6460	46,000 CFM, 7-1/2 HP			2	10.000	Ea.
	6480	51,500 CFM, 10 HP	↓	↓	1.80	11.110	Ea.
	6490	V-belt drive, 115V., residential, whole house					
	6500	Ceiling-wall, 5200 CFM, 1/4 HP, 30" x 30"	1 Shee	1 Sheet Metal Worker	6	1.330	Ea.
	6530	13,200 CFM, 1/3 HP, 48" x 48"			4	2.000	Ea.
	6540	15,445 CFM, 1/2 HP, 48" x 48"			4	2.000	Ea.
	6550	17,025 CFM, 1/2 HP, 54" x 54"	↓	↓	4	2.000	Ea.
	6570	Shutter, automatic, ceiling/wall					
	6580	30" x 30"	1 Shee	1 Sheet Metal Worker	8	1.000	Ea.
	6590	36" x 36"			8	1.000	Ea.
	6600	42" x 42"			8	1.000	Ea.
	6610	48" x 48"			7	1.140	Ea.
	6620	54" x 54"			6	1.330	Ea.
	6630	Timer, shut off, to 12 Hr.	↓	↓	20	.400	Ea.
	6650	Residential, bath exhaust, grille, back draft damper					
	6660	50 CFM	Q-20	1 Sheet Metal Worker / 1 Sheet Metal Apprentice / .5 Electrician	24	.833	Ea.
	6670	110 CFM			22	.909	Ea.
	6680	Light combination, squirrel cage, 100 watt, 70 CFM	↓	↓	24	.833	Ea.
	6700	Light/heater combination, ceiling mounted					
	6710	70 CFM, 1450 watt	Q-20	1 Sheet Metal Worker / 1 Sheet Metal Apprentice / .5 Electrician	24	.833	Ea.
	6800	Heater combination, recessed, 70 CFM			24	.833	Ea.
	6820	With 2 infrared bulbs			23	.870	Ea.
	6900	Kitchen exhaust, grille, complete, 160 CFM			22	.909	Ea.
	6920	344 CFM	↓	↓	18	1.110	Ea.
	7000	Roof exhauster, centrifugal, aluminum housing, 12" galvanized					
	7020	curb, bird screen, back draft damper, 1/4" S.P.					
	7100	Direct drive, 420 CFM, 8" sq. damper	Q-20	1 Sheet Metal Worker / 1 Sheet Metal Apprentice / .5 Electrician	7	2.860	Ea.
	7120	675 CFM, 12" sq. damper			6	3.330	Ea.
	7140	770 CFM, 16" sq. damper			5	4.000	Ea.
	7160	1870 CFM, 20" sq. damper			4.20	4.760	Ea.
	7180	2150 CFM, 20" sq. damper			4	5.000	Ea.
	7200	V-belt drive, 1660 CFM, 12" sq. damper			6	3.330	Ea.
	7220	2830 CFM, 14" sq. damper			5	4.000	Ea.
	7240	4600 CFM, 20" sq. damper			4	5.000	Ea.
	7260	8750 CFM, 26" sq. damper			3	6.670	Ea.
	7280	12,500 CFM, 32" sq. damper			2	10.000	Ea.
	7300	21,600 CFM, 40" sq. damper	↓	↓	1	20.000	Ea.
	7500	Utility set, steel construction, pedestal, 1/4" S.P.					
	7520	Direct drive, 150 CFM, 1/8 HP	Q-20	1 Sheet Metal Worker / 1 Sheet Metal Apprentice / .5 Electrician	6.40	3.130	Ea.
	7540	485 CFM, 1/6 HP			5.80	3.450	Ea.
	7560	1950 CFM, 1/2 HP			4.80	4.170	Ea.
	7580	2410 CFM, 3/4 HP			4.40	4.550	Ea.
	7600	3328 CFM, 1-1/2 HP	↓	↓	3	6.670	Ea.

157 200	System Components	CREW	MAKEUP	DAILY OUTPUT	MAN-HOURS	UNIT
290 7701	Fans, utility set, V-belt drive, 3 ph, 800 CFM, 1/4 HP	Q-20	1 Sheet Metal Worker	6	3.330	Ea.
			1 Sheet Metal Apprentice			
			.5 Electrician			
7720	1300 CFM, 1/3 HP			5	4.000	Ea.
7740	2000 CFM, 1 HP			4.60	4.350	Ea.
7760	2900 CFM, 3/4 HP			4.20	4.760	Ea.
7780	3600 CFM, 3/4 HP			4	5.000	Ea.
7800	4800 CFM, 1 HP			3.50	5.710	Ea.
7820	6700 CFM, 1-1/2 HP			3	6.670	Ea.
7840	11,000 CFM, 3 HP			2	10.000	Ea.
7860	13,000 CFM, 3 HP			1.60	12.500	Ea.
7880	15,000 CFM, 5 HP			1	20.000	Ea.
7900	17,000 CFM, 7-1/2 HP			.80	25.000	Ea.
7920	20,000 CFM, 7-1/2 HP	↓	↓	.80	25.000	Ea.
8000	Ventilation, residential					
8020	Attic, roof type					
8030	Aluminum dome, damper & curb					
8040	6" diameter, 300 CFM	1 Elec	1 Electrician	16	.500	Ea.
8050	7" diameter, 450 CFM			15	.533	Ea.
8060	9" diameter, 900 CFM			14	.571	Ea.
8080	12" diameter, 1000 CFM (gravity)			10	.800	Ea.
8090	16" diameter, 1500 CFM (gravity)			9	.889	Ea.
8100	20" diameter, 2500 CFM (gravity)			8	1.000	Ea.
8110	26" diameter, 4000 CFM (gravity)			7	1.140	Ea.
8120	32" diameter, 6500 CFM (gravity)			6	1.330	Ea.
8130	38" diameter, 8000 CFM (gravity)			5	1.600	Ea.
8140	50" diameter, 13,000 CFM (gravity)	↓	↓	4	2.000	Ea.
8160	Plastic, ABS dome					
8180	930 CFM	1 Elec	1 Electrician	14	.571	Ea.
8200	1600 CFM	"	"	12	.667	Ea.
8240	Attic, wall type, with shutter, one speed					
8250	12" diameter, 1000 CFM	1 Elec	1 Electrician	14	.571	Ea.
8260	14" diameter, 1500 CFM			12	.667	Ea.
8270	16" diameter, 2000 CFM	↓	↓	9	.889	Ea.
8290	Whole house, wall type, with shutter, one speed					
8300	30" diameter, 4800 CFM	1 Elec	1 Electrician	7	1.140	Ea.
8310	36" diameter, 7000 CFM			6	1.330	Ea.
8320	42" diameter, 10,000 CFM			5	1.600	Ea.
8330	48" diameter, 16,000 CFM	↓	↓	4	2.000	Ea.
8350	Whole house, lay-down type, with shutter, one speed					
8360	30" diameter, 4500 CFM	1 Elec	1 Electrician	8	1.000	Ea.
8370	36" diameter, 6500 CFM			7	1.140	Ea.
8380	42" diameter, 9000 CFM			6	1.330	Ea.
8390	48" diameter, 12,000 CFM			5	1.600	Ea.
8450	For 12 hour timer switch, add	↓	↓	32	.250	Ea.
8500	Wall exhausters, centrifugal, auto damper, 1/8" S.P.					
8520	Direct drive , 635 CFM, 1/20 HP	Q-20	1 Sheet Metal Worker	14	1.430	Ea.
			1 Sheet Metal Apprentice			
			.5 Electrician			
8540	845 CFM, 1/12 HP			13	1.540	Ea.
8560	1005 CFM, 1/6 HP			12	1.670	Ea.
8580	1220 CFM, 1/6 HP			12	1.670	Ea.
8600	1575 CFM, 1/4 HP			11	1.820	Ea.
8620	2065 CFM, 1/4 HP			10	2.000	Ea.
8640	2660 CFM, 1/2 HP			9	2.220	Ea.
8660	3260 CFM, 3/4 HP	↓	↓	8	2.500	Ea.

157 | Air Conditioning/Ventilating

157 200 | System Components

		CREW	MAKEUP	DAILY OUTPUT	MAN-HOURS	UNIT
290 9521	Fans, wall exhauster, V-belt drive, 3 ph, 2800 CFM, 1/4 HP	Q-20	1 Sheet Metal Worker	9	2.220	Ea.
			1 Sheet Metal Apprentice			
			.5 Electrician			
9540	3740 CFM, 1/2 HP			8	2.500	Ea.
9560	4400 CFM, 3/4 HP			7	2.860	Ea.
9580	5700 CFM, 1-1/2 HP	↓	↓	6	3.330	Ea.

157 400 | Accessories

		CREW	MAKEUP	DAILY OUTPUT	MAN-HOURS	UNIT
401	AIR FILTERS					
0500	Chemical media filtration type					
1100	Industrial air fume & odor scrubber unit w/pump & motor					
1110	corrosion resistant PVC construction					
1120	Single pack filter, horizontal type					
1130	500 CFM	Q-9	1 Sheet Metal Worker	14	1.140	Ea.
			1 Sheet Metal Apprentice			
1140	1000 CFM			11	1.450	Ea.
1150	2000 CFM			8	2.000	Ea.
1160	3000 CFM			7	2.290	Ea.
1170	5000 CFM			5	3.200	Ea.
1180	8000 CFM			4	4.000	Ea.
1190	12,000 CFM			3	5.330	Ea.
1200	16,000 CFM			2.50	6.400	Ea.
1210	20,000 CFM			2	8.000	Ea.
1220	26,000 CFM	↓	↓	1.50	10.670	Ea.
1230	30,000 CFM	Q-10	2 Sheet Metal Workers	2	12.000	Ea.
			1 Sheet Metal Apprentice			
1240	40,000 CFM	"	"	1.50	16.000	Ea.
1250	50,000 CFM	Q-11	1 Sheet Metal Foreman (ins)	2	16.000	Ea.
			2 Sheet Metal Workers			
			1 Sheet Metal Apprentice			
1260	55,000 CFM			1.80	17.780	Ea.
1270	60,000 CFM	↓	↓	1.50	21.330	Ea.
1300	Double pack filter, horizontal type					
1310	500 CFM	Q-9	1 Sheet Metal Worker	10	1.600	Ea.
			1 Sheet Metal Apprentice			
1320	1000 CFM			8	2.000	Ea.
1330	2000 CFM			6	2.670	Ea.
1340	3000 CFM			5	3.200	Ea.
1350	5000 CFM			4	4.000	Ea.
1360	8000 CFM			3	5.330	Ea.
1370	12,000 CFM			2.50	6.400	Ea.
1380	16,000 CFM			2	8.000	Ea.
1390	20,000 CFM			1.50	10.670	Ea.
1400	26,000 CFM	↓	↓	1	16.000	Ea.
1410	30,000 CFM	Q-10	2 Sheet Metal Workers	1.50	16.000	Ea.
			1 Sheet Metal Apprentice			
1420	40,000 CFM	"	"	1.30	18.460	Ea.
1430	50,000 CFM	Q-11	1 Sheet Metal Foreman (ins)	1.50	21.330	Ea.
			2 Sheet Metal Workers			
			1 Sheet Metal Apprentice			
1440	55,000 CFM			1.30	24.620	Ea.
1450	60,000 CFM	↓	↓	1	32.000	Ea.
1500	Single pack filter, vertical type					
1510	500 CFM	Q-9	1 Sheet Metal Worker	24	.667	Ea.
			1 Sheet Metal Apprentice			
1520	1000 CFM			18	.889	Ea.
1530	2000 CFM			12	1.330	Ea.
1540	3000 CFM	↓	↓	9	1.780	Ea.

			CREW	MAKEUP	DAILY OUTPUT	MAN-HOURS	UNIT
**157 400	Accessories**							
401	1551	Air filters, single pack, vertical type, 5000 CFM	Q-9	1 Sheet Metal Worker	6	2.670	Ea.
				1 Sheet Metal Apprentice			
	1560	8000 CFM			4	4.000	Ea.
	1570	12,000 CFM			3	5.330	Ea.
	1580	16,000 CFM			2	8.000	Ea.
	1590	20,000 CFM			1.80	8.890	Ea.
	1600	24,000 CFM	↓	↓	1.60	10.000	Ea.
	1650	Double pack filter, vertical type					
	1660	500 CFM	Q-9	1 Sheet Metal Worker	22	.727	Ea.
				1 Sheet Metal Apprentice			
	1670	1000 CFM			16	1.000	Ea.
	1680	2000 CFM			10	1.600	Ea.
	1690	3000 CFM			7	2.290	Ea.
	1700	5000 CFM			5	3.200	Ea.
	1710	8000 CFM			3	5.330	Ea.
	1720	12,000 CFM			2.50	6.400	Ea.
	1730	16,000 CFM			2	8.000	Ea.
	1740	20,000 CFM			1.50	10.670	Ea.
	1750	24,000 CFM	↓	↓	1	16.000	Ea.
	2000	Electronic air cleaner, self-contained					
	2050	185 CFM	1 Shee	1 Sheet Metal Worker	2.40	3.330	Ea.
	2100	200 CFM			2.30	3.480	Ea.
	2150	500 CFM			2.30	3.480	Ea.
	2200	1000 CFM			2.20	3.640	Ea.
	2250	1200 CFM			2.10	3.810	Ea.
	2300	2500 CFM	↓	↓	2	4.000	Ea.
	2400	In-line installation, duct or plenum					
	2420	Power pack, one required for each					
	2430	Installation, one or two filter cells	1 Shee	1 Sheet Metal Worker	2	4.000	Ea.
	2440	Filter cell, 2" thick, 1" perimeter offset			4	2.000	Ea.
	2450	20" x 20"			4	2.000	Ea.
	2460	20" x 16"			4	2.000	Ea.
	2470	25" x 20"			3.50	2.290	Ea.
	2480	25" x 16"	↓	↓	3	2.670	Ea.
	420	**CONTROL COMPONENTS**					
	0700	Controller, receiver					
	0730	Panel mount, single input	1 Plum	1 Plumber	8	1.000	Ea.
	0740	With conversion mounting bracket			8	1.000	Ea.
	0750	Dual input, with control point adjustment	↓	↓	7	1.140	Ea.
	0850	Electric, single snap switch	1 Elec	1 Electrician	4	2.000	Ea.
	0860	Dual snap switches	"	"	3	2.670	Ea.
	1000	Enthalpy control, boiler water temperature control					
	1010	governed by outdoor temperature, with timer	1 Elec	1 Electrician	3	2.670	Ea.
	2000	Gauges, pressure or vacuum					
	2100	2" diameter dial	1 Stpi	1 Steamfitter	32	.250	Ea.
	2200	2-1/2" diameter dial			32	.250	Ea.
	2300	3-1/2" diameter dial			32	.250	Ea.
	2400	4-1/2" diameter dial	↓	↓	32	.250	Ea.
	2700	Flanged iron case, black ring					
	2800	3-1/2" diameter dial	1 Stpi	1 Steamfitter	32	.250	Ea.
	2900	4-1/2" diameter dial			32	.250	Ea.
	3000	6" diameter dial	↓	↓	32	.250	Ea.
	3350	Humidistat					
	3390	Electric operated	1 Shee	1 Sheet Metal Worker	8	1.000	Ea.
	3400	Relays					
	3430	Pneumatic/electric	1 Plum	1 Plumber	16	.500	Ea.
	3440	Pneumatic proportioning			8	1.000	Ea.
	3450	Pneumatic switching	↓	↓	12	.667	Ea.

578

157 400	Accessories	CREW	MAKEUP	DAILY OUTPUT	MAN-HOURS	UNIT
420 3461	Relays, selector, 3 point	1 Plum	1 Plumber	6	1.330	Ea.
3470	Time delay	"	"	8	1.000	Ea.
3500	Sensor, air operated					
3520	Humidity	1 Plum	1 Plumber	16	.500	Ea.
3540	Pressure			16	.500	Ea.
3560	Temperature	↓	↓	12	.667	Ea.
3600	Electric operated					
3620	Humidity	1 Elec	1 Electrician	8	1.000	Ea.
3650	Pressure			8	1.000	Ea.
3680	Temperature	↓	↓	10	.800	Ea.
4000	Thermometers					
4100	Dial type, 3-1/2" diameter, vapor type, union connection	1 Stpi	1 Steamfitter	32	.250	Ea.
4120	Liquid type, union connection			32	.250	Ea.
4500	Stem type, 6-1/2" case, 2" stem, 1/2" NPT			32	.250	Ea.
4520	4" stem, 1/2" NPT			32	.250	Ea.
4600	9" case, 3-1/2" stem, 3/4" NPT			28	.286	Ea.
4620	6" stem, 3/4" NPT			28	.286	Ea.
4640	8" stem, 3/4" NPT			28	.286	Ea.
4660	12" stem, 1" NPT	↓	↓	26	.308	Ea.
5000	Thermostats					
5030	1 set back, manual	1 Shee	1 Sheet Metal Worker	8	1.000	Ea.
5040	1 set back, electric, timed			8	1.000	Ea.
5050	2 set back, electric, timed			8	1.000	Ea.
5200	24 hour, automatic, clock	↓	↓	8	1.000	Ea.
5220	Electric, 2 wire	1 Elec	1 Electrician	13	.615	Ea.
5230	3 wire	"	"	10	.800	Ea.
5250	Pneumatic, 2 pipe	1 Plum	1 Plumber	10	.800	Ea.
5300	Transmitter, pneumatic					
5320	Temperature averaging element	Q-1	1 Plumber 1 Plumber Apprentice	8	2.000	Ea.
5350	Pressure differential	1 Plum	1 Plumber	7	1.140	Ea.
5370	Humidity, duct			8	1.000	Ea.
5380	Room			12	.667	Ea.
5390	Temperature, with averaging element	↓	↓	6	1.330	Ea.
5420	Electric operated, humidity	1 Elec	1 Electrician	8	1.000	Ea.
5430	DPST	"	"	8	1.000	Ea.
6000	Valves, motorized zone					
6100	Sweat connections, 1/2" C x C	1 Stpi	1 Steamfitter	20	.400	Ea.
6110	3/4" C x C			20	.400	Ea.
6120	1" C x C			19	.421	Ea.
6140	1/2" C x C, with end switch, 2 wire			20	.400	Ea.
6150	3/4" C x C, with end switch, 2 wire			20	.400	Ea.
6160	1" C x C, with end switch, 2 wire			19	.421	Ea.
6180	1-1/4" C x C, w/end switch, 2 wire			15	.533	Ea.
7000	Threaded connections, 1/2" NPT			20	.400	Ea.
7010	3/4" NPT	↓	↓	20	.400	Ea.
7090	Valves, motor controlled					
7100	Electric motor actuated					
7200	Brass, two way, screwed					
7210	1/2" pipe size	L-6	1 Plumber .5 Electrician	36	.333	Ea.
7220	3/4" pipe size			30	.400	Ea.
7230	1" pipe size			28	.429	Ea.
7240	1-1/2" pipe size			19	.632	Ea.
7250	2" pipe size	↓	↓	16	.750	Ea.
7350	Brass, three way, screwed					
7360	1/2" pipe size	L-6	1 Plumber .5 Electrician	33	.364	Ea.

157 400	Accessories	CREW	MAKEUP	DAILY OUTPUT	MAN-HOURS	UNIT
420 7371	Valves, elec. motor actuated, brass, 3 way, 3/4" pipe size	L-6	1 Plumber	27	.444	Ea.
			.5 Electrician			
7380	1" pipe size			25.50	.471	Ea.
7390	1-1/2" pipe size			17	.706	Ea.
7400	2" pipe size	↓	↓	14	.857	Ea.
7550	Iron body, two way, flanged					
7560	2-1/2" pipe size	L-6	1 Plumber	4	3.000	Ea.
			.5 Electrician			
7570	3" pipe size			3	4.000	Ea.
7580	4" pipe size			2	6.000	Ea.
7590	6" pipe size	↓	↓	1.50	8.000	Ea.
7850	Iron body, three way, flanged					
7860	2-1/2" pipe size	L-6	1 Plumber	3	4.000	Ea.
			.5 Electrician			
7870	3" pipe size			2.50	4.800	Ea.
7880	4" pipe size			2	6.000	Ea.
7890	6" pipe size	↓	↓	1.50	8.000	Ea.
8000	Pneumatic, air operated					
8050	Brass, two way, screwed					
8060	1/2" pipe size	1 Plum	1 Plumber	24	.333	Ea.
8070	3/4" pipe size			20	.400	Ea.
8080	1" pipe size			19	.421	Ea.
8090	1-1/4" pipe size			15	.533	Ea.
8100	1-1/2" pipe size			13	.615	Ea.
8110	2" pipe size	↓	↓	11	.727	Ea.
8180	Brass, three way, screwed					
8190	1/2" pipe size	1 Plum	1 Plumber	22	.364	Ea.
8200	3/4" pipe size			18	.444	Ea.
8210	1" pipe size			17	.471	Ea.
8220	1-1/2" pipe size			11	.727	Ea.
8230	2" pipe size	↓	↓	9	.889	Ea.
8450	Iron body, two way, flanged					
8460	2-1/2" pipe size	Q-1	1 Plumber	5	3.200	Ea.
			1 Plumber Apprentice			
8470	3" pipe size			4.50	3.560	Ea.
8480	4" pipe size	↓	↓	3	5.330	Ea.
8490	6" pipe size	Q-2	2 Plumbers	3	8.000	Ea.
			1 Plumber Apprentice			
8560	Iron body, three way, flanged					
8570	2-1/2" pipe size	Q-1	1 Plumber	4.50	3.560	Ea.
			1 Plumber Apprentice			
8580	3" pipe size			4	4.000	Ea.
8590	4" pipe size	↓	↓	2.50	6.400	Ea.
8600	6" pipe size	Q-2	2 Plumbers	3	8.000	Ea.
			1 Plumber Apprentice			
440	**CURBS/PADS PREFABRICATED**					
6000	Pad, fiberglass reinforced concrete with polystyrene foam core					
6050	Condenser, 2" thick, 20" x 54"	1 Shee	1 Sheet Metal Worker	8	1.000	Ea.
6070	24" x 24"			16	.500	Ea.
6090	24" x 36"			12	.667	Ea.
6110	24" x 48"	↓	↓	8	1.000	Ea.
6150	26" x 56"	Q-9	1 Sheet Metal Worker	8	2.000	Ea.
			1 Sheet Metal Apprentice			
6170	28" x 38"	1 Shee	1 Sheet Metal Worker	8	1.000	Ea.
6190	30" x 30"			12	.667	Ea.
6220	30" x 36"	↓	↓	8	1.000	Ea.
6240	30" x 48"	Q-9	1 Sheet Metal Worker	8	2.000	Ea.
			1 Sheet Metal Apprentice			

			CREW	MAKEUP	DAILY OUTPUT	MAN-HOURS	UNIT
157 400	**Accessories**						
440 6261	Pad, fiberglass reinforced concrete, 30" x 56"		Q-9	1 Sheet Metal Worker	7	2.290	Ea.
				1 Sheet Metal Apprentice			
6280	36" x 36"				8	2.000	Ea.
6300	36" x 48"				7	2.290	Ea.
6320	36" x 60"				7	2.290	Ea.
6340	36" x 72"				6	2.670	Ea.
6360	40" x 42"				7	2.290	Ea.
6400	40" x 72"				6	2.670	Ea.
6430	45" x 50"				7	2.290	Ea.
6460	45" x 58"				6	2.670	Ea.
6490	26" round				10	1.600	Ea.
6550	30" round				9	1.780	Ea.
6600	36" round		↓	↓	8	2.000	Ea.
7500	Heat pump						
7550	16" x 28", 4" thick		1 Shee	1 Sheet Metal Worker	8	1.000	Ea.
7600	16" x 28", 8" thick				6	1.330	Ea.
7650	22" x 36", 4" thick				6	1.330	Ea.
7700	24" round, 6" thick		↓	↓	8	1.000	Ea.
8800	Stand, concrete coated polystyrene foam						
8850	Heat pump, 6" high		1 Shee	1 Sheet Metal Worker	32	.250	Ea.
8870	10" high		"	"	32	.250	Ea.
450	**DIFFUSERS** Aluminum, opposed blade damper unless noted						
0100	Ceiling, linear, also for sidewall						
0120	2" wide		1 Shee	1 Sheet Metal Worker	32	.250	L.F.
0140	3" wide				30	.267	L.F.
0160	4" wide				26	.308	L.F.
0180	6" wide				24	.333	L.F.
0200	8" wide				22	.364	L.F.
0220	10" wide				20	.400	L.F.
0240	12" wide				18	.444	L.F.
0500	Perforated, 24" x 24", panel size 6" x 6"				16	.500	Ea.
0520	8" x 8"				15	.533	Ea.
0540	10" x 10"				14	.571	Ea.
0560	12" x 12"				12	.667	Ea.
0580	15" x 15"				11	.727	Ea.
0600	18" x 18"				10	.800	Ea.
1000	Rectangular, 1 to 4 way blow, 6" x 6"				16	.500	Ea.
1020	12" x 6"				15	.533	Ea.
1040	12" x 9"				14	.571	Ea.
1060	12" x 12"				12	.667	Ea.
1080	18" x 12"				11	.727	Ea.
1100	24" x 12"				10	.800	Ea.
1120	15" x 15"				10	.800	Ea.
1140	18" x 15"				9	.889	Ea.
1160	21" x 21"				8	1.000	Ea.
1180	24" x 24"				7	1.140	Ea.
1500	Round, butterfly damper, 6" diameter				18	.444	Ea.
1520	8" diameter				16	.500	Ea.
1540	10" diameter				14	.571	Ea.
1560	12" diameter				12	.667	Ea.
1580	14" diameter				10	.800	Ea.
1600	18" diameter				9	.889	Ea.
1620	22" diameter				8	1.000	Ea.
2000	T bar mounting, 24" x 24" lay-in frame, 6" x 6"				16	.500	Ea.
2020	9" x 9"				14	.571	Ea.
2040	12" x 12"				12	.667	Ea.
2060	15" x 15"				11	.727	Ea.
2080	18" x 18"		↓	↓	10	.800	Ea.

157 400 | Accessories		CREW	MAKEUP	DAILY OUTPUT	MAN-HOURS	UNIT
450 2501	Diffusers, ceiling, combination supply and return					
2520	21" x 21" supply, 15" x 15" return	Q-9	1 Sheet Metal Worker	10	1.600	Ea.
			1 Sheet Metal Apprentice			
2540	24" x 24" supply, 18" x 18" return			9.50	1.680	Ea.
2560	27" x 27" supply, 18" x 18" return			9	1.780	Ea.
2580	30" x 30" supply, 21" x 21" return			8.50	1.880	Ea.
2600	33" x 33" supply, 24" x 24" return			8	2.000	Ea.
2620	36" x 36" supply, 24" x 24" return	▼	▼	7.50	2.130	Ea.
3000	Baseboard, white enameled steel					
3100	18" long	1 Shee	1 Sheet Metal Worker	20	.400	Ea.
3120	24" long			18	.444	Ea.
3140	48" long	▼	▼	16	.500	Ea.
4000	Floor, steel, adjustable pattern					
4100	2" x 10"	1 Shee	1 Sheet Metal Worker	34	.235	Ea.
4120	2" x 12"			32	.250	Ea.
4140	2" x 14"			30	.267	Ea.
4200	4" x 10"			28	.286	Ea.
4220	4" x 12"			26	.308	Ea.
4240	4" x 14"			25	.320	Ea.
4260	6" x 10"			26	.308	Ea.
4280	6" x 12"			24	.333	Ea.
4300	6" x 14"	▼	▼	22	.364	Ea.
5000	Sidewall, aluminum, 3 way dispersion					
5100	8" x 4"	1 Shee	1 Sheet Metal Worker	24	.333	Ea.
5110	8" x 6"			24	.333	Ea.
5120	10" x 4"			22	.364	Ea.
5130	10" x 6"			22	.364	Ea.
5140	10" x 8"			20	.400	Ea.
5160	12" x 4"			18	.444	Ea.
5180	12" x 8"			16	.500	Ea.
5200	14" x 4"			15	.533	Ea.
5220	14" x 6"			14	.571	Ea.
5240	14" x 8"	▼	▼	13	.615	Ea.
460 0020	GRILLES					
	Aluminum					
0100	Air supply, single deflection, adjustable					
0120	8" x 4"	1 Shee	1 Sheet Metal Worker	30	.267	Ea.
0140	8" x 8"			28	.286	Ea.
0160	10" x 4"			24	.333	Ea.
0180	10" x 10"			23	.348	Ea.
0200	12" x 6"			23	.348	Ea.
0220	12" x 12"			22	.364	Ea.
0240	14" x 8"			23	.348	Ea.
0260	14" x 14"			22	.364	Ea.
0280	18" x 10"			23	.348	Ea.
0300	18" x 18"			21	.381	Ea.
0320	20" x 12"			22	.364	Ea.
0340	20" x 20"			21	.381	Ea.
0360	24" x 14"			18	.444	Ea.
0380	24" x 24"			15	.533	Ea.
0400	30" x 8"			20	.400	Ea.
0420	30" x 10"			19	.421	Ea.
0440	30" x 12"			18	.444	Ea.
0460	30" x 16"			17	.471	Ea.
0480	30" x 18"			17	.471	Ea.
0500	30" x 30"			14	.571	Ea.
0520	36" x 12"			17	.471	Ea.
0540	36" x 16"	▼	▼	16	.500	Ea.

157 400 | Accessories

		Description	CREW	MAKEUP	DAILY OUTPUT	MAN-HOURS	UNIT
460	0561	Grilles, alum. air supply, single deflection, 36" x 18"	1 Shee	1 Sheet Metal Worker	15	.533	Ea.
	0580	36" x 24"			14	.571	Ea.
	0600	36" x 28"			13	.615	Ea.
	0620	36" x 30"			12	.667	Ea.
	0640	36" x 32"			12	.667	Ea.
	0660	36" x 34"			11	.727	Ea.
	0680	36" x 36"			11	.727	Ea.
	1000	Air return, 6" x 6"			26	.308	Ea.
	1020	10" x 6"			24	.333	Ea.
	1040	14" x 6"			23	.348	Ea.
	1060	10" x 8"			23	.348	Ea.
	1080	16" x 8"			22	.364	Ea.
	1100	12" x 12"			22	.364	Ea.
	1120	24" x 12"			18	.444	Ea.
	1140	30" x 12"			16	.500	Ea.
	1160	14" x 14"			22	.364	Ea.
	1180	16" x 16"			22	.364	Ea.
	1200	18" x 18"			21	.381	Ea.
	1220	24" x 18"			16	.500	Ea.
	1240	36" x 18"			15	.533	Ea.
	1260	24" x 24"			15	.533	Ea.
	1280	36" x 24"			14	.571	Ea.
	1300	48" x 24"			12	.667	Ea.
	1320	48" x 30"			11	.727	Ea.
	1340	36" x 36"			13	.615	Ea.
	1360	48" x 36"			11	.727	Ea.
	1380	48" x 48"			8	1.000	Ea.
	2000	Door grilles, 12" x 12"			22	.364	Ea.
	2020	18" x 12"			22	.364	Ea.
	2040	24" x 12"			18	.444	Ea.
	2060	18" x 18"			18	.444	Ea.
	2080	24" x 18"			16	.500	Ea.
	2100	24" x 24"			15	.533	Ea.
	3000	Filter grille with filter, 12" x 12"			24	.333	Ea.
	3020	18" x 12"			20	.400	Ea.
	3040	24" x 18"			18	.444	Ea.
	3060	24" x 24"			16	.500	Ea.
	3080	30" x 24"			14	.571	Ea.
	3100	30" x 30"			13	.615	Ea.
	3950	Eggcrate, framed, 6" x 6" opening			26	.308	Ea.
	3960	10" x 10" opening			23	.348	Ea.
	3970	12" x 12" opening			22	.364	Ea.
	3980	14" x 14" opening			22	.364	Ea.
	3990	18" x 18" opening			21	.381	Ea.
	4020	22" x 22" opening			17	.471	Ea.
	4040	24" x 24" opening			15	.533	Ea.
	4050	48" x 24" opening	↓	↓	12	.667	Ea.
	4060	Eggcrate, lay-in, T-bar system					
	4070	48" x 24" sheet	1 Shee	1 Sheet Metal Worker	40	.200	Ea.
	5000	Transfer grille, vision proof, 8" x 4"			30	.267	Ea.
	5020	8" x 6"			28	.286	Ea.
	5040	8" x 8"			26	.308	Ea.
	5060	10" x 6"			24	.333	Ea.
	5080	10" x 10"			23	.348	Ea.
	5100	12" x 10"			22	.364	Ea.
	5120	14" x 10"			22	.364	Ea.
	5140	16" x 8"			21	.381	Ea.
	5160	18" x 12"	↓	↓	20	.400	Ea.

157 400	Accessories	CREW	MAKEUP	DAILY OUTPUT	MAN-HOURS	UNIT
460 5181	Grilles, aluminum transfer, 20" x 12"	1 Shee	1 Sheet Metal Worker	20	.400	Ea.
5200	20" x 20"			19	.421	Ea.
5220	24" x 12"			17	.471	Ea.
5240	24" x 24"			16	.500	Ea.
5260	30" x 6"			15	.533	Ea.
5280	30" x 8"			15	.533	Ea.
5300	30" x 12"			14	.571	Ea.
5320	30" x 16"			13	.615	Ea.
5340	30" x 20"			12	.667	Ea.
5360	30" x 24"			11	.727	Ea.
5380	30" x 30"	↓	↓	10	.800	Ea.
6200	Plastic, eggcrate, lay-in, T-bar system					
6210	48" x 24" sheet	1 Shee	1 Sheet Metal Worker	50	.160	Ea.
6250	Steel door louver					
6270	With fire link, steel only					
6350	12" x 18"	1 Shee	1 Sheet Metal Worker	22	.364	Ea.
6410	12" x 24"			21	.381	Ea.
6470	18" x 18"			20	.400	Ea.
6530	18" x 24"			19	.421	Ea.
6600	18" x 36"			17	.471	Ea.
6660	24" x 24"			15	.533	Ea.
6720	24" x 30"			15	.533	Ea.
6780	30" x 30"			13	.615	Ea.
6840	30" x 36"			12	.667	Ea.
6900	36" x 36"	↓	↓	10	.800	Ea.
470	**REGISTERS**					
0980	Air supply					
1000	Ceiling/wall, O.B. damper, anodized aluminum					
1010	One or two way deflection, adj. curved face bars					
1020	8" x 4"	1 Shee	1 Sheet Metal Worker	26	.308	Ea.
1040	8" x 8"			24	.333	Ea.
1060	10" x 6"			20	.400	Ea.
1080	10" x 10"			19	.421	Ea.
1100	12" x 6"			19	.421	Ea.
1120	12" x 12"			18	.444	Ea.
1140	14" x 8"			17	.471	Ea.
1160	14" x 14"			18	.444	Ea.
1180	18" x 8"			18	.444	Ea.
1200	18" x 18"			17	.471	Ea.
1220	20" x 4"			19	.421	Ea.
1240	20" x 6"			18	.444	Ea.
1260	20" x 8"			18	.444	Ea.
1280	20" x 20"			17	.471	Ea.
1300	24" x 4"			17	.471	Ea.
1320	24" x 6"			16	.500	Ea.
1340	24" x 8"			13	.615	Ea.
1360	24" x 24"			11	.727	Ea.
1380	30" x 4"			16	.500	Ea.
1400	30" x 6"			15	.533	Ea.
1420	30" x 8"			14	.571	Ea.
1440	30" x 24"			12	.667	Ea.
1460	30" x 30"	↓	↓	10	.800	Ea.
1980	One way deflection, adj. vert. or horiz. face bars					
2000	8" x 4"	1 Shee	1 Sheet Metal Worker	26	.308	Ea.
2020	8" x 8"			24	.333	Ea.
2040	10" x 6"			20	.400	Ea.
2060	10" x 10"			19	.421	Ea.
2080	12" x 6"	↓	↓	19	.421	Ea.

157 400 | Accessories

		CREW	MAKEUP	DAILY OUTPUT	MAN-HOURS	UNIT
470	2101	Registers, air supply, ceiling/wall, 12" x 12"	1 Shee	1 Sheet Metal Worker	18	.444	Ea.
	2120	14" x 8"			17	.471	Ea.
	2140	14" x 12"			18	.444	Ea.
	2160	14" x 14"			18	.444	Ea.
	2180	16" x 6"			18	.444	Ea.
	2200	16" x 12"			18	.444	Ea.
	2220	16" x 16"			17	.471	Ea.
	2240	18" x 8"			18	.444	Ea.
	2260	18" x 12"			17	.471	Ea.
	2280	18" x 18"			16	.500	Ea.
	2300	20" x 10"			18	.444	Ea.
	2320	20" x 16"			16	.500	Ea.
	2340	20" x 20"			16	.500	Ea.
	2360	24" x 12"			15	.533	Ea.
	2380	24" x 16"			14	.571	Ea.
	2400	24" x 20"			12	.667	Ea.
	2420	24" x 24"			10	.800	Ea.
	2440	30" x 12"			13	.615	Ea.
	2460	30" x 16"			13	.615	Ea.
	2480	30" x 24"			11	.727	Ea.
	2500	30" x 30"			9	.889	Ea.
	2520	36" x 12"			11	.727	Ea.
	2540	36" x 24"			10	.800	Ea.
	2560	36" x 36"	↓	↓	8	1.000	Ea.
	3000	Baseboard, hand adj. damper, enameled steel					
	3020	10" x 6"	1 Shee	1 Sheet Metal Worker	24	.333	Ea.
	3040	12" x 5"			23	.348	Ea.
	3060	12" x 6"			23	.348	Ea.
	3080	12" x 8"			22	.364	Ea.
	3100	14" x 6"	↓	↓	20	.400	Ea.
	4000	Floor, toe operated damper, enameled steel					
	4020	4" x 6"	1 Shee	1 Sheet Metal Worker	32	.250	Ea.
	4040	4" x 12"			26	.308	Ea.
	4060	6" x 8"			28	.286	Ea.
	4080	6" x 14"			22	.364	Ea.
	4100	8" x 10"			22	.364	Ea.
	4120	8" x 16"			20	.400	Ea.
	4140	10" x 10"			20	.400	Ea.
	4160	10" x 16"			18	.444	Ea.
	4180	12" x 12"			18	.444	Ea.
	4200	12" x 24"			16	.500	Ea.
	4220	14" x 14"			16	.500	Ea.
	4240	14" x 20"			15	.533	Ea.
	4260	16" x 16"	↓	↓	15	.533	Ea.
	4980	Air return					
	5000	Ceiling or wall, fixed 45° face blades,					
	5010	Adjustable O.B. damper, anodized aluminum					
	5020	8" x 4"	1 Shee	1 Sheet Metal Worker	26	.308	Ea.
	5040	8" x 6"			24	.333	Ea.
	5060	10" x 6"			19	.421	Ea.
	5080	16" x 6"			18	.444	Ea.
	5100	10" x 8"			19	.421	Ea.
	5120	12" x 8"			16	.500	Ea.
	5140	10" x 10"			18	.444	Ea.
	5180	18" x 12"			18	.444	Ea.
	5200	30" x 12"			12	.667	Ea.
	5220	16" x 16"			16	.500	Ea.
	5240	18" x 18"	↓	↓	17	.471	Ea.

157 400 | Accessories

		CREW	MAKEUP	DAILY OUTPUT	MAN-HOURS	UNIT
470 5261	Registers, air return, ceiling/wall, 36" x 18"	1 Shee	1 Sheet Metal Worker	10	.800	Ea.
5280	24" x 24"			11	.727	Ea.
5300	36" x 24"			8	1.000	Ea.
5320	48" x 24"	↓	↓	6	1.330	Ea.
480	**DUCT ACCESSORIES**					
0050	Air extractors, 12" x 4"	1 Shee	1 Sheet Metal Worker	24	.333	Ea.
0100	8" x 6"			22	.364	Ea.
0120	12" x 6"			21	.381	Ea.
0140	16" x 6"			20	.400	Ea.
0160	24" x 6"			18	.444	Ea.
0180	12" x 8"			20	.400	Ea.
0200	20" x 8"			16	.500	Ea.
0240	18" x 10"			14	.571	Ea.
0260	24" x 10"			12	.667	Ea.
0280	24" x 12"			10	.800	Ea.
0300	30" x 12"			8	1.000	Ea.
1000	Duct access door, insulated, 6" x 6"			14	.571	Ea.
1020	10" x 10"			11	.727	Ea.
1040	12" x 12"			10	.800	Ea.
1060	16" x 12"			9	.889	Ea.
1080	24" x 24"			8	1.000	Ea.
2000	Fabrics for flexible connections, with metal edge			100	.080	L.F.
2100	Without metal edge			160	.050	L.F.
3000	Fire damper, curtain type, vertical, 8" x 4"			24	.333	Ea.
3020	12" x 4"			22	.364	Ea.
3040	10" x 6"			22	.364	Ea.
3060	20" x 6"			18	.444	Ea.
3080	12" x 8"			22	.364	Ea.
3100	24" x 8"			16	.500	Ea.
3120	12" x 10"			21	.381	Ea.
3140	24" x 10"			15	.533	Ea.
3160	36" x 10"			12	.667	Ea.
3180	14" x 12"			20	.400	Ea.
3200	24" x 12"			13	.615	Ea.
3220	48" x 12"			10	.800	Ea.
3240	16" x 14"			18	.444	Ea.
3260	24" x 14"			12	.667	Ea.
3280	30" x 14"			11	.727	Ea.
3300	18" x 16"			17	.471	Ea.
3320	24" x 16"			11	.727	Ea.
3340	36" x 16"			10	.800	Ea.
3360	24" x 18"			10	.800	Ea.
3380	48" x 18"			8	1.000	Ea.
3400	24" x 20"			8	1.000	Ea.
3420	36" x 20"			7	1.140	Ea.
3440	24" x 22"			7	1.140	Ea.
3460	30" x 22"			6	1.330	Ea.
3480	26" x 24"	↓	↓	7	1.140	Ea.
3500	48" x 24"	Q-9	1 Sheet Metal Worker 1 Sheet Metal Apprentice	12	1.330	Ea.
3520	28" x 26"			13	1.230	Ea.
3540	30" x 28"			12	1.330	Ea.
3560	48" x 30"			11	1.450	Ea.
3580	48" x 36"			10	1.600	Ea.
3600	44" x 44"			10	1.600	Ea.
3620	48" x 48"	↓	↓	8	2.000	Ea.
4500	Fire/smoke combination damper, louver type, UL					
4510	8" x 8"	1 Shee	1 Sheet Metal Worker	22	.364	Ea.

		CREW	MAKEUP	DAILY OUTPUT	MAN-HOURS	UNIT
**157 400	Accessories**					
480 4521	Fire/smoke combination damper, louver type, 16" x 8"	1 Shee	1 Sheet Metal Worker	20	.400	Ea.
4540	18" x 8"			18	.444	Ea.
4560	20" x 8"			16	.500	Ea.
4580	10" x 10"			21	.381	Ea.
4600	24" x 10"			15	.533	Ea.
4620	30" x 10"			12	.667	Ea.
4640	12" x 12"			20	.400	Ea.
4660	18" x 12"			18	.444	Ea.
4680	24" x 12"			13	.615	Ea.
4700	30" x 12"			11	.727	Ea.
4720	14" x 14"			17	.471	Ea.
4740	16" x 14"			18	.444	Ea.
4760	20" x 14"			14	.571	Ea.
4780	24" x 14"			12	.667	Ea.
4800	30" x 14"			10	.800	Ea.
4820	16" x 16"			16	.500	Ea.
4840	20" x 16"			14	.571	Ea.
4860	24" x 16"			11	.727	Ea.
4880	30" x 16"			8	1.000	Ea.
4900	18" x 18"			15	.533	Ea.
5000	24" x 18"			10	.800	Ea.
5020	36" x 18"			7	1.140	Ea.
5040	20" x 20"			13	.615	Ea.
5060	24" x 20"			8	1.000	Ea.
5080	30" x 20"			8	1.000	Ea.
5100	36" x 20"			7	1.140	Ea.
5120	24" x 24"	↓	↓	8	1.000	Ea.
5140	36" x 24"	Q-9	1 Sheet Metal Worker 1 Sheet Metal Apprentice	12	1.330	Ea.
5180	Mixing box, includes electric or pneumatic motor					
5200	Constant volume, 150 to 270 CFM	Q-9	1 Sheet Metal Worker 1 Sheet Metal Apprentice	12	1.330	Ea.
5210	270 to 600 CFM			11	1.450	Ea.
5230	550 to 1000 CFM			9	1.780	Ea.
5240	1000 to 1600 CFM			8	2.000	Ea.
5250	1300 to 1900 CFM	↓	↓	6	2.670	Ea.
6000	Multi-blade dampers, opposed blade, 12" x 12"	1 Shee	1 Sheet Metal Worker	21	.381	Ea.
6020	12" x 18"			18	.444	Ea.
6040	18" x 24"			12	.667	Ea.
6060	18" x 28"			10	.800	Ea.
6080	24" x 24"			8	1.000	Ea.
6100	24" x 28"	↓	↓	6	1.330	Ea.
6120	28" x 28"	Q-9	1 Sheet Metal Worker 1 Sheet Metal Apprentice	11	1.450	Ea.
6140	36" x 36"			10	1.600	Ea.
6160	44" x 28"			8	2.000	Ea.
6180	48" x 36"			7	2.290	Ea.
6200	56" x 36"			7	2.290	Ea.
6220	60" x 36"			6	2.670	Ea.
6240	60" x 44"	↓	↓	5	3.200	Ea.
7000	Splitter damper assembly, self-locking, 1' rod	1 Shee	1 Sheet Metal Worker	24	.333	Ea.
7020	3' rod			22	.364	Ea.
7040	4' rod			20	.400	Ea.
7060	6' rod	↓	↓	18	.444	Ea.
7500	Variable volume modulating motorized damper					
7520	12" x 12"	1 Shee	1 Sheet Metal Worker	12	.667	Ea.
7540	18" x 12"			10	.800	Ea.
7560	24" x 12"	↓	↓	8	1.000	Ea.

157 400	Accessories	CREW	MAKEUP	DAILY OUTPUT	MAN-HOURS	UNIT
480 7581	Variable volume modulating motorized damper, 28" x 16"	1 Shee	1 Sheet Metal Worker	6	1.330	Ea.
7600	30" x 18"			4	2.000	Ea.
7700	For thermostat, add			8	1.000	Ea.
7800	For transformer 40 VA capacity, add	↓	↓	16	.500	Ea.
8000	Volume control, dampers					
8100	8" x 8"	1 Shee	1 Sheet Metal Worker	24	.333	Ea.
8120	12" x 8"			22	.364	Ea.
8140	16" x 10"			20	.400	Ea.
8160	18" x 12"			18	.444	Ea.
8180	22" x 12"			15	.533	Ea.
8200	24" x 16"			11	.727	Ea.
8220	28" x 16"			10	.800	Ea.
8240	30" x 16"			8	1.000	Ea.
8260	30" x 18"	↓	↓	7	1.140	Ea.
482 0100	**LOUVERS** Aluminum, extruded, with screen, mill finish					
1000	Brick vent, (see also division 041-524)					
1100	Standard, 4" deep, 8" wide, 5" high	1 Shee	1 Sheet Metal Worker	24	.333	Ea.
1200	Modular, 4" deep, 7-3/4" wide, 5" high			24	.333	Ea.
1300	Speed brick, 4" deep, 11-5/8" wide, 3-7/8" high			24	.333	Ea.
1400	Fuel oil brick, 4" deep, 8" wide, 5" high			24	.333	Ea.
2000	Cooling tower and mechanical equip., screens, light weight			40	.200	S.F.
2020	Standard weight			35	.229	S.F.
2500	Dual combination, automatic, intake or exhaust			20	.400	S.F.
2520	Manual operation			20	.400	S.F.
2540	Electric or pneumatic operation			20	.400	S.F.
2560	Motor, for electric or pneumatic	↓	↓	14	.571	Ea.
3000	Fixed blade, continuous line					
3100	Mullion type, stormproof	1 Shee	1 Sheet Metal Worker	28	.286	S.F.
3200	Stormproof			28	.286	S.F.
3300	Vertical line			28	.286	S.F.
3520	Motor, for damper, electric or pneumatic			14	.571	Ea.
4000	Operating, 45°, manual, electric or pneumatic			24	.333	S.F.
4100	Motor, for electric or pneumatic			14	.571	Ea.
4200	Penthouse, roof			56	.143	S.F.
4300	Walls			40	.200	S.F.
5000	Thinline, under 4" thick, fixed blade	↓	↓	40	.200	S.F.
490 0500	**VENTILATORS** Base, damper & bird screen, CFM in 5 MPH wind	Q-9	1 Sheet Metal Worker	16	1.000	Ea.
	Rotary syphon, galvanized, 6" neck diameter, 185 CFM		1 Sheet Metal Apprentice			
0520	8" neck diameter, 215 CFM			14	1.140	Ea.
0540	10" neck diameters, 260 CFM			12	1.330	Ea.
0560	12" neck diameter, 310 CFM			10	1.600	Ea.
0580	14" neck diameter, 500 CFM			10	1.600	Ea.
0600	16" neck diameter, 635 CFM			9	1.780	Ea.
0620	18" neck diameter, 835 CFM			9	1.780	Ea.
0640	20" neck diameter, 1080 CFM			8	2.000	Ea.
0660	24" neck diameter, 1530 CFM			8	2.000	Ea.
0680	30" neck diameter, 2500 CFM			7	2.290	Ea.
0700	36" neck diameter, 3800 CFM			6	2.670	Ea.
0720	42" neck diameter, 4500 CFM	↓	↓	4	4.000	Ea.
1280	Spinner ventilators, wind driven, galvanized					
1300	4" neck diameter, 180 CFM	Q-9	1 Sheet Metal Worker	20	.800	Ea.
			1 Sheet Metal Apprentice			
1320	5" neck diameter, 210 CFM			18	.889	Ea.
1340	6" neck diameter, 250 CFM			16	1.000	Ea.
1360	8" neck diameter, 360 CFM			14	1.140	Ea.
1380	10" neck diameter, 540 CFM	↓	↓	12	1.330	Ea.

157 400 | Accessories

		CREW	MAKEUP	DAILY OUTPUT	MAN-HOURS	UNIT
490 1401	Ventilators, spinner, galv., 12" neck diameter, 770 CFM	Q-9	1 Sheet Metal Worker	10	1.600	Ea.
			1 Sheet Metal Apprentice			
1420	14" neck diameter, 830 CFM			10	1.600	Ea.
1440	16" neck diameter, 1200 CFM			9	1.780	Ea.
1460	18" neck diameter, 1700 CFM			9	1.780	Ea.
1480	20" neck diameter, 2100 CFM			8	2.000	Ea.
1500	24" neck diameter, 3100 CFM			8	2.000	Ea.
1520	30" neck diameter, 4500 CFM			7	2.290	Ea.
1540	36" neck diameter, 5500 CFM	▼	▼	6	2.670	Ea.
2000	Stationary, gravity, syphon, galvanized					
2100	3" diameter, 40 CFM	Q-9	1 Sheet Metal Worker	24	.667	Ea.
			1 Sheet Metal Apprentice			
2120	4" neck diameter, 50 CFM			20	.800	Ea.
2140	5" neck diameter, 58 CFM			18	.889	Ea.
2160	6" neck diameter, 66 CFM			16	1.000	Ea.
2180	7" neck diameter, 86 CFM			15	1.070	Ea.
2200	8" neck diameter, 110 CFM			14	1.140	Ea.
2220	10" neck diameter, 140 CFM			12	1.330	Ea.
2240	12" neck diameter, 160 CFM			10	1.600	Ea.
2260	14" neck diameter, 250 CFM			10	1.600	Ea.
2280	16" neck diameter, 380 CFM			9	1.780	Ea.
2300	18" neck diameter, 500 CFM			9	1.780	Ea.
2320	20" neck diameter, 625 CFM			8	2.000	Ea.
2340	24" neck diameter, 900 CFM			8	2.000	Ea.
2360	30" neck diameter, 1375 CFM			7	2.290	Ea.
2380	36" neck diameter, 2000 CFM			6	2.670	Ea.
2400	42" neck diameter, 3000 CFM			4	4.000	Ea.
3000	Rotating chimney cap, galvanized, 4" neck diameter			20	.800	Ea.
3020	5" neck diameter			18	.889	Ea.
3040	6" neck diameter			16	1.000	Ea.
3060	7" neck diameter			15	1.070	Ea.
3080	8" neck diameter			14	1.140	Ea.
3100	10" neck diameter			12	1.330	Ea.
3600	Stationary chimney rain cap, galvanized, 3" neck diameter			24	.667	Ea.
3620	4" neck diameter			20	.800	Ea.
3640	6" neck diameter			16	1.000	Ea.
3680	8" neck diameter			14	1.140	Ea.
3700	10" neck diameter			12	1.330	Ea.
3720	12" neck diameter			10	1.600	Ea.
3740	14" neck diameter			10	1.600	Ea.
3760	16" neck diameter			9	1.780	Ea.
4200	Stationary mushroom, aluminum, 16" orifice diameter			10	1.600	Ea.
4220	26" orifice diameter			9	1.780	Ea.
4240	38" orifice diameter			8	2.000	Ea.
4260	50" orifice diameter	▼	▼	7	2.290	Ea.
5000	Relief vent					
5500	Rectangular, aluminum, galvanized curb					
5510	intake/exhaust, 0.05" SP					
5600	500 CFM, 12" x 16"	Q-9	1 Sheet Metal Worker	8	2.000	Ea.
			1 Sheet Metal Apprentice			
5620	750 CFM, 12" x 20"			7.20	2.220	Ea.
5640	1000 CFM, 12" x 24"			6.60	2.420	Ea.
5660	1500 CFM, 12" x 36"			5.80	2.760	Ea.
5680	3000 CFM, 20" x 42"			4	4.000	Ea.
5700	6000 CFM, 20" x 84"			2.60	6.150	Ea.
5720	8000 CFM, 24" x 96"			2.30	6.960	Ea.
5740	10,000 CFM, 48" x 60"			1.80	8.890	Ea.
5760	12,500 CFM, 48" x 72"	▼	▼	1.60	10.000	Ea.

157 400 | Accessories

		Item	CREW	MAKEUP	DAILY OUTPUT	MAN-HOURS	UNIT
490	5781	Relief vent, intake/exhaust, 15,000 CFM, 48" x 96"	Q-9	1 Sheet Metal Worker	1.30	12.310	Ea.
				1 Sheet Metal Apprentice			
	5800	20,000 CFM, 48" x 120"			1.20	13.330	Ea.
	5820	25,000 CFM, 60" x 120"			.90	17.780	Ea.
	5840	30,000 CFM, 72" x 120"			.70	22.860	Ea.
	5860	40,000 CFM, 96" x 120"			.60	26.670	Ea.
	5880	50,000 CFM, 96" x 144"	↓	↓	.50	32.000	Ea.
	7500	For power open, spring return damper					
	7600	motor for each S.F. of throat area	Q-9	1 Sheet Metal Worker	100	.160	S.F.
				1 Sheet Metal Apprentice			

157 600 | Miscellaneous

	Item	CREW	MAKEUP	DAILY OUTPUT	MAN-HOURS	UNIT
606	EXHAUST SYSTEMS					
0500	Engine exhaust, garage, in-floor system					
0510	Single tube outlet assemblies					
0520	For transite pipe ducting, self-storing tube	↓	↓			
0530	3" tubing adapter plate	1 Shee	1 Sheet Metal Worker	16	.500	Ea.
0540	4" tubing adapter plate			16	.500	Ea.
0550	5" tubing adapter plate	↓	↓	16	.500	Ea.
0600	For vitrified tile ducting					
0610	3" tubing adapter plate, self-storing tube	1 Shee	1 Sheet Metal Worker	16	.500	Ea.
0620	4" tubing adapter plate, self-storing tube			16	.500	Ea.
0650	4" tube size opening, non-storing tube			16	.500	Ea.
0660	5" tubing adapter plate, self-storing tube	↓	↓	16	.500	Ea.
0700	For vitrified tile & transite pipe ducting					
0710	3" tube size opening, self-storing tube	1 Shee	1 Sheet Metal Worker	16	.500	Ea.
0720	4" tube size opening, self-storing tube	"	"	16	.500	Ea.
0800	Two tube outlet assemblies					
0810	For transite pipe ducting, self-storing tube					
0820	3" tubing, dual exhaust adapter plate	1 Shee	1 Sheet Metal Worker	16	.500	Ea.
0850	For vitrified tile ducting					
0860	3" tubing, dual exhaust, self-storing tube	1 Shee	1 Sheet Metal Worker	16	.500	Ea.
0870	3" tubing, double outlet, non-storing tubes	"	"	16	.500	Ea.
2500	Engine exhaust, thru-door outlet					
2510	3" for up to 1/4" thick door	1 Carp	1 Carpenter	16	.500	Ea.
2520	3" for over 1/4" thick door			16	.500	Ea.
2530	4" for up to 1/4" thick door	↓	↓	16	.500	Ea.
7500	Welding fume elimination accessories for garage exhaust systems					
7600	Cut off (blast gate)					
7610	3" tubing size, 3" x 6" opening	1 Shee	1 Sheet Metal Worker	24	.333	Ea.
7620	4" tubing size, 4" x 8" opening			24	.333	Ea.
7630	5" tubing size, 5" x 10" opening	↓	↓	24	.333	Ea.
7700	Hoods, magnetic, with handle & screen					
7710	3" tubing size, 3" x 6" opening	1 Shee	1 Sheet Metal Worker	24	.333	Ea.
7720	4" tubing size, 4" x 8" opening			24	.333	Ea.
7730	5" tubing size, 5" x 10" opening	↓	↓	24	.333	Ea.

DIVISION 16

ELECTRICAL

DIVISION 16 ELECTRICAL

There are numerous factors that affect electrical construction, but perhaps the most significant is job site conditions. The location of electrical installations can vary to such a degree that before developing productivity figures in this area, parameters such as quality of access, height above floor, complexity of wiring, and specific problems related to materials must be determined or evaluated. It is important to know exactly how many elevated installations are involved, how much access to the inside of walls is to be allowed to the electrician, and exactly what type of service and appliances are planned. Each of these items can add greatly to the time required to get the job done.

Code requirements and standards must always be followed in electrical work. This tends to make productivity figures for straightforward procedures standard from job to job; however, it is important to remember that electrical installation is not the same in concrete buildings as it is in steel or open-web joist buildings.

Since most tasks in this division are performed by electricians, productivity is always directly tied to the level of expertise that workers bring to the job. This varies with location and the quality of the labor force. The productivity figures in the listings assume that the electrical craftsmen on the job are skilled, licensed workmen.

Weather may be a factor when installing electrical items, since much of the work can only be done in a protected area within a reasonable temperature range.

The man-hours involved in assembling electrical systems is directly tied to the time needed for such tasks as: handling materials, securing them, setting supports, and cleaning up.

Productivity figures for the installation of air conditioning and other special systems do not include the installation of items that fall under the mechanical division (such as pipe work) or other related items such as ductwork, diffusers, and mechanical connections between various pieces of equipment.

		160 100 | Cable Trays	CREW	MAKEUP	DAILY OUTPUT	MAN-HOURS	UNIT
105	105	**CABLE TRAY** Ladder type w/ftngs & supports, 4" dp., to 15' elev.					
	0160	Galv. steel tray					
	0170	4" rung spacing, 6" wide	1 Elec	1 Electrician	49	.163	L.F.
	0180	9" wide			46	.174	L.F.
	0200	12" wide			43	.186	L.F.
	0400	18" wide			41	.195	L.F.
	0600	24" wide			39	.205	L.F.
	0650	30" wide			34	.235	L.F.
	0700	36" wide			30	.267	L.F.
	0800	6" rung spacing, 6" wide			50	.160	L.F.
	0850	9" wide			47	.170	L.F.
	0860	12" wide			44	.182	L.F.
	0870	18" wide			42	.190	L.F.
	0880	24" wide			40	.200	L.F.
	0890	30" wide			35	.229	L.F.
	0900	36" wide			32	.250	L.F.
	0910	9" rung spacing, 6" wide			51	.157	L.F.
	0920	9" wide			49	.163	L.F.
	0930	12" wide			47	.170	L.F.
	0940	18" wide			45	.178	L.F.
	0950	24" wide			43	.186	L.F.
	0960	30" wide			40	.200	L.F.
	0970	36" wide			37	.216	L.F.
	0980	12" rung spacing, 6" wide			53	.151	L.F.
	0990	9" wide			52	.154	L.F.
	1000	12" wide			50	.160	L.F.
	1010	18" wide			48	.167	L.F.
	1020	24" wide			47	.170	L.F.
	1030	30" wide			44	.182	L.F.
	1040	36" wide			42	.190	L.F.
	1041	18" rung spacing, 6" wide			54	.148	L.F.
	1042	9" wide			53	.151	L.F.
	1043	12" wide			51	.157	L.F.
	1044	18" wide			49	.163	L.F.
	1045	24" wide			48	.167	L.F.
	1046	30" wide			45	.178	L.F.
	1047	36" wide			43	.186	L.F.
	1051	Elbows, horiz. or vert. 9" rung spacing, 90° 12" radius, 6" wide			4.80	1.670	Ea.
	1060	9" wide			4.20	1.900	Ea.
	1070	12" wide			3.80	2.110	Ea.
	1080	18" wide			3.10	2.580	Ea.
	1090	24" wide			2.70	2.960	Ea.
	1100	30" wide			2.40	3.330	Ea.
	1110	36" wide			2.10	3.810	Ea.
	1120	90°, 24" radius, 6" wide			4.60	1.740	Ea.
	1130	9" wide			4	2.000	Ea.
	1140	12" wide			3.60	2.220	Ea.
	1150	18" wide			2.90	2.760	Ea.
	1160	24" wide			2.50	3.200	Ea.
	1170	30" wide			2.20	3.640	Ea.
	1180	36" wide			1.90	4.210	Ea.
	1190	90°, 36" radius, 6" wide			4.40	1.820	Ea.
	1200	9" wide			3.80	2.110	Ea.
	1210	12" wide			3.40	2.350	Ea.
	1220	18" wide			2.70	2.960	Ea.
	1230	24" wide			2.30	3.480	Ea.
	1240	30" wide			2	4.000	Ea.
	1250	36" wide	↓	↓	1.70	4.710	Ea.

		160 100 Cable Trays	CREW	MAKEUP	DAILY OUTPUT	MAN-HOURS	UNIT
105	1261	Cable tray elbows, 45°, 12" radius, 6" wide	1 Elec	1 Electrician	6.60	1.210	Ea.
	1270	9" wide			5.50	1.450	Ea.
	1280	12" wide			4.80	1.670	Ea.
	1290	18" wide			3.80	2.110	Ea.
	1300	24" wide			3.10	2.580	Ea.
	1310	30" wide			2.70	2.960	Ea.
	1320	36" wide			2.30	3.480	Ea.
	1330	45°, 24" radius, 6" wide			6.40	1.250	Ea.
	1340	9" wide			5.30	1.510	Ea.
	1350	12" wide			4.60	1.740	Ea.
	1360	18" wide			3.60	2.220	Ea.
	1370	24" wide			2.90	2.760	Ea.
	1380	30" wide			2.50	3.200	Ea.
	1390	36" wide			2.10	3.810	Ea.
	1400	45°, 36" radius, 6" wide			6.20	1.290	Ea.
	1410	9" wide			5.10	1.570	Ea.
	1420	12" wide			4.40	1.820	Ea.
	1430	18" wide			3.40	2.350	Ea.
	1440	24" wide			2.70	2.960	Ea.
	1450	30" wide			2.30	3.480	Ea.
	1460	36" wide			1.90	4.210	Ea.
	1740	Tee, horizontal, 9" rung spacing, 12" radius, 6" wide			2.50	3.200	Ea.
	1750	9" wide			2.30	3.480	Ea.
	1760	12" wide			2.20	3.640	Ea.
	1770	18" wide			2	4.000	Ea.
	1780	24" wide			1.80	4.440	Ea.
	1790	30" wide			1.70	4.710	Ea.
	1800	36" wide			1.50	5.330	Ea.
	1810	24" radius, 6" wide			2.30	3.480	Ea.
	1820	9" wide			2.10	3.810	Ea.
	1830	12" wide			2	4.000	Ea.
	1840	18" wide			1.80	4.440	Ea.
	1850	24" wide			1.60	5.000	Ea.
	1860	30" wide			1.50	5.330	Ea.
	1870	36" wide			1.30	6.150	Ea.
	1880	36" radius, 6" wide			2.10	3.810	Ea.
	1890	9" wide			1.90	4.210	Ea.
	1900	12" wide			1.80	4.440	Ea.
	1910	18" wide			1.60	5.000	Ea.
	1920	24" wide			1.40	5.710	Ea.
	1930	30" wide			1.30	6.150	Ea.
	1940	36" wide			1.10	7.270	Ea.
	1980	Tee, vertical, 9" rung spacing 12" radius, 6" wide			2.70	2.960	Ea.
	1990	9" wide			2.60	3.080	Ea.
	2000	12" wide			2.50	3.200	Ea.
	2010	18" wide			2.30	3.480	Ea.
	2020	24" wide			2.20	3.640	Ea.
	2030	30" wide			2	4.000	Ea.
	2040	36" wide			1.80	4.440	Ea.
	2050	24" radius, 6" wide			2.50	3.200	Ea.
	2060	9" wide			2.40	3.330	Ea.
	2070	12" wide			2.30	3.480	Ea.
	2080	18" wide			2.10	3.810	Ea.
	2090	24" wide			2	4.000	Ea.
	2100	30" wide			1.80	4.440	Ea.
	2110	36" wide			1.60	5.000	Ea.
	2120	36" radius, 6" wide			2.30	3.480	Ea.
	2130	9" wide	↓	↓	2.20	3.640	Ea.

160 100	Cable Trays	CREW	MAKEUP	DAILY OUTPUT	MAN-HOURS	UNIT
105	2141	Cable tray, tee, vertical, 12" wide	1 Elec	1 Electrician	2.10	3.810	Ea.
	2150	18" wide			1.90	4.210	Ea.
	2160	24" wide			1.80	4.440	Ea.
	2170	30" wide			1.60	5.000	Ea.
	2180	36" wide			1.40	5.710	Ea.
	2220	Cross, horizontal, 9" rung spacing, 12" radius, 6" wide			2	4.000	Ea.
	2230	9" wide			1.90	4.210	Ea.
	2240	12" wide			1.80	4.440	Ea.
	2250	18" wide			1.70	4.710	Ea.
	2260	24" wide			1.50	5.330	Ea.
	2270	30" wide			1.40	5.710	Ea.
	2280	36" wide			1.30	6.150	Ea.
	2290	24" radius, 6" wide			1.80	4.440	Ea.
	2300	9" wide			1.70	4.710	Ea.
	2310	12" wide			1.60	5.000	Ea.
	2320	18" wide			1.50	5.330	Ea.
	2330	24" wide			1.30	6.150	Ea.
	2340	30" wide			1.20	6.670	Ea.
	2350	36" wide			1.10	7.270	Ea.
	2360	36" radius, 6" wide			1.60	5.000	Ea.
	2370	9" wide			1.50	5.330	Ea.
	2380	12" wide			1.40	5.710	Ea.
	2390	18" wide			1.30	6.150	Ea.
	2400	24" wide			1.10	7.270	Ea.
	2410	30" wide			1	8.000	Ea.
	2420	36" wide			.90	8.890	Ea.
	2460	Reducer, 9" to 6" wide			6.50	1.230	Ea.
	2470	12" to 9" wide tray			6	1.330	Ea.
	2480	18" to 12" wide tray			5.20	1.540	Ea.
	2490	24" to 18" wide tray			4.50	1.780	Ea.
	2500	30" to 24" wide tray			4	2.000	Ea.
	2510	36" to 30" wide tray			3.50	2.290	Ea.
	2511	Reducer, 18" to 6" wide tray			5.20	1.540	Ea.
	2512	24" to 12" wide tray			4.50	1.780	Ea.
	2513	30" to 18" wide tray			4	2.000	Ea.
	2514	30" to 12" wide tray			4	2.000	Ea.
	2515	36" to 24" wide tray			3.50	2.290	Ea.
	2516	36" to 18" wide tray			3.50	2.290	Ea.
	2517	36" to 12" wide tray			3.50	2.290	Ea.
	2520	Dropout or end plate, 6" wide			16	.500	Ea.
	2530	9" wide			14	.571	Ea.
	2540	12" wide			13	.615	Ea.
	2550	18" wide			11	.727	Ea.
	2560	24" wide			10	.800	Ea.
	2570	30" wide			9	.889	Ea.
	2580	36" wide			8	1.000	Ea.
	2590	Tray connector			24	.333	Ea.
	3200	Aluminum tray, 4" deep, 6" rung spacing, 6" wide			67	.119	L.F.
	3210	9" wide			64	.125	L.F.
	3220	12" wide			62	.129	L.F.
	3230	18" wide			57	.140	L.F.
	3240	24" wide			53	.151	L.F.
	3250	30" wide			50	.160	L.F.
	3260	36" wide			47	.170	L.F.
	3270	9" rung spacing, 6" wide			70	.114	L.F.
	3280	9" wide			67	.119	L.F.
	3290	12" wide			65	.123	L.F.
	3300	18" wide	↓	↓	61	.131	L.F.

		160 100 | Cable Trays	CREW	MAKEUP	DAILY OUTPUT	MAN-HOURS	UNIT
105	3311	Cable tray, alum., 9" rung spacing, 24" wide	1 Elec	1 Electrician	58	.138	L.F.
	3320	30" wide			54	.148	L.F.
	3330	36" wide			50	.160	L.F.
	3340	12" rung spacing, 6" wide			73	.110	L.F.
	3350	9" wide			70	.114	L.F.
	3360	12" wide			67	.119	L.F.
	3370	18" wide			64	.125	L.F.
	3380	24" wide			62	.129	L.F.
	3390	30" wide			57	.140	L.F.
	3400	36" wide			53	.151	L.F.
	3401	18" rung, spacing, 6" wide			75	.107	L.F.
	3402	9" wide tray			72	.111	L.F.
	3403	12" wide tray			70	.114	L.F.
	3404	18" wide tray			67	.119	L.F.
	3405	24" wide tray			65	.123	L.F.
	3406	30" wide tray			60	.133	L.F.
	3407	36" wide tray			55	.145	L.F.
	3411	Elbows, horiz. or vert., 9" rung spacing, 90°, 12" radius, 6" wide			4.80	1.670	Ea.
	3420	9" wide			4.20	1.900	Ea.
	3430	12" wide			3.80	2.110	Ea.
	3440	18" wide			3.10	2.580	Ea.
	3450	24" wide			2.70	2.960	Ea.
	3460	30" wide			2.40	3.330	Ea.
	3470	36" wide			2.10	3.810	Ea.
	3480	90°, 24" radius, 6" wide			4.60	1.740	Ea.
	3490	9" wide			4	2.000	Ea.
	3500	12" wide			3.60	2.220	Ea.
	3510	18" wide			2.90	2.760	Ea.
	3520	24" wide			2.50	3.200	Ea.
	3530	30" wide			2.20	3.640	Ea.
	3540	36" wide			1.90	4.210	Ea.
	3550	90°, 36" radius, 6" wide			4.40	1.820	Ea.
	3560	9" wide			3.80	2.110	Ea.
	3570	12" wide			3.40	2.350	Ea.
	3580	18" wide			2.70	2.960	Ea.
	3590	24" wide			2.30	3.480	Ea.
	3600	30" wide			2	4.000	Ea.
	3610	36" wide			1.70	4.710	Ea.
	3620	45°, 12" radius, 6" wide			6.60	1.210	Ea.
	3630	9" wide			5.50	1.450	Ea.
	3640	12" wide			4.80	1.670	Ea.
	3650	18" wide			3.80	2.110	Ea.
	3660	24" wide			3.10	2.580	Ea.
	3670	30" wide			2.70	2.960	Ea.
	3680	36" wide			2.30	3.480	Ea.
	3690	45°, 24" radius, 6" wide			6.40	1.250	Ea.
	3700	9" wide			5.30	1.510	Ea.
	3710	12" wide			4.60	1.740	Ea.
	3720	18" wide			3.60	2.220	Ea.
	3730	24" wide			2.90	2.760	Ea.
	3740	30" wide			2.50	3.200	Ea.
	3750	36" wide			2.10	3.810	Ea.
	3760	45°, 36" radius, 6" wide			6.20	1.290	Ea.
	3770	9" wide			5.10	1.570	Ea.
	3780	12" wide			4.40	1.820	Ea.
	3790	18" wide			3.40	2.350	Ea.
	3800	24" wide			2.70	2.960	Ea.
	3810	30" wide	↓	↓	2.30	3.480	Ea.

		160 100	Cable Trays	CREW	MAKEUP	DAILY OUTPUT	MAN-HOURS	UNIT
105	3821	Cable tray, alum., elbows, 45°, 36" radius, 36" wide	1 Elec	1 Electrician	1.90	4.210	Ea.
	4100	Tee, horizontal, 9" rung spacing, 12" radius, 6" wide			2.50	3.200	Ea.
	4110	9" wide			2.30	3.480	Ea.
	4120	12" wide			2.20	3.640	Ea.
	4130	18" wide			2.10	3.810	Ea.
	4140	24" wide			2	4.000	Ea.
	4150	30" wide			1.80	4.440	Ea.
	4160	36" wide			1.70	4.710	Ea.
	4170	24" radius, 6" wide			2.30	3.480	Ea.
	4180	9" wide			2.10	3.810	Ea.
	4190	12" wide			2	4.000	Ea.
	4200	18" wide			1.90	4.210	Ea.
	4210	24" wide			1.80	4.440	Ea.
	4220	30" wide			1.60	5.000	Ea.
	4230	36" wide			1.50	5.330	Ea.
	4240	36" radius, 6" wide			2.10	3.810	Ea.
	4250	9" wide			1.90	4.210	Ea.
	4260	12" wide			1.80	4.440	Ea.
	4270	18" wide			1.70	4.710	Ea.
	4280	24" wide			1.60	5.000	Ea.
	4290	30" wide			1.40	5.710	Ea.
	4300	36" wide			1.30	6.150	Ea.
	4310	Tee, vertical, 9" rung spacing, 12" radius, 6" wide			2.70	2.960	Ea.
	4320	9" wide			2.60	3.080	Ea.
	4330	12" wide			2.50	3.200	Ea.
	4340	18" wide			2.30	3.480	Ea.
	4350	24" wide			2.20	3.640	Ea.
	4360	30" wide			2.10	3.810	Ea.
	4370	36" wide			2	4.000	Ea.
	4380	24" radius, 6" wide			2.50	3.200	Ea.
	4390	9" wide			2.40	3.330	Ea.
	4400	12" wide			2.30	3.480	Ea.
	4410	18" wide			2.10	3.810	Ea.
	4420	24" wide			2	4.000	Ea.
	4430	30" wide			1.90	4.210	Ea.
	4440	36" wide			1.80	4.440	Ea.
	4450	36" radius, 6" wide			2.30	3.480	Ea.
	4460	9" wide			2.20	3.640	Ea.
	4470	12" wide			2.10	3.810	Ea.
	4480	18" wide			1.90	4.210	Ea.
	4490	24" wide			1.80	4.440	Ea.
	4500	30" wide			1.70	4.710	Ea.
	4510	36" wide			1.60	5.000	Ea.
	4550	Cross, horizontal, 9" rung spacing, 12" radius, 6" wide			2.20	3.640	
	4560	9" wide			2.10	3.810	Ea.
	4570	12" wide			2	4.000	Ea.
	4580	18" wide			1.80	4.440	Ea.
	4590	24" wide			1.70	4.710	Ea.
	4600	30" wide			1.50	5.330	Ea.
	4610	36" wide			1.40	5.710	Ea.
	4620	24" radius, 6" wide			2	4.000	Ea.
	4630	9" wide			1.90	4.210	Ea.
	4640	12" wide			1.80	4.440	Ea.
	4650	18" wide			1.60	5.000	Ea.
	4660	24" wide			1.50	5.330	Ea.
	4670	30" wide			1.30	6.150	Ea.
	4680	36" wide			1.20	6.670	Ea.
	4690	36" radius, 6" wide			1.80	4.440	Ea.

160 100 | Cable Trays

		Description	CREW	MAKEUP	DAILY OUTPUT	MAN-HOURS	UNIT
105	4701	Cable tray, alum., cross, horiz., 36" radius, 9" wide	1 Elec	1 Electrician	1.70	4.710	Ea.
	4710	12" wide			1.60	5.000	Ea.
	4720	18" wide			1.40	5.710	Ea.
	4730	24" wide			1.30	6.150	Ea.
	4740	30" wide			1.10	7.270	Ea.
	4750	36" wide			1	8.000	Ea.
	4790	Reducer, 9" to 6" wide			8	1.000	Ea.
	4800	12" to 9" wide tray			7	1.140	Ea.
	4810	18" to 12" wide tray			6.20	1.290	Ea.
	4820	24" to 18" wide tray			5.30	1.510	Ea.
	4830	30" to 24" wide tray			4.60	1.740	Ea.
	4840	36" to 30" wide tray			4	2.000	Ea.
	4841	Reducer, 18" to 6" wide tray			6.20	1.290	Ea.
	4842	24" to 12" wide tray			5.30	1.510	Ea.
	4843	30" to 18" wide tray			4.60	1.740	Ea.
	4844	30" to 12" wide tray			4.60	1.740	Ea.
	4845	36" to 24" wide tray			4	2.000	Ea.
	4846	36" to 18" wide tray			4	2.000	Ea.
	4847	36" to 12" wide tray			4	2.000	Ea.
	4850	Dropout or end plate, 6" wide			16	.500	Ea.
	4860	9" wide tray			14	.571	Ea.
	4870	12" wide tray			13	.615	Ea.
	4880	18" wide tray			11	.727	Ea.
	4890	24" wide tray			10	.800	Ea.
	4900	30" wide tray			9	.889	Ea.
	4910	36" wide tray			8	1.000	Ea.
	4920	Tray connector			24	.333	Ea.
	9200	Splice plate			48	.167	Pr.
	9210	Expansion joint			48	.167	Pr.
	9220	Horizontal hinged			48	.167	Pr.
	9230	Vertical hinged			48	.167	Pr.
	9240	Ladder hanger, vertical			28	.286	Ea.
	9250	Ladder to channel connector			24	.333	Ea.
	9260	Ladder to box connector 30" wide			19	.421	Ea.
	9270	24" wide			20	.400	Ea.
	9280	18" wide			21	.381	Ea.
	9290	12" wide			22	.364	Ea.
	9300	9" wide			23	.348	Ea.
	9310	6" wide			24	.333	Ea.
	9320	Ladder floor flange			24	.333	Ea.
	9330	Cable roller for tray 30" wide			10	.800	Ea.
	9340	24" wide			11	.727	Ea.
	9350	18" wide			12	.667	Ea.
	9360	12" wide			13	.615	Ea.
	9370	9" wide			14	.571	Ea.
	9380	6" wide			15	.533	Ea.
	9390	Pulley, single wheel			12	.667	Ea.
	9400	Triple wheel			10	.800	Ea.
	9440	Nylon cable tie, 14" long			80	.100	Ea.
	9450	Ladder, hold down clamp			60	.133	Ea.
	9460	Cable clamp			60	.133	Ea.
	9470	Wall bracket for 30" wide tray			19	.421	Ea.
	9480	24" wide tray			20	.400	Ea.
	9490	18" wide tray			21	.381	Ea.
	9500	12" wide tray			22	.364	Ea.
	9510	9" wide tray			23	.348	Ea.
	9520	6" wide tray	▼	▼	24	.333	Ea.

160 100	Cable Trays	CREW	MAKEUP	DAILY OUTPUT	MAN-HOURS	UNIT
110	110	**CABLE TRAY** Solid bottom, w/ftngs & supports, 3" dp, to 15' high					
	0220	Galvanized steel, tray, 6" wide	1 Elec	1 Electrician	60	.133	L.F.
	0240	12" wide			50	.160	L.F.
	0260	18" wide			35	.229	L.F.
	0280	24" wide			30	.267	L.F.
	0300	30" wide			25	.320	L.F.
	0320	36" wide			22	.364	L.F.
	0341	Elbows, horiz. or vert., 90°, 12" radius, 6" wide			4.80	1.670	Ea.
	0360	12" wide			3.40	2.350	Ea.
	0370	18" wide			2.70	2.960	Ea.
	0380	24" wide			2.20	3.640	Ea.
	0390	30" wide			1.90	4.210	Ea.
	0400	36" wide			1.70	4.710	Ea.
	0420	24" radius, 6" wide			4.60	1.740	Ea.
	0440	12" wide			3.20	2.500	Ea.
	0450	18" wide			2.50	3.200	Ea.
	0460	24" wide			2	4.000	Ea.
	0470	30" wide			1.70	4.710	Ea.
	0480	36" wide			1.50	5.330	Ea.
	0500	36" radius, 6" wide			4.40	1.820	Ea.
	0520	12" wide			3	2.670	Ea.
	0530	18" wide			2.30	3.480	Ea.
	0540	24" wide			1.80	4.440	Ea.
	0550	30" wide			1.50	5.330	Ea.
	0560	36" wide			1.30	6.150	Ea.
	0840	Tee, horizontal, 12" radius, 6" wide			2.50	3.200	Ea.
	0860	12" wide			2	4.000	Ea.
	0870	18" wide			1.70	4.710	Ea.
	0880	24" wide			1.40	5.710	Ea.
	0890	30" wide			1.30	6.150	Ea.
	0900	36" wide			1.10	7.270	Ea.
	0940	24" radius, 6" wide			2.30	3.480	Ea.
	0960	12" wide			1.80	4.440	Ea.
	0970	18" wide			1.50	5.330	Ea.
	0980	24" wide			1.20	6.670	Ea.
	0990	30" wide			1.10	7.270	Ea.
	1000	36" wide			.90	8.890	Ea.
	1020	36" radius, 6" wide			2.10	3.810	Ea.
	1040	12" wide			1.60	5.000	Ea.
	1050	18" wide			1.30	6.150	Ea.
	1060	24" wide			1.10	7.270	Ea.
	1070	30" wide			1	8.000	Ea.
	1080	36" wide			.80	10.000	Ea.
	1100	Tee, vertical, 12" radius, 6" wide			2.50	3.200	Ea.
	1120	12" wide			2	4.000	Ea.
	1130	18" wide			1.80	4.440	Ea.
	1140	24" wide			1.70	4.710	Ea.
	1150	30" wide			1.50	5.330	Ea.
	1160	36" wide			1.30	6.150	Ea.
	1180	24" radius, 6" wide			2.30	3.480	Ea.
	1200	12" wide			1.80	4.440	Ea.
	1210	18" wide			1.60	5.000	Ea.
	1220	24" wide			1.50	5.330	Ea.
	1230	30" wide			1.30	6.150	Ea.
	1240	36" wide			1.10	7.270	Ea.
	1260	36" radius, 6" wide			2.10	3.810	Ea.
	1280	12" wide			1.60	5.000	Ea.
	1290	18" wide	↓	↓	1.40	5.710	Ea.

160 100	Cable Trays	CREW	MAKEUP	DAILY OUTPUT	MAN-HOURS	UNIT
110 1301	Cable tray, galv. steel, tee, vert., 36" radius, 24" wide	1 Elec	1 Electrician	1.30	6.150	Ea.
1310	30" wide			1.10	7.270	Ea.
1320	36" wide			1	8.000	Ea.
1340	Cross, horizontal, 12" radius, 6" wide			2	4.000	Ea.
1360	12" wide			1.70	4.710	Ea.
1370	18" wide			1.40	5.710	Ea.
1380	24" wide			1.20	6.670	Ea.
1390	30" wide			1	8.000	Ea.
1400	36" wide			.90	8.890	Ea.
1420	24" radius, 6" wide			1.80	4.440	Ea.
1440	12" wide			1.50	5.330	Ea.
1450	18" wide			1.20	6.670	Ea.
1460	24" wide			1	8.000	Ea.
1470	30" wide			.90	8.890	Ea.
1480	36" wide			.80	10.000	Ea.
1500	36" radius, 6" wide			1.60	5.000	Ea.
1520	12" wide			1.30	6.150	Ea.
1530	18" wide			1	8.000	Ea.
1540	24" wide			.90	8.890	Ea.
1550	30" wide			.80	10.000	Ea.
1560	36" wide			.70	11.430	Ea.
1580	Drop out or end plate, 6" wide			16	.500	Ea.
1600	12" wide			13	.615	Ea.
1610	18" wide			11	.727	Ea.
1620	24" wide			10	.800	Ea.
1630	30" wide			9	.889	Ea.
1640	36" wide			8	1.000	Ea.
1660	Reducer, 12" to 6" wide			6	1.330	Ea.
1680	18" to 12" wide			5.30	1.510	Ea.
1700	18" to 6" wide			5.30	1.510	Ea.
1720	24" to 18" wide			4.60	1.740	Ea.
1740	24" to 12" wide			4.60	1.740	Ea.
1760	30" to 24" wide			4	2.000	Ea.
1780	30" to 18" wide			4	2.000	Ea.
1800	30" to 12" wide			4	2.000	Ea.
1820	36" to 30" wide			3.60	2.220	Ea.
1840	36" to 24" wide			3.60	2.220	Ea.
1860	36" to 18" wide			3.60	2.220	Ea.
1880	36" to 12" wide			3.60	2.220	Ea.
2000	Aluminum, tray, 6" wide			75	.107	L.F.
2020	12" wide			65	.123	L.F.
2030	18" wide			50	.160	L.F.
2040	24" wide			45	.178	L.F.
2050	30" wide			35	.229	L.F.
2060	36" wide			32	.250	L.F.
2081	Elbows, horiz. or vert., 90°, 12" radius, 6" wide			4.80	1.670	Ea.
2100	12" wide			3.80	2.110	Ea.
2110	18" wide			3.40	2.350	Ea.
2120	24" wide			2.90	2.760	Ea.
2130	30" wide			2.50	3.200	Ea.
2140	36" wide			2.20	3.640	Ea.
2160	24" radius, 6" wide			4.60	1.740	Ea.
2180	12" wide			3.60	2.220	Ea.
2190	18" wide			3.20	2.500	Ea.
2200	24" wide			2.70	2.960	Ea.
2210	30" wide			2.30	3.480	Ea.
2220	36" wide			2	4.000	Ea.
2240	36" radius, 6" wide	▼	▼	4.40	1.820	Ea.

160 100 | Cable Trays

		CREW	MAKEUP	DAILY OUTPUT	MAN-HOURS	UNIT
110	2261	Cable tray, alum., elbow, 90°, 36" radius, 12" wide	1 Elec	1 Electrician	3.40	2.350	Ea.
	2270	18" wide			3	2.670	Ea.
	2280	24" wide			2.50	3.200	Ea.
	2290	30" wide			2.10	3.810	Ea.
	2300	36" wide			1.80	4.440	Ea.
	2560	Tee, horizontal, 12" radius, 6" wide			2.50	3.200	Ea.
	2580	12" wide			2.20	3.640	Ea.
	2590	18" wide			2	4.000	Ea.
	2600	24" wide			1.80	4.440	Ea.
	2610	30" wide			1.50	5.330	Ea.
	2620	36" wide			1.20	6.670	Ea.
	2640	24" radius, 6" wide			2.30	3.480	Ea.
	2660	12" wide			2	4.000	Ea.
	2670	18" wide			1.80	4.440	Ea.
	2680	24" wide			1.50	5.330	Ea.
	2690	30" wide			1.20	6.670	Ea.
	2700	36" wide			1.10	7.270	Ea.
	2720	36" radius, 6" wide			2.10	3.810	Ea.
	2740	12" wide			1.80	4.440	Ea.
	2750	18" wide			1.60	5.000	Ea.
	2760	24" wide			1.30	6.150	Ea.
	2770	30" wide			1	8.000	Ea.
	2780	36" wide			.90	8.890	Ea.
	2800	Tee, vertical, 12" radius, 6" wide			2.50	3.200	Ea.
	2820	12" wide			2.20	3.640	Ea.
	2830	18" wide			2.10	3.810	Ea.
	2840	24" wide			2	4.000	Ea.
	2850	30" wide			1.80	4.440	Ea.
	2860	36" wide			1.50	5.330	Ea.
	2880	24" radius, 6" wide			2.30	3.480	Ea.
	2900	12" wide			2	4.000	Ea.
	2910	18" wide			1.90	4.210	Ea.
	2920	24" wide			1.80	4.440	Ea.
	2930	30" wide			1.60	5.000	Ea.
	2940	36" wide			1.30	6.150	Ea.
	2960	36" radius, 6" wide			2.10	3.810	Ea.
	2980	12" wide			1.70	4.710	Ea.
	2990	18" wide			1.70	4.710	Ea.
	3000	24" wide			1.60	5.000	Ea.
	3010	30" wide			1.40	5.710	Ea.
	3020	36" wide			1.10	7.270	Ea.
	3040	Cross, horizontal, 12" radius, 6" wide			2.20	3.640	Ea.
	3060	12" wide			2	4.000	Ea.
	3070	18" wide			1.70	4.710	Ea.
	3080	24" wide			1.40	5.710	Ea.
	3090	30" wide			1.30	6.150	Ea.
	3100	36" wide			1.10	7.270	Ea.
	3120	24" radius, 6" wide			2	4.000	Ea.
	3140	12" wide			1.80	4.440	Ea.
	3150	18" wide			1.50	5.330	Ea.
	3160	24" wide			1.20	6.670	Ea.
	3170	30" wide			1.10	7.270	Ea.
	3180	36" wide			.90	8.890	Ea.
	3200	36" radius, 6" wide			1.80	4.440	Ea.
	3220	12" wide			1.60	5.000	Ea.
	3230	18" wide			1.30	6.150	Ea.
	3240	24" wide			1	8.000	Ea.
	3250	30" wide	↓	↓	.90	8.890	Ea.

160 100 | Cable Trays

		Description	CREW	MAKEUP	DAILY OUTPUT	MAN-HOURS	UNIT
110	3261	Cable tray, alum., cross, horiz., 36" radius, 36" wide	1 Elec	1 Electrician	.80	10.000	Ea.
	3280	Dropout, or end plate 6" wide			16	.500	Ea.
	3300	12" wide			13	.615	Ea.
	3310	18" wide			11	.727	Ea.
	3320	24" wide			10	.800	Ea.
	3330	30" wide			9	.889	Ea.
	3340	36" wide			8	1.000	Ea.
	3380	Reducer, 12" to 6" wide			7	1.140	Ea.
	3400	18" to 12" wide			6	1.330	Ea.
	3420	18" to 6" wide			6	1.330	Ea.
	3440	24" to 18" wide			5.30	1.510	Ea.
	3460	24" to 12" wide			5.30	1.510	Ea.
	3480	30" to 24" wide			4.60	1.740	Ea.
	3500	30" to 18" wide			4.60	1.740	Ea.
	3520	30" to 12" wide			4.60	1.740	Ea.
	3540	36" to 30" wide			4	2.000	Ea.
	3560	36" to 24" wide			4	2.000	Ea.
	3580	36" to 18" wide			4	2.000	Ea.
	3600	36" to 12" wide	↓	↓	4	2.000	Ea.
120		**CABLE TRAY** Trough, vented w/ftngs & supports, 6" dp, to 15' hi					
	0200	Galvanized steel, tray, 6" wide	1 Elec	1 Electrician	45	.178	L.F.
	0240	12" wide			40	.200	L.F.
	0260	18" wide			35	.229	L.F.
	0280	24" wide			30	.267	L.F.
	0300	30" wide			25	.320	L.F.
	0320	36" wide			20	.400	L.F.
	0341	Elbow, vert. or horiz., 90°, 12" radius, 6" wide			3.80	2.110	Ea.
	0360	12" wide			2.80	2.860	Ea.
	0370	18" wide			2.20	3.640	Ea.
	0380	24" wide			1.80	4.440	Ea.
	0390	30" wide			1.60	5.000	Ea.
	0400	36" wide			1.40	5.710	Ea.
	0420	24" radius, 6" wide			3.60	2.220	Ea.
	0440	12" wide			2.60	3.080	Ea.
	0450	18" wide			2	4.000	Ea.
	0460	24" wide			1.60	5.000	Ea.
	0470	30" wide			1.40	5.710	Ea.
	0480	36" wide			1.20	6.670	Ea.
	0500	36" radius, 6" wide			3.40	2.350	Ea.
	0520	12" wide			2.40	3.330	Ea.
	0530	18" wide			1.80	4.440	Ea.
	0540	24" wide			1.40	5.710	Ea.
	0550	30" wide			1.20	6.670	Ea.
	0560	36" wide			1	8.000	Ea.
	0820	Tee, horizontal, 12" radius, 6" wide			2	4.000	Ea.
	0840	12" wide			1.60	5.000	Ea.
	0850	18" wide			1.40	5.710	Ea.
	0860	24" wide			1.20	6.670	Ea.
	0870	30" wide			1.10	7.270	Ea.
	0880	36" wide			1	8.000	Ea.
	0900	24" radius, 6" wide			1.80	4.440	Ea.
	0920	12" wide			1.40	5.710	Ea.
	0930	18" wide			1.20	6.670	Ea.
	0940	24" wide			1	8.000	Ea.
	0950	30" wide			.90	8.890	Ea.
	0960	36" wide			.80	10.000	Ea.
	0980	36" radius, 6" wide			1.60	5.000	Ea.
	1000	12" wide	↓	↓	1.20	6.670	Ea.

160 100	Cable Trays	CREW	MAKEUP		DAILY OUTPUT	MAN-HOURS	UNIT
120 1011	Cable tray trough, tee, horiz., 36" radius, 18" wide	1 Elec	1 Electrician		1	8.000	Ea.
1020	24" wide				.80	10.000	Ea.
1030	30" wide				.70	11.430	Ea.
1040	36" wide				.60	13.330	Ea.
1060	Tee, vertical, 12" radius, 6" wide				2	4.000	Ea.
1080	12" wide				1.60	5.000	Ea.
1090	18" wide				1.50	5.330	Ea.
1100	24" wide				1.40	5.710	Ea.
1110	30" wide				1.30	6.150	Ea.
1120	36" wide				1.10	7.270	Ea.
1140	24" radius, 6" wide				1.80	4.440	Ea.
1160	12" wide				1.40	5.710	Ea.
1170	18" wide				1.30	6.150	Ea.
1180	24" wide				1.20	6.670	Ea.
1190	30" wide				1.10	7.270	Ea.
1200	36" wide				.90	8.890	Ea.
1220	36" radius, 6" wide				1.60	5.000	Ea.
1240	12" wide				1.20	6.670	Ea.
1250	18" wide				1.10	7.270	Ea.
1260	24" wide				1	8.000	Ea.
1270	30" wide				.90	8.890	Ea.
1280	36" wide				.70	11.430	Ea.
1300	Cross, horizontal, 12" radius, 6" wide				1.60	5.000	Ea.
1320	12" wide				1.40	5.710	Ea.
1330	18" wide				1.20	6.670	Ea.
1340	24" wide				1	8.000	Ea.
1350	30" wide				.90	8.890	Ea.
1360	36" wide				.80	10.000	Ea.
1380	24" radius, 6" wide				1.40	5.710	Ea.
1400	12" wide				1.20	6.670	Ea.
1410	18" wide				1	8.000	Ea.
1420	24" wide				.80	10.000	Ea.
1430	30" wide				.70	11.430	Ea.
1440	36" wide				.60	13.330	Ea.
1460	36" radius, 6" wide				1.20	6.670	Ea.
1480	12" wide				1	8.000	Ea.
1490	18" wide				.80	10.000	Ea.
1500	24" wide				.60	13.330	Ea.
1510	30" wide				.50	16.000	Ea.
1520	36" wide				.40	20.000	Ea.
1540	Dropout or end plate, 6" wide				13	.615	Ea.
1560	12" wide				11	.727	Ea.
1580	18" wide				10	.800	Ea.
1600	24" wide				9	.889	Ea.
1620	30" wide				8	1.000	Ea.
1640	36" wide				6.70	1.190	Ea.
1660	Reducer, 12" to 6" wide				4.70	1.700	Ea.
1680	18" to 12" wide				4.20	1.900	Ea.
1700	18" to 6" wide				4.20	1.900	Ea.
1720	24" to 18" wide				3.60	2.220	Ea.
1740	24" to 12" wide				3.60	2.220	Ea.
1760	30" to 24" wide				3.20	2.500	Ea.
1780	30" to 18" wide				3.20	2.500	Ea.
1800	30" to 12" wide				3.20	2.500	Ea.
1820	36" to 30" wide				2.90	2.760	Ea.
1840	36" to 24" wide				2.90	2.760	Ea.
1860	36" to 18" wide				2.90	2.760	Ea.
1880	36" to 12" wide	↓	↓		2.90	2.760	Ea.

160 100	Cable Trays	CREW	MAKEUP	DAILY OUTPUT	MAN-HOURS	UNIT
120 2001	Cable tray trough, aluminum, tray, 6" wide	1 Elec	1 Electrician	60	.133	L.F.
2010	9" wide			55	.145	L.F.
2020	12" wide			50	.160	L.F.
2030	18" wide			45	.178	L.F.
2040	24" wide			40	.200	L.F.
2050	30" wide			35	.229	L.F.
2060	36" wide			30	.267	L.F.
2081	Elbow, vert. or horiz., 90°, 12" radius, 6" wide			3.80	2.110	Ea.
2090	9" wide			3.50	2.290	Ea.
2100	12" wide			3.10	2.580	Ea.
2110	18" wide			2.80	2.860	Ea.
2120	24" wide			2.30	3.480	Ea.
2130	30" wide			2	4.000	Ea.
2140	36" wide			1.80	4.440	Ea.
2160	24" radius, 6" wide			3.60	2.220	Ea.
2180	12" wide			2.90	2.760	Ea.
2190	18" wide			2.60	3.080	Ea.
2200	24" wide			2.10	3.810	Ea.
2210	30" wide			1.80	4.440	Ea.
2220	36" wide			1.60	5.000	Ea.
2240	36" radius, 6" wide			3.40	2.350	Ea.
2260	12" wide			2.70	2.960	Ea.
2270	18" wide			2.40	3.330	Ea.
2280	24" wide			1.90	4.210	Ea.
2290	30" wide			1.70	4.710	Ea.
2300	36" wide			1.40	5.710	Ea.
2560	Tee, horizontal, 12" radius, 6" wide			2	4.000	Ea.
2570	9" wide			1.90	4.210	Ea.
2580	12" wide			1.80	4.440	Ea.
2590	18" wide			1.60	5.000	Ea.
2600	24" wide			1.40	5.710	Ea.
2610	30" wide			1.20	6.670	Ea.
2620	36" wide			1.10	7.270	Ea.
2640	24" radius, 6" wide			1.80	4.440	Ea.
2660	12" wide			1.60	5.000	Ea.
2670	18" wide			1.40	5.710	Ea.
2680	24" wide			1.20	6.670	Ea.
2690	30" wide			1	8.000	Ea.
2700	36" wide			.90	8.890	Ea.
2720	36" radius, 6" wide			1.60	5.000	Ea.
2740	12" wide			1.40	5.710	Ea.
2750	18" wide			1.20	6.670	Ea.
2760	24" wide			1	8.000	Ea.
2770	30" wide			.80	10.000	Ea.
2780	36" wide			.70	11.430	Ea.
2800	Tee, vertical, 12" radius, 6" wide			2	4.000	Ea.
2810	9" wide			1.90	4.210	Ea.
2820	12" wide			1.80	4.440	Ea.
2830	18" wide			1.70	4.710	Ea.
2840	24" wide			1.60	5.000	Ea.
2850	30" wide			1.50	5.330	Ea.
2860	36" wide			1.30	6.150	Ea.
2880	24" radius, 6" wide			1.80	4.440	Ea.
2900	12" wide			1.60	5.000	Ea.
2910	18" wide			1.50	5.330	Ea.
2920	24" wide			1.40	5.710	Ea.
2930	30" wide			1.30	6.150	Ea.
2940	36" wide	↓	↓	1.10	7.270	Ea.

		160 100	Cable Trays	CREW	MAKEUP	DAILY OUTPUT	MAN-HOURS	UNIT
120	2961	Cable tray trough, tee, vert., 36" radius, 6" wide	1 Elec	1 Electrician	1.60	5.000	Ea.
	2980	12" wide			1.40	5.710	Ea.
	2990	18" wide			1.30	6.150	Ea.
	3000	24" wide			1.20	6.670	Ea.
	3010	30" wide			1.10	7.270	Ea.
	3020	36" wide			.90	8.890	Ea.
	3040	Cross, horizontal, 12" radius, 6" wide			1.80	4.440	Ea.
	3050	9" wide			1.70	4.710	Ea.
	3060	12" wide			1.60	5.000	Ea.
	3070	18" wide			1.40	5.710	Ea.
	3080	24" wide			1.20	6.670	Ea.
	3090	30" wide			1.10	7.270	Ea.
	3100	36" wide			.90	8.890	Ea.
	3120	24" radius, 6" wide			1.60	5.000	Ea.
	3140	12" wide			1.40	5.710	Ea.
	3150	18" wide			1.20	6.670	Ea.
	3160	24" wide			1	8.000	Ea.
	3170	30" wide			.90	8.890	Ea.
	3180	36" wide			.70	11.430	Ea.
	3200	36" radius, 6" wide			1.40	5.710	Ea.
	3220	12" wide			1.20	6.670	Ea.
	3230	18" wide			1	8.000	Ea.
	3240	24" wide			.80	10.000	Ea.
	3250	30" wide			.70	11.430	Ea.
	3260	36" wide			.60	13.330	Ea.
	3280	Dropout or end plate, 6" wide			13	.615	Ea.
	3300	12" wide			11	.727	Ea.
	3310	18" wide			10	.800	Ea.
	3320	24" wide			9	.889	Ea.
	3330	30" wide			8	1.000	Ea.
	3340	36" wide			7	1.140	Ea.
	3370	Reducer, 9" to 6" wide			6	1.330	Ea.
	3380	12" to 6" wide			5.70	1.400	Ea.
	3390	12" to 9" wide			5.70	1.400	Ea.
	3400	18" to 12" wide			4.80	1.670	Ea.
	3420	18" to 6" wide			4.80	1.670	Ea.
	3430	18" to 9" wide			4.80	1.670	Ea.
	3440	24" to 18" wide			4.20	1.900	Ea.
	3460	24" to 12" wide			4.20	1.900	Ea.
	3470	24" to 9" wide			4.20	1.900	Ea.
	3480	30" to 24" wide			3.60	2.220	Ea.
	3490	24" to 6" wide			4.20	1.900	Ea.
	3500	30" to 18" wide			3.60	2.220	Ea.
	3520	30" to 12" wide			3.60	2.220	Ea.
	3540	36" to 30" wide			3.20	2.500	Ea.
	3560	36" to 24" wide			3.20	2.500	Ea.
	3580	36" to 18" wide			3.20	2.500	Ea.
	3600	36" to 12" wide			3.20	2.500	Ea.
	3610	Elbow, horizontal, 60°, 12" radius, 6" wide			3.90	2.050	Ea.
	3620	9" wide			3.60	2.220	Ea.
	3630	12" wide			3.20	2.500	Ea.
	3640	18" wide			2.90	2.760	Ea.
	3650	24" wide			2.40	3.330	Ea.
	3680	Elbow, horizontal, 45°, 12" radius, 6" wide			4	2.000	Ea.
	3690	9" wide			3.70	2.160	Ea.
	3700	12" wide			3.30	2.420	Ea.
	3710	18" wide			3	2.670	Ea.
	3720	24" wide	↓	↓	2.50	3.200	Ea.

160 100	Cable Trays	CREW	MAKEUP	DAILY OUTPUT	MAN-HOURS	UNIT
120 3751	Cable tray trough, elbow, horiz., 30°, 12" radius, 6" wide	1 Elec	1 Electrician	4.10	1.950	Ea.
3760	9" wide			3.80	2.110	Ea.
3770	12' wide			3.40	2.350	Ea.
3780	18" wide			3.10	2.580	Ea.
3790	24" wide			2.60	3.080	Ea.
3820	Elbow, vertical, 60°, in/outside, 12" radius, 6" wide			3.90	2.050	Ea.
3830	9" wide			3.60	2.220	Ea.
3840	12" wide			3.20	2.500	Ea.
3850	18" wide			2.90	2.760	Ea.
3860	24" wide			2.40	3.330	Ea.
3890	Elbow, vertical, 45°, in/outside, 12" radius, 6" wide			4	2.000	Ea.
3900	9" wide			3.70	2.160	Ea.
3910	12" wide			3.30	2.420	Ea.
3920	18" wide			3	2.670	Ea.
3930	24" wide			2.50	3.200	Ea.
3960	Elbow, vertical, 30°, in/outside, 12" radius, 6" wide			4.10	1.950	Ea.
3970	9" wide			3.80	2.110	Ea.
3980	12" wide			3.40	2.350	Ea.
3990	18" wide			3.10	2.580	Ea.
4000	24" wide			2.60	3.080	Ea.
4250	Reducer, left or right hand, 24" to 18" wide			4.20	1.900	Ea.
4260	24" to 12" wide			4.20	1.900	Ea.
4270	24" to 9" wide			4.20	1.900	Ea.
4280	24" to 6" wide			4.20	1.900	Ea.
4290	18" to 12" wide			4.80	1.670	Ea.
4300	18" to 9" wide			4.80	1.670	Ea.
4310	18" to 6" wide			4.80	1.670	Ea.
4320	12" to 9" wide			5.70	1.400	Ea.
4330	12" to 6" wide			5.70	1.400	Ea.
4340	9" to 6" wide			6	1.330	Ea.
4350	Splice plate			48	.167	Ea.
4360	Splice plate, expansion joint			48	.167	Ea.
4370	Splice plate, hinged, horizontal			48	.167	Ea.
4380	Vertical			48	.167	Ea.
4390	Trough, hanger, vertical			28	.286	Ea.
4400	Box connector, 24" wide			20	.400	Ea.
4410	18" wide			21	.381	Ea.
4420	12" wide			22	.364	Ea.
4430	9" wide			23	.348	Ea.
4440	6" wide			24	.333	Ea.
4450	Floor flange			24	.333	Ea.
4460	Hold down clamp			60	.133	Ea.
4520	Wall bracket for 24" wide tray			20	.400	Ea.
4530	18" wide tray			21	.381	Ea.
4540	12" wide tray			22	.364	Ea.
4550	9" wide tray			23	.348	Ea.
4560	6" wide tray			24	.333	Ea.
5000	Cable channel, aluminum, vented, 1-1/4" deep, 4" wide, straight			80	.100	L.F.
5010	Elbow, horizontal, 36" radius, 90°			5	1.600	Ea.
5020	60°			5.50	1.450	Ea.
5030	45°			6	1.330	Ea.
5040	30°			6.50	1.230	Ea.
5050	Adjustable			6	1.330	Ea.
5060	Elbow, vertical, 36" radius, 90°			5	1.600	Ea.
5070	60°			5.50	1.450	Ea.
5080	45°			6	1.330	Ea.
5090	30°			6.50	1.230	Ea.
5100	Adjustable	▼	▼	6	1.330	Ea.

160 100	Cable Trays	CREW	MAKEUP	DAILY OUTPUT	MAN-HOURS	UNIT
120 5111	Cable channel, splice plate, hinged, horizontal	1 Elec	1 Electrician	48	.167	Ea.
5120	Splice plate hinged vertical			48	.167	Ea.
5130	Hanger, vertical			28	.286	Ea.
5140	Single			28	.286	Ea.
5150	Double			20	.400	Ea.
5160	Channel to box connector			24	.333	Ea.
5170	Hold down clip			80	.100	Ea.
5180	Wall bracket, single			28	.286	Ea.
5190	Double			20	.400	Ea.
5200	Cable roller			16	.500	Ea.
5210	Splice plate	↓	↓	48	.167	Ea.
130	**CABLE TRAY COVERS AND DIVIDERS** To 15' high					
0100	Covers, ventilated galv. steel, straight, 6" wide tray size	1 Elec	1 Electrician	260	.031	L.F.
0200	9" wide tray size			230	.035	L.F.
0300	12" wide tray size			200	.040	L.F.
0400	18" wide tray size			150	.053	L.F.
0500	24" wide tray size			110	.073	L.F.
0600	30" wide tray size			90	.089	L.F.
0700	36" wide tray size			80	.100	L.F.
1000	Elbow, horizontal, 90°, 12" radius, 6" wide tray size			75	.107	Ea.
1020	9" wide tray size			64	.125	Ea.
1040	12" wide tray size			54	.148	Ea.
1060	18" wide tray size			42	.190	Ea.
1080	24" wide tray size			33	.242	Ea.
1100	30" wide tray size			30	.267	Ea.
1120	36" wide tray size			25	.320	Ea.
1160	24" radius, 6" wide tray size			68	.118	Ea.
1180	9" wide tray size			58	.138	Ea.
1200	12" wide tray size			48	.167	Ea.
1220	18" wide tray size			38	.211	Ea.
1240	24" wide tray size			30	.267	Ea.
1260	30" wide tray size			26	.308	Ea.
1280	36" wide tray size			22	.364	Ea.
1320	36" radius, 6" wide tray size			60	.133	Ea.
1340	9" wide tray size			52	.154	Ea.
1360	12" wide tray size			42	.190	Ea.
1380	18" wide tray size			36	.222	Ea.
1400	24" wide tray size			26	.308	Ea.
1420	30" wide tray size			23	.348	Ea.
1440	36" wide tray size			20	.400	Ea.
1480	Elbow, horizontal, 45°, 12" radius, 6" wide tray size			75	.107	Ea.
1500	9" wide tray size			64	.125	Ea.
1520	12" wide tray size			54	.148	Ea.
1540	18" wide tray size			44	.182	Ea.
1560	24" wide tray size			38	.211	Ea.
1580	30" wide tray size			33	.242	Ea.
1600	36" wide tray size			30	.267	Ea.
1640	24" radius, 6" wide tray size			68	.118	Ea.
1660	9" wide tray size			58	.138	Ea.
1680	12" wide tray size			48	.167	Ea.
1700	18" wide tray size			40	.200	Ea.
1720	24" wide tray size			35	.229	Ea.
1740	30" wide tray size			30	.267	Ea.
1760	36" wide tray size			26	.308	Ea.
1800	36" radius, 6" wide tray size			60	.133	Ea.
1820	9" wide tray size			52	.154	Ea.
1840	12" wide tray size			42	.190	Ea.
1860	18" wide tray size	↓	↓	38	.211	Ea.

160 100 | Cable Trays

		Cable Trays	CREW	MAKEUP	DAILY OUTPUT	MAN-HOURS	UNIT
130	1881	Cable tray cover, elbow, horiz., 45°, 36" radius, 24" wide	1 Elec	1 Electrician	31	.258	Ea.
	1900	30" wide tray size			26	.308	Ea.
	1920	36" wide tray size			24	.333	Ea.
	1960	Elbow, vertical, 90°, 12" radius, 6" wide tray size			75	.107	Ea.
	1980	9" wide tray size			64	.125	Ea.
	2000	12" wide tray size			54	.148	Ea.
	2020	18" wide tray size			44	.182	Ea.
	2040	24" wide tray size			34	.235	Ea.
	2060	30" wide tray size			30	.267	Ea.
	2080	36" wide tray size			25	.320	Ea.
	2120	24" radius, 6" wide tray size			68	.118	Ea.
	2140	9" wide tray size			58	.138	Ea.
	2160	12" wide tray size			48	.167	Ea.
	2180	18" wide tray size			40	.200	Ea.
	2200	24" wide tray size			31	.258	Ea.
	2220	30" wide tray size			26	.308	Ea.
	2240	36" wide tray size			22	.364	Ea.
	2280	36" radius, 6" wide tray size			60	.133	Ea.
	2300	9" wide tray size			52	.154	Ea.
	2320	12" wide tray size			42	.190	Ea.
	2340	18" wide tray size			38	.211	Ea.
	2350	24" wide tray size			27	.296	Ea.
	2360	30" wide tray size			23	.348	Ea.
	2370	36" wide tray size			20	.400	Ea.
	2400	Tee, horizontal, 12" radius, 6" wide tray size			46	.174	Ea.
	2410	9" wide tray size			40	.200	Ea.
	2420	12" wide tray size			34	.235	Ea.
	2430	18" wide tray size			30	.267	Ea.
	2440	24" wide tray size			26	.308	Ea.
	2460	30" wide tray size			18	.444	Ea.
	2470	36" wide tray size			15	.533	Ea.
	2500	24" radius, 6" wide tray size			44	.182	Ea.
	2510	9" wide tray size			38	.211	Ea.
	2520	12" wide tray size			32	.250	Ea.
	2530	18" wide tray size			28	.286	Ea.
	2540	24" wide tray size			24	.333	Ea.
	2560	30" wide tray size			16	.500	Ea.
	2570	36" wide tray size			13	.615	Ea.
	2600	36" radius, 6" wide tray size			42	.190	Ea.
	2610	9" wide tray size			36	.222	Ea.
	2620	12" wide tray size			30	.267	Ea.
	2630	18" wide tray size			26	.308	Ea.
	2640	24" wide tray size			22	.364	Ea.
	2660	30" wide tray size			14	.571	Ea.
	2670	36" wide tray size			11	.727	Ea.
	2700	Cross, horizontal, 12" radius, 6" wide tray size			34	.235	Ea.
	2710	9" wide tray size			32	.250	Ea.
	2720	12" wide tray size			30	.267	Ea.
	2730	18" wide tray size			26	.308	Ea.
	2740	24" wide tray size			18	.444	Ea.
	2760	30" wide tray size			15	.533	Ea.
	2770	36" wide tray size			14	.571	Ea.
	2800	24" radius, 6" wide tray size			32	.250	Ea.
	2810	9" wide tray size			30	.267	Ea.
	2820	12" wide tray size			28	.286	Ea.
	2830	18" wide tray size			24	.333	Ea.
	2840	24" wide tray size			16	.500	Ea.
	2860	30" wide tray size	↓	↓	13	.615	Ea.

160 100 | Cable Trays

		Description	CREW	MAKEUP	DAILY OUTPUT	MAN-HOURS	UNIT
130	2871	Cable tray cover, cross, horiz., 24" radius, 36" wide	1 Elec	1 Electrician	12	.667	Ea.
	2900	36" radius, 6" wide tray size			30	.267	Ea.
	2910	9" wide tray size			28	.286	Ea.
	2920	12" wide tray size			26	.308	Ea.
	2930	18" wide tray size			22	.364	Ea.
	2940	24" wide tray size			14	.571	Ea.
	2960	30" wide tray size			11	.727	Ea.
	2970	36" wide tray size			10	.800	Ea.
	3000	Reducer, 9" to 6" wide tray size			64	.125	Ea.
	3010	12" to 6" wide tray size			54	.148	Ea.
	3020	12" to 9" wide tray size			54	.148	Ea.
	3030	18" to 12" wide tray size			44	.182	Ea.
	3050	18" to 6" wide tray size			44	.182	Ea.
	3060	24" to 18" wide tray size			40	.200	Ea.
	3070	24" to 12" wide tray size			40	.200	Ea.
	3090	30" to 24" wide tray size			35	.229	Ea.
	3100	30" to 18" wide tray size			35	.229	Ea.
	3110	30" to 12" wide tray size			35	.229	Ea.
	3140	36" to 30" wide tray size			32	.250	Ea.
	3150	36" to 24" wide tray size			32	.250	Ea.
	3160	36" to 18" wide tray size			32	.250	Ea.
	3170	36" to 12" wide tray size			32	.250	Ea.
	3250	Covers, aluminum, straight 6" wide tray size			260	.031	L.F.
	3270	9" wide tray size			230	.035	L.F.
	3290	12" wide tray size			200	.040	L.F.
	3310	18" wide tray size			160	.050	L.F.
	3330	24" wide tray size			130	.062	L.F.
	3350	30" wide tray size			100	.080	L.F.
	3370	36" wide tray size			90	.089	L.F.
	3400	Elbow, horizontal, 90°, 12" radius, 6" wide tray size			75	.107	Ea.
	3410	9" wide tray size			64	.125	Ea.
	3420	12" wide tray size			54	.148	Ea.
	3430	18" wide tray size			44	.182	Ea.
	3440	24" wide tray size			35	.229	Ea.
	3460	30" wide tray size			32	.250	Ea.
	3470	36" wide tray size			27	.296	Ea.
	3500	24" radius, 6" wide tray size			68	.118	Ea.
	3510	9" wide tray size			58	.138	Ea.
	3520	12" wide tray size			48	.167	Ea.
	3530	18" wide tray size			40	.200	Ea.
	3540	24" wide tray size			32	.250	Ea.
	3560	30" wide tray size			28	.286	Ea.
	3570	36" wide tray size			24	.333	Ea.
	3600	36" radius, 6" wide tray size			60	.133	Ea.
	3610	9" wide tray size			52	.154	Ea.
	3620	12" wide tray size			42	.190	Ea.
	3630	18" wide tray size			38	.211	Ea.
	3640	24" wide tray size			28	.286	Ea.
	3660	30" wide tray size			25	.320	Ea.
	3670	36" wide tray size			22	.364	Ea.
	3700	Elbow, horizontal, 45°, 12" radius, 6" wide tray size			75	.107	Ea.
	3710	9" wide tray size			64	.125	Ea.
	3720	12" wide tray size			54	.148	Ea.
	3730	18" wide tray size			44	.182	Ea.
	3740	24" wide tray size			40	.200	Ea.
	3760	30" wide tray size			35	.229	Ea.
	3770	36" wide tray size			32	.250	Ea.
	3800	24" radius, 6" wide tray size	↓	↓	68	.118	Ea.

160 100 | Cable Trays

		CREW	MAKEUP	DAILY OUTPUT	MAN-HOURS	UNIT
130 3811	Cable tray cover, elbow, horiz., 24" radius, 9" wide	1 Elec	1 Electrician	58	.138	Ea.
3820	12" wide tray size			48	.167	Ea.
3830	18" wide tray size			40	.200	Ea.
3840	24" wide tray size			36	.222	Ea.
3860	30" wide tray size			32	.250	Ea.
3870	36" wide tray size			28	.286	Ea.
3900	36" radius, 6" wide tray size			60	.133	Ea.
3910	9" wide tray size			52	.154	Ea.
3920	12" wide tray size			42	.190	Ea.
3930	18" wide tray size			38	.211	Ea.
3940	24" wide tray size			32	.250	Ea.
3960	30" wide tray size			28	.286	Ea.
3970	36" wide tray size			25	.320	Ea.
4000	Elbow, vertical, 90°, 12" radius, 6" wide tray size			75	.107	Ea.
4010	9" wide tray size			64	.125	Ea.
4020	12" wide tray size			54	.148	Ea.
4030	18" wide tray size			44	.182	Ea.
4040	24" wide tray size			35	.229	Ea.
4060	30" wide tray size			32	.250	Ea.
4070	36" wide tray size			27	.296	Ea.
4100	24" radius, 6" wide tray size			68	.118	Ea.
4110	9" wide tray size			58	.138	Ea.
4120	12" wide tray size			48	.167	Ea.
4130	18" wide tray size			40	.200	Ea.
4140	24" wide tray size			32	.250	Ea.
4160	30" wide tray size			28	.286	Ea.
4170	36" wide tray size			24	.333	Ea.
4200	36" radius, 6" wide tray size	•		60	.133	Ea.
4210	9" wide tray size			52	.154	Ea.
4220	12" wide tray size			42	.190	Ea.
4230	18" wide tray size			38	.211	Ea.
4240	24" wide tray size			28	.286	Ea.
4260	30" wide tray size			25	.320	Ea.
4270	36" wide tray size			22	.364	Ea.
4300	Tee, horizontal, 12" radius, 6" wide tray size			54	.148	Ea.
4310	9" wide tray size			44	.182	Ea.
4320	12" wide tray size			40	.200	Ea.
4330	18" wide tray size			34	.235	Ea.
4340	24" wide tray size			28	.286	Ea.
4360	30" wide tray size			22	.364	Ea.
4370	36" wide tray size			18	.444	Ea.
4400	24" radius, 6" wide tray size			48	.167	Ea.
4410	9" wide tray size			40	.200	Ea.
4420	12" wide tray size			36	.222	Ea.
4430	18" wide tray size			30	.267	Ea.
4440	24" wide tray size			24	.333	Ea.
4460	30" wide tray size			20	.400	Ea.
4470	36" wide tray size			16	.500	Ea.
4500	36" radius, 6" wide tray size			44	.182	Ea.
4510	9" wide tray size			36	.222	Ea.
4520	12" wide tray size			32	.250	Ea.
4530	18" wide tray size			28	.286	Ea.
4540	24" wide tray size			22	.364	Ea.
4560	30" wide tray size			18	.444	Ea.
4570	36" wide tray size			14	.571	Ea.
4600	Cross, horizontal, 12" radius, 6" wide tray size			40	.200	Ea.
4610	9" wide tray size			36	.222	Ea.
4620	12" wide tray size	▼	▼	32	.250	Ea.

160 | Raceways

160 100 | Cable Trays

		Item	CREW	MAKEUP	DAILY OUTPUT	MAN-HOURS	UNIT
130	4631	Cable tray cover, cross, horiz., 12" radius, 18" wide	1 Elec	1 Electrician	28	.286	Ea.
	4640	24" wide tray size			24	.333	Ea.
	4660	30" wide tray size			20	.400	Ea.
	4670	36" wide tray size			16	.500	Ea.
	4700	24" radius, 6" wide tray size			36	.222	Ea.
	4710	9" wide tray size			32	.250	Ea.
	4720	12" wide tray size			28	.286	Ea.
	4730	18" wide tray size			24	.333	Ea.
	4740	24" wide tray size			20	.400	Ea.
	4760	30" wide tray size			16	.500	Ea.
	4770	36" wide tray size			12	.667	Ea.
	4800	36" radius, 6" wide tray size			32	.250	Ea.
	4810	9" wide tray size			28	.286	Ea.
	4820	12" wide tray size			25	.320	Ea.
	4830	18" wide tray size			22	.364	Ea.
	4840	24" wide tray size			18	.444	Ea.
	4860	30" wide tray size			14	.571	Ea.
	4870	36" wide tray size			11	.727	Ea.
	4900	Reducer, 9" to 6" wide tray size			64	.125	Ea.
	4910	12" to 6" wide tray size			54	.148	Ea.
	4920	12" to 9" wide tray size			54	.148	Ea.
	4930	18" to 12" wide tray size			44	.182	Ea.
	4950	18" to 6" wide tray size			44	.182	Ea.
	4960	24" to 18" wide tray size			40	.200	Ea.
	4970	24" to 12" wide tray size			40	.200	Ea.
	4990	30" to 24" wide tray size			35	.229	Ea.
	5000	30" to 18" wide tray size			35	.229	Ea.
	5010	30" to 12" wide tray size			35	.229	Ea.
	5040	36" to 30" wide tray size			32	.250	Ea.
	5050	36" to 24" wide tray size			32	.250	Ea.
	5060	36" to 18" wide tray size			32	.250	Ea.
	5070	36" to 12" wide tray size			32	.250	Ea.
	5710	Tray cover hold down clamp			60	.133	Ea.
	8000	Divider strip, straight, galvanized, 3" deep			200	.040	L.F.
	8020	4" deep			180	.044	L.F.
	8040	6" deep			160	.050	L.F.
	8060	Aluminum 3" deep			210	.038	L.F.
	8080	4" deep			190	.042	L.F.
	8100	6" deep	↓	↓	170	.047	L.F.
	8110	Divider strip, vertical fitting, 3" deep					
	8120	12" radius, galvanized, 30°	1 Elec	1 Electrician	28	.286	Ea.
	8140	45°			27	.296	Ea.
	8160	60°			26	.308	Ea.
	8180	90°			25	.320	Ea.
	8200	Aluminum 30°			29	.276	Ea.
	8220	45°			28	.286	Ea.
	8240	60°			27	.296	Ea.
	8260	90°			26	.308	Ea.
	8280	24" radius, galvanized, 30°			25	.320	Ea.
	8300	45°			24	.333	Ea.
	8320	60°			23	.348	Ea.
	8340	90°			22	.364	Ea.
	8360	Aluminum, 30°			26	.308	Ea.
	8380	45°			25	.320	Ea.
	8400	60°			24	.333	Ea.
	8420	90°			23	.348	Ea.
	8440	36" radius, galvanized 30°			22	.364	Ea.
	8460	45°	↓	↓	21	.381	Ea.

			CREW	MAKEUP	DAILY OUTPUT	MAN-HOURS	UNIT
	160 100 | Cable Trays						
130	8481	Divider strip, vert. fitting, 3" deep, 36" radius, galv., 60°	1 Elec	1 Electrician	20	.400	Ea.
	8500	90°			19	.421	Ea.
	8520	Aluminum, 30°			23	.348	Ea.
	8540	45°			22	.364	Ea.
	8560	60°			21	.381	Ea.
	8570	90°	↓	↓	20	.400	Ea.
	8590	Divider strip, vertical fitting, 4" deep					
	8600	12" radius, galvanized, 30°	1 Elec	1 Electrician	27	.296	Ea.
	8610	45°			26	.308	Ea.
	8620	60°			25	.320	Ea.
	8630	90°			24	.333	Ea.
	8640	Aluminum, 30°			28	.286	Ea.
	8650	45°			27	.296	Ea.
	8660	60°			26	.308	Ea.
	8670	90°			25	.320	Ea.
	8680	24" radius, galvanized, 30°			24	.333	Ea.
	8690	45°			23	.348	Ea.
	8700	60°			22	.364	Ea.
	8710	90°			21	.381	Ea.
	8720	Aluminum 30°			25	.320	Ea.
	8730	45°			24	.333	Ea.
	8740	60°			23	.348	Ea.
	8750	90°			22	.364	Ea.
	8760	36" radius, galvanized 30°			23	.348	Ea.
	8770	45°			22	.364	Ea.
	8780	60°			21	.381	Ea.
	8790	90°			20	.400	Ea.
	8800	Aluminum 30°			24	.333	Ea.
	8810	45°			23	.348	Ea.
	8820	60°			22	.364	Ea.
	8830	90°	↓	↓	21	.381	Ea.
	8840	Divider strip, vertical fitting, 6" deep					
	8850	12" radius, galvanized, 30°	1 Elec	1 Electrician	24	.333	Ea.
	8860	45°			23	.348	Ea.
	8870	60°			22	.364	Ea.
	8880	90°			21	.381	Ea.
	8890	Aluminum, 30°			25	.320	Ea.
	8900	45°			24	.333	Ea.
	8910	60°			23	.348	Ea.
	8920	90°			22	.364	Ea.
	8930	24" radius, galvanized 30°			23	.348	Ea.
	8940	45°			22	.364	Ea.
	8950	60°			21	.381	Ea.
	8960	90°			20	.400	Ea.
	8970	Aluminum, 30°			24	.333	Ea.
	8980	45°			23	.348	Ea.
	8990	60°			22	.364	Ea.
	9000	90°			21	.381	Ea.
	9010	36" radius, galvanized 30°			22	.364	Ea.
	9020	45°			21	.381	Ea.
	9030	60°			20	.400	Ea.
	9040	90°			19	.421	Ea.
	9050	Aluminum, 30°			23	.348	Ea.
	9060	45°			22	.364	Ea.
	9070	60°			21	.381	Ea.
	9080	90°			20	.400	Ea.
	9120	Divider strip, horizontal fitting, galvanized, 3" deep			33	.242	Ea.
	9130	4" deep	↓	↓	30	.267	Ea.

160 100 | Cable Trays

		Description	CREW	MAKEUP	DAILY OUTPUT	MAN-HOURS	UNIT
130	9141	Divider strip, horiz. fitting, galv., 6" deep	1 Elec	1 Electrician	27	.296	Ea.
	9150	Aluminum 3" deep			35	.229	Ea.
	9160	4" deep			32	.250	Ea.
	9170	6" deep			29	.276	Ea.
	9300	Divider strip protector	↓	↓	300	.027	L.F.
	150	**WIREWAY** to 15' high					
	0100	Screw cover with fittings and supports, 2-1/2" x 2-1/2"	1 Elec	1 Electrician	45	.178	L.F.
	0200	4" x 4"			40	.200	L.F.
	0400	6" x 6"			30	.267	L.F.
	0600	8" x 8"			20	.400	L.F.
	0620	10" x 10"			15	.533	L.F.
	0640	12" x 12"			10	.800	L.F.
	0800	Elbows 90°, 2-1/2"			24	.333	Ea.
	1000	4"			20	.400	Ea.
	1200	6"			18	.444	Ea.
	1400	8"			16	.500	Ea.
	1420	10"			12	.667	Ea.
	1440	12"			10	.800	Ea.
	1500	Elbows, 45°, 2-1/2"			24	.333	Ea.
	1510	4"			20	.400	Ea.
	1520	6"			18	.444	Ea.
	1530	8"			16	.500	Ea.
	1540	10"			12	.667	Ea.
	1550	12"			10	.800	Ea.
	1600	"T" box, 2-1/2"			18	.444	Ea.
	1800	4"			16	.500	Ea.
	2000	6"			14	.571	Ea.
	2200	8"			12	.667	Ea.
	2220	10"			10	.800	Ea.
	2240	12"			8	1.000	Ea.
	2300	Cross, 2-1/2"			16	.500	Ea.
	2310	4"			14	.571	Ea.
	2320	6"			12	.667	Ea.
	2400	Panel adapter,			24	.333	Ea.
	2600	4"			20	.400	Ea.
	2800	6"			18	.444	Ea.
	3000	8"			16	.500	Ea.
	3020	10"			14	.571	Ea.
	3040	12"			12	.667	Ea.
	3200	Reducer, 4" to 2-1/2"			24	.333	Ea.
	3400	6" to 4"			20	.400	Ea.
	3600	8" to 6"			18	.444	Ea.
	3620	10" to 8"			16	.500	Ea.
	3640	12" to 10"			14	.571	Ea.
	3780	End cap, 2-1/2"			24	.333	Ea.
	3800	4"			20	.400	Ea.
	4000	6"			18	.444	Ea.
	4200	8"			16	.500	Ea.
	4220	10"			14	.571	Ea.
	4240	12"			12	.667	Ea.
	4300	U-connector, 2-1/2"			200	.040	Ea.
	4320	4"			200	.040	Ea.
	4340	6"			180	.044	Ea.
	4360	8"			170	.047	Ea.
	4380	10"			150	.053	Ea.
	4400	12"			130	.062	Ea.
	4420	Hanger, 2-1/2"			100	.080	Ea.
	4430	4"	↓	↓	100	.080	Ea.

160 | Raceways

160 100 | Cable Trays

		CREW	MAKEUP	DAILY OUTPUT	MAN-HOURS	UNIT
150 4441	Wireway, hanger, 6"	1 Elec	1 Electrician	80	.100	Ea.
4450	8"			65	.123	Ea.
4460	10"			50	.160	Ea.
4470	12"			40	.200	Ea.
4500	Hinged cover with fittings and supports 2-1/2" x 2-1/2"			60	.133	L.F.
4520	4" x 4"			45	.178	L.F.
4540	6" x 6"			40	.200	L.F.
4560	8" x 8"			30	.267	L.F.
4580	10" x 10"			25	.320	L.F.
4600	12" x 12"			12	.667	L.F.
4700	Elbows 90°, hinged cover 2-1/2" x 2-1/2"			32	.250	Ea.
4720	4"			27	.296	Ea.
4730	6"			23	.348	Ea.
4740	8"			18	.444	Ea.
4750	10"			14	.571	Ea.
4760	12"			12	.667	Ea.
4800	Tee box, hinged cover, 2-1/2"			23	.348	Ea.
4810	4"			20	.400	Ea.
4820	6"			18	.444	Ea.
4830	8"			16	.500	Ea.
4840	10"			12	.667	Ea.
4860	12"			10	.800	Ea.
4880	Cross box, hinged cover, 2-1/2" x 2-1/2"			18	.444	Ea.
4900	4"			16	.500	Ea.
4920	6"			13	.615	Ea.
4940	8"			11	.727	Ea.
4960	10"			10	.800	Ea.
4980	12"			9	.889	Ea.
5000	Flanged, oil tite, w/screw cover, 2-1/2" x 2-1/2"			40	.200	L.F.
5020	4" x 4"			35	.229	L.F.
5040	6" x 6"			30	.267	L.F.
5060	8" x 8"			25	.320	L.F.
5120	Elbows 90°, flanged, 2-1/2"			23	.348	Ea.
5140	4"			20	.400	Ea.
5160	6"			18	.444	Ea.
5180	8"			15	.533	Ea.
5240	Tee box, flanged 2-1/2"			18	.444	Ea.
5260	4"			16	.500	Ea.
5280	6"			15	.533	Ea.
5300	8"			13	.615	Ea.
5360	Cross box, flanged 2-1/2"			15	.533	Ea.
5380	4"			13	.615	Ea.
5400	6"			12	.667	Ea.
5420	8"			10	.800	Ea.
5480	Flange gasket, 2-1/2"			160	.050	Ea.
5500	4"			80	.100	Ea.
5520	6"			53	.151	Ea.
5530	8"	↓	↓	40	.200	Ea.

160 200 | Conduits

		CREW	MAKEUP	DAILY OUTPUT	MAN-HOURS	UNIT
205	**CONDUIT TO 15' HIGH** Includes 2 terminations, 2 elbows and					
0020	11 beam clamps per 100 L.F.					
0300	Aluminum, 1/2" diameter	1 Elec	1 Electrician	100	.080	L.F.
0500	3/4" diameter			90	.089	L.F.
0700	1" diameter			80	.100	L.F.
1000	1-1/4" diameter			70	.114	L.F.
1030	1-1/2" diameter			65	.123	L.F.
1050	2" diameter	↓	↓	60	.133	L.F.

615

		CREW	MAKEUP	DAILY OUTPUT	MAN-HOURS	UNIT
160 200 | Conduits						
1072	Conduit, aluminum, 2-1/2" diameter	1 Elec	1 Electrician	50	.160	L.F.
1100	3" diameter			45	.178	L.F.
1130	3-1/2" diameter			40	.200	L.F.
1140	4" diameter			35	.229	L.F.
1150	5" diameter			25	.320	L.F.
1160	6" diameter			20	.400	L.F.
1170	Elbows, 1/2" diameter			40	.200	Ea.
1200	3/4" diameter			32	.250	Ea.
1230	1" diameter			28	.286	Ea.
1250	1-1/4" diameter			24	.333	Ea.
1270	1-1/2" diameter			20	.400	Ea.
1300	2" diameter			16	.500	Ea.
1330	2-1/2" diameter			12	.667	Ea.
1350	3" diameter			8	1.000	Ea.
1370	3-1/2" diameter			6	1.330	Ea.
1400	4" diameter			5	1.600	Ea.
1410	5" diameter			4	2.000	Ea.
1420	6" diameter			2.50	3.200	Ea.
1750	Galvanized steel, 1/2" diameter			90	.089	L.F.
1770	3/4" diameter			80	.100	L.F.
1800	1" diameter			65	.123	L.F.
1830	1-1/4" diameter			60	.133	L.F.
1850	1-1/2" diameter			55	.145	L.F.
1870	2" diameter			45	.178	L.F.
1900	2-1/2" diameter			35	.229	L.F.
1930	3" diameter			25	.320	L.F.
1950	3-1/2" diameter			22	.364	L.F.
1970	4" diameter			20	.400	L.F.
1980	5" diameter			15	.533	L.F.
1990	6" diameter			10	.800	L.F.
2000	Elbows, 1/2" diameter			32	.250	Ea.
2030	3/4" diameter			28	.286	Ea.
2050	1" diameter			24	.333	Ea.
2070	1-1/4" diameter			18	.444	Ea.
2100	1-1/2" diameter			16	.500	Ea.
2130	2" diameter			12	.667	Ea.
2150	2-1/2" diameter			8	1.000	Ea.
2170	3" diameter			6	1.330	Ea.
2200	3-1/2" diameter			4.20	1.900	Ea.
2220	4" diameter			4	2.000	Ea.
2230	5" diameter			3.50	2.290	Ea.
2240	6" diameter			2	4.000	Ea.
2500	Steel, intermediate conduit (IMC), 1/2" diameter			100	.080	L.F.
2530	3/4" diameter			90	.089	L.F.
2550	1" diameter			70	.114	L.F.
2570	1-1/4" diameter			65	.123	L.F.
2600	1-1/2" diameter			60	.133	L.F.
2630	2" diameter			50	.160	L.F.
2650	2-1/2" diameter			40	.200	L.F.
2670	3" diameter			30	.267	L.F.
2700	3-1/2" diameter			27	.296	L.F.
2730	4" diameter			25	.320	L.F.
2750	Elbows, 1/2" diameter			32	.250	Ea.
2770	3/4" diameter			28	.286	Ea.
2800	1" diameter			24	.333	Ea.
2830	1-1/4" diameter			18	.444	Ea.
2850	1-1/2" diameter			16	.500	Ea.
2870	2" diameter	▼	▼	12	.667	Ea.

205

160 200 | Conduits

			CREW	MAKEUP	DAILY OUTPUT	MAN-HOURS	UNIT
205	2901	Conduit, steel, elbows, 2-1/2" diameter	1 Elec	1 Electrician	8	1.000	Ea.
	2930	3" diameter			6	1.330	Ea.
	2950	3-1/2" diameter			4.20	1.900	Ea.
	2970	4" diameter	↓	↓	4	2.000	Ea.
	4100	Rigid steel, plastic coated, 40 mil. thick					
	4130	1/2" diameter	1 Elec	1 Electrician	80	.100	L.F.
	4150	3/4" diameter			70	.114	L.F.
	4170	1" diameter			55	.145	L.F.
	4200	1-1/4" diameter			50	.160	L.F.
	4230	1-1/2" diameter			45	.178	L.F.
	4250	2" diameter			35	.229	L.F.
	4270	2-1/2" diameter			25	.320	L.F.
	4300	3" diameter			22	.364	L.F.
	4330	3-1/2" diameter			20	.400	L.F.
	4350	4" diameter			18	.444	L.F.
	4370	5" diameter			15	.533	L.F.
	4400	Elbows, 1/2" diameter			28	.286	Ea.
	4430	3/4" diameter			24	.333	Ea.
	4450	1" diameter			18	.444	Ea.
	4470	1-1/4" diameter			16	.500	Ea.
	4500	1-1/2" diameter			12	.667	Ea.
	4530	2" diameter			8	1.000	Ea.
	4550	2-1/2" diameter			6	1.330	Ea.
	4570	3" diameter			4.20	1.900	Ea.
	4600	3-1/2" diameter			4	2.000	Ea.
	4630	4" diameter			3.80	2.110	Ea.
	4650	5" diameter			3.50	2.290	Ea.
	5000	Electric metallic tubing (EMT), 1/2" diameter			170	.047	L.F.
	5020	3/4" diameter			130	.062	L.F.
	5040	1" diameter			115	.070	L.F.
	5060	1-1/4" diameter			100	.080	L.F.
	5080	1-1/2" diameter			90	.089	L.F.
	5100	2" diameter			80	.100	L.F.
	5120	2-1/2" diameter			60	.133	L.F.
	5140	3" diameter			50	.160	L.F.
	5160	3-1/2" diameter			45	.178	L.F.
	5180	4" diameter			40	.200	L.F.
	5200	Field bends, 45° to 90°, 1/2" diameter			89	.090	Ea.
	5220	3/4" diameter			80	.100	Ea.
	5240	1" diameter			73	.110	Ea.
	5260	1-1/4" diameter			38	.211	Ea.
	5280	1-1/2" diameter			36	.222	Ea.
	5300	2" diameter			26	.308	Ea.
	5320	Offsets, 1/2" diameter			65	.123	Ea.
	5340	3/4" diameter			62	.129	Ea.
	5360	1" diameter			53	.151	Ea.
	5380	1-1/4" diameter			30	.267	Ea.
	5400	1-1/2" diameter			28	.286	Ea.
	5420	2" diameter			20	.400	Ea.
	5700	Elbows, 1" diameter			40	.200	Ea.
	5720	1-1/4" diameter			32	.250	Ea.
	5740	1-1/2" diameter			24	.333	Ea.
	5760	2" diameter			20	.400	Ea.
	5780	2-1/2" diameter			12	.667	Ea.
	5800	3" diameter			9	.889	Ea.
	5820	3-1/2" diameter			7	1.140	Ea.
	5840	4" diameter			6	1.330	Ea.
	5900	Slipfit elbows, 1 end, 2-1/2" diameter	↓	↓	13	.615	Ea.

160 200 | Conduits

		CREW	MAKEUP	DAILY OUTPUT	MAN-HOURS	UNIT
205 5921	Conduit, elec. metallic tubing, slipfit elbows, 3" diameter	1 Elec	1 Electrician	10	.800	Ea.
5940	3-1/2" diameter			8	1.000	Ea.
5960	4" diameter			7	1.140	Ea.
6000	Slipfit elbows, 2 end, 2-1/2" diameter			14	.571	Ea.
6020	3" diameter			11	.727	Ea.
6040	3-1/2" diameter			9	.889	Ea.
6060	4" diameter			8	1.000	Ea.
6500	Box connectors, set screw, steel, 1/2" diameter			120	.067	Ea.
6520	3/4" diameter			110	.073	Ea.
6540	1" diameter			90	.089	Ea.
6560	1-1/4" diameter			70	.114	Ea.
6580	1-1/2" diameter			60	.133	Ea.
6600	2" diameter			50	.160	Ea.
6620	2-1/2" diameter			36	.222	Ea.
6640	3" diameter			27	.296	Ea.
6680	3-1/2" diameter			21	.381	Ea.
6700	4" diameter	↓	↓	16	.500	Ea.
6739	Insulated box connectors, same as box connectors					
7000	EMT to conduit adapters, 1/2" diameter (compression)	1 Elec	1 Electrician	70	.114	Ea.
7020	3/4" diameter			60	.133	Ea.
7040	1" diameter			50	.160	Ea.
7060	1-1/4" diameter			40	.200	Ea.
7080	1-1/2" diameter			30	.267	Ea.
7100	2" diameter			25	.320	Ea.
7200	EMT to Greenfield adapters, 1/2" to 3/8" diameter (compression)			90	.089	Ea.
7220	1/2" diameter			90	.089	Ea.
7240	3/4" diameter			80	.100	Ea.
7260	1" diameter			70	.114	Ea.
7270	1-1/4" diameter			60	.133	Ea.
7280	1-1/2" diameter			50	.160	Ea.
7290	2" diameter			40	.200	Ea.
7400	EMT, IB, LR or LL fittings with covers, 1/2" diameter, set screw			24	.333	Ea.
7420	3/4" diameter			20	.400	Ea.
7440	1" diameter			16	.500	Ea.
7450	1-1/4" diameter			13	.615	Ea.
7460	1-1/2" diameter			11	.727	Ea.
7470	2" diameter			9	.889	Ea.
7600	EMT, "T" fittings with covers, 1/2" diameter, set screw			16	.500	Ea.
7620	3/4" diameter			15	.533	Ea.
7640	1" diameter			12	.667	Ea.
7650	1-1/4" diameter			11	.727	Ea.
7660	1-1/2" diameter			10	.800	Ea.
7670	2" diameter			8	1.000	Ea.
8000	EMT, expansion fittings, no jumper, 1/2" diameter			24	.333	Ea.
8020	3/4" diameter			20	.400	Ea.
8040	1" diameter			16	.500	Ea.
8060	1-1/4" diameter			13	.615	Ea.
8080	1-1/2" diameter			11	.727	Ea.
8100	2" diameter			9	.889	Ea.
8110	2-1/2" diameter			7	1.140	Ea.
8120	3" diameter			6	1.330	Ea.
8140	4" diameter			5	1.600	Ea.
8200	Split adapter, 1/2" diameter			110	.073	Ea.
8210	3/4" diameter			90	.089	Ea.
8220	1" diameter			70	.114	Ea.
8230	1-1/4" diameter			60	.133	Ea.
8240	1-1/2" diameter			50	.160	Ea.
8250	2" diameter	↓	↓	36	.222	Ea.

160 | Raceways

160 200 | Conduits

		Conduit	CREW	MAKEUP	DAILY OUTPUT	MAN-HOURS	UNIT
205	8301	Conduit, 1 hole clips, 1/2" diameter	1 Elec	1 Electrician	500	.016	Ea.
	8320	3/4" diameter			470	.017	Ea.
	8340	1" diameter			444	.018	Ea.
	8360	1-1/4" diameter			400	.020	Ea.
	8380	1-1/2" diameter			355	.023	Ea.
	8400	2" diameter			320	.025	Ea.
	8420	2-1/2" diameter			266	.030	Ea.
	8440	3" diameter			160	.050	Ea.
	8460	3-1/2" diameter			133	.060	Ea.
	8480	4" diameter			100	.080	Ea.
	8500	Clamp back spacers, 1/2" diameter			500	.016	Ea.
	8510	3/4" diameter			470	.017	Ea.
	8520	1" diameter			444	.018	Ea.
	8530	1-1/4" diameter			400	.020	Ea.
	8540	1-1/2" diameter			355	.023	Ea.
	8550	2" diameter			320	.025	Ea.
	8560	2-1/2" diameter			266	.030	Ea.
	8570	3" diameter			160	.050	Ea.
	8580	3-1/2" diameter			133	.060	Ea.
	8590	4" diameter			100	.080	Ea.
	8600	Offset connectors, 1/2" diameter			40	.200	Ea.
	8610	3/4" diameter			32	.250	Ea.
	8620	1" diameter			24	.333	Ea.
	8650	90° pulling elbows, female, 1/2" diameter, with gasket			24	.333	Ea.
	8660	3/4" diameter	↓	↓	20	.400	Ea.
	8801	Box connectors, compression, same as set screw					
	8899	Insulated compression, same as compression					
	9100	PVC, #40, 1/2" diameter	1 Elec	1 Electrician	190	.042	L.F.
	9110	3/4" diameter			145	.055	L.F.
	9120	1" diameter			125	.064	L.F.
	9130	1-1/4" diameter			110	.073	L.F.
	9140	1-1/2" diameter			100	.080	L.F.
	9150	2" diameter			90	.089	L.F.
	9160	2-1/2" diameter			65	.123	L.F.
	9170	3" diameter			55	.145	L.F.
	9180	3-1/2" diameter			50	.160	L.F.
	9190	4" diameter			45	.178	L.F.
	9200	5" diameter			35	.229	L.F.
	9210	6" diameter			30	.267	L.F.
	9220	Elbows, 1/2" diameter			50	.160	Ea.
	9230	3/4" diameter			42	.190	Ea.
	9240	1" diameter			35	.229	Ea.
	9250	1-1/4" diameter			28	.286	Ea.
	9260	1-1/2" diameter			20	.400	Ea.
	9270	2" diameter			16	.500	Ea.
	9280	2-1/2" diameter			11	.727	Ea.
	9290	3" diameter			9	.889	Ea.
	9300	3-1/2" diameter			7	1.140	Ea.
	9310	4" diameter			6	1.330	Ea.
	9320	5" diameter			4	2.000	Ea.
	9330	6" diameter			3	2.670	Ea.
	9340	Field bends, 45° & 90°, 1/2" diameter			45	.178	Ea.
	9350	3/4" diameter			40	.200	Ea.
	9360	1" diameter			35	.229	Ea.
	9370	1-1/4" diameter			32	.250	Ea.
	9380	1-1/2" diameter			27	.296	Ea.
	9390	2" diameter			20	.400	Ea.
	9400	2-1/2" diameter	↓	↓	16	.500	Ea.

160 200	Conduits	CREW	MAKEUP	DAILY OUTPUT	MAN-HOURS	UNIT
205 9411	Conduit, PVC, field bends, 45° & 90°, 3" diameter	1 Elec	1 Electrician	13	.615	Ea.
9420	3-1/2" diameter			12	.667	Ea.
9430	4" diameter			10	.800	Ea.
9440	5" diameter			9	.889	Ea.
9450	6" diameter			8	1.000	Ea.
9460	PVC adapters, 1/2" diameter			80	.100	Ea.
9470	3/4" diameter			64	.125	Ea.
9480	1" diameter			53	.151	Ea.
9490	1-1/4" diameter			46	.174	Ea.
9500	1-1/2" diameter			40	.200	Ea.
9510	2" diameter			32	.250	Ea.
9520	2-1/2" diameter			23	.348	Ea.
9530	3" diameter			18	.444	Ea.
9540	3-1/2" diameter			13	.615	Ea.
9550	4" diameter			11	.727	Ea.
9560	5" diameter			8	1.000	Ea.
9570	6" diameter	↓	↓	6	1.330	Ea.
9580	PVC-LB, LR or LL					
9590	1/2" diameter	1 Elec	1 Electrician	20	.400	Ea.
9600	3/4" diameter			16	.500	Ea.
9610	1" diameter			12	.667	Ea.
9620	1-1/4" diameter			9	.889	Ea.
9630	1-1/2" diameter			7	1.140	Ea.
9640	2" diameter			6	1.330	Ea.
9650	2-1/2" diameter			6	1.330	Ea.
9660	3" diameter			5	1.600	Ea.
9670	3-1/2" diameter			4	2.000	Ea.
9680	4" diameter	↓	↓	3	2.670	Ea.
9690	PVC-tee fitting & cover					
9700	1/2"	1 Elec	1 Electrician	14	.571	Ea.
9710	3/4"			13	.615	Ea.
9720	1"			10	.800	Ea.
9730	1-1/4"			9	.889	Ea.
9740	1-1/2"			8	1.000	Ea.
9750	2"	↓	↓	7	1.140	Ea.
210 0200	**CONDUIT TO 15' HIGH** Includes couplings only					
0200	Electric metallic tubing, 1/2"diameter	1 Elec	1 Electrician	435	.018	L.F.
0220	3/4" diameter			253	.032	L.F.
0240	1" diameter			207	.039	L.F.
0260	1-1/4"diameter			173	.046	L.F.
0280	1-1/2" diameter			153	.052	L.F.
0300	2" diameter			130	.062	L.F.
0320	2-1/2" diameter			92	.087	L.F.
0340	3" diameter			74	.108	L.F.
0360	3-1/2" diameter			67	.119	L.F.
0380	4" diameter			57	.140	L.F.
0500	Steel rigid galvanized, 1/2" diameter			146	.055	L.F.
0520	3/4" diameter			125	.064	L.F.
0540	1" diameter			93	.086	L.F.
0560	1-1/4" diameter			88	.091	L.F.
0580	1-1/2" diameter			80	.100	L.F.
0600	2" diameter			65	.123	L.F.
0620	2-1/2" diameter			48	.167	L.F.
0640	3" diameter			32	.250	L.F.
0660	3-1/2" diameter			30	.267	L.F.
0680	4" diameter	↓	↓	26	.308	L.F.

160 200	Conduits	CREW	MAKEUP	DAILY OUTPUT	MAN-HOURS	UNIT
220	**CONDUIT NIPPLES** With locknuts and bushings					
0100	Aluminum, 1/2" diameter, close	1 Elec	1 Electrician	36	.222	Ea.
0101	Aluminum, 1/2" diameter, close, to 12" long			36	.222	Ea.
0341	3/4" diameter, close, to 12" long			32	.250	Ea.
0581	1" diameter, close, to 12" long			27	.296	Ea.
0801	1-1/4" diameter, close, to 12" long			23	.348	Ea.
1021	1-1/2" diameter, close, to 12" long			20	.400	Ea.
1241	2" diameter, close, to 12" long			18	.444	Ea.
1441	2-1/2" diameter, close, to 12" long			15	.533	Ea.
1621	3" diameter, close, to 12" long			12	.667	Ea.
1801	3-1/2" diameter, close, to 12" long			11	.727	Ea.
1941	4" diameter, close, to 12" long			9	.889	Ea.
2081	5" diameter, close, to 12" long			7	1.140	Ea.
2201	6" diameter, close, to 12" long			6	1.330	Ea.
2321	Rigid galvanized steel, 1/2" diameter, close, to 12" long			32	.250	Ea.
2561	3/4" diameter, close, to 12" long			27	.296	Ea.
2781	1" diameter, close, to 12" long			23	.348	Ea.
3001	1-1/4" diameter, close, to 12" long			20	.400	Ea.
3201	1-1/2" diameter, close, to 12" long			18	.444	Ea.
3421	2" diameter, close, to 12" long			16	.500	Ea.
3621	2-1/2" diameter, close, to 12" long			13	.615	Ea.
3801	Conduit nipples, galv., 3" diameter, close, to 12" long			12	.667	Ea.
4041	3-1/2" diameter, close, to 12" long			10	.800	Ea.
4181	4" diameter, close, to 12" long			8	1.000	Ea.
4321	5" diameter, close, to 12" long			6	1.330	Ea.
4441	6" diameter, close, to 12" long			5	1.600	Ea.
4561	Plastic coated, 40 mil thick, 1/2" diameter, 2" to 12" long			32	.250	Ea.
4821	3/4" diameter, 2" to 12" long			26	.308	Ea.
5021	1" diameter, 2" to 12" long			22	.364	Ea.
5221	1-1/4" diameter, 2" to 12" long			18	.444	Ea.
5421	1-1/2" diameter, 2" to 12" long			16	.500	Ea.
5621	2" diameter, 2-1/2" to 12" long			14	.571	Ea.
5801	2-1/2" diameter, 3-1/2" to 12" long			12	.667	Ea.
5941	3" diameter, 3-1/2" to 12" long			11	.727	Ea.
6081	3-1/2" diameter, 4" to 12" long			9	.889	Ea.
6201	4" diameter, 4" to 12" long			7.50	1.070	Ea.
6321	5" diameter, 5" to 12" long			5.50	1.450	Ea.
6421	6" diameter, 5" to 12" long	↓	↓	4.50	1.780	Ea.
230	**CONDUIT IN CONCRETE SLAB** Including terminations,					
0020	fittings and supports					
3230	PVC, schedule 40, 1/2" diameter	1 Elec	1 Electrician	270	.030	L.F.
3250	3/4" diameter			230	.035	L.F.
3270	1" diameter			200	.040	L.F.
3300	1-1/4" diameter			170	.047	L.F.
3330	1-1/2" diameter			140	.057	L.F.
3350	2" diameter			120	.067	L.F.
3370	2-1/2" diameter			90	.089	L.F.
3400	3" diameter			80	.100	L.F.
3430	3-1/2" diameter			60	.133	L.F.
3440	4" diameter			50	.160	L.F.
3450	5" diameter			40	.200	L.F.
3460	6" diameter			30	.267	L.F.
3530	Sweeps, 1' diameter, 30" radius			32	.250	Ea.
3550	1-1/4" diameter			24	.333	Ea.
3570	1-1/2" diameter			21	.381	Ea.
3600	2" diameter			18	.444	Ea.
3630	2-1/2" diameter			14	.571	Ea.
3650	3" diameter	↓	↓	10	.800	Ea.

160 200 | Conduits

		Crew	Makeup	Daily Output	Man-Hours	Unit
230 3671	Conduit in concrete slab, PVC sweeps, 3-1/2" diameter	1 Elec	1 Electrician	8	1.000	Ea.
3700	4" diameter			7	1.140	Ea.
3710	5" diameter			6	1.330	Ea.
4030	End bells 1" diameter, PVC			60	.133	Ea.
4050	1-1/4" diameter			53	.151	Ea.
4100	1-1/2" diameter			48	.167	Ea.
4150	2" diameter			34	.235	Ea.
4170	2-1/2" diameter			27	.296	Ea.
4200	3" diameter			20	.400	Ea.
4250	3-1/2" diameter			16	.500	Ea.
4300	4" diameter			14	.571	Ea.
4310	5" diameter			12	.667	Ea.
4320	6" diameter			9	.889	Ea.
4350	Rigid galvanized steel, 1/2" diameter			200	.040	L.F.
4400	3/4" diameter			170	.047	L.F.
4450	1" diameter			130	.062	L.F.
4500	1-1/4" diameter			110	.073	L.F.
4600	1-1/2" diameter			100	.080	L.F.
4800	2" diameter	↓	↓	90	.089	L.F.
240 0020	**CONDUIT IN TRENCH** Includes terminations and fittings					
	Does not include excavation or backfill, see 022-200					
0200	Rigid galvanized steel, 2" diameter	1 Elec	1 Electrician	150	.053	L.F.
0400	2-1/2" diameter			100	.080	L.F.
0600	3" diameter			80	.100	L.F.
0800	3-1/2" diameter			70	.114	L.F.
1000	4" diameter			50	.160	L.F.
1200	5" diameter			40	.200	L.F.
1400	6" diameter	↓	↓	30	.267	L.F.
250 1130	**CONDUIT FITTINGS** For RGS					
	Bushings, plastic, 1/2" diameter	1 Elec	1 Electrician	40	.200	Ea.
1150	3/4" diameter			32	.250	Ea.
1170	1" diameter			28	.286	Ea.
1200	1-1/4" diameter			24	.333	Ea.
1230	1-1/2" diameter			18	.444	Ea.
1250	2" diameter			15	.533	Ea.
1270	2-1/2" diameter			13	.615	Ea.
1300	3" diameter			12	.667	Ea.
1330	3-1/2" diameter			11	.727	Ea.
1350	4" diameter			9	.889	Ea.
1360	5" diameter			7	1.140	Ea.
1370	6" diameter			5	1.600	Ea.
1390	Steel, 1/2" diameter			40	.200	Ea.
1400	3/4" diameter			32	.250	Ea.
1430	1" diameter			28	.286	Ea.
1450	Steel, insulated, 1-1/4" diameter			24	.333	Ea.
1470	1-1/2" diameter			18	.444	Ea.
1500	2" diameter			15	.533	Ea.
1530	2-1/2" diameter			13	.615	Ea.
1550	3" diameter			12	.667	Ea.
1570	3-1/2" diameter			11	.727	Ea.
1600	4" diameter			9	.889	Ea.
1610	5" diameter			7	1.140	Ea.
1620	6" diameter			5	1.600	Ea.
1630	Sealing locknuts, 1/2" diameter			40	.200	Ea.
1650	3/4" diameter			32	.250	Ea.
1670	1" diameter			28	.286	Ea.
1700	1-1/4" diameter			24	.333	Ea.
1730	1-1/2" diameter	↓	↓	18	.444	Ea.

160 200	Conduits	CREW	MAKEUP	DAILY OUTPUT	MAN-HOURS	UNIT
250 1751	Conduit fittings for RGS, sealing locknuts, 2" diameter	1 Elec	1 Electrician	15	.533	Ea.
1760	Grounding bushing, insulated, 1/2" diameter			32	.250	Ea.
1770	3/4" diameter			28	.286	Ea.
1780	1" diameter			20	.400	Ea.
1800	1-1/4" diameter			18	.444	Ea.
1830	1-1/2" diameter			16	.500	Ea.
1850	2" diameter			13	.615	Ea.
1870	2-1/2" diameter			12	.667	Ea.
1900	3" diameter			11	.727	Ea.
1930	3-1/2" diameter			9	.889	Ea.
1950	4" diameter			8	1.000	Ea.
1960	5" diameter			6	1.330	Ea.
1970	6" diameter			4	2.000	Ea.
1990	Coupling with set screw, 1/2" diameter			50	.160	Ea.
2000	3/4" diameter			40	.200	Ea.
2030	1" diameter			35	.229	Ea.
2050	1-1/4" diameter			28	.286	Ea.
2070	1-1/2" diameter			23	.348	Ea.
2090	2" diameter			20	.400	Ea.
2100	2-1/2" diameter			18	.444	Ea.
2110	3" diameter			15	.533	Ea.
2120	3-1/2" diameter			12	.667	Ea.
2130	4" diameter			10	.800	Ea.
2140	5" diameter			9	.889	Ea.
2150	6" diameter			8	1.000	Ea.
2160	Box connector, with set screw, plain 1/2" diameter			70	.114	Ea.
2170	3/4" diameter			60	.133	Ea.
2180	1" diameter			50	.160	Ea.
2190	Insulated, 1-1/4" diameter			40	.200	Ea.
2200	1-1/2" diameter			30	.267	Ea.
2210	2" diameter			20	.400	Ea.
2220	2-1/2" diameter			18	.444	Ea.
2230	3" diameter			15	.533	Ea.
2240	3-1/2" diameter			12	.667	Ea.
2250	4" diameter			10	.800	Ea.
2260	5" diameter			9	.889	Ea.
2270	6" diameter			8	1.000	Ea.
2280	LB, LR or LL fittings & covers, 1/2" diameter			16	.500	Ea.
2290	3/4" diameter			13	.615	Ea.
2300	1" diameter			11	.727	Ea.
2330	1-1/4" diameter			8	1.000	Ea.
2350	1-1/2" diameter			6	1.330	Ea.
2370	2" diameter			5	1.600	Ea.
2380	2-1/2" diameter			4	2.000	Ea.
2390	3" diameter			3.50	2.290	Ea.
2400	3-1/2" diameter			3	2.670	Ea.
2410	4" diameter			2.50	3.200	Ea.
2420	T fittings with cover, 1/2" diameter			12	.667	Ea.
2430	3/4" diameter			11	.727	Ea.
2440	1" diameter			9	.889	Ea.
2450	1-1/4" diameter			6	1.330	Ea.
2470	1-1/2" diameter			5	1.600	Ea.
2500	2" diameter			4	2.000	Ea.
2510	2-1/2" diameter			3.50	2.290	Ea.
2520	3" diameter			3	2.670	Ea.
2530	3-1/2" diameter			2.50	3.200	Ea.
2540	4" diameter			2	4.000	Ea.
2550	Nipples, chase, plain, 1/2" diameter	∨	∨	40	.200	Ea.

160 200 | Conduits

		CREW	MAKEUP	DAILY OUTPUT	MAN-HOURS	UNIT
250 2561	Conduit fittings for RGS, nipples, chase, plain, 3/4" diameter	1 Elec	1 Electrician	32	.250	Ea.
2570	1" diameter			28	.286	Ea.
2600	Insulated, 1-1/4" diameter			24	.333	Ea.
2630	1-1/2" diameter			18	.444	Ea.
2650	2" diameter			15	.533	Ea.
2660	2-1/2" diameter			12	.667	Ea.
2670	3" diameter			10	.800	Ea.
2680	3-1/2" diameter			9	.889	Ea.
2690	4" diameter			8	1.000	Ea.
2700	5" diameter			7	1.140	Ea.
2710	6" diameter			6	1.330	Ea.
2720	Nipples, offset, plain, 1/2" diameter			40	.200	Ea.
2730	3/4" diameter			32	.250	Ea.
2740	1" diameter			24	.333	Ea.
2750	Insulated, 1-1/4" diameter			20	.400	Ea.
2760	1-1/2" diameter			18	.444	Ea.
2770	2" diameter			16	.500	Ea.
2780	3" diameter			14	.571	Ea.
2850	Coupling, expansion, 1/2" diameter			12	.667	Ea.
2880	3/4" diameter			10	.800	Ea.
2900	1" diameter			8	1.000	Ea.
2920	1-1/4" diameter			6.40	1.250	Ea.
2940	1-1/2" diameter			5.30	1.510	Ea.
2960	2" diameter			4.60	1.740	Ea.
2980	2-1/2" diameter			3.60	2.220	Ea.
3000	3" diameter			3	2.670	Ea.
3020	3-1/2" diameter			2.80	2.860	Ea.
3040	4" diameter			2.40	3.330	Ea.
3060	5" diameter			2	4.000	Ea.
3080	6" diameter			1.80	4.440	Ea.
3100	Expansion deflection, 1/2" diameter			12	.667	Ea.
3120	3/4" diameter			12	.667	Ea.
3140	1" diameter			10	.800	Ea.
3160	1-1/4" diameter			6.40	1.250	Ea.
3180	1-1/2" diameter			5.30	1.510	Ea.
3200	2" diameter			4.60	1.740	Ea.
3220	2-1/2" diameter			3.60	2.220	Ea.
3240	3" diameter			3	2.670	Ea.
3260	3-1/2" diameter			2.80	2.860	Ea.
3280	4" diameter			2.40	3.330	Ea.
3300	5" diameter			2	4.000	Ea.
3320	6" diameter			1.80	4.440	Ea.
3340	Ericson, 1/2" diameter			16	.500	Ea.
3360	3/4" diameter			14	.571	Ea.
3380	1" diameter			11	.727	Ea.
3400	1-1/4" diameter			8	1.000	Ea.
3420	1-1/2" diameter			7	1.140	Ea.
3440	2" diameter			5	1.600	Ea.
3460	2-1/2" diameter			4	2.000	Ea.
3480	3" diameter			3.50	2.290	Ea.
3500	3-1/2" diameter			3	2.670	Ea.
3520	4" diameter			2.70	2.960	Ea.
3540	5" diameter			2.50	3.200	Ea.
3560	6" diameter			2.30	3.480	Ea.
3580	Split, 1/2" diameter			32	.250	Ea.
3600	3/4" diameter			27	.296	Ea.
3620	1" diameter			20	.400	Ea.
3640	1-1/4" diameter	↓	↓	16	.500	Ea.

160 200	Conduits	CREW	MAKEUP	DAILY OUTPUT	MAN-HOURS	UNIT
250	3661	Conduit fittings for RGS, coupling, split, 1-1/2" diameter	1 Elec	1 Electrician	14	.571	Ea.
	3680	2" diameter			12	.667	Ea.
	3700	2-1/2" diameter			10	.800	Ea.
	3720	3" diameter			9	.889	Ea.
	3740	3-1/2" diameter			8	1.000	Ea.
	3760	4" diameter			7	1.140	Ea.
	3780	5" diameter			6	1.330	Ea.
	3800	6" diameter			5	1.600	Ea.
	4600	Reducing bushings, 3/4" to 1/2" diameter			54	.148	Ea.
	4620	1" to 3/4" diameter			46	.174	Ea.
	4640	1-1/4" to 1" diameter			40	.200	Ea.
	4660	1-1/2" to 1-1/4" diameter			36	.222	Ea.
	4680	2" to 1-1/2" diameter			32	.250	Ea.
	4740	2-1/2" to 2"			30	.267	Ea.
	4760	3" to 2-1/2"			28	.286	Ea.
	4800	Through-wall seal, 1/2" diameter			8	1.000	Ea.
	4820	3/4" diameter			7.50	1.070	Ea.
	4840	1" diameter			6.50	1.230	Ea.
	4860	1-1/4" diameter			5.50	1.450	Ea.
	4880	1-1/2" diameter			5	1.600	Ea.
	4900	2" diameter			4.20	1.900	Ea.
	4920	2-1/2" diameter			3.50	2.290	Ea.
	4940	3" diameter			3	2.670	Ea.
	4960	3-1/2" diameter			2.50	3.200	Ea.
	4980	4" diameter			2	4.000	Ea.
	5000	5" diameter			1.50	5.330	Ea.
	5020	6" diameter	↓	↓	1	8.000	Ea.
	5100	Cable supports for 2 or more wires					
	5120	1-1/2" diameter	1 Elec	1 Electrician	8	1.000	Ea.
	5140	2" diameter			6	1.330	Ea.
	5160	2-1/2" diameter			4	2.000	Ea.
	5180	3" diameter			3.50	2.290	Ea.
	5200	3-1/2" diameter			2.60	3.080	Ea.
	5220	4" diameter			2	4.000	Ea.
	5240	5" diameter			1.50	5.330	Ea.
	5260	6" diameter			1	8.000	Ea.
	5280	Service entrance cap, 1/2" diameter			16	.500	Ea.
	5300	3/4" diameter			13	.615	Ea.
	5320	1" diameter			10	.800	Ea.
	5340	1-1/4" diameter			8	1.000	Ea.
	5360	1-1/2" diameter			6.50	1.230	Ea.
	5380	2" diameter			5.50	1.450	Ea.
	5400	2-1/2" diameter			4	2.000	Ea.
	5420	3" diameter			3.40	2.350	Ea.
	5440	3-1/2" diameter			3	2.670	Ea.
	5460	4" diameter			2.70	2.960	Ea.
	5600	Fire stop fittings, to 3/4" diameter			24	.333	Ea.
	5610	1" diameter			22	.364	Ea.
	5620	1-1/2" diameter			20	.400	Ea.
	5640	2" diameter			16	.500	Ea.
	5660	3" diameter			12	.667	Ea.
	5680	4" diameter			10	.800	Ea.
	5700	6" diameter			8	1.000	Ea.
	5750	90° pull elbows, steel, female, 1/2" diameter			16	.500	Ea.
	5760	3/4" diameter			13	.615	Ea.
	5780	1" diameter			11	.727	Ea.
	5800	1-1/4" diameter			8	1.000	Ea.
	5820	1-1/2" diameter	↓	↓	6	1.330	Ea.

160 200	Conduits	CREW	MAKEUP	DAILY OUTPUT	MAN-HOURS	UNIT
250 6000	Explosion proof, flexible coupling					
6011	1/2" diameter, 4" to 36" long	1 Elec	1 Electrician	12	.667	Ea.
6141	3/4" diameter, 4" to 36" long			10	.800	Ea.
6271	1" diameter, 6" to 36" long			8	1.000	Ea.
6391	1-1/4" diameter, 12" to 36" long			6.40	1.250	Ea.
6481	1-1/2" diameter, 12" to 36" long			5.30	1.510	Ea.
6571	2" diameter, 12" to 36" long			4.60	1.740	Ea.
7000	Close up plug, 1/2" diameter, explosion proof			40	.200	Ea.
7010	3/4" diameter			32	.250	Ea.
7020	1" diameter			28	.286	Ea.
7030	1-1/4" diameter			24	.333	Ea.
7040	1-1/2" diameter			18	.444	Ea.
7050	2" diameter			15	.533	Ea.
7060	2-1/2" diameter			13	.615	Ea.
7070	3" diameter			12	.667	Ea.
7080	3-1/2" diameter			11	.727	Ea.
7090	4" diameter			9	.889	Ea.
7091	Elbow, female, 45°, 1/2"			16	.500	Ea.
7092	3/4"			13	.615	Ea.
7093	1"			11	.727	Ea.
7094	1-1/4"			8	1.000	Ea.
7095	1-1/2"			6	1.330	Ea.
7096	2"			5	1.600	Ea.
7097	2-1/2"			4.50	1.780	Ea.
7098	3"			4.20	1.900	Ea.
7099	3-1/2"			4	2.000	Ea.
7100	4"			3.80	2.110	Ea.
7101	90°, 1/2"			16	.500	Ea.
7102	3/4"			13	.615	Ea.
7103	1"			11	.727	Ea.
7104	1-1/4"			8	1.000	Ea.
7105	1-1/2"			6	1.330	Ea.
7106	2"			5	1.600	Ea.
7107	2-1/2"			4.50	1.780	Ea.
7110	Elbows, 90° long, male & female, 1/2" diameter, explosion proof			16	.500	Ea.
7120	3/4" diameter			13	.615	Ea.
7130	1" diameter			11	.727	Ea.
7140	1-1/4" diameter			8	1.000	Ea.
7150	1-1/2" diameter			6	1.330	Ea.
7160	2" diameter			5	1.600	Ea.
7170	Capped elbow, 1/2" diameter, diameter proof			11	.727	Ea.
7180	3/4" diameter			8	1.000	Ea.
7190	1" diameter			6	1.330	Ea.
7200	1-1/4" diameter			5	1.600	Ea.
7210	Pulling elbow, 1/2" diameter, explosion proof			11	.727	Ea.
7220	3/4" diameter			8	1.000	Ea.
7230	1" diameter			6	1.330	Ea.
7240	1-1/4" diameter			5	1.600	Ea.
7250	1-1/2" diameter			5	1.600	Ea.
7260	2" diameter			4	2.000	Ea.
7270	2-1/2" diameter			3.50	2.290	Ea.
7280	3" diameter			3	2.670	Ea.
7290	3-1/2" diameter			2.50	3.200	Ea.
7300	4" diameter			2.20	3.640	Ea.
7310	LB conduit body, 1/2" diameter			11	.727	Ea.
7320	3/4" diameter			8	1.000	Ea.
7330	T conduit body, 1/2" diameter			9	.889	Ea.
7340	3/4" diameter	↓	↓	6	1.330	Ea.

160 200 | Conduits

		CREW	MAKEUP	DAILY OUTPUT	MAN-HOURS	UNIT
7350	Explosionproof, round box w/cover, 3 threaded hubs, 1/2"	1 Elec	1 Electrician	8	1.000	Ea.
7351	3/4"			8	1.000	Ea.
7352	1"			7.50	1.070	Ea.
7353	1-1/4"			7	1.140	Ea.
7354	1-1/2"			7	1.140	Ea.
7355	2"			6	1.330	Ea.
7356	Round box w/cover & mtng flange, 3 threaded hubs, 1/2"			8	1.000	Ea.
7357	3/4"			8	1.000	Ea.
7358	4 threaded hubs, 1"			7	1.140	Ea.
7400	Unions, 1/2" diameter, explosion proof			20	.400	Ea.
7410	3/4" - 1/2" diameter			16	.500	Ea.
7420	3/4" diameter			16	.500	Ea.
7430	1" diameter			14	.571	Ea.
7440	1-1/4" diameter			12	.667	Ea.
7450	1-1/2" diameter			10	.800	Ea.
7460	2" diameter			8.50	.941	Ea.
7480	2-1/2" diameter			8	1.000	Ea.
7490	3" diameter			7	1.140	Ea.
7500	3-1/2" diameter			6	1.330	Ea.
7510	4" diameter			5	1.600	Ea.
7680	Reducer, 3/4" to 1/2"			54	.148	Ea.
7690	1" to 1/2"			46	.174	Ea.
7700	1" to 3/4"			46	.174	Ea.
7710	1 1/4" to 3/4"			40	.200	Ea.
7720	1 1/4" to 1"			40	.200	Ea.
7730	1 1/2" to 1"			36	.222	Ea.
7740	1 1/2" to 1-1/4"			36	.222	Ea.
7750	2" to 3/4"			32	.250	Ea.
7760	2" to 1-1/4"			32	.250	Ea.
7770	2" to 1-1/2"			32	.250	Ea.
7780	2-1/2" to 1-1/2"			30	.267	Ea.
7790	3" to 2"			30	.267	Ea.
7800	3-1/2" to 2-1/2"			28	.286	Ea.
7810	4" to 3"			28	.286	Ea.
7820	Sealing fitting, vertical/horizontal, 1/2"			12	.667	Ea.
7830	3/4"			10	.800	Ea.
7840	1"			8	1.000	Ea.
7850	1-1/4"			7	1.140	Ea.
7860	1-1/2"			6	1.330	Ea.
7870	2"			5	1.600	Ea.
7880	2-1/2"			4.50	1.780	Ea.
7890	3"			4	2.000	Ea.
7900	3-1/2"			3.50	2.290	Ea.
7910	4"			3	2.670	Ea.
7920	Sealing hubs, 1" by 1-1/2"			12	.667	Ea.
7930	1-1/4" by 2"			10	.800	Ea.
7940	1-1/2" by 2"			9	.889	Ea.
7950	2" by 2-1/2"			8	1.000	Ea.
7960	3" by 4"			7	1.140	Ea.
7970	4" by 5"			6	1.330	Ea.
7980	Drain, 1/2"			32	.250	Ea.
7990	Breather, 1/2"	↓	↓	32	.250	Ea.
8000	Plastic coated 40 mil thick					
8010	LB, LR or LL conduit body w/cover, 1/2" diameter	1 Elec	1 Electrician	13	.615	Ea.
8020	3/4" diameter			11	.727	Ea.
8030	1" diameter			8	1.000	Ea.
8040	1-1/4" diameter			6	1.330	Ea.
8050	1-1/2" diameter	↓	↓	5	1.600	Ea.

250

160 200 | Conduits

		CREW	MAKEUP	DAILY OUTPUT	MAN-HOURS	UNIT
250 8061	LB, LR or LL, conduit body w/cover, 2" diameter	1 Elec	1 Electrician	4.50	1.780	Ea.
8070	2-1/2" diameter			4	2.000	Ea.
8080	3" diameter			3.50	2.290	Ea.
8090	3-1/2" diameter			3	2.670	Ea.
8100	4" diameter			2.50	3.200	Ea.
8150	T conduit body with cover, 1/2" diameter			11	.727	Ea.
8160	3/4" diameter			9	.889	Ea.
8170	1" diameter			6	1.330	Ea.
8180	1-1/4" diameter			5	1.600	Ea.
8190	1-1/2" diameter			4.50	1.780	Ea.
8200	2" diameter			4	2.000	Ea.
8210	2-1/2" diameter			3.50	2.290	Ea.
8220	3" diameter			3	2.670	Ea.
8230	3-1/2" diameter			2.50	3.200	Ea.
8240	4" diameter			2	4.000	Ea.
8300	FS conduit body, 1 gang, 3/4" diameter			11	.727	Ea.
8310	1" diameter			10	.800	Ea.
8350	2 gang, 3/4" diameter			9	.889	Ea.
8360	1" diameter			8	1.000	Ea.
8400	Duplex receptacle cover			64	.125	Ea.
8410	Switch cover			64	.125	Ea.
8420	Switch, vaportight cover			53	.151	Ea.
8430	Blank, cover			64	.125	Ea.
8520	FSC conduit body, 1 gang, 3/4" diameter			10	.800	Ea.
8530	1" diameter			9	.889	Ea.
8550	2 gang, 3/4" diameter			8	1.000	Ea.
8560	1" diameter			7	1.140	Ea.
8590	Conduit hubs, 1/2" diameter			18	.444	Ea.
8600	3/4" diameter			16	.500	Ea.
8610	1" diameter			14	.571	Ea.
8620	1-1/4" diameter			12	.667	Ea.
8630	1-1/2" diameter			10	.800	Ea.
8640	2" diameter			8.80	.909	Ea.
8650	2-1/2" diameter			8.50	.941	Ea.
8660	3" diameter			8	1.000	Ea.
8670	3-1/2" diameter			7.50	1.070	Ea.
8680	4" diameter			7	1.140	Ea.
8690	5" diameter			6	1.330	Ea.
8710	Pipe strap, stamped 1 hole, 1/2" diameter			470	.017	Ea.
8720	3/4" diameter			440	.018	Ea.
8730	1" diameter			400	.020	Ea.
8740	1-1/4" diameter			355	.023	Ea.
8750	1-1/2" diameter			320	.025	Ea.
8760	2" diameter			266	.030	Ea.
8770	2-1/2" diameter			200	.040	Ea.
8780	3" diameter			133	.060	Ea.
8790	3-1/2"			110	.073	Ea.
8800	4" diameter			90	.089	Ea.
8810	5" diameter			70	.114	Ea.
8840	Clamp back spacers, 3/4" diameter			440	.018	Ea.
8850	1" diameter			400	.020	Ea.
8860	1-1/4" diameter			355	.023	Ea.
8870	1-1/2" diameter			320	.025	Ea.
8880	2" diameter			266	.030	Ea.
8900	3" diameter			133	.060	Ea.
8920	4" diameter			90	.089	Ea.
8960	Sealing fittings, 1/2" diameter			11	.727	Ea.
8970	3/4" diameter	↓	↓	9	.889	Ea.

160 200 | Conduits

		CREW	MAKEUP	DAILY OUTPUT	MAN-HOURS	UNIT
250 8981	Sealing fittings, 1" diameter	1 Elec	1 Electrician	7.50	1.070	Ea.
8990	1-1/4" diameter			6.50	1.230	Ea.
9000	1-1/2" diameter			5.50	1.450	Ea.
9010	2" diameter			4.80	1.670	Ea.
9020	2-1/2" diameter			4	2.000	Ea.
9030	3" diameter			3.50	2.290	Ea.
9040	3-1/2" diameter			3	2.670	Ea.
9050	4" diameter			2.50	3.200	Ea.
9060	5" diameter			1.70	4.710	Ea.
9070	Unions, 1/2" diameter			18	.444	Ea.
9080	3/4" diameter			15	.533	Ea.
9090	1" diameter			13	.615	Ea.
9100	1-1/4" diameter			11	.727	Ea.
9110	1-1/2" diameter			9.50	.842	Ea.
9120	2" diameter			8	1.000	Ea.
9130	2-1/2" diameter			7.50	1.070	Ea.
9140	3" diameter			6.80	1.180	Ea.
9150	3-1/2" diameter			5.80	1.380	Ea.
9160	4" diameter			4.80	1.670	Ea.
9170	5" diameter	↓	↓	4	2.000	Ea.
260	**CUTTING AND DRILLING**					
0100	Hole drilling to 10' high, concrete wall					
0110	8" thick, 1/2" pipe size	1 Elec	1 Electrician	12	.667	Ea.
0120	3/4" pipe size			12	.667	Ea.
0130	1" pipe size			9.50	.842	Ea.
0140	1-1/4" pipe size			9.50	.842	Ea.
0150	1-1/2" pipe size			9.50	.842	Ea.
0160	2" pipe size			4.40	1.820	Ea.
0170	2-1/2" pipe size			4.40	1.820	Ea.
0180	3" pipe size			4.40	1.820	Ea.
0190	3-1/2" pipe size			3.30	2.420	Ea.
0200	4" pipe size			3.30	2.420	Ea.
0500	12" thick, 1/2" pipe size			9.40	.851	Ea.
0520	3/4" pipe size			9.40	.851	Ea.
0540	1" pipe size			7.30	1.100	Ea.
0560	1-1/4" pipe size			7.30	1.100	Ea.
0570	1-1/2" pipe size			7.30	1.100	Ea.
0580	2" pipe size			3.60	2.220	Ea.
0590	2-1/2" pipe size			3.60	2.220	Ea.
0600	3" pipe size			3.60	2.220	Ea.
0610	3-1/2" pipe size			2.80	2.860	Ea.
0630	4" pipe size			2.50	3.200	Ea.
0650	16" thick 1/2" pipe size			7.60	1.050	Ea.
0670	3/4" pipe size			7	1.140	Ea.
0690	1" pipe size			6	1.330	Ea.
0710	1-1/4" pipe size			5.50	1.450	Ea.
0730	1-1/2" pipe size			5.50	1.450	Ea.
0750	2" pipe size			3	2.670	Ea.
0770	2-1/2" pipe size			2.70	2.960	Ea.
0790	3" pipe size			2.50	3.200	Ea.
0810	3-1/2" pipe size			2.30	3.480	Ea.
0830	4" pipe size			2	4.000	Ea.
0850	20" thick 1/2" pipe size			6.40	1.250	Ea.
0870	3/4" pipe size			6	1.330	Ea.
0890	1" pipe size			5	1.600	Ea.
0910	1-1/4" pipe size			4.80	1.670	Ea.
0930	1-1/2" pipe size	↓	↓	4.60	1.740	Ea.

160 | Raceways

160 200 | Conduits

		CREW	MAKEUP	DAILY OUTPUT	MAN-HOURS	UNIT
260 0951	Hole drilling, concrete wall, 20" thick, 2" pipe size	1 Elec	1 Electrician	2.70	2.960	Ea.
0970	2-1/2" pipe size			2.40	3.330	Ea.
0990	3" pipe size			2.20	3.640	Ea.
1010	3-1/2" pipe size			2	4.000	Ea.
1030	4" pipe size			1.70	4.710	Ea.
1050	24" thick 1/2" pipe size			5.50	1.450	Ea.
1070	3/4" pipe size			5.10	1.570	Ea.
1090	1" pipe size			4.30	1.860	Ea.
1110	1-1/4" pipe size			4	2.000	Ea.
1130	1-1/2" pipe size			4	2.000	Ea.
1150	2" pipe size			2.40	3.330	Ea.
1170	2-1/2" pipe size			2.20	3.640	Ea.
1190	3" pipe size			2	4.000	Ea.
1210	3-1/2" pipe size			1.80	4.440	Ea.
1230	4" pipe size			1.50	5.330	Ea.
1500	Brick wall, 8" thick, 1/2" pipe size			18	.444	Ea.
1520	3/4" pipe size			18	.444	Ea.
1540	1" pipe size			13.30	.602	Ea.
1560	1-1/4" pipe size			13.30	.602	Ea.
1580	1-1/2" pipe size			13.30	.602	Ea.
1600	2" pipe size			5.70	1.400	Ea.
1620	2-1/2" pipe size			5.70	1.400	Ea.
1640	3" pipe size			5.70	1.400	Ea.
1660	3-1/2" pipe size			4.40	1.820	Ea.
1680	4" pipe size			4	2.000	Ea.
1700	12" thick, 1/2" pipe size			14.50	.552	Ea.
1720	3/4" pipe size			14.50	.552	Ea.
1740	1" pipe size			11	.727	Ea.
1760	1-1/4" pipe size			11	.727	Ea.
1780	1-1/2" pipe size			11	.727	Ea.
1800	2" pipe size			5	1.600	Ea.
1820	2-1/2" pipe size			5	1.600	Ea.
1840	3" pipe size			5	1.600	Ea.
1860	3-1/2" pipe size			3.80	2.110	Ea.
1880	4" pipe size			3.30	2.420	Ea.
1900	16" thick, 1/2" pipe size			12.30	.650	Ea.
1920	3/4" pipe size			12.30	.650	Ea.
1940	1" pipe size			9.30	.860	Ea.
1960	1-1/4" pipe size			9.30	.860	Ea.
1980	1-1/2" pipe size			9.30	.860	Ea.
2000	2" pipe size			4.40	1.820	Ea.
2010	2-1/2" pipe size			4.40	1.820	Ea.
2030	3" pipe size			4.40	1.820	Ea.
2050	3-1/2" pipe size			3.30	2.420	Ea.
2070	4" pipe size			3	2.670	Ea.
2090	20" thick, 1/2" pipe size			10.70	.748	Ea.
2110	3/4" pipe size			10.70	.748	Ea.
2130	1" pipe size			8	1.000	Ea.
2150	1-1/4" pipe size			8	1.000	Ea.
2170	1-1/2" pipe size			8	1.000	Ea.
2190	2" pipe size			4	2.000	Ea.
2210	2-1/2" pipe size			4	2.000	Ea.
2230	3" pipe size			4	2.000	Ea.
2250	3-1/2" pipe size			3	2.670	Ea.
2270	4" pipe size			2.70	2.960	Ea.
2290	24" thick, 1/2" pipe size			9.40	.851	Ea.
2310	3/4" pipe size			9.40	.851	Ea.
2330	1" pipe size	↓	↓	7.10	1.130	Ea.

160 200	Conduits	CREW	MAKEUP	DAILY OUTPUT	MAN-HOURS	UNIT
260 2351	Hole drilling, brick wall, 24" thick, 1-1/4" pipe size	1 Elec	1 Electrician	7.10	1.130	Ea.
2370	1-1/2" pipe size			7.10	1.130	Ea.
2390	2" pipe size			3.60	2.220	Ea.
2410	2-1/2" pipe size			3.60	2.220	Ea.
2430	3" pipe size			3.60	2.220	Ea.
2450	3-1/2" pipe size			2.80	2.860	Ea.
2470	4" pipe size	↓	↓	2.50	3.200	Ea.
3000	Knockouts to 8' high, metal boxes & enclosures					
3020	With hole saw, 1/2" pipe size	1 Elec	1 Electrician	53	.151	Ea.
3040	3/4" pipe size			47	.170	Ea.
3050	1" pipe size			40	.200	Ea.
3060	1-1/4" pipe size			36	.222	Ea.
3070	1-1/2" pipe size			32	.250	Ea.
3080	2" pipe size			27	.296	Ea.
3090	2-1/2" pipe size			20	.400	Ea.
4010	3" pipe size			16	.500	Ea.
4030	3-1/2" pipe size			13	.615	Ea.
4050	4" pipe size			11	.727	Ea.
4070	With hand punch set, 1/2" pipe size			40	.200	Ea.
4090	3/4" pipe size			32	.250	Ea.
4110	1" pipe size			30	.267	Ea.
4130	1-1/4" pipe size			28	.286	Ea.
4150	1-1/2" pipe size			26	.308	Ea.
4170	2" pipe size			20	.400	Ea.
4190	2-1/2" pipe size			17	.471	Ea.
4200	3" pipe size			15	.533	Ea.
4220	3-1/2" pipe size			12	.667	Ea.
4240	4" pipe size			10	.800	Ea.
4260	With hydraulic punch, 1/2" pipe size			44	.182	Ea.
4280	3/4" pipe size			38	.211	Ea.
4300	1" pipe size			38	.211	Ea.
4320	1-1/4" pipe size			38	.211	Ea.
4340	1-1/2" pipe size			38	.211	Ea.
4360	2" pipe size			32	.250	Ea.
4380	2-1/2" pipe size			27	.296	Ea.
4400	3" pipe size			23	.348	Ea.
4420	3-1/2" pipe size			20	.400	Ea.
4440	4" pipe size	↓	↓	18	.444	Ea.
270	FLEXIBLE METALLIC CONDUIT					
0050	Greenfield, 3/8" diameter	1 Elec	1 Electrician	200	.040	L.F.
0100	1/2" diameter			200	.040	L.F.
0200	3/4" diameter			160	.050	L.F.
0250	1" diameter			100	.080	L.F.
0300	1-1/4" diameter			70	.114	L.F.
0350	1-1/2" diameter			50	.160	L.F.
0370	2" diameter			40	.200	L.F.
0380	2-1/2" diameter			30	.267	L.F.
0390	3" diameter			25	.320	L.F.
0400	3-1/2" diameter			20	.400	L.F.
0410	4" diameter			15	.533	L.F.
0420	Connectors, plain, 3/8" diameter			100	.080	Ea.
0430	1/2" diameter			80	.100	Ea.
0440	3/4" diameter			70	.114	Ea.
0450	1" diameter			50	.160	Ea.
0490	Insulated, 1" diameter			40	.200	Ea.
0500	1-1/4" diameter			40	.200	Ea.
0550	1-1/2" diameter	↓	↓	32	.250	Ea.
0600	2" diameter			23	.348	Ea.

160 200 | Conduits

		CREW	MAKEUP	DAILY OUTPUT	MAN-HOURS	UNIT
270 0611	Flex. metallic conduit, connectors, insul., 2-1/2" diameter	1 Elec	1 Electrician	20	.400	Ea.
0620	3" diameter			17	.471	Ea.
0630	3-1/2" diameter			13	.615	Ea.
0640	4" diameter			10	.800	Ea.
0650	Connectors 90°, plain, 3/8" diameter			80	.100	Ea.
0660	1/2" diameter			60	.133	Ea.
0700	3/4" diameter			50	.160	Ea.
0750	1" diameter			40	.200	Ea.
0790	Insulated, 1" diameter			40	.200	Ea.
0800	1-1/4" diameter			30	.267	Ea.
0850	1-1/2" diameter			23	.348	Ea.
0900	2" diameter			18	.444	Ea.
0910	2-1/2" diameter			16	.500	Ea.
0920	3" diameter			14	.571	Ea.
0930	3-1/2" diameter			11	.727	Ea.
0940	4" diameter			8	1.000	Ea.
0960	Couplings, to conduit, 1/2" diameter			50	.160	Ea.
0970	3/4" diameter			40	.200	Ea.
0980	1" diameter			35	.229	Ea.
0990	1-1/4" diameter			28	.286	Ea.
1000	1-1/2" diameter			23	.348	Ea.
1010	2" diameter			20	.400	Ea.
1020	2-1/2" diameter			18	.444	Ea.
1030	3" diameter			15	.533	Ea.
1070	Sealtite, 3/8" diameter			140	.057	L.F.
1080	1/2" diameter			140	.057	L.F.
1090	3/4" diameter			100	.080	L.F.
1100	1" diameter			70	.114	L.F.
1200	1-1/4" diameter			50	.160	L.F.
1300	1-1/2" diameter			40	.200	L.F.
1400	2" diameter			30	.267	L.F.
1410	2-1/2" diameter			27	.296	L.F.
1420	3" diameter			25	.320	L.F.
1440	4" diameter			15	.533	L.F.
1490	Connectors, plain, 3/8" diameter			70	.114	Ea.
1500	1/2" diameter			70	.114	Ea.
1700	3/4" diameter			50	.160	Ea.
1900	1" diameter			40	.200	Ea.
1910	Insulated, 1" diameter			40	.200	Ea.
2000	1-1/4" diameter			32	.250	Ea.
2100	1-1/2" diameter			27	.296	Ea.
2200	2" diameter			20	.400	Ea.
2210	2-1/2" diameter			15	.533	Ea.
2220	3" diameter			12	.667	Ea.
2240	4" diameter			8	1.000	Ea.
2290	Connectors 90°, 3/8" diameter			70	.114	Ea.
2300	1/2" diameter			70	.114	Ea.
2400	3/4" diameter			50	.160	Ea.
2600	1" diameter			40	.200	Ea.
2790	Insulated 1" diameter			40	.200	Ea.
2800	1-1/4" diameter			32	.250	Ea.
3000	1-1/2" diameter			27	.296	Ea.
3100	2" diameter			20	.400	Ea.
3110	2-1/2" diameter			14	.571	Ea.
3120	3" diameter			11	.727	Ea.
3140	4" diameter			7	1.140	Ea.
4300	Coupling, sealtite to rigid,			20	.400	Ea.
4500	3/4" diameter	▼	▼	18	.444	Ea.

160 200 | Conduits

		Description	CREW	MAKEUP	DAILY OUTPUT	MAN-HOURS	UNIT
270	4801	Coupling, sealtite to rigid, 1" diameter	1 Elec	1 Electrician	14	.571	Ea.
	4900	1-1/4" diameter			12	.667	Ea.
	5000	1-1/2" diameter			11	.727	Ea.
	5100	2" diameter			10	.800	Ea.
	5110	2-1/2" diameter			9.50	.842	Ea.
	5120	3" diameter			9	.889	Ea.
	5130	3-1/2" diameter			9	.889	Ea.
	5140	4" diameter	▼	▼	8.50	.941	Ea.
275		**MOTOR CONNECTIONS**					
	0020	Flexible conduit and fittings, up to 1 HP motor, 115 volt, 1 phase	1 Elec	1 Electrician	8	1.000	Ea.
	0050	2 HP motor			6.50	1.230	Ea.
	0100	3 HP motor			5.50	1.450	Ea.
	0120	230 volt, 10 HP motor, 3 phase			4.20	1.900	Ea.
	0150	15 HP motor			3.30	2.420	Ea.
	0200	25 HP motor			2.70	2.960	Ea.
	0400	50 HP motor			2.20	3.640	Ea.
	0600	100 HP motor			1.50	5.330	Ea.
	1500	460 volt, 5 HP motor, 3 phase			8	1.000	Ea.
	1520	10 HP motor			8	1.000	Ea.
	1530	25 HP motor			6	1.330	Ea.
	1540	30 HP motor			6	1.330	Ea.
	1550	40 HP motor			5	1.600	Ea.
	1560	50 HP motor			5	1.600	Ea.
	1570	60 HP motor			3.80	2.110	Ea.
	1580	75 HP motor			3.50	2.290	Ea.
	1590	100 HP motor			2.50	3.200	Ea.
	1600	125 HP motor			2	4.000	Ea.
	1610	150 HP motor			1.80	4.440	Ea.
	1620	200 HP motor	▼	▼	1.50	5.330	Ea.
290		**WIREMOLD RACEWAY**					
	0090	Raceway, surface, metal, straight section					
	0100	No. 500	1 Elec	1 Electrician	100	.080	L.F.
	0400	No. 1500, small pancake			90	.089	L.F.
	0600	No. 2000, base & cover			90	.089	L.F.
	0610	Receptacle, 6" O.C.			40	.200	L.F.
	0620	12" O.C.			44	.182	L.F.
	0630	18" O.C.			46	.174	L.F.
	0650	30" O.C.			50	.160	L.F.
	0660	60" O.C.			50	.160	L.F.
	0670	No. 2200, base & cover, blank			80	.100	L.F.
	0700	Receptacle 18" O.C.			36	.222	L.F.
	0720	30" O.C.			40	.200	L.F.
	0730	60" O.C.			40	.200	L.F.
	0800	No. 3000, base & cover			75	.107	L.F.
	0810	Receptacle, 6" O.C.			60	.133	L.F.
	0820	12" O.C.			62	.129	L.F.
	0830	18" O.C.			64	.125	L.F.
	0840	24" O.C.			66	.121	L.F.
	0850	30" O.C.			68	.118	L.F.
	0860	60" O.C.			70	.114	L.F.
	1000	No. 4000, base & cover			65	.123	L.F.
	1010	Receptacle, 6" O.C.			50	.160	L.F.
	1020	12" O.C.			52	.154	L.F.
	1030	18" O.C.			54	.148	L.F.
	1040	24" O.C.			56	.143	L.F.
	1050	30" O.C.			58	.138	L.F.
	1060	60" O.C.			60	.133	L.F.
	1200	No. 6000, base & cover	▼	▼	50	.160	L.F.

			160 200	Conduits	CREW	MAKEUP	DAILY OUTPUT	MAN-HOURS	UNIT
290	1211	Wiremold raceway, No. 6000, receptacle, 6" O.C.	1 Elec	1 Electrician	35	.229	L.F.
	1220	12" O.C.			37	.216	L.F.
	1230	18" O.C.			39	.205	L.F.
	1240	24" O.C.			41	.195	L.F.
	1250	30" O.C.			43	.186	L.F.
	1260	60" O.C.			45	.178	L.F.
	2400	Fittings, elbows, No. 500			40	.200	Ea.
	2800	Elbow cover, No. 2000			40	.200	Ea.
	3000	Switch box, No. 500			16	.500	Ea.
	3400	Telephone outlet, No. 1500			16	.500	Ea.
	3600	Junction box, No. 1500	↓	↓	16	.500	Ea.
	3800	Plugmold wired sections, No. 2000					
	4000	1 circuit, 6 outlets, 3 ft. long	1 Elec	1 Electrician	8	1.000	Ea.
	4100	2 circuits, 8 outlets, 6 ft. long			5.30	1.510	Ea.
	4200	Tele-power poles, aluminum, 4 outlets	↓	↓	2.70	2.960	Ea.
	4300	Overhead distribution systems, 125 volt					
	4400	ODS 2G30 50 ft., 1 circ., 3W #2000 size	1 Elec	1 Electrician	75	.107	L.F.
	4600	ODS 2GA30 50 ft., 2 circ., 4W #2000 size			75	.107	L.F.
	4800	2010A entrance end fitting			20	.400	Ea.
	5000	2010B blank end fitting			40	.200	Ea.
	5200	G2003 supporting clip			40	.200	Ea.
	5400	ODS 3G30 50 ft., 1 circ., 3W #3000 size			65	.123	L.F.
	5600	ODS 3GA30 50 ft., 2 circ., 4W #3000 size			65	.123	L.F.
	5800	G3010A entrance end fitting			20	.400	Ea.
	6000	G3010B blank end fitting			40	.200	Ea.
	6020	G3017 NE internal elbow			20	.400	Ea.
	6030	G3018 AE external elbow			20	.400	Ea.
	6040	G3007 C device bracket			53	.151	Ea.
	6200	G3008TC T-bar clip			40	.200	Ea.
	6400	G3008A hanger clamp			32	.250	Ea.
	7000	4000B base			90	.089	L.F.
	7200	4000D divider			100	.080	L.F.
	7400	G4010D entrance end fitting			16	.500	Ea.
	7600	G4010B blank end fitting			40	.200	Ea.
	7610	G4046 B recp. & tele. cover			53	.151	Ea.
	7620	G4018 external elbow			16	.500	Ea.
	7630	G4001 coupling			53	.151	Ea.
	7640	G4001 D divider clip & coup.			80	.100	Ea.
	7650	G4086 A panel connector			16	.500	Ea.
	7800	G4074 take off connector			16	.500	Ea.
	8000	G6074 take off connector			16	.500	Ea.
	8100	G4046H take off fitting			16	.500	Ea.
	8200	G6008A hanger clamp			32	.250	Ea.
	8240	G6007 C-1 device bracket			53	.151	Ea.
	8250	G6007 C-2 device bracket			40	.200	Ea.
	8260	G6010 B blank end fitting			40	.200	Ea.
	8270	G6017 TX combination elbow			14	.571	Ea.
	8300	G6086 panel connector			16	.500	Ea.
	8400	2321G cable adapter assembly, 6 ft.	↓	↓	32	.250	Ea.
	8500	Chan-L-Wire system installed in 1-5/8" x 1-5/8" strut. Strut					
	8600	not incl., 30 amp, 4 wire, 3 phase	1 Elec	1 Electrician	200	.040	L.F.
	8700	Junction box			8	1.000	Ea.
	8800	Insulating end cap			40	.200	Ea.
	8900	Strut splice plate			40	.200	Ea.
	9000	Tap			40	.200	Ea.
	9100	Fixture hanger	↓	↓	60	.133	Ea.

160 300 | Conduit Support

			CREW	MAKEUP	DAILY OUTPUT	MAN-HOURS	UNIT
320	320	**HANGERS** Steel					
	0030	Conduit supports					
	0050	Strap, 2 hole, rigid conduit					
	0100	1/2" diameter	1 Elec	1 Electrician	470	.017	Ea.
	0150	3/4" diameter			440	.018	Ea.
	0200	1" diameter			400	.020	Ea.
	0300	1-1/4" diameter			355	.023	Ea.
	0350	1-1/2" diameter			320	.025	Ea.
	0400	2" diameter			266	.030	Ea.
	0500	2-1/2" diameter			160	.050	Ea.
	0550	3" diameter			133	.060	Ea.
	0600	3-1/2" diameter			100	.080	Ea.
	0650	4" diameter	↓	↓	80	.100	Ea.
	0701	EMT, same as rigid conduit					
	1400	Hanger, conduit, with bolt, 1/2" diameter	1 Elec	1 Electrician	200	.040	Ea.
	1450	3/4" diameter			190	.042	Ea.
	1500	1" diameter			176	.045	Ea.
	1550	1-1/4" diameter			160	.050	Ea.
	1600	1-1/2" diameter			140	.057	Ea.
	1650	2" diameter			130	.062	Ea.
	1700	2-1/2" diameter			100	.080	Ea.
	1750	3" diameter			64	.125	Ea.
	1800	3-1/2" diameter			50	.160	Ea.
	1850	4" diameter			40	.200	Ea.
	1900	Riser clamps, conduit, 1/2" diameter			40	.200	Ea.
	1950	3/4" diameter			36	.222	Ea.
	2000	1" diameter			30	.267	Ea.
	2100	1-1/4" diameter			27	.296	Ea.
	2150	1-1/2" diameter			27	.296	Ea.
	2200	2" diameter			20	.400	Ea.
	2250	2-1/2" diameter			20	.400	Ea.
	2300	3" diameter			18	.444	Ea.
	2350	3-1/2" diameter			18	.444	Ea.
	2400	4" diameter			14	.571	Ea.
	2500	Threaded rod, 1/4" diameter, painted			260	.031	L.F.
	2600	3/8" diameter			200	.040	L.F.
	2700	1/2" diameter			140	.057	L.F.
	2800	5/8" diameter			100	.080	L.F.
	2900	3/4" diameter			60	.133	L.F.
	3800	Channels, steel, 3/4" x 1-1/2"			80	.100	L.F.
	3900	1-1/2" x 1-1/2"			70	.114	L.F.
	4000	1-7/8" x 1-1/2"			60	.133	L.F.
	4100	3" x 1-1/2"			50	.160	L.F.
	4201	Spring nuts, long or short, 1/4"			120	.067	Ea.
	4250	3/8"			100	.080	Ea.
	4300	1/2"			80	.100	Ea.
	4500	Closure strip			200	.040	L.F.
	4550	End cap			60	.133	Ea.
	4600	End connector 3/4" conduit			40	.200	Ea.
	4650	Junction box, 1 channel			16	.500	Ea.
	4700	2 channel			14	.571	Ea.
	4750	3 channel			12	.667	Ea.
	4800	4 channel			10	.800	Ea.
	4850	Spliceplate			40	.200	Ea.
	4901	Continuous concrete insert, 3/4" and 1-1/2" deep, 1' long			16	.500	Ea.
	4950	2' long			14	.571	Ea.
	5000	3' long			12	.667	Ea.
	5050	4' long	↓	↓	10	.800	Ea.

160 300 | Conduit Support

		CREW	MAKEUP	DAILY OUTPUT	MAN-HOURS	UNIT
320 5101	Channels, cont. concrete insert, 3/4" & 1-1/2" deep, 6' long	1 Elec	1 Electrician	8	1.000	Ea.
5400	90° angle fitting 2-1/8" x 2-1/8"			60	.133	Ea.
5450	Channel supports, suspension rod type, small			60	.133	Ea.
5500	Large			40	.200	Ea.
5550	Beam clamp, small			60	.133	Ea.
5600	Large			40	.200	Ea.
5650	U-support, small			60	.133	Ea.
5700	Large			40	.200	Ea.
5750	Concrete insert, cast, for up to 1/2" threaded rod			16	.500	Ea.
5800	Beam clamp, 1/4" clamp, 1/4" threaded drop rod			32	.250	Ea.
5900	3/8" clamp, 3/8" threaded drop rod			32	.250	Ea.
6000	Channel strap for rigid conduit, 1/2" diameter			540	.015	Ea.
6050	3/4" diameter			440	.018	Ea.
6100	1" diameter			420	.019	Ea.
6150	1-1/4" diameter			400	.020	Ea.
6200	1-1/2" diameter			400	.020	Ea.
6250	2" diameter			267	.030	Ea.
6300	2-1/2" diameter			267	.030	Ea.
6350	3" diameter			160	.050	Ea.
6400	3-1/2" diameter			133	.060	Ea.
6450	4" diameter			100	.080	Ea.
6500	5" diameter			80	.100	Ea.
6550	6" diameter	↓	↓	60	.133	Ea.
6601	EMT, same as rigid conduit					
7000	Clip, 1 hole for rigid conduit, 1/2" diameter	1 Elec	1 Electrician	500	.016	Ea.
7050	3/4" diameter			470	.017	Ea.
7100	1" diameter			440	.018	Ea.
7150	1-1/4" diameter			400	.020	Ea.
7200	1-1/2" diameter			355	.023	Ea.
7250	2" diameter			320	.025	Ea.
7300	2-1/2" diameter			266	.030	Ea.
7350	3" diameter			160	.050	Ea.
7400	3-1/2" diameter			133	.060	Ea.
7450	4" diameter			100	.080	Ea.
7500	5" diameter			80	.100	Ea.
7550	6" diameter			60	.133	Ea.
7820	Conduit hangers, with bolt & 12" rod, 1/2" diameter			150	.053	Ea.
7830	3/4" diameter			145	.055	Ea.
7840	1" diameter			135	.059	Ea.
7850	1-1/4" diameter			120	.067	Ea.
7860	1-1/2" diameter			110	.073	Ea.
7870	2" diameter			100	.080	Ea.
7880	2-1/2" diameter			80	.100	Ea.
7890	3" diameter			60	.133	Ea.
7900	3-1/2" diameter			45	.178	Ea.
7910	4" diameter			35	.229	Ea.
7920	5" diameter			30	.267	Ea.
7930	6" diameter			25	.320	Ea.
7950	Jay clamp, 1/2" diameter			32	.250	Ea.
7960	3/4" diameter			32	.250	Ea.
7970	1" diameter			32	.250	Ea.
7980	1-1/4" diameter			30	.267	Ea.
7990	1-1/2" diameter			30	.267	Ea.
8000	2" diameter			30	.267	Ea.
8010	2-1/2" diameter			28	.286	Ea.
8020	3" diameter			28	.286	Ea.
8030	3-1/2" diameter			25	.320	Ea.
8040	4" diameter	↓	↓	25	.320	Ea.

160 300 | Conduit Support

		CREW	MAKEUP	DAILY OUTPUT	MAN-HOURS	UNIT
320 8051	Jay clamp, 5" diameter	1 Elec	1 Electrician	20	.400	Ea.
8060	6" diameter			16	.500	Ea.
8070	Channels, 3/4" x 1-1/2" w/12" rods for 1/2" to 1" conduit			30	.267	Ea.
8080	1-1/2" x 1-1/2" w/12" rods for 1-1/4" to 2" conduit			28	.286	Ea.
8090	1-1/2" x 1-1/2" w/12" rods for 2-1/2" to 4" conduit			26	.308	Ea.
8100	1-1/2" x 1-7/8" w/12" rods for 5" to 6" conduit			24	.333	Ea.
8110	Beam clamp, conduit, plastic coated, 1/2" diameter			30	.267	Ea.
8120	3/4"			30	.267	Ea.
8130	1"			30	.267	Ea.
8140	1-1/4"			28	.286	Ea.
8150	1-1/2"			28	.286	Ea.
8160	2"			28	.286	Ea.
8170	2-1/2"			26	.308	Ea.
8180	3"			26	.308	Ea.
8190	3-1/2"			23	.348	Ea.
8200	4"			23	.348	Ea.
8210	5"	↓	↓	18	.444	Ea.
8220	Channels, plastic coated					
8250	3/4" x 1-1/2", w/12" rods for 1/2" to 1" conduit	1 Elec	1 Electrician	28	.286	Ea.
8260	1-1/2" x 1-1/2", w/12" rods for 1-1/4" to 2" conduit			26	.308	Ea.
8270	1-1/2" x 1-1/2", w/12" rods for 2-1/2" to 3-1/2" cond.			24	.333	Ea.
8280	1-1/2" x 1-7/8", w/12" rods for 4" to 5" conduit			22	.364	Ea.
8290	1-1/2" x 1-7/8", w/12" rods for 6" conduit			20	.400	Ea.
8320	Conduit hangers plastic coated, with bolt & 12" rod, 1/2" diam.			140	.057	Ea.
8330	3/4"			135	.059	Ea.
8340	1"			125	.064	Ea.
8350	1-1/4"			110	.073	Ea.
8360	1-1/2"			100	.080	Ea.
8370	2"			90	.089	Ea.
8380	2-1/2"			70	.114	Ea.
8390	3"			50	.160	Ea.
8400	3-1/2"			35	.229	Ea.
8410	4"			25	.320	Ea.
8420	5"			20	.400	Ea.
9010	3/4"			32	.250	Ea.
9020	1"			32	.250	Ea.
9030	1-1/4"			30	.267	Ea.
9040	1-1/2"			30	.267	Ea.
9050	2"			30	.267	Ea.
9060	2-1/2"			28	.286	Ea.
9070	3"			28	.286	Ea.
9090	4"			25	.320	Ea.
9350	Combination conduit hanger, 3/8"			32	.250	Ea.
9360	Adjustable flange 3/8"	↓	↓	32	.250	Ea.

160 500 | Ducts

		CREW	MAKEUP	DAILY OUTPUT	MAN-HOURS	UNIT
540	TRENCH DUCT Steel with cover					
0020	Standard adjustable, depths to 4"					
0100	Straight, single compartment, 9" wide	1 Elec	1 Electrician	120	.067	L.F.
0200	12" wide			16	.500	L.F.
0400	18" wide			13	.615	L.F.
0600	24" wide			11	.727	L.F.
0700	27" wide			10.50	.762	L.F.
0800	30" wide			10	.800	L.F.
1000	36" wide			8	1.000	L.F.
1020	Two compartment, 9" wide			19	.421	L.F.
1030	12" wide			15	.533	L.F.
1040	18" wide	↓	↓	12	.667	L.F.

160 500 | Ducts

		Description	CREW	MAKEUP	DAILY OUTPUT	MAN-HOURS	UNIT
540	1051	Trench duct, straight, 2 compartment, 24" thick	1 Elec	1 Electrician	10	.800	L.F.
	1060	30" wide			9	.889	L.F.
	1070	36" wide			7	1.140	L.F.
	1090	Three compartment, 9" wide			18	.444	L.F.
	1100	12" wide			14	.571	L.F.
	1110	18" wide			11	.727	L.F.
	1120	24" wide			9	.889	L.F.
	1130	30" wide			8	1.000	L.F.
	1140	36" wide			6	1.330	L.F.
	1201	Horiz. or vert. elbow, 9" wide			2.70	2.960	Ea.
	1400	12" wide			2.30	3.480	Ea.
	1600	18" wide			2	4.000	Ea.
	1800	24" wide			1.60	5.000	Ea.
	1900	27" wide			1.50	5.330	Ea.
	2000	30" wide			1.30	6.150	Ea.
	2200	36" wide			1.20	6.670	Ea.
	2221	Horiz. elbow, two compartment, 9" wide			1.90	4.210	Ea.
	2230	12" wide			1.50	5.330	Ea.
	2240	18" wide			1.20	6.670	Ea.
	2250	24" wide			1	8.000	Ea.
	2260	30" wide			.90	8.890	Ea.
	2270	36" wide			.80	10.000	Ea.
	2290	Three compartment, 9" wide			1.80	4.440	Ea.
	2300	12" wide			1.40	5.710	Ea.
	2310	18" wide			1.10	7.270	Ea.
	2320	24" wide			.90	8.890	Ea.
	2330	30" wide			.80	10.000	Ea.
	2350	36" wide			.70	11.430	Ea.
	3600	Cross, 9" wide			2	4.000	Ea.
	3800	12" wide			1.60	5.000	Ea.
	4000	18" wide			1.30	6.150	Ea.
	4200	24" wide			1.10	7.270	Ea.
	4300	27" wide			1.10	7.270	Ea.
	4400	30" wide			1	8.000	Ea.
	4600	36" wide			.90	8.890	Ea.
	4620	Two compartment, 9" wide			1.90	4.210	Ea.
	4630	12" wide			1.50	5.330	Ea.
	4640	18" wide			1.20	6.670	Ea.
	4650	24" wide			1	8.000	Ea.
	4660	30" wide			.90	8.890	Ea.
	4670	36" wide			.80	10.000	Ea.
	4690	Three compartment, 9" wide			1.80	4.440	Ea.
	4700	12" wide			1.40	5.710	Ea.
	4710	18" wide			1.10	7.270	Ea.
	4720	24" wide			.90	8.890	Ea.
	4730	30" wide			.80	10.000	Ea.
	4740	36" wide			.70	11.430	Ea.
	4800	End closure, 9" wide			7.20	1.110	Ea.
	5000	12" wide			6	1.330	Ea.
	5200	18" wide			5	1.600	Ea.
	5400	24" wide			4	2.000	Ea.
	5500	27" wide			3.50	2.290	Ea.
	5600	30" wide			3.30	2.420	Ea.
	5800	36" wide			2.90	2.760	Ea.
	6000	Tees, 9" wide			2	4.000	Ea.
	6200	12" wide			1.80	4.440	Ea.
	6400	18" wide			1.60	5.000	Ea.
	6600	24" wide	↓	↓	1.50	5.330	Ea.

160 500 | Ducts

		CREW	MAKEUP	DAILY OUTPUT	MAN-HOURS	UNIT
540 6701	Trench duct, tees, 27" wide	1 Elec	1 Electrician	1.40	5.710	Ea.
6800	30" wide			1.30	6.150	Ea.
7000	36" wide			1	8.000	Ea.
7020	Two compartment, 9" wide			1.90	4.210	Ea.
7030	12" wide			1.70	4.710	Ea.
7040	18" wide			1.50	5.330	Ea.
7050	24" wide			1.40	5.710	Ea.
7060	30" wide			1.20	6.670	Ea.
7070	36" wide			.95	8.420	Ea.
7090	Three compartment, 9" wide			1.80	4.440	Ea.
7100	12" wide			1.60	5.000	Ea.
7110	18" wide			1.40	5.710	Ea.
7120	24" wide			1.30	6.150	Ea.
7130	30" wide			1.10	7.270	Ea.
7140	36" wide			.90	8.890	Ea.
7200	Riser and cabinet connector, 9" wide			2.70	2.960	Ea.
7400	12" wide			2.30	3.480	Ea.
7600	18" wide			2	4.000	Ea.
7800	24" wide			1.60	5.000	Ea.
7900	27" wide			1.50	5.330	Ea.
8000	30" wide			1.30	6.150	Ea.
8200	36" wide			1	8.000	Ea.
8400	Insert assembly, cell to conduit adapter, 1-1/4"			16	.500	Ea.
8500	Adjustable partition			320	.025	L.F.
8700	Support post	↓	↓	240	.033	L.F.
560	**UNDERFLOOR DUCT**					
0100	Duct, 1-3/8" x 3-1/8" blank, standard	1 Elec	1 Electrician	80	.100	L.F.
0200	1-3/8" x 7-1/4" blank, super duct			60	.133	L.F.
0400	7/8" or 1-3/8" insert type, 24" O.C., 1-3/8", x 3-1/8", std.			70	.114	L.F.
0600	1-3/8" x 7-1/4", super duct			50	.160	L.F.
0800	Junction box, single duct, 1 level, 3-1/8"			4	2.000	Ea.
0820	3-1/8" x 7-1/4"			4	2.000	Ea.
0840	2 level, 3-1/8" upper & lower			3.20	2.500	Ea.
0860	3-1/8" upper, 7-1/4" lower			2.70	2.960	Ea.
0880	Carpet pan for above			80	.100	Ea.
0900	Terrazzo pan for above			67	.119	Ea.
1000	Junction box, single duct, 1 level, 7-1/4"			2.70	2.960	Ea.
1020	2 level, 7-1/4" upper & lower			2.70	2.960	Ea.
1040	2 duct, two 3-1/8" upper & lower			3.20	2.500	Ea.
1200	1 level, 2 duct, 3-1/8"			3.20	2.500	Ea.
1220	Carpet pan for above boxes			80	.100	Ea.
1240	Terrazzo pan for above boxes			67	.119	Ea.
1260	Junction box, 1 level, two 3-1/8" x one 3-1/8" + one 7-1/4"			2.30	3.480	Ea.
1280	2 level, two 3-1/8" upper, one 3-1/8" + one 7-1/4" lower			2	4.000	Ea.
1300	Carpet pan for above boxes			80	.100	Ea.
1320	Terrazzo pan for above boxes			67	.119	Ea.
1400	Junction box, 1 level, 2 duct, 7-1/4"			2.30	3.480	Ea.
1420	Two 3-1/8" + one 7-1/4"			2	4.000	Ea.
1440	Carpet pan for above			80	.100	Ea.
1460	Terrazzo pan for above			67	.119	Ea.
1580	Junction box, 1 level, one 3-1/8" + one 7-1/4" x same			2.30	3.480	Ea.
1600	Triple duct, 3-1/8"			2.30	3.480	Ea.
1700	Junction box, 1 level, one 3-1/8" + two 7-1/4"			2	4.000	Ea.
1720	Carpet pan for above			80	.100	Ea.
1740	Terrazzo pan for above			67	.119	Ea.
1800	Insert to conduit adapter, 3/4" & 1"			32	.250	Ea.
2000	Support, single cell			27	.296	Ea.
2200	Super duct	↓	↓	16	.500	Ea.

160 | Raceways

160 500 | Ducts

		CREW	MAKEUP	DAILY OUTPUT	MAN-HOURS	UNIT
560 2401	Underfloor duct support, double cell	1 Elec	1 Electrician	16	.500	Ea.
2600	Triple cell			11	.727	Ea.
2800	Vertical elbow, standard duct			10	.800	Ea.
3000	Super duct			8	1.000	Ea.
3200	Cabinet connector, standard duct			32	.250	Ea.
3400	Super duct			27	.296	Ea.
3600	Conduit adapter, 1" to 1-1/4"			32	.250	Ea.
3800	2" to 1-1/4"			27	.296	Ea.
4000	Outlet, low tension (tele, computer, etc.)			8	1.000	Ea.
4200	High tension, receptacle (120 volt)			8	1.000	Ea.
4300	End closure, standard duct			160	.050	Ea.
4310	Super duct			160	.050	Ea.
4350	Elbow, horiz., standard duct			26	.308	Ea.
4360	Super duct			26	.308	Ea.
4380	Elbow, offset, standard duct			26	.308	Ea.
4390	Super duct			26	.308	Ea.
4400	Marker screw assembly for inserts			50	.160	Ea.
4410	Y take off, standard duct			26	.308	Ea.
4420	Super duct			26	.308	Ea.
4430	Box opening plug, standard duct			160	.050	Ea.
4440	Super duct			160	.050	Ea.
4450	Sleeve coupling, standard duct			160	.050	Ea.
4460	Super duct			160	.050	Ea.
4470	Conduit adapter, standard duct, 3/4"			32	.250	Ea.
4480	1" or 1-1/4"			32	.250	Ea.
4500	1-1/2"	↓	↓	32	.250	Ea.

161 | Conductors and Grounding

161 100 | Conductors

		CREW	MAKEUP	DAILY OUTPUT	MAN-HOURS	UNIT
105	**ARMORED CABLE**					
0050	600 volt, copper (BX), #14, 2 wire	1 Elec	1 Electrician	2.40	3.330	C.L.F.
0100	3 wire			2.20	3.640	C.L.F.
0120	4 wire			2	4.000	C.L.F.
0150	#12, 2 wire			2.30	3.480	C.L.F.
0200	3 wire			2	4.000	C.L.F.
0220	4 wire			1.80	4.440	C.L.F.
0240	#12, 19 wire, stranded			1.10	7.270	C.L.F.
0250	#10, 2 wire			2	4.000	C.L.F.
0300	3 wire			1.60	5.000	C.L.F.
0320	4 wire			1.40	5.710	C.L.F.
0350	#8, 3 wire			1.30	6.150	C.L.F.
0370	4 wire			1.10	7.270	C.L.F.
0380	#6, 2 wire, stranded			1.30	6.150	C.L.F.
0400	3 conductor with PVC jacket, in cable tray, #6			3.10	2.580	C.L.F.
0450	#4			2.70	2.960	C.L.F.
0500	#2			2.30	3.480	C.L.F.
0550	#1			2	4.000	C.L.F.
0600	1/0			1.80	4.440	C.L.F.
0650	2/0			1.70	4.710	C.L.F.
0700	3/0			1.60	5.000	C.L.F.
0750	4/0	↓	↓	1.50	5.330	C.L.F.

161 100 | Conductors

		CREW	MAKEUP	DAILY OUTPUT	MAN-HOURS	UNIT
105 0801	Armored cable, 3 conductor, in cable tray, 250 MCM	1 Elec	1 Electrician	1.20	6.670	C.L.F.
0850	350 MCM			1.10	7.270	C.L.F.
0900	500 MCM			1	8.000	C.L.F.
0910	4 conductor with PVC jacket in cable tray, #6			2.70	2.960	C.L.F.
0920	#4			2.30	3.480	C.L.F.
0930	#2			2	4.000	C.L.F.
0940	#1			1.80	4.440	C.L.F.
0950	1/0			1.70	4.710	C.L.F.
0960	2/0			1.60	5.000	C.L.F.
0970	3/0			1.50	5.330	C.L.F.
0980	4/0			1.20	6.670	C.L.F.
0990	250 MCM			1.10	7.270	C.L.F.
1000	350 MCM			1	8.000	C.L.F.
1010	500 MCM	↓	↓	.90	8.890	C.L.F.
1050	5 KV, copper, 3 conductor with PVC jacket,					
1060	non-shielded, in cable tray, #4	1 Elec	1 Electrician	190	.042	L.F.
1100	#2			180	.044	L.F.
1200	#1			150	.053	L.F.
1400	1/0			145	.055	L.F.
1600	2/0			130	.062	L.F.
2000	4/0			120	.067	L.F.
2100	250 MCM			110	.073	L.F.
2150	350 MCM			105	.076	L.F.
2200	500 MCM	↓	↓	90	.089	L.F.
2400	15 KV, copper, 3 conductor with PVC jacket,					
2500	grounded neutral, in cable tray, #2	1 Elec	1 Electrician	150	.053	L.F.
2600	#1			140	.057	L.F.
2800	1/0			130	.062	L.F.
2900	2/0			110	.073	L.F.
3000	4/0			95	.084	L.F.
3100	250 MCM			90	.089	L.F.
3150	350 MCM			80	.100	L.F.
3200	500 MCM	↓	↓	70	.114	L.F.
3400	15 KV, copper, 3 conductor with PVC jacket,					
3450	ungrounded neutral, in cable tray, #2	1 Elec	1 Electrician	130	.062	L.F.
3500	#1			115	.070	L.F.
3600	1/0			100	.080	L.F.
3700	2/0			95	.084	L.F.
3800	4/0			80	.100	L.F.
4000	250 MCM			70	.114	L.F.
4050	350 MCM			65	.123	L.F.
4100	500 MCM	↓	↓	60	.133	L.F.
4200	600 volt, aluminum, 3 conductor in cable tray with PVC jacket					
4300	#2	1 Elec	1 Electrician	270	.030	L.F.
4400	#1			230	.035	L.F.
4500	#1/0			200	.040	L.F.
4600	#2/0			180	.044	L.F.
4700	#3/0			170	.047	L.F.
4800	#4/0			160	.050	L.F.
4900	250 MCM			150	.053	L.F.
5000	350 MCM			120	.067	L.F.
5200	500 MCM			110	.073	L.F.
5300	750 MCM	↓	↓	95	.084	L.F.
5400	600 volt, aluminum, 4 conductor in cable tray with PVC jacket					
5410	#2	1 Elec	1 Electrician	260	.031	L.F.
5430	#1			220	.036	L.F.
5450	1/0			190	.042	L.F.
5470	2/0	↓	↓	170	.047	L.F.

161 100	Conductors	CREW	MAKEUP	DAILY OUTPUT	MAN-HOURS	UNIT
105 5481	Armored cable, 600 volt, alum., 4 conductor in cable tray, 3/0	1 Elec	1 Electrician	160	.050	L.F.
5500	4/0			150	.053	L.F.
5520	250 MCM			140	.057	L.F.
5540	350 MCM			110	.073	L.F.
5560	500 MCM			100	.080	L.F.
5580	750 MCM			90	.089	L.F.
5600	5 KV, aluminum, unshielded in cable tray, #2			190	.042	L.F.
5700	#1			180	.044	L.F.
5800	1/0			150	.053	L.F.
6000	2/0			145	.055	L.F.
6200	3/0			130	.062	L.F.
6300	4/0			120	.067	L.F.
6400	250 MCM			110	.073	L.F.
6500	350 MCM			105	.076	L.F.
6600	500 MCM			100	.080	L.F.
6800	750 MCM			90	.089	L.F.
7000	15 KV, aluminum, shielded grounded, #1 with PVC jacket			150	.053	L.F.
7200	1/0			140	.057	L.F.
7300	2/0			130	.062	L.F.
7400	3/0			120	.067	L.F.
7500	4/0			110	.073	L.F.
7600	250 MCM			100	.080	L.F.
7700	350 MCM			90	.089	L.F.
7800	500 MCM			80	.100	L.F.
8000	750			68	.118	L.F.
8200	15 KV, aluminum, shielded-ungrounded, #1 with PVC jacket			125	.064	L.F.
8300	1/0			115	.070	L.F.
8400	2/0			105	.076	L.F.
8500	3/0			100	.080	L.F.
8600	4/0			95	.084	L.F.
8700	250 MCM			90	.089	L.F.
8800	350 MCM			80	.100	L.F.
8900	500 MCM			70	.114	L.F.
9200	750 MCM	↓	↓	58	.138	L.F.
135	CONTROL CABLE					
0020	600 volt, copper, #14 THWN wire with PVC jacket, 2 wires	1 Elec	1 Electrician	9	.889	C.L.F.
0030	3 wires			8	1.000	C.L.F.
0100	4 wires			7	1.140	C.L.F.
0150	5 wires			6.50	1.230	C.L.F.
0200	6 wires			6	1.330	C.L.F.
0300	8 wires			5.30	1.510	C.L.F.
0400	10 wires			4.80	1.670	C.L.F.
0500	12 wires			4.30	1.860	C.L.F.
0600	14 wires			3.80	2.110	C.L.F.
0700	16 wires			3.50	2.290	C.L.F.
0800	18 wires			3.30	2.420	C.L.F.
0810	19 wires			3.10	2.580	C.L.F.
0900	20 wires			3	2.670	C.L.F.
1000	22 wires	↓	↓	2.80	2.860	C.L.F.
140	MINERAL INSULATED CABLE					
0100	1 conductor, #12	1 Elec	1 Electrician	1.60	5.000	C.L.F.
0200	#10			1.60	5.000	C.L.F.
0400	#8			1.50	5.330	C.L.F.
0500	#6			1.40	5.710	C.L.F.
0600	#4			1.20	6.670	C.L.F.
0800	#2			1.10	7.270	C.L.F.
0900	#1			1.05	7.620	C.L.F.
1000	1/0	↓	↓	1	8.000	C.L.F.

161 100	Conductors	CREW	MAKEUP	DAILY OUTPUT	MAN-HOURS	UNIT
140 1101	Mineral insul. cable, 1 conductor, 2/0	1 Elec	1 Electrician	.95	8.420	C.L.F.
1200	3/0			.90	8.890	C.L.F.
1400	4/0			.80	10.000	C.L.F.
1500	2 conductor, #12			1.40	5.710	C.L.F.
1600	#10			1.20	6.670	C.L.F.
1800	#8			1.10	7.270	C.L.F.
2000	#6			1.05	7.620	C.L.F.
2100	#4			1	8.000	C.L.F.
2200	3 conductor,			1.20	6.670	C.L.F.
2400	#10			1.10	7.270	C.L.F.
2600	#8			1.05	7.620	C.L.F.
2800	#6			1	8.000	C.L.F.
3000	#4			.90	8.890	C.L.F.
3100	4 conductor,			1.20	6.670	C.L.F.
3200	#10			1.10	7.270	C.L.F.
3400	#8			1	8.000	C.L.F.
3600	#6			.90	8.890	C.L.F.
3620	7 conductor,			1.10	7.270	C.L.F.
3640	#10			1	8.000	C.L.F.
3800	M.I. terminations, 600 volt, 1 conductor, #12			8	1.000	Ea.
4000	#10			7.60	1.050	Ea.
4100	#8			7.30	1.100	Ea.
4200	#6			6.70	1.190	Ea.
4400	#4			6.20	1.290	Ea.
4600	#2			5.70	1.400	Ea.
4800	#1			5.30	1.510	Ea.
5000	1/0			5	1.600	Ea.
5100	2/0			4.70	1.700	Ea.
5200	3/0			4.30	1.860	Ea.
5400	4/0			4	2.000	Ea.
5500	2 conductor,			6.70	1.190	Ea.
5600	#10			6.40	1.250	Ea.
5800	#8			6.20	1.290	Ea.
6000	#6			5.70	1.400	Ea.
6200	#4			5.30	1.510	Ea.
6400	3 conductor, #12			5.70	1.400	Ea.
6500	#10			5.50	1.450	Ea.
6600	#8			5.20	1.540	Ea.
6800	#6			4.80	1.670	Ea.
7200	#4			4.60	1.740	Ea.
7400	4 conductor, #12			4.60	1.740	Ea.
7500	#10			4.40	1.820	Ea.
7600	#8			4.20	1.900	Ea.
8400	#6			4	2.000	Ea.
8500	7 conductor,			3.50	2.290	Ea.
8600	#10	↓	↓	3	2.670	Ea.
145	**NON-METALLIC SHEATHED CABLE** 600 volt					
0100	Copper with ground wire, (Romex)					
0150	#14, 2 wire	1 Elec	1 Electrician	2.70	2.960	C.L.F.
0200	3 wire			2.40	3.330	C.L.F.
0220	4 wire			2.20	3.640	C.L.F.
0250	#12, 2 wire			2.50	3.200	C.L.F.
0300	3 wire			2.20	3.640	C.L.F.
0320	4 wire			2	4.000	C.L.F.
0350	#10, 2 wire			2.20	3.640	C.L.F.
0400	3 wire			1.80	4.440	C.L.F.
0420	4 wire			1.60	5.000	C.L.F.
0450	#8, 3 wire	↓	↓	1.50	5.330	C.L.F.

161 100 | Conductors

		CREW	MAKEUP	DAILY OUTPUT	MAN-HOURS	UNIT
145 0481	Non-metallic sheathed cable, 600 volt, #8, 4 wire	1 Elec	1 Electrician	1.40	5.710	C.L.F.
0500	#6, 3 wire			1.40	5.710	C.L.F.
0520	#4, 3 wire			1.20	6.670	C.L.F.
0540	#2, 3 wire	↓	↓	1.10	7.270	C.L.F.
0550	SE type SER aluminum cable, 3 RHW and					
0600	1 bare neutral, 3 #8 & 1 #8	1 Elec	1 Electrician	1.60	5.000	C.L.F.
0650	3 #6 & 1 #6			1.40	5.710	C.L.F.
0700	3 #4 & 1 #6			1.20	6.670	C.L.F.
0750	3 #2 & 1 #4			1.10	7.270	C.L.F.
0800	3 #1/0 & 1 #2			1	8.000	C.L.F.
0850	3 #2/0 & 1 #1			.90	8.890	C.L.F.
0900	3 #4/0 & 1 #2/0			.80	10.000	C.L.F.
1450	UF underground feeder cable, copper with ground, #14-2 cond.			4	2.000	C.L.F.
1500	#12-2 conductor			3.50	2.290	C.L.F.
1550	#10-2 conductor			3	2.670	C.L.F.
1600	#14-3 conductor			3.50	2.290	C.L.F.
1650	#12-3 conductor			3	2.670	C.L.F.
1700	#10-3 conductor			2.50	3.200	C.L.F.
1750	#14-1 conductor			13	.615	C.L.F.
1800	#12-1 conductor			11	.727	C.L.F.
1850	#10-1 conductor			10	.800	C.L.F.
1900	#8-1 conductor			8	1.000	C.L.F.
1950	#6-1 conductor			6.50	1.230	C.L.F.
2000	#4-1 conductor			5.30	1.510	C.L.F.
2100	#2-1 conductor			4.50	1.780	C.L.F.
2400	SEU service entrance cable, copper 2 conductors, #8 + #8 neut.			1.50	5.330	C.L.F.
2600	#6 + #8 neutral			1.30	6.150	C.L.F.
2800	#6 + #6 neutral			1.30	6.150	C.L.F.
3000	#4 + #6 neutral			1.10	7.270	C.L.F.
3200	#4 + #4 neutral			1.10	7.270	C.L.F.
3400	#3 + #5 neutral			1.05	7.620	C.L.F.
3600	#3 + #3 neutral			1.05	7.620	C.L.F.
3800	#2 + #4 neutral			1	8.000	C.L.F.
4000	#1 + #1 neutral			.95	8.420	C.L.F.
4200	1/0 + 1/0 neutral			.90	8.890	C.L.F.
4400	2/0 + 2/0 neutral			.85	9.410	C.L.F.
4600	3/0 + 3/0 neutral			.80	10.000	C.L.F.
4800	Aluminum, 2 conductors #8 + #8 neutral			1.60	5.000	C.L.F.
5000	#6 + #6 neutral			1.40	5.710	C.L.F.
5100	#4 + #6 neutral			1.25	6.400	C.L.F.
5200	#4 + #4 neutral			1.20	6.670	C.L.F.
5300	#2 + #4 neutral			1.15	6.960	C.L.F.
5400	#2 + #2 neutral			1.10	7.270	C.L.F.
5450	1/0 + #2 neutral			1.05	7.620	C.L.F.
5500	1/0 + 1/0 neutral			1	8.000	C.L.F.
5550	2/0 + #1 neutral			.95	8.420	C.L.F.
5600	2/0 + 2/0 neutral			.90	8.890	C.L.F.
5800	3/0 + 1/0 neutral			.85	9.410	C.L.F.
6000	3/0 + 3/0 neutral			.85	9.410	C.L.F.
6200	4/0 + 2/0 neutral			.80	10.000	C.L.F.
6400	4/0 + 4/0 neutral	↓	↓	.80	10.000	C.L.F.
6500	Service entrance cap for copper SEU					
6600	100 amp	1 Elec	1 Electrician	12	.667	Ea.
6700	150 amp			10	.800	Ea.
6800	200 amp	↓	↓	8	1.000	Ea.

161 100 | Conductors

		CREW	MAKEUP		DAILY OUTPUT	MAN-HOURS	UNIT
150	**150**	**SHIELDED CABLE** Splicing & terminations not included					
	0050	Copper, CLP shielding, 5KV #4	1 Elec	1 Electrician		2.20	3.640	C.L.F.
	0100	#2				2	4.000	C.L.F.
	0200	#1				2	4.000	C.L.F.
	0400	1/0				1.90	4.210	C.L.F.
	0600	2/0				1.80	4.440	C.L.F.
	0800	4/0				1.60	5.000	C.L.F.
	1000	250 MCM				1.50	5.330	C.L.F.
	1200	350 MCM				1.30	6.150	C.L.F.
	1400	500 MCM				1.20	6.670	C.L.F.
	1600	15 KV, ungrounded neutral, #1				2	4.000	C.L.F.
	1800	1/0				1.90	4.210	C.L.F.
	2000	2/0				1.80	4.440	C.L.F.
	2200	4/0				1.60	5.000	C.L.F.
	2400	250 MCM				1.50	5.330	C.L.F.
	2600	350 MCM				1.30	6.150	C.L.F.
	2800	500 MCM				1.20	6.670	C.L.F.
	3000	25 KV, grounded neutral, #1/0				1.80	4.440	C.L.F.
	3200	2/0				1.70	4.710	C.L.F.
	3400	4/0				1.50	5.330	C.L.F.
	3600	250 MCM				1.40	5.710	C.L.F.
	3800	350 MCM				1.20	6.670	C.L.F.
	3900	500 MCM				1.10	7.270	C.L.F.
	4000	35 KV, grounded neutral, #1/0				1.70	4.710	C.L.F.
	4200	2/0				1.60	5.000	C.L.F.
	4400	4/0				1.40	5.710	C.L.F.
	4600	250 MCM				1.30	6.150	C.L.F.
	4800	350 MCM				1.10	7.270	C.L.F.
	5000	500 MCM				1	8.000	C.L.F.
	5050	Aluminum, CLP shielding, 5KV, #2				2.50	3.200	C.L.F.
	5070	#1				2.20	3.640	C.L.F.
	5090	1/0				2	4.000	C.L.F.
	5100	2/0				1.90	4.210	C.L.F.
	5150	4/0				1.80	4.440	C.L.F.
	5200	250 MCM				1.60	5.000	C.L.F.
	5220	350 MCM				1.50	5.330	C.L.F.
	5240	500 MCM				1.30	6.150	C.L.F.
	5260	750 MCM				1.20	6.670	C.L.F.
	5300	15 KV aluminum, CLP, #1				2.20	3.640	C.L.F.
	5320	1/0				2	4.000	C.L.F.
	5340	2/0				1.90	4.210	C.L.F.
	5360	4/0				1.80	4.440	C.L.F.
	5380	250 MCM				1.60	5.000	C.L.F.
	5400	350 MCM				1.50	5.330	C.L.F.
	5420	500 MCM				1.30	6.150	C.L.F.
	5440	750 MCM	↓	↓		1.20	6.670	C.L.F.
155		**SPECIAL WIRES & FITTINGS**						
	0100	Fixture, TFFN, 600 volt, 90°, stranded #18	1 Elec	1 Electrician		13	.615	C.L.F.
	0150	#16				13	.615	C.L.F.
	0200	AF, 300 volt, 150°, stranded #18				13	.615	C.L.F.
	0250	#16				13	.615	C.L.F.
	0300	#14				12	.667	C.L.F.
	0350	#12				11	.727	C.L.F.
	0400	#10				10	.800	C.L.F.
	0500	Thermostat, no jacket, twisted, #18-2 conductor				8	1.000	C.L.F.
	0550	#18-3				7	1.140	C.L.F.
	0600	#18-4				6.50	1.230	C.L.F.
	0650	#18-5	↓	↓		6	1.330	C.L.F.

161 100 | Conductors

			CREW	MAKEUP	DAILY OUTPUT	MAN-HOURS	UNIT
155	0701	Thermostat, no jacket, twisted, #18-6	1 Elec	1 Electrician	5.50	1.450	C.L.F.
	0750	#18-7			5	1.600	C.L.F.
	0800	#18-8			4.80	1.670	C.L.F.
	0900	TV, antenna lead-in, 300 ohm #20-2 conductor			7	1.140	C.L.F.
	0950	Coaxial, feeder outlet			7	1.140	C.L.F.
	1000	Coaxial, main riser			6	1.330	C.L.F.
	1100	Sound, shielded with drain, #22-2 conductor			8	1.000	C.L.F.
	1150	#22-3 conductor			7.50	1.070	C.L.F.
	1200	#22-4 conductor			6.50	1.230	C.L.F.
	1250	Nonshielded #22-2 conductor			10	.800	C.L.F.
	1300	#22-3 conductor			9	.889	C.L.F.
	1350	#22-4 conductor			8	1.000	C.L.F.
	1400	Microphone cable	↓	↓	8	1.000	C.L.F.
	1500	Fire alarm, FEP teflon, 150 volt, 200° centigrade					
	1550	#22, 1 pair	1 Elec	1 Electrician	10	.800	C.L.F.
	1600	2 pair			8	1.000	C.L.F.
	1650	4 pair			7	1.140	C.L.F.
	1700	6 pair			6	1.330	C.L.F.
	1750	8 pair			5.50	1.450	C.L.F.
	1800	10 pair			5	1.600	C.L.F.
	1850	#18, 1 pair			8	1.000	C.L.F.
	1900	2 pair			6.50	1.230	C.L.F.
	1950	4 pair			4.80	1.670	C.L.F.
	2000	6 pair			4	2.000	C.L.F.
	2050	8 pair			3.50	2.290	C.L.F.
	2100	10 pair			3	2.670	C.L.F.
	2200	Telephone, twisted, PVC insulation, #22-2 conductor			10	.800	C.L.F.
	2250	#22-3 conductor			9	.889	C.L.F.
	2300	#22-4 conductor			8	1.000	C.L.F.
	2350	#19-2 conductor			9	.889	C.L.F.
	2500	Tray cable type TC, copper #14, 2 conductor			9	.889	C.L.F.
	2520	3 conductor			8	1.000	C.L.F.
	2540	4 conductor			7	1.140	C.L.F.
	2560	5 conductor			6.50	1.230	C.L.F.
	2580	6 conductor			6	1.330	C.L.F.
	2600	8 conductor			5.30	1.510	C.L.F.
	2620	10 conductor	↓	↓	4.80	1.670	C.L.F.
	2640	300V, copper braided shield, PVC jacket					
	2650	2 conductor #18 stranded	1 Elec	1 Electrician	7	1.140	C.L.F.
	2660	3 conductor #18	"	"	6	1.330	C.L.F.
	3000	Strain relief grip for cable					
	3050	Cord, top, #12-3	1 Elec	1 Electrician	40	.200	Ea.
	3060	#12-4			40	.200	Ea.
	3070	#12-5			39	.205	Ea.
	3100	#10-3			39	.205	Ea.
	3110	#10-4			38	.211	Ea.
	3120	#10-5			38	.211	Ea.
	3200	Bottom, #12-3			40	.200	Ea.
	3210	#12-4			40	.200	Ea.
	3220	#12-5			39	.205	Ea.
	3230	#10-3			39	.205	Ea.
	3300	#10-4			38	.211	Ea.
	3310	#10-5	↓	↓	38	.211	Ea.
	3500	Coaxial, connectors 50 ohm impedance quick disconnect					
	3540	BNC plug, for RG A/U #58 cable	1 Elec	1 Electrician	42	.190	Ea.
	3550	RG A/U #59 cable			42	.190	Ea.
	3560	RG A/U #62 cable			42	.190	Ea.
	3600	BNC jack for RG A/U #58 cable	↓	↓	42	.190	Ea.

	161 100	Conductors	CREW	MAKEUP	DAILY OUTPUT	MAN-HOURS	UNIT
155	3611	Coaxial connectors, BNC jack for RG A/U #59 cable	1 Elec	1 Electrician	42	.190	Ea.
	3620	RG A/U #62 cable			42	.190	Ea.
	3660	BNC panel jack for RG A/U #58 cable			40	.200	Ea.
	3670	RG A/U #59 cable			40	.200	Ea.
	3680	RG A/U #62 cable			40	.200	Ea.
	3720	BNC bulkhead jack for RG A/U #58 cable			40	.200	Ea.
	3730	RG A/U 59 cable			40	.200	Ea.
	3740	RG A/U 62 cable			40	.200	Ea.
	3850	Coaxial cable, RG A/U 58, 50 ohm			8	1.000	C.L.F.
	3860	RG A/U 59, 75 ohm			8	1.000	C.L.F.
	3870	RG A/U 62, 93 ohm			8	1.000	C.L.F.
	3950	RG A/U 58, 50 ohm fire rated			8	1.000	C.L.F.
	3960	RG A/U 59, 75 ohm fire rated			8	1.000	C.L.F.
	3970	RG A/U 62, 93 ohm fire rated	↓	↓	8	1.000	C.L.F.
	160	**UNDERCARPET**					
	0020	Power System					
	0100	Cable flat, 3 conductor, #12, w/attached bottom shield	1 Elec	1 Electrician	982	.008	L.F.
	0200	Shield, top, steel			1,768	.005	L.F.
	0250	Splice, 3 conductor			48	.167	Ea.
	0300	Top shield			96	.083	Ea.
	0350	Tap			40	.200	Ea.
	0400	Insulating patch, splice, tap, & end			48	.167	Ea.
	0450	Fold			230	.035	Ea.
	0500	Top shield, tap & fold			96	.083	Ea.
	0700	Transition, block assembly			77	.104	Ea.
	0750	Receptacle frame & base			32	.250	Ea.
	0800	Cover receptacle			120	.067	Ea.
	0850	Cover blank			160	.050	Ea.
	0860	Receptacle, direct connected, single			25	.320	Ea.
	0870	Dual			16	.500	Ea.
	0880	Combination Hi & Lo, tension			21	.381	Ea.
	0900	Box, floor with cover			20	.400	Ea.
	0920	Floor service w/barrier			4	2.000	Ea.
	1000	Wall, surface, with cover			20	.400	Ea.
	1100	Wall, flush, with cover			20	.400	Ea.
	1450	Cable, flat, 5 conductor #12, w/attached bottom shield			800	.010	L.F.
	1550	Shield, top, steel			1,768	.005	L.F.
	1600	Splice, 5 conductor			48	.167	Ea.
	1650	Top shield			96	.083	Ea.
	1700	Tap			48	.167	Ea.
	1750	Insulating patch, splice tap, & end			83	.096	Ea.
	1800	Transition, block assembly			77	.104	Ea.
	1850	Box, wall, flush with cover			20	.400	Ea.
	1900	Cable, flat, 4 conductor, #12			933	.009	L.F.
	1950	3 conductor #10			982	.008	L.F.
	1960	4 conductor #10			933	.009	L.F.
	1970	5 conductor #10	↓	↓	884	.009	L.F.
	2500	Telephone System					
	2510	Transition fitting wall box, surface	1 Elec	1 Electrician	24	.333	Ea.
	2520	Flush			24	.333	Ea.
	2530	Flush, for PC board			24	.333	Ea.
	2540	Floor service box			4	2.000	Ea.
	2700	Floor fitting w/duplex jack & cover			21	.381	Ea.
	2720	Low profile			53	.151	Ea.
	2740	Miniature w/duplex jack			53	.151	Ea.
	2760	25 pair kit			21	.381	Ea.
	2780	Low profile			53	.151	Ea.
	2800	Call director kit for 5 cable	↓	↓	19	.421	Ea.

161 100 | Conductors

		CREW	MAKEUP	DAILY OUTPUT	MAN-HOURS	UNIT
160 2821	Undercarpet transition floor fitting, 4 pair kit	1 Elec	1 Electrician	19	.421	Ea.
2840	3 pair kit			19	.421	Ea.
2860	Comb. 25 pair & 3 cond power			21	.381	Ea.
2880	5 cond power			21	.381	Ea.
2900	PC board, 8-3 pair			161	.050	Ea.
2920	6-4 pair			161	.050	Ea.
2940	3 pair adapter			161	.050	Ea.
2950	Plug			77	.104	Ea.
2960	Couplers			321	.025	Ea.
3000	Bottom shield for 25 pr. cable			4,420	.002	L.F.
3020	4 pair			4,420	.002	L.F.
3040	Top shield for 25 pr. cable			4,420	.002	L.F.
3100	Cable assembly, double-end, 50', 25 pr.			11.80	.678	Ea.
3110	3 pair			23.60	.339	Ea.
3120	4 pair			23.60	.339	Ea.
3140	Bulk 3 pair			1,473	.005	L.F.
3160	4 pair	↓	↓	1,473	.005	L.F.
3500	Data System					
3520	Cable 25 conductor w/conn. 40', 75 ohm	1 Elec	1 Electrician	14.50	.552	Ea.
3530	Single lead			22	.364	Ea.
3540	Dual lead			22	.364	Ea.
3590	BNC coax connectors, Plug			40	.200	Ea.
3600	TNC coax connectors, Plug	↓	↓	40	.200	Ea.
3700	Cable-bulk					
3710	Single lead	1 Elec	1 Electrician	1,473	.005	L.F.
3720	Dual lead			1,473	.005	L.F.
3790	Data cable notching 90°			97	.082	Ea.
3800	180°			60	.133	Ea.
8100	Drill floor			160	.050	Ea.
8200	Marking floor			1,600	.005	L.F.
8300	Tape, hold down			6,400	.001	L.F.
8350	Tape primer, 500 ft. per can	↓	↓	96	.083	Ea.
165 WIRE						
0021	600 volt types THW, THWN, TW, XHHW, copper, solid, #14	1 Elec	1 Electrician	13	.615	C.L.F.
0030	#12			11	.727	C.L.F.
0040	#10			10	.800	C.L.F.
0050	Stranded #14			13	.615	C.L.F.
0100	#12			11	.727	C.L.F.
0120	#10			10	.800	C.L.F.
0140	#8			8	1.000	C.L.F.
0160	#6			6.50	1.230	C.L.F.
0180	#4			5.30	1.510	C.L.F.
0200	#3			5	1.600	C.L.F.
0220	#2			4.50	1.780	C.L.F.
0240	#1			4	2.000	C.L.F.
0260	1/0			3.30	2.420	C.L.F.
0280	2/0			2.90	2.760	C.L.F.
0300	3/0			2.50	3.200	C.L.F.
0350	4/0			2.20	3.640	C.L.F.
0400	250 MCM			2	4.000	C.L.F.
0420	300 MCM			1.90	4.210	C.L.F.
0450	350 MCM			1.80	4.440	C.L.F.
0480	400 MCM			1.70	4.710	C.L.F.
0490	500 MCM			1.60	5.000	C.L.F.
0500	600 MCM			1.30	6.150	C.L.F.
0510	750 MCM			1.10	7.270	C.L.F.
0520	1000 MCM	↓	↓	.90	8.890	C.L.F.
0521						

161 | Conductors and Grounding

161 100 | Conductors

			CREW	MAKEUP	DAILY OUTPUT	MAN-HOURS	UNIT
165	0531	Wire, aluminum, types THW, XHHW, stranded, #8	1 Elec	1 Electrician	9	.889	C.L.F.
	0540	#6			8	1.000	C.L.F.
	0560	#4			6.50	1.230	C.L.F.
	0580	#2			5.30	1.510	C.L.F.
	0600	#1			4.50	1.780	C.L.F.
	0620	1/0			4	2.000	C.L.F.
	0640	2/0			3.60	2.220	C.L.F.
	0680	3/0			3.30	2.420	C.L.F.
	0700	4/0			3.10	2.580	C.L.F.
	0720	250 MCM			2.90	2.760	C.L.F.
	0740	300 MCM			2.70	2.960	C.L.F.
	0760	350 MCM			2.50	3.200	C.L.F.
	0780	400 MCM			2.30	3.480	C.L.F.
	0800	500 MCM			2	4.000	C.L.F.
	0850	600 MCM			1.90	4.210	C.L.F.
	0880	700 MCM			1.70	4.710	C.L.F.
	0900	750 MCM			1.60	5.000	C.L.F.
	1450	#3			5	1.600	C.L.F.
	1500	#2			4.50	1.780	C.L.F.
	1550	#1			4	2.000	C.L.F.
	1600	1/0			3.30	2.420	C.L.F.
	1650	2/0	↓	↓	2.90	2.760	C.L.F.

161 500 | Terminations

			CREW	MAKEUP	DAILY OUTPUT	MAN-HOURS	UNIT
510		CABLE CONNECTORS					
	0100	600 volt, nonmetallic, #14-2 wire	1 Elec	1 Electrician	160	.050	Ea.
	0200	#14-3 wire to #12-2 wire			133	.060	Ea.
	0300	#12-3 wire to #10-2 wire			114	.070	Ea.
	0400	#10-3 wire to #14-4 and #12-4 wire			100	.080	Ea.
	0500	#8-3 wire to #10-4 wire			80	.100	Ea.
	0600	#6-3 wire			40	.200	Ea.
	0800	SER, aluminum 3 #8 insulated + 1 #8 ground			32	.250	Ea.
	0900	3 #6 + 1 #6 ground			24	.333	Ea.
	1000	3 #4 + 1 #6 ground			22	.364	Ea.
	1100	3 #2 + 1 #4 ground			20	.400	Ea.
	1200	3 1/0 + 1 #2 ground			18	.444	Ea.
	1400	3 2/0 + 1 #1 ground			16	.500	Ea.
	1600	3 4/0 + 1 # 2/0 ground			14	.571	Ea.
	1800	600 volt, armored , #14-2 wire			80	.100	Ea.
	2200	#14-4, #12-3 and #10-2 wire			40	.200	Ea.
	2400	#12-4, #10-3 and #8-2 wire			32	.250	Ea.
	2600	#8-3 and #10-4 wire			26	.308	Ea.
	2650	#8-4 wire			22	.364	Ea.
	2700	PVC jacket connector, #6-3 wire, #6-4 wire			16	.500	Ea.
	2800	#4-3 wire, #4-4 wire			16	.500	Ea.
	2900	#2-3 wire			12	.667	Ea.
	3000	#1-3 wire, #2-4 wire			12	.667	Ea.
	3200	1/0-3 wire			11	.727	Ea.
	3400	2/0-3 wire, 1/0-4 wire			10	.800	Ea.
	3500	3/0-3 wire, 2/0-4 wire			9	.889	Ea.
	3600	4/0-3 wire, 3/0-4 wire			7	1.140	Ea.
	3800	250 MCM-3 wire, 4/0-4 wire			6	1.330	Ea.
	4000	350 MCM-3 wire, 250 MCM-4 wire			5	1.600	Ea.
	4100	350 MCM-4 wire			4	2.000	Ea.
	4200	500 MCM-3 wire			4	2.000	Ea.
	4250	500 MCM-4 wire, 750 MCM-3 wire			3.50	2.290	Ea.
	4400	5 KV, armored, #4			8	1.000	Ea.
	4600	#2	↓	↓	8	1.000	Ea.

161 500 | Terminations

		CREW	MAKEUP	DAILY OUTPUT	MAN-HOURS	UNIT
510 4801	Cable connectors, 5 KV, armored, #1	1 Elec	1 Electrician	8	1.000	Ea.
5000	1/0			6.40	1.250	Ea.
5200	2/0			5.30	1.510	Ea.
5500	4/0			4	2.000	Ea.
5600	250 MCM			3.60	2.220	Ea.
5650	350 MCM			3.20	2.500	Ea.
5700	500 MCM			2.50	3.200	Ea.
5720	750 MCM			2.20	3.640	Ea.
5750	1000 MCM			2	4.000	Ea.
5800	15 KV, armored,			4	2.000	Ea.
5900	1/0			4	2.000	Ea.
6000	3/0			3.60	2.220	Ea.
6100	4/0			3.40	2.350	Ea.
6200	250 MCM			3.20	2.500	Ea.
6300	350 MCM			2.70	2.960	Ea.
6400	500 MCM	↓	↓	2	4.000	Ea.
520	**CABLE TERMINATIONS**					
0050	Terminal lugs, solderless, #16 to #10	1 Elec	1 Electrician	50	.160	Ea.
0100	#8 to #4			30	.267	Ea.
0150	#2 to #1			22	.364	Ea.
0200	1/0 to			16	.500	Ea.
0250	3/0			12	.667	Ea.
0300	4/0			11	.727	Ea.
0350	250 MCM			9	.889	Ea.
0400	350 MCM			7	1.140	Ea.
0450	500 MCM			6	1.330	Ea.
0500	600 MCM			5.80	1.380	Ea.
0550	750 MCM			5.20	1.540	Ea.
0600	Split bolt connectors, tapped, #6			16	.500	Ea.
0650	#4			14	.571	Ea.
0700	#2			12	.667	Ea.
0750	#1			11	.727	Ea.
0800	1/0			10	.800	Ea.
0850	2/0			9	.889	Ea.
0900	3/0			7.20	1.110	Ea.
1000	4/0			6.40	1.250	Ea.
1100	250 MCM			5.70	1.400	Ea.
1200	300 MCM			5.30	1.510	Ea.
1400	350 MCM			4.60	1.740	Ea.
1500	500 MCM	↓	↓	4	2.000	Ea.
1600	Crimp, 1 hole lugs, copper or aluminum, 600 volt					
1620	#14	1 Elec	1 Electrician	60	.133	Ea.
1630	#12			50	.160	Ea.
1640	#10			45	.178	Ea.
1780	#8			36	.222	Ea.
1800	#6			30	.267	Ea.
2000	#4			27	.296	Ea.
2200	#2			24	.333	Ea.
2400	#1			20	.400	Ea.
2600	2/0			15	.533	Ea.
2800	3/0			12	.667	Ea.
3000	4/0			11	.727	Ea.
3200	250 MCM			9	.889	Ea.
3400	300 MCM			8	1.000	Ea.
3500	350 MCM			7	1.140	Ea.
3600	400 MCM			6.50	1.230	Ea.
3800	500 MCM			6	1.330	Ea.
4000	600 MCM	↓	↓	5.80	1.380	Ea.

		161 500 | Terminations	CREW	MAKEUP	DAILY OUTPUT	MAN-HOURS	UNIT
520	4201	Cable terminations, crimp, 1 hole lugs, 700 MCM	1 Elec	1 Electrician	5.50	1.450	Ea.
	4400	750 MCM	"	"	5.20	1.540	Ea.
	4500	Crimp, 2-way connectors, copper or alum., 600 volt,					
	4510	#14	1 Elec	1 Electrician	60	.133	Ea.
	4520	#12			50	.160	Ea.
	4530	#10			45	.178	Ea.
	4540	#8			27	.296	Ea.
	4600	#6			25	.320	Ea.
	4800	#4			23	.348	Ea.
	5000	#2			20	.400	Ea.
	5200	#1			16	.500	Ea.
	5400	1/0			13	.615	Ea.
	5420	2/0			12	.667	Ea.
	5440	3/0			11	.727	Ea.
	5460	4/0			10	.800	Ea.
	5480	250 MCM			9	.889	Ea.
	5500	300 MCM			8.50	.941	Ea.
	5520	350 MCM			8	1.000	Ea.
	5540	400 MCM			7.30	1.100	Ea.
	5560	500 MCM			6.20	1.290	Ea.
	5580	600 MCM			5.50	1.450	Ea.
	5600	700 MCM			4.50	1.780	Ea.
	5620	750 MCM			4	2.000	Ea.
	7000	Compression equipment adapter for aluminum wire, #6			30	.267	Ea.
	7020	#4			27	.296	Ea.
	7040	#2			24	.333	Ea.
	7060	#1			20	.400	Ea.
	7080	1/0			18	.444	Ea.
	7100	2/0			15	.533	Ea.
	7140	4/0			11	.727	Ea.
	7160	250 MCM			9	.889	Ea.
	7180	300 MCM			8	1.000	Ea.
	7200	350 MCM			7	1.140	Ea.
	7220	400 MCM			6.50	1.230	Ea.
	7240	500 MCM			6	1.330	Ea.
	7260	600 MCM			5.80	1.380	Ea.
	7280	750 MCM	↓	↓	5.20	1.540	Ea.
	525	CABLE TERMINATIONS, 5 KV to 35 KV					
	0100	Indoor, insulation diameter range .525" to 1.025"					
	0300	Padmount, 5 KV	1 Elec	1 Electrician	8	1.000	Ea.
	0400	15 KV			6.40	1.250	Ea.
	0500	25 KV			6	1.330	Ea.
	0600	35 KV	↓	↓	5.60	1.430	Ea.
	0700	.975" to 1.570"					
	0800	Padmount, 5 KV	1 Elec	1 Electrician	8	1.000	Ea.
	0900	15 KV			6	1.330	Ea.
	1000	25 KV			5.60	1.430	Ea.
	1100	35 KV	↓	↓	5.30	1.510	Ea.
	1200	1.540" to 1.900"					
	1300	Padmount, 5 KV	1 Elec	1 Electrician	7.40	1.080	Ea.
	1400	15 KV			5.60	1.430	Ea.
	1500	25 KV			5.30	1.510	Ea.
	1600	35 KV	↓	↓	5	1.600	Ea.
	1700	Outdoor systems, #4 stranded to 1/0 stranded					
	1800	5 KV	1 Elec	1 Electrician	7.40	1.080	Ea.
	1900	15KV			5.30	1.510	Ea.
	2000	25 KV			5	1.600	Ea.
	2100	35 KV	↓	↓	4.80	1.670	Ea.

161 | Conductors and Grounding

161 500 | Terminations

		CREW	MAKEUP	DAILY OUTPUT	MAN-HOURS	UNIT
525 2201	Cable terminations, outdoor, #1 solid to 4/0 stranded, 5 KV	1 Elec	1 Electrician	6.90	1.160	Ea.
2300	15 KV			5	1.600	Ea.
2400	25 KV			4.80	1.670	Ea.
2500	35 KV			4.60	1.740	Ea.
2600	3/0 solid to 350 MCM stranded, 5 KV			6.40	1.250	Ea.
2700	15 KV			4.80	1.670	Ea.
2800	25 KV			4.60	1.740	Ea.
2900	35 KV			4.40	1.820	Ea.
3000	400 MCM compact to 750 MCM stranded, 5 KV			6	1.330	Ea.
3100	15 KV			4.60	1.740	Ea.
3200	25 KV			4.40	1.820	Ea.
3300	35 KV			4.20	1.900	Ea.
3400	1000 MCM, 5 KV			5.60	1.430	Ea.
3500	15 KV			4.40	1.820	Ea.
3600	25 KV			4.20	1.900	Ea.
3700	35 KV	↓	↓	4	2.000	Ea.
540	**CABLE SPLICING** URD or similar, ideal conditions					
0100	#6 stranded to #1 stranded, 5 KV	1 Elec	1 Electrician	4	2.000	Ea.
0120	15 KV			3.60	2.220	Ea.
0140	25 KV			3.20	2.500	Ea.
0200	#1 stranded to 4/0 stranded, 5 KV			3.60	2.220	Ea.
0210	15 KV			3.20	2.500	Ea.
0220	25 KV			2.80	2.860	Ea.
0300	4/0 stranded to 500 MCM stranded, 5 KV			3.30	2.420	Ea.
0310	15 KV			2.90	2.760	Ea.
0320	25 KV			2.50	3.200	Ea.
0400	500 MCM, 5 KV			3.20	2.500	Ea.
0410	15 KV			2.80	2.860	Ea.
0420	25 KV			2.30	3.480	Ea.
0500	600 MCM, 5 KV			2.90	2.760	Ea.
0510	15 KV			2.40	3.330	Ea.
0520	25 KV			2	4.000	Ea.
0600	750 MCM, 5 KV			2.60	3.080	Ea.
0610	15 KV			2.20	3.640	Ea.
0620	25 KV			1.90	4.210	Ea.
0700	1000 MCM, 5 KV			2.30	3.480	Ea.
0710	15 KV			1.90	4.210	Ea.
0720	25 KV	↓	↓	1.60	5.000	Ea.

161 800 | Grounding

		CREW	MAKEUP	DAILY OUTPUT	MAN-HOURS	UNIT
810	**GROUNDING**					
0030	Rod, copper clad, 8' long, 1/2" diameter	1 Elec	1 Electrician	5	1.600	Ea.
0040	5/8" diameter			5.50	1.450	Ea.
0050	3/4" diameter			5.30	1.510	Ea.
0080	10' long, 1/2" diameter			4.80	1.670	Ea.
0090	5/8" diameter			4.60	1.740	Ea.
0100	3/4" diameter			4.40	1.820	Ea.
0130	15' long, 3/4" diameter			4	2.000	Ea.
0230	Clamp, bronze, 1/2" diameter			32	.250	Ea.
0240	5/8" diameter			32	.250	Ea.
0250	3/4" diameter			32	.250	Ea.
0260	Wire, ground, bare armored, #8-1 conductor			2	4.000	C.L.F.
0270	#6-1 conductor			1.80	4.440	C.L.F.
0280	#4-1 conductor			1.60	5.000	C.L.F.
0320	Bare copper wire #14 solid			14	.571	C.L.F.
0330	#12			13	.615	C.L.F.
0340	#10			12	.667	C.L.F.
0350	#8	↓	↓	11	.727	C.L.F.

161 800 | Grounding

		Description	CREW	MAKEUP	DAILY OUTPUT	MAN-HOURS	UNIT
810	0361	Grounding, clamp, bare copper wire, #6	1 Elec	1 Electrician	10	.800	C.L.F.
	0370	#4			8	1.000	C.L.F.
	0380	#2			5	1.600	C.L.F.
	0390	Bare copper wire #8 stranded			11	.727	C.L.F.
	0410	#6			10	.800	C.L.F.
	0450	#4			8	1.000	C.L.F.
	0600	#2			5	1.600	C.L.F.
	0650	#1			4.50	1.780	C.L.F.
	0700	1/0			4	2.000	C.L.F.
	0750	2/0			3.60	2.220	C.L.F.
	0800	3/0			3.30	2.420	C.L.F.
	1000	4/0			2.85	2.810	C.L.F.
	1200	250 MCM			2.40	3.330	C.L.F.
	1210	300 MCM			2.20	3.640	C.L.F.
	1220	350 MCM			2	4.000	C.L.F.
	1230	400 MCM			1.90	4.210	C.L.F.
	1240	500 MCM			1.70	4.710	C.L.F.
	1250	600 MCM			1.30	6.150	C.L.F.
	1260	750 MCM			1.20	6.670	C.L.F.
	1270	1000 MCM			1	8.000	C.L.F.
	1350	Bare aluminum, #8 stranded			10	.800	C.L.F.
	1360	#6			9	.889	C.L.F.
	1370	#4			8	1.000	C.L.F.
	1380	#2			6.50	1.230	C.L.F.
	1390	#1			5.30	1.510	C.L.F.
	1400	1/0			4.50	1.780	C.L.F.
	1410	2/0			4	2.000	C.L.F.
	1420	3/0			3.60	2.220	C.L.F.
	1430	4/0			3.30	2.420	C.L.F.
	1440	250 MCM			3.10	2.580	C.L.F.
	1450	300 MCM			2.90	2.760	C.L.F.
	1460	400 MCM			2.50	3.200	C.L.F.
	1470	500 MCM			2.30	3.480	C.L.F.
	1480	600 MCM			2	4.000	C.L.F.
	1490	700 MCM			1.90	4.210	C.L.F.
	1500	50 MCM			1.70	4.710	C.L.F.
	1510	1000 MCM	↓	↓	1.60	5.000	C.L.F.
	1800	Water pipe ground clamps, heavy duty					
	2000	Bronze, 1/2" to 1" diameter	1 Elec	1 Electrician	8	1.000	Ea.
	2100	1-1/4" to 2" diameter			8	1.000	Ea.
	2200	2-1/2" to 3" diameter			6	1.330	Ea.
	2730	Cadweld, 4/0 wire to 1" ground rod			7	1.140	Ea.
	2740	4/0 wire to building steel			7	1.140	Ea.
	2750	4/0 wire to motor frame			7	1.140	Ea.
	2760	4/0 wire to 4/o wire			7	1.140	Ea.
	2770	4/0 wire to #4 wire			7	1.140	Ea.
	2780	4/0 wire to #8 wire			7	1.140	Ea.
	2800	Brazed connections, #6 wire			12	.667	Ea.
	3000	#2 wire			10	.800	Ea.
	3100	3/0 wire			8	1.000	Ea.
	3200	4/0 wire			7	1.140	Ea.
	3400	250 MCM wire			5	1.600	Ea.
	3600	500 MCM wire			4	2.000	Ea.
	3700	Insulated ground wire, copper #14			13	.615	C.L.F.
	3710	#12			11	.727	C.L.F.
	3720	#10			10	.800	C.L.F.
	3730	#8			8	1.000	C.L.F.
	3740	#6	↓	↓	6.50	1.230	C.L.F.

161 800 | Grounding

810			CREW	MAKEUP	DAILY OUTPUT	MAN-HOURS	UNIT
	3751	Grounding, brazed connections, insul. ground wire, copper, #4	1 Elec	1 Electrician	5.30	1.510	C.L.F.
	3770	#2			4.50	1.780	C.L.F.
	3780	#1			4	2.000	C.L.F.
	3790	1/0			3.30	2.420	C.L.F.
	3800	2/0			2.90	2.760	C.L.F.
	3810	3/0			2.50	3.200	C.L.F.
	3820	4/0			2.20	3.640	C.L.F.
	3830	250 MCM			2	4.000	C.L.F.
	3840	300 MCM			1.90	4.210	C.L.F.
	3850	350 MCM			1.80	4.440	C.L.F.
	3860	400 MCM			1.70	4.710	C.L.F.
	3870	500 MCM			1.60	5.000	C.L.F.
	3880	600 MCM			1.30	6.150	C.L.F.
	3890	750 MCM			1.10	7.270	C.L.F.
	3900	1000 MCM			.90	8.890	C.L.F.
	3950	Insulated ground wire, aluminum #8			9	.889	C.L.F.
	3960	#6			8	1.000	C.L.F.
	3970	#4			6.50	1.230	C.L.F.
	3980	#2			5.30	1.510	C.L.F.
	3990	#1			4.50	1.780	C.L.F.
	4000	1/0			4	2.000	C.L.F.
	4010	2/0			3.60	2.220	C.L.F.
	4020	3/0			3.30	2.420	C.L.F.
	4030	4/0			3.10	2.580	C.L.F.
	4040	250 MCM			2.90	2.760	C.L.F.
	4050	300 MCM			2.70	2.960	C.L.F.
	4060	350 MCM			2.50	3.200	C.L.F.
	4070	400 MCM			2.30	3.480	C.L.F.
	4080	500 MCM			2	4.000	C.L.F.
	4090	600 MCM			1.90	4.210	C.L.F.
	4100	700 MCM			1.70	4.710	C.L.F.
	4110	750 MCM	↓	↓	1.60	5.000	C.L.F.
	5000	Copper Electrolytic ground rod system					
	5010	Includes augering hole, mixing clay electrolyte,					
	5020	Installing tube, and terminating ground wire					
	5100	Straight Vertical type, 2" Dia.					
	5120	8.5' long, Clamp Connection	1 Elec	1 Electrician	2.67	3.000	Ea.
	5130	With Cadweld Connection			1.95	4.100	Ea.
	5140	10' long			2.35	3.400	Ea.
	5150	With Cadweld Connection			1.78	4.490	Ea.
	5160	12' long			2.16	3.700	Ea.
	5170	With Cadweld Connection			1.67	4.790	Ea.
	5180	20' long			1.74	4.600	Ea.
	5190	With Cadweld Connection	↓	↓	1.40	5.710	Ea.
	5200	L-Shaped, 2" Dia.					
	5220	4' Vert. x 10 Horz., Clamp Connection	1 Elec	1 Electrician	5.33	1.500	Ea.
	5230	With Cadweld Connection	"	"	3.08	2.600	Ea.
	5300	Protective Box at grade level, with breather slots					
	5320	Round, 12" long, Plastic	1 Elec	1 Electrician	32	.250	Ea.
	5330	Concrete	"	"	16	.500	Ea.

162 | Boxes and Wiring Devices

		162 100	Boxes	CREW	MAKEUP	DAILY OUTPUT	MAN-HOURS	UNIT
110	110	OUTLET BOXES						
	0020	Pressed steel, octagon, 4"	1 Elec	1 Electrician	20	.400	Ea.
	0040	For Romex or BX			20	.400	Ea.
	0050	For Romex or BX, with bracket			20	.400	Ea.
	0100	Extension			40	.200	Ea.
	0150	Square 4"			20	.400	Ea.
	0160	Romex or BX			20	.400	Ea.
	0170	For Romex or BX, with bracket			20	.400	Ea.
	0200	Extension			40	.200	Ea.
	0220	2-1/8" deep, 1" KO			20	.400	Ea.
	0250	Covers, blank			64	.125	Ea.
	0260	Raised device			64	.125	Ea.
	0300	Plaster rings			64	.125	Ea.
	0350	Square, 4-11/16"			20	.400	Ea.
	0370	2-1/8" deep, 3/4" to 1-1/4" KO			20	.400	Ea.
	0400	Extension			40	.200	Ea.
	0450	Covers, blank			53	.151	Ea.
	0460	Raised device			53	.151	Ea.
	0500	Plaster rings			53	.151	Ea.
	0550	Handy box			27	.296	Ea.
	0560	Covers, device			64	.125	Ea.
	0600	Extension			54	.148	Ea.
	0650	Switchbox			27	.296	Ea.
	0660	Romex or BX			27	.296	Ea.
	0670	Romex or BX, with bracket			27	.296	Ea.
	0680	Partition, metal			27	.296	Ea.
	0700	Masonry, 1 gang, 2-1/2" deep			27	.296	Ea.
	0710	3-1/2" deep			27	.296	Ea.
	0750	2 gang, 2-1/2" deep			20	.400	Ea.
	0760	3-1/2" deep			20	.400	Ea.
	0800	3 gang, 2-1/2" deep			13	.615	Ea.
	0850	4 gang, 2-1/2" deep			10	.800	Ea.
	0860	5 gang, 2-1/2" deep			9	.889	Ea.
	0870	6 gang, 2-1/2" deep			8	1.000	Ea.
	0881	Masonry thru-the-wall box, 1 gang, 4" to 8" block			16	.500	Ea.
	0920	2 gang, 6" block			16	.500	Ea.
	0940	Bar hanger with 3/8" stud, for wood and masonry boxes			53	.151	Ea.
	0950	Concrete, set flush, 4" deep			20	.400	Ea.
	1000	Plate with 3/8" stud			80	.100	Ea.
	1100	Concrete, floor, 1 gang			5.30	1.510	Ea.
	1150	2 gang			4	2.000	Ea.
	1200	3 gang			2.70	2.960	Ea.
	1250	For duplex receptacle, pedestal mounted, add			24	.333	Ea.
	1270	Flush mounted, add			27	.296	Ea.
	1300	For telephone, pedestal mounted, add			30	.267	Ea.
	1350	Carpet flange, 1 gang			53	.151	Ea.
	1400	Cast, 1 gang, FS (2" deep), 1/2" hub			12	.667	Ea.
	1410	3/4" hub			12	.667	Ea.
	1420	FD (2-11/16" deep), 1/2" hub			12	.667	Ea.
	1430	3/4" hub			12	.667	Ea.
	1450	2 gang, FS, 1/2" hub			10	.800	Ea.
	1460	3/4" hub			10	.800	Ea.
	1470	FD, 1/2" hub			10	.800	Ea.
	1480	3/4" hub			10	.800	Ea.
	1500	3 gang, FS, 3/4" hub			9	.889	Ea.
	1510	Switch cover, 1 gang, FS			64	.125	Ea.
	1520	2 gang			53	.151	Ea.
	1530	Duplex receptacle cover, 1 gang, FS			64	.125	Ea.

162 100 | Boxes

		Description	CREW	MAKEUP	DAILY OUTPUT	MAN-HOURS	UNIT
110	1541	Outlet box, cast, duplex receptacle cover, 2 gang, FS	1 Elec	1 Electrician	53	.151	Ea.
	1550	Weatherproof switch cover			64	.125	Ea.
	1600	Weatherproof receptacle cover			64	.125	Ea.
	1750	FSC, 1 gang, 1/2" hub			11	.727	Ea.
	1770	2 gang, 1/2" hub			9	.889	Ea.
	1780	3/4" hub			9	.889	Ea.
	1790	FDC, 1 gang, 1/2" hub			11	.727	Ea.
	1800	3/4" hub			11	.727	Ea.
	1810	2 gang, 1/2" hub			9	.889	Ea.
	1820	3/4" hub			9	.889	Ea.
	2000	Poke-thru fitting, fire rated, for 3-3/4" floor			6.80	1.180	Ea.
	2040	For 7" floor			6.80	1.180	Ea.
	2100	Pedestal, 15 amp, duplex receptacle & blank plate			5.25	1.520	Ea.
	2120	Duplex receptacle and telephone plate			5.25	1.520	Ea.
	2140	Pedestal, 20 amp, duplex recept. & phone plate			5	1.600	Ea.
	2160	Telephone plate, both sides			5.25	1.520	Ea.
	2200	Abandonment plate	↓	↓	32	.250	Ea.
120		**OUTLET BOXES, PLASTIC**					
	0050	4", round, with 2 mounting nails	1 Elec	1 Electrician	25	.320	Ea.
	0100	Bar hanger mounted			25	.320	Ea.
	0200	Square with 2 mounting nails			25	.320	Ea.
	0300	Plaster ring			64	.125	Ea.
	0400	Switch box with 2 mounting nails, 1 gang			30	.267	Ea.
	0500	2 gang			25	.320	Ea.
	0600	3 gang			20	.400	Ea.
	0700	Old work box	↓	↓	30	.267	Ea.
130		**PULL BOXES & CABINETS**					
	0100	Sheet metal, pull box, NEMA 1, type SC, 6"W x 6"H x 4"D	1 Elec	1 Electrician	8	1.000	Ea.
	0180	6"W x 8"H x4"D			8	1.000	Ea.
	0200	8"W x 8"H x 4"D			8	1.000	Ea.
	0210	10"W x 10"H x 4"D			7	1.140	Ea.
	0220	12"W x 12"H x 4"D			6	1.330	Ea.
	0230	15"W x 15"H x 4"D			5.20	1.540	Ea.
	0240	18"W x 18"H x 4"D			4.40	1.820	Ea.
	0250	6"W x 6"H x 6"D			8	1.000	Ea.
	0260	8"W x 8"H x 6"D			7.50	1.070	Ea.
	0270	10"W x 10"H x 6"D			5.50	1.450	Ea.
	0300	10"W x 12"H x 6"D			5.30	1.510	Ea.
	0310	12"W x 12"H x 6"D			5.20	1.540	Ea.
	0320	15"W x 15"H x 6"D			4.60	1.740	Ea.
	0330	18"W x 18"H x 6"D			4.20	1.900	Ea.
	0340	24"W x 24"H x 6"D			3.20	2.500	Ea.
	0350	12"W x 12"H x 8"D			5	1.600	Ea.
	0360	15"W x 15"H x 8"D			4.50	1.780	Ea.
	0370	18"W x 18"H x 8"D			4	2.000	Ea.
	0380	24"W x 18"H x 6"D			3.70	2.160	Ea.
	0400	16"W x 20"H x 8"D			4	2.000	Ea.
	0500	20"W x 24"H x 8"D			3.20	2.500	Ea.
	0510	24"W x 24"H x 8"D			3	2.670	Ea.
	0600	24"W x 36"H x 8"D			2.70	2.960	Ea.
	0610	30"W x 30"H x 8"D			2.70	2.960	Ea.
	0620	36"W x 36"H x 8"D			2	4.000	Ea.
	0630	24"W x 24"H x 10" D			2.50	3.200	Ea.
	0650	Hinged cabinets, type A, 6"W x 6"H x 4"D			8	1.000	Ea.
	0660	8"W x 8"H x 4"D			8	1.000	Ea.
	0670	10"W x 10"H x 4"D			7	1.140	Ea.
	0680	12"W x 12"H x 4"D			6	1.330	Ea.
	0690	15"W x 15"H x 4"D	↓	↓	5.20	1.540	Ea.

162 100 | Boxes

		Description	CREW	MAKEUP	DAILY OUTPUT	MAN-HOURS	UNIT
130	0701	Sheet metal hinged cabinet, type A, 18"W x 18"H x 4"D	1 Elec	1 Electrician	4.40	1.820	Ea.
	0710	6"W x 6"H x 6"D			8	1.000	Ea.
	0720	8"W x 8"H x 6"D			7.50	1.070	Ea.
	0730	10"W x 10"H x 6"D			5.50	1.450	Ea.
	0740	12"W x 12"H x 6"D			5.20	1.540	Ea.
	0800	12"W x 16"H x 6"D			4.70	1.700	Ea.
	0810	15"W x 15"H x 6"D			4.60	1.740	Ea.
	0820	18"W x 18"H x 6"D			4.20	1.900	Ea.
	1000	20"W x 20"H x 6"D			3.60	2.220	Ea.
	1010	24"W x 24"H x 6"D			3.20	2.500	Ea.
	1020	12"W x 12"H x 8"D			5	1.600	Ea.
	1030	15"W x 15"H x 8"D			4.50	1.780	Ea.
	1040	18"W x 18"H x 8"D			4	2.000	Ea.
	1200	20"W x 20"H x 8"D			3.20	2.500	Ea.
	1210	24"W x 24"H x 8"D			3	2.670	Ea.
	1220	30"W x 30"H x 8"D			2.70	2.960	Ea.
	1400	24"W x 36"H x 8"D			2.70	2.960	Ea.
	1600	24"W x 42"H x 8"D			2	4.000	Ea.
	1610	36"W x 36"H x 8"D	↓	↓	2	4.000	Ea.
	2100	NEMA 3R, raintight & weatherproof					
	2150	6"L x 6"W x 6"D	1 Elec	1 Electrician	10	.800	Ea.
	2200	8"L x 6"W x 6"D			8	1.000	Ea.
	2250	10"L x 6"W x 6"D			7	1.140	Ea.
	2300	12"L x 12"W x 6"D			5	1.600	Ea.
	2350	16"L x 16"W x 6"D			4.50	1.780	Ea.
	2400	20"L x 20"W x 6"D			4	2.000	Ea.
	2450	24"L x 18"W x 8"D			3	2.670	Ea.
	2500	24"L x 24"W x 10"D			2.50	3.200	Ea.
	2550	30"L x 24"W x 12"D			2	4.000	Ea.
	2600	36"L x 36"W x 12"D	↓	↓	1.50	5.330	Ea.
	2800	Cast iron, pull boxes for surface mounting					
	3000	NEMA 4, watertight & dust tight					
	3050	6"L x 6"W x 6"D	1 Elec	1 Electrician	4	2.000	Ea.
	3100	8"L x 6"W x 6"D			3.20	2.500	Ea.
	3150	10"L x 6"W x 6"D			2.50	3.200	Ea.
	3200	12"L x 12"W x 6"D			2	4.000	Ea.
	3250	16"L x 16"W x 6"D			1.30	6.150	Ea.
	3300	20"L x 20"W x 6"D			.80	10.000	Ea.
	3350	24"L x 18"W x 8"D			.70	11.430	Ea.
	3400	24"L x 24"W x 10"D			.50	16.000	Ea.
	3450	30"L x 24"W x 12"D			.40	20.000	Ea.
	3500	36"L x 36"W x 12"D			.20	40.000	Ea.
	3510	NEMA 4 clamp cover, 6"L x 6"W x 4"D			4	2.000	Ea.
	3520	8"L x 6"W x 4"D	↓	↓	4	2.000	Ea.
	4000	NEMA 7, explosionproof					
	4050	6"L x 6"W x 6"D	1 Elec	1 Electrician	2	4.000	Ea.
	4100	8"L x 6"W x 6"D			1.80	4.440	Ea.
	4150	10"L x 6"W x 6"D			1.60	5.000	Ea.
	4200	12"L x 12"W x 6"D			1	8.000	Ea.
	4250	16"L x 14"W x 6"D			.60	13.330	Ea.
	4300	18"L x 18"W x 8"D			.50	16.000	Ea.
	4350	24"L x 18"W x 8"D			.40	20.000	Ea.
	4400	24"L x 24"W x 10"D			.30	26.670	Ea.
	4450	30"L x 24"W x 12"D			.20	40.000	Ea.
	5000	NEMA 9, dust tight 6"L x 6"W x 6"D			3.20	2.500	Ea.
	5050	8"L x 6"W x 6"D			2.70	2.960	Ea.
	5100	10"L x 6"W x 6"D			2	4.000	Ea.
	5150	12"L x 12"W x 6"D	↓	↓	1.60	5.000	Ea.

162 100 | Boxes

		CREW	MAKEUP	DAILY OUTPUT	MAN-HOURS	UNIT
130 5201	Pull box, NEMA 9, 16"L x 16"W x 6"D	1 Elec	1 Electrician	1	8.000	Ea.
5250	18"L x 18"W x 8"D			.70	11.430	Ea.
5300	24"L x 18"W x 8"D			.60	13.330	Ea.
5350	24"L x 24"W x 10"D			.40	20.000	Ea.
5400	30"L x 24"W x 12"D	↓	↓	.30	26.670	Ea.
6000	J.I.C. wiring boxes, NEMA 12, dust tight & drip tight					
6050	6"L x 8"W x 4"D	1 Elec	1 Electrician	10	.800	Ea.
6100	8"L x 10"W x 4"D			8	1.000	Ea.
6150	12"L x 14"W x 6"D			5.30	1.510	Ea.
6200	14"L x 16"W x 6"D			4.70	1.700	Ea.
6250	16"L x 20"W x 6"D			4.40	1.820	Ea.
6300	24"L x 30"W x 6"D			3.20	2.500	Ea.
6350	24"L x 30"W x 8"D			2.90	2.760	Ea.
6400	24"L x 36"W x 8"D			2.70	2.960	Ea.
6450	24"L x 42"W x 8"D			2.30	3.480	Ea.
6500	24"L x 48"W x 8"D	↓	↓	2	4.000	Ea.
7000	Cabinets, current transformer					
7050	Single door, 24"H x 24"W x 10"D	1 Elec	1 Electrician	1.60	5.000	Ea.
7100	30"H x 24"W x 10"D			1.30	6.150	Ea.
7150	36"H x 24"W x 10"D			1.10	7.270	Ea.
7200	30"H x 30"W x 10"D			1	8.000	Ea.
7250	36"H x 30"W x 10"D			.90	8.890	Ea.
7300	36"H x 36"W x 10"D			.80	10.000	Ea.
7500	Double door, 48"H x 36"W x 10"D			.60	13.330	Ea.
7550	24"H x 24"W x 12"D	↓	↓	1	8.000	Ea.
7600	Telephone with wood backboard					
7620	Single door, 12"H x 12"W x 4"D	1 Elec	1 Electrician	5.30	1.510	Ea.
7650	18"H x 12"W x 4"D			4.70	1.700	Ea.
7700	24"H x 12"W x 4"D			4.20	1.900	Ea.
7720	18"H x 18"W x 4"D			4.20	1.900	Ea.
7750	24"H x 18"W x 4"D			4	2.000	Ea.
7780	36"H x 36"W x 4"D			3.60	2.220	Ea.
7800	24"H x 24"W x 6"D			3.60	2.220	Ea.
7820	30"H x 24"W x 6"D			3.20	2.500	Ea.
7850	30"H x 30"W x 6"D			2.70	2.960	Ea.
7880	36"H x 30"W x 6"D			2.50	3.200	Ea.
7900	48"H x 36"W x 6"D			2.20	3.640	Ea.
7920	Double door, 48"H x 36"W x 6"D	↓	↓	2	4.000	Ea.
140 0080	**PULL BOXES & CABINETS** Nonmetallic Enclosures fiberglass NEMA 4X					
0100	Wall mount, quick release latch door, 20"H x 16"W x 6"D	1 Elec	1 Electrician	4.80	1.670	Ea.
0110	20"H x 20"W x 6"D			4.50	1.780	Ea.
0120	24"H x 20"W x 6"D			4.20	1.900	Ea.
0130	20"H x 16"W x 8"D			4.50	1.780	Ea.
0140	20"H x 20"W x 8"D			4.20	1.900	Ea.
0150	24"H x 24"W x 8"D			3.80	2.110	Ea.
0160	30"H x 24"W x 8"D			3.20	2.500	Ea.
0170	36"H x 30"W x 8"D			3	2.670	Ea.
0180	20"H x 16"W x 10"D			3.50	2.290	Ea.
0190	20"H x 20"W x 10"D			3.20	2.500	Ea.
0200	24"H x 20"W x 10"D			3	2.670	Ea.
0210	30"H x 24"W x 10"D			2.80	2.860	Ea.
0220	20"H x 16"W x 12"D			3	2.670	Ea.
0230	20"H x 20"W x 12"D			2.80	2.860	Ea.
0240	24"H x 24"W x 12"D			2.60	3.080	Ea.
0250	30"H x 24"W x 12"D			2.40	3.330	Ea.
0260	36"H x 30"W x 12"D			2.20	3.640	Ea.
0270	36"H x 36"W x 12"D	↓	↓	2.10	3.810	Ea.

162 | Boxes and Wiring Devices

162 100 | Boxes

			CREW	MAKEUP	DAILY OUTPUT	MAN-HOURS	UNIT
140	0281	Pull box, fiberglass, wall mount, 48"H x 36"W x 12"D	1 Elec	1 Electrician	2	4.000	Ea.
	0290	60"H x 36"W x 12"D			1.80	4.440	Ea.
	0300	30"H x 24"W x 16"D			1.40	5.710	Ea.
	0310	48"H x 36"W x 16"D			1.20	6.670	Ea.
	0320	60"H x 36"W x 16"D			1	8.000	Ea.
	0480	Freestanding, one door, 72"H x 25"W x 25"D			.80	10.000	Ea.
	0490	Two doors with two panels, 72"H x 49"W x 24"D			.50	16.000	Ea.
	0500	Floor stand kits, for NEMA 4 & 12, 20"W or more			24	.333	Ea.
	0510	6"H x 10"D			24	.333	Ea.
	0520	6"H x 12"D			24	.333	Ea.
	0530	6"H x 18"D			24	.333	Ea.
	0540	12"H x 8"D			22	.364	Ea.
	0550	12"H x 10"D			22	.364	Ea.
	0560	12"H x 12"D			22	.364	Ea.
	0570	12"H x 16"D			22	.364	Ea.
	0580	12"H x 18"D			22	.364	Ea.
	0590	12"H x 20"D			22	.364	Ea.
	0600	18"H x 8"D			20	.400	Ea.
	0610	18"H x 10"D			20	.400	Ea.
	0620	18"H x 12"D			20	.400	Ea.
	0630	18"H x 16"D			20	.400	Ea.
	0640	24"H x 8"D			16	.500	Ea.
	0650	24"H x 10"D			16	.500	Ea.
	0660	24"H x 12"D			16	.500	Ea.
	0670	24"H x 16"D	↓	↓	16	.500	Ea.

162 300 | Wiring Devices

			CREW	MAKEUP	DAILY OUTPUT	MAN-HOURS	UNIT
310		LOW VOLTAGE SWITCHING					
	3600	Relays, 120V or 277V standard	1 Elec	1 Electrician	12	.667	Ea.
	3800	Flush switch, standard			40	.200	Ea.
	4000	Interchangeable			40	.200	Ea.
	4100	Surface switch, standard			40	.200	Ea.
	4200	Transformer 115V to 25V			12	.667	Ea.
	4400	Master control, 12 circuit, manual			4	2.000	Ea.
	4500	25 circuit, motorized			4	2.000	Ea.
	4600	Rectifier, silicon			12	.667	Ea.
	4800	Switchplates, 1 gang, 1, 2 or 3 switch, plastic			80	.100	Ea.
	5000	Stainless steel			80	.100	Ea.
	5400	2 gang, 3 switch, stainless steel			53	.151	Ea.
	5500	4 switch, plastic			53	.151	Ea.
	5600	2 gang, 4 switch, stainless steel			53	.151	Ea.
	5700	6 switch, stainless steel			53	.151	Ea.
	5800	3 gang, 9 switch, stainless steel			32	.250	Ea.
	5900	Receptacle, triple, 1 return, 1 feed			26	.308	Ea.
	6000	2 feed			20	.400	Ea.
	6100	Relay gang boxes, flush or surface, 6 gang			5.30	1.510	Ea.
	6200	12 gang			4.70	1.700	Ea.
	6400	18 gang			4	2.000	Ea.
	6500	Frame, to hold up to 6 relays			12	.667	Ea.
	7200	Control wire,			6.30	1.270	C.L.F.
	7400	3 conductor			5	1.600	C.L.F.
	7600	19 conductor			2.50	3.200	C.L.F.
	7800	26 conductor			2	4.000	C.L.F.
	8000	Weatherproof, 3 conductor	↓	↓	5	1.600	C.L.F.

162 300 | Wiring Devices

		CREW	MAKEUP		DAILY OUTPUT	MAN-HOURS	UNIT
320	320	**WIRING DEVICES**					
	0200	Toggle switch, quiet type, single pole, 15 amp	1 Elec	1 Electrician	40	.200	Ea.
	0500	20 amp			27	.296	Ea.
	0510	30 amp			23	.348	Ea.
	0520	Mercury, 15 amp			40	.200	Ea.
	0530	Lock handle, 20 amp			27	.296	Ea.
	0540	Security key, 20 amp			26	.308	Ea.
	0600	3 way, 15 amp			23	.348	Ea.
	0800	20 amp			18	.444	Ea.
	0810	30 amp			9	.889	Ea.
	0820	Mercury, 15 amp			23	.348	Ea.
	0830	Lock handle, 20 amp			18	.444	Ea.
	0840	Security key, 20 amp			17	.471	Ea.
	0900	4 way, 15 amp			15	.533	Ea.
	1000	20 amp			11	.727	Ea.
	1020	Lock handle, 20 amp			11	.727	Ea.
	1100	Toggle switch, quiet type, double pole, 15 amp			15	.533	Ea.
	1200	20 amp			11	.727	Ea.
	1210	30 amp			9	.889	Ea.
	1230	Lock handle, 20 amp			11	.727	Ea.
	1250	Security key, 20 amp			10	.800	Ea.
	1420	Toggle switch, quiet type, 1 pole, 2 throw, center off, 15 amp			23	.348	Ea.
	1440	20 amp			18	.444	Ea.
	1460	Lock handle, 20 amp			18	.444	Ea.
	1480	Momentary contact, 15 amp			23	.348	Ea.
	1500	20 amp			18	.444	Ea.
	1520	Momentary contact, lock handle, 20 amp			18	.444	Ea.
	1650	Dimmer switch, 120 volt, incandescent, 600 watt, 1 pole			16	.500	Ea.
	1700	600 watt, 3 way			12	.667	Ea.
	1750	1000 watt, 1 pole			16	.500	Ea.
	1800	1000 watt, 3 pole			12	.667	Ea.
	2000	1500 watt, 1 pole			11	.727	Ea.
	2100	2000 watt, 1 pole			8	1.000	Ea.
	2110	Fluorescent, 600 watt			15	.533	Ea.
	2120	1000 watt			15	.533	Ea.
	2130	1500 watt			10	.800	Ea.
	2160	Explosionproof, toggle switch, wall, single pole			5.30	1.510	Ea.
	2180	Receptacle, single outlet, 20 amp			5.30	1.510	Ea.
	2190	30 amp			4	2.000	Ea.
	2290	60 amp			2.50	3.200	Ea.
	2360	Plug, 20 amp			16	.500	Ea.
	2370	30 amp			12	.667	Ea.
	2380	60 amp			8	1.000	Ea.
	2410	Furnace, thermal cutoff switch with plate			26	.308	Ea.
	2460	Receptacle, duplex, 120 volt, grounded, 15 amp			40	.200	Ea.
	2470	20 amp			27	.296	Ea.
	2480	Ground fault interupting, 15 amp			27	.296	Ea.
	2490	Dryer, 30 amp			15	.533	Ea.
	2500	Range, 50 amp			11	.727	Ea.
	2601	Wall plates, stainless steel or brown plastic, 1 gang			80	.100	Ea.
	2800	2 gang			53	.151	Ea.
	3000	3 gang			32	.250	Ea.
	3100	4 gang			27	.296	Ea.
	3170	Switch cover, weatherproof, 1 gang			60	.133	Ea.
	3180	Vandal proof lock, 1 gang			60	.133	Ea.
	3200	Lampholder, keyless			26	.308	Ea.
	3400	Pullchain with receptacle			22	.364	Ea.
	3500	Pilot light, neon with jewel			27	.296	Ea.

162 300 | Wiring Devices

		CREW	MAKEUP	DAILY OUTPUT	MAN-HOURS	UNIT
320	3601	Receptacle, 20 amp, 250 volt, NEMA 6-7-10	1 Elec	1 Electrician	27	.296	Ea.
	3681	125/250 volt NEMA 14-15-18			25	.320	Ea.
	3741	30 amp, 125 volt NEMA 5-6-7			15	.533	Ea.
	3821	125/250 volt NEMA 14-15			14	.571	Ea.
	3881	Receptacle, 50 amp, 125 volt NEMA 5-6-7			11	.727	Ea.
	3961	125/250 volt NEMA 14-15			10	.800	Ea.
	4021	60 amp, 125/250 volt, NEMA 14-15-18			8	1.000	Ea.
	4101	Receptacle locking, 15 or 20 amp, 125 volt NEMA L5-L6-L7-L11			27	.296	Ea.
	4161	20 amp, 480 volt NEMA L8-L9-L10			27	.296	Ea.
	4231	125/250 volt NEMA L12-L14-L15-L16-L18			25	.320	Ea.
	4341	277/280 volt NEMA L19-L20			25	.320	Ea.
	4381	120/208 volt NEMA L21-L22-L23			23	.348	Ea.
	4441	30 amp, 125 volt NEMA L5-L6-L7-L8-L9-L10-L11-L12-L13			15	.533	Ea.
	4621	125/250 volt NEMA L14-L15-L16-L17-L18-L19-L20			14	.571	Ea.
	4761	120/208 volt NEMA L21-L22-L23			13	.615	Ea.
	4841	Receptacle corrosion resistant, 15/20 amp, 125 volt NEMA L5-L6			27	.296	Ea.
	4901	Receptacle cover plate, phenolic plastic, NEMA 5-6-7-23			80	.100	Ea.
	4921	Stainless steel, NEMA 5-6-7-23			80	.100	Ea.
	4941	Brushed brass NEMA 5-6-7-23			80	.100	Ea.
	4961	Anodized aluminum, NEMA 5-6-7-23			80	.100	Ea.
	5100	Plug, 20 amp, 250 volt, NEMA 6			30	.267	Ea.
	5110	277 volt NEMA 7			30	.267	Ea.
	5120	3 pole, 120/250 volt, NEMA 10			26	.308	Ea.
	5130	125/250 volt NEMA 14			26	.308	Ea.
	5140	250 volt NEMA 15			26	.308	Ea.
	5150	120/208 volt NEMA 8			26	.308	Ea.
	5160	30 amp, 125 volt NEMA 5			13	.615	Ea.
	5170	250 volt NEMA 6			13	.615	Ea.
	5180	277 volt NEMA 7			13	.615	Ea.
	5190	125/250 volt NEMA 14			13	.615	Ea.
	5200	3 pole, 250 volt NEMA 15			12	.667	Ea.
	5210	50 amp, 125 volt NEMA 5			9	.889	Ea.
	5220	250 volt NEMA 6			9	.889	Ea.
	5230	277 volt NEMA 7			9	.889	Ea.
	5240	125/250 volt NEMA 14			9	.889	Ea.
	5250	3 pole, 250 volt NEMA 15			8	1.000	Ea.
	5260	60 amp, 125/250 volt NEMA 14			7	1.140	Ea.
	5270	3 pole, 250 volt NEMA 15			7	1.140	Ea.
	5280	120/208 volt NEMA 18			7	1.140	Ea.
	6000	Connector, 20 amp, 250 volt NEMA 6			30	.267	Ea.
	6010	277 volt NEMA 7			30	.267	Ea.
	6020	3 pole, 120/250 volt NEMA 10			26	.308	Ea.
	6030	125/250 volt nema 14			26	.308	Ea.
	6040	250 volt NEMA 15			26	.308	Ea.
	6050	120/208 volt NEMA 18			26	.308	Ea.
	6060	30 amp, 125 volt NEMA 5			13	.615	Ea.
	6070	250 volt NEMA 6			13	.615	Ea.
	6080	277 volt NEMA 7			13	.615	Ea.
	6110	50 amp, 125 volt NEMA 5			9	.889	Ea.
	6120	250 volt NEMA 6			9	.889	Ea.
	6130	277 volt NEMA 7	↓	↓	9	.889	Ea.

163 100	**Starters & Controls**	CREW	MAKEUP	DAILY OUTPUT	MAN-HOURS	UNIT
110	110	**MOTOR CONTROL CENTER** Consists of starters & structures					
	0050	Starters, class 1, type B, comb. MCP, FVNR, with					
	0100	control transformer, 10 HP, size 1, 12" high	1 Elec	1 Electrician	2.70	2.960	Ea.
	0200	25 HP, size 2, 18" high			2	4.000	Ea.
	0300	50 HP, size 3, 24" high			1	8.000	Ea.
	0350	75 HP, size 4, 24" high			.80	10.000	Ea.
	0400	100 HP, size 4, 30" high			.70	11.430	Ea.
	0500	200 HP, size 5, 48" high			.50	16.000	Ea.
	0600	400 HP, size 6, 72" high	↓	↓	.40	20.000	Ea.
	0800	Structures, 300 amp, 22,000 rms, takes any					
	0900	combination of starters up to 72" high	1 Elec	1 Electrician	.80	10.000	Ea.
	1000	Back to back, 72" front & 66" back			.60	13.330	Ea.
	1700	For pilot lights, add per starter			16	.500	Ea.
	1800	For push button, add per starter			16	.500	Ea.
	1900	For auxilliary contacts, add per starter	↓	↓	16	.500	Ea.
120		**MOTOR CONTROL CENTER COMPONENTS**					
	0101	Starter, size 1, FVNR, NEMA 1, type A or B, fusible or breaker	1 Elec	1 Electrician	2.70	2.960	Ea.
	0181	NEMA 12, type A or B, fusible or circuit breaker			2.60	3.080	Ea.
	0301	Starter, size 1, FVR, NEMA 1, type A or B, fusible or breaker			2	4.000	Ea.
	0381	NEMA 12, type A or B, fusible or circuit breaker	↓	↓	1.90	4.210	Ea.
	0490	Starter size 1, 2 speed, separate winding					
	0501	NEMA 1, type A or B, fusible or circuit breaker	1 Elec	1 Electrician	2.60	3.080	Ea.
	0581	NEMA 12, type A or B, fusible or circuit breaker	"	"	2.50	3.200	Ea.
	0650	Starter size 1, 2 speed, consequent pole					
	0661	NEMA 1, type A or B, fusible or circuit breaker	1 Elec	1 Electrician	2.60	3.080	Ea.
	0741	NEMA 12, type A or B, fusible or circuit breaker	"	"	2.50	3.200	Ea.
	0810	Starter size 1, 2 speed, space only					
	0821	NEMA 1, type A or B, fusible or circuit breaker	1 Elec	1 Electrician	16	.500	Ea.
	0901	NEMA 12, type A or B, fusible or circuit breaker			15	.533	Ea.
	1101	Starter size 2, FVNR, NEMA 1, type A or B, fusible or breaker			2	4.000	Ea.
	1181	NEMA 12, type A or B, fusible or circuit breaker			1.90	4.210	Ea.
	1301	Starter size 2, FVR, NEMA 1, type A or B, fusible or breaker			1.60	5.000	Ea.
	1381	NEMA 12, type A or B, fusible or circuit breaker	↓	↓	1.50	5.330	Ea.
	1490	Starter size 2, 2 speed, separate winding					
	1501	NEMA 1, type A or B, fusible or circuit breaker	1 Elec	1 Electrician	1.90	4.210	Ea.
	1571	NEMA 12, type A or B, fusible or circuit breaker	"	"	1.80	4.440	Ea.
	1630	Starter size 2, 2 speed, consequent pole					
	1641	NEMA 1, type A or B, fusible or circuit breaker	1 Elec	1 Electrician	1.90	4.210	Ea.
	1721	NEMA 12, type A or B, fusible or circuit breaker	"	"	1.80	4.440	Ea.
	1830	Starter size 2, autotransformer					
	1841	NEMA 1, type A or B, fusible or circuit breaker	1 Elec	1 Electrician	1.70	4.710	Ea.
	1921	NEMA 12, type A or B, fusible or circuit breaker	"	"	1.60	5.000	Ea.
	2030	Starter size 2, space only					
	2041	NEMA 1, type A or B, fusible or circuit breaker	1 Elec	1 Electrician	16	.500	Ea.
	2121	NEMA 12, type A or B, fusible or circuit breaker			15	.533	Ea.
	2301	Starter size 3, FVNR, NEMA 1, type A or B, fusible or breaker			1	8.000	Ea.
	2381	NEMA 12, type A or B, fusible or circuit breaker			.95	8.420	Ea.
	2501	Starter size 3, FVR, NEMA 1, type A or B, fusible or breaker			.80	10.000	Ea.
	2581	NEMA 12, type A or B, fusible or circuit breaker	↓	↓	.75	10.670	Ea.
	2690	Starter size 3, 2 speed, separate winding					
	2701	NEMA 1, type A or B, fusible or circuit breaker	1 Elec	1 Electrician	1	8.000	Ea.
	2781	NEMA 12, type A or B, fusible or circuit breaker	"	"	.95	8.420	Ea.
	2850	Starter size 3, 2 speed, consequent pole					
	2861	NEMA 1, type A or B, fusible or circuit breaker	1 Elec	1 Electrician	1	8.000	Ea.
	2941	NEMA 12, type A or B, fusible or circuit breaker			.95	8.420	Ea.
	3101	Starter size 3, autotransformer, NEMA 1, type A-B, fusible or c.b.			.80	10.000	Ea.
	3181	NEMA 12, type A or B, fusible or circuit breaker	↓		.75	10.670	Ea.
	3261	Starter size 3, space only, NEMA 1, type A-B, fusible or breaker	↓	↓	15	.533	Ea.

			CREW	MAKEUP	DAILY OUTPUT	MAN-HOURS	UNIT
120	3341	Starter size 3, nEMA 12, type A/B, fusible/circ. breaker	1 Elec	1 Electrician	14	.571	Ea.
	3501	Starter size 4, FVNR, NEMA 1, type A or B, fusible or breaker			.80	10.000	Ea.
	3581	NEMA 12, type A or B, fusible or circuit breaker			.75	10.670	Ea.
	3701	Starter size 4, FVR, NEMA 1, type A or B, fusible or breaker			.60	13.330	Ea.
	3781	NEMA 12, type A or B, fusible or circuit breaker	↓	↓	.58	13.790	Ea.
	3890	Starter size 4, 2 speed, separate windings					
	3901	NEMA 1, type A or B, fusible or circuit breaker	1 Elec	1 Electrician	.80	10.000	Ea.
	3981	NEMA 12, type A or B, fusible or circuit breaker	"	"	.75	10.670	Ea.
	4050	Starter size 4, 2 speed, consequent pole					
	4061	NEMA 1, type A or B, fusible or circuit breaker	1 Elec	1 Electrician	.80	10.000	Ea.
	4141	NEMA 12, type A or B, fusible or circuit breaker			.75	10.670	Ea.
	4301	Starter size 4, autotransformer, NEMA 1, type A-B, fusible or c.b.			.65	12.310	Ea.
	4381	NEMA 12, type A or B, fusible or circuit breaker			.62	12.900	Ea.
	4501	Starter size 4, space only, NEMA 1, type A-B, fusible or breaker			14	.571	Ea.
	4581	NEMA 12, type A or B, fusible or circuit breaker			13	.615	Ea.
	4801	Starter size 5, FVNR, NEMA 1, type A or B, fusible or breaker			.50	16.000	Ea.
	4881	NEMA 12, type A or B, fusible or circuit breaker			.48	16.670	Ea.
	5001	Starter size 5, FVR, NEMA 1, type A or B, fusible or breaker			.40	20.000	Ea.
	5081	NEMA 12, type A or B, fusible or circuit breaker	↓	↓	.38	21.050	Ea.
	5190	Starter size 5, 2 speed, separate windings					
	5201	NEMA 1, type A or B, fusible or circuit breaker	1 Elec	1 Electrician	.50	16.000	Ea.
	5281	NEMA 12, type A or B, fusible or circuit breaker			.48	16.670	Ea.
	5401	Starter size 5, autotransformer, NEMA 1, type A-B, fusible or c.b.			.35	22.860	Ea.
	5481	NEMA 12, type A or B, fusible or circuit breaker			.34	23.530	Ea.
	5601	Starter size 5, space only, NEMA 1, type A-B, fusible or breaker			12	.667	Ea.
	5681	NEMA 12, type A or B, fusible or circuit breaker			11	.727	Ea.
	5801	Fuse, light contact, NEMA 1, type A or B, 30 amp			2.70	2.960	Ea.
	5820	60 amp			2	4.000	Ea.
	5840	100 amp			1	8.000	Ea.
	5860	200 amp			.80	10.000	Ea.
	5961	NEMA 12, type A or B, 30 amp			2.60	3.080	Ea.
	5980	60 amp			1.90	4.210	Ea.
	6000	100 amp			.95	8.420	Ea.
	6020	200 amp			.75	10.670	Ea.
	6201	Circuit breaker, light contact, NEMA 1, type A or B, 30 amp			2.70	2.960	Ea.
	6220	60 amp			2	4.000	Ea.
	6240	100 amp			1	8.000	Ea.
	6260	200 amp			.80	10.000	Ea.
	6361	NEMA 12, type A or B, 30 amp			2.60	3.080	Ea.
	6380	60 amp			1.90	4.210	Ea.
	6400	100 amp			.95	8.420	Ea.
	6420	200 amp			.75	10.670	Ea.
	6601	Fusible switch or circuit breaker, NEMA 1, type A, 30 amp			5.30	1.510	Ea.
	6620	60 amp			5	1.600	Ea.
	6640	100 amp			4	2.000	Ea.
	6641	Fusible switch, NEMA 1, type A, 100 amp			4	2.000	Ea.
	6660	200 amp			3.20	2.500	Ea.
	6680	400 amp			2.30	3.480	Ea.
	6700	600 amp			1.60	5.000	Ea.
	6720	800 amp			1.30	6.150	Ea.
	6740	NEMA 12, type A, 30 amp			5.20	1.540	Ea.
	6760	60 amp			4.90	1.630	Ea.
	6780	100 amp			3.90	2.050	Ea.
	6800	200 amp			3.10	2.580	Ea.
	6820	400 amp			2.20	3.640	Ea.
	6840	600 amp			1.50	5.330	Ea.
	6860	800 amp			1.20	6.670	Ea.
	7300	Incoming line, main lug only, 600 amp, alum, NEMA 1	↓	↓	.80	10.000	Ea.

163 100	Starters & Controls	CREW	MAKEUP	DAILY OUTPUT	MAN-HOURS	UNIT
120 7321	Incoming line, main lug only, 600 amp, alum., NEMA 12	1 Elec	1 Electrician	.75	10.670	Ea.
7340	Copper, NEMA 1			.80	10.000	Ea.
7360	800 amp, alum., NEMA 1			.75	10.670	Ea.
7380	NEMA 12			.70	11.430	Ea.
7400	Copper, NEMA 1			.75	10.670	Ea.
7420	1200 amp, copper, NEMA 1			.70	11.430	Ea.
7441	Incoming line, fusible switch or circ breaker, 400 amp, alum., NEMA 1			.60	13.330	Ea.
7460	NEMA 12			.55	14.550	Ea.
7480	Copper, NEMA 1			.60	13.330	Ea.
7500	600 amp, alum., NEMA 1			.55	14.550	Ea.
7520	NEMA 12			.50	16.000	Ea.
7540	Copper, NEMA 1			.55	14.550	Ea.
7840	For 1/4" x 1" ground bus, add			16	.500	Ea.
7860	For 1/4" x 2" ground bus, add			12	.667	Ea.
7880	Main rating, basic section, alum., NEMA 1, 600 amp			.80	10.000	Ea.
7900	800 amp			.70	11.430	Ea.
7920	1200 amp			.60	13.330	Ea.
8060	Unit devices, pilot light, standard			16	.500	Ea.
8080	Pilot light, push to test			16	.500	Ea.
8100	Pilot light, standard, and push button			12	.667	Ea.
8120	Pilot light, push to test, and push button			12	.667	Ea.
8140	Pilot light, standard, and select switch			12	.667	Ea.
8160	Pilot light, push to test, and select switch	↓	↓	12	.667	Ea.
130	**MOTOR STARTERS & CONTROLS**					
0050	Magnetic, FVNR, with enclosure and heaters, 480 volt					
0080	2 HP, size 00	1 Elec	1 Electrician	3.50	2.290	Ea.
0100	5 HP, size 0			2.30	3.480	Ea.
0200	10 HP, size 1			1.60	5.000	Ea.
0300	25 HP, size 2			1.10	7.270	Ea.
0400	50 HP, size 3			.90	8.890	Ea.
0500	100 HP, size 4			.60	13.330	Ea.
0600	200 HP, size 5			.45	17.780	Ea.
0610	400 HP, size 6			.40	20.000	Ea.
0620	NEMA 7, 5 HP, size 0			1.60	5.000	Ea.
0630	10 HP, size 1			1.10	7.270	Ea.
0640	25 HP, size 2			.90	8.890	Ea.
0650	50 HP, size 3			.60	13.330	Ea.
0660	100 HP, size 4			.45	17.780	Ea.
0670	200 HP, size 5			.25	32.000	Ea.
0700	Combination, with motor circuit protectors, 5 HP, size 0			1.80	4.440	Ea.
0800	10 HP, size 1			1.30	6.150	Ea.
0900	25 HP, size 2			1	8.000	Ea.
1000	50 HP, size 3			.66	12.120	Ea.
1200	100 HP, size 4			.40	20.000	Ea.
1220	NEMA 7, 5 HP, size 0			1.30	6.150	Ea.
1230	10 HP, size 1			1	8.000	Ea.
1240	25 HP, size 2			.66	12.120	Ea.
1250	50 HP, size 3			.40	20.000	Ea.
1260	100 HP, size 4			.30	26.670	Ea.
1270	200 HP, size 5			.20	40.000	Ea.
2710	Magnetic, FVR, control circuit transformer, NEMA 1, size 1			1.30	6.150	Ea.
2720	Size 2			1	8.000	Ea.
2730	Size 3			.66	12.120	Ea.
2740	Size 4			.40	20.000	Ea.
2760	NEMA 4, size 1			1.10	7.270	Ea.
2770	Size 2			.80	10.000	Ea.
2780	Size 3			.60	13.330	Ea.
2790	Size 4	↓	↓	.35	22.860	Ea.

163 100	Starters & Controls	CREW	MAKEUP	DAILY OUTPUT	MAN-HOURS	UNIT
130	2821	Motor starter, magnetic, FVR, NEMA 12, size 1	1 Elec	1 Electrician	1.10	7.270	Ea.
	2830	Size 2			.80	10.000	Ea.
	2840	Size 3			.60	13.330	Ea.
	2850	Size 4			.35	22.860	Ea.
	3010	Manual, single phase, w/pilot, 1 pole 120V NEMA 1			6.40	1.250	Ea.
	3020	NEMA 4			4	2.000	Ea.
	3030	2 pole, 230V, NEMA 1			6.40	1.250	Ea.
	3040	NEMA 4			4	2.000	Ea.
	3050	3 phase, 3 pole 600V, NEMA 1			5.50	1.450	Ea.
	3060	NEMA 4			3.50	2.290	Ea.
	3070	NEMA 12	▼	▼	3.50	2.290	Ea.
	3500	Magnetic FVNR with NEMA 12, enclosure & heaters, 480 volt					
	3600	5 HP, size 0	1 Elec	1 Electrician	2.20	3.640	Ea.
	3700	10 HP, size 1			1.50	5.330	Ea.
	3800	25 HP, size 2			1	8.000	Ea.
	3900	50 HP, size 3			.80	10.000	Ea.
	4000	100 HP, size 4			.50	16.000	Ea.
	4100	200 HP, size 5	▼	▼	.40	20.000	Ea.
	5200	Factory installed controls, adders to size 0 thru 5					
	5300	Start-stop push button	1 Elec	1 Electrician	32	.250	Ea.
	5400	Hand-off-auto-selector switch			32	.250	Ea.
	5810	Magnetic FVR, NEMA 7 w/heaters, size 1			.66	12.120	Ea.
	5830	Size 2			.55	14.550	Ea.
	5840	Size 3			.35	22.860	Ea.
	5850	Size 4			.30	26.670	Ea.
	5860	Combination w/circuit breakers, heaters, control xfmr PB size 1			.60	13.330	Ea.
	5870	Size 2			.40	20.000	Ea.
	5880	Size 3			.25	32.000	Ea.
	5890	Size 4			.20	40.000	Ea.
	5900	Manual, 240 volt, .75 HP motor			4	2.000	Ea.
	5910	2 HP motor			4	2.000	Ea.
	6000	Magnetic, 240 volt, 1 or 2 pole, .75 HP motor			4	2.000	Ea.
	6020	2 HP motor			4	2.000	Ea.
	6040	5 HP motor			3	2.670	Ea.
	6060	10 HP motor			2.30	3.480	Ea.
	6100	3 pole, .75 HP motor			3	2.670	Ea.
	6120	5 HP motor			2.30	3.480	Ea.
	6140	10 HP motor			1.60	5.000	Ea.
	6160	15 HP motor			1.60	5.000	Ea.
	6180	20 HP motor			1.10	7.270	Ea.
	6200	25 HP motor			1.10	7.270	Ea.
	6210	30 HP motor			.90	8.890	Ea.
	6220	40 HP motor			.90	8.890	Ea.
	6230	50 HP motor			.90	8.890	Ea.
	6240	60 HP motor			.60	13.330	Ea.
	6250	75 HP motor			.60	13.330	Ea.
	6260	100 HP motor			.60	13.330	Ea.
	6270	125 HP motor			.45	17.780	Ea.
	6280	150 HP motor			.45	17.780	Ea.
	6290	200 HP motor			.45	17.780	Ea.
	6400	Starter & nonfused disconnect, 240 volt, 1-2 pole, .75 HP motor			2	4.000	Ea.
	6410	2 HP motor			2	4.000	Ea.
	6420	5 HP motor			1.80	4.440	Ea.
	6430	10 HP motor			1.40	5.710	Ea.
	6440	3 pole, .75 HP motor			1.60	5.000	Ea.
	6450	5 HP motor			1.40	5.710	Ea.
	6460	10 HP motor			1.10	7.270	Ea.
	6470	15 HP motor	▼	▼	1	8.000	Ea.

163 100	Starters & Controls	CREW	MAKEUP	DAILY OUTPUT	MAN-HOURS	UNIT
130 6481	Starter, 3 pole, 20 HP motor	1 Elec	1 Electrician	.75	10.670	Ea.
6490	25 HP motor			.75	10.670	Ea.
6500	30 HP motor			.65	12.310	Ea.
6510	40 HP motor			.62	12.900	Ea.
6520	50 HP motor			.56	14.290	Ea.
6530	60 HP motor			.45	17.780	Ea.
6540	75 HP motor			.38	21.050	Ea.
6550	100 HP motor			.35	22.860	Ea.
6560	125 HP motor			.30	26.670	Ea.
6570	150 HP motor			.26	30.770	Ea.
6580	200 HP motor			.25	32.000	Ea.
6600	Starter & fused disconnect, 240 volt, 1-2 pole, .75 HP motor			2	4.000	Ea.
6610	2 HP motor			2	4.000	Ea.
6620	5 HP motor			1.80	4.440	Ea.
6630	10 HP motor			1.40	5.710	Ea.
6640	3 pole, .75 HP motor			1.60	5.000	Ea.
6650	5 HP motor			1.40	5.710	Ea.
6660	10 HP motor			1.10	7.270	Ea.
6690	15 HP motor			1	8.000	Ea.
6700	20 HP motor			.80	10.000	Ea.
6710	25 HP motor			.80	10.000	Ea.
6720	30 HP motor			.70	11.430	Ea.
6730	40 HP motor			.60	13.330	Ea.
6740	50 HP motor			.60	13.330	Ea.
6750	60 HP motor			.45	17.780	Ea.
6760	75 HP motor			.45	17.780	Ea.
6770	100 HP motor			.35	22.860	Ea.
6780	125 HP motor	▼	▼	.27	29.630	Ea.
7190	Combination starter & circuit breaker disconnect					
7200	240 volt, 1-2 pole, .75 HP motor	1 Elec	1 Electrician	2	4.000	Ea.
7210	2 HP motor			2	4.000	Ea.
7220	5 HP motor			1.50	5.330	Ea.
7230	10 HP motor			1.20	6.670	Ea.
7240	3 pole, .75 HP motor			1.80	4.440	Ea.
7250	5 HP motor			1.30	6.150	Ea.
7260	10 HP motor			1	8.000	Ea.
7270	15 HP motor			1	8.000	Ea.
7280	20 HP motor			.66	12.120	Ea.
7290	25 HP motor			.66	12.120	Ea.
7300	30 HP motor			.66	12.120	Ea.
7310	40 HP motor			.40	20.000	Ea.
7320	50 HP motor			.40	20.000	Ea.
7330	60 HP motor			.40	20.000	Ea.
7340	75 HP motor			.35	22.860	Ea.
7350	100 HP motor			.35	22.860	Ea.
7360	125 HP motor			.35	22.860	Ea.
7370	150 HP motor			.30	26.670	Ea.
7380	200 HP motor	▼	▼	.30	26.670	Ea.
7400	Magnetic FVNR with enclosure & heaters, 2 pole,					
7410	230 volt, 1 HP size 00	1 Elec	1 Electrician	4	2.000	Ea.
7420	2 HP, size 0			4	2.000	Ea.
7430	3 HP, size 1			3	2.670	Ea.
7440	5 HP, size 1p			3	2.670	Ea.
7450	115 volt, 1/3 HP, size 00			4	2.000	Ea.
7460	1 HP, size 0			4	2.000	Ea.
7470	2 HP, size 1			3	2.670	Ea.
7480	3 HP, size 1P			3	2.670	Ea.
7500	3 pole, 480 volt, 600 HP, size 7	▼	▼	.35	22.860	Ea.

163 200	Boards	CREW	MAKEUP	DAILY OUTPUT	MAN-HOURS	UNIT
205	**205 CIRCUIT BREAKERS** (in enclosure)					
0100	Enclosed (NEMA 1), 600 volt, 3 pole, 30 amp	1 Elec	1 Electrician	3.20	2.500	Ea.
0200	60 amp			2.80	2.860	Ea.
0400	100 amp			2.30	3.480	Ea.
0600	225 amp			1.50	5.330	Ea.
0700	400 amp			.80	10.000	Ea.
0800	600 amp			.60	13.330	Ea.
1000	800 amp			.47	17.020	Ea.
1200	1000 amp			.42	19.050	Ea.
1220	1200 amp			.40	20.000	Ea.
1240	1600 amp			.36	22.220	Ea.
1260	2000 amp			.32	25.000	Ea.
1400	1200 amp with ground fault			.40	20.000	Ea.
1600	1600 amp with ground fault			.36	22.220	Ea.
1800	2000 amp with ground fault			.32	25.000	Ea.
2000	Disconnect, 240 volt 3 pole, 5 HP motor			3.20	2.500	Ea.
2020	10 HP motor			3.20	2.500	Ea.
2040	15 HP motor			2.80	2.860	Ea.
2060	20 HP motor			2.30	3.480	Ea.
2080	25 HP motor			2.30	3.480	Ea.
2100	30 HP motor			2.30	3.480	Ea.
2120	40 HP motor			2	4.000	Ea.
2140	50 HP motor			1.50	5.330	Ea.
2160	60 HP motor			1.50	5.330	Ea.
2180	75 HP motor			1	8.000	Ea.
2200	100 HP motor			.80	10.000	Ea.
2220	125 HP motor			.80	10.000	Ea.
2240	150 HP motor			.60	13.330	Ea.
2260	200 HP motor			.60	13.330	Ea.
2300	Enclosed (NEMA 7), explosion proof, 600 volt, 3 pole, 50 amp			2.30	3.480	Ea.
2350	100 amp			1.50	5.330	Ea.
2400	150 amp			1	8.000	Ea.
2450	250 amp			.80	10.000	Ea.
2500	400 amp	↓	↓	.60	13.330	Ea.
220	**220 FUSES**					
0020	Cartridge, nonrenewable					
0050	250 volt, 30 amp	1 Elec	1 Electrician	50	.160	Ea.
0100	60 amp			50	.160	Ea.
0150	100 amp			40	.200	Ea.
0200	200 amp			36	.222	Ea.
0250	400 amp			30	.267	Ea.
0300	600 amp			24	.333	Ea.
0400	600 volt, 30 amp			40	.200	Ea.
0450	60 amp			40	.200	Ea.
0500	100 amp			36	.222	Ea.
0550	200 amp			30	.267	Ea.
0600	400 amp			24	.333	Ea.
0650	600 amp			20	.400	Ea.
0800	Dual element, time delay, 250 volt, 30 amp			50	.160	Ea.
0850	60 amp			50	.160	Ea.
0900	100 amp			40	.200	Ea.
0950	200 amp			36	.222	Ea.
1000	400 amp			30	.267	Ea.
1050	600 amp			24	.333	Ea.
1300	600 volt, 15 to 30 amp			40	.200	Ea.
1350	35 to 60 amp			40	.200	Ea.
1400	70 to 100 amp			36	.222	Ea.
1450	110 to 200 amp	↓	↓	30	.267	Ea.

163 200 | Boards

		Description	CREW	MAKEUP	DAILY OUTPUT	MAN-HOURS	UNIT
220	1801	Fuses, class K5, high capacity, 250 volt, 30 amp	1 Elec	1 Electrician	50	.160	Ea.
	1850	60 amp			50	.160	Ea.
	1950	200 amp			36	.222	Ea.
	2000	400 amp			30	.267	Ea.
	2050	600 amp			24	.333	Ea.
	2200	600 volt, 30 amp			40	.200	Ea.
	2250	60 amp			40	.200	Ea.
	2300	100 amp			36	.222	Ea.
	2350	200 amp			30	.267	Ea.
	2400	400 amp			24	.333	Ea.
	2450	600 amp			20	.400	Ea.
	2700	Class J, CLF, 250 or 600 volt, 30 amp			40	.200	Ea.
	2750	60 amp			40	.200	Ea.
	2800	100 amp			36	.222	Ea.
	2850	200 amp			30	.267	Ea.
	2900	400 amp			24	.333	Ea.
	2950	600 amp			20	.400	Ea.
	3100	Class L, 250 or 600 volt, 601 to 1200 amp			16	.500	Ea.
	3150	1500-1600 amp			13	.615	Ea.
	3200	1800-2000 amp			10	.800	Ea.
	3250	2500 amp			10	.800	Ea.
	3300	3000 amp			8	1.000	Ea.
	3350	3500-4000 amp			8	1.000	Ea.
	3400	4500-5000 amp			6.70	1.190	Ea.
	3450	6000 amp			5.70	1.400	Ea.
	3600	Plug, 120 volt, 1 to 10 amp			50	.160	Ea.
	3650	15 to 30 amp			50	.160	Ea.
	3700	Dual element 0.3 to 14 amp			50	.160	Ea.
	3750	15 to 30 amp			50	.160	Ea.
	3800	Fustat, 120 volt, 15 to 30 amp			50	.160	Ea.
	3850	0.3 to 14 amp			50	.160	Ea.
	3900	Adapters .3 to 10 amp			50	.160	Ea.
	3950	15 to 30 amp	↓	↓	50	.160	Ea.
	225	**FUSE CABINETS**					
	0050	120/240 volts, 3 wire, 30 amp branches,					
	0200	4 circuits	1 Elec	1 Electrician	4	2.000	Ea.
	0300	6 circuits			3.20	2.500	Ea.
	0400	8 circuits			2.70	2.960	Ea.
	0500	12 circuits	↓	↓	2	4.000	Ea.
	230	**LOAD CENTERS** (residential type)					
	0100	3 wire, 120/240V, 1 phase, including 1 pole plug-in breakers					
	0200	100 amp main lugs, indoor, 8 circuits	1 Elec	1 Electrician	1.40	5.710	Ea.
	0300	12 circuits			1.20	6.670	Ea.
	0400	Rainproof, 8 circuits			1.40	5.710	Ea.
	0500	12 circuits			1.20	6.670	Ea.
	0600	200 amp main lugs, indoor, 16 circuits			.90	8.890	Ea.
	0700	20 circuits			.75	10.670	Ea.
	0800	24 circuits			.65	12.310	Ea.
	0900	30 circuits			.60	13.330	Ea.
	1000	42 circuits			.40	20.000	Ea.
	1200	Rainproof, 16 circuits			.90	8.890	Ea.
	1300	20 circuits			.75	10.670	Ea.
	1400	24 circuits			.65	12.310	Ea.
	1500	30 circuits			.60	13.330	Ea.
	1600	42 circuits			.40	20.000	Ea.
	1800	400 amp main lugs, indoor, 42 circuits			.36	22.220	Ea.
	1900	Rainproof, 42 circuit	↓	↓	.36	22.220	Ea.

163 200	Boards	CREW	MAKEUP	DAILY OUTPUT	MAN-HOURS	UNIT
230 2200	Plug in breakers with 20 amp, 1 pole, 4 wire, 120/208 volts					
2210	125 amp main lugs, indoor, 12 circuits	1 Elec	1 Electrician	1.20	6.670	Ea.
2300	18 circuits			.80	10.000	Ea.
2400	Rainproof, 12 circuits			1.20	6.670	Ea.
2500	18 circuits			.80	10.000	Ea.
2600	200 amp main lugs, indoor, 24 circuits			.65	12.310	Ea.
2700	30 circuits			.60	13.330	Ea.
2800	36 circuits			.50	16.000	Ea.
2900	42 circuits			.40	20.000	Ea.
3000	Rainproof, 24 circuits			.65	12.310	Ea.
3100	30 circuits			.60	13.330	Ea.
3200	36 circuits			.50	16.000	Ea.
3300	42 circuits			.40	20.000	Ea.
3500	400 amp main lugs, indoor, 42 circuits			.36	22.220	Ea.
3600	Rainproof, 42 circuits	▼	▼	.36	22.220	Ea.
3700	Plug-in breakers with 20 amp, 1 pole, 3 wire, 120/240 volts					
3800	100 amp main breaker, indoor, 12 circuits	1 Elec	1 Electrician	1.20	6.670	Ea.
3900	18 circuits			.80	10.000	Ea.
4000	200 amp main breaker, indoor, 20 circuits			.75	10.670	Ea.
4200	24 circuits			.65	12.310	Ea.
4300	30 circuits			.60	13.330	Ea.
4400	40 circuits			.45	17.780	Ea.
4500	Rainproof, 20 circuits			.75	10.670	Ea.
4600	24 circuits			.65	12.310	Ea.
4700	30 circuits			.60	13.330	Ea.
4800	40 circuits			.45	17.780	Ea.
5000	400 amp main breaker, indoor, 42 circuits			.36	22.220	Ea.
5100	Rainproof, 42 circuits	▼	▼	.36	22.220	Ea.
5300	Plug in breakers with 20 amp, 1 pole, 4 wire, 120/208 volts					
5400	200 amp main breaker, indoor, 30 circuits	1 Elec	1 Electrician	.60	13.330	Ea.
5500	42 circuits			.40	20.000	Ea.
5600	Rainproof, 30 circuits			.60	13.330	Ea.
5700	42 circuits	▼	▼	.40	20.000	Ea.
240	METER CENTERS AND SOCKETS					
0100	Sockets, single position, 4 terminal, 100 amp	1 Elec	1 Electrician	3.20	2.500	Ea.
0200	150 amp			2.30	3.480	Ea.
0300	200 amp			1.90	4.210	Ea.
0400	20 amp			3.20	2.500	Ea.
0500	Double position, 4 terminal, 100 amp			2.80	2.860	Ea.
0600	150 amp			2.10	3.810	Ea.
0700	200 amp			1.70	4.710	Ea.
0800	Trans-socket, 13 terminal, 3 CT mounts, 400 amp			1	8.000	Ea.
0900	800 amp	▼	▼	.60	13.330	Ea.
2000	Meter center, main fusible switch, 1P 3W 120/240V					
2030	400 amp	1 Elec	1 Electrician	8	1.000	Ea.
2040	600 amp			.55	14.550	Ea.
2050	800 amp			.45	17.780	Ea.
2060	Rainproof 1P 3W 120/240V, 400 amp			.80	10.000	Ea.
2070	600 amp			.55	14.550	Ea.
2080	800 amp			.45	17.780	Ea.
2100	3P 4W 120/208V, 400 amp			.80	10.000	Ea.
2110	600 amp			.55	14.550	Ea.
2120	800 amp			.45	17.780	Ea.
2130	Rainproof 3P 4W 120/208V, 400 amp			.80	10.000	Ea.
2140	600 amp			.55	14.550	Ea.
2150	800 amp	▼	▼	.45	17.780	Ea.
2170	Main circuit breaker, 1P 3W 120/240V					
2180	400 amp	1 Elec	1 Electrician	.80	10.000	Ea.

			CREW	MAKEUP	DAILY OUTPUT	MAN-HOURS	UNIT
**163 200	Boards**							
240	2191	Meter center, main C.B., 1P 3W 120/240V, 600 amp	1 Elec	1 Electrician	.55	14.550	Ea.
	2200	800 amp			.45	17.780	Ea.
	2210	1000 amp			.40	20.000	Ea.
	2220	1200 amp			.38	21.050	Ea.
	2230	1600 amp			.34	23.530	Ea.
	2240	Rainproof 1P 3W 120/240V, 400 amp			.80	10.000	Ea.
	2250	600 amp			.55	14.550	Ea.
	2260	800 amp			.45	17.780	Ea.
	2270	1000 amp			.40	20.000	Ea.
	2280	1200 amp			.38	21.050	Ea.
	2300	3P 4W 120/208V, 400 amp			.80	10.000	Ea.
	2310	600 amp			.55	14.550	Ea.
	2320	800 amp			.45	17.780	Ea.
	2330	1000 amp			.40	20.000	Ea.
	2340	1200 amp			.38	21.050	Ea.
	2350	1600 amp			.34	23.530	Ea.
	2360	Rainproof 3P 4W 120/208V, 400 amp			.80	10.000	Ea.
	2370	600 amp			.55	14.550	Ea.
	2380	800 amp			.45	17.780	Ea.
	2390	1000 amp			.38	21.050	Ea.
	2400	1200 amp	↓	↓	.34	23.530	Ea.
	2590	Basic meter device					
	2600	1P 3W 120/240V 4 jaw 125A sockets, 3 meter	1 Elec	1 Electrician	.50	16.000	Ea.
	2610	4 meter			.45	17.780	Ea.
	2620	5 meter			.40	20.000	Ea.
	2630	6 meter			.30	26.670	Ea.
	2640	7 meter			.28	28.570	Ea.
	2650	8 meter			.26	30.770	Ea.
	2660	10 meter	↓	↓	.24	33.330	Ea.
	2680	Rainproof 1P 3W 120/240V 4 jaw 125A sockets					
	2690	3 meter	1 Elec	1 Electrician	.50	16.000	Ea.
	2700	4 meter			.45	17.780	Ea.
	2710	6 meter			.30	26.670	Ea.
	2720	7 meter			.28	28.570	Ea.
	2730	8 meter	↓	↓	.26	30.770	Ea.
245		**PANELBOARDS** (Commercial use)					
	0050	NQOB, w/20 amp 1 pole bolt-on circuit breakers					
	0100	3 wire, 120/240 volts, 100 amp main lugs					
	0150	10 circuits	1 Elec	1 Electrician	1	8.000	Ea.
	0200	14 circuits			.88	9.090	Ea.
	0250	18 circuits			.75	10.670	Ea.
	0300	20 circuits			.65	12.310	Ea.
	0350	225 amp main lugs, 24 circuits			.60	13.330	Ea.
	0400	30 circuits			.45	17.780	Ea.
	0450	36 circuits			.40	20.000	Ea.
	0500	38 circuits			.36	22.220	Ea.
	0550	42 circuits			.33	24.240	Ea.
	0600	4 wire, 120/208 volts, 100 amp main lugs, 12 circuits			1	8.000	Ea.
	0650	16 circuits			.75	10.670	Ea.
	0700	20 circuits			.65	12.310	Ea.
	0750	24 circuits			.60	13.330	Ea.
	0800	30 circuits			.53	15.090	Ea.
	0850	225 amp main lugs, 32 circuits			.45	17.780	Ea.
	0900	34 circuits			.42	19.050	Ea.
	0950	36 circuits			.40	20.000	Ea.
	1000	42 circuits			.34	23.530	Ea.
	1040	225 amp main lugs, NEMA 7, 12 circuits			.50	16.000	Ea.
	1100	24 circuits	↓	↓	.20	40.000	Ea.

		CREW	MAKEUP	DAILY OUTPUT	MAN-HOURS	UNIT
163 200	**Boards**					
1200	NEHB,w/20 amp, 1 pole bolt-on circuit breakers					
1300	20 circuits	1 Elec	1 Electrician	.60	13.330	Ea.
1350	225 amp main lugs, 24 circuits			.45	17.780	Ea.
1400	30 circuits			.40	20.000	Ea.
1450	36 circuits			.36	22.220	Ea.
1500	42 circuits			.30	26.670	Ea.
1510	225 amp main lugs, NEMA 7, 12 circuits			.45	17.780	Ea.
1590	24 circuits	↓	↓	.15	53.330	Ea.
1600	NQOB panel, w/20 amp, 1 pole, circuit breakers					
1650	3 wire, 120/240 volt with main circuit breaker					
1700	100 amp main, 12 circuits	1 Elec	1 Electrician	.80	10.000	Ea.
1750	20 circuits			.60	13.330	Ea.
1800	225 amp main, 30 circuits			.34	23.530	Ea.
1850	42 circuits			.26	30.770	Ea.
1900	400 amp main, 30 circuits			.27	29.630	Ea.
1950	42 circuits	↓	↓	.25	32.000	Ea.
2000	4 wire, 120/208 volts with main circuit breaker					
2050	100 amp main, 24 circuits	1 Elec	1 Electrician	.47	17.020	Ea.
2100	30 circuits			.40	20.000	Ea.
2200	225 amp main, 32 circuits			.36	22.220	Ea.
2250	42 circuits			.28	28.570	Ea.
2300	400 amp main, 42 circuits	↓	↓	.24	33.330	Ea.
2400	NEHB, with 20 amp, 1 pole circuit breaker					
2450	4 wire, 227/480 volts with main circuit breaker					
2500	100 amp main, 24 circuits	1 Elec	1 Electrician	.42	19.050	Ea.
2550	30 circuits			.38	21.050	Ea.
2600	225 amp main, 30 circuits			.36	22.220	Ea.
2650	42 circuits			.28	28.570	Ea.
2700	400 amp main, 42 circuits			.23	34.780	Ea.
2750	600 amp main, 42 circuits			.19	42.110	Ea.
3010	Main lug, no main breaker, 240 volt, 1 pole, 3 wire, 100 amp			2.30	3.480	Ea.
3020	225 amp			1.20	6.670	Ea.
3030	400 amp			.90	8.890	Ea.
3060	3 pole, 3 wire, 100 amp			2.30	3.480	Ea.
3070	225 amp			1.20	6.670	Ea.
3080	400 amp			.90	8.890	Ea.
3090	600 amp			.80	10.000	Ea.
3110	3 pole, 4 wire, 100 amp			2.30	3.480	Ea.
3120	225 amp			1.20	6.670	Ea.
3130	400 amp			.90	8.890	Ea.
3140	600 amp			.80	10.000	Ea.
3160	480 volt, 3 pole, 3 wire, 100 amp			2.30	3.480	Ea.
3170	225 amp			1.20	6.670	Ea.
3180	400 amp			.90	8.890	Ea.
3190	600 amp			.80	10.000	Ea.
3210	277/480 volt, 3 pole, 4 wire, 100 amp			2.30	3.480	Ea.
3220	225 amp			1.20	6.670	Ea.
3230	400 amp			.90	8.890	Ea.
3240	600 amp			.80	10.000	Ea.
3260	Main circuit breaker, 240 volt, 1 pole, 3 wire, 100 amp			2	4.000	Ea.
3270	225 amp			1	8.000	Ea.
3280	400 amp			.80	10.000	Ea.
3310	3 pole, 3 wire, 100 amp			2	4.000	Ea.
3320	225 amp			1	8.000	Ea.
3330	400 amp			.80	10.000	Ea.
3360	120/208 volt, 3 pole, 4 wire, 100 amp			2	4.000	Ea.
3370	225 amp			1	8.000	Ea.
3380	400 amp	↓	↓	.80	10.000	Ea.

245

163 | Starters, Boards and Switches

163 200 | Boards

		Description	CREW	MAKEUP	DAILY OUTPUT	MAN-HOURS	UNIT
245	3411	Main C.B., 480 volt, 3 pole, 3 wire, 100 amp	1 Elec	1 Electrician	2	4.000	Ea.
	3420	225 amp			1	8.000	Ea.
	3430	400 amp			.80	10.000	Ea.
	3460	277/480 volt, 3 pole, 4 wire, 100 amp			2	4.000	Ea.
	3470	225 amp			1	8.000	Ea.
	3480	400 amp			.80	10.000	Ea.
	3510	Main circuit breaker, HIC, 240 volt, 1 pole, 3 wire, 100 amp			2	4.000	Ea.
	3520	225 amp			1	8.000	Ea.
	3530	400 amp			.80	10.000	Ea.
	3560	3 pole, 3 wire, 100 amp			2	4.000	Ea.
	3570	225 amp			1	8.000	Ea.
	3580	400 amp			.80	10.000	Ea.
	3610	120/208 volt, 3 pole, 4 wire, 100 amp			2	4.000	Ea.
	3620	225 amp			1	8.000	Ea.
	3630	400 amp			.80	10.000	Ea.
	3660	480 volt, 3 pole, 3 wire, 100 amp			2	4.000	Ea.
	3670	225 amp			1	8.000	Ea.
	3680	400 amp			.80	10.000	Ea.
	3710	277/480 volt, 3 pole, 4 wire, 100 amp			2	4.000	Ea.
	3720	225 amp			1	8.000	Ea.
	3730	400 amp			.80	10.000	Ea.
	3760	Main circuit breaker with shunt trip, 100 amp			1.20	6.670	Ea.
	3770	225 amp			.80	10.000	Ea.
	3780	400 amp	↓	↓	.70	11.430	Ea.
	250	**PANELBOARD & LOAD CENTER CIRCUIT BREAKERS**					
	0050	Bolt-on, 10,000 amp I.C., 120 volt, 1 pole					
	0100	15 to 50 amp	1 Elec	1 Electrician	10	.800	Ea.
	0200	60 amp			8	1.000	Ea.
	0300	70 amp	↓	↓	8	1.000	Ea.
	0350	240 volt, 2 pole					
	0400	15 to 50 amp	1 Elec	1 Electrician	8	1.000	Ea.
	0500	60 amp			7.50	1.070	Ea.
	0600	80 to 100 amp			5	1.600	Ea.
	0700	3 pole, bolt-on, 15 to 60 amp			6.20	1.290	Ea.
	0800	70 amp			5	1.600	Ea.
	0900	80 to 100 amp			3.60	2.220	Ea.
	1000	22,000 amp I.C., 240 volt, 2 pole, 70 to 225 amp			2.70	2.960	Ea.
	1100	3 pole, 70 to 225 amp			2.30	3.480	Ea.
	1200	14,000 amp I.C., 277 volts, 1 pole, 15 to 30 amp			8	1.000	Ea.
	1300	22,000 amp I.C., 480 volts, 2 pole, 70 to 225 amp			2.70	2.960	Ea.
	1400	3 pole, 70 to 225 amp			2.30	3.480	Ea.
	2000	Plug-in, panel or load center, 120/240 volt, to 60 amp, 1 pole			12	.667	Ea.
	2010	2 pole			9	.889	Ea.
	2020	3 pole			7.50	1.070	Ea.
	2030	100 amp, 2 pole			6	1.330	Ea.
	2040	3 pole			4.50	1.780	Ea.
	2050	150 amp, 2 pole			3	2.670	Ea.
	2100	High interrupting capacity, 120/240 volt, plug-in, 30 amp, 1 pole			12	.667	Ea.
	2110	60 amp, 2 pole			9	.889	Ea.
	2120	3 pole			7.50	1.070	Ea.
	2130	100 amp, 2 pole			6	1.330	Ea.
	2140	3 pole			4.50	1.780	Ea.
	2150	125 amp, 2 pole			3	2.670	Ea.
	2200	Bolt-on, 30 amp, 1 pole			10	.800	Ea.
	2210	60 amp, 2 pole			7.50	1.070	Ea.
	2220	3 pole			6.20	1.290	Ea.
	2230	100 amp, 2 pole			5	1.600	Ea.
	2240	3 pole	↓	↓	3.60	2.220	Ea.

163 200 | Boards

		CREW	MAKEUP	DAILY OUTPUT	MAN-HOURS	UNIT
250 2301	Panelboard, ground fault, 240 volt, 30 amp, 1 pole	1 Elec	1 Electrician	7	1.140	Ea.
2310	2 pole			6	1.330	Ea.
2350	Key operated, 240 volt, 1 pole, 30 amp			7	1.140	Ea.
2360	Switched neutral, 240 volt, 30 amp, 2 pole			6	1.330	Ea.
2370	3 pole			5.50	1.450	Ea.
2400	Shunt trip for 240 volt breaker, 60 amp, 1 pole			4	2.000	Ea.
2410	2 pole			3.50	2.290	Ea.
2420	3 pole			3	2.670	Ea.
2430	100 amp, 2 pole			3	2.670	Ea.
2440	3 pole			2.50	3.200	Ea.
2450	150 amp, 2 pole			2	4.000	Ea.
2500	Auxiliary switch for 240 volt, breaker, 60 amp, 1 pole			4	2.000	Ea.
2510	2 pole			3.50	2.290	Ea.
2520	3 pole			3	2.670	Ea.
2530	100 amp, 2 pole			3	2.670	Ea.
2540	3 pole			2.50	3.200	Ea.
2550	150 amp, 2 pole			2	4.000	Ea.
2600	Panel or load center, 277/480 volt, plug-in, 30 amp, 1 pole			12	.667	Ea.
2610	60 amp, 2 pole			9	.889	Ea.
2620	3 pole			7.50	1.070	Ea.
2650	Bolt-on, 60 amp, 2 pole			7.50	1.070	Ea.
2660	3 pole			6.20	1.290	Ea.
2700	I-line, 277/480 volt, 30 amp, 1 pole			8	1.000	Ea.
2710	60 amp, 2 pole			7.50	1.070	Ea.
2720	3 pole			6.20	1.290	Ea.
2730	100 amp, 1 pole			7.50	1.070	Ea.
2740	2 pole			5	1.600	Ea.
2750	3 pole			3.50	2.290	Ea.
2800	High interrupting capacity, 277/480 volt, plug-in, 30 amp, 1 pole			12	.667	Ea.
2810	60 amp, 2 pole			9	.889	Ea.
2820	3 pole			7	1.140	Ea.
2830	Bolt-on, 30 amp, 1 pole			8	1.000	Ea.
2840	60 amp, 2 pole			7.50	1.070	Ea.
2850	3 pole			6.20	1.290	Ea.
2900	I-line, 30 amp, 1 pole			8	1.000	Ea.
2910	60 amp, 2 pole			7.50	1.070	Ea.
2920	3 pole			6.20	1.290	Ea.
2930	100 amp, 1 pole			7.50	1.070	Ea.
2940	2 pole			5	1.600	Ea.
2950	3 pole			3.60	2.220	Ea.
2960	Shunt trip, 277/480V breaker, remote oper., 30 amp, 1 pole			4	2.000	Ea.
2970	60 amp, 2 pole			3.50	2.290	Ea.
2980	3 pole			3	2.670	Ea.
2990	100 amp, 1 pole			3.50	2.290	Ea.
3000	2 pole			3	2.670	Ea.
3010	3 pole			2.50	3.200	Ea.
3050	Under voltage trip, 277/480 volt breaker, 30 amp, 1 pole			4	2.000	Ea.
3060	60 amp, 2 pole			3.50	2.290	Ea.
3070	3 pole			3	2.670	Ea.
3080	100 amp, 1 pole			3.50	2.290	Ea.
3090	2 pole			3	2.670	Ea.
3100	3 pole			2.50	3.200	Ea.
3150	Motor operated 277/480 volt breaker, 30 amp, 1 pole			4	2.000	Ea.
3160	60 amp, 2 pole			3.50	2.290	Ea.
3170	3 pole			3	2.670	Ea.
3180	100 amp, 1 pole			3.50	2.290	Ea.
3190	2 pole			3	2.670	Ea.
3200	3 pole	↓	↓	2.50	3.200	Ea.

163 200	Boards	CREW	MAKEUP	DAILY OUTPUT	MAN-HOURS	UNIT
255 0100	**SUBSTATIONS,** Require switch with cable connections, transformer, & Low Voltage section					
0200	Load interrupter switch, 600 amp, 2 position					
0300	NEMA 1, 4.8 KV, 300 KVA & below w/CLF fuses	R-3	1 Electrician Foreman	.40	50.000	Ea.
			1 Electrician			
			.5 Equip. Oper. (crane)			
			.5 S.P. Crane, 5 Ton			
0400	400 KVA & above w/CLF fuses			.38	52.630	Ea.
0500	Non fusible			.41	48.780	Ea.
0600	13.8 KV, 300 KVA & below			.38	52.630	Ea.
0700	400 KVA & above			.36	55.560	Ea.
0800	Non fusible	↓	↓	.40	50.000	Ea.
0900	Cable lugs for 2 feeders 4.8 KV or 13.8 KV	1 Elec	1 Electrician	8	1.000	Ea.
1000	Pothead, one 3 conductor or three 1 conductor			4	2.000	Ea.
1100	Two 3 conductor or six 1 conductor			2	4.000	Ea.
1200	Key interlocks	↓	↓	8	1.000	Ea.
1300	Lightning arrestors-Distribution class (no charge)					
1400	Intermediate class or line type 4.8 KV	1 Elec	1 Electrician	2.70	2.960	Ea.
1500	13.8 KV			2	4.000	Ea.
1600	Station class, 4.8 KV			2.70	2.960	Ea.
1700	13.8 KV	↓	↓	2	4.000	Ea.
1800	Transformers, 4800 volts to 480/277 volts, 75 KVA	R-3	1 Electrician Foreman	.68	29.410	Ea.
			1 Electrician			
			.5 Equip. Oper. (crane)			
			.5 S.P. Crane, 5 Ton			
1900	112.5 KVA			.65	30.770	Ea.
2000	150 KVA			.57	35.090	Ea.
2100	225 KVA			.48	41.670	Ea.
2200	300 KVA			.41	48.780	Ea.
2300	500 KVA			.36	55.560	Ea.
2400	750 KVA			.29	68.970	Ea.
2500	13,800 volts to 480/277 volts, 75 KVA			.61	32.790	Ea.
2600	112.5 KVA			.55	36.360	Ea.
2700	150 KVA			.49	40.820	Ea.
2800	225 KVA			.41	48.780	Ea.
2900	300 KVA			.37	54.050	Ea.
3000	500 KVA			.31	64.520	Ea.
3100	750 KVA	↓	↓	.26	76.920	Ea.
3200	Forced air cooling & temperature alarm	1 Elec	1 Electrician	1	8.000	Ea.
3300	Low voltage components					
3900	Breakers, 2 pole, 15 to 60 amp, type FA	1 Elec	1 Electrician	5.60	1.430	Ea.
4000	70 to 100 amp, FA			4.20	1.900	Ea.
4100	15 to 60 amp, FH			5.60	1.430	Ea.
4200	70 to 100 amp, FH			4.20	1.900	Ea.
4300	125 to 225 amp, KA			3.40	2.350	Ea.
4400	125 to 225 amp, KH			3.40	2.350	Ea.
4500	125 to 400 amp, LA			2.50	3.200	Ea.
4600	125 to 600 amp, MA			1.80	4.440	Ea.
4700	700 & 800 amp, MA			1.50	5.330	Ea.
4800	3 pole, 15 to 60 amp, FA			5.30	1.510	Ea.
4900	70 to 100 amp, FA			4	2.000	Ea.
5000	15 to 60 amp, FH			5.30	1.510	Ea.
5100	70 to 100 amp, FH			4	2.000	Ea.
5200	125 to 225 amp, KA			3.20	2.500	Ea.
5300	125 to 225 amp, KH			3.20	2.500	Ea.
5400	125 to 400 amp, LA			2.30	3.480	Ea.
5500	125 to 600 amp, MA			1.60	5.000	Ea.
5600	700 & 800 amp, MA	↓	↓	1.30	6.150	Ea.

255

		163 200 | **Boards**	CREW	MAKEUP	DAILY OUTPUT	MAN-HOURS	UNIT
260	260	**SWITCHBOARDS** Incoming main service section,					
	0100	Aluminum bus bars, not including CT's or PT's					
	0200	No main disconnect, includes CT compartment					
	0300	120/208 volt, 4 wire, 600 amp	1 Elec	1 Electrician	.50	16.000	Ea.
	0400	800 amp			.44	18.180	Ea.
	0500	1000 amp			.40	20.000	Ea.
	0600	1200 amp			.36	22.220	Ea.
	0700	1600 amp			.33	24.240	Ea.
	0800	2000 amp			.31	25.810	Ea.
	1000	3000 amp			.28	28.570	Ea.
	1200	277/480 volt, 4 wire, 600 amp			.50	16.000	Ea.
	1300	800 amp			.44	18.180	Ea.
	1400	1000 amp			.40	20.000	Ea.
	1500	1200 amp			.36	22.220	Ea.
	1600	1600 amp			.33	24.240	Ea.
	1700	2000 amp			.31	25.810	Ea.
	1800	3000 amp			.28	28.570	Ea.
	1900	4000 amp	↓	↓	.26	30.770	Ea.
	2000	Fused switch & CT compartment					
	2100	120/208 volt, 4 wire, 400 amp	1 Elec	1 Electrician	.56	14.290	Ea.
	2200	600 amp			.47	17.020	Ea.
	2300	800 amp			.42	19.050	Ea.
	2400	1200 amp			.34	23.530	Ea.
	2500	277/480 volt, 4 wire, 400 amp			.57	14.040	Ea.
	2600	600 amp			.47	17.020	Ea.
	2700	800 amp			.42	19.050	Ea.
	2800	1200 amp	↓	↓	.34	23.530	Ea.
	2900	Pressure switch & CT compartment					
	3000	120/208 volt, 4 wire, 800 amp	1 Elec	1 Electrician	.40	20.000	Ea.
	3100	1200 amp			.33	24.240	Ea.
	3200	1600 amp			.31	25.810	Ea.
	3300	2000 amp			.28	28.570	Ea.
	3310	2500 amp			.25	32.000	Ea.
	3320	3000 amp			.22	36.360	Ea.
	3330	4000 amp			.20	40.000	Ea.
	3400	277/480 volt, 4 wire,			.40	20.000	Ea.
	3600	1200 amp, with ground fault			.33	24.240	Ea.
	4000	1600 amp, with ground fault			.31	25.810	Ea.
	4200	2000 amp, with ground fault	↓	↓	.28	28.570	Ea.
	4400	Circuit breaker, molded case & CT compartment					
	4600	3 pole, 4 wire, 600 amp	1 Elec	1 Electrician	.47	17.020	Ea.
	4800	800 amp			.42	19.050	Ea.
	5000	1200 amp	↓	↓	.34	23.530	Ea.
	262	**SWITCHBOARD** (in plant distribution)					
	0100	Main lugs only, to 600 volt, 3 pole, 3 wire, 200 amp	1 Elec	1 Electrician	.60	13.330	Ea.
	0110	400 amp			.60	13.330	Ea.
	0120	600 amp			.60	13.330	Ea.
	0130	800 amp			.54	14.810	Ea.
	0140	1200 amp			.46	17.390	Ea.
	0150	1600 amp			.43	18.600	Ea.
	0160	2000 amp			.41	19.510	Ea.
	0250	To 480 volt, 3 pole, 4 wire, 200 amp			.60	13.330	Ea.
	0260	400 amp			.60	13.330	Ea.
	0270	600 amp			.60	13.330	Ea.
	0280	800 amp			.54	14.810	Ea.
	0290	1200 amp			.46	17.390	Ea.
	0300	1600 amp			.43	18.600	Ea.
	0310	2000 amp	↓	↓	.41	19.510	Ea.

163 200	Boards	CREW	MAKEUP		DAILY OUTPUT	MAN-HOURS	UNIT
262 0400	Main circuit breaker, to 600 volt, 3 pole, 3 wire, 200 amp	1 Elec	1 Electrician		.60	13.330	Ea.
0410	400 amp				.57	14.040	Ea.
0420	600 amp				.55	14.550	Ea.
0430	800 amp				.52	15.380	Ea.
0440	1200 amp				.44	18.180	Ea.
0450	1600 amp				.42	19.050	Ea.
0460	2000 amp				.40	20.000	Ea.
0550	277/480 volt, 3 pole, 4 wire, 200 amp				.60	13.330	Ea.
0560	400 amp				.57	14.040	Ea.
0570	600 amp				.55	14.550	Ea.
0580	800 amp				.52	15.380	Ea.
0590	1200 amp				.44	18.180	Ea.
0600	1600 amp				.42	19.050	Ea.
0610	2000 amp				.40	20.000	Ea.
0700	Main fusible switch w/fuse, 208/240 volt, 3 pole, 3 wire, 200 amp				.60	13.330	Ea.
0710	400 amp				.57	14.040	Ea.
0720	600 amp				.55	14.550	Ea.
0730	800 amp				.52	15.380	Ea.
0740	1200 amp				.44	18.180	Ea.
0800	120/208, 120/240 volt, 3 pole, 4 wire, 200 amp				.60	13.330	Ea.
0810	400 amp				.57	14.040	Ea.
0820	600 amp				.55	14.550	Ea.
0830	800 amp				.52	15.380	Ea.
0840	1200 amp				.44	18.180	Ea.
0900	480 or 600 volt, 3 pole, 3 wire, 200 amp				.60	13.330	Ea.
0910	400 amp				.57	14.040	Ea.
0920	600 amp				.55	14.550	Ea.
0930	800 amp				.52	15.380	Ea.
0940	1200 amp				.44	18.180	Ea.
1000	277 or 480 volt, 3 pole, 4 wire, 200 amp				.60	13.330	Ea.
1010	400 amp				.57	14.040	Ea.
1020	600 amp				.55	14.550	Ea.
1030	800 amp				.52	15.380	Ea.
1040	1200 amp				.44	18.180	Ea.
1120	1600 amp				.38	21.050	Ea.
1130	2000 amp				.34	23.530	Ea.
1150	Pressure switch, bolted, 3 pole, 208/240 volt, 3 wire, 800 amp				.48	16.670	Ea.
1160	1200 amp				.40	20.000	Ea.
1170	1600 amp				.38	21.050	Ea.
1180	2000 amp				.34	23.530	Ea.
1200	120/208 or 120/240 volt, 3 pole, 4 wire, 800 amp				.48	16.670	Ea.
1210	1200 amp				.40	20.000	Ea.
1220	1600 amp				.38	21.050	Ea.
1230	2000 amp				.34	23.530	Ea.
1300	480 or 600 volt, 3 wire, 800 amp				.48	16.670	Ea.
1310	1200 amp				.40	20.000	Ea.
1320	1600 amp				.38	21.050	Ea.
1330	2000 amp				.34	23.530	Ea.
1400	277-480 volt, 4 wire, 800 amp				.48	16.670	Ea.
1410	1200 amp				.40	20.000	Ea.
1420	1600 amp				.38	21.050	Ea.
1430	2000 amp				.34	23.530	Ea.
1500	Main ground fault protector, 1200-2000 amp				2.70	2.960	Ea.
1600	Bus way connection, 200 amp				2.70	2.960	Ea.
1610	400 amp				2.30	3.480	Ea.
1620	600 amp				2	4.000	Ea.
1630	800 amp	▼	▼		1.60	5.000	Ea.

163 200 | Boards

		Description	CREW	MAKEUP	DAILY OUTPUT	MAN-HOURS	UNIT
262	1641	Bus way connection, 1200 amp	1 Elec	1 Electrician	1.30	6.150	Ea.
	1650	1600 amp			1.20	6.670	Ea.
	1660	2000 amp			1	8.000	Ea.
	1700	Shunt trip for remote operation 200 amp			4	2.000	Ea.
	1710	400 amp			4	2.000	Ea.
	1720	600 amp			4	2.000	Ea.
	1730	800 amp			4	2.000	Ea.
	1740	1200-2000 amp			4	2.000	Ea.
	1800	Motor operated main breaker 200 amp			4	2.000	Ea.
	1810	400 amp			4	2.000	Ea.
	1820	600 amp			4	2.000	Ea.
	1830	800 amp			4	2.000	Ea.
	1840	1200-2000 amp			4	2.000	Ea.
	1900	Current/potential transformer metering compartment 200-800 amp			2.70	2.960	Ea.
	1940	1200 amp			2.70	2.960	Ea.
	1950	1600-2000 amp			2.70	2.960	Ea.
	2000	With watt meter 200-800 amp			2	4.000	Ea.
	2040	1200 amp			2	4.000	Ea.
	2050	1600-2000 amp			2	4.000	Ea.
	2100	Split bus 60-200 amp			5.30	1.510	Ea.
	2130	400 amp			2.30	3.480	Ea.
	2140	600 amp			1.80	4.440	Ea.
	2150	800 amp			1.30	6.150	Ea.
	2170	1200 amp			1	8.000	Ea.
	2250	Contactor control 60 amp			2	4.000	Ea.
	2260	100 amp			1.50	5.330	Ea.
	2270	200 amp			1	8.000	Ea.
	2280	400 amp			.50	16.000	Ea.
	2290	600 amp			.42	19.050	Ea.
	2300	800 amp			.36	22.220	Ea.
	2500	Modifier for two distribution sections, add			.40	20.000	Ea.
	2520	Three distribution sections, add			.20	40.000	Ea.
	2560	Auxiliary pull section, 20", add			1	8.000	Ea.
	2580	24", add			.90	8.890	Ea.
	2600	30", add			.80	10.000	Ea.
	2620	36", add			.70	11.430	Ea.
	2640	Dog house, 12", add			1.20	6.670	Ea.
	2660	18", add	↓	↓	1	8.000	Ea.
	3000	Transition section between switchboard and transformer					
	3050	or motor control center, 4 wire, alum. bus, 600 amp	1 Elec	1 Electrician	.57	14.040	Ea.
	3100	800 amp			.50	16.000	Ea.
	3150	1000 amp			.44	18.180	Ea.
	3200	1200 amp			.40	20.000	Ea.
	3250	1600 amp			.36	22.220	Ea.
	3300	2000 amp			.33	24.240	Ea.
	3350	2500 amp			.31	25.810	Ea.
	3400	3000 amp			.28	28.570	Ea.
	4000	Weatherproof construction, per vertical section	↓	↓	.88	9.090	Ea.
264		**DISTRIBUTION SECTION**					
	0100	Aluminum bus bars, not including breakers					
	0160	Subfeed lug-rated at 60 amp	1 Elec	1 Electrician	.65	12.310	Ea.
	0170	100 amp			.63	12.700	Ea.
	0180	200 amp			.60	13.330	Ea.
	0190	400 amp			.55	14.550	Ea.
	0200	120/208 or 277/480 volt, 4 wire, 600 amp			.50	16.000	Ea.
	0300	800 amp			.44	18.180	Ea.
	0400	1000 amp			.40	20.000	Ea.
	0500	1200 amp	↓	↓	.36	22.220	Ea.

163 200 | Boards

		Description	CREW	MAKEUP	DAILY OUTPUT	MAN-HOURS	UNIT
264	0601	Alum. bus bars, 120/208 or 277/480 volt, 4 wire, 1600 amp	1 Elec	1 Electrician	.33	24.240	Ea.
	0700	2000 amp			.31	25.810	Ea.
	0800	2500 amp			.30	26.670	Ea.
	0900	3000 amp			.28	28.570	Ea.
	0950	4000 amp	↓	↓	.26	30.770	Ea.
266		FEEDER SECTION Group mounted devices					
	0030	Circuit breakers					
	0160	FA frame, 15 to 60 amp, 240 volt, 1 pole	1 Elec	1 Electrician	8	1.000	Ea.
	0170	2 pole			7	1.140	Ea.
	0180	3 pole			5.30	1.510	Ea.
	0210	480 volt, 1 pole			8	1.000	Ea.
	0220	2 pole			7	1.140	Ea.
	0230	3 pole			5.30	1.510	Ea.
	0260	600 volt, 2 pole			7	1.140	Ea.
	0270	3 pole			5.30	1.510	Ea.
	0280	FA frame, 70 to 100 amp, 240 volt, 1 pole			7	1.140	Ea.
	0310	2 pole			5	1.600	Ea.
	0320	3 pole			4	2.000	Ea.
	0330	480 volt, 1 pole			7	1.140	Ea.
	0360	2 pole			5	1.600	Ea.
	0370	3 pole			4	2.000	Ea.
	0380	600 volt, 2 pole			5	1.600	Ea.
	0410	3 pole			4	2.000	Ea.
	0420	KA frame, 70 to 225 amp			3.20	2.500	Ea.
	0430	LA frame, 125 to 400 amp			2.30	3.480	Ea.
	0460	MA frame, 450 to 600 amp			1.60	5.000	Ea.
	0470	700 to 800 amp			1.30	6.150	Ea.
	0480	1000 amp			1	8.000	Ea.
	0490	PA frame, 1200 amp			.80	10.000	Ea.
	0500	Branch circuit, fusible switch, 600 volt, double 30/30 amp			4	2.000	Ea.
	0550	60/60 amp			3.20	2.500	Ea.
	0600	100/100 amp			2.70	2.960	Ea.
	0650	Single, 30 amp			5.30	1.510	Ea.
	0700	60 amp			4.70	1.700	Ea.
	0750	100 amp			4	2.000	Ea.
	0800	200 amp			2.70	2.960	Ea.
	0850	400 amp			2.30	3.480	Ea.
	0900	600 amp			1.80	4.440	Ea.
	0950	800 amp			1.30	6.150	Ea.
	1000	1200 amp	↓	↓	.80	10.000	Ea.
	1080	Branch circuit, circuit breakers, high interrupting capacity					
	1100	60 amp, 240, 480 or 600 volt, 1 pole	1 Elec	1 Electrician	8	1.000	Ea.
	1120	2 pole			7	1.140	Ea.
	1140	3 pole			5.30	1.510	Ea.
	1150	100 amp, 240, 480 or 600 volt, 1 pole			7	1.140	Ea.
	1160	2 pole			5	1.600	Ea.
	1180	3 pole			4	2.000	Ea.
	1200	225 amp, 240, 480 or 600 volt, 2 pole			3.50	2.290	Ea.
	1220	3 pole			3.20	2.500	Ea.
	1240	400 amp, 240, 480 or 600 volt, 2 pole			2.50	3.200	Ea.
	1260	3 pole			2.30	3.480	Ea.
	1280	600 amp, 240, 480 or 600 volt, 2 pole			1.80	4.440	Ea.
	1300	3 pole			1.60	5.000	Ea.
	1320	800 amp, 240, 480 or 600 volt, 2 pole			1.50	5.330	Ea.
	1340	3 pole			1.30	6.150	Ea.
	1360	1000 amp, 240, 480 or 600 volt, 2 pole			1.10	7.270	Ea.
	1380	3 pole			1	8.000	Ea.
	1400	1200 amp, 240, 480 or 600 volt, 2 pole	↓	↓	.90	8.890	Ea.

163 200	**Boards**	CREW	MAKEUP	DAILY OUTPUT	MAN-HOURS	UNIT
266 1422	Branch circuit, 1200 amp, 240, 480 or 600 volt, 3 pole	1 Elec	1 Electrician	.80	10.000	Ea.
1700	Fusible switch, 240 V, 60 amp, 2 pole			3.20	2.500	Ea.
1720	3 pole			3	2.670	Ea.
1740	100 amp, 2 pole			2.70	2.960	Ea.
1760	3 pole			2.50	3.200	Ea.
1780	200 amp, 2 pole			2	4.000	Ea.
1820	400 amp, 2 pole			1.50	5.330	Ea.
1840	3 pole			1.30	6.150	Ea.
1860	600 amp, 2 pole			1	8.000	Ea.
1880	3 pole			.90	8.890	Ea.
1900	240-600 V, 800 amp, 2 pole			.70	11.430	Ea.
1920	3 pole			.60	13.330	Ea.
2000	600 V, 60 amp, 2 pole			3.20	2.500	Ea.
2040	100 amp, 2 pole			2.70	2.960	Ea.
2080	200 amp, 2 pole			2	4.000	Ea.
2120	400 amp, 2 pole			1.50	5.330	Ea.
2160	600 amp, 2 pole			1	8.000	Ea.
2500	Branch circuit, circuit breakers, 60 amp, 600 volt, 3 pole			5.30	1.510	Ea.
2520	240, 480 or 600 volt, 1 pole			8	1.000	Ea.
2540	240 volt, 2 pole			7	1.140	Ea.
2560	480 or 600 volt, 2 pole			7	1.140	Ea.
2580	240 volt, 3 pole			5.30	1.510	Ea.
2600	480 volt, 3 pole			5.30	1.510	Ea.
2620	100 amp, 600 volt, 2 pole			5	1.600	Ea.
2640	3 pole			4	2.000	Ea.
2660	480 volt, 2 pole			5	1.600	Ea.
2680	240 volt, 2 pole			5	1.600	Ea.
2700	3 pole			4	2.000	Ea.
2720	480 volt, 3 pole			4	2.000	Ea.
2740	225 amp, 240, 480 or 600 volt, 2 pole			3.50	2.290	Ea.
2760	3 pole			3.20	2.500	Ea.
2780	400 amp, 240, 480 or 600 volt, 2 pole			2.50	3.200	Ea.
2800	3 pole			2.30	3.480	Ea.
2820	600 amp, 240 or 480 volt, 2 pole			1.80	4.440	Ea.
2840	3 pole			1.60	5.000	Ea.
2860	800 amp, 240, 480 volt or 600 volt, 2 pole			1.50	5.330	Ea.
2880	3 pole			1.30	6.150	Ea.
2900	1000 amp, 240, 480 or 600 volt, 2 pole			1.10	7.270	Ea.
2920	480 volt, 600 volt, 3 pole			1	8.000	Ea.
2940	1200 amp, 240, 480 or 600 volt, 2 pole			.90	8.890	Ea.
2960	3 pole			.80	10.000	Ea.
2980	600 volt, 3 pole	↓	↓	.80	10.000	Ea.
268	**SWITCHBOARD INSTRUMENTS** 3 phase, 4 wire					
0100	AC indicating, ammeter & switch	1 Elec	1 Electrician	8	1.000	Ea.
0200	Voltmeter & switch			8	1.000	Ea.
0300	Wattmeter			8	1.000	Ea.
0400	AC recording, ammeter			4	2.000	Ea.
0500	Voltmeter			4	2.000	Ea.
0600	Ground fault protection, zero sequence			2.70	2.960	Ea.
0700	Ground return path			2.70	2.960	Ea.
0800	3 current transformers, 5 to 800 amp			2	4.000	Ea.
0900	1000 to 1500 amp			1.30	6.150	Ea.
1200	2000 to 4000 amp			1	8.000	Ea.
1300	Fused potential transformer, maximum 600 volt	↓	↓	8	1.000	Ea.

163 300	Switches	CREW	MAKEUP	DAILY OUTPUT	MAN-HOURS	UNIT
310	**CONTACTORS, AC** Enclosed (NEMA 1)					
0050	Lighting, 600 volt 3 pole, electrically held					
0100	20 amp	1 Elec	1 Electrician	4	2.000	Ea.
0200	30 amp			3.60	2.220	Ea.
0300	60 amp			3	2.670	Ea.
0400	100 amp			2.50	3.200	Ea.
0500	200 amp			1.40	5.710	Ea.
0600	300 amp			.80	10.000	Ea.
0800	Mechanically held, 30 amp			3.60	2.220	Ea.
0900	60 amp			3	2.670	Ea.
1000	75 amp			2.80	2.860	Ea.
1100	100 amp			2.50	3.200	Ea.
1200	150 amp			2	4.000	Ea.
1300	200 amp			1.40	5.710	Ea.
1500	Magnetic with auxiliary contact, size 00, 9 amp			4	2.000	Ea.
1600	Size 0, 18 amp			4	2.000	Ea.
1700	Size 1, 27 amp			3.60	2.220	Ea.
1800	Size 2, 45 amp			3	2.670	Ea.
1900	Size 3, 90 amp			2.50	3.200	Ea.
2000	Size 4, 135 amp			2.30	3.480	Ea.
2100	Size 5, 270 amp			.90	8.890	Ea.
2200	Size 6, 540 amp			.60	13.330	Ea.
2300	Size 7, 810 amp			.50	16.000	Ea.
2310	Size 8, 1215 amp	↓	↓	.40	20.000	Ea.
320	**CONTROL STATIONS**					
0050	NEMA 1, heavy duty, stop/start	1 Elec	1 Electrician	8	1.000	Ea.
0100	Stop/start, pilot light			6.20	1.290	Ea.
0200	Hand/off/automatic			6.20	1.290	Ea.
0400	Stop/start/reverse			5.30	1.510	Ea.
0500	NEMA 7, heavy duty, stop/start			6	1.330	Ea.
0600	Stop/start, pilot light			4	2.000	Ea.
0700	NEMA 7 or 9, 1 element			6	1.330	Ea.
0800	2 element			6	1.330	Ea.
0900	3 element			4	2.000	Ea.
0910	Selector switch, 2 position			6	1.330	Ea.
0920	3 position			4	2.000	Ea.
0930	Oiltight, 1 element			8	1.000	Ea.
0940	2 element			6.20	1.290	Ea.
0950	3 element			5.30	1.510	Ea.
0960	Selector switch, 2 position			6.20	1.290	Ea.
0970	3 position	↓	↓	5.30	1.510	Ea.
350	**RELAYS** Enclosed (NEMA 1)					
0050	600 volt AC, 1 pole, 12 amp	1 Elec	1 Electrician	5.30	1.510	Ea.
0100	2 pole, 12 amp			5	1.600	Ea.
0200	4 pole, 10 amp			4.50	1.780	Ea.
0500	250 volt DC, 1 pole, 15 amp			5.30	1.510	Ea.
0600	2 pole, 10 amp			5	1.600	Ea.
0700	4 pole, 4 amp	↓	↓	4.50	1.780	Ea.
360	**SAFETY SWITCHES**					
0100	General duty, 240 volt, 3 pole, fused, 30 amp	1 Elec	1 Electrician	3.20	2.500	Ea.
0200	60 amp			2.30	3.480	Ea.
0300	100 amp			1.90	4.210	Ea.
0400	200 amp			1.30	6.150	Ea.
0500	400 amp			.90	8.890	Ea.
0600	600 amp			.60	13.330	Ea.
0610	Non fused, 30 amp			3.20	2.500	Ea.
0650	60 amp			2.30	3.480	Ea.
0700	100 amp	↓	↓	1.90	4.210	Ea.

310

163 | Starters, Boards and Switches

163 300 | Switches

			CREW	MAKEUP	DAILY OUTPUT	MAN-HOURS	UNIT
360	0751	Safety switches, general duty, 240 volt, non fused, 200 amp	1 Elec	1 Electrician	1.30	6.150	Ea.
	0800	400 amp			.90	8.890	Ea.
	0850	600 amp			.60	13.330	Ea.
	8310	Fused heavy duty, 600 volt, 3 pole, NEMA 4, 30 amp			3	2.670	Ea.
	8320	60 amp			2.20	3.640	Ea.
	8330	100 amp			1.80	4.440	Ea.
	8340	200 amp			1.20	6.670	Ea.
	8350	400 amp			.80	10.000	Ea.
	8360	Non fused, heavy duty, 600 volt, 3 pole, NEMA 4, 30 amp			3	2.670	Ea.
	8370	60 amp			2.20	3.640	Ea.
	8380	100 amp			1.80	4.440	Ea.
	8390	200 amp			1.20	6.670	Ea.
	8400	400 amp			.80	10.000	Ea.
	8490	Motor starters, manual, single phase, NEMA 1			6.40	1.250	Ea.
	8500	NEMA 4			4	2.000	Ea.
	8700	NEMA 7			4	2.000	Ea.
	8900	NEMA 1 with pilot			6.40	1.250	Ea.
	8920	3 pole, NEMA 1, 230/460 volt, 5 HP, size 0			3.50	2.290	Ea.
	8940	10 HP, size 1			2	4.000	Ea.
	9010	Disc. switch, 600V, 3 pole, fused, 30 amp, to 10 HP motor			3.20	2.500	Ea.
	9050	60 amp, to 30 HP motor			2.30	3.480	Ea.
	9070	100 amp, to 60 HP motor			1.90	4.210	Ea.
	9100	200 amp, to 125 HP motor			1.30	6.150	Ea.
	9110	400 amp, to 200 HP motor	↓	↓	.90	8.890	Ea.
370		TIME SWITCHES					
	0100	Single pole, single throw, 24 hour dial	1 Elec	1 Electrician	4	2.000	Ea.
	0200	24 hour dial with reserve power			3.60	2.220	Ea.
	0300	Astronomic dial			3.60	2.220	Ea.
	0400	Astronomic dial with reserve power			3.30	2.420	Ea.
	0500	7 day calendar dial			3.30	2.420	Ea.
	0600	7 day calendar dial with reserve power			3.20	2.500	Ea.
	0700	Photo cell 2000 watt			8	1.000	Ea.
	1080	Load management device, 2 loads			4	2.000	Ea.
	1100	Load management device, 8 loads	↓	↓	1	8.000	Ea.

163 500 | Motors

			CREW	MAKEUP	DAILY OUTPUT	MAN-HOURS	UNIT
510		HANDLING					
	5000	Motors					
	5100	1/2 HP, approximately 23 pounds	1 Elec	1 Electrician	4	2.000	Ea.
	5110	3/4 HP, approximately 28 pounds			4	2.000	Ea.
	5120	1 HP, approximately 33 pounds			4	2.000	Ea.
	5130	1-1/2 HP, approximately 44 pounds			3.20	2.500	Ea.
	5140	2 HP, approximately 56 pounds			3	2.670	Ea.
	5150	3 HP, approximately 71 pounds			2.30	3.480	Ea.
	5160	5 HP, approximately 82 pounds			1.90	4.210	Ea.
	5170	7-1/2 HP, approximately 124 pounds			1.50	5.330	Ea.
	5180	10 HP, approximately 144 pounds			1.20	6.670	Ea.
	5190	15 HP, approximately 185 pounds	↓	↓	1	8.000	Ea.
	5200	20 HP, approximately 214 pounds	2 Elec	2 Electricians	1.50	10.670	Ea.
	5210	25 HP, approximately 266 pounds			1.40	11.430	Ea.
	5220	30 HP, approximately 310 pounds			1.20	13.330	Ea.
	5230	40 HP, approximately 400 pounds			1	16.000	Ea.
	5240	50 HP, approximately 450 pounds			.90	17.780	Ea.
	5250	75 HP, approximately 680 pounds	↓	↓	.80	20.000	Ea.
	5260	100 HP, approximately 870 pounds	3 Elec	3 Electricians	1	24.000	Ea.
	5270	125 HP, approximately 940 pounds			.80	30.000	Ea.
	5280	150 HP, approximately 1200 pounds			.70	34.290	Ea.
	5290	175 HP, approximately 1300 pounds	↓	↓	.60	40.000	Ea.

		163 500 | Motors	CREW	MAKEUP	DAILY OUTPUT	MAN-HOURS	UNIT
520	520	**MOTORS** 230/460 volts, 60 HZ					
	0050	Dripproof, Class B, 1.15 service factor					
	0100	1800 RPM, 1 HP	1 Elec	1 Electrician	4.50	1.780	Ea.
	0150	2 HP			4.50	1.780	Ea.
	0200	3 HP			4.50	1.780	Ea.
	0250	5 HP			4.50	1.780	Ea.
	0300	7.5 HP			4.20	1.900	Ea.
	0350	10 HP			4	2.000	Ea.
	0400	15 HP			3.20	2.500	Ea.
	0450	20 HP			2.60	3.080	Ea.
	0500	25 HP			2.50	3.200	Ea.
	0550	30 HP			2.40	3.330	Ea.
	0600	40 HP			2	4.000	Ea.
	0650	50 HP			1.60	5.000	Ea.
	0700	60 HP			1.40	5.710	Ea.
	0750	75 HP			1.20	6.670	Ea.
	0800	100 HP			.90	8.890	Ea.
	0850	125 HP			.70	11.430	Ea.
	0900	150 HP			.60	13.330	Ea.
	0950	200 HP			.50	16.000	Ea.
	1000	1200 RPM, 1 HP			4.50	1.780	Ea.
	1050	2 HP			4.50	1.780	Ea.
	1100	3 HP			4.50	1.780	Ea.
	1150	5 HP			4.50	1.780	Ea.
	1200	3600 RPM, 2 HP			4.50	1.780	Ea.
	1250	3 HP			4.50	1.780	Ea.
	1300	5 HP	↓	↓	4.50	1.780	Ea.
	1350	Totally enclosed, Class B, 1.0 service factor					
	1400	1800 RPM, 1 HP	1 Elec	1 Electrician	4.50	1.780	Ea.
	1450	2 HP			4.50	1.780	Ea.
	1500	3 HP			4.50	1.780	Ea.
	1550	5 HP			4.50	1.780	Ea.
	1600	7.5 HP			4.20	1.900	Ea.
	1650	10 HP			4	2.000	Ea.
	1700	15 HP			3.20	2.500	Ea.
	1750	20 HP			2.60	3.080	Ea.
	1800	25 HP			2.50	3.200	Ea.
	1850	30 HP			2.40	3.330	Ea.
	1900	40 HP			2	4.000	Ea.
	1950	50 HP			1.60	5.000	Ea.
	2000	60 HP			1.40	5.710	Ea.
	2050	75 HP			1.20	6.670	Ea.
	2100	100 HP			.90	8.890	Ea.
	2150	125 HP			.70	11.430	Ea.
	2200	150 HP			.60	13.330	Ea.
	2250	200 HP			.50	16.000	Ea.
	2300	1200 RPM, 1 HP			4.50	1.780	Ea.
	2350	2 HP			4.50	1.780	Ea.
	2400	3 HP			4.50	1.780	Ea.
	2450	5 HP			4.50	1.780	Ea.
	2500	3600 RPM, 2 HP			4.50	1.780	Ea.
	2550	3 HP			4.50	1.780	Ea.
	2600	5 HP	↓	↓	4.50	1.780	Ea.

164 100	Transformers	CREW	MAKEUP	DAILY OUTPUT	MAN-HOURS	UNIT
110	**BUCK-BOOST TRANSFORMER**					
0100	Single phase, 120/240 volt primary, 12/24 volt secondary					
0200	0.10 KVA	1 Elec	1 Electrician	8	1.000	Ea.
0400	0.25 KVA			5.70	1.400	Ea.
0600	0.50 KVA			4	2.000	Ea.
0800	0.75 KVA			3.10	2.580	Ea.
1000	1.0 KVA			2	4.000	Ea.
1200	1.5 KVA			1.80	4.440	Ea.
1400	2.0 KVA			1.60	5.000	Ea.
1600	3.0 KVA			1.40	5.710	Ea.
1800	5.0 KVA			1.20	6.670	Ea.
2000	3 phase, 240/208 volt, 15 KVA			1.20	6.670	Ea.
2200	30 KVA			.80	10.000	Ea.
2400	45 KVA			.70	11.430	Ea.
2600	75 KVA			.60	13.330	Ea.
2800	112.5 KVA			.57	14.040	Ea.
3000	150 KVA			.45	17.780	Ea.
3200	225 KVA			.40	20.000	Ea.
3400	300 KVA	↓	↓	.36	22.220	Ea.
120	**DRY TYPE TRANSFORMER**					
0050	Single phase, 240/480 volt primary 120/240 volt secondary					
0100	1 KVA	1 Elec	1 Electrician	2	4.000	Ea.
0300	2 KVA			1.60	5.000	Ea.
0500	3 KVA			1.40	5.710	Ea.
0700	5 KVA			1.20	6.670	Ea.
0900	7.5 KVA			1.10	7.270	Ea.
1100	10 KVA	↓	↓	.80	10.000	Ea.
1300	15 KVA	2 Elec	2 Electricians	1.20	13.330	Ea.
1500	25 KVA			1	16.000	Ea.
1700	37.5 KVA			.80	20.000	Ea.
1900	50 KVA			.70	22.860	Ea.
2100	75 KVA	↓	↓	.65	24.620	Ea.
2110	100 KVA	R-3	1 Electrician Foreman 1 Electrician .5 Equip. Oper. (crane) .5 S.P. Crane, 5 Ton	.90	22.220	Ea.
2120	167 KVA	"	"	.80	25.000	Ea.
2190	480V primary 120/240V secondary, nonvent., 15 KVA	2 Elec	2 Electricians	1.20	13.330	Ea.
2200	25 KVA			.90	17.780	Ea.
2210	37 KVA			.75	21.330	Ea.
2220	50 KVA			.65	24.620	Ea.
2230	75 KVA			.60	26.670	Ea.
2240	100 KVA			.50	32.000	Ea.
2250	Low operating temperature(80°C), 25 KVA			1	16.000	Ea.
2260	37 KVA			.80	20.000	Ea.
2270	50 KVA			.70	22.860	Ea.
2280	75 KVA			.65	24.620	Ea.
2290	100 KVA	↓	↓	.55	29.090	Ea.
2300	3 phase, 240/480 volt primary, 120/208 volt secondary					
2310	3 KVA	1 Elec	1 Electrician	1	8.000	Ea.
2700	6 KVA			.80	10.000	Ea.
2900	9 KVA	↓	↓	.70	11.430	Ea.
3100	15 KVA	2 Elec	2 Electricians	1.10	14.550	Ea.
3300	30 KVA			.90	17.780	Ea.
3500	45 KVA			.80	20.000	Ea.
3700	75 KVA	↓	↓	.70	22.860	Ea.

164 100	Transformers	CREW	MAKEUP	DAILY OUTPUT	MAN-HOURS	UNIT
120 3903	Dry type transformer, 3 phase, 112.5 KVA	R-3	1 Electrician Foreman	.90	22.220	Ea.
			1 Electrician			
			.5 Equip. Oper. (crane)			
			.5 S.P. Crane, 5 Ton			
4100	150 KVA			.85	23.530	Ea.
4300	225 KVA			.65	30.770	Ea.
4500	300 KVA			.55	36.360	Ea.
4700	500 KVA			.45	44.440	Ea.
4800	750 KVA			.35	57.140	Ea.
4820	1000 KVA	↓	↓	.32	62.500	Ea.
5020	480 volt primary, 120/208 volt secondary,					
5030	Nonventilated, 15 KVA	2 Elec	2 Electricians	1.10	14.550	Ea.
5040	30 KVA			.80	20.000	Ea.
5050	45 KVA			.70	22.860	Ea.
5060	75 KVA	↓	↓	.65	24.620	Ea.
5070	112 KVA	R-3	1 Electrician Foreman	.85	23.530	Ea.
			1 Electrician			
			.5 Equip. Oper. (crane)			
			.5 S.P. Crane, 5 Ton			
5081	150 KVA			.85	23.530	Ea.
5090	225 KVA			.60	33.330	Ea.
5100	300 KVA			.50	40.000	Ea.
5200	Low operating temperature (80°C), 30 KVA			.90	22.220	Ea.
5210	45 KVA			.80	25.000	Ea.
5220	75 KVA			.70	28.570	Ea.
5230	112 KVA			.90	22.220	Ea.
5240	150 KVA			.85	23.530	Ea.
5250	225 KVA			.65	30.770	Ea.
5260	300 KVA			.55	36.360	Ea.
5270	500 KVA	↓	↓	.45	44.440	Ea.
5591	5 or 15 KV primary, 277/480 volt secondary					
5600	High voltage, 112 KVA	R-3	1 Electrician Foreman	.85	23.530	Ea.
			1 Electrician			
			.5 Equip. Oper. (crane)			
			.5 S.P. Crane, 5 Ton			
5610	150 KVA			.65	30.770	Ea.
5620	225 KVA			.55	36.360	Ea.
5630	300 KVA			.45	44.440	Ea.
5640	500 KVA			.35	57.140	Ea.
5650	750 KVA			.32	62.500	Ea.
5660	1000 KVA			.30	66.670	Ea.
5670	1500 KVA			.27	74.070	Ea.
5680	2000 KVA			.25	80.000	Ea.
5690	2500 KVA			.20	100.000	Ea.
5700	3000 KVA			.18	111.000	Ea.
6000	2400V primary, 480V secondary 300 KVA			.45	44.440	Ea.
6010	500 KVA			.35	57.140	Ea.
6020	750 KVA	↓	↓	.32	62.500	Ea.
140	ISOLATING PANELS used with isolating transformers					
0100	Critical care area, 8 circuit, 3 KVA	1 Elec	1 Electrician	.58	13.790	Ea.
0200	5 KVA			.54	14.810	Ea.
0400	7.5 KVA			.52	15.380	Ea.
0600	10 KVA			.44	18.180	Ea.
0800	Operating room power & lighting, 8 circuit, 3 KVA			.58	13.790	Ea.
1000	5 KVA			.54	14.810	Ea.
1200	7.5 KVA			.52	15.380	Ea.
1400	10 KVA			.44	18.180	Ea.
1600	X-ray systems, 15 KVA, 90 amp	↓	↓	.44	18.180	Ea.

164 100	Transformers	CREW	MAKEUP	DAILY OUTPUT	MAN-HOURS	UNIT
150	150	**ISOLATING TRANSFORMER**					
0100		Single phase, 120/240 volt primary, 120/240 volt secondary					
0200		0.50 KVA	1 Elec	1 Electrician	4	2.000	Ea.
0400		1 KVA			2	4.000	Ea.
0600		2 KVA			1.60	5.000	Ea.
0800		3 KVA			1.40	5.710	Ea.
1000		5 KVA			1.20	6.670	Ea.
1200		7.5 KVA			1.10	7.270	Ea.
1400		10 KVA			.80	10.000	Ea.
1600		15 KVA			.60	13.330	Ea.
1800		25 KVA	↓	↓	.50	16.000	Ea.
1810		37.5 KVA	2 Elec	2 Electricians	.80	20.000	Ea.
1820		75 KVA	"	"	.65	24.620	Ea.
1830		3 phase, 120/240 to 120/208V secondary, 112.5 KVA	R-3	1 Electrician Foreman	.90	22.220	Ea.
				1 Electrician			
				.5 Equip. Oper. (crane)			
				.5 S.P. Crane, 5 Ton			
1840		150 KVA			.85	23.530	Ea.
1850		225 KVA			.65	30.770	Ea.
1860		300 KVA			.55	36.360	Ea.
1870		500 KVA			.45	44.440	Ea.
1880		750 KVA	↓	↓	.35	57.140	Ea.
1881							
160		**OIL FILLED TRANSFORMER** Pad mounted, Primary delta or Y,					
0050		5 KV or 15 KV, with taps, 277/480 secondary, 3 phase					
0100		150 KVA	R-3	1 Electrician Foreman	.65	30.770	Ea.
				1 Electrician			
				.5 Equip. Oper. (crane)			
				.5 S.P. Crane, 5 Ton			
0110		225 KVA			.55	36.360	Ea.
0200		300 KVA			.45	44.440	Ea.
0300		500 KVA			.40	50.000	Ea.
0400		750			.38	52.630	Ea.
0500		1000 KVA			.26	76.920	Ea.
0600		1500 KVA			.23	86.960	Ea.
0700		2000 KVA			.20	100.000	Ea.
0710		2500 KVA			.19	105.000	Ea.
0720		3000 KVA			.17	118.000	Ea.
0800		3750 KVA	↓	↓	.16	125.000	Ea.
170		**TRANSFORMER, SILICON FILLED** Pad mounted					
0020		5 KV or 15 KV primary 277/480 volt secondary, 3 phase					
0050		225 KVA	R-3	1 Electrician Foreman	.55	36.360	Ea.
				1 Electrician			
				.5 Equip. Oper. (crane)			
				.5 S.P. Crane, 5 Ton			
0100		300 KVA			.45	44.440	Ea.
0200		500 KVA			.40	50.000	Ea.
0250		750 KVA			.38	52.630	Ea.
0300		1000 KVA			.26	76.920	Ea.
0350		1500 KVA			.23	86.960	Ea.
0400		2000 KVA			.20	100.000	Ea.
0450		2500 KVA	↓	↓	.19	105.000	Ea.
190		**HANDLING** Add to normal labor cost in restricted areas					
5000		Transformers					
5150		15 KVA, approximately 200 pounds	2 Elec	2 Electricians	2.70	5.930	Ea.
5160		25 KVA, approximately 300 pounds			2.50	6.400	Ea.
5170		37.5 KVA, approximately 400 pounds			2.30	6.960	Ea.
5180		50 KVA, approximately 500 pounds	↓	↓	2	8.000	Ea.

164 | Transformers and Bus Ducts

164 100 | Transformers

		Description	CREW	MAKEUP	DAILY OUTPUT	MAN-HOURS	UNIT
190	5191	Handling transformers, 75 KVA, approximately 600 pounds	2 Elec	2 Electricians	1.80	8.890	Ea.
	5200	100 KVA, approximately 700 pounds	"	"	1.60	10.000	Ea.
	5210	112.5 KVA, approximately 800 pounds	3 Elec	3 Electricians	2.20	10.910	Ea.
	5220	125 KVA, approximately 900 pounds			2	12.000	Ea.
	5230	150 KVA, approximately 1000 pounds			1.80	13.330	Ea.
	5240	167 KVA, approximately 1200 pounds			1.60	15.000	Ea.
	5250	200 KVA, approximately 1400 pounds			1.40	17.140	Ea.
	5260	225 KVA, approximately 1600 pounds			1.30	18.460	Ea.
	5270	250 KVA, approximately 1800 pounds			1.10	21.820	Ea.
	5280	300 KVA, approximately 2000 pounds			1	24.000	Ea.
	5290	500 KVA, approximately 3000 pounds			.75	32.000	Ea.
	5300	600 KVA, approximately 3500 pounds			.67	35.820	Ea.
	5310	750 KVA, approximately 4000 pounds			.60	40.000	Ea.
	5320	1000 KVA, approximately 5000 pounds	↓	↓	.50	48.000	Ea.

164 200 | Bus Ducts

		Description	CREW	MAKEUP	DAILY OUTPUT	MAN-HOURS	UNIT
210		**ALUMINUM BUS DUCT**					
	0050	3 pole 4 wire, plug-in/indoor, straight section, 225 amp	1 Elec	1 Electrician	22	.364	L.F.
	0100	400 amp			18	.444	L.F.
	0150	600 amp			16	.500	L.F.
	0200	800 amp			13	.615	L.F.
	0250	1000 amp			12	.667	L.F.
	0300	1350 amp			11	.727	L.F.
	0310	1600 amp			9	.889	L.F.
	0320	2000 amp			8	1.000	L.F.
	0330	2500 amp			7	1.140	L.F.
	0340	3000 amp			6	1.330	L.F.
	0350	Feeder, 600 amp			17	.471	L.F.
	0400	800 amp			14	.571	L.F.
	0450	1000 amp			13	.615	L.F.
	0500	1350 amp			12	.667	L.F.
	0550	1600 amp			10	.800	L.F.
	0600	2000 amp			9	.889	L.F.
	0620	2500 amp			7	1.140	L.F.
	0630	3000 amp			6	1.330	L.F.
	0640	4000 amp			5	1.600	L.F.
	0650	Elbow, 225 amp			2.20	3.640	Ea.
	0700	400 amp			1.90	4.210	Ea.
	0750	600 amp			1.70	4.710	Ea.
	0800	800 amp			1.50	5.330	Ea.
	0850	1000 amp			1.40	5.710	Ea.
	0900	1350 amp			1.30	6.150	Ea.
	0950	1600 amp			1.20	6.670	Ea.
	1000	2000 amp			1	8.000	Ea.
	1020	2500 amp			.90	8.890	Ea.
	1030	3000 amp			.80	10.000	Ea.
	1040	4000 amp			.70	11.430	Ea.
	1100	Cable tap box, end, 225 amp			1.80	4.440	Ea.
	1150	400 amp			1.60	5.000	Ea.
	1200	600 amp			1.30	6.150	Ea.
	1250	800 amp			1.10	7.270	Ea.
	1300	1000 amp			1	8.000	Ea.
	1350	1350 amp			.80	10.000	Ea.
	1400	1600 amp			.70	11.430	Ea.
	1450	2000 amp			.60	13.330	Ea.
	1460	2500 amp			.50	16.000	Ea.
	1470	3000 amp			.40	20.000	Ea.
	1480	4000 amp	↓	↓	.30	26.670	Ea.

164 200 | Bus Ducts

		CREW	MAKEUP	DAILY OUTPUT	MAN-HOURS	UNIT
210 1501	Aluminum bus duct, switchboard stub, 225 amp	1 Elec	1 Electrician	2.90	2.760	Ea.
1550	400 amp			2.70	2.960	Ea.
1600	600 amp			2.30	3.480	Ea.
1650	800 amp			2	4.000	Ea.
1700	1000 amp			1.60	5.000	Ea.
1750	1350 amp			1.50	5.330	Ea.
1800	1600 amp			1.30	6.150	Ea.
1850	2000 amp			1.20	6.670	Ea.
1860	2500 amp			1.10	7.270	Ea.
1870	3000 amp			1	8.000	Ea.
1880	4000 amp			.90	8.890	Ea.
1890	Tee fittings, 225 amp			1.60	5.000	Ea.
1900	400 amp			1.40	5.710	Ea.
1950	600 amp			1.30	6.150	Ea.
2000	800 amp			1.20	6.670	Ea.
2050	1000 amp			1.10	7.270	Ea.
2100	1350 amp			1	8.000	Ea.
2150	1600 amp			.80	10.000	Ea.
2200	2000 amp			.60	13.330	Ea.
2220	2500 amp			.50	16.000	Ea.
2230	3000 amp			.40	20.000	Ea.
2240	4000 amp			.30	26.670	Ea.
2300	Wall flange, 600 amp			10	.800	Ea.
2310	800 amp			8	1.000	Ea.
2320	1000 amp			6.50	1.230	Ea.
2330	1350 amp			5.40	1.480	Ea.
2340	1600 amp			4.50	1.780	Ea.
2350	2000 amp			4	2.000	Ea.
2360	2500 amp			3.30	2.420	Ea.
2370	3000 amp			2.70	2.960	Ea.
2380	4000 amp			2	4.000	Ea.
2390	5000 amp			1.50	5.330	Ea.
2400	Vapor barrier			4	2.000	Ea.
2420	Roof flange kit			2	4.000	Ea.
2600	Expansion fitting, 225 amp			5	1.600	Ea.
2610	400 amp			4	2.000	Ea.
2620	600 amp			3	2.670	Ea.
2630	800 amp			2.30	3.480	Ea.
2640	1000 amp			2	4.000	Ea.
2650	1350 amp			1.80	4.440	Ea.
2660	1600 amp			1.60	5.000	Ea.
2670	2000 amp			1.40	5.710	Ea.
2680	2500 amp			1.20	6.670	Ea.
2690	3000 amp			1	8.000	Ea.
2700	4000 amp			.80	10.000	Ea.
2800	Reducer, unfused, 400 amp			4	2.000	Ea.
2810	600 amp			3	2.670	Ea.
2820	800 amp			2.30	3.480	Ea.
2830	1000 amp			2	4.000	Ea.
2840	1350 amp			1.80	4.440	Ea.
2850	1600 amp			1.60	5.000	Ea.
2860	2000 amp			1.40	5.710	Ea.
2870	2500 amp			1.20	6.670	Ea.
2880	3000 amp			1	8.000	Ea.
2890	4000 amp			.80	10.000	Ea.
2950	Reducer, fuse included, 225 amp			2.20	3.640	Ea.
2960	400 amp			2.10	3.810	Ea.
2970	600 amp	↓	↓	1.80	4.440	Ea.

164 200	Bus Ducts	CREW	MAKEUP		DAILY OUTPUT	MAN-HOURS	UNIT
210 2981	Aluminum bus duct, reducer, w/fuse, 800 amp	1 Elec	1 Electrician		1.60	5.000	Ea.
2990	1000 amp				1.50	5.330	Ea.
3000	1200 amp				1.40	5.710	Ea.
3010	1600 amp				1.10	7.270	Ea.
3020	2000 amp				.90	8.890	Ea.
3100	Reducer, circuit breaker, 225 amp				2.20	3.640	Ea.
3110	400 amp				2.10	3.810	Ea.
3120	600 amp				1.80	4.440	Ea.
3130	800 amp				1.60	5.000	Ea.
3140	1000 amp				1.50	5.330	Ea.
3150	1200 amp				1.40	5.710	Ea.
3160	1600 amp				1.10	7.270	Ea.
3170	2000 amp				.90	8.890	Ea.
3250	Reducer, circuit breaker, 75,000 AIC, 225 amp				2.20	3.640	Ea.
3260	400 amp				2.10	3.810	Ea.
3270	600 amp				1.80	4.440	Ea.
3280	800 amp				1.60	5.000	Ea.
3290	1000 amp				1.50	5.330	Ea.
3300	1200 amp				1.40	5.710	Ea.
3310	1600 amp				1.10	7.270	Ea.
3320	2000 amp				.90	8.890	Ea.
3400	Reducer, circuit breaker CLF 225 amp				2.20	3.640	Ea.
3410	400 amp				2.10	3.810	Ea.
3420	600 amp				1.80	4.440	Ea.
3430	800 amp				1.60	5.000	Ea.
3440	1000 amp				1.50	5.330	Ea.
3450	1200 amp				1.40	5.710	Ea.
3460	1600 amp				1.10	7.270	Ea.
3470	2000 amp				.90	8.890	Ea.
3550	Ground bus added to bus duct, 225 amp				160	.050	L.F.
3560	400 amp				160	.050	L.F.
3570	600 amp				140	.057	L.F.
3580	800 amp				120	.067	L.F.
3590	1000 amp				100	.080	L.F.
3600	1350 amp				90	.089	L.F.
3610	1600 amp				80	.100	L.F.
3620	2000 amp				80	.100	L.F.
3630	2500 amp				70	.114	L.F.
3640	3000 amp				60	.133	L.F.
3650	4000 amp				50	.160	L.F.
3810	High short circuit, 400 amp				18	.444	L.F.
3820	600 amp				16	.500	L.F.
3830	800 amp				13	.615	L.F.
3840	1000 amp				12	.667	L.F.
3850	1350 amp				11	.727	L.F.
3860	1600 amp				9	.889	L.F.
3870	2000 amp				8	1.000	L.F.
3880	2500 amp				7	1.140	L.F.
3890	3000 amp				6	1.330	L.F.
3920	Cross, 225 amp				2.80	2.860	Ea.
3930	400 amp				2.30	3.480	Ea.
3940	600 amp				2	4.000	Ea.
3950	800 amp				1.70	4.710	Ea.
3960	1000 amp				1.50	5.330	Ea.
3970	1350 amp				1.40	5.710	Ea.
3980	1600 amp				1.10	7.270	Ea.
3990	2000 amp				.90	8.890	Ea.
4000	2500 amp	↓	↓		.80	10.000	Ea.

164 | Transformers and Bus Ducts

			164 200	Bus Ducts	CREW	MAKEUP	DAILY OUTPUT	MAN-HOURS	UNIT
210	4012	Aluminum bus duct, cross, 3000 amp	1 Elec	1 Electrician	.60	13.330	Ea.
	4020	4000 amp			.50	16.000	Ea.
	4040	Cable tap box, center, 225 amp			1.80	4.440	Ea.
	4050	400 amp			1.60	5.000	Ea.
	4060	600 amp			1.30	6.150	Ea.
	4070	800 amp			1.10	7.270	Ea.
	4080	1000 amp			1	8.000	Ea.
	4090	1350 amp			.80	10.000	Ea.
	4100	1600 amp			.70	11.430	Ea.
	4110	2000 amp			.60	13.330	Ea.
	4120	2500 amp			.50	16.000	Ea.
	4130	3000 amp			.40	20.000	Ea.
	4140	4000 amp			.30	26.670	Ea.
	4500	Weatherproof, feeder, 600 amp			15	.533	L.F.
	4520	800 amp			12	.667	L.F.
	4540	1000 amp			11	.727	L.F.
	4560	1350 amp			10	.800	L.F.
	4580	1600 amp			8.50	.941	L.F.
	4600	2000 amp			8	1.000	L.F.
	4620	2500 amp			6	1.330	L.F.
	4640	3000 amp			5	1.600	L.F.
	4660	4000 amp			4	2.000	L.F.
	5000	3 pole, 3 wire, feeder, 600 amp			20	.400	L.F.
	5010	800 amp			16	.500	L.F.
	5020	1000 amp			15	.533	L.F.
	5030	1350 amp			14	.571	L.F.
	5040	1600 amp			12	.667	L.F.
	5050	2000 amp			10	.800	L.F.
	5060	2500 amp			8	1.000	L.F.
	5070	3000 amp			7	1.140	L.F.
	5080	4000 amp			6	1.330	L.F.
	5200	Plug-in type, 225 amp			25	.320	L.F.
	5210	400 amp			21	.381	L.F.
	5220	600 amp			18	.444	L.F.
	5230	800 amp			15	.533	L.F.
	5240	1000 amp			14	.571	L.F.
	5250	1350 amp			13	.615	L.F.
	5260	1600 amp			10	.800	L.F.
	5270	2000 amp			9	.889	L.F.
	5280	2500 amp			8	1.000	L.F.
	5290	3000 amp			7	1.140	L.F.
	5300	4000 amp			6	1.330	L.F.
	5330	High short circuit, 400 amp			21	.381	L.F.
	5340	600 amp			18	.444	L.F.
	5350	800 amp			15	.533	L.F.
	5360	1000 amp			14	.571	L.F.
	5370	1350 amp			13	.615	L.F.
	5380	1600 amp			10	.800	L.F.
	5390	2000 amp			9	.889	L.F.
	5400	2500 amp			8	1.000	L.F.
	5410	3000 amp			7	1.140	L.F.
	5440	Elbow, 225 amp			2.50	3.200	Ea.
	5450	400 amp			2.20	3.640	Ea.
	5460	600 amp			2	4.000	Ea.
	5470	800 amp			1.70	4.710	Ea.
	5480	1000 amp			1.60	5.000	Ea.
	5490	1350 amp			1.50	5.330	Ea.
	5500	1600 amp	▼	▼	1.40	5.710	Ea.

164 200	Bus Ducts	CREW	MAKEUP	DAILY OUTPUT	MAN-HOURS	UNIT
210 5512	Aluminum bus duct, 3 pole, 3 wire, elbow, 2000 amp	1 Elec	1 Electrician	1.20	6.670	Ea.
5520	2500 amp			1	8.000	Ea.
5530	3000 amp			.90	8.890	Ea.
5540	4000 amp			.80	10.000	Ea.
5560	Tee fittings, 225 amp			1.80	4.440	Ea.
5570	400 amp			1.60	5.000	Ea.
5580	600 amp			1.50	5.330	Ea.
5590	800 amp			1.40	5.710	Ea.
5600	1000 amp			1.30	6.150	Ea.
5610	1350 amp			1.20	6.670	Ea.
5620	1600 amp			.90	8.890	Ea.
5630	2000 amp			.70	11.430	Ea.
5640	2500 amp			.60	13.330	Ea.
5650	3000 amp			.50	16.000	Ea.
5660	4000 amp			.35	22.860	Ea.
5680	Cross, 225 amp			3.20	2.500	Ea.
5690	400 amp			2.70	2.960	Ea.
5700	600 amp			2.30	3.480	Ea.
5710	800 amp			2	4.000	Ea.
5720	1000 amp			1.80	4.440	Ea.
5730	1350 amp			1.60	5.000	Ea.
5740	1600 amp			1.30	6.150	Ea.
5750	2000 amp			1.10	7.270	Ea.
5760	2500 amp			.90	8.890	Ea.
5770	3000 amp			.70	11.430	Ea.
5780	4000 amp			.60	13.330	Ea.
5800	Expansion fitting, 225 amp			5.80	1.380	Ea.
5810	400 amp			4.60	1.740	Ea.
5820	600 amp			3.50	2.290	Ea.
5830	800 amp			2.60	3.080	Ea.
5840	1000 amp			2.30	3.480	Ea.
5850	1350 amp			2.10	3.810	Ea.
5860	1600 amp			1.80	4.440	Ea.
5870	2000 amp			1.60	5.000	Ea.
5880	2500 amp			1.40	5.710	Ea.
5890	3000 amp			1.20	6.670	Ea.
5900	4000 amp			.90	8.890	Ea.
5940	Reducer, nonfused, 400 amp			4.60	1.740	Ea.
5950	600 amp			3.50	2.290	Ea.
5960	800 amp			2.60	3.080	Ea.
5970	1000 amp			2.30	3.480	Ea.
5980	1350 amp			2.10	3.810	Ea.
5990	1600 amp			1.80	4.440	Ea.
6000	2000 amp			1.60	5.000	Ea.
6010	2500 amp			1.40	5.710	Ea.
6020	3000 amp			1.10	7.270	Ea.
6030	4000 amp			.90	8.890	Ea.
6050	Reducer, fuse included, 225 amp			2.50	3.200	Ea.
6060	400 amp			2.40	3.330	Ea.
6070	600 amp			2.10	3.810	Ea.
6080	800 amp			1.80	4.440	Ea.
6090	1000 amp			1.70	4.710	Ea.
6100	1350 amp			1.60	5.000	Ea.
6110	1600 amp			1.30	6.150	Ea.
6120	2000 amp			1	8.000	Ea.
6160	Reducer, circuit breaker, 225 amp			2.50	3.200	Ea.
6170	400 amp			2.40	3.330	Ea.
6180	600 amp	↓	↓	2.10	3.810	Ea.

		164 200	Bus Ducts	CREW	MAKEUP	DAILY OUTPUT	MAN-HOURS	UNIT
210	6192	Aluminum bus duct, reducer, circuit breaker, 800 amp		1 Elec	1 Electrician	1.80	4.440	Ea.
	6200	1000 amp				1.70	4.710	Ea.
	6210	1350 amp				1.60	5.000	Ea.
	6220	1600 amp				1.30	6.150	Ea.
	6230	2000 amp				1	8.000	Ea.
	6270	Cable tap box, center, 225 amp				2.10	3.810	Ea.
	6280	400 amp				1.80	4.440	Ea.
	6290	600 amp				1.50	5.330	Ea.
	6300	800 amp				1.30	6.150	Ea.
	6310	1000 amp				1.20	6.670	Ea.
	6320	1350 amp				.90	8.890	Ea.
	6330	1600 amp				.80	10.000	Ea.
	6340	2000 amp				.70	11.430	Ea.
	6350	2500 amp				.60	13.330	Ea.
	6360	3000 amp				.50	16.000	Ea.
	6370	4000 amp				.35	22.860	Ea.
	6390	Cable tap box, end, 225 amp				2.10	3.810	Ea.
	6400	400 amp				1.80	4.440	Ea.
	6410	600 amp				1.50	5.330	Ea.
	6420	800 amp				1.30	6.150	Ea.
	6430	1000 amp				1.20	6.670	Ea.
	6440	1350 amp				.90	8.890	Ea.
	6450	1600 amp				.80	10.000	Ea.
	6460	2000 amp				.70	11.430	Ea.
	6470	2500 amp				.60	13.330	Ea.
	6480	3000 amp				.50	16.000	Ea.
	6490	4000 amp				.35	22.860	Ea.
	7000	Weatherproof, feeder, 600 amp				17	.471	L.F.
	7020	800 amp				14	.571	L.F.
	7040	1000 amp				13	.615	L.F.
	7060	1350 amp				12	.667	L.F.
	7080	1600 amp				10	.800	L.F.
	7100	2000 amp				9	.889	L.F.
	7120	2500 amp				7	1.140	L.F.
	7140	3000 amp				6	1.330	L.F.
	7160	4000 amp	▼	▼		5	1.600	L.F.
215		**BUS DUCT** 100 amp and less, aluminum or copper, plug-in						
	0080	Bus duct, 3 pole 3 wire, 100 amp	1 Elec	1 Electrician		42	.190	L.F.
	0110	Elbow				4	2.000	Ea.
	0120	Tee				2	4.000	Ea.
	0130	Wall flange				8	1.000	Ea.
	0140	Ground kit				16	.500	Ea.
	0180	3 pole 4 wire, 100 amp				40	.200	L.F.
	0200	Cable tap box				3.10	2.580	Ea.
	0300	End closure				16	.500	Ea.
	0400	Elbow				4	2.000	Ea.
	0500	Tee				2	4.000	Ea.
	0600	Hangers				10	.800	Ea.
	0700	Circuit breakers, 15 to 50 amp, 1 pole				8	1.000	Ea.
	0800	15 to 60 amp, 2 pole				6.70	1.190	Ea.
	0900	3 pole				5.30	1.510	Ea.
	1000	60 to 100 amp, 1 pole				6.70	1.190	Ea.
	1100	70 to 100 amp, 2 pole				5.30	1.510	Ea.
	1200	3 pole				4.50	1.780	Ea.
	1220	Switch, nonfused				8	1.000	Ea.
	1240	Fused, 3 fuses, 4 wire, 30 amp				8	1.000	Ea.
	1260	60 amp				5.30	1.510	Ea.
	1280	100 amp	▼	▼		4.50	1.780	Ea.

		CREW	MAKEUP	DAILY OUTPUT	MAN-HOURS	UNIT
164 200	**Bus Ducts**					
215 1301	Bus duct, plug, fusible, 3 pole 250 volt, 30 amp	1 Elec	1 Electrician	5.30	1.510	Ea.
1310	60 amp			5.30	1.510	Ea.
1320	100 amp			4.50	1.780	Ea.
1330	3 pole 480 volt, 30 amp			5.30	1.510	Ea.
1340	60 amp			5.30	1.510	Ea.
1350	100 amp			4.50	1.780	Ea.
1360	Circuit breaker, 3 pole 250 volt, 60 amp			5.30	1.510	Ea.
1370	3 pole 480 volt, 100 amp			4.50	1.780	Ea.
2000	Bus duct, 2 wire, 250 volt 30 amp			60	.133	L.F.
2100	60 amp			50	.160	L.F.
2200	300 volt, 30 amp			60	.133	L.F.
2300	60 amp			50	.160	L.F.
2400	3 wire, 250 volt, 30 amp			60	.133	L.F.
2500	60 amp			50	.160	L.F.
2600	480/277 volt, 30 amp			60	.133	L.F.
2700	60 amp			50	.160	L.F.
2750	End feed, 300 volt, 2 wire, max. 30 amp			6	1.330	Ea.
2800	60 amp			5.50	1.450	Ea.
2850	30 amp miniature			6	1.330	Ea.
2900	3 wire, 30 amp			6	1.330	Ea.
2950	60 amp			5.50	1.450	Ea.
3000	30 amp miniature			6	1.330	Ea.
3050	. Center feed, 300 volt 2 wire, 30 amp			6	1.330	Ea.
3100	60 amp			5.50	1.450	Ea.
3150	3 wire, 30 amp			6	1.330	Ea.
3200	60 amp			5.50	1.450	Ea.
3220	Elbow, 30 amp			6	1.330	Ea.
3240	60 amp			5.50	1.450	Ea.
3260	End cap			40	.200	Ea.
3280	Strength beam, 10 ft.			15	.533	Ea.
3300	Hanger			24	.333	Ea.
3320	Tap box, nonfusible			6.30	1.270	Ea.
3340	Fusible, 30 amp, 1 fuse			6	1.330	Ea.
3360	2 fuse			6	1.330	Ea.
3380	3 fuse			6	1.330	Ea.
3400	Circuit breaker, handle on cover, 1 pole			6	1.330	Ea.
3420	2 pole			6	1.330	Ea.
3440	3 pole			6	1.330	Ea.
3460	Circuit breaker, external operhandle, 1 pole			6	1.330	Ea.
3480	2 pole			6	1.330	Ea.
3500	3 pole			6	1.330	Ea.
3520	Terminal plug, only			16	.500	Ea.
3540	Terminal with receptacle			16	.500	Ea.
3560	Fixture plug			16	.500	Ea.
4000	Copper bus duct, lighting, 2 wire 300 volt, 20 amp			70	.114	L.F.
4020	35 amp			60	.133	L.F.
4040	50 amp			55	.145	L.F.
4060	60 amp			50	.160	L.F.
4080	3 wire 300 volt, 20 amp			70	.114	L.F.
4100	35 amp			60	.133	L.F.
4120	50 amp			55	.145	L.F.
4140	60 amp			50	.160	L.F.
4160	Feeder in box, end, 1 circuit			6	1.330	Ea.
4180	2 circuit			5.50	1.450	Ea.
4200	Center, 1 circuit			6	1.330	Ea.
4220	2 circuit			5.50	1.450	Ea.
4240	End cap			40	.200	Ea.
4260	Hanger, surface mount	↓	↓	24	.333	Ea.

164 200	Bus Ducts	CREW	MAKEUP	DAILY OUTPUT	MAN-HOURS	UNIT
220	**220**	**COPPER BUS DUCT** Plug-in, indoor				
0050	3 pole 4 wire, bus duct, straight section, 225 amp	1 Elec	1 Electrician	20	.400	L.F.
1000	400 amp			16	.500	L.F.
1500	600 amp			13	.615	L.F.
2400	800 amp			10	.800	L.F.
2450	1000 amp			9	.889	L.F.
2500	1350 amp			8	1.000	L.F.
2510	1600 amp			6	1.330	L.F.
2520	2000 amp			5	1.600	L.F.
2530	2500 amp			4	2.000	L.F.
2540	3000 amp			3	2.670	L.F.
2550	Feeder, 600 amp			14	.571	L.F.
2600	800 amp			11	.727	L.F.
2700	1000 amp			10	.800	L.F.
2800	1350 amp			9	.889	L.F.
2900	1600 amp			7	1.140	L.F.
3000	2000 amp			6	1.330	L.F.
3010	2500 amp			4	2.000	L.F.
3020	3000 amp			3	2.670	L.F.
3030	4000 amp			2	4.000	L.F.
3040	5000 amp			1	8.000	L.F.
3100	Elbows, 225 amp			2	4.000	Ea.
3200	400 amp			1.80	4.440	Ea.
3300	600 amp			1.60	5.000	Ea.
3400	800 amp			1.40	5.710	Ea.
3500	1000 amp			1.30	6.150	Ea.
3600	1350 amp			1.20	6.670	Ea.
3700	1600 amp			1.10	7.270	Ea.
3800	2000 amp			.90	8.890	Ea.
3810	2500 amp			.80	10.000	Ea.
3820	3000 amp			.70	11.430	Ea.
3830	4000 amp			.60	13.330	Ea.
3840	5000 amp			.50	16.000	Ea.
4000	End box, 225 amp			17	.471	Ea.
4100	400 amp			16	.500	Ea.
4200	600 amp			14	.571	Ea.
4300	800 amp			13	.615	Ea.
4400	1000 amp			12	.667	Ea.
4500	1350 amp			11	.727	Ea.
4600	1600 amp			10	.800	Ea.
4700	2000 amp			9	.889	Ea.
4710	2500 amp			8	1.000	Ea.
4720	3000 amp			7	1.140	Ea.
4730	4000 amp			6	1.330	Ea.
4740	5000 amp			5	1.600	Ea.
4800	Cable tap box, end, 225 amp			1.60	5.000	Ea.
5000	400 amp			1.30	6.150	Ea.
5100	600 amp			1.10	7.270	Ea.
5200	800 amp			1	8.000	Ea.
5300	1000 amp			.80	10.000	Ea.
5400	1350 amp			.70	11.430	Ea.
5500	1600 amp			.60	13.330	Ea.
5600	2000 amp			.50	16.000	Ea.
5610	2500 amp			.40	20.000	Ea.
5620	3000 amp			.30	26.670	Ea.
5630	4000 amp			.20	40.000	Ea.
5640	5000 amp	▼	▼	.10	80.000	Ea.

164 200	Bus Ducts	CREW	MAKEUP		DAILY OUTPUT	MAN-HOURS	UNIT
220 5701	Copper bus duct, switchboard stub, 225 amp	1 Elec	1 Electrician		2.70	2.960	Ea.
5800	400 amp				2.30	3.480	Ea.
5900	600 amp				2	4.000	Ea.
6000	800 amp				1.60	5.000	Ea.
6100	1000 amp				1.50	5.330	Ea.
6200	1350 amp				1.30	6.150	Ea.
6300	1600 amp				1.20	6.670	Ea.
6400	2000 amp				1	8.000	Ea.
6410	2500 amp				.90	8.890	Ea.
6420	3000 amp				.80	10.000	Ea.
6430	4000 amp				.70	11.430	Ea.
6440	5000 amp				.60	13.330	Ea.
6490	Tee fittings, 225 amp				1.20	6.670	Ea.
6500	400 amp				1	8.000	Ea.
6600	600 amp				.90	8.890	Ea.
6700	800 amp				.80	10.000	Ea.
6750	1000 amp				.70	11.430	Ea.
6800	1350 amp				.60	13.330	Ea.
7000	1600 amp				.50	16.000	Ea.
7100	2000 amp				.40	20.000	Ea.
7110	2500 amp				.30	26.670	Ea.
7120	3000 amp				.25	32.000	Ea.
7130	4000 amp				.20	40.000	Ea.
7140	5000 amp				.10	80.000	Ea.
7200	Plug-in switches, 600 volt, 3 pole, 30 amp				4	2.000	Ea.
7300	60				3.60	2.220	Ea.
7400	100 amp				2.70	2.960	Ea.
7500	200 amp				1.60	5.000	Ea.
7600	400 amp				.70	11.430	Ea.
7700	600 amp				.45	17.780	Ea.
7800	800 amp				.33	24.240	Ea.
7900	1200 amp				.25	32.000	Ea.
7910	1600 amp				.22	36.360	Ea.
8000	Plug-in circuit breakers, molded case, 15 to 50 amp				4.40	1.820	Ea.
8100	70 to 100 amp				3.10	2.580	Ea.
8200	150 to 225 amp				1.70	4.710	Ea.
8300	250 to 400 amp				.70	11.430	Ea.
8400	500 to 600 amp				.50	16.000	Ea.
8500	700 to 800 amp				.32	25.000	Ea.
8600	900 to				.28	28.570	Ea.
8700	1200 amp				.22	36.360	Ea.
8720	1400 amp				.20	40.000	Ea.
8730	1600 amp				.20	40.000	Ea.
8750	Circuit breakers with current limiting fuse, 15 to 50 amp				4.40	1.820	Ea.
8760	70 to 100 amp				3.10	2.580	Ea.
8770	150 to 225 amp				1.70	4.710	Ea.
8780	250 to 400 amp				.70	11.430	Ea.
8790	500 to 600 amp				.50	16.000	Ea.
8800	700 to 800 amp				.32	25.000	Ea.
8810	900 to 1000 amp				.28	28.570	Ea.
8850	Combination starter FVNR, fusible switch, NEMA size 0, 30 amp				2	4.000	Ea.
8860	NEMA size 1, 60 amp				1.80	4.440	Ea.
8870	NEMA size 2, 100 amp				1.30	6.150	Ea.
8880	NEMA size 3, 200 amp				1	8.000	Ea.
8900	Circuit breaker, NEMA size 0, 30 amp				2	4.000	Ea.
8910	NEMA size 1, 60 amp				1.80	4.440	Ea.
8920	NEMA size 2, 100 amp				1.30	6.150	Ea.
8930	NEMA size 3, 200 amp	▼	▼		1	8.000	Ea.

164 200	Bus Ducts	CREW	MAKEUP		DAILY OUTPUT	MAN-HOURS	UNIT
220 8950	Combination contactor, fusible switch, NEMA size 0, 30 amp	1 Elec	1 Electrician		2	4.000	Ea.
8960	NEMA size 1, 60 amp				1.80	4.440	Ea.
8970	NEMA size 2, 100 amp				1.30	6.150	Ea.
8980	NEMA size 3, 200 amp				1	8.000	Ea.
9000	Circuit breaker, NEMA size 0, 30 amp				2	4.000	Ea.
9010	NEMA size 1, 60 amp				1.80	4.440	Ea.
9020	NEMA size 2, 100 amp				1.30	6.150	Ea.
9030	NEMA size 3, 200 amp				1	8.000	Ea.
9050	Control transformer for above, NEMA size 0, 30 amp				8	1.000	Ea.
9060	NEMA size 1, 60 amp				8	1.000	Ea.
9070	NEMA size 2, 100 amp				7	1.140	Ea.
9080	NEMA size 3, 200 amp				7	1.140	Ea.
9100	Comb. fusible switch & lighting control, electrically held, 30 amp				2	4.000	Ea.
9110	60 amp				1.80	4.440	Ea.
9120	100 amp				1.30	6.150	Ea.
9130	200 amp				1	8.000	Ea.
9150	Mechanically held, 30 amp				2	4.000	Ea.
9160	60 amp				1.80	4.440	Ea.
9170	100 amp				1.30	6.150	Ea.
9180	200 amp				1	8.000	Ea.
9200	Ground bus added to bus duct, 225 amp				160	.050	L.F.
9210	400 amp				120	.067	L.F.
9220	600 amp				120	.067	L.F.
9230	800 amp				80	.100	L.F.
9240	1000 amp				80	.100	L.F.
9250	1350 amp				70	.114	L.F.
9260	1600 amp				60	.133	L.F.
9270	2000 amp		ı		55	.145	L.F.
9280	2500 amp				50	.160	L.F.
9290	3000 amp				45	.178	L.F.
9300	4000 amp				40	.200	L.F.
9310	5000 amp	▼	▼		35	.229	L.F.
225	**COPPER BUS DUCT**						
0100	3 pole 4 wire, weatherproof, feeder duct, 600 amp	1 Elec	1 Electrician		12	.667	L.F.
0110	800 amp				9	.889	L.F.
0120	1000 amp				8.50	.941	L.F.
0130	1350 amp				8	1.000	L.F.
0140	1600 amp				6	1.330	L.F.
0150	2000 amp				5	1.600	L.F.
0160	2500 amp				3.50	2.290	L.F.
0170	3000 amp				2.50	3.200	L.F.
0180	4000 amp				1.80	4.440	L.F.
0200	Plug-in/indoor, bus duct, high short circuit, 400 amp				16	.500	L.F.
0210	600 amp				13	.615	L.F.
0220	800 amp				10	.800	L.F.
0230	1000 amp				9	.889	L.F.
0240	1350 amp				8	1.000	L.F.
0250	1600 amp				6	1.330	L.F.
0260	2000 amp				5	1.600	L.F.
0270	2500 amp				4	2.000	L.F.
0280	3000 amp				3	2.670	L.F.
0310	Cross, 225 amp				1.50	5.330	Ea.
0320	400 amp				1.40	5.710	Ea.
0330	600 amp				1.30	6.150	Ea.
0340	800 amp				1.10	7.270	Ea.
0350	1000 amp				1	8.000	Ea.
0360	1350 amp				.90	8.890	Ea.
0370	1600 amp	▼	▼		.85	9.410	Ea.

164 200 | Bus Ducts

		Description	CREW	MAKEUP	DAILY OUTPUT	MAN-HOURS	UNIT
225	0382	Copper bus duct, plug-in/indoor, cross, 2000 amp	1 Elec	1 Electrician	.80	10.000	Ea.
	0390	2500 amp			.70	11.430	Ea.
	0400	3000 amp			.60	13.330	Ea.
	0410	4000 amp			.50	16.000	Ea.
	0430	Expansion fitting, 225 amp			2.70	2.960	Ea.
	0440	400 amp			2.30	3.480	Ea.
	0450	600 amp			2	4.000	Ea.
	0460	800 amp			1.70	4.710	Ea.
	0470	1000 amp			1.50	5.330	Ea.
	0480	1350 amp			1.40	5.710	Ea.
	0490	1600 amp			1.30	6.150	Ea.
	0500	2000 amp			1.10	7.270	Ea.
	0510	2500 amp			.90	8.890	Ea.
	0520	3000 amp			.80	10.000	Ea.
	0530	4000 amp			.60	13.330	Ea.
	0550	Reducer, nonfused, 225 amp			2.70	2.960	Ea.
	0560	400 amp			2.30	3.480	Ea.
	0570	600 amp			2	4.000	Ea.
	0580	800 amp			1.70	4.710	Ea.
	0590	1000 amp			1.50	5.330	Ea.
	0600	1350 amp			1.40	5.710	Ea.
	0610	1600 amp			1.30	6.150	Ea.
	0620	2000 amp			1.10	7.270	Ea.
	0630	2500 amp			.90	8.890	Ea.
	0640	3000 amp			.80	10.000	Ea.
	0650	4000 amp			.60	13.330	Ea.
	0670	Reducer, fuse included, 225 amp			2.20	3.640	Ea.
	0680	400 amp			2.10	3.810	Ea.
	0690	600 amp			1.80	4.440	Ea.
	0700	800 amp			1.60	5.000	Ea.
	0710	1000 amp			1.50	5.330	Ea.
	0720	1350 amp			1.40	5.710	Ea.
	0730	1600 amp			1.10	7.270	Ea.
	0740	2000 amp			.90	8.890	Ea.
	0790	Reducer, circuit breaker, 225 amp			2.20	3.640	Ea.
	0800	400 amp			2.10	3.810	Ea.
	0810	600 amp			1.80	4.440	Ea.
	0820	800 amp			1.60	5.000	Ea.
	0830	1000 amp			1.50	5.330	Ea.
	0840	1350 amp			1.40	5.710	Ea.
	0850	1600 amp			1.10	7.270	Ea.
	0860	2000 amp			.90	8.890	Ea.
	0910	Cable tap box, center, 225 amp			1.60	5.000	Ea.
	0920	400 amp			1.30	6.150	Ea.
	0930	600 amp			1.10	7.270	Ea.
	0940	800 amp			1	8.000	Ea.
	0950	1000 amp			.80	10.000	Ea.
	0960	1350 amp			.70	11.430	Ea.
	0970	1600 amp			.60	13.330	Ea.
	0980	2000 amp			.50	16.000	Ea.
	1040	2500 amp			.40	20.000	Ea.
	1060	3000 amp			.30	26.670	Ea.
	1080	4000 amp			.20	40.000	Ea.
	1800	3 pole 3 wire, feeder duct, weatherproof, 600 amp			14	.571	L.F.
	1820	800 amp			11	.727	L.F.
	1840	1000 amp			10	.800	L.F.
	1860	1350 amp			9	.889	L.F.
	1880	1600 amp	↓	↓	7	1.140	L.F.

164 | Transformers and Bus Ducts

164 200 | Bus Ducts

		CREW	MAKEUP		DAILY OUTPUT	MAN-HOURS	UNIT
225 1901	Copper bus duct, feeder duct, 2000 amp	1 Elec	1 Electrician		6	1.330	L.F.
1920	2500 amp				4	2.000	L.F.
1940	3000 amp				3	2.670	L.F.
1960	4000 amp				2	4.000	L.F.
2000	Feeder duct, 600 amp				16	.500	L.F.
2010	800 amp				13	.615	L.F.
2020	1000 amp				12	.667	L.F.
2030	1350 amp				10	.800	L.F.
2040	1600 amp				8	1.000	L.F.
2050	2000 amp				7	1.140	L.F.
2060	2500 amp				5	1.600	L.F.
2070	3000 amp				4	2.000	L.F.
2080	4000 amp				3	2.670	L.F.
2200	Bus duct plug-in, 225 amp				23	.348	L.F.
2210	400 amp				18	.444	L.F.
2220	600 amp				15	.533	L.F.
2230	800 amp				12	.667	L.F.
2240	1000 amp				10	.800	L.F.
2250	1350 amp				9	.889	L.F.
2260	1600 amp				7	1.140	L.F.
2270	2000 amp				6	1.330	L.F.
2280	2500 amp				5	1.600	L.F.
2290	3000 amp				4	2.000	L.F.
2330	High short circuit, 400 amp				18	.444	L.F.
2340	600 amp				15	.533	L.F.
2350	800 amp				12	.667	L.F.
2360	1000 amp				10	.800	L.F.
2370	1350 amp				9	.889	L.F.
2380	1600 amp				7	1.140	L.F.
2390	2000 amp				6	1.330	L.F.
2400	2500 amp				5	1.600	L.F.
2410	3000 amp				4	2.000	L.F.
2440	Elbows, 225 amp				2.30	3.480	L.F.
2450	400 amp				2.10	3.810	Ea.
2460	600 amp				1.80	4.440	Ea.
2470	800 amp				1.60	5.000	Ea.
2480	1000 amp				1.50	5.330	Ea.
2490	1350 amp				1.40	5.710	Ea.
2500	1600 amp				1.30	6.150	Ea.
2510	2000 amp				1	8.000	Ea.
2520	2500 amp				.90	8.890	Ea.
2530	3000 amp				.80	10.000	Ea.
2540	4000 amp				.70	11.430	Ea.
2560	Tee fittings, 225 amp				1.40	5.710	Ea.
2570	400 amp				1.20	6.670	Ea.
2580	600 amp				1	8.000	Ea.
2590	800 amp				.90	8.890	Ea.
2600	1000 amp				.80	10.000	Ea.
2610	1350 amp				.70	11.430	Ea.
2620	1600 amp				.60	13.330	Ea.
2630	2000 amp				.50	16.000	Ea.
2640	2500 amp				.35	22.860	Ea.
2650	3000 amp				.30	26.670	Ea.
2660	4000 amp				.25	32.000	Ea.
2680	Cross, 225 amp				1.80	4.440	Ea.
2690	400 amp				1.60	5.000	Ea.
2700	600 amp				1.50	5.330	Ea.
2710	800 amp	↓	↓		1.30	6.150	Ea.

			Bus Ducts	CREW	MAKEUP	DAILY OUTPUT	MAN-HOURS	UNIT
225	2722		Copper bus duct, plug-in, cross, 1000 amp	1 Elec	1 Electrician	1.20	6.670	Ea.
	2730		1350 amp			1.10	7.270	Ea.
	2740		1600 amp			1	8.000	Ea.
	2750		2000 amp			.90	8.890	Ea.
	2760		2500 amp			.80	10.000	Ea.
	2770		3000 amp			.70	11.430	Ea.
	2780		4000 amp			.50	16.000	Ea.
	2800		Expansion fitting, 225 amp			3.20	2.500	Ea.
	2810		400 amp			2.70	2.960	Ea.
	2820		600 amp			2.30	3.480	Ea.
	2830		800 amp			2	4.000	Ea.
	2840		1000 amp			1.80	4.440	Ea.
	2850		1350 amp			1.60	5.000	Ea.
	2860		1600 amp			1.50	5.330	Ea.
	2870		2000 amp			1.30	6.150	Ea.
	2880		2500 amp			1.10	7.270	Ea.
	2890		3000 amp			.90	8.890	Ea.
	2900		4000 amp			.70	11.430	Ea.
	2920		Reducer, nonfused, 225 amp			3.20	2.500	Ea.
	2930		400 amp			2.70	2.960	Ea.
	2940		600 amp			2.30	3.480	Ea.
	2950		800 amp			2	4.000	Ea.
	2960		1000 amp			1.80	4.440	Ea.
	2970		1350 amp			1.60	5.000	Ea.
	2980		1600 amp			1.50	5.330	Ea.
	2990		2000 amp			1.30	6.150	Ea.
	3000		2500 amp			1.10	7.270	Ea.
	3010		3000 amp			.90	8.890	Ea.
	3020		4000 amp			.70	11.430	Ea.
	3040		Reducer, fuse included, 225 amp			2.50	3.200	Ea.
	3050		400 amp			2.40	3.330	Ea.
	3060		600 amp			2.10	3.810	Ea.
	3070		800 amp			1.80	4.440	Ea.
	3080		1000 amp			1.70	4.710	Ea.
	3090		1350 amp			1.60	5.000	Ea.
	3100		1600 amp			1.30	6.150	Ea.
	3110		2000 amp			1	8.000	Ea.
	3160		Reducer, circuit breaker, 225 amp			2.50	3.200	Ea.
	3170		400 amp			2.40	3.330	Ea.
	3180		600 amp			2.10	3.810	Ea.
	3190		800 amp			1.80	4.440	Ea.
	3200		1000 amp			1.70	4.710	Ea.
	3210		1350 amp			1.60	5.000	Ea.
	3220		1600 amp			1.30	6.150	Ea.
	3230		2000 amp			1	8.000	Ea.
	3280		Cable tap box, center, 225 amp			1.80	4.440	Ea.
	3290		400 amp			1.50	5.330	Ea.
	3300		600 amp			1.30	6.150	Ea.
	3310		800 amp			1.20	6.670	Ea.
	3320		1000 amp			.90	8.890	Ea.
	3330		1350 amp			.80	10.000	Ea.
	3340		1600 amp			.70	11.430	Ea.
	3350		2000 amp			.60	13.330	Ea.
	3360		2500 amp			.50	16.000	Ea.
	3370		3000 amp			.35	22.860	Ea.
	3380		4000 amp			.25	32.000	Ea.
	3400		Cable tap box, end, 225 amp			1.80	4.440	Ea.
	3410		400 amp	↓	↓	1.50	5.330	Ea.

164 200	Bus Ducts	CREW	MAKEUP	DAILY OUTPUT	MAN-HOURS	UNIT
225 3422	Copper bus duct, cable tap box, end, 600 amp	1 Elec	1 Electrician	1.30	6.150	Ea.
3430	800 amp			1.20	6.670	Ea.
3440	1000 amp			.90	8.890	Ea.
3450	1350 amp			.80	10.000	Ea.
3460	1600 amp			.70	11.430	Ea.
3470	2000 amp			.60	13.330	Ea.
3480	2500 amp			.50	16.000	Ea.
3490	3000 amp			.35	22.860	Ea.
3500	4000 amp			.25	32.000	Ea.
4600	Plugs, fusible, 3 pole 250 volt, 30 amp			4	2.000	Ea.
4610	60 amp			3.60	2.220	Ea.
4620	100 amp			2.70	2.960	Ea.
4630	200 amp			1.60	5.000	Ea.
4640	400 amp			.70	11.430	Ea.
4650	600 amp			.45	17.780	Ea.
4700	4 pole 120/208 volt, 30 amp			3.90	2.050	Ea.
4710	60 amp			3.50	2.290	Ea.
4720	100 amp			2.60	3.080	Ea.
4730	200 amp			1.50	5.330	Ea.
4740	400 amp			.65	12.310	Ea.
4750	600 amp			.40	20.000	Ea.
4800	3 pole 480 volt, 30 amp			4	2.000	Ea.
4810	60 amp			3.60	2.220	Ea.
4820	100 amp			2.70	2.960	Ea.
4830	200 amp			1.60	5.000	Ea.
4840	400 amp			.70	11.430	Ea.
4850	600 amp			.45	17.780	Ea.
4860	800 amp			.33	24.240	Ea.
4870	1000 amp			.30	26.670	Ea.
4880	1200 amp			.25	32.000	Ea.
4890	1600 amp			.22	36.360	Ea.
4900	4 pole 277/480 volt, 30 amp			3.90	2.050	Ea.
4910	60 amp			3.50	2.290	Ea.
4920	100 amp			2.60	3.080	Ea.
4930	200 amp			1.50	5.330	Ea.
4940	400 amp			.65	12.310	Ea.
4950	600 amp			.40	20.000	Ea.
5050	800 amp			.30	26.670	Ea.
5060	1000 amp			.28	28.570	Ea.
5070	1200 amp			.24	33.330	Ea.
5080	1600 amp			.21	38.100	Ea.
5150	Fusible with starter, 3 pole 250 volt, 30 amp			3.50	2.290	Ea.
5160	60 amp			3.20	2.500	Ea.
5170	100 amp			2.50	3.200	Ea.
5180	200 amp			1.40	5.710	Ea.
5200	3 pole 480 volt, 30 amp			3.50	2.290	Ea.
5210	60 amp			3.20	2.500	Ea.
5220	100 amp			2.50	3.200	Ea.
5230	200 amp			1.40	5.710	Ea.
5300	Fusible with contactor, 3 pole 250 volt, 30 amp			3.50	2.290	Ea.
5310	60 amp			3.20	2.500	Ea.
5320	100 amp			2.50	3.200	Ea.
5330	200 amp			1.40	5.710	Ea.
5400	3 pole 480 volt, 30 amp			3.50	2.290	Ea.
5410	60 amp			3.20	2.500	Ea.
5420	100 amp			2.50	3.200	Ea.
5430	200 amp			1.40	5.710	Ea.
5450	Fusible with capacitor, 3 pole 250 volt, 30 amp	↓	↓	3	2.670	Ea.

164 200	Bus Ducts	CREW	MAKEUP	DAILY OUTPUT	MAN-HOURS	UNIT
225 5461	Plugs, fusible, w/capacitor, 3 pole, 250 volt, 60 amp	1 Elec	1 Electrician	2	4.000	Ea.
5500	3 pole 480 volt, 30 amp			3	2.670	Ea.
5510	60 amp			2	4.000	Ea.
5600	Circuit breaker, 3 pole 250 volt, 60 amp			4.50	1.780	Ea.
5610	100 amp			3.20	2.500	Ea.
5650	4 pole 120/208 volt, 60 amp			4.40	1.820	Ea.
5660	100 amp			3.10	2.580	Ea.
5700	3 pole 4 wire 277/480 volt, 60 amp			4.30	1.860	Ea.
5710	100 amp			3	2.670	Ea.
5720	225 amp			1.60	5.000	Ea.
5730	400 amp			.60	13.330	Ea.
5740	600 amp			.48	16.670	Ea.
5750	700 amp			.30	26.670	Ea.
5760	800 amp			.30	26.670	Ea.
5770	900 amp			.27	29.630	Ea.
5780	1000 amp			.27	29.630	Ea.
5790	1200 amp			.21	38.100	Ea.
5810	Circuit breaker w/HIC fuses, 3 pole 480 volt, 60 amp			4.40	1.820	Ea.
5820	100 amp			3.10	2.580	Ea.
5830	225 amp			1.70	4.710	Ea.
5840	400 amp			.70	11.430	Ea.
5850	600 amp			.50	16.000	Ea.
5860	700 amp			.32	25.000	Ea.
5870	800 amp			.32	25.000	Ea.
5880	900 amp			.28	28.570	Ea.
5890	1000 amp			.28	28.570	Ea.
5950	3 pole 4 wire, 277/480 volt, 60 amp			4.30	1.860	Ea.
5960	100 amp			3	2.670	Ea.
5970	225 amp			1.50	5.330	Ea.
5980	400 amp			.55	14.550	Ea.
5990	600 amp			.47	17.020	Ea.
6000	700 amp			.29	27.590	Ea.
6010	800 amp			.29	27.590	Ea.
6020	900 amp			.26	30.770	Ea.
6030	1000 amp			.26	30.770	Ea.
6040	1200 amp			.20	40.000	Ea.
6100	Circuit breaker with starter, 3 pole 250 volt, 60 amp			3.20	2.500	Ea.
6110	100 amp			2.50	3.200	Ea.
6120	225 amp			1.50	5.330	Ea.
6130	3 pole 480 volt, 60 amp			3.20	2.500	Ea.
6140	100 amp			2.50	3.200	Ea.
6150	225 amp			1.50	5.330	Ea.
6200	Circuit breaker with contactor, 3 pole 250 volt, 60 amp			3.20	2.500	Ea.
6210	100 amp			2.50	3.200	Ea.
6220	225 amp			1.50	5.330	Ea.
6250	3 pole 480 volt, 60 amp			3.20	2.500	Ea.
6260	100 amp			2.50	3.200	Ea.
6270	225 amp			1.50	5.330	Ea.
6300	Circuit breaker with capacitor, 3 pole 250 volt, 60 amp			2	4.000	Ea.
6310	3 pole 480 volt, 60 amp			2	4.000	Ea.
6400	Add control transformer with pilot light to starter			16	.500	Ea.
6410	Switch, fusible, mechanically held contactor optional			16	.500	Ea.
6430	Circuit breaker, mechanically held contactor optional			16	.500	Ea.
6450	Ground neutralizer, 3 pole	↓	↓	16	.500	Ea.

164 200 Bus Ducts	CREW	MAKEUP	DAILY OUTPUT	MAN-HOURS	UNIT
230 COPPER OR ALUMINUM BUS DUCT FITTINGS					
0100 Flange, wall, with vapor barrier, 225 amp	1 Elec	1 Electrician	3.10	2.580	Ea.
0110 400 amp			3	2.670	Ea.
0120 600 amp			2.90	2.760	Ea.
0130 800 amp			2.70	2.960	Ea.
0140 1000 amp			2.50	3.200	Ea.
0150 1350 amp			2.30	3.480	Ea.
0160 1600 amp			2.10	3.810	Ea.
0170 2000 amp			2	4.000	Ea.
0180 2500 amp			1.80	4.440	Ea.
0190 3000 amp			1.60	5.000	Ea.
0200 4000 amp			1.30	6.150	Ea.
0300 Roof, 225 amp			3.10	2.580	Ea.
0310 400 amp			3	2.670	Ea.
0320 600 amp			2.90	2.760	Ea.
0330 800 amp			2.70	2.960	Ea.
0340 1000 amp			2.50	3.200	Ea.
0350 1350 amp			2.30	3.480	Ea.
0360 1600 amp			2.10	3.810	Ea.
0370 2000 amp			2	4.000	Ea.
0380 2500 amp			1.80	4.440	Ea.
0390 3000 amp			1.60	5.000	Ea.
0400 4000 amp			1.30	6.150	Ea.
0420 Support, floor mounted, 225 amp			10	.800	Ea.
0430 400 amp			10	.800	Ea.
0440 600 amp			9	.889	Ea.
0450 800 amp			8	1.000	Ea.
0460 1000 amp			6.50	1.230	Ea.
0470 1350 amp			5.30	1.510	Ea.
0480 1600 amp			4.60	1.740	Ea.
0490 2000 amp			4	2.000	Ea.
0500 2500 amp			3.20	2.500	Ea.
0510 3000 amp			2.70	2.960	Ea.
0520 4000 amp			2	4.000	Ea.
0540 Weather stop, 225 amp			6	1.330	Ea.
0550 400 amp			5	1.600	Ea.
0560 600 amp			4.50	1.780	Ea.
0570 800 amp			4	2.000	Ea.
0580 1000 amp			3.20	2.500	Ea.
0590 1350 amp			2.70	2.960	Ea.
0600 1600 amp			2.30	3.480	Ea.
0610 2000 amp			2	4.000	Ea.
0620 2500 amp			1.60	5.000	Ea.
0630 3000 amp			1.30	6.150	Ea.
0640 4000 amp			1	8.000	Ea.
0660 End closure, 225 amp			17	.471	Ea.
0670 400 amp			16	.500	Ea.
0680 600 amp			14	.571	Ea.
0690 800 amp			13	.615	Ea.
0700 1000 amp			12	.667	Ea.
0710 1350 amp			11	.727	Ea.
0720 1600 amp			10	.800	Ea.
0730 2000 amp			9	.889	Ea.
0740 2500 amp			8	1.000	Ea.
0750 3000 amp			7	1.140	Ea.
0760 4000 amp			6	1.330	Ea.
0780 Switchboard stub, 3 pole 3 wire, 225 amp	↓	↓	3	2.670	Ea.
0790 400 amp			2.60	3.080	Ea.

164 200 | Bus Ducts

		CREW	MAKEUP		DAILY OUTPUT	MAN-HOURS	UNIT
230	0801	Bus duct fitting, switchboard stub, 3 pole, 3 wire, 600 amp	1 Elec	1 Electrician	2.30	3.480	Ea.
	0810	800 amp			1.80	4.440	Ea.
	0820	1000 amp			1.70	4.710	Ea.
	0830	1350 amp			1.50	5.330	Ea.
	0840	1600 amp			1.40	5.710	Ea.
	0850	2000 amp			1.20	6.670	Ea.
	0860	2500 amp			1	8.000	Ea.
	0870	3000 amp			.90	8.890	Ea.
	0880	4000 amp			.80	10.000	Ea.
	0900	3 pole 4 wire, 225 amp			2.70	2.960	Ea.
	0910	400 amp			2.30	3.480	Ea.
	0920	600 amp			2	4.000	Ea.
	0930	800 amp			1.60	5.000	Ea.
	0940	1000 amp			1.50	5.330	Ea.
	0950	1350 amp			1.30	6.150	Ea.
	0960	1600 amp			1.20	6.670	Ea.
	0970	2000 amp			1	8.000	Ea.
	0980	2500 amp			.90	8.890	Ea.
	0990	3000 amp			.80	10.000	Ea.
	1000	4000 amp			.70	11.430	Ea.
	1050	Service head, weatherproof, 3 pole 3 wire, 225 amp			1.50	5.330	Ea.
	1060	400 amp			1.40	5.710	Ea.
	1070	600 amp			1.30	6.150	Ea.
	1080	800 amp			1.20	6.670	Ea.
	1090	1000 amp			1	8.000	Ea.
	1100	1350 amp			.90	8.890	Ea.
	1110	1600 amp			.80	10.000	Ea.
	1120	2000 amp			.70	11.430	Ea.
	1130	2500 amp			.60	13.330	Ea.
	1140	3000 amp			.45	17.780	Ea.
	1150	4000 amp			.35	22.860	Ea.
	1200	3 pole 4 wire, 225 amp			1.30	6.150	Ea.
	1210	400 amp			1.20	6.670	Ea.
	1220	600 amp			1.10	7.270	Ea.
	1230	800 amp			1	8.000	Ea.
	1240	1000 amp			.85	9.410	Ea.
	1250	1350 amp			.75	10.670	Ea.
	1260	1600 amp			.70	11.430	Ea.
	1270	2000 amp			.60	13.330	Ea.
	1280	2500 amp			.50	16.000	Ea.
	1290	3000 amp			.40	20.000	Ea.
	1300	4000 amp			.30	26.670	Ea.
	1350	Flanged end, 3 pole 3 wire, 225 amp			3	2.670	Ea.
	1360	400 amp			2.60	3.080	Ea.
	1370	600 amp			2.30	3.480	Ea.
	1380	800 amp			1.80	4.440	Ea.
	1390	1000 amp			1.70	4.710	Ea.
	1400	1350 amp			1.50	5.330	Ea.
	1410	1600 amp			1.40	5.710	Ea.
	1420	2000 amp			1.20	6.670	Ea.
	1430	2500 amp			1	8.000	Ea.
	1440	3000 amp			.90	8.890	Ea.
	1450	4000 amp			.80	10.000	Ea.
	1500	3 pole 4 wire, 225 amp			2.70	2.960	Ea.
	1510	400 amp			2.30	3.480	Ea.
	1520	600 amp			2	4.000	Ea.
	1530	800 amp			1.60	5.000	Ea.
	1540	1000 amp	▼	▼	1.50	5.330	Ea.

164 | Transformers and Bus Ducts

			164 200	Bus Ducts	CREW	MAKEUP	DAILY OUTPUT	MAN-HOURS	UNIT
230	1551	Bus duct fitting, flanged end, 3 pole, 4 wire, 1350 amp	1 Elec	1 Electrician	1.30	6.150	Ea.
	1560	1600 amp			1.20	6.670	Ea.
	1570	2000 amp			1	8.000	Ea.
	1580	2500 amp			.90	8.890	Ea.
	1590	3000 amp			.80	10.000	Ea.
	1600	4000 amp			.70	11.430	Ea.
	1650	Hanger, standard, 225 amp			32	.250	Ea.
	1660	400 amp			24	.333	Ea.
	1670	600 amp			20	.400	Ea.
	1680	800 amp			16	.500	Ea.
	1690	1000 amp			12	.667	Ea.
	1700	1350 amp			10	.800	Ea.
	1710	1600 amp			10	.800	Ea.
	1720	2000 amp			9	.889	Ea.
	1730	2500 amp			8	1.000	Ea.
	1740	3000 amp			8	1.000	Ea.
	1750	4000 amp			8	1.000	Ea.
	1800	Spring type, 225 amp			8	1.000	Ea.
	1810	400 amp			7	1.140	Ea.
	1820	600 amp			7	1.140	Ea.
	1830	800 amp			7	1.140	Ea.
	1840	1000 amp			7	1.140	Ea.
	1850	1350 amp			7	1.140	Ea.
	1860	1600 amp			6	1.330	Ea.
	1870	2000 amp			6	1.330	Ea.
	1880	2500 amp			6	1.330	Ea.
	1890	3000 amp			5	1.600	Ea.
	1900	4000 amp	↓	↓	5	1.600	Ea.
	240	FEEDRAIL , 12 foot mounting					
	0050	Trolley busway, 3 pole					
	0100	300 volt 60 amp, plain, 10 ft. lengths	1 Elec	1 Electrician	50	.160	L.F.
	0300	Door track			50	.160	L.F.
	0500	Curved track			30	.267	L.F.
	0900	Center feed			5.30	1.510	Ea.
	1100	End feed			5.30	1.510	Ea.
	1300	Hanger set			24	.333	Ea.
	1501	Aluminum bus duct, switchboard stub, 225 amp			2.90	2.760	Ea.
	3000	600 volt 100 amp, plain, 10 ft. lengths			35	.229	L.F.
	3300	Door track			35	.229	L.F.
	4000	End cap			40	.200	Ea.
	4200	End feed			4	2.000	Ea.
	4500	Trolley, 600 volt, 20 amp			5.30	1.510	Ea.
	4700	30 amp			5.30	1.510	Ea.
	4900	Duplex, 40 amp			4	2.000	Ea.
	5000	60 amp			4	2.000	Ea.
	5300	Fusible, 20 amp			4	2.000	Ea.
	5500	30 amp			4	2.000	Ea.
	5900	300 volt, 20 amp			5.30	1.510	Ea.
	6000	30 amp			5.30	1.510	Ea.
	6300	Fusible, 20 amp			4.70	1.700	Ea.
	6500	30 amp			4.70	1.700	Ea.
	7300	Busway, 250 volt, 50 amp, 2 wire			70	.114	L.F.
	7340	Center feed			6	1.330	Ea.
	7350	End feed			6	1.330	Ea.
	7360	End cap			40	.200	Ea.
	7370	Hanger set			24	.333	Ea.
	7400	125/250 volt, 3 wire			60	.133	L.F.
	7430	Coupling	↓	↓	6	1.330	Ea.

164 200 | Bus Ducts

		CREW	MAKEUP	DAILY OUTPUT	MAN-HOURS	UNIT
240 7440	Feedrail, busway, 125/250 volt, 3 wire, center feed	1 Elec	1 Electrician	6	1.330	Ea.
7451	End feed			6	1.330	Ea.
7460	End cap			40	.200	Ea.
7470	Hanger set			24	.333	Ea.
7480	Trolley, 250 volt, 20 amp, 2 pole			6	1.330	Ea.
7490	30 amp			6	1.330	Ea.
7500	125/250 volt, 20 amp, 3 pole			6	1.330	Ea.
7510	30 amp	↓	↓	6	1.330	Ea.

164 300 | Computer Pwr Supplies

		CREW	MAKEUP	DAILY OUTPUT	MAN-HOURS	UNIT
305	AUTOMATIC VOLTAGE REGULATORS					
0100	Computer grade, solid state, variable trans. volt. regulator					
0110	Single-phase, 120 V, 8.6 KVA	2 Elec	2 Electricians	1.33	12.030	Ea.
0120	17.3 KVA			1.14	14.040	Ea.
0130	208/240 V, 7.5/8.6 KVA			1.33	12.030	Ea.
0140	13.5/15.6 KVA			1.33	12.030	Ea.
0150	27.0/31.2 KVA			1.14	14.040	Ea.
0210	Two-phase, single control, 208/240 V, 15.0/17.3 KVA			1.14	14.040	Ea.
0220	Individual phase control, 15.0/17.3 KVA	↓	↓	1.14	14.040	Ea.
0230	30.0/34.6 KVA	3 Elec	3 Electricians	1.33	18.050	Ea.
0310	Three-phase, single control, 208/240 V, 26/30 KVA	2 Elec	2 Electricians	1	16.000	Ea.
0320	380/480 V, 24/30 KVA	"	"	1	16.000	Ea.
0330	43/54 KVA	3 Elec	3 Electricians	1.33	18.050	Ea.
0340	Individual phase control, 208 V, 26 KVA	"	"	1.33	18.050	Ea.
0350	52 KVA	R-3	1 Electrician Foreman 1 Electrician .5 Equip. Oper. (crane) .5 S.P. Crane, 5 Ton	.91	21.980	Ea.
0360	340/480 V, 24/30 KVA	"	"	.91	21.980	Ea.
0370	43/54 KVA	2 Elec	2 Electricians	1	16.000	Ea.
0380	48/60 KVA	3 Elec	3 Electricians	1.33	18.050	Ea.
0390	86/108 KVA	R-3	1 Electrician Foreman 1 Electrician .5 Equip. Oper. (crane) .5 S.P. Crane, 5 Ton	.91	21.980	Ea.
0500	Standard grade, solid state, variable transformer volt. regulator					
0510	Single-phase, 115 V, 2.3 KVA	1 Elec	1 Electrician	2	4.000	Ea.
0520	4.2 KVA			2.29	3.490	Ea.
0530	6.6 KVA			1.14	7.020	Ea.
0540	13.0 KVA	↓	↓	1.14	7.020	Ea.
0550	16.6 KVA	2 Elec	2 Electricians	1.23	13.010	Ea.
0610	230 V, 8.3 KVA			1.33	12.030	Ea.
0620	21.4 KVA			1.23	13.010	Ea.
0630	29.9 KVA			1.23	13.010	Ea.
0710	460 V, 9.2 KVA			1.33	12.030	Ea.
0720	20.7 KVA	↓	↓	1.23	13.010	Ea.
0810	Three-phase, 230 V, 13.1 KVA	3 Elec	3 Electricians	1.41	17.020	Ea.
0820	19.1 KVA			1.41	17.020	Ea.
0830	25.1 KVA	↓	↓	1.60	15.000	Ea.
0840	57.8 KVA	R-3	1 Electrician Foreman 1 Electrician .5 Equip. Oper. (crane) .5 S.P. Crane, 5 Ton	.95	21.050	Ea.
0850	74.9 KVA	"	"	.91	21.980	Ea.
0910	460 V, 14.3 KVA	3 Elec	3 Electricians	1.41	17.020	Ea.
0920	19.1 KVA			1.41	17.020	Ea.
0930	27.9 KVA	↓	↓	1.50	16.000	Ea.

		CREW	MAKEUP	DAILY OUTPUT	MAN-HOURS	UNIT
164 300	**Computer Pwr Supplies**					
305 0941	Automatic voltage regulator, std. grade, 3 ph, 460V, 59.8 KVA	R-3	1 Electrician Foreman	1	20.000	Ea.
			1 Electrician			
			.5 Equip. Oper. (crane)			
			.5 S.P. Crane, 5 Ton			
0950	79.7 KVA	↓	↓	.95	21.050	Ea.
0960	118 KVA	↓	↓	.95	21.050	Ea.
1000	Laboratory grade, precision, electronic voltage regulator					
1110	Single-phase, 115 V, .5 KVA	1 Elec	1 Electrician	2.29	3.490	Ea.
1120	1.0 KVA	↓	↓	2	4.000	Ea.
1130	3.0 KVA	↓	↓	.80	10.000	Ea.
1140	6.0 KVA	2 Elec	2 Electricians	1.46	10.960	Ea.
1150	10.0 KVA	3 Elec	3 Electricians	1	24.000	Ea.
1160	15.0 KVA	"	"	1.50	16.000	Ea.
1210	230 V, 3.0 KVA	1 Elec	1 Electrician	.80	10.000	Ea.
1220	6.0 KVA	2 Elec	2 Electricians	1.46	10.960	Ea.
1230	10.0 KVA	3 Elec	3 Electricians	1.71	14.040	Ea.
1240	15.0 KVA	"	"	1.60	15.000	Ea.
310	**ISOLATION TRANSFORMER**					
0100	Computer grade, isolation transformer					
0110	Single-phase, 120/240 V, .5 KVA	1 Elec	1 Electrician	4	2.000	Ea.
0120	1.0 KVA			2.67	3.000	Ea.
0130	2.5 KVA			2	4.000	Ea.
0140	5 KVA	↓	↓	1.14	7.020	Ea.
315	**TRANSIENT VOLTAGE SUPPRESSOR TRANSFORMER**					
0110	Single-phase, 120 V, 1.8 KVA	1 Elec	1 Electrician	4	2.000	Ea.
0120	3.6 KVA			4	2.000	Ea.
0130	7.2 KVA			3.20	2.500	Ea.
0150	240 V, 3.6 KVA			4	2.000	Ea.
0160	7.2 KVA			4	2.000	Ea.
0170	14.4 KVA			3.20	2.500	Ea.
0210	Plug-in unit, 120 V, 1.8 KVA	↓	↓	8	1.000	Ea.
320	**TRANSIENT SUPPRESSOR/VOLTAGE REGULATOR** (without isolation)					
0110	Single-phase, 115 V, 1.0 KVA	1 Elec	1 Electrician	2.67	3.000	Ea.
0120	2.0 KVA			2.29	3.490	Ea.
0130	4.0 KVA			2.13	3.760	Ea.
0140	220 V, 1.0 KVA			2.67	3.000	Ea.
0150	2.0 KVA			2.29	3.490	Ea.
0160	4.0 KVA			2.13	3.760	Ea.
0210	Plug-in unit, 120 V, 1.0 KVA			8	1.000	Ea.
0220	2.0 KVA	↓	↓	8	1.000	Ea.
325	**COMPUTER REGULATOR TRANSFORMER**					
0100	Ferro-resonant, constant voltage, variable transformer					
0110	Single-phase, 240 V, .5 KVA	1 Elec	1 Electrician	2.67	3.000	Ea.
0120	1.0 KVA			2	4.000	Ea.
0130	2.0 KVA			1	8.000	Ea.
0210	Plug-in unit, 120 V, .14 KVA			8	1.000	Ea.
0220	.25 KVA			8	1.000	Ea.
0230	.5 KVA			8	1.000	Ea.
0240	1.0 KVA			5.33	1.500	Ea.
0250	2.0 KVA	↓	↓	4	2.000	Ea.
330	**POWER CONDITIONER TRANSFORMER**					
0100	Electronic solid state, buck-boost, transformer, w/tap switch					
0110	Single-phase, 115 V, 3.0 KVA, + or - 3% accuracy	2 Elec	2 Electricians	1.60	10.000	Ea.
0120	208, 220, 230, or 240 V, 5.0 KVA, + or - 1.5% accuracy	3 Elec	3 Electricians	1.60	15.000	Ea.
0130	5.0 KVA, + or - 6% accuracy	2 Elec	2 Electricians	1.14	14.040	Ea.
0140	7.5 KVA, + or - 1.5% accuracy	3 Elec	3 Electricians	1.50	16.000	Ea.
0150	7.5 KVA, + or - 6% accuracy			1.60	15.000	Ea.
0160	10.0 KVA, + or - 1.5% accuracy	↓	↓	1.33	18.050	Ea.

164 | Transformers and Bus Ducts

164 300	Computer Pwr Supplies	CREW	MAKEUP	DAILY OUTPUT	MAN-HOURS	UNIT
335	UNINTERRUPTABLE POWER SUPPLY/CONDITIONER TRANSFORMERS					
0100	Volt. regulating, isolating trans., w/invert. & 10 min. battery pack					
0110	Single-phase, 115 V, .2 KVA	1 Elec	1 Electrician	2.29	3.490	Ea.
0120	.5 KVA			2	4.000	Ea.
0130	For additional 55 min. battery, add to .2 KVA			2.29	3.490	Ea.
0140	Add to .5 KVA			1.14	7.020	Ea.
0150	Single-phase, 120 V, .8 KVA			.80	10.000	Ea.
0160	1.0 KVA	↓	↓	.80	10.000	Ea.

165 | Power Systems and Capacitors

165 100	Power Systems	CREW	MAKEUP	DAILY OUTPUT	MAN-HOURS	UNIT
110	AUTOMATIC TRANSFER SWITCHES					
0100	Switches, enclosed 480 volt, 3 pole, 30 amp	1 Elec	1 Electrician	2.30	3.480	Ea.
0200	60 amp			1.90	4.210	Ea.
0300	100 amp			1.30	6.150	Ea.
0400	150 amp			1.20	6.670	Ea.
0500	225 amp			1	8.000	Ea.
0600	260 amp			1	8.000	Ea.
0700	400 amp			.80	10.000	Ea.
0800	600 amp			.50	16.000	Ea.
0900	800 amp			.40	20.000	Ea.
1000	1000 amp			.38	21.050	Ea.
1100	1200 amp			.35	22.860	Ea.
1200	1600 amp			.30	26.670	Ea.
1300	2000 amp	↓	↓	.25	32.000	Ea.
115	NON-AUTOMATIC TRANSFER SWITCHES enclosed					
0100	Fuses included, 480 volt 3 pole, 30 amp	1 Elec	1 Electrician	2.30	3.480	Ea.
0150	60 amp			1.90	4.210	Ea.
0200	100 amp			1.30	6.150	Ea.
0250	200 amp			1	8.000	Ea.
0300	400 amp			.80	10.000	Ea.
0350	600 amp			.50	16.000	Ea.
1000	250 volt 3 pole, 30 amp			2.30	3.480	Ea.
1100	60 amp			1.90	4.210	Ea.
1150	100 amp			1.30	6.150	Ea.
1200	200 amp			1	8.000	Ea.
1300	600 amp			.50	16.000	Ea.
1500	Nonfused 480 volt 3 pole, 60 amp			1.90	4.210	Ea.
1600	100 amp			1.30	6.150	Ea.
1650	200 amp			1	8.000	Ea.
1700	400 amp			.80	10.000	Ea.
1750	600 amp			.50	16.000	Ea.
2000	250 volt 3 pole, 30 amp			2.30	3.480	Ea.
2050	60 amp			1.90	4.210	Ea.
2150	200 amp			1	8.000	Ea.
2200	400 amp			.80	10.000	Ea.
2250	600 amp			.50	16.000	Ea.
2500	NEMA 3R, 480 volt 3 pole, 60 amp			1.80	4.440	Ea.
2550	100 amp			1.20	6.670	Ea.
2600	200 amp	↓	↓	.90	8.890	Ea.

165 | Power Systems and Capacitors

165 100 | Power Systems

		CREW	MAKEUP	DAILY OUTPUT	MAN-HOURS	UNIT
115 2651	Transfer switch, non-auto., NEMA 3R, 480V 3 pole, 400 amp	1 Elec	1 Electrician	.70	11.430	Ea.
2800	250 volt 3 pole, solid neutral, 100 amp			1.20	6.670	Ea.
2850	200 amp			.90	8.890	Ea.
2900	250 volt, 2 pole, solid neutral, 100 amp			1.30	6.150	Ea.
2950	200 amp	↓	↓	1	8.000	Ea.
120	**GENERATOR SET**					
0020	Gas or gasoline operated, includes battery,					
0050	charger, muffler & transfer switch					
0200	3 phase, 4 wire, 277/480 volt, 7.5 KW	R-3	1 Electrician Foreman 1 Electrician .5 Equip. Oper. (crane) .5 S.P. Crane, 5 Ton	.83	24.100	Ea.
0300	10 KW			.71	28.170	Ea.
0400	15 KW			.63	31.750	Ea.
0500	30 KW			.55	36.360	Ea.
0520	55 KW			.50	40.000	Ea.
0600	70 KW			.40	50.000	Ea.
0700	85 KW			.33	60.610	Ea.
0800	115 KW			.28	71.430	Ea.
0900	170 KW	↓	↓	.25	80.000	Ea.
2000	Diesel engine, including battery, charger,					
2010	muffler, transfer switch & fuel tank, 30 KW	R-3	1 Electrician Foreman 1 Electrician .5 Equip. Oper. (crane) .5 S.P. Crane, 5 Ton	.55	36.360	Ea.
2100	50 KW			.42	47.620	Ea.
2200	75 KW			.35	57.140	Ea.
2300	100 KW			.31	64.520	Ea.
2400	125 KW			.29	68.970	Ea.
2500	150 KW			.26	76.920	Ea.
2600	175 KW			.25	80.000	Ea.
2700	200 KW			.24	83.330	Ea.
2800	250 KW			.23	86.960	Ea.
2900	300 KW			.22	90.910	Ea.
3000	350 KW			.20	100.000	Ea.
3100	400 KW			.19	105.000	Ea.
3200	500 KW			.18	111.000	Ea.
3220	600 KW			.19	105.000	Ea.
3240	750 KW	↓	↓	.16	125.000	Ea.

165 200 | Capacitors

		CREW	MAKEUP	DAILY OUTPUT	MAN-HOURS	UNIT
210	**CAPACITORS** Indoor					
0020	240 volts, single & 3 phase, 0.5 KVAR	1 Elec	1 Electrician	2.70	2.960	Ea.
0100	1.0 KVAR			2.70	2.960	Ea.
0150	2.5 KVAR			2	4.000	Ea.
0200	5.0 KVAR			1.80	4.440	Ea.
0250	7.5 KVAR			1.60	5.000	Ea.
0300	10 KVAR			1.50	5.330	Ea.
0350	15 KVAR			1.30	6.150	Ea.
0400	20 KVAR			1.10	7.270	Ea.
0450	25 KVAR			1	8.000	Ea.
1000	480 volts, single & 3 phase, 1 KVAR			2.70	2.960	Ea.
1050	2 KVAR			2.70	2.960	Ea.
1100	5 KVAR			2	4.000	Ea.
1150	7.5 KVAR			2	4.000	Ea.
1200	10 KVAR			2	4.000	Ea.
1250	15 KVAR			2	4.000	Ea.
1300	20 KVAR	↓	↓	1.60	5.000	Ea.

165 | Power Systems and Capacitors

165 200 | Capacitors

		CREW	MAKEUP	DAILY OUTPUT	MAN-HOURS	UNIT
210	1351	Capacitors, indoor, 480 volt, single & 3 phase, 30 KVAR	1 Elec	1 Electrician	1.50	5.330	Ea.
	1400	40 KVAR			1.20	6.670	Ea.
	1450	50 KVAR			1.10	7.270	Ea.
	2000	600 volts, single & 3 phase, 1 KVAR			2.70	2.960	Ea.
	2050	2 KVAR			2.70	2.960	Ea.
	2100	5 KVAR			2	4.000	Ea.
	2150	7.5 KVAR			2	4.000	Ea.
	2200	10 KVAR			2	4.000	Ea.
	2250	15 KVAR			1.60	5.000	Ea.
	2300	20 KVAR			1.60	5.000	Ea.
	2350	25 KVAR			1.50	5.330	Ea.
	2400	35 KVAR			1.40	5.710	Ea.
	2450	50 KVAR	↓	↓	1.30	6.150	Ea.

166 | Lighting

166 100 | Lighting

		CREW	MAKEUP	DAILY OUTPUT	MAN-HOURS	UNIT
110	**EXIT AND EMERGENCY LIGHTING**					
0080	Exit light, ceiling or wall mount, incandescent, single face	1 Elec	1 Electrician	8	1.000	Ea.
0100	Double face			6.70	1.190	Ea.
0120	Explosion proof			3.80	2.110	Ea.
0150	Fluorescent, single face			8	1.000	Ea.
0160	Double face	↓	↓	6.70	1.190	Ea.
0300	Emergency light units, battery operated					
0350	Twin sealed beam light, 25 watt, 6 volt each					
0500	Lead battery operated	1 Elec	1 Electrician	4	2.000	Ea.
0700	Nickel cadmium battery operated			4	2.000	Ea.
0780	Additional remote mount, sealed beam, 25 W6V			26.70	.300	Ea.
0790	Twin sealed beam light, 25 W6V each			26.70	.300	Ea.
0900	Self-contained fluorescent lamp pack	↓	↓	10	.800	Ea.
115	**EXTERIOR FIXTURES** With lamps					
0200	Wall mounted, incandescent, 100 watt	1 Elec	1 Electrician	8	1.000	Ea.
0400	Quartz, 500 watt			5.30	1.510	Ea.
0420	1500 watt			4.20	1.900	Ea.
0600	Mercury vapor, 100 watt			5.30	1.510	Ea.
0800	Wall pack, mercury vapor, 175 watt			4	2.000	Ea.
1000	250 watt			4	2.000	Ea.
1100	Low pressure sodium, 35 watt			4	2.000	Ea.
1150	55 watt			4	2.000	Ea.
1160	High pressure sodium, 70 watt			4	2.000	Ea.
1170	150 watt			4	2.000	Ea.
1180	Metal Halide, 175 watt			4	2.000	Ea.
1190	250 watt	↓	↓	4	2.000	Ea.
1200	Floodlights with ballast and lamp,					
1400	pole mounted, pole not included					
1500	Mercury vapor, 250 watt	1 Elec	1 Electrician	2.40	3.330	Ea.
1600	400 watt			2.20	3.640	Ea.
1800	1000 watt			2	4.000	Ea.
1950	Metal halide, 175 watt			2.70	2.960	Ea.
2000	400 watt			2.20	3.640	Ea.
2200	1000 watt			2	4.000	Ea.
2210	1500 watt	↓	↓	1.85	4.320	Ea.

166 100	Lighting	CREW	MAKEUP	DAILY OUTPUT	MAN-HOURS	UNIT
115 2251	Floodlights, pole mounted, low pressure sodium, 55 watt	1 Elec	1 Electrician	2.70	2.960	Ea.
2270	90 watt			2	4.000	Ea.
2290	180 watt			2	4.000	Ea.
2340	High pressure sodium, 70 watt			2.70	2.960	Ea.
2360	100 watt			2.70	2.960	Ea.
2380	150 watt			2.70	2.960	Ea.
2400	400 watt			2.20	3.640	Ea.
2600	1000 watt			2	4.000	Ea.
2610	Incandescent, 300 watt			4	2.000	Ea.
2620	500 watt			4	2.000	Ea.
2630	1000 watt			3	2.670	Ea.
2640	1500 watt			3	2.670	Ea.
2650	Roadway area luminaire, low pressure sodium, 135 watt			2	4.000	Ea.
2700	180 watt			2	4.000	Ea.
2720	Mercury vapor, 400 watt			2.20	3.640	Ea.
2730	1000 watt			2	4.000	Ea.
2750	Metal halide, 400 watt			2.20	3.640	Ea.
2760	1000 watt			2	4.000	Ea.
2780	High pressure sodium, 400 watt			2.20	3.640	Ea.
2790	1000 watt	↓	↓	2	4.000	Ea.
2800	Light poles, anchor base,					
2820	not including concrete bases					
2840	Aluminum pole, 8' high	1 Elec	1 Electrician	4	2.000	Ea.
2850	10' high			4	2.000	Ea.
2860	12' high			3.80	2.110	Ea.
2870	14' high			3.40	2.350	Ea.
2880	16' high	↓	↓	3	2.670	Ea.
3000	20' high	R-3	1 Electrician Foreman 1 Electrician .5 Equip. Oper. (crane) .5 S.P. Crane, 5 Ton	2.90	6.900	Ea.
3200	30' high			2.60	7.690	Ea.
3400	35' high			2.30	8.700	Ea.
3600	40' high	↓	↓	2	10.000	Ea.
3800	Bracket arms, 1 arm	1 Elec	1 Electrician	8	1.000	Ea.
4000	2 arms			8	1.000	Ea.
4200	3 arms			5.30	1.510	Ea.
4400	4 arms			5.30	1.510	Ea.
4500	Steel pole, galvanized, 8' high			3.80	2.110	Ea.
4510	10' high			3.70	2.160	Ea.
4520	12' high			3.40	2.350	Ea.
4530	14' high			3.10	2.580	Ea.
4540	16' high			2.90	2.760	Ea.
4550	18' high	↓	↓	2.70	2.960	Ea.
4600	20' high	R-3	1 Electrician Foreman 1 Electrician .5 Equip. Oper. (crane) .5 S.P. Crane, 5 Ton	2.60	7.690	Ea.
4800	30' high			2.30	8.700	Ea.
5000	35' high			2.20	9.090	Ea.
5200	40' high	↓	↓	1.70	11.760	Ea.
5400	Bracket arms, 1 arm	1 Elec	1 Electrician	8	1.000	Ea.
5600	2 arms			8	1.000	Ea.
5800	3 arms			5.30	1.510	Ea.
6000	4 arms	↓	↓	5.30	1.510	Ea.

166 100	Lighting	CREW	MAKEUP	DAILY OUTPUT	MAN-HOURS	UNIT
115 6100	Fiberglass pole for 1 or 2 fixtures, 20' high	R-3	1 Electrician Foreman	4	5.000	Ea.
			1 Electrician			
			.5 Equip. Oper. (crane)			
			.5 S.P. Crane, 5 Ton			
6200	30' high			3.60	5.560	Ea.
6300	35' high			3.20	6.250	Ea.
6400	40' high	↓	↓	2.80	7.140	Ea.
6420	Wood pole, 4-1/2" x 5-1/8", 8' high	1 Elec	1 Electrician	6	1.330	Ea.
6430	10' high			6	1.330	Ea.
6440	12' high			5.70	1.400	Ea.
6450	15' high			5	1.600	Ea.
6460	20' high	↓	↓	4	2.000	Ea.
6500	Bollard light, lamp & ballast, 42" high with polycarbonate lens					
6700	Mercury vapor, 175 watt	1 Elec	1 Electrician	3	2.670	Ea.
6800	Metal Halide, 175 watt			3	2.670	Ea.
6900	High pressure sodium, 70 watt			3	2.670	Ea.
7000	100 watt			3	2.670	Ea.
7100	150 watt			3	2.670	Ea.
7200	Incandescent, 150 watt	↓	↓	3	2.670	Ea.
120	**FIXTURE HANGERS**					
0200	Explosionproof, box	1 Elec	1 Electrician	8	1.000	Ea.
0220	Hub cover			32	.250	Ea.
0240	Canopy			12	.667	Ea.
0260	Connecting block			40	.200	Ea.
0280	Cushion hanger			16	.500	Ea.
0300	Box hanger, with mounting strap			8	1.000	Ea.
0320	Connecting block			40	.200	Ea.
0340	Flexible, 1/2" diameter, 4" long			12	.667	Ea.
0360	6" long			12	.667	Ea.
0380	8" long			12	.667	Ea.
0400	10" long			12	.667	Ea.
0420	12" long			12	.667	Ea.
0440	15" long			12	.667	Ea.
0460	18" long			12	.667	Ea.
0480	3/4" diameter, 4" long			10	.800	Ea.
0500	6" long			10	.800	Ea.
0520	8" long			10	.800	Ea.
0540	10" long			10	.800	Ea.
0560	12" long			10	.800	Ea.
0580	15" long			10	.800	Ea.
0600	18" long	↓	↓	10	.800	Ea.
125	**FIXTURE WHIPS**					
0080	3/8" Greenfield, 2 connectors, 6' long					
0100	TFFN wire, three #18	1 Elec	1 Electrician	32	.250	Ea.
0150	Four #18			28	.286	Ea.
0200	Three #16			32	.250	Ea.
0250	Four #16			28	.286	Ea.
0300	THHN wire, three #14			32	.250	Ea.
0350	Four #14			28	.286	Ea.
0500	AF wire, three #18			32	.250	Ea.
0550	Three #16			32	.250	Ea.
0600	Three #14	↓	↓	32	.250	Ea.
130	**INTERIOR LIGHTING FIXTURES** Including lamps, mounting					
0030	hardware and connections					
0100	Fluorescent, C.W. lamps, troffer, recess mounted in grid, RS					
0200	Acrylic lens, 1'W x 4'L, two 40 watt	1 Elec	1 Electrician	5.70	1.400	Ea.
0210	1'W x 4'L, three 40 watt			5.40	1.480	Ea.
0300	2'W x 2'L, two U40 watt	↓	↓	5.70	1.400	Ea.

166 100	Lighting	CREW	MAKEUP	DAILY OUTPUT	MAN-HOURS	UNIT
130 0401	Interior fluorescent lamps, 2'W x 4'L, two 40 watt	1 Elec	1 Electrician	5.30	1.510	Ea.
0500	2'W x 4'L, three 40 watt			5	1.600	Ea.
0600	2'W x 4'L, four 40 watt			4.70	1.700	Ea.
0700	4'W x 4'L, four 40 watt			3.20	2.500	Ea.
0800	4'W x 4'L, six 40 watt			3.10	2.580	Ea.
0900	4'W x 4'L, eight 40 watt	↓	↓	2.90	2.760	Ea.
1000	Surface mounted, RS					
1030	Acrylic lens with hinged & latched door frame					
1100	1'W x 4'L, two 40 watt	1 Elec	1 Electrician	7	1.140	Ea.
1110	1'W x 4'L, three 40 watt			6.70	1.190	Ea.
1200	2'W x 2'L, two U40 watt			7	1.140	Ea.
1300	2'W x 4'L, two 40 watt			6.20	1.290	Ea.
1400	2'W x 4'L, three 40 watt			5.70	1.400	Ea.
1500	2'W x 4'L, four 40 watt			5.30	1.510	Ea.
1600	4'W x 4'L, four 40 watt			3.60	2.220	Ea.
1700	4'W x 4'L, six 40 watt			3.30	2.420	Ea.
1800	4'W x 4'L, eight 40 watt			3.10	2.580	Ea.
1900	2'W x 8'L, four 40 watt			3.20	2.500	Ea.
2000	2'W x 8'L, eight 40 watt	↓	↓	3.10	2.580	Ea.
2010	Acrylic wrap around lens					
2020	6"W x 4'L, one 40 watt	1 Elec	1 Electrician	8	1.000	Ea.
2030	6"W x 8'L, two 40 watt			4	2.000	Ea.
2040	11"W x 4'L, two 40 watt			7	1.140	Ea.
2050	11"W x 8'L, four 40 watt			3.30	2.420	Ea.
2060	16"W x 4'L, four 40 watt			5.30	1.510	Ea.
2070	16"W x 8'L, eight 40 watt			3.20	2.500	Ea.
2080	2'W x 2'L, two U40 watt	↓	↓	7	1.140	Ea.
2100	Strip fixture					
2200	4' long, one 40 watt RS	1 Elec	1 Electrician	8.50	.941	Ea.
2300	4' long, two 40 watt RS			8	1.000	Ea.
2400	4' long, one 40 watt, SL			8	1.000	Ea.
2500	4' long, two 40 watt, SL			7	1.140	Ea.
2600	8' long, one 75 watt, SL			6.70	1.190	Ea.
2700	8' long, two 75 watt, SL			6.20	1.290	Ea.
2800	4' long, two 60 watt, HO			6.70	1.190	Ea.
2900	8' long, two 110 watt, HO			5.30	1.510	Ea.
2910	4' long, two 115 watt, VHO			6.50	1.230	Ea.
2920	8' long, two 215 watt, VHO	↓	↓	5.20	1.540	Ea.
3000	Pendent mounted, industrial, white porcelain enamel					
3100	4' long, two 40 watt, RS	1 Elec	1 Electrician	5.70	1.400	Ea.
3200	4' long, two 60 watt, HO			5	1.600	Ea.
3300	8' long, two 75 watt, SL			4.40	1.820	Ea.
3400	8' long, two 110 watt, HO			4	2.000	Ea.
3410	Acrylic finish, 4' long, two 40 watt, RS			5.70	1.400	Ea.
3420	4' long, two 60 watt, HO			5	1.600	Ea.
3430	4' long, two 115 watt, VHO			4.80	1.670	Ea.
3440	8' long, two 75 watt, SL			4.40	1.820	Ea.
3450	8' long, two 110 watt, HO			4	2.000	Ea.
3460	8' long, two 215 watt, VHO			3.80	2.110	Ea.
3470	Troffer, air handling, 2'W x 4'L with four 40 watt, RS			4	2.000	Ea.
3480	2'W x 2'L with two U40 watt RS			5.50	1.450	Ea.
3490	Air connector insulated, 5" diameter			20	.400	Ea.
3500	6" diameter			20	.400	Ea.
3510	Troffer parabolic lay-in, 1'W x 4'L with one F40			5.70	1.400	Ea.
3520	1'W x 4'L with two F40			5.30	1.510	Ea.
3530	2'W x 4'L with three F40	↓	↓	5	1.600	Ea.

166 100	Lighting	CREW	MAKEUP	DAILY OUTPUT	MAN-HOURS	UNIT
130 3580	Mercury vapor, integral ballast, ceiling, recess mounted,					
3590	prismatic glass lens, floating door					
3600	2'W x 2'L, 250 watt DX lamp	1 Elec	1 Electrician	3.20	2.500	Ea.
3700	2'W x 2'L, 400 watt DX lamp			2.90	2.760	Ea.
3800	Surface mtd., prismatic lens, 2'W x 2'L, 250 watt DX lamp			2.70	2.960	Ea.
3900	2'W x 2'L, 400 watt DX lamp	↓	↓	2.40	3.330	Ea.
4000	High bay, aluminum reflector					
4030	Single unit, 400 watt DX lamp	1 Elec	1 Electrician	2.30	3.480	Ea.
4100	Single unit, 1000 watt DX lamp			2	4.000	Ea.
4200	Twin unit, two 400 watt DX lamps			1.60	5.000	Ea.
4210	Low bay, aluminum reflector, 250W DX lamp	↓	↓	3.20	2.500	Ea.
4220	Metal halide, integral ballast, ceiling, recess mounted					
4230	prismatic glass lens, floating door					
4240	2'W x 2'L, 250 watt	1 Elec	1 Electrician	3.20	2.500	Ea.
4250	2'W x 2'L, 400 watt			2.90	2.760	Ea.
4260	Surface mounted, 2'W x 2'L, 250 watt			2.70	2.960	Ea.
4270	2'W x 2'L, 400 watt	↓	↓	2.40	3.330	Ea.
4280	High bay, aluminum reflector,					
4290	Single unit, 400 watt	1 Elec	1 Electrician	2.30	3.480	Ea.
4300	Single unit, 1000 watt			2	4.000	Ea.
4310	Twin unit, 400 watt			1.60	5.000	Ea.
4320	Low bay, aluminum reflector, 250W DX lamp			3.20	2.500	Ea.
4330	400 watt lamp	↓	↓	2.50	3.200	Ea.
4340	High pressure sodium integral ballast ceiling, recess mounted					
4350	prismatic glass lens, floating door					
4360	2'W x 2'L, 150 watt lamp	1 Elec	1 Electrician	3.20	2.500	Ea.
4370	2'W x 2'L, 400 watt lamp			2.90	2.760	Ea.
4380	Surface mounted, 2'W x 2'L, 150 watt lamp			2.70	2.960	Ea.
4390	2'W x 2'L, 400 watt lamp	↓	↓	2.40	3.330	Ea.
4400	High bay, aluminum reflector,					
4410	Single unit, 400 watt lamp	1 Elec	1 Electrician	2.30	3.480	Ea.
4430	Single unit, 1000 watt lamp			2	4.000	Ea.
4440	Low bay, aluminum reflector, 150 watt lamp	↓	↓	3.20	2.500	Ea.
4450	Incandescent, high hat can, round alzak reflector, prewired					
4470	100 watt	1 Elec	1 Electrician	8	1.000	Ea.
4480	150 watt			8	1.000	Ea.
4500	300 watt			6.70	1.190	Ea.
4520	Round with reflector and baffles, 150 watt			8	1.000	Ea.
4540	Round with concentric louver, 150 watt PAR	↓	↓	8	1.000	Ea.
4600	Square glass lens with metal trim, prewired					
4630	100 watt	1 Elec	1 Electrician	6.70	1.190	Ea.
4700	200 watt	"	"	6.70	1.190	Ea.
6300	Explosionproof					
6310	Metal halide, ballast, ceiling, surface mounted, 175 watt	1 Elec	1 Electrician	2.90	2.760	Ea.
6320	250 watt			2.70	2.960	Ea.
6330	400 watt			2.40	3.330	Ea.
6340	Ceiling, pendent mounted, 175 watt			2.60	3.080	Ea.
6350	250 watt			2.40	3.330	Ea.
6360	400 watt			2.10	3.810	Ea.
6370	Wall, surface mounted, 175 watt			2.90	2.760	Ea.
6380	250 watt			2.70	2.960	Ea.
6390	400 watt			2.40	3.330	Ea.
6400	High pressure sodium, ceiling surface mounted, 70 watt			3	2.670	Ea.
6410	100 watt			3	2.670	Ea.
6420	150 watt			2.70	2.960	Ea.
6430	Pendent mounted, 70 watt			2.70	2.960	Ea.
6440	100 watt			2.70	2.960	Ea.
6450	150 watt	↓	↓	2.40	3.330	Ea.

166 | Lighting

		166 100	Lighting	CREW	MAKEUP	DAILY OUTPUT	MAN-HOURS	UNIT
130	6461	Int. lighting, explosionproof, high pres. sodium, 70 watt		1 Elec	1 Electrician	3	2.670	Ea.
	6470	100 watt				3	2.670	Ea.
	6480	150 watt				2.70	2.960	Ea.
	6510	Incandescent, ceiling mounted, 200 watt				4	2.000	Ea.
	6520	Pendent mounted, 200 watt				3.50	2.290	Ea.
	6530	Wall mounted, 200 watt				4	2.000	Ea.
	6600	Fluorescent, RS, 4' long, ceiling mounted, two 40 watt				2.70	2.960	Ea.
	6610	Three 40 watt				2.20	3.640	Ea.
	6620	Four 40 watt				1.90	4.210	Ea.
	6630	Pendent mounted, two 40 watt				2.30	3.480	Ea.
	6640	Three 40 watt				1.90	4.210	Ea.
	6650	Four 40 watt				1.70	4.710	Ea.
	6700	Mercury vapor with ballast, surface mounted, 175 watt				2.70	2.960	Ea.
	6710	250 watt				2.70	2.960	Ea.
	6740	400 watt				2.40	3.330	Ea.
	6750	Pendent mounted, 175 watt				2.40	3.330	Ea.
	6760	250 watt				2.40	3.330	Ea.
	6770	400 watt				2.10	3.810	Ea.
	6780	Wall mounted, 175 watt				2.70	2.960	Ea.
	6790	250 watt				2.70	2.960	Ea.
	6820	400 watt				2.40	3.330	Ea.
	6850	Vandalproof, surface mounted, fluorescent, two 40 watt				3.20	2.500	Ea.
	6860	Incandescent, one 150 watt				8	1.000	Ea.
	6900	Mirror light, fluorescent, RS, acrylic enclosure, two 40 watt				8	1.000	Ea.
	6910	One 40 watt				8	1.000	Ea.
	6920	One 20 watt				12	.667	Ea.
	7000	Low bay, aluminum reflector. 70 watt, high pressure sodium				4	2.000	Ea.
	7010	250 watt, high pressure sodium				3.20	2.500	Ea.
	7020	400 watt, high pressure sodium		▼	▼	2.50	3.200	Ea.
	7500	Ballast replacement, by weight of ballast, to 15' high						
	7520	Indoor fluorescent, less than 2 lbs.		1 Elec	1 Electrician	10	.800	Ea.
	7540	2 40W, watt reducer, 2 to 5 lbs.				9.40	.851	Ea.
	7560	2 F96 slimline, over 5 lbs.				8	1.000	Ea.
	7580	Vaportite ballast, less than 2 lbs.				9.40	.851	Ea.
	7600	2 lbs. to 5 lbs.				8.90	.899	Ea.
	7620	Over 5 lbs.		▼	▼	7.60	1.050	Ea.
	135	**INTERIOR LIGHTING FIXTURES** Incl. lamps, and mounting hardware						
	0100	Mercury vapor, recessed, round, 250 watt		1 Elec	1 Electrician	3.20	2.500	Ea.
	0120	400 watt				2.90	2.760	Ea.
	0140	1000 watt				2.40	3.330	Ea.
	0200	Square, 1000 watt				2.40	3.330	Ea.
	0220	Surface, round, 250 watt				2.70	2.960	Ea.
	0240	400 watt				2.40	3.330	Ea.
	0260	1000 watt				1.80	4.440	Ea.
	0320	Square, 1000 watt				1.80	4.440	Ea.
	0340	Pendent, round, 250 watt				2.70	2.960	Ea.
	0360	400 watt				2.40	3.330	Ea.
	0380	1000 watt				1.80	4.440	Ea.
	0400	Square, 250 watt				2.70	2.960	Ea.
	0420	400 watt				2.40	3.330	Ea.
	0440	1000 watt				1.80	4.440	Ea.
	0460	Wall, round, 250 watt				2.70	2.960	Ea.
	0480	400 watt				2.40	3.330	Ea.
	0500	1000 watt				1.80	4.440	Ea.
	0520	Square, 250 watt				2.70	2.960	Ea.
	0540	400 watt				2.40	3.330	Ea.
	0560	1000 watt				1.80	4.440	Ea.
	0700	High pressure sodium, recessed, round, 70 watt		▼	▼	3.50	2.290	Ea.

166 | Lighting

166 100 | Lighting

		Description	CREW	MAKEUP	DAILY OUTPUT	MAN-HOURS	UNIT
135	0721	Int. lighting, high pres. sodium, recessed, round, 100 watt	1 Elec	1 Electrician	3.50	2.290	Ea.
	0740	150 watt			3.20	2.500	Ea.
	0760	Square, 70 watt			3.60	2.220	Ea.
	0780	100 watt			3.60	2.220	Ea.
	0820	250 watt			3	2.670	Ea.
	0840	1000 watt			2.40	3.330	Ea.
	0860	Surface round, 70 watt			3	2.670	Ea.
	0880	100 watt			3	2.670	Ea.
	0900	150 watt			2.70	2.960	Ea.
	0920	Square, 70 watt			3	2.670	Ea.
	0940	100 watt			3	2.670	Ea.
	0980	250 watt			2.50	3.200	Ea.
	1040	Pendent, round, 70 watt			3	2.670	Ea.
	1060	100 watt			3	2.670	Ea.
	1080	150 watt			2.70	2.960	Ea.
	1100	Square, 70 watt			3	2.670	Ea.
	1120	100 watt			3	2.670	Ea.
	1140	150 watt			2.70	2.960	Ea.
	1160	250 watt			2.50	3.200	Ea.
	1180	400 watt			2.40	3.330	Ea.
	1220	Wall, round, 70 watt			3	2.670	Ea.
	1240	100 watt			3	2.670	Ea.
	1260	150 watt			2.70	2.960	Ea.
	1300	Square, 70 watt			3	2.670	Ea.
	1320	100 watt			3	2.670	Ea.
	1340	150 watt			2.40	3.330	Ea.
	1360	250 watt			2.50	3.200	Ea.
	1380	400 watt			2.40	3.330	Ea.
	1400	1000 watt			1.80	4.440	Ea.
	1500	Metal halide, recessed, round, 175 watt			3.40	2.350	Ea.
	1520	250 watt			3.20	2.500	Ea.
	1540	400 watt			2.90	2.760	Ea.
	1580	Square, 175 watt			3.40	2.350	Ea.
	1640	Surface, round, 175 watt			2.90	2.760	Ea.
	1660	250 watt			2.70	2.960	Ea.
	1680	400 watt			2.40	3.330	Ea.
	1720	Square, 175 watt			2.90	2.760	Ea.
	1800	Pendent, round, 175 watt			2.90	2.760	Ea.
	1820	250 watt			2.70	2.960	Ea.
	1840	400 watt			2.40	3.330	Ea.
	1880	Square, 175 watt			2.90	2.760	Ea.
	1900	250 watt			2.70	2.960	Ea.
	1920	400 watt			2.40	3.330	Ea.
	1980	Wall, round, 175 watt			2.90	2.760	Ea.
	2000	250 watt			2.70	2.960	Ea.
	2020	400 watt			2.40	3.330	Ea.
	2060	Square, 175 watt			2.90	2.760	Ea.
	2080	250 watt			2.70	2.960	Ea.
	2100	400 watt			2.40	3.330	Ea.
	2500	Vaporproof, mercury vapor, recessed, 250 watt			3.20	2.500	Ea.
	2520	400 watt			2.90	2.760	Ea.
	2540	1000 watt			2.40	3.330	Ea.
	2560	Surface, 250 watt			2.70	2.960	Ea.
	2580	400 watt			2.40	3.330	Ea.
	2600	1000 watt			1.80	4.440	Ea.
	2620	Pendent, 250 watt			2.70	2.960	Ea.
	2640	400 watt			2.40	3.330	Ea.
	2660	1000 watt	▼	▼	1.80	4.440	Ea.

166 100	Lighting	CREW	MAKEUP	DAILY OUTPUT	MAN-HOURS	UNIT
135	2681	Int. lighting, vaporproof, mercury vapor, wall, 250 watt	1 Elec	1 Electrician	2.70	2.960	Ea.
	2700	400 watt			2.40	3.330	Ea.
	2720	1000 watt			1.80	4.440	Ea.
	2800	High pressure sodium, recessed, 70 watt			3.50	2.290	Ea.
	2820	100 watt			3.50	2.290	Ea.
	2840	150 watt			3.20	2.500	Ea.
	2900	Surface, 70 watt			3	2.670	Ea.
	2920	100 watt			3	2.670	Ea.
	2940	150 watt			2.70	2.960	Ea.
	3000	Pendent, 70 watt			3	2.670	Ea.
	3020	100 watt			3	2.670	Ea.
	3040	150 watt			2.70	2.960	Ea.
	3100	Wall, 70 watt			3	2.670	Ea.
	3120	100 watt			3	2.670	Ea.
	3140	150 watt			2.70	2.960	Ea.
	3200	Metal halide, recessed, 175 watt			3.40	2.350	Ea.
	3220	250 watt			3.20	2.500	Ea.
	3240	400 watt			2.90	2.760	Ea.
	3260	1000 watt			2.40	3.330	Ea.
	3280	Surface, 175 watt			2.90	2.760	Ea.
	3300	250 watt			2.70	2.960	Ea.
	3320	400 watt			2.40	3.330	Ea.
	3340	1000 watt			1.80	4.440	Ea.
	3360	Pendent, 175 watt			2.90	2.760	Ea.
	3380	250 watt			2.70	2.960	Ea.
	3400	400 watt			2.40	3.330	Ea.
	3420	1000 watt			1.80	4.440	Ea.
	3440	Wall, 175 watt			2.90	2.760	Ea.
	3460	250 watt			2.70	2.960	Ea.
	3480	400 watt			2.40	3.330	Ea.
	3500	1000 watt	↓	↓	1.80	4.440	Ea.
140		LAMPS					
	0080	Fluorescent, rapid start, cool white, 2' long, 20 watt	1 Elec	1 Electrician	1	8.000	C
	0100	4' long, 40 watt			.90	8.890	C
	0120	3' long, 30 watt			.90	8.890	C
	0150	U-40 watt			.80	10.000	C
	0170	4' long, 35 watt energy saver			.90	8.890	C
	0200	Slimline, 4' long, 40 watt			.90	8.890	C
	0300	8' long, 75 watt			.80	10.000	C
	0350	8' long, 60 watt energy saver			.80	10.000	C
	0400	High output, 4' long, 60 watt			.90	8.890	C
	0500	8' long, 110 watt			.80	10.000	C
	0520	Very high output, 4' long, 110 watt			.90	8.890	C
	0550	8' long, 215 watt			.70	11.430	C
	0600	Mercury vapor, mogul base, deluxe white, 100 watt			.30	26.670	C
	0650	175 watt			.30	26.670	C
	0700	250 watt			.30	26.670	C
	0800	400 watt			.30	26.670	C
	0900	1000 watt			.20	40.000	C
	1000	Metal halide, mogul base, 175 watt			.30	26.670	C
	1100	250 watt			.30	26.670	C
	1200	400 watt			.30	26.670	C
	1300	1000 watt			.20	40.000	C
	1320	1000 watt, 125,000 initial lumens			.20	40.000	C
	1330	1500 watt			.20	40.000	C
	1350	Sodium high pressure, 70 watt			.30	26.670	C
	1360	100 watt			.30	26.670	C
	1370	150 watt	↓	↓	.30	26.670	C

166 100	Lighting	CREW	MAKEUP	DAILY OUTPUT	MAN-HOURS	UNIT
140 1381	Lamps, sodium high pressure, 250 watt	1 Elec	1 Electrician	.30	26.670	C
1400	400 watt			.30	26.670	C
1450	1000 watt			.20	40.000	C
1500	Low pressure, 35 watt			.30	26.670	C
1550	55 watt			.30	26.670	C
1600	90 watt			.30	26.670	C
1650	135 watt			.20	40.000	C
1700	180 watt			.20	40.000	C
1750	Quartz line, clear, 500 watt			1.10	7.270	C
1760	1500 watt			.20	40.000	C
1800	Incandescent, interior, A21, 100 watt			1.60	5.000	C
1900	A21, 150 watt			1.60	5.000	C
2000	A23, 200 watt			1.60	5.000	C
2200	PS 30, 300 watt			1.60	5.000	C
2210	PS 35, 500 watt			1.60	5.000	C
2230	PS 52, 1000 watt			1.30	6.150	C
2240	PS 52, 1500 watt			1.30	6.150	C
2300	R30, 75 watt			1.30	6.150	C
2400	R40, 150 watt			1.30	6.150	C
2500	Exterior, PAR 38, 75 watt			1.30	6.150	C
2600	PAR 38, 150 watt			1.30	6.150	C
2700	PAR 46, 200 watt			1.10	7.270	C
2800	PAR 56, 300 watt			1.10	7.270	C
3000	Guards, fluorescent lamp, 4' long			1	8.000	C
3200	8' long	↓	↓	.90	8.890	C
145	**RESIDENTIAL FIXTURES**					
0400	Fluorescent, interior, surface, circline, 32 watt & 40 watt	1 Elec	1 Electrician	20	.400	Ea.
0500	2' x 2', two U 40 watt			8	1.000	Ea.
0700	Shallow under cabinet, two 20 watt			16	.500	Ea.
0900	Wall mounted, 4'L, one 40 watt, with baffle			10	.800	Ea.
2000	Incandescent, exterior lantern, wall mounted, 60 watt			16	.500	Ea.
2100	Post light, 150W, with 7' post			4	2.000	Ea.
2500	Lamp holder, weatherproof with 150W PAR			16	.500	Ea.
2550	With reflector and guard			12	.667	Ea.
2600	Interior pendent, globe with shade, 150 watt	↓	↓	20	.400	Ea.
150	**TRACK LIGHTING**					
0080	Track, 1 circuit, 4' section	1 Elec	1 Electrician	6.70	1.190	Ea.
0100	8' section			5.30	1.510	Ea.
0200	12' section			4.40	1.820	Ea.
0300	3 circuits, 4' section			6.70	1.190	Ea.
0400	8' section			5.30	1.510	Ea.
0500	12' section			4.40	1.820	Ea.
1000	Feed kit, surface mounting			16	.500	Ea.
1100	End cover			24	.333	Ea.
1200	Feed kit, stem mounting, 1 circuit			16	.500	Ea.
1300	3 circuit			16	.500	Ea.
2000	Electrical joiner for continuous runs, 1 circuit			32	.250	Ea.
2100	3 circuit			32	.250	Ea.
2200	Fixtures, spotlight, 150 PAR			16	.500	Ea.
3000	Wall washer, 250 watt tungsten halogen			16	.500	Ea.
3100	Low voltage, 25/50 watt, 1 circuit			16	.500	Ea.
3120	3 circuit	↓	↓	16	.500	Ea.

167 100 | Electric Utilities

		Description	CREW	MAKEUP	DAILY OUTPUT	MAN-HOURS	UNIT
110	110	**ELECTRIC & TELEPHONE SITEWORK** Not including excavation,					
	0200	backfill and cast in place concrete					
	0400	Hand holes, precast concrete with concrete cover					
	0600	2' x 2' x 3' deep	R-3	1 Electrician Foreman	2.40	8.330	Ea.
				1 Electrician			
				.5 Equip. Oper. (crane)			
				.5 S.P. Crane, 5 Ton			
	0800	3' x 3' x 3' deep	↓	↓	1.90	10.530	Ea.
	1000	4' x 4' x 4' deep			1.40	14.290	Ea.
	1200	Manholes, precast, with iron racks, pulling irons, C.I. frame					
	1400	and cover, 4' x 6' x 7' deep	R-3	1 Electrician Foreman	1.20	16.670	Ea.
				1 Electrician			
				.5 Equip. Oper. (crane)			
				.5 S.P. Crane, 5 Ton			
	1600	6' x 8' x 7' deep			1	20.000	Ea.
	1800	6' x 10' x 7' deep			.80	25.000	Ea.
	2000	Poles, wood, creosoted, see also division 166-115, 20' high			3.10	6.450	Ea.
	2400	25' high			2.90	6.900	Ea.
	2600	30' high			2.60	7.690	Ea.
	2800	35' high			2.40	8.330	Ea.
	3000	40' high			2.30	8.700	Ea.
	3200	45' high	↓	↓	1.70	11.760	Ea.
	3400	Cross arms with hardware & insulators					
	3600	4' long	1 Elec	1 Electrician	2.50	3.200	Ea.
	3800	5' long			2.40	3.330	Ea.
	4000	6' long	↓	↓	2.20	3.640	Ea.
	4200	Underground duct, banks ready for concrete fill, min. of 1-1/2"					
	4401	between ducts					
	4580	PVC, type EB, 1 @ 2" diameter	1 Elec	1 Electrician	240	.033	L.F.
	4600	2 @ 2" diameter			120	.067	L.F.
	4800	4 @ 2" diameter			60	.133	L.F.
	4900	1 @ 3" diameter			200	.040	L.F.
	5000	2 @ 3" diameter			100	.080	L.F.
	5200	4 @ 3" diameter			50	.160	L.F.
	5300	1 @ 4" diameter			160	.050	L.F.
	5400	2 @ 4" diameter			80	.100	L.F.
	5600	4 @ 4" diameter			40	.200	L.F.
	5800	6 @ 4" diameter			27	.296	L.F.
	5810	1 @ 5" diameter			130	.062	L.F.
	5820	2 @ 5" diameter			65	.123	L.F.
	5840	4 @ 5" diameter			35	.229	L.F.
	5860	6 @ 5" diameter			25	.320	L.F.
	5870	1 @ 6" diameter			100	.080	L.F.
	5880	2 @ 6" diameter			50	.160	L.F.
	5900	4 @ 6" diameter			25	.320	L.F.
	5920	6 @ 6" diameter			15	.533	L.F.
	6200	Rigid galvanized steel, 2 @ 2" diameter			90	.089	L.F.
	6400	4 @ 2" diameter			45	.178	L.F.
	6800	2 @ 3" diameter			50	.160	L.F.
	7000	4 @ 3" diameter			25	.320	L.F.
	7200	2 @ 4" diameter			35	.229	L.F.
	7400	4 @ 4" diameter			17	.471	L.F.
	7600	6 @ 4" diameter			11	.727	L.F.
	7620	2 @ 5" diameter			30	.267	L.F.
	7640	4 @ 5" diameter			15	.533	L.F.
	7660	6 @ 5" diameter			9	.889	L.F.
	7680	2 @ 6" diameter			20	.400	L.F.
	7700	4 @ 6" diameter	↓	↓	10	.800	L.F.

		167 100	Electric Utilities	CREW	MAKEUP	DAILY OUTPUT	MAN-HOURS	UNIT
110	7800	For Cast-in-place Concrete - Add						
	7810	Under 1 c.y.	C-6	1 Labor Foreman (outside)	16	3.000	C.Y.
				4 Building Laborers			
				1 Cement Finisher			
				2 Gas Engine Vibrators			
	7820	1 c.y. - 5 c.y.	↓	↓	19.20	2.500	C.Y.
	7830	Over 5 c.y.			24	2.000	C.Y.
	7850	For Reinforcing Rods - Add					
	7860	#4 to #7	2 Rodm	2 Rodman, (Reinf.)	7	2.290	Ton
	7870	#8 to #14	"	"	4	4.000	Ton
	8000	Fittings, PVC type EB, elbow, 2" diameter	1 Elec	1 Electrician	16	.500	Ea.
	8200	3" diameter			14	.571	Ea.
	8400	4" diameter			12	.667	Ea.
	8420	5" diameter			10	.800	Ea.
	8440	6" diameter			9	.889	Ea.
	8800	Adapter, 2" diameter			26	.308	Ea.
	9000	3" diameter			20	.400	Ea.
	9200	4" diameter			16	.500	Ea.
	9220	5" diameter			13	.615	Ea.
	9240	6" diameter			10	.800	Ea.
	9400	End bell, 2" diameter			16	.500	Ea.
	9600	3" diameter			14	.571	Ea.
	9800	4" diameter			12	.667	Ea.
	9810	5" diameter			10	.800	Ea.
	9820	6" diameter			8	1.000	Ea.
	9830	5° angle coupling, 2" diameter			26	.308	Ea.
	9840	3" diameter			20	.400	Ea.
	9850	4" diameter			16	.500	Ea.
	9860	5" diameter			13	.615	Ea.
	9870	6" diameter			10	.800	Ea.
	9880	Expansion joint, 2" diameter			16	.500	Ea.
	9890	3" diameter			18	.444	Ea.
	9900	4" diameter			12	.667	Ea.
	9910	5" diameter			10	.800	Ea.
	9920	6" diameter	↓	↓	8	1.000	Ea.
120		**FIBRE DUCT**					
	0080	Type 1, 2" diameter	1 Elec	1 Electrician	200	.040	L.F.
	0100	3" diameter			160	.050	L.F.
	0200	4" diameter			110	.073	L.F.
	0220	5" diameter			100	.080	L.F.
	0240	6" diameter			80	.100	L.F.
	0300	Fittings elbow, 2" diameter			12	.667	Ea.
	0400	3" diameter			12	.667	Ea.
	0600	4" diameter			10	.800	Ea.
	0620	5" diameter			9	.889	Ea.
	0640	6" diameter			8	1.000	Ea.
	1300	Adapter, 2" diameter			26	.308	Ea.
	1400	3" diameter			20	.400	Ea.
	1500	4" diameter			16	.500	Ea.
	1520	5" diameter			13	.615	Ea.
	1540	6" diameter			10	.800	Ea.
	1600	End bell, 2" diameter			13	.615	Ea.
	1800	3" diameter			11	.727	Ea.
	1900	4" diameter			10	.800	Ea.
	1920	5" diameter			9	.889	Ea.
	1940	6" diameter			7.50	1.070	Ea.
	2000	Bends, 5°, 2" diameter	↓	↓	26	.308	Ea.

167 | Electric Utilities

167 100 | Electric Utilities

		CREW	MAKEUP	DAILY OUTPUT	MAN-HOURS	UNIT
120 2201	Fibre duct, bends, 5°, 3" diameter	1 Elec	1 Electrician	20	.400	Ea.
2400	4" diameter			16	.500	Ea.
2420	5" diameter			13	.615	Ea.
2440	6" diameter			10	.800	Ea.
2500	Expansion joint, 2" diameter			13	.615	Ea.
2550	3" diameter			11	.727	Ea.
2600	4" diameter			10	.800	Ea.
2650	5" diameter			9	.889	Ea.
2700	6" diameter			7.50	1.070	Ea.
2800	Bends, flexible 2" diameter			12	.667	Ea.
2850	3" diameter			12	.667	Ea.
2900	4" diameter			10	.800	Ea.
2950	5" diameter			9	.889	Ea.
3000	Plastic spacers, 3" diameter			100	.080	Ea.
3050	3-1/2" diameter			100	.080	Ea.
3100	4" diameter	↓	↓	100	.080	Ea.

168 | Special Systems

168 100 | Special Systems

		CREW	MAKEUP	DAILY OUTPUT	MAN-HOURS	UNIT
105	**CLOCKS**					
0080	12" diameter, single face	1 Elec	1 Electrician	8	1.000	Ea.
0100	Double face	"	"	6.20	1.290	Ea.
110	**CLOCK SYSTEMS**					
0100	Time system components, master controller	1 Elec	1 Electrician	.33	24.240	Ea.
0200	Program bell			8	1.000	Ea.
0400	clock & speaker			3.20	2.500	Ea.
0600	Frequency generator			2	4.000	Ea.
0800	Job time automatic stamp recorder, minimum			4	2.000	Ea.
1000	Maximum	↓	↓	4	2.000	Ea.
1600	Master time clock system, clocks & bells, 20 room	4 Elec	4 Electricians	.20	160.000	Ea.
1800	50 room	"	"	.08	400.000	Ea.
2000	Time clock, 100 cards in & out, 1 color	1 Elec	1 Electrician	3.20	2.500	Ea.
2200	2 colors			3.20	2.500	Ea.
2400	With 3 circuit program device, minimum			2	4.000	Ea.
2600	Maximum			2	4.000	Ea.
2800	Metal rack for 25 cards			7	1.140	Ea.
3000	Watchman's tour station			8	1.000	Ea.
3200	Annunciator with zone indication			1	8.000	Ea.
3400	Time clock with tape	↓	↓	1	8.000	Ea.
115	**DOCTORS IN-OUT REGISTER**					
0050	Register, 200 names	4 Elec	4 Electricians	.64	50.000	Ea.
0100	Combination control and recall, 200 names	"	"	.64	50.000	Ea.
0200	Recording register	1 Elec	1 Electrician	.50	16.000	Ea.
0300	Transformers	"	"	4	2.000	Ea.
120	**DETECTION SYSTEMS**					
0100	Burglar alarm, battery operated, mechanical trigger	1 Elec	1 Electrician	4	2.000	Ea.
0200	Electrical trigger			4	2.000	Ea.
0400	For outside key control, add			8	1.000	Ea.
0800	Card reader, flush type, standard			2.70	2.960	Ea.
1000	Multi-code			2.70	2.960	Ea.
1200	Door switches, hinge switch	↓	↓	5.30	1.510	Ea.

			CREW	MAKEUP	DAILY OUTPUT	MAN-HOURS	UNIT
168 100		**Special Systems**					
120	1401	Detection systems, burglar alarm, door switches, magnetic	1 Elec	1 Electrician	5.30	1.510	Ea.
	1600	Exit control locks, horn alarm			4	2.000	Ea.
	1800	Flashing light alarm			4	2.000	Ea.
	2000	Indicating panels, 1 channel			2.70	2.960	Ea.
	2200	10 channel			1.60	5.000	Ea.
	2400	20 channel			1	8.000	Ea.
	2600	40 channel			.57	14.040	Ea.
	2800	Ultrasonic motion detector, 12 volt			2.30	3.480	Ea.
	3000	Infrared photoelectric detector			2.30	3.480	Ea.
	3200	Passive infrared detector			2.30	3.480	Ea.
	3400	Glass break alarm switch			8	1.000	Ea.
	3420	Switchmats, 30" x 5'			5.30	1.510	Ea.
	3440	25'			4	2.000	Ea.
	3460	Police connect panel			4	2.000	Ea.
	3480	Telephone dialer			5.30	1.510	Ea.
	3500	Alarm bell			4	2.000	Ea.
	3520	Siren			4	2.000	Ea.
	3540	Microwave detector, 10' to 200'			2	4.000	Ea.
	3560	10' to 350'			2	4.000	Ea.
	3600	Fire, sprinkler & standpipe alarm, control panel, 4 zone			2	4.000	Ea.
	3800	8 zone			1	8.000	Ea.
	4000	12 zone			.66	12.120	Ea.
	4020	Alarm device			8	1.000	Ea.
	4050	Actuating device			8	1.000	Ea.
	4200	Battery and rack			4	2.000	Ea.
	4400	Automatic charger			8	1.000	Ea.
	4600	Signal bell			8	1.000	Ea.
	4800	Trouble buzzer or manual station			8	1.000	Ea.
	5000	Detector, rate of rise			8	1.000	Ea.
	5100	Fixed temperature			8	1.000	Ea.
	5200	Smoke detector, ceiling type			6.20	1.290	Ea.
	5400	Duct type			3.20	2.500	Ea.
	5600	Light and horn			5.30	1.510	Ea.
	5800	Fire alarm horn			6.70	1.190	Ea.
	6000	Door holder, electro-magnetic			4	2.000	Ea.
	6200	Combination holder and closer			3.20	2.500	Ea.
	6400	Code transmitter			4	2.000	Ea.
	6600	Drill switch			8	1.000	Ea.
	6800	Master box			2.70	2.960	Ea.
	7000	Break glass station			8	1.000	Ea.
	7800	Remote annunciator, 8 zone lamp			1.80	4.440	Ea.
	8000	12 zone lamp			1.30	6.150	Ea.
	8200	16 zone lamp	↓	↓	1.10	7.270	Ea.
125		**DOORBELL SYSTEM** Incl. transformer, button & signal					
	0100	6" bell	1 Elec	1 Electrician	4	2.000	Ea.
	0200	Buzzer			4	2.000	Ea.
	1000	Door chimes, 2 notes, minimum			16	.500	Ea.
	1020	Maximum			12	.667	Ea.
	1100	Tube type, 3 tube system			12	.667	Ea.
	1180	4 tube system			10	.800	Ea.
	1900	For transformer & button, minimum add			5	1.600	Ea.
	1960	Maximum, add			4.50	1.780	Ea.
	3000	For push button only, minimum			24	.333	Ea.
	3100	Maximum			20	.400	Ea.
	3200	Bell transformer	↓	↓	16	.500	Ea.

	168 100	Special Systems	CREW	MAKEUP	DAILY OUTPUT	MAN-HOURS	UNIT
130	130	**ELECTRIC HEATING**					
	0200	Snow melting for paved surface embedded mat heaters & controls	1 Elec	1 Electrician	130	.062	S.F.
	0400	Cable heating, radiant heat plaster, no controls, in South			130	.062	S.F.
	0600	In North			90	.089	S.F.
	0800	Cable on 1/2" board, not incl. controls, tract housing			90	.089	S.F.
	1000	Custom housing			80	.100	S.F.
	1100	Rule of thumb: Baseboard units, including control			4.40	1.820	KW
	1200	Duct heaters, including controls			5.30	1.510	KW
	1300	Baseboard heaters, 2' long, 375 watt			8	1.000	Ea.
	1400	3' long, 500 watt			8	1.000	Ea.
	1600	4' long, 750 watt			6.70	1.190	Ea.
	1800	5' long, 935 watt			5.70	1.400	Ea.
	2000	6' long, 1125 watt			5	1.600	Ea.
	2200	7' long, 1310 watt			4.40	1.820	Ea.
	2400	8' long, 1500 watt			4	2.000	Ea.
	2600	9' long, 1680 watt			3.60	2.220	Ea.
	2800	10' long, 1875 watt	↓	↓	3.30	2.420	Ea.
	2950	Wall heaters with fan, 120 to 277 volt					
	2970	surface mounted, residential, 750 watt	1 Elec	1 Electrician	7	1.140	Ea.
	2980	1000 watt			7	1.140	Ea.
	2990	1250 watt			6	1.330	Ea.
	3000	1500 watt			5	1.600	Ea.
	3010	2000 watt			5	1.600	Ea.
	3040	2250 watt			4	2.000	Ea.
	3050	2500 watt			4	2.000	Ea.
	3070	4000 watt			3.50	2.290	Ea.
	3080	Commercial, 750 watt			7	1.140	Ea.
	3090	1000 watt			7	1.140	Ea.
	3100	1250 watt			6	1.330	Ea.
	3110	1500 watt			5	1.600	Ea.
	3120	2000 watt			5	1.600	Ea.
	3130	2500 watt			4.50	1.780	Ea.
	3140	3000 watt			4	2.000	Ea.
	3150	4000 watt			3.50	2.290	Ea.
	3161	Recessed, residential or commercial, 750 watt			6	1.330	Ea.
	3170	1000 watt			6	1.330	Ea.
	3180	1250 watt			5	1.600	Ea.
	3190	1500 watt			4	2.000	Ea.
	3210	2000 watt			4	2.000	Ea.
	3230	2500 watt			3.50	2.290	Ea.
	3240	3000 watt			3	2.670	Ea.
	3250	4000 watt			2.70	2.960	Ea.
	3600	Thermostats, integral			16	.500	Ea.
	3800	Line voltage, 1 pole			8	1.000	Ea.
	3810	2 pole			8	1.000	Ea.
	3820	Low voltage, 1 pole	↓	↓	8	1.000	Ea.
	4000	Heat trace system, 400 degree					
	4020	115V, 2.5 watts per L.F.	1 Elec	1 Electrician	530	.015	L.F.
	4030	5 watts per L.F.			530	.015	L.F.
	4050	10 watts per L.F.			530	.015	L.F.
	4060	220V, 4 watts per L.F.			530	.015	L.F.
	4080	480V, 8 watts per L.F.	↓	↓	530	.015	L.F.
	4200	Heater raceway					
	4220	5/8"w x 3/8" H	1 Elec	1 Electrician	200	.040	L.F.
	4240	5/8"w x 1/2" H	"	"	190	.042	L.F.
	4320	Snap band, clamp					
	4340	3/4" pipe size	1 Elec	1 Electrician	470	.017	Ea.
	4360	1" pipe size	"	"	444	.018	Ea.

		Special Systems	CREW	MAKEUP	DAILY OUTPUT	MAN-HOURS	UNIT
		168 100 Special Systems					
130	4381	Electric, heat trace system, snap band, clamp, 1-1/4" pipe size	1 Elec	1 Electrician	400	.020	Ea.
	4400	1-1/2" pipe size			355	.023	Ea.
	4420	2" pipe size			320	.025	Ea.
	4440	3" pipe size			160	.050	Ea.
	4460	4" pipe size			100	.080	Ea.
	4480	Single pole thermostat NEMA 4, 30 amp			8	1.000	Ea.
	4500	NEMA 7, 30 amp			7	1.140	Ea.
	4520	Double pole, NEMA 4, 30 amp			7	1.140	Ea.
	4540	NEMA 7, 30 amp	↓	↓	6	1.330	Ea.
	4560	Thermostat/contactor combination, NEMA 4					
	4580	30 amp 4 pole	1 Elec	1 Electrician	3.60	2.220	Ea.
	4600	50 amp 4 pole			3	2.670	Ea.
	4620	75 amp 3 pole			2.50	3.200	Ea.
	4640	75 amp 4 pole			2.30	3.480	Ea.
	4680	Control transformer, 50 VA			4	2.000	Ea.
	4700	75 VA			3.10	2.580	Ea.
	4720	Expediter fitting			11	.727	Ea.
	5000	Radiant heating ceiling panels, 2' x 4', 500 watt			16	.500	Ea.
	5050	750 watt			16	.500	Ea.
	5200	For recessed plaster frame, add			32	.250	Ea.
	5300	Infra-red quartz heaters, 120 volts, 1000 watts			6.70	1.190	Ea.
	5350	1500 watt			5	1.600	Ea.
	5400	240 volts, 1500 watt			5	1.600	Ea.
	5450	2000 watt			4	2.000	Ea.
	5500	3000 watt			3	2.670	Ea.
	5550	4000 watt			2.60	3.080	Ea.
	5570	Modulating control	↓	↓	.80	10.000	Ea.
	5600	Unit heaters, heavy duty, with fan & mounting bracket					
	5650	Single phase, 208-240-277 volt, 3 KW	1 Elec	1 Electrician	3.20	2.500	Ea.
	5700	4 KW			2.80	2.860	Ea.
	5750	5 KW			2.40	3.330	Ea.
	5800	7 KW			1.90	4.210	Ea.
	5850	10 KW			1.30	6.150	Ea.
	5900	13 KW			1	8.000	Ea.
	5950	15 KW			.90	8.890	Ea.
	6000	480 volt, 3KW			3.30	2.420	Ea.
	6020	4 KW			3	2.670	Ea.
	6040	5 KW			2.60	3.080	Ea.
	6060	7 KW			2	4.000	Ea.
	6080	10 KW			1.40	5.710	Ea.
	6100	13 KW			1.10	7.270	Ea.
	6120	15 KW			1	8.000	Ea.
	6140	20 KW			.90	8.890	Ea.
	6300	3 phase, 208-240 volt, 5 KW			2.40	3.330	Ea.
	6320	7 KW			1.90	4.210	Ea.
	6340	10 KW			1.30	6.150	Ea.
	6360	15 KW			.90	8.890	Ea.
	6380	20 KW			.70	11.430	Ea.
	6400	25 KW			.50	16.000	Ea.
	6500	480 volt, 5 KW			2.60	3.080	Ea.
	6520	7 KW			2	4.000	Ea.
	6540	10 KW			1.40	5.710	Ea.
	6560	13 KW			1.10	7.270	Ea.
	6580	15 KW			1	8.000	Ea.
	6600	20 KW			.90	8.890	Ea.
	6620	25 KW			.60	13.330	Ea.
	6630	30 KW			.70	11.430	Ea.
	6640	40 KW	↓	↓	.60	13.330	Ea.

		CREW	MAKEUP	DAILY OUTPUT	MAN-HOURS	UNIT
168 100	**Special Systems**					
130 6800	Vertical discharge heaters, with fan					
6820	Single phase, 208-240-277 volt, 10 KW	1 Elec	1 Electrician	1.30	6.150	Ea.
6840	15 KW			.90	8.890	Ea.
6900	3 phase, 208-240 volt, 10 KW			1.30	6.150	Ea.
6920	15 KW			.90	8.890	Ea.
6940	20 KW			.70	11.430	Ea.
6960	25 KW			.50	16.000	Ea.
6980	30 KW			.40	20.000	Ea.
7000	40 KW			.36	22.220	Ea.
7020	50 KW			.32	25.000	Ea.
7100	480 volt, 10 KW			1.40	5.710	Ea.
7120	15 KW			1	8.000	Ea.
7140	20 KW			.90	8.890	Ea.
7160	25 KW			.60	13.330	Ea.
7180	30 KW			.50	16.000	Ea.
7200	40 KW			.40	20.000	Ea.
7220	50 KW			.35	22.860	Ea.
7410	Sill height convector heaters, 5" high x 2' long, 500 watt			6.70	1.190	Ea.
7420	3' long, 750 watt			6.50	1.230	Ea.
7430	4' long, 1000 watt			6.20	1.290	Ea.
7440	5' long, 1250 watt			5.50	1.450	Ea.
7450	6' long, 1500 watt			4.80	1.670	Ea.
7460	8' long, 2000 watt			3.60	2.220	Ea.
7470	10' long, 2500 watt	↓	↓	3	2.670	Ea.
7900	Cabinet convector heaters, 240 volt					
7920	2' long, 1000 watt	1 Elec	1 Electrician	5.30	1.510	Ea.
7940	1500 watt			5.30	1.510	Ea.
7960	2000 watt			5.30	1.510	Ea.
7980	3' long, 1500 watt			4.60	1.740	Ea.
8000	2250 watt			4.60	1.740	Ea.
8020	3000 watt			4.60	1.740	Ea.
8040	4' long, 2000 watt			4	2.000	Ea.
8060	3000 watt			4	2.000	Ea.
8080	4000 watt	↓	↓	4	2.000	Ea.
8081						
8200	Cabinet unit heaters, 120 to 277 volt, 1 pole,					
8220	wall mounted, 2000 watt	1 Elec	1 Electrician	4.60	1.740	Ea.
8230	3000 watt			4.60	1.740	Ea.
8240	4000 watt			4.40	1.820	Ea.
8250	5000 watt			4.40	1.820	Ea.
8260	6000 watt			4.20	1.900	Ea.
8270	8000 watt			4	2.000	Ea.
8280	10,000 watt			3.80	2.110	Ea.
8290	12,000 watt			3.50	2.290	Ea.
8300	13,500 watt			2.90	2.760	Ea.
8310	16,000 watt			2.70	2.960	Ea.
8320	20,000 watt			2.30	3.480	Ea.
8330	24,000 watt			1.90	4.210	Ea.
8350	Recessed, 2000 watt			4.40	1.820	Ea.
8370	3000 watt			4.40	1.820	Ea.
8380	4000 watt			4.20	1.900	Ea.
8390	5000 watt			4.20	1.900	Ea.
8400	6000 watt			4	2.000	Ea.
8410	8000 watt			3.80	2.110	Ea.
8420	10,000 watt			3.50	2.290	Ea.
8430	12,000 watt			2.90	2.760	Ea.
8440	13,500 watt			2.70	2.960	Ea.
8450	16,000 watt	↓	↓	2.30	3.480	Ea.

168 | Special Systems

			CREW	MAKEUP	DAILY OUTPUT	MAN-HOURS	UNIT
	168 100 | Special Systems						
130	8461	Cabinet unit heaters, recessed, 20,000 watt	1 Elec	1 Electrician	1.90	4.210	Ea.
	8470	24,000 watt			1.60	5.000	Ea.
	8490	Ceiling mounted, 2000 watt			3.20	2.500	Ea.
	8510	3000 watt			3.20	2.500	Ea.
	8520	4000 watt			3	2.670	Ea.
	8530	5000 watt			3	2.670	Ea.
	8540	6000 watt			2.80	2.860	Ea.
	8550	8000 watt			2.40	3.330	Ea.
	8560	10,000 watt			2.20	3.640	Ea.
	8570	12,000 watt			2	4.000	Ea.
	8580	13,500 watt			1.50	5.330	Ea.
	8590	16,000 watt			1.30	6.150	Ea.
	8600	20,000 watt			.90	8.890	Ea.
	8610	24,000 watt			.60	13.330	Ea.
	8960	4000 watt	↓	↓	3	2.670	Ea.
	140	**LIGHTNING PROTECTION**					
	0200	Air terminals, copper					
	0400	3/8" diameter x 10" (to 75' high)	1 Elec	1 Electrician	8	1.000	Ea.
	0500	1/2" diameter x 12" (over 75' high)			8	1.000	Ea.
	1000	Aluminum, 1/2" diameter x 12" (to 75' high)			8	1.000	Ea.
	1100	5/8" diameter x 12" (over 75' high)			8	1.000	Ea.
	2000	Cable, copper, 220 lb. per thousand ft. (to 75' high)			320	.025	L.F.
	2100	375 lb. per thousand ft. (over 75' high)			230	.035	L.F.
	2500	Aluminum, 101 lb. per thousand ft. (to 75' high)			280	.029	L.F.
	2600	199 lb. per thousand ft. (over 75' high)			240	.033	L.F.
	3000	Arrestor, 175 volt AC to ground			8	1.000	Ea.
	3100	650 volt AC to ground	↓	↓	6.70	1.190	Ea.
	145	**NURSE CALL SYSTEMS**					
	0100	Single bedside call station	1 Elec	1 Electrician	8	1.000	Ea.
	0200	Ceiling speaker station			8	1.000	Ea.
	0400	Emergency call station			8	1.000	Ea.
	0600	Pillow speaker			8	1.000	Ea.
	0800	Double bedside call station			4	2.000	Ea.
	1000	Duty station			4	2.000	Ea.
	1200	Standard call button			8	1.000	Ea.
	1400	Lights, corridor, dome or zone indicator	↓	↓	8	1.000	Ea.
	1600	Master control station for 20 stations	2 Elec	2 Electricians	.65	24.620	Total
	150	**PUBLIC ADDRESS SYSTEM**					
	0100	Conventional, office	1 Elec	1 Electrician	5.33	1.500	Speaker
	0200	Industrial	"	"	2.70	2.960	Speaker
	155	**SOUND SYSTEM**					
	0100	Components, outlet, projector	1 Elec	1 Electrician	8	1.000	Ea.
	0200	Microphone			4	2.000	Ea.
	0400	ceiling or wall			8	1.000	Ea.
	0600	Trumpets			4	2.000	Ea.
	0800	Privacy switch			8	1.000	Ea.
	1000	Monitor panel			4	2.000	Ea.
	1200	Antenna, AM/FM			4	2.000	Ea.
	1400	Volume control			8	1.000	Ea.
	1600	Amplifier, 250 watts			1	8.000	Ea.
	1800	Cabinets			1	8.000	Ea.
	2000	Intercom, 25 station capacity, master station			1	8.000	Ea.
	2020	11 station capacity			2	4.000	Ea.
	2200	Remote station			8	1.000	Ea.
	2400	Intercom outlets			8	1.000	Ea.
	2600	Handset			4	2.000	Ea.
	2800	Emergency call system, 12 zones, annunciator			1.30	6.150	Ea.
	3000	Bell	↓	↓	5.30	1.510	Ea.

168 | Special Systems

168 100	Special Systems	CREW	MAKEUP	DAILY OUTPUT	MAN-HOURS	UNIT
155 3201	Emergency call system, 12 zones, light or relay	1 Elec	1 Electrician	8	1.000	Ea.
3400	Transformer			4	2.000	Ea.
3600	House telephone, talking station			1.60	5.000	Ea.
3800	Press to talk, release to listen			5.30	1.510	Ea.
4200	Door release			4	2.000	Ea.
4400	Combination speaker and microphone			8	1.000	Ea.
4600	Termination box			3.20	2.500	Ea.
4800	Amplifier or power supply			5.30	1.510	Ea.
5000	Vestibule door unit			16	.500	Name
5200	Strip cabinet			27	.296	Ea.
5400	Directory	↓	↓	16	.500	Ea.
160	T.V. SYSTEMS					
0100	Master TV antenna system					
0200	VHF reception & distribution, 12 outlets	1 Elec	1 Electrician	6	1.330	Outlet
0400	30 outlets			10	.800	Outlet
0600	100 outlets			13	.615	Outlet
0800	VHF & UHF reception & distribution, 12 outlets			6	1.330	Outlet
1000	30 outlets			10	.800	Outlet
1200	100 outlets			13	.615	Outlet
1400	School and deluxe systems, 12 outlets			2.40	3.330	Outlet
1600	30 outlets			4	2.000	Outlet
1800	80 outlets			5.30	1.510	Outlet
1900	Amplifier			4	2.000	Ea.
1910	Antenna			2	4.000	Ea.
2000	Closed circuit, surveillance, one station (camera & monitor)			1.30	6.150	Total
2200	For additional camera stations, add			2.70	2.960	Ea.
2400	Industrial quality, one station (camera & monitor)			1.30	6.150	Total
2600	For additional camera stations, add			2.70	2.960	Ea.
2610	For low light, add			2.70	2.960	Ea.
2620	For very low light, add			2.70	2.960	Ea.
2800	For weatherproof camera station, add			1.30	6.150	Ea.
3000	For pan and tilt, add			1.30	6.150	Ea.
3200	For zoom lens - remote control, add, minimum			2	4.000	Ea.
3400	Maximum			2	4.000	Ea.
3410	For automatic iris for low light, add	↓	↓	2	4.000	Ea.
3600	Educational T.V. studio, basic 3 camera system, black & white,					
3800	electrical & electronic equip. only, minimum	4 Elec	4 Electricians	.80	40.000	Total
4000	Maximum (full console)			.28	114.000	Total
4100	As above, but color system, minimum			.28	114.000	Total
4120	Maximum	↓	↓	.12	267.000	Total
4200	For film chain, black & white, add	1 Elec	1 Electrician	1	8.000	Ea.
4250	Color, add			.25	32.000	Ea.
4400	For video tape recorders, add, minimum	↓	↓	1	8.000	Ea.
4600	Maximum	4 Elec	4 Electricians	.40	80.000	Ea.
170	RESIDENTIAL WIRING					
2130	EMT & wire	1 Elec	1 Electrician	5.71	1.400	Ea.
4550	Air conditioner outlet, 20 amp-240 volt recpt.					
4560	30' of #12/2, 2 pole circuit breaker					
4570	Type NM cable	1 Elec	1 Electrician	10	.800	Ea.
4580	Type MC cable			9	.889	Ea.
4590	EMT & wire			4	2.000	Ea.
4600	Decorator style, type NM cable			10	.800	Ea.
4620	Type MC cable			9	.889	Ea.
4630	EMT & wire	↓	↓	4	2.000	Ea.
4650	Dryer outlet, 30 amp-240 volt recpt., 20' of #10/3					
4660	2 pole circuit breaker					
4670	Type NM cable	1 Elec	1 Electrician	6.41	1.250	Ea.
4680	Type MC cable	"	"	5.71	1.400	Ea.

168 100	Special Systems	CREW	MAKEUP	DAILY OUTPUT	MAN-HOURS	UNIT
170 4691	Dryer outlet, 2 pole circuit breaker, EMT & wire	1 Elec	1 Electrician	3.48	2.300	Ea.
4700	Range outlet, 50 amp-240 volt recpt., 30' of #8/3					
4710	Type NM cable	1 Elec	1 Electrician	4.21	1.900	Ea.
4720	Type MC cable			4	2.000	Ea.
4730	EMT & wire			2.96	2.700	Ea.
4750	Central vacuum outlet			6.40	1.250	Ea.
4770	Type MC cable			5.71	1.400	Ea.
4780	EMT & wire	↓	↓	3.48	2.300	Ea.
4800	30 amp-110 volt locking recpt., #10/2 circ. bkr.					
4810	Type NM cable	1 Elec	1 Electrician	6.20	1.290	Ea.
4820	Type MC cable			5.40	1.480	Ea.
4830	EMT & wire	↓	↓	3.20	2.500	Ea.
4900	Low voltage outlets					
4910	Telephone recpt., 20' of 4/C phone wire	1 Elec	1 Electrician	26	.308	Ea.
4920	TV recpt., 20' of RG59U coax wire, F type connector	"	"	16	.500	Ea.
4950	Door bell chime, transformer, 2 buttons, 60' of bellwire					
4970	Economy model	1 Elec	1 Electrician	11.50	.696	Ea.
4980	Custom model			11.50	.696	Ea.
4990	Luxury model, 3 buttons	↓	↓	9.50	.842	Ea.
6000	Lighting outlets					
6050	Wire only (for fixture) type NM cable	1 Elec	1 Electrician	32	.250	Ea.
6070	Type MC cable			24	.333	Ea.
6080	EMT & wire			10	.800	Ea.
6100	Box (4") and wire (for fixture), type NM cable			25	.320	Ea.
6120	Type MC cable			20	.400	Ea.
6130	EMT & wire	↓	↓	11	.727	Ea.
6200	Fixtures (use with lines 6050 or 6100 above)					
6210	Canopy style, economy grade	1 Elec	1 Electrician	40	.200	Ea.
6220	Custom grade			40	.200	Ea.
6250	Dining room chandelier, economy grade			19	.421	Ea.
6260	Custom grade			19	.421	Ea.
6270	Luxury grade			15	.533	Ea.
6310	Kitchen fixture (fluorescent), economy grade			30	.267	Ea.
6320	Custom grade			25	.320	Ea.
6350	Outdoor, wall mounted, economy grade			30	.267	Ea.
6360	Custom grade			30	.267	Ea.
6370	Luxury grade			25	.320	Ea.
6410	Outdoor Par floodlights, 1 lamp, 150 watt			20	.400	Ea.
6420	2 lamp, 150 watt each			20	.400	Ea.
6430	For infrared security sensor, add			32	.250	Ea.
6450	Outdoor, quartz-halogen, 300 watt flood			20	.400	Ea.
6600	Recessed downlight, round, pre-wired, 50 or 75 watt trim			30	.267	Ea.
6610	With shower light trim			30	.267	Ea.
6620	With wall washer trim			28	.286	Ea.
6630	With eye-ball trim			28	.286	Ea.
6700	Porcelyn lamp holder			40	.200	Ea.
6710	With pull switch			40	.200	Ea.
6750	Fluorescent strip, 1-20 watt tube, wrap around diffuser, 24"			24	.333	Ea.
6760	1-40 watt tube, 48"			24	.333	Ea.
6770	2-40 watt tubes, 48"			20	.400	Ea.
6780	With 0° ballast			20	.400	Ea.
6800	Bathroom heat lamp, 1-250 watt			28	.286	Ea.
6810	2-250 watt lamps	↓	↓	28	.286	Ea.
6900	Outdoor post lamp, incl. post, fixture, 35' of #14/2					
6910	Type NMC cable	1 Elec	1 Electrician	3.50	2.290	Ea.
6920	Photo-eye, add			27	.296	Ea.
6950	Clock dial time switch, 24 hr., w/enclosure, type NM cable	↓	↓	11.43	.700	Ea.
6970	Type MC cable	↓	↓	11	.727	Ea.

168 100	Special Systems	CREW	MAKEUP	DAILY OUTPUT	MAN-HOURS	UNIT
170 6981	Clock dial time switch, 24 hr., EMT & wire	1 Elec	1 Electrician	4.85	1.650	Ea.
7000	Alarm systems					
7050	Smoke detectors, box, #14/3 type NM cable	1 Elec	1 Electrician	14.55	.550	Ea.
7070	Type MC cable	↓	↓	12.31	.650	Ea.
7080	EMT & wire	↓	↓	5	1.600	Ea.
8000	Residential equipment					
8050	Disposal hook-up, incl. switch, outlet box, 3' of flex					
8060	20 amp-1 pole circ. bkr., and 25' of #12/2					
8070	Type NM cable	1 Elec	1 Electrician	10	.800	Ea.
8080	Type MC cable	↓	↓	8	1.000	Ea.
8090	EMT & wire	↓	↓	5	1.600	Ea.
8100	Trash compactor or dishwasher hook-up, incl. outlet box,					
8110	3' of flex, 15 amp-1 pole circ. bkr., and 25' of #14/2					
8120	Type NM cable	1 Elec	1 Electrician	10	.800	Ea.
8130	Type MC cable	↓	↓	8	1.000	Ea.
8140	EMT & wire	↓	↓	5	1.600	Ea.
8150	Hot water sink dispensor hook-up, use line 8100					
8200	Vent/exhaust fan hook-up, type NM cable	1 Elec	1 Electrician	32	.250	Ea.
8220	Type MC cable	↓	↓	24	.333	Ea.
8230	EMT & wire	↓	↓	10	.800	Ea.
8250	Bathroom vent fan, 50 CFM (use with above hook-up)					
8260	Economy model	1 Elec	1 Electrician	15	.533	Ea.
8270	Low noise model	↓	↓	15	.533	Ea.
8280	Custom model	↓	↓	12	.667	Ea.
8300	Bathroom or kitchen vent fan, 110 CFM					
8310	Economy model	1 Elec	1 Electrician	15	.533	Ea.
8320	Low noise model	↓	↓	15	.533	Ea.
8330	Type MC cable	↓	↓	3.50	2.290	Ea.
8350	Paddle fan, variable speed (w/o lights)					
8360	Economy model (AC motor)	1 Elec	1 Electrician	10	.800	Ea.
8370	Custom model (AC motor)			10	.800	Ea.
8380	Luxury model (DC motor)			8	1.000	Ea.
8390	Remote speed switch for above, add	↓	↓	12	.667	Ea.
8500	Whole house exhaust fan, ceiling mount, 36", variable speed					
8510	Remote switch, incl. shutters, 20 amp-1 pole circ. bkr.					
8520	30' of #12/2/ type NM cable	1 Elec	1 Electrician	4	2.000	Ea.
8530	Type MC cable	↓	↓	3.50	2.290	Ea.
8540	EMT & wire	↓	↓	3	2.670	Ea.
8600	Whirlpool tub hook-up, incl. timer switch, outlet box					
8610	3' of flex, 20 amp-1 pole GFI circ. bkr.					
8620	30' of #12/2 type NM cable	1 Elec	1 Electrician	10	.800	Ea.
8630	Type MC cable	↓	↓	8	1.000	Ea.
8640	EMT & wire	↓	↓	4	2.000	Ea.
8650	Hot water heater hook-up, incl. 1-2 pole circ. bkr. box;					
8660	3' of flex, 20' of #10/2 type NM cable	1 Elec	1 Electrician	10	.800	Ea.
8670	Type MC cable	↓	↓	8	1.000	Ea.
8680	EMT & wire	↓	↓	5	1.600	Ea.
9000	Heating/air conditioning					
9050	Furnace/boiler hook-up, incl. firestat, local on-off switch					
9060	Emergency switch, and 40' of type NM cable	1 Elec	1 Electrician	4	2.000	Ea.
9070	Type MC cable	↓	↓	3.50	2.290	Ea.
9080	EMT & wire	↓	↓	1.50	5.330	Ea.
9100	Air conditioner hook-up, incl. local 60 amp disc. switch					
9110	3' Sealtite, 40 amp, 2 pole circuit breaker					
9130	40' of #8/2 type NM cable	1 Elec	1 Electrician	3.50	2.290	Ea.
9140	Type MC cable	↓	↓	3	2.670	Ea.
9150	EMT & wire	↓	↓	1.30	6.150	Ea.

168 100	Special Systems		CREW	MAKEUP	DAILY OUTPUT	MAN-HOURS	UNIT
170	9200	Heat pump hook-up, 1-40 & 1-100 amp 2 pole circ. bkr.					
	9210	Local disconnect switch, 3' Sealtite					
	9220	40' of #8/2 & 30' of #3/2					
	9230	Type NM cable	1 Elec	1 Electrician	1.30	6.150	Ea.
	9240	Type MC cable	↓	↓	1.08	7.410	Ea.
	9250	EMT & wire			.94	8.510	Ea.
	9500	Thermostat hook-up, using low voltage wire					
	9520	Heating only	1 Elec	1 Electrician	24	.333	Ea.
	9530	Heating/cooling	"	"	20	.400	Ea.

APPENDIX

Abbreviations

A	Area Square Foot; Ampere	Cab.	Cabinet	Demob.	Demobilization
ABS	Acrylonitrile Butadiene Styrene; Asbestos Bonded Steel	Cair.	Air Tool Laborer	d.f.u.	Drainage Fixture Units
		Calc	Calculated	D.H.	Double Hung
A.C.	Alternating Current ; Air Conditioning; Asbestos Cement	Cap.	Capacity	DHW	Domestic Hot Water
		Carp.	Carpenter	Diag.	Diagonal
		C.B.	Circuit Breaker	Diam.	Diameter
A.C.I.	American Concrete Institute	C.C.F.	Hundred Cubic Feet	Distrib.	Distribution
Addit.	Additional	cd	Candela	Dk.	Deck
Adj.	Adjustable	cd/sf	Candela per Square Foot	D.L.	Dead Load; Diesel
af	Audio-frenquency	CD	Grade of Plywood Face & Back	Do.	Ditto
A.G.A.	American Gas Association	CDX	Plywood, grade C&D, exterior glue	Dp.	Depth
Agg.	Aggregate	Cefi.	Cement Finisher	D.P.S.T.	Double Pole, Single Throw
A.H.	Ampere Hours	Cem.	Cement	Dr.	Driver
A hr	Ampere-hour	CF	Hundred Feet	Drink.	Drinking
A.I.A.	American Institute of Architects	C.F.	Cubic Feet	D.S.	Double Strength
AIC	Ampere Interrupting Capacity	CFM	Cubic Feet per Minute	D.S.A.	Double Strength A Grade
Allow.	Allowance	c.g.	Center of Gravity	D.S.B.	Double Strength B Grade
alt.	Altitude	CHW	Chilled Water	Dty.	Duty
Alum.	Aluminum	C.I.	Cast Iron	DWV	Drain Waste Vent
a.m.	Ante Meridiem	C.I.P.	Cast in Place	DX	Deluxe White, Direct Expansion
Amp.	Ampere	Circ.	Circuit	dyn	Dyne
Approx.	Approximate	C.L.	Carload Lot	e	Eccentricity
Apt.	Apartment	Clab.	Common Laborer	E	Equipment Only; East
Asb.	Asbestos	C.L.F.	Hundred Linear Feet	Ea.	Each
A.S.B.C.	American Standard Building Code	CLF	Current Limiting Fuse	Econ.	Economy
Asbe.	Asbestos Worker	CLP	Cross Linked Polyethylene	EDP	Electronic Data Processing
A.S.H.R.A.E.	American Society of Heating, Refrig. & AC Engineers	cm	Centimeter	E.D.R.	Equiv. Direct Radiation
		CMP	Corr. Metal Pipe	Eq.	Equation
A.S.M.E.	American Society of Mechanical Engineers	C.M.U.	Concrete Masonry Unit	Elec.	Electrician; Electrical
		Col.	Column	Elev.	Elevator; Elevating
A.S.T.M.	American Society for Testing and Materials	CO₂	Carbon Dioxide	EMT	Electrical Metallic Conduit; Thin Wall Conduit
		Comb.	Combination		
Attchmt.	Attachment	Compr.	Compressor	Eng.	Engine
Avg.	Average	Conc.	Concrete	EPDM	Ethylene Propylene Diene Monomer
A.W.G.	American Wire Gauge	Cont.	Continuous;		
Bbl.	Barrel		Continued	Eqhv.	Equip. Oper., heavy
B.&B.	Grade B and Better; Balled & Burlapped	Corr.	Corrugated	Eqlt.	Equip. Oper., light
		Cos	Cosine	Eqmd.	Equip. Oper., medium
B.&S.	Bell and Spigot	Cot	Cotangent	Eqmm.	Equip. Oper., Master Mechanic
B.&W.	Black and White	Cov.	Cover	Eqol.	Equip. Oper., oilers
b.c.c.	Body-centered Cubic	CPA	Control Point Adjustment	Equip.	Equipment
BE	Bevel End	Cplg.	Coupling	ERW	Electric Resistance Welded
B.F.	Board Feet	C.P.M.	Critical Path Method	Est.	Estimated
Bg. Cem.	Bag of Cement	CPVC	Chlorinated Polyvinyl Chloride	esu	Electrostatic Units
BHP	Brake Horse Power	C. Pr.	Hundred Pair	E.W.	Each Way
B.I.	Black Iron	CRC	Cold Rolled Channel	EWT	Entering Water Temperature
Bit.;		Creos.	Creosote	Excav.	Excavation
Bitum.	Bituminous	Crpt.	Carpet & Linoleum Layer	Exp.	Expansion
Bk.	Backed	CRT	Cathode-ray Tube	Ext.	Exterior
Bkrs.	Breakers	CS	Carbon Steel	Extru.	Extrusion
Bldg.	Building	Csc	Cosecant	f.	Fiber stress
Blk.	Block	C.S.F.	Hundred Square Feet	F	Fahrenheit; Female; Fill
Bm.	Beam	C.S.I.	Construction Specification Institute	Fab.	Fabricated
Boil.	Boilermaker			FBGS	Fiberglass
B.P.M.	Blows per Minute	C.T.	Current Transformer	F.C.	Footcandles
BR	Bedroom	CTS	Copper Tube Size	f.c.c.	Face-centered Cubic
Brg.	Bearing	Cu	Cubic	f'c.	Compressive Stress in Concrete; Extreme Compressive Stress
Brhe.	Bricklayer Helper	Cu. Ft.	Cubic Foot		
Bric.	Bricklayer	cw	Continuous Wave	F.E.	Front End
Brk.	Brick	C.W.	Cool White; Cold Water	FEP	Fluorinated Ethylene Propylene (Teflon)
Brng.	Bearing	Cwt.	100 Pounds		
Brs.	Brass	C.W.X.	Cool White Deluxe	F.G.	Flat Grain
Brz.	Bronze	C.Y.	Cubic Yard (27 cubic feet)	F.H.A.	Federal Housing Administration
Bsn.	Basin	C.Y./Hr.	Cubic Yard per Hour	Fig.	Figure
Btr.	Better	Cyl.	Cylinder	Fin.	Finished
BTU	British Thermal Unit	d	Penny (nail size)	Fixt.	Fixture
BTUH	BTU per Hour	D	Deep; Depth; Discharge	Fl. Oz.	Fluid Ounces
BX	Interlocked Armored Cable	Dis.;		Flr.	Floor
c	Conductivity	Disch.	Discharge	F.M.	Frequency Modulation; Factory Mutual
C	Hundred; Centigrade	Db.	Decibel		
		Dbl.	Double	Fmg.	Framing
C/C	Center to Center	DC	Direct Current	Fndtn.	Foundation

731

Fori.	Foreman, inside	I.P.	Iron Pipe	Max.	Maximum
Fount.	Fountain	I.P.S.	Iron Pipe Size	MBF	Thousand Board Feet
FPM	Feet per Minute	I.P.T.	Iron Pipe Threaded	MBH	Thousand BTU's per hr.
FPT	Female Pipe Thread	I.W.	Indirect Waste	M.C.F.	Thousand Cubic Feet
Fr.	Frame	J	Joule	M.C.F.M.	Thousand Cubic Feet
F.R.	Fire Rating	J.I.C.	Joint Industrial Council		per Minute
FRK	Foil Reinforced Kraft	K	Thousand; Thousand Pounds;	M.C.M.	Thousand Circular Mils
FRP	Fiberglass Reinforced Plastic		Heavy Wall Copper Tubing	M.C.P.	Motor Circuit Protector
FS	Forged Steel	K.A.H.	Thousand Amp. Hours	MD	Medium Duty
FSC	Cast Body; Cast Switch Box	K.D.A.T.	Kiln Dried After Treatment	M.D.O.	Medium Density Overlaid
Ft.	Foot; Feet	kg	Kilogram	Med.	Medium
Ftng.	Fitting	kG	Kilogauss	MF	Thousand Feet
Ftg.	Footing	kgf	Kilogram force	M.F.B.M.	Thousand Feet Board Measure
Ft. Lb.	Foot Pound	kHz	Kilohertz	Mfg.	Manufacturing
Furn.	Furniture	Kip.	1000 Pounds	Mfrs.	Manufacturers
FVNR	Full Voltage Non Reversing	KJ	Kiljoule	mg	Milligram
FXM	Female by Male	K.L.	Effective Length Factor	MGD	Million Gallons per Day
Fy.	Minimum Yield Stress of Steel	Km	Kilometer	MGPH	Thousand Gallons per Hour
g	Gram	K.L.F.	Kips per Linear Foot	MH	Manhole; Metal Halide; Man Hour
G	Gauss	K.S.F.	Kips per Square Foot	MHz	Megahertz
Ga.	Gauge	K.S.I.	Kips per Square Inch	Mi.	Mile
Gal.	Gallon	K.V.	Kilo Volt	MI	Malleable Iron; Mineral Insulated
Gal./Min.	Gallon Per Minute	K.V.A.	Kilo Volt Ampere	mm	Millimeter
Galv.	Galvanized	K.V.A.R.	Kilovar (Reactance)	Mill.	Millwright
Gen.	General	KW	Kilo Watt	Min.	Minimum
Glaz.	Glazier	KWh	Kilowatt-hour	Misc.	Miscellaneous
GPD	Gallons per Day	L	Labor Only; Length; Long;	ml	Milliliter
GPH	Gallons per Hour		Medium Wall Copper Tubing	M.L.F.	Thousand Linear Feet
GPM	Gallons per Minute	Lab.	Labor	Mo.	Month
GR	Grade	lat	Latitude	Mobil.	Mobilization
Gran.	Granular	Lath.	Lather	Mog.	Mogul Base
Grnd.	Ground	Lav.	Lavatory	MPH	Miles per Hour
H	High; High Strength Bar Joist;	lb.; #	Pound	MPT	Male Pipe Thread
	Henry	L.B.	Load Bearing; L Conduit Body	MRT	Mile Round Trip
H.C.	High Capacity	L. & E.	Labor & Equipment	ms	Millisecond
H.D.	Heavy Duty; High Density	lb./hr.	Pounds per Hour	M.S.F.	Thousand Square Feet
H.D.O.	High Density Overlaid	lb./L.F.	Pounds per Linear Foot	Mstz.	Mosaic & Terrazzo Worker
Hdr.	Header	lbf/sq in.	Pound-force per Square Inch	M.S.Y.	Thousand Square Yards
Hdwe.	Hardware	L.C.L.	Less than Carload Lot	Mtd.	Mounted
Help.	Helper average	Ld.	Load	Mthe.	Mosaic & Terrazzo Helper
HEPA	High Efficiency Particulate Air Filter	L.F.	Linear Foot	Mtng.	Mounting
Hg	Mercury	Lg.	Long; Length; Large	Mult.	Multi; Multiply
H.O.	High Output	L. & H.	Light and Heat	M.V.A.	Million Volt Amperes
Horiz.	Horizontal	L.H.	Long Span High Strength Bar Joist	M.V.A.R.	Million Volt Amperes Reactive
H.P.	Horsepower; High Pressure	L.J.	Long Span Standard Strength	MV	Megavolt
H.P.F.	High Power Factor		Bar Joist	MW	Megawatt
Hr.	Hour	L.L.	Live Load	MXM	Male by Male
Hrs./Day	Hours Per Day	L.L.D.	Lamp Lumen Depreciation	MYD	Thousand yards
HSC	High Short Circuit	lm	Lumen	N	Natural; North
Ht.	Height	lm/sf	Lumen per Square Foot	nA	Nanoampere
Htg.	Heating	lm/W	Lumen Per Watt	NA	Not Available; Not Applicable
Htrs.	Heaters	L.O.A.	Length Over All	N.B.C.	National Building Code
HVAC	Heating, Ventilating &	log	Logarithm	NC	Normally Closed
	Air Conditioning	L.P.	Liquefied Petroleum;	N.E.M.A.	National Electrical
Hvy.	Heavy		Low Pressure		Manufacturers Association
HW	Hot Water	L.P.F.	Low Power Factor	NEHB	Bolted Circuit Breaker to 600V.
Hyd.;		L.S.	Lump Sum	N.L.B.	Non-Load-Bearing
Hydr.	Hydraulic	Lt.	Light	nm	Nanometer
Hz.	Hertz (cycles)	Lt. Ga.	Light Gauge	No.	Number
I.	Moment of Inertia	L.T.L.	Less than Truckload Lot	NO	Normally Open
I.C.	Interrupting Capacity	Lt. Wt.	Lightweight	N.O.C.	Not Otherwise Classified
ID	Inside Diameter	L.V.	Low Voltage	Nose.	Nosing
I.D.	Inside Dimension;	M	Thousand; Material; Male;	N.P.T.	National Pipe Thread
	Identification		Light Wall Copper Tubing	NQOB	Bolted Circuit Breaker to 240V.
I.F.	Inside Frosted	m/hr	Man-hour	N.R.C.	Noise Reduction Coefficient
I.M.C.	Intermediate Metal Conduit	mA	Milliampere	N.R.S.	Non Rising Stem
In.	Inch	Mach.	Machine	ns	Nanosecond
Incan.	Incandescent	Mag. Str.	Magnetic Starter	nW	Nanowatt
Incl.	Included; Including	Maint.	Maintenance	OB	Opposing Blade
Int.	Interior	Marb.	Marble Setter	OC	On Center
Inst.	Installation	Mat.	Material	OD	Outside Diameter
Insul.	Insulation	Mat'l.	Material	O.D.	Outside Dimension

ODS	Overhead Distribution System	Rofp.	Roofer, Precast	Thn.	Thin
O & P	Overhead and Profit	Rohe.	Roofer Helpers (Composition)	Thrded	Threaded
Oper.	Operator	Rots.	Roofer, Tile & Slate	Tilf.	Tile Layer Floor
Opng.	Opening	R.O.W.	Right of Way	Tilh.	Tile Layer Helper
Orna.	Ornamental	RPM	Revolutions per Minute	THW.	Insulated Strand Wire
O.S.&Y.	Outside Screw and Yoke	R.R.	Direct Burial Feeder Conduit	THWN;	
Ovhd.	Overhead	R.S.	Rapid Start	THHN	Nylon Jacketed Wire
OWG	Oil, Water or Gas	RT	Round Trip	T.L.	Truckload
Oz.	Ounce	S.	Suction; Single Entrance;	Tot.	Total
P.	Pole; Applied Load; Projection		South	T.S.	Trigger Start
p.	Page	Scaf.	Scaffold	Tr.	Trade
Pape.	Paperhanger	Sch.;		Transf.	Transformer
PAR	Weatherproof Reflector	Sched.	Schedule	Trhv.	Truck Driver, Heavy
Pc.	Piece	S.C.R.	Modular Brick	Trlr.	Trailer
P.C.	Portland Cement;	S.D.R.	Standard Dimension Ratio	Trlt.	Truck Driver, Light
	Power Connector	S.E.	Surfaced Edge	TV	Television
P.C.F.	Pounds per Cubic Foot	S.E.R.;		T.W.	Thermoplastic Water
P.E.	Professional Engineer;	S.E.U.	Service Entrance Cable		Resistant Wire
	Porcelain Enamel; Polyethylene;	S.F.	Square Foot	UCI	Uniform Construction Index
	Plain End	S.F.C.A.	Square Foot Contact Area	UF	Underground Feeder
Perf.	Perforated	S.F.G.	Square Foot of Ground	U.H.F.	Ultra High Frequency
Ph.	Phase	S.F. Hor.	Square Foot Horizontal	U.L.	Underwriters Laboratory
P.I.	Pressure Injected	S.F.R.	Square Feet of Radiation	Unfin.	Unfinished
Pile.	Pile Driver	S.F.Shlf.	Square Foot of Shelf	URD	Underground Residential
Pkg.	Package	S4S	Surface 4 Sides		Distribution
Pl.	Plate	Shee.	Sheet Metal Worker	V	Volt
Plah.	Plasterer Helper	Sin.	Sine	V.A.	Volt Amperes
Plas.	Plasterer	Skwk.	Skilled Worker	V.A.T.	Vinyl Asbestos Tile
Pluh.	Plumbers Helper	SL	Saran Lined	VAV	Variable Air Volume
Plum.	Plumber	S.L.	Slimline	Vent.	Ventilating
Ply.	Plywood	Sldr.	Solder	Vert.	Vertical
p.m.	Post Meridiem	S.N.	Solid Neutral	V.F.	Vinyl Faced
Pord.	Painter, Ordinary	S.P.	Static Pressure; Single Pole;	V.G.	Vertical Grain
pp	Pages		Self Propelled	V.H.F.	Very High Frequency
PP; PPL	Polypropylene	Spri.	Sprinkler Installer	VHO	Very High Output
P.P.M.	Parts per Million	Sq.	Square; 100 square feet	Vib.	Vibrating
Pr.	Pair	S.P.D.T.	Single Pole, Double Throw	V.L.F.	Vertical Linear Foot
Prefab.	Prefabricated	S.P.S.T.	Single Pole, Single Throw	Vol.	Volume
Prefin.	Prefinished	SPT	Standard Pipe Thread	W	Wire; Watt; Wide; West
Prop.	Propelled	Sq. Hd.	Square Head	w/	With
PSF; psf	Pounds per Square Foot	S.S.	Single Strength; Stainless Steel	W.C.	Water Column; Water Closet
PSI; psi	Pounds per Square Inch	S.S.B.	Single Strength B Grade	W.F.	Wide Flange
PSIG	Pounds per Square Inch Gauge	Sswk.	Structural Steel Worker	W.G.	Water Gauge
PSP	Plastic Sewer Pipe	Sswl.	Structural Steel Welder	Wldg.	Welding
Pspr.	Painter, Spray	St.; Stl.	Steel	W. Mile	Wire Mile
Psst.	Painter, Structural Steel	S.T.C.	Sound Transmission Coefficient	W.R.	Water Resistant
P.T.	Potential Transformer	Std.	Standard	Wrck.	Wrecker
P. & T.	Pressure & Temperature	STP	Standard Temperature & Pressure	W.S.P.	Water, Steam, Petroleum
Ptd.	Painted	Stpi.	Steamfitter, Pipefitter	WT, Wt.	Weight
Ptns.	Partitions	Str.	Strength; Starter; Straight	WWF	Welded Wire Fabric
Pu	Ultimate Load	Strd.	Stranded	XFMR	Transformer
PVC	Polyvinyl Chloride	Struct.	Structural	XHD	Extra Heavy Duty
Pvmt.	Pavement	Sty.	Story	Y	Wye
Pwr.	Power	Subj.	Subject	yd	Yard
Q	Quantity Heat Flow	Subs.	Subcontractors	yr	Year
Quan.; Qty.	Quantity	Surf.	Surface	Δ	Delta
Q.C.	Quick Coupling	Sw.	Switch	%	Percent
r	Radius of Gyration	Swbd.	Switchboard	~	Approximately
R	Resistance	S.Y.	Square Yard	Ø	Phase
R.C.P.	Reinforced Concrete Pipe	Syn.	Synthetic	@	At
Rect.	Rectangle	Sys.	System	#	Pound; Number
Reg.	Regular	t.	Thickness	<	Less Than
Reinf.	Reinforced	T	Temperature; Ton	>	Greater Than
Req'd.	Required	Tan	Tangent		
Resi	Residential	T.C.	Terra Cotta		
Rgh.	Rough	T & C	Threaded and Coupled		
R.H.W.	Rubber, Heat & Water Resistant	T.D.	Temperature Difference		
	Residential Hot Water	TFE	Tetrafluoroethylene (Teflon)		
rms	Root Mean Square	T. & G.	Tongue & Groove;		
Rnd.	Round		Tar & Gravel		
Rodm.	Rodman	Th.; Thk.	Thick		
Rofc.	Roofer, Composition				

733

Index

Index

Index

Index

Index

Index

746

Index

Index

Index

Index

Index

Index